SOCIOLOGY

FOURTH EDITION

SOCIOLOGY

ROBERT VAN KRIEKEN
DAPHNE HABIBIS
PHILIP SMITH
BRETT HUTCHINS
GREG MARTIN
KARL MATON

PEARSON

FOURTH EDITION

Copyright © Pearson Australia (a division of Pearson Australia Group Pty Ltd) 2010

Pearson Australia
Unit 4, Level 3
14 Aquatic Drive
Frenchs Forest NSW 2086

www.pearson.com.au

The *Copyright Act 1968* of Australia allows a maximum of one chapter or 10% of this book, whichever is the greater, to be copied by any educational institution for its educational purposes provided that that educational institution (or the body that administers it) has given a remuneration notice to Copyright Agency Limited (CAL) under the Act. For details of the CAL licence for educational institutions contact: Copyright Agency Limited, telephone: (02) 9394 7600, email: info@copyright.com.au

All rights reserved. Except under the conditions described in the *Copyright Act 1968* of Australia and subsequent amendments, no part of this publication may be reproduced, stored in a retrieval system or transmitted in any form or by any means, electronic, mechanical, photocopying, recording or otherwise, without the prior permission of the copyright owner.

Editor-in-Chief: Frances Eden
Acquisitions Editor: Joanne Stanley
Project Editor: Melissa Read
Development Editor: Rebecca Cornell
Production Administrator: Rochelle Deighton
Copy Editor: Caroline Hunter, Burrumundi Pty Ltd
Proofreader: Annie Kewe, AQ Editorial Services
Copyright and Pictures Editor: Jodie Streckeisen
Indexer: Frances Paterson, Olive Grove Indexing
Cover and internal design by Liz Nicholson, Design Bite
Cover image: *Head on Sand,* coloured etching 88 x 215 cm by Graham Fransella © Graham Fransella.
Typeset by Midland Typesetters, Australia

Printed in Malaysia (CTP-VP)

2 3 4 5 14 13 12 11

National Library of Australia Cataloguing-in-Publication Data

Title:	Sociology / Robert van Krieken ... [et al.]
Edition:	4th ed.
ISBN:	9780733993862 (pbk.)
Notes:	Includes index.
	Bibliography.
Subjects:	Sociology--Textbooks.
Other Authors/Contributors:	
	Van Krieken, Robert.
Dewey Number:	301

Every effort has been made to trace and acknowledge copyright. However, should any infringement have occurred, the publishers tender their apologies and invite copyright owners to contact them.

PEARSON AUSTRALIA
is a division of
PEARSON

Brief Contents

DETAILED CONTENTS	VI
PREFACE	XVI
ABOUT THE AUTHORS	XVII
ACKNOWLEDGEMENTS	XIX
1. WHAT IS SOCIOLOGY?	1
2. GLOBALISATION	27
3. POPULAR CULTURE AND THE MEDIA	75
4. FAMILY LIFE	111
5. EDUCATION AND KNOWLEDGE	161
6. LEISURE, SPORT, TOURISM AND WORK	193
7. CLASS AND INEQUALITY	221
8. IDENTITIES: INDIGENOUS, NATIONAL, ETHNIC AND RACIAL	255
9. GENDER AND SEXUALITY	283
10. HEALTH	319
11. RELIGION	349
12. POWER AND THE STATE	377
13. CRIME AND DEVIANCE	407
14. METHODS OF SOCIAL RESEARCH	441
15. SOCIOLOGICAL THEORY	465
BIBLIOGRAPHY	491
GLOSSARY	533
AUTHOR INDEX	545
SUBJECT INDEX	555

Contents

Preface	xvi
About the authors	xvii
Acknowledgements	xix

CHAPTER 1
WHAT IS SOCIOLOGY?

Introduction	2
The sociological imagination	2
The self and social change	4
Some basic concepts	4
Social construction	5
Structure and system	5
Culture	6
Agency	7
Socialisation, the self and identity	8
Modernity and colonialism	9
Globalisation and deglobalisation	10
Sociological perspectives	10
Science, politics or interpretation	11
Sociology as science	12
Sociology as politics and critical theory	12
Sociology as interpretation	13
Gender and feminism	13
The question of postmodernity	14
The development of sociology and social change	15
Sociology's European origins in the age of revolutions, 1840s–1870s	15
Sociology's establishment as an academic discipline, 1880s–1910	16
The development of interpretivist sociology, 1920s–1930s	17
The dominance of functionalist theory, 1940s–1960s	17
The rise of conflict theory, 1970s	19
Feminist and interactionist sociology, 1970s–1980s	19
Postmodernity and globalisation, 1980s–2000s	20
Public sociology	20
Australian sociology	22
History	22
Australian sociological research	23
Tutorial exercises	25
Further reading	25
Websites	25

CHAPTER 2
GLOBALISATION

Introduction	28
'Society' beyond the nation-state	30
Measuring globalisation	31
The sociology of globalisation	33
World-systems theory—Immanuel Wallerstein	35
The compression of the world—Roland Robertson	35
The consequences of late-modernity—Anthony Giddens	36
Techno-capitalism and inequality—Manuel Castells	37
Technology and inequality	38
A history of globalisation	38
Six waves of globalisation—Göran Therborn	39
The first wave, 300–600	39
The second wave, 1500–1600	39
The third wave, 1700–1850	40
The fourth wave, 1850–1918	40
The fifth wave, 1940–70	40
The sixth wave, 1980–present	40
Technological and economic globalisation	42
International economy and globalised economy	43
The size and scope of the global economy	44
Class and global capitalism	44
Neoliberalism	45
A brief history of neoliberalism	45
Neoliberalism and globalisation	47
The limits of global capitalism	48
The brink of a global economy	48
Beyond benign economism	49
The poverty debate	49

The globalisation of poverty	49
Wealth for whom?	51

Political and legal globalisation — 51
- The withering away of the state? — 52
- Global governance — 53
- The globalisation of law — 55
  - Law and globalisation — 55
  - Global law — 55
- American hegemony — 57
  - The limitations of hegemony — 57
  - The decline of American hegemony—Wallerstein — 57

Cultural globalisation — 58
- Cultural homogenisation — 58
  - The McDonalisation of society—George Ritzer — 59
  - The Starbuckisation of society — 61
  - Jihad vs McWorld — 61
  - Clash of civilisations — 61
- Cultural heterogeneity — 62
  - The global production of difference and hybridity — 62
- Glocalisation — 64

In search of deglobalisation — 64
- The anti-capitalist movement—Alex Callinicos — 65
  - The emergence of anti-capitalism — 65
- *No logo*—Naomi Klein — 66
  - Brands not products — 66
  - Promoting the superbrand — 67
  - Culture jamming — 68
- The World Social Forum and deglobalisation — 69

Critiques of globalisation theory — 70
- Globalisation as northern theory—Raewyn Connell — 70
  - Mechanisms of exclusion, projection and erasure — 71
  - Globalisation beyond the metropole — 71

Conclusion — 72
- Tutorial exercises — 73
- Further reading — 73
- Websites — 73

Chapter 3
Popular culture and the media

Introduction — 76
- Modernity — 77
- *The Media and Modernity*—Thompson — 78
  - The rise of the printing industry — 79
  - The emergence of periodical publications — 80
  - The transformation of media institutions into large-scale commercial concerns — 80
  - The globalisation of communication — 80
- Conceptual tools — 81
  - Face-to-face interaction — 81
  - Mediated interaction — 82
  - Mediated quasi-interaction — 82
  - Computer-mediated interaction — 83

Media rituals — 84
- Habitual action — 84
- Formalised action — 84
- Action involving transcendent values — 84
- Media as social practice—Couldry — 85

Media events — 86
- Beyond media events—the 2008 Beijing Olympic Games — 88

The public sphere — 89
- *The Structural Transformation of the Public Sphere*—Habermas — 90
- The global public sphere—Volkmer — 94

Celebrity: the private meets the public — 94
- Celebrity and religion — 97

The internet, the Web and mobile phones — 98
- The network society — 99
- The culture of real virtuality — 101
- Community and networked individualism — 102
- The digital divide — 103
- The mobile network society — 104

The sociology of the media into the future — 106
- Tutorial exercises — 108
- Further reading — 108
- Websites — 108

Chapter 4
Family life

Introduction — 112
The modern, Western family — 113
- The Western nuclear family — 113
- Industrialisation and modern family life — 114
- The Christian Church and the European Family—Jack Goody — 114
  - The Church, property and kinship — 114

Marriage and parental control	114
Australian colonial family life	115
The Symmetrical Family—Michael Young and Peter Willmott	116

Sociological perspectives on family life — 116
Marxism—the family and the reproduction of capitalism	116
The family as a social construction	117
The contradictory relationship between family life and capitalism	117
Positive and negative aspects of familial 'irrationality'	117
Undermining patriarchal power	118
The family in permanent crisis	118
Weber's theory of the family	118
The structure of family life	118
Sex and marriage	119
The historical development of kin group and household	119
Functionalism—the nuclear family as the foundation of society	119
Primary socialisation and personality stabilisation—Talcott Parsons	120
The transfer of functions	120
Feminism and the 'antisocial family'	120

Gender and domestic labour — 121
Gender inequality in rural Australia—Ken Dempsey	121
The gender division of household labour—Janeen Baxter	122
How Australians Use Their Time—ABS	122
Domestic violence	123
Inequality within marriage	124

Culture, ethnicity and family diversity — 125
Aboriginal family life	125
Traditional Aboriginal family life	125
Rural and urban Aboriginal family life	127
Aboriginal family change in Adelaide, 1966–80—Fay Gale	128
Aboriginal families and state intervention: the Stolen Generations	128
Migrant family structure and values	129
Greek families in Australia	130
Lebanese Muslim families in Australia	131
Ethnicity and family diversity: conclusion	132

Structural change in family life — 132
The fertility decline in Australia	133
The decline in household size	133
From the 'proper time to marry' to the 'proper time to reproduce'—John Caldwell and Lado Ruzicka	134
Baby boom or marriage boom?	136
The post-1970s fertility decline	136
Women's participation in the workforce	138
Causes and effects of increased female participation in the workforce	139
Marriage, cohabitation and divorce	141
The marriage rate and ex-nuptial child-bearing	142
Cohabitation	144
Single-parent families	145
Divorce	145

Children and childhood — 149
Centuries of Childhood—Phillippe Ariès	150
Regulation and rights	150
The social construction of childhood	151
Children's lives beyond the family	152
Children and divorce	153
Child abuse and neglect	153

Towards the 'post-familial family'? — 154
Family 'decline'	155
Democratisation and egalitarianism—Giddens, Beck and Beck-Gernsheim	155
The Transformation of Intimacy—Anthony Giddens	156
The Normal Chaos of Love—Ulrich Beck and Elisabeth Beck-Gernsheim	156
Continuity and enduring power relations	158

Conclusion—the future of family life — 158
Tutorial exercises	160
Further reading	160
Websites	160

CHAPTER 5
EDUCATION AND KNOWLEDGE

Introduction	162

Education in Australia: evolving structures and ideas — 162
Liberal humanism and the formation of education	163
Social democracy and educational expansion	164
New economism and marketisation	165
Contemporary education	167

Three giants—the problems of class, gender and ethnicity 168
  Social class 168
  Gender 169
  Ethnicity 170
  Explanations of education—a map of the field 171

Naturalism—'nothing to declare but my genes' 171
  Criticisms of naturalism 172

Externalism—fulfilling others' needs 173
  Economic needs—structural functionalism 173
    Criticisms of structural functionalism 173
  Capitalist needs—reproduction theories 174
    Criticisms of reproduction theories 175
  Patriarchal needs—gender 175
  'The Australian way of life'—ethnicity 176
  Criticisms of externalism 176

Internalism—looking inside classrooms 177
  Labelling theory and classroom practices 177
  Gender and identity 178
    The underperformance of boys 179
  Ethnicities 180
  Criticisms of internalism 180

Culturalism—integrating insights into education 182
  Learning to Labour—Paul Willis 182
  Making the Difference—Connell et al. 183
  Pierre Bourdieu's field theory 184
    Habitus and cultural capital 184
    Limitations of Bourdieu's approach 185
  Basil Bernstein's code theory 186
    Educational knowledge codes 187

Future trends: the rise of knowledge 188
  Social realism 189
  Legitimation code theory 189
  Tutorial exercise 191
  Further reading 191
  Websites 191

Chapter 6
Leisure, sport, tourism and work

Introduction 194
Leisure 194
  Leisure in our lives 194
  Leisure, power and inequality 196
    Taste and cultural capital—Pierre Bourdieu 196
    Leisure and social capital 197
  Power and conflict over leisure 198
  Gender and leisure 198
    Women reading—Janice Radway 198
    Gender and leisure time—Michael Bittman and Judy Wajcman 199

Sport 199
  Australian participation in sport 199
  Sport and modernity 200
    From Ritual to Record—Allen Guttmann 200
    The civilising process in sports—Eric Dunning 200
  Sport and the gender order 202
    Gendered patterns of participation in Australia 202
    Gender order in Australia 202
    Sporting ideology and gender in Australia 203
    Sport and sexual violence in Australia—Peter Mewett and Kim Toffoletti 204
  David Beckham and the 'new man' 205
  Sport, class and race 205

Tourism 206
  The importance of tourism 207
  Sociological perspectives on tourism 208
    'Escaping the real'— Daniel Boorstin 208
    The search for the 'authentic'—Dean MacCannell 208
    The tourist gaze—John Urry 208
  The social impacts of tourism—Jennifer Craik 209
  Future directions in tourism studies 209

Work 211
  The work and employment profile of Australia 211
  The experience of work 211
  Multiple factors influencing militancy and strikes—Claire Williams 213
  Work, modernity and postmodernity 214
  Gender, inequality and work 215
    The emotional labour of Australian magistrates—Sharyn Roach Anleu and Kathy Mack 216
    Emotional labour in the airline industry—Claire Williams 216
  Unemployment 217
  Unemployment in Australia—a profile 218

Conclusion 218
  Tutorial exercise 219
  Further reading 219
  Websites 219

Chapter 7
Class and inequality

Introduction	222
Key concepts	223
Does social inequality matter?	224
Inequality in a changing world	225
Class, stratification and modernity	225
Locating class in late modernity	226
Understanding contemporary inequality	227
Theories of inequality	227
Marx's theory of class	227
Positivism	228
Marx's evolutionary theory of social change	228
Historical materialism	228
Modes of production and evolutionary social change	229
Class, class consciousness and the state	229
Criticisms of Marx	230
The legacy of Marx	230
Weber's multidimensional theory of inequality	230
Class as market position	231
Status groups and social closure	231
Parties	231
The legacy of Weber	232
Durkheim and the division of labour	232
The legacy of Durkheim: the functions of inequality	232
Pierre Bourdieu: class and culture	233
The legacy of Bourdieu	234
Material inequality in Australia	234
Measuring economic resources	235
The social wage	235
Changes in economic inequality	235
Winners and losers	240
International comparisons of social inequality	241
Poverty and social exclusion	242
Poverty, social exclusion and citizenship	242
Measuring poverty	243
Classes in Australian society	244
Changes in the occupational structure	244
Mapping the class structure	245
Weberian maps—Goldthorpe	246
Wright's models of contradictory class locations	246
The upper class	247
Interlocks and networks	247
Unity and division	248
The middle class	249
Middle or working class?	250
The professions and cultural power	250
The working class	251
Social mobility	251
Measuring social mobility	252
Social mobility in Australia	252
Strategies for social reproduction	253
Tutorial exercise	254
Further reading	254
Websites	254

Chapter 8
Identities: indigenous, national, ethnic and racial

Introduction	256
Australian Aborigines and Aboriginality	257
Australian Aborigines and racial oppression since 1788—a brief history	257
Australian Aborigines and Torres Strait Islanders as 'fourth world peoples'	258
The survival of Australian Aboriginal culture in everyday life	258
Whitefella Comin'—David Trigger	259
The camp at Wallaby Cross—Basil Sansom	259
Kinship ties among Adelaide Aborigines—Fay Gale and Joy Wundersitz	260
Aboriginal life in a rural small town—Gillian Cowlishaw	260
Aboriginal culture and everyday life—summary	260
Australian Aboriginal land rights, Mabo, Wik and the new cultural identity	261
The Mabo decision and other issues in Aboriginal politics	261
Social disadvantage and Australian Aboriginality today	262
Employment, income and education	262
The criminal justice system	263
Ethnicity	265
Migration	266
Migrant decision making	266
Structural aspects of migration	266
Outcomes of migration	266
Migration to Australia—a historical overview	267
Migration and multiculturalism	270
Postmodern ethnicity	271

Nationalism and national identity — 272
  Ethnic and civic nationalism — 273
  Australian national identity — 273
    Australian national identity in historical perspective — 274
    Popular culture and national identity—Fiske, Hodge and Turner: *Myths of Oz* — 274
    Quantitative research on Australian national identity — 275
    Multiculturalism and the end of traditional nationalism—Castles et al. — 277

Racism — 278
  Old and new racism—historical shifts — 278
  Institutional racism — 279
  Racism in Australia — 279
    Racism and Australia's Indigenous communities — 280
    Racism in the Australian media — 280
  Tutorial exercise — 282
  Further reading — 282
  Websites — 282

CHAPTER 9
GENDER AND SEXUALITY

Introduction — 284
  Sex, gender and sexuality — 285
Biology, culture, sex and gender — 285
  Sociobiology—the evolution of human behaviour — 286
    Criticisms of sociobiological theories — 286
  Sex roles—Talcott Parsons — 287
  Sigmund Freud — 288
  The problem of cultural diversity — 289
  Gender as 'expression'—Erving Goffman — 289
  Sociology, biology and the body — 290
Gender identity — 291
  Role theory — 291
    Criticisms of role theory — 292
  The Reproduction of Mothering— Nancy Chodorow — 293
    Male gender personality — 293
    Female gender personality — 293
    Criticisms of Chodorow — 294
  Frogs and Snails and Feminist Tales— Bronwyn Davies — 295
  Masculinities—Raewyn Connell — 296
    Active bodies — 296
    Hegemonic masculinity — 297
    Men's life histories — 297
    The history of masculinities — 299
    The 'gender order' — 301
Transforming gender and sexuality — 301
  The women's movement/feminism — 302
  The gay and lesbian movement — 302
Sexual identity and beyond— heterosexual, homosexual, queer — 303
  Criticisms of 'categorical' theory — 303
  Compulsory heterosexuality—Adrienne Rich — 304
    Criticisms of Rich — 304
  Continuums of sexual behaviour— Alfred Kinsey et al. — 305
    Criticisms of Kinsey — 306
  The psychology of gender and sexuality after Kinsey — 307
  Sexual conduct—John Gagnon and William Simon — 308
    Sexual scripts — 308
    Sex as a powerful 'natural' drive — 310
    Scripting theory — 310
  An ethnomethodological approach— Suzanne Kessler and Wendy McKenna — 311
  Sexuality and power—Michel Foucault — 312
  Beyond sexual 'identity'—queer sexuality — 312
    Critiques of queer theory — 313
    Queer sexual politics — 314
Sociology and the future of gender and sexuality — 315
  Tutorial exercises — 317
  Further reading — 317
  Websites — 317

CHAPTER 10
HEALTH

Introduction — 320
The rise of modern medicine — 320
The sociological critique of modern medicine — 321
  Michel Foucault and the medical gaze — 321
  Marxist views on health, class and capitalism — 322
  Feminist perspectives—controlling women's bodies — 322
  Micro-perspectives — 323
    Erving Goffman on the asylum — 324
    The moral evaluation of patients—Julius Roth — 324

XI

The hospital	324
Doctor–patient interaction	326
Empirical studies on doctor–patient interaction	327
Health, welfare and the community	328
Community ties and health	329
The decision to see a doctor—Irving Zola	329
Lay definitions of disease	330
The political economy of health and welfare	330
Types of health-care systems	330
The health care system in the United States	331
The Australian health-care system	332
The unexpected consequences of Medicare	332
The medical occupations—doctors, nurses and allied health professions	333
Doctors	334
Nurses and allied health professions	335
Recent changes to the medical professions	335
Medical training	336
Death and dying	337
Dealing with death	337
Epidemiology and the social correlates of health and illness	338
Causes of death	338
Health in the developing world	339
Sickness, health and social inequality	339
Sickness, health and gender	341
Sickness, health, ethnicity and migration	342
Sickness, health and Aboriginal people	342
Current trends—the end of biomedicine and medical dominance?	343
The rise of alternative therapies	343
Feminist interventions and the women's health movement	345
Health promotion and preventive medicine	345
Self-help movements	346
Managerialism, consumerism and the end of medical autonomy	346
Conclusion	347
Tutorial exercise	348
Further reading	348
Websites	348

CHAPTER 11
RELIGION

Introduction	350
Definitions of religion	351
Religion and spirituality	351
Theories of religion	352
Functionalist theories of religion	352
Durkheim	352
Civil religion	353
Materialist theories of religion	353
Marx	353
Phenomenological theories of religion	355
Religion as a sacred canopy	355
Criticisms of Berger and Luckmann	356
Feminist theories of religion	356
The deconstruction of religious traditions	356
Religion as an instrument for the oppression of women	356
The feminist reconstruction of religion	357
The influence of feminism on the Christian Church	357
Science and religion	357
Religion and social change	358
Religion as the source of social change	358
The Protestant Ethic and the Spirit of Capitalism—Max Weber	359
Religion as a conservative influence on society	359
The effects of religious beliefs on political and social attitudes	360
Religion as a radical influence on society	361
Liberation theology	361
Secularisation	361
Evidence in support of secularisation	362
Problems with the secularisation thesis	363
Secularisation or post-secularisation?	365
Explaining the resurgence of religion	366
The search for moral guidance	366
Contemporary religious expression	367
Fundamentalism	367
Christian fundamentalism in the United States	367
Islamic fundamentalism	368
Explanations of the appeal of fundamentalism	370
New forms of religiosity	371
New Age movements	371
Neo-paganism	372
Locating new forms of religiosity in modernity	373

The future of religion	373
Tutorial exercise	375
Further reading	375
Websites	375

CHAPTER 12
POWER AND THE STATE

Introduction	378
Defining power	378
Max Weber	378
Charismatic authority	378
Traditional authority	379
Rational–legal authority	379
Types of social action	380
Elite theory	380
The power elite—C. Wright Mills	380
Elite theory in Australia	381
Power is like money—Talcott Parsons	382
Pluralism	383
Who governs?—Robert Dahl	385
Bureaucracy, discipline and the state	386
The 'technical superiority' of bureaucracy, or TINA	386
Bureaucracy, discipline and power	386
Stateless societies	387
The emergence of the modern state and bureaucracy	387
The sources of social power—Michael Mann	388
The Australian state	388
The Constitution and the High Court	388
The federal structure	389
A Weberian approach to the Australian state—Sol Encel	389
Rethinking power	390
The three faces of power—Steven Lukes	390
Neo-pluralism	391
The power of hegemony—Antonio Gramsci	391
Class and the Australian state—Raewyn Connell	392
Power and the self	394
The Civilising Process—Norbert Elias	394
Court society—representational power	395
Power and meetings	396
A micro-ritual theory of power—Randall Collins	396
Knowledge, discipline and government—Michel Foucault	397
Knowledge, discourses and power	397
The history of sexuality	397

Modern individuality and power	398
Disciplinary power	399
Governmentality	400
Power as effect—Bruno Latour	402
Beyond the state?	402
New social movements and postmodernisation	402
Critique—how 'new' is the new politics?	403
Australian social movements and globalisation—Verity Burgmann	404
Tutorial exercise	406
Further reading	406
Websites	406

CHAPTER 13
CRIME AND DEVIANCE

Introduction	408
Defining crime and deviance	409
The social construction of official criminal statistics	409
The dark figure of crime—undetected and unreported crime	409
Changing definitions of crime	410
Changing resources of law and order	410
The influence of discretionary decisions within the criminal justice system	410
Theories of crime and deviance	411
Biological and psychological theories of crime and deviance	411
Sociological theories of crime and deviance	411
Deviance—a functionalist perspective	412
Traditional functionalists	412
Anomie theory	412
The Chicago School	413
The ecology of deviance	413
The ethnography of deviance	413
Criticisms of the Chicago School	413
Social control theory	414
Wilson and Herrnstein	414
Social control theory—an assessment	415
Crime control and the New Right	415
Deviance—an interactionist perspective	416
Primary and secondary deviance—Edwin Lemert	416
Labelling theory—Howard Becker	416
Deviance amplification; moral panics and collective reactions	417
Deviance and the interactionist perspective—criticisms and evaluation	417

Deviance and power—conflict perspectives	417
Deviance—the conventional Marxist perspective	418
The second wave—neo-Marxist and 'socialist' perspectives	418
Left realism—the new reformism?	419
Feminist theories of crime and deviance	419
Women and social control—Heidensohn	419
Masculinities and the accomplishment of gender through crime—Messerschmidt	420
Feminist theory—an evaluation	420
Crime, shame and reintegration	420

The future of the sociology of crime and deviance — 421

Patterns of crime in Australia — 422

Crime rates in Australia over time	424
Community attitudes towards crime	426
Offenders	426
Young people and crime	428
Young people and gangs	429
Young people and the police	430
Offending women	431
Victims	432
Violence against women	433
Indigenous people and crime	433
The Royal Commission into Aboriginal Deaths in Custody	434
Crimes of the powerful	435
Class and crime	436
The costs of crimes of the powerful	437
Class and the criminal justice system	438
Tutorial exercise	440
Further reading	440
Websites	440

CHAPTER 14
METHODS OF SOCIAL RESEARCH

Introduction	442
Positivism and quantitative methodology	443
Positivist sociology	443
Social facts as 'things'	443
Statistics	443
Laws of human society and inductive methodology	443
Falsification and the hypothetico-deductive model—Karl Popper	444
Paradigms and scientific revolutions—Thomas Kuhn	444
Paradigms	445
Scientific revolutions	445
Anti-positivism and relativism—Peter Winch	445
The comparative method	446

The sociology of suicide — 446

Suicide rates	446
Types of suicide	447
Criticisms of Durkheim's study	448
Categorising death as suicide—J. Maxwell Atkinson	449
Suicide in Australia—Riaz Hassan	450

Interpretive and qualitative methodology — 450

Qualitative data and the interpretive approach	451
Verstehen sociology—Max Weber	452
Symbolic interactionism	452
Applications and criticisms of symbolic interactionism	453
Phenomenology	454
Ethnomethodology	454
The realist view of science	455
Scientific research 'systems'	455
Studying the unobservable	455
Causation	455
Sociology as science	456
Feminist research	456
Triangulation or methodological pluralism	457

Street corner society — 459

Cornerville revisited	460
Boelen's critique of Whyte	460
Whyte's reply	461
The wider significance of street corner society	461
Possibilities for action research	462
A note on representation	462
Tutorial exercises	464
Further reading	464
Websites	464

CHAPTER 15
SOCIOLOGICAL THEORY

Introduction	466
Durkheim and the social	468
Social facts	468
The collective conscience and moral order	468

The division of labour, differentiation of society and social solidarity	469
Anomie and justice	469
Talcott Parsons and the problem of social order	469

Marx and Western Marxism — 470
- Ideology — 470
- Alienation — 471
- Social change — 471
- Western Marxism — 472
  - Antonio Gramsci — 472
  - The Frankfurt School — 473
- Weber and conflict sociology — 474
- Capitalism and ascetic Protestantism — 475
  - The Protestant ethic — 475
  - The spirit of capitalism — 476
- Conflict sociology — 476
  - Authority and conflict—Ralf Dahrendorf — 477
  - *Conflict Sociology*—Randall Collins — 477

Simmel and social interactionism — 477
- Simmel's concept of society and sociology — 478
  - Relationism and reciprocal working — 478
  - Social relations—forms and types — 479
- The philosophy of money and objective culture — 480
- Simmel—an evaluation — 481
- Interactionism and interpretive sociology — 481
  - Symbolic interactionism — 482
  - Ethnomethodology — 483

Beyond classical sociology? — 484
- Feminist sociology — 484
  - Beyond public and private—Anna Yeatman — 484
- Modernity, the Enlightenment and beyond — 485
  - Postmodernism and knowledge—Jean-François Lyotard — 485
  - *Simulations*—Jean Baudrillard — 486
  - Second modernity and 'zombie' sociology—Ulrich Beck — 487

Sociology today — 488
- Tutorial exercises — 490
- Further reading — 490
- Websites — 490

Bibliography — 491
Glossary — 533
Author index — 545
Subject index — 555

Preface

This fourth Australian edition of *Sociology* follows the first three Australian (1996, 2000 and 2005) revisions and adaptations of the UK textbook, *Sociology: Themes and Perspectives*. The strengths of the earlier editions, which made them invaluable texts and source books, included clear presentation and expression, breadth and depth of coverage, and up-to-date discussions of both theoretical debates and empirical research. As well as retaining these strengths, the revision of the book has here been extended to make it a completely distinct book from the UK edition, a stand-alone Australian guide to sociological thought and research. We say farewell to Michael Haralambos and Martin Holborn as co-authors, with warm thanks for the opportunity to collaborate in the production of the first three Australian revisions.

NEW TO THIS EDITION

Latest social science research

In revising this fourth edition, the team of authors drew upon the published scholarship of hundreds of Australian sociologists as well as many working in related fields such as criminology, cultural studies, gender studies and political science. It covers the landscape of intellectual inquiry in the Australian social sciences today, drawing on findings from both established and early-career scholars, and research projects ranging from low-budget observational studies to big-budget surveys. Each chapter has been thoroughly revised to keep abreast of current developments in Australian and international sociology, including updated and improved figures and tables.

Global orientation

Two new authors, both from the University of Sydney, have joined the writing team: Karl Maton, who has taken over Chapter 5, *Education and Knowledge*, and Greg Martin, who has become responsible for Chapter 14, *Methods of Social Research*. All the authors have, at the same time, also made an effort to make each chapter as 'global' as possible, locating the Australian experience in the context of other parts of the world. Philip Smith is currently at Yale University, and Robert van Krieken is currently at University College Dublin, where both are developing the linkages between sociology in Australia, Europe and North America.

Continued improvement

The globalisation chaper has been thoroughly reworked, and Chapter 3, *Popular Culture and the Media*, has been expanded to include more discussion of popular culture. The fourth edition has an illustrative opening vignette to set the scene for every chapter, a thought-provoking set of in-text reflective questions, as well as tutorial exercises at the end of the chapter, and the lists of useful Web sites, Key Terms and Further Reading sections have been retained. Every chapter has been shortened and organised more tightly.

Supporting resources

For the students the Companion Website—www.pearson.com.au/highered/vankrieken4e—is also much improved. The site remains an excellent resource for all Australian sociology students, offering extensive links to sociology sites of interest, key definitions, and self-assessment activities including multiple-choice and short answer questions.

For lecturers the new edition includes a computerised test bank of questions and an instructor's manual containing chapter summaries, classroom activities and further discussion topics.

Thanks to the anonymous reviewers for their critical and supportive commentary. Our respective colleagues, friends and significant others are also to be thanked for their support and forbearance as we struggled with what, as we say for every edition, was a much more time-consuming and demanding task than anyone anticipated. All the authors owe a debt of gratitude to a number of people at Pearson: Joy Whitton, for enduring our stubbornness about the contract; Joanne Davis, who also made important contributions in the early stages; Joanne Stanley, Rebecca Cornell and Michael Stone for guiding the manuscript's completion, their encouragement and their patience in having to keep their procrastinating and recalcitrant authors in harness; and Michael Young, also for his unwavering support for the project.

Robert van Krieken, Daphne Habibis, Philip Smith, Brett Hutchins, Karl Maton, Greg Martin

About the authors

ROBERT VAN KRIEKEN

Robert van Krieken received both his BA Honours and PhD in Sociology from the University of New South Wales, and also has a Law degree from the University of Sydney. He has taught and researched for many years at the University of Sydney, where he played a central role in establishing a distinct sociology program from 1991 onwards, as well as setting up a program in socio-legal studies in 2006. He has done research on the historical sociology of child welfare in Australia, the Stolen Generations, processes of civilisation and decivilisation, the question of cultural genocide, and the sociology of recent changes in family law in Australia, the USA and Europe, as well contributing to the theoretical debates around the work of Elias, Foucault, Luhmann and Latour. He is currently Professor of Sociology at University College Dublin, where he aims to develop the linkages between sociology in Australia and Europe.

DAPHNE HABIBIS

Daphne Habibis is a senior lecturer with the School of Sociology and Social Work at the University of Tasmania. She is a qualitative researcher who has collaborated frequently with quantitative researchers. Her research is in the area of social justice and has focused on housing, mental illness and Indigenous peoples. She completed her BSc (Sociology) and PhD at the London School of Economics and holds a BSW from the University of Tasmania.

Daphne has recently published, with Maggie Walter, *Social Inequality in Australia: Discourses, Realities and Futures* (2008 Oxford University Press). She is currently completing a large AHURI grant examining how housing services can improve responses to Indigenous mobility practices. Evaluations have included programs funded by the National Homelessness Strategy and community sector tenancy support programs. Other large, funded research projects have focused on issues relating to tenancy sustainment and the impact of community mental health teams on consumer and relative outcomes.

PHILIP SMITH

Philip Smith has an MA in Anthropology from Edinburgh and a PhD in Sociology from UCLA. He worked at the University of Queensland from 1993-2002 where for a time he was head of both the sociology and criminology programs. He is currently Associate Professor in Sociology at Yale University and Co-Chair of the International Sociological Association's Research Committee on Sociological Theory. Known as a member of Yale's Strong Program in Cultural Sociology (see http://ccs.research.yale.edu/). Smith's work argues for the role of deep meanings in shaping cultural life. *Why War?* (University of Chicago Press, 2005) suggested that military conflict today is driven by narratives of evil. *Punishment and Culture* (Chicago, 2008) explored the history of the prison and execution through themes of purification and sacrifice. His most recent study, *Incivility* (Cambridge, 2010, co-written with T. Phillips and R. King) is a systematic investigation of the everyday encounters with rude strangers in Australia.

BRETT HUTCHINS

Brett Hutchins is a Senior Lecturer in Communications and Media Studies in the School of English, Communications and Performance Studies at Monash University. He holds a PhD in Sociology from the University of

Queensland, graduating in 2001 and receiving the Dean's Commendation for Outstanding Research Higher Degree Thesis (PhD). His thesis was published as *Don Bradman: Challenging the Myth* by Cambridge University Press in 2002, receiving significant media and critical attention and appearing in paperback in 2005.

Brett's research and teaching interests are in the areas of sports media, digital media and environmental media, with his most recent publications appearing in high-profile international journals such as *Media, Culture & Society*, *New Media & Society*, *Television & New Media* and *Journalism: Theory, Practice & Criticism*. He is presently working on a three-year Australian Research Council funded project investigating the transition of sports media content from broadcast to online environments, and the cultural, social and economic implications of this shift.

Karl Maton

Karl Maton is a Senior Lecturer in sociology at the School of Social and Political Sciences, University of Sydney. He holds three degrees in economics, social and political science and Education from the University of Cambridge and has taught at the University of Cambridge, the Open University (UK), Keele University and Wollongong University. His sociological theory of knowledge and education is now being internationally used by researchers in sociology, education, philosophy and linguistics (see www.karlmaton.com). Karl has published extensively in sociology, cultural studies, education, linguistics and philosophy. He is currently working on two major projects funded by the Australian Research Council, titled *Living and Learning in a Knowledge Society* (on young people and digital technology) and *Disciplinarity, Knowledge and Schooling* (on building students' knowledge over time). He recently conducted the biggest study of its kind in the world on students' experiences and expectations of technology in higher education. Karl's book, *Knowledge and Knowers: Towards a realist sociology of education*, was published in 2010 by Routledge.

Greg Martin

Greg Martin is a Lecturer on the Socio-Legal Studies programme in the Department of Sociology and Social Policy at the University of Sydney. After obtaining his degree in sociology from the University of Exeter, Greg conducted ethnographic fieldwork amongst New Age Travellers for his PhD, which he also completed at Exeter. He then did a Postgraduate Certificate in Education, taught in the Department of Sociology and Social Anthropology at Keele University and was a Research Fellow in the Department of Sociology and Social Policy at the University of Leeds. Subsequently, Greg travelled the world, completed a law degree at the University of Western Australia, worked in legal publishing and was employed as a Lecturer in Criminology at the University of Western Sydney. He has several international publications in areas as diverse as sociology, social policy, politics, criminology and law. His main research interests are in social movements and youth culture.

Acknowledgements

Copyright holders for material used in this book are shown below.

CHAPTER 1
2, Courtesy of the National Archives/Newsmakers/Getty Images
18, Artwork – 'The Passage of Venus', digital print on polyester screen by Guy Dempster. Exhibited in 2008 NSW Art Express Competition.

CHAPTER 2
28, Daily Telegraph
46, © Bettman/Corbis
Extracts from speech by Paul Keating reproduced with permission of Hon P J Keating.
Extracts from *No Logo: No Space, No Choice, No Jobs* © N. Klein (2000), reprinted by permission of Harper-Collins Publishers Ltd

CHAPTER 3
76, AAP Image/Network Ten
93, iStockphoto.com/©Kyle Maass

CHAPTER 4
112, iStockphoto.com/©Sheryl Griffin
141, iStockphoto.com/©Leah Marshall

CHAPTER 5
162, Photo by Phil Walter/Getty Images
187, iStockphoto.com/©Jacob Wackerhausen

CHAPTER 6
194, iStockphoto.com/©David Joyner
200, Timothy A. Clary/AFP/Getty Images

CHAPTER 7
222, iStockphoto.com/© Catherine Yeulet
224, From *World History Connections to Today: Guide to Essential World History.* © 1999 Pearson Education Inc., or its affiliates. Used with permission. All rights reserved.

CHAPTER 8
256, AAP Image/Paul Miller
276, Jay Mallin/Bloomberg/Getty Images

CHAPTER 9
284, Michael Ochs Archives/Getty Images
308, George Marks/Getty Images
Extracts from *Frogs and Snails and Feminists Tales* © B. Davies (1989), reprinted by permission of Allen & Unwin (Sydney), www.allenandunwin.com
Extracts from *Masculinities* © R.W. Connell (1995), reprinted by permission of Allen & Unwin (Sydney), www.allenandunwin.com.
Extracts from *Sexual Conduct* © Aldine Publishers (1973), reprinted by permission of Aldine Transaction, a division of Transaction Publishers.

CHAPTER 10
320, courtesy Claude Ho
341, iStockphoto.com/©Simone van den Berg

CHAPTER 11
350, iStockphoto.com/© Alexander Copeland
360, *Sydney Morning Herald* photograph by Ben Rushton
Extracts from Reaction, Introspection and Exploration: Diversity in Journeys out of Faith by Zina O'Leary. Christian Research Association Paper No. 4, 1999, reprinted by permission of the Christian Research Association, Melbourne.

CHAPTER 12
378, iStockphoto.com/©Fernando Celescuekci
383, Keystone/Hulton Archive/Getty Images

CHAPTER 13
408, AAP Image/ABC TV
439, iStockphoto.com/©Rich Legg

CHAPTER 14
442, courtesy Pitt Rivers Museum, University of Oxford
451, iStockphoto.com/webphotopheer

CHAPTER 15
466, iStockphoto.com/©David Freund
473, iStockphoto.com/©contour99

What is Sociology?

This chapter provides an introduction to the study of sociology and gives you an overview of some of the basic concepts you are likely to encounter in your reading in sociology. It explains how and why developing a 'sociological imagination' in thinking about social life is useful if you would like to understand the world you live in and how it is changing. It also outlines, very briefly, the ways in which sociology has changed over time in connection with historical changes in the surrounding social context, ending up with some observations on the more recent concerns of sociologists in the 21st century, with particular reference to Australia.

By the end of the chapter, you should have a better understanding of a number of concepts, topics and issues, including:
— the sociological imagination
— social construction, structure, culture and action
— socialisation and identity, modernity and colonialism, globalisation and deglobalisation
— the range of sociological perspectives: sociology as science, politics or interpretation
— feminism
— postmodernity
— the historical development of sociology within changing social contexts
— public sociology
— Australian sociology in the world.

INTRODUCTION	**2**
The sociological imagination	2
The self and social change	4
SOME BASIC CONCEPTS	**4**
Social construction	5
Structure and system	5
Culture	6
Agency	7
Socialisation, the self and identity	8
Modernity and colonialism	9
Globalisation and deglobalisation	10
SOCIOLOGICAL PERSPECTIVES	**10**
Science, politics or interpretation	11
Sociology as science	12
Sociology as politics and critical theory	12
Sociology as interpretation	13
Gender and feminism	13
The question of postmodernity	14
THE DEVELOPMENT OF SOCIOLOGY AND SOCIAL CHANGE	**15**
Sociology's European origins in the age of revolutions, 1840s–1870s	15
Sociology's establishment as an academic discipline, 1880s–1910	16
The development of interpretivist sociology, 1920s–1930s	17
The dominance of functionalist theory, 1940s–1960s	17
The rise of conflict theory, 1970s	19
Feminist and interactionist sociology, 1970s–1980s	19
Postmodernity and globalisation, 1980s–2000s	20
Public sociology	20
AUSTRALIAN SOCIOLOGY	**22**
History	22
Australian sociological research	23
Tutorial exercises	25
Further reading	25
Websites	25

INTRODUCTION

The Holocaust was an event that defined the 20th century. The attempted genocide of the Jewish people of Europe by the German Nazis and their allies during World War II resulted in the deaths of an estimated six million Jewish people and a further seven to 11 million others deemed undesirable because of their sexual orientation, ethnic background or political or religious views. In the aftermath of the war the scale and spread of the Holocaust across Nazi-occupied Europe, its state-sponsored nature and the complicity of the population seemed incomprehensible. Since then the Holocaust has been subjected to intense scrutiny in an effort to understand how such events could take place.

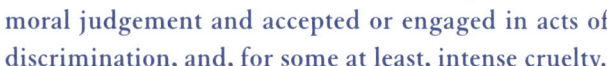

For many observers the Holocaust represents the loss of civilisation, but for the sociologist Zygmunt Bauman it is its result. He links the conditions that gave rise to the Holocaust with the principles of **modernity** (Bauman 1989). These include rational technical organisation, scientific efficiency and self-interest. This achieves expression in the state bureaucracy's concern to classify and order. Like a gardener, the modern administrator cultivates society, putting everything in its rightful place and weeding out 'undesirables'. Modern virtues of efficiency and regulation cancel out human values of compassion and concern for others.

The Third Reich of Nazi Germany was an expression of this. It was characterised by an obsession with efficiency and documentation. Problems of human suffering were reduced to technical problems that could be solved through a feat of engineering. Following orders became the new moral code. The result was that millions of ordinary men and women suspended their moral judgement and accepted or engaged in acts of discrimination, and, for some at least, intense cruelty.

1. Is the term 'modernity' still relevant as an accurate description of contemporary social life? If not, identify two features of life today that do not fit this depiction.
2. What features of Bauman's analysis demonstrate the application of the sociological imagination? How does Bauman's argument differ from (a) historical and (b) psychological accounts of the Holocaust?

The main reason that people study **sociology** is because it helps them to understand the social world around them, especially how it is changing. There are patterns to the ways we relate to each other that are difficult to identify and explain without looking at them closely over a period of time and experimenting with different possible explanations. There often appear to be processes and institutions to be studied over and above the individuals who form them, and this means you need concepts and ways of thinking that can capture those aspects of the world around you, concepts such as 'society', 'culture', 'modernity' and 'globalisation'. At the very least, you need to gather information ('data') about what people do, how they think and feel about it, and how their relationships with each other are shaped, in order to come to an informed understanding of any problem or issue. This is what sociological research is concerned with.

THE SOCIOLOGICAL IMAGINATION

A useful starting point for seeing why it is worthwhile to develop a **sociological imagination** has for some time been C. Wright Mills' (1959) observation on the differences between our everyday knowledge of our social environment and a sociological understanding of it. In Western societies, with the high value placed on ideas of individual 'autonomy' and 'freedom', we tend towards a psychological orientation in our understanding of what happens to ourselves and others. There is a strong tendency in liberal democracies towards seeing human behaviour in terms of individual characteristics, abilities, choices and preferences. Often, people think it is too 'deterministic' to talk about restrictions placed on individual choices. We tend to experience whatever happens in our own lives as unique and private, and also to interpret what happens to other people as unique and private to them, as *private troubles*.

What sociologists, on the other hand, are more interested in, is establishing the relationship between what happens to individuals in their lives and the larger processes of social, economic and political change that might be said to lie underneath or behind those happenings. The discipline of sociology encourages you to look for the social processes and structures that give a generalised pattern to those private troubles and thus turn them into *public issues*. Mills gave the example of unemployment: when one person is unemployed, that is a private trouble; when three million are unemployed, that is a public issue. Another example would be fertility: when one couple never has a baby, that is a private issue. When ever-increasing numbers of couples are in this situation, that is a public issue referred as the 'declining fertility rate'. Sociologists are responsive to the times when it is useful to step outside of our individual experience and see ourselves 'from the outside', as social creatures, part of groups and larger institutions. The sociological imagination, wrote Mills, 'enables us to grasp history and biography and the relations between the two in society' (1959, p. 6).

> ... *sociology is justified by the belief that it is better to be conscious than unconscious and that consciousness is a condition of freedom. To attain a greater measure of awareness, and with it of freedom, entails a certain amount of suffering and even risk. An educational process that would avoid this becomes simple technical training and ceases to have any relationship to the civilizing of the mind.* (Peter Berger, 1963, p. 175)

Anthony Giddens (1986, p. 13) argues that there are three distinct forms of sensibility that together make up the sociological imagination: first, a *historical sensibility*, an appreciation of how the world we live in today is the product of a number of historical processes of social transformation that we need to understand if we are to grasp how and why social life takes the form that it does today; second, *anthropological insight*, which refers to a sensitivity to what is culturally specific about the social world in which any individual lives, and the significant variability in what humans value, how they see the world and how they do things in everyday life; and third, the capacity for *critical thought*, which is underpinned by both of these sensibilities and involves questioning everyday thinking and commonsense assumptions about human behaviour and social life.

Critical thought in sociology is an invitation to look beyond everyday perspectives so that we see the world in a different light, as if we had come from another culture, another period in history or even another planet. It involves challenging the taken-for-granted in order to create new insights and understandings of our experiences. By standing outside our cultural and historical 'skin', we can make new, often unexpected, connections between social phenomena. This can lead to new and more penetrating interpretations of social life which have the potential, at least, of contributing to changes in the way we relate to the world around us.

> *One could say that the main service the art of thinking sociologically may render to each and every one of us is to make us more sensitive; it may sharpen up our senses, open our eyes wider so that we can explore human conditions which thus far had remained all but invisible. Once we understand better how the apparently neutral, inevitable, immutable, eternal aspects of our lives have been brought into being through the exercise of human power and human resources, we will find it hard to accept once more that they are immune and impenetrable to human action—our own action included.* (Bauman 1990, p. 16)

This does not mean that sociologists simply gather information that exposes flaws and contradictions in commonsense ideas: the relationship between sociological knowledge and our commonsense beliefs about the social world is more complex than that. You could probably say that we are all amateur sociologists, and we go through most of our lives at least partially conscious of the rules and structures within which they are embedded, such as our sense of time, our experience of masculinity and femininity, and our adherence to manners and etiquette. The US television series *Seinfeld* is a good example of a sociological way of seeing the world; much of its humour stems from its exposure of rules of behaviour and social interaction that are usually left hidden and unconscious. At the same time, when we do consciously reflect on social processes— say, the relationship between changing economic forces and family life—sociology has also contributed to and even formed that everyday knowledge. The information and knowledge gathered in social research and the associated analyses of social change often filter throughout society to become part of the commonsense of most of its members. Examples would include the 'lay theories' we all hold about how crime is best prevented, the role that education plays in society and the impact of the mass media on the way we think about the world.

THE SELF AND SOCIAL CHANGE

The list of changes that our apparently 'intimate' and 'personal' lives have undergone over time is long and constantly expanding. The fact that these changes are as widespread, patterned and systematic as they often are means that the only way to explain these changes properly is in terms of changing social structures and social relations; in terms of broader social arrangements. For example:

- *Our sense of time:* clocks and watches became widespread only relatively recently, and before their emergence people felt very differently about the passage of time, which played a different role in their lives. This is closely related to the increasing complexity of modern societies and the ever-increasing need to coordinate a growing variety of activities.
- *Manners, emotions and etiquette:* our sense of what is acceptable and desirable behaviour is constantly changing, and is intimately linked to the way our social relationships are organised. For example, it is now much less acceptable to express anger in the workplace; the spread of mobile phones has produced different concerns about phone etiquette; and the management of anger while driving has become a new social problem.
- *Gender relations and sexuality:* what it means to be a man or a woman, and what is acceptable dating or courting behaviour, has been transformed enormously as broader social relations between men and women have changed.
- *Family relations:* what it means to be a mother/father/child, when to have children and how many, and how to balance work and family life are all concerns that we think about differently compared to our parents or grandparents.
- *Mass media and the internet:* the role played by the mass media and more recently the internet in providing us with information and 'ways of thinking' about ourselves, society and politics is constantly changing, and this also has an impact on our social relationships and our sense of identity.

The example of the emergence and spread of McDonald's fast-food restaurants is a useful illustration of what can be done with a sociological imagination. In *The McDonaldization of Society* (2008), the American sociologist George Ritzer argues that going to McDonald's or Starbucks is about more than eating hamburgers or drinking coffee. His analysis shows how the manufacture and sale of hamburgers actually characterises a much broader range of organised social activity. For example, he notes that every step in the process is carefully measured and controlled, from the size of the hamburger to the positioning of the cheese. The way that each outlet is organised and run conforms to a precise formula, including the phrases and facial expressions used when serving customers, as well as the furnishings. The amount of time taken to perform each action is carefully calculated and organised for maximum efficiency.

Ritzer argues that the McDonald's phenomenon reflects one of the key features of social organisation today. Building on the ideas of one of the founders of sociology, Max Weber, Ritzer suggests that the principles behind the McDonald's chain reflect contemporary demands for the *rational organisation of social life*. By this he means the process by which the principles of efficiency, control, predictability and calculability are applied to human endeavours, usually with the aim of financial profit. Not only has this technique allowed McDonald's to be a global success, but its impact as a model beyond the world of eating hamburgers means that it is possible to speak of a much more general process of 'McDonaldization', in which this type of rational organisation of social life is spreading throughout society, not just in the United States, but also across the globe. In this sense, it is also a leading example of a particular way of organising our activities: it is about the **globalisation** of culture and everyday life, and the impact that the rational pursuit of profit has on the everyday human experience.

Like Weber, Ritzer argues that this development is essentially 'tragic', because it creates a sense of meaninglessness within our culture and stifles human creativity and freedom. Although our commonsense approach to understanding eating at McDonald's is to treat it simply as somewhere to have a meal, from a sociological perspective it is also a window onto our culture's tendency to measure, calculate and control human experience in the pursuit of individual and corporate wealth.

SOME BASIC CONCEPTS

The aim of most sociological research, writing and argument is to encourage and develop what is called a **reflexive** consciousness of the ways we are socialised within particular cultural contexts, the social construction of individual behaviour, and the cultural norms underlying what we regard as 'normality', in order to approach social life more intelligently and above all actively, rather than existing as the passive object of surrounding social forces. As you read through this book, you will encounter a wide range of concepts and ideas that are either new or being used in new ways. Much of the process of learning to 'think sociologically' is like learning a new language: the first step is to acquire the vocabulary and grammar.

This section begins the process of acquiring a sociological vocabulary by introducing some of the discipline's basic concepts: social construction, structure, culture, agency, socialisation and identity, modernity and colonialism, and globalisation. Many equally important concepts—especially power and inequality—will be discussed in later chapters.

> **Reflective questions:** What is meant by the idea that sociology is a reflexive discipline? How has this been illustrated by the historical development of sociology?

Social construction

A vital element of the critical analysis of social life that sociologists pursue is the idea of the 'social construction of reality' (Berger & Luckmann 1971). Instead of seeing the social world as 'natural', god-given or based on relatively unchangeable dimensions of human individuals such as their biology, sociologists generally prefer to place more emphasis on the ways in which human behaviour, interaction and social institutions change over time and vary across different social and cultural contexts. For example, to argue that gender is 'socially constructed' is, to begin with, to say that what humans understand and experience as masculinity and femininity is based not only on biology, for the simple reason that the ideas, practices and institutions surrounding gender are different in different historical periods and cultural settings.

The role of language is central to the social construction of reality. It makes an enormous difference, first, whether a name for a phenomenon exists at all and, second, how it is defined. For example, the term 'child abuse' is relatively recent, becoming widespread only in relation to physical abuse in the 1960s and sexual abuse from the 1980s onwards, although the behaviours it refers to have always existed. Another example is what it means to be a refugee or an asylum seeker. This is determined not just by the raw facts of the experience itself, but also by the particular form taken by the concept 'refugee' or 'asylum seeker' and how it is linked to other concepts such as 'migrant', 'dole bludger', 'terrorist' or 'queue-jumper'. Individuals in that situation will adjust their behaviour and choices in relation to such socially determined definitions.

To the extent that any event or thing only exists *in the human world* subject to human perception and forms of knowledge, which are in turn socially organised, the strong version of the argument is that everything is socially constructed, because everything has to pass through the—essentially social—filter of human knowledge production.

Structure and system

The concept of social structure expresses the idea that social formations are organised along patterned lines that endure over time and that act as a constraint on those living within them, even though those people may not be aware of this. When we are born we are not born into a social vacuum but into an existing set of social arrangements that carry with them expectations of how we should behave and that we transgress at our peril. The term 'structure' implies something relatively hard, concrete and immovable, and this association reflects its meaning in sociology.

The recognition of the existence of social structure was central to the emergence of sociology as a distinct discipline. Structuralist perspectives in sociology rest on the assumption that human action should be understood primarily as a product of an underlying *social structure* (or *social system*) composed of a variety of *social institutions*, such as the education system, the family, the economic system, the political system, the mass media, the military and the legal system. A structuralist perspective was nicely captured by the German philosopher Karl Marx when he wrote 'It is not the consciousness of men that determines their being, but, on the contrary, their social being that determines their consciousness' (Marx & Engels 1951, p. 329). The French sociologist Emile Durkheim (1858–1917) agreed, writing that:

> *I consider extremely fruitful this idea that social life should be explained, not by the notions of those who participate in it, but by more profound causes which are unperceived by consciousness, and I think also that these causes are to be sought mainly in the manner according to which the associated individuals are grouped. Only in this way, it seems, can history become a science, and sociology itself exist.* (1897 in Winch 1990, pp. 23–4)

Durkheim used the term *social fact* to express the notion of social structure. He stressed that who we are and how we behave in society necessarily operates within the framework of obligations, expectations and patterns that exist outside of us as individuals. Even if the performance of his duties as a brother, husband or citizen 'conform to my own sentiments, and I feel their reality subjectively, such reality is still objective, for I did not create them; I merely inherited them through my education' (1938, p. 1). He defined social facts as 'ways of acting, thinking, and feeling, external to the individual, and endowed with a power of coercion' (1938, p. 3; see also Chapter 15, pp. 468–9). This did not mean, for Durkheim, that we are all the same; social life is in fact characterised by 'a whole scale of individual gradations'. Nonetheless, 'the area of variations that are possible and tolerated is always and everywhere more or less restricted ... sooner or later, we encounter ... a limit that we cannot transcend' (Durkheim 1964, p. 368).

Structuralist sociology generally makes use of some variety of *functionalist analysis* (so that you may encounter the term 'structural-functionalism'), and it can be divided into *consensus* and *conflict* versions. Often only consensus approaches are seen as functionalist, but in fact there are considerable similarities in the ways in which functionalist and conflict theories approach the understanding and explanation of society; the main difference concerns the way they *evaluate* the existing social order. The question of whether or not a sociological approach is functionalist is really quite different from whether it falls within a consensus or conflict perspective.

CULTURE

Understanding culture—what it is, how it changes, who shapes it and how it relates to other aspects of social life—is central to the sociological imagination. It encompasses much of what sociologists mean by the terms 'social' and 'society', and sociologists will often use the concept of culture as an alternative to biological or psychological explanations of social phenomena. Cultural factors have a great deal to do with both how societies change and how societies are maintained. Cultural dynamics at global, national and local levels contribute both to the establishment of communal feeling within groups and to conflict between them.

The concept of culture has its origins in anthropology, where it was used to refer to human artefacts or creations. The 19th-century anthropologist Edward Tylor defined it as 'that complex whole which includes knowledge, belief, art, morals, law, custom and any other capabilities and habits acquired by man as a member of society' (1891, p. 1). More recently, Abercrombie et al. have described it as 'the symbolic and learned, non-biological aspects of human society, including language, custom and convention, by which human behaviour can be distinguished from that of other primates' (1994, p. 98). This meaning of the word 'culture' is broader than when it is used to refer only to activities associated with refinement, manners and art, or 'high culture'. It stresses the importance of the processes by which meaning is created within a community, which is expressed in a set of values and a way of life that is unique to that community and distinguishes it from other communities. The German sociologist Georg Simmel, for example, analysed what it was that was specific about the cultural life of people living in complex, modern, urban, industrial societies as opposed to life in smaller, traditional, rural settings.

At one level, the importance of culture is obvious. The kind of activities people engage in, the tools they use, the way they earn their living, and their mannerisms and expectations are all shaped by their cultural environment, the ways in which particular meanings are given to all aspects of their lives. At another level, the influence of culture is less apparent. This is the way in which culture shapes our view of the world, influencing the ways in which we think and feel, the outlook we have on life and the meanings we give to situations. Emile Durkheim (1912) pointed this out when he noted that every culture makes assumptions about fundamental phenomena such as relations of time, space and number. These form a framework for the experience of the world and, although they are relative to each culture, they are experienced as absolute, unquestioned truths.

The beliefs that organise people's lives can be seen as constituted by both values and norms. The *values* people hold identify what is worthwhile in life, what they ought to aspire towards—this could include a good education; a well-paid job; having children; living in a city (or a particular part of it); being kind to strangers; a happy childhood; preventing global warming; social equality across lines of gender, class, race and ethnicity; and the fairer distribution of income or wealth around the world. Norms are the translation of values into rules of behaviour about how people should behave, such as that one should not steal, kill other human beings, neglect children or use more energy than one needs to. Sometimes there is general consensus about values and norms, but often there is not, with greater or fewer differences across different social and cultural groups. Values and norms can also be inconsistent and contradictory, and there is not always a direct relationship between values and norms on the one hand and actual behaviour on the other—people often act in ways that contradict their own values and norms. These nuances and complexities about values and norms are an important topic of sociological research.

More recently, sociologists influenced by theories of language have emphasised the way that social life is based on a system of signs and symbols that we unconsciously learn and that give meaning to our world (Baudrillard 1983). These symbols (or signifiers) include language, clothes, smells, physical gestures such as hand waving and images such as traffic lights. The words of a language are symbols that have meaning only in so far as we distinguish them from other symbols, rather than having a direct relationship to the external object to which they are meant to refer. The French sociologist Pierre Bourdieu (1973, 1984) organises much of his work on contemporary social life around the concept of culture, approaching the symbolic realm of language and meaning as central to the sociological analysis of power, inequality and social change. In a wide variety of fields—education, art, sport, the media, politics, social movements, status differences, even warfare—it is clear that power relations operate as much in the world of symbolic interaction as they do through more objective material means. Just as we can speak of the accumulation and unequal distribution of *economic* capital—money, property, stocks and shares—it makes as much sense to speak of the accumulation and unequal distribution of *cultural* capital—education, status, legitimacy, knowledge, information, recognition and fame.

AGENCY

One problem with structuralist accounts is that they tend to suggest that human beings have no control over their lives but simply act according to the requirements of the social structure. Moreover, we need to explain where the structure itself comes from. After all, individuals and groups make up the social structure and it is their decisions and activities that keep the structure going, not some invisible hand pulling the strings of human puppets. The changing position of women during the last century is a good example of this. We can certainly identify structural forces creating opportunities for women—the effects of World War II, the influence of new forms of contraception and the growth of the service industry—but women themselves acted in ways that influenced that change. On the whole, they tended to embrace the opportunity to move out of

> A more adequate representation of social reality would be the puppet theatre, with the curtain rising on the little puppets jumping about on the ends of their invisible strings, cheerfully acting out the little parts that have been assigned to them in the tragi-comedy to be enacted ... We see the puppets dancing on their miniature stage, moving up and down as the strings pull them around, following the prescribed course of their various little parts. We learn to understand the logic of this theatre and we find ourselves in its motions. We locate ourselves in society and thus recognize our own position as we hang from its subtle strings. For a moment we see ourselves as puppets indeed. But then we grasp a decisive difference between the puppet theatre and our own drama. Unlike the puppets, we have the possibility of stopping in our movements, looking up and perceiving the machinery by which we have been moved. In this act lies the first step towards freedom.
>
> (Peter Berger 1963, p. 199)

the home, and a minority of them actively encouraged women's rights, including their freedom to work as equals with men. There was no objective necessity for this to happen, no iron rule forcing women to change their roles.

If the human world is a world of socially constructed meaning in which our actions take place on the basis of shared understandings, this suggests that we are not mechanical dolls blindly following the dictates of social forces, but are reasoning, thinking beings. As the American sociologist Harold Garfinkel argued, the tendency in sociology is often to treat people as 'cultural dopes', by which he meant an individual 'who produces the stable features of society by acting in compliance with pre-established and legitimate alternatives of action that the common culture provides' (1967, p. 68). Garfinkel believed that we construct our own interpretation of our situation and often respond in ways that cannot be reduced to the dull weight of external social forces. These behaviours can be fully explained only by turning to the concept of **human agency**, by understanding how people interpret their situation and negotiate with those around them according to that interpretation and the opportunities available to them. This concern is clear in the sociology of Max Weber and the American symbolic interactionists and ethnomethodologists, and was later given further emphasis by Stuart Hall (1981) and Anthony Giddens (1979b).

In 1970, Alan Dawe argued that there are in fact 'two sociologies': one that asserts the priority of a social system over its participants, organised around the concepts of 'system' and 'structure'; and one that sees social systems as the creation of their members, organised around the concepts of 'action' and 'interaction'. Anthony Giddens (1984) subsequently popularised seeing this distinction between sociologies of structure and action as a central problem in social theory, and this led many sociology textbooks to highlight the difference between the relative emphasis placed on *social structure* as opposed to *social action*. Giddens proposed a way of transcending this dichotomy with his theory of *structuration*, in which he argued that humans are knowledgeable agents who impose their meaning on the world although they are simultaneously constrained by structural forces.

This idea that people are both created by, and the creators of, society is not in itself new, and in many respects Giddens' theory of structuration was a long footnote to Karl Marx's (1818–83) observation that:

> *Men make their own history, but they do not make it just as they please; they do not make it under circumstances chosen by themselves, but under circumstances directly encountered, given and transmitted from the past.* (Marx & Engels 1951, p. 225)

In other words, social formations are the result of human activity and choice, but at the same time this activity and choice is limited by prevailing social arrangements. Or the other way round: human action is constrained by prevailing social arrangements, but those arrangements are themselves the ongoing product of human activity and choice.

Reflective question: Do you think the most important changes going on around you are primarily structural or cultural? What has been the role of human agency in those changes?

SOCIALISATION, THE SELF AND IDENTITY

The concept of socialisation is used to refer to the transmission or reproduction of culture from one generation to the next. It captures the way in which human beings learn to develop patterns of behaviour, experiences and identities relevant to their culture. It is a continuous process that takes place from the moment of every individual's birth until their death.

Both sociologists and psychologists are interested in the process of socialisation, but their level of analysis differs. Psychologists tend to focus on the immediate environment of the individual, such as the influence of the family, whereas sociologists focus on broader social forces operating at the level of institutions and systems, such as the education system, the state, the economy and the media. They are also concerned to demonstrate that socialisation is not a one-way street in which individuals are moulded into a pattern determined by society. Instead, they see it as a complex process in which individuals make choices, react and respond to the influences around them. They emphasise the way we make our world as well as the way we are shaped by it.

Socialisation takes place at many different levels, from learning the characteristics that make us recognisable members of the species to absorbing the patterns of sexuality that are regarded as normal within the community in which we live. At the most basic level, socialisation is about learning to act like a member of the species. Although we take it for granted that communicating through words and walking upright are an essential component of being a human, there is evidence that suggests that these skills are not inherent but are learned through interaction in human communities. This form of learning is universal. Cases of children brought up with limited human contact (feral or 'wolf' children) suggest that without social interaction, human beings lose most of the qualities we associate with our species (Davis 1940). The basic faculties of speech, reason, human posture and movement are discovered only as a result of contact with other human beings through a process of transmission or unconscious imitation. It is only through living in social groups that we become recognisably human.

However, the type of person we become is dependent on the particular cultural context into which we are born. Sociologists use the term **identity** to refer to the constellation of characteristics that people regard as part of their self, including the way they present themselves to others. It is often assumed that our identities are derived from a combination of our genetic inheritance and our psychological development, especially during our first years of life. This assumption is challenged by sociologists who, although they do not deny the role of genetic inheritance, argue that a substantial part of our identity is derived from our social environment. For example, we tend to take it for granted that our education system encourages us to compete with one another and assesses us according to our individual abilities. Yet this **individualism**, which is so pervasive in the social life of Western countries such as Australia, is culturally specific in the same way that our notions of time and space are. Our experience of being male or female is also filtered through a cultural prism. Aspects of our personality that we unquestioningly accept as part of our innermost being have nonetheless been profoundly influenced by our culture's expectations of what it means to be a man or a woman.

In *Ways of Seeing*, John Berger (1972) argued that the portrayal of the nude in classical European painting unconsciously reflects Western cultural attitudes towards women. The women are portrayed as passive objects who are there for the pleasure of the male observer. They present with the self-consciousness and self-awareness of their bodies that is normal for women in our culture. Berger writes: 'Men act and women appear. Men look at women. Women watch themselves being looked at' (p. 47). This is quite different from the portrayal of men, whose bodies are displayed in very different ways, and who are constructed as observers of objects external to them, rather than as being the object of observation. This suggests that women's sense of themselves as objects of desire and men's sense of assertiveness and power are cultural norms, reflected in Western art and culture. It contrasts with the imagery of other cultures, such as Taoist and Hindu societies, in which nudes of both genders are active participants. The way in which this cultural norm regarding the female body has persisted and evolved in response to the feminist movement is analysed by Naomi Wolf (1991) in her book *The Beauty Myth*. Wolf points out how young women today are subjected to ever-stricter standards of beauty, and she examines the linkages between this cultural expectation and the changing expression of power relations between men and women, as well as the functions of the never-ending search for the perfect body and face for a capitalist consumer economy.

MODERNITY AND COLONIALISM

Sociology's concern to understand the social forces that shape contemporary life has led to an ongoing focus on the description and analysis of the key features of contemporary societies, the social trends that have shaped them in the past and that are likely to shape them in the future, as well as the problems and conflicts that they generate. These issues were central concerns of the classical sociologists, including Comte, Marx, Weber, Durkheim and Simmel, all of whom set out to understand what it was that was distinctive about the societies of their time (that is, Western societies, especially Britain, Western Europe and North America), how those societies had developed from their pre-industrial origins and what the destructive effects of that development were, as well as what its likely future direction was.

Sociologists generally use the term **modernity** to describe the complex range of phenomena associated with the historical process, commencing in the 17th century, which saw Western societies change from an agricultural to an industrial foundation, from a feudal to a capitalist economic framework, with most of their populations migrating from rural, village settings to towns and cities, as well as moving beyond Western Europe in the process of colonising much of the rest of the world. The origins of modernity are usually seen as lying roughly in 17th-century Europe before becoming the dominant form of social organisation in the 20th century, radically transforming people's lives—sometimes for the better, but often for the worse—in virtually every part of the globe. Sociologists identify the following features as some of the central components of modernity:

- An economic structure that is both *industrial*—organised around mass production, the increasing use of machines, the ever more efficient use of large reserves of energy—and *capitalist*—based on the never-ending accumulation of *profit* and ever-increasing levels of *consumption*.
- The *nation-state* becomes the principal form of political organisation. The emergence of geographic regions with fixed, stable borders and strong, centralised governments that held ultimate military power within their borders was vital for the development of industry and **capitalism**.
- An increasing adherence to the principles of *rationality*, rather than those of tradition or emotion. Rational principles are those that emphasise the use of logic, observation and experimentation as the basis of what to believe in and what actions to take. This was accompanied by a faith in the power of science to solve society's problems.
- A belief in *progress*. Both human beings and human society are believed to be evolving into a more perfected state in which injustice, poverty and inequality will be eliminated.
- A growing focus on *individuals* as bearers of rights and freedoms, and an increasing recognition of a private sphere of individual choice and preference.
- Paradoxically accompanied by the development of *bureaucracy* and the growing intrusion of the state and other organisations into the daily lives of its citizens.

- The 'export' of all these characteristics of modern society beyond Western Europe through the dynamics of *colonialism*, including to North and South America, India, Africa, Australia and South-East Asia.

The concept of 'modernity', therefore, can be used to capture the whole complex of ideas, political forms, economic structures and cultural patterns that have dominated the first Western societies since the Industrial Revolution and then the rest of the world through colonialism and other mechanisms of modernisation. Sociology is often described as essentially a 'critique of modernity'. (See also the discussion of *postmodernity* below, p. 14.)

GLOBALISATION AND DEGLOBALISATION

Globalisation can be described as the process by which people's daily lives are increasingly influenced by the growing technological and economic, political and legal, social and cultural integration of people and communities around the world. It includes ideas about mass culture, the effects of information technology, the power of global corporations and the growing web of international agreements that change the nature of national sovereignty. Deglobalisation refers to the ways in which globalisation processes can also change direction and go into reverse, so that there are times when the world can become *less* integrated across the dimensions of economics, politics and culture. The period between the two world wars is one example of a period of deglobalisation.

At the cultural level, globalisation is expressed in the idea that today people everywhere are networked into a 'global village' (McLuhan 1962) as a result of mass communication. The World Wide Web is only the most recent example of a set of technologies that have made it possible for people to communicate instantaneously across vast distances, to share ideas, information and feelings. The mass media seem to have created a common culture, with television programs such as *The Simpsons*, *The Bold and the Beautiful* and *Neighbours* being received into the homes of people around the world, from Nepal to Israel. Everywhere roughly the same consumer goods can be purchased: Coca-Cola and Nike are as well-known in Thailand as they are in the United States.

At the political and economic level, the integrity of the nation-state is increasingly challenged by a variety of transnational arrangements and organisations, such as the United Nations, the World Bank and the International Monetary Fund, as well as global corporations like Exxon Mobil, the Industrial & Commercial Bank of China, Walmart, Microsoft, Royal Dutch Shell, BHP Billiton, McDonald's and IKEA. These political and economic organisations all influence the decisions of national governments in ways that directly affect their citizens. A growing number of sociologists such as Wallerstein (1979), Robertson (1992a), Giddens (1990, 2000), Beck (2000d; 2005) and Castells (2000a) have argued that we need to pay more attention to the way that global as well as national forces shape social life. Sociologists generally argue that the trend towards globalisation is today so strong that any understanding of how society works must place it within the global context.

One of the conceptual consequences of this argument is that sociologists need to move beyond the conception of 'society' being contained within the boundaries of the nation-state, so that we speak of 'Australian' or 'French' society. There is an increasingly complex relationship between the global and the local. We need to acknowledge *both* the growing cultural, economic and political integration of contemporary social formations across the globe, *and* the apparently paradoxical strengthening of local ties. While on the one hand our everyday actions are linked to a global environment in which what we do, how we live and even what we think are related to global forces, our actions at the local level also have global implications. The way in which globalisation disrupts local cultures and customs and creates material instability has also led to a reassertion of local traditions and identities. This is reflected in phenomena such as the rise of nationalist movements around the world, the development of community-based organisations, and the shift to regions as the basis for economic development. At the cultural level, the same goods may be consumed by people across the globe (e.g. McDonald's, IKEA, Coca-Cola), but it is possible to argue that their local meaning and significance may be very different. The concept of globalisation is examined in more detail in Chapter 2.

Reflective questions: What do you think are the main differences between the way you have been socialised throughout your childhood and the way your parents were socialised? What does this tell you about the way that society has changed?

SOCIOLOGICAL PERSPECTIVES

We have said that the study of sociology will encourage you to achieve a critical and systematic understanding of the society around you and your place in it. At the same time, it is important to be aware that there is no single, 'correct' way of 'thinking sociologically'. Sociological analysis takes place through an ongoing conversation or debate between a variety of different *perspectives* on any given issue or problem. Sociology, like any science, cannot provide the truth about human society, only a way of understanding it. This may sound surprising or disheartening if you are looking for 'the' truth about anything, but final answers are beyond the reach of any intellectual discipline, including the natural sciences. This is an important aspect of what makes sociology a particularly modern way of thinking about the world, with its constant testing of its knowledge against different ways of gathering and explaining data.

> All knowledge of cultural reality ... is always knowledge from particular points of view.
>
> (Max Weber 1949, p. 81)

In 1962 Thomas Kuhn published a book called *The Structure of Scientific Revolutions*, in which he analysed how sciences change over time. His argument was that scientific activity operates within a single, shared frame of reference, known as a *paradigm*. A scientific paradigm tells us what the problems are, what the solutions are likely to look like, their central characteristics and the methods by which we can go about looking for them. In other words, scientists set problems before they go about solving them, and the type of problem—as well as the way it is defined—establishes the matrix within which scientific activity occurs. A paradigm constitutes a 'way of seeing' the world that affects both what is seen and how it is seen. As time goes by, scientists tend to accumulate evidence or research results that don't seem to fit their understanding of what they should be, until eventually it becomes clear to someone that the basic framework requires reconstruction—what Kuhn called 'scientific revolutions'. The source of scientific dispute is usually the fact that the old paradigm still works reasonably well most of the time and it is not absolutely clear that the new one will work better.

What is true for the natural sciences is even more true for the social sciences, in that a number of paradigms, or what we are here calling 'perspectives', coexist. Although it is possible to distinguish good and bad sociological reasoning and analysis, no one 'way of understanding' the social world can definitively claim superiority over the others. Sociology is best approached not as a single set of undisputed truths (laws, explanations) but as a set of multiple 'ways of seeing', each of which has something useful to say about human beings and social relations, and each with different and distinctive vocabulary, concepts, modes of analysis, explanations and conclusions.

Throughout this book, in every chapter we will familiarise you with the theoretical perspectives that are most important and influential in relation to that particular topic, and they will not always be the same. There are, however, a number of conceptual standpoints that you will encounter more frequently than others, and in this next section we give you an outline of some major issues and debates running through differing sociological perspectives that you are most likely to need to familiarise yourself with.

There are a number of ways, often overlapping, in which we can divide up the field of differing sociological perspectives. For example, a threefold distinction is often made in sociology textbooks between (1) consensus or functionalist theories, (2) conflict theories and (3) interactionist approaches. Recently Michael Burawoy (2004, 2005a) has mapped out four different orientations to the production of sociological knowledge: (1) professional, (2) policy, (3) critical and (4) public sociology (discussed below). In *Perspectives in Sociology*, Cuff, Sharrock and Francis (1990/1979) distinguished between two umbrella perspectives: (1) structuralism and (2) sociological theories of meaning. The first was in turn divided into three sub-perspectives (consensus, conflict and critical theories) and the second into two (symbolic interactionism and ethnomethodology). These theoretical orientations are discussed in Chapter 15, which distinguishes between the foundations of four traditions in sociological theory flowing from Durkheim, Marx, Weber and Simmel, and then explores some more recent developments.

In the following section we will examine Peter Hamilton's (2002) 'mapping' of the field of sociology, where he outlines what he considers to be the three central 'traditions' in sociology—although we could also call them 'perspectives' or simply 'ways of doing of thinking sociologically'.

SCIENCE, POLITICS OR INTERPRETATION

Hamilton distinguishes between three sociological traditions:

1. a 'rational-scientific' tradition, in which sociology is seen as a 'science of society' and 'an intellectual

practice designed to elicit objective information open to scrutiny and debate' (2002, p. 6)
2. a 'political' tradition, in which sociology is seen as 'inherently political because it deals with the organization of society' and the validity of the knowledge produced by sociologists can be established only in practice, in the real world
3. an 'expressionistic' or interpretive tradition, adopting a position detached from both science and politics, taking a more literary or humanities-based approach towards grasping the meaning of human social life, without making any appeal either to the objective validity of its knowledge or to its political effects.

These three perspectives, traditions or approaches are also reflected in the different settings in which sociological work takes place: differing university contexts with varying national intellectual traditions, contract research, and policy research in government and administration. They are not mutually exclusive, in the sense that any particular sociologist or sociological study will often span more than one perspective.

Sociology as science

The question of whether sociology should be approached as the 'science of society' is not entirely settled, but a sociological analysis of any issue or problem is scientific to the extent that it is systematic, by which we mean based on the collection and analysis of information and data, the making of observations that are recorded and compared with each other, the development of theories and generalisations to explain the data, and an overall concern to relate whatever is said by one sociological researcher to the work of other researchers in the same field.

Sociologists often study the same kinds of topics and issues that are dealt with in novels, television series and films, but their claim to be listened to and taken seriously have a different basis. We experience a work of literature as 'good' or 'true' for reasons that are hard to define, on the basis of how well written it is and how well it resonates with our intuitive understanding and feelings. On the other hand, although the quality of writing of a work of science will make a difference to its persuasiveness, the work bases its claim to having any authority on different qualities: how comprehensive, systematic and well-designed its research is, and how well its analysis and arguments stack up against those of competing explanations.

In this perspective, although sociologists have values and normative preferences like everybody else, if they are to mount persuasive arguments in public debate, they need to appeal to different sorts of legitimisation of their ideas. Key figures in this tradition include Emile Durkheim, Max Weber, Robert Merton, Norbert Elias and Pierre Bourdieu. A strong emphasis is placed on providing support for sociological analysis with empirical evidence, and there is sometimes an inclination to see an affinity between the social and the natural sciences. A core aim in this perspective is *value-freedom*, although the exact meaning of this can range from pure objectivity and complete detachment from any conceptual constraints arising from one's social position or value orientation to the more modest version articulated by Weber, which aims for 'little more than that the sociologists should not openly proclaim their personal views on matters of social fact'.

Sociology as politics and critical theory

The critique of the idea of value-freedom is essentially that it simply is not possible—that is, whether social scientists are aware of it or not, they cannot avoid their value orientations structuring the kinds of questions they ask, the topics they choose to research, the silent premises and presuppositions they place beyond discussion, the approaches they adopt, the answers they are more likely to be responsive to, the audiences they direct their work towards, the debates and issues they choose to highlight and so on. A central example here was the tendency to research social life and social history only in terms of the experiences of men, which was always presented as a neutral, objective perspective to adopt, rather than taking the trouble to examine the experiences of women.

From this perspective, the role of sociology is not simply one of accumulating knowledge, but 'one of emancipation and change'. Important inspirations for this approach are two of Karl Marx's Theses on Feuerbach: the eighth, 'All social life is essentially practical. All mysteries which lead theory to mysticism find their rational solution in human practice and in the comprehension of this practice'; and the eleventh, 'The philosophers have only interpreted the world, in various ways; the point is to change it' (Marx & Engels 1970). A key proponent of this approach to sociology was the American sociologist Alvin W. Gouldner (1920–80), beginning with his 1962 article 'Anti-Minotaur: the myth of value-free sociology', where he suggested that 'the only choice is between an expression of one's values, as open and honest as it can be, this side of the psychoanalytical couch, and a vain ritual of moral neutrality which, because it invites men to ignore the vulnerability of reason to bias, leaves it at the mercy of irrationality' (1962, p. 212). The current proponents of this perspective are more likely to refer to their work as 'critical theory', organised around the idea that all social scientific knowledge is produced from a particular value position and social standpoint, and that this always has to be taken into account in assessing its validity and persuasiveness.

Sociology as interpretation

The third perspective is more influenced by anthropology and literature, aiming to interpret and give expression to interesting aspects of social life 'without pretensions to offer scientific knowledge or to claims of political significance' (Hamilton 2002, p. 27). Although in practice sociology and literature have generally been competitors for authority in interpreting the human condition (Lepenies 1988), this approach moves close to the position of the humanities, simply providing a range of possible perceptions of human social experience, distinguished primarily by a variety of narrative orientations. For Hamilton, philosopher Jean Baudrillard's approach to circulating his work 'articles in newspapers, books, lectures, photographs, exhibitions and interviews' is a central feature of the 'expressionistic tradition'. Hamilton sees the work of Georg Simmel and Erving Goffman as key representatives of this perspective and the prevalence of qualitative methods such as ethnography as an indicator of its ongoing presence in sociological research, even if sometimes combined with claims either to scientific validity or critical impact.

Hamilton suggests that these three traditions 'really exhaust the range of possible perspectives about sociology' (2002, p. 27), but invites us to decide for ourselves whether we agree with his interpretation. There are certainly other ways of mapping the sociological field, as indicated earlier, and next we outline two additional important areas of debate that affect the distinctions between different sociological perspectives.

> **Reflective question:** For one example of an important aspect of recent social change, explain how it would be approached differently from the perspectives of sociology as science, as politics and as interpretation. Is there a way of combining all three perspectives?

Gender and feminism

Until the advent of feminist theory in the 1960s, sociology had virtually ignored half of the population—women. This was reflected in the male-centred nature of research as well as the domination of males within the discipline. Despite the presence of female sociologists such as Harriet Martineau (1802–76) in the early days of sociology, as well as the continuing contribution made by women to sociological thought, no women could be found in the sociology hall of fame until relatively recently. Even today it is rare to find a woman in a position of strong influence within the discipline. Professors, writers of textbooks, presidents of sociological associations, journal editors and thesis examiners—the 'gatekeepers'—are overwhelmingly male.

Until recently this gender bias could also be found in sociological thought itself: when sociologists referred to 'people' or 'individuals' they were often referring only to men and leaving women's experience out of the picture. For example, studies of class focused exclusively on men. The position of women was presumed to be determined by their male partner so that stratification studies dealt only with the husband's occupation. The sociology of work and industry ignored the contribution of women's work—both in the workforce and in the home.

The 1960s saw the re-emergence of the women's movement and with it a new generation of female sociologists who placed women at the centre of their analyses of society. In so doing they not only sought to describe the position of women but also provided a range of different explanations for the structured nature of female inequality. This resulted in feminist theory making a major contribution to both sociological theory and sociological methods of research.

Feminist sociologists focus on a range of issues, including:

- the way in which women experience their particular position in social formations, including how they understand and respond to their social situation
- the ways in which women are disadvantaged compared with men
- how gender intersects with other forms of social inequality, including race, class and ethnicity
- the development of concepts and theories that explain how this disadvantage occurs, paying particular attention to the analysis of the power relationships and ideologies that structure gendered social relations.

Feminist sociological theory is examined in more detail in Chapter 15.

> **Reflective question:** Explore the possibilities for developing a feminist sociological analysis of an aspect of the world around you that has changed recently and that does not at first glance appear to be amenable to feminist arguments—say, the 2008/2009 global financial crisis or global warming.

THE QUESTION OF POSTMODERNITY

The perspective known as 'postmodernism' first emerged in architecture, where it was used to describe the transition from the ever-progressing rational application of scientific knowledge to one of playful and ironic mixtures of apparently incompatible elements. The influence of postmodernist arguments now extends to the humanities and social sciences. Although there is not unanimity about how concepts like 'postmodernism' and 'postmodernity' should be understood and used, there is, nonetheless, a common core of ideas that relate to the changes that have taken place in society from about the 1960s onwards.

The concept of **postmodernity** refers to the form of social life in which the enlightenment belief in science, rationality and the idea of progress characterising earlier stages of modernity is no longer unquestioningly accepted. People are less likely to believe in 'grand narratives', such as that reason can conquer superstition, that human beings can be perfected or that political change can produce a perfect society (Lyotard 1984, p. xxiv). Inequality can be explained as an unavoidable component of postmodern society, the pursuit of its elimination often generating different, sometimes even worse problems. This is associated with growing cynicism about the benefits of science, a questioning of the authority of experts, and an associated rise in 'alternative' lifestyles and beliefs. The supposed boundary between science and literature is questioned, and scientific explanation is often approached as another story or 'narrative', a 'truth claim' rather than 'the truth'.

In sociology, this questioning of the directions being taken by modern societies can be understood as centring on the following core observations about how social life works today. First, sociologists need to re-evaluate the importance of the *symbolic* or *cultural* dimensions of the social. Structuralists tend to see the symbolic world of culture and ideology as reflecting the social structures underpinning them, with the latter somehow more 'real' and determining the nature and dynamics of the former. One of the central observations of postmodernism is that this placement of greater weight and significance on structures and material relations has not applied to social life since the middle of the 20th century. Indeed, it is possible to argue that the representations of social reality, particularly in the mass media, have become more 'real', in the sense of more significant, than what they are supposed to represent. This also means that the role of consumption is much more important in postmodernity than it was in modern society: it is no longer our occupation or profession that defines our identity, but the clothes we wear, the beer we drink and the mobile phone we use. The old modernist concepts of the subject, meaning, truth and reality have been replaced by a new world of information, communication and signs (Baudrillard 1983).

Second, it is important to be sensitive to the way that social life today is characterised by the plurality and fragmentation of social forces, making notions of a unified 'society' or 'social structure' difficult to sustain. Class relations may be important in their own terms, but they need not have any influence at all on politics or culture. A structuralist and modernist would assume that someone with a working-class background would present themselves as a unified 'package': this person would vote for the Australian Labor Party, enjoy going to the footy, drink beer (and dislike people that drank wine) and watch *Neighbours* and *The Footy Show* on television. Structuralist theories had assumed that every individual contained a coherent core that responded to external influences in a consistent fashion. As individuals, it was assumed we had a fixed identity that had integrity and uniformity. A **postmodernist,** on the other hand, would see the possible identity 'package' as much more variable and diverse, with no assumed linkages between different aspects of a person's identity. In a postmodern society, a person can be working class, go to the opera, drink wine, and watch both *The Footy Show* and subtitled SBS movies.

The reception of postmodernist ideas in sociology has not, however, been entirely uncritical, and many sociologists see themselves as combining the insights of both modernist and postmodernist sociology. Jürgen Habermas (1996), for example, sees postmodernism as a form of neo-conservatism—its rejection of the metanarratives of rationality and science as a recipe for surrender to existing power relations, and a removal of any basis for genuine critical analysis of social life. (Postmodern sociological perspectives and other approaches to the development of modernity are discussed in greater detail in Chapter 15.)

Reflective questions: Using today's newspaper, which of the perspectives examined above seems most relevant to the material it contains? How would you explain in sociological terms the difference between modernity and postmodernity?

THE DEVELOPMENT OF SOCIOLOGY AND SOCIAL CHANGE

The problems and issues that sociologists engage with are closely related to their particular social and historical context. Sociological thinking changes in association with the development of society itself, not least because sociologists are subject to the same dynamic interplay between the forces of human agency and social structure as are all human beings.

The development of sociology can be divided into a number of phases:

- its origins in the mid-18th century when it was met with optimism as a new science that would help humanity's progress
- its establishment as an academic discipline at the beginning of the 20th century—this phase is associated with the pessimism of this *fin de siècle* (end-of-the-century) period
- an interactionist phase between World War I and World War II
- a functionalist phase from World War II to the early 1960s
- a conflict phase from the mid-1960s to the early 1970s
- the influence of feminism from the 1970s onwards
- increased concern with postmodernity and globalisation
- the question of 'public sociology'.

Each phase can be distinguished by its relationship with the prevailing social, economic and political climate, its key concerns and its view of its status as a science.

SOCIOLOGY'S EUROPEAN ORIGINS IN THE AGE OF REVOLUTIONS, 1840s–1870s

The roots of the sociological imagination in Europe are often seen as lying in the 18th century, in the writings of philosophers such as Hume (1711–76), Smith (1723–90) and Ferguson (1723–1815) in Scotland, Locke (1632–1704) in England, and Montesquieu (1689–1755), Rousseau (1712–78) and Voltaire (1694–1778) in France. However, its 'take-off' period is generally regarded as lying later in the 18th century, when the French philosophers Claude Henri Saint-Simon (1760–1825) and August Comte (1798–1857), who coined the term 'sociology', argued for a 'science of society'.

Two revolutions in this period, the Industrial Revolution and the French Revolution, radically transformed Western societies. Alongside momentous technological changes, the process of industrialisation triggered massive population movements, rapid urbanisation, changing family structures, enormous changes in social relationships and a range of new ideas. It was associated with an increased responsiveness to science and reason as the legitimate foundations for authority, as opposed to the authority of the Church.

The French Revolution paralleled at the political level the effect of industrialisation, shaking the 18th-century European world to its foundations. The slogans of the French Revolution, 'Liberty, Equality, Fraternity', expressed ideals that were to become embedded in Western political culture. Their roots can be traced back to the Enlightenment, which questioned traditional beliefs and prejudices, especially religious ones, and emphasised the importance of reason, strict scientific method and the possibility of progress to a new and better society. This is why this period in European history is often described as the 'Age of Reason'. It was closely associated with the growing secularisation of social life, in which religious thinking and religious institutions ceased to dominate all aspects of life. Until this period, all knowledge had been located within the framework of a Christian understanding of life, its meaning, values and concerns. Most areas of life were also closely tied to the Church, either directly as in the case of education, or indirectly as in the case of the family. Enlightenment thinking challenged both the institutional dominance of the Church and these religious-based ways of thinking. It sought answers to questions of causation (what causes phenomena to happen) by asking *how* they worked, instead of questions of meaning (*why* they worked). This shifted attention from transcendental, supernatural explanations to worldly, material ones.

The impact of a rational, materialist approach to the study of phenomena was not limited to the natural sciences, but began to pervade many other areas of human thought. Karl Marx (1818–83), Herbert Spencer

(1820–1903) and Auguste Comte (1798–1857) sought to apply this rational approach to the analysis of how society worked. The chaos and violence of this period led some people, such as Claude Saint-Simon (1766–1825) and Comte in France, and Marx in Germany, to enquire into the nature and causes of stability and change. They sought to discover the underlying principles behind what they called 'the social' or 'society' in the hope that they could control human destiny more effectively. This attempt to understand the dynamics of social stability and change has remained a central theme in contemporary sociological thought. The aim of a 'science of society' was to facilitate the emergence of a new era based on reason and equality, one that both transcended the superstition and oppression of the past, and developed a form of social organisation that effectively replaced the positive social bonds of pre-modern social life. From its beginnings, sociology has been both a product and a critique of modernity and Enlightenment thought.

This was reflected in the work of the key social theorists including Marx, Spencer and Comte, who each developed evolutionary theories of social change that argued that all societies went through a series of step-like stages of development. In the work of both Marx and Comte, these stages culminated in a utopian or ideal stage in which inequality would be eliminated and humanity would achieve its full potential. They conceived of sociology as a scientific discipline, modelled on the principles of the natural sciences—that is, the use of objective observation, experimentation and measurement of the phenomena being studied. This approach is called positivism and it has remained an important, although criticised, approach to the study of social life (for a discussion of positivism, see Chapter 14). It was closely tied to the expectation that society was subject to the same universal laws that natural scientists had discovered applied in the physical world. For the sociologists of this period, their task was to discover these laws in order to enable people to better understand how they should act. Comte believed that the new scientists of sociology would serve as guides and replace the role played by priests in the past.

Sociology's establishment as an academic discipline, 1880s–1910

In the 1850s sociology had not yet found any academic home. No-one was employed to undertake sociological research and there was no systematic attempt to study society. 'Sociology' existed only in the minds of a handful of brilliant, innovative and sometimes eccentric individuals. In France, Durkheim was appointed to the first Chair of Social Science at the University of Bordeaux in France in 1887, while the German lawyer and economist Max Weber pursued his sociological studies from his position as Professor of Economics at the University of Heidelberg.

The Age of Reason had given way to a more realistic assessment of the benefits of industrialisation and a *fin de siècle* pessimism about the direction society was taking. Although industrialisation had brought material benefits to the population, it was accompanied by an increasing regulation of social life. Industrial development required a high degree of organisation, which was expressed in the *bureaucratisation* of large areas of existence, with their increasing subjection to organisation arranged along fixed, hierarchical lines with written rules and regulations. Weber wrote about the dominance of instrumental rationality in all areas of social life and argued that the price of the fruits of industrial capitalism was that the human spirit was placed within an 'iron cage' of discipline and regulation.

Despite this rather bleak picture of life in the industrialising West at the turn of the 19th century, there remained an expectation that sociology could shed light on what made society work, how it changed and what we needed to do to improve it. The grand evolutionary theories of Marx, Spencer and Comte gave way to an empirically grounded positivism that sought to establish a systematic method for the study of social formations. For Durkheim, society existed *sui generis*—independently of the meanings people brought to a situation. Sociology was about the scientific study of the objective, observable social facts of society. It need not concern itself with how individuals and groups experienced their world. Their *subjective* interpretations of society were of little analytical significance to the sociologist, and in this sense he continued the positivist tradition of his predecessors.

Weber agreed with Durkheim that sociology was the disinterested study of objectively observable phenomena. However, unlike Durkheim, he argued that sociologists should also account for the *meanings* people brought to their situation. Weber's *The Protestant Ethic and the Spirit of Capitalism* (1930) was an example of how a social group's interpretation of the world shaped social development, how Protestantism 'meshed' with the emergence of capitalism. The pessimism of this period also forms the backdrop to Weber's recognition of the limitations of knowledge. He was one of the first writers to point out that all science (including sociology) could do was to tell us *how* something had occurred and what we might do to influence its occurrence in the future. It could not answer the more important questions of what we *should* do or any other question involving a value judgement about what was best for society (Weber 1949).

This period of sociology's development can, therefore, be characterised as one in which sociology established itself as an academic discipline with realistic, achievable claims about its value to society. Its concerns remained those of the earlier period—how societies change, how order is maintained, the nature and causes of inequality, the relationship between culture and economy—but these were set against a backdrop of disillusionment with industrialisation and a concern with its dehumanising effects.

THE DEVELOPMENT OF INTERPRETIVIST SOCIOLOGY, 1920s–1930s

The early decades of the 20th century saw sociology being only slowly introduced into university departments in the United Kingdom and Europe. Where it was introduced, for example into the London School of Economics in 1904, it was closely linked to a reformist political agenda. Most English sociologists saw the discipline as a means of improving the human condition by describing social problems and discovering solutions to them.

Sociology was introduced earlier and more rapidly into the United States, the University of Chicago's Department of Sociology being founded in 1892 and growing rapidly in the 1920s as a result of a generous endowment from the Rockefeller Foundation. This department attracted some of the best social thinkers of the time, including Albion Small, W. I. Thomas, Robert Park and Ernest Burgess. These writers shared a similar social background to their overseas counterparts and, like them, they were concerned with the problems of poverty and urbanisation. Most of them also came from rural areas, and the disorder they encountered in Chicago was in sharp contrast to their previous experiences.

At this time Chicago was a rapidly expanding city, taking in migrants from Europe as well as from the countryside. Rapid industrialisation and urbanisation had created serious social problems, including juvenile delinquency, vagrancy, organised crime and corruption. Gangs operated by crime figures such as Al Capone ran illegal gambling and drinking businesses, often with the cooperation of corrupt police.

Their belief that sociology was an objective science meant that the sociologists at the University of Chicago sought to develop knowledge for its own sake rather than linking it with the direct improvement of social life. In the seamy underside of Chicago city life in the 1920s they had the perfect social laboratory in which to investigate their ideas and develop their theories. The rapid expansion of Chicago resulted from the migration of groups from a diverse range of backgrounds. They included rural Anglo-Saxon Americans, Italians from cities such as Naples as well as from rural regions, Hispanics and Blacks. These subcultures had values and beliefs that were often distinct from those of mainstream society. In order to understand the existence and behaviour of these groups, the Chicago sociologists developed research methodologies that allowed the investigator to experience and give credence to the world of subcultures.

This development was helped by their incorporation of the work of the social psychologist and philosopher George Herbert Mead, as well as other psychologists and philosophers located at the University of Chicago. Mead made a major contribution to the theory of symbolic interaction, which emphasised the way in which the meanings people bring to a situation are socially relevant. He also made the seminal observation that we live in a world of meaning that is socially constructed by active agents through the use of symbols, the most important of which is language (see p. 482). Mead emphasised the extent to which social life is the outcome of an ongoing process of negotiation in which people actively construct their lives and the lives of those around them. This perspective has continued to surface in many forms, including labelling and postmodern theory.

THE DOMINANCE OF FUNCTIONALIST THEORY, 1940s–1960s

The United States continued to dominate developments in sociology after World War II, but the focus shifted from the micro-perspective, which is concerned with social interactions at the level of individuals and small groups, to a macro-perspective, which focuses on large-scale institutions and structures.

The person who dominated sociology in the post–World War II era up until the late 1960s was Talcott

Case Study
Transformations of gender and identity

This image is one of three representing student artist Guy Dempster's 21st century reimagining of the 15th century artist Sandro Botticelli's famous painting *The Birth of Venus*. Botticelli's *Venus* emerges from the sea perched delicately on a seashell. Her femininity is conveyed through the modest placement of her hands and hair, the flowers, the ocean and her passive stance as supernatural beings gather round to guide and protect her.

In recreating a contemporary *Venus*, Dempster not only portrays her as an assertive, self-consciously sexy woman, set against a globalised, urban backdrop, but he also shows how she reinvents herself. In one image from the triptych she is androgynous, in another contemplative and feminine.

Botticelli's nude is located in the cultural context of a male observer and the associated gender inequalities of the time. Dempster's cool and powerful young woman captures contemporary concerns with image and self-invention through fashion. Contrasting his *Venus* with Botticelli's, Dempster explains that his work 'signifies our ability to experience multiple births or "rebirths" during our lives, fuelled by drastic change or transition such as I am currently experiencing in my own birth of independence'.

Dempster's insight is derived from sociological arguments that in the past social identity was largely fixed by collective determinants such as gender, class and ethnicity. Today, globalisation has transformed identity construction to a highly individuated and fluid process, with consumption playing a key role in its establishment. Dempster's understanding illustrates how sociological ideas are absorbed into contemporary thinking and help people to interpret their experiences. This is why sociology must always keep one step ahead of contemporary understandings.

A sociological analysis of Dempster's work provides insights into contemporary social life that go well beyond understanding the transformation of gender and identity. Its display in a public gallery reveals the democratisation of culture compared with the elite status of art in Renaissance Europe, the use of technology in the creation of art, the role of signifiers in conveying social meaning and the *bricolage* quality of contemporary culture where all materials and ideas are acceptable, regardless of their source or original purpose.

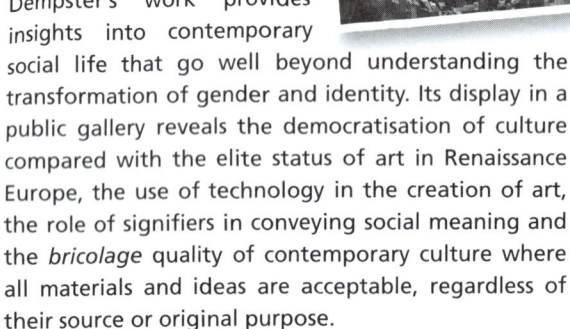

1. Go online to find an image of Botticelli's *Venus* and compare it with Dempster's image. What do the different portrayals suggest about the transformation of gender today, referring especially to the ideas of John Berger and Naomi Wolf? Do you agree with these analyses?
2. Why must sociology 'always keep one step ahead of contemporary understandings'?
3. How are individualisation and consumption linked to the social construction of identity today?

Parsons (1902–79). His dominance and that of the functionalist theory he helped to develop can be explained by locating it within the social context of this period. Parsons' sociology was developed in the economic upheaval of the Depression of the 1930s and the trauma of World War II that followed it. At one of the darkest periods of the 20th century, Parsons sounded an optimistic note with his prediction that the social system not only would survive but also would recover to its former strength. His optimism appeared to be vindicated by the success of the Allies and the prolonged period of affluence that followed. This period was the closest that sociology ever came to having a single set of theoretical principles for the study of social life, leading Kingsley Davis (1959) to assert that **functionalism** was indistinguishable from sociology itself.

Functionalist theories about questions such as the family, politics and social inequality reinforced the values and beliefs of conventional, white, male middle-class America. Parsons argued that in Western democracies, the answer to the question 'How is order maintained?' lay in the existence of a social consensus in which there was widespread agreement on the fundamental social arrangements. His views coincided with a period of political stability and economic security, when few doubted that the enemy was communism and that the United States had God on its side.

THE RISE OF CONFLICT THEORY, 1970s

The political and social conservativism of the two decades following World War II began to crumble in the 1960s. The United States' complacent view of itself was shattered in the face of protest movements that pointed to the continued existence of deep, structural poverty and disadvantage. The black civil rights movement was only one of a number of similar movements that challenged the image of the United States as a land of equality and freedom. The environmental movement pointed out the damage caused by the Western world's high levels of consumption and its technological exploitation of the land. Youth movements in the form of the hippie movement also transformed the cultural scene. These rebelled against the conservative social values of the previous generation and rejected the materialism of American culture. They reacted against the alienation of industrial life, stressing instead human spirituality and creativity. Many of these movements were associated with left-wing politics. They reached their fullest expression in the anti-Vietnam War movement, which drew the American left together in a concerted attempt to get the United States government to withdraw its troops from Vietnam.

These social movements made it very difficult for sociologists to maintain that society was characterised by consensus. The prevailing cultural atmosphere was one of division and disagreement, and it was against this background that different theories began to dominate sociology. This development was fed by the increased availability of Marx's writings, many of which had not previously been available to Western thinkers. These writings were humanistic, emphasising the alienating effects of the capitalist mode of production and stressing human creative self-expression. This, together with Marx's emphasis on inequality and disadvantage, had a powerful resonance with the cultural climate of the day, in sharp contrast to functionalism.

Conflict theory suggests that contemporary Western societies should be seen as based on the exploitation of the many by the few rather than on harmonious consensus, and that they produce social problems that affect everyone. Although conflict theory shared functionalism's focus on social structure as the explanation of social phenomena, it focused on the question of how society changed rather than how order was maintained. It answered this question in terms of structural arrangements for inequality, especially economic inequality in the form of class. It also criticised positivism, arguing that sociologists were part of society and, therefore, could never be disinterested, objective observers.

Many sociologists were influenced by Marxism and were generally critical of the status quo in Western democracies. Its iconoclastic tendencies made sociology popular among young people who were also rebelling against mainstream social values. For the same reason it was often criticised by conservative politicians and public servants who saw it as an irrational and destabilising influence on society. Nonetheless, it was during this period that the discipline underwent its most rapid expansion in universities. This included its establishment in Australia, where Morven Brown was appointed to the first chair in 1959, at the University of New South Wales.

This period can therefore be characterised as one in which sociology both reflected and contributed to the radicalism of the late 1960s and 1970s. The primary focus of sociology was on issues relating to power and social inequality in which the Marxist idea of class was the principal explanatory tool. Consequently, the sociology of this period focused on the male world of work and, from the mid-1970s onwards, on the role of the state in the creation and maintenance of unequal access to resources.

FEMINIST AND INTERACTIONIST SOCIOLOGY, 1970s–1980s

The 1960s saw the resurgence of feminism in many Western societies, including Australia. It was associated with an increasing number of women entering the workforce and higher levels of education. By the 1970s this was reflected in a growing number of female academics whose commitment to feminism was expressed in their work. The work of Oakley (1972; 1974a) and Mitchell (1971) in the United Kingdom, Firestone (1972) and Chodorow (1978) in the United States, and Bryson (1972) in Australia formed part of a growing chorus of voices that pointed to the gender blindness of sociology. Until this time women had rarely figured as either objects of study or producers of knowledge. Their interests, concerns and experiences had been disregarded as irrelevant and unimportant by male academics throughout the history of the discipline. The error of this view was demonstrated by a series of studies on such questions as women's housework, their involvement in crime and their relationship to the state. These offered the discipline a rich seam of knowledge that not only identified new and important areas of interest, but also challenged many of the 'malestream' assumptions about how society worked. Formerly the dynamics of class had been seen as the primary cause of social change. Feminist sociology pointed out that gender was a far more deep-rooted source of inequality affecting all levels of all societies. The concept of class itself was modified. Previously its measurement had treated women as irrelevant, considering only the activities of men. Today most measures of class seek to take into account both women's and men's economic position.

Initially feminist sociology developed within the framework of Marxist conflict theory, partly as a critique of its male orientation and partly as a way of extending and refining it. Over time, however, radical feminist theory developed theoretical concepts of its own, such as patriarchy, which were recognised as making an important independent contribution to our understanding of how society works. The impact of feminist theory has been such that sociology today is no longer gender blind. If either gender is excluded from a study the reasons for this are usually examined and acknowledged as a limitation.

This period can therefore be characterised as one in which women's inclusion in the expansion of higher education, together with their growing involvement in the paid labour force, contributed to sociology's recognition of women's contribution to social life. Sociologists' concerns shifted from asking how men experienced the world to asking how women experienced it, what social forces shaped women's lives and how they made meaning of it. The previous decades' focus on inequality was expanded to include women.

Postmodernity and globalisation, 1980s–2000s

Both Marxist and feminist sociologists had developed critiques of positivist sociology, arguing that because human beings are members of the societies they are studying, they can make no claim to objectivity. The attention of sociologists had also been shifted away from a preoccupation with the economy towards a greater concern with the cultural and symbolic dimensions of society in their own right. If social formations are never static, but are ongoing social constructions resulting from the creative acts of individuals and groups, Durkheim's dictum to treat social life as a social fact is an impossibility. It seemed, then, that the subject of sociological endeavours is not an objectively observable phenomenon, but a world of socially constructed meaning, expressed in symbols.

The concepts of modernity, postmodernity and globalisation have become central to sociological theory and research. Sociology's ongoing concern with understanding the social forces shaping contemporary social life has led to a debate about whether this period, at the turn of the 21st century, is a continuation of modernity or whether the transformations that have taken place since World War II are so great that we are now in a postmodern age. Sociology is about *contemporary* social life and is only of value if its concerns reflect this. Just as the founding figures of sociology such as Marx, Weber and Durkheim concerned themselves with the transformation from an agricultural to an industrial society, sociologists today such as Bauman and Beck are concerned with analysing what is happening now and where current social trends are taking us. This interest shifts the focus of attention from the economy to culture, with the media and entertainment industry and the world of subjective meanings becoming subjected to equally close scrutiny.

Reflective question: What have been the main stages in the development of sociology in Western Europe and North America, and how has this development been linked to surrounding social changes?

Public sociology

The question of differing sociological perspectives and what Peter Hamilton called the 'political tradition' in sociology and the concept of value-freedom has been reinvigorated following Michael Burawoy's 2004 addresses to the North Carolina Sociological Association (Burawoy 2004) and the American Sociological Association (Burawoy 2005a). In these addresses, and a number of subsequent articles developing his argument and engaging in the extensive debate that has been generated, Burawoy outlined his own fourfold typology of sociological perspectives across two dimensions: (1) the question of whether sociological knowledge is seen as *instrumental*—focusing on 'providing solutions to predefined problems' (2004, p. 1606)—or *reflexive*—being 'concerned explicitly with the goals for which our research may be mobilized, and with the values that underpin and guide our research' (p. 1606); and (2) the question of the audience for sociological theory and research, which can be either other sociologists, a purely academic audience or various groups outside the academic world, such as policy makers, contract research clients, interest groups, NGOs, social movements or the general public.

Across these two dimensions, it becomes possible to identify four different sociological orientations, traditions or perspectives—professional, critical, policy and public sociology—each with a distinct approach to the nature and legitimation of valid knowledge, to the audience to which its regards itself as accountable, and with its own characteristic forms of politics and pathologies (see Table 1.1).

For Burawoy, the challenge is not to identify which perspective is to be preferred, but rather to establish an ongoing dialogue between all four. As he puts it, 'I look forward to a unity based on diversity—a unity that incorporates a plurality of perspectives' (2004, p. 1612). However, the bulk of the attention has been paid, including by Burawoy himself, to the concept of public sociology—a dialogue between sociologists and the wider public—partly because Burawoy sees the current sociological world as dominated by professional and policy sociology. Highlighting the key American books that fall into this category, he mentions W. E. B. Du Bois (1903), *The Souls of Black Folk*, Gunnar Myrdal (1994), *An American Dilemma*, David Riesman (1950), *The Lonely Crowd* and Robert Bellah et al. (1985), *Habits of the Heart*, saying what they all have in common is that '[t]hey are written by sociologists, they are read beyond the academy, and they become the vehicle of a public discussion about the nature of US society—the nature of its values, the gap between its promise and its reality, its malaise, its tendencies' (2005a, p. 7).

Burawoy also distinguishes between 'traditional' public sociology, with sociologists simply having a say in public debate or having their research discussed in the media, and 'organic' public sociology, with 'sociologists working with a labor movement, neighborhood associations, communities of faith, immigrant rights groups, human rights organizations' (pp. 7–8). He notes that his particular mapping of the sociological field is particular to the United States and the global North. For example, he notes in relation to this issue: 'When I travel to South Africa, however, to talk about public sociology—and this would be true of many countries in the world—my audiences look at me nonplussed. What else could sociology be, if not an engagement with diverse publics about public issues?' (2005a, p. 21). But for Burawoy this only emphasises the importance for American sociologists at least to exert more effort to institutionalise various forms of public sociology, enabling the discipline to play a more significant and meaningful role in processes of social transformation.

In a world tending toward market tyranny and state unilateralism, civil society is at once threatened with extinction and at the same time a major possible hold-out against deepening inequalities and multiplying threats to all manner of human rights. The interest of sociology in the very existence, let alone expansion, of civil society (even with all its warts) becomes the interest of humanity—locally, nationally and globally. If we can transcend our parochialism and recognize our distinctive relation to diverse publics within and across borders, sociologists could yet create the fulcrum around which a critical social science might evolve, one responsive to public issues while at the same time committed to professional excellence. (Burawoy 2004, p. 1616)

Burawoy's typology of sociological perspectives

	Academic audience	Extra-academic audience
Instrumental knowledge	**Professional sociology**	**Policy sociology**
Knowledge	Theoretical/empirical	Concrete
Legitimacy	Scientific norms	Effectiveness
Accountability	Peers	Clients/patrons
Politics	Professional self-interest	Policy intervention
Pathology	Self-referentiality	Servility
Reflexive knowledge	**Critical sociology**	**Public sociology**
Knowledge	Foundational	Communicative
Legitimacy	Moral vision	Relevance
Accountability	Critical intellectuals	Designated publics
Politics	Internal debate	Public dialogue
Pathology	Dogmatism	Faddishness

Source: Burawoy (2005a, p. 16).

TABLE 1.1

The idea of public sociology has been the subject of considerable debate, and not everyone agrees that it is the best or the only way to understand sociology's position in the world. John Braithwaite (2005), for example argues that the best 'sociology' is in fact profoundly interdisciplinary. Charles Tittle (2004) thinks that public sociology is 'a bad idea because it endangers what little legitimacy sociology currently has, which is precious little' (2004, p. 1641). Tittle argues that by aligning themselves with particular political or normative projects, sociologists lose the one claim they have to intellectual authority and persuasiveness, which is precisely the production of knowledge that is autonomous from politics and morality. Tittle gives the example of a debate in a US state legislature to restore the death penalty, where it became clear that the legislature 'did not regard sociologists or criminologists as scientists, did not believe their research, and most of all, did not trust their motives in interpreting accumulated research and setting forth its implications' (p. 1642). John Holmwood (2007) generally agrees, suggesting that 'political neutrality is central to the corporate organization of sociology, not because social inquiry can, or should be, value-neutral, but because corporate political neutrality creates the space for dialogue and is the condition for any sociology to have a voice' (p. 46). Nonetheless, the basic issue to which Burawoy has drawn attention remains a central concern—for whom and for what purposes is sociological knowledge actually useful, and to what extent do sociologists need to converse with more people than just each other?

> **Reflective questions:** How do you see the relationship between the four approaches to sociology identified by Michael Burawoy: professional, policy, critical and public? What are the arguments for and against the idea of public sociology?

AUSTRALIAN SOCIOLOGY

Sociologists form an international community, sharing a vocabulary, broad conceptual frameworks and research concerns. However, there are also specific features of the types of sociology practised in different parts of the world that make it possible to distinguish between the different sociological perspectives within that international community.

Specific features of Australian history and society make it possible to examine sociological theories, developed in different social and historical contexts, in ways that generate a uniquely Australian sociology. The history of white Australian society as invading and dominating Aboriginal society, the country's period as a British penal colony and then a colony of British immigrants, the particular relationship between state and society in Australia, the multiculturalism generated by successive waves of migration, the particular pattern of urbanisation and suburbanisation, class and gender relations, Australia's geopolitical and cultural relationship with other countries—all these characteristics of Australian culture, history and society are arenas in which sociological arguments can be developed and, at times, challenged.

HISTORY

Sociology first gained a significant presence in Australian universities in its own right as late as 1959, when the first chair in sociology was filled by Morven Brown at the University of New South Wales in Sydney. In 1961, the Australian National University in Canberra established a sociology department in its Research School of Social Sciences, after a period of growth in sociological research in the Research School of Pacific Studies since 1950. The professional organisation for Australian sociologists was formed in 1963, initially as the Sociological Association of Australia and New Zealand and taking its present form of The Australian Sociological Association (TASA) in 1988. The discipline's Australian journal, originally the *Australian and New Zealand Journal of Sociology* and now the *Journal of Sociology*, was founded in 1965.

The philosopher Francis Anderson introduced sociology to the University of Sydney in 1909, teaching it as part of the Bachelor of Arts course in 1909 and 1910, and then as part of the master's program until 1925; and the economist R. F. Irvine argued along positivist lines for the establishment of sociology in Australia. The Workers' Educational Association (WEA) began teaching sociology in 1913, when Meredith Atkinson was appointed director of tutorial classes at the University of Sydney. Atkinson moved to the University of Melbourne in 1918 where he taught sociology as part of the WEA program until his resignation in 1922. He was followed by John Gunn, who taught a version of sociology increasingly oriented towards psychology and eugenics.

Throughout the 1920s, Australian universities continued to ignore the example of their American counterparts and made no serious attempt to develop sociological teaching and research. In some sense this reflected Australia's ties to the British university system, where sociology was also growing only slowly. Jerzy Zubrzycki (1971), however, argued that the relative stability of Australian society generated less interest in the study of social problems and social policy. Leading economists such as D. B. Copland had little respect for sociology as a discipline in general, or for the work of Atkinson and especially Gunn, thus laying the foundations of a dispute between economics and sociology that continues to this day. While on an international tour, Copland wrote that he found 'great scepticism about sociology' (cited in Bourke 1988, p. 58), and on his return the course was dismantled at the University of Melbourne. At the University of Sydney, however, the anthropologist A. P. Elkin supported sociology and, between 1945 and 1950, a significant component of sociological theory and research methods was taught as part of the anthropology program, producing a number of graduates who later came to be employed as sociologists. Sociology has also been part of the social work, education and law curriculums at a number of universities, and these three professions can be counted among the important stimulants for sociology teaching in Australia.

Helen Bourke pointed out that economists dominated the social sciences throughout the first half of the 20th century, being far more successful in responding to the dominant political discourse. Economists, she wrote, 'achieved their ascendancy in the social sciences and in national life because they did serve the existing and growing needs of central government' (Bourke 1988, p. 60). The sociologists who did attempt to have a broader impact on public life found that their discipline failed to engage with the current political concerns.

Australian society, and particularly university education, was to change dramatically in the 1960s, enabling the interests of university students to play a greater role in determining the character of university teaching and research. As a result, the teaching of sociology and sociological research expanded considerably during the 1960s and 1970s, coinciding with the general growth in universities during this period. The growth of sociology in the 1960s and 1970s was concentrated in the newer universities and colleges: the University of Adelaide and the University of Western Australia still have no distinct sociology program, the University of Sydney began its program in 1991, and the University of Melbourne began teaching sociology in first year in 1995, based in the Department of Political Science. Sociology also forms an important part of a number of professional programs, including education, social work, nursing and the allied health professions. In this relatively short period, sociology has established a fairly secure place in Australian intellectual life, producing a steady stream of graduates and postgraduates and, at times, influencing public debates.

AUSTRALIAN SOCIOLOGICAL RESEARCH

The range of research interests that engage Australian sociologists has developed over time: a core of topics that continue to attract attention is accompanied by new areas developed in response to changes in Australian society. The core topics include class, gender and ethnicity; the Australian state, social welfare and social policy; health and illness; patterns of migration and settlement; the family, childhood, domestic labour and fertility; the media, communications and culture; and urban, rural and community studies.

One way to get a sense of the scope of the work undertaken by Australian sociologists is to look over the list of the 10 most influential books in Australian sociology that emerged from a survey of the members of TASA in 2003 (Skrbis & Germov 2004). Out of 66 nominated books, the following were the top 10, in rank order:

1. R.W. Connell (1977), *Ruling Class, Ruling Culture: Studies of Conflict, Power and Hegemony in Australian Life*: on class and class consciousness in Australia
2. M. Pusey (1991), *Economic Rationalism in Canberra: A Nation-building State Changes its Mind*: a study of Canberra's senior public servants and the way in which state bureaucrats had shifted from a welfare-state discourse to economic rationalism
3. A. Summers (1975, 1994 and 2002), *Damned Whores and God's Police: The Colonization of Women in Australia*: on the hidden role of women in Australian history, and the cultural duality between 'damned whores' and 'God's police'
4. R. W. Connell (1987), *Gender and Power: Society, the Person, and Sexual Politics*: an analysis of the power relations built into gender and sexuality
5. R. W. Connell (1995), *Masculinities*: a study of masculinity as a social construction and its intersection with class, ethnicity and race
6. R. W. Connell, D. W. Ashenden, S. Kessler and G. W. Dowsett (1982), *Making the Difference: Schools, Families and Social Division*: a study of the class dimensions of the school system
7. B. Turner (1984 and 1996), *The Body and Society: Explorations in Social Theory*: an outline of how

individual concerns and social dynamics are experienced through our bodies; the role of the body in identity formation
8. A. Game and R. Pringle (1983), *Gender at Work*: on the way in which the workplace is a central site for the social construction of gender and gender relations
9. E. Willis (1983 and 1989), *Medical Dominance: The Division of Labour in Australian Health Care*: a study of the medical profession and its relationship to various forms of inequality
10. J. Braithwaite (1989), *Crime, Shame and Reintegration*: on the role of shame in crime control and the possibilities of less punitive forms of social integration.

The size of Australia's population relative to that of the United States, the United Kingdom and Western Europe produces a comparatively small marketplace for sociological writing and research, making it more difficult to find publication outlets for studies that focus specifically on Australian society. Consequently, Australian sociologists often look to Europe, the United Kingdom and, to a lesser extent, the United States for new and leading theoretical developments.

However, the traffic is not all one way. Sociologists located in Australia who have an impact on theoretical developments in sociology worldwide include:

- Raewyn (formerly R. W.) Connell on class, education, gender and social theory, especially 'southern theory'
- Stephen Castles on migration, citizenship and multiculturalism
- Jack Barbalet on the sociology of emotions and economic sociology
- Anna Yeatman on citizenship, public policy and state formation
- John Braithwaite on corporate crime, punishment, new modes of regulation and restorative justice
- Bryan Turner on sociological theory, religion, globalisation and the body
- Sharyn Roach Anleu on deviance and social control, as well as the sociology of law
- Gary Wickham on Foucault and law, sociology and politics, and state formation
- Anthony Elliott on social theory, psychoanalysis, cosmetic surgery, and self and identity in a globalised world
- Michael Pusey on the state, economic rationalism and the middle class
- Stewart Clegg on power and organisations
- Jan Pakulski, Stephen Crook and Malcolm Waters on postmodernity, Pakulski and Waters on class and Waters on globalisation
- Mitchell Dean on poverty and contemporary forms of government
- Barry Hindess on power, governance and colonialism
- Peter Beilharz on social theory.

There are also many Australian sociologists who make less visible but nonetheless important contributions to international sociological discussions. (For a useful overview of sociology in Australia and New Zealand, see Baldock 1994.)

Sociologists have stopped talking about 'society' in a general, abstract sense and are giving increasing recognition to the specifics of geographical location, history and culture. As we move further into the 21st century, the old divisions between the core and periphery of the sociological community are likely to become increasingly irrelevant, so that Australian sociologists will continue to develop their presence in the world sociological community.

Connell provided perhaps the best perspective on how Australian sociologists can and should see themselves in relation to the rest of the world when she argued for a 'locally based social science with the capacity to speak globally ... both internationally, and between or across social locations in a region' (1991, pp. 74–5).

Reflective question: In what ways do you think Australian sociology should be different from the sociological research undertaken in other countries? In what ways should it be the same?

Tutorial exercises

1. Outline the main features of modernity and give a 'balance sheet' of its positive and negative effects. Include a reference to globalisation and deglobalisation.
2. Australia can be described as a settler-colonial society. What aspects of its history as a British colony, and as a colonised continent occupied by Aboriginal people, do you think distinguishes social life in Australia from that in other countries?
3. Create a table with two columns. Think of a social issue that interests you, such as youth homelessness, mobile phone etiquette, body piercing or internet dating. In one column identify some commonsense explanations for the social issue and in the other identify some of the ways a sociologist would examine and explain it.
4. Give some other examples of private troubles/public issues and explain what difference it makes to analyse them as public issues.
5. Sociologists often claim that their discipline can help comprehend a changing world. What are some of the more important changes currently taking place, and how might sociology contribute to a different understanding of them?
6. Do you think the world is being 'McDonaldised'?

For activity suggestions, learning aids, revision of key concepts and access to self-study material, visit: **www.pearson.com.au/highered/vankrieken4e**

Further reading

Abercrombie, N., Hill, S. & Turner, B. 2006, *The Penguin Dictionary of Sociology*, 5th edn, Penguin, Harmondsworth.

Bauman, Z. & May, T. 2001, *Thinking Sociologically*, 2nd edn, Blackwell, Oxford.

Charon, J. M. and Vigilant, L. G. 2009, *The Meaning of Sociology*, 8th edn, Pearson/Prentice Hall, Upper Saddle River, NJ.

Hamilton, P. & Thompson, K. 2002, *The Uses of Sociology*, Blackwell Publishing, Oxford.

Hodgson, D. 2008, *Pressing Questions: Explorations in Sociology*, 5th edn, Pearson, Sydney.

Mills, C. W. 2000, *The Sociological Imagination*, Oxford University Press, New York.

Willis, E, 2004, *The Sociological Quest*, Allen & Unwin, Sydney.

Sociology Writing Group, 2007, *A Guide to Writing Sociology Papers*, 6th edn, Worth Publishers, New York.

Websites

Australian Bureau of Statistics (ABS):
www.abs.gov.au
The website of Australia's official statistical data collection agency contains social surveys of Australia and some analyses of many different aspects of Australian social life, including social trends as well as some helpful articles. Some of the information is free, some involves a fee. Many libraries subscribe to the ABS, so full access to ABS material can be gained through them.

Australian Institute of Family Studies:
www.aifs.gov.au
This is the website of Australia's agency for research into family matters. It contains research, publications and links on the family and related areas of Australian social life.

Australian Social Science Data Archive:
http://assda.anu.edu.au
This is the social science data archive, which is the main repository of sociological survey research in Australia. Data from quantitative studies and reports are available, although sometimes there is a fee.

International Sociological Association (ISA):
www.isa-sociology.org
The site for the international professional association of all the world's sociologists, providing information about forthcoming conferences, the activities of all the ISA's research committees, fellowships, grants and prizes, the Junior Sociologists network and publication opportunities.

Intute Social Sciences: Sociology (UK):
www.intute.ac.uk/socialsciences/sociology
This useful gateway site collects Web resources in a wide range of sociological subject areas such as communication and work, as well as internet material covering many sociologists.

Reinvention: a Journal of Undergraduate Research:
www2.warwick.ac.uk/fac/soc/sociology/rsw/undergrad/cetl/ejournal
This online, peer-reviewed journal is dedicated to the publication of high-quality undergraduate student research. It is produced, edited and managed by students and staff at Oxford Brookes University and the University of Warwick. It is published bi-annually and only houses papers written by undergraduate students.

Sociosite: Social Science Information System based at the University of Amsterdam:
www.sociosite.net
Run by Albert Benschop in Amsterdam, this site presents the resources and information that are important for the

international sociological scene. It links students of sociology to many interesting sociologically relevant locations in cyberspace. The site offers a comprehensive information system that is very easy to use and has become a popular guide for social scientists all over the world.

The Australian Sociological Association:
www.tasa.org.au
This site has information about the professional association of Australian sociologists, as well as helpful links to sociology resources in Australia and overseas.

WWW Virtual Library: Sociology:
http://socserv2.mcmaster.ca/w3virtsoclib
This website provides summaries of major sociological theories, sociology newsgroups and chat rooms and has a huge number of links to sociological resources throughout the world.

2
Globalisation

Globalisation is a term that has captured the popular and academic imagination since the 1980s. It is often used to explain a multitude of social and other phenomena and it is therefore difficult to specify with any clarity exactly what globalisation means or refers to. This chapter addresses the key themes, concepts and debates that characterise sociological and other discussions on globalisation.

By the end of the chapter, you should have a better understanding of:
— the key elements of the sociology and history of globalisation
— the technological and economic, political and legal, and social and cultural dimensions of globalisation
— the social movements that contest and resist globalisation
— the critiques of globalisation discourse.

INTRODUCTION	**28**
'SOCIETY' BEYOND THE NATION-STATE	**30**
Measuring globalisation	31
THE SOCIOLOGY OF GLOBALISATION	**33**
World-systems theory—Immanuel Wallerstein	35
The compression of the world—Roland Robertson	35
The consequences of late-modernity—Anthony Giddens	36
Techno-capitalism and inequality—Manuel Castells	37
Technology and inequality	38
A HISTORY OF GLOBALISATION	**38**
Six waves of globalisation—Göran Therborn	39
The first wave, 300–600	39
The second wave, 1500–1600	39
The third wave, 1700–1850	40
The fourth wave, 1850–1918	40
The fifth wave, 1940–70	40
The sixth wave, 1980–present	40
TECHNOLOGICAL AND ECONOMIC GLOBALISATION	**42**
International economy and globalised economy	43
The size and scope of the global economy	44
Class and global capitalism	44
Neoliberalism	45
A brief history of neoliberalism	45
Neoliberalism and globalisation	47
The limits of global capitalism	48
The brink of a global economy	48
Beyond benign economism	49
The poverty debate	49
The globalisation of poverty	49
Wealth for whom?	51
POLITICAL AND LEGAL GLOBALISATION	**51**
The withering away of the state?	52
Global governance	53
The globalisation of law	55
Law and globalisation	55
Global law	55
American hegemony	57
The limitations of hegemony	57
The decline of American hegemony—Wallerstein	57
CULTURAL GLOBALISATION	**58**
Cultural homogenisation	58
The McDonaldisation of Society—George Ritzer	59
Efficiency	59
Calculability	59
Predictability	60
Control	60
The irrationality of rationality	60
The Starbuckisation of society	61
Jihad vs McWorld	61
Clash of civilisations	61
Cultural heterogeneity	62
The global production of difference and hybridity	62
Glocalisation	64
IN SEARCH OF DEGLOBALISATION	**64**
The anti-capitalist movement—Alex Callinicos	65
The emergence of anti-capitalism	65
No Logo—Naomi Klein	66
Brands not products	66
Promoting the superbrand	67
Culture jamming	68
The World Social Forum and deglobalisation	69
CRITIQUES OF GLOBALISATION THEORY	**70**
Globalisation as Northern Theory—Raewyn Connell	70
Mechanisms of exclusion, projection and erasure	71
Globalisation beyond the metropole	71
CONCLUSION	**72**
Tutorial exercises	73
Further reading	73
Websites	73

INTRODUCTION

In August 2007, the *Daily Telegraph* published an article explaining the ways in which the fate of the Seed family in the southern Sydney suburb of Rockdale is bound to that of the Smith family in Little Rock, Arkansas, in the southern United States. Alongside a photograph of the Smith family, the article said: 'This American family's mortgage is one of the reasons you face a home loan rate rise—regardless of what the Reserve Bank does.'

The Smiths wanted to buy a house, but the banks would not loan them the money, because Mr Smith runs a removalist business and his income fluctuates. So, the Smiths borrowed the money from a subprime mortgage broker instead. It is not clear from the article whether the Smiths then defaulted on their loan, but the implication is that they did (as did many others), playing their part in the collapse of the US mortgage market, with all its flow-on effects to financial institutions around the world, including the Commonwealth Bank and RAMS Home Loans in Australia. It didn't make much difference whether an institution had direct linkages with the US subprime mortgage market, as RAMS did, or not, like the Commonwealth Bank: the cost of lending money had risen. This in turn affected the interest rate that the Seed family paid on their mortgage. Mrs Seed was quoted as saying: 'It's not our fault, what is happening in America; it shouldn't have anything to do with what is happening to us. We're in a totally different country.'

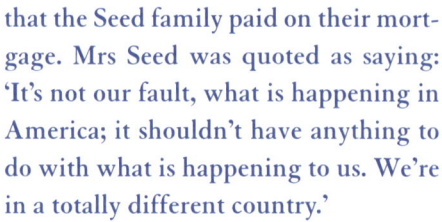

Perhaps this is globalisation at work, when what is happening in the United States or China or Venezuela *does* have a lot to do with what happens to a family living in a suburb of Sydney.

1. When people talk about globalisation, they are often concerned with both the positive and negative effects of this intensified interconnectedness of many parts of the world's population. Can you think of other examples of such interconnectedness around the world? Or counter-examples, where groups of people are isolated and insulated from what is going on in the rest of the world?
2. Is there any kind of relationship between connectedness and isolation?

Source: Balogh, S. & Jones, G. 2007, 'Stars and gripes over US loans', *Daily Telegraph*, 16 August 2007.

Today, it is difficult to give serious consideration to any issue or question to do with human social, political, cultural or economic life that does not include at least some engagement with its global dimensions and with its location within ongoing longer term processes of globalisation. Even many people who are sceptical about global warming accept that 'climate change' is an urgent issue requiring coordinated worldwide action, because no part of the world can isolate itself from the effects of activities elsewhere. If a new strain of influenza appears in one part of the world, the extent and intensity of global travel is such that it spreads around the whole world in a matter of days. When the American economy sneezes, the whole world catches a financial cold. Germs, carbon emissions, information, money, people, goods and services now move around the world at such speed that it is difficult to think of any aspects of social life in purely local or national terms.

We have become used to thinking of economic activity as global, but many families are also spread around the world, political action takes place as much in world forums as it does in national parliaments or congresses, and cultural innovations spread around the world as quickly as viruses.

Thinking globally is not in itself especially new. The 'world religions' are so-called for a reason: Islam and Christianity have a long history of universalistic ambitions to encompass the whole world's population. The various political ideologies—liberalism, socialism, communism, fascism—have also never confined their aims to any particular nation-state. Karl Marx and Friedrich Engels famously exhorted: 'Workers of the world, unite!'

But the concept of *globalisation* is more recent, and it has become, at least since the end of the Cold War, central to our way of thinking about social life, poli-

- 'Formerly the things which happened in the world had no connection among themselves. Each action interested only the locality where it happened. But since then all events are united in a common bundle.'
  (Polybius, 2nd century BC, *Universal History*, cited in Kohn 1971, p. 121)

- 'Inexorably, hesitantly, terrible as fate, the great task and question is approaching: how shall the earth as a whole be governed? And *for what* shall "man" as a whole—no longer as just one people, one race—be raised and bred?'
  (Friedrich Nietzsche 2003, section 37[8], p. 31)

- 'With the improvement of communication and the growth of commerce, Humanity is rapidly becoming, physically speaking, a single society—single in the sense that what affects one part tends to affect the whole.'
  (LT Hobhouse 1906, p. 331)

- 'All distances in time and space are shrinking. Man now reaches overnight, by plane, places which formerly took weeks and months of travel. He now receives information, by radio, of events which he formerly learned about only years later, if at all … The peak of this abolition of every possibility of remoteness is reached by television, which will soon pervade and dominate the whole machinery of communication.'
  (Martin Heidegger 1971, p. 165)

- 'No one, I think, will dispute the fact of a global system.'
  (Niklas Luhmann 1997)

In 1996, Paul Keating (Federal Treasurer 1983–1991, Prime Minister 1991–1996) was attempting to understand the feelings of discontent that appeared to lend support to the rise of Pauline Hanson and the One Nation party when he spelled out what he called the 'price we pay' for globalisation:

At its core is the loss of identity and spiritual frameworks wrought by the rolling tide of forces we wrap up in convenient catch-alls like 'globalisation': the feeling that many of us have that our lives are increasingly beyond our individual control, that our cultural signposts are changing without our consent; that old definitions and boundaries are blurring; that the world is becoming an alarmingly small place, but also, paradoxically, moving beyond a human scale. Essentially, the old certainties are passing. There is a feeling that … modern life is leading to a greater sense of isolation … that employment is insecure; that structural change leaves uncompensated losers in its wake; that the absence of widely shared and binding social and national values leaves people feeling disconnected and searching for some greater meaning in their lives. (Keating 1999)

1. Do you think Keating's description of the world today rings true for you and the people you know?
2. Are some people more comfortable with globalisation than others? Why?

tics and economics. The concept has transformed every social science discipline, becoming the new all-purpose conceptual container for almost every idea, argument or ideal—a kind of social scientific Swiss Army knife. In many respects this has itself become a problem: although globalisation can be a useful social scientific concept, its self-evident character can lead to intellectual laziness, and it is often used in an *ideological* way—as an argument for a particular kind of globalisation, for free trade and neoliberalism (see below, p. 45), but also for the environmental movement in encouraging people to heighten their awareness of their ecological interconnectedness.

Much of the public discussion of globalisation is marked by the idea that individuals and local, regional and even national bodies and authorities are being increasingly deprived of control over their own affairs—the idea that it inevitably means loss of sovereignty and loss of control to impersonal, large-scale abstract forces manipulated by an unknown power.

If globalisation is often understood as though it is something done *to* people by forces that are beyond human intervention, this feeling is not surprising, given that many of the key decisions and events that affect our lives are indeed made by people and processes far removed from our direct experience. But in fact it is possible to understand what globalisation entails, its history, its structure and dynamics, and its various strands and themes.

How, then, can we think about globalisation sociologically? How do we explain the forms taken by the globalisation process? How should we think about some of the major debates and issues, themselves also global, which affect us all? Is globalisation a good or a bad thing for social life, for the pursuit of fairness and justice around the world, indeed for happiness itself? Does it really mean a loss of sovereignty to shadowy groups of faceless power brokers? Does it ever change direction and become deglobalisation? Where does all the opposition to globalisation come from?

'SOCIETY' BEYOND THE NATION-STATE

The first sociology textbook published in Australia, in 1965, was *Australian Society: A Sociological Introduction*, written by A. F. Davies and Sol Encel. The focus on Australian society captures an essential feature of sociological thinking throughout most of the 20th century, what Ulrich Beck and Nathan Sznaider (2006) have called **methodological nationalism**, which they describe as follows:

> ... it equates societies with nation-state societies and sees states and their governments as the primary focus of social-scientific analysis. It assumes that humanity is naturally divided into a limited number of nations, which organize themselves internally as nation-states and externally set boundaries to distinguish themselves from other nation-states. And it goes further: this outer delimitation as well as the competition between nation-states, represent the most fundamental category of political organization. (p. 3)

They argue that the mistake is to equate the fact that social life has been organised into the 'container' of the nation-state form with a core category of sociological analysis, 'society'. All the central concepts in social science—class, family, the state, power, democracy, law, history, politics and, of course, 'society' itself—need to be rethought on a global scale. They must 'be released from the fetters of methodological nationalism, re-conceptualized, and empirically established within the framework of a new cosmopolitan social and political science' (2006, p. 6).

The concept 'global' is at least 400 years old and most likely emerged around the time of the Copernican revolution, when the view of the world as a globe emerged (Waters 2001, p. 2). More recent use of the word 'globalisation' in terms of a process (*isation*) did not emerge with any real academic significance until the mid- to late 1980s, with few academic articles published before the mid-1990s referring to globalisation as a process. The word was first used in English in 1962 in an article in *The Spectator* discussing American anxiety about Britain joining the European Economic community, where Charles A. Cerami wrote: 'After so long privately chiding the French for their fear of *mondialisation*, the Americans are struck by the thought that globalisation is, indeed, a staggering concept' (1962, p. 495).

Robbie Robertson (2003) suggests that a form of conscious awareness and intent to globalise, which is referred to as **globalism**, did not really emerge until just after World War II. Since the early 1980s, and more

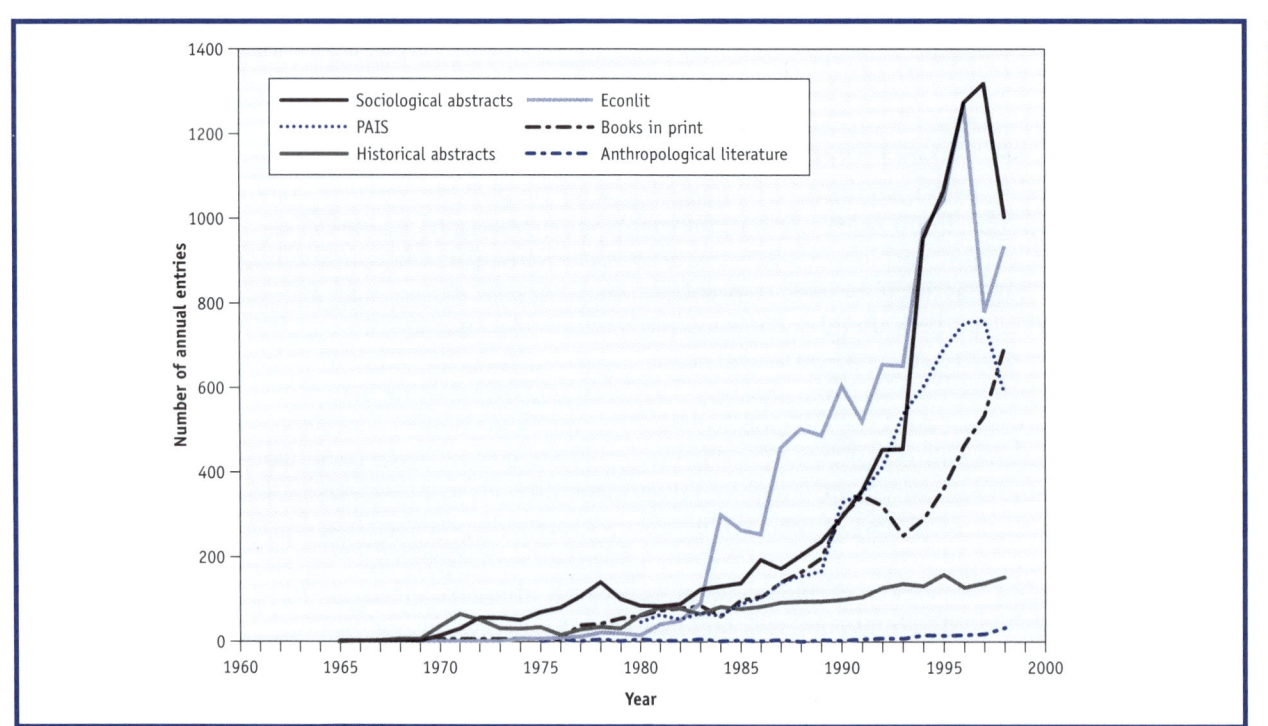

FIGURE 2.1

Social science publications on globalisation Source: Guillén (2001, p. 241). Reprinted, with permission, from the *Annual Review of Sociology*, Volume 27 © 2001 by Annual Reviews www.annualreviews.org.

Definitions of globalisation

- 'the processes by which the world is being made into a single place with systemic properties'
  (Robertson & Lechner 1985, p. 103)

- 'the intensification of worldwide social relations which link distant localities in such a way that local happenings are shaped by events occurring many miles away and vice versa'
  (Giddens 1990, p. 64)

- 'the increasing acceleration in both concrete global interdependence and consciousness of the global whole in the 20th century'
  (Robertson 1992a, p. 8)

- 'simply the intensification of global interconnectedness ... the multiplicity of linkages and interconnections that transcend the nation-states (and by implication the societies) which make up the modern world system'
  (McGrew 1992, pp. 63, 65)

- 'tendencies to a worldwide reach, impact, or connectedness of social phenomena or to a world-encompassing awareness among social actors'
  (Therborn 2000, p. 154)

- 'the process through which an ever-expanding free flow of goods, services, capital, peoples and social customs leads to further integration of economies and societies worldwide'
  (Sharma 2008, p. 1)

- 'an achievement of advanced capitalism and technological innovation seeking a world free from restraints on the opportunity to invent and to invest ... in which size and scale in terms of numbers of persons (who can produce), and in numbers of outlets (to disseminate and place the products), and capital (to purchase both labor and land) determine the capacity to saturate local cultures'
  (Silbey 1997, pp. 219–20)

- 'a process (or set of processes) which embodies a transformation in the spatial organization of social relations and transactions, generating transcontinental or interregional flows and networks of activity, interaction and power ... the widening, intensifying, speeding up, and growing impact of world-wide interconnectedness'
  (Held et al., n.d.)

- 'the process of creating networks of connections among actors at multi-continental distances, mediated through a variety of flows including people, information and ideas, capital and goods ... a process that erodes national boundaries, integrates national economies, cultures, technologies and governance and produces complex relations of mutual interdependence'
  (Dreher 2006, p. 1092)

prolifically the 1990s, the volume of publications referring to globalisation has increased dramatically. The volume of publications referring to the dramatic increase in publications on globalisation has increased dramatically too—including this one, of course (see Figure 2.1).

Reflective question: How would you define globalisation?

Measuring globalisation

There are a number ways in which we can measure globalisation. For example, the AT Kearney/*Foreign Policy* Globalisation Index identifies four dimensions of globalisation: political engagement, personal contact, technological connectivity and economic integration. It gathers data on international travel, international phone calls, cross-border remittances and other transfers, the number of internet users, the number of internet hosts and secure servers, the changing share of international trade in each country, the convergence of domestic and international prices, inward- and outward-directed foreign investment and portfolio capital flows, and income payments and receipts. Another widely used measure, the KOF Index of Globalisation, has been developed by Swiss economist Axel Dreher and his colleagues (see http://globalization.kof.ethz.ch). Following Keohane and Nye (2000b, p. 4), Dreher (2006, p. 1092) divides globalisation into three distinct but interrelated dimensions:

- *economic globalisation*, characterised as long-distance flows of goods, capital and services, as well as information and perceptions that accompany market exchanges. Its measurement is divided into two categories: (1) actual economic flows—data on trade (the sum of a country's exports and imports), foreign direct investment and portfolio investment (the sum of a country's stock of assets and liabilities), income payments to foreign nationals and capital; and (2) restrictions to trade and capital—hidden import barriers, mean tariff rates, taxes on international trade (as a share of current revenue) and capital controls.

- *social globalisation*, expressed as the spread of ideas, information, images and people. Its measurement is divided into three categories: (1) *personal contacts*—international telecom traffic (traffic in minutes per person), the amount of tourism (incoming and outgoing), government and workers' transfers received and paid (in percentage of GDP), the stock of foreign population, and the number of international letters sent and received; (2) *information flows*—the number of internet users (per 1000 people), the share of households with a television set, and international newspapers traded (in percentage of GDP); and (3) *cultural proximity*— imported and exported books (relative to GDP), the number of McDonald's restaurants and the number of IKEA stores.
- *political globalisation*, characterised by a diffusion of government policies. It is measured by the number of embassies and high commissions in a country, the number of international organisations to which the country is a member, the number of UN peace missions the country has participated in and the number of treaties it has signed with one or more states since 1945.

The KOF Index indicates a gradual increase in the extent of aggregate globalisation according to these measures since 1970 (see Figure 2.2). This shows the degree of political **deglobalisation** in the period between 1983 and 1991, as well as the broader general trends across all dimensions.

The KOF Index also ranks countries according to their degree of globalisation, and this highlights the enormous diversity and disparities that the aggregate figures conceal, although the overall trend is generally similar. The difference in rankings of a selection of countries for 2009 is shown in Table 2.1.

There are clear disparities across the dimensions in which particular countries and regions are more or less globalised. The United States, for example, ranks quite low overall—only 59th for economic globalisation, below Kazakhstan (40th), Botswana (46th) and Mongolia (55th), and 56th for social globalisation below the United Arab Emirates (31st), Samoa (39th) and Belarus (54th). Over time, the trends have been different for different parts of the world (see Figure 2.3).

The more important general principles that you need to keep in mind when thinking about globalisation, then, include:

- The most recent phases of globalisation processes involve a significant increase in both the scope and intensity of interconnectedness and interdependence, with the following characteristics: deterritorialisation, interconnectedness, speed, depth and **multidimensionality**.
- Globalisation is not a state, but a set of processes that need not be aligned with each other.
- Globalisation processes can change direction, so that there are also processes of deglobalisation.
- The time frame makes a difference. An upward trend from a particular point in time, such as the 1970s or World War II, needs to be placed in the context of what went before, and trends can move in waves—downwards as well as upwards.

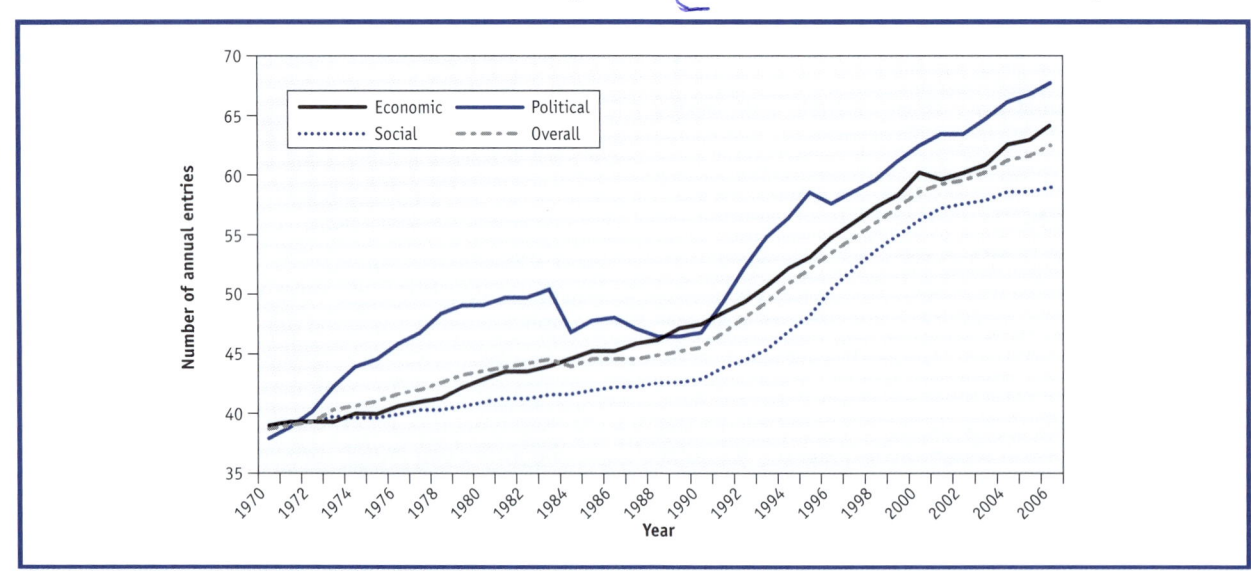

FIGURE 2.2

KOF Index of Globalisation, 1970–2006 *Source*: KOF Index of Globalization (http://globalization.kof.ethz.ch/).

TABLE 2.1

Degree of globalisation according to the KOF Index of Globalisation, selected countries, 2009

	Overall	Economic	Social	Political
Ireland	2	3	3	36
The Netherlands	3	6	15	11
France	16	35	28	1
New Zealand	12	15	12	57
Australia	26	33	37	23
United Kingdom	27	29	19	77
United States	38	59	56	9
China	91	83	118	38
Indonesia	100	67	136	44
India	122	120	137	20

Source: KOF Index of Globalization (http://globalization.kof.ethz.ch/).

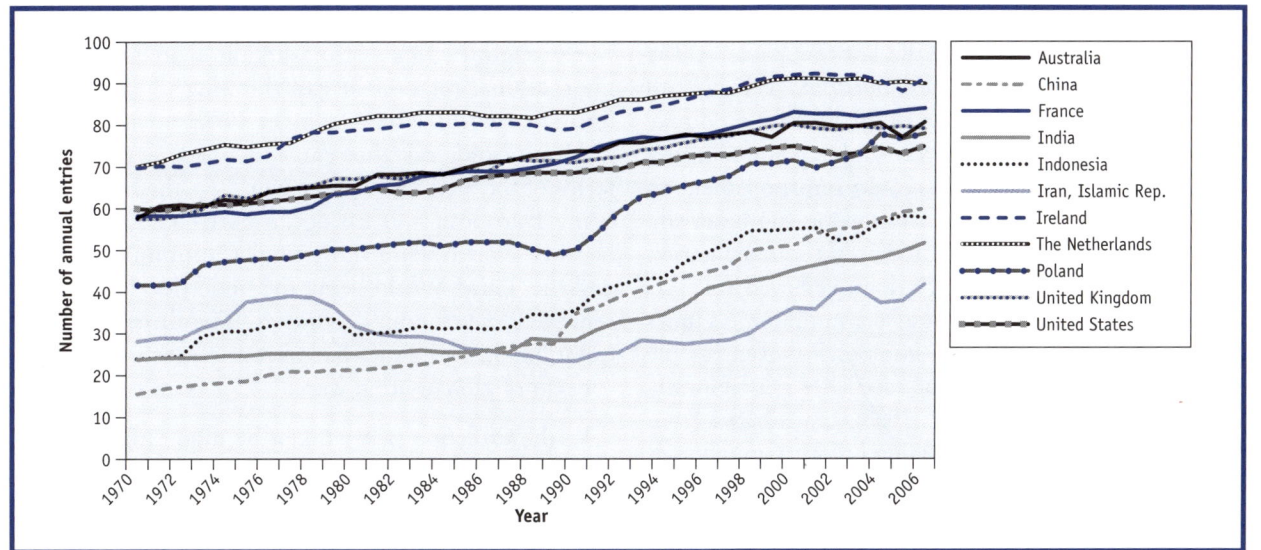

FIGURE 2.3

KOF Index of Globalisation, ranking trends for selected countries, 1970–2006 *Source:* KOF Index of Globalization (http://globalization.kof.ethz.ch/).

THE SOCIOLOGY OF GLOBALISATION

Bryan Turner (1990) and Roland Robertson (1992a) have pointed out that the early sociologists (Marx, Durkheim, Saint-Simon and Weber) centred much of their work on what is now referred to as globalisation, but in ways quite different from how it is presently understood. They made only tacit reference to the *globalising* potentials of modernity we now experience, despite the sweeping social and industrial changes of their own societies that they attempted to understand. Globalisation was conceived largely in terms of the internationalisation or the universalisation of existing nation-states. The primary boundaries of their investigations remained within the confines of the nation-state, particularly as nationalisation was a powerful project of the time (Robertson 1992a, pp. 15–17). This emphasis on the nation as the boundary of analysis was largely due to the dual processes of globalisation (understood as internationalisation or cosmopolitanism) and nationalisation. Robertson refers to this as the 'Janus-faced problem' confronting early sociology. In other words, given the salience of the idea of a bounded nation-state, it was only when the divisions between internal and external started to significantly blur that an interdisciplinary sociology of the global emerged (Robertson 1992a, p. 16).

Nonetheless, contemporary sociological analysis of the global owes a lot to the early sociologists' work, which outlined important ideas, concepts and a clear paradigm of thinking and framing the concept of society and social change at a global level. Durkheim's comparative studies of suicide, religion and the state, and Simmel's emphasis on the micro-social, cultural, interpersonal and symbolic, for example, are not in principle imprisoned within methodological nationalism.

There is much, then, in the history of sociology that can be invigorated to analyse the global present. Two examples stand out, and there are repeated references to their work in many discussions of globalisation. The first is Max Weber, who recognised that aspects of modernity, such as bureaucracy and rationality, would inevitably come to dominate all human activity, with largely undesirable consequences. In the last few pages of *The Protestant Ethic and the Spirit of Capitalism*, Weber (1930) considers that the mechanisms of the modern economic order involved forcing people into a dehumanising bureaucratic machinery that would imprison them in a cage of repetitive work and mundane consumerism. These themes resonate even today: the rationalisation and bureaucratisation of work is dominant even in a post-Fordist economy, and righteous consumption occupies most people's lives in Western societies. For example, the bureaucratic rationalisation of social life is graphically portrayed by George Ritzer (2008), who draws from Weber to explain the globalisation of a certain mode of doing business and sociality, which Ritzer refers to as McDonaldisation (see below, p. 59).

Second, the globalising potential of an expanding capitalist economy did not go unnoticed by Karl Marx and Frederick Engels, who observed in *The Communist Manifesto*:

> *The need for a constantly expanding market for its products chases the bourgeoisie over the surface of the whole globe. It must nestle everywhere, settle everywhere, establish connections everywhere.* (1967, p. 83)

Since the collapse of the Soviet Union in 1991, it appears that capitalism has triumphed in the ideological war against socialism and can now enfold the entire globe in its embrace, in many respects fulfilling Marx and Engels' prediction. Wallerstein (1979) draws heavily from Marx in conceptualising a capitalist world-system, and Sklair (1995; 1999; 2002) also mobilises a Marxist conceptualisation of class and an ideology of consumerism to explain the global. Indeed, drawing from the roots of Marxist and Weberian traditions in sociology can be useful to develop a strong conception and, in fact, a reconsideration of the political, economic, hegemonic, ideological, democratic and individual aspects of modernity and globalisation (Nash 2000).

In 1966 the American sociologist Wilbert Moore wrote an article titled 'Global sociology: the world as a singular system', where he argued that there were two reasons why sociologists should pay more attention to what different parts of the world had in common: first, the 'rather remarkable concurrence in the ideology of economic development, despite differences in technique and, often, despite differences in the more ultimate goals to which this essentially instrument goal is to be directed'; and second, Moore felt that the diversity that one could observe resulted from 'accidental *and eclectic* combinations from pools of options that are essentially worldwide in scope' (1966, p. 481).

Although the fields of marketing, management and international relations began thinking increasingly in terms of a world-system from the 1970s onwards (Levitt 1983), sociological thought remained structured in terms of the concept of 'three worlds'—the First World being European and European-derived countries, the Second World being those with Communist regimes and the Third World being the underdeveloped (later renamed 'developing') countries. The three dominant questions in sociology that were the precursors to the concept of globalisation were:

1. the direction being taken by modernisation, and whether it should be understood as post or late modernity
2. the notion of the convergence of industrial societies and whether socialist and communist countries should be understood in terms of state capitalism
3. the question of pathways to modernisation and the 'development' of the Third World.

In 1985, Robertson and Lechner observed that although there had been some steps taken towards thinking in terms of the whole world, sociologists were 'still struggling analytically towards a fully global paradigm' and on the whole 'the concern with modernity (or, in slightly different but still very significant form, modernism) has not been coordinated analytically with the phenomenon of globalism' (1985, pp. 104, 106). Immanuel Wallerstein's 'world-systems theory' was the notable exception. At around the same time, Scott Lash and John Urry's *The End of Organized Capitalism* (1987) was published which, even though their primary theme was the nature of capitalism rather than globalisation, drew attention to many of the core features of the globalisation process. But it took until the demise of communism in the 1990s before most sociologists were persuaded that fundamental distinctions should not continue to be made between the basic social, economic, political and cultural orders of each of the 'three worlds'.

WORLD-SYSTEMS THEORY— IMMANUEL WALLERSTEIN

American sociologist Immanuel Wallerstein traces the historical development of the world-system, from feudalism to capitalism, and sees the world as a total system that has historically (back as far as the 16th century) and more so presently (from the 19th century onwards) been driven by an evolution of capitalism (Wallerstein 1979). Capitalism, for Wallerstein, is a 'historical social system' (1983, p. 13) and the history of that system will eventually culminate in its demise. Drawing heavily from Marx, he sees the world as comprising the structural components of capitalism that have their own evolutionary logic. For Wallerstein, even in 1979 there was only one world and that world was capitalist:

> *There are today no socialist systems in the world-economy any more than there are feudal systems because there is only one world-system. It is a world-economy and is by definition capitalist in form. (Wallerstein 1979, p. 35, original emphasis)*

For Wallerstein (1979; 1983; 1984), the world can be analysed in terms of a single global economic system that comprises a number of interdependent, but unequal, elements: the core, the periphery and the semi-periphery. The movement from feudalism to capitalism involved the development of regional placement in the world-economy. Those regions at the core of the capitalist economy benefit most from the world-system. They are those nations/regions that are most developed technologically and governmentally. The less-developed periphery acts as a feeder of raw materials and cheap labour into the core, which further enhance the core's economic and political power. In short, the core exploits those nations on the periphery of the capitalist system. The semi-periphery lies between the two extremes of core and periphery and, while it is exploited by the core, it also exploits the periphery. Tensions, inequalities and system-wide contradictions are therefore *inherent* in the world-system due to its structural design, a design that benefits certain component parts of the system while disadvantaging others. The development of the global capitalist system does not, and perhaps cannot, advantage all equally; it is inherently biased towards advantaging the core. By seeing the world as a whole, and one that is connected by a world-economy, Wallerstein is able to analyse its historical development, which includes the struggles and tensions between classes, states, race etc. and the process of progressive accumulation and exploitation (Hopkins & Wallerstein 1996).

According to Wallerstein (1996) and true to the Marxist foundation he draws from, the crisis and future demise of the capitalist world-system will be brought about by the inherent contradictions in the system. Wallerstein examines the historical nature of capitalism as a world-system, and out of that he attempts to trace a couple of present and future scenarios. Although Wallerstein does concede that predictions of the future are not inevitable, even those based on good social science, his analysis can be useful for attempting to explain the complexities of the present moment.

Wallerstein argues that global capitalism moves in *Kondratieff* cycles of expansion and contraction, each cycle lasting between 45 and 60 years (Hopkins & Wallerstein 1996, p. 9). The most recent expansion phase occurred between World War II and the early 1970s, after which it entered into a contraction phase. Hegemonic cycles follow this pattern but lag behind and tend to last longer. Using the concept of *Kondratieff*, which refers to waves or cyclic patterns in the economy, Wallerstein (1996) attempts to map possible trajectories for the world-system up to the year 2025. He argues that one possibility is that the *Kondratieff* phase would begin to swing upwards into an economic boom period, carrying with it the existing hegemony, contradictions, tensions and inequalities inherent in the system. The second and more likely possibility is the 'burgeoning of a systemic crisis or bifurcation, which would manifest itself as a period of systemic chaos, the outcome of which would be uncertain' (p. 226). Either way, Wallerstein's work provides a strong theoretical critique against the view that progressive economic liberalisation will bring lasting prosperity and peace to the world. Wallerstein's theory suggests that such a view is inherently false. As such, it provides a theoretical basis for anti-capitalist politics.

THE COMPRESSION OF THE WORLD—ROLAND ROBERTSON

Although Wallerstein argued that sociological thought should be organised in terms of a world-system, he did use the term globalisation. The American sociologist Roland Robertson (Nettl & Robertson 1968; Robertson 1983; Robertson & Lechner 1985) was an important early pioneer in the sociology of world society and processes of globalisation, and his work is widely quoted in the literature. Robertson emphasises that globalisation is a complex phenomenon that cannot be reduced to any particular or easy-to-grasp idea, force, framework or perspective. He argues that globalisation must be appreciated in terms of consciousness, culture, the relationship between the universal and the particular, nostalgia, and increases in interconnectedness that are a part of (but not reducible to) modernity.

Robertson conceives globalisation as referring 'both to the compression of the world and the intensification of consciousness of the world as a whole' (1992a, p. 8). The central concepts 'compression of the world' and 'intensification of consciousness' are important ideas that Robertson indicates operate within a 'global field' (p. 25) or 'global human condition' (p. 27) that contains 'four major reference points' (p. 25). These reference points are:

1. national societies
2. selves
3. world-system of societies
4. humankind (pp. 25–7).

These reference points are held within the global field in terms of the 'problematics' of:

1. shifting complexities rather than fixed interdependency
2. relativisation rather than stability
3. discontinuities rather than integration of the relationships.

These reference points, Robertson argues, comprise complex interrelationships and he is critical of any sort of one-dimensional account of globalisation. For example, he feels it should not be seen 'simply as an aspect of outcome of the Western "project" of modernity or, except in very broad terms, enlightenment' (p. 27). For Robertson, seeing globalisation as complex and dynamic, as totalising and, at the same time, particular poses the greatest challenge and opportunity for a study of the global (p. 188).

The consequences of late-modernity— Anthony Giddens

In *The Consequences of Modernity* (1990), Anthony Giddens locates globalisation within the context of 'late'

Global shrinkage?

The image in Figure 2.4 is frequently used to represent the 'shrinkage' of the world as the costs associated with travel and the time required for travel have declined. However, it is based on the optimum speeds for land, sea and air travel, and critics have pointed out that transportation improvements are not equally distributed around the world (Knowles 2006). It is possible that some parts of the world may have shrunk more than this, whereas others may have stayed the same or even 'expanded' in terms of their time/space and cost/space relationships.

Can you think of any examples of parts of the world that have come closer together than others, and parts that may have experienced far less time/space compression?

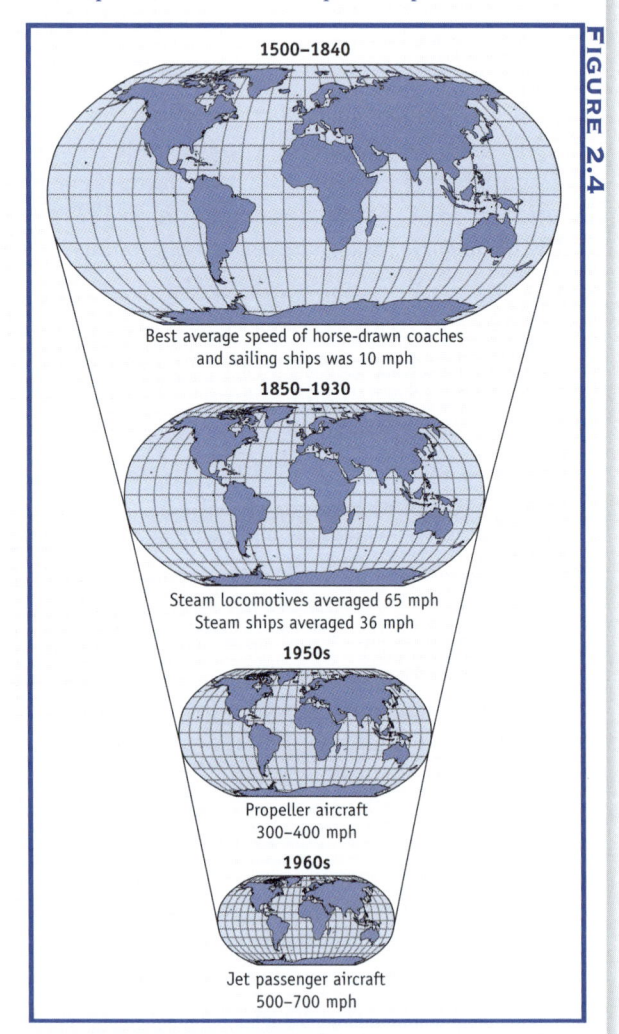

FIGURE 2.4

1500–1840
Best average speed of horse-drawn coaches and sailing ships was 10 mph

1850–1930
Steam locomotives averaged 65 mph
Steam ships averaged 36 mph

1950s
Propeller aircraft 300–400 mph

1960s
Jet passenger aircraft 500–700 mph

Global shrinkage: the effects of changing transport technologies *Source:* Dicken (1992, p. 102, Figure 4.3). Reproduced by permission of SAGE Publications, London, Los Angeles, New Delhi and Singapore. © PC Chapman, London, 1992.

or 'high' modernity. Giddens' overall thesis is that globalisation is an extension of modernity. He rejects the idea that we have entered a purely postmodern era in terms of a distinct break or the superseding of modernity. Rather, Giddens sees that the period of modernity, originating from the 17th century in Europe, has in recent times intensified and become more universal and intentional (pp. 3–4). He argues that traditional sociological theories have as yet failed to fully grasp or explain modernity; and to fully understand modernity requires a more robust appreciation of the dynamics of globalisation (p. 16). For Giddens, late modernity and globalisation are characterised by an intensification of the following:

- *The separation of time and space.* Giddens refers to this in terms of developing a uniformity of time, which allows a 'precise time-space "zoning" of social life' (p. 16). Another way to think about this idea is in terms of 'a phenomenology of contraction' (Waters 2001, p. 15), in which increases in the speed and scope of transport and communication tend to render the world a 'smaller' place, and concepts of time, such as the calendar year, become generalised (Waters 2001, p. 15; Giddens 1990, p. 18).
- *Disembeddedness.* By this Giddens means the '"lifting out" of social relations from local context of interaction and their restructuring across indefinite spans of space-time' (p. 21). The local and contained is now subjected to processes of reconstruction that transcend time and space. What was once perhaps a confined local activity is now penetrated by and, as such, reconstructed by distant events.
- *Reflexivity.* This is the process whereby 'thought and action are constantly refracted back upon one another', so that 'social practices are routinely altered in the light of discoveries which feed into them' (p. 38). The enlightenment goals of untainted and undiluted knowledge that lead to progress, order and predictability can never truly be attained, for the very process of coming to that knowing is its undoing, and certainty and predictability are not possible.

By drawing from these particular features of late modernity, Giddens then explains the transactional and dialectical nature of globalisation:

Globalisation can thus be defined as the intensification of worldwide social relations which link distant localities in such a way that local happenings are shaped by events occurring many miles away and vice versa. This is a dialectical process because such happenings may move in an obverse direction from the very distanciated relationships that shape them. Local transformation is as much a part of globalisation as the lateral extension of social connections across time and space (p. 64).

Such intensification and speed of local and global transformations, as well as the dimensions of late modernity Giddens outlines, means that social life is experienced increasingly as becoming out of control, fraught with risk and yet, at the same time, full of opportunity and potential. Giddens' view of late or high modernity is relatively optimistic, in the sense of still believing in the possibilities of being able to 'steer the juggernaut' (p. 154) that is late modernity. He argues for a 'utopian realism' (pp. 154–8) that involves a politicisation of the local and the global in relation to an emancipatory politics or, as he states, a *'life politics or a politics of self-actualisation'* (p. 156, original italics). These politics would ideally be achieved through a range of social movements, which would potentially temper the emerging risks of high modernity: risks such as the 'collapse of economic growth mechanisms, growth of totalitarian power, nuclear conflict or large-scale warfare, ecological decay or disaster' (Giddens 1990, p. 171, from Figure 7).

TECHNO-CAPITALISM AND INEQUALITY—MANUEL CASTELLS

A different kind of emphasis can be found in *The Rise of the Network Society*, where Manuel Castells (2000a) explores the rise and development of information and communications technologies in relation to the globalisation of the economy. Castells explains that a new economy has emerged based on information, globalisation and networking. He argues that capitalism has moved from a world economy to a global economy through the development of technological innovation, along with the privatisation and deregulation of economic policies under the general banner of neoliberalism. For Castells, a global economy is 'an economy whose core components have the institutional, organizational, and technological capacity to work as a unit in real time, or in chosen time, on a planetary scale' (p. 102). This informationalism 'alters, but does not replace, the dominant mode of production' (p. 211). Capitalism is still alive and well. Rather than the basic unit of capitalist organisation being the individual or nation-state, however, it is the network of disparate but interconnected individuals and organisations—a 'virtual culture' (p. 214)—that will transform the nature of work and employment. Under these conditions, work becomes 'post-industrial'. It becomes specialised yet diversified, technical and high skills based, service and retail oriented, fragmented, flexible and unstable, and managerial. Some industries will be retrenched while new ones will be generated. However, this retrenchment/generation process will proceed unequally and there will be concentrated unemployment in some areas and growth in others as the labour force becomes increasingly polarised.

Technology and inequality

It is the extent of this polarisation and destabilisation that is explained in Castells' *End of Millennium* (2000b; see also Harvey 1990). Castells argues that the Information Age is beyond state control and new tensions are emerging between state power and the power of global capital. We now see a new and rapacious form of global capitalism that is capable of encompassing all parts of the globe, but at the same time excluding millions of people from the potential of economic growth and informationalism. Riding on the back of the Information Age, global capitalism is 'intertwined with rising inequality and social exclusion throughout the world' (p. 68). In particular, these social inequalities involve a deepening polarisation between the haves and the have-nots and a deepening of poverty and misery. It occurs especially in regions that have recently had their economies and peoples devastated by war, famine, economic decline etc., but also in the generation of fourth-world conditions in the most wealthy and economically advanced countries such as the United States. As Castells explains:

> *Globalisation proceeds selectively, including and excluding segments of economies and societies in and out of the networks of information, wealth, and power that characterize the new, dominant system. (p. 165)*

As he concludes *End of Millennium*, Castells emphasises how information technology underpins socioeconomic structures and dynamics, and sees it as 'allowing the development of networking as a dynamic, self-expanding form of organization of human activity. This prevailing, networking logic transforms all domains of social and economic life' (pp. 367–8).

Clearly, technological development is an important dynamic in how we understand and experience globalisation. It would be wrong to simply conclude that technology is the only force behind globalisation and, as such, the single explanatory variable behind a host of social, political and economic changes. Castells demonstrates that technological developments need to be seen in historical and social context and in *relation to* the unfolding of a global economy, including the relative shifts and reconstructions of power, politics and the state.

> **Reflective question:** How would you outline and compare the approaches of the four main theorists examined here: Wallerstein, Robertson, Giddens and Castells?

A HISTORY OF GLOBALISATION

One of the central points of debate about globalisation is the extent to which it should be seen as a new or recent phenomenon, and whether we should see ourselves as entering an entirely new kind of society. Many of the more breathless accounts will proclaim the uniqueness of contemporary global society, but there is considerable dispute about whether we are witnessing the unfolding of very long-term processes of development or are experiencing a sharp rupture with past ways of organising human social, political and economic life.

There are now a number of accounts of the history of globalisation, including Robbie Robertson's (2003) *The Three Waves of Globalisation*, Roland Robertson's (1992a) discussion of five phases of globalisation and Christopher Chase-Dunn et al.'s (2000) analysis of three waves of trade globalisation since 1795.

Robbie Robertson's account identifies three waves: (1) from the 16th century to the end of the 18th century, (2) the Industrial Revolution of the 19th century and (3) the period after the end of World War II in 1945. Roland Robertson's history sees the first 'germinal' phase as running from the 15th century to the mid-18th century, the second 'incipient' phase from the mid-18th century to the late 19th century, the third 'take-off' phase from the late 19th century to the 1920s, the fourth 'struggle for hegemony' phase from the mid-1920s to the 1960s, and the fifth 'uncertainty' phase from the late 1960s to the present. Chase-Dunn and his colleagues identify three post-1795 waves of trade globalisation, the first running from the middle of the 19th century to peak in the 1880s, the second a smaller wave between 1905 and 1929, and the third running from 1945 to the present (see Figure 2.5).

However, the account we focus on here is the one presented by Swedish sociologist Göran Therborn, partly because he looks also to the period before 1500,

FIGURE 2.5

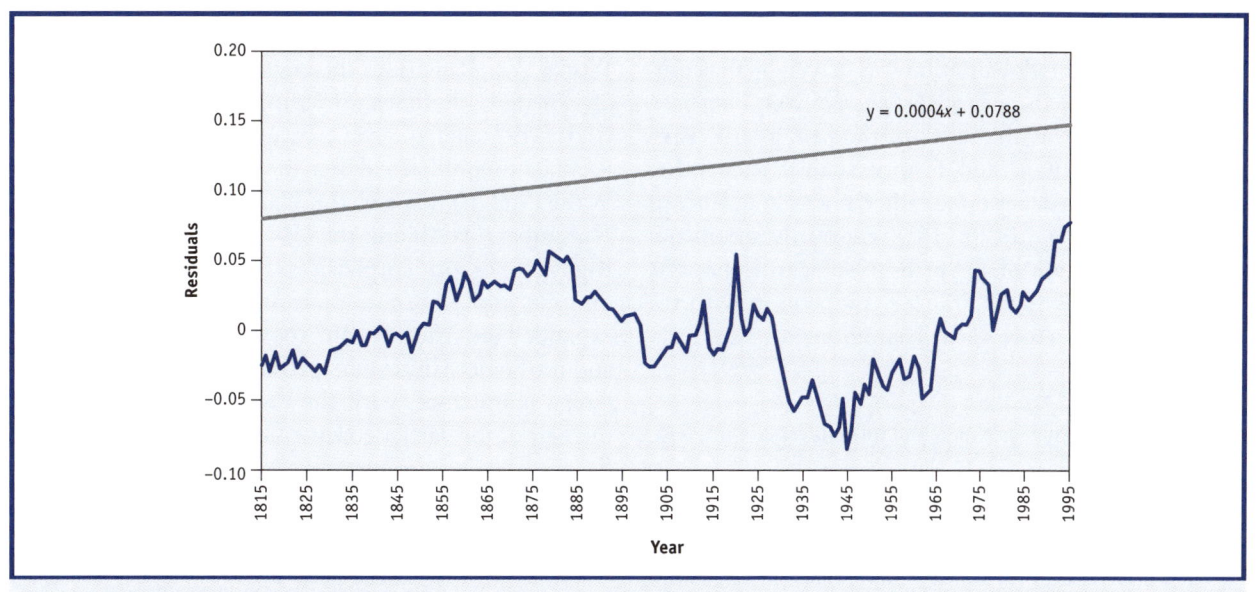

Trade globalisation, 1815–1995 *Source:* Chase-Dunn et al. (2000, p. 87).

but mostly because he takes into account the ways in which globalisation processes do not always go in the same direction—they can also go into reverse and turn into processes of *deglobalisation*. It is especially important to be aware of this when trying to understand the future of globalisation and all the possible permutations of the relationship between the global and the local.

Six waves of globalisation—Göran Therborn

Therborn suggests that globalisation should be seen as a plural phenomenon and that it is useful to use the term in the plural as well, to speak of differing globalisations—distinct modes of globalisation in different dimensions of social, economic, political and cultural life. The dynamics of any particular globalisation process is the result of its emergence over time, which Therborn sees as running across six historical 'waves'.

The first wave, 300–600

The first wave consisted of 'the diffusion of world religions and the establishment of transcontinental civilizations' (Therborn 2000, p. 158). Christianity became established in Europe (via the Roman Empire), Hinduism was taken up in the South East, and Buddhism spread from India to China, Korea and Japan. By the end of this period, Islam governed Spain and the Arab world from Morocco to what are now Iran and Pakistan. 'These were cultures', writes Therborn, 'which were not only a set of beliefs and ritual practices but also included a trans-tribal, trans-monarchical literary language—Latin, Sanskrit, Pali or Arabic specific architecture and esthetics as well as social norms' (p. 160).

The developments were followed by movements of deglobalisation, in which distinct language forms crystallised in local scripts, alphabets and spoken languages. This process of cultural deglobalisation was accompanied by the emergence of distinct political regimes, with the exception of the Islamic world, which remained structured as a large empire.

The second wave, 1500–1600

The second wave of globalisation, suggests Therborn, ran from 1500 to 1600, driven by European naval exploration and colonial conquest, beginning with the Portuguese and the Spanish, then the Dutch, the British and to a lesser extent the French. This world system revolved around exotic high-value goods such as spices, the exploitation of raw materials, metals and minerals, and slave labour. 'For two continents of the world', emphasises Therborn, 'this was an epoch of full-scale disaster: the genocidal depopulation of the Americas and the opening up of Africa to a trans-Atlantic slave trade' (p. 161). Commerce and trade, then, drove a massive expansion in the interlinkages between peoples, cultures and economies, with Europe at the centre and holding the whip-hand, although the cultural influences were not one-way, moving as much, perhaps more, towards Europe as from Europe to its colonial empires.

The third wave, 1700–1850

The third wave of globalisation was driven by the competition between the European powers. As Therborn observes, 'This was the series of the first global wars, which pitted Britain and France against each other with shifting constellations of allies, not only in Europe but all over the world' (p. 161). Especially significant was the occupation of Egypt by Napoleon Bonaparte in 1798, which brought France's competition with the English right to centre of the Islamic world.

> 22 June 1798, Napoleon's speech to his soldiers en route to Egypt:
>
> *Soldiers! You are undertaking a conquest with incalculable consequences for civilization and world trade. You will inflict a decisive and significant blow on England ...*

The fourth wave, 1850–1918

The fourth wave was centred on domination of the world by the European empires, driven by large-scale trade and transcontinental migration 'sustained by new and faster means of transport and communication' (Therborn 2000, p. 161). It began with the forced opening up of China by the British for the international trade in opium, followed by the Americans doing the same favour for Japan. European domination of Asia and Africa was tightened, and there was mass migration from Europe to the Americas, Australia and New Zealand. Millions of Chinese and Indian labourers migrated to North America and Australia. Gold governed transnational financial transactions and global markets in commodities and capital emerged. World War I marked the end of this wave, arising from conflicts between the European powers and resulting in a range of global organisations, including the League of Nations and the International Labour Organization.

This wave was followed, especially after the Wall Street stock market crash of 29 October 1929 and the ensuing global Great Depression, by another period of deglobalisation, involving the abandonment of the gold standard, the contraction of world trade and the rise of Keynesian economic policies. Bankers were so unpopular and money was in such short supply that the bank robbers Bonnie Parker and Clyde Barrow became popular heroes in the United States during this time.

The fifth wave, 1940–70

World War II marked the beginning of the next wave of globalisation, first in drawing Asia, Oceania, North Africa, Ethiopia and the Caucus as well as Europe and Russia into conflict, and then in the aftermath of the war, in the establishment of the United Nations (UN), the Nuremberg Trials and the UN Declaration of Human Rights. Therborn emphasises that the costs of communication and transport plummeted, and world trade expanded enormously. But above all, the United States and the Soviet Union engaged in worldwide rivalry for global dominance, with the Cold War between them the heir of the earlier competition between Britain and France. As Therborn writes:

> *The Cold War had its origins in Europe, and it might be seen as a global projection of the internal, deep ideological cleavages characteristic of European modernity, but it entered everywhere into all parts of Asia, from Korea and Japan to Arab West Asia, into sub-Saharan Africa, the Caribbean and South America. It brought dramatic and highly controversial Communist-hunting into Australia and New Zealand.* (2000, p. 162)

This wave reached its peak in the late 1970s, when the collapse of the postwar world economic system and new technological developments in communications and transport led to new forms of global economic integration.

The sixth wave, 1980–present

For Therborn, the most recent wave of globalisation constitutes a replacement of the political and military dynamic of the previous wave with one of finance and culture. It is marked by an enormous growth in foreign currency trading following the breakdown of the Bretton Woods system, the emergence of derivatives and securitisation, the reconfiguration of corporate activity in almost all fields on a global scale to take advantage of world markets, and the decline of the welfare state model of the relationship between the state and the market. Governments of all persuasions shifted towards neoliberal economic and political policies (see below, pp. 45–48), revolving around the severe reduction of state regulation of capital movements, the privatisation of public enterprises and the general opening up of national economies to worldwide activity and competition.

New streams of migration emerged—especially after the collapse of the Soviet Union and the fall of the Berlin Wall in 1989—from South to North America, from Africa, the Middle East and Asia to Europe and

A useful sense of the deglobalisation of the inter-war period is conveyed by the figures concerning legal migration to the United States, which declined sharply in 1915 and rose again in 1946. The number of legal migrants fell by 75 per cent from 1.2 million in 1914 to just over 300 000 in 1915, and then rose from 38 000 in 1945 to 108 000 in 1946 (see Figure 2.6).

1. Can you think of other examples of deglobalisation?
2. To what extent is the current global financial crisis a possible expression of deglobalisation?

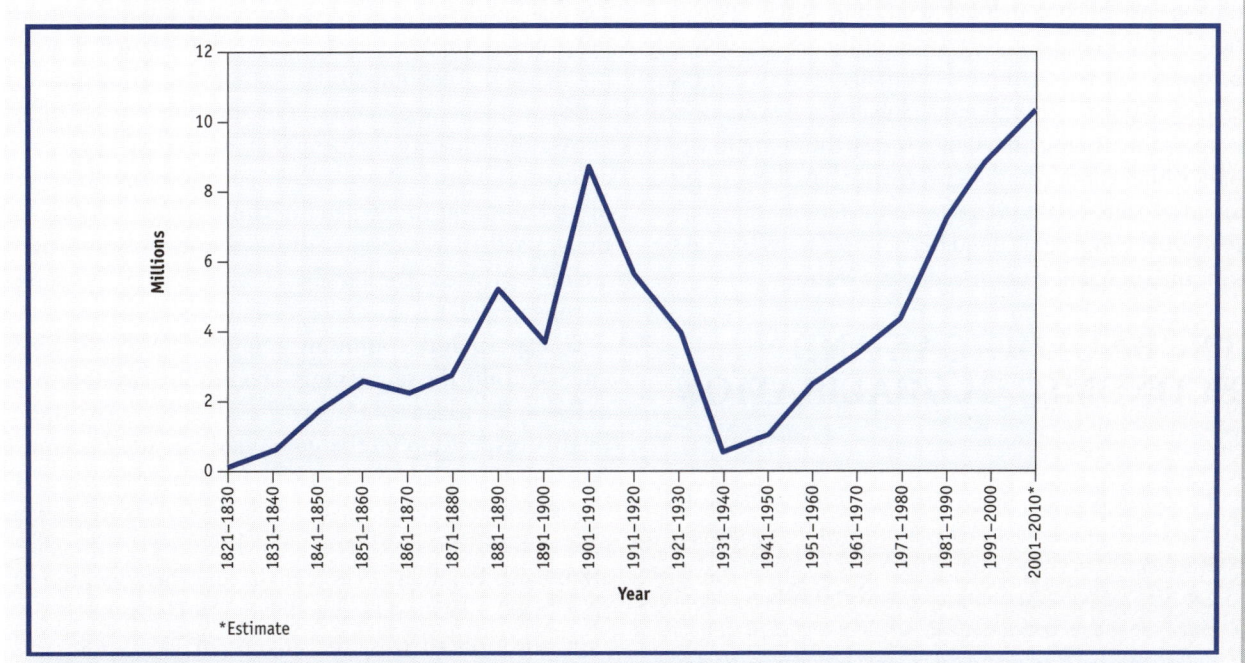

FIGURE 2.6

Number of migrants obtaining legal permanent resident status in the United States, 1821–2010 (million)
Source: United States Department of Homeland Security (2009, p. 5).

Australasia, and from Asia to North America. Europe itself has been transformed, from a region of emigration to one of immigration, and Europeans have had to learn how to be multicultural and deal with the mixture of Christianity with Islam, Hinduism and Buddhism.

Global media enterprises such as CNN have turned public communication and indeed culture itself into a worldwide phenomenon. The impact of the internet has been enormous, enabling the easy constitution of worldwide virtual communities and intensifying the disembedding of all forms of activity—social, cultural, economic and political. It is now probably easier to acquire a book, either new or second-hand, from Amazon.com than it is to visit your local bookshop. The English language is increasingly functioning as the world *lingua franca*, although at the same time generating countertendencies towards the reinvigoration of local languages. Therborn suggests the collapse of the Soviet Union and the end of the Cold War meant a deglobalisation of world politics, although one could argue the opposite—that as the world was no longer divided into at least two competing models of economic and political organisation, it became even more possible to think of the world as a single political, economic, social and cultural system. In any case, at the same time, the tendencies in the economic and communications fields remained towards increased globalisation. Therborn notes that 'finance and mass communication reached higher levels of global extension, building upon economic and technological developments coinciding with post-Second World War Cold War politics' (2000, pp. 165–6).

Therborn argues that each wave has run its own course, sometimes followed by waves of deglobalisation. The waves sometimes overlapped, with one wave beginning before the previous one had come to an end. Globalisation and deglobalisation processes also need not be synchronised with each other across different fields, so that it would be possible for economic globalisation to coincide with political deglobalisation—although lack of synchronisation does slow down any particular globalisation process.

It is important, then, to keep the multidimensional character of processes of globalisation and deglobalisation in view. Many of the disputes about the nature of globalisation are the product of focusing on one aspect at the expense of the others. The argument that globalisation leads to the withering away of the nation-state (see below, p. 52), for example, is in many respects the result of concentrating on equating globalisation with its economic dimensions and failing to grasp the extent to which nation-states and forms of governance have become globalised and altered the character of the nation-state so that, in its increasingly globalised form, it retains its central significance in relation to the economic realm.

TECHNOLOGICAL AND ECONOMIC GLOBALISATION

> *The bourgeoisie has, through its exploitation of the world market, given a cosmopolitan character to production and consumption in every country. To the great chagrin of reactionaries, it has drawn from under the feet of industry the national ground on which it stood. All old-established national industries have been destroyed or are daily being destroyed. They are dislodged by new industries, whose introduction becomes a life and death question for all civilised nations, by industries that no longer work up indigenous raw material, but raw material drawn from the remotest zones; industries whose products are consumed, not only at home, but in every quarter of the globe. In place of the old wants, satisfied by the production of the country, we find new wants, requiring for their satisfaction the products of distant lands and climes. In place of the old local and national seclusion and self-sufficiency, we have intercourse in every direction, universal inter-dependence of nations ... The intellectual creations of individual nations become common property. National one-sidedness and narrow-mindedness become more and more impossible, and from the numerous national and local literatures, there arises a world literature ... In one word, it creates a world after its own image. (Marx & Engels, The Communist Manifesto, 1848)*

Before we can understand the nature of economic globalisation, it is important to get a sense of the central technological changes that have taken place since the 1960s. Dicken (1992, p. 97), for example, suggests that technology is 'at the heart of the process of economic growth and economic development'. Advances in communications and transport technologies, in particular, have made global movements and connections far more accessible and frequent. These advances are fundamentally changing the nature and processes of production (Dicken 1992, pp. 110–19). The whole basis of economic production and reproduction, including its social and subjective dimensions, is moving from Fordist to post-Fordist modalities, or economies and labour markets now based on flexible accumulation (Harvey 1990, pp. 141–72). Technological developments also allow for reflexive identity practices. The internet, for example, allows the capacity for people to use 'virtual spaces to construct identity' (Turkle 2000, p. 230). Many observers of globalisation suggest that technological transformations, particularly recent advances in communications technology, are at the very heart of globalising processes (Aronson 2001).

Transport and communications technologies were once basically the same thing—communications moved as fast as the means of transport available to carry them. In this respect alone, the globe had already become a much smaller place by the 1950s as forms of transportation speeded up with the development of steam power, steel for rail and shipping, the building of the Suez (1869) and Panama (1914) canals, and the advent of jet travel in the 1950s (Dicken 1992, pp. 103–4).

In addition to this, the advent of electronic communications has meant that the two technologies have, for all intents and purposes, separated (Dicken 1992). The development of communications technologies such as intercontinental cables, satellites and the internet means that communication can occur more or less instantaneously over vast distances. The most recent globalising technologies include breakthroughs in 'micro-electronics, computing (machines and software), telecommunications/broadcasting, and opto-electronics ... genetic engineering ... energy sources' (Castells 2000a, p. 29). For Castells, it is clear that technology, particularly information technology, transforms the global political, economic and social landscape (Castells 2000a; 2000b).

Some simple examples of the transformative power of technological networking can be found in Aronson (2001). According to Aronson, the recent advances and developments of communications technologies, particularly the internet, impact on nations and people in a number of ways, both politically and socially. First, Aronson states that informationalism leads to 'information overload' on government decision making and the capacity to make policy in various ways:

1. Governments now have so much information at their disposal (often contradictory information)

that they often cannot make decisions and potentially become 'paralysed'.
2. Governments may attempt to centralise information and decision making, while other forms of information are being decentralised, meaning that other key political stakeholders (e.g. media, non-governmental organisations and corporations) may have better or faster access to information than most formal policy makers.
3. Global networks increase the transparency of information, meaning that global issues such as terrorism and global warming are not able to be dealt with unilaterally but must occur in an international alliance and often to greater public scrutiny.

Second, Aronson argues that the information revolution has facilitated the rapid rise in size of many companies. Access to information and networks, coupled with a lack of economic regulation, has allowed large corporations to balloon in size to the point that many now have more economic and political clout than many nations. As Cohen and Kennedy (2000, p. 123) indicate, 'of the 100 most important economic units in the world today, half are nation-states and half are TNCs [**transnational corporations**]' and of all the recognised nation-states in the world 130 out of 180 'have economies smaller than the first 50 TNCs'. Moreover, Willetts (2001, p. 357) explains that while there may be fewer than 200 governments in the world, there are 60 000 major TNCs that individually and collectively potentially wield significant political and economic power.

Third, Aronson explains how **non-governmental organisations (NGOs)** have also proliferated among the global communication networks, taking advantage of an increase in communications technology and information and, as such, they too are shaping up as powerful political actors on the global scene. These include a range of NGOs that deal with issues of environment, weapons proliferation, human rights and so on, but also a range of right-wing or conservative NGOs, including 10 000 single-country NGOs, 250 intergovernmental organisations such as the United Nations and 5800 international organisations such as Amnesty International and the International Red Cross (Willetts 2001, p. 357).

Finally, Aronson states that global communications networks can empower people and bring together collective social movements. The very structure of the internet, for example, is horizontal, designed specifically in the early 1970s by the United States Defense Department to make the 'network independent of command and control centres, so that the message units would find their own routes along the network, being reassembled in coherent meaning at any point in the network' (Castells 2000a, p. 45). The communicated message of the internet is not subject to centralisation in the way that can be achieved with television, for example. Cohen and Kennedy (2000, p. 255) argue that these less controlled and decentralised approaches to communications are opening up possibilities of greater democracy, activism and, possibly, a counter-hegemony of media (see also Aronson 2001, p. 253; Klein 2000).

INTERNATIONAL ECONOMY AND GLOBALISED ECONOMY

Hirst et al. (2009) suggest that it is useful to make a conceptual distinction between two 'ideal types' of international economy: an international economy and a globalised economy. An *international* economy is one where nation-states, still operating within a relatively bounded domestic economy, trade with each other at an international level. It is 'still fundamentally characterized by exchange between relatively distinct national economies and in which many outcomes...are substantially determined by processes occurring at the national level' (p. 19). The interdependence between nation-states 'implies the continued relative separation of the domestic and the international frameworks for policy-making and the management of economic affairs, and also a relative separation in terms of economic effects' (p. 19).

Within a *globalised* economy, in contrast, the extent, speed and intensity of the economic interactions themselves are raised to such an extent that national economies are 'subsumed and rearticulated by genuinely global processes and transactions into a new structure' (Hirst et al. 2009, p. 20). This 'rearticulation' (1) makes domestic governance more challenging and (2) provides greater opportunities for TNCs to develop greater financial and geographical mobility and, ultimately, power. Such a view provides the basis for the theory that economic globalisation diminishes the power of the nation-state and therefore, by definition, diminishes the power of the citizen. (This argument will be examined later in this chapter.)

The two types of economies that Hirst et al. emphasise are not necessarily mutually exclusive: it is possible for 'a complex combination of features of both types of economy' to coexist. The problem then becomes how 'to identify the dominant trends: either the growth

> *Nobody is safe from global reach and the irresistible economies of scale ... Given what is everywhere the purpose of commerce, the global company will shape the vectors of technology and globalization into its great strategic fecundity. It will systematically push these vectors toward their own convergence, offering everyone simultaneously high-quality, more or less standardized products at optimally low prices, thereby achieving for itself vastly expanded markets and profits. Companies that do not adapt to the new global realities will become victims of those that do. (Levitt 1983, p. 102)*

of globalization or the continuation of the existing international patterns' (p. 20), although, despite their willingness to raise the question, their own diagnosis is that 'such a process of hybridization is not taking place' (p. 21). Their central point is that the alternative to a globalised economy is not a set of inward-looking, entirely national economies isolated from each other, but 'an open world market based on trading nations and regulated to a greater or lesser extent by both the public policies and nation-states and supranational agencies' (p. 20), which is more or less the kind of world economy that has been in place since the 1870s.

THE SIZE AND SCOPE OF THE GLOBAL ECONOMY

It is the concept of the global economy and the sense that it has shifted into overdrive that forms the basis of the easy-to-grasp and frequently espoused argument that economic globalisation now dominates nearly all aspects of international and domestic life (Prigoff 2000, p. 1). Many people seem at the very least vaguely aware that there has been a distinct shift in the prominence and politicisation of the economy in most aspects of social life. Money, budgets, finance, the economy, the stock market and the 'nervous' market: these are often treated as things in themselves—things that in many cases are afforded moral consideration and status equal to, and even higher than, that of people (Stone 2002). The privileging of the market and money over people is one thing, but the rapid growth in financial outputs and trade that constitutes the sheer volume and size of the global economy gives it both prominence and significance (see Figure 2.7). For example:

- World imports and exports went from US$126 billion in 1950 to US$4109 billion in 1980 and US$32542 billion in 2008 (World Trade Organization).
- Global GDP roughly doubled in the 30 years between 1950 and 1980, from US$5336 billion to US$11 805, but increased five-fold in the next 30 years, to US$64 168 billion in 2009.
- Inward foreign direct investment increased 17 times from US$58 billion in 1985 to US$1 036 billion in 2006 (UNCTAD 2007).
- The number of major TNCs grew from 44 000 in 1996 to 65 000 in 2001, with their assets growing from US$8.3 trillion in 1996 to US$25 trillion in 2000 (Mishra 2004, paragraph 1).
- Ten of the world's largest TNCs have an income greater than that of the 100 poorest countries.
- Two-thirds of world trade is conducted by 500 companies.
- In the ten years between 1990 and 2000, daily turnover of foreign exchange markets went from US$500 billion to US$1.2 trillion (Ryman & Kean 2002, p. 2).
- Even though trade slowed during the 1970s and 1980s, 'between 1950 and 2000 trade had increased twentyfold while world product increased only sixfold' (Waters 2001, p. 69).

CLASS AND GLOBAL CAPITALISM

The concept of class is relevant in analysing and explaining economic globalisation. The dominant global class is referred to by Sklair (1991, p. 8) as a 'transnational capitalist' class who, according to Sklair, dominate and control the major hegemonic institutions of consumerism, media, political parties and cultural ideological practices. He points to the enormous wealth of many corporations and the crucial role they have in most national economies. According to Sklair, the transnational capitalist class is the driver of the global system. This class consists of executives of TNCs, 'globalising state bureaucrats', 'capitalist-inspired politicians and professionals' and 'consumerist elites (merchants, media)'. This group is seen as making system-wide decisions that affect the whole of the global system, and it attempts to make decisions that further its own interests within the system. Although it includes some politicians based in particular nation-states, the class opposes protectionism, which would put national interests above those of the class as a whole.

It is perhaps not so much capitalism per se that infuriates many commentators and anti-globalisation activists as it is the establishment and domination of self-interested hegemonic institutions by a privileged

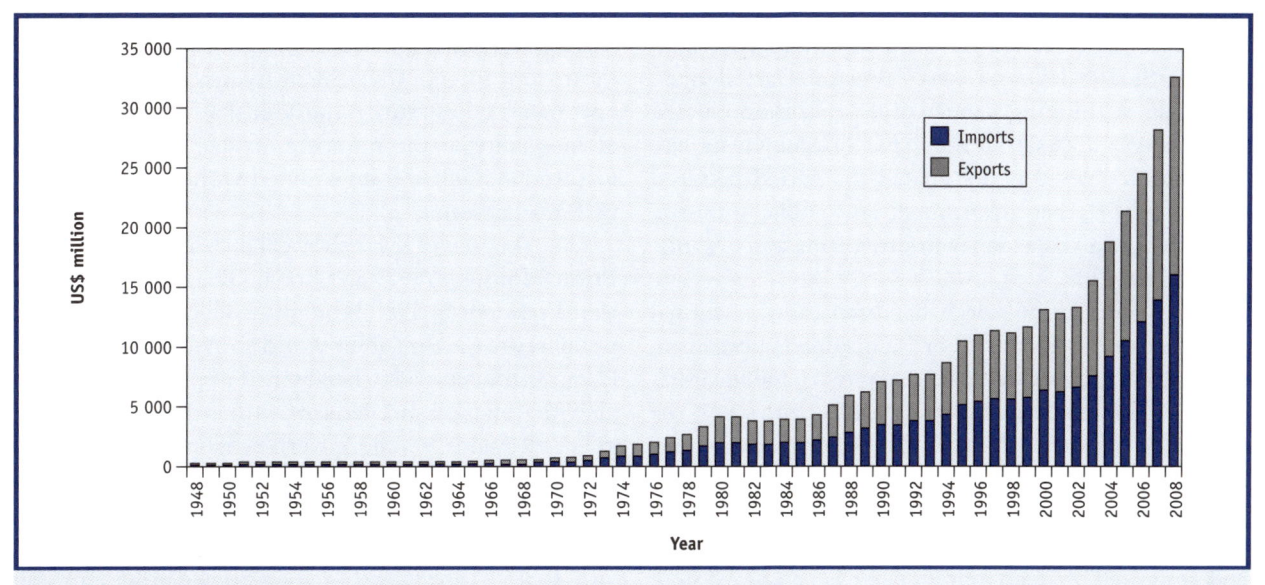

World trade, 1948–2008 *Source:* World Trade Organization (http://stat.wto.org/StatisticalProgram/WSDBViewData.aspx?Language=E).

class of people (Sklair 2002). For example, according to Prigoff (2000, pp. 129–49), the development of the **World Trade Organization (WTO)** in 1994, the **North American Free Trade Agreement (NAFTA)**, the yet-to-be- realised **Multilateral Agreement on Investment (MAI)**, the **World Economic Forum (WEF)** and the Group of Eight industrial nations (G8) can be seen as nothing less than attempts at plunging the world into a new corporate global **hegemony**. Under such hegemony, financial organisations and corporations will dominate global affairs with ruinous effects for the majority of the world's peoples. The power of corporations and finance institutions is not a particularly new phenomenon, however, (Prigoff 2000) but the prominence of corporate power at the political level perhaps is. It is certainly not insignificant.

Greider (2004/1997), for example, sees global integration as driven by the market, but these market processes are supported or made possible through political arrangements. Such arrangements are, rather bluntly, analogous to an auctioning or bidding process. A nation's economic needs for development and investment may be facilitated through political 'deals' between the spheres of national governance and an economic entity, such as a TNC, which holds the promise of jobs, growth and prosperity (Greider 2004/1997). The lack of formal control of economic policy is therefore significant, with 'half the people and two-thirds of the countries of the world' lacking the capacity to control their economic policies (Pieper & Taylor 1998, p. 37). Even so, Chang (1998) dismisses the wholesale power of TNCs, suggesting that the bargaining power of TNCs must be seen on a continuum of which absolute power might be only one possible position.

NEOLIBERALISM

'We must distinguish sharply and clearly', writes John Gray, 'between globalisation as an historical process and globalisation as a particular international economic regime.' He goes on insist that 'the current regime of free trade and unrestricted capital flows in world markets' should be seen as 'a specific phase of globalisation, not globalisation itself' (Gray 2002b, p. 191).

In order to make this distinction, it is important to specify the nature of the particular economic regime that has tended to accompany globalisation processes since the 1970s and that is often confused with globalisation itself. The term most often used to refer to the policy orientation characterising this specific, recent phase of globalisation is **neoliberalism**, and it is useful to get a sense of what this concept means in arriving at a more general understanding of globalisation itself.

A brief history of neoliberalism

In *A Brief History of Neoliberalism*, David Harvey (2005) explains how a particular model for understanding the relationships between state, economy and society emerged, from the 1970s onwards, at first in the United States and the United Kingdom, but then driving politics and economic policy to an increasing extent throughout the rest of the world. The term 'neoliberalism' is meant to capture the fusion of a liberal political orientation with neoclassical economics, developed in the work of economists such as Alfred Marshall, William Stanley Jevons, Leon Walras and Carl Menger. As a way of thinking about politics and economics it was strongly opposed to the views of economists like Maynard Keynes that dominated the period between 1945 and 1970, that government and public authority had a significant role to play in structuring and organising economic life.

This Keynesian approach has been called 'national capitalism' (Block 1977) or 'embedded liberalism' (Ruggie 1983; Ikenberry 1992), to refer to the idea that market mechanisms and corporate action are seen to be embedded in 'a web of social and political constraints' (Harvey 2005, p. 11) which guide and restrain economic and political policy. It characterised economic policy in the industrialised world after the Depression, which had indicated that an unregulated economic system was highly unstable. One key element of the 'embedded liberalist' approach can be seen in the Bretton Woods system of monetary management established in 1944, when currency exchange values were set in relation to the value of gold by the respective governments as a policy decision.

The critique of this approach, mounted by the Austrian philosopher Friedrich von Hayek and American economist Milton Friedman, was that state intervention in the marketplace should be kept to a minimum, for the simple reason that 'the state cannot possibly possess enough information to second-guess market signals (prices) and because powerful interest groups will inevitably distort and bias state interventions (particularly in democracies) for their own benefit' (Harvey 2005, p. 2). The more social and political life is governed by the logic of the marketplace, the wealthier and happier we will all be. This remained a minority view, Harvey observes, until the Bretton Woods system began to break down in the late 1960s and 1970s, accompanied by a combination of rising unemployment and rising inflation, referred to as 'stagflation'.

The adoption of neoliberal policies came first in Chile, notes Harvey, when General Augusto Pinochet executed a coup in 1973, backed and supported by the United States, against the democratically elected social democrat Salvadore Allende. Pinochet's military dictatorship ran from 1973 to 1990, drawing on the assistance of 'the Chicago boys', a group of economists at the University of Chicago, to facilitate foreign investment, privatise public assets and services, allow foreign corporations to repatriate their profits and open up the country's primary resources to exploitation by the world's—in fact, the United States'—corporations.

This generated high levels of economic growth and returns on foreign investment, which neoliberal theorists regarded as more important than the rising levels of inequality or the numbers of people killed (3200), tortured (30 000) and imprisoned without trial (80 000) by Pinochet's junta.

The election of Margaret Thatcher as the British Prime Minister in 1979 and Ronald Reagan as the American President in 1980 brought neoliberalism from the periphery to the core of the world economic system. Both led governments with a heightened responsiveness to the view that market mechanisms, rather than government policy decisions, should govern economic and political life, and made continuing efforts to reduce government economic regulation, privatise as much of the state's activities as possible, reduce expenditure on public services (with a view to encouraging private provision), and

Case Study
General Pinochet and global law

Pinochet's own fate is an interesting example of the globalisation of law (see pp. 55–56). While visiting the United Kingdom in 1998, he was arrested on charges of murder, torture, illegal detention and forced disappearance brought by a Spanish court under the principle of universal jurisdiction, meaning that certain crimes are so fundamentally contrary to all principles of human justice that they can be prosecuted in any of the world's jurisdictions. The case went to the House of Lords, which declined to extradite Pinochet because most of the events had taken place before 1988, when the United Kingdom implemented the UN Convention against Torture, but it nonetheless affirmed the principle of universal jurisdiction and refused to extend former head-of-state immunity for the crime of torture.

1. Do you think that Pinochet should have been prosecuted for war crimes?
2. Are there other crimes by heads of state that you can think of that have been punished by the international community?
3. Does this sort of development of international law mean that the nation-state is in decline and losing its sovereignty?

reduce trade union power and influence. As the Australian Prime Minister, Kevin Rudd, has put it:

The ideology of the unrestrained free market, discredited by the Great Depression, re-emerged in the 1970s amid a widespread belief that the prevailing economic woes of high inflation and low growth were exclusively the result of excessive government intervention in the market. In the '80s, the Reagan and Thatcher governments gave political voice to this neo-liberal movement of anti-tax, anti-regulation, anti-government conservatives. (Rudd 2009)

In the United States, just to pick one of Harvey's examples, a crucial turning point was the 1979 decision by Paul Volcker, then Chairman of the US Federal Reserve Bank, to prioritise the reduction of inflation above reducing unemployment.

> *Economics are the method; the object is to change the heart and soul. (Margaret Thatcher, in Butt 1981, p. 35)*

The 2008/2009 global financial crisis has come to be seen by many commentators as closely linked to the workings of neoliberal economic policy. Kevin Rudd (2009) describes it as follows:

The time has come ... to proclaim that the great neo-liberal experiment of the past 30 years has failed, that the emperor has no clothes. Neo-liberalism, and the free-market fundamentalism it has produced, has been revealed as little more than personal greed dressed up as an economic philosophy. And, ironically, it now falls to social democracy to prevent liberal capitalism from cannibalising itself.

David Harvey's analysis goes into more detail into what the concept of 'personal greed' should be seen as referring to, arguing that the emergence of neoliberalism should be understood in terms of the power relations between the wealthy and the rest of society, as an attempt to 'restore class power' after the postwar welfare state's emphasis on reducing inequality, and as a deliberate project to improve the capacity of the wealthy to accumulate increasing proportions of society's total wealth. He refers to the work of Gérard Duménil and Dominique Lévy, saying that they concluded

that neoliberalization was from the very beginning a project to achieve the restoration of class power. After the implementation of neoliberal policies in the late 1970s, the share of national income of the top 1 per cent of income earners in the US soared, to reach 15 per cent (very close to its pre-Second World War share) by the end of the century. The top 0.1 per cent of income earners in the US increased their share of the national income from 2 per cent in 1978 to over 6 per cent by 1999. (p. 16)

One central mechanism by which wealth is concentrated, suggests Harvey, is what he calls 'accumulation by dispossession'. In countries like Mexico, the reform of land ownership has often meant simply dispossessing small farmers in favour of large-scale agribusiness enterprises. Debt also is a mechanism by which people become dispossessed of their assets, when they are encouraged to borrow more than they can afford and are forced to sell out at far lower prices, losing what little they already possessed. Superannuation entitlements, for which people have in fact 'paid' in the course of their working lives, can simply disappear when their employer goes bankrupt.

Harvey points out that the critique of the neoliberal approach to government and economics had already been articulated by Karl Polanyi in *The Great Transformation* (1944), where he indicated the need to distinguish different types of 'freedom'. Polanyi noted that, on the one hand, the supposed restriction of freedom entailed by government regulation could generate other kinds of freedoms, such as security and leisure. On the other hand, there were also 'freedoms' that were less likely to attract universal support, such as:

the freedom to exploit one's fellows, or the freedom to make inordinate gains without commensurable service to the community, the freedom to keep technological inventions from being used for public benefit, or the freedom to profit from public calamities secretly engineered for private advantage. (pp. 256–8)

For Polanyi, the concept of freedom promoted by Hayek 'degenerates into a mere advocacy of free enterprise'—that is:

the fullness of freedom for those whose income, leisure and security need no enhancing, and a mere pittance of liberty for the people, who may in vain attempt to make use of their democratic rights to gain shelter from the power of the owners of property.

The 'freedom' that neoliberalism promotes, argues Harvey, should be seen as 'nothing more than the convenient means to spread corporate monopoly power and Coca Cola everywhere without constraint' (Harvey 2005, p. 38).

Neoliberalism and globalisation

This is not, however, the only way of putting it. Marion Fourcade-Gourinchas (2002), for example, argues that neoliberalism should not be seen simply as a financial regime within a process of globalisation that 'happens' to have been preferred over social democracy simply for ideological or instrumental reasons. She suggests that the globalisation process itself was 'the driving force behind the worldwide spread of market-friendly policies after the 1970s'. Once technological developments had made financial transactions and production processes much more fluid, mobile and globalised, 'the economy is increasingly perceived as exogenous—and therefore relatively uncontrollable' (p. 535).

Eric Helleiner makes a related observation, noting that the mobility of capital makes it difficult for governments to regulate it, tempting them to 'liberalize external capital controls as well as domestic financial regulations as a means of luring international capital and financial business to their own markets' (1994, p. 301). And once a significant-enough group of states goes down this road and gains its economic advantages—in fact, it was the United States and the United Kingdom—it is almost impossible for the rest of the world to avoid doing the same.

So, the perception of economic forces as independent of state control was not simply an ideological preference, but had some basis in real changes taking place in the relationship between economic mechanisms and the political sphere. As Fourcade-Gourinchas puts it:

Following the disciplining logic dictated by international market forces thus comes to be understood as the only way to achieve growth—whether such course of action is rationalized in negative terms (e.g. "If we don't adapt to the global economy by making labor more flexible and opening our capital markets, we will fall behind") or more positive ones (e.g. "If we want to reap the benefits of economic and financial globalisation, then we have to be more free trade and market oriented"). (2002, p. 535)

Eric Helleiner similarly points out:

Many policymakers began to embrace neoliberal ideas for the practical reason that they found it increasingly difficult to continue to support embedded liberal policies in the increasingly open financial environment of the 1970s and 1980s. (1996, p. 15)

This interpretation and Harvey's do not, however, need to be seen as opposing each other—they each capture different aspects of neoliberalism. On the one hand, the globalisation of economic activity did raise particular new challenges for the nation-state to manage increasingly complex and large-scale financial mechanisms, so neoliberal market-oriented economic policies did not spring simply from the minds of greedy capitalists such as Hayek, Friedman, Thatcher, Reagan—and, it should be added, Paul Keating in Australia. On the other hand, there are different ways in which the new problems of regulating a globalising financial system were responded to, as Fourcade-Gourinchas' comparison of the differing trajectories of Chile, Britain, Mexico and France shows; and Harvey is right to point to the central role played by the wealthy in pushing government policy in the directions that most suited their interest in accumulating ever-increasing shares of society's wealth. In short, neoliberalism is indeed inherently globalising, and globalisation does give enormous impetus to neoliberal tendencies, but that does not exhaust all the possible forms that globalisation can and does take.

Reflective question: How would you explain what neoliberalism is? How does it relate to globalisation?

THE LIMITS OF GLOBAL CAPITALISM

It is easy to read the above in terms of seeing economic globalisation as a totalising and unstoppable dominating force. How far we extend the concept of global is important to how far we see economic globalisation reaching and transforming social life. Hirst et al. (2009) believe that arguments of the world's economy being globalised are often overstated, precisely because many countries are marginal or on the periphery of the bulk of international economic transactions, which occur mainly among the economic triad of North America, Europe and Japan. Second, Hirst et al. offer a more tempered view of Prigoff's (2000) concerns regarding the loss of financial control of many countries (e.g. developing countries with **International Monetary Fund (IMF) Structural Adjustment Programs (SAPs)**). They state that there are local and domestic explanations for swings in unemployment or poverty, and these local conditions are meaningful even in advanced countries that may be wired to the global economy. In other words, it is misleading to always link local issues to the global context. At the same time, we should not assume that local experiences have nothing to do with the global. Careful analysis is required to avoid falling too heavily into either binary.

The brink of a global economy

For example, Waters (2001) suggests that a total global economic system, while close, is not yet complete.

Waters adopts an approach that argues that a global economic totality, where the economic reach of capitalism penetrates every corner of the world rendering the nation-state obsolete, has not yet come to pass, but it may be near. Waters does concede that in the past 25 years the world economy has more or less shifted into 'overdrive', which may signal that 'the planet is entering a final globalisation phase' (p. 61). For Waters, the world is on the *brink* of becoming a truly global economy (pp. 88–92).

In demonstrating this, he draws attention to the 'Asian meltdown' in the late 1990s, which began with Thailand and subsequently flowed onto other countries in the region. A contagion metaphor was widely used to describe this process of economic collapse (Lechner & Boli 2004, p. 157). Attempts to halt the spread of the crisis involved massive IMF loans of US$5 billion to Indonesia and US$57 billion to Korea to bail out their economies. Despite this intervention, the systemic flow-on effects of falling demand and falling value of commodities impacted on the devaluing of the Russian and Brazilian economies. This was followed by further IMF bailouts. This example, according to Waters, illustrates the depth and extent of the globalised economy in several different ways.

1. Economies of the entire planet are in many ways systemically connected, and in many ways this connectedness exacerbates the extent of the global economic crisis far more than what was experienced in the economic depression of the 1920s.
2. Global economic booms and slumps have real-life consequences for the wellbeing of many of the world's citizens—such as job losses, starvation and hardships.
3. The speed at which an economic crisis infiltrates surrounding economies is phenomenal, meaning that the intensity of an economic crisis is abrupt and deep.
4. Despite this, the globalisation of the economy is not out of control because the intervention of the IMF and the **World Bank**, financed from the United States, effectively managed and resolved the crisis.

Beyond benign economism

A focus on the economy as an abstract, yet central, dimension of globalisation misses a crucial point. Axford (2001/1995) states that even if we accept the idea of a borderless world dominated by corporations, capital and consumption, we risk treating this as a *benign* process and this then ignores the continued production of winners and losers: the global production of poverty and wealth. Emphasising the creative possibilities of reflexive consumerism or the potentials of clever technology and situating these at the centre of what is understood to be globalisation may all be very interesting, but it ignores a vital and nagging problem: the continuation and entrenchment of poverty and misery on a planetary scale. The persistent and what is argued to be the exacerbation of poverty throughout the world (Chossudovsky 1998a; 1998b) is a major blight on the celebrations of economic globalisation. One of the key debates in the literature on globalisation is between those who see globalisation as bringing new levels of wealth and increases in standards of living to the world's poor (e.g. Dollar 2002) and those who argue that globalisation brings enormous wealth to the few, while exploiting and impoverishing the many (e.g. Chossudovsky 1998a; 1998b; Prigoff 2000).

THE POVERTY DEBATE

Anyone living on more than US$1.25 a day is considered by the World Bank as 'nonpoor'. The US$1.25 per day formula is equated in terms of *purchasing power parity* (PPP), which is benchmarked against 2005 values. Although there are a number of criticisms of using such a conservative and blunt measure, the statistics and indicators of poverty and inequality that are based on the US$1.25 per day formula illustrate the scope and depth of global poverty: in 2005 1.4 billion people, or one-quarter of the population in the developing world, lived on less than US$1.25 per day (Chen & Ravallion 2008). See Figures 2.8 and 2.9.

The globalisation of poverty

Joseph Stiglitz (2004/2002), once the Chief Economist of the World Bank and now one of its sharpest critics, argues that it is not globalisation per se that accounts for world poverty, but how globalisation is managed. He levels responsibility for the problem of poverty at international finance agencies such as the IMF, specifically for pushing an ideology of market fundamentalism onto countries where such approaches do not and cannot work.

'Structural Adjustment Programs (SAPs) are designed by the IMF, supported by the World Bank, and based on "neoliberal" monetary policies' (Prigoff 2000, p. 121). They are more often than not used in developing countries. According to Prigoff, SAPs typically involve a range of policy measures such as privatisation,

SOCIOLOGY

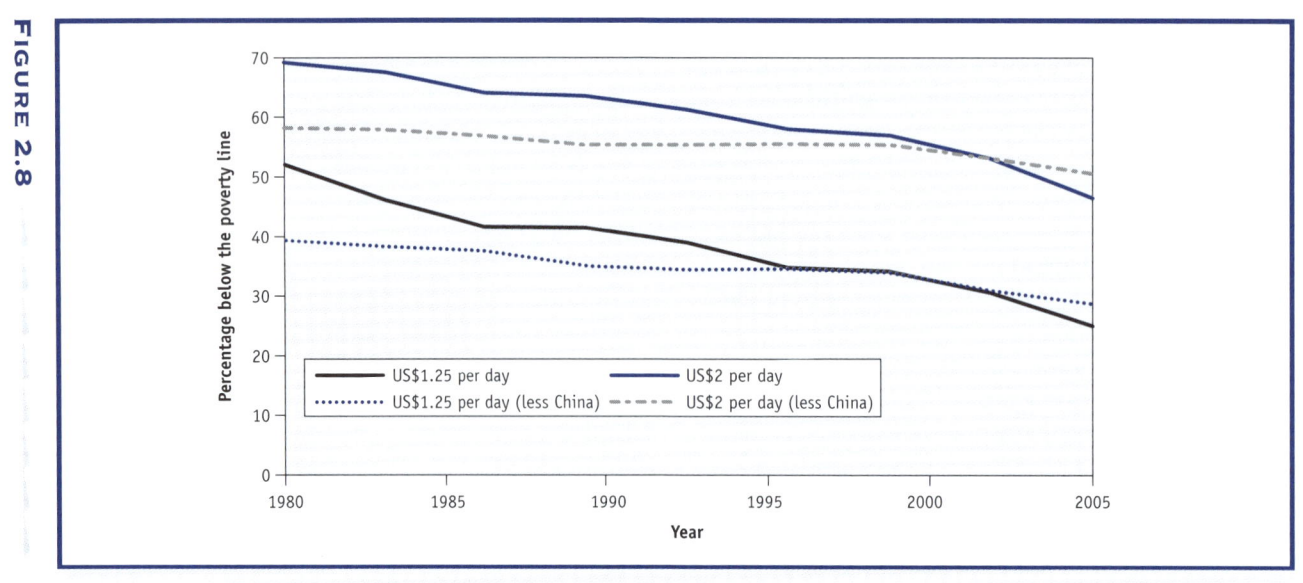

FIGURE 2.8

Headcount indices for the developing world, 1981–2005 *Source:* Chen & Ravallion (2008). *Note:* poverty lines in 2005 prices.

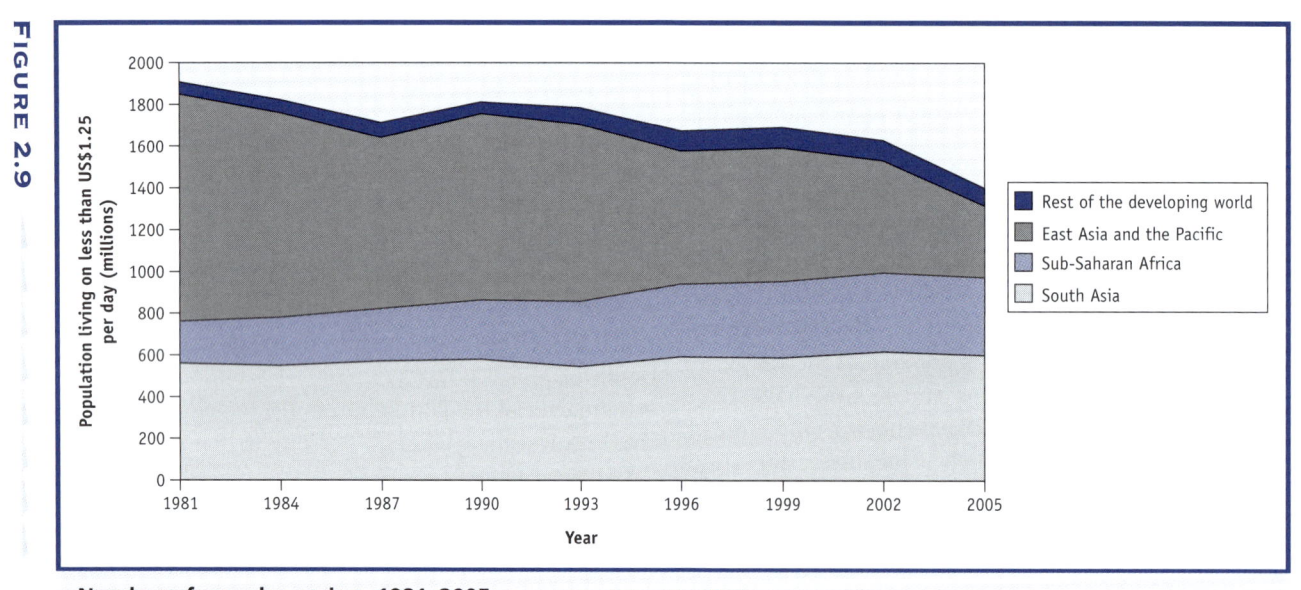

FIGURE 2.9

Number of poor by region, 1981–2005 *Source:* Chen & Ravallion (2008).

deregulation, tax breaks, retrenching 'expensive' welfare, devaluing national currency and terminating indigenous land rights or environmental protections. These policies aim at mobilising a region's economic and other resources to pay back SAP loans quickly, while at the same time fostering free market principles in policy and practice.

Philosophically, such approaches are aimed at encouraging economic growth which, it is argued by the World Bank, will alleviate poverty. Such an approach, argues Stiglitz (2004/2002), does not work in certain areas because the levels of volatility associated with market liberalisation exacerbate existing levels of poverty, particularly where there are underdeveloped safety nets. In addition, investors tend to demand higher than normal concessions to offset the risks of this instability, further stunting local growth possibilities and cutting short the time it takes for sustainable capital building. Finally, under a liberalised context, capital flees if the host country attempts to tax or regulate the development too heavily, which rapidly thrusts people back into poverty. As Stiglitz argues, the volatility of market liberalisation in some countries carries excessive risk, which Prigoff explains as including: increases in polarising political and economic power; sell-offs of national assets; increases in poverty; forced prostitution; drug and weapons trafficking; health and mental health problems; cultural fragmentation; forced migration; environmental decay; debt; loss of political confidence; and loss of a sense of security or hope for the future (Prigoff 2000, pp. 122–3).

Michael Chossudovsky (1998a) links poverty directly to globalisation. His study demonstrates how global economic developments are 'regulated by "a worldwide process of debt collection" which constricts the institutions of the national state and contributes to destroying employment and economic activity' (p. 15). Such a process is driven by the contradictory forces of searching for both cheap labour and new markets (p. 17). Chossudovsky argues that the world economy is more and more controlled by a handful of financial monopolies, corporations, and financial institutions and regulators, which all yield enormous political power, are largely self-interested, feed off debt and exacerbate poverty.

A contrasting view is contained in the essay, 'Growth is good for the poor', by Dollar and Kraay (2004/2002). They argue that the evidence does not support the view that globalisation exacerbates poverty: in fact, the opposite is true. Dollar has elsewhere (2002) written that there is a discord between academics in the affluent 'North' who see globalisation exacerbating poverty and academics in the poorer 'South' who take the opposite view. Dollar and Kraay argue that while there may have been trends towards global inequality over the past 200 years, these trends have begun to reverse in the past 30 years, particularly in China and India. These countries have managed to take advantage of rising economic growth. In particular, Dollar and Kraay state that inequality is more of a domestic issue than one derived from global processes, and individual nations therefore need better policy frameworks to enable globalisation to work better for them. Rather ironically, Dollar (2002, pp. 18–32) cites five trends of global poverty reduction, implying that while economic globalisation cannot be causally associated with increasing poverty, it can be linked to decreasing it. First, Dollar argues that the growth rates of the world's poorest countries have accelerated and this growth leads to higher living standards. Second, there has been a net reduction in the numbers of world poor since 1980. Third, measures of global inequality have also declined. Fourth, there is no clear pattern of rising inequality within countries. Finally, although there may be general patterns of increasing wage inequality, the overall increases in wages mean that household inequality is not as pronounced as it was in the past. Overall, Dollar states that globalisation since 1980 'has been a powerful force for equality and poverty reduction' (p. 32).

Wealth for whom?

However, a paper by Oxfam (2004) titled 'Growth with equity is good for the poor' asks the question: good for whom? Oxfam does not explicitly dispute the idea that growth can be beneficial; what it does dispute is the way that Dollar and Kraay conflate the benefits of growth with globalisation, liberalisation and the free market. The data presented by Oxfam demonstrate the opposite conclusion from that reached by Dollar and Kraay, making it hard to answer the question of globalisation and poverty with any empirical definitiveness. For example, Wade (2002) suggests that there are multiple reasons to be critical of the World Bank's point-blank claim that globalisation reduces poverty, because it relies on data that are infected with serious conceptual and methodological flaws. Second, as Birdsall (2002) argues, an open and globally integrated economy is not by definition always good for alleviating poverty; it actually depends on the specific situation, as some developing countries are more vulnerable to the risks associated with an open economic policy than others. Third, while economic globalisation may be productive, integrative and growth-generating, this is not necessarily evenly distributed, nor is it a sufficient condition on its own to alleviate poverty (Coeuré 2002; Gramlich 2002; Kawai 2002).

The benefits and costs of economic globalisation appear to be 'mixed' (Tisdell, Svizzero & Lasselle 2004, p. 73). A blanket approach of market liberalisation may produce excellent results in some places and disasters in others. The liberalisation of the market, SAPs, economic growth and global integration is neither the panacea for global poverty, in many cases compounding and even creating poverty, nor necessarily a driving force behind it.

Reflective question: Does globalisation make the world richer or poorer, or both?

POLITICAL AND LEGAL GLOBALISATION

The idea of the nation-state refers to the claim to sovereignty over a particular territory in which there is agreement as to the demarcation of its borders. The definition of the modern state was eloquently characterised by Max Weber in the following way:

It possesses an administrative and legal order subject to change by legislation, to which the organized corporate activity of the administrative staff, which is also regulated by legislation, is oriented. This system of order claims binding authority, not only over members of the state, the citizens, most of whom have obtained membership by birth, but also to a very large extent, over all action taking place of its jurisdiction. It is thus a compulsory association with a territorial basis. Furthermore, today, the use of force is regarded as legitimate only so far as it is permitted by the state or prescribed by it. (1964, p. 156)

Many of the commentators on globalisation argue that the actual distinction of this territory has become blurred and that economic globalisation has weakened the state's ability to exercise legitimate authority over a specific jurisdiction, to the point of collapse. When the inevitability of the market becomes 'God', the status of the citizen is then potentially reduced to that of a servant of that market and therefore no longer a citizen of the community and polis (Stone 2002). The question that is then raised is: does globalisation, particularly its economic dimensions, undermine national sovereignty?

THE WITHERING AWAY OF THE STATE?

A number of sociologists of globalisation think that globalisation does undermine national sovereignty, referring to the 'demise' or 'withering away' of the nation-state (Albrow 1996; Castells 1996b, p. ii; Lash & Urry 1994, p. 325; Beck 2000d, pp. 139–42). Castells believes that 'globalisation … undermines the autonomy and decision-making power of nation-states' (1996b, pp. ii, 261). Zygmunt Bauman (1998) similarly suggests that nation-states are indeed withering away under the weight and speed of 'transnationality' and under such conditions the capacity for 'deliberate, purposeful and potentially rational action' (p. 56) gives way to a 'new world disorder' in which no-one in particular appears to be at the helm (p. 57). Bauman argues that globalisation is more about disorder and confusion than coherency or universalism, and what remains of the nation-state is merely its threadbare capacity to facilitate the business of economic growth.

Overall, as James Fulcher (2000) has summed it up, the arguments concerning the erosion of the nation-state revolve around the following five points:

- The expansion of international law and global organisations undermines national sovereignty.
- Global economic integration reduces nation-states' control over their own economies.
- Global social and religious movements have undermined the authority and legitimacy of national governments.
- The development of global communication reduces states' power to police their territory and borders.
- Ethnic and religious identity has been reconfigured on a global scale to cut across national boundaries and undermine the authority of the nation-state (pp. 523–4).

For many sociologists of globalisation, then, the constantly increasing global integration of economic enterprises and activity occurs, by definition, at the expense of the sovereignty of the nation-state.

In these approaches to globalisation, the view is that subsequent to the weakening power of the state and the disorder of the global context, it is TNCs that will emerge triumphantly and come to dominate national and global policy (Klein 2000). This idea is also central to much of the anti-globalisation movement—the view that corporations now, or at least at some time in the near future, will dominate the globe, rendering democracy meaningless.

However, Paul Hirst, Graeme Thompson and Simon Bromley (2009; see also Hirst & Thompson 1995; 1996) suggest that the understanding of globalisation 'as conceived by the more extreme globalisers'—that is, as driven by autonomous economic processes rendering the nation-state powerless and irrelevant—'is largely unfounded' (p. 3). They see the division of the world between the advanced industrial economies and the developing economies as having lost none of its salience, and they give five main reasons for their scepticism about the supposedly radical changes that globalisation is seen as having brought about:

1. The internationalisation of the economy is not really new, and 'the current international economy has only recently become as open and integrated as the regime that prevailed from 1870 to 1914'.
2. Genuine TNCs are in fact rare, with most corporations being based nationally and trading regionally or multinationally.
3. Foreign direct investment remains 'highly concentrated in the advanced industrial economies, and the Third World remains marginal in both investment and trade, a small minority of newly industrializing countries apart'.
4. What is considered 'the global economy' is therefore really only the economy of the North America/Europe/Japan triad.

5. Contrary to ideas of the market being out of control, the major economic powers and players, 'centred on the G8 with China and India', can and do regulate and control global markets. For Hirst, Thompson and Bromley, 'global markets are ... by no means beyond regulation and control' (p. 3).

None of this implies that the materiality of international travel, communication, economics, transport, international treaties, **non-governmental organisations (NGOs)**, TNCs, media, poverty and so on is irrelevant or somehow not real. But, at the same time, the capacity for domestic governance of TNCs still exists, meaning that TNCs are not always in positions to dictate the policy conditions of their operations. Given the fluidity and chaos of the global environment, some (such as Garrett 2004) argue that under conditions of global and mobile capital, nations will actually attempt to *strengthen* their sovereignty in order to manage such fluidity. Globalisation is therefore seen as potentially good for national sovereignty and actually provides an incentive for social democracy.

The 'driver' of social transformation is also often the nation-state rather than processes of globalisation. John Zysman, for example, argues that '[n]ational developments have ... driven changes in the global economy; even more than a so-called "globalisation" has driven national evolutions' (1996, p. 164). As Kofi Annan argued in a keynote address on globalisation and international relations, 'the sovereign state remains a highly relevant and necessary institution; indeed, the very linchpin of human security' (2004, p. 240). Paul Hirst similarly observed that: 'Nation states are linchpins in the art of distributing power, ordering government by giving it legitimacy' (2000, p. 243).

Few would consider the state as always benevolent, but as Annan (2004) suggests, even though globalisation will present a challenge to the state, that challenge ought to be met by states through robust policy measures that claim legitimate authority to protect and provide for their citizens. One of the problems, however, is how to reconcile what appear to be mutually exclusive concepts of the boundedness of statism with borderless globalisation. For example, realists argue that internally nation-states need to operate within strict principles of legitimacy, authority, law and regard for their members. However, outside the confines of the nation-state there is, according to realists, international anarchy. This means that there is no overall international authority or government that presides over the collection of disparate and competitive states (Dunne & Schmidt 2001). One way out of this problem perhaps is to see the state as having a legitimate, even symbiotic, role with the global and therefore aim to avoid unhelpful state/global oppositional dichotomies. As Fulcher argues:

As the range of social relationships expands and new, larger-scale units emerge, lower-level ones do not disappear but persist in a changed form. We must also make room for the existence of distinct regional groupings between the national and the global. The only solution is to recognise that we live in a multi-level society with communal, national, regional, and global levels of organization. (2000, p. 540)

The state is, after all, a 'site of cultural politics' (Nash 2000, p. 47) and these politics are not being rendered obsolete but are being 'redefined and restructured in light of global processes' (Nash 2000, p. 47). The task for sociologists, concludes Fulcher, 'is not to argue about whether society is global or national but to analyse and understand the complex interaction between the various levels of a multi-level society' (2000, p. 541; see also Weiss 1997; 2003).

It is clear that the nation-state is being altered and reconstructed, particularly by the power and scope of economic and technological globalisation. As Jan Nederveen Pieterse put it:

... state power remains extremely strategic, but it is no longer the only game in town. The tide of globalization reduces states' room for manoeuvre, while international institutions, transnational transactions, regional co-operation, subnational dynamics and non-governmental organizations expand in impact and scope. (1994, p. 179)

However, this does not mean that the nation-state is withering away or being rendered obsolete. Instead, there is argument to say that under the fluidity and uncertainty of globalisation, states will actually strengthen their position of authority through strong governance and policy. Drawing on the strength and infrastructure of existing states, as well as the potential that globalisation presents for integration, provides possibilities for uniting nation-states around common global problems.

GLOBAL GOVERNANCE

Christopher Chase-Dunn and his colleagues have pointed out that economic globalisation in fact 'creates a great demand for political globalization because markets are unable to resolve the problems of distributive justice and uneven development that they create' (2000, p. 83). Rather than undermining the nation-state, the effect of economic globalisation is more likely to be stimulation of political and cultural globalisation—what many analyses refer to as the formation of global civil society. More than this, as Fulcher emphasises, state-formation has taken place *through* globalisation and not in *opposition* to it. It was the protective and regulatory 'shell' provided by international alignments and organisations that made the construction of national identity and the autonomy and sovereignty of the nation-state possible. A key foundation stone of the modern system of states was the Peace of Westphalia in 1648, which constituted a multi-state agreement between all the powers of Western Europe to recognise each state's sovereignty over religious belief, as well as the right of Christians of other denominations to practise their religion in private or in public at particular times. 'Thus to a significant degree', write Hirst, Thompson and Bromley, 'the capacity for sovereignty came from without, through agreements between states in the newly emerging society of states' (2009, p. 221).

> 'There can be no doubt that politics is becoming more polycentric, with states as merely one level in a complex system of overlapping and often competing agencies of governance.' (Hirst et al. 2009, pp. 233–4)

This Westphalian model of national sovereignty has been put under strain by the processes of globalisation, because many governance functions are increasingly difficult to contain within national borders. The regulation of trade, finance, labour, migration and refugee movements, the environment and crime all require supra-nationally coordinated activities. Hirst, Thompson and Bromley explain the new role that states take on in a post-Westphalian system:

> ... *states will come to function less as all-purpose providers of governance and more as the authors and legitimators of an international 'quasi-polity'; the central functions of the nation-state will become those of providing legitimacy for and ensuring the accountability of supranational and subnational governance mechanisms which exercise various forms of 'private' authority'. (2009, p. 220)*

Even in those areas that remain clearly the domestic responsibility of sovereign states, such as the regulation of populations and population movement, the ways in which such tasks are addressed still need to be globally coordinated and aligned.

Hirst, Thompson and Bromley suggest that the management of economic globalisation takes place at three levels of global *economic* governance, but they also constitute difference levels of global *political* governance:

1. international, multilateral regulatory agencies designed for specific purposes, including a significant number of states: the WTO, IMF, World Bank, ILO and environmental agencies (Whaling Commission, etc.)
2. agreements on global imbalances, exchange-rate movements, regulation of short-term financial transactions and so on by the major political entities: G3 (United States, Japan, European Union), G8, G20
3. regional trade and investment blocs: European Union, NAFTA, APEC (2009, pp. 190–1).

To these three they add:

4. national and supranational regional policies balancing social interests with corporate competition and cooperation
5. subnational regional provision of services to particular industries (2009, p. 238).

A variety of legal arenas are also bound up with political globalisation, and the key institutions managing the globalisation of the political domain are identified by Lechner (2009, p. 138) as including the UN General Assembly, the UN Security Council, the International Court of Justice, the International Criminal Court, the International Criminal Tribunal for the former Yugoslavia and the Permanent Court of Arbitration.

The expansion of global forms of governance across a number of levels—transnational, international, macro-regional, national, micro-regional, municipal, local—all 'criss-crossed by functional networks of corporations, international organisations, non-governmental organisations as well as professionals and computer users' (Nederveen Pieterse 2004, p. 166), generates a new form of global governance that does not replace national sovereignty, but transforms it into a form that Michael Hardt and Antonio Negri refer to as 'Empire':

> *Our basis hypothesis is that sovereignty has taken a new form, comprised of a series of national and supranational organizations united under a simple logic of rule. The new global order of sovereignty is what we call Empire.* (2000, pp. xi–xii)

Hardt and Negri see the constitution of this globalised ordering of political institutions and relationships in the form of a pyramid with three tiers, each subdivided into a number of levels. At the top of the first tier is the United States, ' a superpower that can act alone but prefers to act in collaboration with others under the umbrella of the United Nations' (p. 309). On the levels below, but still within the first tier, are the next-most important nation-states, the G8, and 'a heterogeneous set of associations … [which] … deploy cultural and biopolitical power on a global level' (p. 310), which would include bodies such as the UN, WTO, IMF and World Bank. The second tier consists of transnational corporations, 'productive organizations that … extend transversally under the umbrella and guarantee of the central power that constitutes the first tier of global power' (p. 310), together with the smaller nation-states and their associated NGOs. The third tier comprises 'groups that represent popular interests in the global power arrangement' (p. 311), nation-states in their capacity as representing their constituencies and those NGOs 'that strive to represent the least among us, those who cannot represent themselves … [to] … defend human life against torture, starvation, massacre, imprisonment, and political assassination' (p. 313), which includes Amnesty International, Human Rights Watch, Oxfam and Médecines San Frontières.

THE GLOBALISATION OF LAW

Both economic and political globalisation are dependent on transformations in the structure and functioning of legal institutions and practices. As Frank Lechner observes, 'international law is steadily expanding into "world law" … a configuration of rules that govern more than state relations and anchor diverse and significant forms of governance' (2009, p. 126).

There are two senses in which we can speak of the globalisation of law:

1. In relation to the central role that law plays in all processes of globalisation, especially economic globalisation. As Halliday and Osinsky argue, 'law is heavily implicated in the process of globalisation' (2006, p. 447). Economic relations depend on business regulation and the legal definition of markets; the integration of global economic activity across national borders is based on the formulation of standardised, legally enforceable rules, principles and practices; and intellectual property rights regimes are central to cultural globalisation.
2. In terms of the increasingly global nature of legal institutions, ideas and practices, generating the expansion of global law in areas such as transnational governance, human rights and international criminal law. In response to this line of development, the practice of law is also becoming increasingly transglobal, with law firms, like corporations, taking on a global scale and operating across national borders.

Law and globalisation

A central element of the deterritorialisation of economic activity and its disembedding from the context of the nation-state is the creation of what Halliday and Osinsky refer to as 'an international financial architecture and global norms, model laws, regulatory frameworks, and institutions of dispute resolution to facilitate economic development within countries and across the world' (2006, p. 457). Law is a vital vehicle for economic globalisation in three senses:

1. in the form of legislation that harmonises corporate, commercial, tax and administrative law to facilitate the globalisation of trade and finance
2. in a variety of transnational forms of regulating business activity
3. in a proliferating range of semi-formal and informal dispute-resolution forums.

Halliday and Osinsky note that the legal arena 'reflects and expresses the conflict in competition among nation-states and market actors for economic advantage' (p. 460). Law is also used by a variety of global political actors to 'enforce' globalisation processes in relation to recalcitrant nation-states, often leading to changes in national legislation constituting a gradual convergence in legal standards, norms, principles and procedures across the whole range of legal arenas (p. 452). The globalisation of legal norms can be seen in areas such as 'international policing, human rights, citizenship, environmental politics, and women's rights' (p. 453). But law is also used as the vehicle for what can be regarded as 'postmodern colonialism' (Silbey 1997) or 'capitalist imperialism' (Callinicos 2007), by utilising the law's claim to objectivity, rationality and universality as a Trojan horse for the reduction of local political control over global economic processes that generally favour the global North (de Sousa Santos 1995).

Global law

The other side of the coin to law's mobilisation in support of a range of globalisation processes is its increasingly globalised character, the convergence of national bodies of law around global norms, and the shifting of the balance between international and domestic law towards the former, albeit with the United States holding on most tightly to its status as the global exception. This expansion in the significance of international legal regimes can be seen in a variety of areas, including human rights, children's rights, women's rights, crimes against humanity, war crimes, genocide, all forms of crime, corruption, human trafficking and prostitution, constitutions, environmental regulation, agricultural standards, intellectual property, regulation of labour conditions and tax regulation.

In relation to human rights, for example, we can observe over recent decades 'the persistence and increasingly global spread of rights, despite vast cultural, economic, and political differences' (Klug 2005, p. 99). Continuing a line of development that began with the Nuremberg and Tokyo trials and various other military tribunals at the end of World War II, the pursuit of crime against humanity and genocide has superimposed global legal norms onto national jurisdictions that would not necessarily have pursued such concerns if left to their own devices. The United Nations International Criminal Tribunal for the former Yugoslavia, for example, made it possible to define the ethnic cleansing of Bosnia, Kosovo and Serbia as crimes against humanity and for prosecution to reach right to President Milosevic to bring him to the Tribunal in The Hague.

However, the United States does not see itself as subject to this sort of war crimes jurisdiction and it remains consistently opposed to the International Criminal Court. As Halliday and Osinsky observe, in stark contrast to its agitation for globalisation in other arenas, 'the United States is working hard against global integration on war crimes. Not only has the United States steadfastly resisted ratification, but it is also pursuing values of ad hoc legalism and legal exceptionalism to undermine the legal liberalism that most of its allies advocate' (2006, p. 463).

The globalisation of human rights norms and the significance of legal frameworks for economic globalisation have also underpinned a strong concern with constitutionalism, in the aftermath of the disintegration of the Soviet Union and in other parts of the world engaged in state-formation efforts. The World Bank and the IMF, for example, have been keen to agitate for the strengthening of a variety of aspects of the rule of law around the world. The principles of this 'rise in world constitutionalism', as Halliday and Osinsky refer to it, generally 'include the separation of powers, a strong and independent judiciary, a constitutional court that appeals to higher-order norms than statutes, the expansion of human rights that are protected or expanded by courts, a separation of religious and secular power, and some kind of majoritarian or popular democracy' (2006, p. 464). Klug (2005, p. 96) points out that in the decade after the end of the Cold War in 1989, more than 56 per cent of UN member states made major amendments to their constitutions, and more than 70 per cent of these adopted entirely new constitutions. And by the turn of the millennium, the constitutions of roughly half the member states included bills of rights or some form of fundamental rights, so that this new world constitutionalism has become a significant vehicle for the spread of globalised conceptions of human rights.

The practice of the legal profession itself has also become significantly globalised, with the expansion of mega-law firms, dominated overwhelmingly by American lawyers and staffed, as Yves Dezalay observed, by

> ... a new kind of lawyer, distinguished from their predecessors as much by their appetite for success as by the resources that they are able to mobilize: they rely less on social connections and the reciprocal granting of favors, classical characteristics of the insulated world of the law, and present themselves more as technical experts who are sure of their competence and quite ready to put it into practice. (1990, p. 287)

Dezalay described this aspect of the emergence of global law as an ongoing 'recomposition of the legal field' (p. 280), allowing legal practice both to improve its alignment with its clients in the corporate world and to retain its autonomy. The new forms of global legal practice underpin what is referred to as the revival of the medieval 'lex mercatoria'—'law merchants' operating outside the framework of state-managed legal regimes to establish principles of contract and commerce and to settle disputes (Cutler 2001; Dezalay & Garth 1996). The argument, as Lawrence Friedman outlines it, is that 'the transnational lawyers of today have their own customs, norms, and practices, and a sort of merchant law is emerging, without benefit of legislation, from their patterns of behavior' (2001, p. 356). These new legal entrepreneurs are primarily at the service of their wealthy and powerful clients, focused on 'working towards the construction of increasingly more sophisticated juridical mechanisms for the framing and regulation of international economic exchange' (Dezalay 1990, p. 282).

Reflective questions: Can you think of how to approach other possible examples of the globalisation of law, such as intellectual property law, or the control of copyright in songs and music?

Are there sometimes reasons to be critical of law's globalisation? What are its negative effects?

AMERICAN HEGEMONY

The global ordering of politics and governance is often seen as being subject to the hegemonic power of the United States. For example, Noam Chomsky (1999) claims that the United States has used and abused international institutions such as the United Nations and the WTO to its own advantage by imposing tariffs and subsidising American industries, imposing SAPs on some countries through the IMF and the World Bank, empowering American corporations and aggressively spreading American values, particularly those associated with neoliberalism, 'democracy' and the market.

The United States certainly did capitalise on its strong economy to play a central role after World War II in designing and controlling an infrastructure for managing the international economy. Its own economy grew fantastically from 1991 to 2000 (Cox 2001), and the country has continued to develop and use its overwhelming military superiority against regimes or countries deemed hostile to its interests, further attempting to establish itself as a global superpower. It has been argued that the United States effectively 'won' the Cold War between its greatest military and ideological opponent, the former USSR and other Eastern Bloc countries. American confidence subsequently grew and the country has recently begun to act unilaterally in the international arena. To many it seems as if American cultural products—from films to sports shoes, McDonald's and bombs—are flooding the world, hand in hand with an American brand of free market democracy.

More alarmingly, however, in *Hegemony or Survival* Chomsky (2003) notes that the United States has recently made a number of quite aggressive inroads towards achieving *permanent and total* global dominance. Using intense forms of propaganda within the United States (such as controlling the media and limiting the range of political options open to its citizens) and using even more overt and aggressive means abroad (such as 'preventative' rather than pre-emptive military force), the United States, Chomsky explains, is presently attempting to dismantle international laws, agreements and protocols that prevent its reaching its hegemonic goals. Such goals are, of course, not consensually shared by citizens of the United States, but remain the province of the state and elite power. Chomsky refers to this as 'enforcing hegemony' (p. 12) and says that the scope and indignity of this hegemony is edging the world towards a precarious future: global hegemony on a powder-keg of nuclear weapons is a genuine threat to human survival, and as such the fate of the world hangs in the balance.

The limitations of hegemony

Whereas some commentators equate globalisation with **Americanisation** (e.g. Taylor 2000; Barber 2004 [1995]), others disagree. Taylor (2000), for example, does indeed link globalisation and modernisation with Americanisation and with the process of American hegemony that extended after World War II. However, he also argues that the strength of this hegemony has been declining since the 1970s. The very word 'Americanisation' implies a process that is practically guaranteed; it describes both the 'being' and the 'becoming' as immutable. The being, of course, is America and the becoming is the rest of the world. However, as Taylor explains, 'pure end states *never* come into being' (p. 50, emphasis added) and so what we might witness as Americanisation is more or less mere 'tendencies' rather than total end points.

Hegemony, which is never complete, is however more than economic or military dominance. Using Gramsci's concept of hegemony, Taylor argues that American hegemony is as much to do with the cultural and the social as it is to do with politics and economics. Thus, American hegemony is not just about its superpower status—it is about Western American culture and its *relationship* to political and economic power. Taylor argues that American hegemony is not a linear process, but can be identified in phases: incipient, capacious and resonant. These phases culminated in a period of high hegemony during the times in history in which the embracement of modernity was strongest. The strength of American hegemony exists in tandem with the strength of a coherent form of modernity. Globalisation, then, as a recasting of modernity, signals the demise of American hegemony, alongside the demise of everything else promised by progressive modernity (Taylor 2000). This argument suggests that far from globalisation being the opportune moment for total American hegemony, it is in fact the vehicle for its decline.

The decline of American hegemony—Wallerstein

Immanuel Wallerstein (2002) takes this view one step further and argues strongly that the period of **Pax Americana** is actually over and the United States is now in the throes of a progressive decline as a global superpower. Wallerstein argues that:

> The economic, political, and military factors that contributed to U.S. hegemony are the same factors that will inexorably produce the coming U.S. decline. (2002, paragraph 1)

Wallerstein made this point as early as 1979, indicating that this decline is evidence of a crisis in the capitalist system generally. According to Wallerstein, the United States consolidated its hegemonic position up to and just after World War II by:

- dominating newly formed international governance and economic agreements
- attempting to monopolise the use of force through superior military power
- supporting the growth and modernisation of regions in Western Europe and Japan that would provide a fertile bed for market demand for United States products
- cultivating a global ideological and cultural hegemony of free market democracy in the style of the United States.

All this, Wallerstein (2002; 2006) argues, has been eroded since 1968 by the following:

- *The Vietnam War.* This exhausted the American economy, and the corresponding 1968 revolutions reflected a loss of faith in the righteousness of American ideological dominance.
- *The collapse of communism.* This was sudden and largely unanticipated. The loss of an ideological opponent contributed to a 'loss of legitimacy' behind American hegemony. Wallerstein argues that the Gulf War in Iraq in 1990 aimed to fill this gap and provided in many ways a reason for the United States to continue to exist as a world superpower in the absence of communism.
- *Eastern European and Middle Eastern conflict.* The United States has failed to manage this conflict, despite its best efforts to do so.
- *The response to 9/11 and the invasion of Iraq.* The terrorist attacks on the World Trade Center and the Pentagon in September 2001 made it possible for American neoconservatives to mobilise their agenda to restore American global power. In their pursuit of the 'New American Century', the aim was to intimidate the three major sources of challenge to American hegemony: (1) Western Europe, (2) potential nuclear proliferators such as North Korea and Iran, and (3) the Arab states, which were continuing to resist Israel's legitimacy. The invasion of Iraq came nowhere near to achieving any part of this aim, and the net result, argues Wallerstein, has been 'to accelerate the decline of U.S. hegemony rather than reverse it' (2006, p. 92).

The world has entered into a relatively unstructured, multilateral division of geopolitical power, with a number of regional centres of varying strength manoeuvring for advantage—the United States, the United Kingdom, Western Europe, Russia, China, Japan, India, Iran and Brazil at the very least. There is no overwhelming superiority— economic, political, military or ideological-cultural—in any one of these centres. And there is no strong set of alliances for the moment, although one is likely to emerge.

Wallerstein suggests that the military is the United States' *only* strength, but that it is at the same time its major weakness, given its enormous expense. As long as the United States pours money into its military complex it makes its economy and social infrastructure progressively weaker, as the recent global financial crisis has highlighted. In all, Wallerstein anticipates that the world 'has entered into a relatively unstructured, multilateral division of geopolitical power' (2006, p. 92), with the United States one of a number of regional centres of power, as outlined above, none of which will have clear economic, political, cultural or even military superiority.

Reflective question: What are the arguments for and against seeing the globalised world as basically America writ large?

CULTURAL GLOBALISATION

Arjan Appadurai suggests that a central theme in the discussions of the cultural dimensions of globalisation has been the question of 'the tension between cultural homogenization and cultural heterogenization' (1990, p. 295). So, some observers will draw attention to processes of McDonaldisation or Americanisation (Barber 1992), whereas others will see globalisation processes as being far more complex, generating greater diversity as much as greater standardisation (Appadurai 1990; 1996; Hannerz 1992; 1996; Nederveen Pieterse 2004). Nederveen Pieterse (2004, p. 178) outlines the different vocabularies that characterise these two contrasting approaches to cultural globalisation: 'globalisation-as-homogenisation' and 'globalisation-as-hybridisation' (see Table 2.2).

Cultural homogenisation

Leslie Sklair (1991) has argued that a central element of global economic transactions is a pervasive culture and ideology of consumerism. Corporations may exercise

Table 2.2 Two contrasting approaches to cultural globalisation

Globalisation-as-homogenisation	Globalisation-as-diversification
Cultural imperialism	Cultural planetarisation
Cultural dependence	Cultural interdependence
Cultural hegemony	Cultural interpenetration
Autonomy	Syncretism, synthesis, hybridity
Modernisation	Modernisation
Westernisation	Global mélange
Cultural synchronisation	Creolisation, cross-over
World civilisation	Global ecumene

control not only over political or economic spheres, but also over the cultural mechanisms that foster demand. For example, Korzeniewicz's (2004/1994) study of Nike shows how Nike was able to advance its position by developing control and expertise, not only at the level of production (of shoes), but also at other levels of the 'commodity chain' (p. 170). These include controlling the capacities not only to import and export its products, but also to market and advertise its product, contributing in some way towards raising the social and cultural importance of fitness and athleticism at a 'global' level. So powerful is this ideology in maintaining global economism, that Sklair argues that a counter-hegemony of the global can exist only through dismantling the cultures and ideologies of consumerism or, as Sklair states, by rejecting any commitment to 'continuous capitalist accumulation' (p. 82). The commitment to consumerism is, for Sklair, crucial to global economic, political and cultural hegemony, which, as he says, is an almost complete hegemonic process.

One of the key areas in which consumption has been globalised is that of fast food, and the ubiquitous presence of McDonald's around the world provides a good insight in the mechanics of globalisation processes.

The McDonaldisation of society—George Ritzer

A useful discussion of the globalisation of everyday life is American sociologist George Ritzer's *The McDonaldization of Society* (2008; orig 1993). *McDonaldisation* is a term coined by Ritzer to refer to 'the process by which the principles of the fast-food restaurant are coming to dominate more and more sectors of American society as well as the rest of the world' (p. 1). For Ritzer, it is important to understand the extent to which the nature of social and cultural life is formed by its *organisation*, leading to a global standardisation of important aspects of everyday life.

McDonaldisation does not simply refer to the spread and global proliferation of McDonald's restaurants or, indeed, the global franchising of countless other industries; instead, Ritzer identifies McDonald's as the paradigm example of modern bureaucratic rationality. Ritzer identifies four interconnected dimensions in the McDonaldisation process: efficiency, calculability, predictability and control (pp. 13–15). Paradoxically, such apparent rationality produces its own forms of irrationality, which he believes should lead us to develop a more critical understanding of the McDonaldisation process.

Efficiency

Like all bureaucracies, the emphasis in McDonaldised organisations is on efficiency, on striving to find the best possible means of achieving particular goals. In his analysis of bureaucracy, Weber contrasted the concept of 'substantive' rationality, which is based on the particular value positions used to determine goals, with 'instrumental' rationality, which determines the optimum means of achieving those goals. Ritzer argues that instrumental rationality seems to overwhelm substantive rationality. Making various service organisations more efficient has in fact involved a considerable transfer of labour to the consumer. The most obvious examples include supermarkets, service stations, salad bars and automatic teller machines (ATMs), but it extends to medical consultations, automated telephone answering systems and booking airline tickets. 'The modern consumer', writes Ritzer, 'spends an increasingly significant amount of time and energy doing unpaid labour' (2008, p. 78).

Calculability

Part of the process of increasing efficiency is to make organisations, their work processes and the human resources and raw materials they work with as quantifiable and calculable as possible. The effect is a focus on quantity and **calculability**, with concern for quality becoming secondary and reduced to its 'predictability'. Ritzer mentioned the example of Kentucky Fried Chicken (KFC): the original gravy was excellent quality but, when Colonel Sanders sold the business, the new owners decided 'it was too complex, too time-consuming, too expensive ... It wasn't fast food'. Colonel Sanders said:

> *That friggin'... outfit ... They prostituted every goddam thing I had. I had the greatest gravy in the world and those sons of bitches they dragged it out and extended and watered it down that I'm so goddamn mad. (quoted in Ritzer 2008, p. 83)*

Television programs are also increasingly oriented towards the sheer number of viewers (ratings), which results in their being targeted at the 'lowest common denominator' in the potential audience. In universities, too, both teaching and research are increasingly defined in purely quantifiable terms—of students graduating, of papers published, of citations listed—often at the expense of quality, which is much harder to measure. The social world thus becomes oriented around what is quantifiable, measurable and calculable, at the expense of anything that is more difficult to calculate.

Predictability

Calculability is greatly enhanced by **predictability**: if the work done by organisations is predictable and standardised, so that work processes, the organisation's products and even workers themselves remain as similar as possible no matter what the context. McDonald's thus claims that its hamburgers are exactly the same whether they are bought in Beijing or Paris, Texas. Australian homes filled with IKEA furniture look identical to their counterparts in Sweden, and a Holiday Inn in Amsterdam is the same as one in Rio de Janeiro. Camping grounds are also increasingly standardised across the world, as are clothes, cars, music, most foods—in fact, almost any product of consumption one chooses to mention. Disneyland is an example of routinised, McDonaldised recreation, and it works as a model for clones throughout the world, such as Dreamworld in Australia.

Control

These processes in turn rely on a maximum **control** over everything that organisations deal with: human beings and their labour, raw materials, labour processes, sometimes animals. This control is best achieved through the maximum substitution of non-human technology for human skills—robotisation—or the imposition of a military-like discipline with little room for anything as inefficient as 'democracy'. Labour processes are routinised and their skill content reduced ('deskilled') as much as possible in order to maximise the elimination of human error, variability, inefficiency and lack of calculability. The use of non-human technologies is becoming increasingly widespread as a means of exercising total control, effectively turning the remaining human beings into robots and machines, much as Frederick Taylor and Henry Ford aimed for. Ritzer quotes one airline employee as saying: 'My body became an extension of the computer terminal that I type the reservations into. I came to feel emptied of self' (2008, p. 123).

The irrationality of rationality

In reality, the pursuit of efficiency often creates other inefficiencies, such as queues outside ATMs and in recreation parks, the refuse produced by fast-food packaging or the traffic generated by people travelling to McDonald's, Pizza Hut or KFC. A strong focus on instrumental rationality can make it difficult to grasp issues to do with substantive rationality, such as when social change occurs.

The processes of routinisation and standardisation characteristic of McDonaldisation can also reflect in an inefficient way the regional and local differences in the way organisations, their workers and their clients operate. Standardisation aims to iron out local differences, when sensitivity to such differences can be what is necessary to make an organisation's activities rational.

Ritzer also argues that McDonaldisation is dehumanising, in that a range of important features of human social life and interaction tend to be eliminated. He quotes Bob Garfield's comments on a visit to Disneyland, in which he emphasised how little fun and fantasy there actually was in an organisation aiming precisely at encouraging fun and fantasy:

> *From the network of chutes and corrals channeling people into attractions, to the chillingly programmed Stepford Wives demeanour of the employees, to the compulsively litter-free grounds, to the generalized North Korean model Socialist Society sense of totalitarian order, to the utterly passive nature of the entertainment itself, Disney turns out to be the very antithesis of fantasy ... Disney is a plodding, precise, computer controlled mechanism pulling an estimated 30 million visitors along the same calculated, unvarying, meticulously engineered entertainment experience ... Imagine, for example, a fake*

submergence in a fake submarine for a fake voyage past fake coral and fake seafood, knowing full well that there are two magnificent aquariums within a 70-minute drive of your house. (cited in Ritzer 2004, p. 155)

The irrationality of McDonaldisation, and more broadly cultural globalisation to the extent that it follows these principles, argues Ritzer, is that it undermines the human capacity for thought and the exercise of imagination, skill and creativity, because these qualities are difficult to quantify, routinise, calculate, predict and control.

The Starbuckisation of society

There are a range of linked examples of McDonaldisation in processes of globalising social and economic life, such as the spread of IKEA and Walmart, but recently Ritzer (2008, pp. 211–31) has raised the possibility that the spread of Starbucks coffee shops might have taken over from McDonald's as the model for the organisational form taken by globalisation processes, so that it may be more accurate today to speak of the Starbuckisation of society. Although Starbucks currently has fewer outlets worldwide than McDonald's, Ritzer observes that its rate of expansion is much more rapid (p. 212), and Starbucks is 'not only the current star of the fast-food industry and a model for businesspeople everywhere, but it is also increasingly seen as an important cultural force and cultural phenomenon' (p. 213).

Starbucks is pursuing a strategy of denser occupation of parts of some cities, on the principle that it is more likely that the average consumer will buy one or more cups of coffee four or five times a week than buy a Big Mac and fries every day. The spread of Starbucks has actively transformed many aspects of everyday life in the countries where it operates—in some respects positively, such as improving the quality of coffee available on a large scale in countries like the United States and the United Kingdom. But Ritzer concludes that although Starbuckisation takes the McDonaldisation process into different directions—addressing a different section of the market, stressing the quality of its coffee, offering a more congenial atmosphere and so on—it is still essentially the same process, offering, in the main, 'coffees for those who don't really like coffee' (p. 228). Indeed, the two are merging, with McDonald's offering higher quality coffee and Starbucks offering breakfast that is a copy of McDonald's Egg McMuffin. Ritzer predicts that 'in the not-too distant future, McDonald's and Starbucks will *both* offer the same food for breakfast—a decent-tasting egg-and-cheese on an English muffin sandwich and high(er)-quality coffee' (p. 230).

Australia, however, seems to be offering some local resistance to the Starbuckisation of the world. In July 2008, Starbucks decided to close 61 of its 84 Australian outlets. The company's lack of success in Australia as well as other parts of the world may be related to the kind of 'irrationality of rationalisation' to which Ritzer has drawn attention, and as expressed in the concerns of Starbucks' founder, Howard Schultz, who worried in 2007 that 'some people even call our stores sterile, cookie cutter, no longer reflecting the passion our partners [i.e. employees] feel about our coffee' (cited in Ritzer 2008, p. 230).

Jihad vs McWorld

For Benjamin Barber (2004), the future appears to have only two competing possibilities. On the one hand, we can look forward to a future of a multicultural 'Jihad' in which 'culture is pitted against culture, people against people, tribe against tribe' (p. 29) in countless attempts to resist unfolding modernity. On the other hand, we can expect the bland homogenising spectacle of 'McWorld', of fast food, computers and MTV (p. 29). Paradoxically, both exist in tandem, in a dialect, so to speak, and together they force the world into chaos as they erode the nation-state, democracy and any hope for a civil society. For Barber, 'McWorld' is a euphemism for the corporatisation and Americanisation of the planet. The product on sale is American culture and ideology, and it is 'driven by expansionist commerce' (p. 33) into every corner of the world. According to Barber, while 'Jihad' may dominate the headlines with 'microwars' (p. 34), it is 'McWorld' that will eventually homogenise the planet.

Clash of civilisations

In a similar style, Huntington (2004) argues that *the conflicts of the future will be not so much ideological or economic between nation-states as they will be cultural between civilisations.* He argues that the great conflicts of the past have been ideological wars within the corpus of Western society. Like some other theorists of globalisation, he believes the increasing contact between different groups can sometimes have the effect of intensifying the emphasis on differences rather than bringing groups closer together. In Huntington's theory, the groups are civilisations rather than nation-states or religions as such. However, there are often close relationships between religions and civilisations.

'The fault lines between civilizations will be the battle lines of the future', writes Huntington (p. 36). These 'fault lines' are divided between 'Western, Confucian,

Japanese, Islamic, Hindu, Slavic-Orthodox, Latin American and possibly African American civilizations' (p. 37). Huntington argues that the clash of civilisations will play itself out between the West and the Rest. Despite the power of the West, or perhaps because of it, Huntington can see five reasons for believing that a clash of civilisations will occur:

1. The differences between civilisations are marked.
2. Globalisation is thrusting these civilisations together faster than these marked differences can be accommodated.
3. Economic modernisation weakens regional identity, with fundamentalist religion filling a newly created ideological and identity gap.
4. The power of the West is accompanied by corresponding anti-Western trends.
5. The international economy is concentrated in regional areas, forcing once ideological rivals into closer partnerships of interdependence and also potential conflict.

Huntington does not argue that sources of conflict and identity other than civilisations and their religions will disappear or become insignificant. However, he does believe that civilisations will become more important than ideology and other sources of conflict. The implication is that religion will become more rather than less important in global terms. Although at the moment Western Christian civilisation is dominant, in the future it will increasingly be challenged. China, for example, has developed nuclear weapons, and Islamic countries such as Pakistan, India, Iran and Iraq have been trying to develop them (India carried out underground nuclear tests in 1998). There is also the possibility of an arms race between Eastern civilisations based on Islamic and Confucian religions. However, as there is no likelihood of a world or global civilisation developing, the different civilisations will have to learn to live with one another. Huntington does not have much to say about how this might be achieved.

Cultural heterogeneity

Much of Ritzer's argument could be read as indicating that McDonaldisation is a process of homogenisation: of turning the world into a bland, predictable and, ultimately, boring place. Even if we take the busiest McDonald's in the world as an example, which is in Hong Kong, it would be wrong to simply conclude that Hong Kong has been McDonaldised because it is extraordinarily popular and well patronised. The extent of popularity and patronage alone does not mean that people in Hong Kong have had their cultural heritage subsumed by transnational corporations (Watson 2004). Ritzer is aware of this and does note the way that McDonald's has reflexively adapted to many cultural contexts, contributing in many ways to its global success. For example, McDonald's modifies and customises its menus, changes the aesthetics of its venues and reflexively reconstructs the expectations of its customers according to the cultural context in which it operates (Ritzer 2008, pp. 172–4). It does this as well as transforming the context it operates within (pp. 174–6).

Waters (2001) also sees any homogenising tendencies as always mediated by a process of reflexivity. Rather than complete cultural homogenisation (a virtual transplant of one culture onto or over another), cultural spaces adapt, modify and counteract new cultural forms. Jan Nederveen Pieterse, in an influential 1994 article titled 'Globalization as hybridization', explains that hybridisation refers to the 'ways in which forms become separated from existing practices and recombine with new forms in new practices' (quoted from Rowe & Schelling 1991, p. 231). Cultural hybridisation concerns 'the mixing of Asian, African, American, European cultures: hybridization is the making of global culture as a global mélange' (Nederveen Pieterse 1994, pp. 175–6), and its extent and reach is seriously underestimated by the globalisation-as-homogenisation arguments. The concept 'global cultural synchronisation', writes Nederveen Pieterse,

> ... overrates the homogeneity of Western culture and overlooks the fact that many of the standards exported by the West and its cultural industries themselves turn out to be of culturally mixed character if we examine their cultural lineages. Centuries of South–North cultural osmosis have resulted in an intercontinental cross-over culture. European and Western culture are part of this global mélange. (1994, p. 169)

Waters (2001) agrees, saying that under the conditions of globalisation, 'local homogeneity [is not replaced] by global homogeneity but by *global diversity*' (p. 228, emphasis added).

The global production of difference and hybridity

Scholars working from an anthropological perspective (Appadurai 1990; 1996; Nederveen Pieterse 1994; 2004) have noted how the relationship between globality and localism is often paradoxical. Globalisation processes often do not simply erase or replace local identities, but in fact encourage and generate new forms. Processes of cultural globalisation 'unleash intense nostalgia politics and mobilization drives, of which ethnic upsurges, ethnicization of nations, and religious revivalism form part' (Nederveen Pieterse 1994, pp. 178–9). The homogenising effects of global culture rarely 'sit still'; just as often as not they are 'absorbed into local political and cultural economies, only to be repatriated as heterogeneous dialogues of national sovereignty, free enterprise, fundamentalism' (Appadurai 1990, p. 307). As Birgit Meyer and Peter Geschiere observed in 1999:

> ... in many parts of Africa, accumulation of Western goods is regarded as a sure sign of witchcraft and thus as a way to distinguish between trustworthy and dangerous people; modern technical devices, such as tape recorders, played a crucial role in the spread of Muslim fundamentalism in North Africa and the Middle East, creating a huge market for cassettes of the latest star imam; the recent economic boom of Eastern Asia's newly industrialized countries was accompanied by an equally vibrant boom of spirit cults; Westerners' desire for an encounter with the 'exotic' during their holidays incorporates people all over the world into global relations by requiring them to produce local 'authenticity' as a commodity for global tourism. (p. 7)

In the subsequent decade we have seen ever-proliferating examples of such hybrid cultural mixtures, in which what is claimed as local or national is in many respects the product of global cultural interactions. The mechanisms of global economic, political and social life are often precisely the stimulus and vehicles for the production of an expanding array of localised identities, rather than a standardised template to which everyone in the world is converging.

For Arjan Appadurai, the contemporary world is characterised by a unique combination of mass migration and powerful mass media, which produces diasporic communities that are physically spread around the world, but are linked together by television, telecommunications and the internet. Global networking leads to the regeneration of local languages and forms of cultural production, and new communications technologies such as the internet enable the formation of virtual communities that maintain but also transform and in many respects create forms of 'local' culture. In this sense, Appadurai feels that '[t]he new global cultural economy has to be understood as a complex, overlapping, disjunctive order, which cannot any longer be understood in terms of existing center–periphery models' (1990, p. 296).

Appadurai proposes an alternative conceptual framework that breaks globalisation down into five different dimensions: (1) ethnicity and cultural identity, (2) technology, (3) financial flows, (4), media and (5) ideas and knowledge. He refers to them as 'scapes' structuring the imagination of people living in the contemporary world:

1. *Ethnoscapes:* 'the landscape of persons who constitute the shifting world in which we live: tourists, immigrants, refugees, exiles, guestworkers, and other moving groups and persons' (p. 297), all of whom destabilise and diversify the ethnic and cultural composition of the social world.
2. *Technoscapes:* the global configuration of flow of technology, 'increasingly driven not by obvious economies of scale, of political control, or of market rationality, but of increasingly complex relationships between money flows, political possibilities and the availability of both low and highly-skilled labor' (pp. 297–8).
3. *Finanscapes:* the increasingly rapid flow of money around the world, 'as currency markets, national stock exchanges, and commodity speculations move mega-monies through national turnstiles at blinding speed, with vast absolute implications for small differences in percentage points and time units' (p. 298).
4. *Mediascapes:* the production of images and ideas through newspapers, magazines, television, film, radio and the internet, available to growing

---

> How do we come to terms with phenomena such as Thai boxing in Amsterdam, Mardi Gras Indians in the United States, Asian rap in London, Irish bagels, Chinese tacos or Mexican schoolgirls dressed in Greek togas dancing in the style of Isadora Duncan? How do we interpret Peter Brook directing the Mahabharata, or Ariane Mnouchkine staging a Shakespeare play in Japanese Kabuki style for a Paris audience in the Theatre Soleil? 'Cultural experiences, past or present, have not been simply moving in the direction of cultural uniformity and standardisation' (Nederveen Pieterse 1994, p. 169).
> 1. Are there examples in your own life of this kind of cultural hybridity, a mixing of cultural influences from around the world?
> 2. How does this actually encourage changing forms of local identities?

proportions of the world's population, which 'provide (especially in television film and cassette forms) large and complex repertoires of images, narratives and "ethnoscapes" to viewers throughout the world, in which the world of commodities and the world of "news" and politics are profoundly mixed' (p. 299).

5. *Ideoscapes:* the discursive realm of ideas, images and ideologies around which political action is organised, 'composed of elements of the Enlightenment world-view, which consists of a concatenation of ideas, terms and images, including "freedom", "welfare", "rights", "sovereignty", "representation" and the master-term "democracy"' (p. 299).

For Appadurai, the 'deterritorialisation' and 'disembedding' that writers such as Giddens see as characteristic of globalisation processes take place unevenly across these five different dimensions, producing outcomes that are far too complex and multilayered to be seen as simply universalising a standardising global culture.

GLOCALISATION

One of the ways in which the relationship between the global and the local, and between homogeneity and heterogeneity, has been conceptualised is with the term glocalisation or the expression 'think global, act local'. The concepts 'glocal' and 'glocalisation' were introduced into sociological discussions of globalisation by Roland Robertson, who attributes the origins of glocalisation to its emergence in Japanese marketing discourse, from the word *dochakuka*, meaning 'global localisation', in particular refashioning global products to resonate with local tastes and preferences (Robertson 1992a, pp. 173–4). George Ritzer has defined glocalisation as 'the interpenetration of the global and the local, resulting in unique outcomes in different geographic areas' (2008, p. 166).

The discussion above of McDonald's in Hong Kong is a good example of glocalisation, and Rick Fantasia (1995) also makes similar observations about how the consumption of McDonald's is 'localised' in France, resonating with young, mostly working-class French people's desire for a less formal and less expensive food experience than that of the 'traditional' French restaurant or café. The glocalisation of McDonald's is also evident in the company's replacement of Ronald McDonald in France in 2002 with Asterix the Gaul, largely in response to French resistance to McDonaldisation. As Tony Karon observed in relation to the company's adoption of Asterix:

> 'Indigenizing' McDonald's has been a major component of adapting the brand to its global role—more of the company's earnings today come from abroad than from its U.S. outlets. As former McDonald's President James Cantalupo had said in 1991, the company's strategy was to make itself 'as much part of the local culture as possible'. (Karon 2002)

Rather than seeing global standardisation and localised hybridity as mutually exclusive, the sociological usage of the term 'glocalisation' aims to capture the coexistence 'of both universalizing and particularizing tendencies in globalization; that is, the commonly interconnected processes of homogenization and heterogenization' (Giulianotti & Robertson 2007, p. 134).

Reflective question: Does globalisation produce cultural homogeneity or cultural hybridity, or some combination of the two? Give some examples.

IN SEARCH OF DEGLOBALISATION

Globalisation processes have also generated a number of social and political movements resistant to many of their features, especially to the extent that globalisation processes are harnessed to the pursuit of profit and increased inequality. They are often referred to as anti-globalisation movements, but it is probably more accurate to refer to them as anti-capitalist, alter-globalisation or deglobalisation movements (Callinicos 2003; Bello 2002; 2004). If we ask what it is exactly that underpins these debates, and what it is that has proliferated through the academy, media and political and cultural consciousness filling countless pages of books, journals, articles and papers (Busch 2000), it may not be globalisation per se that occupies people's worries (or celebrations for that matter) but everything that globalisation is considered to represent. As Burgmann argues, 'it is not globalisation in the obvious sense—the greater interconnectedness of the world economy—that is being contested, but the way that this interconnectedness currently operates' (2003, p. 244). The protesters demonstrating in Seattle and Melbourne in 1999 (see below) were clearly concerned about what they saw as the ills of globalisation, but the targets of their critique defended themselves by characterising them instead as anti-globalisation, anti-progress and anti-cosmopolitan (Burgmann 2003, p. 248).

THE ANTI-CAPITALIST MOVEMENT—ALEX CALLINICOS

Alex Callinicos (2003) argues that in the late 1990s a distinctive new social movement began to take shape. Although sometimes called *anti-globalisation*, he suggests it is more accurate to see it as *anti-capitalist*. Many of those involved welcome some aspects of globalisation, such as increased global sharing of culture, resources and even styles of cooking. Callinicos suggests that it is specifically the influence of global capitalism that its supporters are opposed to. The most obvious manifestations of this movement have been demonstrations that have taken place at meetings of leading politicians from Western capitalist countries or influential capitalist organisations. For example, in Seattle in 1999 some 40 000 demonstrators focused on a meeting of the WTO; during protests in Genoa in 2001 there was serious violence in which a local youth was shot dead (Callinicos 2003); and there were major protests at the G8 summit (a meeting of the leaders of the eight principal industrial/capitalist countries) at Edinburgh in July 2005.

Although the movement involves a wide range of groups, each of which has slightly different concerns, it is possible to see it as a single movement because of an overarching hostility to capitalism and the effects of globalisation. It involves elements of peace movements, ecological movements and labour movements, but is characterised more by informal alliances than by any hierarchical organisation. Unlike conventional labour movements, it does not represent particular groups of workers, but is concerned with issues that affect people throughout the world.

The movement brings together those campaigning about a variety of issues. What these issues share in common is that the problems involved can all be seen as produced by global capitalism in general, and the power of global corporations in particular. Callinicos suggests that the movement does not campaign over particular issues, but is guided by a spirit of the interconnection between many different injustices and dangers. For example, the movement is concerned about the way that rich countries prevent the importation of agricultural goods from poor countries (e.g. through the European Union Common Agriculture Policy), which contributes to leading poor countries into debt, causing increased poverty. It is concerned with the way that large corporations systematically exploit workers in the Third World, damage the environment and support repressive regimes that allow the easy exploitation of workers.

Callinicos admits that the movement embraces a wide variety of political positions, from those who support relatively moderate reforms to revolutionaries. Some want better controls of global capitalism to reduce the harm it does, while others advocate the complete overthrow of capitalism. Those who support revolution disagree over what to replace it with. Some are socialists, others anarchists and some are mostly influenced by the environmental movement.

Nevertheless, Callinicos believes that they can work together because of the loose-knit nature of the movement, as there are no overall leaders, no single statement of the movement's aims and no formal organisation; it is often possible for participants to cooperate on the basis of the aims they share rather than be divided by differences.

The emergence of anti-capitalism

Callinicos sees the emergence of the anti-capitalist movement as being a significant new development in thinking about society. The 1990s witnessed the increasing dominance of neoliberalism. Communism in the Soviet Union and Eastern Europe had collapsed, and many Western politicians and social scientists argued there was no longer any alternative to free-market capitalism.

In the United States a set of policy prescriptions that became known as the **Washington Consensus** emerged, arguing for worldwide fiscal discipline; rethinking the priorities in public spending; tax reform; liberalisation of interest rates, trade and inward foreign investment; privatisation; deregulation; and the extension of property rights—supported if necessary by the use of military power. Politicians such as President Bill Clinton in the United States and Prime Minister Tony Blair in the United Kingdom and sociologists such as Anthony Giddens claimed to offer a Third Way (between capitalism and socialism), but to Callinicos this was not significantly different from neoliberalism. Callinicos argues that the Third Way involves an acceptance of economic globalisation, free markets and a belief that nothing can be done about inequality. As such it is little different from neoliberalism.

In the United States, Francis Fukuyama (1992) declared 'the end of history'. He believed that major ideological disputes were a thing of the past—everybody now accepted there was no alternative to capitalism. In sociology and other social sciences, postmodernism became increasingly popular. Postmodernists such as

Baudrillard argued that politics had become meaningless because the social world was increasingly constituted by images rather than reality.

However, the 1999 Seattle protests were a turning point and marked the revival of radical politics and radical social science that stress issues such as inequality and injustice. Callinicos believes this shift back towards radical social science theories such as Marxism was largely stimulated by the development of protest movements, particularly the anti-capitalist movement. But why did this movement appear with apparent suddenness at the end of the 1990s? Callinicos attributes this development to a number of factors:

1. In part, the movement was a response to globalisation. The increased prominence of global or transnational institutions such as the United Nations, the European Union and the G8 has prompted more of a global outlook from protest movements. In addition, campaigning NGOs such as Amnesty International and Greenpeace have developed and linked together local campaigns. They have gained prominence through involvement in conferences such as the 1992 Rio Summit on global warming.
2. The network of activists throughout the world has developed as a result of specific campaigns such as Jubilee 2000, a campaign to alleviate Third World poverty by cancelling Third World debt owed to the richer nations.
3. In 1997–98 East Asia experienced an acute financial crisis that raised questions about the sustainability of prosperity through global capitalism. Even capitalist financiers such as George Soros began to question the viability of global capitalism in its existing form. For many future protestors, the crisis in East Asia showed the dangers of a deregulated world economy.
4. In 1993 the North American Free Trade Agreement was concluded. This established new and more liberal trade between the United States, Canada and Mexico. There was considerable opposition to the agreement. After it was implemented in 1994, south-eastern Mexico experienced a Zapatista uprising. The Zapatistas were protesting about their loss of access to common land as a result of the agreement. This highlighted the effect of neoliberal policies on indigenous peoples and the opposition to the agreement was a precursor of later protest movements.
5. Neoliberal economic policies also met resistance in some richer countries. For example, in France there were public sector strikes in late 1995; these contributed to the development of a new left group in that country that was opposed to aspects of globalisation.

Together, these various events stimulated the development of an anti-capitalist movement that was beginning to develop loose networks across the globe. It was further encouraged through the writings of leading radicals such as Noam Chomsky (1996a; 1996b; 1999; 2003) in the United States and Pierre Bourdieu (1999) in France. According to Callinicos, another important influence was the work of Naomi Klein and her best-selling book *No Logo* (2000).

NO LOGO—NAOMI KLEIN

In *No Logo*, Klein offers a radical critique of global or transnational corporations. The main focus of her study is the development of marketing and branding by corporations such as Coca-Cola and Nike. She also examines what she sees as the negative impact of such corporations and the development of anti-capitalist social movements opposed to their activities. Because of its popularity, her work has encouraged the further development of the anti-capitalist movement.

Brands not products

Klein argues that the 'astronomical growth in the wealth and cultural influence of multinational corporations over the last fifteen years can arguably be traced back to a single, seemingly innocuous idea developed by management theorists in the mid-1980s: that successful corporations must primarily produce brands as opposed to products' (2000, p. 3).

Since the second half of the 19th century, companies have mass-marketed products. However, it was only in the 1940s that marketing experts began to realise the importance of branding. From that time on, it was not so much the product as the brand that was marketed. Thus most jeans, cola drinks and cigarettes are very similar products, but companies need to persuade consumers that their brand is the best. Consequently, corporations have put a tremendous amount of resources into promoting brands such as Levi Strauss, Coca-Cola and Marlboro. Each tried to develop a distinctive brand image that would appeal to consumers throughout the world.

By the 1980s, however, corporations were discovering that rather than promoting the product as a brand, it was possible to promote the company, or the logo of the company, as a brand in its own right. Once the company itself and its logo were sufficiently well established in the minds of the public, the company could diversify and sell a wider variety of products through their association with the logo. In the United Kingdom, for example, Richard Branson's Virgin company has used its logo not just to promote its original products (records and music shops) but also to sell cola, mobile phones, airline and rail services, financial services and so on. Particular symbols such as Nike's *swoosh*, the golden arches of McDonald's and the Coca-Cola logos have become globally recognisable and powerful marketing tools for promoting the respective businesses.

For consumers, it is increasingly the logo that it is important for them to buy rather than the product it relates to. Often logos are associated with particular lifestyles. For example, Nike has tried to associate the *swoosh* with the ideal of sport. Nike has branched far beyond its original business (selling trainers and sports footwear) to encompass all aspects of sport. Nike now not only sells a whole range of sports goods but also bought the Ben Hogan golf tour in 1992 (renaming it the Nike tour) and has its own agency for managing sports stars. It has particularly benefited from promoting its association with the world's greatest basketball player, Michael Jordan, to establish itself as a 'superbrand'. Klein says that Nike is 'a shoe company that is determined to unseat pro sports, the Olympics and even star athletes, to become the very definition of sport itself' (p. 51).

Promoting the superbrand

As companies try to become superbrands, they start to compete with other superbrands. Ideally, they want their logo to be the most recognisable logo on earth. Nike's competitors are no longer just other sportswear companies such as Adidas and Reebok; the company is also competing with Coca-Cola, McDonald's and many others for global recognition of its brand. To maintain and enhance the position of their brands, global corporations are prepared to go to almost any lengths. For example:

- They are willing to spend vast amounts of money on advertising and marketing. In 1997 Nike alone spent some US$500 million on advertising compared with less than US$50 million in 1987. Between 1979 and 1998, overall advertising expenditure in the United States rose from US$50 billion to just under US$200 billion, and from 1985 to 1998 there was a 700 per cent increase in corporate sponsorship spending.
- Corporations are willing to extend advertising and marketing into virtually every area of social life. They sponsor television programs, sporting events and rock music tours, and they are increasingly involved in sponsoring education and advertising in schools and universities. Klein suggests that the activities of corporations are beginning to limit freedom of inquiry within education. For example, corporations have threatened to withdraw funds from universities whose academics publish anything critical of the corporation or its products.
- Corporations also try to make use of every trend in youth culture to make their products seem more 'cool'. Nike is so focused on 'borrowing style, attitude and imagery from black urban youth that the company has its own word for the practice: *bro-ing*' (Klein 2000, p. 75, original italics). The corporations try to incorporate anything that could be seen as anti-capitalist or against their interests into their marketing. Lou Reed of the Velvet Underground has done advertisements for Honda; the Beatles' song 'Revolution' and John Lennon's 'Instant Karma' have both been used in Nike advertisements; the image of Cuban revolutionary Che Guevara has been used to sell soft drinks; and Red or Dead has used the communist leaders Mao and Lenin to sell handbags. In these circumstances, even radical messages tend to be drowned out by the pervasive manipulation of images by corporations.
- Companies that wish to establish their brand as predominant often try to put the opposition out of business. According to Klein, Starbucks sometimes tries to buy up independent cafés in an area or outbid independent café owners for the leases on their properties.
- Takeovers and mergers are frequently used to ensure the promotion and predominance of a particular brand. Klein gives some examples:
  - *Disney buys ABC, which then broadcasts its movies and cartoons.*
  - *Time Warner purchases Turner Broadcasting, which then cross-promotes its magazines and films on CNN.*
  - *George Lucas buys block stocks in Hasbro and Galoob before he sells the toy companies the licensing rights for the new Star Wars films, at which point Hasbro promptly buys Galoob to consolidate its hold on the toy market. (2000 p. 147)*
- Corporations use various forms of censorship to block messages that are critical of their activities or

that pose even the slightest threat to the exclusivity of their brand. McDonald's took two environmental protestors (the McLibel two; see below) to court in the United Kingdom for criticising its environmental record and claiming its product was unhealthy. McDonald's also 'continues busily to harass small shopkeepers and restaurateurs of Scottish descent for that nationality's uncompetitive predisposition towards the Mc prefix in its surnames' (2000, pp. 177–8). For example, it sued both a sandwich shop called McMunchies in Buckinghamshire and a Ronald McDonald who owned a restaurant in Illinois.

So far, Klein's work suggests a world in which branding by multinational corporations has become the dominant cultural force across the globe. In Klein's words there appears to be no space for alternative or oppositional messages and no choice but to buy the products and services sold by the corporations.

Furthermore, Klein argues that the activities of corporations have a damaging effect on employment. The more that is spent on advertising and promotion, the less there is to pay the workers who make their products. Jobs are moved from the richer First World countries to sweatshops in the Third World, where workers are paid very low wages. Many of the jobs that remain in the richer countries are temporary, part-time or insecure.

Nevertheless, as well as exploring the rise of branding and the power of corporations, Klein also examines the rise of social movements opposing corporations.

Culture jamming

One of the oppositional movements has been what Klein refers to as *culture jamming* (changing an advertisement to reveal what the protestor sees as the true meaning of the ad). In the late 1990s, culture jamming revived and became increasingly prominent. Graffiti artists such as New Yorker Rodriguez de Gerada began openly to change billboards in public spaces.

By creating a society obsessed with logos, the large corporations set themselves up as targets. Klein says: 'We are a celebrity-obsessed culture, and such a culture is never in finer form than when one of its most loved icons is mired in scandal' (2000, p. 351). Any association with prominent logos is glamorous and attractive, even for those who are undermining the logos through culture jamming. Attacking logos is also appealing for culture jammers because it is so effective. Modern corporations may not rely on particular workers or factories to make their products (they can easily move production somewhere else), but they do rely on the positive appeal of their logos.

Companies such as Nike, Shell and McDonald's have been the subject of quite effective campaigns that have provided their logos with less appealing associations than those promoted by the companies. For example, the Nike *swoosh* has been dubbed the 'Swooshstika' and associated with very poor pay and conditions in the Third World factories where the company's products are largely made. Shell has been linked by its critics to the 1995 execution of the Nigerian Ken Saro Wiwa by the Nigerian Government. Wiwa had campaigned against Shell's operations that had damaged the land of the Ogoni people of the Niger delta. Some culture jammers hung dummies from Shell logos at petrol stations with the slogan 'Shell Kills Ogoni'. And in June 1997, pickets at 500 McDonald's outlets distributed leaflets critical of many aspects of McDonald's business. At one outlet there was 'a street performance featuring an axe-wielding Ronald McDonald, a cow and lots of ketchup' (p. 391). McDonald's attempts to silence its critics by suing two protestors for libel backfired: the 'McLibel' case simply drew attention to the accusations made by the protestors.

Klein is, however, aware of the limitations of this sort of resistance to globalisation. It might inconvenience particular multinational companies, but the 'conduct of the individual multinationals is simply a by-product of a broader global economic system that has steadily been removing almost all barriers and conditions to trade, investment and outsourcing' (p. 422). When one company loses business because of the bad publicity that it has received, another company that may be little better is usually the beneficiary. For example, Adidas has benefited from campaigns against Nike, although, as Klein argues, it has followed similar exploitative employment practices. Furthermore, anti-branding campaigns can do little to embarrass companies that do not rely on brands—for example, mining companies and steel factories that have poor safety records but no brand image.

Despite its limitations, Klein believes that the anti-branding, culture-jamming movement has laid the foundation for wider global social movements. It has drawn attention to links between politically repressive regimes, the exploitation of workers and the activities of corporations and brands. As such, it has stimulated the development of broad coalitions between different campaigners. This has been evident in the various types of protests at meetings of world leaders and organisations of economic globalisation such as the WTO, the IMF and the World Bank.

> *Among better known events that would be included in anyone's highlights of peripheral movements of resistance against global neoliberalism are: the unrest in Amman that followed the doubling of the price of bread as part of an IMF-supervised reform plan (August 1996); protests in Quito against the dollarisation of the economy (August 1999–December 2000); the general strike in Asunción against the government's plans to privatise telephone, water and railroad companies (June 2000); and anti-IMF near riots in Lusaka (April 2000). Others include the 'Switch On' campaign in Johannesburg against the privatisation of gas and electricity (2000); protests in Jakarta against the IMF-coordinated increase of oil prices (April 2001, January 2003); protests in Caracas against the privatisation of public transport (December 2001); the 'water war' in Cochabamba, Bolivia (February 2003); the gas war in La Paz (February–October 2003); and anti-IMF protests in Santo Domingo (November 2003) and Cartagena (May 2004). (Drainville 2008, p. 239)*

THE WORLD SOCIAL FORUM AND DEGLOBALISATION

In addition to the protests organised at events such as meetings of the World Bank and the G8, a central focus for the movements critical of neoliberal globalisation has been the World Social Forum (WSF) (Wallerstein 2004, p. 634), a gathering of organisations and individuals that usually forms alongside its rival, the World Economic Forum (an annual meeting of business and political leaders, NGO representatives, diplomats, selected intellectuals and journalists, which is often accompanied by protests). The WSF is described on its website as:

> … an open meeting place where social movements, networks, NGOs and other civil society organizations opposed to neo-liberalism and a world dominated by capital or by any form of imperialism come together to pursue their thinking, to debate ideas democratically, formulate proposals, share their experiences freely and network for effective action. (Source: World Social Forum, www.forumsocialmundial.org.br/index.php?cd_language=2, reproduced with permission)

The first WSF meeting was held in Porto Alegre, Brazil, in 2001 with 25 000 participants; the 2007 meeting had 66 000 participants. As Tom Bramble observes: 'The sheer scale of the WSF is astounding, and it is by far the largest event of its type in the world' (2006, p. 288). Regional social forums are also held regularly around the world, and the Australian social forum has been taking place annually in both Brisbane and Sydney since 2002 (Bramble 2006).

There is an enormous diversity of aims and concerns at the WSF meetings, and one of the criticisms of this type of activity is the question of its coherence and practical effectiveness. Within the collection of alter-globalisation movements, for example, there is enormous difference of opinion about the approach to the environment and climate change. Pigman illustrates this by pointing to the diversity of groups that come together in opposing globalisation in Asia alone, where 'the opposition ranges from Islamist movements, Hindu nationalist factions in India such as the RSS (Rashtriya Swayamsevak Sangh), right-wing nationalists in Japan, to Marxist and Maoist agriculturalists and artisanal produced movements from Nepal to the Philippines' (2006, p. 198).

However, what draws them all together is an overall concern to constrain neoliberal economic and political policies and to strengthen the voice of the South, the Third World or the developing countries in the determination of genuinely globalised processes of transformation that do justice to the concerns of the South, rather than merely being imperialism or postmodern colonialism by another name (Silbey 1997). As Walden Bello, director of *Focus on the Global South* and Professor of Sociology and Public Administration at the University of the Philippines, sums it up:

> *The primordial principle is that instead of the economy driving society the market must be … 're-embedded' in society and governed by the overarching values of community, solidarity, justice and equity. At the international level, the global economy must be deglobalized or rid of the distorting, disfiguring logic of corporate profitability and truly internationalized, meaning that participation in the international economy must serve to strengthen and develop rather than disintegrate and destroy local and national economies. (Bello 2007)*

The concern of deglobalisation activists, then, is to reverse many of the changes brought about by neoliberal globalisation, to 're-empower the local and the national' (Bello 2004). Rather than assuming that global always trumps local, deglobalisers seek a restoration of the balance towards the local, re-establishing the principle of subsidiarity in economic action 'by encouraging production of goods to take place at the community and national level if it can be done so at reasonable cost in order to preserve community' (Bello 2004).

> **Reflective questions:** How would you describe the emergence and aims of the social and political movements critical of globalisation?
> Is deglobalisation a realistic and desirable objective?

CRITIQUES OF GLOBALISATION THEORY

> *The literature stemming from the debate on globalization has grown in the last decade beyond any individual's capacity of extracting a workable definition of the concept. In a sense the meaning of the concept is self evident, in another, it is as vague and obscure as its reaches are wide and constantly shifting. Perhaps, more than any other concept, globalization is the debate about it. (Poppi 1997, p. 300)*

We have seen that there are a number of critiques of particular concepts of globalisation, which are effectively internal critiques. They mostly constitute arguments about *how* we should understand globalisation, rather than whether we *should* be speaking about globalisation at all. And there are a number of intellectual orientations they still continue to share about which we can also be critical.

For example, Jens Bartelson (2000) argues that the concept has become increasingly abstract and intangible, detached from empirical investigation. Rather than referring to a particular domain or field, it has come to constitute the conceptual conditions of possibility for analysing any particular domain. By this he means that globalisation does not necessarily describe anything in particular, it simply becomes the central possible way of describing anything. In this sense, it 'seems as if the concept of globalization has attained a life of its own' (2000, p. 192). Like the concepts 'civilisation' and 'revolution', observed Bartelson, it is very easy for globalisation to move from being an idea referring to something about the real world or its possible future to being 'a prophecy in quest for self-fulfilment'.

Susan Silbey (1997) has suggested that the concept has functioned to disguise relations of power and exploitation, especially to the extent that globalisation is presented as a TINA ('there is no alternative') process that just 'happens' and about which there is little to be done. In reality, globalisation processes produce such a concentration of power, such a standardisation of work practices and institutional forms that favour the rich and the powerful in the core advanced industrial economies, that use of the term 'globalisation', like 'modernisation' before it, hinders rather than aids the capacity for genuinely useful social scientific analysis. 'By entitling our narratives "globalisation" rather than "capitalism," "late capitalism," or "postmodern colonialism," we camouflage the organization of power and thus misrepresent the targets of, and impede the struggles for, justice' (Silbey 1997, p. 233).

The critique we focus on here is Raewyn Connell's analysis of the close relationship that globalisation theory has to the theories of modernisation that preceded it and with which it shares many of the problems of being the product of the metropole or the global 'North'—what Wallerstein calls the 'core' countries, concentrated on, but not confined to, Western Europe and North America.

GLOBALISATION AS NORTHERN THEORY— RAEWYN CONNELL

In *Southern Theory* (2007), Connell observes that the shift in the 1990s to thinking in terms of globalisation and moving away from methodological nationalism was in many respects a return to the sociology of classical sociologists such as Spencer, who suddenly 'had come back to life, and sociology was speaking once more about the world as a whole' (p. 52). However, this move 'back to the future' had some important features. Connell suggests that the accounts of writers like Beck and Giddens did not really change their explanatory form very much at all; they simply shifted their analysis of risk society or late modernity to the global level.

Connell also argues that the sociological study of globalisation tends to remain wedded to a conception of the global as European modernity writ large, so that '[t]he idea of modernity spreading from its heartland in Europe and North America to cover the whole world is probably the most widespread of all views of global society' (2007, p. 53). In other words, the analysis of global social life is undertaken with a 'metropolitan conceptual apparatus and way of seeing things', what Connell calls an 'intellectual strategy', which was itself the product of methodological nationalism and which has merely been tinkered with rather than sufficiently rethought in order to understand sociological issues in global terms (p. 55). As Connell puts it, '[m]etropolitan sociology in the 1990s constructed its narratives of global society mostly by scaling up its existing conceptual tools, rather than by launching a fresh research agenda on a global scale', which means that the sociology of globalisation 'produced in the metropole, was constituted in a way that ... concealed the conditions of its own existence and set internal limits to its own development' (p. 60).

Among the more important effects of this is that in many respects the old distinction between tradition and modernity has simply been mapped onto the distinction between the pre-globalised and the globalised world, with the same normative assumption that the second is inherently superior and 'better' and obviously the direction in which we all want or should want to travel.

One central feature of the globalisation literature that demonstrates the problematic character of this neglect of more far-reaching conceptual reconstruction is the notion that globalisation is a relatively blind, autonomous process with little possibility for human control and binds the whole of humanity together in a more or less similar way. The image is one of everyone in the same boat, and it is a boat with no captain. A universal, undifferentiated 'we' is often the subject of globalisation discussions, with risks related to the environment, job loss or health distributed over the whole world. The question of their distribution tends to remain in the background, which in effect generates the unspoken inference that they are in fact distributed evenly.

The question of the nature of the power relations structuring globalisation processes also tends to be pushed into the background by the idea that 'no one seems now to be in control' (Bauman 1998, p. 58). As Connell suggests, analyses of globalisation written in this way 'put a metaphorical arm around the reader's shoulder and speak confidently about the problems "we" now face' (p. 62). This supposedly shared experience does not 'include much of the sharp end of global social processes' (p. 63). It remains confined within the perspective of those oriented towards life in Europe, North America and Australia, rather than including the views of those living in, say, South Africa, Brazil or Iran. Much of the real character of globalisation gets left out of consideration, or is left to the alter-globalisation movement to rally behind as indicators that it is fundamentally flawed.

Mechanisms of exclusion, projection and erasure

Connell identifies three mechanisms at play in the 'Northernness' of the sociology of globalisation.

- The first is simply the *exclusion* of the perspective of non-Northern scholarship. The reading lists of writers on globalisation hardly ever include the work of writers from Delhi, Durban or Sao Paulo, and almost always include the thoughts of intellectuals based in Paris, Munich or Chicago.
- The second is that of the *projection* of all the concerns of the metropole onto the rest of the world— the presumption that whatever is true of experience in Lyons or Dortmund is universally true, so that one can speak grandly of 'global modernity' or 'the capitalist economy' today, without needing to identify the specifics of the situation beyond the metropole.
- The third is that of *erasure*, by which Connell means the removal from view of the central place occupied by colonialism in the emergence of both the modern and the globalised world. As Connell writes, '[t]he fact that the majority world has deep prior experience of subjection to globalising powers is surely known to all the theorists. But this experience of subjection does not surface as a central issue in *any* of the theories of globalisation considered here' (p. 65). European and North American dominance of processes of modernisation and globalisation generally gets casually overlooked, and the response of Northern intellectuals to having their attention drawn to it is often irritation verging on outrage (see Collins 1997).

Globalisation beyond the metropole

For Connell, then, there are some clear pointers to the direction in which the study of globalisation can and should go, addressing each of these three mechanisms. It can work towards undoing exclusion by broadening the field of scholarship that is drawn upon in analysing globalisation—to go beyond the metropole, to include, for example, al-Afghani rather than concentrating solely on Weber. As Connell observes, the inhabitants of the world beyond the metropole 'are not just the objects of theory, the data mine for social science. They are also the subjects—the *producers* of theory about the social world and their own place in it' (p. 68; just one recent example is Mauricio Domingues 2009).

It can realise that the world is indeed a highly diverse and differentiated place, and that the concept of 'global society' does not mean simply European societies writ large upon the rest of the world—even if that can also be viewed critically, as an indicator of American imperialism or capitalism taking over the world. It can also pay considerably more attention to the relationship between processes of globalisation and deglobalisation on the one hand, and mechanisms and strategies of colonisation (including their aftermath and continued effects) on the other—to see the colonial dimensions of globalisation not as inherent to globalisation in itself, but as central to the way that globalisation processes have in fact unfolded, and as requiring recognition to avoid their resurrection in new, harder-to-recognise forms.

Reflective questions: What does it mean to describe globalisation theory as 'Northern theory'? What would 'Southern' globalisation theory entail?

CONCLUSION

This chapter has introduced only some of the main ideas, debates and emerging dilemmas in studying and understanding globalisation. There are many more aspects of globalisation that we have not had the opportunity to discuss, such as the globalisation of sport, food, organisations and the mass media; the role of violence in processes of globalisation; and the structure and dynamics of cosmopolitanism (e.g. Beck 2000d; 2006). But the chapter will have given you a good foundation to begin exploring the future of the sociology of globalisation and deglobalisation processes—a possibility that is daunting but also exciting. Jan Nederveen Pieterse suggests that:

A global sociology is taking shape, around notions such as social networks (rather than 'societies'), border zones, boundary crossing and global society. In other words, a sociology conceived within the framework of nations/ societies is making place for a post-inter/national sociology of hybrid formations, times and spaces. (1994, p. 179)

As we have discussed throughout this chapter, this may be overly enthusiastic about the novelty of globalisation. Nonetheless, it is true that there is some very interesting and useful work to be done in sociological theory and research to make sense of the ways in which globalisation can be understood and engaged with. The question of how to understand globalisation from a sociological perspective will emerge, one way or another, in all the topics that we will be exploring throughout this book.

Tutorial exercises

1. Visit the 'Focus on the Global South' website (**http://focusweb.org**) and outline the various components of the approach to globalisation that you find there. Is there a consistent concept of globalisation that this group uses? What is the rationale for being critical of globalisation processes?
2. Select one of the following examples of global organisations—McDonald's, Starbucks or IKEA—and identify the different dimensions of its role in the processes of globalisation (technological, economic, political and cultural). How do you think the company has changed your own day-to-day life?
3. Look at some recent daily newspapers and identify a selection of articles that best exemplify what you could call globalisation. Do the articles consciously understand things in terms of globalisation, or is this more implicit in their accounts? Do they present things in a positive or negative light, and what kind of 'theory' of globalisation can you see in their approach?

For activity suggestions, learning aids, revision of key concepts and access to self-study material, visit: **www.pearson.com.au/highered/vankrieken4e**

Further reading

Bello, W. 2004, *Deglobalisation: Ideas for a New World Economy*, Zed Books, London.
Chase-Dunn, C. & Babones, S. J. (eds) 2006, *Global Social Change: Historical and Comparative Perspectives*, Johns Hopkins University Press, Baltimore.
Hardt, M. & Negri, A. 2000, *Empire*, Harvard University Press, Cambridge, Mass.
Held, D. & McGrew, A. (eds) 2003, *The Global Transformations Reader: An Introduction to the Globalization Debate*, 2nd edn, Polity Press, Cambridge.
Held, D. & McGrew, A. (eds) 2007, *Globalization Theory: Approaches and Controversies*, Polity Press, Cambridge.
Hirst, P., Thompson, G. & Bromley, S. 2009, *Globalization in Question*, 3rd edn, Polity Press, Cambridge.
Jones, A. 2006, *Dictionary of Globalization*, Polity Press, Cambridge.
Klein, N. 2002, *Fences and Windows: Dispatches from the Front Lines of the Globalisation Debate*, Flamingo, London.
Lechner, F. 2009, *Globalisation: The Making of World Society*, Wiley-Blackwell, Chichester.
Ritzer, G. (ed.) 2007, *The Blackwell Companion to Globalisation*, Blackwell Publishing, Oxford.
Robertson, R. 1992, *Globalisation, Social Theory and Global Culture*, Sage, London.
Robertson, R. T. 2003, *Three Waves of Globalization: A History of a Developing Global Consciousness*, Zed Books, New York.
Schirato, T. & Webb, J. 2003, *Understanding Globalisation*, Sage, London.
Waters, M. 2001, *Globalisation*, 2nd edn, Routledge, London.

Websites

Amnesty International Australia:
www.amnesty.org.au

Anthony Giddens' Reith Lecture, Runaway World:
http://news.bbc.co.uk/hi/english/static/events/reith_99

Australian Government Department of Foreign Affairs and Trade:
www.dfat.gov.au

Corporate Watch:
www.corporatewatch.org

Focus on the Global South:
http://focusweb.org

Globalisation Guide:
www.globalisationguide.org

Global Transformations (maintained by David Held and Anthony McGrew):
www.polity.co.uk/global

International Forum on Globalization:
www.ifg.org

International Institute for Sustainable Development:
www.iisd.org

International Monetary Fund:
www.imf.org

Interview with Stuart Hall, 2006:
www.youtube.com/watch?v=fBfPtRaGZPM

KOF Index of Globalization:
http://globalization.kof.ethz.ch

Multilateral Agreement on Investment (MAI):
www.ifg.org/maiinfo.html

New Internationalist:
www.newint.org

North American Free Trade Agreement (NAFTA):
www.naftanow.org

Organisation for Economic Cooperation and Development:
www.oecd.org/home

The Australian APEC Study Centre:
www.apec.org.au

The Economist:
www.economist.com

The Globalisation Debate, Anthony Giddens and Leslie Sklair, Columbia University's Fathom Archive:
www.fathom.com/course/10701014/index.html

The Globalization Website (maintained by Frank Lechner, Emory University):
www.sociology.emory.edu/globalization/index.html

The Global Policy Forum:
www.globalpolicy.org

The World Bank:
www.worldbank.org

United Nations:
www.un.org

United Nations Conference on Trade and Development:
www.unctad.org

What is globalization? Auburn University students interviewed:
www.youtube.com/watch?v=4Vy9TjhzYdY

World Economic Forum:
www.weforum.org

World Social Forum:
www.forumsocialmundial.org.br

World Trade Organization:
www.wto.org

Popular Culture and the Media

3

Drawing on a range of theories, concepts and well-known examples, this chapter traces the historical emergence of the media and the press at the onset of modernity, travels through the 20th century and the era of the mass media, and finishes by discussing the emergence of the internet and mobile communications in the network society. The chapter reflects the fact that sociology as a discipline is expert at investigating and evaluating the state of contemporary social relations, which are increasingly organised around media, communications and information flows.

By the end of the chapter, you should have a better understanding of:

— the social and technological developments that gave form to the mass media and communications technologies of the 20th century
— the role of the media industries in the generation of collective social identities such as the public and the nation, especially through media rituals and media events
— the historical emergence and political function of the public sphere
— the rise and enduring significance of celebrities and celebrity culture
— the significance of the internet, the Web and mobile phones in creating new forms of social interaction and identities, as well as the impact of these technologies on patterns of social inequality.

INTRODUCTION	**76**
MODERNITY	**77**
The Media and Modernity—Thompson	78
The rise of the printing industry	79
The emergence of periodical publications	80
The transformation of media institutions into large-scale commercial concerns	80
The globalisation of communication	80
Conceptual tools	81
Face-to-face interaction	81
Mediated interaction	82
Mediated quasi-interaction	82
Computer-mediated interaction	83
MEDIA RITUALS	**84**
Habitual action	84
Formalised action	84
Action involving transcendent values	84
Media as social practice—Couldry	85
MEDIA EVENTS	**86**
Beyond media events—the 2008 Beijing Olympic Games	88
THE PUBLIC SPHERE	**89**
The Structural Transformation of the Public Sphere—Habermas	90
The global public sphere—Volkmer	94
CELEBRITY: THE PRIVATE MEETS THE PUBLIC	**94**
Celebrity and religion	97
THE INTERNET, THE WEB AND MOBILE PHONES	**98**
The network society	99
The culture of real virtuality	101
Community and networked individualism	102
The digital divide	103
The mobile network society	104
THE SOCIOLOGY OF THE MEDIA INTO THE FUTURE	**106**
Tutorial exercises	108
Further reading	108
Websites	108

INTRODUCTION

Reality television is both a popular culture and a sociological phenomenon. This flexible genre of television offers a range of content, alternately serious, titillating, humorous and puerile in character. A cursory examination of the weekly television program guide reveals shows such as *Australian Idol*, *Australia's Got Talent*, *The Biggest Loser*, *Bondi Rescue*, *Aussie Ladette to Lady* and *Australia's Next Top Model*, the likes of which have become a staple for commercial television networks and their audiences. Built upon a cost-effective production model and varying appeals to nation and national culture, these shows offer engaging unscripted drama that produces a sense of 'predictable unpredictability' (Ruddock 2007) as contestants are placed in situations unfamiliar to them.

It is worth revisiting the recently cancelled but once global sensation, *Big Brother*, for insight into why networks screen so much reality television. *Big Brother* and its host Gretel Killeen may have become unfashionable in the show's final seasons, but the imprint left by the show's previous success as a 'pop culture moment' is evident by its many imitators offering variations on a common theme—people competing in a manufactured setting to win a prize by appealing to viewers or judges.

Each season of *Big Brother* ran daily for almost three months. Viewers watched highlight packages of the contestants living in a house under 24-hour-a-day audiovisual surveillance. In her 2002 study, Johnson-Woods provides a range of facts about the first series of *Big Brother*. In 2001, the show occupied six of Australia's top 20 television program rating slots (including two of the top three). Nearly three million people watched the final eviction program and almost two million logged onto the official website. Media coverage of the show included more than 1000 newspaper articles, while ABC's *Four Corners*, the epitome of serious current affairs, devoted an entire program to this reality television spectacle. Worldwide in 2002, more than two billion people watched versions of *Big Brother* in countries as varied as Argentina, France, Germany, Norway, South Africa, Russia and the United States. Most surprising of all, according to Britain's *Guardian* newspaper (cited in Bauman 2002, p. 61), an estimated 10 million 18–25-year-olds cast votes for *Big Brother* contestants yet only 1.5 million in the same age group voted in the British general election.

These facts are a challenge to anyone who dismisses reality television or popular media in general as trivial and unworthy of serious consideration. Sociology is ideally placed to provide commentary on issues related to reality television and media more generally. For example, sociologists investigating *The Biggest Loser*—a program premised on competitive weight loss and public reflections on the relationship between self-esteem and body image—would not focus specifically on the inner workings of the program, although this would be part of their analysis. They would be more interested in how this popular **media text** and the pervasive technological medium on which it is presented (television) inform and reflect the wider social world. For example, what does *The Biggest Loser* tell us about ideals of the male and female body, community attitudes towards health and obesity, the social function and power of the health and fitness industries, gender identity, the manufacture of 'ordinary' people as minor celebrities, competitive individualism, the global circulation of program formats and the uses of the internet in relation to the program's partner website?

The examples discussed above underline one of sociology's primary concerns about the media: how the media structures, informs and reflects social life. It is almost impossible to imagine a life devoid of the media industry and communications technologies. The biographies of individuals are filled with programs, websites, movies, books, games, songs, documentaries, stories and spectacles that change people's lives by impacting on how they think about themselves and relate to the world around them. Couldry (2003, p. 20) points out that, for better or worse, almost all possibilities of collective social action pass through media forms, which provide important communicative links between our private lives and markets, governments and institutions (Pusey 2003, pp. 126–7).

The sociological significance of the media and communications is also supported by an array of statistical evidence and estimates, such as:

- 99 per cent of Australian homes own one or more television sets
- 27 per cent of Australian homes subscribe to pay television
- when it comes to assessing political and economic matters, newspapers are the most influential medium according to survey respondents to Pusey's national study of 'middle Australia' (Pusey 2003, p. 127)
- as of mid-2006, there were 699 licensed commercial, community and public radio broadcast operations in Australia
- 65 per cent of Australians attended the cinema at least once in 2005–06
- there were approximately 7.23 million internet subscribers in Australia in June 2008, with 55 per cent of Australians using the internet more than eight times a week
- there are 22.12 million mobile phone services in Australia, which exceeds the official population of the country
- in 2008, an estimated 88 per cent of Australian homes possessed a device for playing computer games—the average age of computer and video gamers is estimated to be 30 years, and females make up 46 per cent of the player population.

Such statistics emphasise the importance for students of sociology in understanding the media and its role in society.

Using a range of examples from newspapers, radio, television, the internet and mobile communications, this chapter considers:

- the media's role in modernity
- the relationship between social rituals and media events such as the Olympics
- the public sphere and the rise of celebrity culture
- the emergence and development of 'the network society'.

These topics provide an introduction to an important range of theories, concepts and issues. Each section chooses a key topic and develops it in depth, thereby allowing the reader to 'think through' the material presented. By reading this chapter, either in its entirety or a particular section, it is hoped that students will acquire knowledge of this area and are prompted to initiate their own research projects. An appealing feature of media sociology is that almost everyone is familiar with the media and telecommunications industries, their products and technologies, which provide fertile ground for research ideas. The reward of sociology when done successfully is that it transforms this familiarity into systematic understanding about the social world in which we live.

MODERNITY

The future has a hold on people's attention. Innovation in the media and communications sectors generates interest in the introduction and applications of 3G mobile devices such as the Apple iPhone and internet-enabled game consoles like the PlayStation 3, which doubles as a home entertainment centre. But gazing towards an ever-receding horizon obscures the fact that the antecedents for both these items can be found in technologies that include a 19th-century electric communications network (the telegraph) and an invention of the 1970s (the microprocessor) (Winston 1998). The neglected issue here is how new communications technologies contribute to social change by altering the ways in which people interact and communicate over time. Historical perspective, an essential part of the sociological imagination (Mills 1959), is a useful resource when considering this issue. Looking to the past makes it possible to assess the impact of media technologies that now seem old or unexceptional, such as the printed word and the landline telephone. This perspective then provides a context with which to contemplate the social effects of recently introduced media and communications.

John Hartley (1996, 1999) argues that modernity has two parents: the Enlightenment and journalism. Modernity flowed from the Enlightenment and the ideals of this modernising process (science, truth, reason and progress) and from the system that popularised these ideals and communicated them to the public at large—journalism and media. Both the Enlightenment and journalism were born and developed in the 17th and 18th centuries, both claimed fealty to notions of truth and progress, and both sought to engage and empower self-determining sovereign citizens. Situating the French Revolution of 1789 as a pivotal historical moment, Hartley argues that journalism helped spread and communicate revolutionary ideals such as 'liberty, fraternity and equality for all'. Journalism and pamphlet writing served to rework the 'horizons of possibility' (Hartley 1996, p. 84), making political participation for all subjects of the nation appear not just desirable but an inviolable right. The *Ancien Régime* and the crown of Louis XVI fell as the modernising impulse found its voice through print media.

Journals of news began appearing weekly in Western Europe during the first two decades of the 17th century. It was at this time that journalism began to affirm its role as a 'modernising discourse': 'the service industry of truth, the communicator of reason, the populariser of modernity' (Hartley 1999, p. 26). News and journalism gathered strength in this regard into the 19th and 20th centuries in many developed economies, symbolically organising the social and cultural changes occurring with the increased democratisation of political life, the expansion of capitalism and large-scale urbanisation (Schudson 1979). As well as being a 'journal of record' for daily political and social life, newspapers are situated historically as the fourth estate, whose duty it is to communicate truth and defend reason by reporting and critiquing the activities of the state. An affirmation made in France in 1790 on the role of the press summarises this function:

One of the greatest benefits of press freedom is the constant surveillance of government officials, opening up their conduct of affairs to public scrutiny, exposing their intrigues and warning society of the danger; it acts like a watchful sentry, guarding the state day and night. (Jerome Petion, quoted in Hartley 1996, p. 86)

Ideally, investigative journalism as practised by the ABC's *Four Corners* and *The Australian* and *Sydney Morning Herald* newspapers is focused on uncovering corruption and finding the truth. People who do not adhere to proper standards of conduct and honesty, be they powerful or powerless, are publicly identified, condemned and (sometimes) shamed. In other words, journalism is 'a sense-making practice' of modernity that serves to maintain social order (Hartley 1996, pp. 32–3).

Hartley makes a provocative argument. But why did the advent of the newspaper and journalism have the impact that he suggests, and why does the media continue to exert such marked influence on the collective imagination? Part of the answer to this question is by routine social practice, which is an issue touched upon by Benedict Anderson (1991) in *Imagined Communities* (discussed in Chapter 8 in relation to national identity). Anderson traces a similar pattern of development to Hartley. The newspaper was a print technology made available to ever-larger audiences by the advent of the commercial printing press, improvements in transport and communications, the expansion of capitalist markets and the unification of languages throughout Europe. Anderson suggests that the newspaper gave the 'imagined community' of the nation textual form. The habitual practice of reading a newspaper was a powerful social act and in terms of identity formation:

We know that particular morning and evening editions will overwhelmingly be consumed between this hour and that ... The significance of this mass ceremony—Hegel observed that newspapers serve modern man as a substitute for modern prayers—is paradoxical. It is performed in silent privacy, in the lair of the skull. Yet each communicant is well aware that the ceremony he performs is being replicated simultaneously by thousands (or millions) of others of whose existence he is confident, yet of whose identity he has not the slightest notion. (Anderson 1991, p. 35)

A newspaper is a symbolic and social unifier. The daily act of reading one announces implicitly, but persuasively, that issues of common concern, as well as language, politics and national identity, connect people. The mass consumption of print media has helped to construct a sense of shared identity and common interest among previously divided populations and regions. The unfolding of modernity has demonstrated that Anderson's imagined communities (nation-states) grew and were consolidated parallel to the continuing development of the media.

THE MEDIA AND MODERNITY—THOMPSON

British sociologist John B. Thompson (1990; 1995; 2000; 2005) uses a combination of structuralist and symbolic interactionist perspectives to develop a theory of the media's role in modernity. He too argues that the development of modernity cannot be understood without reference to the media but, in making his case, he adds much-needed sociological flesh to the theoretical provocations of Hartley and the historical analysis of Anderson. Thompson focuses on the way that media and communications technologies have reordered space and time, structuring social life by enabling specific patterns and types of interaction. Since the 15th century, face-to-face communication has been displaced by communication-at-a-distance, via technologies such as the

Audiences

There are many different approaches to the study of media audiences and you should consult Ruddock (2001, 2007) for a comprehensive explanation and critique. The concepts and strategies used to study audiences shape how we understand them and their behaviours. There are a wide range of approaches and traditions, including the following:

- *Media effects research.* In the United States, American sociologists set out to study the effects of the media empirically. The central idea to emerge from the research of Merton (1946) and Lazarsfeld (Lazarsfeld, Berelson & Gaudet 1968) was that the reception of media messages was an active, not a passive, process, as messages received from the media are discussed and mediated by personal networks. Since the 1960s, media effects research has focused on the capacity of the media to influence what people think about. One consistent conclusion has emerged from this type of research (Rogers & Dearing 1987): the media's ability to influence a person is greatest in cases where that person has little knowledge of the issues involved. This approach still influences debates on the relationship between television and videogame violence and social behaviour. No conclusive link between the two has been established, even after decades of research (McKay 2002), although it should never be assumed that no relationship exists, however indirect it may be.
- *Audience ethnographies.* Attempts to move beyond the limitations of the media effects model saw the development of an ethnographic approach. This method attempts to locate media use within lived experience. The research path chosen is often participant observation, with the aim being to get inside the viewing experience and reconstruct it from the perspective of those who watch television.

  One of the earliest and most influential of these studies was Morley's (1980) exploration of audience reaction to a popular 1970s British current affairs show, Nationwide. In a method that has since become widely used, Morley showed a videotaped episode of Nationwide to 29 groups of five to ten people of different racial, age and gender composition. Each of these audiences 'decoded' the same show in different ways—some contesting the worldview presented in the show, others refusing to acknowledge it, others adopting it. Studies of this type have been criticised for the fact that they are not ethnographies as practised in anthropology. The researcher is not engaging with another culture, but a disconnected fragment of activity that is removed from the general social life of the viewer. Nonetheless, this approach remains useful. In moving attention away from media texts, it focuses on the social practices of everyday life and the ways in which people consume and understand the media (Turner 1996, pp. 147–51).
- *Cross-cultural studies.* Use of anthropological insights and methods informs a growing body of research that investigates cross-cultural consumption of media texts (Askew & Wilk 2002). Studies attempt to come to terms with the meanings that particular national, racial and ethnic audiences take from media texts that are produced in other cultural contexts, and with the emergence of cross-cultural audiences. This research is particularly useful in an age of globalisation where large bodies of people emigrate to other countries and form new and hybrid cultural identities, and where cultural products such as media texts are consumed in multiple cultural contexts (Turnbull 2000; 2002).

Studies of this type have looked at the reception of various programs, including the following:

- *Neighbours* among Punjabi communities in London (Gillespie 1995) and the United Kingdom (Wober & Fazal 1994)
- *Dynasty* in Norway (Gripsrud 1995)
- *Paradise Beach* and *The Flying Doctors* in the Netherlands and the United States, respectively (Cunningham & Jacka 1996)
- *Dallas* in the Netherlands, Israel, Japan, Peru and Algeria (Ang 1985; Liebes & Katz 1990; Silj 1988)
- television programs produced by and for Iranian exiles in Los Angeles (Naficy 1993).

printed word, the telegraph, the telephone, radio, television and networked computers. This transformation is a defining feature of social relations in modernity.

Thompson (1995, 2000, 2005) identifies a set of historical developments from the second half of the 15th century onwards that have resulted in the 'mediazation of culture' (Thompson 1995, p. 46). These developments are: (1) the rise of the printing industry; (2) the emergence of periodical publications; (3) the transformation of media institutions into large-scale commercial concerns; (4) the globalisation of communication; and (5) the rise of computer-mediated interaction and the proliferation of internet usage in the public domain. The first four are discussed below, and the impact of the internet and the Web are discussed later in the chapter.

The rise of the printing industry

The invention and successful development of the printing press for commercial applications took place within an infant capitalist economy during the 15th century. While techniques of printing had existed for centuries, it was not until the 1450s that Johan Gutenberg, a German goldsmith, managed to create the first commercially viable press. His technique of printing allowed large quantities of type to be produced for extended texts. With this technology he printed the Gutenberg Bible. Gutenberg's innovation triggered an increase in demand for the printed book and contributed to the continuing growth of a capitalist economy. Printers began to multiply throughout Europe, underlining the growing market for the 'commodification of symbolic forms' (i.e. language). By 1500, at least 20 million books had been printed. A century later, it is estimated that as many as 200 million volumes had been produced (Anderson 1991, p. 37).

The emergence of periodical publications

Thompson (1995, p. 65) explains that the production and dissemination of journals of regular news in Europe from the 1600s onwards had a profound impact on networks of communication. These journals reported occurrences in distant places and were translated for sale in other markets, cities and countries throughout Europe. Previously uninformed communities were informed about the deaths of political leaders, wars, trade disputes and the issues surrounding such conflicts. Recalling the arguments of Anderson, Thompson states:

> *The circulation of the early forms of newspaper helped to create a sense of a world of events which lay beyond the individual's immediate milieu, but which had some relevance to, and potentially some bearing on, his or her life. (1995, p. 66)*

One effect of these weekly newspapers was to help embed a principle of the modern democratic state: the freedom of the press. Newspapers began to devote more space to events and government at home, provoking an ongoing battle between the threat of state regulation and press independence. Periodicals determined to inform their readers and be vigilant in covering the affairs of government had the potential to embarrass or threaten those in power. Depending on the national context, this threat resulted in special taxes, censorship, licensing regimes and the jailing of publishers (Thompson 2000, pp. 41–50). Nevertheless, in the face of such restrictions and ongoing legal battles, the legitimate status of an independent press emerged intact. Under the conditions of modernity and democracy, independent and self-determining citizens effectively delegated the right to seek out information in their name to the press (Hartley 2000, p. 41), a notion that is encapsulated in the journalist's clarion call, 'the public has a right to know'.

The transformation of media institutions into large-scale commercial concerns

In the 17th and 18th centuries newspapers were operated on a small scale, with print runs sometimes limited to 400 copies (Thompson 1995, p. 66), but improving literacy levels, continuing innovations in printing technology and increasing advertising revenues saw publications targeted at wider readerships. Gradually, newspapers became large-scale operations that competed intensely for readers and advertising dollars and concentrated resources via mergers and takeovers (Thompson 1995, pp. 76–8). This trajectory of marketisation continued in the radio and television industries during the 20th century and has culminated in multinational corporations dominating the global mediascape. Examples of these conglomerates include Time Warner, Viacom, Bertelsmann Media Worldwide, Disney and Rupert Murdoch's News Corporation.

The media in Australia exemplify the concentration of both resources and power. In 1923, Australia had 26 metropolitan daily newspapers that were owned by 21 companies. By 2008, these publications had shrunk to just two national and ten state or territory daily newspapers, all owned by either News Limited, a subsidiary of News Corporation, or Fairfax Media. This situation is the product of market pressures and political decisions made by both Labor and Coalition federal governments. Parallel, albeit shifting, patterns of concentration are observable in radio, television and telecommunications markets (e.g. Telstra), confounding misguided assumptions that the rise of the digital media would revolutionise the media landscape in Australia by offering unlimited choice to audiences. Certainly, innumerable websites, blogs, podcasts and vodcasts are now available, but these display highly uneven rates of resourcing, credibility, profitability and popularity. One of the few exceptions is Crikey.com, which has managed to establish a recognised role in the reporting of politics and election campaigns in Australia.

The globalisation of communication

A series of technological developments, economic relations and social processes in its own right, globalisation has provided the structural capacity for communications media to connect distant parts of the globe on an unprecedented scale. Thompson (1995) traces the beginnings of this process to the 19th century, while others suggest that its origins lie in the 1400s with the establishment of trade routes between different parts of Europe (Wolf 1982). In outlining the origins of the globalisation of communication, Thompson (1995, pp. 149–78) details three major developments. These can be summarised as follows:

- First was the laying of submarine cables throughout the world from the 1850s, which constituted 'the first global system of communication in which the capacity to transmit messages was clearly separated from the time-consuming processes of transportation' (Thompson 1995, p. 154). These cables allowed the telegraphing of messages and were used for business, political and military purposes. By 1900, about 306 000 kilometres of submarine cable had been laid connecting Great Britain, Europe, Asia, Australia, South America and the coasts of Africa. The impact of the telegraph was to compress both time and space. In *The Tyranny of Distance*, Blainey (1966, pp. 224–7) explains that prior to the 1870s news from England could take up to two months to reach Australia. Following the introduction of the telegraph this time span was reduced to between 24 and 48 hours, allowing a more effective integration of Australian business into international markets.
- Second, Thompson nominates the founding of international news agencies in the 19th century. After a period of competition, the agencies strategically divided up the world into mutually exclusive geopolitical spheres of operation. During the 1870s, the three spheres accorded with the European imperial powers of the time: the British Empire and the Far East; the French Empire, Italy, Spain and Portugal; and Germany, Austria, Scandinavia and Russia. Capitalising on the telegraph cable systems, agencies collected and disseminated news throughout the globe and supplied content and information to newspapers. Some of these agencies maintain dominant positions in the international news market in the present day (e.g. Reuters, Associated Press (AP), United Press International (UPI) and Agence France-Presse (AFP)).
- Third, Thompson discusses the transmission of information via electromagnetic waves. The initial media technology using this type of transmission was radio. Electromagnetic waves avoided the expense of laying submarine cables and made it possible to transmit information over vast distances almost instantaneously. The ability to send signals literally through the air—'the ether was buzzing' (Miller & Turner 2002, p. 135)—was a symbol of technological progress that seemed almost magical. Johnson (1988, p. 15) states: 'Radio came to stand for modernity and universal progress.' The impact of this technology in Australia was immense, with the 1930s regarded as the golden age of radio. By 1934, more than one million wireless receivers were licensed and audiences were growing at almost 8000 listeners per month (Hutchins 2002, p. 22; Miller & Turner 2002, p. 136).

Radio is representative of a collective ambition to transcend space and time via communications technologies during the 20th century. Television, introduced to Australia in 1956 to coincide with the Melbourne Olympic Games, intensified this process. Television and communications satellites saw the mass media flourish. The dynamics of the mass media are still evident today despite the impact of digital technologies in the network society.

Conceptual tools

Thompson offers a set of conceptual tools that explain the social effects of the historical transformations that he details. Fundamental to his case is that the unfolding of modernity has seen face-to-face communication displaced by communication-at-a-distance, reorganising relations of time and space and changing the character of social interaction. In explaining this process, Thompson nominates four different types of interaction: (1) face-to-face interaction; (2) mediated interaction; (3) mediated quasi-interaction; and (4) computer-mediated interaction (1995, pp. 81–118; 2005). These categories are summarised in Table 3.1.

Face-to-face interaction

Face-to-face communication between people has taken place throughout human history. Examples of this type of interaction include a town-hall meeting, a university lecture, a face-to-face chat and a group of people surrounding a person telling a story. Participants share 'a context of co-presence'; they can see and hear one another as they are in close proximity. They can see who they are directing their speech at or, as Thompson puts it, orient their interaction 'towards specific others'.

TABLE 3.1

Types of interaction				
Interaction characteristics	Face-to-face interaction	Mediated interaction	Mediated quasi-interaction	Computer-mediated interaction
Space–time constitution	Context of co-presence	Separation of contexts	Separation of contexts	Separation of contexts
Range of symbolic cues	Multiplicity of symbolic cues	Narrowing of the range of symbolic cues	Narrowing of the range of symbolic cues	Varying range of symbolic cues depending on the use of particular audio and visual digital media
Action orientation	Oriented towards specific others	Oriented towards specific others	Oriented towards an indefinite range of potential recipients	Oriented towards specific others and an indefinite range of potential recipients
Dialogical/ monological	Dialogical	Dialogical	Monological	Dialogical and monological

Source: Thompson (1995, p. 85; 2005). Reproduced with permission.

Participants can observe facial expressions, gestures and body language, providing a 'multiplicity of symbolic cues' when interpreting the messages of others and responding in turn. Face-to-face interaction is also dialogical, involving 'a two-way flow of information and communication' (Thompson 1995, p. 83). Participants can respond to one another and build a conversation.

Mediated interaction

This interaction involves the use of a technical medium (e.g. paper or a telephone) to communicate with someone who may be far away in terms of time and/or space. Examples include telephone conversations and letter writing. This 'separation of contexts' narrows the 'range of symbolic cues' available to participants in the exchange. A person using a telephone cannot see the facial expressions or body language of the person with whom he or she is speaking, which changes the nature of the exchange when compared with face-to-face interaction. For instance, a listener cannot see the smile of the person with whom she is speaking. It may then be necessary for the speaker to state that she is joking in order to avoid misinterpretation. Greater effort is required by both parties to communicate effectively and accurately. Just as with face-to-face interaction, mediated interaction is directed 'towards specific others' and is dialogical.

Mediated quasi-interaction

Mediated quasi-interaction (quasi- meaning 'seemingly' but not 'actually') is a form of interaction that is a dominant feature of the 20th century and the new millennium. It is associated with the media of mass communication (Thompson 1995, p. 84) and is specific to modernity, altering people's understanding of what it is to communicate. Television, newspapers, radio, magazines and books—everyday popular items—extend the availability of information across both space and time. For example, a television program can be watched months or years after it is produced in countries around the globe. Re-runs of *The Muppet Show*, *Hogan's Heroes*, *Gilligan's Island* and *The Young Ones* on pay television in Australia typify this phenomenon.

As with mediated interaction, this type of interaction involves a 'separation of contexts' and narrows 'the range of symbolic cues'. However, the number of potential recipients that these cues are available to is indefinite. Unlike a telephone conversation that occurs between two people, a television broadcast is available to an audience of thousands or millions. Also, the interaction is not dialogical but monological: the flow of communication is mainly one way. For example, a newsreader speaks to an audience, not another individual from whom she elicits a direct response and constructs a conversation. She does not hear or see the reaction of audience members, and she is never sure how many people are in the audience.

The impact of mediated quasi-interaction on social life has been immense. If 99 per cent of Australian homes own a television set, the vast majority of the population are engaged in mediated quasi-interaction on a daily basis. This mode of communication has saturated social relations and undermined the clear-cut dominance of face-to-face and mediated interaction. The cumulative effect of this communicative practice has been to reshape collective perceptions of time and space, and to naturalise a technological mode of interaction that is actually quasi-interaction. The difference between the mediated quasi-interaction of the electronic age and the almost exclusively face-to-face interaction of feudal times should not be underestimated, although it is difficult to imagine. Bauman attempts to illustrate the experience of the past:

> *For the overwhelming majority of the pre-modern population, the tasks of status definition and maintenance ... were performed on the local level and grounded in local institutions—parishes, village and town councils, craft guilds. The parish and the guild were not specialized organizations, assigned clearly defined jobs; for most people they were total worlds.* (1982, p. 5)

People relate differently to time and space now. A combination of television, satellite technology and mediated quasi-interaction has resulted in people's perceptions of the world extending beyond the horizon, making events on the other side of the planet immediate and relevant. When the events of an American presidential election or the Academy Awards are broadcast on television in Australia they exist in the 'here and now', despite the vast distance between the two countries. The 'total world' of viewers is exactly that—the total world. There is almost no space on the globe that is immune from the camera in modernity.

Computer-mediated interaction

Technological convergence, pervasive hardware and software infrastructures, and the varying types of interaction afforded by networked communications have led Thompson to update his conceptual schema. Computer-mediated interaction offers a range of experiences that encompass both dialogical (email and real-time chat) and monological (streaming video and audio, podcasting) communication, with the distinction between these categories shifting according to the purpose and functionality of the program or site in question. Text messaging, email and online social networking have also produced entirely new or repurposed 'symbolic cues', such as emoticons (☺), avatars, profiles and text speak that enable communicative interaction (as well as confusing those unfamiliar with them). The uncertainty caused by the internet and the Web is evident through sites such as YouTube and Vimeo. The clips that are available for viewing range enormously, from user-generated compilations to professional productions, and may elicit comments by one or thousands of viewers. This variability means that YouTube can be categorised in many ways in terms of interaction characteristics (see Table 3.1).

Accepting a degree of uncertainty, Thompson (2005) moves to explain what has clearly changed with the mass availability and use of computer-mediated interaction. He identifies four cascading dimensions:

1. Computer-mediated interaction affords great 'temporal compression', or speed of communication.
2. Conditions of use and access in digital networked environments like the internet and the Web are very different to print and analogue broadcast technologies. As YouTube demonstrates, users can now regularly and relatively easily both produce *and* consume digital content (Bruns 2008).
3. Compared to only 20 years ago, information flows are now *more intensive* in quantity and volume; networks of communication are *more extensive* in terms of individuals connected and geography, extending globally; and information is *less controllable* with the reduced capacity of individuals and organisations to restrict the circulation of images and information (Thompson 2005, pp. 48–9).
4. Computer-mediated interaction has changed the functioning of political power, giving rise to a new 'mediated visibility'. Using the 2004 Abu Ghraib prison torture scandal in Iraq as an example, Thompson (2005) discusses how the character of visibility has acutely shifted, bringing into public view what was previously hidden due to spatial–temporal limitations. This change was enabled by digitised images, email, web-casts and audio and video files that overcame the distance between citizen and event, as well as circumventing the control of capital and government. These images of torture moved faster via email and the Web than the US military or the Bush administration could cope with, revealing previously private and disturbing practices in the public domain.

All citizens, employees, families, organisations, corporations and governments are knowingly and unknowingly implicated in this changed world of mediated visibility and its accompanying positive and negative consequences. Personal digital photos, webcams, Facebook, Skype, laptops, email, internet banking, mobile phones and PDAs, GPS devices, closed circuit cameras, and records and images in official (e.g. government and universities) and private (e.g. marketers) databases are all evidence of an internet-enabled information environment. If you need convincing that this new mediated visibility is real, check out a high-resolution colour image of your house or apartment on Google Maps' 'Street View'.

MEDIA RITUALS

Classical sociologist Emile Durkheim's emphasis on meaning and symbolism in social interaction makes him a useful source in the study of media and culture. The following discussion focuses on his notion of social ritual (Durkheim [1912] 1965), which has been used by numerous scholars to study media events. According to Nick Couldry (2003, p. 3), there are three broad approaches to the term 'ritual' in the anthropology literature: (1) habitual action; (2) formalised action; and (3) action involving transcendent values. They are explained here in relation to the media.

Habitual action

Habitual action is any habit or repeated pattern that may or may not have specific meaning for the social actor. This is evident in how people consume the media each day in its various forms. Sometimes this consumption is purposive, paying close attention to a program or publication. At other times, consumption is an almost absent-minded experience, with the media serving as little more than a welcome distraction or background noise to other activities in domestic and other contexts. For example, flicking through a magazine in the waiting room of a doctor's surgery rarely involves close reading. And many people leave the television on when they are at home, even when they are not sitting in front of it, or listen to the radio while driving. When they get in the car the radio is automatically turned on, their attention shifting from the road to the sound and back again. Getting out of the car with uneven recollection of what was broadcast is a common experience.

Formalised action

Formalised action involves a regular and meaningful pattern of action (e.g. the way a table is laid for food in a particular culture). This approach is about more than habit, involving a recognisable shape or pattern that gives meaning to action. For example, formalised action is observable in how television news is programmed and presented. The news is both regular and meaningful. It is on every night and forms a permanent part of the television schedule—this is the appointed time of the day for the broadcast of up-to-date information about local, national and international events. The news is rarely rescheduled or stopped for other programs, although other programs are occasionally interrupted for significant 'breaking news'. The news is a purposively reliable television program, allowing viewers to keep in touch and feel connected with the wider social, cultural and political environments.

The news is also distinctive in terms of formalised presentation conventions. It stands in stark contrast to entertainment genres such as game shows. No-one confuses the news with a game show such as *Wheel of Fortune*. Newsreaders are usually seated in a studio, dressed soberly and with sensible haircuts, and they speak in a formal tone. These conventions reinforce the message that news—a meaningful, serious matter—is being broadcast. Even when travelling overseas, television news is still recognisable, despite the fact that it may be in another language. Tone of voice, the way the newsreader is dressed and the rhythm of presentation—newsreader speaking, visual footage with captions, newsreader speaking again, visual footage and so on—inform the viewer that this is the case. The reliability and rigidity of this format are fuel for parody and comedy shows, such as Jon Stewart's exceptionally popular *The Daily Show* and *Naked News* (featuring naked newsreaders), which has appeared on Foxtel in Australia and is also broadcast in Japan, Spain and Italy.

Action involving transcendent values

This category overlaps with formalised action, but contains additional significance. To demonstrate action involving transcendent values, Couldry (2003, p. 3) uses the example of Holy Communion, a Christian religious ritual that symbolises and embodies a connection with God. The experience of transcendence and connection was a key concern of Durkheim (1965). He was interested in religion in order to understand how people imagine and figure themselves as connected to others as a group. This sense of connectedness contributes to the creation of social order. Media events (see below) are instances of this category, hence sociologists such as Couldry (2003), and Dayan and Katz (1992; see also Price & Dayan 2008) are interested in them. In *Media Rituals: A Critical Approach* (2003), Couldry concentrates on the category of actions involving transcendent values, updating, contesting and critiquing theories relating to **media rituals**.

> **Reflective questions:** What is the relationship between the media and social ritual? Provide your own examples of how the media relates to habitual action, formalised action and action involving transcendent values.

MEDIA AS SOCIAL PRACTICE—COULDRY

Nick Couldry (2000; 2003; 2006; Couldry & Curran 2003; Couldry & McCarthy 2004; Couldry et al. 2007) stands out as an innovative and increasingly influential example of how to apply the traditions of sociology to the study of media. He moves attention away from the study of particular media texts and industry structures, posing a crucial question: what does it mean to live in 'a society dominated by large-scale media institutions'? (Couldry 2000; 2006). Wisely, media are located here within the broader social field, used as a window onto how society reproduces itself and how the social world is represented. Couldry is interested in how the media fits into people's everyday lives as a social practice, seeking to understand 'the types of things people do in relation to media', as well as what they say. A rudimentary example of this approach is to consider (1) how reading the newspaper or watching television news influences or 'mediates' how people relate their private lives to the public world of government, the legal system and educational institutions; and (2), in turn, how people working in these institutions use media to think about their role and respond to members of the public. *Media are implicated in how practices across a range of social contexts are defined, ordered and thought about.* This means that media play a central role as a ritual space in which 'the details of social life make sense' (Couldry 2003, pp. 2–3), thereby helping give shape to what people think of as 'society' (Cottle 2006).

Couldry's arguments are important given the routine consumption of media and the fact that many possibilities for acting together socially are realised through the media (Couldry 2003, p. 20). The generation of collective emotional excitement and belonging—Durkheim's collective effervescence—is often mediated. The media industries do more than create a product in order to sell advertising or serve the public. Coverage of the Olympic Games, football grand finals and the results night of a federal election enable people to come together and *imagine* themselves as a collective. Individuals support an athlete, a team or a party and in doing so join with others physically and/or psychologically. When Cathy Freeman ran the 400-metre track race at the Sydney Olympics in 2000, 'the nation' stopped for the race. At these moments, the Australian public is momentarily figured in the imagination of the viewer. The media offers these ritual moments at regular intervals:

> *The term 'media rituals' refers to the whole range of situations where media themselves 'stand in', or appear to 'stand in', for something wider, something linked to the fundamental organisational level on which we are, or imagine ourselves to be, connected as members of a society.* (Couldry 2003, p. 4; see also p. 29)

Couldry moves beyond Durkheim by critiquing his emphasis on the creation of social order through ritual. He adopts a neo-Durkheimian approach, arguing that media create only the *appearance* of generating social order and connectedness. The extraordinary reach of media communications technologies and the size of audiences make this appearance convincing, suggesting that principles of order rather than disorder are the foundation of society. Couldry (2003, p. 10) argues that this suggestion is illusory. The media provide no more than temporary coherence. The fact that this coherence exists temporarily is mistakenly read as proof of something more permanent and unalterable at the heart of social relations and identities.

The belief that media rituals generate social order means two things. First, it demonstrates the extent to which principles of order are embedded in the way that people perceive the world, even when there is evidence suggesting otherwise. Second, this appearance of order may well compensate for an underlying disorder, and the inevitable existence of conflict, change and fragmentation. 'Everything works *as if* there were a functioning whole', thereby helping states and societies to hold together (Couldry 2003, pp. 10–11).

Couldry's arguments in relation to media rituals and practices make sense in theory, but legitimate doubts can be raised about the available evidence to back his claims. *Media Consumption and Public Engagement: Beyond the Presumption of Attention* (Couldry et al. 2007) is a convincing response to this concern, demonstrating what people both do and say in relation to media. Extensive data are provided to support the arguments presented, drawn from semi-structured interviews, focus groups, a nationwide survey involving more than 1000 British citizens and media diaries kept by 42 volunteers over a three-month period. The study starts from two widely held assumptions about democratic societies. First, citizens share an 'orientation' to the public world where issues of common concern are, or at least should be, dealt with. Contrary to claims of a generalised collapse in political and public life, a sense of 'public connection' is found to exist among the study's participants and is strong in many cases. Prudently, the investigators make few assumptions about what constitutes a public issue from the perspective of participants, instead allowing the data to 'speak'. Public concerns range from serious matters (formal politics, international relations and war) to the lightweight and ephemeral (celebrities, entertainment and sport). People draw important and sometimes surprising political and ethical conclusions from *both* the serious and the lightweight as they make sense of the public sphere.

The second assumption is that a sense of public connection is generated primarily via mediated versions of the public world. This assumption is confirmed, although varying strengths and consistencies of mediated public connection are reported. (An interesting contradiction was found to exist here: those participants with the heaviest television viewing habits are among the *most disengaged* from public issues and affairs.) A notable finding of the study is that although many citizens are interested in public life and politics, often expressing strong feelings and opinions, few opportunities exist to turn this 'talk to action' (Couldry et al. 2007, p. 121). People want to engage with governments and public issues, but the mechanisms to achieve this involvement are lacking and require development.

Discussion now turns to media events, moments during which the orientation of private citizens to the wider social world is thought to be particularly intense.

MEDIA EVENTS

Media events are an example of the third category of ritual listed by Couldry, action involving transcendent values. In their widely cited book, *Media Events: The Live Broadcasting of History*, Daniel Dayan and Elihu Katz (1992, pp. 1–2) deploy a Durkheimian perspective in bringing 'the anthropology of ceremony to bear on the process of mass communication'. Television, they contend, changed the conditions and scope of social ritual via the form of its content, the size of its audiences and its geographical reach. Televised media events help to integrate nations as political and social communities.

Examples of media events include the broadcast of man landing on the moon in 1969, the funerals of John F. Kennedy in 1963 and Diana, Princess of Wales, in 1997, the wedding of Prince Charles and Diana in 1982, Australia's Bicentennial in 1988, the first anniversary of September 11 in 2002, the 2005 funeral of Pope John Paul II, Kevin Rudd's apology to the Stolen Generations in 2008, the Olympic Games and the Football World Cup. The difference between these events and an occurrence such as the planes hitting the Twin Towers on 11 September 2001 or a natural disaster such as the 2009 Victorian bushfires is that the latter are unexpected and unplanned from the perspective of broadcasters. Such events are major news, political and humanitarian occurrences, but they are not media events in the sociological sense. There is no opportunity to create a sense of anticipation among viewers in the weeks preceding the event by the promotion of special programming.

According to Dayan and Katz (1992, pp. 1–53; Dayan 2008), media events fit into three broad genres: contests (sport and politics), conquests (giant leaps of humankind) and coronations (parades with strong ceremonial content). Each of these relates to Weber's three types of authority: rationality, charisma and tradition. Media events are said to have the following characteristics:

- *Planning.* They are pre-planned. Audiences are given advance notice via advertising and publicity. In an effort to create a sense of anticipation among audiences, this publicity may begin weeks prior to the event.
- *Routine.* They interrupt media routine, as they are one-off or irregular events. Networks present them as 'special events' and 'must-see TV'.
- *Broadcast.* They are often broadcast live, offering the viewer the appearance of unmediated access to a real event. They attempt to harness the potential of media and communication technologies in terms of geographical reach. Service delivery platforms such as Star TV, CNN and BBC World TV span the globe, offering the possibility of a genuinely global audience. A factor preventing the realisation of such an audience is the fact that not all regions of the globe attribute uniform significance to events. For instance, British reaction to the death of the Pope in 2005 was obviously not mirrored throughout much of Asia and the Middle East.
- *Presentation.* Media events use three main themes in their presentation: celebration, reconciliation and commemoration. Celebrations are ceremonies of respect and festivity such as

a royal wedding or a historical landmark such as a bicentenary. Reconciliatory events invite people to overcome conflict or at least postpone it. The Olympic truce, an invitation to suspend warfare and foster world peace through sport, is a quixotic attempt at such reconciliation. Commemorations honour or preserve the memory of people or events that contain great symbolic value. The anniversaries of September 11 and Anzac Day serve this function.

- *Audiences*. When successful, these broadcasts are watched by large audiences, possibly the biggest in the history of the world. It is estimated, for example, that the Beijing Olympics in 2008 had an audience of more than four billion people. In addition, these events privilege 'the home'. Whereas some commentators have blamed television for a decline in people's engagement with family and community, these events are moments when friends and family gather together to 'witness history'.
- *Organisation*. They are often run by powerful public organisations located within the political establishment. The Returned Services League (RSL) is primarily responsible for Anzac Day, while Australia's 1988 Bicentennial celebrations and the 2008 national apology to the Stolen Generations were federal government initiatives. They are important events that evoke mainstream and conservative political meanings, stressing the unity and importance of the nation and public.

Dayan and Katz (1992) argue that these events are primarily integrative in the way that they foster an 'upsurge of fellow feeling, an epidemic of communitas' (p. 196): 'These broadcasts *integrate* societies in a collective heartbeat and evoke a *renewal of loyalty* to the society and its legitimate authority' (p. 9). Media events are figured as expressions of social order, symbolising both renewal and reaffirmation of this order among viewers and citizens. A national viewing public stands witness to the legitimacy of the state, the experience of social unity and the emotional pull of nation. The media sit at the middle of this process, as a launching pad for the expression of national culture. Dayan and Katz make an original and widely discussed case. Instead of treating television as a technology that serves to isolate people from one another, contributing to the individualisation of society, they argue that it offers collective ceremonies that bring people together across multiple locations and constitutes them as communities and nations.

Despite its originality and strength, the problem with Dayan and Katz's case is threefold. First, they place too much faith in the existence and unity of the viewing public. The literature on media audiences informs us that the diversity of ways that people receive and interpret media texts demands we think in terms of multiple and subaltern publics (Fiske 1987; Fraser 1999). Many people may accept and enjoy the dominant messages contained within a commemorative media event, but others will negotiate or oppose these messages, creating their own readings of what they see and hear (Hall 1990). A broadcast of Anzac Day commemorations, for example, can be read in several ways: as honouring fallen soldiers and the Anzac spirit; as a reminder of the futility of war; as a ceremony that needlessly glorifies the destructive, masculine character of war; or as a dull march with boring commentary. Depending on the historical, political and cultural mood of the time, the hardening of difference, the achievement of unity and palpable indifference are all possible outcomes of witnessing media events.

Second, the idea that media events serve a large-scale socially integrative function is more assumption than fact. Media events are representations—constructions—of social order that obscure conflict or a lack of consensus. Couldry states, 'The fact that societies are stable ... does not necessarily mean that they have a shared set of values' (2003, p. 65). Nonetheless, qualified credence should be granted to the arguments of Dayan and Katz on this point. Even if media events do not integrate people to the degree that Dayan and Katz suggest, the representation of social unity and connection may help people to live with and accept the inevitably of conflict and difference. Media events *promote*, but do not *consummate* or *guarantee*, social unity.

Third, there is a flaw in the arguments of both Dayan and Katz (1992) and Couldry (2003) in regard to the function of media events. Dayan and Katz's overemphasis on social unity and order has already been discussed. In seeking to rectify the problems in their argument, Couldry states that media events obscure a 'conflictual reality': 'we must *look beyond* the claims of order ... and concentrate instead on the conflictual reality with which they are entangled' (2003, p. 74). Couldry is right to highlight the need to look beyond the unifying rhetoric of media events. But to imply that reality is primarily conflictual is to overcorrect Dayan and Katz's case. Social relations are not about either/or choices. Following the example of Simmel (1968), it is better to engage with the 'restlessness' of social life and culture. Both order *and* conflict (not order *or* conflict) are the reality that people live with daily. Order and disorder, agreement and conflict, assembly and disassembly coexist, side by side. At different times and in specific social contexts, one condition may achieve greater coherence than the other in relation to a media ritual, but this coherence will erode. People relate to events differently as time passes and history and culture change, which is a point supported in the next section.

Beyond media events: the 2008 Beijing Olympic Games

Daniel Dayan (2008; Price & Dayan 2008) updated his theorising of media events recently by using the megaevent of the Beijing Olympic Games as a focal point. Written prior to the staging of the Beijing Olympics, *Owning the Olympics: Narratives of the New China* is an edited collection that uses the Olympics to revisit media events, treating the Olympics as a 'media platform' that attracts massive audiences (Price 2008). The meanings attached to this platform in Beijing were contested keenly by a range of actors—organisers, sponsors, NGOs, protestors, political groups—all of whom were attempting to inscribe it with their preferred meanings in the public mind. As highlighted by protests and civil disobedience during the Olympic torch relay in the lead-up to Beijing, the Beijing Olympics were the most politically charged Games in 25 years, with acute sensitivity surrounding the issues of freedom of expression and human rights in the host nation. Therefore, the contest over the media platform was particularly fierce.

Dayan (2008) acknowledges in the opening sections of his essay, 'Beyond media events: disenchantment, derailment, disruption', that many years have passed since *Media Events* was first published with Katz in 1992 and that 'the world has changed' (p. 392). Judging by his arguments, this change has not been for the better. He makes the point that the multiplying range of technologies delivering media content means that 'television-as-we-knew-it' is disappearing.

In departing momentarily from Dayan's analysis, this disappearance signals the emergence of a 'convergence culture' (Jenkins 2006a), in which the distinctions between broadcast, print and online media have partly dissolved with the growth of digital content distribution. This has contributed to a radical expansion and intensification in media coverage of the Olympic Games since the early 1990s. For example, NBC's coverage of the 1992 Barcelona Olympic Games for its American audience totalled approximately 161 hours. The browser that popularised the Web, Mosaic (which became Netscape) was not available to the public until 1994, meaning that online coverage was almost non-existent in 1992. By way of comparison, NBC claims to have supplied 'an unprecedented 3600 hours of Beijing Olympic Games coverage, the most ambitious single media project in history' over the 17 days of the event, with the seven NBC-Universal networks cumulatively offering more than 212 hours of coverage *per day* (NBC 2008). This coverage included in excess of 2000 hours of live broadband streaming on NBCOlympics.com.

Even making allowance for self-promoting exaggeration, these are incredible figures, which help us to understand why, in Dayan's mind, Beijing was a useful 'laboratory' (p. 394) to rethink media events in their contemporary guise. Dayan identifies three main changes in the character of media events and explores these under the semiotic headings of semantics, syntactics and pragmatics. While these terms may at first appear confusing, they are worth considering (or at least tolerating) given the significance of the arguments presented.

- *The semantics of conflictualisation* (Dayan 2008, p. 395). The end of the Cold War following the collapse of the Communist Bloc in 1989 meant that 'the end of conflicts' and 'the waning of feuds' were dominant ideas resonating globally when *Media Events* was published in 1992. It was a new era with warfare on a worldwide scale momentarily appearing a most unlikely prospect for the first time since World War II. The Beijing Olympic Games, by contrast, occurred in a post-September 11 environment in which 'war rituals multiply' (Iraq, Afghanistan, Sudan, the Arab–Israeli conflict), accompanied by 'televised ordeals, punishments, and torture'. The concept of sporting contests now conjures the 'brutality of conflict' in the popular imagination. The implication of this argument is that media events may now provoke hostility and divide populations, which is a considerable shift in argument given the emphasis on unity and social integration that ran throughout the original study. It is interesting to contemplate whether the Beijing Olympic Games acted to either foster unity or entrench divides for both the Chinese population and between nations.
- *The syntactics of banalisation* (pp. 395–6). Dayan is analysing here the ways in which media events are organised and received. In connecting to the previous point made about conflict, he argues that

the 'social and political polarization and its effect on media mean it is harder to achieve a broad consensus about the importance of particular events' (p. 396). This broader political culture is exemplified by the emergence and influence of international cable news networks such as Fox News and Al Jazeera, which regularly offer different interpretations and footage when covering the same events. These networks are also indicative of the fact that media and media events travel beyond the frame of the nation-state to a far greater extent than in 1992. These developments have coincided with a confusion of the line between media events and news, particularly given the increasing technical capacity and frequency of the 'live cross' by networks to a journalist or commentator who may be presenting in another country via a digital camera or portable satellite video phone.

Put simply, live events are no longer as special as they once were, with audiovisual footage from afar just a click away on the Web nowadays. Moments of high ceremony have been reduced to an everyday, banal occurrence. All these developments have created what Dayan calls a banalisation of the format following from the proliferation of 'almost media events' (p. 396). Again, he is describing a different world and media setting compared to the early 1990s when nationally based broadcast television was still the dominant audiovisual medium and the impact of digital media was only beginning to be felt.

- *The pragmatics of media events* (p. 396). Media events have lost their enchantment, or at least a large part of it (p. 397). They no longer generate a sense of communitas in the way they once did, with reality television co-opting the live communal experience and digital media reintroducing 'individualised reception', meaning that the tacit collective agreement to 'suspend disbelief' and bear witness to history is at risk.

Confirming the individualistic dimension of media reception is the fact that the 2008 Beijing Olympic Games were experienced in a multitude of forms, all affording different perspectives on the same media event. A month *prior* to the games (13 July), there were 23 800 YouTube videos prompted by the keywords '2008 Olympics'. Moreover, idiosyncratic Olympic discourses and images were accessible via innumerable blogs, Facebook, MySpace, Bebo, Twitter and Flickr. Even when watching the Olympics live on television at home with family and friends, audience members now carry a mobile phone, which threatens to disengage their attention from those around them. Since media events are stripped of their transcendent qualities, this leads Dayan to conclude pessimistically that they are now an 'exploited resource within a political economy of collective attention' (p. 397).

Dayan's arguments about the broader global political conditions of conflict and war are powerful and his understanding of the interplay between individualised and collective reception, be it experienced as banal or transcendent, remains impressive. His attitude, however, arguably has as much to do with the approaching redundancy of the theoretical model that he presented with Katz in *Media Events* in 1992. What his essay, and the edited collection of which it is a part, offers is a thought-provoking foundation to reflect on how collective experiences and identities are enacted, felt and consummated through media events in a convergence culture. A failure to continue thinking, discussing and writing about these issues will lead to a sense that little exists beyond the spectacle of an event, which is, in effect, to live in a social world minus the sensation of social connection with others.

THE PUBLIC SPHERE

'I am a member of the Australian public.' This claim raises a number of questions, revealing how much is taken for granted in this statement. How do you become a member of the public? Who permits you membership and what is the cost? What rights and responsibilities flow from membership? How long does your membership last and can it be taken away? Most importantly, what are you a member of exactly?

It is commonsense to believe that the public—a grouping of rational, self-determining, mutually recognising citizens linked by common interests—exists. Yet consider the range of terms where the public and variations of it appear—public opinion, public interest, public policy, publicity, publicise, public relations, public sector, public space, public school, public impact. 'The public' and its relationship to media and society are anything but straightforward, especially when it comes to the right to communicate—both in terms of means and expression—which is considered a key component in contemporary cultural citizenship (Miller 2007).

One approach to understanding the public is to treat the media as both participatory and creative in character. Journalists and producers believe in the public as much as their audiences do, invoking it via presentation techniques and modes of address. Their activities help to figure the public, but audience participation is required for consummation of the relationship. By responding to invitations from the media to watch, listen, read and respond, individuals turn themselves into an audience: a volatile, transitory grouping that gives form to 'the public'. In the case of television, this grouping may last as long as the next ad break, before wandering attention and its behavioural expression, channel surfing, reduce its size and/or reform it around another media text. Viewers never stop believing that they are members of a permanently present Australian public, but this public keeps shifting, reconfiguring, gaining power, losing power, appearing and disappearing; 'the belief in the public's existence is much more real than the public is' (Hartley 1992, p. 119).

The public cannot be imagined without the media industries. These industries use the public for financial survival and the maintenance of their cultural legitimacy, and people use the media to bring them together and contribute to the generation of collective identity. These industries fulfil their duty relentlessly, calling the public into being 24 hours a day, seven days a week. People respond by reading, watching, listening and logging on. But the public created and structured by the media in myriad texts and technologies is not fixed or whole; it is multiple and mobile in terms of identity and practices, sometimes dispersing as quickly as it was formed. Identities, politics, values and beliefs are all thrown into the melting pot of the public, magically making the irreducibility of all these things somehow reducible. The media manages this task

on a mass scale, in the form of vox-pops, opinion polls, feedback shows, letters pages, agony columns, ratings and audience surveys. Now it's our civic duty to state, vote or tick our opinion of, preference for, or assent to scenarios, choices or questions to which we have been invited to respond in the media we read, see or hear. By such means various publics are created, circulated, adjusted and supplanted, in competition or coexistence with each other, available for media readers to slip on and off like a jacket as the need arises. (Hartley 1992, p. 4)

The media and its publics are situated within large-scale social forces that exist beyond the control of any individual. The effects of institutions, such as broadcasting and publishing organisations, and discourses of national identity and citizenship create a range of ever-changing publics (Hermes 2006). Therefore, sociology has much to offer in understanding how the public is socially constructed, with influential German social theorist Jürgen Habermas featuring prominently in the literature.

THE STRUCTURAL TRANSFORMATION OF THE PUBLIC SPHERE—HABERMAS

Habermas' *The Structural Transformation of the Public Sphere* (1989) is a book grounded in the critical theory tradition of Western Marxism and is indirectly related to the work produced by the Frankfurt School (see box) (Pusey 1987). One of Habermas' early books, originally published in 1962, it introduced the concept of the public sphere, which has become an enduring feature of commentaries on the media, journalism, politics and public life. Habermas has since reworked and expanded his arguments in his theorising of communicative rationality (Habermas 1984, 1987) and a range of other studies. But the relevance of the concept of the public sphere remains, having produced a wealth of critique and analyses. It is an essential tool for those wanting to understand the interrelated character of communication processes, political dialogue and civil society.

The public sphere is a historical ideal used to assess the health of public discourse and democratic politics in contemporary society. Habermas argues that the bourgeois public sphere took root in Western Europe during the late 17th and early 18th centuries. Prior to this time the feudal system had denied open political discussion among subjects of the crown. The development of nation-states, parliaments, commerce, printing and an expanding capitalist class changed this situation. The public sphere emerged in the space that opened up between the state and formal politics, and the economic, personal and family relationships of individuals. The physical setting for this space was coffee houses, salons and clubs where educated citizens gathered to exchange information and debate issues of common concern. The mediation of these issues occurred through political journals, pamphlets and newspapers. This is the time and space where the media become central to the operation of political culture. In principle, the public sphere was universally accessible, with the primary qualification for participation being the ability to discuss the affairs of the state, the economy and society in a rational manner. Citizens gathered to discuss and further their own interests, affect the state and practices of government, and improve the conditions of public life. The public sphere:

THE FRANKFURT SCHOOL (AND *THE MATRIX*)

The Frankfurt School sociologists are pioneers in the field of critical theory. Despite their approach and arguments having dated, they remain an influential school of thought, setting the terms for debate and discussion about popular culture for the second half of the 20th century. Originally from Germany, they emigrated to the United States in the 1930s seeking exile from Nazism. The emerging Nazi regime had made extensive use of the media in its rise to power. Theodor Adorno, one of the School's founders, believes that radio played a pivotal role in Hitler's ascendancy and the development of an emerging authoritarian mass society. This belief relates to the school of thought's criticism of the mass media and its role in the creation of political and social alienation.

In *Dialectic of Enlightenment*, Adorno and Max Horkheimer (1972) argue that the promise of the Enlightenment had been betrayed, with scientific principles and rationality no longer creating knowledge and freedom, but rather subverting and denying these ideals (Strinati 1995, p. 54). The most famous essay from this book, 'The culture industry: enlightenment as mass deception', is a damning indictment of the mass media and its products (movies, soap operas, jazz music). They argue that these cultural forms function to secure the economic and political ascendancy of capital, with media corporations more interested in maximising profit than enhancing human freedom. The culture industries are central to patterns of social and political domination that characterise industrial capitalist societies.

This system of domination produces 'mindless' social subjects and a relentlessly amused mass society. The citizen-turned-consumer is suffering under a condition of false consciousness that blinds them from the injustices of the capitalist system and prevents effective political action: 'The individual who supported society bore its disfiguring mark; seemingly free, he was actually the product of its economic and social apparatus.'

A very loose and modified version of this argument is presented in the storyline of the movie *The Matrix* (1999) and its many sequels and spin-offs. The character of Neo undergoes a process of self-realisation that the 'system' within which he exists is exploitative and deadly. He is joined in his quest as 'the chosen one'—the person who will reveal the true nature of the system and liberate humanity from the tyranny of technology and the machines—by a group of similarly aware and motivated dissidents, led by Morpheus and Trinity. Ironically, *The Matrix* movies have grossed hundreds of millions of dollars for Rupert Murdoch's Twentieth Century Fox studios.

designates a theatre in modern societies in which political participation is enacted through the medium of talk. It is the space in which citizens deliberate about their common affairs, and hence an institutionalized arena of discursive interaction. This arena is conceptually distinct from the state; it is a site for the production and circulation of discourses that can in principle be critical of the state. (Fraser 1999, p. 519)

The function of this social domain is to give expression to public opinion by allowing people to express their views openly and equally (Habermas 1997).

The idealised historical moment of the bourgeois public sphere is used as a measure for whether the conditions for effective democracy exist and to critique the media's role in facilitating this condition. The capacity of the media to sustain democracy, public dialogue and the political participation of citizens is seen as more important now than it was in the coffee houses and salons of the 18th century. The sheer scale of present-day politics, the media and society makes it impossible for even small portions of the public to gather together physically and enter into meaningful dialogue. The historical measure of the public sphere and the role of the print media in it produce two common claims, which are discussed in more detail below. The first is that the contemporary media are comparatively commercialised and trivialised, and that this character has led to social fragmentation and apathy among members of the public about the state of liberal democracy. The second is the overly optimistic predictions that technologies such as the internet will breathe life into the public sphere as Habermas imagined it, creating genuinely open and democratic public discourse.

There are difficulties with using Habermas' conception of the public sphere when assessing the current state of the media and political culture, three of which stand out. First, Habermas' historical analysis is arguably faulty because the bourgeois public sphere never existed as he describes it. Fraser (1999) and Dahlgren (2002) both dispute his claims that universal access to the public sphere existed in the salons and coffee houses. Those who participated in these spaces were mostly male, educated and wealthy. There was limited suspension of 'status hierarchies' such as class, gender and ethnicity for the purpose of rational discussion. The men who participated in this sphere may well have viewed themselves as representing universal interests, but this was an erroneous assumption of privileged men who enjoyed and exercised social power. The bourgeois public sphere was an exclusionary space just as much as a participatory space. Habermas ignores alternative and subaltern publics, such as women, workers and people of colour. He has acknowledged the validity of these and other criticisms in subsequent writings (Habermas 1992).

The second problem is that Habermas idealises the role of pamphlets, journals and newspapers in sustaining the public sphere. He misrepresents the diversity of the media during the 17th, 18th and 19th centuries. He depicts a small-scale press whose primary function is to generate public dialogue about politics. According to Habermas, this function is betrayed by the gradual transformation of the press into large-scale commercial concerns and then the later rise of electronic media, which 're-feudalise' the public sphere and deny the public a voice. Public dialogue is now administered by commercial media organisations that impose themselves upon the masses in the pursuit of profit and with little regard for politics or reason (Habermas 1989, pp. 170–1). The critical and political faculties of the public are impaired as commercial imperatives, advertising and image management dominate the operation of the media. This case appeals to those who dislike the excesses of the commercial media, but it also underplays the long-term commercial character of the media and the agency of audiences.

Thompson (1995, p. 72; 2000, pp. 41–59) highlights that the press of the 18th century was both commercial in character and devoted to more than just political discussion and reporting. In particular, the cheaper newspapers of the 18th and 19th centuries are evidence of notable interest in sensational content and sex scandals. The hegemony of 'serious' political reporting and public discussion was not as great as Habermas suggests: 'there never was a "golden age" when public communication was generally "quality", serious and rational' (McKee 2005, p. 25). Furthermore, Habermas assumes that as commercialisation of the press and the media proceeds, readers are transformed from active political subjects into passive consumers. As he expresses it, 'impersonal indulgence in stimulating relaxation' overtakes 'a public use of reason' (Habermas 1989, p. 170). This case underplays the capacity of readers and audiences to receive, resist and respond critically to media messages.

Third, the fact that Habermas talks of *the* public sphere implies that a functioning, democratic singular public sphere is the key to democracy. The problem with this idea is that *the* public sphere has never existed. Open access for all to a public dialogue forum free from the distorting effects of social repression and hierarchy is a worthy ideal, but needs to be tempered by the realities of the social world in which people live. Fraser's influential case tells us that acknowledging and working through political difference and conflict requires the open acknowledgment of multiple publics—some more powerful than others—that need to communicate with one another for democracy to be realised:

> *In stratified societies, arrangements that accommodate contestation among a plurality of competing publics better promote the ideal of participatory parity than does a single, comprehensive, overarching public.* (1999, p. 527)

Habermas fails to come to terms with social and cultural inequality and, to restate a point made earlier, ignores women, people of colour, religious minorities, the poor, and gays and lesbians. Not all publics are equal in terms of legal rights, political representation, economic resources and cultural legitimacy, and the temporary suspension of difference for the purpose of political dialogue is unlikely. It is more worthwhile to think in terms of multiple and alternative public spheres, especially in an age of globalisation where access to information and media differs between social groups, communities, regions, cities, countries and continents.

The three problems discussed here are well recognised. The important issue is how they have impacted on subsequent studies of public communication and politics by media researchers and sociologists. Dahlgren (2002; Gregory & Hutchins 2004, pp. 188–9) suggests that Habermas' idealised conception of the public sphere, which was a short-lived and unique historical moment, has led to an unhelpful analytical polarisation. Either the analyst (1) agrees with Habermas' tragic and 'dismally ideological' conclusions, concurring that the media's role in public disengagement from politics is cause for grave concern (Bauman 1999; Postman 1986) or (2) seeks to disprove Habermas' case and falls into the trap of overcompensating for the excesses of his argument, leading to a 'blatantly Utopian' diagnosis of public life and communication. For instance, the democratising potential of a communication technology such as the Web is cause for excitement and hope (cf. Dahlgren 2001; 2005; Papacharissi 2002), but the Web is yet to deliver a new age of democratic politics (although it has affected practices in party politics, election campaigning and social movements; see Dahlberg & Siapera 2007; Sey & Castells 2004). The diagnosis for this unwanted choice is to exercise analytical caution:

> *And like the concept of democracy, to use the notion of the public sphere does not suggest that what we see today is its consummate embodiment. Again, we would be advised to try to position ourselves between 'dismally ideological' and 'blatantly Utopian' views.* (Dahlgren 2002, p. 196)

Case Study
Letters to the editor

To properly appreciate the operation of a public sphere, it is necessary to survey the empirical conditions and social actions that produce public communication. In a study published by *Media International Australia*, Gregory and Hutchins (2004) examined the letters-to-the-editor page of an Australian daily regional newspaper in an effort to understand how everyday editorial practices create this public discussion and debate forum. Their approach was informed by the fact that institutions, organisations and individuals actively administer the communication forums made available by the media, such as letters-to-the-editor pages, influencing both the form and content of public discourse (cf. Mikosza 2003).

The newspaper had a circulation of above 20 000 copies daily. The research site was chosen because the region in question had almost no other local media outlets facilitating public discussion, with both radio and television services having closed or scaled back operations in recent years. Readers appreciate the letters page because it offers an opportunity to express opinions about issues of common concern, which include environmental and farming issues, politics and religion. The newspaper receives about 20 letters per day, a high amount for a regional newspaper, reflecting this appreciation. Of these letters, between 30 and 60 per cent are published depending on the day of the week.

Rather than seeking to analyse the letters page after its publication, the investigation sought to understand the processes and decisions that shape discourse *before* it enters the formal public domain. Using a combination of in-depth interviews with editorial staff and content analysis, this methodological approach attempted to understand how public dialogue was influenced and controlled by decisions of staff in the newsroom, thereby helping to shape the public sphere of the region in question. The findings of the study were as follows:

- When choosing letters for publication, editors use both formal and informal practices. Formal practices include avoiding letters that contain false claims and/or are legally questionable. Writers must also supply their contact details. Space limitations mean that concise and well-written letters are more likely to be published. Informal practices include a preference for letters that are connected to the current news agenda and are written by people living in the region. Editorial staff express a dislike of letters that are responding to other letter writers ('table tennis' or 'ping-pong' letters).
- Editors make sincere attempts to facilitate open and constructive public dialogue, while admitting that they deal with unavoidable technical (e.g. space and legal issues), organisational (e.g. the economic interests of the newspaper) and cultural constraints and parameters (e.g. the news agenda that best fits the concerns of readers and whether correspondents reside in the region). The fact that these constraints exist, however, does not debilitate public dialogue. Letters continue to arrive at the offices of the newspaper, and circulation figures and reader feedback suggest that people continue to read and respond to the letters that are published. The study reveals that the operation of public discourse is an ongoing process of mediation and negotiation grounded in everyday social practices.

Habermas' notion of an *ideal* public sphere has masked the practical and organisational conditions that mediate public dialogue. An empirical examination of these conditions helps to overcome the unnecessary dichotomisation of public communication analysis between the 'dismally ideological' and the 'blatantly Utopian'. The type of communication occurring on the letters page is not completely open or free, but nor is it unfairly restrictive or anti-democratic.

This case study demonstrates the benefit of a sociological approach to the operation of the public sphere.

Sociologists are well placed to find this middle ground. Empirical research into specific social contexts and media organisations makes it possible to move beyond an ideological/utopian binary. The above case study is an example of an approach that follows Dahlgren's advice.

THE GLOBAL PUBLIC SPHERE—VOLKMER

Ingrid Volkmer (1999; 2002; 2003; Volkmer & Heinrich 2009) has provided a helpful addition to the literature on the public sphere, analysing its operation in a global age. Describing the historical evolution of this sphere since the 19th century sees her covering similar ground to Thompson and Habermas, describing a process of ever-expanding '"transborder" communication and distribution of political news' across nations, regions and continents, a process intensified by the birth of international news agencies like Reuters and API in the nineteenth century (Volkmer 2003, pp. 9–10). Her contribution is to use this historical context to explain the emergence and operation of the global public sphere in contemporary society.

Since the 1980s, communications satellites, such as Australia's AUSSAT series, and cable technologies have accelerated transcontinental and transregional information flows in the broadcast television sector. About 400 of the 900 satellites in orbit transmit entertainment and political content, as well as telecommunications services (Volkmer 2003, p. 11). Influential, genuinely global news hubs such as CNN International, BBC World, Al Jazeera, Zee-TV and Fox News have entered this transnational space, which represents the establishment of a transnational political news sphere. The advent of the syndicated 'world report', or variations on it, during news broadcasts is a barometer of this change, with journalism taking on ever-more important political functions in reporting complex stories with implications for global geopolitical relations (p. 14). Dispersed expatriate and diasporic communities reinforce the reality of a worldwide audience, unlike during the 20th century, when addresses to a peculiarly national audience dominated. The internet further complicates this picture, adding a 'multi-channelled, multi-layered information network fed by numerous news deliverers' (Volkmer & Heinrich 2009, p. 55), with all the aforementioned news providers possessing a significant Web presence.

Volkmer presents a range of sophisticated arguments in explaining the operation and dynamics of the global public sphere. Two are discussed here. First, the significance of these global news hubs lies not in their popularity as reflected in daily ratings—on a day-to-day basis, these are not especially high when compared with much of commercial television. Rather, their power is related to their impact on national and global political discourse at times of crisis and war—moments when confusion and uncertainty reign in the immediate aftermath of a major incident. Prime ministers, presidents, defence leaders and many members of the public turn to CNN and the BBC when attempting to make sense of unfolding events or take decisive action. The bombings and attacks in New York (2001), Bali (2002 and 2005), Mombasa (2002), Madrid (2004), Jakarta (2004), London (2005) and Mumbai (2008) bear this out. In their immediate aftermath—sometimes literally minutes later—people around the world turn to their television sets and computer screens to make sense of the bewildering events, which awards the news networks considerable political power in defining the 'reality of the situation' for leaders and citizens throughout the world. In Australia, Channels Seven, Nine and Ten, the ABC and SBS all source real-time reports from global news providers when broadcasting breaking international news, while those households with pay television have additional dedicated news channels to choose from (Sky News, Fox News, BBC World and CNN).

Second, the global public sphere is one of globalised differentiation and diversity, with news networks and audiences 'increasingly polarized around political ideologies and topical contexts' (Volkmer 2003, p. 12). This conflictual news space is typified by coverage of the Iraq invasion and conflict (2003–present). The differences between the editorial attitudes and storylines presented by the British publicly owned BBC World, Rupert Murdoch's Fox News and Qatar-based Al Jazeera are not only marked, but sometimes opposing and contradictory. A 'dialectical space' then opens up between the local and the global in the reception of news, as conflicting images and stories flow into nations, regions and cultures. These dynamics have significant consequences for the reconfiguration of political identity, public participation, citizenship, journalism and news in a global age (Volkmer 2002, 2003). A primary challenge of our age is:

> How best to establish a global discourse, to make events from different 'micro-spheres' comprehensible to everyone—these are the issues which will determine the future of crisis journalism in the global public sphere of the twenty-first century. (Volkmer 2002, p. 245)

It is essential to reflect upon and analyse how or whether this challenge is being met, particularly as democracy, capitalism and journalism march in lockstep, just as they have for the past three centuries.

CELEBRITY: THE PRIVATE MEETS THE PUBLIC

The changing character of public communications and media institutions over the past four decades has blurred the lines between the public and private spheres. The increasing reach of audio and visual technologies, the growth of media organisations and audiences, and the insatiable demand of both producers and consumers for media content have made information flows more intensive and pervasive (Thompson 2000). One outcome of this process is that people's private lives have become increasingly public. The proliferation of American chat shows discussing adultery, sexual dysfunction and eating disorders indicates that matters once thought shameful, secret or unfit for open discussion are now material for public entertainment. The private sphere has invaded and conquered the public sphere (Bauman 2000, p. 69). At the least, private affairs have become legitimate issues for public discussion and spectacle, as demonstrated by a daily diet of (quasi-) news stories dealing with the triumphs and travails of celebrities.

Media scandals often involve celebrities. Reality television creates them and tabloid media gossip about them. Their presence infuses public life, as evidenced by the television and movie industries, sport, music, business, video and computer games, and increasingly politics. Cate Blanchett, Kylie Minogue, Peter Garrett, George Clooney, Tony Hawk, Jennifer Hawkins, Brad Pitt, Chris Martin, Kyle Sandilands, Eddie McGuire, Snoop Dog and Paris Hilton—the famous, infamous and absurd—are the lingua franca of the popular media. Magazines such as *Australian Women's Weekly* (still the highest-selling magazine in Australia), *Woman's Day*, *New Idea* and *Girlfriend!* are dedicated to **celebrity** stories and gossip, while innumerable websites and blogs cover similar territory. The male version of this gossip tends to occur in the sports pages of newspapers, in men's lifestyle magazines like *Ralph* and *FHM*, or on online message boards. Moreover, media surveys demonstrate that celebrity reporting is not limited to popular or tabloid media, but has flowed through into 'quality' news media such as the *Sydney Morning Herald*, *Time* magazine, the ABC's *7.30 Report* and Channel Nine's *Sunday* program (Turner et al. 2000, pp. 16–23).

The analysis of prominent public figures has a long history. For instance, the Scottish essayist Thomas Carlyle authored the influential *On Heroes, Hero-Worship, and the Heroic in History* in 1841. Another of the founding fathers of sociology, Max Weber, offers the idea of charismatic authority to help explain the special qualities embodied by military and political leaders and religious prophets. Charismatic authority is viewed as a special gift of mind and spirit, an internal rather than external affair:

Its [charismatic authority's] 'objective' law emanates concretely from the highly personal experience of heavenly grace and from the god-like strength of the hero. Charismatic domination means a rejection of all ties to any external order in favor of the exclusive glorification of the genuine mentality of the prophet and hero. Hence, its attitude is revolutionary and transvalues everything; it makes a sovereign break with all traditional or rational norms: 'It is written, but I say unto you.' (Weber 1968, p. 24)

Those who possess this authority transcend the strictures of everyday life and have the capacity to puncture the rationalising logic of bureaucratic norms and institutional structures. By their power and authority, these exceptional figures help to determine history (Gerth & Mills 1948, 'Introduction', pp. 1–74). The subjective and contingent character of this authority, however, means that it cannot reverse the disenchantment of the world, a generalised social trend of rationalisation and bureaucratisation that Weber theorised.

Belief in extraordinary personal qualities is relevant in the case of some but not all celebrities. Deceased figures such as Marilyn Monroe, Jim Morrison, Elvis Presley, Bruce Lee, Kurt Cobain, Tupac Shakur and Michael Jackson have fans and admirers who believe that they possessed 'matchless, God-given, creative gifts' (Rojek 2001, pp. 32–3). Weber's insights also intimate the evolution of an industry built around the systematic deification and commodification of celebrity representations and memorabilia. Yet the usefulness of the theory of charismatic authority should not be overstated. It cannot account for the manufactured and inexplicable fame of David Hasselhoff, or the intersections between cultural identity, media consumption and celebrity. The social world of Weber at the turn of the 20th century was different from the media-saturated society of the 21st century.

Hollywood's star system dates back to the early 20th century, situating celebrity firmly within modernity and the development of the mass media (Braudy 1986; Rojek 2001). Writing in 1961, Daniel Boorstin (1987, p. 57) offered one of the best known critiques of celebrity when he argued that the age of mass media had helped to create 'the human pseudo event': a person who is known for their 'well-knownness' and who is the manifestation of a contrived reality in which images now have more dignity than originals. Boorstin's savage critique argued that American culture had lost its way and was no longer capable of recognising genuine achievement. The simulation had become the real. This argument resembles the tragic narratives about the media and public life offered by Habermas and the Frankfurt School and hints at the postmodern theory of Baudrillard and his concept of the simulacrum (see Chapter 15). Boorstin's polemic is compelling despite being dated. What it misses is that representations and images have played a major role in social life since at least the advent of print culture more than 500 years ago, and that people draw satisfaction and enjoyment from celebrities despite their constructed character. Discussing and decoding a celebrity's representational construction is part of the fun of media consumption.

A celebrity's wealth, fame and/or achievement are often admired (sometimes grudgingly), with their visibility and promotion in the media making a range of market and cultural choices available to consumers. These choices might include buying a celebrity's latest special edition DVD, purchasing a magazine where the celebrity appears on the front cover, emulating the celebrity's style of dress, repeating a figure of speech used by them in a movie, reading their biography or buying an autographed photo of them on an internet auction website.

A chain of industry linkages extends from the representation and activities of celebrities. They are both brand names and cultural icons (Turner et al. 2000, p. 13). This seamless connection of culture, the market and consumer choice awards celebrities social and economic power. An indication of the recognised function of celebrity in the formal economy is the fact that *Forbes* business magazine publishes a 'Celebrity 100', mirroring its annual list of the 400 richest Americans. This list ranks celebrities according to the value of their brand franchise, rather than simply their wealth (Turner 2004, p. 34). Along similar lines, but with a more playful intent, is Celebdaq: Celebrity Stock Exchange. Mirroring the National Association of Securities Dealers Automated Quotation system (NASDAQ) Stock Market and run by the BBC, this online game allows people to buy and sell celebrities as stock, build trading portfolios and follow the fortunes of famous figures as their 'value' rises and falls according to their successes, failures and the level of publicity that they attract.

Celebrities are more than commodities that serve to reproduce and legitimise consumer markets. Fans and audiences identify with and relate to celebrities in a range of ways: admiringly, associatively, sympathetically, cathartically and ironically (Marshall 1997, p. 69). An examination of this range makes it clear that people form real social and emotional connections with famous figures. The widespread and emotional reaction to the 1997 death of celebrity royal Princess Diana demonstrates this fact. In appreciating the media's role in the production of the social world, it would be a mistake to dismiss the intense reactions to her death as illegitimate or manufactured. Turner (2004, pp. 23–4, 96–102) highlights that the collective outpouring of grief at this time was literally constitutive of the media coverage and produced unexpected reactions for many people:

> *As one man said in a radio talkback session, 'I didn't cry this much when my wife died'. His remark illustrates a strange possibility: that the vast media coverage of Diana rendered her more real to many people than real life itself.* (Lumby, quoted in Turner, Bonner & Marshall 2000, p. 8)

The tens of thousands of mourners at Diana's funeral procession and the millions who watched the television broadcast did not know her personally. But many had formed a definite connection with her, or the Diana that was constructed by media representations of, and discourses about, the 'people's Princess'.

The connections that people feel for media figures can be understood as 'para-social interaction': relations of intimacy constructed through the media rather than face-to-face contexts (Rojek 2001, p. 52; Horton & Wohl 1956). Rojek points out that it is hardly surprising that relations of intimacy are constructed through the media when many people admit to subclinical feelings of loneliness and isolation. Celebrities offer a personalised connection, albeit with a distant other. Turner (2004, pp. 23–4, 92–4) suggests that this type of connection is not necessarily unhealthy or pathological, and in fact may be becoming increasingly important:

> *As the research on para-social interaction suggests, many people use television as a way of combating loneliness; with a trend towards single living, particularly among young people, the uses and gratifications of para-social relationships may become increasingly important as society fragments further.* (Giles, quoted in Turner 2004, p. 93)

Processes of individualisation (Bauman 2001b) and the atomisation of social relationships (Castells 1999a) have impacted on the workplace, family life, sexual relations, religious practice, and rural and urban communities. The rise of celebrity culture coincides with these changes.

The strengths of the para-social interaction argument are that it embeds growing identification with celebrities in broader processes of social change, and avoids condemning those who enjoy or gain emotional satisfaction from celebrity consumption as aberrant or strange. The weakness of this case is that celebrity consumption is viewed primarily as a compensatory practice for things that are otherwise lacking in social life. This bias draws attention away from the idea that celebrity relations are not compensatory, but thoroughly social in character (Turner 2004, p. 100). They are real relations, not second-order artificial substitutes. This perspective entails a focus on the emergence of new social practices and relations connected to the production, representation and consumption of media.

Celebrity and religion

Discussion of para-social interaction and celebrity raises the issue of religion (Turner 2004, p. 94). It is arguable that there is a spiritual dimension to the devotion exhibited by fans of musicians such as Elvis Presley, Patsy Kline, John Lennon, Janis Joplin, Jimi Hendrix, Kurt Cobain, Jeff Buckley and Tupac Shakur. Spiritual connection and transcendence is imaginable if a person believes that Cobain, for instance, possessed 'matchless, God-given, creative gifts' (Rojek 2001, pp. 32–3). John Frow (1998) examines the religious dimension of stardom and the connections that people form with famous figures, asking an apparently silly question—Is Elvis a god?—that reveals a thought-provoking set of conclusions. The problem, as he sees it, is that the discipline of cultural studies is theoretically ill-equipped to deal with this matter, despite the fact that religion in both its organised and disorganised forms is 'perhaps the most important set of popular cultural systems in the contemporary world' (Frow 1998, p. 207). This is a shortcoming that sociology rectifies, given its long history of studying the religious and sacred dimensions of social life.

It is reasonable to claim that famous celebrities and stars are god-like figures to their followers. Rojek (2001, p. 74) explains that celebrity culture is secular, but that the roots of secular society lie in Christianity. Religious forms and rituals provide an important frame through which people express devotion and worship. A short examination of one of the most famous rock'n'roll stars of all time, Elvis Presley, is instructive here. Table 3.2 provides a list of religious characteristics associated with 'the King' taken from Frow (1998) and Rojek (2001). The table details a combination of serious worship, canny commercialism and parody. It does not seek to prove that Elvis is a deity, even if he is god-like from the perspective of some fans. Rather, its purpose is to highlight the interconnections between celebrity dedication and religious rituals and expression.

Rojek (2001, pp. 51–99) is one of the only sociologists to have addressed the topic of celebrity and religion. He provides an overview of this multifaceted relationship, discussing Durkheim's collective effervescence, shamanism, death, and processes of ascension and descent. He concludes that celebrity culture stimulates a 'faux ecstasy' and is no substitute for religion (Rojek 2001, pp. 90–9). Celebrity worship and consumption is fragmented, unstable and constantly changing. It is not capable of generating the unifying beliefs and practices, or the general view of social and spiritual order, that is central to religious belief. The actions of fans

TABLE 3.2

Religious dimensions of fan devotion to Elvis Presley	
Religious dimension	**Elvis Presley**
Pilgrimage	Visitors to Graceland, Elvis' former Tennessee home, number more than 750 000 annually. Many of these people describe their visit as a form of pilgrimage to a shrine devoted to Elvis. Movies such as *Finding Graceland*, starring Harvey Keitel, fictionalise such journeys.
Reliquaries	Displays of sacred relics/items devoted to Elvis are evident at Graceland, by the possession and arrangement of Elvis memorabilia and artefacts by devoted fans, at the First Presleyterian Church of Elvis the Divine and in virtual form by various 'Web shrines'.
Immortality	Elvis has overcome death. Despite dying from a heart attack in 1977, there have been countless Elvis sightings. Many fans see him as living on through his music and movies, the symbols that he has left behind for people to honour and worship. These things have made him immortal.
Worship	Various Elvis impersonators see their act as a form of worship. 'Religious worship is not just a handy metaphor … The impersonator is often considered a medium who channels the spirit of Elvis' (Spiegel, quoted in Frow 1998, p. 203). Elvis conventions and festivals serve as sites of worship.

Source: Based on information in Frow (1998) and Rojek (2001).

gathering around Elvis are matched by countless others forming around other dead or living stars, none of whom can sustain a generally accepted sacred status. Celebrity culture is, nonetheless, a fascinating milieu to observe the adaptation of religious rites and recognition around venerated figures in popular culture.

By using religion in their analyses, Rojek (2001) and Frow (1998) are both making the point that the ubiquity of celebrity culture is a key issue requiring attention. This culture is inescapable, its tentacles spreading ever further throughout social life. Even organised religion is not immune. American evangelists use the stances and methods of celebrity presentation, while many churches have adopted the forms and styles of retailing and media communications strategies used by the celebrity promotion and public relations industries (Rojek 2001, p. 98). In Australia, the popular Sydney-based Pentecostal church, Hillsong, is an example of the latter, possessing its own music label and retailing operation, and producing a television program that is screened in more than 180 countries and is available for streaming online. More applied and in-depth research is required into these issues, as well as case studies of specific celebrities and their devotees.

Reflective question: What are the similarities and differences between celebrity worship and religious forms and rituals?

THE INTERNET, THE WEB AND MOBILE PHONES

About 15 years ago, media theorist Mark Poster (1995) presented a widely cited argument that is worth revisiting briefly despite the passage of time and its subsequent development (Poster 2001, 2006): a second age of mass media has arrived. The first media age unfolded during the 20th century and was dominated by broadcast media and a broadcast model of communication. This was the age of mass production, mass consumption and the culture industries, which raised the ire of Habermas and the Frankfurt School. Film, television and radio are media through which a small and powerful number of producers create and transmit information to a large number of consumers (Poster 1995, p. 3). A one-way flow of communication where 'the few speak to the many' dominates, with media moguls such as William Randolph Hearst, Rupert Murdoch and Kerry Packer symbolising this centralised and demagogic form of power.

In Poster's mind, circa 1995, the second media age involves the decline of the broadcast media and the subsequent democratisation of communication. This process is made possible by interactive digital technologies such as the internet and the Web. These are networked technologies that potentially enable 'an entirely new configuration of communication relations' based on multiple producers/distributors/consumers in which the 'boundaries between those terms collapse' (Poster 1995, pp. 3–4). This is a two-way, decentralised model of communication in which the grip of 'the few' on media power is loosened by 'the many' who assume greater control over what they watch, listen to and read, as well as the range of people with whom they interact. Rather than serving as objects of passive consumption, digital media communications technologies offer a range of interactive possibilities. Reorganisation of the cultural and media industries is required as the power structures of broadcast media are transformed in the wake of these changes.

Downloadable music and video files and peer-to-peer file-sharing programs, such as BitTorrent, are an example of this challenge to the traditional model of media power and control. Instead of relying primarily on multinational media companies to produce, package and distribute CDs and DVDs, as was the case for many decades, Web users with sufficient knowledge and technical skills select their preferred content in any combination, download it for free, swap files with other users, produce and upload their own files, and engage in online commentary and debate via email, chatrooms, bulletin boards and blogs that bypass the mainstream news media. This level of interactivity is beyond what was thought possible for much of the 20th century.

Massive increases in internet usage and Web content help to explain the emphasis on renewal and possibility in Poster's argument. The internet has the second-fastest penetration rate of any communications technology in history, surpassed only by the mobile phone (which is discussed below). Television took 15 years to reach 60 million people. After the development of the Web, the internet achieved this figure in three years (Castells 2000a, p. 382). As of December 2008, there were an estimated 1 581 571 589 internet users worldwide, compared to 360 985 492 in 2000 (Internet World Stats 2009). In developed economies, the internet has become an increasingly taken-for-granted communications 'backbone' for most public, private and social organisations, be they local public libraries, health clinics, sports clubs or major corporations. Indeed, enrolling or working in a university is now almost impossible without Web access. Two-thirds (67 per cent) of Australian households have access to the internet (ABS 2008f).

SALAM PAX AND BLOGGING

An interesting and unusual example of the complex relationship between blogging and the news media occurred during the 2003 invasion of Iraq by American forces. Balnaves, Mayrhofer & Shoesmith (2004) discuss the weblog of Salam Pax and its relationship to news media and public relations sources covering the war. In the months preceding the invasion, a 29-year-old architect living at home with his parents and brothers in Baghdad began using a blog to talk about life under the repressive regime of Saddam Hussein and the threat of impending invasion. His online identity was Salam Pax, which means 'peace' in both Arabic and Latin. Keeping a blog was a risky exercise for him. If discovered by Saddam's security or intelligence agents, his life and that of his family would have been jeopardised.

His site was registering around 20 hits per day in the months leading up to the war. Just prior to the invasion in April 2003, this number had risen to 3000. The increase was achieved by links from other blogs and a growing number of regular readers. Unlike pro- or anti-war media 'cheerleaders' in Australia, the United States and the United Kingdom, Salam Pax provided an intimate, occasionally amusing first-hand account of life in Baghdad. Entries on his site detailed the pain of watching your home city being bombed and the relief associated with the fall of Saddam, condemned Western media coverage of the invasion, and criticised the way the invasion was conducted and managed by the American forces and their allies on the ground. As the invasion proceeded, an increasing amount of broadcast media reports began to appear in the United States and the United Kingdom about the content of Salam Pax's blog. These reports generated speculation over who he was, whether he was actually in Baghdad and the possibility that he was a Central Intelligence Agency (CIA) agent.

A fascinating dimension of this story is the way in which major news media outlets such as Reuters used Salam Pax's blog to source and generate stories. His blog offered the opportunity to bypass both defence force information sources and embedded journalists working with military units. It provided a unique and independent first-hand account of conditions in Baghdad. This example also highlights the growing use of blogs and websites by professional journalists to generate stories.

The story of Salam Pax has been committed to a book titled *The Baghdad Blog* (Salam Pax 2003). He also made an appearance on Australian television when Andrew Denton interviewed him on ABC's *Enough Rope* in May 2004. He left Iraq in 2007, living in London and Beirut, before returning to Baghdad in 2009. He presently maintains a blog (http://salampax.wordpress.com) and a Flickr photostream (www.flickr.com/photos/salam_pax) and 'tweets' regularly (http://twitter.com/Salam).

Manuel Castells is the leading sociologist internationally who investigates this incredible growth and the evolution of what he terms 'the network society'. Communication is not as democraticised as Poster's vision of the future once was, but it has involved large-scale social change requiring serious and extensive sociological investigation.

THE NETWORK SOCIETY

Castells is not the only sociologist to investigate and theorise the relationship between social relations and the internet (see, for example, Holmes 2005; Slevin 2000), but he is the most prominent. He has, for example, been a member of several advisory boards for the United Nations and the European Commission, as well as serving as an advisor for the World Bank and the governments of Chile, Russia, South Africa, China and Spain (see Castells & Ince 2003). His masterful information age trilogy (Castells 2000a; 2000b; 2004a) and edited collections (Castells 2004b; Castells & Cardoso 2006) analysing cross-cultural phenomena in the network society are seminal sources for those interested in the economy, society, politics and culture. Castells situates the internet and networked communications as a crucial technology in the emergence of the network society. *The Internet Galaxy* (Castells 2001) specifically develops his ideas and arguments about this communications technology, while his most recent co-authored book deals with the ubiquity of mobile phones and wireless communication (Castells et al. 2007). Given the scale and range of Castells' scholarship—which includes analysis of the environment, crime, gender, work, business, time, politics, social movements and nationalism—discussion here is necessarily limited to the internet and mobile phones. Readers are encouraged to engage with the full range of Castells' writing, given its diverse array of insights and applications. His is a genuine attempt to develop a comprehensive social theory of the contemporary age.

Castells' *The Internet Galaxy* references the title of a book written by Marshall McLuhan. McLuhan's 1962 volume, *The Gutenberg Galaxy*, offers 107 separate pieces, ranging from one to five pages in length, probing the impact of writing and the printing press on society and culture from ancient times to the middle of the 20th century. McLuhan's point is that printed language and communication gradually eroded the dominance of oral modes of communication and story-telling and, in the process, changed the very appearance and collective understanding of the world. The thoughts and actions of people were recast, with print language subsequently constituting an important component of rational perception. By his choice of title, Castells is attempting to convey a related message: that the internet is the technological foundation of the society that we live in, with digital communications and (hyper-)text now challenging the printed word. Moreover, just as electricity made the Industrial Age possible, so information technology and advances arising from the micro-electronics 'revolution' have made the network society possible (Castells 1996a, p. 15)—the network being the organisational form that makes the internet possible. The origins of this so-called revolution are the 1970s and the early stages of mass-produced microprocessors, which made the personal computer (PC) a growing concern for businesses and households (Winston 1998). While it may be difficult to imagine now, 40 years ago the idea that people would want a computer for their personal use was generally thought to be unlikely. Castells' voluminous books are making sense of this recently realised 'galaxy' and the social implications flowing from its manifestation.

Castells' theory is about much more than technology. He argues that the *social* structure of present-day society is based on networks and, more specifically, adaptable information and communications technology (ICT) networks. His term, 'the network society', captures this reality. It is the power of networks, networking and network logic that is enabling a fundamental transformation of the social world, exponentially increasing the capacity for human communication and productivity. Networks are very old forms and patterns (e.g. transport, social and telephone networks), but the internet and the Web have accelerated and intensified communication across time and space, changing the ways in which information is represented, produced, consumed, circulated, valued and traded within and across territorial borders (see Hutchins et al. 2009; Maxwell 2003).

Social institutions—markets, communities, media and political systems—are increasingly organised in, and connected by, a series of flexible and ever-changing nodes and hubs. This is the mode of development that has made a genuinely global capitalist and social system possible and

MARSHALL MCLUHAN (1911–80)

McLuhan was a student of another Canadian theorist and historian who specialised in the sociology of media, Harold Innis (1950; 1951; 2004). McLuhan's work has a range of applications in the analysis of the internet (Levinson 1999). Following the example of Innis, McLuhan demonstrated the analytical distinction between media and *the* media. Rather than focusing on the content and messages communicated by television networks and media corporations, McLuhan was interested in the social and cultural effects of the technological medium that delivers the message, such as paper, radio and television. He argued that the technical apparatus of the media—the medium—is constitutive of social relations, fundamentally shaping social interactions, sensory perception and human thinking. Carey (1968, p. 289) sums up this approach, 'Communications media, then, determine not only what one thinks about but literally how one thinks'. Media are 'extensions' of man and the mind (Carey 1968; Cohen 2000; McLuhan 1967; Theall 2000).

A distinctive feature of McLuhan's scholarship is its form. Much to the frustration of sociologists such as Robert Merton, he did not produce systematic, evidentially based studies, preferring analytical 'probes' based on metaphor, pun and aphorism. The playfulness of his writing stands out. For the reader, this style lends itself to both engagement and irritation.

His probes can be illuminating and thought-provoking, as well as overly general and obtuse. 'The medium is the message' is the most famous of McLuhan's probes. It underlines the idea that how humans use and perceive a communication medium is of most importance: 'The "content" of a medium is like the juicy piece of meat carried by the burglar to distract the watchdog of the mind'.

McLuhan also coined the term 'the global village' to describe the way in which electronic media connect distant parts of the globe. This connection restores the simultaneity of access to information that defined the village of feudal times, where all members of the community heard the town crier at once. First offered in 1960, McLuhan's metaphor was criticised for the fact that television's reach did not actually connect all parts of the globe. The advent of the internet and the Web, however, has seen the global village achieve renewed relevance. The spread of computer-mediated communication holds out the potential for a simultaneously connected global village (Levinson 1999, pp. 65–79).

A distinctive feature of McLuhan's career and life was that he was a minor media celebrity. He made an appearance in Woody Allen's 1977 film, *Annie Hall*, Stanley Kubrick sought him out for a private screening of *2001: A Space Odyssey*, he was interviewed by *Playboy* magazine in 1969, had documentaries and biographies produced about his life and work (Marchand 1989), and apparently even had a musical written about him in 1994.

given rise to unpredictable and decentralised power relations (Castells 2000a; 2000c; Flew & McElhinney 2002). Both space and time are reshaped as communication and human consciousness extend over great distances in both online and offline contexts. The structural logic of networks is also evident by the organisation and operation of global identity-based social movements. In their positive manifestations, these movements include environmentalism and feminism, while reactionary and occasionally destructive movements include the various permutations of religious fundamentalism and reactionary nationalism (Castells 2004a; Hutchins & Lester 2006; Lester & Hutchins 2009).

THE CULTURE OF REAL VIRTUALITY

The spectacular increase in internet usage and the information storage and retrieval capacity of networked computers has had both cultural and social effects. The impact on social life will be discussed shortly. Culturally, Castells outlines a series of possible changes related to the technological capabilities of the internet and the communicative practices of users. He houses these changes within the concept of 'the culture of real virtuality', which was initially presented in 1996 in the first volume of the first edition of the information age trilogy, *The Rise of the Network Society* (Castells 2000a, pp. 355–406). Castells has since backed away from this concept and its related arguments. It is, however, worth discussing because it captures a present-day anxiety felt by some individuals and groups—that we know less than ever before, especially about the past, despite having more information easily available to us via the Web than at any point in history. By way of demonstration, Yahoo! indexed a total of 19.2 billion web pages in 2005, which is roughly three times the world's population. It is speculated that the gaps between data, information, knowledge and wisdom are widening, thereby inhibiting mutual understanding and cooperation.

The culture of real virtuality is an early attempt by Castells to come to terms with the logic and impact of the internet. For the first time ever, written, oral and audiovisual modes of communication have converged into a hypertext or electronic meta-language (Castells 2000a, p. 356). Whereas media technologies such as the book, radio and television were once discrete mediums that appealed to different senses, the Web has fused them together digitally. Diverse cultural expressions have been captured within one digital domain. The fusion of past, present and future modes of communi-

THE HISTORY OF THE INTERNET

What has become a free-flowing and decentralised communications technology with myriad applications began life as a project situated within the United States Defense Department, one of the most secretive and authoritarian state structures imaginable (Morton 2004, p. 182). The internet was developed within the Advanced Research Projects Agency (ARPA), which was formed in 1958 and based within the Defense Department. The aim of this agency was to build military superiority over the Soviet Union in the wake of its launching the first Sputnik satellite in 1957. ARPA set up a computer network (ARPANET) designed to be both decentralised and flexible. A rationale for this design was to avoid a communication breakdown in the event of a nuclear attack. ARPANET contained no command centre—no single point of control—so if one point in the network was destroyed or malfunctioning, information would be re-routed via other links in the network. This flexibility was achieved by 'packet switching', the most significant innovation of ARPA in the 1960s:

> Packet switching meant that long messages could be broken down into smaller 'packets'; messages could be re-routed if there was a blockage at one message route or point of interconnection between two computers; and messages would be sent in an asynchronous mode, meaning that the receiver would not receive the message until some time after the message was originally sent. (Flew 2005, p. 5)

While conceived for military application, ARPANET was never implemented for this purpose. During the 1970s, the network came to be used and developed by the American computer science research community, with electronic mail being the most popular application (Castells 2001, p. 18). (It continues to be popular: in 2008, according to Nielsen (2009), more than 65.1 per cent of internet users accessed email, which was surpassed only by social networking sites at 66.8 per cent.) The development of a common set of networking protocols enabled computers and computer mainframes to communicate with one another. By 1990, the formal transition of the network from military to civilian use had occurred and the development of the Web followed shortly afterwards.

See Castells (2000a; 2001), Flew (2005), Leiner et al. (2000) and Winston (1998) for a more detailed account of the internet's evolution.

cation and every conceivable cultural expression have created a new symbolic environment. Virtuality is now our reality (Castells 2001, p. 403).

This is a worrying development in Castells' mind. Reality and virtuality have fused, leaving people adrift in a sea of digitised information. Every way a person looks reveals only more hypertext, and a search engine is of little use when each direction leads to the same destination: more information that adds to the blurring of the boundaries between reality and virtuality. The problem here is one of navigation and guidance. The internet has made more information available to humans than ever before, but it is difficult to ascertain what segments of this information are significant and trustworthy, or whether they can be used as an effective guide to social action. The transformation of information into reliable knowledge is a fraught and uncertain process. The logic of the internet, at least superficially, weakens traditional forms of communication and sources of authority that have performed this task, such as religion, history, political ideology and community. Social interaction in online environments is about constructed image worlds, blinding people to the realities of politics, social inequality and injustice as they submit to the virtual logic of the Web.

The drawback with Castells' thinking in this instance is that it lacks supporting evidence. While engaging, the idea of the culture of real virtuality is speculative. It is an attempt to project the dynamics of computer-mediated interaction in terms of cultural outcomes. The conclusions Castells draws about the internet, society and culture in his subsequent scholarship are not as dire.

COMMUNITY AND NETWORKED INDIVIDUALISM

The Internet Galaxy (Castells 2001) argues that the internet is a communications technology that reinforces and intensifies existing social patterns. Online sociability complements and augments offline sociability. Those who are active within their 'real-world' communities use the Web to maintain and expand their range of social activities and contacts. Moral panics about the breakdown of community and family life as lonely and disenfranchised 'netizens' become addicted to online interaction appear baseless, a point also confirmed by recent research (Purcell 2006). Castells (2001, p. 117) reports that such dystopian scenarios are based on an insufficient body of empirical evidence and nostalgia for the supposedly tight-knit communities of a past that never actually existed.

By surveying the growing literature, Castells provides a range of facts and estimates that dispel the popular notion that the internet causes reduced social interaction and increased isolation (Castells 2001, pp. 118–25):

- A British study of 2600 individuals living in 1000 households found that there was no evidence to suggest that internet access in the home reduced the amount of time people spent watching television, reading books, listening to the radio or engaging in social activity in comparison with people in households without access. The only changes that can be associated with internet access in the home are more time spent emailing and surfing the Web.
- A United States study based on national telephone surveys found higher or equal levels of community and political involvement among internet users compared with non-users. It also found that users were more likely than non-users to meet with friends and have a social life away from the home.
- Another United States study using surveys of public participation found that internet users attended more arts events, read more literature, went to more movies, watched more sports and played more sports than non-users.
- A survey of 40 000 internet users in North America found that the use of email added to social interaction, face-to-face and by telephone, and was not a substitute for other forms of social interaction.
- A loss of sociability is reported only among the most frequent users. Those individuals who pass a particular usage threshold substitute this activity for housework, sleep and family care.

These studies offer comfort to those concerned about the detrimental social consequences of internet use. Nevertheless, even given this evidence, it should not be forgotten that there are negative social behaviours associated with the internet. It is a technology designed and used by humans, meaning that its applications can be good, bad and negligible. In addition to facilitating interaction between family members and friends, the internet is utilised by networks of child pornographers, racists and scam artists. However, the available evidence presented by Castells suggests that the *majority* of users are going about legitimate everyday affairs in both online and offline environments.

The temptation here is to conclude that the social effects of the internet and computer-mediated interaction have been minimal. This is to misread Castells' argument. The initial fear was that the internet would replace traditional social communication and relations and that a culture of real virtuality would take hold, which has not been the case. Rather, the widespread use of this technology has provided an *additional layer* to social life. This addition is changing the boundaries and meanings of social relationships, particularly those centred on work, family, business and leisure.

The concept offered by Castells (2001, p. 131) to describe these changes is **networked individualism**. This is a social pattern, one in which individuals organise both their online and offline interactions according to tastes, affinities and values. This emphasis on selectivity is empowered by the flexibility and adaptability of the internet. The increasing role played by online interaction in social life provides material support to this pattern, which may become the dominant form of sociability generally (Castells 2001, p. 132). It is highly individualistic, favouring diversity and plurality as people engage in flexible and mobile relations with multiple 'communities of choice'. For instance, an online session may see a user visit their Facebook profile and post on the wall of a 'friend', follow their favourite 'tweet', read a news story and family email, receive the RSS feed (Really Simple Syndication feed: a Web feed that offers automatic updates to users) from a political blog, check the result of a sports fixture and post on an online message board devoted to discussion of Battlestar Galactica. At no point is the user made to engage or participate in any of these forums or reveal their identity—it is always a matter of choice. The Web offers the opportunity for social, civic, political and popular discussion and interaction, but no more. Networked individualism prioritises choice over commitment and taste over responsibility.

Castells acknowledges that the internet and the Web afford a massively expanded range of social contacts and opportunities for dialogue compared with offline social life. He extends his inquiry by asking a critical question about relationships specifically formed and conducted online: are these meaningful or enduring relationships? He answers in the negative, concluding that many online groups are ephemeral communities of 'variable geometry and changing composition' (Castells 2001, p. 130). As a basis for social relationships, online interaction favours the creation of weak social ties over strong lasting ones. It offers quantity and variety rather than quality and durability. This situation presents a challenge for those who hope that the Web can energise the political and civic engagement of citizens on a local, national and global scale (Freeman & Hutchins 2009).

Discussion now turns to the relationship between the internet and social inequality, a topic about which the available evidence leads to firm conclusions.

THE DIGITAL DIVIDE

The early to mid-1990s saw the spruiking of much over-hyped 'cyberole' (Woolgar 2002), offering the utopian promise of online equality and democracy in the dissemination, access and control of information. The empirical reality has proved otherwise in the respect of an emergent **digital divide** (Castells 2001, p. 247). Internet access and use have become important indicators of social inequality over the past decade, particularly when measured against variables such as age, education, income, employment, race, ethnicity, gender and geographical location (see, for example, Baker & Coleman 2004). Information and communications technologies have become a fundamental source of productivity and power in the global economy (Castells 2000a, p. 21), meaning that those individuals and groups without access to them are triply debilitated. They are left without the following:

1. *The education and skills to generate information that is considered valuable within the networks of economic and social power.* The relationship between education and internet use is worth considering here. In the United Kingdom, approximately 64.4 per cent of people with a secondary education qualification access the internet, but this figure rises to 88.1 per cent for those who possess a university qualification. The same comparison in the United States produces figures of 61 per cent and 87.1 per cent, respectively, and in Singapore the figures are 66.3 per cent and 92.2 per cent, respectively (Cardoso 2006, p. 36). Below these two categories sit those people without secondary qualifications, who are even less likely to access the internet (Baker & Coleman 2004; Castells et al. 2004).

2. *Access to the technological tools and computing equipment used in the production and circulation of this information.* Mundane evidence of this pattern can be found in British government policy supporting online access points in public libraries, kiosks and internet cafés, targeted at helping the socially and economically disadvantaged (Woolgar 2004, p. 138). However, providing equipment and facilities has not equated with likelihood of use. A high number of people using these spaces already have internet access at home, meaning that many of those on the wrong side of the 'divide' are not using these facilities or gaining computer literacy skills.

3. *Information of relevance to their lives.* Evidence is emerging that disenfranchised populations are

offered little online information of direct relevance to their experiences, communities and cultures (Servon & Pinkett 2004). Content is produced and controlled by those populations possessing high levels of technological and digital literacy, creating additional disenfranchisement.

At a macro-scale, recent years have seen the digital divide between nations and continents closing, albeit unevenly, promoting some to think in terms of a 'digital continuum' as opposed to a digital divide (Servon & Pinkett 2004). This welcome development counters Castells' (2000b, p. 165) fear that many regions, nations or continents risk becoming 'black holes of informational capitalism' from which there is limited hope of escape, although the global economic crisis may reverse some of the advances made. The available figures, taken from Internet World Stats (2009), present a mixed picture:

- Only 5.6 per cent (an estimated 54 million people) of the most populous continent in the world, Africa, has access to the internet, although internet use there grew at a rate of 1000 per cent between 2000 and 2008.
- The online user population of Asia (more than 650 million people) has now overtaken the combined total of Europe and North America, which was not the case during the 1990s.
- An estimated 23.6 per cent of the world's population have access to the internet, with a growth rate of 338 per cent between 2000 and 2008. Per capita penetration rates across regions are as follows: North America 73.1 per cent, Oceania/Australia 59.9 per cent, Europe 48.5 per cent, Latin America/Caribbean 29.9 per cent, Middle East 23.3 per cent, Asia 17.2 per cent and Africa 5.6 per cent.

Patterns of exclusion also exist *within* developed nations and major cities (Baker & Coleman 2004). The nation-state is no longer a satisfactory analytical unit to understand the character of social inequality. Castells (2000b, pp. 68–168) uses the term 'The Fourth World' to explain this situation. Poverty and deprivation are not limited to the developing world, such as Africa and sections of Latin America and Asia. Similar conditions are experienced by an entrenched underclass in wealthy countries such as the United States, the United Kingdom, Japan and Australia. Under the conditions of the network society, developed nations have produced conditions of social inequality within their own borders, albeit in less proportion to developing nations (Castells 1999b, p. 400). Examples of this phenomenon include many Australian Indigenous communities, African-American and Latino inner-city ghettos in the United States, and Kamagasaki, the south-end slum in Osaka, Japan. Located in ostensibly wealthy nations, these are informational black holes where unemployment, illiteracy, poverty, crime and homelessness are almost permanent features of the social landscape. The chances of connecting these places to the global networks of wealth, power and knowledge are almost nonexistent, particularly given the instrumental logic that dominates the operation of the network society.

Global and managerial elites, multinational corporations and governments are locked into this instrumentality. A consequence of this commitment is the exploitation of workers (e.g. sweatshop labour) and conditions of chronic poverty in both developing and developed nations. An observation made by Castells about the business world applies equally to the state of humanity in the new millennium: 'Inside the networks, new possibilities are relentlessly created. Outside the networks, survival is increasingly difficult' (2000a, p. 187). In simple terms, this means that an indicator of social disadvantage in the network society is an inability, in terms of either technological infrastructure or knowledge, to access the internet and surf the Web.

Reflective question: Discuss the relationship between social inequality and internet access. Suggest some social and/or political measures that might help to redress the digital divide.

THE MOBILE NETWORK SOCIETY

Nokia estimates that two-thirds of the world's population will be mobile phone users by 2015. At present the number of users is thought to be about two billion, which is double the number in 2004. Young people in the United Kingdom reportedly believe that their mobile phone is more important to them than their television (see Urry 2007, pp. 171–2). This massive growth in mobile phone usage and the implications of a historically unprecedented *mobility* of communications and communicative acts are key research challenges now and into the future, having already contributed to the establishment of John Urry's (2007) broad-ranging 'mobilities paradigm' for sociological investigation.

The implications of mobile communications are manifold, having increased markedly the capacity for flexible, on-the-move communication (e.g. PDAs and

SMART MOBS

The term 'Smart mobs' was coined by technology writer and critic Howard Rheingold in his 2002 book, *Smart Mobs: The Next Social Revolution*. Smart mobs 'consist of people who are able to act in concert even if they don't know each other' (p. xii), and this collective action is enabled by communications and computing devices such as the Web, mobile phones, laptops and mobile internet devices. Rheingold's concept encapsulates how these devices are catalysts and amplifiers of human talents for cooperation, enabling large-scale coordinated action and innovation. Rheingold suggests that smart mobs are representative of broader social, cultural and economic processes that are 'beginning to change the way people meet, mate, work, fight, buy, sell, govern, and create' (p. xiii). His accessible approach moves the focus away from the individualising and atomising effects of networked communications technologies such as mobile phones and the Web and instead he enthusiastically identifies the ways in which these technologies enable collective actions that enrich people's capacities for social cooperation.

Several examples are used to support Rheingold's arguments, which include both beneficial and malignant uses of communications technologies to achieve things not previously thought possible. This includes anti-globalisation coalitions using regularly updated websites, text messaging and mobile phones to coordinate highly mobile and flexible protest actions at meetings of the WTO, enabling the quick gathering of crowds that then melt away. In 2001, with the use of text messaging, it took just a few hours for one million Manila residents to gather in the centre of the city to protest against and overthrow the corrupt regime of President Estrada. Rheingold also points out that terrorists and organised crime have used smart mob tactics to achieve terrible outcomes. An Australian example of undesirable smart mob behaviour is hundreds of uninvited teenage guests using their mobile phones and texting to converge on a house party in the suburbs, creating a major problem for the host and police.

Rheingold's concept also relates to inexplicable mob action, or flash mobs. These usually involve people using social networking media, viral email, chatrooms and texting to gather in a designated public space, perform an unusual act and then disperse again. The largest known flash mob action occurred in March 2008 when 'International Pillow Fight Day' (www.pillowfightday.com) took place. This involved a coordinated day of pillow fights in 25 cities worldwide, including Melbourne and Sydney. According to the *Wall Street Journal* (http://s.wsj.net/article/SB120814163599712081.html), around 5000 people participated in New York. Footage is available on YouTube.

Goggin (2006) provides a short, but useful summary and critique of Rheingold's smart mobs concept. Resources and information relating to smart mobs can be found at the 'Smart Mobs: The Next Social Revolution' website (www.smartmobs.com).

---

iPhones) and 24/7 'perpetual contact' with others (Katz & Aakhus 2002). The 'always-on, always connected' connectivity of mobile communications has complicated the boundaries between work, home and leisure activities, especially given the popularity of devices such as the Blackberry (or Crackberry, as it is anecdotally referred to because of its apparently addictive properties) (Middleton 2008). Camera-phones have helped to produce an unprecedented level of mediated visibility (Thompson 2005), with any event or incident occurring in a public space likely to be digitally recorded. There have been moral panics involving the use of mobiles in school bullying incidents (Goggin 2006). The pervasiveness of mobile phones in pockets, handbags and palms has reconfigured human–technology relations and the body, as mobiles have become an extension of the body and self (Richardson 2008; Urry 2007). In the case of the disabled coping with immobility, mobile communications have, in selected cases, offered connectivity and increased communicative capacity (Castells et al. 2007). 'Smart mobs' have emerged, text messaging is a new linguistic practice with its own codes and conventions, and a powerful sector in the global telecommunications industry has flourished (cf. Goggin 2006, 2008).

At the heart of all these changes is the reorganisation of both private and public social interactions. The dynamics of face-to-face communications and communication-at-a-distance have been reorganised via mobile communications. The idea of urban space minus mobile phones has become difficult to imagine, and the ever-present threat or promise of someone calling from afar is an ineradicable feature of face-to-face discussion (Urry 2007, p. 177) (which is why your lecturers and tutors demand you turn off your mobile!).

The developments outlined here have created what Castells terms 'the mobile network society', which refers to the 'diffusion of networking logic in all domains of social life by means of wireless communication technology' (Castells et al. 2007, p. 6). These wireless technologies—of which the mobile phone is the most obvious and most popular—have enhanced the networked structure and logic of social relations, both intensifying and mobilising social networks. These arrangements constitute a 'new spatiotemporal [space-time] configuration' (p. 178) that further embeds the network as the dominant social structure of the age.

Wireless communications have diffused faster than any previous communications technology (p. 7). This diffusion is, however, distinctive for its widespread, albeit highly uneven penetration across regions and continents. Widely differing usage rates are reported. In Oceania, Australia's 82.6 per cent mobile phone penetration rate in 2004 exceeded all other countries in the region. Samoa, for instance, did not even introduce mobile telephony until 1997 (pp. 23–4). In the Middle East, Bahrain had an 88 per cent mobile phone penetration rate in 2004 compared to Syria's 13 per cent (p. 10). Africa is an interesting example in terms of addressing the digital divide. A 1800 per cent increase in mobile phone subscribers across the continent occurred between 1999 and 2004, despite a low overall penetration rate—just nine mobile phones per 100 inhabitants (pp. 22–3). This increase is attributable to changes in telecommunications policy by governments, the cost-effectiveness of handsets and pre-paid systems of payment, and an inability of fixed-line telephone providers to meet demand.

Mobiles have also been used to combat the spread of malaria and AIDS in Mali and Kenya, respectively (Katz et al. 2006, p. 199). In Kenya, free text messaging services are available whereby users can send questions about HIV and AIDS and receive free answers, with daily messages also offering tips on prevention and treatment. In the case of malaria in Mali, health slogans are sent out via text messages and prevention slogans are printed on pre-paid phone cards.

Mobile wireless communications pose a series of sociological challenges, in addition to the obvious environmental problem of disposing of and recycling millions of used handsets and devices. In terms of social interaction, Castells et al. (2007, pp. 250–1) identify the strengthening of 'the culture of individualism' as a trend requiring particular attention because of the ways mobile technologies and 'm-etiquette' enable individuals to build their own private space, even when surrounded by others or moving through a public space. Norms of courtesy and civility around the dinner table, in the classroom and on the train are being reworked individually and collectively through action, response, debate and reflection. These matters are important, as they represent the blurring of pre-existing norms of communication that form the basis of social interaction. While it may not appear to be the case, an individual speaking on a mobile phone repeatedly each day is contributing to social transformation—the individual is a symbolic and material actor involved in an ongoing negotiation of their relationship with groups, organisations, institutions and social norms in both immediate and distant contexts.

THE SOCIOLOGY OF THE MEDIA INTO THE FUTURE

Sociology offers an effective set of perspectives and methods that address the deepest, most intractable problems and issues of contemporary life, many of which involve the media (Carey 2004, p. xx). Leading figures such as John B. Thompson, Nick Couldry and Manuel Castells offer compelling studies demonstrating this fact, which is moving the discipline as a whole forward. Australia does not, however, have a strong tradition of the sociology of media scholarship. This is explainable on three levels. First, it is a relatively recent occurrence that cultural spheres such as the media and popular culture are viewed as legitimate matters for serious sociological research (de la Fuente & West 2008). Second, the study of media in universities has long been informed by a 'deep anti-intellectualism' (Lewis 2009). There exists a widely held suspicion that those who study media only do so because they enjoy media and, as a result, the task requires little specialist knowledge or training given that we all consume media in one form or another. Third, pressure from government and industry demands that graduates emerge equipped with vocational skills that they can apply in the ever-expanding media industries that are the backbone of the so-called (and over-hyped) knowledge economy. In these scenarios, critical sociological inquiry is situated as unlikely, all-too-easy or an undesirable afterthought.

The emergence and development of cultural sociology as a subdiscipline is opening new directions that may help to remove some of these obstacles. A recent 'Cultural sociology' special issue of *Journal of Sociology*, edited by Eduardo de la Fuente and Brad West (2008), highlights how issues of representation, politics, identity, nationalism and cosmopolitanism intersect clearly and subtly with media texts and representation. Offering approaches that avoid the 'media-centric' abstraction of a great deal of media and cultural studies in which 'the social' effectively disappears, the research presented emphasises the complex interdependence of culture, social relations, practices and material forms such as the media. This special issue also highlights the fact that in contemporary society—at least to a degree—all sociologists must be sociologists of the media and all areas of sociology must engage with the media and communications.

In travelling from the Enlightenment to the network society and the printing press to the mobile phone, this chapter has presented a series of broad themes and topics that orient the reader to the state of the field of the sociology of the media. Other topics that could have been covered include theories of social performance, news and media production, media scandals and the growing area of computer and videogame studies. Readers are encouraged to pursue their own interests in an effort to continue building sociological understanding of how media texts, practices, technologies and industries structure, inform and reflect social life.

Tutorial exercises

1. Check your mobile phone or 3G mobile smartphone to see how many messages you have sent and received in the past three days. Then check how many calls you have sent and received. Compare your results with others in your class.
2. Reflect on and discuss the following questions:
   (a) What would be your reaction if your mobile phone was taken away from you for a month?
   (b) How would you go about replacing your sms and call activities?
   (c) How is your use of mobile communications related to your self-image and reputation among your peer group and friends?
   (d) Do you believe that mobile communications help and/or hinder your professional and personal relationships?

For activity suggestions, learning aids, revision of key concepts and access to self-study material, visit: **www.pearson.com.au/highered/vankrieken4e**

Further reading

Bruns, A. 2008, *Blogs, Wikipedia, Second Life, and Beyond: From Production to Produsage*, Peter Lang, New York.
Butsch, R. 2007, *Media and Public Spheres*, Palgrave Macmillan, Basingstoke.
Castells, M. & Ince, M. 2003, *Conversations with Manuel Castells*, Polity Press, Cambridge.
Couldry, N. 2006, *Listening Beyond the Echoes: Media, Ethics, and Agency in an Uncertain World*, Paradigm Publishers, Boulder, CO.
Couldry, N. & Curran, J. (eds) 2003, *Contesting Media Power: Alternative Media Power in a Networked World*, Rowan & Littlefield, Lanham, MD.
Goggin, G. 2006, *Cell Phone Culture: Mobile Technologies in Everyday Life*, Routledge, London.
Goggin, G. (ed.) 2008, *Mobile Phone Cultures*, Routledge, London.
Holmes, D. 2005, *Communication Theory: Media, Technology and Society*, Sage, London.
Jenkins, H. 2006, *Convergence Culture: Where Old and New Media Collide*, New York University Press, New York.
Price, M. & Dayan, D. (eds) 2008, *Owning the Olympics: Narratives of the New China*, University of Michigan Press, Ann Arbor.
Purcell, P. (ed.) 2006, *Networked Neighbourhoods: The Connected Community in Context*, Springer, London.
Redmond, S. & Holmes, S. 2007, *Stardom and Celebrity: A Reader*, Sage, London.
Thompson, J. B. 2000, *Political Scandal: Power and Visibility in the Media Age*, Polity Press, Cambridge.
Winston, B. 1998, *Media Technology and Society. A History: From the Telegraph to the Internet*, Routledge, London.

Websites

'A Brief History of the Internet':
www.isoc.org/internet/history/brief.shtml

Annual Weblog Awards:
http://bloggies.com

Australian Communications and Media Authority (ACMA):
www.acma.gov.au

Australian Media History Database:
www.amhd.org.au

BBC's Celebdaq Celebrity Stock Exchange:
www.bbc.co.uk/celebdaq

ClickZ Internet Statistics and Web Trends:
www.clickz.com/stats

Content Makers: Commentary on Australian Media:
http://blogs.crikey.com.au/contentmakers

Cultural Sociology Group:
www.culturalsociology.org

Gutenberg and the Gutenberg Press:
www.mainz.de/gutenberg/english/index.htm

Henry Jenkins (convergence culture):
http://henryjenkins.org

International Telecommunication Union (resources and information):
www.itu.int/net/home/index.aspx

Internet World Stats. Usage and Population Statistics:
www.internetworldstats.com/stats.htm

Manuel Castells:
www.manuelcastells.info/en

Marshall McLuhan:
www.mcluhan.utoronto.ca and www.marshallmcluhan.com

Media Ownership in Australia:
www.aph.gov.au/library/intguide/SP/Media_Regulation.htm

Media Theory Resources:
www.theory.org.uk

Mobile Information Society:
www.itu.int/osg/spu/ni/futuremobile

Public Sphere Project:
www.publicsphereproject.org

Salam Pax, the Baghdad Blogger:
http://salampax.wordpress.com

Smart Mobs: The Next Social Revolution:
www.smartmobs.com

4
Family Life

This chapter looks at what is possibly the most fundamental arena for the organisation of human social relationships and interdependency: family life.

By the end of the chapter, you should have a better understanding of the following dimensions of the sociology of the family:
— the emergence of the modern, Western family form, revolving around the separation of family and work life, the preference for a smaller, nuclear family and uncoupling of marriage from parental control
— the key sociological perspectives on family life, including Marxism, Weber's approach to the family, functionalism, and Marxist feminism and other feminist approaches
— the gendered division of domestic labour and domestic violence as an aspect of power relations within family life
— the role of culture and ethnicity in the diversity of family forms
— the 'discovery of childhood' over time, the regulation of children's lives and the emergence of the concept of children's rights, the social construction of childhood, children and divorce, and child abuse and neglect
— the ongoing structural changes in family life, especially the fertility decline, the changing approach to marriage, bearing and raising children, cohabitation and divorce, and women's workforce participation.

INTRODUCTION	**112**
THE MODERN, WESTERN FAMILY	**113**
The Western nuclear family	113
Industrialisation and modern family life	114
The Christian Church and the European family— Jack Goody	114
The Church, property and kinship	114
Marriage and parental control	114
Australian colonial family life	115
The Symmetrical Family—Michael Young and Peter Willmott	116
SOCIOLOGICAL PERSPECTIVES ON FAMILY LIFE	**116**
Marxism—the family and the reproduction of capitalism	116
The family as a social construction	117
The contradictory relationship between family life and capitalism	117
Positive and negative aspects of familial 'irrationality'	117
Undermining patriarchal power	118
The family in permanent crisis	118
Weber's theory of the family	118
The structure of family life	118
Sex and marriage	119
The historical development of kin group and household	119
Functionalism—the nuclear family as the foundation of society	119
Primary socialisation and personality stabilisation— Talcott Parsons	120
The transfer of functions	120
Feminism and the 'antisocial family'	120
GENDER AND DOMESTIC LABOUR	**121**
Gender inequality in rural Australia—Ken Dempsey	121
The gender division of household labour—Janeen Baxter	122
How Australians Use Their Time—ABS	122
Domestic violence	123
Inequality within marriage	124
CULTURE, ETHNICITY AND FAMILY DIVERSITY	**125**
Aboriginal family life	125
Traditional Aboriginal family life	125
Rural and urban Aboriginal family life	127
Aboriginal family change in Adelaide, 1966–80—Fay Gale	128
Aboriginal families and state intervention: the Stolen Generations	128
Migrant family structure and values	129
Greek families in Australia	130
Lebanese Muslim families in Australia	131
Ethnicity and family diversity: conclusion	132
STRUCTURAL CHANGE IN FAMILY LIFE	**132**
The fertility decline in Australia	133
The decline in household size	133
From the 'proper time to marry' to the 'proper time to reproduce'—John Caldwell and Lado Ruzicka	134
Baby boom or marriage boom?	136
The post-1970s fertility decline	136
Women's participation in the workforce	138
Causes and effects of increased female participation in the workforce	139
Marriage, cohabitation and divorce	141
The marriage rate and ex-nuptial child-bearing	142
Cohabitation	144
Single-parent families	145
Divorce	145
CHILDREN AND CHILDHOOD	**149**
Centuries of Childhood—Phillippe Ariès	150
Regulation and rights	150
The social construction of childhood	151
Children's lives beyond the family	152
Children and divorce	153
Child abuse and neglect	153
TOWARDS THE 'POST-FAMILIAL FAMILY'?	**154**
Family 'decline'	155
Democratisation and egalitarianism—Giddens, Beck and Beck-Gernsheim	155
The Transformation of Intimacy—Anthony Giddens	156
The Normal Chaos of Love—Ulrich Beck and Elisabeth Beck-Gernsheim	156
Continuity and enduring power relations	158
CONCLUSION—THE FUTURE OF FAMILY LIFE	**158**
Tutorial exercises	160
Further reading	160
Websites	160

INTRODUCTION

A woman (let's call her Alice) born in Ireland, aged 31, comes to Australia in 1990 for a holiday, falls in love with an Australian (say, Jack), and they travel around the country before heading to Europe to work for a while. Alice falls pregnant and they return to Australia to live. They have a second child. Jack has bouts of violence, mostly directed at Alice, but sometimes at the children, too. Alice decides she has had enough and goes back to Ireland with the children. Jack takes the matter to court, where it is decided that the children's best interests would be better realised if they stayed with their mother in Ireland. Jack is not happy: he thinks it is important for children to stay in contact with both their parents, and he will miss them. He thinks that divorce should not mean that one parent loses contact with their children.

Much of the nature of family life today is bundled up in this kind of story—the globalisation of family relationships, the increased emotional significance of children, uncertainty about gender roles, violence in family life, the prevalence of divorce in children's lives and the difficulty of sustaining parent–child relations over time.

There are many ways in which human beings organise their social relationships and interdependency, but the realm of family life is probably the most basic. The study of family life deals with many of the most fundamental aspects of human sociability.

Most people go through their infancy and childhood in one type of family setting or another, and they generally continue to have lasting and meaningful—even if not always harmonious—relationships with those people they define as their family. They form their own household arrangements and some sort of family of their own, even if that means redefining their relationships as 'family-like'. Many will become parents and over time possibly grandparents.

Family life is also an important arena where the public and the private spheres intersect. For example, in the early years of the 21st century, the question of declining fertility rates is one that has broad policy significance, because today's children are tomorrow's school and university students, doctors, scientists, builders and taxpayers. But it also has much more personal meanings, connected with how and when we form lasting intimate relationships, the role that children play in our lives and how adults' relationships with children relate to their relationships with each other.

It is often thought natural and normal in Western societies for the social organisation of residence and reproduction to be based on the **nuclear family**—mum, dad and the two kids. This view has discouraged serious and detailed consideration of the very different forms taken by 'the family' in different cultures and different social and economic settings, or of the variety of ways in which people live together and raise children. It has also made it difficult to understand the ways in which family life has changed in association with broader social change as anything other than 'decline'.

We will examine, then, the critical perspectives on the family that have developed since the 1960s, providing critical scrutiny of the idea that there has been, is and should be only one form of 'the family'. Specific attention will also be given to the changes in people's actual behaviour—marrying less and at later ages, divorcing more, cohabiting instead of marrying and having fewer children at later ages.

It is useful to keep two distinctions in mind when looking at family life in sociological terms: first, Max Weber's distinction between 'the family' as a **household** or **domestic group**, sharing a roof and meals, and as a **kinship group**, an organisation of people according to prevailing rules of kinship; and, second, the distinction emphasised by William J. Goode (1963, p. 2) between *ideal* family patterns ('the family' as some would like it to be) and *real* family behaviour and values (the actual family relationships that people enter into). In any one society it is quite possible for a particular ideal to coexist with a very different reality, especially during periods of significant social change.

THE MODERN, WESTERN FAMILY

Before we examine how sociologists have approached the structure and dynamics of family life from a variety of perspectives, it will be useful to spend a little time looking at the emergence of a specifically modern, Western form of the family. Three issues in particular stand out in sociological and historical discussions of how a particular form of family life arose in Western Europe:

1. the question of the size of family formations, how many generations lived together as single households and whether the dominant form was 'nuclear' or 'extended'
2. the relationship between home and work life, particularly the impact of industrialisation and urbanisation
3. the role of the parents of young couples in family formation, especially the authority wielded by the parents over the choice of a marriage partner.

THE WESTERN NUCLEAR FAMILY

The French social scientist, social reformer and engineer Frédéric Le Play (1806–82) was among the first to argue that pre-industrial family structure was originally 'extended', encompassing three generations at a time, and that nuclear families were a 'modern' creation (Zimmerman & Frampton 1966). This view of the history of the family as being centred on a transition from a traditional, pre-industrial 'extended' form to a modern, industrialised 'nuclear' form also became quite popular in sociology in the 1950s, especially in the work of Talcott Parsons (Wilensky & Lebeaux 1958).

However, a number of sociologists have pointed out that Le Play's **extended family** was not at all typical of pre-industrial Western Europe and North America. Sidney Greenfield (1961), for example, argues that the smaller nuclear family predated the Industrial Revolution, and that the notion of the close functional interdependence between **industrialisation** and the nuclear family was contradicted by the counter-examples of pre-industrial societies with nuclear family structures (Barbados) and industrial societies without the nuclear family (Japan).

Marion Levy (1965) went on to develop the argument that, although the extended family might have been the family ideal prior to industrialisation, the demographic constraints on pre-industrial Western Europe and North America made such a family improbable. In other words, mortality rates were such that it was highly unlikely that many people would live to see their grandchildren for any significant length of time, if at all.

The work of historian Peter Laslett also lent support to the view that family life has been 'nuclear' for much longer than thought by Le Play and Parsons. Between 1564 and 1821, Laslett (1972) found that 90 per cent of households consisted only of the nuclear family. The same is true of America (Hareven 1987). This structure is the product of a number of factors, including late marriage and short life expectancy. Laslett concluded: 'There is no sign of the large, extended co-residential family group of the traditional peasant world giving way to the small, nuclear conjugal household of modern industrial society' (p. 126).

Laslett (1983; 1984) came to the view that there was a typical 'Western' nuclear form of family life in Britain, northern France, the Netherlands, Belgium, Scandinavia and parts of Italy and Germany, in contrast to a more extended family form in Eastern Europe, Russia and Japan. Laslett and his colleagues refined their approach by distinguishing four sets of areas in pre-industrial Europe:

1. West and Northwest—high proportion of simple family households, very low proportion of complex family households
2. West-Central—high simple, low complex
3. Mediterranean—low simple, high complex
4. Eastern—low simple, very high complex.

An important contrast with contemporary nuclear families, however, was that a large number of pre-industrial families contained servants, as well as boarders and lodgers. 'Servants' in pre-industrial Europe were something very different from what we currently understand the word to mean—they were also, often primarily, workers in the household's system of production. It was considered an appropriate form of preparation for adult life to send children into service or apprenticeship in other people's households, making it, as John Hajnal (1982) argued, 'a stage for young people between leaving home and marriage, that is, a stage in the life-cycle' (p. 471). They would appear in households either as 'servants', living and working within the household, or as boarders, working outside the household.

There was a constant circulation of young people between households from roughly the age of seven onwards, establishing them as independent workers and preparing them for the establishment of their own household, separate from their parents. Hajnal and Laslett argued that the nuclear family should be seen as one of the foundations of the process of industrialisation, rather than one its consequences (see also Berger & Berger 1983; Macfarlane 1986).

INDUSTRIALISATION AND MODERN FAMILY LIFE

In most pre-industrial societies, kinship and family ties are the principal basis of social organisation. Societies are often divided into a number of kinship groups such as lineages, which are groups descended from a common ancestor. The needs of kinship groups are to a large extent met by their own production of key goods and services. For example, a lineage may own agricultural land that is worked by members of the lineage, who then share its produce.

Members of kinship groups are united by a network of mutual rights and obligations. In some cases, if an individual is insulted or injured by someone from outside the group, he or she has the right to call on the support of members of the group to seek reparation or revenge. Many areas of an individual's behaviour are shaped by kinship status. For example, an uncle may have binding obligations to be involved with aspects of his nephew's socialisation and may be responsible for the welfare of his nieces and nephews should their father die.

In Western societies, the role of kinship gradually became more narrowly defined, and came to operate alongside other social institutions with competing claims to authority and loyalty. For example, a particularly important change in family life was associated with industrialisation: production had been organised largely around the household, whereas with industrialisation production took place outside the home or farm, resulting in what is often referred to as 'the separation of home and work'. This, in turn, is often seen as radically altering the relationships between the sexes—patriarchal power is greater in a household-based production system.

THE CHRISTIAN CHURCH AND THE EUROPEAN FAMILY—JACK GOODY

Historical anthropologist Jack Goody (1983) has suggested that the most formative period in the history of the European family was that of the Christian Church's dominance of social and cultural life between the 4th and 16th centuries. This is not to say that the Industrial Revolution had no impact at all, but that most of the definitive features of the 'Western' family either were in place during the Roman Empire or were the product of the Church's impact on family life. So significant was this impact that John Goldthorpe (1987) referred to it as the 'Christian Revolution' in family life.

The Church, property and kinship

After Christianity turned from a sect into a Church and became the official state religion of the Roman Empire and, later, of all Europe, the Church set about changing a number of common practices in European family life—marriage between close kin, remarriage with affinal kin (those of their former spouse), remarriage after divorce, concubinage (the practice of men taking a 'child-bearing wife', often in addition to a childless first wife), adoption and fostering.

The Church also exerted a strong influence on the way property was inherited. Land had been held in 'folkland', normally transmitted to the kin of the deceased, but the Church brought about the introduction of 'bookland', with land tenure held under a written title deed and disposed of through the use of wills, usually written by those rare people who could read and write—the clergy.

The significance of these changes, argued Goody, was that they all weakened kinship ties beyond the immediate nuclear family and had the effect of vastly increasing the property that came into the Church's hands. All the practices it prohibited were what Goody called 'strategies of heirship', ways of ensuring that accumulated property and wealth stayed within the kinship network in the face of the usual barriers to the transmittal of inheritance from one generation to the next—childlessness, absence of male heirs, death of one parent and separation of parents.

Marriage and parental control

In addition, the insistence that marriage depend on the consent of the two partners, rather than on arrangements between their parents or other older kin, weakened the control of parents over familial wealth and inheritance, and possibly resulted in some children being disinherited. This further increased the Church's acquisitions. The Church's doctrine of consensual marriage was, argued David Herlihy (1985), 'a damaging blow to paternal authority within the medieval household, and by itself assured that the medieval family could never develop into a true patriarchy' (p. 81). This does not mean that fathers lost control over their children's marriage patterns altogether; on the contrary, their command over familial resources meant that they continued to exert considerable effective influence. But the Church's marriage doctrine did mean that fathers could neither force a daughter or son into a marriage nor prevent one.

Most of the key features of the 'Western' family—the relative independence of the married couple from their parents and older kin, greater equality (relatively) between the sexes within marriage and a focus on the immediate nuclear family with no real authority exercised by the extended family—are thus seen by Goody as:

> *intrinsic to the whole process whereby the Church established its position as a power in the land, a spiritual power certainly, but also a worldly one, the owner of property, the largest landowner, a position it obtained by gaining control of the system of marriage, gifts and inheritance.* (1983, p. 154)

The reduction in the influence of wider kinship networks and patriarchal authority had thus taken place quite early in Western Europe's history, during the entire course of Christianity's influence on European society throughout the Middle Ages. As Göran Therborn puts it, 'the Western European family was by far the least patriarchal in a very patriarchal world' (2004, p. 297).

AUSTRALIAN COLONIAL FAMILY LIFE

This family system was transported to Australia alongside the English and Irish convicts and settlers, but with some modifications, especially in the convict and colonial periods.

1. In the early years of the 19th century men greatly outnumbered women and Australian popular culture was correspondingly male-dominated. It gained an element of hostility to family life and domesticity that persisted well into the 20th century.
2. The settlers who came to Australia were removed from their normal networks of extended kin, although they would often do their best to encourage other members of their family to join them later. As Patricia Grimshaw and Graham Willett summarise it, the usual pattern was that 'a single individual or a small family of parents and one or two young children would face colonial life in isolation for a period of years, and if they found the environment a hopeful one, would encourage other family members or groups to join them' (1981, pp. 137–8). They concluded that if one defines the 'modern' family as restricted to a narrow range of kin, 'the Australian family was "born modern" in that respect' (p. 146). Some did develop relatively dense extended family networks quite quickly, but those who did not turned for social support to those they might have known from home, those they shared the voyage with or neighbours.
3. Emotional and instrumental ties within the nuclear family were strong. The lack of an extended family network made members of the nuclear family more dependent on each other than they might have been in Europe, as well as more independent and self-sufficient as a unit. For most of the colonial period, state Grimshaw and Willett:

   > *The dominant family patterns closely resembled the traditional family of pre-industrial Europe, if analysed in terms of instrumental bonds ... Nearly all women were involved in production for exchange, in production for domestic use, as well as in their roles in reproduction and child-socialization.* (pp. 146–7)

   Children were also expected to work and contribute to the family economy, and this increased the importance of women's reproductive role, 'because of the vital unpaid labour the children could provide' (p. 148). Grimshaw and Willett also argued that the shortage of women and the importance of their work for their family's economic survival had the effect of enhancing their social status in comparison with their counterparts in Europe.
4. This economic significance of women's work, combined with the relative independence from extended kin, 'had nurtured both a relatively democratic and affectionate family unit' (p. 153). Since children did not depend on their parents and family for the provision of land, they did not have to seek their approval for marriage and were generally more independent. The shortage of marriageable women also made young women less dependent on their family of origin. The overall consequence was a weakened patriarchal control and a more egalitarian style of family relationships.

By the end of the 19th century, family life among white Australians was becoming more clearly organised around the model of men as breadwinners, women as homemakers and children as non-working dependants engaged in full-time schooling. The home became less a place of economically productive activity and more one of consumption, and the two spheres became more clearly separated, with the public world of work defined as a male sphere and the home defined as the realm of women and young children. This became the family ideal among the working class as well as the middle class; as Grimshaw and Willett put it:

> *In Australia, with its strong trade union movement and its fight for reasonable wages, working-class families also adopted this demarcation of roles, probably more widely than was possible in the more impoverished European proletariat of the time. (1981, pp. 149–50)*

A central focus of labour movement activity was the attainment of a *family wage*—a wage sufficient for a man to support a wife and children—which in turn rested on the assumption that women would play only a marginal role in the workforce. (See also the discussion of women's workforce participation, pp. 138–141.)

The Symmetrical Family—Michael Young and Peter Willmott

In Michael Young and Peter Willmott's (1973) studies of family life in London, they suggested that the development of family life can be seen as characterised by three main types, with some overlap across the different family stages: (1) the pre-industrial family, up to the early 19th century; (2) the early industrial family, from the Industrial Revolution to the early 20th century; and (3) the *symmetrical family*, from the early 20th century onwards, characterised by 'the separation of the immediate, or nuclear, family from the extended family' (1973, p. 91).

They saw the contemporary form of family life as symmetrical because it is regarded as a shared project between husband and wife, both of whom provide companionship for each other, with the home seen as the basis of shared activity (p. 94). There is still a division of labour between men and women, but an attempt is made to establish some sort of equivalence or balance between different types of contribution to the household, and there is a presumption, in principle at least, of shared decision making. Above all, the family home is seen as relatively self-contained and independent from the wider kin network or extended family, certainly in relation to decision making.

Young and Willmott saw the shift towards increased symmetry as driven by a number of other social changes, including the increased financial independence of couples from their extended family, increased geographical mobility, the fertility decline (see p. 133) and a rise in living standards making the home a more comfortable and attractive place for men to spend time with their families. (For a critique of the symmetrical family thesis, see p. 121.)

SOCIOLOGICAL PERSPECTIVES ON FAMILY LIFE

Marxism—the Family and the Reproduction of Capitalism

Marx did not give any systematic attention to the family, although there are a few passing comments on the effect of industrial capitalism on pre-industrial family patterns that anticipated later analyses, such as the following passage from *Capital*:

> *However terrible and disgusting the dissolution, under the capitalist system, of the old family ties may appear, nevertheless modern industry, by assigning as it does an important part in the process of production, outside the domestic sphere, to women, to young children of both sexes, creates a new economical foundation for a higher form of the family and of the relations between the sexes. (1954, pp. 459–60)*

This was the beginning of an argument concerning the impact on the family of the separation of production from the domestic sphere, of the power relations between women and men that were built into pre-industrial family life, and of the possibility of changed gender relations emerging from industrial society. The first extensive Marxist discussion of family life appeared in Friedrich Engels' 'The origin of the family, private property and the state', published in 1884, in which he argued for a linkage between changes in the form taken by the family and changes in the mode of production.

The importance of Engels' work on the family lies, as David Morgan (1975, pp. 137–40) has emphasised, less in the details of its evolutionary argument than its general orientation towards seeing the contemporary nuclear family as:

- a historically changing institution
- closely related to the form taken by economic relations
- based on an unequal and exploitative relationship between women and men.

A more developed Marxist analysis of the family can be found in the work of a group of Marxist social scientists working in the Frankfurt Institute of Social Research between the 1920s and the 1950s. Collectively they have become known as the Frankfurt School and their better known members include Max Horkheimer, Theodor Adorno and Herbert Marcuse, although it was Horkheimer who wrote most extensively on the sociology of the family. They developed the following arguments.

The family as a social construction

The structure of the family should be regarded as socially constructed, as the product of the society the family belongs to. This meant that it was not possible to see the family as something 'natural' or as having an existence prior to society. Rather, the family should be seen as 'socially mediated down to its innermost structure'. Horkheimer and his colleagues felt that it was not possible to regard family life as a kind of 'haven in a heartless world', because the structures of the surrounding society would inevitably affect whatever went on within family life. It was, therefore, impossible to pursue emancipation or equality within the family if the surrounding society was characterised by oppressive and unequal social relations: 'There can be no emancipation of the family without the emancipation of the whole' (Frankfurt Institute for Social Research 1973, p. 145).

The contradictory relationship between family life and capitalism

The Frankfurt sociologists saw the relationship between family life and the surrounding society in modern capitalist societies as profoundly *contradictory*. On the one hand, they regarded the family as an essential part of the social order in that it adapted every individual to conform to authority. The family, wrote Horkheimer:

> as one of the most important formative agencies, sees to it that the kind of human character emerges which social life requires, and gives this human being in great measure the indispensable adaptability for a specific authority oriented conduct on which the existence of the bourgeois order largely depends. (1982, p. 98)

Like Engels, Horkheimer recognised the significance of the basic economic inequality between men on the one hand and women and children on the other. If men are the sole breadwinners, argued Horkheimer, this 'makes wife, sons and daughters, even in modern times, "his", puts their lives in large measure into his hands, and forces them to submit to his order and guidance' (p. 105). However, he went on to point out the permanent socialising effect this had on children.

The development of obedience to the authority of one's own father was a preparation for obedience to the authority of the state and one's employer. Horkheimer also saw family life as imposing conformity on men, in that the dependence of their wife and children made them more conservative about radical social change that might undermine their ability to support their families. In this sense the nuclear family can be seen as an integral part of modern capitalist society, and Horkheimer's perspective was similar to that of the functionalist theorists, who also saw the family as performing an essential socialising function.

On the other hand, however, Horkheimer and his colleagues also pointed out that there was a fundamental opposition between the logic of family life, the principles governing its operation, and that of a market-based capitalist society. Family life is not based on economic exchange or the rational pursuit of self-interested gain, but rather on relations of kinship and emotional bonds of love, altruism and care.

This makes the family essentially a pre-capitalist, feudal institution because 'it has held fast to an irrational moment in the midst of an industrial society which aims at rationality, the exclusive domination of the principle that all relations must be calculable' (Frankfurt Institute for Social Research 1973, p. 134). In this sense, the 'bourgeois family' is an impossibility, because the logic of rationally self-interested individualism contradicts the apparent irrationality of family life.

Positive and negative aspects of familial 'irrationality'

This familial 'irrationality' has both positive and negative aspects. Its positive sense is that family life allows the expression of emotions that otherwise have little place in a rational, calculating capitalist society, where the measure of all things is economic gain and loss. Its negative aspect is that relations of domination and oppression continue to exist, especially of the father over the rest of the family, but also generally of males over females. In relation to the capitalist society beyond the family, the unpaid **domestic labour** of women is above all an irrational feature of family life, because it operates outside the rules of the market, where work is exchanged for money.

Undermining patriarchal power

The separation of work and home has therefore led to an undermining of patriarchal power, because it was through control over the primary means of economic production—land—that fathers exercised their power. The spread of wage labour meant increased ability for younger family members to achieve economic independence, and the Frankfurt School theorists saw this as the beginning of the end for patriarchy, which would increasingly be 'presented with the reckoning … for the economic injustice in the exploitation of domestic labour within a society which in all other respects obeyed the laws of the market' (Frankfurt Institute for Social Research 1973, p. 137).

The family in permanent crisis

All the various crises in the family—the changing relations between men and women, increasing divorce and the focus on children's rights—are in fact permanent crises because they can be traced back to this fundamental opposition, in which the market is destined to be the winner. Marriage, the Frankfurt School theorists argue, will shrink into 'a relationship of exchange serving purely practical ends', women as a group 'exploit' their monopoly over child-bearing 'to gain a certain security … [in] the institution of divorce', and individuals 'become interchangeable here too as they do in business life, where one leaves a position as soon as a better one offers itself' (Frankfurt Institute for Social Research 1973, p. 139).

WEBER'S THEORY OF THE FAMILY

Max Weber is not usually known as a family sociologist, and there has never been a 'Weberian' approach to the family. However, he dealt with a number of important issues concerning family life that anticipated many later debates and are still to be improved upon. Perhaps the most important contribution that Weber (1978) made was his general conceptualisation of family life. Rather than treating 'the family' as a pre-existing entity that acts upon or is acted upon by surrounding social structures, Weber saw family structure itself as the product of prevailing social, economic and political conditions. He opposed Engels' evolutionary approach, preferring to identify the particular constellations of social circumstances that produced different types of family structure throughout history and in different cultures. Instead of being concerned about the relative size of 'the family' and whether it was extended or nuclear, Weber focused on the changing size and political position of the household and the kin group in relation to wider political structures such as the state. His analysis also established the centrality of family life to the development of other social institutions such as the state and the economy.

The structure of family life

Weber analysed family life in terms of two main structures—the *household* and the *kin group*—and saw what others term 'the family' as produced by interaction of these two structures. The household is the group sharing a roof and meals, but it need not coincide with 'the family'. Husbands and wives, for example, may eat and sleep in separate households, and households often contain members with no kinship relationship. The kin group is the larger network of those related by 'blood', either biological or fictitious (e.g. in-laws).

Weber argued that, in addition to being an *economic* unit, this wider kin group has often been a *political* unit, serving to organise military protection, revenge and expansion. This control over the means of violence often gave the kin group a clear advantage over the household. In situations where military activity became the province of specialised elite groups of warriors, and eventually the state, this wresting of control over violence and military activity from kin groups had the effect of strengthening the household.

Neither the household nor the kin group arose prior to the other and, unlike most family sociologists, Weber argued that there was a *power relation* between them. Rather than seeing the household or nuclear family as benignly nestled within a wider, more diffuse network of extended kin, Weber argued that the household and the kin group were different, often opposing, forms of organising marriage, sexuality and inheritance. The conflict between household and the wider kin group would then also interact in varying ways with surrounding economic and political structures, which may provide more or less support for the household head, kin group leaders or individuals within households. For Weber, an important aspect of this power relation was that the kinship group protected the interests of *individuals* within households in conflict with the interests of the household patriarch. Exactly how this operated depended on the given economic and political conditions.

Sex and marriage

For Weber, marriage was essentially a way of distinguishing between legitimate and illegitimate sexual unions. This distinction reflected on the relationship itself between husband and wife, and on the social position of the children produced from that relationship. Marriage distinguishes between those relationships approved of by the wider kin group and those requiring revenge or some form of atonement. It also identifies which children will be treated as equal members of the wider community—village, kin group, religious group, ethnic group—and which will not be granted the full benefits of legitimate community identity.

Weber saw marriage as a similar form of management of female sexuality to prostitution, differing in degree rather than in kind. Women's sexuality has often been exchanged by male household heads for other services, and marriage in general is a form of exchange of sexual for economic resources. Weber regarded prostitution itself as possibly the more liberal version of women's sexual exploitation, because the economic exchange is made explicit and put to some extent under the control and management of women themselves.

The historical development of kin group and household

Weber stressed that no one form of family life can be regarded as more 'primitive' than or prior to another. Rather than there being a 'basic' nuclear family with various 'extensions', he argued that households arose with the development of agriculture and were not present in nomadic hunting societies. The relationship of the household to the kin group was dependent on the particular constellation of political conditions prevailing in the local community, village or region. Because the kin group was the only basis for the organisation of hunting and fighting, its position would rise and fall depending on the role played by those activities. Where a community was heavily dependent on collective hunting or engaged in constant feuding and warfare, the kin group's power would rise in relation to the household. When these functions were either taken over by a more specialised group—trained warriors or the state—or made redundant by the sudden outbreak of peace, this would weaken the kin group's position and correspondingly reinforce that of the patriarchal household and its male head. This was what happened in Western Europe, and less so in Eastern Europe, China and India.

Randall Collins (1986) pointed out that Weber saw two stages in the development of family life in Western Europe:

1. the decline of the kin group relative to the patriarchal household (patrimonial domination)
2. a reduction in the significance of the patriarchal household in relation to the bureaucratic state and industrial capitalist production.

Because the household became the basis of social, economic and political organisation, the wealthier a household was the larger it would be, including apprentices, servants, slaves and soldiers. Weber referred to this type of society as being characterised by **patrimonial domination**. The members of households linked by kinship ties had shrunk to that of the nuclear family, but the size of a household would be as large as its wealth permitted. As Collins summed it up, Weber showed:

that the dominant households of the societies immediately preceding our own were large precisely because the more remote links of kinship were now forgotten or at least supplemented by relationships that were not based on kinship. (1986, p. 289)

The accelerated development of the state and bureaucracy from about the 16th century onwards gradually broke down the power of patrimonial households. Western European states increasingly separated their own administration from that of the family-centred household, attempting to free bureaucracy from family ties and obligations. With the development of factory production, economic activity also came to be increasingly separated from family life. In addition, the state gradually monopolised the means of violence, making individuals less dependent on their households for security and protection, and this also weakened the authority of patriarchal household heads.

FUNCTIONALISM—THE NUCLEAR FAMILY AS THE FOUNDATION OF SOCIETY

Functionalist analyses of family life address three main questions:

1. *What are the functions of the family?* Answers to this question deal with the contributions made by the family to the maintenance of the social system. It is assumed that society has certain functional prerequisites or basic needs that must be met if it is to survive and operate efficiently. The family is examined in terms of the degree to which it meets these functional prerequisites.
2. *What are the functional relationships between the family and other parts of the social system?* It is

assumed that there must be a certain degree of fit, integration and harmony between the parts of the social system if society is going to function efficiently. For example, the family must be integrated to some extent with the economic system. This question is examined in detail in a later section when the relationships between the family and industrialisation are considered.

3. *What are the functions performed by an institution or a part of society for the individual?* In the case of the family, this question considers the functions of the family for its individual members.

Primary socialisation and personality stabilisation—Talcott Parsons

For Parsons the 'basic and irreducible' functions of the family were the 'primary socialization of children' and the 'stabilization of the adult personalities of the population of the society' (1955a, p. 16). **Primary socialisation** is simply the development of a child's personality, which takes place within the family, as opposed to secondary socialisation, which takes place later in settings beyond the family, such as the peer group and the school. Parsons saw primary socialisation as the arena where a child internalises the culture of the surrounding adult society and where the structure of their personality is established. He suggested that families 'are "factories" which produce human personalities' (1955a, p. 16), and thought that there was no other plausible social arena where these functions could be fulfilled.

The central function of the family for its adult members, in contrast, was the **stabilisation of adult personalities**. Marriage and family life are seen as providing emotional security and support, and a haven from the stress and demands of working life. Child-rearing, too, provides an outlet for parents to express the child-like aspects of their personalities in a safe and non-threatening context, by participating in their children's activities.

The transfer of functions

Parsons believed that a number of the family's functions had, in modern industrial society, been transferred to other social institutions. Institutions such as businesses, political parties, schools and welfare organisations now specialised in functions formerly performed by the family. In itself, Parsons argued, the family does not play a significant role in society—its members all contribute to social life as individuals rather than as part of the family (1955a, p. 16). This did not mean, however, that Parsons saw the family as being in decline, but simply as more specialised:

the family is more specialized than before, but not in any general sense less important, because society is dependent more exclusively on it for the performance of certain of its vital functions. (1955a, pp. 9–10)

For Parsons as well as later functionalist sociologists of the family, such as Ronald Fletcher (1966), while it is true that the family has changed, this is seen as a process of adaptation to a changed social environment, rather than a process of decline.

FEMINISM AND THE 'ANTISOCIAL FAMILY'

Marxist writers on the family generally acknowledge that the subordinate position of women within family life is an important aspect of what they see as its harmful effects. However, the emphasis is on the relationship between the family and capitalism, and its effects on women tend to be seen as derived from the more primary economic inequality between capitalists and wage labourers. The feminist analysis of the family began with a use of Marxist concepts to explain and analyse the way in which they believe the family leads to the specific exploitation of women.

Margaret Benston (1972), for example, argued that:

The amount of unpaid labor performed by women is very large and very profitable to those who own the means of production. To pay women for their work, even at minimum wage scales, would involve a massive redistribution of wealth. At present, the support of the family is a hidden tax on the wage earner—his wage buys the labor power of two people. (p. 127)

To give an Australian example, Duncan Ironmonger has estimated that the inclusion of the labour involved in household production in 1975–76 would have boosted Australia's GDP by 48 per cent, and that 'Australian households demanded and supplied more labour for their own purposes in production within the household than they supplied to the whole of the rest of the economy' (Ironmonger 1989, p. 8).

Echoing the Frankfurt School's arguments, Benston (1972) suggested that:

The nuclear family is a valuable stabilizing force in capitalist society. Since the production which is done in the home is paid for by the husband–father's earnings, his ability to withhold his labor from the market is much reduced. (p. 125)

The family can thus be regarded as performing a number of important functions for employers and the capitalist class—including feeding and maintaining the current cohort of workers, as well as producing the next generation of workers—at little to no cost.

Such accounts of family life tend to overlook the great variety of family forms across cultures and classes and over time. However, there is an important strand in feminist thought on family life that takes greater account of variations in family life. Juliet Mitchell (1966), for example, argued that the family should not be understood as a unified entity, but in terms of the separate structures from which it is composed and which can be combined in various patterns in differing cultures or at different points in history. The underlying structures that she saw as manifesting themselves in a condensed fashion in particular forms of 'the family' are those of production, reproduction, sexuality and the socialisation of children.

Similarly, Michèle Barrett and Mary McIntosh (1982) said that more attention should be paid to the diversity of family and household forms, making it difficult to pin down what the functions or social role of 'the' family actually are. They also highlighted the effect of attaching too much importance to the family, because 'The family ideal makes everything else seem pale and unsatisfactory' (p. 77). The idealisation of family life, they wrote:

> ... has made the outside world cold and friendless, and made it harder to maintain relationships of security and trust except with kin. Caring, sharing and loving would all be more widespread if the family did not claim them for its own. (Barrett & McIntosh 1982, p. 80)

An additional problem is that the idealised view of the family is a barrier to perceiving its darker side—domestic violence, rape within marriage and child abuse (see pp. 123–4, 153–4).

GENDER AND DOMESTIC LABOUR

An important concern in the sociology of family life has been the questions of the degree of inequality between husband and wife within marriage. Different researchers have measured different aspects of domestic inequality. Some concentrated on the division of labour in the home, examining the allocation of responsibility for domestic work between husband and wife and the amount of time spent by each spouse on particular tasks. Others examined the role played by domestic violence in the distribution of power within marriage.

As we saw earlier, Young and Willmott (1973) maintained that conjugal roles could increasingly be described as 'joint'. They suggested that family life was becoming more 'symmetrical' because of the degree to which spouses increasingly share domestic work and leisure activities. However, most sociologists working in this area have found little evidence for such a reduction of inequality within marriage. Ailsa Burns observed that 'even the most resourceful wife and best-intentioned husband find it difficult to avoid a slippage towards "traditional" roles' (1986, p. 227). As Bittman and Pixley (1997) point out, the major stumbling block facing the symmetrical family thesis 'has been to demonstrate that where wives do paid work, husbands do correspondingly more domestic work'. However, the evidence on domestic labour shows that when women do take on more paid employment, there is little by way of a compensating increase in men's domestic labour (see also the discussion of time use on pp. 122–3).

GENDER INEQUALITY IN RURAL AUSTRALIA—KEN DEMPSEY

In his studies of family relations in a small rural town in the north-west of Victoria, Ken Dempsey found a marked division of labour between males and females that started in early adolescence. Dempsey and his colleagues conducted two surveys, one in 1974 and another in 1984. Both studies 'failed to produce any evidence whatsoever of the blurring of the old distinctions between "women's work" and "men's work"' (1992, p. 96). They showed that women 'have entire responsibility for household management and major responsibility for child care' (1988, p. 420).

Dempsey concentrated on the most time-consuming routine domestic tasks such as vacuuming and washing and ironing clothes, and found in 1984 that '75 per cent of the husbands never performed any of these three tasks, and over 90 per cent never ironed or washed clothes' (1992, p. 96). If men engaged in domestic tasks they usually did so as 'helpers', rather than taking responsibility for the initiation and completion of the task. When their wives were absent from home for any reason, other female relatives would intervene to ensure that meals were cooked and clothes washed and ironed. Cooking by men generally meant turning over the meat at a barbecue or heating up a tin of baked beans.

Men were more inclined to contribute to child care, but would ensure that it did not interfere with their own paid work or leisure activities. For example, children would be taken along to a football match that the father was attending in any case. Child care, wrote Dempsey, 'is yet another area in which men help or assist their wives rather than share responsibility and in which their participation has a voluntary character' (1992, p. 101). Children's wellbeing is still seen as primarily the mother's responsibility.

This gendered division of labour begins to be established in early adolescence, when girls 'begin preparing for their future subordinate and servant activities as wives by servicing brothers and fathers' (1988, p. 420). Young males then 'enter their own marriages committed to the view that women exist primarily to serve as carers and nurturers of men and their offspring' (1988, p. 420). Dempsey pointed out that, even if males undertake other tasks in and around the home, the nature of the tasks makes them easier to postpone or to fit around the men's leisure and paid work activities. The allocation of the most routine and time-consuming tasks to girls and women, on the other hand, interferes far more with their leisure and paid work, and places them in 'a subordinate and servant-like role' (1988, p. 422) in comparison with their brothers, husbands and sons.

THE GENDER DIVISION OF HOUSEHOLD LABOUR— JANEEN BAXTER

In Australia, Bettina Cass suggested that Young and Willmott's notion of the symmetrical family is 'visionary' (1987, p. 204) rather than an accurate description of real family relationships. More recently, Janeen Baxter (2002) outlined the current trends in the gendered division of domestic labour by analysing the data from three national surveys—the 1986 and 1993 Class Structure of Australia Projects and the 1997 Negotiating the Lifecourse Project.

Baxter found, on the one hand, that 'men are doing an increasing share of some domestic chores' (p. 411). The increases were in meal preparation, up 12 per cent for men and down 4 per cent for women, and cleaning up after meals (+7 per cent), house cleaning (+7 per cent), washing (+7 per cent) and ironing (+10 per cent). Overall there was an increase of 5 per cent in men's share of household labour.

On the other hand, 'women still spend at least twice as much time on selected routine housework chores' (p. 411). In relation to preparation of meals and cleaning up after meals, for example, women spent 14 hours per week on this task in 1986 and 10 hours in 1997, compared with men's 7 hours in 1986 and 5 hours in 1997. Women also spend twice as much time on grocery shopping, with no change between 1986 and 1997.

Baxter concluded that 'the gender division of labour, in terms of both the gender gap in time spent on childcare and housework and gender differences in the kinds of tasks men and women do in the home, is still clearly evident' (p. 419). If men are doing a greater share of the food preparation, this does not equate with spending greater actual time. Baxter argues that this shift has a lot to do with a decline in overall time spent on food preparation, which is in turn likely to be related to greater use of pre-prepared meals. As Baxter puts it:

It is possible that changes in the kinds of food eaten and the level of preparation necessary have not only led to a reduction in time spent on cooking but also to a reorganization of men's and women's responsibilities for certain tasks. For example, men may be more inclined to do meal preparation if it involves heating a jar of pasta sauce and cooking spaghetti than if it involves more elaborate or time consuming preparation. (2002, p. 420)

The effect of women being in paid employment seems to be largely that they reduce the amount of domestic work they do, and Baxter concludes that this is probably the primary force behind the slight shift towards greater symmetry between 1986 and 1997.

HOW AUSTRALIANS USE THEIR TIME—ABS

The Australian Bureau of Statistics (ABS) has conducted three nationwide surveys of time use (in 1992, 1997 and 2006) that collected detailed information on people's daily activities. Activities were divided into the following categories:

1. *personal care:* sleeping, sleeplessness, personal hygiene, health care, eating and drinking, associated travel
2. *employment-related:* main job, other job, unpaid work in family business or farm, work breaks, job search, associated travel
3. *education:* attendance at education courses, job-related training, homework/study/research, breaks at place of education, associated travel
4. *domestic activities:* housework (food and drink preparation/clean-up, laundry and clothes care, housework), other housework (grounds and animal care, home maintenance, household management, associated travel)

5. *child care:* care of children, teaching/helping/reprimanding, playing/reading/talking with child, minding child, visiting childcare establishment/school, associated travel
6. *purchasing goods and services:* purchasing goods, purchasing services, associated travel
7. *voluntary work and care:* support for adults, unpaid voluntary work, associated travel
8. *social and community interaction:* socialising, visiting entertainment and cultural venues, attendance at sports events, religious activities/ritual ceremonies, community participation, negative social activities, associated travel
9. *recreation and leisure:* sport and outdoor activities, games/hobbies/arts/crafts, reading, audio/visual media, attendance at recreation courses, talking (including phone), writing/reading own correspondence, associated travel.

The main findings (see Table 4.1 and Figure 4.1) included that the average time spent by men on activities such as cooking, laundry and other cleaning (1 hour 37 minutes per day) did not change between 1992 and 2006. In 1992, the time spent by women on domestic labour was 3 hours 2 minutes per day, and in 2006 this declined by 10 minutes to 2 hours 52 minutes per day. Men spent around 30 minutes per day more than women on other household tasks, such as home maintenance. 'Women spent much less time on recreation and leisure ... nearly double the time spent by men on domestic activities ... and about half the time that men spent on employment related activities' (ABS 2006a, p. 2) Women also spent more time on the direct care of their children, while men spent more time on activities such as teaching and playing with their children.

Reflective question: How would you describe and explain the domestic division of labour between men and women?

DOMESTIC VIOLENCE

The tendency to idealise the family has made it difficult to perceive and analyse its less pleasant aspects, such as physically abusive relationships within family life. On average, in any given couple the male is usually physically stronger than his female partner, and this can play an important role in the power relations within family

Table 4.1 Time use, by gender, 2006

	Weekday (%) Men			Weekday (%) Women			Weekend (%) Men			Weekend (%) Women		
	1992	1997	2006	1992	1997	2006	1992	1997	2006	1992	1997	2006
Sleeping	36.0	35.1	34.4	34.1	35.1	34.7	36.3	38.0	37.8	35.9	37.5	37.5
Personal hygiene	3.3	3.0	3.0	3.7	3.5	3.7	3.1	3.0	3.1	3.8	3.7	3.8
Eating and drinking	4.3	6.2	5.8	4.4	6.4	6.0	4.7	6.8	6.7	4.5	7.0	6.9
Education	2.6	2.1	2.6	2.4	2.4	2.6	0.5	0.6	0.8	0.7	0.9	0.9
Employment-related	25.3	22.6	23.5	11.1	11.5	12.4	7.2	7.0	7.5	2.5	3.5	3.5
Housework	2.4	2.6	2.8	10.1	9.5	8.8	2.5	3.0	3.6	10.4	13.3	9.6
Other housework	3.2	2.9	2.6	1.5	2.3	2.2	5.1	5.0	4.3	2.6	3.0	2.9
Child care	0.5	1.0	1.4	3.7	3.3	4.3	1.0	1.5	1.9	2.7	2.6	3.7
Purchasing goods and services	2.6	2.3	2.5	4.2	3.8	4.0	2.5	2.8	3.1	2.6	3.6	4.0
Voluntary work and care	1.1	1.2	0.9	1.6	1.7	1.7	1.9	1.7	1.4	1.6	1.7	1.7
Social and community interaction	5.1	2.1	1.9	6.6	2.6	2.5	12.2	5.0	4.9	13.0	4.9	5.1
Recreation and leisure	15.9	17.7	16.9	15.3	16.5	15.4	21.4	24.4	23.1	16.3	20.3	19.0

Source: ABS (1998g; 2008b).

FIGURE 4.1

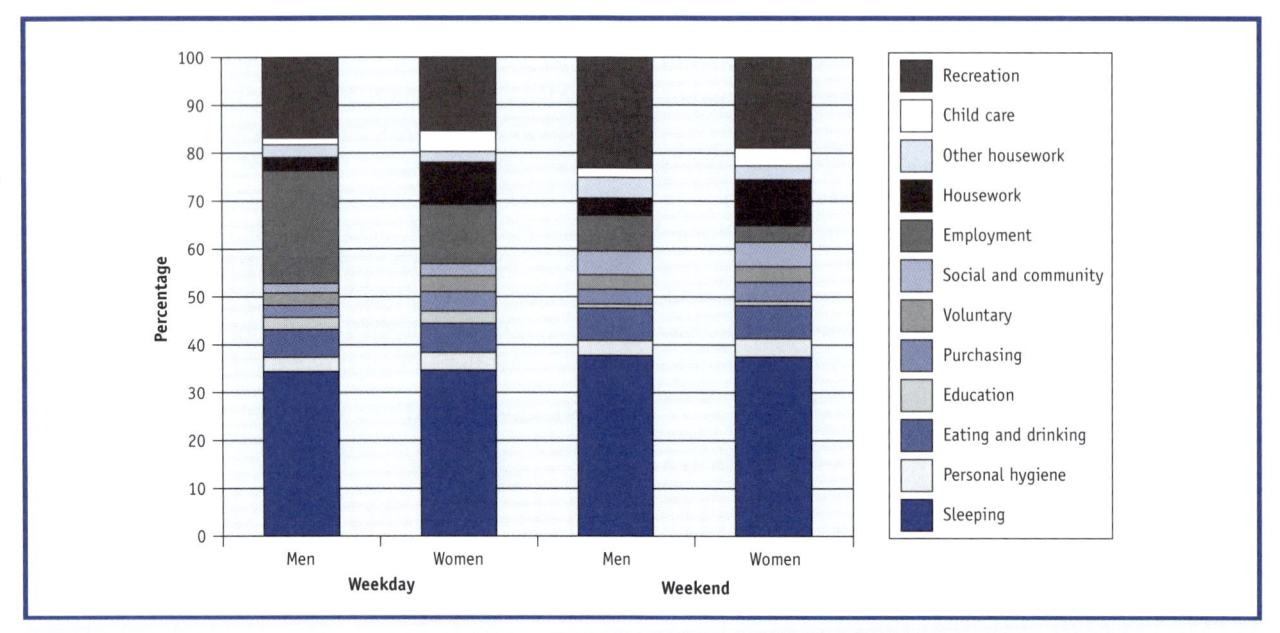

Time use, by gender, 2006 *Source:* ABS (2006a).

life. From the 1970s onwards, it has been primarily feminist researchers who have drawn attention to the ways in which domestic violence and child abuse are, in fact, quite widespread throughout society, rather than being simply a marginal and unusual aspect of family relations.

The concept of domestic violence encompasses a wide range of behaviour. It was defined in 1991 by the National Committee on Violence against Women as 'behaviour adopted by the man to control his victim which results in physical, sexual and/or psychological damage, forced social isolation, or economic deprivation, or behaviour which leaves a woman living in fear' (cited in Easteal 1994, p. 86).

Michael Gilding has pointed out that 'there is an unambiguous gender pattern in domestic violence' (1997, p. 184). Men are overwhelmingly the perpetrators and women overwhelmingly the victims. Research into domestic violence conducted since the 1970s has been significant in that it has shown domestic violence to be prevalent in all social spheres, in apparently 'happy' marriages and across all social classes. The class differences, Gilding emphasises, lay more in the response to violence. Middle-class wives would first consult a lawyer, whereas working-class wives would more immediately call the police—if they took any action at all (Gilding 1997, p. 186).

Gilding summarises the feminist explanation of domestic violence as having the following three key components:

1. *Gender socialisation*. It is not just a question of physical strength, because one can use weapons to inflict violence, but more the greater emphasis on the use of violence to respond to problems among males (p. 187).
2. *The effect of economic inequality*. 'Men's control over the larger part of the household income, especially when there were children, limited women's capacity to bargain or leave' (p. 188).
3. *Implicit social acceptance*. The response to victims of domestic violence can often be unsympathetic or ambivalent. This is based on an underlying presumption of male dominance over females.

Overall, the feminist argument is that family life is inevitably coloured by broader gender inequality, which underpins the threat of some form of violence in all women's lives, to a greater or lesser extent. British sociologist Liz Kelly has suggested that 'sexual violence exists in most women's lives', but also that 'the form it takes, how women define events, and its impact on them at the time and over time varies' (1987, p. 52).

INEQUALITY WITHIN MARRIAGE

The sociological evidence appears to suggest, then, that if marriage relations in contemporary Western societies have made any moves towards equality or 'symmetry' between men and women, these moves have been rather modest (see also p. 121). Women still do the majority of the housework and child care, and within marriage many women are still subjected to their partner's physical violence.

The underlying structural change since the second half of the 20th century has been that the division between the public and private spheres is becoming less rigid with women's increased workforce participation. However, the effect of that within family life seems to have been to produce a 'double burden' for women, rather than dramatically changing either the domestic division of labour or the power relations between men and women within marriage.

> **Reflective question:** Does it make any sense to see the family as a 'haven in a heartless world', given the degree of inequality, violence and abuse that characterises many family relationships?

CULTURE, ETHNICITY AND FAMILY DIVERSITY

It is often assumed that a single type of family is the dominant one in any particular era. Whether the modern family is regarded as nuclear, modified extended, modified elementary or dispersed extended, the assumption has been that only one type of family lies at the centre of people's experiences in modern industrial societies.

However, as Robert and Rhona Rapoport (1982) have argued, culture, religion and ethnicity constitute an important dimension of diversity in family forms. In Australia, for example, there are differences between families of Aboriginal and Torres Strait Islander, Anglo-Saxon, Southern European, Middle-Eastern and Asian origin, not to mention other ethnic groups. Lifestyle differences related to religion may also be an important element of diversity.

Australian family sociologists have paid increasing attention to the family patterns of different cultural and ethnic groups. They have been concerned to establish the extent to which Australian social institutions such as education and the law might assume a particular family structure, thus disadvantaging different family forms, as well as whether the family relationships typical of the societies of origin of immigrants have been modified within the Australian context. Thus sociologists have compared ethnic families in Australia with families in their country of origin and also with other Australian families.

Although some changes in the traditional family life of these groups might be expected, the degree to which they change could provide important evidence about the theory of increasing family diversity. If it is true that cultural diversity is becoming increasingly accepted in Australia, then these families could be expected to change little. If, however, the families of ethnic minorities are becoming more similar to those of other members of Australian society, family diversity might ultimately be based more on responses to general social and economic conditions than on ethnic differences. Apart from Aboriginal and Torres Strait Islander peoples, there are many different ethnic groups in Australia; this chapter examines two—the Greeks and the Lebanese Muslims—as examples of the impact of cultural diversity on family form.

ABORIGINAL FAMILY LIFE

There are a variety of family forms among the Aboriginal people themselves, characterised primarily by the opposition between traditional family structure and the degree to which that has been modified through contact with Western culture and social institutions. The best way to understand Aboriginal family life is, first, to draw a picture of the family in traditional Aboriginal societies and, second, to identify how that family form has changed since European invasion and settlement.

Traditional Aboriginal family life

In traditional Aboriginal society the extended family formed the basis for virtually all aspects of society. One was not considered an adult until married, it was expected that families would produce large numbers of children and the extended family was the central form of social organisation. Extended families or clans were themselves organised into larger territorial and linguistic groups, called 'tribes'. All political, economic and religious activities were coordinated around what Hart, Pillig and Goodale (1988) term the 'master system' of the household structure. In addition to a concern with marriage and raising children, the family and kinship system in traditional Aboriginal societies regulated education, political relations, economic activity and the legal–moral–religious system, all of which are differentiated into separate spheres of social life in modern Western societies. This also meant that Aboriginal households generally contained a larger number of extended family members, extended horizontally (across the same generation: aunts, uncles, cousins) as well as vertically.

Men were in a dominant position over women; they could reject their wives simply on inclination, whereas wives could leave only by eloping, leaving their husbands free to take action against them and their new partner—and the partnership was not regarded as valid until the husband relinquished his rights, often after receiving compensation. A man could also 'dispose of his wife's sexual favours as he pleases, with or without her consent' without losing his rights over her (Berndt & Berndt 1968, p. 207).

The system of marriage, around which family life was organised, had several characteristics. Victoria Burbank described the ideal marriage system as follows (1988, p. 51):

- All women are married.
- Females join their husbands before puberty.
- The arrangement of a marriage is not the sole concern of potential partners. A female's marriage is ideally arranged by her mother's kin.
- The selection of partners is governed by rules that define which partners are acceptable (i.e. 'straight').
- Females are exchanged in marriage—that is, the marriage of any female generates a reciprocal obligation on the part of the husband's family to bestow a female in marriage to a male in the wife's family.
- Marriages may be polygynous—that is, men may have multiple wives.

Burbank gave an example of how marriages were arranged, ideally, in the Aboriginal community she studied:

In the past, or so say older people at Mangrove today, two women and their mothers and mothers' brothers might decide that they would make their respective children, a 'little boy' and a 'little girl' gajali, that is, mother-in-law and son-in-law together. In a brief ritual, one or another of these people would rub white clay into the children's hair. The clay ensured that the 'promise' the relationship entailed would not be forgotten. When the little girl grew, married and had children, she would give all of her daughters to this son-in-law as his wives. Ideally, this son-in-law was an eldest son and if, or when, he died, these women were to go to his surviving brothers. This act also entailed reciprocity. If the son-in-law had a sister, she was to give all her daughters as wives to her brother's mother-in-law's brother. (1988, pp. 51–2)

The relationships and obligations established in the marriage system between the families of those marrying were thus of greater social consequence than the relationships between the partners themselves, which was the basis of the pivotal role played by marriage and family life in Aboriginal society.

One of the central features of traditional Aboriginal marriage that distinguishes it from the European marriage pattern is the ability of men to acquire multiple wives, and considerable attention has been paid to developing an explanation for the male interest in more than one wife. Burbank (1988) distinguished four possible explanations:

1. *Economics.* The family is the primary site of economic activity, and multiple wives ensured that sufficient food would be gathered and that it would be well prepared. Hart, Pillig and Goodale quoted the head of a large Tiwi household responding to a missionary preaching on the evils of **polygyny**: 'If I only had one or two wives I would starve, but with my present 10 or 12 wives I can send them out in all directions in the morning and at least two or three of them are likely to bring back something with them at the end of the day, and then we can all eat' (1988, p. 38). The ideal combination included both energetic younger wives and experienced, knowledgeable and skilled wives to supervise their activities. Hart, Pillig and Goodale stated that almost all households contained at least one experienced older woman and that those rare 'uneconomic' households with only younger wives were most likely to go hungry. This was the basis for the inclination among the Tiwi young men towards 'laying the foundation of their household by marrying an elderly widow usually long before there was any young wife in sight' (1988, p. 39).

2. *Reproduction.* A number of writers have suggested that Aboriginal men have an interest in accumulating as many wives as possible in order to produce the maximum number of children. Burbank found in her study that the desire for children was often the reason given for men wanting more than one wife, although she stopped short of embracing Hiatt's (1985) sociobiological argument that polygyny is integral to a broader biologically programmed concern for reproductive success.

3. *Exchange value.* Maddock (1972) also argued, following Lévi-Strauss (1969), that polygyny maximises the political advantages of exchanging women within an increasing network of families and tribes, so that women exchanged in marriage are the basis for networks of reciprocal obligation. However, this approach has been heavily criticised, largely because 'its inherent assumptions about Aboriginal social organization are not

supported by the evidence of Aboriginal ethnography' (Burbank 1988, p. 49). The central concern in traditional marriage was less to establish alliances than to maintain the correct kinship relationships and to avoid incestuous marriages between actual or classificatory kin (Healy, Hassan & McKenna 1985, p. 306).

4. *Play.* Burbank herself also argued that polygyny can be more simply regarded as one of the 'games people play', so that 'men might value women for the status and prestige that accrues for simply doing well in a game where women are the stakes' (1988, p. 50). Once polygyny is established at all, perhaps to some extent the product of female concerns for co-wives to help with domestic labour, then men may simply want to maximise their efforts in the game to enhance their overall social status.

However, two qualifications need to be made concerning this 'ideal marriage pattern'. First, the extent of polygyny varied considerably in different parts of Aboriginal Australia. Among the Tiwi in the north of Australia it was well established, with younger men initially marrying older wives who had lost their husbands and gradually accumulating younger wives, totalling 20 in some cases. However, Berndt and Berndt (1968) pointed out that there are also disadvantages to having more than one wife, in the form of additional cares and responsibilities and a need for greater domestic political skill. It is usually, they argued, the 'forceful person with entrepreneurial leanings' who collects numerous wives, and today in most desert regions of Australia two or three wives is the norm, up to a maximum of six. The majority of marriages among Aboriginal people throughout Australia are now monogamous.

Second, although marriages were usually arranged, this did not mean that girls and women had no influence on their marriage futures. Their preferences could exert pressure on their Elders' choice, and there were often 'incorrect' marriages; women could elope with or be captured by a more appealing suitor, and such practices modified and softened the socially approved marriage rules. The injured 'correct' husband and his family might inflict some form of punishment on the couple or accept a payment of some kind to waive his rights in the matter (Berndt & Berndt 1968, pp. 200–1).

Rural and urban Aboriginal family life

Although family and kinship remain a central feature of Aboriginal social organisation, much of this traditional family system has been changed, sometimes dramatically, by contact with European culture and social institutions—often by the deliberate intervention of white Australian state agencies and religious bodies. Generally, Aboriginal families living in or near country towns will have retained more of the traditional ideal family structure than those living in larger cities.

Two of the most striking contrasts between the traditional Aboriginal marriage pattern and that of Western Europeans are:

1. the possibility of polygyny
2. the organisation and control of marriage by an extended kin group, particularly the betrothal of women at a young age, frequently to much older men.

Both of these features of the traditional marriage system have been radically transformed since European settlement, partly under the onslaught of Christian missionaries, and partly as a result of contact and integration with European culture and social institutions. Young Aboriginal women themselves, to the extent that they are influenced by Western ideologies of individualism, freedom and the notion of love as the basis for marriage, now tend to resist their family's attempts to keep them to the marriage rules. They marry the man of their choice, perhaps a non-Aboriginal man, or avoid marriage altogether. There is certainly little tolerance among Aboriginal women of polygyny, which now survives only in remote regions.

These changes are partly a response to contact with Western culture, and partly the consequence of changed social relations within the family resulting from social institutions such as the school. Much of the control that traditional Aboriginal families were able to exert over their daughters was based on a tight regulation of their physical movement and social contacts. Girls often spent time with their intended husband and would usually be living with him before menarche. Ideally, by the time they struck adolescence, stated Burbank, 'their sexual impulses had been directed toward men deemed appropriate husbands by their society' (1988, p. 115). However, participation in schooling radically transformed relations between young Aborigines and their families. It provided a forum for mixed-sex social interaction free from familial supervision, a peer group whose influence could outweigh that of the family and the practical means for arranging liaisons, with peers carrying messages and helping to evade adult scrutiny (pp. 104–6).

The transition to a more Western marriage pattern has resulted in the greater freedom of Aboriginal women to choose their partners, but that has been only one of its effects. Bell and Ditton pointed out that women are no longer protected by the network of reciprocal obligations that characterised the traditional marriage system, and 'many women express horror at the incidence of rape and violent abuse of women which sometimes occurs today' (1980, p. 17). Polygynous marriage also enabled relations of mutual support among co-wives, whereas monogamous marriage makes a wife more dependent on her husband, although this dependence is often tempered by the presence of other female kin in the household.

Aboriginal family change in Adelaide, 1966–80—Fay Gale

Many of the processes of change occurring in Aboriginal family life through increased contact with white Australian society have been well illustrated in a study of the migration of Aborigines in the city of Adelaide. Gale (1981) found that the movement from a rural to an urban context had a number of significant consequences for the structure and dynamics of Aboriginal family life:

- *Increased intermarriage.* Gale found that mixed marriages in Adelaide increased from 26.6 per cent of all Aboriginal marriages in 1966 to 43.6 per cent in 1973, and 57.9 per cent in 1980. Non-mixed marriages had correspondingly decreased from 73.4 per cent in 1966 to 42.1 per cent in 1980. Gale found that Aboriginal men and women perceive unions with white Australians as providing them with greater security and freedom from the restrictions of the strict Aboriginal kinship system. The rules governing Aboriginal marriage are so complex and extensive, argued Gale, that young people often cannot comprehend them and attempt to avoid them; so it appears that 'the extent and strength of the kinship bonds may in fact be militating against their continuance' (p. 295).

  Gale also identified the economic factors encouraging intermarriage: for the white partner, increased benefits including subsidised housing and special educational allowances for children during the marriage; for the Aboriginal partner, increased financial security in the case of marriage breakdown, when the house and other benefits automatically go to the Aboriginal partner.

- *Declining marriage rate.* At the same time, overall marriage rates declined considerably. On the Aboriginal reserves, marriage was the norm; in the city, Gale found that de facto, separated and single (never married) households were becoming increasingly widespread. Such households were too infrequent to be identified separately in 1966 but, by 1973, 26.4 per cent of dual-head households were de facto, increasing to 51.4 per cent in 1980. In 1973, single-parent households made up 8.4 per cent of the study population aged over 15 years, increasing to 12.4 per cent in 1980.

  The increase in de facto unions was also concentrated in non-mixed partnerships, so that by 1980 most mixed couples were married, while non-mixed couples were more likely to be de facto. Gale's explanation for this is that the welfare system positively discourages marriage by limiting the benefits available when married. The age pension is reduced, and unemployment, supporting mother's and invalid pensions are withdrawn from one partner upon marriage.

- *Household structure and mobility.* Three aspects of urban Aboriginal family organisation continued to distinguish it from white Australian families. The first was the strength of the multiple or extended family household. In 1976, households containing two or more families accounted for 20.4 per cent of Aboriginal households, as opposed to 4.9 per cent in the general population. The 1991 Census found that, for the whole of Australia, 11.9 per cent of Aboriginal and Torres Strait Islander households contained two or more families, and the figure was 1.5 per cent for the non-Aboriginal households, suggesting a decline between 1976 and 1991 among both Aboriginals and non-Aboriginals. Aboriginal household size is also generally larger, 4.6 persons on average, compared with an average of 2.6 persons for non-Aboriginal households; and the number living alone was 3 per cent, less than half the non-Aboriginal figure of 6.8 per cent (ABS 1993b, pp. 7–8).

Second, Gale found that there was above-average mobility between Aboriginal households. Roughly one-third of her sample had relatives staying in the house and 10 per cent had three or more visitors.

Third, there was a high ratio of females to males in 1973, and 62.3 per cent females to 37.7 per cent males in 1980. Gale's interpretation of these figures was that Aboriginal males are more likely to be able to marry white women; and single-parent females have access to welfare and housing benefits unavailable to single men.

Aboriginal families and state intervention: the Stolen Generations

Traditional Aboriginal family life, and traditional culture in general, was subjected to systematic attempts at eradi-

> The 2006 Census found that, for the whole of Australia, 5 per cent of Aboriginal and Torres Strait Islander households contained two or more families, and the figure was 1 per cent for non-Aboriginal households, suggesting a decline between 1976 and 2006 among both Aboriginal and non-Aboriginal households. Aboriginal household size was still generally larger, 3.3 persons on average (down from 4.6 in 1991), compared with an average of 2.5 persons for non-Aboriginal households; and the number living alone was 14 per cent (up from 3 per cent in 1991), a little more than half the non-Aboriginal figure of 23 per cent (also up from 6.8 per cent in 1991) (ABS 1993b, pp. 7–8; 2006c, pp. 27–9).

cation by the euphemistically named state Aborigines Protection Boards. From the early 1900s onwards every state in Australia passed various Aborigines Protection Acts, giving authority to Aborigines Protection (or Welfare) Boards to 'care' for Aboriginal children. In practice, the legislation was used to remove as many children as possible from their families in order to facilitate their absorption into European culture and family values, with the aim of completely eliminating Aboriginal culture and society. 'In the course of a few years', hoped one welfare official in 1909, 'there will be no need for the camps and stations; the old people will have passed away, and their progeny will be absorbed in the industrial classes of the country' (cited in Edwards & Read 1989, p. xiv).

Simply being Aboriginal was regarded as sufficient reason to define children as 'neglected'. The definition of neglect automatically encompassed almost all Aboriginal families, because it included central features of the social position of Aborigines in European Australian society—features such as having 'no visible means of support or fixed place of abode', a situation often forced upon Aboriginal families; and illegitimacy, which applied to all Aborigines retaining traditional marriage customs. In 1915 the New South Wales Aborigines Protection Act was amended to allow children to be removed without parental consent:

if the Board considered it to be in the interests of the child's moral or physical welfare, placing the onus on the parents to show that their child was not neglected. (Read 1983, p. 6)

In Western Australia in 1936 the West Australian Commissioner for Aboriginal Affairs was made the legal guardian of all Aboriginal children up to age 21, and the Native Administration Act empowered the state to take all Aboriginal children from their families by force and place them in government institutions to be trained in the ways of 'white civilisation' and 'society'

(Haebich 1988, p. 350). The flavour of state officials' attitudes towards Aboriginal family life is captured by this typical comment by a leading welfare reformer, Charles Mackellar, on 'the Aboriginal problem' in 1915:

Paternity is casual and conjectural, and promiscuous association is the rule; sanitation is ignored. Dirt is the dominating element. In this mire of moral and physical abasement, tended by semi-imbecile mothers, children are allowed to wallow through the imitative stages of childhood. (cited in van Krieken 1991, p. 97)

More than 5000 Aboriginal children were removed from their families between 1909 and 1969 in New South Wales alone (Read 1983) and, unlike white children, great care was taken to ensure that they neither said goodbye nor ever saw their parents or family again. Often they were given new names, and the isolation of Aboriginal settlements made it more difficult for parents and children to trace each other. Deceit was often used to remove children, on the pretext of a brief court hearing or hospital stay.

The Australian Bureau of Statistics found that one in ten Aboriginal people aged 25 or over in 1994 stated that they had been removed from their natural families (ABS 1996b, p. 115). Peter Read's overall estimate was slightly higher: about one in six Aboriginal children were removed from their families during this time, compared with one in 300 white children. He saw this as the basis of much of the disintegration of Aboriginal culture and family life, especially the violence and alcohol dependency often encountered in Aboriginal communities. Read concluded: 'Perhaps in time the whites will suffer in the knowledge of what they have done. But they cannot expect forgiveness' (1983, p. 20).

MIGRANT FAMILY STRUCTURE AND VALUES

Peter McDonald (1991) has argued that many of Australia's migrants come from societies where family life more closely approximates what in Western European cultures is regarded as the 'traditional' **patriarchal family**: an extended kinship network exerting a strong influence over marriage and family life, relatively high fertility, early marriage, infrequent divorce, women's work concentrated in and around the home, and strong paternal authority over women and children. The perception of a particular family structure as a defining feature of cultural identity seems to produce greater resistance to more general economic and social forces producing changes in family life both among Western

European Australians and in the country of origin. The maintenance of the type of family life prevalent in the country of origin when the last family member migrated to Australia often 'represents centuries of valuable tradition, the source of rich and meaningful culture and a field that contains primary contacts and reference groups' (Bottomley 1979, p. 180). This pertains even though family life in the country of origin will in fact have changed in response to different social and economic conditions (Peristiany 1976, p. 2). The cultural isolation of migrant groups from mainstream Australian society accentuates this tendency by intensifying each individual's dependence on the family network for support, social interaction and a basis for social identity (McDonald 1991, p. 118).

There is general agreement among Australian sociologists that migrants retain what they perceive to be a 'core culture' (Bottomley 1979) (irrespective of whether it corresponds to the real family forms currently found in their country of origin), which provides a clear sense of cultural distinctiveness in their family life, and also adapt their family forms where necessary to Australian social and economic conditions. However, there is disagreement on where the emphasis should be placed. Gillian Bottomley argued, for example, that Greek family values and structure are generally resistant to change, because of the centrality of Greek familialism to Greek culture and the relative ease with which a separate cultural identity can be maintained in the private sphere of the family, in contrast to more public political and economic behaviour. On the other hand, McDonald argued that the overall tendency is towards a reduction of the influence of traditional family forms, listing the main forces of change as:

> *counter-socialisation of children through peers, the media and school; involvement of migrant women in the workforce outside the family circle; direct intervention of Australian institutions in the daily life of migrants [e.g. schools and courts]; economic difficulties; urban lifestyles; and isolation from the wider kin group. (1991, p. 118)*

Two ethnic groups will be examined to illustrate these arguments: the Greek and Lebanese Muslim communities in Australia.

Greek families in Australia

After the Odyssey: a study of Greek Australians—Gillian Bottomley

Between 1969 and 1971, Gillian Bottomley studied the Sydney Greek community in order to identify the forms taken by Greek migrants' ethnic identity, the extent to which that identity had changed in response to Australian society, and the possible sociological explanations for both stability and change. Her description of traditional Greek family structure emphasised the role played by the extended kin network, especially fathers, in controlling adolescent sexual and social behaviour and in determining marriage partners. Greek marriage is a matter of honour for the whole family network, in contrast to the more individualist emphasis on romantic love as the primary basis for marriage among Western European Australian adolescents.

There was a strong emphasis on the authority of fathers and husbands, and on the relative subservience of wives and daughters. Greek women and children were thus more likely to be economically dependent on the male family head (1979, p. 88). Kin networks also played a substantial role in organising everyday life, and Bottomley cited one informant as speaking of Greek 'family bonds the strength of which the average Australian cannot conceive' (1979, p. 146). Greek family networks served economic and moral purposes that in Western European Australian families have come to belong to a separate, public sphere. One point of similarity was the orientation towards the family of procreation rather than the family of origin; obligations to their family did not disappear after the birth of children, stated Bottomley, but the emphasis was on responsibility for their own children (p. 82).

She found there was a general tendency among the Greek community to maintain a separate ethnic identity. The preservation of specifically patterned forms of social interaction and primary relationships such as marriage and family was central to that identity.

Australian Family Formation Project—Greek families in Melbourne

A study conducted in 1976 as part of the Australian Family Formation Project by Packer, Caldwell and Caldwell among Greek women of various ages, educational levels and date of arrival in Australia found a range of changes in Greek family patterns, but also considerable stability. Although Greek mothers did admit a preference for their daughters marrying Greek men, they felt they had no real control over their daughters' choice of partner and that marriages were arranged to a decreasing extent. However, university-educated girls especially felt that their parents still played a larger role in relationships and marriage than among their non-Greek Australian counterparts. They felt their parents wanted to meet and know about prospective sons-in-law and retained tight control over their social encounters with males until they were engaged. Parents still attempted to prohibit all unsupervised dates, assuming that boys had only one thing on their minds. The Greek girls took this for granted and explained that they would lie to their parents in order to meet with boyfriends. In fact, 'there would probably have been suspicion of parents who showed little concern about their daughters' doings' (1976, p. 128). Generally, there was still a strong linkage in the girls' minds between sexuality, or loss of virginity, and marriage. They believed that their non-Greek peers were far more likely to be sexually active while still single and that 'Australian girls have no hang-ups at all about remaining virgins' (p. 134).

Once married, however, the study found that Greek couples were as likely as non-Greeks to defer the birth of their first child, and all generations agreed that a couple should begin acquiring a house, establish careers and have a few years going out and enjoying themselves— roughly two to four years at least after marriage. Their ideal family size was at least two children, but no more than three.

Greek mothers in Greece and Australia—Smyrnios and Tonge

In 1981 Kosmas Smyrnios and Bruce Tonge conducted a survey that compared the attitudes of Greek mothers living in Australia with those of Greek mothers in Greece. They found that 73 per cent of the Australian sample reported that either a parent or relative had played a significant role in arranging their marriage, whereas only 25 per cent of the Greek sample said that their marriage was arranged. The researchers also found that no Australian Greek mother reported a pre-marital pregnancy, whereas 17.6 per cent of the Greek mothers had conceived their first child before marriage. The first child had been conceived within six months of marriage among 75 per cent of the Australian mothers, and 41.2 per cent of the Greek mothers.

Smyrnios and Tonge concluded that, in the attempt to retain a distinctive cultural identity, aspects of Greek family life had been 'frozen', especially the role played by parents in arranging marriages and restricting pre-marital sexuality, despite changes in those family patterns in Greece itself.

Lebanese Muslim families in Australia

Family life also plays a central role in both traditional and contemporary Lebanese society, serving economic, social and welfare purposes. Although contemporary Lebanese society is becoming more individualistic, Hassan, Healy and McKenna argue that individuals are 'still dependent on kinship structure for identity protection, economic advancement or security' (1985, p. 180). They described the role of the extended family in society as adaptable and 'elastic', since Lebanese society and family life have been changing for some time. Nonetheless, a source of stress in Lebanese family life is still the unity and honour of the family as a whole, centred on male dominance and authority, and emphasising familial responsibility and reciprocity. Hassan, Healy and McKenna found that in Australia 'marriages were generally arranged, and "unsuitable" marriages rarely occurred. If such unions seemed likely, parental or familial counter-influence was said to be decisive' (1985, p. 189).

In Lebanese society there has never been any civil law concerning marriage and divorce. They come under the exclusive authority of Lebanon's 17 different Christian, Muslim and Jewish religious groupings (Humphrey 1984, p. 184). The pivotal role of religion in family life contrasts with Australian society, where the state is regarded as having almost complete jurisdiction over family matters. This has far-reaching consequences for the Lebanese Muslim community, because Islamic family law conflicts with Australian civil family law on a number of important points: permissible age at marriage, the authority of sheikhs to perform marriage, bridewealth provisions in marriage contracts and custody of children after divorce, as well as division of property and men's entitlement to declare divorce (Humphrey 1984, p. 183).

The most intense conflict between Islamic and Australian civil family law arises from divorce and subsequent custody and property settlement issues. In Islamic law, the concept of 'fault' and its impact on questions of family honour is central to the resolution of disputes, whereas Australian family law ignores such issues, focusing instead on the future welfare of all the individuals in the dispute, particularly that of the custodial parent and children. Australian family law can remove full custody and control from the male parent, whereas:

> *in Islamic law husbands are entitled to the custody of boys at seven years and girls at nine years and to all property not brought to the marriage by the wife, or given to her as bridewealth.* (Humphrey 1984, p. 192)

A husband can also refuse to grant his wife a divorce, or repudiate her (*talaq*), so that, while she may be divorced in the eyes of Australian courts, under Islamic law she remains married and unable to remarry. The husband may do so, as Islamic law allows him to have up to four wives (Hassan, Healy & McKenna 1985, p. 190).

The Australian Family Law Court thus provides an avenue for Lebanese Muslim women and their kin to challenge the claims and authority of their husbands and their kin under Islamic law. Michael Humphrey found that 75 per cent of the divorces he studied were initiated by the wife and that such court action establishes the support of the wife's kin, since she would rarely go to a solicitor alone (1984, p. 193). There are two important consequences emerging from migration to Australia:

1. The Islamic courts, which in the Middle East temper the power of husbands, are largely absent in the Australian Muslim community. This enhances men's ability to declare divorce unilaterally (Humphrey 1984, p. 192), and increases the influence of the Lebanese sheikhs, who are concerned to reinforce their authority in the Australian Lebanese community through regulation of marital disputes.
2. Their Muslim identity is experienced as being threatened in a predominantly non-Muslim, secular society. The drawing of most family members into education and work means that 'the relations which are governed by honour tend to contract to the members of the household, which increasingly become the focus of cultural and social continuity' (p. 194).

In the migrant context, then, the maintenance of family customs assumes the extra burden of ensuring cultural and ethnic continuity, and increases the resistance to any accommodation to the Australian civil legislation covering marriage and divorce. Lebanese Muslim husbands are inclined to regard the impact of the Australian Family Law Court on their family affairs as an illegitimate attack on their position within the traditional moral order of Lebanese family life, and as an assault on the very foundations of Lebanese ethnic identity. Their response most often ranges from being uncooperative with the court and their estranged wives and children and refusing to grant a religious divorce (making it impossible for their wives to remarry) to physical threats or assaults (p. 193).

Ethnicity and family diversity: conclusion

The general picture provided by these studies suggests that immigrants and their descendants have in many ways adapted their family life to fit Australian circumstances, yet maintain many of the relationships on which their traditional family life was based. Despite considerable changes since the 1970s, families originating in Mediterranean cultures maintain a relatively high rate of endogamy (marrying within the ethnic group). They also experience lower rates of divorce and tend to marry earlier; and they are less likely to live in households apart from their families, more likely to form multiple-family households and less likely to enter into de facto relationships (McDonald 1991).

This would suggest that the existence of a variety of ethnic groups has indeed contributed to the diversity of family types to be found in Australia. These migrant groups have succeeded in retaining many of the culturally distinctive features of their family life. Nevertheless, there is also evidence of changes taking place in migrant families that may continue in future generations. As McDonald argued, 'their children are deeply exposed to the dominant Australian social environment' (p. 120). The sociological question here is whether migrant groups will sustain the diversity in family values in the face of the many economic, social and institutional forces that challenge the basis of their distinctive familial identities.

Reflective question: Can we continue to speak of 'the family', given the enormous diversity of family types and forms?

STRUCTURAL CHANGE IN FAMILY LIFE

'Marriage is a wonderful institution ... but who would want to live in an institution?' (H. L. Mencken)

The idea of 'the' family suggests a single model for all intimate and child-rearing relationships. However, there is now considerable social research establishing that contemporary societies are characterised by a plurality of household and family types, and the idea of a typical family is misleading. Over two decades ago, in a report entitled *What's Happening to the Australian Family?*, the National Population Council declared that 'Australian society has been passing through a transition from being dominated by one family type, parents and their offspring, to being one of diversity, where a wide range of different family and non-family types are common' (National Population Council 1987, p. 1). Thus it is becoming more and more problematic to think in terms of a typical, normal or conventional family.

In Australia today, only about 13 per cent of Australians live in families with dependent children in which the husband is in paid work and the wife is not (McDonald 2003). Table 4.2 shows the proportions of different family and household types in 1986 and 2003. The overall long-term trends in all Western countries, despite occasional variations and fluctuations, are towards:

- a steady decline in fertility
- increasing female workforce participation, irrespective of their marital status
- increasing numbers of single-parent families
- increasing rates of divorce, de facto cohabitation before or instead of marriage, and births outside of marriage.

THE FERTILITY DECLINE IN AUSTRALIA

Although family life can be regarded as having been 'nuclear', and relatively constant in size, through most of the history of Western Europe, there has been a dramatic change in the size and structure of families and households in all Western societies over the past century. These changes have had, and continue to have, profound and far-reaching social and economic consequences, both for family life itself and for the place of the family within the broader society.

John Caldwell and Lado Ruzicka argued that fertility decline was probably the major cause of 'the collapse of the domestic society in the modern era' (1978, p. 95), by which they mean the demise of the conventional nuclear family with a clear division of labour between a male breadwinner and a female houseworker. The consequences of family size are felt in the short term through the immediate economic and social impact of fewer children, but they also echo down through history as the reproductive choices made by one generation set the demographic, economic and social scene for the actions of the following generation.

The decline in household size

The overall size of European Australian households has dropped since white settlement in 1788 from over ten to a little over 2.5 in 2006 (Figure 4.2). In the convict period and colonial period up to the 1850s convicts were housed in dormitories, in households and on farms as servants, and the unbalanced gender ratio meant that many males were living in hotels and boarding houses. These conditions led to large households of about ten people, roughly double the average British size.

TABLE 4.2 Family and household types, 1986 and 2003

	1986 (%)	2003 (%)
All two-parent families with dependent children	39	35
All families with dependent children	33	25
All families	18	11
All households	13	8

Source: Kilmartin (1989); ABS (2004f, p. 5).

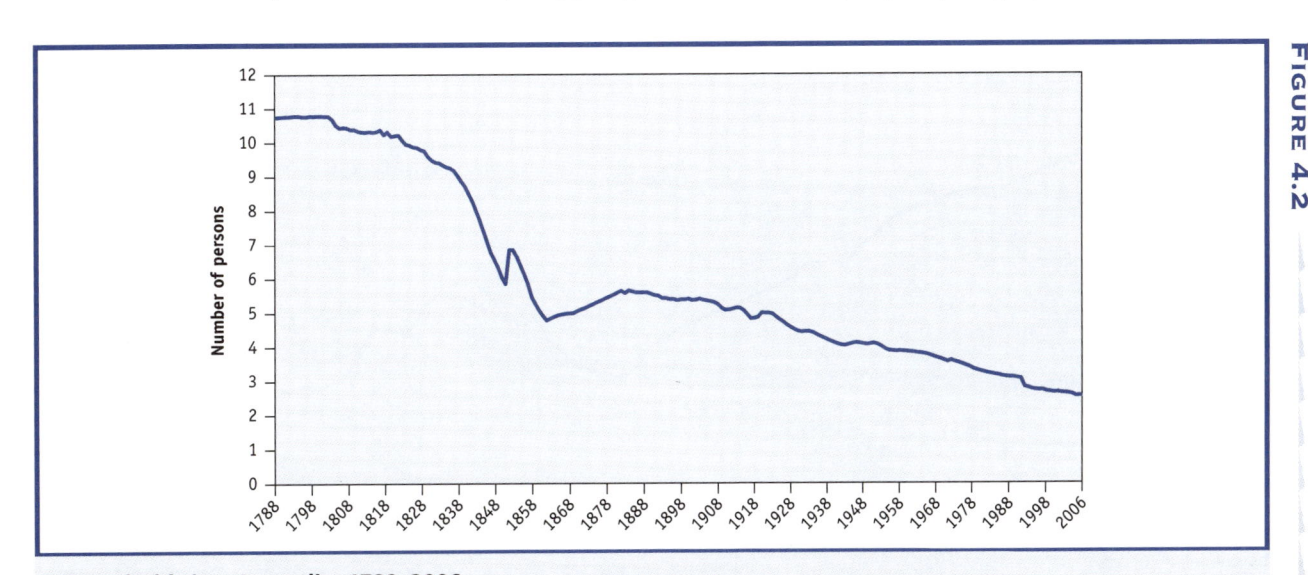

FIGURE 4.2 Household size, Australia, 1788–2006 Source: Snooks (1994); ABS *Year Book*, various years.

SOCIOLOGY

After the gold rushes in the 1850s, Australian household size remained relatively constant at around five persons until World War I. It then declined, first slowly and then more rapidly after the 1930s to around three persons in 1990 and an average of 2.5 in 2002. Graeme Snooks emphasised that this 'was part of the first major change in average household size in Western society in 1000 years' and that 'its importance cannot be exaggerated' (1994, p. 66). As Caldwell put it:

The study of fertility transition is the study of the transformation of familial production into production through the labour market, of traditional society into modern society. (1982, p. 231)

This change in household size was the result of a drastic reduction in the number of children borne by Australian women, producing what some observers see as the most significant impact on women's lives over the last century. In 1891, over 40 per cent of Australian families had six or more children, whereas today the most common size is two or three. This decline is reflected in the total fertility rate, which indicates approximately the total number of children born in any given year.

The fertility rate of Australian women, like their counterparts throughout the Western world, began to decline in the 1870s, recovered again in the post-World War II 'baby boom', declined significantly again in the 1970s and showed some signs of modest recovery in the 1990s and early 2000s (see Figure 4.3).

There are three transitions to be explained—the dramatic fertility decline since the 1870s, which has remained the longer term trend; the 'baby boom' following World War II; and the strong decline in the 1970s. These are discussed below.

From the 'proper time to marry' to the 'proper time to reproduce'— John Caldwell and Lado Ruzicka

The general framework most commonly used to analyse fertility changes is the model of **demographic transition**, which is summarised in the diagram developed by Graeme Hugo (see Figure 4.4).

Caldwell and Ruzicka argued that the economics of child-bearing for most of the 19th century (Stage 2 in the model) were that children were economically beneficial at best and cheap to raise at worst. Clothes were handmade, food was freely available on farms, a frugal life was regarded as good for children and 'neither children not parents believed that the former should have parity with the latter in consumption or pleasures or even that such a comparison should be made' (1978, p. 85). Children were expected to work and contribute to the family income as soon as possible. Fertility was generally high within marriage, and although deferring marriage had the effect of reducing fertility, marriage was not deferred for this reason, but because of the costs involved in the establishment of a new household. There was a strong sense of the 'proper time to marry' but, once married, fertility was high, and little relationship was seen between family size and economic welfare.

Caldwell also suggested that this familial ideology, 'teaching its less powerful members that it was good for them to live austerely and that there should

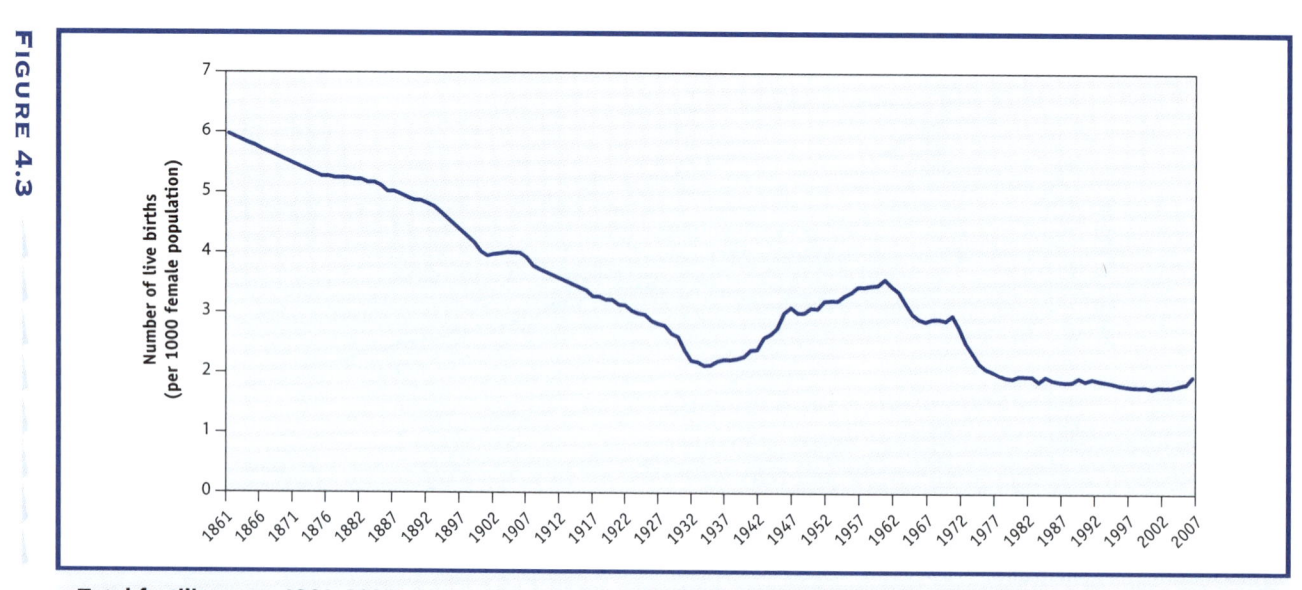

FIGURE 4.3

Total fertility rate, 1861–2007 *Source:* Hugo (1992); ABS, *Australian Historical Population Statistics*.

FIGURE 4.4

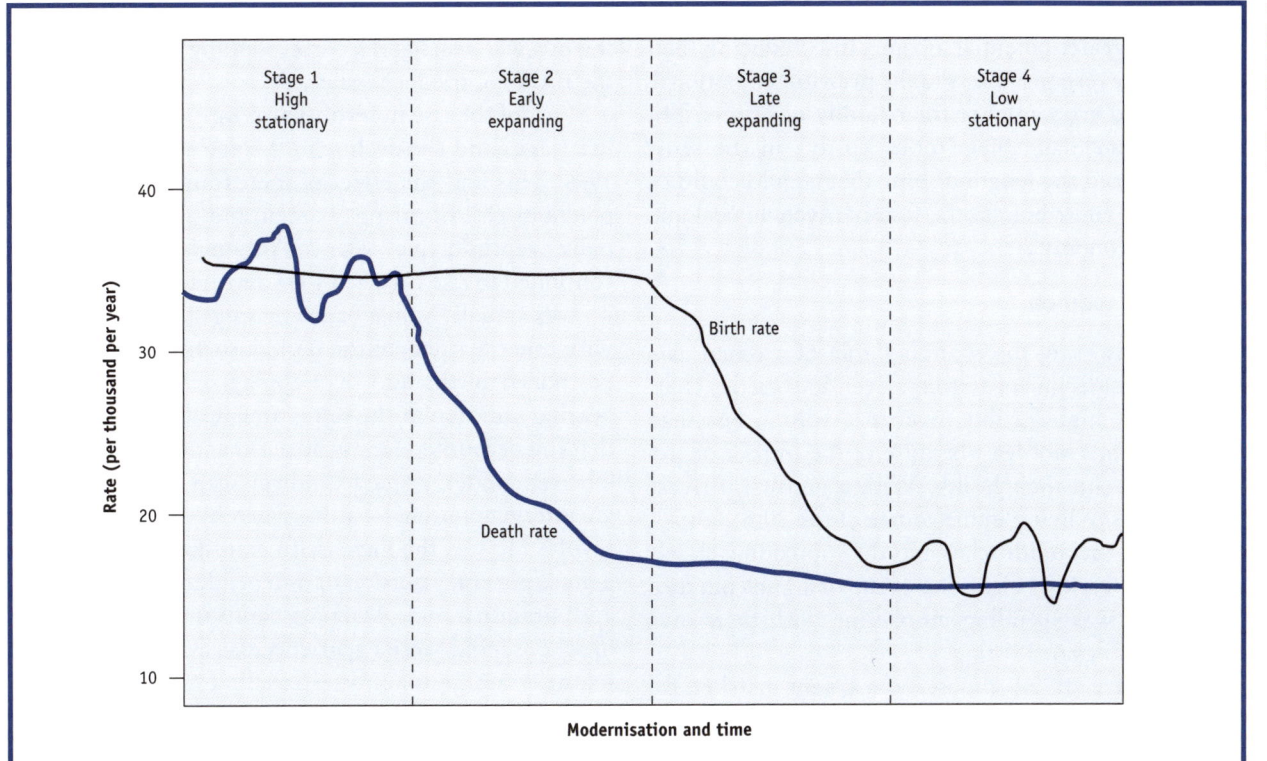

Traditional form of the demographic transition model *Source:* Hugo (1986, p. 43).

be no resentment of differential treatment and privilege' (1982, p. 212), fitted well with an early capitalist economy, which required considerable unskilled labour and little consumption, and where familial, household production still played an important economic role. This all changed, according to Caldwell and Ruzicka, with the dramatic change in parent–child relations brought about by mass compulsory schooling towards the end of the 19th century; and Australian family structure moved to Stage 3.

Schooling and fertility decline

The expansion of the market for wage labour, the changing nature of work requiring workers with greater levels of skill and the increasing orientation towards consumption turned children into different sorts of creatures and changed fundamentally their relations with their parents. Caldwell and Ruzicka summarised the change with the concept of a reversal of the 'net intergenerational flow of wealth'. Schooling turned children into investments in the future, rather than resources to be drawn upon in the present.

As Philippe Ariès (1980) put it, the 19th-century decline 'was unleashed by an enormous sentimental and financial investment in the child' (p. 649), an investment that required the planning of births and 'introduced foresight and organization where formerly there had been only automatic, unplanned behaviour and resigned surrender to impulses and destiny' (1980, p. 646).

A central feature of this investment is its uncertain, unbounded nature, so that a strong temptation arises to maximise the investment—one never knows what the return might be. The knowledge provided in schools expanded the range of consumer items a child would be interested in, as well as the pleasure adults would derive from introducing their children to the delights of, say, music, sewing machines or cameras, all of which became increasingly available from the 1880s onwards. Rather than being a source of economic input into the family economy, children became an ever-increasing cost, giving rise to an interest in fertility limitation.

The increasing 'cost' of children was not only economic but also psychological and emotional. The school diminished the control parents had over their children, because of the additional authority figure of the teacher and the network of peers it provided. This required greater effort on the part of parents to maintain their relationships with their children. Schooling and its effects made children more independent of their parents, providing them with greater labour market skills and greater potential income, thus reducing their likely future responsiveness to the priorities (emotional, cultural and economic) of their family of origin. The situation also made them more 'costly', in the sense that it reduced the length of time that a child could be expected to contribute to the family psychological and financial 'economy'.

The role of women

Caldwell also saw the changing role of women as a factor in the decline of fertility. Even in societies characterised by high fertility, women favour it less than their husbands, not least because of the impact of frequent births on their health. With a gradual increase in standards of living in the course of the 20th century, first among the middle class and then spreading slowly among the working class, one of the first aims pursued by women was spending more time with their own children (Quiggan 1988).

In the face of an almost nonexistent market for female labour, the nuclear family became a source of women's individuality and their rights against their parents, parents-in-law and husbands. Wives forged 'a powerful weapon for weakening their husbands' bonds with their parents by arguing that the children must come first, that they are their children' (Caldwell 1982, p. 241).

Economic conditions and fertility

Once children are perceived as a cost rather than a resource, some part in a declining birth rate is also played by general economic conditions and the prospects for being able to support greater fertility. Pat Quiggan argued that women had a particular interest in fertility control, being more directly faced, as housekeepers, with the task of feeding and clothing their children, especially problematic if their husbands were unemployed. She pointed out that the role of economic conditions is reflected in the interstate differences in fertility, which corresponded to the different onsets of depressed economic conditions in New South Wales and Victoria (1988, p. 119).

Baby boom or marriage boom?

The long-term trend towards fertility decline was interrupted dramatically and significantly by the post-World War II 'baby boom' in all Western countries, including Australia. The increase in the crude birth rate has been attributed to two main causes—a marriage boom and a particular cultural and ideological climate, characterised by a 'youth revolt' against the prudence of the pre-war years and a corresponding optimism about the future of modern society.

Much of the rise in fertility was due to the increase in marriages and the decline in the age at marriage after 1946. This had the effect of increasing the number of potential child-bearing women and also their potentially reproductive years. Although total fertility continued to rise between 1947 and 1961, marital fertility was actually stable or decreasing slightly. Together with other features of the period, such as a catch-up of postponed births and overlapping cohorts of women bearing children at the same time, Caldwell estimated that this accounted for 30–50 per cent of the baby boom. The remainder, argued Caldwell, can be explained by an intergenerational battle, what he calls the 'youth revolt'. He sees the increase in child-bearing as part of a more general assertion of independence from parents and grandparents. Marriage and the establishment of a household were experienced as a manifestation of maturity and autonomy, especially for young women. Also:

A lesser care about the containment of fertility was necessary, defiantly so, to proclaim the absoluteness of their control over their relations with their spouses and the children who were the products of their union. (1982, p. 250)

The post-1970s fertility decline

The Australian decline in fertility after 1970 was 'one of the world's most dramatic' (Hugo 1992, p. 13)—a drop of 45 per cent in the 20 years between 1961 and 1981 (see Figure 4.5).

This decline has been the product of social and economic changes, which Peter McDonald (1984; 2000) explained as follows:

- The depressed economic conditions of the 1970s made couples more cautious about child-bearing.
- In part, the baby boom itself was a factor. By the 1970s, the children born in the baby boom era were competing with each other in the workforce and also entering their prime child-bearing years. They formed a generation who 'have, throughout their lives, faced relative deprivation and fierce competition, relative … to the preceding generations born in the 1930s and early 1940s' (1984, p. 19).
- There is a lack of synchronisation across different social institutions in a shift away from the 'male breadwinner' towards the 'gender equity' model. McDonald argues that if those social institutions connected with education and work have moved

FIGURE 4.5

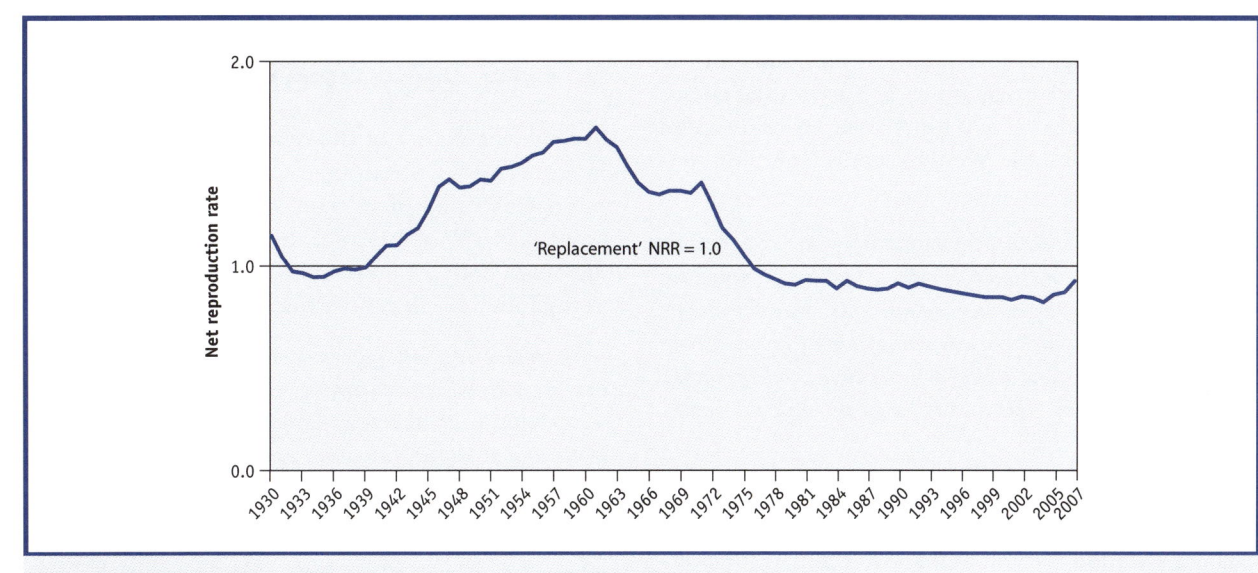

Net reproduction rate, 1930–2007 *Source:* ABS, *Australian Historical Population Statistics.*

a great deal towards increased gender equity, while those related to the family and parenthood are still more aligned to the 'male breadwinner' model, this is having a crucial dampening effect on fertility. The contradictions and tensions across different social spheres lead both men and women to be more cautious about having children, to delay child-bearing and to reduce the number of children they have.

The clear trend since the 1970s is that women are having their first child later in life. The median age of mothers has risen from around 25 years old in 1972 to nearly 31 in 2007 (see Figure 4.6).

The age-specific fertility rates also provide a useful picture of the change that is taking place: the fertility rates of women between 20 and 30 years have steadily declined from 1961 to the present, while those of women between 30 and 40 years have gradually increased, albeit at a much lower level, since the mid-1970s (see Figure 4.7).

Another long-term trend is the changing role played by children within overall family economies, particularly in competition with other ways of consuming

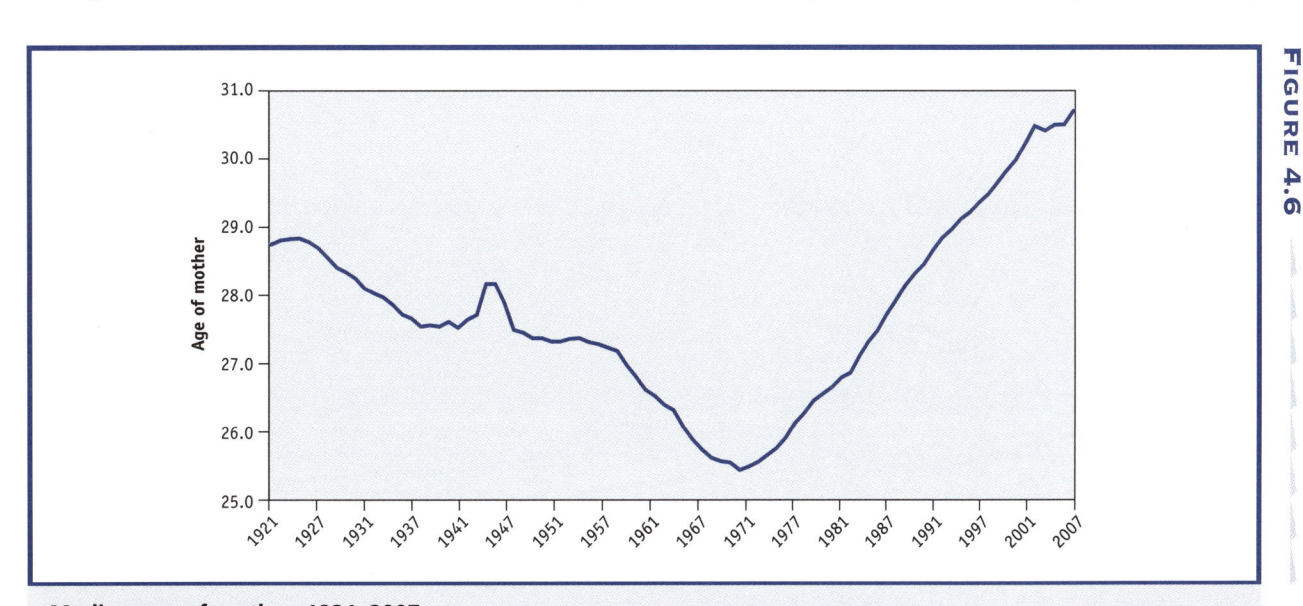

FIGURE 4.6

Median age of mother, 1921–2007 *Source:* ABS, *Australian Historical Population Statistics.*

disposable income. For Snooks, the historical evidence on the relationship between family income and number of children indicated that, when faced with the choice between procreation and increased consumption, families throughout the Western world opted for consumption:

> *What has been substituted for family time is a bewildering array of consumer durables, fast foods, domestic service, cars, larger homes, restaurants, entertainment, exotic holidays, travel, holiday houses, hobby farms, motor launches, yachts, four-wheel drive vehicles, together with expensive clothing and a vast range of personal goods.* (Snooks 1994, p. 145)

This supports Ariès' argument that, while a greater investment in children produced the first decline in the birth rate around the end of the 19th century, the post-1970s decline was caused by exactly the opposite—a greater investment in alternative forms of consumption. 'The days of the child-king are over. The under-40s generation is leading us into a new epoch, one in which the child occupies a smaller place, to say the least' (1980, p. 649). Not that children have no place at all, but they now have to fit in 'as one of the various components that make it possible for adults to blossom as individuals' (1980, p. 649).

Reflective questions: Give an explanation of the social dynamics behind the falling fertility rate in European societies since the late 19th century. Do you think that Australian family life has followed the same trends? If so, has this been for the same reasons?

WOMEN'S PARTICIPATION IN THE WORKFORCE

Although the nature of the relationship is not clear, a related change is the dramatic increase in the workforce participation of women, and especially married women, since World War II. Before 1939, the division of labour in both the household and the paid workforce was organised along gender lines:

> *with males specializing in the acquisition of market human capital and working full-time in the market sector, and with married females acquiring household skills and working full-time in the household.* (Snooks 1994, p. 82)

However, Caldwell and Ruzicka argued that, because the baby boom took place within the framework of the preceding fertility decline, along with various other social changes such as suburbanisation, the spread of the motor car and the development of shopping centres, the basic infrastructure for such an expansion of domesticity and child-rearing was disappearing from beneath the nuclear family's feet. Parents, especially mothers, had fewer siblings to call on for support and the remote nature of the Australian suburbs made parenting an even more isolating task. The changing nature of work and the gradual increase in women's wages after 1946 made entering the workforce a more attractive option for women, one that they took up in increasing numbers. Once they started working outside the home, the process became self-sustaining, because 'it

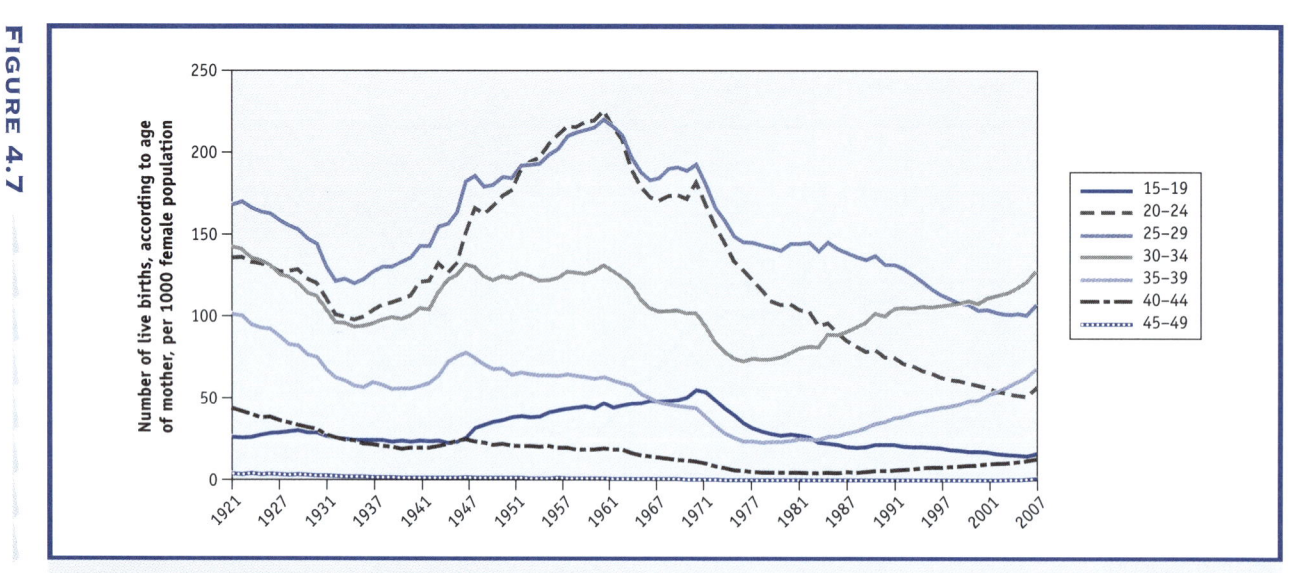

FIGURE 4.7

Age-specific fertility rates, 1921–2007 *Source:* ABS, *Australian Historical Population Statistics.*

reinforced the isolation of wives who were not working and the downgrading of the domestic virtues' (1978, p. 95).

The employment available to women had changed significantly, with more jobs in offices, shops and light manufacturing. The increasing participation of girls in education after World War II also led to an interest in careers and self-development beyond the family, as well as opening up more work opportunities. Caldwell and Ruzicka pointed out that women's increased entry into the paid workforce preceded by almost ten years the reappearance of a women's movement in the 1970s. They argued that this change produced the women's movement, rather than the other way round. Once the process was in motion, the two phenomena became mutually reinforcing, so that the effects of feminism were to further facilitate and accelerate women's workforce participation.

The change in the proportion of women in the paid workforce since 1950 has been dramatic, more than doubling from 25 per cent in 1945 to 57.5 per cent in 2009 (see Figure 4.8). Much of the increase can be attributed to married women, who went from 6.5 per cent in 1947 to 62.3 per cent in 2009, rising above the rate for all women. About 90 per cent of the increase has been in part-time work.

The pattern of change becomes clearer when we look at workforce participation for different age groups at each of the censuses (see Figures 4.9 and 4.10). Australian women have moved from a pattern of doing paid work between the ages of 15 and 19 and then working full-time in the home, to staying longer at school, entering the workforce, either leaving for increasingly brief intervals of child-rearing and full-time domestic labour during their peak child-bearing years or somehow combining work and child-rearing, and then returning to the workforce until their mid-50s.

One important qualification is that these figures do not capture the distinction between part-time and full-time work. The proportion of women working part-time increased in the years between 1982 and 2009 from 35 per cent of total female employment to 45.9 per cent (ABS 2009b). The issue simmering underneath these changes is how the predominance of part-time work among women is to be explained—whether it is a choice they make, enabling them to keep one foot in the domestic sphere; or whether it is a choice forced upon them by husbands who are either openly or furtively reluctant to increase their share of the domestic duties. (For a discussion of these issues, see the section on gender and domestic labour, p. 121.)

Causes and effects of increased female participation in the workforce

Various explanations have been offered for the increase in female participation in the workforce, including declining family size, higher average education levels, greater equality in personal relationships, easier divorce, increased numbers of single-mother families and greater life expectancy (Eccles 1984; Richmond

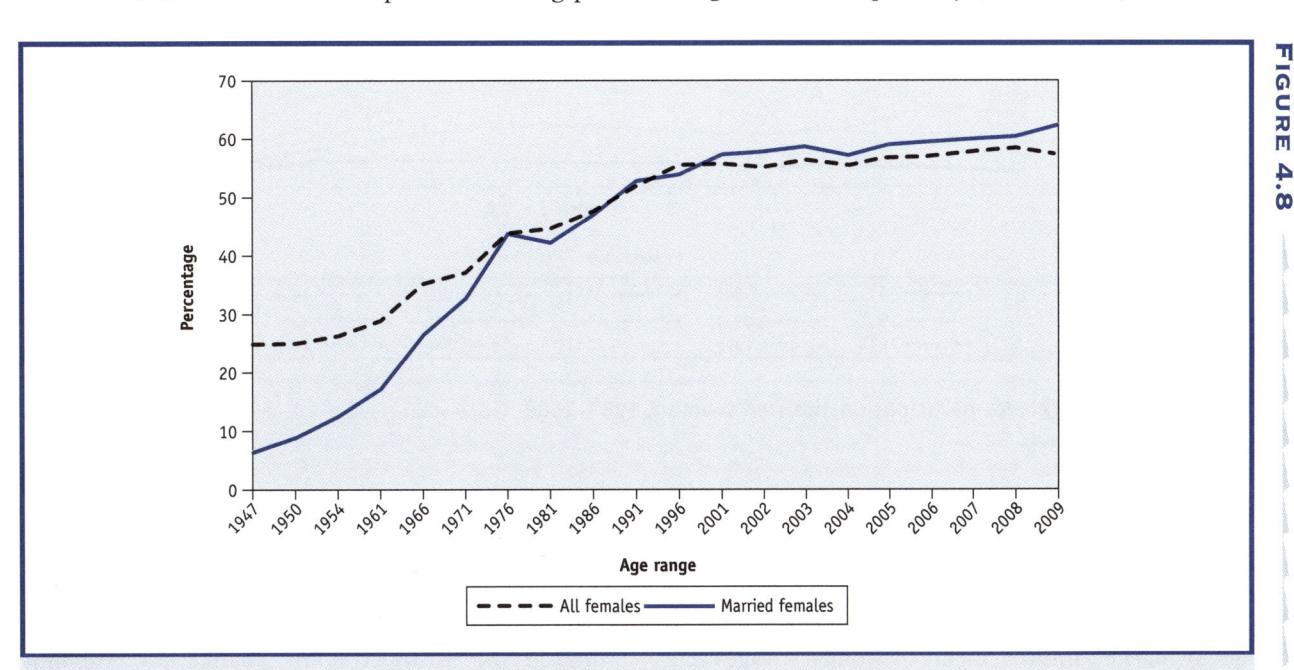

FIGURE 4.8

Women's participation in the workforce, 1947–2009 *Source:* Young (1990, p. 71); Eccles (1984, p. 81), ABS, *Labour Force* (pp. 15–16).

SOCIOLOGY

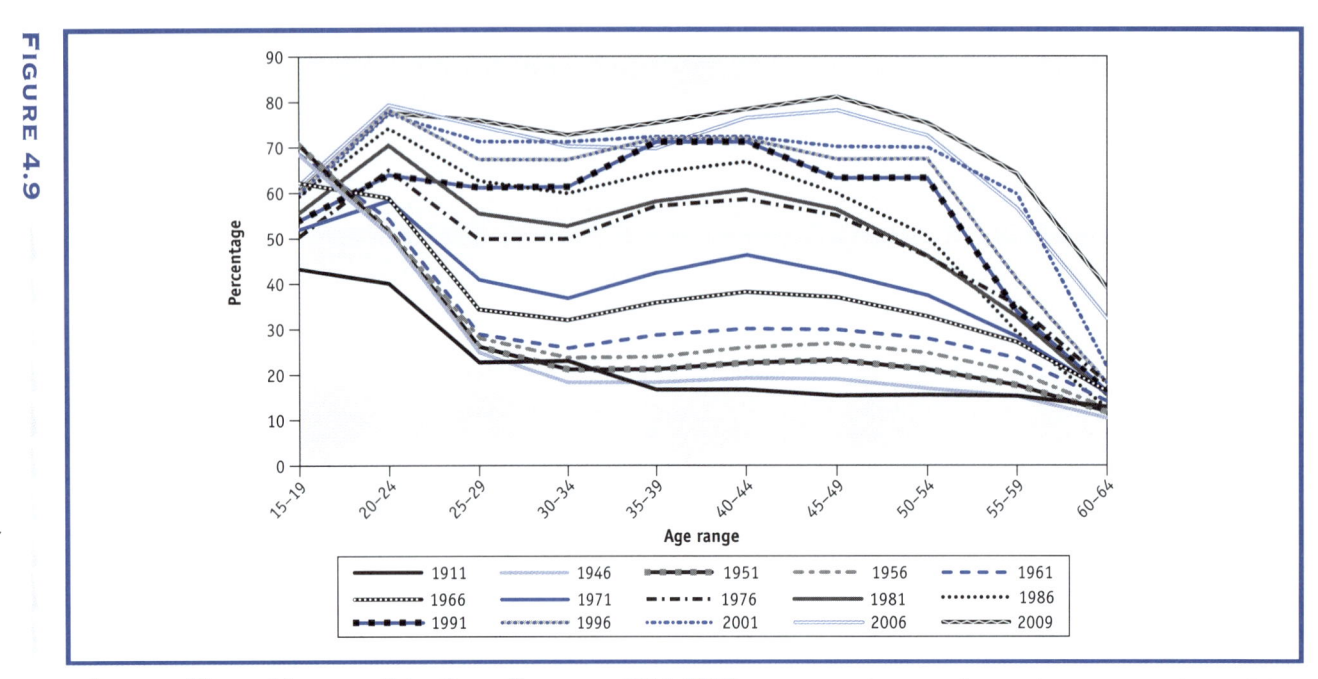

FIGURE 4.9

Age-specific workforce participation, all women, 1911–2009 Source: Young (1990, p. 71); ABS, *Labour Force, Australia, Detailed*.

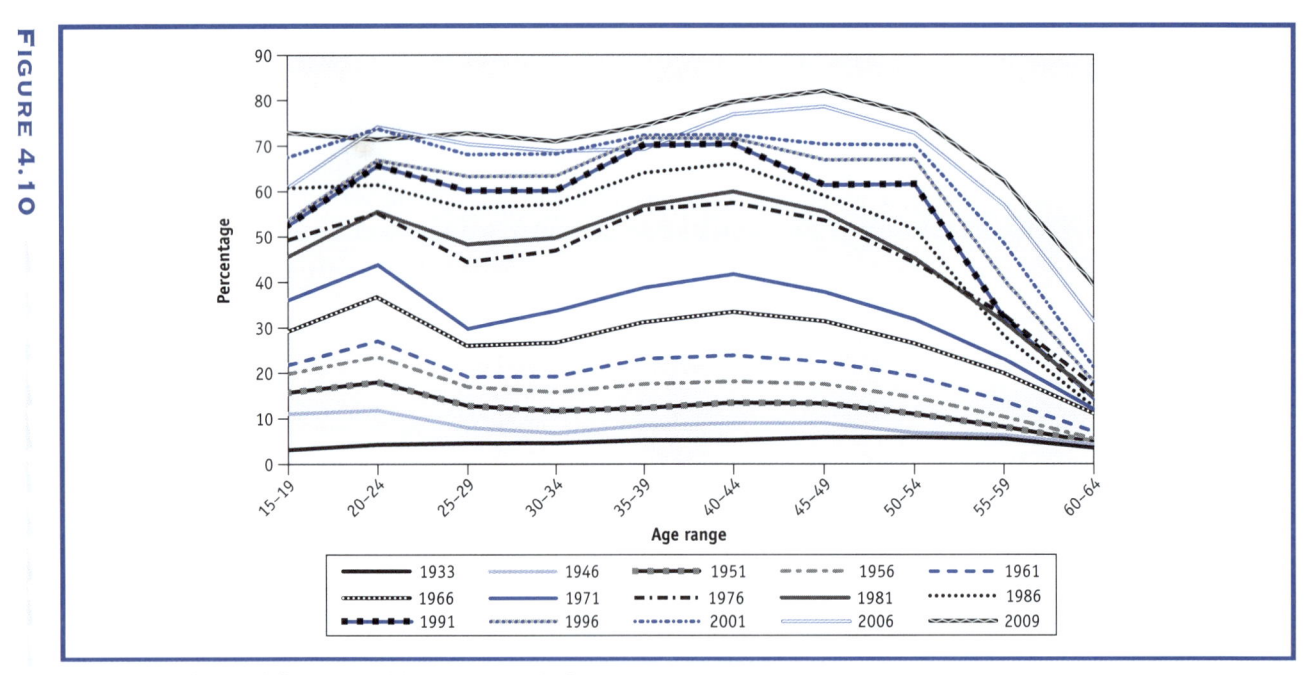

FIGURE 4.10

Age-specific workforce participation, married women, 1933–2009 Source: Young (1990, p. 72); ABS, *Labour Force, Australia, Detailed*; McDonald (1994).

1974). Snooks believed that the most significant changes were those in the technological character of the economy—rises in the costs of labour relative to capital, the deskilling and 'de-physicalisation' of large sectors of the labour market, improvements in women's wages relative to men's and the substitution of capital for labour in the household (1994, p. 83). 'No amount of political rhetoric, social rationalization, or sexual discrimination ... no amount of male chauvinism' could resist these economic developments, argued Snooks, because 'social values are forged by economic change, not economic change by social values' (p. 83). Snooks saw increased female workforce participation as 'largely a function of the changing technological base, and the emerging post-industrial structure of the market economy, rather than of an exogenous change in institutional or "cultural" forces' (p. 104; see also Harris 1983, pp. 92–3). This type of perspective is often referred to as emphasising 'demand-side' factors, because it concentrates on the demands or requirements of the economy rather than on the characteristics of the 'supply' of workers.

Kingsley Davis (1984) pointed out how the separation of the spheres of economic production and familial reproduction that was characteristic of Western societies after the Industrial Revolution was historically unprecedented, rather than 'normal' or 'traditional'. He called the family structure based on the man as breadwinner and the woman as homemaker the **breadwinner system** and saw it as associated with a very particular stage of development: the transitional period when agriculture gradually gave way to industrial production (around 1850–1920 in the United States).

The separation of home and work took this particular form because of the existing levels of fertility; women were still having too many children to work outside the home as well. These fertility levels changed over the next half-century, partly because of the economic changes mentioned by Snooks, but also because the breadwinner system had 'internal contradictions that make its ultimate demise a foregone conclusion' (Davis 1984, p. 406). In most of human history, argued Davis, except during this relatively brief period, 'women have rivalled men in economic production and are now returning to that condition and will not give it up' (1984, p. 415).

In the breadwinner system, women's income lay beyond their control, yet they were expected to behave as fully mature managers and executors of familial finances (Zelizer 1994). Family income was funnelled through husbands who had minimal personal contact with the family it was supposed to support, or at the very least they struggled with a constant opposition between the spheres of home and work. The financial dependency that characterised women's position made choosing the 'right' partner a decision fraught with significance and consequences; it made marriage a heavy responsibility for men, and family life an extremely good recipe for conflict and a yearning by both parties for escape (Ehrenreich 1994). For Goode (1963), the increasing workforce participation of married women, increasing divorce rates and declining fertility were manifestations of this tension lodged at the heart of the breadwinner system.

Case Study
Work/life balance

As women have increasingly taken up paid work outside the home, this does not seem to have had much impact on the division of domestic labour between men and women. Although women do more paid work than they used to, men do not seem to be making up the difference in housework. In addition, many people feel constantly torn between the demands of the workplace and being able to spend time with family and friends.

A recent study of the relationship between work and family life found that 'women are now as annoyed as men at the extent work encroaches on the other facets of life' (Narushima 2009).

1. What effect do you think that the amount of paid work people do these days has on the character of family relationships?
2. Does it make people less inclined to have children or to have fewer children?
3. Does it change the relationships between family members?

MARRIAGE, COHABITATION AND DIVORCE

Important changes have been taking place in family life in all Western industrialised countries, including Australia—changes that are challenging the dominance of the 'conventional family' in society. Part of this change is that marriage appears to be decreasingly central to family life. Fewer people are getting married, they are marrying later, they are having fewer children or none at all, and more people are cohabiting and having children without getting married. The increase in marital breakdown is reflected in rises in the divorce rate.

In 2007, about 87 per cent of the Australian population lived in households consisting of some type of family (88 per cent in 1992), 85 per cent of family households consisted of one-couple families and 14 per cent were single-parent families (ABS 2007b) (see Figure 4.11).

SOCIOLOGY

FIGURE 4.11

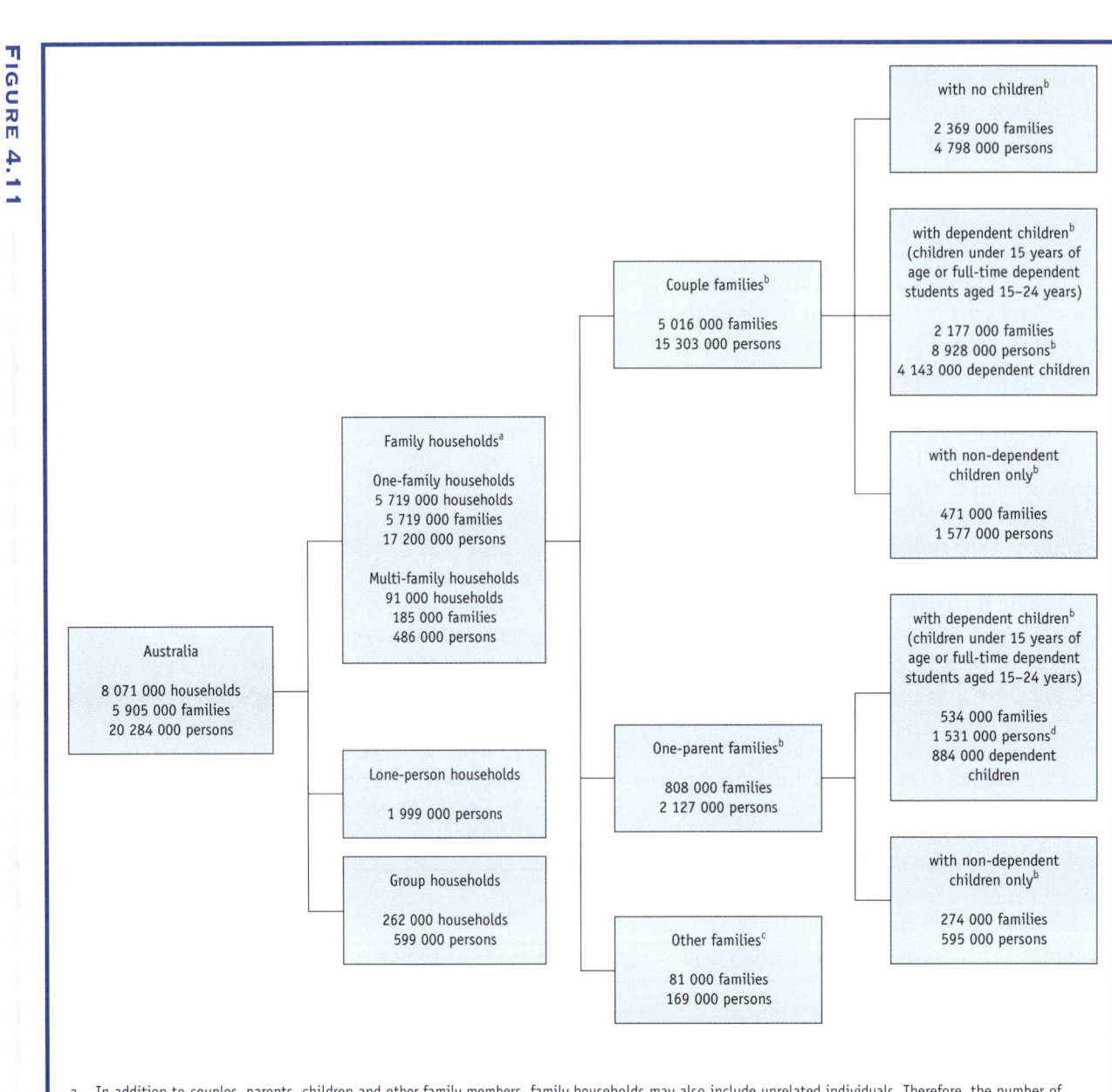

```
Australia
8 071 000 households
5 905 000 families
20 284 000 persons
├── Family households[a]
│   ├── One-family households
│   │   5 719 000 households
│   │   5 719 000 families
│   │   17 200 000 persons
│   └── Multi-family households
│       91 000 households
│       185 000 families
│       486 000 persons
│       ├── Couple families[b]
│       │   5 016 000 families
│       │   15 303 000 persons
│       │   ├── with no children[b]
│       │   │   2 369 000 families
│       │   │   4 798 000 persons
│       │   ├── with dependent children[b]
│       │   │   (children under 15 years of age or full-time dependent students aged 15–24 years)
│       │   │   2 177 000 families
│       │   │   8 928 000 persons[b]
│       │   │   4 143 000 dependent children
│       │   └── with non-dependent children only[b]
│       │       471 000 families
│       │       1 577 000 persons
│       ├── One-parent families[b]
│       │   808 000 families
│       │   2 127 000 persons
│       │   ├── with dependent children[b]
│       │   │   (children under 15 years of age or full-time dependent students aged 15–24 years)
│       │   │   534 000 families
│       │   │   1 531 000 persons[d]
│       │   │   884 000 dependent children
│       │   └── with non-dependent children only[b]
│       │       274 000 families
│       │       595 000 persons
│       └── Other families[c]
│           81 000 families
│           169 000 persons
├── Lone-person households
│   1 999 000 persons
└── Group households
    262 000 households
    599 000 persons
```

a In addition to couples, parents, children and other family members, family households may also include unrelated individuals. Therefore, the number of persons in family households will not equal the number of persons in families.
b These families may include 'other unrelated individuals', but excludes 'unrelated individuals'.
c Refers to families where there are no partners or children (e.g. adult siblings living together without a parent), but excludes unrelated individuals.
d Includes non-dependent children in families with dependent children as well as other related individual and unrelated individuals.

Households, families and persons, June 2007 *Source:* ABS, *Family Characteristics*.

The marriage rate and ex-nuptial child-bearing

Marriage rates among young adults have declined in all Western countries since World War II. Figure 4.12 shows the crude marriage rate (per 1000 mean population, including both remarriages and first marriages) in Australia between 1860 and 2003. Apart from the wartime peaks—World Wars I and II, and the Vietnam War—the overall tendency has been downwards.

These figures should not, however, be interpreted simply as indicating a decline in marriage as a social institution. Gordon Carmichael pointed out that in historical terms 'it is the carefree approach to marriage that peaked around 1970 that is aberrant; statistically,

FIGURE 4.12

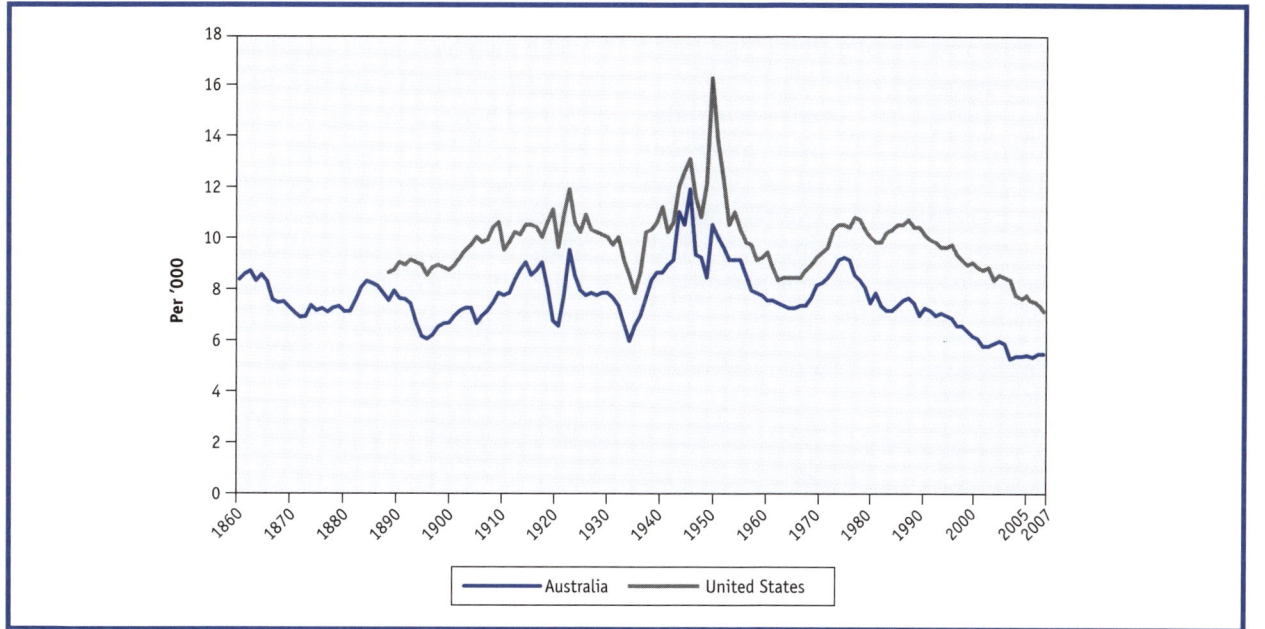

Crude marriage rate, 1860–2007 *Source:* ABS 2007c.

marriage patterns nowadays bear similarities to those of the 1940s' (Carmichael 1990, p. 53).

Australian couples are also marrying at a later age; in 1975 the median age at first marriage was 23.4 years for males and 21.0 years for females; in 2007 this had increased to 29.6 years for males and 27.6 years for females (see Figure 4.13).

Apart from the age at which Australians marry, it is also possible to gauge the general popularity of marriage by looking at the percentage of women who never marry. Peter McDonald pointed out that the proportion of Australian women who never marry moved from a high point of around 15 per cent for those born in the late 1800s, dropped to a low of around 5 per cent

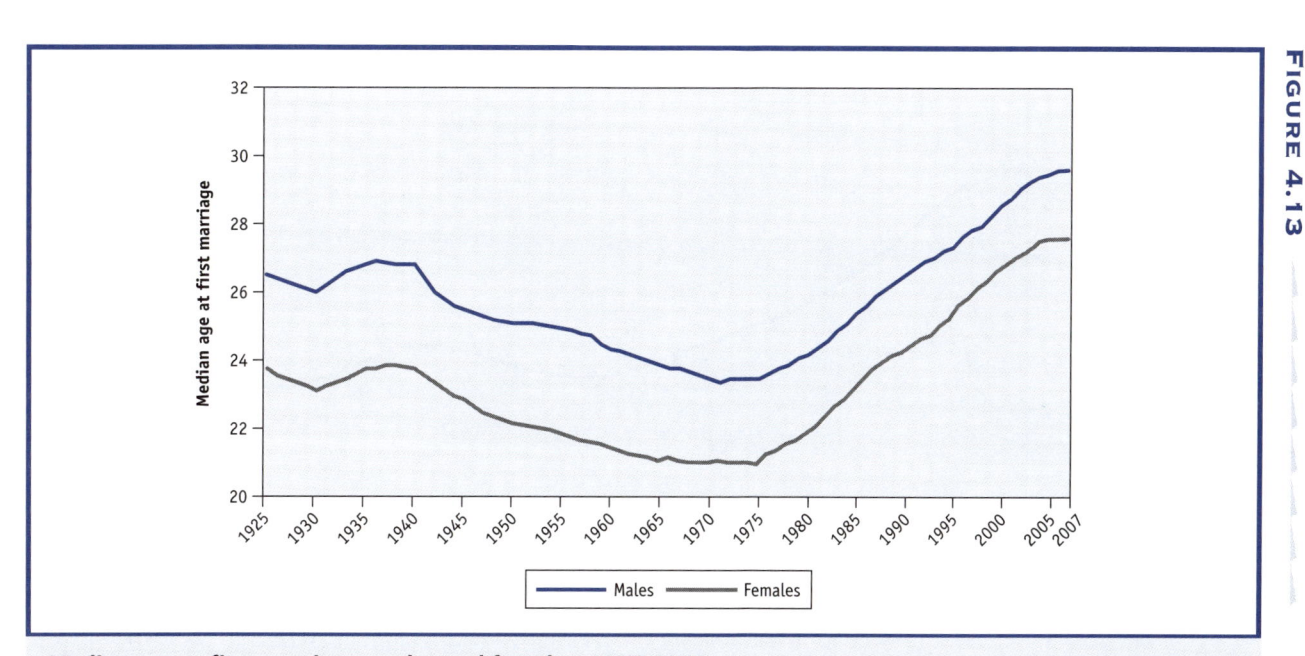

FIGURE 4.13

Median age at first marriage, males and females, 1925–2007 *Source:* ABS, *Marriages and Divorces, Australia* (various years).

for those born between 1920 and 1950, and has since increased towards the formerly high levels for those born since 1950 (see Figures 4.14 and 4.15).

The link between marriage and child-bearing also appears to be weakening over time, with more and more children being born outside marriage. Up until the mid-1960s, the proportion of ex-nuptial births remained roughly steady at around 5 per cent of all births, but since then it has been climbing steadily, to 33.4 per cent in 2007 (see Figure 4.16).

Cohabitation

Cohabitation in 'consensual unions' by couples who are not legally married has increasingly become a form of preparation for marriage, an alternative to marriage itself or a living arrangement following divorce or widowhood (Carmichael 1990; ABS 1995e, p. 135). With the greater tolerance of pre-marital sexuality from the 1960s onwards, marriage has lost its role in legitimising regular sexual activity, making cohabitation before, or instead of, marriage an acceptable lifestyle.

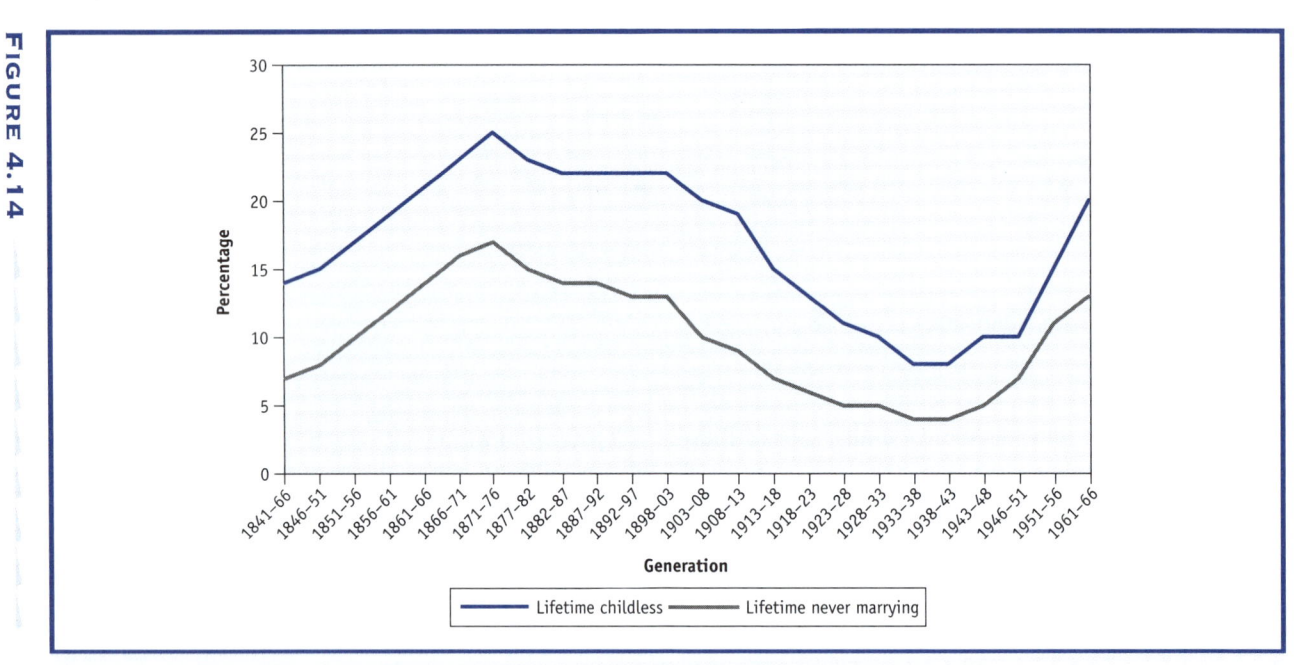

FIGURE 4.14

Lifetime childless, never marrying *Source:* McDonald (1984, p. 44; 1994, p. 155).

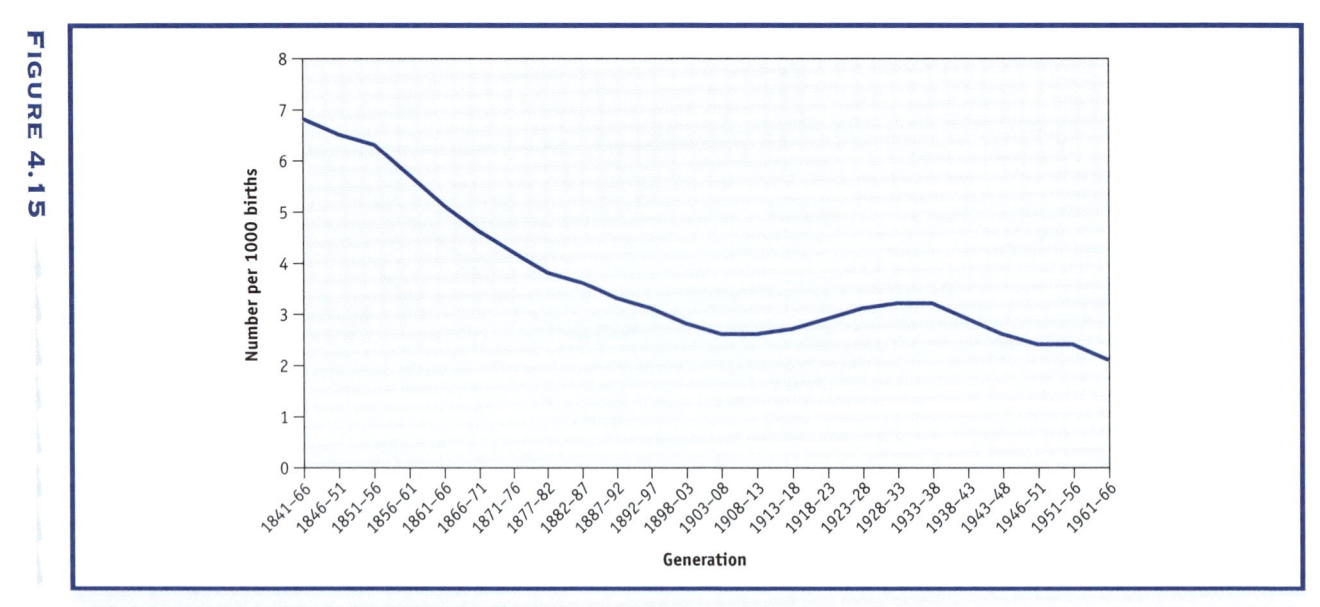

FIGURE 4.15

Births per never-married woman *Source:* McDonald (1984, p. 44; 1994, p. 155).

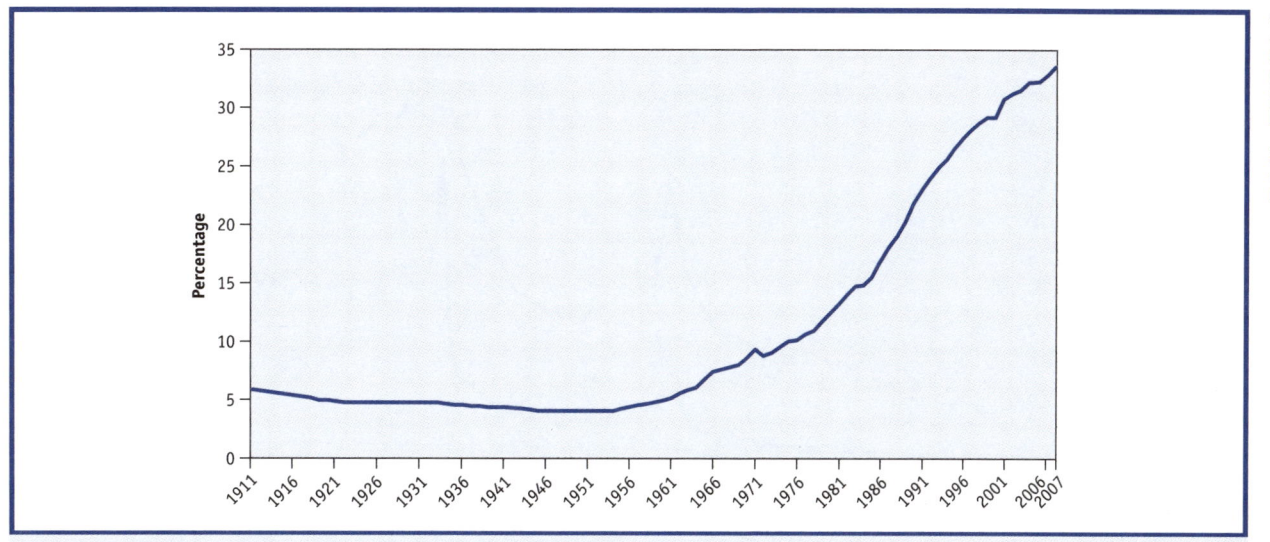

Ex-nuptial births, percentage of total births, 1911–2007 *Source:* ABS, *Births, Australia* (various years).

The proportion of marriages preceded by the couple living together has steadily increased since the 1970s, from around 16 per cent in 1975 to 27 per cent in 1983, nearly 56 per cent in 1992, 75 per cent in 2003, and 76.8 per cent in 2007 (ABS 1995g; 2004h; 2007c). The proportion of people over 15 living as 'socially married' without actually marrying has also gradually increased from 8 per cent in 1991 to 10 per cent in 1996, 12 per cent in 2001 and 15 per cent in 2006 (ABS 2005g, p. 135; 2008a, p. 212).

Single-parent families

Single parenthood became increasingly common in all Western countries from the 1970s onwards. Single-parent families result from the death of one spouse, marriage breakdown or births to unmarried women. The majority of single-parent families are headed by women (83.4 per cent in 2007, down from 86 per cent in 2003) (ABS 2004f, p. 29; 2006d, p. 20).

In Australia in 2007, single-parent families constituted 15 per cent of all families with children under 17, slightly up from 14 per cent in 1989 (ABS 1999c, p. 28; 2002a, p. 30; 2004d, p. 28; 2004f, p. 6; 2006d). However, it is important to note that the proportion of single-parent families was similar a century ago; Peter McDonald noted, for example, that in Victoria in 1891, 16.7 per cent of families with dependent children had only one parent (1995, p. 22).

Divorce

Despite occasional fluctuations, there was a steady rise in the divorce rate in Western industrial societies throughout the 20th century up to the 1980s, after which it began to decline in the United States and Australia (see Figure 4.17). The sudden increase in the divorce rate in Australia in 1976 was due in large part to new family legislation, releasing a backlog of couples with divorces in train, separated couples deciding to proceed to divorce and unstable marriages breaking down earlier than was usual under the previous divorce legislation. However, the divorce rate had already doubled in the ten years before the change in legislation and the figures indicate a general trend towards increasing divorce. As Alan Tapper stated, the divorce rate 'appears to represent a social trend operating relatively independently of the state of the law' (1990, p. 158). He suggested that 'the legal change was as much a response to a social change as it was a cause of social change' (p. 158).

In 1995 Peter McDonald suggested that roughly 1 per cent of children are likely to experience their parents' separation for each year of their life. In other words, 10 per cent of children aged 10 will have divorced or separated parents and 15 per cent of children aged 15 will have divorced or separated parents (McDonald 1995, p. 55).

A slightly different picture is drawn by David de Vaus and Matthew Gray (2004) in their analysis of data from the 2001 Household, Income and Labour Dynamics in Australia (HILDA) household panel survey, which also outlines the extent to which children are more likely to experience parental separation (see Figure 4.18). They observe that 'since 1946, an increasing proportion of children have been experiencing parental separation by the age of 5', although that proportion has remained

SOCIOLOGY

FIGURE 4.17

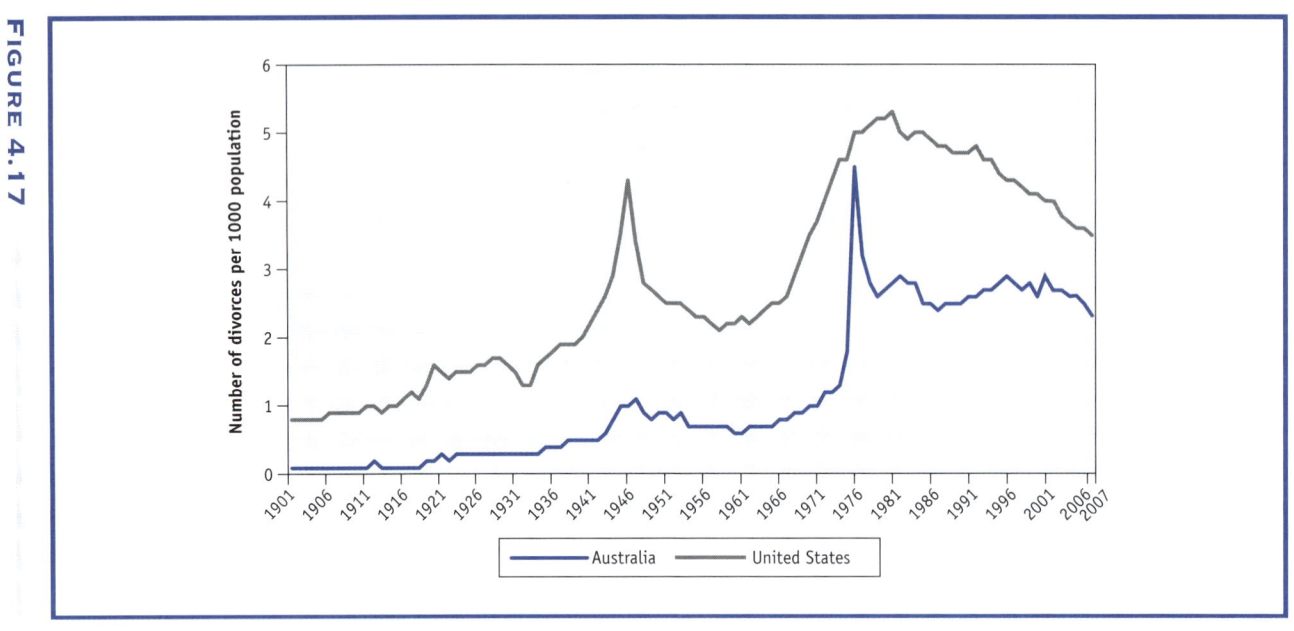

Crude divorce rate, 1901–2007 *Source:* ABS, *Australian Historical Population Statistics*; ABS, *Divorces, Australia* (various years).

roughly steady since the late 1970s (2004, p. 14). For children born between 1981 and 1985, 7.8 per cent of children under 5, 17.1 per cent of children under 10 and 23.4 per cent of children under 15 had experienced parental separation.

This also means that an increasing proportion of children are experiencing a type of family life other than 'mum, dad and the two kids'—they are experiencing more blended or step-families, and more of them spend at least some time with a single parent (see Figure 4.19). For the generation born 1946–55, 94 per cent would only ever live with both their parents, whereas for the generation born 1981–95 that proportion had dropped to 82 per cent. The other 17 per cent would have lived with either step-parents or a single parent by the time they reached the age of 15 (de Vaus & Gray 2004, p. 17).

It is important, however, to put the increase in divorce rates into historical perspective, especially if it leads to the conclusion that family life might be less stable than in the past. McDonald (1995) pointed out that two aspects of the history of divorce tend to be overlooked:

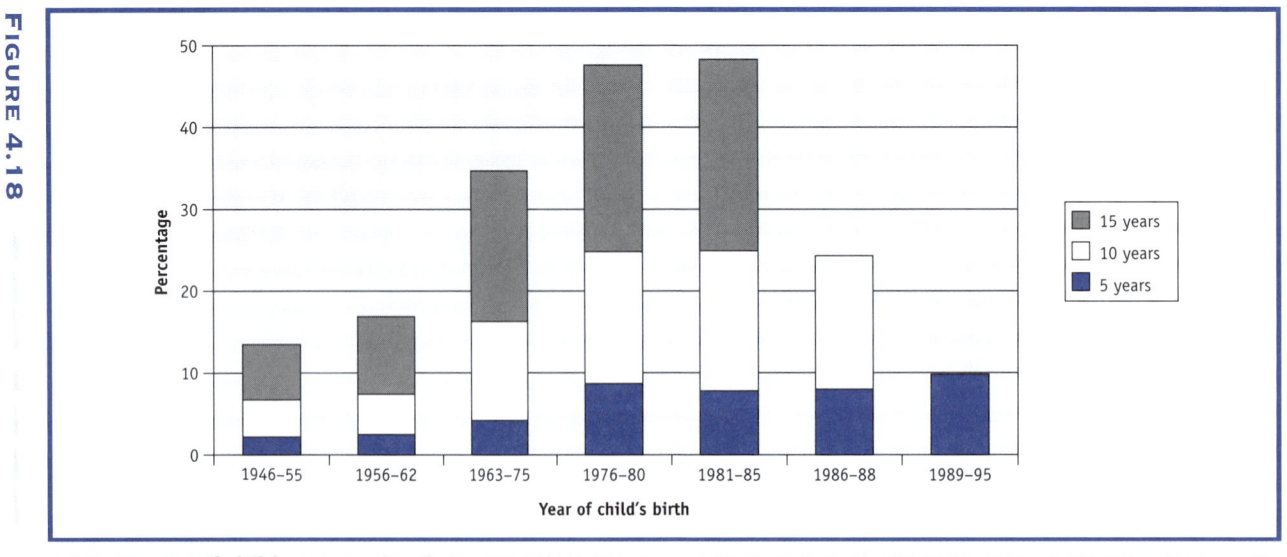

FIGURE 4.18

Percentage of children experiencing separation *Source:* de Vaus & Gray (2004, p. 15) © 1995–2010 eContent Management.

146

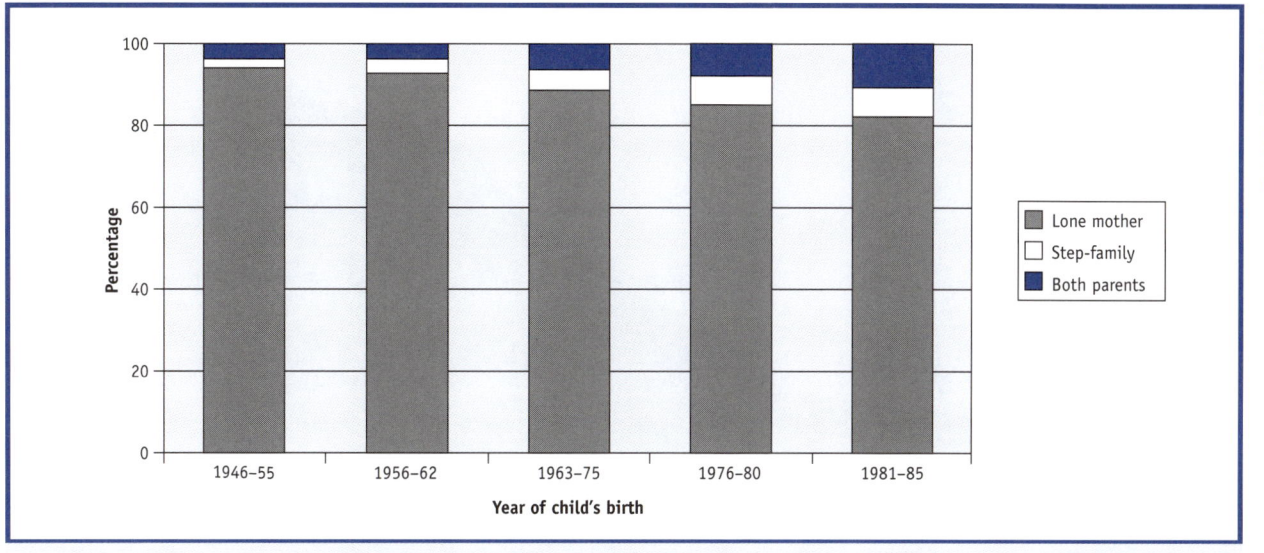

Percentage of time spent in family type by age 15 *Source:* de Vaus & Gray (2004, p. 17) © 1995–2010 eContent Management.

1. A century ago, the death of one spouse, usually the husband, frequently disrupted a marriage. This indicates that at least some of the current divorce rate can be attributed to greater life expectancy.
2. Although formal divorce rates were very low, marriages still broke down. Given that the divorce rate rose slowly to reach about 10 per cent in the mid-1960s, it is reasonable to estimate a separation rate of roughly 10 per cent, with the increasing divorce rate simply reflecting a formalisation of marriage breakdown.

Taking both widowhood and separation into account, McDonald calculated that, in 1991, 53 per cent of couples would be still together after 30 years, whereas, in 1891, 41 per cent of couples were still together after 30 years (1995, pp. 52–3). In this sense, marriage is in fact more stable now than it was a century ago.

Several writers have also pointed out that, although the Australian divorce rate was low compared with that of Sweden and the United States, it did not capture the true extent of marital breakdown, particularly the large number of marriages that effectively ended in desertion and separation, and the often very lengthy period before a separation when one or both partners experienced the marriage as essentially at an end. In 1975, for example, Ailsa Burns (1980) found that only 40 per cent of the men and women in her sample of divorcees who felt that their marriage had broken down in the first five years actually separated in that period. Between 1947 and 1991 a relatively constant proportion of 3–4 per cent of married people regarded themselves as permanently separated (ESCAP 1982, p. 192; ABS 1989; 1991a) (see Figure 4.20). This 'separated but not divorced' group made up 71 per cent of the total divorced and separated population in 1947, 64 per cent in 1961, 58 per cent in 1971, 41 per cent in 1981, 35 per cent in the decade between 1986 and 1996 and 31 per cent in 2001 (ABS 1989; 1991a; 1999i, p. 62; 2003h, p. 9; Burns 1980, p. 21).

The enactment of the *Family Law Act 1975* (Cwlth) and the rising divorce rate are thus partly manifestations of the increasing formalisation of marital breakdown and are insufficient as an indicator of the extent of marital stability. The divorce rate 'tells us more about the society's acceptance of divorce as a feasible solution to marital discord than about the level of discord prevailing in the society' (ESCAP 1982, p. 192).

Explaining divorce

Although divorce is usually associated with a decline in the values attached to marriage and family life, it may in fact be the result of precisely the opposite—higher expectations about the way that marriage is meant to be experienced, with greater intimacy, no domestic violence or abuse of children and lasting over a longer period of time. Ronald Fletcher, for example, argued that 'a relatively high divorce rate may be indicative not of lower but of higher standards of marriage in society' (1966, p. 213).

It is also important to remember that until relatively recently, more marriages were dissolved by death than by divorce, and increasing divorce rates have some connection with increasing life expectancy. As David

FIGURE 4.20

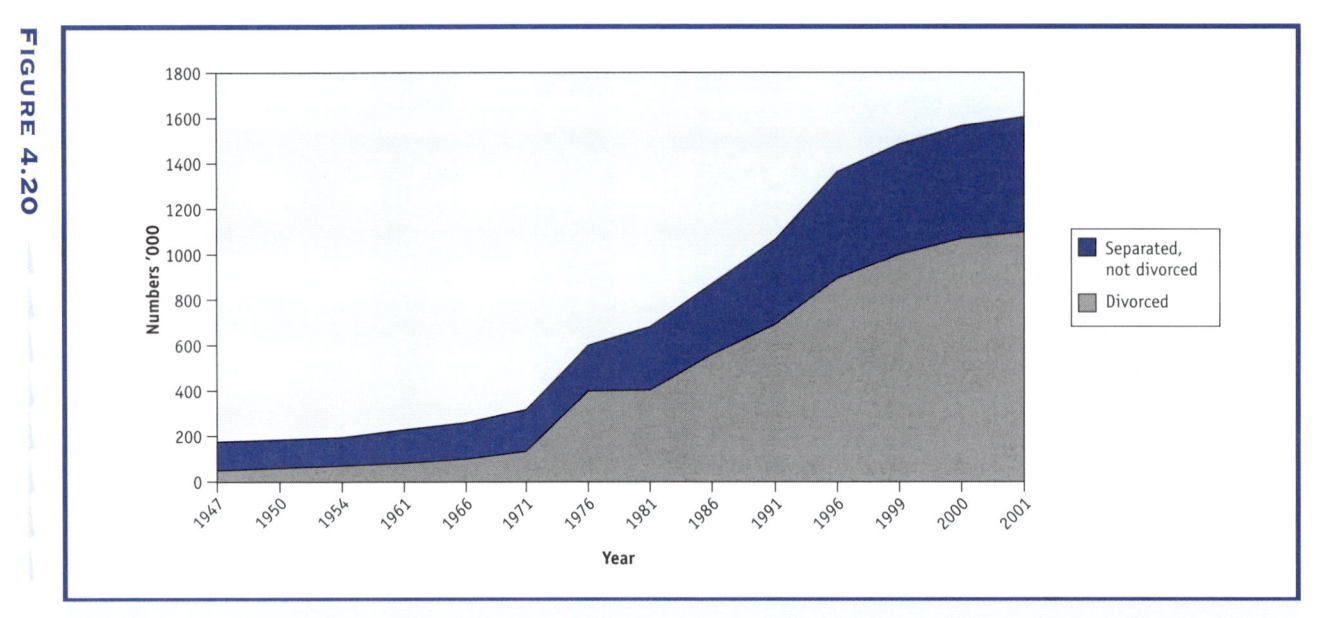

Divorces and separated, not divorced, 1947–2001 *Source:* ESCAP (1982, p. 192) and ABS (1989; 1991a; 1999h, p. 62).

Popenoe observed, 'a landmark of sorts was passed in 1974, when for the first year in American history more marriages ended in divorce than in death' (1993, p. 532).

Australian demographer Lincoln Day has argued that emotional bonds are the primary basis for family life, and family life has become almost the only place where emotional needs can be met. Under present demographic, economic and social conditions—fewer siblings, fewer or no children, increased geographic mobility, greater workforce participation by women— the number of people in a position to respond to those needs has declined. Given this increasing emotional dependence on the family, Day stated:

especially upon the husband–wife relationship within it as a haven of refuge from the pressures and lack of emotional supports in the outside world—one is seriously tempted to ask not why, at current rates, about one-fifth of Australian marriages can be expected to end in divorce, but rather why it is that some four-fifths of them can be expected not to. (1979, pp. 30–1)

Changing attitudes towards divorce have been institutionalised by various changes in the law, which have made divorce much easier to obtain. Australian divorce law was based on the English Divorce Act of 1857, eventually codified in separate legislation for each colony, from South Australia in 1858 to New South Wales in 1873. Over time, each state modified its legislation without reference to the other states, producing a patchwork of legislation that was standardised by the *Matrimonial Causes Act 1959* (Cwlth). This legislation provided for divorce on a range of grounds of 'fault'— such as mental cruelty, adultery, drunkenness, desertion for more than three years—or a five-year separation (ESCAP 1982, p. 184).

The *Family Law Act 1975* abolished the concept of fault and allowed for no-fault divorce on only one ground, 'irretrievable breakdown', established after a separation of 12 months. The Act is based on the idea that the sorts of conduct formerly regarded as indications of fault are symptoms rather than causes of marital breakdown, and that the breakdown of a marriage cannot be attributed to only one of the partners (Harrison 1989). Resolution of conflicts concerning custody of children and property is now based primarily on considerations of the welfare and best interests of the child.

The concern with individual autonomy has filtered through to family life, so that marriage is no longer regarded as an institutionalised, non-negotiable lifelong commitment, but as only one way among many of meeting more fundamental emotional and psychological needs, and one that should be abandoned if those needs are not being met (McDonald 1988).

The economics of marriage and separation have changed in a number of ways that make separation, at the same time, a less unattractive option for women but, in some senses, a desirable choice for both partners. Single parents are still highly likely to be destined for relative poverty or, at the very least, a significant decline in living standards. However, Carmichael and McDonald argued that the increased workforce participation of women since World War II, accelerating after the 1960s, made it more possible for women, especially if they had not yet had children, to be economically independent. The introduction of the supporting mother's (now supporting parent's) benefit in 1973 also provided welfare support to women leaving a marriage, whereas previously they were only entitled to support as deserted wives if the divorce was initiated by the husband (1986, p. 23). The overall decline in fertility also made it easier to end marriages that were found to be unsatisfactory at an early stage, before children were born (p. 25).

There have been gender differences in relation to who takes the initiative in seeking divorce. The portrait painted in the book edited by Dale Spender, *Weddings and Wives* (Spender 1994), shows that women are more unhappy with married life than men, wanting to leave husbands who are unable or unwilling to adjust to a different division of domestic labour and changing gender roles. There is some basis to this picture. Ailsa Burns, for example, found in 1975, before the passage of the Family Law Act, that 37 per cent of wives said that their marriage had begun to break down in its first year, compared with 24 per cent of husbands, and 15 per cent of wives felt that the breakdown had begun in the first three months of the marriage (Burns 1980, p. 42).

However, this pattern has been changing since the early 1980s. The applications filed by females have dropped from 59 per cent in 1984 to 39 per cent in 2007; applications filed by males have also dropped, from 40 per cent in 1984 to 27 per cent in 2007; while joint applications have increased from 0.4 per cent in 1984, when they were first made possible, to 34 per cent in 2007 (ABS 1993d; 2005c; 2007d) (see Figure 4.21). The decision to divorce appears increasingly to be one that both partners make together.

> **Reflective question:** Why do people get married, and why do they divorce?

CHILDREN AND CHILDHOOD

Until the 1980s, there was not really a distinct sociology of childhood. Within sociology itself, children were subsumed within the family as a whole; they were more or less the province of developmental psychology and education, and were generally subsumed within studies of the family, socialisation and perhaps youth. In 1950, Erik Erikson complained about the absence of 'reference to the fact that all people start as children and that all peoples begin in their nurseries' (1950, p. 16). In 1973, the anthropologist Charlotte Hardman proposed that children should be 'studied in their own right, and not just as receptacles of adult teaching', aiming to reveal 'whether there is in childhood a self-regulating, autonomous world which does not necessarily reflect early development of adult culture' and suggesting that 'at the level of behaviour, values, symbols, games, beliefs and oral traditions, there may be a dimension exclusive to the child' (p. 87).

The dominance of the concept of socialisation (Alanen 1988, pp. 57–61) meant that until the 1980s the sociological approach to children was framed in terms of their 'becoming' adult and as 'productions' of the

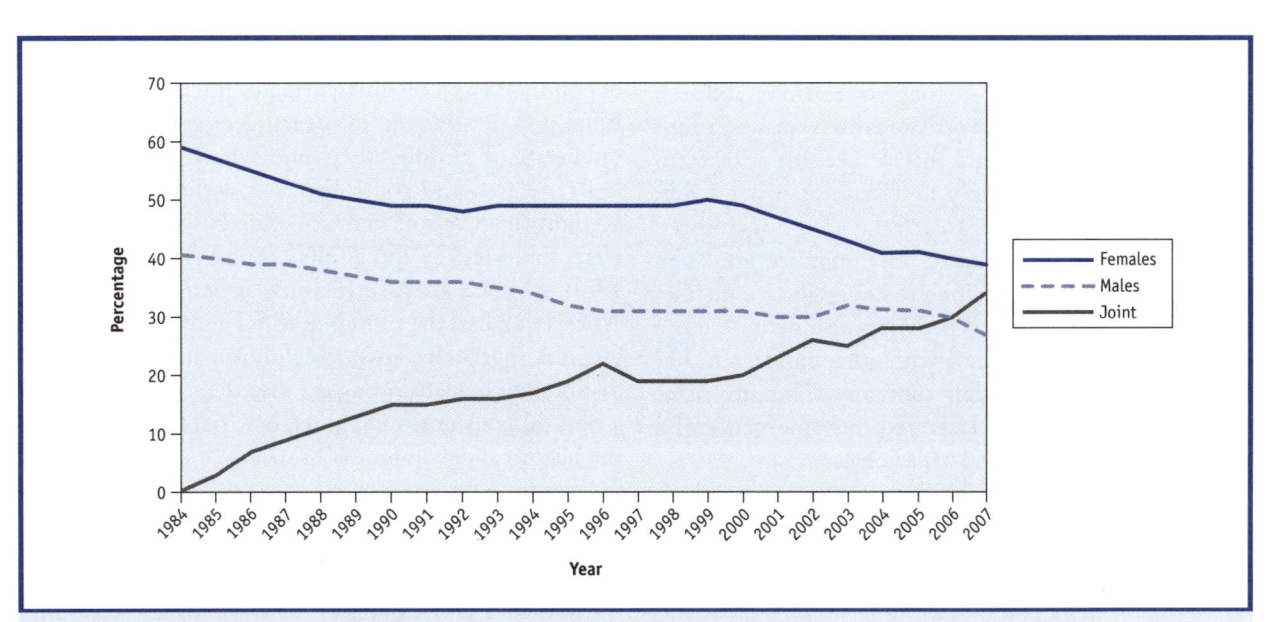

FIGURE 4.21

Applications for divorce, 1984–2007 *Source:* ABS, *Marriages and Divorces* (various years); *Divorces, Australia* (2003–2007).

family and the school (Alanen 1988; Qvortrup 1993b; James & Prout 1997; Lee 1998). The broader concern in sociology with class, inequality and social mobility led to a concentration on the structural constraints exercised by children's familial background. In the 1960s and 1970s socialisation research concentrated on the ways in which a 'proper' childhood functioned to (re-)produce and legitimate social inequality. The statistics on participation in education since the 1960s have made it clear that the social position of the family of origin—and initially also other variables of inequality such as gender, region and religion—has a very clear influence on children's educational chances (Coleman 1966; Bourdieu & Passeron 1977; Jencks 1972; Boudon 1974; Halsey, Heath & Ridge 1980; Connell 1994).

CENTURIES OF CHILDHOOD— PHILLIPPE ARIÈS

French historian Phillippe Ariès' 1960 book *L'enfant et la vie familiale sous l'Ancien Régime* (published in English in 1962 as *Centuries of Childhood*) played a central role in the shift away from a focus on socialisation. Also influential was Lloyd de Mause's (1974) *The History of Childhood*. Ariès established childhood as having a history and children as having been understood and treated differently in different historical periods. Ariès spoke of both the 'invention' of childhood as a distinct phase of life and the emergence of a particular 'sentiment' towards children, in association with particular social conditions and particular configurations of power relations between different social groups.

Ariès showed that the language concerning children shifted, with the range of words and different age groups gradually expanding. Until the 18th century, the term 'childhood' referred simply to a state of dependence, rather than a stage of life. In art, the image of children shifted from being portrayed as miniature adults in ancient and medieval painting to being given a distinct identity as children. Their activities also became more distinct, spending more time with other children rather than always being in adult company. The advent of mass schooling clearly accelerated this emergence of a distinct arena of childhood experience.

Thus, the very idea of childhood as a separate phase of life was a particularly modern phenomenon. As Ariès wrote:

In medieval society, the idea of childhood did no exist; this is not to suggest that children were neglected, forsaken or despised. The idea of childhood is not to be confused with affection for children: it corresponds to an awareness of the particular nature of childhood, that particular nature which distinguishes the child from the adult, even the young adult. In medieval society, this awareness was lacking. This is why, as soon as the child could live without the constant solicitude (care) of his mother, his nanny or his cradle-rocker, he belonged to adult society. (1962, p. 125)

Children increasingly became the object of a number of contradictory concerns, ideas and feelings—coddled as being in need of love and care, a source of amusement and entertainment, a source of fear and anxiety, and an object of regulation and control. This challenge to the idea of childhood as 'natural' paved the way for the concept of the *social construction of childhood* and contributed to the mobilisation of this concept in a number of different contexts and situations, in relation to a variety of questions and issues.

There have been extensive critiques of Ariès' methods and his interpretation of the evidence (e.g. Pollock 1983; Luke 1989; Burton 1989). The core themes in the criticisms are, first, that Ariès assumes rather than shows the relationships between the development of language and art and the social reality of childhood experience. The fact that children were portrayed as miniature adults, for example, might have had more to do with conventions and techniques in painting than with the way people felt about children. Second, it is not clear how *ideas* about childhood relate to the *social organisation* of childhood. Is Ariès really talking about the second rather than the first? Third, there is a range of contrary historical evidence indicating a clear sense of childhood as a distinct period of life in earlier times. Finally, Ariès seemed to regard the period before the discovery of childhood as one where children were less regulated and controlled, but without taking into account the levels of violence and abuse to which they were subjected by the adults around them (de Mause 1974). Despite these criticisms, it remains true that Ariès' book laid the foundations for contemporary sociological approaches towards children and generational distinctions by developing the idea that childhood is not a natural constant, but rather is variable according to the historical development of society.

REGULATION AND RIGHTS

From the middle of the 19th century, with the gradual introduction and expansion of compulsory schooling, children came to be seen as requiring at least temporary isolation from the labour market in order to undergo the discipline of various types of school and become 'good and useful men and women' (van Krieken 1989), so that the length of time spent in institutionalised education gradually continued to increase. At around the same time, the distinct position occupied by children in relation to the law, especially with respect to crime and punishment, was given additional institutional shape (Platt 1969) and their exposure to violence and adult sexuality came to be understood as a social problem requiring various forms of organised intervention. The notion that children can be and are abused by their parents and other adults is now broadly accepted in a way that it was not prior to World War II (Parton 1985). Thus, in many respects the Swedish pedagogue Ellen Key (1909) was correct to declare the 20th century 'the century of the child'.

In *Pricing the Priceless Child*, Viviana Zelizer (1985) showed how one can see a shift in the ideologies surrounding childhood in Western societies between the 1870s and 1930s, from a conception of children as 'useful' to a much more sentimental and emotional one of the 'priceless' child. The shift was a contentious one. The construction of childhood as a sphere cordoned off from the labour market made most sense for middle-class and 'respectable working-class' parents, but was deeply problematic for many working-class families (Olsen 2000), so that it was not until after World War II that one could speak more or less genuinely of 'universal' primary education. The shift that Zelizer identifies was heavily dependent on state intervention—mainly policing ever-expanding legislation against children's employment and truancy, and gradually raising the minimum school-leaving age—which is why Therborn speaks of modern childhood as 'a creation by the nation-state, against the threatening encroachments of the market (for child labour) and against the sovereignty of *patria potestas*, of paternal power and the seclusion of the family' (1996, p. 30).

Beginning with the League of Nations' Declaration of Children's Rights in 1924, and decisively reinforced by the UN Convention on the Rights of the Child (UNCRC) in 1989, an essential element of the social and political discourses surrounding children is now that they have certain kinds of rights specific to them, even if the actual meaning and effect of the idea varies enormously (Roche 1999; Freeman 1983; 1997; 1998; Alston, Parker & Seymour 1992; Guggenheim 2005). For example, the process of adoption used to be seen simply as an arrangement between the relevant adults, but now children who are adopted are seen as being entitled to a certain kind of relationship with their biological parents. When parents divorce, the 'best interests' of their children play an increasingly significant role in the identification of post-custody arrangements, although different countries adopt a more or less participatory approach to the construction of those 'best interests' (van Krieken 2005; Bühler-Niederberger 2003; James, James & McNamee 2004).

THE SOCIAL CONSTRUCTION OF CHILDHOOD

In line with these broader developments, in the last few decades there has been an upsurge in the interest in what is specific about childhood and the experiences of children. In the development of sociological thinking and research, the identification of a distinct field for the study of childhood began to take off in the 1980s (Jenks 1982; Synnott 1983; Thorne 1987; Alanen 1988) and in the United Kingdom this stream of sociological thought has been called 'the new sociology of childhood' (James & Prout 1997).

Recent developments in social theory and the methodology of the social sciences have contributed to the greater visibility of children's issues and childhood among sociologists. The weakening of the centrality of conceptions of class and economic production processes in sociological research was linked to the greater visibility of various other types of social groups, such as women and then children. The feminist critique of sociological thought had the effect of disaggregating and decomposing 'the family', making it possible to render first women, but then also inevitably children, visible to social researchers (Thorne 1987). The 'return of the actor' in sociology (Touraine 1988) also had the effect of drawing attention to every type of social actor and opened the door to the inclusion of children as actors.

The question of changing relations of power and authority between adults and children has led many childhood scholars towards the concept of a 'generational order/ordering' to capture the significance of adult–child relationships for the social production of both adulthood and childhood. In this sense childhood is seen as a having a social-structural character similar to class, race or gender. As Leena Alanen put it:

Hence childhood, too, is a relational concept: childhood only exists in relation to adulthood ... This leads to the suggestions that parallel to a 'gender agenda' we can also imagine a 'generational agenda' being at work—a particular social order that organizes children's relations to the world in a systematic way, allocates them positions from which to act and a view and knowledge about themselves and their social relations. (1994, p. 37)

In one sense every generational order is one of conflict (or at least potential conflict), to the extent that there is a power relation between adults and children, and constant cooperation between the two age groups, without which the daily practices of 'growing up' could not be realised.

The organisation of sociological thinking around the concept of 'socialisation' has had two important effects: first, it blocks an adequate view of children's capacity for agency in relation to the structural demands of socialisation processes (Speier 1976; James & Prout 1997; Lee 1998); and second, it approaches children primarily in terms of what they are in the process of *becoming*—adults-in-the-making—rather than what they actually *are*, subsuming the category of childhood to those of class, gender and race (Qvortrup 1985). The 'new sociology of childhood' is primarily an extended effort to address these two deficits and to develop a range of research programs that follow through the conceptual and empirical consequences of examining what it means to see children as 'actors' and to pay greater attention to the 'generational order'.

Against this background, it is possible to distinguish, very roughly, three different types of theoretical approach in the field:

- The *structural approach* studies the statistical distribution of poverty, wealth, life chances, health conditions, educational outcomes and so on (Scraton 1997; Sgritta, 1996; Bradshaw & Mayhew 2005).
- The *historical and constructivist approach* analyses discourses and practices concerning childhood, including the construction of expertise and scientific knowledge concerning children and the emergence of particular strategies of governance in relation to childhood (Ambert 1986; Donzelot 1979; Hendrick 1997; Zelizer 1985; Nelson 1984; Best 1990; Bühler-Niederberger 1998; James, Jenks & Prout 1998; McGillivray 1997).
- In an *ethnographic approach* one studies interaction and communication in children's everyday experiences, in the family and at school, on the street, among peers, at play, etc. (Mehan 1974; 1979; Alanen & Mayall, 2001; Corsaro 1992).

The central empirical concerns in sociological studies of childhood today can be grouped, very roughly, into the following areas:

1. children's actual experiences, particularly their active participation in family life, the public sphere and schooling, children's play and use of space
2. children's rights, citizenship, and legal processes and institutions more broadly, especially in relation to criminal law
3. children's lives beyond family and school, especially working and on the street, and particularly in developing countries
4. inequality, in terms of gender, class, race, ethnicity, the rural/urban divide and globally
5. children and divorce
6. the different dimensions and effects of particular institutional contexts such as health, education and welfare.

There are also a range of other fields of study that are important, such as children's experiences of war (as child soldiers and as civilians), children as refugees, the impact of television and the media, and cultural constructions and representations of childhood. Here we take a closer look at three of these topics: children's lives beyond the family, children and divorce, and children and child abuse (for a detailed discussion of the others, see van Krieken & Bühler-Niederberger 2009).

> **Reflective questions:** How would you say that your experience of childhood was different from that of your parents' experiences? What do you think are the negatives and positives of the changes that have taken place?

Children's lives beyond the family

One problem with Zelizer's account of the changing adult conceptions of childhood, as Zelizer herself has written recently, is that it does not have much to say about 'children's own experiences of economic change' (2002, p. 377; see also Zelizer 2005; Miller 2005). The concept of a 'normal childhood' tends to disguise not only very basic competencies of social action, but also what has to be considered as informal or even formal work.

Zelizer pleads, accordingly, for an accompanying consideration of 'children as active economic agents, and adults as simply one category of persons with whom children carry on economic activities' (2002, p. 377). She argues against analysing modern children simply as consumers, in favour of seeing them as also playing pivotal roles in production and distribution across three types of social relations with: (1) other members of their households; (2) organisations outside their own families; and (3) other children. In her review of the relevant literature on children as economic agents, she finds that children's activities in the spheres of production, distribution and consumption show significant autonomy from those of adults, although they generally experience their relationship with adults as one of the unequal exercise of power (2002, p. 379). Children's contribution to domestic labour, for example, is now extensively 'monetarised' in the form of allowances which generate complex household economies.

The question of children's work becomes still more significant when we look beyond Western societies. Some of the central critiques of the 'priceless child' thesis were that most families across the globe do not have the luxury of excluding their children from economically productive activities, that the analysis really only accounts for developments in economically highly developed countries and that increasing levels of poverty and inequality endanger the argument even in the advanced industrial parts of the world. Zelizer suggests, then, that social scientific research into children's economic activity needs to be developed in the following three directions:

> ... towards the variable and unequal experiences of children within high-income capitalist countries; towards the enormous variety of children's circumstances in the lower-income regions where most of the world's kids actually live; towards the historical changes that are transforming children's economic relations in rich and poor countries alike. (2002, p. 393)

This is now one of the most important areas of research in the sociology of childhood, examining the nature, structure and dynamics of children's economic activity in developed as well as developing countries (Lavalette 1994; 1996), the relationship between child labour and the concept of children's rights (Myers 1999) and broader labour relations standards (Blagbrough & Glynn 1999), the role of organisations such as trades unions (Myrstad 1999) and working children themselves (Liebel 2003).

Children and divorce

A significant amount of research has been done over the last few decades on differing approaches to the parent–child relationship, changing expectations of both mothers and fathers, changing authority relations between parents and children (with the 'discipline' question only the most obvious one), the impact of divorce and how it is managed, the role that children should play in divorce arrangements and the question of children's 'voice' in separation and divorce proceedings (Smart, Neale & Wade 2001).

A central conceptual problem that all researchers in the area are compelled to address in one way or another is that of the real meaning of the catch-all term 'the best interests of the child' (van Krieken 2005). This concept is relied upon heavily in political and legal terms to resolve ambiguities and contradictions in family conflicts, to function as a sort of 'trump card' cutting through the knots of contemporary family life, but at the cost of leaving unresolved a number of other problems, some normative and some empirical—such as exactly why the interests of children should outweigh those of their parents, how a child's interests might align with those of their parents or their community, and how the interests of a child at one time should be related to some hypothetical assessment of their interests in the future.

In practice the identification of 'the best interests of the child' is actually a matter of weighing up some interests against others, and in this process a variety of other concerns come into play invisibly and behind the scenes. These mechanisms then become an important topic of research in the sociology of childhood, to go beyond the 'naturalised' presentation of children's 'best interests' and uncover the social forces constituting their conceptualisation. As Carol Smart and her colleagues have observed, children's experiences of separation and divorce are often 'about resilience, transformations, growing self-reflexiveness, and the development of a new set of perspectives on parenting and family practices' (Smart, Neale & Wade 2001, p. 173). The research and policy problem then becomes one of identifying the ways in which children manage 'the personal and social transformations associated with family change' (p. 173).

Child abuse and neglect

The experience that is now referred to as child abuse and neglect has a history to it, in the sense that the concepts used to capture the phenomenon have only gradually emerged in the course of the 20th century, along with shifting attitudes to the treatment of children. Much that we now regard as clearly abusive has in the past been seen as a normal part of childhood experience, or at worst something at which one simply shrugged one's shoulders. Girls who were raped by their uncles, fathers or step-fathers would be sent to reformatories as being 'in moral danger', and boys who were the target of their parents' physical violence or sexual abuse would be sent to industrial schools for being 'uncontrollable' (van Krieken 1991). Carol Smart observes that there was no single concept for everything we now call child abuse and neglect: it was termed 'unlawful carnal knowledge, incest, criminal assault, indecent assault, an outrage, an unnatural act, a slip and so on. It was not conceptualized as abuse, and hence was not referred to as such until the 1970s' (Smart, C. 1999, p. 393).

Simulated to a large extent by feminist critiques of family life, the attitude to the treatment of children shifted in all Western countries in the 1960s and 1970s, focusing first on physical abuse (Kempe et al. 1962) and then on sexual abuse, so that we can speak of the 'discovery' of child (and spousal) abuse in that period (Bala 2008; Parton 1985). Numerous approaches were taken to explaining child abuse and neglect, but as Michael Gilding (1997) sums it up, there were three main lines of argument pursued by sociologists: the first was to link physical abuse with the broader use of physical punishment in society; the second was to see child abuse 'as an extension of gender relations in the family' (p. 231), especially the power relations between men and women within family life; and the third was to pay attention to the role of social inequality 'in creating the conditions for child abuse; hence the association between child abuse and poverty' (p. 231). This was particularly relevant for the understanding of child abuse and neglect among Aboriginal families. Overall, the core concern was to move beyond seeing the abuse and neglect of children simply as a manifestation of individual psychological pathology, to see how 'abuse was embedded in wider familial and social processes' (p. 232).

In Australia today child abuse and neglect is differentiated into the following four categories:

1. *physical abuse:* any non-accidental physical act inflicted on a child by a person having the care of a child
2. *sexual abuse:* any act by a person having the care of the child that exposes the child to, or involves the child in, sexual processes beyond his or her understanding or contrary to accepted community standards
3. *emotional abuse:* any act by a person having the care of a child that results in the child suffering any kind of significant emotional deprivation or trauma
4. *neglect:* any serious omissions or commissions by a person having the care of a child which, within the bounds of cultural tradition, constitute a failure to provide conditions that are essential for the healthy, physical and emotional development of a child (Australian Institute of Health and Welfare 2009, pp. 99–100).

The Australian Institute of Health and Welfare (2009, pp. viii–ix) highlights four aspects of the more recent trends in the incidence of child abuse and neglect. First, the number of child protection notifications increased by 26 per cent over the four years from 2004–05 to 2007–08, from 252 831 to 317 526. Second, the number of substantiate notifications rose from 46 154 in 2004–05 to 60 230 in 2006–07, before falling to 55 120 in 2007–08. Third, there was significant variation across the different states in the rates of children who were the subject of notification, between 20.9 per thousand in Western Australia to 11.9 in the Northern Territory. Finally, the rates among Indigenous children on care and protection orders were more than seven times those of non-Indigenous children.

TOWARDS THE 'POST-FAMILIAL FAMILY'?

All the changes in family life discussed throughout this chapter have posed a challenge to sociological theory to develop appropriate conceptual tools to understand and explain them. One useful outline of the range of perspectives is that there are essentially three theoretical orientations running through the research in changes in family life, which Gillies (2003) characterises as:

1. breakdown and demoralisation
2. democratisation and egalitarianism
3. continuity and enduring power relations (p. 15).

The first two perspectives see family relationships as having been subjected to significant transformations, with the 'breakdown' approach seeing the changes in negative terms and the 'democratisation' approach placing a more positive evaluation on how family life

> *Marriage and the family used to be firmly embedded in a matrix of wider community relationships ... There were few separating barriers between the world of the individual family and the wider community ... The same social life pulsated through the house, the street and the community ... In our contemporary society, by contrast, each family constitutes its own segregated sub-world ... This fact requires a much greater effort on the part of the marriage parties. Unlike in earlier situations in which the establishment of the new marriage simply added to the differentiation and complexity of an already existing social world, the marriage partners now are embarked on the often difficult task of constructing for themselves the little world in which they live. (Berger & Kellner 1974, pp. 162–3)*

has changed. The 'continuity' approach, in contrast, is critical of the idea that family life has been radically altered, placing much more emphasis on the contrary evidence showing how family relations have remained more or less stable, with especially the power relations between men and women and between adults and children being slow to change.

Family 'decline'

For some observers of family life since the 1960s, changes such as rising divorce rates, declining fertility, increased extra-marital cohabitation, increased rates of illegitimacy and single parenthood, and the spread of non-traditional family forms are all indications of a decline of the family, which is linked to a range of other social problems such as truancy, unemployment, mental illness, juvenile delinquency and crime, and child abuse. Gillies (2003, p. 7) gives the example of Charles Murray's (1994) theory of the underclass, which links illegitimacy and single parenthood to crime rates and economic decline based on a 'culture of dependency'.

One of the more detailed presentations of this perspective is the work of American sociologist David Popenoe (1988; 1993), who sees the current state of family life as the end point of a long historical process of losing its functions to other social institutions, to such an extent that family life is becoming decreasingly able to fulfil the last two functions left to it: raising children, and providing affection and companionship. Popenoe defines the family fairly broadly as 'a relatively small domestic group of kin (or people in a kin-like relationship) consisting of at least one adult and one dependent person' (1993, p. 529). It thus includes single-parent families, step-families, non-married and homosexual couples, and all other family types in which dependents are involved (p. 529), with dependency including the elderly and the handicapped. The functions that the family fulfils, or the needs that it meets, are defined by Popenoe as including:

> ... procreation (reproduction) and the socialization of children; the provision to its members of care, affection, and companionship; economic cooperation (the sharing of economic resources, especially shelter, food, and clothing); and sexual regulation (so that sexual activity in a society is not completely permissive and people are made responsible for the consequences of their sexuality). (1993, p. 529)

It is what Popenoe and others observe as the decreasing ability of family life to meet these needs that constitutes their sense of family life being in decline.

As Popenoe sees it, the decline in fertility indicates a decreasing valuation of children, especially in relation to other concerns such as occupational success, leisure, consumption and self-fulfilment. People have 'become less willing to invest time, money, and energy in family life, turning instead to investments in themselves' (p. 528). For Popenoe, separation, divorce and single parenthood primarily constitute instability in family life. The same is true of the changed evaluation of marriage itself, in which it is seen less as a stable obligation for life and more as a route to self-fulfilment, from which one departs if it is no longer achieving that end.

The issue at the core of Popenoe's argument that the changes in family life should be seen as problematic is that of the effects on children's lives and wellbeing. The rise of individualism and the fluidity in interpersonal relationships that underpin the fundamental transformations of family life have reached a 'saturation point' for Popenoe and other like-minded observers of family change in relation to the care of children. The perceived danger is that the sense of mutual obligation characterising all relations of dependency, but especially between adults and children, might become so overwhelmed by the desire for individual self-fulfilment that people lose the capacity to care for each other adequately.

> A representation of the kind of lifestyle that Popenoe fears constitutes the fatal decline of family life would be that found in the television series *Seinfeld*, where the characters spend all of their time with each other, with other adults, at work or in leisure activities. Their only real interpersonal obligations are to their parents, whom they see as little as possible and regard primarily as a rather irritating, albeit unavoidable burden. The possibility that they might sacrifice any of their self-gratification to that of a child is not even remotely entertained in the program's worldview.

However, the same characteristics of family life can also be viewed through a different conceptual lens and be presented in a more positive light.

Democratisation and egalitarianism— Giddens, Beck and Beck-Gernsheim

Two of the most influential versions of the 'democratisation' approach are Anthony Giddens' account of the increasing *reflexivity* of personal and family life in what he calls 'high modernity', and Ulrich Beck and Elisabeth Beck-Gernsheim's analysis of the 'normal chaos of love' in the context of increasing *individualisation*. As one commentary emphasises, it is particularly within the field of family studies that 'the use of Beck's and Giddens' theories are extensive, often both as broad, sweeping framing statements about what world "we" live in and as tools for interpreting empirical accounts' (Mulinari & Sandell 2009, p. 494).

Both approaches centre on an account of modern societies having moved, from about the 1970s onwards, to a new stage of 'high', 'late' or 'second' modernity, characterised by heightened *reflexivity* and *individualisation*. These two processes, in turn, are central, accelerated aspects of the overall transition from tradition to modernity, or 'de-traditionalisation'—the gradual emancipation of individuals from the constraints of tradition, culture, social status, occupational position, gender, race, ethnicity, community, church dogma or kin network. The election of Barack Obama as President of the United States would be seen from this perspective as a leading illustration of de-traditionalisation and 'second' modernity (and President *Michelle* Obama would be an even better example).

The Transformation of Intimacy—Anthony Giddens

The analysis of 'high' modernity that Giddens develops more generally (1990; 1991b) is extended in *The Transformation of Intimacy* to the realm of personal relations, love, sexuality and intimacy, based to a large extent on his reading of the whole genre of self-help literature concerning personal development and relationships. For Giddens, the expansion of this personal development genre—in books, magazines and television programs hosted by Oprah Winfrey, Dr Phil and so on—should be seen as an indicator of greater knowledge about an ongoing reflection on love, intimacy, relationships and sexuality. Extending Young and Willmott's (1973) observations on the rise of the symmetrical family, Giddens argues that one can see an ongoing democratisation of gender and relations, which become increasingly egalitarian and organised around negotiated agreement based on consent and choice, and a minimisation of compulsion of any sort.

With the spread of easier techniques and methods of contraception and the uncoupling of sexuality from reproduction, this has been especially liberating for female sexuality, suggests Giddens, because women can be sexually active without being concerned about unwanted pregnancy and childbirth. He uses the term *'plastic' sexuality* to capture the sense in which sexuality has become increasingly malleable, freed from the constraints of its implications for one's social and economic responsibility for children, and able to serve a range of different needs, including pleasure and self-expression (Giddens 1991b, p. 164). This kind of sexuality is also central to what Giddens refers to as a shift to the *'pure' relationship*, which refers to:

> ...a situation where a social relation is entered into for its own sake, for what can be derived by each person from a sustained association with another; and which is continued only in so far as it is thought by both parties to deliver enough satisfaction for each individual to stay within it'. (1992, p. 58; see also 1991b, p. 6)

Consistent with the overall tendency towards de-traditionalisation, the 'pure' relationship has only itself as a justification and a foundation, rather than any sense of obligation or commitment to each other or to others such as children, kin, the church or the community, or to the demands of religious and moral belief.

The nature of love also shifts for Giddens, from romantic love, which is centred on a relatively permanent valorisation of one's partner as an ideal object of love, to what he calls *'confluent' love*. 'Confluent' love is both 'pure' in the sense of being entirely self-contained and situated in a closer relationship to sexuality, with sexual satisfaction being a more central element to its constitution than it is for romantic love. As Giddens suggests:

> *Confluent love for the first time introduces the ars erotica into the core of the conjugal relationship and makes the achievement of reciprocal sexual pleasure a key element in whether the relationship is sustained or dissolved. The cultivation of sexual skills, the capability of giving and experiencing sexual satisfaction, on the part of both sexes, become organized reflexively via a multitude of sources of sexual information, advice and training'.* (1992, pp. 62–3).

This form of love distinguishes itself, writes Giddens, from 'the "for-ever", "one-and-only" qualities of the romantic love complex' and should be seen as one of the causes of the increased inclination for couples to separate and divorce. But for Giddens, unlike for Popenoe, this is simply part of the price one pays for greater democracy and equality in personal relationships.

The Normal Chaos of Love—Ulrich Beck and Elisabeth Beck-Gernsheim

The German sociologists Ulrich Beck and Elisabeth Beck-Gernsheim (Beck & Beck-Gernsheim 1995;

2002; Beck-Gernsheim 1998; 2002) have developed a similar analysis focusing on the increased degree of individual choice producing greater variety and complexity in family relations within an ongoing process of individualisation.

Individualisation refers to 'a historical process that increasingly questions and tends to break up people's traditional rhythms of life—what sociologists call the normal biography' (Beck & Beck-Gernsheim 2002, p. 88) A core aspect of this long-term process is that 'more people than ever before are being forced to piece together their own biographies and fit in the components as best they can … the normal life history is giving way to the do-it-yourself life history' (2002, p. 88).

They characterise the pre-industrial family as bound together by non-negotiable obligations—a 'community of need', held together by mutual interdependence. People lived within the framework of families because they needed to, because that was simply how the world was structured; the question of individual choice was simply irrelevant. 'To go one's own way', writes Beck-Gernsheim, 'was possible (if at all) only at a high personal cost' (1998, p. 57). In the course of the 20th century, however, it became more and more of an 'elective relationship' (2002, p. 85), in which 'more and more things must be negotiated, planned, personally brought about' (2002, p. 91). One key element in this shift was the expansion of social welfare provision, which was accompanied by a loosening of economic dependence on family and kin. Beck and Beck-Gernsheim see the causal relationship as being that welfare provision enabled individuals to be financially independent of their families. It is also possible to see the causal connection as working in the opposite direction, so that it was the decreased capacity of family and kin to support various categories of dependency in the context of industrialisation and urbanisation that produced a demand for support from public authorities (Zaretsky 1982).

They also see the growing impact of feminist thought on social and economic policy as playing an important role: women became increasingly independent from their husbands in relation to economic security and social status, and so the family became disaggregated into its component parts—the individual men, women and children that make it up. Whereas 'the family' always used to occupy the whole field of vision, now men and women are becoming visible as separate individuals, each linked to the family through different expectations and interests, each experiencing different opportunities and burdens. In short, the contours of distinctively male and distinctively female lives are now becoming apparent within the family (Beck-Gernsheim 1998, p. 59).

This type of family life produces a range of particular demands and expectations of its members. It requires greater coordination to keep individual lives together, more decisions and choices have to be made, and it is decreasingly possible to rely on established rules and codes of behaviour. As Beck-Gernsheim writes, 'More and more things must be negotiated, planned, personally brought about' (1998, p. 59). The physical locations of the family's activities are spread out, between home, school (often quite a distance away), sporting fields, dance schools, concert halls, workplaces, all with different temporal rhythms. The freedom from community constraints also requires greater effort to construct a shared intimate world, which is both a freedom and a new demand, so that in contemporary marriage, 'the partners are not only expected to construct their own form of togetherness; they *must* do so' (1998, p. 61).

This makes 'the family bond' increasingly fragile, and 'there is a greater danger of collapse if attempts to reach agreements are not successful' (Beck-Gernsheim 2002, p. 98). Divorce becomes normal, the complexity of post-separation step-parenting and blended families becomes a standard aspect of family life, and life becomes a 'planning project' requiring constant discussion, negotiation and re-negotiation and above all the knowledge produced by a growing array of experts on relationships, love, child-rearing and personal happiness.

The impact of these processes of individualisation is not to bring about the death of the family, but simply to increase the diversity and complexity of family forms. As Beck-Gernsheim puts it, the answer to the question, 'What comes after the family?' is thus quite simple, 'the family!'

Only different, more, better: the negotiated family, the alternating family, the multiple family, new arrangements after divorce, remarriage, divorce again, new assortments from you, my children, our past and present families. It will be the expansion of the nuclear family and its extension over time; it will be the alliance between individuals that it represents; and it will be glorified largely because it represents an image of refuge in the chilly environment of our affluent, impersonal, uncertain society, which has been stripped of its traditions and exposed to all kinds of risk. (Beck-Gernsheim 2002, p. 8)

Families will be 'without a formal marriage or without children; single parenting, conjugal succession, or same-sex partnerships; part-time relationships and companionships lasting for some period in life;

living between more than one home or between different towns' (Beck & Beck-Gernsheim 2002, p. 98). It is this increasingly diverse range of family forms that Beck and Beck-Gernsheim see as constituting the 'post-familial family'.

Continuity and enduring power relations

In contrast to the emphasis placed on the radical transformation of the family, whether it is seen in a negative or positive way, it is also possible to see family life as displaying a number of enduring continuities. In fact, the account of family relationships as being radically different has a much longer history and is not as closely tied to 'high' or 'second' modernity as Giddens, Beck and Beck-Gernsheim seem to assume. Lynn Jamieson (1999) points out that these sorts of descriptions of changes in marriage and intimate relations can be found in the 1940s, and 'are part of the orthodox account of how the "modern family" developed' (p. 480). Earlier we also looked at the arguments of Young and Willmott (1973) concerning the symmetrical family.

The empirical research that is done on men's and women's attitudes and practices in family life also shows a very different picture, with far fewer changes in the structure and dynamics of family relationships than either the pessimistic or the optimistic accounts of family transformation. Although Jamieson's discussion is now more than ten years old, it provides a useful overview of the relevant research up to that point (more recently, see Smart & Shipman 2004). A variety of studies of couples show very little support for the idea of the 'pure' relationship. Women continue to complain about lack of intimacy, while men complain about lack of sex; and men continue to exercise more power than women in their relationships in relation to decision making and control of finances. Rather than Giddens' 'pure' relationship, what the empirical studies show is more a greater effort to reconcile actually continued inequality with the ideals of equality and of a perception of their partner as mutually caring and responsible.

Although it is true, wrote Jamieson, that a sense of equality, perhaps even the *idea* of the 'pure' relationship, is significant in intimate relationships, the effort deployed in those relationships is directed primarily at the *reconciliation* of that ideal with continued inequality and constraints characterising the model of romantic love that Giddens sees as having been replaced by 'confluent' love. As Jamieson wrote, people's 'creative energy is deployed in disguising inequality, not in undermining it' (1999, p. 485, referring to the Australian study by Bittman & Lovejoy 1993). This is why Bittman and Pixley refer to the 'double life' of the family, where particular normative ideals concerning family life are simply made to cohabit with a contradictory reality, and 'the evidence that the domestic division of labour is not an equal division, does not shake people's belief in equal partnership or in the value of nuclear families' (1997, p. 15).

In another study of step-parenting, McCarthy, Edwards and Gillies (2000; 2003) found that parents and step-parents were still strongly motivated to place the interests of their children ahead of their own and saw their family relationships as stable, ongoing and non-negotiable. They thus found little support for the concept of the 'pure' relationship, or for increased egalitarianism, observing that their commitment to children remained 'deeply gendered, with men concentrating on providing for children's needs financially and eschewing individual pleasures, and women focusing on accepting an inescapable responsibility for children and creating a stable family environment for them' (McCarthy, Edwards & Gillies 2000, p. 800). They conclude, in contrast to the picture drawn by those emphasising radical changes in family relationships, that 'we still appear to be living in a modernist, morally absolute, society. The moral imperative around taking responsibility for putting children's needs first may be one of the few remaining unquestionable moral assertions' (p. 800). From this perspective, as Gillies writes, 'personal values and practices of trust and caring have remained relatively steady over the years, reflecting ingrained identities and power relationships' (2003, p. 16).

CONCLUSION—THE FUTURE OF FAMILY LIFE

Regardless of whether one sees the organisation of child-rearing and sexual and intimate relationships around marriage as in 'decline', or even whether it is changing in its fundamentals, its *meaning* and the way it is experienced is certainly being transformed. In his detailed analysis of the development of family life around the world over the course of the 20th century, Swedish sociologist Göran Therborn sums up the question of its possible future direction as follows:

For the Western European family in particular, what happened did not lead to some 'aftermath of the family', but rather to a return to its modern historical complexity, including non-marriage as well as marriage, variable age at marriage, informal cohabitation and extra-marital births … Complexity is likely to remain, and with it a contingency of sexual relations, partnerships and family forms, around a modal pattern of long-term, institutionalized heterosexual coupling. (2004, p. 314)

There is general agreement among sociologists of the family that family life is caught up in a number of significant contradictions and tensions, such as between the world of intimate relations of interdependency and the world of work and increasingly globalised economic relations, and between love and consumption. For American sociologist Kingsley Davis, these contradictions run so deep that it was obvious in 1937 that 'the nature of the family … is unavoidably incompatible with the nature of modern society' (p. 294). As Therborn observes, 'All surveys point to there being a strong desire both to embark on a career and to form a family, including having children. But how to combine them is a difficult task, which many people have not yet been able to solve satisfactorily' (2004, p. 314).

Leading American sociologist of the family Andrew J. Cherlin has also argued that marriage has been 'deinstitutionalised', which refers to 'the weakening of social norms that define people's behaviour in a social institution such as marriage' (2004, p. 848). Cherlin suggests that the meaning of marriage has shifted from being simply the presumed, universal context for living together or having and raising children to being a symbol of status and success. He writes that marriage has 'evolved from a marker of conformity to a marker of prestige' (2004, p. 855), and this has a significant effect on the diversity of possible family forms, gender relations within the family and fertility rates.

Cherlin believes that it is unlikely that marriage will be 'reinstitutionalised'—that is, returning to 'a rise in the proportion who ever marry, a rise in the proportion of births born to married couples, and a decline in divorce' (2004, p. 857). This would be possible only if many of the core broad social trends characterising contemporary society—increasing reflexivity, individualisation, women's workforce participation, egalitarian gender roles—were reversed, and Cherlin thinks that this is unlikely. He also thinks that it is unlikely that marriage will simply fade away, because of its continuing symbolic significance. Although he is not entirely sure, overall he appears to think that the current situation will continue in a variety of ways—increasing proportions of people living in family forms other than the ideal nuclear family, but with that family model still retaining a distinctive place in the organisation of how people live together and raise children.

One thing that the sociology of the family does make clear is that the variety of forms that family life will take in the future is not fixed or predetermined, and it will be given shape by the exact ways in which people and a range of social institutions navigate their way through these contradictions, tensions and complexities.

Tutorial exercises

1. Discuss the extent to which we now relate to each other in 'post-familial' families, as Beck and Beck-Gernsheim suggest. What is the evidence against this argument—for continuing stability in the ways people relate to each other in family life?
2. Draw up a list of all the differences between your own childhood and that of your parents, and identify the ways in which you can use the approaches to the sociology of the family discussed in this chapter to explain the differences. Is it possible to predict how the childhoods of the next generation of Australians will be different from your own?

For activity suggestions, learning aids, revision of key concepts and access to self-study material, visit: **www.pearson.com.au/highered/vankrieken4e**

Further reading

Beck-Gernsheim, E. 2002, *Reinventing the Family: In Search of New Lifestyles*, Polity Press, Cambridge.

Bittman, M. & Pixley, J. 1997, *The Double Life of the Family*, Allen & Unwin, Sydney.

Pocock, B. 2003, *The Work/Life Collision*, The Federation Press, Sydney.

Scott, J., Treas, J. & Richards, M. (eds) 2004, *The Blackwell Companion to the Sociology of Families*, Blackwell, Malden, Mass.

Silva, E. B. & Smart, C. (eds) 1999, *The New Family?*, Sage, London.

Smart, C. 2007, *Personal Life*, Polity Press, Cambridge.

Websites

American Sociological Association Section on the Family:
www2.asanet.org/sectionfamily

Australian Institute of Family Studies:
www.aifs.org.au

WWW Virtual Library—Demography & Population Studies:
http://adsri.anu.edu.au/VirtualLibrary

Education and Knowledge

In this chapter we explore the nature, role and structure of education. First, we outline key stages in the history of Australian education and the policy thinking that drove its development. We examine the issues this history has raised for sociology, in particular differences in the educational outcomes of different social classes, genders and ethnicities. We then set out the principal ways that sociological theories have explained the role of education in creating and changing social inequalities. Finally, we discuss the role of knowledge and outline new ways in which sociologists are exploring forms taken by knowledge and their significance for education and society.

By the end of the chapter, you should have a better understanding of:
— the evolving structure of education in Australia
— key ideologies of education that have shaped the development of Australian education
— the central problems addressed by the sociology of education
— the differential educational achievements of different social classes, genders and ethnicities and their role in reproducing or changing social inequalities
— the insights and limitations of different broad ways of analysing education, specifically externalism, internalism and culturalism
— a range of significant sociological theories and key studies of education
— recent work rethinking the role of knowledge in education and society.

INTRODUCTION 162	**INTERNALISM: LOOKING INSIDE CLASSROOMS** 177
EDUCATION IN AUSTRALIA: EVOLVING STRUCTURES AND IDEAS 162	Labelling theory and classroom practices 177
Liberal humanism and the formation of education 163	Gender and identity 178
Social democracy and educational expansion 164	The underperformance of boys 179
New economism and marketisation 165	Ethnicities 180
Contemporary education 167	Criticisms of internalism 180
THREE GIANTS: THE PROBLEMS OF CLASS, GENDER AND ETHNICITY 168	**CULTURALISM: INTEGRATING INSIGHTS INTO EDUCATION** 182
Social class 168	*Learning to Labour*—Paul Willis 182
Gender 169	*Making the Difference*—Connell et al. 183
Ethnicity 170	Pierre Bourdieu's field theory 184
Explanations of education—a map of the field 171	Habitus and cultural capital 184
	Limitations of Bourdieu's approach 185
NATURALISM: 'NOTHING TO DECLARE BUT MY GENES' 171	Basil Bernstein's code theory 186
Criticisms of naturalism 172	Educational knowledge codes 187
EXTERNALISM: FULFILLING OTHERS' NEEDS 173	**FUTURE TRENDS: THE RISE OF KNOWLEDGE** 188
Economic needs—structural functionalism 173	Social realism 189
Criticisms of structural functionalism 173	Legitimation Code Theory 189
Capitalist needs—reproduction theories 174	Tutorial exercise 191
Criticisms of reproduction theories 175	Further reading 191
Patriarchal needs—gender 175	Websites 191
'The Australian way of life'–ethnicity 176	
Criticisms of externalism 176	

INTRODUCTION

In November 2007, Kevin Rudd launched the Australian Labor Party's successful federal election campaign by calling for an 'education revolution':

I believe passionately in the power of education. I believe education is the engine room of equity. The engine room of opportunity. And the engine room of the economy. I would not be standing here before you today were it not for the encouragement, instruction and opportunity provided to me by the teachers who shaped my life. They made it possible for a kid like me from country Queensland to finish school, go to university, become a diplomat and stand here today seeking to lead our nation into the future. I know the difference a great education can make.

I want every child growing up in Australia to have the opportunity of fulfilling their potential. My vision for Australia is to build the best education system in the world—so that we produce the most innovative, the most skilled and the best trained workforce in the world.

1. From this perspective, education plays a key role in shaping Australia's future economic, political and cultural success. Why is education so important?
2. Is education only a positive force in society, or might it also be a source of social inequalities?
3. What obstacles might there be to achieving Kevin Rudd's vision of every child fulfilling their potential?

Why look at education and knowledge? Intellectually, education was one of the founding areas of sociology and has remained a key area for research. Experientially, consider how many months of the year, days of the week and hours of the day you have spent at school, college or university. Education is a formative experience and when we realise that formal schooling is only one aspect of education, its significance to our sense of ourselves and our view of the world becomes obvious.

Moreover, education and knowledge form a central part of the activities of modern life. Over the past century, educational expansion has been meteoric. This represents a dramatic change not only in the proportion of the planet's population who are literate, but also in the position of formal education in modern societies. Indeed, education has been guaranteed as a basic human right by the United Nations since 1966 (as Article 13 of the International Covenant on Economic, Social and Cultural Rights).

Education is also big business; it is Australia's third-largest export industry (Bradley et al. 2008, p. 12). Education is a crucial part of the economy of industrialised societies and is viewed by policymakers as key for development in the rest of the world. In short, more people are being taught than ever before, more people are teaching them and more money is being spent doing so. Without an understanding of education, we cannot understand society.

EDUCATION IN AUSTRALIA: EVOLVING STRUCTURES AND IDEAS

It is easy to forget that formal education as we understand it today is a relatively recent creation. Our commonsense picture of education—universal, compulsory and formalised—only began to emerge in Australia from the mid-19th century onwards. Since then, our understanding of the role and purpose of education has changed. It is thus important to understand education from a historical perspective. We can identify at least three principal phases of change and three associated perspectives on education: from the mid-19th century to World War II (influenced principally by liberal humanism); from World War II to the late 1970s (shaped by social democratic beliefs); and since the 1980s (under neoliberalism).

LIBERAL HUMANISM AND THE FORMATION OF EDUCATION

Prior to the mid-19th century, informal learning was practised by voluntary groups, often church organisations. However, through state legislation such as the Primary Education Bill (Queensland, 1860), the Common Schools Bill (Victoria, 1862) and the Public Schools Bill (New South Wales, 1866), state governments became increasingly involved in organising education, although government schools were often set up in addition to church schools rather than replacing them. In subsequent decades, legislation such as the *Public Instruction Act 1880* (NSW) gradually led to the creation of a secular and public primary school system.

Underpinning these moves was a wider concern with educating a working class that was growing rapidly as industrialisation progressed. The ruling elites in Britain, whose influence in shaping Australian thinking on education remained strong at this time, were increasingly concerned that they faced a choice between what Matthew Arnold (1869) famously called 'culture and anarchy'. It was argued that, if left to their own devices, the working class could come under the influence of radical ideas and fail to understand the value of the current social order and their rightful place within it. They needed to be inculcated into the right kinds of values and beliefs. In outlining how to do so, such arguments drew on liberal humanist ideas. According to liberal humanism, 'education' should comprise the pursuit of 'knowledge for knowledge's sake', as opposed to 'training' in technical knowledge for vocational ends. Education was held to be inherently civilising and focused on shaping people's general attitudes, outlooks and beliefs. Expanding education would enable more members of society to appreciate what Arnold (1869) called 'the best that has been known and thought in the world'. This emphasis on its intrinsic value implied a need for formal education to be secular, funded by the state rather than economic or religious interests, and run by educational experts rather than politicians or businessmen.

Despite governmental attempts to establish such an education system, children often did not attend school regularly and most left before they completed their primary education (McCallum 1990). During the early 20th century, state governments tried keeping children in school for longer by raising the minimum leaving age, introducing legislation against truancy, prohibiting employment of children under the age of 14 and creating more secondary schooling. Although raising the school-leaving age achieved more participation, up until World War II nearly half of Australian children still did not reach secondary school (Connell et al. 1982). However, after the war things were different. As Figure 5.1 shows, school enrolments rose slowly until the late 1940s and early 1950s, but then grew far more rapidly. By then, circumstances had changed and a different view of the social role of education had come to dominate policy thinking.

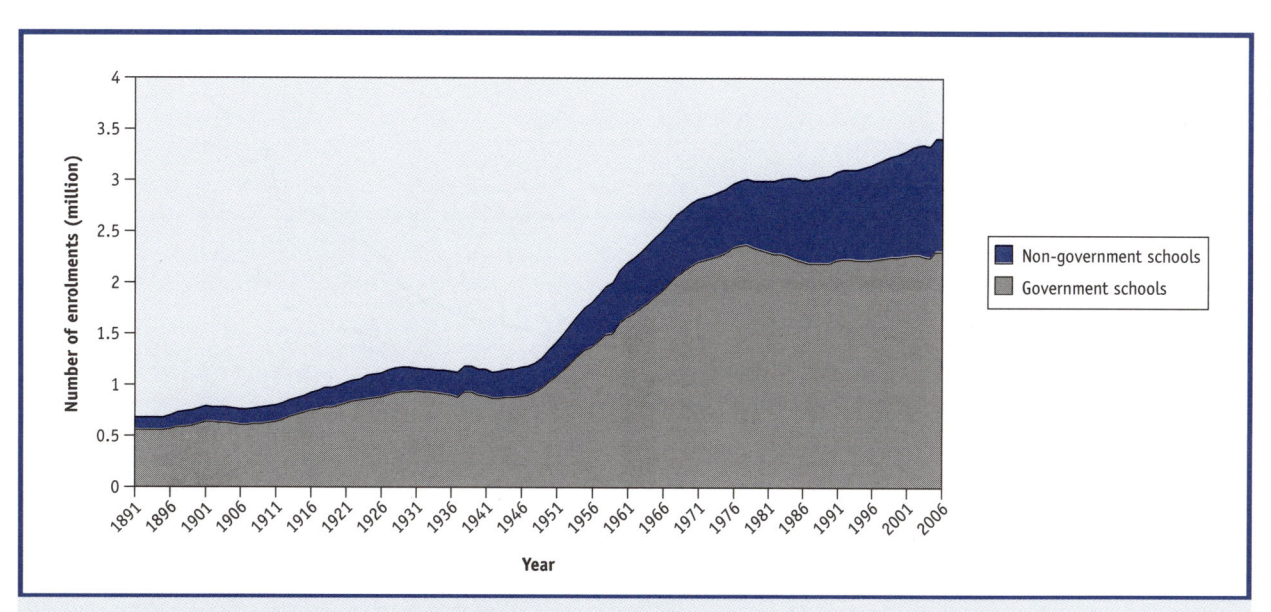

FIGURE 5.1

Enrolments in Australian schools, 1891–2006 *Source:* ABS, *Year Book Australia and Australian Historical Population Statistics,* various years.

SOCIAL DEMOCRACY AND EDUCATIONAL EXPANSION

In Australia, unlike the United Kingdom and France, compulsory education is a state rather than a federal responsibility. However, during the postwar period the federal government became increasingly involved in education, particularly at the tertiary level. This shift was related to a combination of factors encouraging rapid expansion:

- Demographically, the postwar baby-boom generation was working its way through the education system. Their entry into schools at the start of the 1950s created a need for more university-trained teachers and by the late 1950s this population bulge was swelling the number of university entrants.
- Economically, state governments were finding it increasingly difficult to fund higher education.
- Politically, there was a growing desire among politicians to enable more potential students to enrol in higher education.

The change in political will reflected a wider shift towards ideas of social democracy, which emphasised the role education could play in social progress. In the 1940s, critiques of Australian education by writers such as Norman Henderson and L. A. La Nauze argued that the system of education was not overcoming 'artificial' barriers to the 'natural' distribution of ability, especially the effects of poverty. Henderson showed how many poor pupils left school at 14, while La Nauze highlighted that while 10 per cent of the school population possessed the level of intelligence required for university study, only 1 per cent was enrolled in university in 1939, arguing that the principal barrier to university study was financial hardship (McCallum 1990, p. 114). Moreover, evidence showed that if measures of ability were the only criteria, many pupils who later proceeded to university would not have gained entry.

In short, by the late 1950s a widely shared view among policymakers, employers and academic commentators was that of a growing youth population, more would be qualified to enter university, more would want to enter and, crucially, more should be able to enter. This reflected the growing influence of social democratic beliefs in universalism (everyone has a right to be included in society), equality of opportunity (inclusion should be on a fair and equal basis) and meritocracy (the basis should be merit, not inherited privilege). These ideas became enshrined in the 1957 Murray Report as the principle that all those qualified by ability and attainment to pursue higher education should be able to do so. In response, existing universities expanded their enrolments, universities of technology were converted to full universities, and new universities and colleges were created.

The 1964 Martin Report argued for the provision of a second tier of higher education, alongside the Colleges of Technical and Further Education (TAFE). These technological colleges, later called Colleges of Advanced Education (CAEs), were intended to tap the neglected pool of talent among working-class children. Between

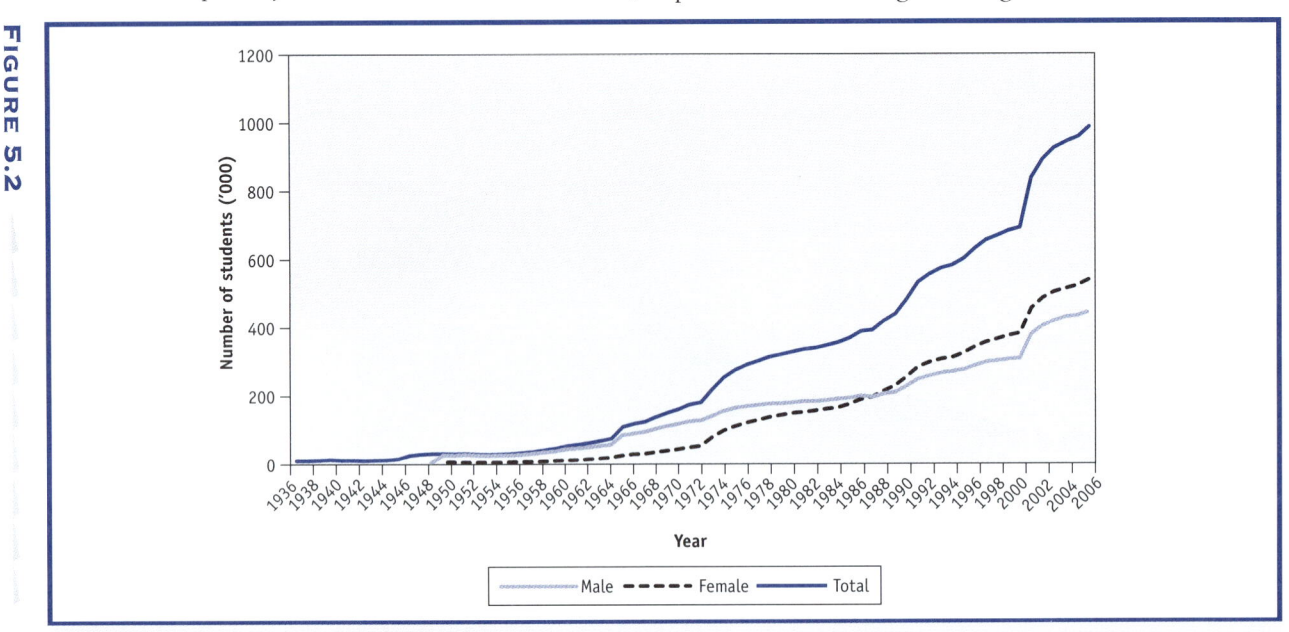

FIGURE 5.2

Higher education students, 1936–2006 *Source:* ABS, *Year Book Australia* and *Australian Historical Population Statistics,* various years.

1956 and 1966 the number of Australian universities grew from nine to 14, reaching 19 in 1975, and the number of CAEs increased from 11 in 1965 to more than 100 in 1977, before dropping back to 70 by 1979. As Figure 5.2 shows, by the mid-1960s growth in the number of students in higher education was accelerating. The rise of social democratic ideas was thereby accompanied by a greater role for the state in determining policy and expansion of provision, to enable more people to attend.

Education more generally remained caught between a desire to enable greater equality of educational opportunity and the reluctance of federal governments to invest sufficient funding to achieve this goal. The key exception to this reluctance was the Whitlam Government of 1972–75. It commissioned the Karmel Report of 1973, *Schools in Australia*, which was underpinned by a commitment to promoting equality of outcomes in schooling by making the 'overall circumstances of children's education as nearly equal as possible' (Karmel 1973, p. 139). The Karmel Report revealed huge deficiencies in the resourcing of many schools and argued for Commonwealth provision of funding. The subsequent creation of the Commonwealth Schools Commission saw federal spending on schools grow dramatically within two years, from $364 million to nearly $1.1 billion (Marginson 1997, p. 46), and the creation of targeted attempts to reshape schooling, such as the Disadvantaged Schools Program (Foster & Harman 1992).

These reforms, as well as the abolition of tuition fees for university students in 1974, were aimed at levelling the educational playing field. Their focus was primarily on the social and cultural benefits of education; the economic benefits of schooling were deemed of far less significance (Karmel 1973, p. 11). All these changes, however, were also the swansong of social democratic educational policies. The belief that the social benefits of education should outweigh its economic benefits was to change in the 1980s with the rise of neoliberal perspectives on education.

NEW ECONOMISM AND MARKETISATION

Expansion of education continued during the 1980s (see Figures 5.1 and 5.2), but the trend for more government spending came to be reversed (see Figure 5.3). Rising numbers of students and declining funding were accompanied by a new vision of education that emphasised economic and vocational issues. An emphasis on the role of education in training for trades and professions and its value for national economy prosperity has long been part of educational thinking. However, vocational training has traditionally been of lower status to humanist education and is typically conducted in different institutions. For example, between 1965 and 1989 the higher education sector in Australia was divided between universities and CAEs, which were established specifically to provide vocationally focused education and training and whose staff were not expected to engage in research.

However, over the past three decades a new form of vocationalism and economism has become increas-

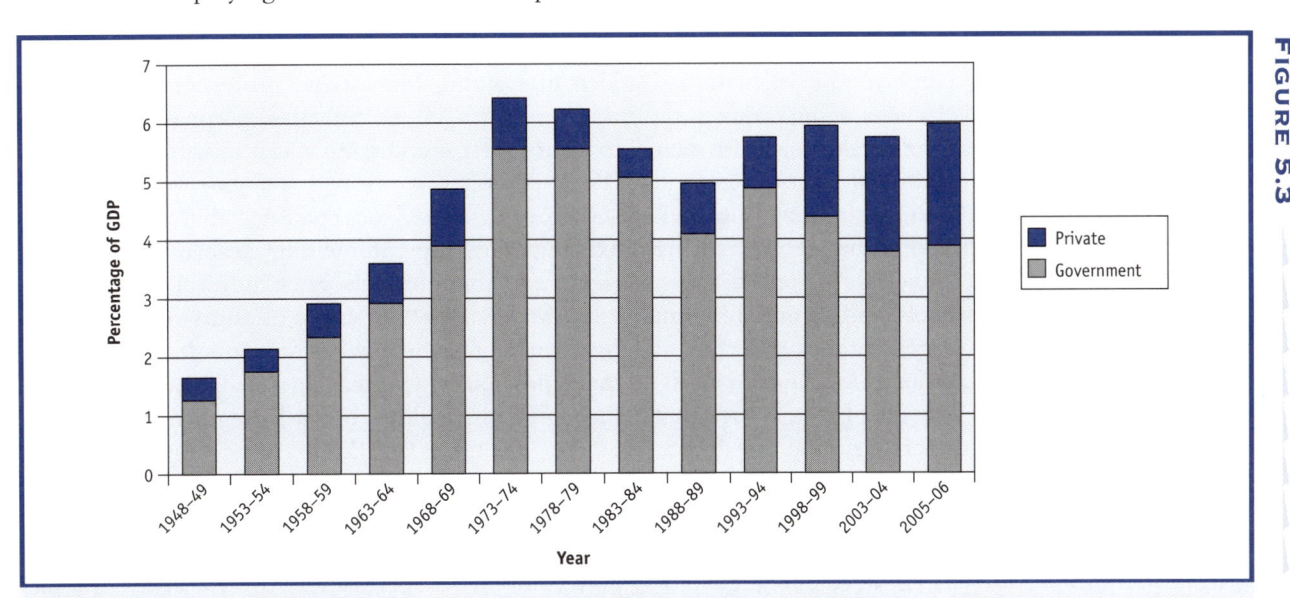

FIGURE 5.3

Final expenditure on education as a percentage of GDP, 1948–49 to 2005–06 *Source:* Compiled from Mathews (1968), ABS (1999g; 2002b; 2008a), Burke & Spaull (2001).

ingly influential in policymaking. Whereas liberal humanism views knowledge as intrinsically valuable and civilising, and social democracy emphasises the capacity of education to enable progressive social change, this **new economism** judges its value in economic terms. Instead of relations between education and *society*, by the late 1980s government policymakers were preoccupied with relations between education and *economy* and 'a new utilitarianism, a new economism, had permeated Australian education at all levels. Schools ... were viewed in an instrumental light' (Barcan 1990, p. 4).

Central to this new perspective is *economic rationalism*, the assumption that competitiveness improves financially defined performance, which has underpinned a focus on efficiency (D'Cruz & Langford 1990). This shift of focus from 'equality' in the 1970s to 'equity' and 'efficiency' in the 1980s was accompanied by growing state management of the education system and marketisation. As D'Cruz and Langford put it, governments throughout the Western world can be seen as:

attempting, in all areas of their activity, including education, to turn some operations over to the market to make them more efficient and to subject those that remain within the state sector to more direct central control with the aim of increasing efficiency. (1990, p. xiv)

Education was restructured by encouraging the development of market-like mechanisms *within* education systems and market-like relations *between* education systems and their 'clientele', which could refer to students, students' employers or their families. Such marketisation included: encouraging competition among schools, such as enabling parents to choose their children's schools; self-government of budgets and staffing at the local school level and training principals in financial management; and corporate sponsorship of schooling. In Australia, 'choice' for parents between government and private schools, and among different private schools, became a catchword of government policy, especially after the election of the Howard Coalition Government in 1996. It could also be argued that marketisation underpins the one exception to declining government funding: private schooling. In the late 1970s and early 1980s government funding of private schools rose faster than any other item in the federal budget (Marginson 1997 p. 154). In so doing, governments are helping privatise education through public money, as well as being engaged in what Marginson calls 'an electoral bidding war [in which] Coalition and Labor vie for support in private school communities' (1997, p. 153).

Another dimension to the marketisation of education comprises attempts by governments to shift the financial burden of education from the state onto individuals. As a proportion of GDP, government spending on education in Australia has decreased since the late 1970s, whereas private spending has risen (see Figure 5.3). For example, in higher education more funding has come from students themselves, through increasing Higher Education Contribution Scheme (HECS) payments and an increase in the number of full-fee-paying places. The traditional liberal ideal of education as enabling personal growth has been increasingly replaced by a neo-liberal ideal of 'education as a process of private investment, and students as self-managing investors in themselves' (Marginson 1997 p. 65). In this image, education and knowledge are simply commodities in a marketplace. As Bernstein describes, from this perspective:

Knowledge should flow like money to wherever it can create advantage and profit. Indeed knowledge is not like money, it is money. Knowledge is divorced from persons, their commitments, their personal dedications. (2000, p.87)

Underpinning these ideas is a particular vision of contemporary social and economic change. Policymakers in industrialised countries argue that workers now need to retrain continually, change careers many times during their lifetime and be flexible as economic conditions change. Rather than the traditional vocational idea of training for specific professions and trades, this new form of vocationalism emphasises the need to train future workers to be (re)trainable. As Sennett (1998) describes, its ideal is someone oriented to the short term, focused on potential ability rather than existing knowledge, and willing to abandon past experience and commitments. Such an ideal is reflected in what Maton (2009) describes as shifts from 'cumulative learning', where what students learn builds on their previously learned knowledge as they move through a curriculum, towards 'segmented learning', where new ideas or skills are accumulated alongside, rather than built on, past knowledge. This can be seen, for example, in the growing modularisation of curricula in university education, where students may combine an increasingly diverse array of topics and areas in different sequences to create their own individual educational pathways.

CHAPTER 5 EDUCATION AND KNOWLEDGE

CONTEMPORARY EDUCATION

The contemporary structure of the Australian education system that has emerged from this history is complex. For every general statement we can make about its nature, there are exceptions. However, in outline, its current features are:

- roughly three-quarters of primary and secondary schools are public, the rest being Catholic and other private schools
- private schools receive a considerable proportion of their funding from state and Commonwealth governments
- public education at primary and secondary levels is primarily administered and funded by state and territory governments (although the Commonwealth also plays a role)
- different states have slightly different systems—for example, different numbers of years of compulsory primary and secondary schooling
- tertiary education is structured into technical and further education (VET/TAFE) and universities
- the federal government is primarily responsible for tertiary education (universities are administered by the states but the Commonwealth is their primary and, since 1992, direct funder and de facto administrator).

Figure 5.4 sets out the structure of Australian educational qualifications. This complex structure has evolved within a relatively short period of time. The three major undercurrents of thinking we have discussed have each helped shape this evolution in different ways. As a new

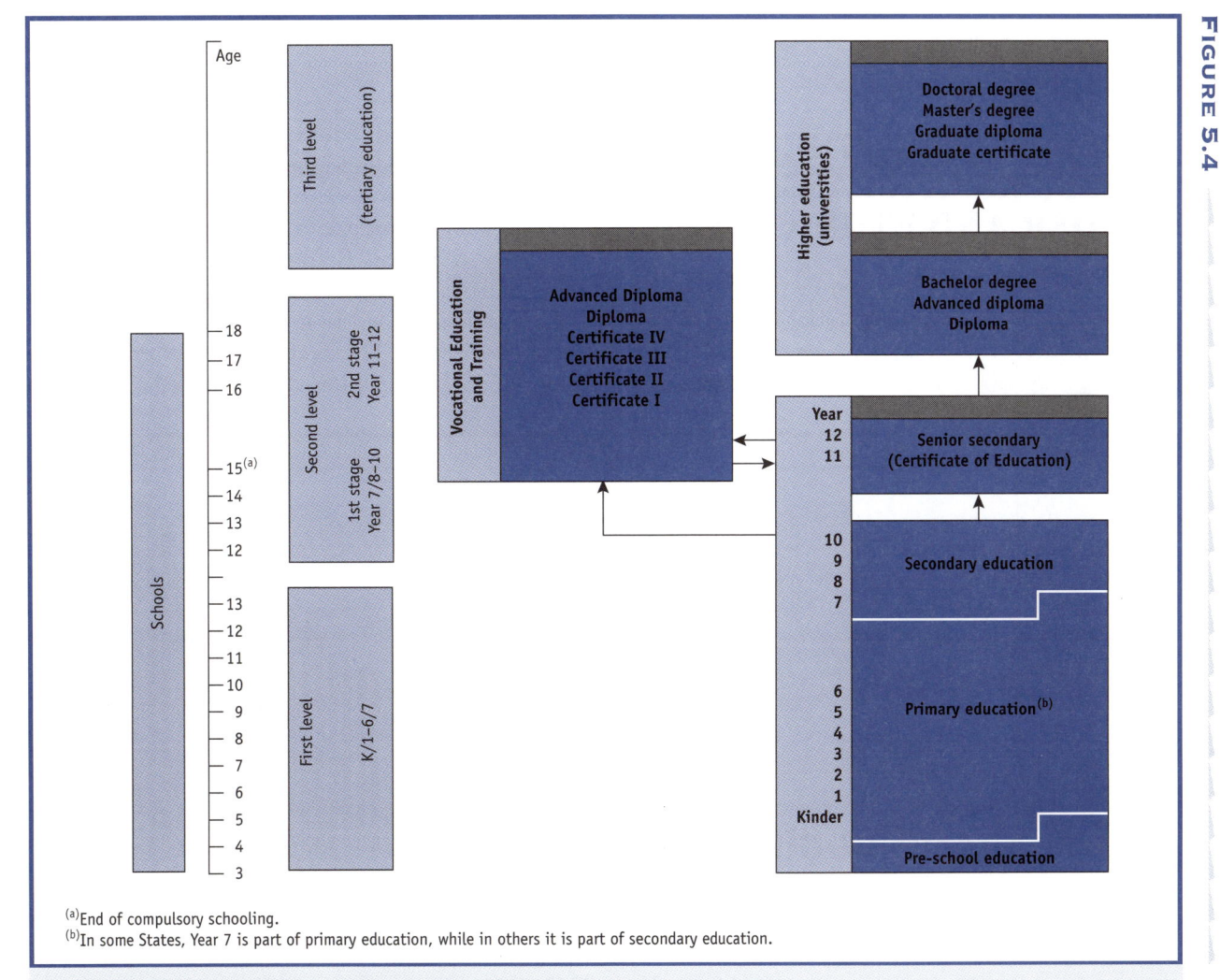

FIGURE 5.4

(a) End of compulsory schooling.
(b) In some States, Year 7 is part of primary education, while in others it is part of secondary education.

The structure of Australian educational qualifications *Source:* www.backingaustraliasfuture.gov.au/publications/crossroads/pdf/crossroads_attach_a_1.pdf. © Commonwealth of Australia, reproduced with permission.

167

set of ideas emerges and rises to prominence, existing perspectives do not simply vanish, although they may become relatively less powerful. Indeed, every phase of the development of education is characterised by debate and contest within and beyond education. The influence of these ideas is more than simply party political—the social democratic perspective was widely shared across the political spectrum and new economism continues to hold sway despite a change of federal government. The sociology of education has played an important role in this public sphere, particularly since the growth of educational provision in the 1950s. Above all, it has focused on questions of educational inequality and their role in reproducing and changing social inequality.

> **Reflective questions:** What features of education as we know it today are relatively recent developments? What have been the key characteristics of changes in education over the past century? How has education been seen by policymakers at different stages of its development?

THREE GIANTS—THE PROBLEMS OF CLASS, GENDER AND ETHNICITY

Education has often been viewed by policymakers as a means of enabling progressive social change. Indeed, a key characteristic of education over the past century has been its expansion, which has been accompanied by increasing participation rates. For example, the number of higher education students as a percentage of the Australian population has risen from 0.16 per cent in 1936 to 4.75 per cent in 2006 (see Figure 5.5). In short, more Australians are now spending greater proportions of their lives in education and gaining more qualifications than ever before.

Despite this expansion, social inequalities in educational participation persist. As Halsey et al. state: 'Class, gender and ethnicity are now the three giants in the path of aspirations towards equity' (1997, p. 638). Other markers of social difference, such as sexuality and disability, have been increasingly researched and discussed over recent years. Nonetheless, the 'three giants' remain central concerns of both research and policy discussion over differences in educational participation and achievement.

SOCIAL CLASS

Research in Australia, the United Kingdom and the United States has consistently shown that social class correlates with educational achievement. The children of parents in higher social classes are more likely to stay on in post-compulsory education, achieve examination passes when at school and gain university entrance. Evidence shows that despite many policies aimed at changing class differentials, expansion has not led to greater equality of educational experience. The average level of educational achievement of working-class pupils has risen in

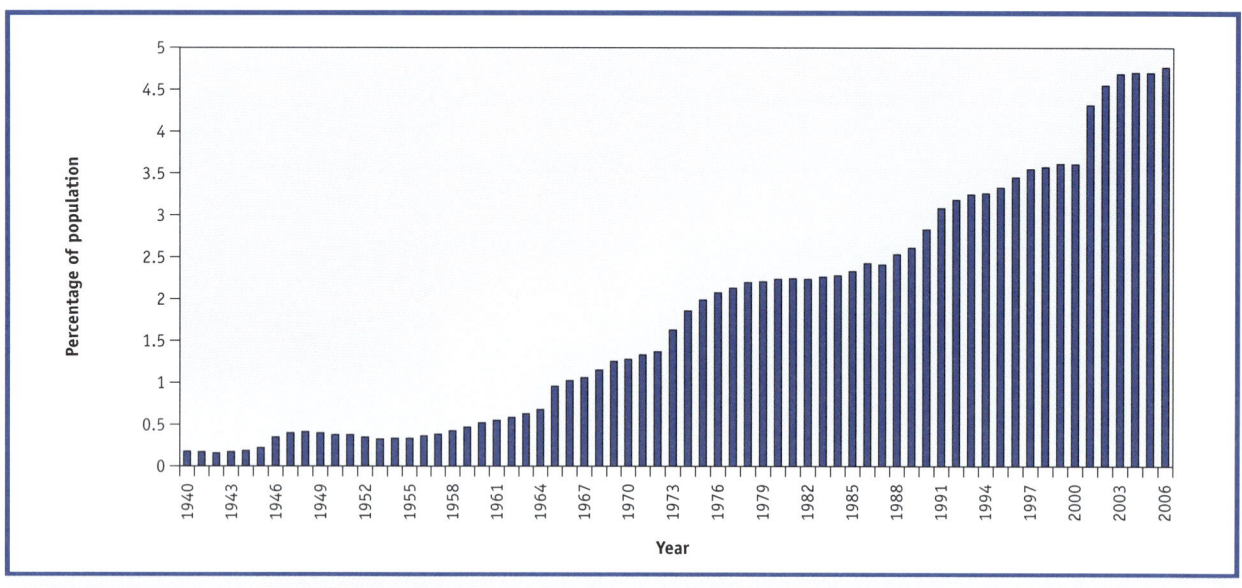

FIGURE 5.5

Higher Education Students as percentage of population 1940–2006 Source: ABS, *Year Book Australia* and *Australian Historical Population Statistics*, various years.

absolute terms—they achieve more and at higher levels of the education system—but has changed little in *relative* terms. So, differences in educational attainment among the classes have remained the same.

Taking higher education as an example, current studies show that in Australia the student population over-represents higher social economic status (SES) backgrounds and under-represents lower SES backgrounds. These differences have remained virtually unchanged over the past two decades, despite rapid expansion of the sector (James et al. 2004). For example, in 2007 students from low SES backgrounds had a participation rate of 15 per cent in higher education, but represented 25 per cent of the general population (see Table 5.1). In other words, for every ten students from this group who should be at university (if participation was equitable), only six are attending. In contrast, students from higher SES backgrounds are three times more likely to attend higher education (Bradley et al. 2008, p. 30).

Studies show that retention rates and pass rates for different SES groups are not dramatically different once students are at university (Marks 2007), so there is little evidence that inability to benefit lies behind this under-representation. The main reasons are lower Year 12 completion rates for students from low SES backgrounds (59 per cent) compared with students from high SES backgrounds (78 per cent) and the tendency of students from low SES backgrounds to progress to work or to the vocational education and training sector rather than higher education (James et al. 2008).

This highlights a second issue: different social classes are differently represented in different institutions. Students from lower SES backgrounds tend to go to newer universities, while those from higher SES backgrounds attend more established and higher status institutions. Figure 5.6 shows access rates for students from low SES backgrounds according to type of university—five of the seven lowest access rate institutions are from the high-status 'Group of Eight' universities.

GENDER

Until the late 1980s, most sociologists would have agreed that there are 'real differences in the school experiences of boys and girls which reflect and help to maintain the unequal positions of men and women in society' (Henry et al. 1988, p. 149). Such 'differences' would have been understood as including superior educational attainment by boys, with the exception of some female-dominated subjects and occupations. However, since then, there has been a **gender revolution** (Arnot, David & Weiner 1999). As the Australian Bureau of Statistics noted in the late 1990s:

> *Girls have both extended their lead in the subjects they had previously dominated, and have begun to perform better than boys in some of the areas of mathematics and science. There is now a growing concern over the significant shift in educational achievement of boys relative to girls and a recognition of the need for programs to enhance the participation and performance of boys as well as girls.* (ABS 1998c, p. 81)

By 2000, an Australian report on educational performance found that in Year 12 the average girl was outperforming the average boy in more subjects than vice versa (Collins et al. 2000, p. 2). The difference between the average tertiary entrance scores of girls

TABLE 5.1

Degree of under-representation of various groups, 2007

Group	Participation rate in higher education (%)	Proportion in general population[a]	Participation ratio[b]
Non–English-speaking background	3.8	3.7	1.02
Students with disabilities	4.1	8.0[c]	0.51
Rural/regional	18.1	25.4	0.71
Remote	1.1	2.5	0.44
Low SES	15.0	25.0	0.60
Indigenous	1.3	2.2	0.59

Notes: (a) Based on ABS 2007 data. (b) A participation ratio of 1 indicates appropriate representation of the equity group in the student population. (c) Excludes profound and severe core activity limitation.
Source: Bradley et al. (2008, p. 28).

SOCIOLOGY

FIGURE 5.6

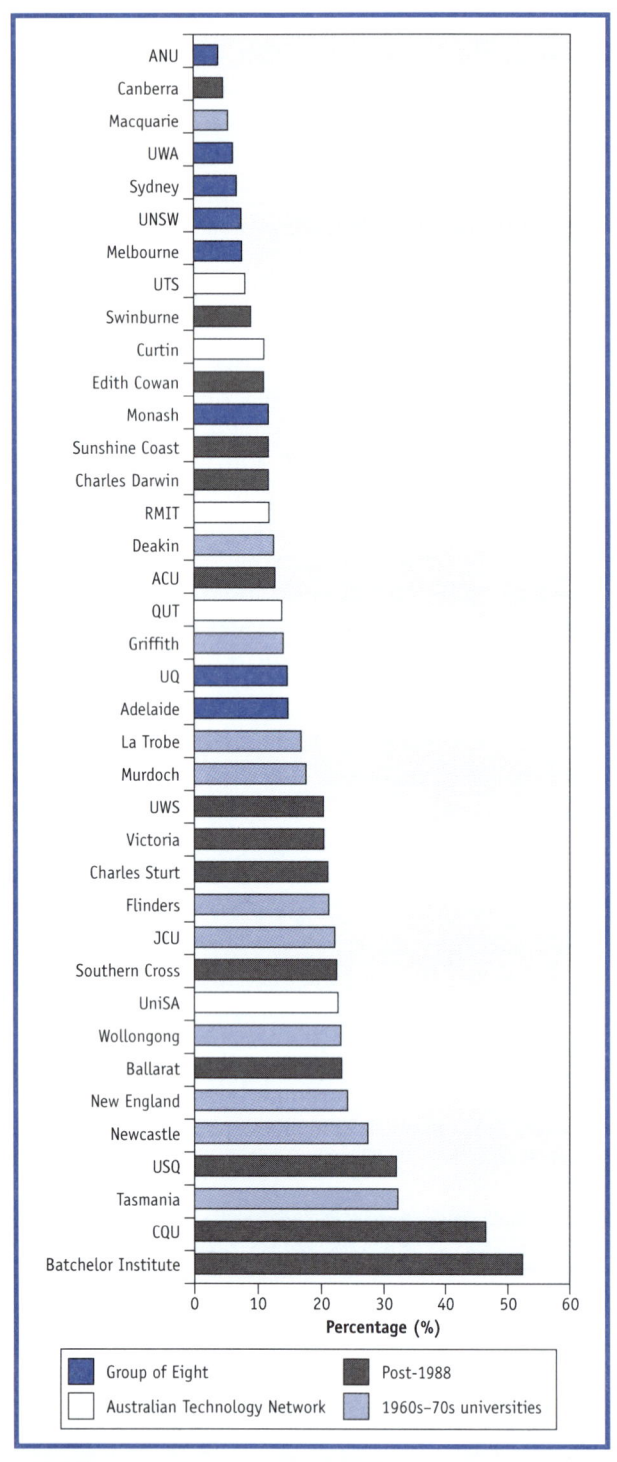

Access rates for low SES students by type of university, 2007

Note: Low SES is determined using a postcode methodology. Students from low SES backgrounds are those whose permanent home address falls within the lowest 25 per cent of postcodes as coded by the *ABS SEIFA Index of Education and Occupation (Census 2006)*.
Source: DEEWR Students (Selected Higher Education Statistics, Institutional Assessment Framework) 2007. © Commonwealth of Australia, reproduced with permission.

and boys in New South Wales rose from 0.6 marks in 1981 to 19.4 marks in 1996 (ABS 1998c, p. 83).

This issue has increasingly attracted the attention of policymakers. In 2002 the federal government's House of Representatives Standing Committee on Education and Training presented to Parliament the findings of an inquiry into the education of boys (*Boys: Getting it Right*) and two major reports were released by the federal government (Alloway et al. 2002; Lingard et al. 2002). By 2003 Brendan Nelson, then Minister for Education, Science and Training, could describe 'the urgent need for action to also address the educational needs of boys in our schools' (CGA 2003, p. 1). A similar story is told in countries such as England, Scotland, Canada and the United States—from a previous position of trailing behind boys in educational performance, girls have begun surpassing them.

A second issue concerns the subjects studied by girls and boys. An Australian report has shown that although most post-compulsory students take English, mathematics, a science and a social science, there are clear gendered differences among Year 12 students. Boys outnumber girls at a ratio of 7:4 in physical science and information technology subjects, while girls outnumber boys in biological science subjects (5:3) and home science (5:1). In addition, twice as many girls as boys take a non-English language and one-third of girls study an arts subject compared to only one-quarter of boys (Collins, Kenway & McLeod 2000, pp. 36–7). Taken as a group, girls study a broader range of subjects than boys, although they are relatively under-represented in information technology and vocational education. Boys, however, are over-represented in mathematics, physical science, technology, computing and accounting. At the level of higher education, a recent review concluded that women now participate in higher numbers than men but remain under-represented in higher degree research programs and in areas such as engineering and information technology (Bradley et al. 2008, p. 27).

ETHNICITY

In terms of ethnicity, there are two principal points concerning differences in educational experiences. First, when discussing ethnicity it is difficult to make any generalisations. Some ethnic groups have higher levels of attainment and others have lower levels, and these positions change over time and can vary depending on geographical location. Migrant families' backgrounds vary from middle-class, urban central European, to rural southern European, to urban South-East Asian entrepreneurs. As research in the United Kingdom has shown, such differences are further complicated by interactions with social class and gender (Gillborn & Mirza 2000). In addition, there are differences between more or less traditionally oriented Aborigines. This diversity means we cannot describe either a unified 'ethnic' experience of schooling or an undifferentiated 'Aboriginal' experience and should be wary of generalisations.

Nonetheless, there are significant patterns to the rates of Indigenous participation and attainment. This is the second point: Indigenous students are significantly under-represented at higher levels of education. Retention rates to Year 12 are improving but remain low compared to the total population (Universities Australia 2008, p. 47). This is reflected in higher education: Indigenous students are one of the most under-represented groups in Australian universities (see Table 5.1). For Indigenous students who do attend higher education, both their success and retention rates remain significantly below those for non-Indigenous students (Universities Australia 2008, p. 44). In 2006, for example, Indigenous students had a 23 per cent lower success rate, and during the 2000s their retention rate was roughly 19 to 26 per cent lower than for non-Indigenous students (Bradley et al, 2008, p. 27). Many Indigenous students leave university without receiving an award.

Explanations of education—a map of the field

In summary, three key issues concerning inequality have served as inspirations for the development of sociological accounts of education:

1. the enduring differences in participation and attainment between social classes, where the working class remain under-represented despite educational expansion
2. the 'gender gap', which has shifted over time from boys outperforming girls to girls outperforming boys
3. the varied nature of the influence of ethnicity and the under-representation of Indigenous students.

This is by no means an exhaustive list of the issues facing the sociology of education. There is a range of other social factors, including disability and sexuality, as well as issues specific to particular countries. Australia, for example, has the significant issue of remote and regional populations: Year 12 completion rates for remote students are 53 per cent compared to 69 per cent for metropolitan students (James et al. 2008), and students from rural/regional and especially remote areas are extremely under-represented in higher education (see Table 5.1). Nonetheless, in terms of understanding the development of the sociology of education as an intellectual field, these three issues provide a broad-brushed picture of concerns around which theories and studies have often gravitated.

There are a number of ways to describe the different approaches that have tried to address these problems. No single map of the field is definitive and it can never be as detailed, rich and complex as the terrain itself. Nonetheless, a useful means of distinguishing the different approaches is in terms of where they place most emphasis in accounting for the role, shape, practices and outcomes of education. In this way, we can distinguish naturalist, externalist, internalist and culturalist approaches:

- **Naturalism** looks beyond education, such as to biological differences among social groups, in order to explain differences in educational experiences and outcomes.
- **Externalism** emphasises the significance of the relations of education to its social context, such as to the economy, in shaping what goes on within education.
- **Internalism** emphasises the significance of educational processes themselves and foreground interactional practices in classrooms and educational institutions.
- **Culturalism** attempts to integrate the insights of externalist and internalist accounts. They emphasise the significance of relations between the beliefs and practices of different social groups and those associated with educational institutions.

Reflective questions: What are the key problems that the sociology of education is attempting to explain? What is the difference between the problem of social class and the issue of gender in terms of different educational outcomes? What is the 'gender revolution' in education?

Naturalism—'nothing to declare but my genes'

Before addressing sociological explanations, it is valuable to consider non-sociological accounts that have gripped educational thinking and that can resonate with commonsensical understandings. These 'naturalistic' explanations explain differences in educational achievement between social classes, genders and ethnic groups in terms of innate or biological differences among social groups.

An influential version of this explanation reflects the influence of psychology in defining achievement in terms of individual 'intelligence'. One commentator describes the 'psychological capture' of education that by the 1940s had allowed 'the problems which earlier had belonged explicitly to sub-ordinate social groups to be posed as problems relating to individuals, and which now demanded educational attention along individual lines' (McCallum 1990, pp. 126–7). This focus on the individual became centred on the notion of individual intelligence as measured by **intelligence quotient** (IQ) tests focused on abstract reasoning ability. Eysenck (1971) and Jensen (1973) argued that about 80 per cent of intelligence is genetically based and that this largely accounts for differences in educational attainment between social groups. Jensen, for example, claimed:

Today there is virtually no uncertainty among those who have attended to the evidence that individual variation in intelligence is predominantly conditioned by genetic factors. (1973, p. 373)

Cultural differences, social discrimination and inequalities of opportunity, he argued, were less significant. Jensen (1969) also argued that the higher average IQ score of white compared to black Americans was genetically based and justified different approaches in educating the two groups.

A similarly naturalistic argument was made by Herrnstein and Murray in *The Bell Curve* (1994). They claimed that the class structure of American society reflected differences of IQ and that the lower intelligence of lower class people is expressed through crime, violence, family breakdown, poor parenting and other socially inadequate behaviour. This account sparked off a passionate debate because the class structure of the United States is often associated with ethnicity. Although they focused on class, the claims of Herrnstein and Murray were understood as expressing a racist position of innate white superiority and black inferiority (a position they denied). The book caused a huge controversy and there were vigorous criticisms of the logic of their argument, in particular the attribution of causal efficacy to genetic differences (Fraser 1995). Similar arguments have also been made to explain differences in educational attainment between the genders in terms of genetic differences.

CRITICISMS OF NATURALISM

Naturalistic explanations resonate with the commonsense notion that those who succeed at education do so because they are naturally bright. However, these explanations have been subject to extensive critique along two fronts. First, the notion that IQ scores are a culture-neutral measure of intelligence has been strongly criticised. Commentators have highlighted how it is impossible to determine the degree to which IQ scores are shaped by genetic or environmental factors (e.g. Kamin 1974). Moreover, IQ tests have been described as biased towards Western, middle-class culture and unable to address patterns of thinking and decision making based on different social structures, such as those of traditional Aboriginal culture (Porteus 1931). Second, the notion that IQ scores explain differences in educational attainment has been thoroughly undermined. Differences in scores *within* social groups vary just as much as *between* groups, and studies show that educational achievement varies between pupils of different social classes even when their IQ scores are the same.

This is not to dismiss naturalistic explanations entirely, but rather to state that innate or biological differences alone cannot explain educational differences. As Powles (1987) points out with respect to gender differences, there is always a large overlap in the distributions of male and female scores for various types of tasks, and gendered patterns of achievement vary across countries and over time, making the notion that such differences are biologically determined implausible. The revolution in the nature of the 'gender gap' is one such example of variation through time that suggests sociological rather than biological issues are at play. Nonetheless, some researchers highlight that biological differences can *potentially* affect educational achievement and whether they come into play or are counteracted depends on socialisation. For example, Rogers proposed that girls' superior performance on verbal tasks may be attributable to mothers talking more to daughters than to sons at earlier ages, and that this early development of verbal ability may in turn influence the brain's development and functioning (1981, p. 55).

We can therefore move beyond the longstanding 'nature versus nurture' debate to hold that biological and cultural factors may interrelate and interact in complex ways. Nonetheless, sociological explanations show that we cannot simply posit 'natural ability' as the sole basis of social patterns of difference in educational attainment, something that has become widely accepted. For example, summarising research into educational attainment, a recent OECD report made clear the significance of the social:

> The most solidly based finding from research on school learning is that the largest source of variation in school achievement is attributable to differences in what students bring to school—their abilities and attitudes, and family and community background. Educational inequalities linked to family background tend to persist. The likelihood of staying on after the compulsory school-leaving age is linked to family background and social disadvantage in many countries. (OECD 2008, Vol. 2, p. 36)

EXTERNALISM—FULFILLING OTHERS' NEEDS

Externalist approaches look beyond classrooms, schools and universities for their explanations of education. We can identify a wide range of approaches as externalist, including accounts that are highly critical of each other's fundamental assumptions. However, what they share is a tendency to highlight something from outside the realm of education as the key driver of practices within the field. All sociological accounts of education involve an externalist dimension because of their concern with such issues as social class, gender and ethnicity. However, here we focus on examples of approaches that give especial emphasis to factors beyond the field. In the postwar period, the first such explanation to dominate understanding of education was structural functionalism, which emphasised the needs of the economy.

Economic needs—structural functionalism

Social democratic beliefs, dominant in policymaking during the 1950s and 1960s, held that a fairer educational system would create a more meritocratic society (see pp. 164–5). This optimism was reflected in the dominant sociological understanding of education at the time: *structural functionalism*. Epitomised by the work of Talcott Parsons (1951), structural functionalism focused on the functions served by education in enabling the social order to be maintained. Parsons (1961) described schools as both a means of socialising children—'it is an agency through which individual personalities are trained to be motivationally and technically adequate to the performance of adult roles' (p. 434)—and 'an agency of "manpower" allocation' (p. 435). In other words, education involved instilling within the young commitment to the broad values of society and preparing them for a specific kind of role within the structure of that society. Additionally, education was viewed as providing training. Overall, structural functionalism emphasised three key functions or needs met by education:

1. the development of 'human capital'—education provides training in skills and competences to meet the needs of industry for human resources
2. an allocative function—the development of the division of labour in advanced industrial societies requires workers trained for a variety of different occupations and so, in turn, a means for selecting, sorting and assigning individuals into different places within the economy on the basis of their talents
3. inculcating a common culture—to enable everyone in society to share the same basic values and so ensure social cohesion.

Structural functionalism explained differences in educational access and attainment among social classes in terms of relations between the talents of individuals and the needs of the economy. As Davis and Moore summarised:

> Social inequality is thus an unconsciously evolved device by which societies insure that the most important positions are conscientiously filled by the most qualified persons. (1953, p. 48)

In other words, the achievements of different social groups rest upon the abilities they bring to education and the kind of education required for them to fulfil the role best suited to those abilities.

Criticisms of structural functionalism

Structural functionalism was subjected to a range of criticisms, particularly in terms of the assumptions underlying the functions education was held to serve:

- Critics argued there was little evidence that education provides training in the skills required by industry, and particularly for the degree of fit between these two assumed by the notion of 'human capital'.
- Studies showed that the allocative function of education could be said to be based on social class, gender, ethnicity or other ascribed characteristics rather than on individual talents.

- Content analyses of curriculums revealed they exhibited biases of class, race and gender rather than a common cultural heritage, and educational studies showed many pupils felt alienated from rather than integrated into the school curriculum.

Above all, despite the growth of education and social democratic belief in widening equality of opportunity during the 1960s, it became increasingly clear that free universal education was not by itself creating equality of attainment and outcomes in the labour market. For one thing, social class clearly remained significant in determining educational chances. As discussed above, although the number of working-class students was rising, so were total numbers from all social classes, so they remained under-represented.

As such evidence mounted, the optimistic notion of education as an ability-based allocative machine gave way to more 'critical' theories that focused on how education was maintaining rather than abolishing socially based inequalities.

Capitalist needs—reproduction theories

Social class was the first focus of 'critical' approaches in the form of 'reproduction' or 'correspondence' theories that came to prominence in the 1970s. Though ideologically opposed to structural functionalism, reproduction theories shared an emphasis on the needs of the economy. The difference lay in how the economy and its needs were defined. Structural functionalism emphasised the technical dimensions of economic organisation—what Goldthorpe (2000) called the 'logic of industrialism'. In contrast, reproduction theories described needs in terms of social class interests—the 'logic of capitalism'. This focus on class divisions and their basis in Marxist ideas are reflected in another name by which they became known: 'conflict theories' of education.

Perhaps the best-known reproduction or correspondence theory is that presented by Bowles and Gintis in *Schooling in Capitalist America* (1976). This looked at how experiences and social relations are structured in the workplace and argued that *correspondences* to these can be found in education, which is thereby preparing students for their future working lives. Bowles and Gintis argued that the education system exists in the 'long shadow of work' and reflects the organisation of production in capitalist society. They highlighted that school experiences are not all alike:

> ... schools do different things to different children. Boys and girls, blacks and whites, rich and poor are treated differently. Affluent suburban schools, working-class schools, and ghetto schools all exhibit a distinctive pattern. (1976, p. 42)

Bowles and Gintis argued that schooling for working-class children is structured so that their experiences prepare them to become the kinds of workers required for capitalism to function successfully: hard-working, obedient, docile, motivated and divided among themselves. For pupils from more privileged backgrounds, schooling is organised to 'favour greater student participation, less direct supervision, more student electives, and, in general, a values system stressing internalised standards of control' (p. 132).

These different values are imparted, they argued, not through the explicit content of lessons but through the forms taken by teaching, learning and school organisation. Such forms represent a hidden curriculum that pupils learn through attending schools that are organised in particular ways. According to Bowles and Gintis, by focusing on the form taken by education we can identify a number of correspondences between the hidden curriculum and future work experiences for working-class pupils:

- The school curriculum and timetable is broken down into individual subjects and classes between which few connections are made, so pupils' experience of knowledge as a whole is fragmented. This corresponds to the organisation of work into specific, isolated tasks where workers experience only a fragment of the overall process. Such experiences also help reduce any sense of shared experience, making the workforce less likely to unite in opposition to authority.
- Schooling involves continuous monitoring of pupils by teachers and parents, through homework, examination scores and report cards, just as their future work will involve close and regular supervision by management through timesheets, appraisals and so on.
- Pupils have little control over what they learn, when and how, encouraging an acceptance of hierarchy and authority in the workplace.
- Future experiences of doing unfulfilling work in exchange for pay correspond to an emphasis on learning to achieve grades rather than learning for its own sake.

- Pupils are awarded higher grades for perseverance, dependability, punctuality and consistency rather than creativity and independence, encouraging the adoption of an attitude of unquestioning passivity and docility.

Education is thus, from this perspective, less about training pupils to possess particular knowledge and skills and concerned more with shaping how they think and act.

Structural functionalism argued that education selects individuals on the basis of their talents and allocates them to suitable positions in the economy. In contrast, reproduction theories posited that education helps reproduce inequality between generations by grooming pupils for different parts of the labour force based on their social backgrounds. Against naturalist accounts, Bowles and Gintis argued that IQ was far less important to educational attainment than social class background. Indeed, IQ was the result rather than the cause of attainment: the higher one's social class background, the longer one stays in education and so the higher one's IQ becomes and the more qualifications one acquires. At the same time, and just as importantly, education legitimates the resulting inequalities by promoting the belief that equality of opportunity is providing everyone with similar chances. This ideology thereby constructs inequalities of outcome as based on differences in personal ability and effort. One's success or failure is viewed as being one's own individual responsibility rather than resulting from the structure of the educational system itself.

Criticisms of reproduction theories

This correspondence explanation of differences in educational attainment exercised considerable influence, particularly during the late 1970s. For example, the author of an influential Australian inquiry into poverty and education proclaimed:

People who are poor and disadvantaged are victims of a societal confidence trick. They have been encouraged to believe that a major goal of schooling is to increase equality while, in reality, schools reflect society's intention to maintain the present unequal distribution of status and power. (Fitzgerald 1976, p. 231)

However, during the late 1970s and 1980s, reproduction theories were subjected to growing criticism, particularly concerning relations between the economy and education and between education and the consciousnesses of pupils (Hickox 1982; Arnot & Whitty 1982).

First, critics argued that reproduction theories overemphasised the determining effects of economic relations on education. It is unclear how the economy could shape education in the ways suggested given that many educational systems grant considerable control over schools to local authorities and autonomy over their affairs to universities, and teachers often have room for discretion in their teaching practices. Close relations between the economy and education are also unclear historically. The origins of the modern school system, as Hunter (1994) highlights, lie in 18th-century Prussia and Austria, countries with agricultural rather than capitalist economies, and compulsory education in societies like Australia was created well after the beginnings of industrialisation.

Second, there is little evidence for the claims Bowles and Gintis make for the degree to which schooling shapes the personality of pupils. Indeed, studies show that pupils may actively resist the rules and values of schooling. Paul Willis (1977), for example, showed how working-class boys could form a counter-school culture that actively aims to undermine the values associated with schooling (see pp. 182–3). The 'fit' between education and the economy was not as neat as they claimed. Indeed, Willis argued that often it was the very sense of alienation from and rejection of the values of schooling by working-class pupils that aided the process of social reproduction. The model thereby exaggerates the extent to which education can be said to provide a docile, pliant workforce. Moreover, as Connell argued, the model 'had curiously little to say about teachers' who are assumed 'to be more or less well-controlled agents of the capitalist system' (1985, p. 2).

PATRIARCHAL NEEDS—GENDER

Reproduction theories were criticised for overly focusing on social class to the neglect of other forms of social inequality. Some commentators argued that thanks to changes in the family (see Chapter 4), the nature of work (see Chapter 6), multiculturalism (see Chapter 8) and the role of women (see Chapter 9) this emphasis on social class left such theories outdated as other aspects of social structure and identity became more important in shaping people's lives. Feminists critiqued reproduction theories for neglecting gender. One needs, however, to distinguish feminisms from one another. Arnot, David and Weiner (1999) describe 'liberal' and 'critical' educational feminisms. In terms of education, the former principally focus on issues of equality of access, experience and opportunity, while the latter (including Marxist, black, lesbian, radical and post-structuralist feminisms) are more concerned with the gendered basis of schooling itself and its relations to patriarchal domination in society.

Each of these different approaches has its own research questions and agendas and views the role of education in society differently (see Moore 2004, p. 22). As we shall discuss, most feminist research on education has been internalist and focused on practices and interactions within education. Marxist and socialist feminisms, however, have often displayed externalist preoccupations with broader social structures. They have argued that reproduction theories neglect the ways education works to serve the needs not only of *capitalist* society but also of *patriarchal* society. Education is providing pupils with the practices and beliefs appropriate to their future roles in both the social division and the sexual division of labour. A gendered hidden curriculum prepares girls for their future position in the labour force, in lower paid and lower status positions and careers, and in the sexual division of labour, including receptivity to doing unpaid and unrecognised domestic labour (Wolpe 1988). Though a valuable corrective to the tendency of internalist feminist research to neglect wider structural issues, Marxist and socialist feminist arguments have been criticised for being overly theoretical and having an insufficient empirical basis (Acker 1994).

'THE AUSTRALIAN WAY OF LIFE'—ETHNICITY

It could be argued that educational policy in Australia towards pupils from non–English-speaking and Indigenous backgrounds was shaped by the needs of the nation-state for a shared sense of national identity and belonging. Between World War II and the 1970s, Australian education typically emphasised assimilation. Newly arrived migrants and their children were expected to assimilate into Australian society, to 'become Australian' by shedding their old languages and cultural practices and acquiring both English and 'the Australian way of life'. It was often a humiliating and unproductive experience. The distance between this mainstream 'Australian' culture and that of Indigenous communities was particularly marked. As Gale et al. emphasise, there is a powerful tension:

> between a society with an oral tradition that perceives knowledge as private and oral language as a mark of distinction and a society with a tradition of literacy, that perceives literacy as a fundamental right; that uses literacy as an indicator of the just distribution of a society's resources; that values literacy as an attribute of a 'citizen' and that views literacy as a means of free access to knowledge. (1987, p. 279)

The emphasis on Indigenous assimilation reached its zenith in policies that resulted in the Stolen Generations. In education it could be understood as an externalist emphasis on the need for national integration into a common culture.

During the 1970s, after mounting evidence that assimilation was failing children educationally, a more multicultural approach to policy emerged (Martin 1978). This has tended towards either 'ethnic politics', where the identification of ethnic disadvantage leads to argument for changed educational policies, structure and practices, or 'cultural pluralism', where cultural diversity is identified, celebrated and cherished but in practical terms is left alone as much as possible—'the do-nothing-except-be-nice solution' (Kalantzis & Cope 1984, p. 86). In both cases, multiculturalism highlights differences between the cultural identities of non–English-speaking cultures and mainstream culture. Multicultural courses were introduced in Australian schools in 1973, aiming at improving students' understanding of cultural diversity in Australian society and responding to language diversity. This general movement of policy and educational debate has thus shifted from its earlier externalist concerns with the need to maintain a common Australian culture towards a more interactional emphasis on how migrant and Indigenous pupils view themselves and are viewed by others.

CRITICISMS OF EXTERNALISM

Externalist approaches have done much to highlight the wider social relations of power within which education is situated. They draw attention to the demands placed upon education, such as meeting the needs of national economies for an educated workforce. Despite often being ideologically opposed, externalist approaches share a logic of explanation. As Moore puts it, they:

> operate with a particular kind of social causality in which it can be argued: 'because of this in society, then that in education' or, alternatively, 'change education thus and these things will follow in society'. (2004, p. 40)

Externalist accounts thereby neglect the interactional classroom practices of teaching and learning and the formal curriculum or content of education. They have often been criticised for being overly abstract and distanced from empirical studies of concrete educational practices. The lack of autonomy afforded to education by externalist theories also makes problematic the possibility of change for the better. If the cause of educational inequalities lies in the unequal structuring of the surrounding society, then changing education requires a social revolution. Moreover, externalist accounts have often emphasised the ideological justification provided by education for the social status quo, making such a social revolution less likely.

Externalism can also be understood as a useful corrective to much educational research. As we shall discuss, internalist approaches have often overplayed the possibilities for wider social change enabled by change within education. In contrast, to use a phrase from Basil Bernstein (1970b), externalism highlights that 'education cannot compensate for society'. In addition, we should not dismiss the significance of external relations. As Connell et al. (1982, p. 189) put it, the account of Bowles and Gintis was 'the simplest, and not the silliest, answer' to the question of why educational inequality persists. The challenge is to provide more subtle accounts of how education relates to its social context. Within the tradition of reproduction theory this challenge was taken up by drawing on Gramsci's notion of hegemony to describe power and ideology (Morrow & Torres 1995). However, as we shall discuss, it is culturalist approaches that have most successfully attempted to build on the insights afforded by externalism.

INTERNALISM—LOOKING INSIDE CLASSROOMS

Internalist explanations look primarily within education to explain differences in educational attainment. They focus on the organisation of the education system and institutions and on educational processes or interactions. The reason for this focus flows from three factors. First, what goes on inside schools and universities is significant to education. This may seem obvious but externalist approaches, often operating at the macrolevel of analysis of the whole education system, have at times neglected the fine-grained reality of everyday life in education. Second, educational institutions and practices are more amenable to intervention by educationalists and policymakers. It is harder to shape external relations and such factors as the influence of the economy or the family. Third, the expansion of universal, compulsory and free education did not by itself diminish social inequalities of educational attainment, even when pupils were attending similar kinds of school. One response by educational researchers was to explore whether pupils were being interacted with differently within education: might they be attending similar schools and in similar classrooms but receiving different kinds of schooling?

In looking at such issues, internalist studies often share a focus on the self-image and sense of identity of pupils. This builds on symbolic interactionism, which holds that our sense of ourselves is constructed in relation to how other people view us. The images of others and their actions towards us, it is argued, shape how we see ourselves and so shape our actions and beliefs. In education, a pupil's sense of self—for example, as sporty or academic, successful or failing—may be shaped by the image projected by teachers and fellow pupils. Pupils might encounter positive or negative images of themselves or of the social groups to which they belong that challenge or reinforce their own sense of themselves and so their behaviour, level of commitment to schooling, attitudes and so forth. This view thereby holds that the identities of pupils are malleable and result from the multiple interactions with teachers and other pupils they encounter on a daily basis during extended periods of schooling. So, explanations of educational achievement should explore how individuals are constructed and the subjective meanings they attach to these constructions. For example, educational failure might be understood by different pupils as resulting from a lack of ability or due to a lack of effort on their own part, meanings that could lead to resignation and disengagement on the one hand or renewed commitment and effort on the other.

Labelling theory and classroom practices

One example of an interactional approach is labelling theory. This suggests that the ways teachers define pupils, in particular their predictions of future success or failure, create a *self-fulfilling prophecy* through the way they shape classroom interactions. Teachers are said to implicitly define students as being of varying degrees of capability, such as 'bright', 'mediocre' or 'less able', and this influences their interactions with pupils. For example, they might expect higher quality work from pupils they view as 'bright' and offer them greater support and encouragement. Classroom observation studies suggest that teachers often spend more time with and give more attention to pupils they believe to be bright. Pupils who see themselves as good at particular tasks, thanks to these positive images, may work harder, while other pupils may become disengaged, believing that they will not succeed. So, the self-image of pupils will be shaped by interactions in ways that reflect teachers' views. 'Bright' pupils may work harder and 'less able' pupils may become less engaged, committed and willing. Their different levels of educational achievement will thus reflect the expectations held by teachers, whose predictions of their future attainment appear to be accurate. So, teachers' expectations shape what they are judging: they become self-fulfilling prophecies.

A well-known attempt to test this argument was the study of an American elementary school by Rosenthal and Jacobson (1968). They chose a random sample of 20 per cent of pupils and informed teachers that these pupils were expected to demonstrate rapid improvement. IQ tests of all pupils were conducted at the outset of the study and after one year. These showed that, overall, the 20 per cent sample experienced greater improvement than their peers. Moreover, teachers' report cards of pupils showed that they believed this group had improved their reading skills more. The researchers concluded that changing the expectations of teachers helped improve the achievements of pupils and suggested this happened through the myriad ways teachers interact with pupils in classrooms, including manner, posture, friendliness and encouragement.

Rosenthal and Jacobson's research was widely criticised for its dependence on IQ tests and lack of study of actual classroom interactions. However, studies of classrooms that focus on identities in terms of social class, gender and ethnicity suggest that the attitudes of teachers towards pupils do have an impact on pupils' behaviour and achievement. Here we primarily focus on gender as an example, because explanations of the recent gender revolution highlight well the strengths and limitations of internalist accounts.

Gender and identity

Until the 1970s comparatively little attention was paid to gender differences (Arnot, David & Weiner 1999). Feminist researchers and teachers played a significant role in highlighting gender issues in education (Arnot 2002). They raised questions about the role of educational institutions and practices in reproducing gender relations in wider society.

Early concerns with gender inequality focused on the underachievement of girls relative to boys. Feminist scholars proposed a number of causes for this gender gap. First, they pinpointed the male-dominated nature of the academic hierarchy: the more senior and higher status the position in education, the more likely it is to be occupied by a man. For example, primary schools have many female teachers but often male managers, and universities have relatively fewer female than male professors and senior managers. Interactional notions of the significance of our encounters with others for our sense of self suggest that it might affect educational attainment; feminists highlight that the role models encountered by young people are ones where women occupy positions of less power and status, encouraging pupils of both genders to view their own future positions in society differently.

Second, alongside other educational researchers, feminists highlighted differences in the subjects that pupils study, particularly the under-representation of girls in science, technology and computing. Different subject choices help shape future employment prospects. For example, boys are thought to be more willing to choose 'high pay-off' subjects even when they may not do well in those areas, while girls are less inclined to gamble on higher status subjects if they anticipate less success (Collins, Kenway & McLeod 2000, p. 2). This has been attributed to a variety of causes, including socialisation into gender stereotypes from an early age (Sharpe 1976), opportunities to play with construction toys (Sharpe 1995), lack of female role models and the construction of different subject areas as belonging to different genders (Kelly 1981).

A third focus of feminist concern has been how the curriculum, and in particular textbooks, embody assumptions concerning gender identities that portray girls and women in a negative light. Feminists argue that curricular materials continue to either portray the genders in stereotyped ways or ignore the contribution of women (Skelton 1993; Abrahams 1995). This, it is held, shapes the way children view each other and themselves, as well as their future roles in society.

Lastly, interactionist studies of classrooms have focused on the gendered attitudes and practices of teachers and their effects on pupils. Green (1985), for example, analysed classroom interactions in three junior schools and three middle schools and showed that teachers with ethnocentric attitudes differed in their relations with pupils of different ethnicities. Similarly, feminists have argued that teachers can possess stereotyped attitudes that reinforce wider gender divisions in society. Disruptive behaviour by girls is said to be viewed more negatively; for example, Clarricoates (1980, p. 161) found that:

If boys get out of hand they are regarded as 'boisterous', 'rough', 'aggressive', 'assertive', 'rowdy', 'adventurous', etc. For girls the adjectives used were 'funny', 'bitchy', 'giggly', 'catty', 'silly'.

Clarricoates argued that the terms applied to boys implied positive masculine behaviour and those applied to girls were derogatory. Subsequent studies have also argued that:

- boys often dominate classroom talk and interaction and are perceived as more active learners than girls (Goddard-Spear 1989)
- girls have lower self-esteem than boys, whatever the level of their achievements, and that the nature of teaching encourages girls to be passive (Powles 1987)
- pupils of both genders underestimated girls' academic performance and teachers judged ability in terms of verbal contributions in the classroom—an arena dominated by boys (Stanworth 1983)
- teachers more often interrupt girls than boys (Lindroos 1995)
- teachers focus on trying to interest boys in order to maintain order because they need more controlling (Skelton 2002).

This is by no means an exhaustive discussion of feminist concerns involving education. As discussed above, different forms of feminism have different research agendas. Nonetheless, they illustrate an ongoing tradition of internalism within educational studies of gender. In particular, they reflect an emphasis, echoing symbolic interactionism, on the capacity of educational structures and practices to shape the attitudes, behaviours, achievements and future lives of children and young people.

The underperformance of boys

The gender revolution in educational attainment has come to dominate research and policy discussion over gender and education. A traditional concern with the 'gender gap' has swung from focusing on the underachievement of girls to emphasising the underachievement of boys. Moreover, differences in subject choices have also come to be viewed as being detrimental to boys. Although boys typically choose groupings of subjects likely to provide greater returns in the labour market, researchers highlight that this means boys are clustered in subjects providing knowledge belonging to only two or three of the eight Australian 'key learning areas'—meaning a restricted set of knowledges and capacities (Collins, Kenway & McLeod 2000, p. 39).

Feminist scholars argue that the relative improvement of girls represents at least in part gains made by feminist critiques of education (Wright et al. 1998, pp. 77–8). Moreover, it is claimed that 'girls are still disadvantaged in that they are channelled into particular subject areas and their participation is not taken seriously' because of the ongoing influence of the 'hidden curriculum' of curriculum content, teacher expectations, school organisation and classroom interactions (Abbott, Wallace & Tyler 2005, p. 107).

This internalist focus also dominates wider research and policy debate. For example, the 'feminisation' of the teaching profession and lack of male teachers as role models for boys has been identified by both policymakers and teachers as crucial to the relative underachievement of boys in recent years (Tinklin et al. 2001). Policymakers have accordingly focused their concern on the under-representation of men in teaching, particularly in primary or elementary schools (Mills, Martino & Lingard 2004), and there have been drives in a number of countries to recruit and retain more male teachers. However, research is calling into question the notion that gendered role models (male teachers for boys, female teachers for girls) helps improve pupil achievement. For example, in an Australian study by Lingard et al. (2002) involving a survey of 641 boys and girls, interviews and focus groups, pupils did not identify the gender of their teachers as significant for their capacity to learn. Another recent Australian study of 964 pupils from five co-educational government schools also contested the value of gendered role models (Martin & Marsh 2005). The study involved a survey aimed at assessing academic motivation and engagement, and results showed that neither of these varied substantially for boys and girls according to their teacher's gender.

A range of other explanations have been advanced for the underachievement of boys, including notions of masculinity discouraging boys from educational success and a general trend towards coursework-based assessment coupled with lesser freedom for girls in how they spend their leisure time (Warrington & Younger 2000). However, a crucial point that is easily forgotten is that advantage and disadvantage cannot simply be read off from educational qualifications. As an Australian report on gender differences in education puts it, if pupils achieve better qualifications but are unable to convert these 'into further training, education or secure work or indeed into other aspects of a meaningful life', then their apparent advantage is limited and short-lived (Collins, Kenway & McLeod 2000, pp. 60–1).

This point highlights a potential weakness of internalism. By focusing on classroom practices at the expense of wider issues, such as future destinations in the workforce, internalist accounts are in danger of missing the bigger picture. In this case, female 'advantage' in education does not necessarily lead to social and economic advantages. This is important from an interactionist perspective, because anticipation of their future beyond school may shape the behaviour of pupils while at school. As Moore (2004, p. 13) puts it:

> ... boys might not do so well as girls because they don't have to given the advantages that males enjoy in the labour market! An implication of this is that if boys did achieve educational parity with girls, then females would be even more disadvantaged in the world of work. Increasing equality between the sexes inside education would increase inequalities outside it. Educational advantages do not translate straightforwardly into social and economic advantages, and pupils are aware of this.

ETHNICITIES

Similar interactional studies have been undertaken into how different ethnic groups are viewed. In an overview of the literature, Gale et al. (1987) showed that all studies have found that non-Aboriginal people generally perceive Aborigines in negative terms, and also that Aboriginal pupils themselves shared those perceptions. 'It is clear', they argued, 'that negative stereotypes of Aboriginal people persist as part of what the white world holds as "knowledge" about Aborigines' (p. 273). For example, in one study 15 teachers were asked to indicate their main difficulties in teaching Aboriginal students (Green 1982). They typically identified aspects external to the school: 'child deficit', 'family deficit', 'environment deficit' and 'other agencies not supporting the school'. Green argued that teachers begin to build up a negative image of Aboriginal pupils even before they reach the classroom, on the basis of gossip, physical appearance, language and their assumption of Aboriginal social disadvantage. This low expectation then reinforces poor school performance by Aboriginal pupils.

In a similar fashion to issues of gender, emphasis has also been placed on the nature of the curriculum, specifically the exclusion or devaluing of Indigenous knowledge. The Bradley Review of Australian higher education emphasised:

> It is critical that Indigenous knowledge is recognised as an important, unique element of higher education, contributing economic productivity by equipping graduates with the capacity to work across Australian society and in particular with Indigenous communities. (Bradley et al. 2008, p. 32)

CRITICISMS OF INTERNALISM

Internalist approaches have been significant for bringing the everyday business of education—teaching pupils in classrooms—back to the centre of research. They have also highlighted the significance of identity for pupils' educational experiences. The tradition of symbolic interactionism is also being built on by current post-structuralist approaches that argue differential educational outcomes reflect the degrees to which different social groups experience education as relevant to and valuing their identity and experience. For example, Weiner, Arnot and David describe discourse theory and Foucault's work as follows:

> Discourses are structuring mechanisms for social institutions (such as schools), modes of thought, and individual subjectivities: they are 'practices that systematically form the objects of which they speak'. (1997, pp. 621–2)

As Moore (2004, p. 25) argues, the quote from Foucault 'indicates the force of the effectivity being attributed to educational discursive processes'—they *form* pupils. Though post-structuralist approaches use the more encompassing notion of 'discourse' rather than classroom practices, they continue the interactional tradition of focusing on identities, beliefs and self-images.

Internalist accounts have been subject to a range of criticisms. Although symbolic interactionism holds that the subjective meanings of individuals should be taken into account, this has not always been the case in research, leading to a sense that labels deterministically shape how pupils behave. Studies have been criticised for projecting a passive model of pupils. Maureen Stone (1981), for example, reviewed research data on the issue of ethnicity and concluded that there is little difference in the self-images of black and white pupils. She argued that to view black pupils as unduly influenced by racist views might encourage teachers to view these pupils as requiring therapeutic help, such as multicultural education aimed at boosting their self-esteem, rather than focusing on their educational needs and enabling them to gain academic qualifications. A passive image of pupils fails to recognise how they can reject or subvert external pressures. For example, a study of a small group of black girls at a London comprehensive school showed that they felt many people expected them to fail but they chose to prove such views wrong by working harder (Fuller 1984). Moreover, interactionist accounts depend on the notion of 'significant others' through which pupils build up a self-image—and teachers may not be significant for pupils (see the discussion of *Learning to Labour* on p. 182). In short, although teachers' views do seem to help shape the way pupils see themselves, their effects are not as straightforward as a deterministic understanding might suggest.

A second limitation of internalist approaches can be their small scale. It is not always clear whether findings reflect the experiences of girls in classrooms or just *these* girls in *this* classroom. Moreover, caution is required concerning claims of how teachers behave differently to pupils. Randall (1987) observed classes involving practical work in workshops and laboratories in a comprehensive school for 11–18-year-olds. She found in one class (that was almost evenly split between the genders) that the boys occupied the central position more often when teachers were giving demonstrations of the work they would be required to undertake. However, in the observed lessons she found that girls actually had more contact time with teachers than boys did. Though again small scale, Randall's results highlight that one needs healthy scepticism when considering claims made by some researchers on the basis of limited evidence.

Third, an emphasis on the significance of identity can lead to proliferation and fragmentation of research and findings. For example, black feminists have been critical of the way feminist theories are assumed to apply to women of all ethnicities (Abbott, Wallace & Tyler 2005). As social realist thinkers have highlighted, emphasising differences of identity makes it difficult to generalise about any group (Maton & Moore 2010b). This also raises the question of how different social factors interact: are some aspects of identity more significant than others? For example, Abbott, Wallace and Tyler point out:

It is also important to recognise that, despite the moral panic about girls outperforming boys in gaining educational credentials, social class and race/ethnicity are much more powerful determinants of educational success. (2005, p. 94)

As Gillborn & Mirza (2000) show in their discussion of how class, gender and ethnicity interact, relations between social factors are complex. There are also other dimensions of identity that could be included, such as religion, sexuality, marital status and age. The multidimensional nature of our social identities thereby makes problematic any attempts to place it at the centre of explanations for differential educational outcomes.

Lastly, an internalist focus can lose sight of wider issues. By showing how the actions and beliefs of teachers and peers, whether intentionally or unintentionally, may influence the success or failure of pupils from different social groups, studies in the interactionist tradition have shown the significance of the processes and practices within education for differential educational attainment. They have brought the classroom itself to the centre of the picture, an arena often neglected by externalist accounts of education. However, by doing so, the classroom can become not simply the central focus but the only focus. Wider social structures and practices can become bracketed out of the analysis or, at best, relegated to the role of background scenery.

As Moore (2004, p. 30) highlights, the significance of wider processes can be illustrated by the gender revolution along at least four fronts:

1. Though it became the object of policy concern only when girls began surpassing the achievements of boys, the gradually improving relative position of girls in education was a long-term trend throughout the second half of the 20th century. It did not correlate with specific periods or episodes of change *within* education.
2. Governmental programs promoting anti-sexist education have been unevenly implemented and often met with official hostility. They have not been extensive enough or long-term enough to have generated such a long-term and widespread trend.
3. There is no simple correlation between the implementation of such policies and girls' educational attainments.
4. Improvements in the performance of girls have been most pronounced at higher levels of the education system, which have been described as more 'masculinist'.

In summary, changes *within* education cannot by themselves account for the gender revolution in education. This is not to say that education makes no difference. Studies in the tradition of 'school effectiveness research' conclude that roughly 10 per cent of variance between students can be accounted for by the school—a percentage that translates into significant differences in opportunities for pupils (Mortimore 1997). However, improving the effectiveness of schools would not improve the position of disadvantaged groups because it would raise attainments for all pupils at the school and so differences between groups would remain. In other words, while classroom interactions and practices do make a difference, they cannot by themselves account for the systematic differences between social groups, such as the persistence of the class gap or the gender revolution.

> **Reflective questions:** What are the differences between 'externalist' and 'internalist' approaches to education? What key strengths might we wish to take away from these approaches in order to develop a fuller understanding of education?

CULTURALISM—INTEGRATING INSIGHTS INTO EDUCATION

Externalist and internalist accounts of education have both been criticised for placing too much emphasis on one dimension of education—externalism on issues beyond education and internalism on practices within schools and universities—and various studies and theories have attempted to bring these two dimensions together. Such an approach has typically focused on the cultures that pupils bring to education, the cultures of different schools and the future occupational cultures into which pupils will go after education. In its more theorised forms, *culturalism* also embodies a relational and structural approach: it explores the structuring principles underlying family backgrounds and school and the degrees to which these match or clash. The basic idea is that different family backgrounds socialise young people into acting and thinking in ways that resonate to different degrees with underlying patterns of schooling.

LEARNING TO LABOUR— PAUL WILLIS

One of the most widely discussed culturalist studies of education is *Learning to Labour* by Paul Willis (1977). On the one hand, like externalist 'reproduction' theories, Willis focused on the ways that education helps prepare pupils for their future role in the workforce and class structure (the book's subtitle is *How Working Class Kids Get Working Class Jobs*). However, he also showed that this is not a simple matter of smooth and successful socialisation into future positions but rather involves contestation and unintended consequences. On the other hand, like internalist studies influenced by symbolic interactionism, Willis' study focused on the concrete practices of the participants in the study and attempted to understand experiences of schooling from their perspectives. It involved a wide variety of research methods, including: observation in class, around the school and during leisure activities; regular recorded group discussions; informal interviews; and diaries kept by the participants.

The study centred on a school in a working-class part of a small industrial town in England. Willis followed a group of 12 working-class boys over their last 18 months at school and first few months of paid employment. These 'lads' formed a friendship group with their own set of values that ran counter to those espoused by the school. This counter-school culture viewed school as boring and valorised and instead they preferred 'having a laff' and partaking of symbolically adult activities, such as alcohol and cigarettes. They expressed little interest in gaining academic qualifications, looked down on teachers and more conformist pupils (whom they called 'ear'oles'), attempted to avoid attending classes wherever possible and when in class did as little schoolwork as possible. The lads denigrated academic success and the 'pen pusher' jobs that they led to as effeminate, and celebrated manual labour or 'graft' as real work.

Contrary to the ideas of reproduction theories (see pp. 174–5), the lads were not being groomed by schooling into deference to authority, obedience and docility. However, their rejection of schooling did make them ideally suited to unskilled or semi-skilled manual labour, and the lads continued the same kinds of attitudes and behaviours in their first jobs, attempting to gain a little freedom but without directly confronting authority. Willis argued that the education system *does* reproduce the kind of class-structured labour force required by capitalism, but neither directly nor intentionally. The ways working-class kids get working-class jobs are often the unintended consequences of their agency in creating a subculture of their own, one opposed to the values of the education system and more aligned with the masculinity of adult working-class culture. It is the *rejection* of schooling rather than its acceptance that prepares them for their future social positions. Moreover, contrary to the externalist argument that education provides ideological justification for social inequality through inculcating beliefs in equality of opportunity, Willis showed that the lads recognised capitalist society was not meritocratic and that they had limited chance of upward social mobility. However, Willis emphasised that though they could see through notions of equality, their antipathy towards non-manual labour illustrated that their understanding of capitalism was restricted to their own personal experience rather than a view of the system as a whole.

Willis has been criticised for extrapolating from a study of 12 atypical pupils to an entire social class, for ignoring subcultural groupings in schools that are neither 'lads' nor conformists, and for overstating the continuity between the lads' attitudes to work and those of their fathers' generation (Blackledge & Hunt 1985). For example, Walker's (1988) study of an inner-city, working-class school in Australia found a variety of male youth subcultures and noted that sport and ethnicity played a stronger role in defining subcultures in this school than in Willis' English study. However, a contribution of Willis' study is how it highlights the cultures that pupils bring to school, by virtue of their upbringing and family backgrounds, and how these relate to the culture of the school. Unlike internalist accounts, this ensures wider social relations do not become backgrounded, but unlike externalist accounts it also includes the study of classroom practices within education.

MAKING THE DIFFERENCE— CONNELL ET AL.

In the late 1970s a major Australian study, *Making the Difference*, by Connell et al. (1982) explored the relationships between school and family background by interviewing pupils, parents, teachers and school principals. Rather than focusing exclusively on wider social structures or classroom interactions, Connell et al. highlighted the mediating role played by families as 'the main link between school students and the larger social structure' (1982, p. 34). In a similar fashion to Willis, they also emphasised the contextualised but active nature of actors. However, in contrast to the over-determined model of individuals to be found in reproduction theory, they argued that actors make choices, although within structured contexts not of their own making.

The study was based on a distinction between the working class (engaged in manual and semi-manual waged labour) and what the researchers termed the 'ruling class' (managers, businesspeople and professionals). In total 424 interviews were conducted with families from both groups and with teachers and principals from state-run and fee-paying independent schools that were located within and catered to each of these classes, respectively. The authors argued that this division into state and independent schools created two different kinds of educational experiences for pupils and their families: 'the ruling class and its schools are articulated mainly *through a market*, while the working class and its schools are articulated mainly *through a bureaucracy* (or, to put it very strictly, through the state via a bureaucracy)' (Connell et al. 1982, p. 133).

According to the study, the 'ruling-class' schools were situated in a market and a social network. Parents tended to view teachers as their paid agents, shopped around for schools, and withdrew their children if dissatisfied. Moreover, school was interlinked with kinship and friendship through socialising among parents and teachers that was facilitated by ancillary organisations such as mothers' clubs and sports associations. The school was thus both responsive to ruling-class families and active in helping shape their relations with other members of the class.

In contrast, working-class families were in a weaker position in relation to the school, whose teachers viewed themselves as working for the state rather than for a clientele of parents. In general, the researchers argued that teachers in working-class schools, as representatives of the 'state' and dismissive of working-class parents' knowledge of schooling, 'stand in a significantly more authoritative relation to working-class families than the teachers in private schools do to ruling-class families' (1982, p. 138). Working-class schools were also said to be less responsive to pupils' needs and consistently described as suffering from 'arbitrary authority, poor teaching, inconsistent discipline, favouritism, lack of respect for the kids' (1982, p. 85). The attitude of parents, however, was not anti-school: aware that schooling helps in the labour market, they wanted their children to receive as much education as possible. In short, where ruling-class families were enmeshed in a reciprocal relationship with their schools, working-class families were less well integrated with a school culture that seemed neither to reach out to them nor understand their concerns.

Both *Learning to Labour* and *Making the Difference* were extremely influential and have remained touchstones for subsequent research. Willis' study has become a classic in both educational and youth studies; and Connell et al.'s study is unsurpassed for its rich and detailed insight into the experiences of its interviewees and their different relationships with schools. Despite this shaping influence on the field of study, neither gave rise to a developing framework of the kind exemplified by perhaps the two most significant theorists in the sociology of education of the past 40 years: Pierre Bourdieu and Basil Bernstein.

PIERRE BOURDIEU'S FIELD THEORY

In a series of studies, including *The Inheritors* (Bourdieu & Passeron 1979), *Reproduction in Education, Society and Culture* (Bourdieu & Passeron 1977), *Homo Academicus* (1988) and *The State Nobility* (1996), Pierre Bourdieu set forward a detailed account of the role of education in modern societies. His approach can be described as 'culturalist' in two senses: the central role that cultural and symbolic products (art, literature, music etc.) plays in the theory, and the significance it affords to 'culture' in the anthropological sense of established practices, beliefs and ways of working. Bourdieu's intellectual project 'amounts to nothing less than an attempt to construct a theory of social practice and society' (Jenkins 1992, p. 67).

Like structural functionalism and reproduction theories (see pp. 173, 174), Bourdieu argues that education has an allocative function: it takes individuals from particular backgrounds, classifies them and assigns them to positions in the social structure. Bourdieu accounts for these external relations in a less reductive manner. As Maton (2005) highlights, for Bourdieu education has its own **relative autonomy** from economic and political power. It is a social field of practice located within wider relations of power but with its own ways of working, beliefs and values—its own (anthropological) culture. The 'autonomy' of education means (against externalism) that one cannot view educational practices as a reflection of industrial or political needs. However, the 'relative' nature of this autonomy means (against internalism) that one cannot understand educational practices in isolation from wider factors in society.

For Bourdieu, education helps to reproduce social inequalities in two principal ways. First, it provides an ideological justification for the way things are. It does so through its role of cultural reproduction: the reproduction of the beliefs and ideas of dominant social classes (Bourdieu & Passeron 1977). This involves 'symbolic violence' or the imposition of a set of ideas in such a way that its selection and valuation are experienced as legitimate and natural. The culture that is valued highly by education is, for Bourdieu, arbitrary and reflects social power rather than cultural value—it is a 'dominant cultural arbitrary' (p. 30). Thanks to education, this arbitrary culture becomes misrecognised as legitimate by those upon whom it is imposed. In doing so, it helps buttress those relations of power, because one vision of reality is taught as if it were the only possible legitimate vision. By reproducing the dominant arbitrary culture, education thereby has a crucial 'social reproduction function' (p. 10). The relative autonomy of education enables this ideological underpinning of social domination to go unnoticed because of its seeming independence from the dominant social classes whose interests it serves: 'dependence through independence' (p. 67).

The second social reproduction function of education is its capacity to transform social inequalities into seemingly neutral educational inequalities. Individuals from different social groups enter education from a social hierarchy (e.g. upper and lower social classes). When they leave education they represent a hierarchy of educational outcomes, thanks to different levels of achieved qualifications. These qualifications shape their future career opportunities and social positions, owing to the value of educational qualifications in the occupational marketplace. However, this educational or cultural hierarchy largely mirrors the initial social hierarchy—for example, lower social groups achieve less educationally. Moreover, academic qualifications have an air of neutrality because education is ostensibly based on meritocratic principles where achievements represent an objective evaluation of the intellectual capacities of individuals. Thus education translates social inequalities into cultural inequalities, which in turn legitimate further social inequalities.

Habitus and cultural capital

For Bourdieu, education achieves this social reproduction function not through 'correspondences' to the needs of capitalist or patriarchal society (reproduction theory), or through classroom practices shaping pupils' self-images (interactional theory), but through **habitus** and **cultural capital**. These concepts integrate insights from externalist and internalist approaches by analysing the attributes pupils bring to education and their relations to practices within education. Briefly put, Bourdieu (1990) argues that our experiences as we grow up shape our ways of acting, feeling, thinking and being—or habitus. This system of dispositions in turn shapes the ways in which we act. These dispositions are *durable* in that they last over time and *transposable* in that they are capable of becoming active within a wide variety of theatres of social action (Bourdieu 1993, p. 87).

The habitus, however, does not act alone. Bourdieu is not suggesting that we are pre-programmed automatons acting out the implications of our upbringing. Rather, practices result from the relationship between one's habitus and the state of play of the field in which one is an actor, such as the field of education. Faced with an array of choices within a particular context, actors will tend to choose some choices rather than others—the habitus is thus a *'predisposition, tendency, propensity or inclination'* (Bourdieu 1977, p. 214). So, it is the *relations* between an individual's habitus and the structure of the social field that together shape practices.

How does this translate into explaining educational inequalities? In *The Inheritors* and *Reproduction in Education, Society and Culture*, for example, Bourdieu and Passeron (1979; 1977) address the question of why actors from middle-class backgrounds are more likely than those from working-class backgrounds to attend university. They describe how innumerable stimuli during their upbringing shape actors' outlooks, beliefs and practices in ways that impact on their educational careers. Rather than the educational system blocking access to actors from non-traditional backgrounds, these actors relegate themselves out of the system, seeing university as 'not for the likes of me'. Much like 'the lads' in Willis' *Learning to Labour*, they do not value education. Thanks to their habituses, when faced with educational choices they either do not see furthering their education as a feasible option or opt out because it does not seem a natural progression—they would feel like 'a fish out of water'. In contrast, middle-class actors are more likely to consider university education as a 'natural' step, as part of their inheritance. They have been brought up to assume that a university education would be an almost inevitable part of their life and so continue their studies for longer. Moreover, when at university they are also more likely to feel 'at home', as the underlying principles generating practices within the university field—its unwritten 'rules of the game'—are homologous to their own habituses.

Bourdieu also argues that different social classes arrive at school already equipped with different levels of the knowledge and know-how required for success. This 'cultural capital' comprises the tacit codes required for understanding culture (Moore 2008). Cultural taste in art, for example, requires the knowledge of how to look at a painting, how to discuss its significance, what forms of art should be appreciated and so on. Similarly, educational knowledge requires understanding of and familiarity with a specific culture. As discussed above, knowledge of this 'dominant cultural arbitrary' is not evenly distributed: what is taught in education and how it is taught reflects the culture of the dominant class. Students from upper-class backgrounds thereby have an advantage; they 'hold the code making it possible to decipher' the cultural content of schooling (Bourdieu 1973, p. 73). Bourdieu posits that this cultural capital can behave like money: it can be earned, stored, passed on, inherited and exchanged. All that is required for this inequality to play out is for education not to counteract this advantage. So, an ideology of equal opportunity enables social inequalities to become differential educational achievements simply by treating all pupils as the same. As researchers such as Lareau (1997) and Brown (1997) argue, drawing on Bourdieu, schools translate working-class culture into working-class educational failure. For Bourdieu, the culture of one's family background is thus crucial for explaining educational and social inequalities.

Limitations of Bourdieu's approach

Bourdieu's 'field theory' represents an advance on externalist accounts that tend to reduce education to the needs of economic and political power, while attempting to retain the insights into classroom practices of internalist accounts and the significance of the mediation of the family highlighted by studies such as *Learning to Labour* and *Making the Difference*. Bourdieu's approach has proven a fertile ground for further work and it is the basis for a wide-ranging and growing number of research studies of all aspects of education (e.g. Grenfell & James 1998).

The approach is not, of course, without its limitations. These spring from the extent to which Bourdieu's concepts enable his intentions to be realised. His approach embodies a *relational* and *structural* mode of thinking. Practices are understood as emerging from relations between the structures of social class habituses and the structure of educational contexts and practices. So we need to analyse these structures in order to discover who holds the 'code' to decipher educational knowledge and so succeed within particular forms of education and whose dispositions make it difficult for them to grasp the code and so fail. As sympathetic critics have argued (Maton 2005; 2008; Moore 2004), this requires analysing the different structures of different habituses and practices so that we can compare them. Without being able to say 'these practices represent a habitus with structure X, and those represent Y', there is a danger of circularity. Bourdieu acknowledged that one could state '"why does someone make petty-bourgeois choices? Because he has a petty bourgeois habitus!'" and he claimed to be 'keenly aware of this danger' (Bourdieu & Wacquant 1992, p. 129). However, critics reply, vigilance is not enough.

Similarly, we need a means of describing educational practices in terms of their underlying structuring principles—that is, the 'code' that makes it 'possible to decipher' the cultural content of schooling. Bourdieu's concepts highlight these key issues to be analysed, but do not fully provide the means for analysing these relational structures. This problem is played out in many uses of the framework, where concepts like 'habitus' have sometimes become a theoretical veneer over empirical description. Moreover, as Maton (2008) argues, although Bourdieu emphasised that the three concepts are inextricably interlinked, many studies have adopted the concept of 'habitus' separate from the framework, often as little more than a synonym for 'socialisation' or 'class background'. Nonetheless, Bourdieu's approach represents one of the most fruitful sociological frameworks designed for understanding education's role in society.

Basil Bernstein's code theory

In a similar fashion to Bourdieu, Basil Bernstein's approach theorises the role of symbolic control in social reproduction by analysing the dispositions that pupils bring to schooling by virtue of their upbringing and the nature of the contexts and practices they encounter in education, in order to explore relations between the two. For Bernstein, actors who experience different material conditions of life are typically socialised into different *orientations to meaning*—that is, different ways of understanding, being, acting and thinking (what Bourdieu calls 'habituses'). These, Bernstein argues, are differently 'valued by the school and differentially effective in it, because of the school's values, modes of practice and relations with its different communities' (1996, p. 91). Bourdieu and Bernstein, who were contemporaries, offer similar ideas on these issues. What distinguishes Bernstein's approach is that he theorises the issues in terms of **coding orientations** (pupils' habituses) and **educational knowledge codes** (educational practices) in a way that more fully enables a structural and relational analysis.

Bernstein's theory began by focusing primarily on how these orientations to meaning were expressed through the linguistic choices people make. In short, actors from working-class backgrounds are predisposed to more context-dependent meanings, or a **'restricted code'**, while those from the middle class are additionally predisposed to more context-independent meanings, or an **'elaborated code'**. Language can be more context-dependent when those conversing have so much in common that there is little need to make meanings explicit; this allows for rich meanings to be expressed in an economical way. Bernstein and colleagues found this form of discourse to be available to pupils from both working-class and middle-class homes. In contrast, an elaborated code makes many of these taken-for-granted meanings explicit, and in so doing often involves abstraction, generalisation, logic and explicating relationships—that is, meanings that are less tied to a specific local context. Research, such as Holland (1981), showed that this code was more to be found among middle-class pupils. Bernstein explained the differential access to the codes in terms of the forms taken by family relationships that reflect the nature of different kinds of occupations. Put simply, working-class jobs often provide little variety, offer few opportunities for participation in decision making and involve manual more than linguistic skills, while middle-class occupations offer greater variety and more negotiation in decision making and require more linguistic skills. These relations are reflected in the form taken by family relations. Bernstein (1971) distinguished between 'positional' forms of authority, where the roles of family members are clear-cut and based on one's position (such as 'father' or 'eldest child'), and 'personal' forms, where relationships are discussed more and negotiated, and thus meanings are made more explicit and rules and decisions are discussed more and explained (rather than 'Because I told you to!' or 'Because I'm your father').

Bernstein's early work was more sophisticated than can be relayed in a brief summary. (For example, he argued that variations within classes, particularly between members of the industrial and cultural middle classes, can be just as great as differences between classes.) Nonetheless, the concepts of elaborated code and restricted code contain the seeds of many of Bernstein's later ideas, especially the significance of differences in the context-dependence of meaning (see p. 189). They were, however, the subject of considerable misunderstanding. Some critics assumed Bernstein was being derogatory about working-class language, although he had stated:

Clearly one code is not better than another; each possesses its own aesthetic, its own possibilities. Society, however, may place different values on the orders of experience elicited, maintained and progressively strengthened through the different coding systems. (1971, p. 135).

What is crucial is thus how society values these codes or, more specifically, how they are differently valued in school. Bernstein and his colleagues showed that schooling values more highly the elaborated code and that success in education depends on the capacity to operate with context-independent meanings, such as abstractions and generalisations.

Educational knowledge codes

Having analysed the nature of pupils' dispositions, Bernstein turned to conceptualise further the nature of the school these pupils encounter. He argued that there exists what could be described as a *hidden curriculum* in the ways knowledge is selected, assembled and sequenced into a curriculum, then taught and assessed. Rather than the *content* of culture, it is the *forms* taken by that culture that are significant for shaping the vision of reality of pupils. Details of the content may fade from pupils' minds, but the pattern or structure underlying its arrangement shapes the way they see the world and their future ways of thinking. To analyse this structure Bernstein introduced the concepts of 'classification' and 'framing' (1975), where:

- strength of *classification* (C) refers to the relative strength of boundaries *between* contexts or categories (such as academic subjects in a curriculum)
- strength of *framing* (F) refers to the relative strength of control *within* these contexts or categories (relatively strong framing indicating strong control 'from above', such as by a teacher in a classroom).

Classification and framing can vary independently as stronger (+) or weaker (–), giving 'educational knowledge codes' underlying school practices. These are (to adopt a phrase from Bourdieu) the 'rules of the game', the unwritten principles shaping practices.

Bernstein described two principal codes: a 'collection code' (+C, +F) of stronger boundaries and stronger control; and an 'integrated code' (–C, –F) where boundaries between disciplines and between educational and everyday knowledge are blurred and where pupils have more control over the selection, sequencing and pacing of their learning. Each code is associated with different forms of school organisation, curriculum, pedagogy and evaluation; and each has its own attributes. For example, the basis of teachers' identities tends to be their subject areas under a collection code ('I teach history') and their understanding of children under an integrated code

> ## Case Study
> ### Kevin Rudd
>
> This chapter opened with a quote from a speech by Kevin Rudd, in which he argued that education is crucial to Australia's future as a nation for a variety of reasons. Looking again at the quote, make a list of the roles that he sees education as fulfilling. Are these roles compatible with one another?
>
> He also talked of the role education played in his own rise to become prime minister. Teachers were crucial to the trajectory of his life story. What kinds of sociological explanations would emphasise the role of teachers? Kevin Rudd is a Caucasian male who grew up in regional Australia. What other possible explanations could there be for his success? How might these different educational theories account for why he was successful but people from different social backgrounds are often less so?

('I teach children'). Importantly for our focus, different social groups arrive at school differentially equipped to understand and carry out what is required of them within each code. Those pupils who have not already been socialised into the code may struggle to succeed when they arrive.

An insightful example to explore with these concepts is 'progressive' or 'constructivist' pedagogy. Since at least the 1970s many educational researchers have argued that weakening boundaries between subject areas, appealing to everyday experiences and student-centred learning, will help pupils from working-class families to succeed. In Bernstein's terms, this represents weaker classification and weaker framing, or an integrated code. Using these concepts, studies by a range of scholars, including Bourne (2003), Morais, Neves & Pires (2004) and Moss (2006), show that such well-intentioned claims are often misguided: such educational practices disadvantage the very groups they are assumed to help. Put simply, pupils from working-class backgrounds have been less socialised into possessing the keys to the integrated code than pupils from cultural middle-class families. The coding orientations of working-class pupils are typically based on a collection code or stronger boundaries and forms of control (what Bernstein previously termed 'positional' forms of authority). When faced with weaker classification and framing they can struggle to recognise what is required of them and/or to provide the correct kind of performances. They are 'fish out of water'. Unless these pupils are clearly and explicitly taught the 'rules of the game' of schooling—which necessitates stronger classification and framing rather than weaker—they are likely to become disengaged and alienated.

Educational knowledge codes are only one dimension of Bernstein's framework for analysing school practices. However, they illustrate how his approach provides concepts that fully enable analysis of the key factors highlighted by other culturalist thinkers: the dispositions pupils bring to schooling; the structure of the educational contexts and practices they encounter there; and relations between the two. In his later work Bernstein also laid the groundwork for sociologically analysing knowledge itself. It is to the question of knowledge, a key theme in contemporary sociology, that we now turn.

FUTURE TRENDS: THE RISE OF KNOWLEDGE

A challenge to established approaches has emerged in recent years in the form of the issue of 'knowledge'. This reflects a wider **knowledge paradox** at the heart of sociological understandings of contemporary societies. According to a range of thinkers we are entering a fundamentally new era, the Information Age (Castells 1996b), characterised by the advent of 'knowledge societies' (Stehr 1994) based on 'knowledge economies' that require their citizens to actively engage in 'lifelong learning' (Field 2006). Though they differ in their emphases, such accounts share two principal features:

1. *Knowledge is central to social change.* Knowledge has become viewed as permeating all areas of social life, from the market, social structure and political sphere to the family, identity and individual consciousness. The rise of new information and communications technologies (ICTs) and their increasingly global reach are said to be rapidly expanding and democratising knowledge, moving its creation and circulation outside formal schooling. Moreover, economic changes are making knowledge central to our lives. Bernstein (2001), for example, argued that we are entering a 'Totally Pedagogised Society' where workers are expected to change skills at a moment's notice, constantly retraining and learning throughout their lives. Much of this retraining is for jobs in the knowledge economy, in which handling information is more significant than the production of material goods.

2. *Knowledge remains largely undefined.* Although knowledge is central to modern societies, most accounts of social changes lack a theory of knowledge. For example, in Manuel Castells' three-volume work, *The Information Age*, the definition of knowledge is relegated to a footnote as 'a set of organized statements of facts or ideas' (1996b, p. 17). Knowledge is typically treated as homogeneous and having no inner structure with properties, powers or tendencies of its own. So, the very thing that is supposedly now central to every aspect of our lives is itself not theorised or understood.

This knowledge-blindness extends to much educational research. As Bernstein (1990) highlights, analyses of education have tended to focus on one of two issues:

- *relations to* knowledge, such as the relations of class, gender and ethnicity to the curriculum
- *relations within* knowledge or the forms taken by knowledge itself, its internal structures.

Since the issue of knowledge was brought to the foreground of sociological thinking in the early 1970s by the 'new sociology of education' (Young 1971), a focus on 'relations to' knowledge has dominated the field. The work of Bowles and Gintis argued that educational knowledge reflects the needs of capitalism (see pp. 174–5); feminists and multiculturalists revealed the ways seemingly neutral curriculums reflected the experiences of white, European men; and post-structuralists have excavated how knowledge constructs subjects in ways that reflect the interests of the powerful. This focus has been adopted by researchers drawing on a diverse range of thinkers and theories, including symbolic interactionism, social phenomenology, cultural anthropology, Bourdieu, Foucault, Derrida and Lyotard, among others. As a number of writers have argued in recent years (Maton & Moore 2010b), these different approaches share a tendency to ask questions of 'whose knowledge?' and obscure questions of 'what form of knowledge?'. 'Relations within' knowledge has typically been viewed as irrelevant and suggestions that it may play a role in understanding education have been dismissed as essentialist. As Maton & Moore (2010a) argue, this reflects a belief that *either* knowledge must be decontextualised, value-free and 'objective' (essentialism) *or* it is nothing but socially and historically constructed and reflects relations of power (relativism). Faced with this dichotomy, sociologists of education have typically opted for focusing on how knowledge reflects the interests of dominant social groups. The result has been a tendency towards relativism and treating knowledge as if it were little more than a mirror of social power.

SOCIAL REALISM

Over the past decade a new approach to understanding knowledge and its role in education has emerged that builds primarily on the work of Bernstein (see p. 186) and Bourdieu (see p. 184). Social realism highlights that knowledge is the basis of education as a social field of practice; it is the production, recontextualisation, teaching and learning of *knowledge* that makes education a distinct field. To reduce knowledge to power is thus to obscure a defining feature of education. Moreover, it argues that the choice between essentialism and relativism is false: we can say that knowledge is historically and socially constructed without saying this means all knowledge is equal and merely reflects social power. Social realism acknowledges that knowledge changes and is shaped by relations of power but maintains that this is not the whole story. Not all knowledge claims are equal—some are more epistemologically powerful and give us a stronger grip on the world than others. Exploring the collective procedures whereby judgements of the comparative value of knowledge claims are made by academics or teachers has been a central focus of social realist thinking.

Above all, social realism argues that different forms of knowledge have different effects for intellectual and educational practices. One way of analysing these draws on Basil Bernstein's description of two different forms of discourse (1999):

- *Horizontal discourse* refers to everyday or 'commonsense' knowledge, where meaning is largely dependent on the context, so knowledges may be strongly segmented from one another; for example, learning to tie up your shoes bears little relation to learning how to use the lavatory correctly.
- *Vertical discourse* refers to educational, formal or 'official' knowledge and 'takes the form of a coherent, explicit, and systematically principled structure' (1999, p. 159) where meanings are related to other meanings rather than to a specific social context. (Here Bernstein is reformulating and revising his earlier distinction between restricted and elaborated codes; see p. 186.)

Bernstein then makes a second distinction within vertical discourse between:

- *hierarchical knowledge structures*, such as physics, which develop through integrating past knowledge within more overarching ideas that attempt to explain a greater number of phenomena than previously achieved, and
- *horizontal knowledge structures*, such as the humanities and sociology, which develop through the addition of a new approach or theory alongside existing approaches and from which it is strongly bounded.

This model of different forms of knowledge is proving fruitful in analysing issues concerning the nature of both academic inquiry and teaching and learning in classrooms. In particular, it highlights the different ways in which knowledge develops over time and the issue of the context-dependence of meaning. Maton (2009), for example, builds on Bernstein's model to analyse examples of teaching in professional education at university and in school English in Australia. He shows how many pupils are experiencing 'segmented learning', where new ideas and skills are failing to build on their previous knowledge, rather than 'cumulative learning', where new knowledge is integrated. Wheelahan (2007) shows how the forms of knowledge taught in vocational education and training in Australia are often less powerful because they are highly dependent on their context. Rather than being taught principles of knowledge, so that ideas can be used in any context, students are typically learning knowledge and skills that are useful for specific tasks and less able to be transferred to other tasks and contexts in future. Working-class students are overrepresented in vocational education, so forms of knowledge of differing capacities are being taught to different social classes. Bringing knowledge into the equation thereby makes the basis of differential educational outcomes a question not simply of access to education or to the highest status institutions and qualifications, but also of access to the most powerful forms of knowledge.

LEGITIMATION CODE THEORY

One example of social realism is Karl Maton's Legitimation Code Theory (or LCT). LCT explores the ways that knowledge claims are legitimated. One dimension of the theory explores what makes a claim to insight special or worthy of distinction. Maton (2000; 2007) begins from the premise that every practice, belief or

SOCIOLOGY

knowledge claim is about or oriented towards something and by someone, and so sets up an *epistemic relation* (ER) to an object and a *social relation* (SR) to a subject. Simply put, each relation may be more strongly (+) or weakly (–) emphasised in practices and beliefs, and these two relative strengths of emphasis together give the code. Thus, a claim to insight can be viewed as specialised by its epistemic relation, by its social relation, by both, or by neither. Figure 5.7 outlines four such codes:

- a *knowledge code* (ER+, SR–), where possession of specialised knowledge, skills or procedures is emphasised as the basis of achievement and the dispositions of authors or actors are downplayed
- a *knower code* (ER–, SR+), where specialist knowledge or skills are less significant and instead the dispositions of the subject as a knower are emphasised as the measure of achievement, whether these are viewed as natural (e.g. 'genius'), cultivated (such as an educated artistic gaze) or socially based (such as a specific gender, e.g. being female)
- an *elite code* (ER+, SR+), where legitimacy is based on both possessing specialist knowledge and being the right kind of knower ('elite' does not mean 'socially exclusive' but rather highlights the necessity of possessing *both* legitimate knowledge *and* legitimate dispositions)
- a *relativist code* (ER–, SR–), where legitimate insight is ostensibly determined by neither specialist knowledge nor specific dispositions.

These legitimation codes of specialisation conceptualise the 'rules of the game'—the dominant basis of success in any particular social context. Like Bernstein's concepts of codes, on which they build, these concepts provide a means for conducting research into the dispositions brought by pupils to education, the nature of educational practices and relations between the two.

Chen, Bennett and Maton (2010), for example, explore why Chinese students studying at a university in Australia struggle with certain forms of teaching. They analyse the educational dispositions these students bring with them in terms of a knowledge code: an emphasis on states of knowledge and a desire for clear, explicit procedures for achieving success. In contrast, the courses they were studying in Australia represented a knower code: teachers downplayed explicit instruction and emphasised that students already possessed legitimate insights and should create their own knowledge based on their experiences. The students did not understand the rules of the game—they saw personal experience as not legitimate knowledge and felt they were not being taught. In other words, there was a 'code clash' between the expectations and dispositions of these students and the educational practices they encountered. The result in this case was that the students felt abandoned, lost, inferior, helpless, guilty and depressed.

Another study explores why school qualifications in music have an extremely low take-up rate among pupils (Lamont & Maton 2008). The study highlights how pupils experience a 'code shift': the rules of the game change from being a knower code at primary school, where the emphasis is on personal expression and creativity at music, to a knowledge code at secondary school, where the emphasis shifts to technical and theoretical knowledge of music. Crucially, in school music a second shift then occurs as pupils near qualifications at the age of 16, which require pupils to demonstrate not only musical knowledge but also musical dispositions—an elite code. In other words, pupils are then judged in two ways, making school qualifications in music potentially less attractive than other subjects, especially when their relative value in the job market is taken into consideration.

What such studies are showing is how the forms taken by knowledge claims can shape the educational experiences and outcomes of different groups of pupils. Approaches like LCT are beginning to unpick the complex nature of knowledge and the role it plays in all aspects of our lives. They are also attempting to integrate the insights of past approaches, so that the sociology of education builds on the past in order to understand the future. However, there is still much to be explored and explained: educational inequalities persist and the role played by education in society remains a source of intense debate within contemporary sociology.

FIGURE 5.7

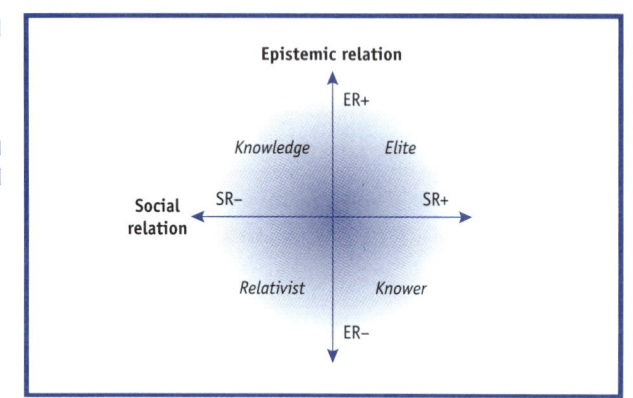

Legitimation codes of specialisation Source: Maton (2007, p. 97).

Tutorial exercise

Consider this sociology textbook. Read through the contents page and think about the narrative within the chapters. Do the various areas of sociology relate to each other, or are they often separate? How do new theories relate to older theories? In your group, make a case for seeing sociology as integrating past ideas within newer, more encompassing theories. Then make a case for describing sociology as being segmented into a series of theories and topics in which newer ideas replace but largely fail to build on older ones. What are the gains and losses to be had from sociology being either of these forms of knowledge?

For activity suggestions, learning aids, revision of key concepts and access to self-study material, visit: **www.pearson.com.au/highered/vankrieken4e**

Further reading

Arnot, M., David, M. & Weiner, G. 1999, *Closing the Gender Gap: Post-war Education and Social Change*, Polity Press, Cambridge.

Grenfell, M. & James, J. 1998, *Bourdieu and Education: Acts of Practical Theory*, Falmer Press, London.

Halsey, A. H., Lauder, H. Brown, P. & Wells, A. S. (eds) 1997, *Education, Culture, Economy, Society*, Oxford University Press, Oxford.

Maton, K. & Moore, R. (eds.) 2010, *Social Realism, Knowledge and the Sociology of Education: Coalitions of the Mind*, Continuum, London.

Moore, R. 2004, *Education and Society: Issues and Explanations in the Sociology of Education*, Polity Press, Cambridge.

Websites

Australian Association for Research in Education:
www.aare.edu.au/live

Bourdieu and Bernstein:
http://groups.google.com/group/Bourdieu and **http://tech.groups.yahoo.com/group/B_Bernstein**
At these websites you can join in email discussion on the culturalist approaches of Bourdieu and Bernstein with researchers.

Department of Education, Employment and Workplace Relations:
www.deewr.gov.au/Pages/default.aspx
This website provides insights into the current political discourse surrounding education.

International Sociological Association's special-interest group on sociology of education:
www.isa-sociology.org/rc04.htm

The Australian Sociological Association:
www.tasa.org.au/web-links/sociology-of-education
This website lists resources on the sociology of education.

Leisure, Sport, Tourism and Work

By the end of the chapter, you should have a better understanding of:
— the reasons why the study of leisure, sport and tourism is central to sociology and to contemporary social life
— the diverse sociological perspectives on leisure, sport and tourism and the ability to think critically about these
— some major sociological findings about work and unemployment.

INTRODUCTION	**194**
LEISURE	**194**
Leisure in our lives	194
Leisure, power and inequality	196
Taste and cultural capital—Pierre Bourdieu	196
Leisure and social capital	197
Power and conflict over leisure	198
Gender and leisure	198
Women reading—Janice Radway	198
Gender and leisure time—Michael Bittman and Judy Wajcman	199
SPORT	**199**
Australian participation in sport	199
Sport and modernity	200
From Ritual to Record—Allen Guttmann	200
The civilising process in sports—Eric Dunning	202
Sport and the gender order	202
Gendered patterns of participation in Australia	202
Gender order in Australia	202
Sporting ideology and gender in Australia	203
Sport and sexual violence in Australia—Peter Mewett and Kim Toffoletti	204
David Beckham and the 'new man'	205
Sport, class and race	205
TOURISM	**206**
The importance of tourism	207
Sociological perspectives on tourism	208
'Escaping the real'—Daniel Boorstin	208
The search for the 'authentic'—Dean MacCannell	208
The tourist gaze—John Urry	208
The social impacts of tourism—Jennifer Craik	209
Future directions in tourism studies	209
WORK	**211**
The work and employment profile of Australia	211
The experience of work	211
Multiple factors influencing militancy and strikes—Claire Williams	213
Work, modernity and postmodernity	214
Gender, inequality and work	215
The emotional labour of Australian magistrates—Sharyn Roach Anleu and Kathy Mack	216
Emotional labour in the airline industry—Claire Williams	216
Unemployment	217
Unemployment in Australia—a profile	218
CONCLUSION	**218**
Tutorial exercise	219
Further reading	219
Websites	219

INTRODUCTION

For many years sociology textbooks such as this would have had special chapters dedicated to the sociology of 'work'. This reflected the agenda-setting by some of the founding figures in sociology, such as Karl Marx and Emile Durkheim. They saw 'work' as the really fundamental thing in social organisation. For years, sociologists often talked as if real work was 'man's work'—in particular, wage-earning industrial work or desk-driven bureaucratic work. The impression they gave was that everything in society was built upon and around the factory floor.

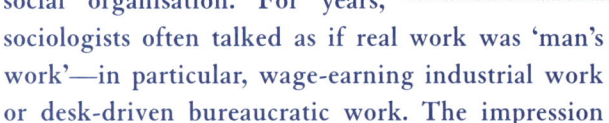

1. Today's textbooks have a very different feel. Leisure, sport and tourism now take up many of the pages that were once given over to 'work'. Why is this so?
2. Does this shift reflect changes in sociological thinking, or changes in the world itself?

Work and leisure make up much of our lives—in fact, along with sleep they comprise most of how we spend our time on this planet, so it is not surprising that they are so central in the research field of sociology. Work drives the economy—and so does leisure. Billions of dollars change hands in wages and in consumer spending on fun.

Furthermore, survey responses show that the way we define ourselves is often through our jobs, as well as through our involvement in sports and leisure activities. For example, some people say that their 'true' self can be found in leisure activities, whereas others point to their jobs as more central to their self-concept. Tourism and sport in particular play a major role in our cultural life. They have a role in defining gender and national identity, in spreading new ideas about selfhood and tolerance for other cultures, and in reinforcing older entrenched beliefs. Likewise, the world of work is not just about generating useful goods and services—it is also an arena where identities, hierarchies and struggles over power take place.

For these reasons, sociologists study work, leisure, sport and tourism not simply as commonplace activities but also as arenas of meaningful social life that have hidden and profound consequences for the organisation of our society.

LEISURE

For many years sociologists did not spend much time looking at leisure. It was assumed to be little more than the optional and trivial stuff that people did once the really important things like earning a wage had been accomplished. What could possibly be interesting or sociologically relevant about people watching television, going for a walk or collecting postage stamps? Shouldn't we be studying coalmining, ship building and government bureaucracies?

Today, things have changed. Leisure is understood to be pivotal to how people spend their time and money, how they think about themselves and their social networks, and how inequality is reproduced in society. This new perspective finds plenty of support in Australia, where leisure has long been seen as an important aspect of everyday life. Indeed, Australians like to think of the 'lucky country' in terms of images of outdoor leisure—the beach, barbecues, fishing and sport are all central components of Australian national identity. Systematic data collection has enabled sociologists to test this myth of an egalitarian leisure-based society and to see exactly what we do.

LEISURE IN OUR LIVES

One of our first tasks should be to see how people spend their time and to answer the question 'How much leisure is there in Australia?' The 2006 Time Use Survey, conducted by the Australian Bureau of Statistics, enables us to address this issue (ABS 2008b). It argues that there are four main kinds of time:

- *Necessary time*. This includes things that are required for personal survival, such as eating and sleeping.
- *Contracted time*. This includes paid work, but also schooling and other activities where certain specified hours belong to an employer or institution.

CHAPTER 6 LEISURE, SPORT, TOURISM AND WORK

- *Committed time.* This includes things that people do for others, such as volunteering or family care work. It also includes housework and shopping.
- *Free time.* This is what is left over.

Figure 6.1 shows how Australians spent their time in 2006 (data are not routinely collected on this issue). We can see that about 46 per cent of time was spent on necessary time activities (8 hours of sleep is 33 per cent of the 24-hour cycle, after all), 17 per cent was spent on committed time, 16 per cent on contracted time and 21 per cent on free time. Looking at the figure we might reflect on the fact that 'work', a form of contracted time, takes up only a small proportion of life despite its importance for traditional sociology and economics. The same survey also revealed some important gender differences. Men had nearly twice as much contracted time (21 per cent) as women (12 per cent), but women had nearly twice as much committed time (22 per cent) as men (12 per cent). To some extent this reflects a gendered division of labour. Men tend to do more full-time paid jobs, whereas women do more unpaid caring work and housework.

As for leisure itself, the survey showed that the average amount of time spent per day on leisure activities is 4 hours and 13 minutes. Those aged 25–64 tend to have less leisure time than people aged under 25 and over 65. Involvement in the paid labour force (contracted time) and with family responsibilities (committed time) eats into available leisure time. In general, men have slightly more leisure time than women, a pattern that might reflect the open-ended nature of housework, child-care and elder-care activities, and the deeply cemented gendered expectations that these are 'women's work'.

Many sociologists argue that the movement towards a postindustrial or postmodern economy has seen the field of leisure, broadly defined, become more and more central to the economy itself. Certainly Australian labour force statistics are consistent with this picture. A remarkable number of people are involved in jobs that provide leisure services and infrastructure for consumers. According to the Australian Bureau of Statistics (2007a), in 2007 some three-and-a-half million Australians, 22 per cent of adults, had undertaken paid or unpaid work in culture and leisure fields in the previous 12 months. Around 8 per cent had been paid for their involvement in culture and leisure. The sorts of jobs counted here were amazingly diverse. They included working or volunteering in a museum, zoo, botanic gardens or art gallery; working in the visual arts such as photography or print making; craft-making such as pottery or jewellery; writing and publishing; working as a live performer/artist; and working in cinema, web design, video-game design, radio or television. This is not an exhaustive list, but it does provide an indication of the huge scope and range of cultural and leisure activities at play.

Furthermore, the statistics tend to underestimate the size of the leisure field. For example, they do not include those engaged in a personal hobby activity. Almost 2.1 million Australians are engaged in art and craft as a hobby, 356 000 in writing as a hobby and 265 000 in music as a hobby. Nor do the statistics include jobs in tourism or sports that we might think of as leisure

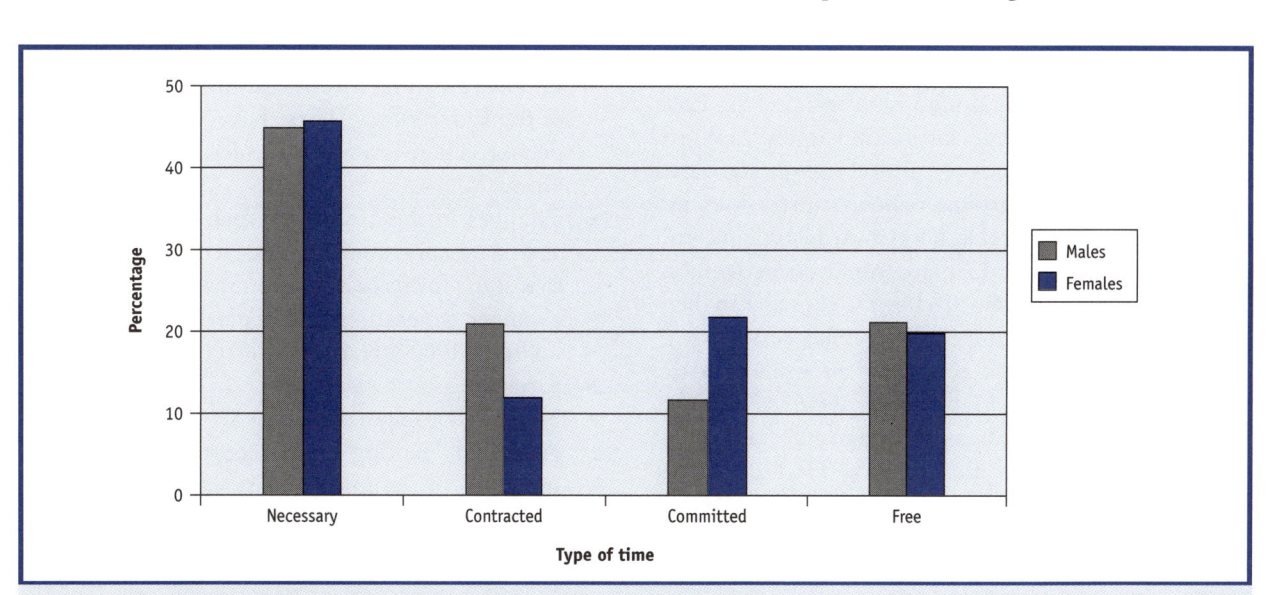

FIGURE 6.1

How Australians spend their time *Source:* ABS (2008b).

195

sector employment, or people visiting cultural centres or merely consuming cultural experiences.

The importance of the arts and leisure fields to the Australian economy has not gone unnoticed in the education sector. Many universities offer courses aiming to prepare graduates for work in the 'culture industries'. By this they mean production and policy in the areas of film, television, museums and arts.

Leisure, power and inequality

Commonsense would tell us that leisure is only weakly related to inequality. We might speculate that rich people have more free time or do things that cost more, such as yachting or playing polo. Perhaps they even have more fun than the average person because they can afford better holidays, hotel rooms, personal trainers and high-end equipment. Sociological research suggests a more profound connection between leisure and life opportunities, especially in the field of cultural consumption. The films we watch, the books we read, the music we play in our free time—all have implications for the reproduction of the wider social structure.

Taste and cultural capital—Pierre Bourdieu

The French sociologist Pierre Bourdieu (2007) suggests that leisure is a major source of cultural capital. This has many dimensions, including knowledge, taste/preferences and skills. So knowing about Beethoven, liking Beethoven's music and being able to play Beethoven's music on the piano are all forms of cultural capital. Bourdieu insists that such knowledge is not trivial. Forms of cultural capital map onto social class. Love and knowledge of opera, classical music and high art, for example, are all kinds of cultural capital associated with dominant social groups. Schools, universities and teachers show subtle preferences towards students with high cultural capital, as do many employers in the more prestigious fields. In short, cultural capital can help people to get ahead by impressing gatekeepers.

Bourdieu's own work conducted in France in the 1960s was published in his book *Distinction*. This showed strong correlations between cultural capital and objective social location or class. He argued that students from middle- and upper-class backgrounds were able to translate this into good jobs and powerful institutional positions. By contrast, students from working-class backgrounds were excluded. Much of what they 'need' to know is not taught in the formal curriculum of schools but rather in the informal world of the family. There was no way for them to catch up.

Critiques of Bourdieu

Bourdieu's work has stimulated a massive effort at replication and testing around the world. A major modification of his argument has come from the work of Richard Peterson in the United States. According to Peterson and his various collaborators (e.g. Peterson & Kern 1996), Bourdieu's work might simply reflect the realities of 1960s France with its more rigid and class-bound society.

Bourdieu found that the taste of the middle and professional classes was upscale, that of the working classes more populist. Peterson argues that in the United States particularly, there is an asymmetry in cultural consumption. The middle classes consume a wider variety of cultural genres than do the working class. They like exclusive cultural products as well as those of the working class. For example, a judge might like opera, rock and blues music. A factory worker, by contrast, might like only country and western music or rock music. The higher status person dips into different genres and has some competence at understanding a range of cultural products. Peterson dubs such a person the omnivore. Using time series data, Peterson and Kern argue that high-brow consumers have become increasingly omnivorous over time. They give several reasons for this:

- The expansion of higher education has made high-brow culture more widely known. Other ways of gaining distinction are required by those who seek it.
- Snobbery is linked to hierarchical value systems of the 19th century. These have been in empirical decline. There is now more tolerance and universalism.
- Changes in the art world, such as 'pop art' and abstract expressionism, undercut the argument that some forms of art were superior to others.
- Younger generations, particularly those growing up in the 1960s, were anti-elitist compared to their parents.
- Elements of popular culture are often tamed and gentrified, making them acceptable and understandable to the middle classes. Non-violent rap music might be a case in point.

The most advanced work on cultural consumption in Australia has been conducted by the noted sociologist Michael Emmison (2003). In a wide-ranging replication of Bourdieu's study, Emmison and his colleagues discovered that the pattern detected by Peterson broadly held good. The Australian middle classes were omnivores. However, they also detected something else going on that Peterson might have missed. What people knew about was different from what they liked. For example, in a survey project Emmison and his collaborators asked people to identify the artists associated with different songs and compositions over a range of genres (Bennett, Emmison & Frow 1999). They were also asked about what they themselves listened to. To be sure the Australian middle classes had omnivorous knowledge. They could name the bands and singers associated with hit records. They knew, for example, about the output of Madonna, Nirvana and Slim Dusty—all important artists at the time of the survey. Yet they did not necessarily like this material. The professionals in the study (doctors, lawyers, etc.) were magpies for information, not omnivorous consumers. They knew a lot about everything but their taste remained somewhat upscale and discriminating. Managers, paraprofessionals and small-business owners were closer to the ideal type of omnivore who likes or consumes material from both high-status and popular genres.

Emmison suggests that the diverse knowledge base of the middle classes gives them a considerable advantage in a complex and culturally diverse world. Higher status individuals are able to move easily across social spheres and to deploy their knowledge as needed in divergent social settings. Emmison (2003) calls this adaptive advantage 'cultural mobility'.

Another important finding of their Australian study was the prevalence of the 'low-brow omnivore' who enjoyed products from a number of popular genres. This group numerically far outnumbered (26 per cent) the Peterson ideal type of the complete omnivore (8 per cent) who had both high and low tastes. These low-brow omnivores tended to be younger. Students, for example, might like rap and rock but also listen occasionally to classical music. Older Australians seemed more likely to be locked into one or two genres of choice.

A further critique of Bourdieu has been made by Ian Woodward (2003; 2006). He conducted an interview study in Brisbane in which he visited people's houses and talked to them about their purchases, favourite objects and interior design choices. Woodward found that the quest for distinction seemed not to be very important for issues of purchase and display. His critique has several dimensions.

- When asked what was 'good taste', people spoke about civility and the need not to offend others. Wearing revealing or age-inappropriate clothing like muffin-top trousers, for example, might be seen as 'bad taste'. Ian Woodward and Michael Emmison (2001) argue that this kind of moral evaluation differs from Bourdieu's understanding of a quest for exclusivity and distinction.
- The objects that people liked or showed to others were tied in particular ways to their biographies. They might come from a special holiday, for example, or be an heirloom.
- People often expressed anxiety and guilt over their consumption activity. They were worried that they were showing off to others or—in the case of a woman who had bought a stove for $5000—that they had become shallow consumers.
- Within the middle class itself there were two different ways of imaging and shaping the home. One was about comfort and relaxation; the other was more concerned with aesthetics, style and display.

The overall picture we get from Ian Woodward's work is of consumption as a complex and deeply meaningful activity that cannot be fully explained as a competitive game that is driven mostly by the quest for status. Rather, consumption is caught up in a personal, moral and emotionally loaded world.

Leisure and social capital

If leisure is seen by Bourdieu as producing negative social outcomes, others have asserted that the right kind of leisure time can have pro-social outcomes. According to Robert Putnam (2001), leisure can play a core role in the formation of **social capital**. At the individual level, social capital gives us trust in others and extensive social networks that can be mobilised in times of trouble. At the community level, improved social capital can translate into low crime rates, better educational attainment, lower unemployment and lower levels of inequality. In addition, Putnam argues that social capital can lead to happier and more interesting lives.

According to Putnam, however, there has been a net decline in social capital over recent decades and leisure has played a role in this fall. Putnam gives particular attention to the role of clubs and societies in bringing people together, often with reference to a shared leisure interest such as gardening, photography or bowling. These clubs and societies bond people together and the common interest allows bridges to be built between sections of the community that might not otherwise meet. But if people used to do such things together, now they do them alone. More and more leisure time is spent at home, watching television for example. Social capital has been eroded. Putnam sums up the situation in his famous analogy to 'bowling alone', by which he means that whereas people used to belong to ten-pin bowling leagues where they would meet strangers, now they simply show up at the bowling ally and play by themselves.

Power and conflict over leisure

Leisure can also connect to power as a sphere where meanings are contested and practices are subject to social control. Often this process involves social movements, moral evaluations and fears about disorder. The sociological literature documents numerous struggles over whether or not certain forms of leisure are legitimate or should be subject to legal regulation. Traditionally, forms of working-class leisure have been subject to regulation and control. The opening hours of pubs and working men's clubs, for example, were closely restricted for many years. This reflected worries about an unruly and drunken workforce as well as paternalistic sentiment—the working class didn't know what was in their own best interests. Sometimes efforts at regulation go up the social scale. The movement to ban foxhunting in England is a classic example. The anti-foxhunting social movement managed to define this as a cruel activity rather than as a healthy and useful sport that was a valuable countryside tradition.

Chris Rojek (1989) usefully suggests that interest groups will battle over the definition and legal regulation of leisure time and leisure space. In looking at *leisure time*, Rojek explores the issue of dispute over Sunday trading (shops opening on Sundays) in the United Kingdom in 1986. Moves to allow Sunday trading were supported by the press, consumer groups and retailers' organisations. But they were opposed by an alliance of trade unions and religious groups. Rojek argues that opponents of Sunday trading mobilised discourses of Sunday as a special time. This understanding was of Sunday as a day for contemplation, home and family life. This vision of Sunday has been historically dominant and responsible for more than restrictions on Sunday trading. Other places such as betting shops, discos, clubs and even museums have limited opening hours on Sundays. As a result there is a paradoxical situation where on the day of the week that the fewest people work, there are the most limited opportunities for leisure.

In exploring *leisure space*, Rojek looks at contestation over the meanings of Stonehenge, the world-famous megalithic stone circle in rural England. Dominant meanings have framed Stonehenge as a place of scientific and heritage interest. However, marginal groups such as hippies and 'new-age travellers' see it not as a museum piece but as a spiritual place that should be available for festivals and gatherings. During the mid-1980s, a series of confrontations took place in which the police, responding to pressure from the Department of the Environment and the National Trust, tried to stop or divert convoys of travellers. Things came to a head in 1985, when a violent confrontation erupted at a roadblock 10 kilometres from Stonehenge at which the police, equipped with riot gear, arrested 537 people.

Rojek concludes that leisure time and leisure space are created by the actions of people. These actions often take on a political and conflictual character when particular times and places have different meanings for various social groups.

Gender and leisure

Feminist theorists have argued that women's leisure is compromised by their domestic responsibilities. They are rarely able to have quiet time alone and are burdened by expectations about never-ending domestic duties. Whereas for men the home is a place of leisure, for women it is also and always a workplace where they can never quite relax. If women have paid work outside the home, when they get home they have a so-called 'second shift' of domestic duties. Public places offer women little practical alternative. Fear of sexual assault is said to reduce options such as walking in the park. Women often cannot go to the pub or gym alone without worrying about sexual harassment or negative innuendo. As a result of constraints in both public and private arenas, women have evolved creative strategies for generating leisure. One of these is reading.

Women reading—Janice Radway

Janice Radway (1991) connected leisure to gender in an interesting book about women's reading activity. Using interviews and ethnography, Radway looked at ordinary women who read romantic fiction. These are the kinds of books, for example, where the heroine gets to marry a tall dark stranger—who turns out to be rich. Radway argued that the plot lines of such works are conservative. To a large extent these works reinforce traditional gender norms and do not offer positive or useful instruction on how to become an independent, non-married female. Radway's interviews showed that her readers were aware of this value bias. They were also aware that the books were escapist. Nevertheless, Radway argued that a gender/power dynamic was at play. Simply by sitting down with a book the women were opting out of never-ending housework demands and claiming their own 'me-time'.

Gender and leisure time—Michael Bittman and Judy Wajcman

Radway used qualitative methods. Another way to investigate women's access to leisure opportunities is through quantitative studies of time use. We might perhaps compare men and women rather than looking at just women's perspectives. Michael Bittman and Judy Wajcman (2000) did just this, making use of data from time-use diaries from cross-national research in developed nations. In order to address theoretical concerns about the 'second shift' (housework responsibilities mentioned above) disadvantaging women's access to leisure, they focused in particular on married couples who were both employed full-time. Their findings demonstrated that in such contexts men and women both do about 50 hours of total work per week on average. However, men tend to do more paid work and women more unpaid work (housework and other chores). Typically, women do about 25 hours of paid work and 25 hours of unpaid work. Men do 42 hours of paid work and 8 hours of unpaid work. The gender gap in free time was remarkably small—usually only two or three hours. There was, however, some variation. Italian men were advantaged to the tune of 6 hours, perhaps reflecting the familial ideologies of their nation, whereas women in Norway had *more* leisure time than their male partners.

Looking at the quality of leisure time provides yet another way of thinking about gender differentials. Bittman and Wajcman usefully distinguished between high-quality (uninterrupted or dedicated) leisure and low-quality (interrupted or combined activity) leisure. They found that men had about 3 hours more quality leisure than women every week. This is a significant finding, although again the gender gap is hardly as dramatic as many advocates of the 'second shift' hypothesis would predict. Where they do find a more striking gender gap is in the case of families with young children. Here, both parents had their leisure time substantially diminished thanks to child-care obligations. However, men still enjoyed substantially more 'adult leisure' (child-free relaxation) than women. For example, in the case of parents of children under age two, the man would typically enjoy nearly 8 hours of adult leisure per week whereas the woman had only 2.5 hours of such time. Much of their leisure was of a poor-quality kind and involved activities with their children. By the time the children had become teenagers this gap in the quality of leisure was substantially reduced.

So Bittman and Wajcman were able to conclude that 'second shift' arguments are a little overdrawn because they assume that women simply add paid working hours onto their existing unpaid housework obligations. Their data suggest that not only is there little difference, on average, between the total work time of men and women, but also there is little difference in leisure time. Taken as a whole, women are only modestly disadvantaged in terms of the *quantity* of leisure available to them. Where differences creep in is in terms of *quality*. Bittman and Wajcman argue that their quantitative findings are consistent with qualitative research, indicating that women's leisure is compromised by multiple and overlapping task obligations that prevent it from being truly relaxing. Most importantly, they suggest that being the mother of young children is a particularly strong predictor of leisure inequity.

> **Reflective questions:** In what ways is leisure socially consequential? Is leisure just about people having fun? Indicate some ways that leisure maps onto social inequality.

SPORT

As with leisure, we might think of sport as something peripheral or trivial in social life. Just the opposite is true. Sociologists have documented:

- the profound impact of sport on our culture as a channel through which personal and collective identities are formed
- the powerful role of major sporting corporations in economic life, often in conjunction with the mass media and in a wider context of globalisation
- the role of sport in perpetuating inequality and, much more rarely, opportunity.

AUSTRALIAN PARTICIPATION IN SPORT

When we think of sport, we tend to think first of sports stars—the world-class athletes and professionals we see on television. It is easy to forget that sport is closely linked to everyday life for ordinary people as both spectators and participants. Many of us spend money on sporting gear, read newspapers and Web pages

Case Study
The Sydney Olympic Games: worthwhile or a waste of money?

The Sydney Olympic Games in 2000 were hailed by the International Olympic Committee President Juan Antonio Samaranch as 'the best Games ever'. A total of 10 651 athletes attended from 199 countries; ticket sales amounted to $780 million; some 47 000 people volunteered to help; four billion people watched around the world; and millions of Australians cheered on their national sporting heroes (ABS 2002a). Yet in the run-up to the Games the media had a field day reporting a litany of bungles, scandals and mismanagement. As the Sydney Olympic Games made clear, sport is simultaneously big business, big politics and an important part of contemporary cultural life.

Like work, sport and leisure are seen as something that brings net benefits to society. They are said to be fun, to encourage a healthy lifestyle and to foster achievement. Perhaps for these reasons our attitudes towards sport are often curiously unreflexive. We rarely think about the negatives. For example, discussion of the financial burden of the Sydney Games was never encouraged. It is believed that they cost about $3 billion to stage. Years later, the under-utilised sporting venues were still being bailed out with taxpayers' money. Critics suggest that these resources could have been better spent on schools, hospitals or grassroots sporting activities from which ordinary Australians could obtain a direct benefit, year after year.

A sociological perspective can help us understand such issues. We can look at the social distribution of leisure time and at rates of everyday sports participation, for example, and see whether sport really does deliver social goods. We can also begin to gain a critical distance by exploring sports mythologies and subcultures and the ways that these might be implicated in the construction of identities and inequalities.

on sport, go to games and competitions, hire coaches, belong to sports clubs that double as community clubs where social networks are built, and spend a lot of time talking about sport with friends and colleagues.

Sport permeates life for a substantial proportion of the population. One way to begin to understand this is to look at some basic statistics. In June 2005 some 100 000 people were employed in sports clubs, horse- and dog-racing venues, gymnasia, sports administration and sports and recreation services. The income of these organisations was more than $7 billion. Australia employs an amazing 12 000 greenkeepers on golf courses. More than 87 000 people receive some kind of payment in cash or goods and services as sports players. Around 11 per cent of Australians volunteer every year for a sports or physical recreation organisation. Some 7.1 million people—or 44 per cent of the adult population—attend a sporting event every year, the most popular of these being Australian Rules Football, horse racing, rugby league and motor sport (ABS 2008a).

Australian participation in sport is shown in Table 6.1. Walking is the most popular activity for both genders, followed by aerobics and fitness workouts. Other activities such as swimming, running and cycling follow. It is interesting to reflect that the activities that people do themselves often are not, as a general rule, the same as the ones that they pay to watch (see ABS 2008a, Table 14.35). People watch events that are expensive to participate in, are complex to organise, perhaps involve some physical risk and require competent teams (e.g. rugby league, motor racing). By contrast, they tend to participate in activities that they can do by themselves at the drop of a hat or that require only one or two other people to be available at the same moment in time (e.g. swimming, golf). This reflects busy lifestyles and ordinary budgets. Soccer, netball, tennis and cricket, it should be noted, are minor exceptions to this rule—between 1 and 5 per cent of Australians attend such sporting events and a roughly similar number participate in them.

SPORT AND MODERNITY

Authors like Johan Huizinga (2003), in his famous book *Homo Ludens*, have pointed to the fact that all known human cultures have games that people love to play. Some of these games are competitive and take the form of sports. However, sports are more than arbitrary activities that have come down to us as the result of custom and tradition. In fact, any historical analysis of sport will show the same slow movement towards modernity that we find in other spheres of social life.

From Ritual to Record—Allen Guttmann

The sociologist Allen Guttmann (1978) uses a Weberian perspective in his analysis of the history of sport entitled *From Ritual to Record*. Writing about 100 years ago, Max Weber argued that over the centuries society has become more rational and bureaucratic, and at the same time less religious. Guttmann traces this path in the evolution of sport. Guttmann claims that modern sports have seven key characteristics:

- *Secularism.* Sports used to be tied to religion. An example is the games played by the ancient Aztecs, which would end in human sacrifice (of the losers), or the Olympic Games in ancient Greece, which were a kind of ritual tribute to the gods. Today, this religious component has been stripped out.
- *Equality of opportunity to compete.* This marks the triumph of the value pattern of universalism. In the past, certain sports could be played only by people of a certain social status. Today, there might be financial or opportunity barriers, yet in theory at least we are all allowed to take part.
- *Specialisation of roles.* Here we see the triumph of the division of labour and the importance of role differentiation, aspects of modernity we also find in the field of work. Sports in the Middle Ages were something of a free for all. Old English football, for example, involved people running around and fighting as they tried to get a ball from one village to the next one. Today there are specified tasks—think of the players in American Football (NFL) whose sole job is to kick the ball through the goal posts.
- *Rationalisation.* This refers to the standardisation of sports and the erosion of small local traditions. In the past, each village might have had its own unique games or rules, maintained by oral tradition. Today sports like soccer have globally agreed on standards that are controlled by central organisations. Furthermore, these are written down in rule books. We might also note the importance of rationalisation for training, medicine and strategy in sports. A visit to the Australian Institute of Sport's website gives some idea of the depth of this process (www.ausport.gov.au/ais).
- *Bureaucratic organisation.* Large-scale sports bureaucracies can be found in professional clubs, administrative bodies and government ministries. They keep records, resolve disputes and allocate resources. Informal local organisations have been displaced.
- *Quantification.* This refers to the rise of statistics and objective performance measures that try to document quality and to go beyond subjective impressions. They match the general triumph of a scientific worldview. In Australia we can see the triumph of quantification in cricket, where new statistical measures emerge every season—the average number of wickets with an old ball, for example.
- *Quest for records.* This reflects a changing time orientation in society and the fact that individuals measure themselves not against the best person in their village or immediate circle, but rather against abstract and universal standards of achievement.

TABLE 6.1

Australian participation in selected sports and physical recreation activities*

	Number ('000)	Participation rate (%)
MALES		
Walking for exercise	1298.6	16.5
Aerobics/fitness	744.5	9.4
Golf	695.6	8.8
Cycling	691.0	8.8
Swimming	633.3	8.0
Running	425.9	5.4
Tennis	389.5	4.9
Soccer (outdoor)	311.5	3.9
Cricket (outdoor)	309.7	3.9
Bush walking	248.1	3.1
FEMALES		
Walking for exercise	2659.7	32.8
Aerobics/fitness	1271.5	15.7
Swimming	814.0	10.0
Netball	387.5	4.8
Tennis	379.4	4.7
Cycling	320.7	3.9
Bush walking	271.4	3.3
Running	255.4	3.1
Yoga	248.7	3.1
Golf	179.9	2.2

*Relates to persons aged 15 years and over who participated in sports or physical recreation as a player at least once during the 12 months prior to the 2005–06 survey.
Source: ABS (2008a, Table 14.29).

The example of Trobriand cricket

To gain an insight into the kinds of processes that Guttmann speaks about it is useful to look at the example of Trobriand cricket (Kildea & Leach 1979). In the

Trobriand Islands near New Guinea a form of cricket is played that seems like a parody of the Western game. Cricket was introduced by missionaries in the hope of reducing feuds between tribes and islands. The modern game was quickly modified to suit a different cultural context.

In Trobriand cricket, singing and dancing seem to be as important as the match itself, which is often interrupted for an impromptu performance after each man is out. Ritual spells are used to bless equipment and improve the odds of victory. The teams feature pretty much any male who wants to take part—inclusion is more important than having just the best players. Similarly, having a good time is considered more important than winning or losing—indeed, the home team must always win because they are the hosts. The rules are only loosely interpreted by local umpires. Trobriand cricket is only nominally a sport—it is more of a bonding ritual for the community in general and the men in particular.

The civilising process in sports— Eric Dunning

Another way to look at the qualities of sports as thoroughly 'social' is through the lens provided by Norbert Elias (1994). Looking over the centuries Elias noted that there were extreme levels of cruelty in the Middle Ages. Public torture, for example, was common. Yet this slowly came to be seen as abhorrent. If we were to watch someone being burned alive today, most of us would feel sick and traumatised. This understanding about the changing threshold for acceptable violence has influenced the work of many sports historians such as Eric Dunning (1999). They note that legislation has progressively eliminated sports such as bear-baiting (where a chained bear is attacked by dogs), ratting (where a dog kills as many rats as it can in a pit), bare-knuckle prize-fighting and duelling with swords. Each of these activities came to be associated with cruelty and excessive, disgusting violence. Often sports were modified to make them socially acceptable. Boxing, for example, now requires the use of gloves and the presence of a doctor. In ice hockey and basketball, players might be required to go to the 'blood bin' if they have a cut. Football hooligans are seen as a major problem, in part because they continue 'pre-modern' violent practices in the sports arena—in the Middle Ages it would have been quite normal for fans or rival teams to have a jolly good fight. Today, Dunning notes, the control of emotions and violent urges is a fundamental expectation of athletes and spectators alike.

Sport and the gender order

Aside from mirroring long-term historical trends, another way in which sport is tied to wider social and cultural patterns is in maintaining ongoing social boundaries and power relations. With regard to gender, this relationship has been explored by sociologists in the following ways:

- gendered patterns of participation and non-participation and barriers to equity
- the role of sport in perpetuating idealised masculinity and femininity
- the ways that sporting figures 'perform' gendered identities
- the connection between sport and sexual violence.

Gendered patterns of participation in Australia

Turning to the first of these points, research has shown that female athletes are generally paid less than male athletes and have to struggle for their rights. Professional tennis is a case in point, with women for years having less prize money than men at events like the Australian Open and Wimbledon. Furthermore, the sports leagues and contests dominated by men—such as rugby, AFL and soccer—tend to dominate newspaper and television reporting. Only in a few sports, such as swimming and maybe netball, can women get much attention. Female leagues in 'male' sports such as soccer and rugby tend to be ignored. Sponsors are rarely interested in female teams. Equity has occasionally been forced by non-market regulation and legal challenge. Famously, in the United States, a ruling known as Title IX compelled colleges to spend money on women's sports programs. Still, the sum picture from sociological research has been of female sports being marginalised.

Gender order in Australia

Perhaps the reason for this second-class status can be found in the second bullet point above. Sociological research suggests that female sport is ideologically problematic for the dominant gender order. The work of Mike Messner, Jim McKay and their collaborators has highlighted the ambiguous and contested status of female athletes relative to male athletes (McKay, Messner & Sabo 2000). They argue that in contemporary society the gender order associates men with physical strength, toughness, muscular bodies and competitiveness. To be a 'man' and to be good at sports is not a contradiction. Rather, their sporting display helps confirm the existing gender order of R.W. Connell's 'hegemonic masculinity'. For women this is not the case. Women who exhibit 'male' virtues, such as a muscular physique or an aggressive personality, potentially challenge the gender order. They are often subject to homophobic innuendo and sanction. Pressures eventuate, perhaps from sponsors, to display a feminine side. This is one reason why female athletes often appear in glamorous magazine photo spreads, perhaps wearing a swimsuit. They might also be photographed with a husband or partner or in a conventional home setting. Although none of this is relevant to sport in and of itself, all of it is relevant to ideology.

Sporting ideology and gender in Australia

Like other countries, Australia has powerful gender myths that are reinforced by sport. Strongly influenced by cultural studies, many scholars have tried to decode the meanings of elite sports activities and their common representations. Brett Hutchins (2002), for example, made a study of the cultural complex that has arisen around Australian cricket legend Donald Bradman. 'The Don' was arguably the greatest cricketer of all time. However, Hutchins is not particularly interested in his cricket skills or even who Bradman was as a 'real' person outside of the sporting world. Hutchins is not out to cut down a tall poppy but rather seeks to understand Bradman as a signifier who has been used by others to reinforce particular values and cultural codes. Using biographies and media reportage on Bradman as his data, Hutchins shows that Bradman has been influential for Australian culture as an icon of middle-class masculine respectability, as an illustration of the individualist ethos that anyone can make it if they try hard, and as an embodiment of solidaristic, manly mateship and the spirit of fair play. According to Hutchins, these various discourses serve politically conservative ends. They reproduce a complacent and nostalgic national culture, exclude women, trivialise the structural barriers to achievement in sport and elsewhere, and celebrate the civic virtues of male sporting activity without reflecting on the dark side of sporting life.

In another study Brett Hutchins and Janine Mikosza (1998) decoded the less genteel world of Australian rugby league, looking in particular at media accounts of this activity. Here there is a slightly different cultural pattern from that in cricket. They argue that rugby league has a gender order that valorises and rewards the use of violence and physical domination. Players who are able to inflict or take pain are treated with respect. They are real men. This cultural complex reinforces male brutality as a 'natural' quality of true Australian masculinity—especially for working-class men. Hutchins and Mikosza show that women and women's sports are marginalised in this homosocial world and that occasional challenges to such a hegemonic order have been repeatedly and skilfully neutralised.

It is important to stress that the gender order of sport does not exist only at the elite level, in the mass media or among fit younger people. Maree Boyle and Jim McKay (1995) undertook an ethnographic study of an Australian bowls club, a place inhabited by older, retired people. The findings suggest that male domination is extended over women in leisure settings and in everyday interaction. Boyle and McKay argue that we tend to see retirement as a time of life when the exploitation of women ends. This is not so. Using a framework derived from R.W. Connell's (1987) work on gender relations, Boyle and McKay claim that inequality in the bowls club is structured along three dimensions—labour, power and cathexis. Broadly speaking, 'labour' refers to the role of the economy and work in maintaining inequality; 'power' to the role of politics; and 'cathexis' to psychological and cultural processes relating to sexuality and sexual identity.

- *Labour.* Work duties concerned with the upkeep of the club were divided on a gendered basis. Men were mostly concerned with the upkeep of the greens and clubhouse. Women's work included catering and the vast majority of fundraising activities. Women were expected to contribute this revenue to the men's branch of the club, even though the men did not reciprocate. This division of labour was based on perceptions about what it was 'natural' for men and women to do. Women who did not contribute enough 'voluntary' labour were liable to ostracism from both male and female members.
- *Power.* The men had control of the club assets, including the land and clubhouse. Women were not encouraged to attend club meetings, at which the decisions were made. Men had control of women's space and time. Women's bowling tended to be confined to weekdays, with men's fixtures being held in the more desirable and prestigious weekend time slots. In some cases, the men would

verbally harass the women, trivialising their style of play and subjecting them to verbal abuse.
- *Cathexis*. The 'ideal' woman bowler had been married for a long time and had conservative views on issues such as parenting, housework and abortion. It was regarded as highly improper for friendships to be formed with persons of the opposite sex, unless the friendship was between married couples. This made it difficult for women without partners to play. Women were also expected to be asexual. They had to wear four layers of clothing even in the middle of summer, including regulation undergarments that provided excess coverage of the crotch area. Men's dress codes, on the other hand, allowed for greater freedom of expression.

Boyle and McKay conclude that:

The women in this study did not 'retire' from unpaid domestic work, and, in some cases, the amount of labour they performed actually increased … The subordinate status of women in the gender regime of lawn bowls is similar to their lifelong experiences of sex segregation in the paid workforce, the family and leisure in the wider gender order. (1995, p. 373)

In a subsequent study McKay and his collaborator Yvonne Lafferty applied Connell's model to women who took up boxing. This is a theoretically interesting topic. Boxing has long been a sporting domain where hegemonic masculinity has ruled in its purest form. Is this gender order subverted by women who seemingly reject traditional female comportment, who empower themselves through violence and who enter the sacrosanct male domain of the boxing gym? Many feminists have made such theoretical claims. Yet Lafferty and McKay (2004) report down-beat findings. Lafferty's ethnographic research in an urban Australian gym suggests that women are excluded from the more prestigious activities (access to the trainer, punching bags). The belief is widespread that they are more interested in keeping fit than in fighting and that female bodies cannot be developed in the same ways as men's for fighting. The presence of sexually attractive women in the gym is understood by men to be a potential danger to the ascetic mental discipline required for training. Moreover, women who box are perceived as in some ways monstrous. The existing gender order inscribes a deep incommensurability between the controlled aggression and violence of boxing and 'true' femininity. In sum, women are marginalised and contained by practices and discourses that trivialise and oppose their participation in this male domain.

Sport and sexual violence in Australia— Peter Mewett and Kim Toffoletti

In Australia as elsewhere, sport is associated not only with sexism, but also with sexual violence. Allegations of rape and sexual assault against sportsmen and sports teams are common, especially for the various football codes in Australia. Peter Mewett and Kim Toffoletti (2008) suggest that convictions rarely eventuate due to problems of evidence. Often the claim can be made that the sex that took place, say, in a hotel room, was consensual. In explaining the prevalence of the sport/sexual assault nexus, sports sociologists have often pointed to 'jock culture' and its associated aggressive masculinity and misogyny. This leaves an interesting open question: what do female fans feel? As Mewett and Toffoletti put it, 'given that the victims of sexual assault by male athletes are overwhelmingly women, how do female supporters of male-dominated sports make sense of sexual misconduct allegations?' (2008, p. 166).

In order to find out they conducted in-depth interviews with female AFL fans. A pattern emerged of the contradictory ways that the fans understood the situation:

- The fans spoke of predatory women and groupies who might approach the men, for example, in nightclubs. The women were understood as hanging around the men and 'not giving them any space' (p. 169).
- Men's biology was interpreted as responsible for their behaviour. They were believed to have uncontrollable desires and high levels of testosterone. When approached by available women there was little they could do to hold themselves back.
- The clubs were blamed for not doing more to control their players.
- The women did recognise some sociocultural drivers of aggressive sexuality. These included the use of alcohol as a component of team bonding, status competition between players, a sense of sexual entitlement and a culture that was derogatory towards women.

The overall picture uncovered by Mewett and Toffoletti is complex. On the one hand, the women blamed other women and used essentialist arguments to excuse men. Yet they were also aware of a larger organisational, situational and cultural context.

David Beckham and the 'new man'

While a good deal of scholarship still focuses on the role of sport in reproducing conventional gender ideologies—and we have looked at this in recent pages—in the past decade attention has shifted somewhat towards sports personalities who confuse or confound these ideologies. Perhaps new role models are emerging?

The literature on soccer star David Beckham is perhaps the most elaborated to explore this issue. Beckham seems to be something of a test case for whether or not the times are changing. A former player with Manchester United, Real Madrid, AC Milan and the somewhat weaker Los Angeles Galaxy, Beckham has moved from the sports pages into magazines and the internet. The sociologist Ellis Cashmore (2002) offers a number of social and cultural reasons for Beckham's global fame. He notes that recent years have seen the rise of celebrity culture more generally. Beckham is a symptom of this. More specifically, the singer Madonna had already pioneered a new style of celebrity involving gender-bending images, fame in multiple spheres and relentless fashion innovation. Beckham was able to follow in her footsteps. Furthermore, 'Beckham' was made possible by the emergence of a 'new masculinity' in the 1990s that was less rugged and macho than that which had gone before. Themes about caring and fathering, for example, were central to this reconfiguration. Other reasons for Beckham's rise are more structural. These include the commodification and marketing of Beckham by sports equipment manufacturers, media conglomerates and his own image team. Put another way, there is money to be made.

According to Momin Rahman (2004), Beckham presents a commodified image that has contradictory elements and has expanded the meanings of masculinity itself. Some things about Beckham's image are consistent with traditional or hegemonic masculinity. He is good at sport, comes from a working-class background but has become wealthy, and is a family man. Other aspects of Beckham are more gender-ambivalent in terms of dominant codes. He is interested in fashion and hairstyles. He often appears in photo spreads in quasi-erotic poses. He has been known to wear pink nail varnish. Rahman argues that rather than leading to a recoding of Beckham as gay, these trends have been ideologically absorbed by enlarging the terrain covered by the idea of masculinity. Rahman writes:

the constant media fascination with Beckham derives from the knowledge that representations around him centre on an attractive and controversial dynamic of masculinity: he can be made to represent the dislocation of masculinity from its traditional moorings but simultaneously to shore up traditional masculine identity. (2004, p. 229)

There is a sense of tension and of boundaries being pushed, but not too far. For Rahman, Beckham does not destabilise masculinity but rather pushes the sign of masculinity into new domains.

Sport, class and race

Much as we did for gender, we can explore the relationship of class to sport in terms of participation (who does what) and the reproduction of class hierarchies. A useful starting point is Pierre Bourdieu's (1978) essay on 'Sport and social class'. According to Bourdieu, sports make up a 'field'. By this he means an area of society that has its own hierarchies, rules and struggles. Bourdieu argues that participation in sports is rigorously structured by class. This determines the kinds of economic, social and cultural capital available to individuals. The cultural capital of a given class will determine what it thinks is meaningful and also the kinds of body that individuals will want to develop through sports activity. Bourdieu argues that working-class males seek to have strong, visibly muscular bodies, while members of the dominant class seek to be 'athletic' and 'toned'. Hence the working-class attraction to tough, physical sports and the middle-class penchant for activities like jogging or yoga. Aside from developing the body and confirming self-identity, Bourdieu suggests that participation in sport is also driven by the quest for distinction. Certain sports are attractive because of their expense or rarity and the opportunities they provide for meeting others who hold valuable social capital. Golf, sailing and polo events held in exclusive clubs are a case in point.

Bourdieu's argument that sports participation is structured by class has been augmented over recent years by cultural studies that focus less on participation and more on the role of sport in reproducing capitalism or offering ideological cover for differential social achievement. Representative of this literature are the diverse analyses of the hugely popular sporting goods company Nike. A look at *Sociological Abstracts* will uncover an astonishing number of research papers exploring what is 'wrong' with Nike. Aside from the company's involvement in sweat shops in Asia, a particular ambition has been to unpick the ideology behind Nike's influential advertising campaigns. The 'Just Do

It 'slogan, in particular, is said to individualise success and failure, in effect hiding the social and structural barriers to success. An analysis of the charismatic US distance runner Steven Prefontaine, who died young in 1975, serves as a case in point. According to Theresa Walton (2004), he was originally a working-class rebel. A 1990s Nike reinvention of Prefontaine transformed him into a white, classless individualist, a generic and depoliticised version of himself. This strategy is often known as 'co-optation'.

When it comes to sport and race, the topic of racism is always in the foreground. Themes investigated have included:

- exclusion, tokenism, harassment and discrimination
- racialised representations of sports personalities
- the myths and realities of racial social mobility through sport
- confronting genetic explanations of sporting excellence.

The general picture that has emerged is not good news. A good deal of research conducted in the United States has shown that black players and coaches are paid less that their white equivalents; that pivotal positions in teams tend to be occupied by whites; and that blacks are often included in tokenistic ways. One study of the American National Football League (Gridiron or NFL) showed that 91 per cent of the players in the glamorous quarterback slot were white, while in the low-profile cornerback position 99 per cent were black (Lapchick 1999). As for upwards mobility, this is often a dangerous myth. An often-cited statistic is that the odds of an American high school athlete making it to the professional level are 10 000 to 1. Many minority students obtain scholarships to college on the strength of their sporting abilities, but unrealistic expectations, pressure from coaches for results and dreams of becoming the next NBA star can see them neglect study and put too much effort into college sport.

Influenced by cultural studies, some of the more interesting work in the race/sport sociology field has explored the images and representations of sports and sports stars and the ways that even when well-intentioned these tend to reinforce conventional or dangerous understandings of race. A major theme here has been the perhaps unwitting association of black athletes with innate or genetic advantage, with animality and sexuality, and in a romanticised way with gangs and inner-city crime. Matthew Soar (2001), for example, shows that Nike's advertising campaigns make extensive use of black bodies. Athletes are framed in very physical terms as the producers of energy and sweat rather than as interesting personalities. White athletes, by contrast, tend to be seen as training for their success or as succeeding by virtue of their intellectual skills. Even positive role models like golfing star Tiger Woods are said to reproduce the illusion of a race-free, achievement-possible society. The multicultural society for which Woods is emblematic in Nike advertisements is a safe one dominated by conventional ideas about whiteness and race—think golf clubhouse (Cole & Andrews 2000). According to leading Australian sports sociologist Jim McKay (1995), Nike's use of black athletes in advertising has been especially dangerous precisely because it appeals to the value placed on athletic sports skill among young black men themselves. He claims what is needed is a comprehensive demythologisation, one that focuses on real-world inequalities and that can lead to a serious discourse about race, class and gender in sports.

Reflective questions: How does sport reflect the rise of modernity? What are some of the negative impacts of sport on our society?

TOURISM

As the literature discussed above exemplifies, research on leisure by sociologists has traditionally looked at involvement in sport and hobbies, at cultural consumption and at time-use patterns. The rapidly growing field of tourism research is one in which sociologists have also staked out a claim. They recognise that tourism too is not a trivial topic for investigation, but should be seen as one of the most important processes of the modern world. Tourism as an activity and industry has grown massively over the past 200 years. Before the 19th century, few people travelled anywhere more than a few kilometres away from their homes unless they were traders, migrants, soldiers, sailors and missionaries, whose primary motives were task-related rather than cultural or recreational. Notable exceptions were:

- *Members of the upper classes who went on the Grand Tour.* This extended trip was intended to enhance their levels of cultural capital—for example, through visiting antiquities in Rome or Greece or by developing skills in a foreign language. A successful Grand Tour could enhance social networks or marriage prospects and consolidate the identity of a 'gentleman'.

- *Pilgrims.* Here the aim of travel was religious and centred around themes such as enlightenment, duty, expiation or atonement.

During the 19th century the invention of the railway, the growth of specialised resort towns, the emergence of new expectations among workers about annual summer holidays and the evolution of infrastructure organised around moving large numbers of people (e.g. booking and ticketing systems) saw mass holiday-making become a real possibility for ordinary citizens. The overall picture, then, is of tourism evolving alongside modernity. That said, it is clear that elements of earlier forms of travel remain. In places such as Italy or France a good proportion of tourism is still devoted to high-cultural pursuits such as visiting museums, galleries and churches. Religious pilgrimage remains important—especially in the Islamic and Hindu worlds where travel to holy sites is a central part of faith. Even in apparently secular contexts we can detect elements of pilgrimage. A visit to Uluru, for example, often evokes feelings of awe and wonder.

The importance of tourism

Travel now occupies about 40 per cent of free time, is growing worldwide at 5–6 per cent per annum, is the world's biggest industry and is already the largest single source of employment in many countries. In Australia tourism is a major component of economic and social life. It is calculated by the Australian Bureau of Statistics (2008a) that in 2005–06 inbound (visitor) tourists consumed $20 billion in goods and services in Australia, or about 11 per cent of the national total. Some 464 000 people were employed in the tourism field. There are about 5.5 million short-term international visitor arrivals every year, many from New Zealand, the United Kingdom, Japan and the United States. China, Hong Kong and Korea are providing increasing numbers of visitors.

When we think of tourism in Australia, we tend to conjure up images of long-haul jet passengers from overseas coming for a dedicated holiday. This is not quite accurate. Many of those foreign visitors are visiting friends or relatives or are here on business. They might take a holiday too, but this could be secondary to their main intention. It is important also to remember the powerful role of domestic tourism, often to low-key places that are off the global tourist circuit—perhaps a bushwalking spot, a country town or a simple beach. Australians made 134 million day trips in 2006 (defined as travelling at least 50 kilometres, being away from home for four or more hours, but then sleeping at home) and spent 285 million nights away from home (ABS 2008a). This adds up to a lot of money and a significant proportion of leisure time.

The industrial sectors that gain income and jobs substantially and in a direct way from tourism include transportation and accommodation services, retailing, education and restaurants. There are also knock-on effects for suppliers of goods and services to these organisations. In other words, even if a company does not have a direct interface with tourists, it might still benefit

The death of a tourist: a sociological approach

In October 2004 a British tourist died in the outback. Ethel Hetherington, aged 52, was found on a remote track leading to the Mutitjulu Aboriginal community near Uluru. She appeared to have died of heat exhaustion and dehydration. It was believed that she had been drinking alcohol and had got lost as she tried to walk back to her hotel after visiting the community.

But let's step back and ask a more radical question about the background social and cultural factors that made this death possible. Why was a middle-aged mother from Cumbria in the middle of the Australian outback? Her grandmother would probably have taken an annual vacation to the British seaside—perhaps Blackpool. To explain why Ethel Hetherington died in the red dust under a scorching desert sun and not in her bed in England we should think sociologically about the tourist experience. We need to be able to theorise why destinations such as Uluru and encounters with Indigenous Australians are considered today to be desirable objectives for holiday travel. These are goals strong enough to justify an expensive trip halfway round the world and then into the inhospitable desert. We might also think a little about the cultural expectation that a holiday involves bodily pleasures, such as the drinking of the alcohol that might have clouded Ethel Hetherington's judgement.

More structurally, the growth of the global travel industry in late modernity has been an enabling factor in Ethel Hetherington's death, as it has been for the numerous tourists and backpackers who have unfortunately made the headlines after being murdered by predatory criminals, drowned in our surf or eaten by our protected wildlife species over recent years. Put simply, the more people who come through Australia, the more likely it is that regrettable events will happen.

from the tourist industry. It is estimated that 900 000 jobs are created directly and indirectly through tourism in this way (about 10 per cent of total employment) and that tourism contributes directly and indirectly 9 per cent to Australia's GDP (Bureau of Tourism Research 2003; 2004; ABS 2004m).

Sociological perspectives on tourism

Much research in the field of tourism is concentrated on applied and policy issues. For example, students in a tourism studies degree might study the marketing of attractions, quality assurance or how to run a hotel. Such a vocational focus fails to take a step back and consider tourism sociologically, using social and cultural theory to make sense of tourists and the tourist industry. As Adrian Franklin and Mike Crang (2001, p. 5) point out, the field of 'tourist studies' has been 'dominated by policy led and industry sponsored work so the analysis tends to internalize industry led priorities and perspectives'. Efforts at a more creative and critical understanding of tourism usually start with three key thinkers: Boorstin, MacCannell and Urry.

'Escaping the real'—Daniel Boorstin

Boorstin's early work (1964) on American tourism was influential in getting the sociology of tourism started. He takes a rather dim and negative view of the tourist. In his hypothesis, tourists seek to escape the 'real' and everyday. What they are looking for is the pleasure to be derived from contrived and unauthentic pseudo-events and spectacles. For this reason they are attracted to theme parks where they do not have to confront the real. They like to travel in large groups and stay in modern hotels that insulate them from contact with real people and events.

The search for the 'authentic'—Dean MacCannell

The American sociologist Dean MacCannell (1976) argues against Boorstin and asserts that all tourists are looking for 'authenticity' rather than the fake and spectacular. In MacCannell's view, tourism is a serious activity. It is a kind of sacred quest to understand and experience other lives and times. People do not try to escape reality, but to come closer to it. Even trips around sewer systems, factories and other workplaces are popular, as people try to find out how society really works. MacCannell agrees with Boorstin that many tourist experiences, such as Aboriginal dancers performing in a five-star hotel, are staged pseudoevents. However, he sees this 'staged authenticity' as arising from social relations rather than a desire for the artificial. Given the volume of contemporary tourism, it would be too disruptive and intrusive if tourists invaded every aspect of real everyday life. Hence the need for tourist experiences to be routinised and stage-managed. Tensions exist, then, between the tourist desire for the authentic and the very processes of tourism themselves.

MacCannell argues that a process of sacralisation constructs tourist attractions as worth visiting. They are framed by cultural processes as being especially sacred or as particularly interesting places where contact with the authentic can be made. An example of this process in Australia is Uluru (discussed in Chapter 8). Uluru is seen as an embodiment of the mysterious primal power of the Australian outback and a link to authentic Aboriginal traditions and legends. Similarly, tourists to Australia often purchase Aboriginal artefacts or bush hats as a way of connecting with the 'authentic' Australia.

The tourist gaze—John Urry

John Urry (1990) agrees that tourist researchers such as Boorstin and MacCannell have some important points to make, but says they have not linked tourism to wider social and economic currents. Urry argues that the societal shift from Fordist to post-Fordist production (see discussion p. 214) has had implications for the tourist industry. During the era of Fordist production in the early and middle 20th century, tourism had a particular set of characteristics. It provided a mass product with little consumer choice—the package holiday often associated with holiday camps and group excursions. This product was frequently clearly tied to class and was undertaken collectively by the family. In the post-Fordist era the nature of holiday-making has changed. Consumer preferences are more flexible and consumers have reacted against being part of a 'mass'. Holidays have become more customised and specialised, directed at particular market segments. Urry claims that today tourists are keen to avoid the group experience, associating it with unauthenticity. Holidays are being marketed as unique 'travel (not tourist) experiences' and are tailored to individual needs rather than to class and family types.

Urry sees the postmodernisation of culture as important in changing the face of tourism today. This process has collapsed conventional definitions and behaviours associated with tourism. According to Urry, the objects of the contemporary tourist gaze are of two types: nature, and heritage or history. Both can be understood as aspects of a postmodern reaction against modern industrial society (see also the discussion of alternative medicine in Chapter 10). In Urry's view, both carry ideological effects, tending to favour the reproduction of an aristocratic and nostalgic view of the landscape, and a sanitised and nostalgic view of the past. Meanwhile, the distinctions between tourist and non-tourist experiences and places are breaking down. Urry argues that shopping centres, movie studios and workplaces are becoming tourist venues. In the Australian context, this process is perhaps most apparent on the Gold Coast. Over half the money spent at Pacific Fair Shopping Centre is spent by tourists, and the centre is said to attract more visitors than the theme parks in the area, such as Water World, Movie World and Dreamworld. Similarly, the very ordinary suburban street where the television program *Neighbours* is shot is one of Melbourne's most popular attractions.

Urry also argues that the distinctions between escape and tourism, and education and tourism, have become blurred. Whereas in the past tourists sought to escape from grimy industrial cities and just have fun, today they flock to museums dedicated to long-gone industries. Former industrial cities such as Glasgow have emerged as popular tourist destinations. Museums, meanwhile, have become more like theme parks. They have interactive displays and performers re-creating life in the past.

THE SOCIAL IMPACTS OF TOURISM—JENNIFER CRAIK

Like John Urry, Jennifer Craik takes a critical perspective on tourism and in so doing engages with the optimistic vision that is often found in policy schools. Craik argues that tourism is not the panacea for Australia's economy that it is often claimed to be. She points out that tourism 'produces benefits for a few but also brings with it major structural imbalances and redistributions of wealth away from the interests of local communities and governments' (1991, p. xi). Craik's analysis is that government policies and poor planning, along with the greed of multinational corporations, are responsible for this situation. Craik suggests that although it emphasises economic benefits, 'tourism policy rarely considers other dimensions' (p. 79) such as community impacts and environmental issues. Craik argues that the negative impacts of tourism in these areas are often overlooked by planners and decision makers. Such negative impacts might include:

- the privatisation of public land by resorts
- the destruction of traditional cultures
- commodification of local culture
- hostility between locals and tourists
- escalating costs of living for locals
- social problems, with tourism correlated with 'increases in gambling, prostitution, drunkenness, drug use, theft and petty crime' (1991, p. 88)
- environmental degradation
- the creation of low-wage and part-time jobs.

Craik is particularly critical of tourism development in Australia. She argues that government policies have been too favourable to big business and 'have yet to guarantee wider public interests against private interests in the push to expand the tourist industry' (p. 235). Moreover, tourism policy has often looked to short-term gains rather than long-term interests. Craik warns that unless tourism planning improves to take a longer term and less economistic view, the sector will remain vulnerable to swings in the market and the boom–bust cycles that occur as destinations move in and out of fashion.

FUTURE DIRECTIONS IN TOURISM STUDIES

Adrian Franklin and Mike Crang (2001) suggest a number of emerging areas for tourism research. These reflect not only shifting intellectual agendas but also the ways that tourism has itself been reconfigured. Theoretical and empirical investigations have been overwhelmingly centred on the stereotyped, short-term package tour and resort holiday characteristic of modernity. Yet as Urry's work suggests, we are moving towards a far more complex field of activity and meaning.

- *Exploring the linkages between tourism and the everyday.* The idea here is to investigate the ways that commonplace life has been shaped by tourism. Many people, for example, live near to or work at tourist attractions. Our holiday experiences—or perhaps the circulation of tourists through our home areas—impact upon daily tastes and activities in such areas as food, movies or romantic opportunities. Consider, for example, how everyday life for residents of Queensland's Gold Coast might be positively or negatively influenced by the choice of golf courses and

restaurants, job opportunity structures, land values and high rents, shopping venues, dating markets and traffic congestion that have arisen as a result of its tourism-driven lifestyle.
- *The ties between tourism, cosmopolitanism and global migration need to be unpacked.* For example, many people do not live or work in the country of their birth. These people are strangers abroad, but they are not tourists in the conventional sense of people who travel from a home (familiar) to a holiday destination (strange). Rather they inhabit a curious in-between space. Roberta Julian (1998) reports that Hmong women in Tasmania experience a sense of excitement about daily life in their adopted land and find many things exotic—even driving a car. When we look only at people on holiday we miss out on the quasi-touristic experiences of migrants and rootless cosmopolitans.
- *Bodies and sexualities.* As Urry's book *The Tourist Gaze* (1990) suggests, much of the tourism literature has been driven by a focus on the visual mode of consumption. According to this paradigm we travel to see some interesting things (waterfalls, monuments, indigenous people, landscapes), we look at these and then—our curiosity satisfied—we go home. Franklin and Crang (2001) point out that much tourism is about participation rather than just looking. Activity holidays such as hiking or skiing involve doing things with the body for long periods of time. This is usually interpreted as enjoyable. Large numbers of tourists are bored with the gaze and seek extreme bodily sensations—perhaps through bungee jumping or jet boating or surfing. Others look for gastronomical satisfactions by seeking out top restaurants or touring vineyards. Clubbing tourism in Ibiza or Bali is about the excitement of dance, music, drink, drugs and sex. This can be an exhausting physical regime. Clearly a sociology of the gaze would not get us very far in understanding these types of energetic, body-testing holidays.
- *Tourism objects.* More attention needs to be given to the material culture produced for and used by tourists. What kind of sense do souvenirs make? Why do people take photographs and insist on showing them to others? How come tourism is not just about having experiences, but also having something to remember them by?
- *Tourism as performance.* Rather than explore how tourists experience performances that are staged for them, we could ask how people accomplish being a tourist. In other words, what are the kinds of interactional competencies that allow tourists to enjoy their holiday? We might think, for example, of the times when they need to dramatise their tourist status (at the immigration desk) and when they might wish to hide this (in the crowded bazaar), or the ways in which particular kinds of tourist identity require particular embodied skills and attitudes (the silent bird-watching tourist or the agile, brash snowboarder, for example).

We might add to this list some other interesting variations on tourism that need further research. Often volunteer and charity work are rolled up with tourist experiences. Westerners working to build a new school in Kenya, for example, may go on a hike up Kilimanjaro. It would be difficult to argue that the hike was the only 'tourist experience' of the trip. The literature also speaks sometimes of 'ironic tourists' and 'post-tourists'. These are people who visit familiar tourist destinations, but with a sense of disengagement. Perhaps they mock or ideologically decode the exhibits. This has long been the case with intellectuals visiting Disneyland. Finally, we could note the global importance of sport tourism, involving the movement of fans who travel to major events like the soccer World Cup or who follow their teams overseas.

Yet another future direction for tourism research is suggested by Brad West (2008). Most sociological accounts of tourism are somewhat critical and ironic. Influenced by critical theory, writers such as Urry and Craik point to tourism as a bad thing—something that provides shallow experiences, reproduces ideologies and generates social harms. Brad West's work suggests this is not necessarily the case. West has investigated battlefield tourism in the United States, Turkey and Vietnam. He notes that this can lead to increased cross-cultural sensitivity rather than prejudice. Visitors come to understand the suffering of others and to appreciate the possibilities for multiple perspectives. West argues that tourism is often 'dialogical'. By this he means that the experience can set up an exchange of views and a dialogue that can question taken-for-granted assumptions. In the case of backpackers visiting Gallipoli, for example, he shows young Australians coming to appreciate the Turkish point of view as they are taken on a tour of the battlefields by Turkish guides. Furthermore, they experience strong emotions of sadness and pride rather than any simplistic Australian patriotism. The overall impression we get from reading West's work is of tourism as cosmopolitan, instructive and educational.

CHAPTER 6 LEISURE, SPORT, TOURISM AND WORK

Reflective questions: Why is tourism important in our society? 'Tourism is all about meaning': discuss the contending ways that this statement could be expanded.

WORK

THE CULTURAL CENTRALITY OF WORK IN AUSTRALIA

In November 2004 the Australian government triumphantly declared that unemployment stood at only 5.3 per cent—the lowest for 26 years. Then Treasurer Peter Costello saw this as a vindication of the Liberal Party's economic strategies. Critics suggested that there was no cause for celebration: the official figures obscured the true rate of unemployment; people were being forced to take jobs with poor pay and benefits as a result of the government's pro-business and anti-union policies; and we should not rest or be satisfied until there was 0 per cent unemployment and every Australian had access to meaningful and well-remunerated full-time work.

Regardless of who was right and who was wrong, such debates demonstrate the centrality of work to our definitions of the good society and human dignity. A working society is seen as a healthy society and as an indication that the government is doing its job. Unemployment statistics are emblematic and contested for this very reason. A sociological understanding of work can help us to think critically about such issues. We might ask how work and unemployment are actually experienced. What does research tell us about the features of a 'meaningful' or rewarding job? Are jobs in our 'postindustrial' society likely to be better or worse than those in the past?

THE WORK AND EMPLOYMENT PROFILE OF AUSTRALIA

In Australia in 2006–2007 there were 10.3 million people in the workforce, 72 per cent of whom worked full-time (ABS 2008a). Figure 6.2 shows the percentage of employed persons by occupation and industry in Australia today. We can use the figure to track both the current distribution of the workforce and the way that this has changed since the mid-1990s as the economy takes on new properties. Today the retail trade is the largest employment sector, followed by property and business services, manufacturing, and health and community services. Note the reductions since 1997 in employment in manufacturing and commodity-based industries such as agriculture, forestry and fishing. Observe also the increasing levels of employment in the service-based industries. This changing profile is typical of developed nations as they undergo a transition to a postindustrial economy organised around leisure, services and knowledge.

Figure 6.3 provides information demonstrating horizontal and vertical segregation of the Australian workforce by gender. You can see here that men dominate managerial positions (this is circumstantial evidence for 'glass-ceiling' effects excluding women), as well as the blue-collar areas of production, transport, trades and labouring. Women outnumber men in the professions and in clerical and service work. Their dominance in the latter in part reflects women's occupation of positions that allow for part-time employment, such as being a sales clerk in a store.

THE EXPERIENCE OF WORK

Sociologists have long been interested in the meanings given to work by the workers themselves. Famously Karl Marx, in works such as *Das Kapital*, suggested that work within the capitalist context was 'alienating'. For Marx, the process of **alienation** had two key dimensions:

- Work was objectively alienating as workers were paid back for only some of the labour that they put into making things—the rest was taken by the factory owner or capitalist as profit. Put another way, workers were exploited.
- Subjectively work was alienating because it was perceived as meaningless, as dull and as separating workers from the experience of authentic community, which Marx called 'species being'. Marx argued that in traditional and artisanal modes of production this was less the case. Here people could have a meaningful connection to the thing they were making and to the community around them.

With his work on alienation Marx set an agenda for sociology that has persisted for more than 150 years. There have been some broadly consistent findings in the literature.

- By and large, studies have shown that workers experience less alienation when they have more control over their work process or a financial stake in the enterprise where they work. By contrast, feelings of alienation increase when workers

FIGURE 6.2

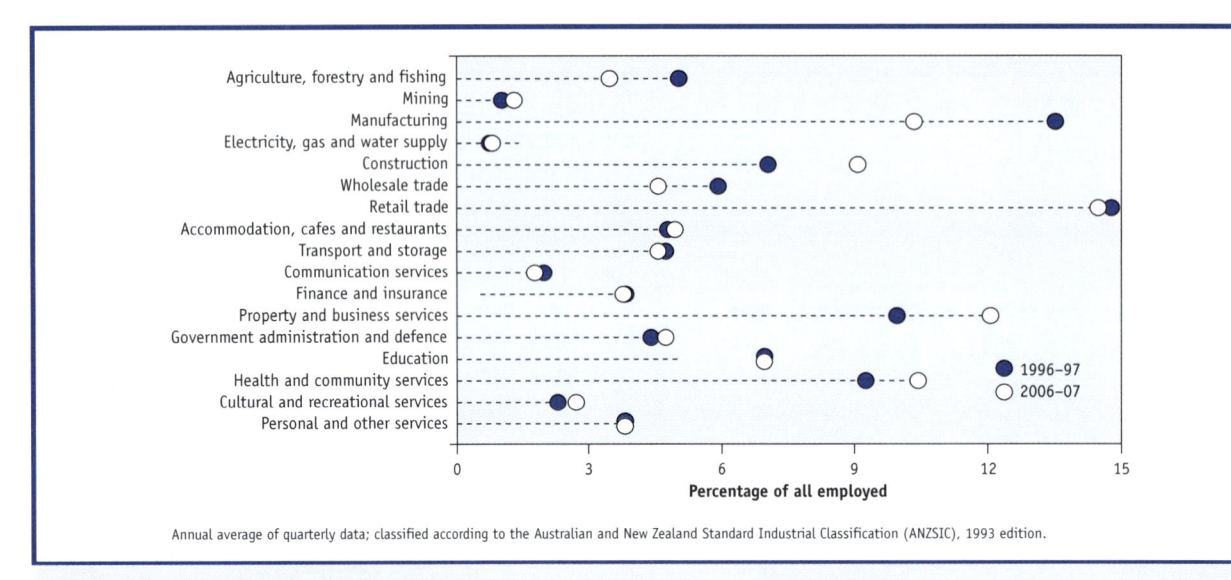

Employed persons by industry Source: ABS, *Labour Force, Australia, Detailed, Quarterly*, cat. no. 6291.

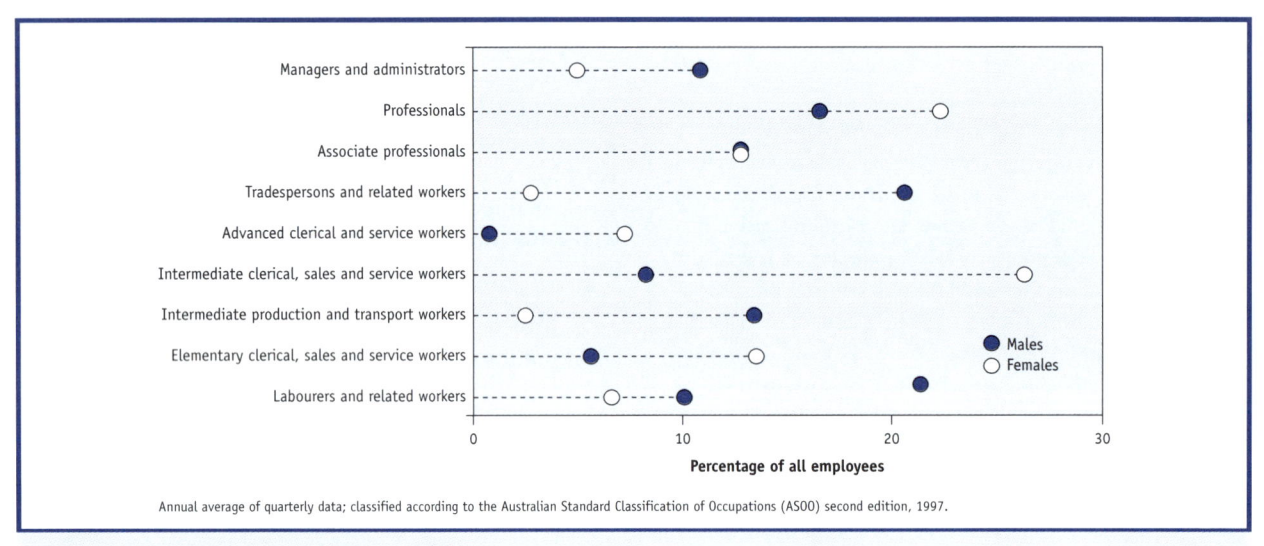

FIGURE 6.3

Employed persons by occupation, 2006–07 Source: ABS, *Labour Force, Australia, Detailed, Quarterly*, cat. no. 6291.

are subject to surveillance and have little ability to make decisions. Pay is important, but not as important as we might at first think in determining overall work satisfaction.

- Workers cope with alienating or disempowering work situations in various ways. Often they have informal cultures and solidarities that run against the official company line. These do not necessarily interfere with productivity. One study of this nature was by Michael Burawoy (1979). In an ethnographic investigation of a Chicago machine shop he noticed that workers worked much harder than they had to. Their objective best interest was in working as little as possible without being fired. Yet Burawoy found workers taking risks and thinking creatively in order to solve problems. He interprets this as a creative response to the broadly alienating work setting. In her study of workers in a luxury hotel, Rachel Sherman (2007) found that the staff had various strategies for dealing with the fact that their guests were super-rich and that they were on regular wages. These included gossip and grumbling behind the backs of the guests and management.

- Strikes and protests emerge as a response not simply to disputes about pay but also to a more general sense of injustice. Often they are triggered by management efforts to increase levels of control and supervision or to break the power of trade unions. When Australian academics strike, for example, a major factor has been a general feeling of dissatisfaction with the ways the universities are run. These might include the encroachment of market principles into higher education or unrealistic expectations about workload.

Multiple factors influencing militancy and strikes—Claire Williams

The classic work of Claire Williams in Australia illustrates the complex social causes of strike action. She argues that in any specific case the causes of worker militancy are complex and overlapping, and should include the impact of technology, management decisions and the workers' culture. In *Open Cut* (1981), an ethnographic study of life in a central Queensland mining town, Williams shows that a number of factors contributed to a militarisation of the workers. Workers experienced dissatisfaction over close supervision by management, who sometimes timed them with stopwatches. They also considered that they had insufficient job control and that automation of the mine had reduced their amount of autonomy. Aggressive company policy further contributed to worker hostility. The company suspended shifts of workers for 24 hours as a disciplinary measure against strikes, and sent letters to the workers' homes threatening to withdraw a recently agreed pay award. Hostility towards the Utah Mining Company (which owned the mine) was compounded by the fact that it was a multinational with no loyalty to Australia, and with only a temporary connection to the area in which it was mining.

Interestingly, Williams suggests that the strongly masculine character of the workplace may have contributed to militancy. The open-cut mine was an almost exclusively male environment where aggression and independence were core values among the workforce and a major source of solidarity. Negotiation and compromise might be seen as a sign of weakness and a threat to this masculinity.

In a subsequent study, *Blue, White and Pink Collar Workers in Australia* (1988), Williams expanded her research to look at industrial relations in non-manual occupations: Telecom (now Telstra) technicians, mostly female Qantas flight attendants and bank employees. Her particular interest was the impact of new technology on work and industrial relations.

During the 1970s new telecommunications technology was introduced by Telecom. The technicians took industrial action because they had the necessary skills and knowledge to anticipate what the consequences of the technology would be for job skills and employment levels. Militancy was further generated by Telecom management plans to reform the career opportunities structure and to exclude technicians from the career ladder. After an industrial dispute, the technicians gained considerable concessions. The new technology was implemented in a way that encouraged re-skilling and the opening up of career paths. Williams argues that the main casualties of the whole process were 'the generation of young workers whose labour is no longer needed' (1988, p. 177)—in other words, school leavers for whom there are no vacancies thanks to the efficient new technology.

In her study of female flight attendants, the technology of interest was the jet aeroplane. Improvements in technology (especially servicing and reliability) had meant that the flight attendants had limited stopovers between flights, and there was a general speeding-up of operations which resulted in increased job stress. Militancy by the flight attendants was further promoted by the attitude of Qantas management towards them. Flight attendants were subject to strict rules and personal surveillance and were treated as peripheral workers of no great importance. Female workers were also outraged by gender discrimination and the fact that (male) flight stewards had better access to the promotions structure than they did. Industrial action by the Qantas flight attendants was broadly successful in winning better pay, conditions and promotion prospects.

There was little militancy in the Queensland bank that Williams studied. New computer technology had brought an upgrading of skills rather than deskilling. Despite poor pay and lack of promotion prospects, the largely female bank tellers were not as militant as the Qantas flight attendants. There were two main reasons for this. First, their union was controlled by men, and so women's issues tended to be placed lower on the agenda. In contrast, the Qantas flight attendants had a female-dominated union that was more responsive to their demands. Second, female bank workers tended to be more conservative in attitude than flight attendants. Women selected banking as a job because it was 'safe', while flight attendants were looking for travel and independence. As a result, the two groups of women tended to have different attitudes towards industrial relations.

Williams' overall finding is that although technology can be important in generating worker militancy, its impact is highly uneven and contingent upon the outcome of particular struggles between workers and management. The effects of technology are mediated by gender relations, management style and policy, the structure of job control and the form of trade union activity.

WORK, MODERNITY AND POSTMODERNITY

A substantial effort by sociologists has gone into identifying how work has changed over time as the wider organisation of society changes. Even at the risk of stereotyping, it is useful to summarise this huge literature with some broad brush strokes, as follows.

- *Work in traditional society.* In small-scale hunting and gathering societies, people foraged for food. Here the pattern seemed to be working for four or five hours collecting what was needed, then spending the rest of the day on social activities. In such traditional societies we are not really certain that there was a concept of 'work' as we know it. Productive activity was integrated into the totality of life and might be accompanied by ritual, joking, drinking, singing or dancing. The anthropologist Marshall Sahlings (1972) describes hunting and gathering as 'the original affluent society'. This is due not to wealth in goods, but rather wealth measured in free time. With the emergence of agriculture people seem to have worked harder, in part to support non-agricultural elites in cities such as those of ancient Egypt or Rome. Still, such work often followed the seasons, in part because these societies had largely agrarian economies. People worked very hard at crucial times of year, such as planting and harvesting times, but often they did not work so hard at other times. In Medieval Europe, for example, there is quite a bit of evidence that people slept a lot during the winter. This hibernation lifestyle would conserve energy. People would often work for food rather than money, or tend their own fields. Work duties were determined by custom rather than contract.
- *Work in industrial modernity.* With the Industrial Revolution we saw the emergence of the traditional working day determined by the clock and the modern concept of 'work'. Wage labour determined by contract became more common. A conceptual distinction between working time and free time started to emerge. By the early 20th century production-line methods were widely established. Scholars in the sociology of work field often speak of Fordism (after Henry Ford). This refers to standardised products manufactured cheaply and in huge numbers; tasks being broken down into boring repetitive activities; huge levels of hierarchy, surveillance and supervision; and efforts at increasing productivity through experimentation and the measurement of output. Another term used alongside Fordism is Taylorism. This refers mostly to the micro-management of tasks and bodily motions, often through time and motion studies such as those conducted by Frederick Winslow Taylor. Critical sociologists have written extensively on the negative aspects of Fordism, associating this with deskilling, intensive alienation and control of workers by management. Scholars associated with the analysis of this kind of work include Karl Marx, Harry Braverman and Michael Burawoy.
- *Work in postmodernity.* Other terms used here that are roughly equivalent in economic sociology are 'post-Fordism', 'postindustrial', 'flexible accumulation' and 'knowledge economy'. Now workers are said to become more skilled as we transition into an economy based less around goods and more around information, finance, cultural products and services. The requirement for the rapid development of new ideas and to reach small niche markets sees Fordism outdated. Hierarchies in corporations are said to be flattened into a 'matrix model', in part because hierarchy impedes the flow of information. The globalisation of the economy assists this process, with new ideas and products circulating at ever-increasing speeds. The boundaries between work and leisure, and work and home become blurred, especially for those in the professions and knowledge industries who keep increasingly irregular working hours and use the internet. Scholars who have written on this transition to a 'postmodern economy' include David Harvey, Scott Lash and John Urry, and Michael Piore.

Such typologies are useful as a starting point. We must remember, however, that they often generalise from the developmental experiences of affluent Western nations.

In many parts of the world people still live in peasant economies. Fordism remains entrenched wherever goods are mass-produced. We can often detect complex and mixed economies. China, for example, currently has a peasant economy, a Fordist economy producing electronics and whitegoods, and aspects of a globally leading-edge postmodern economy. Nevertheless, these sorts of distinctions do capture the trend in many places, most notably in tracking the declining proportion of economic life that revolves around agriculture and manufacturing in developed nations.

Gender, inequality and work

The study of 'work' has traditionally been the study of men at work. Feminist scholarship in sociology has done much to change this over the past three decades. Most feminists believe that the position of women in the labour market is an important source of female disadvantage. Historically women were often paid only a fraction of the male wage for the equivalent job and were openly excluded from some occupations by virtue of their gender. Feminist lobbying and changing attitudes to women and work saw legislation to address such issues. The *Sex Discrimination Act 1984* came into force throughout Australia in 1984, barring discrimination on the ground of sex in employment, education and the provision of goods, services and premises. In employment, women were to be given equal access to jobs and equal chances for promotion. The *Affirmative Action (Equal Employment for Women) Act 1986* was passed in 1986 and took full effect in 1989. Such legal changes have been a positive step for women, as has the considerable increase in the proportion of women who work.

Yet despite this progress, gender inequality persists along several dimensions:

1. Women are not equally represented throughout the occupational structure. There is both horizontal and vertical segregation between men and women in terms of their employment profiles. Horizontal segregation refers to the extent to which men and women do different jobs. Vertical segregation concerns the extent to which men have higher status and higher paid jobs than women. Women are usually concentrated in the lowest reaches of the occupational structure, often taking part-time and marginal work. This is the so-called 'secondary labour market' where pay is low and benefits minimal. Even in the so-called pink-collar occupations in which women predominate (such as primary school teaching, nursing or secretarial work), the senior posts are often taken by men.

2. When we think of 'work', our commonsense tells us to think of paid work. Feminists have resisted this understanding, asserting that much of the most important and arduous work takes the form of unpaid housework and child care. The vast majority of this activity is carried out by women. Even when women have paid work outside the home their domestic responsibilities are little diminished. They experience a 'double burden' or 'second shift'.

3. Even if they have a good job women might be subject to sexual harassment. This term covers a range of activities from 'jokes' in poor taste and unwanted comments, to bullying, demands for sexual favours by superiors and physical assault.

4. Workplaces might also be generally unsympathetic to women's needs in such areas as pregnancy and maternity leave or unresponsive to the familial or caring obligations they might have. A woman could be disadvantaged in arenas such as promotion if the supposition is made that she puts family before company loyalty. 'Evidence' for this might be that she doesn't stay behind after hours for drinks or needs to take time off to look after a sick child. There might also be simple infrastructural disadvantages for women—perhaps they might have to share toilets and changing facilities with their male colleagues.

5. Women are often involved in service-oriented jobs requiring emotional labour such as nursing, hairdressing, waitressing or counselling. Developed by sociologist Arlie Hochschild (1983) in her book *The Managed Heart*, this very influential concept refers to the need to manage felt emotions and emotion displays such that these are consistent with organisational, job or employer norms. For example, if you are hired to dress up as Ronald McDonald, you are required to be jolly; nurses must look as if they care about their patients; and hairdressers are expected to chat to their customers and take an interest in their lives and personal problems. Sometimes this emotion display is organised so as to generate compliance among customers or clients. Flight attendants need to appear relaxed and happy so that passengers do not panic when a flight gets bumpy. Hochschild argues that this demand can be stressful if the worker does not deeply internalise their role and the emotions that go with it. Put

215

another way, if they have to fake being happy or concerned, this can lead to a sense of being phony, inauthentic and emotionally exploited.

The emotional labour of Australian magistrates—Sharyn Roach Anleu and Kathy Mack

Research on emotional labour typically looks at women in service occupations who are subject to supervision and control. More recently, efforts have been made to apply the concept more widely and emotional labour is being detected in unlikely places. Sharyn Roach Anleu and Kathy Mack (2005), for example, used interview and survey methods in a study of Australian magistrates and discovered that emotional labour is a major feature of the job of being a magistrate—a job that is not usually considered to be 'gendered' and where there is considerable power and autonomy of action.

They argue that in higher courts legal representatives such as barristers often do much of the talking. They are paid professionals who are emotionally distant from the concerns of any given dispute. The result is an environment in which 'facts' and legal issues are centre stage in somewhat analytic discussions. This contrasts with the situation in magistrates courts, where people often represent themselves. They might be angry or upset. They might not know how to behave or understand what exactly is going on. In such situations, the magistrate has to engage in various kinds of emotional labour. One of the most important of these is appearing to be fair and impartial. The magistrate might be deeply moved by an item of testimony about a personal event or a tragic life history, yet they cannot show this. In their written opinions and judgements they have to retain a sense of emotional detachment too. Magistrates also have to manage the emotions of those in the court. For example, they might need to find ways to have people cool down or gain the self-control required to give evidence. Often they will find themselves the target of abuse from members of the public, and so need to stay aloof and not retaliate. Anleu and Mack quote one magistrate as follows:

> *So you're always trying to calm the situation down, try and get everybody to have their own say, work within time limits that are reasonable but also let the parties feel like they've walked out knowing that they've said what they wanted to ... (pp. 609–10).*

The emotional labour of being a magistrate can result in stress, just as it does in service professions. For many magistrates being emotionally connected to their work makes it rewarding at a human level. They do not want to develop a thick skin because 'distance and depersonalization ... can have a negative effect on job satisfaction' (p. 613). Yet remaining sensitive can lead to a sense of sadness and emotional exhaustion.

Emotional labour in the airline industry—Claire Williams

In the case of flight attendants we have a more conventional example of emotional labour. Claire Williams (2003) conducted a survey of nearly 3000 Australian flight attendants in 1994. She found that some 44 per cent described the emotional labour component of their job as stressful, although 34 per cent found it added to job satisfaction. Several sources of stress were reported:

- *The role tension between being in charge of passenger safety and yet also being in a service position.* The former required a projection of authority, the latter subservience. It was hard to generate passenger compliance with the service role in the foreground.
- *Soaking up passenger abuse.* This could eventuate if there were disputes over cabin baggage, seatbelts, free drinks or smoking. The policy that the 'customer is always right' did not allow the flight attendants to answer back—they felt that they would not be backed up by management if they did so. They had to remain humiliated.
- *Dealing with sexual harassment.* This was especially common from travelling sports teams, but was also not infrequent with business travellers. Stereotypes of the female flight attendant as single and sexually available are often propagated by airlines in their advertising. Female flight attendants had to fend off unwanted propositions, but again without being rude to passengers. Sometimes they were stalked to their hotels and cars. Other forms of sexual harassment involved groping and grabbing, dirty jokes, and reading and commenting on pornographic magazines on the flight. Whether straight or gay, male flight attendants often had to deal with homophobic behaviour and innuendos.

Williams argues that the attitude of the airline is crucial in determining whether the emotional labour component of work is pleasurable or stressful. She writes:

> *Management can mitigate the quasi-servant aspect of the abuse by letting flight attendants know they are valued, providing training on handling abuse and enforcing policies against passenger anger, bullying and inappropriate behaviour in the workplace. (2003, pp. 544–5).*

Reflective questions: What are the factors that might influence worker feelings of alienation or work satisfaction? How has the nature of work changed over time?

UNEMPLOYMENT

In addition to researching work, sociologists have also researched unemployment. It is important to realise that being 'unemployed' is not the same as 'not working'. Many people are not in the paid labour force, but cannot really be described as unemployed—such as full-time students, homemakers, the retired, children and the long-term sick. The category of the unemployed most accurately refers to people who want to have paid work, but are unable to find it. Operational definitions of 'the unemployed' or 'the unemployment rate' almost invariably make use of official government statistics. These are generally derived from the numbers applying for government benefits. Several problems exist in interpreting these as a true indicator of the level of unemployment:

- Some people want to work and cannot find work, but are not legally eligible for benefits. Thus these people never show up in official statistics.
- Some people are claiming benefits, but are really working in the hidden labour market for cash or goods.
- Others claim benefits but do not seriously seek work—in Australia, such people are known as 'dole bludgers'.
- Governments massage statistics and change definitions of 'unemployment' over time.
- Many people who would consider themselves 'unemployed' are diverted into training and community service programs or go back to the education system to obtain some qualifications. Thus they are counted in a different statistical pool.
- In some countries, most notably the United States, large numbers of people are in prison. The argument has been made that the penal system is a structural alternative to welfare as both systems deal with the socially marginal. If this is the case, then our count should include prison numbers.

Figuring out the prevalence of unemployment, then, is much harder than we might think. That said, we can identify some general implications of being unemployed. These include financial hardship, poor health, stress and loss of self-esteem. We can also identify some of the factors contributing to unemployment. Common-sense tells us that people remain unemployed if they lack skills, experience and motivation, but the picture is a little more complicated. Figure 6.4 reports the reasons that unemployed Australians gave for their difficulties in finding work.

Some patterns stand out. Women cited unsuitable hours and child care as problems, perhaps reflecting their gendered role in the household or worries about travel at night. Women also saw themselves as lacking experience, again perhaps reflecting the problem of entering the labour force after a long period of time

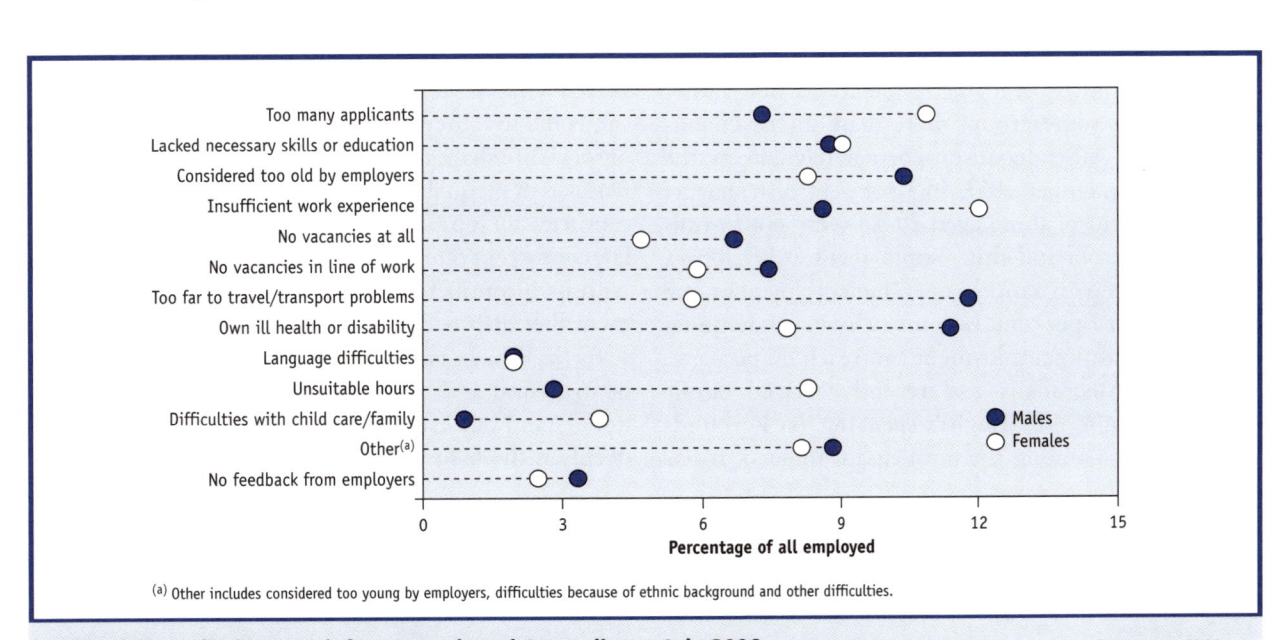

FIGURE 6.4

(a) Other includes considered too young by employers, difficulties because of ethnic background and other difficulties.

Difficulties in finding work for unemployed Australians, July 2006 *Source: ABS, Job Search Experience, Australia, cat. no. 6222.*

involved with bringing up a family. For men, the problems mentioned were transport/distance, age discrimination, ill health and skills. It is interesting to note that qualifications, skills and experience are only part of the picture. Although government labour force policies oriented around 'training' often focus on these, the real problems preventing people from finding work might well lie elsewhere. Affordable housing near to where the jobs are, after-hours child care, safe late-night public transport and so forth might all make a real contribution to reducing unemployment.

Survey data asking people why they are having trouble finding work tell only part of the story. From a more macro perspective we need to think about the structural causes of unemployment. The unemployment rate can change as the economy goes through upturns and downturns. Whole industries and economic sectors, such as fisheries or steel production, can disappear due to international competition, resource exhaustion or a broader shift in the economic profile of a nation. The shift to a postindustrial economy, in particular, can be traumatic. In Britain in the 1980s, for example, the unemployment rate soared as old industrial sectors like coalmining and car manufacturing were scaled back. The 'rustbelt' states in the northern United States are currently experiencing such a slump, even as the 'sunbelt' states further south open up new opportunities linked to the growth of a knowledge and services economy.

Unemployment in Australia—a profile

It is generally agreed that unemployment is not randomly distributed over the population, but rather disadvantages some groups more than others. Unemployment in Australia disproportionately affects the young. In September 2003, 15.3 per cent of teenagers and 23 per cent of those aged 20–24 were not in full-time education or full-time employment (ABS 2003f). This contrasts with a more general unemployment rate of around 6 or 7 per cent. In country towns undergoing recession youth unemployment can reach 60 per cent. Aboriginal Australians and recently arrived ethnic minorities from non–English-speaking backgrounds also tend to be among the most disadvantaged. It has been argued that high levels of youth unemployment are linked to various social problems such as drugs, crime and suicide. For these sorts of reasons youth unemployment is a highly political issue. Recently proposed schemes such as 'work for the dole' and compulsory literacy training have engendered controversy. Critics argue that these pick on young people, while advocates suggest they will provide skills and inculcate a work ethic and sense of social responsibility.

While youth unemployment has long been recognised as a critical issue, in recent years the plight of the older unemployed has been receiving attention. The problem here is one of long-term unemployment. People in their 40s and 50s who have been laid off can find it very difficult to obtain further suitable work. Reasons for this include lack of up-to-date skills, ageism by potential employers and a lack of positions at a level similar to that of their previous job. Often they will find themselves forced into compulsory early retirement.

CONCLUSION

In this chapter we have covered a lot of familiar material—'familiar' in the sense that work, leisure, sport and holidays are things that most of us care about: we talk about them with friends; we dream of time on the beach or scoring a winning goal; we love or hate Monday mornings according to the way we see our jobs, or we wonder why we are unemployed. We think we know a lot about these issues, yet our knowledge is the practical knowledge of the person going through life from day to day. Sociology helps us to understand this everyday experience in a different way and to gain a critical distance so that what was familiar becomes less so. In so doing we can come to understand why each of these dimensions of social life shapes our identities and how it reproduces patterns of inequality. Furthermore, we can see how the centuries-long process of modernity has led to particular, contingent outcomes: cricket with its rules, tourism with its incomplete search for authenticity, unemployment that disproportionately affects rust belt areas and so forth. What seems 'natural' is revealed as the product of structural and historical processes. This capacity to understand our everyday experiences just a little more deeply is the hallmark of the sociological imagination.

Tutorial exercise

Many sociologists spend a lot of time arguing that something is seriously 'wrong' with tourism, that it is superficial and does not encourage creative thinking. Working in groups, pick a local tourist spot and apply these insights. When you have finished your critique, suggest some changes that could lead to an 'improved' tourist experience and more constructive tourist industry.

For activity suggestions, learning aids, revision of key concepts and access to self-study material, visit: **www.pearson.com.au/highered/vankrieken4e**

Further reading

Dunning, E. 2003, *Sport (Critical Concepts in Sociology)*, Routledge, London.
Edgell, S. 2006, *The Sociology of Work*, Sage, London.
Franklin, A. 2003, *Tourism: An Introduction*, Sage, London.
Miller, T., Lawrence, G., McKay J. & Rowe, D. 2001, *Globalization and Sport*, Sage, London.
Urry, J. 1990, *The Tourist Gaze*, Sage, London.
Washington, R. E. & Karen, D. 2001, 'Sport and society', *Annual Review of Sociology*, 27, 187–212.

Websites

Australian Bureau of Statistics:
www.abs.gov.au
The ABS collects information on all the topics covered in this chapter, including work, unemployment, tourism and leisure. By clicking around and using the right search terms you can locate all kinds of useful information.

Australian Council of Trade Unions:
http://actu.asn.au
Here you can look at information on a range of contemporary industrial relations and workplace issues in Australia—from the union perspective. There are links to research reports, speeches and conference papers.

National Institute of Labour Studies:
http://nils.flinders.edu.au
Located at Flinders University, at this site you can find various items on industrial relations, employment and industry.

SocioSite:
www.sociosite.net
This very useful website has links to various sources of information and opinion, including other websites and clearinghouses run by specialist academics. By clicking around you can find reading lists, research reports and academic articles on sport, tourism, work and leisure.

Tourism Australia:
www.tourism.australia.com
This site contains recent Australian tourism statistics and brief research reports. Over the years it has become increasingly devoted to promoting and supporting the tourism industry.

7

Class and Inequality

This chapter considers questions about inequality and social division in contemporary society. As well as exploring debates about how to conceptualise and measure inequality, the chapter provides data on patterns and trends in relation to income and wealth in Australia.

By the end of the chapter, you should have a better understanding of:
— debates about how the transition to a service economy has effected social inequality
— the main theoretical perspectives on class and inequality
— patterns and trends in the distribution of income and wealth in Australia
— the class structure in Australia and debates about the main classes that comprise it
— debates about poverty and social exclusion
— the nature and extent of social mobility in Australia.

INTRODUCTION	**222**
Key concepts	223
Does social inequality matter?	224
INEQUALITY IN A CHANGING WORLD	**225**
Class, stratification and modernity	225
Locating class in late modernity	226
Understanding contemporary inequality	227
THEORIES OF INEQUALITY	**227**
Marx's theory of class	227
Positivism	228
Marx's evolutionary theory of social change	228
Historical materialism	228
Modes of production and evolutionary social change	229
Class, class consciousness and the state	229
Criticisms of Marx	230
The legacy of Marx	230
Weber's multidimensional theory of inequality	230
Class as market position	231
Status groups and social closure	231
Parties	231
The legacy of Weber	232
Durkheim and the division of labour	232
The legacy of Durkheim: the functions of inequality	232
Pierre Bourdieu: class and culture	233
The legacy of Bourdieu	234
MATERIAL INEQUALITY IN AUSTRALIA	**234**
Measuring economic resources	235
The social wage	235
Changes in economic inequality	235
Winners and losers	240
International comparisons of social inequality	241
Poverty and social exclusion	242
Poverty, social exclusion and citizenship	242
Measuring poverty	243
CLASSES IN AUSTRALIAN SOCIETY	**244**
Changes in the occupational structure	244
Mapping the class structure	245
Weberian maps—Goldthorpe	246
Wright's models of contradictory class locations	246
The upper class	247
Interlocks and networks	247
Unity and division	248
The middle class	249
Middle or working class?	250
The professions and cultural power	250
The working class	251
SOCIAL MOBILITY	**251**
Measuring social mobility	252
Social mobility in Australia	252
Strategies for social reproduction	253
Tutorial exercise	254
Further reading	254
Websites	254

INTRODUCTION

This account of a parent's wishes to send her child to a private school, but not being able to afford to, reveals how the existence of private education challenges the claim to equality of opportunity central to liberal democracies. It also highlights how knowledge is a resource that is central to social advancement in contemporary society.

I've been wanting to write this column all year, but dreading it, too. Because I don't want to be misunderstood and I don't want to offend. But the truth is that there is something horribly rotten going on in my personal world and—because the personal is political—this nation. The rot comes from the way we fund our schools. And it is making me so angry (or is it so grief-stricken and guilty?) that I can hardly breath.

The federal government's education policy, and that of the Rudd Opposition, waxes lyrical about parental choice. But while most of the parents I have known since our babies napped side by side at crèche ummed and ahed between private schools A, B and C—and the one local public school—our finances meant that even though several of the independent schools are just down the street from our house, my choice was between the local public school and well, the local public school. Some choice ... But what I really want to talk about is how it feels to be a parent who, week after week, and—as I look into the future—year after year watches her child trek out the door to spend all day in an institution that try as it might (and it does really try) cannot meet his needs. A parent who struggles daily with the worst of all parental emotions: the feeling that she is letting her child—this beautiful, intelligent, eminently worthy creature whom she loves more than life itself—down ...

'I want to go to Private School A,' he said a few months ago, after hearing his closest friend rave about his school camp, curriculum options and sporting tutelage. 'We can't afford it,' I replied. He won't ask again. He can see how frustrated I am at my inability to give him the wonderful educational opportunities we both see dispensed like lollies all round us; how sad and guilty I feel that despite the fact that we are doing the best we can, our best isn't good enough. He knows I need to stop thinking about it, so I can breathe.

Source: Leslie Cannold, 'I feel guilty my son is at a public school', www.onlineopinion.com.au/view.asp?article=6606, posted Thursday 8 November 2007.

Social inequality is a core focus of sociology because in examining questions about the distribution of social goods within a community it raises issues of what kinds of goods are valued, which groups have the greatest control over this, how they achieve this and what effects differences in opportunity and outcome have on people's lives and on the institutions and organisations of society. The field is concerned with questions of social justice, the dominant values within a society and the way different groups understand and relate to one another.

For the classical theorists the way in which a society distributed material and symbolic resources was central to sociology itself. Theorists such as Karl Marx believed that it was these arrangements that caused social conflict and social change. The arrangements for social inequality are central to sociology's core question of what causes social conflict and what causes social cohesion. Today, in an age of affluence, social inequality generates less attention but it still remains a fundamental social issue, especially on a global level. There is enough wealth for everyone to enjoy a high standard of living, yet a substantial proportion of humanity has insufficient to meet its basic needs.

Social inequality is a fact of life, something that has always existed. Even in societies that produce little surplus wealth the distribution of social honour is unevenly distributed, according to such things as skin colour or gender. Sociology argues that this is not something to be treated as a 'given': it requires the application of the sociological imagination to understand why and how this is so. The idea of a truly egalitarian nation may be regarded as utopian, but this does not mean that we should not ask questions about how much inequality is acceptable, and who benefits from existing arrangements.

Key concepts

The term **social inequality** refers to the unequal distribution of social, political and economic resources within a social collective, such as a nation. **Social stratification** refers to an enduring hierarchy of inequality in which groups are positioned according to the systematic, unequal distribution of a particular variable or combination of variables, such as class, ethnic group membership or gender. It refers to the arrangements for inequality embedded in a society's institutions that are practised and experienced in everyday life. **Life chances** are opportunities associated with social positions that give rise to different material, political, cultural and social outcomes. Stratification systems are meaningful because they can be linked to the role of key variables such as class or ethnicity in shaping the life chances of different groups in society.

Underlying the meaning of the terms *equality* and *inequality* are two distinct ideas. *Distributive equality* refers to how resources are distributed—who gets what. **Meritocracy** refers to equality of opportunity. Critics have described meritocracy as having an equal opportunity to be unequal. Distributive understandings of inequality are associated with left-wing perspectives that suggest that the state should intervene to reduce high levels of economic inequality. Meritocratic understandings are concerned with ensuring that a minimal standard of living is provided so that everyone has an equal chance to compete for rewards.

The variables identified by sociologists as especially important in influencing inequality are class, status, power, social capital and cultural capital. **Class** refers to a social group, defined in terms of its economic position in a hierarchy of inequality and with material interests that differentiate it from other classes. The position of the middle class, for example, who possess intellectual skills, is different from that of the working class, who possess manual skills.

Status refers to differences in social honour or prestige that becomes the basis of social hierarchy as a result of processes of social exclusion. Throughout history, and still today, differences in race, ethnicity and gender have formed the basis of unequal access to resources. This is usually legitimated through arguments about the superiority of one group over another—for example, the cultural or biological superiority of white people over black people, or the innate inferiority of women compared with men. These claims are often supported by religious and political social groups.

Weber defined **power** as the capacity of an individual or a group of individuals to achieve their objectives, even if opposed by others (in Gerth & Mills 1948, p. 180). Power may be physical, in the sense of physical force; material, as in access to wealth; or symbolic, in the sense of influence over cultural symbols such as media imagery. For many social theorists it is differential access to power that ultimately underpins all forms of inequality, including class.

Social capital and cultural capital are ways of understanding the role of social networks and cultural knowledge in arrangements for inequality. **Social capital** refers to the social networks and sources of support that are available to people, whereas **cultural capital** refers to a form of value associated with consumption patterns, lifestyle choices, social attributes and formal qualifications (Bourdieu 1990).

Systems of stratification are particular arrangements for inequality that have existed historically. Caste, feudal, capitalist, socialist and communist systems are the systems sociologists have discussed in greatest depth.

Since the late 1990s the idea of social division has to some extent replaced that of stratification. Stratification refers to a vertical hierarchy of inequality and takes no account of differences between social groups occupying parallel positions in the hierarchy of resources. **Social division** can be defined as those aspects of inequality that include both horizontal and vertical boundaries between social groups. Stratification is especially associated with class and economic differences, while social division acknowledges the coexistence of multiple variables influencing social differentiation, including gender, ethnicity, age and place (Bottero 2005, p. 27). The concept also acknowledges the fluidity of contemporary arrangements for social inequality and permits exploration of the processes and practices involved. Closely associated with the idea of social division are ideas of social distance and social exclusion. **Social distance** refers to relational aspects of inequality in which different groups form positive or negative moral judgements about others. **Social exclusion** refers to the process by which some groups exclude or include others from participation in the activities and rewards considered to be an essential feature of citizenship.

Case Study
The caste system in India

Traditional Indian society was divided into four main castes. Brahmins were regarded as the most privileged group, while a fifth, least-privileged group, the Untouchables (or Dalits) were excluded from the caste system altogether and regarded as outsiders. These main groupings were further divided into Jatis, which linked to occupations such as jeweller or leather worker.

Hindu religious beliefs established a system of stratification based on notions of religious purity and pollution. Dharma is the moral code according to which Hindus should live, while kharma refers to the effects of living according to dharma on the individual's life and future incarnations.

In traditional India, occupation, social position and social relations were determined by caste position. This included the physical distance members from different Jatis had to maintain between one another, who they could marry, where they could live, the kind of food they could eat and who was permitted to touch it. Even today, in many parts of India, it is difficult for a Brahmin to share food with an Untouchable.

> *The whole Jat village of Balla in India, a couple of hours drive from the national capital of New Delhi, is proud of the 'honour killing' of a young couple. It was a ghastly killing: 21-year-old Sunitha who was three weeks pregnant and her 22-year-old husband Jasbir Singh were strangled to death recently. Their bodies, half-stripped, were laid out on the dirt outside Sunita's father's house for all to see, a sign that the family's 'honour' had been restored by her cold-blooded murder.*
>
> *A week later the entire village stands united behind the act, proud, defiant almost to a man, writes a horrified Simon Denyer of Reuters. Among the Jat caste of the conservative northern state of Haryana, it is taboo for a man and woman of the same village to marry. Although the couple were not related, they were seen in this deeply traditional society as brother and sister ...*
>
> *Growing economic opportunities for young people and lower castes in Haryana have made 'love marriages' more common, experts say, and the violent repression of them has risen in tandem as upper caste Jat men fight to hold on to power, status and property ... The relatively prosperous northern state of Haryana is one of India's most conservative when it comes to caste, marriage and the role of women. Deeply patriarchal, caste purity is paramount and marriages are arranged to sustain the status quo.*
> (Media India 2008)

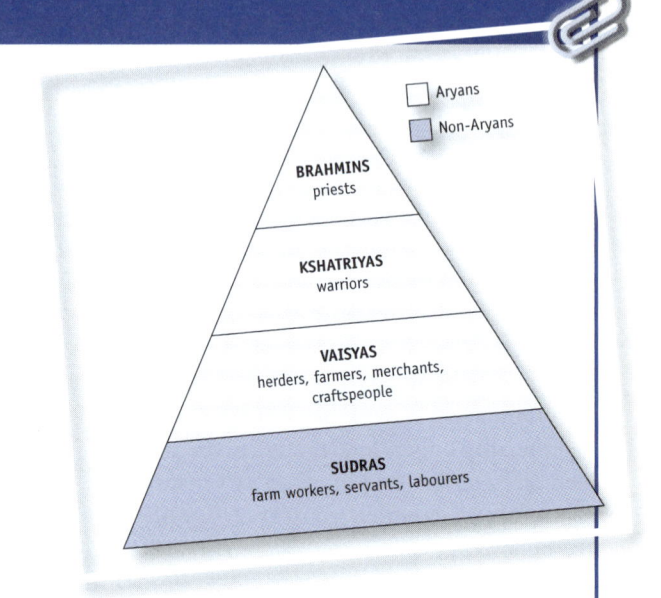

Social mobility refers to the capacity of individuals to move up or down the hierarchy of inequality either within a single person's lifetime or across generations. The more movement up and down the hierarchy, the more open the system is. In a closed system, where there is little movement, it is possible to predict with some certainty the position and therefore the life chances of individuals from the position of their parents. But in an open system, where mobility is based on individual characteristics such as intelligence rather than inheritance, the system is described as meritocratic. The degree of social mobility that exists within a nation indicates how stable the system is across generations.

DOES SOCIAL INEQUALITY MATTER?

The existence of social inequality is not something that arises naturally or from some innate characteristic of human beings. Inequality is a human creation, although we may feel that we have little control over its appearance and effects. Even though humans differ in characteristics such as intelligence, creativity and motivation, there is no direct correspondence between this and the distribution of resources in society. Social inequality derives from social conditions that reflect historical arrangements, values and the capacity for some groups to dominate others. Evidence for this claim can be found in the wide range of arrangements for inequality that have existed historically. As individuals we have the capacity to influence the direction and shape of arrangements for inequality. This is especially true in liberal democracies where people have many avenues for influencing the political process.

From a social justice perspective, social inequality is morally wrong because it violates fundamental human rights. A society that divides its citizens into 'haves' and 'have nots' is unfair because an accident of birth determines who is, and who is not, privileged. This violates the meritocratic principles that are the moral foundation of contemporary democracies. Even if the claim to meritocracy can be supported through measures such as open access to good-quality education, it is still hard to justify the extremes of wealth and privilege that prevail in most nations. Inequality also tends to become perpetuated down the generations, as dominant groups are well-placed to ensure that their children duplicate their own social position. They can afford to buy the best education and can use their connections to help their offspring obtain well-paid jobs with good career potential.

The view that inequality is socially harmful is not universal. The economist and philosopher F.A. Hayek (1899–1992) challenged the idea of human rights that had become prominent following the atrocities of World War II (1976). Hayek argued that egalitarian ideals were arbitrary human inventions and harmed rather than benefited society. Hayek was a social libertarian and believed that human society was best organised by permitting market forces to operate without human interference.

Adherents of this view often also suggest that it is political, not material, inequality that matters. So long as the law operates in an unbiased manner and all citizens are treated equally, then the level of economic inequality is unimportant. The difficulty with this is that it ignores the links between political and economic power. The power generated by wealth tends to extend to the political arena, so that wealthy people can usually have some influence over the political process and use this to defend and develop their interests, often at the expense of those who are less advantaged. Their advantage contrasts with the political exclusion of people living in poverty. High levels of inequality are also associated with corruption, wastage of human capital, significant public expense, conflict and the abuse of human rights. This affects everyone, rich and poor alike (Wilkinson & Pickett 2009).

> **Reflective question:** What arguments would you use against someone who suggested that social inequality is universal and therefore must be inevitable and natural?

INEQUALITY IN A CHANGING WORLD

Until the 1970s the analysis of inequality was dominated by structural approaches that viewed arrangements for social hierarchy as relatively fixed. The transformations wrought by globalisation and the dominance of the service economy in the second half of the 20th century required new understandings about arrangements for inequality. Structuralist accounts emphasise the way social arrangements determine life chances. The difficulty is that such approaches tend to treat society as if its arrangements are fixed and individuals have no control over what happens to them. There is often an overemphasis on one variable that explains everything else, usually class.

The notion of distinct social groups with clear, fixed relationships sits uneasily in a world of **'liquid modernity'** (Bauman 2000) in which boundaries between social groups have become blurred and permeable. Individualisation has heightened the significance of identity construction through consumption rather than class. Self-identity is expressed through taste preferences in clothing, music and entertainment rather than class position. Cultural differences are as important as economic ones in creating a sense of who we recognise as belonging to 'our' group and who we regard as distant and 'other'. This has brought the role of culture into prominence and a concern with how inequality is subjectively experienced and practised.

Multiculturalism and the entrance of large numbers of women into the workforce have also made it difficult not to acknowledge ethnicity and gender as important aspects of inequality. This requires a multidimensional understanding of inequality that acknowledges differences both within and between groups even if they share the same economic position.

CLASS, STRATIFICATION AND MODERNITY

The idea of class as the most important organising principle shaping social formations was one of the metanarratives of modernity. It provided an overarching conceptual framework for understanding large areas of social life.

The concept of class made sense in the industrial period of modernity when many people worked in factories, most workers were male, and the material and social divisions between middle, upper and working class were clear. The **working class** was the largest social group and was distinguished by manual labour. Workers relied on their labour for their income and earned much less than those in the classes above them. The **middle class** and upper class depended on professional qualifications or ownership of productive property for their living and social standing. The **upper class** was distinguished by its political and economic dominance.

The stability of the classes in the industrial age gave rise to a strong sense of class identity, especially among the working class. Social and geographical stability and a shared work experience brought a sense of community with common values and beliefs. Until the 1960s, working-class children left school as soon as they could for a lifetime of work in a factory or another area of primary or secondary industry. In some regions, such as mining and fishing areas, occupations were handed down between the generations. Most working-class people belonged to trade unions and relied on the collective action of this social movement as the best way of improving their economic circumstances. Industrial plants were visible and geographically concentrated, giving economic division a physical presence. Although the divisions of gender and ethnicity were present, neither public nor academic consciousness had accounted for the presence of women, migrants and Indigenous peoples in Australian social life.

Throughout most of the 20th century sociology's main concern was to unravel the links between class, inequality and power. This involved:

- mapping out the boundaries and sizes of different social classes
- exploring the connections between class position and life chances, such as health, education and occupational outcomes
- measuring social mobility between classes
- exploring the role of class in promoting social cohesion and class conflict
- examining how class was used to both usurp and maintain power
- understanding the relationship between class and social and political movements.

Although important, this focus ignored other areas that are equally implicated in processes of social division. Class was a masculine construct, researched and conceptualised by men and defined in male terms; the position of women, and that of migrant groups and Indigenous peoples, was ignored.

LOCATING CLASS IN LATE MODERNITY

By the late 1970s there developed an argument that, as a concept, class had had its day (Bell 1973). The industrial economy is based on heavy industries such as coal-mining and the manufacture of goods such as cars. The service economy of contemporary society is based on the production of ideas and knowledge, such as information, financial products and tourism. Labour power has given way to mental power and the occupational structure has seen a considerable reduction in the size of the traditional working class.

The shift to a service economy has been accompanied by an increase in social mobility with the growth of positions in knowledge-based industries. As the offspring of manual workers entered the middle class, working-class culture and cohesion were eroded. Traditional working-class districts disappeared as manufacturing industries moved offshore and people left for new jobs or became marginalised in the long-term unemployed or under-employed secondary labour market of casual, low-paid, insecure positions.

The growth of the service sector has been accompanied by the entrance of women into the workforce, causing further changes to the workplace. Their experience and motivations are different from men's. Often they are casual and part-time, juggling housework alongside their day job. Their motivations for employment are based as much on social relationships as they are on increasing income (Crompton & Mann 1986, p. 156). They are less likely to go to the pub or club after work and they are less politically active than men. Many do not belong to a trade union. Although gender has always divided the workforce, the increased number of women workers fragmented the labour market.

Modernity was associated with class politics that revolved around industrial conflict between unions and employers, sometimes spilling over into strikes and political protest. By the 1980s industrial conflict had reduced, partly because the strength of trade unionism was declining along with the diminishing size of the working class and partly because of industrial reforms that reduced collective bargaining arrangements in favour of individual or workplace agreements. Identity politics began to replace class politics. This is based around notions of citizenship, such as the demand for Aboriginal land rights and the women's movement, or values such as environmental and peace movements. The class basis of political movements has also changed. Originally working class, the Labor Party today is as much middle class as it is working class. Conversely, many working-class people vote Liberal, which originally was the party of the rich and powerful.

The second half of the 20th century brought the expansion of educational opportunities, greater social mobility and the establishment of the welfare net to support those at the bottom of the hierarchy. Rising living standards mean that nearly everyone owns a car, a DVD and a computer. Most people own their own home, take holidays overseas and enjoy a wide range of consumer goods. Against this background, class distinctions no longer seem so relevant.

Globalisation has also changed the nature of work, making a job for life a thing of the past. The linear path of school, work, retirement has been exchanged for one in which people can expect to undertake education and training at any point in their life and to develop more than one career pathway. As individuals are freed from the constraints of tradition and ascribed social position, identity rather than class becomes the source of social identity. The sociologist Beck observes:

> People with the same income level, or put it in the old-fashioned way, within the same 'class', can or even must choose between different lifestyles, subcultures, social ties and identities. From knowing one's 'class' position one can no longer determine one's personal outlook, relations, family position, social and political ideas or identity. (1992, p. 131)

These changes have transformed the study of inequality, extending it beyond the study of white men operating in the public sphere. Class remains a core variable, but its meaning has been expanded to take account of the role of culture in shaping hierarchy and social division.

Understanding contemporary inequality

To accommodate these changes, the concept of class has undergone a metamorphosis, shedding some of its structuralist baggage and permitting a more individualised understanding of inequality.

The main theorist behind this new wave of class analysis is Bourdieu. For Bourdieu, culture is a resource that is just as implicated in the creation and maintenance of inequality as material resources. Bourdieu draws attention to the way differences in cultural knowledge mark the boundaries within groups even when they share the same economic position. This approach offers theorists of inequality a new framework that links economic position with cultural practices to explain how consumption contributes to social exclusion and domination (Devine & Savage 2000, p. 195). Achieving this has involved a major paradigm shift from:

- the economy to culture
- class to identity
- production to consumption
- life chances to lifestyles
- institutional structures to everyday social practices.

THEORIES OF INEQUALITY

Theories of inequality vary according to their political and moral stance and the emphasis they give to the significance of economic, biological and cultural factors as the causes of inequality. In this section four major theorists of inequality are examined, each of which has given rise to major perspectives on inequality. Marx, Weber and Durkheim form the classical triumvirate, whose ideas dominated theories of inequality in the 20th century. Bourdieu represents the new wave of social theorising and forms a bridge between modern and postmodern understandings of inequality. All these theories are to some degree structuralist, although Weber and Bourdieu also emphasise the importance of non-economic factors. They differ in their views on the prospects for a truly egalitarian society and on how much inequality should be tolerated. The ideas of Marx, Weber and Durkheim represent the starting point for any sociological account of how inequality is developed and maintained. Bourdieu's ideas build on the classical theorists while providing a bridge to contemporary sociology's emphasis on culture and subjectivities.

Marx's theory of class

Karl Marx was born into a period of dramatic social change. He witnessed the aftermath of the American and French revolutions, and lived through the Industrial Revolution. He was influenced by the ideals of the Enlightenment, which emphasised progress, evolutionary theory and a utopian idealism suggesting that industrial production would make possible a just and egalitarian society. Marx's influence on political leaders such as Lenin and Mao Zedong provided the ideological framework for the communist and socialist movements that influenced the political direction of numerous nations in the 20th century.

Positivism

Marx was a positivist and attempted to apply the principles of the natural sciences to discover laws of development in the social world. He believed that societies develop progressively, in a way similar to evolution in the plant and animal world. His belief in underlying laws of social development gives his work a tendency to overemphasise external social forces as if they operate independently of the humans that create them. Although he recognised the importance of agency and subjectivity and acknowledged the interpretations people give to their experience and the choices that result from this, this understanding tended to disappear from his grand theory of social change.

Marx's evolutionary theory of social change

Marx's evolutionary theory was based on a belief that society progresses as a result of a process of conflict, revolution and resolution between different social groups he called classes. He argued that humans had an innate tendency to improve what they did and so were always seeking to innovate, especially in relation to the production of wealth. Eventually a conflict takes place between the groups attached to the old ways of creating wealth and those attached to the new ways, and out of this new, more efficient technologies emerge. Marx used the term **mode of production** to describe how a society produces its wealth, and argued that societies could be classified according to this. The mode of production includes both the means of production, comprising the technological knowledge used to produce goods such as food and clothing, and social relationships between groups involved in production, such as bosses and workers. He argued that it is the economic base of society, or **infrastructure** that shapes the **superstructure**, a term he used to describe all other non-economic aspects of society, including politics and culture.

Historical materialism

Marx believed that inequality occurs as soon as a society produces a surplus of wealth beyond what its members need for mere physical survival. He used the term class to describe the different interest groups that arise out of the unequal distribution of economic resources. This forms the foundation of relationships of domination and exploitation, which become entrenched over time. The struggle to change this situation of inequality leads to class conflict because the disadvantaged will always seek to improve their position. Resolution and progress are only possible through revolution because the economically advantaged group will never relinquish their wealth and power willingly. Where this is successful a new social order is created. Where it is unsuccessful the society stagnates and slowly disintegrates.

Marx described this principle of social change as *dialectical materialism* because of its emphasis on the clash between opposing forces, and the material basis of this. It was also known as *historical materialism* because of the emphasis Marx gave to the role of pre-existing conditions in shaping the future.

The key components of Marx's theory of historical materialism are contained in the following statement from his study *The Critique of Political Economy* (1859):

In the social production of their existence, men inevitably enter into definite relations, which are independent of their will, namely relations of production appropriate to a given stage in the development of their material forces of production. The totality of these relations of production constitutes the economic structure of society, the real foundation, on which arises a legal and political superstructure, and to which correspond definite forms of consciousness. The mode of production of material life conditions the general process of social, political, and intellectual life. It is not the consciousness of men that determines their existence, but their social existence that determines their consciousness. At a certain stage of development, 7 material productive forces of society come into conflict with the existing relations of production or—this merely expresses the same thing in legal terms—with the property relations within the framework of which they have operated hitherto. From forms of development, of the productive forces, these relations turn into their fetters. Then begins an era of social revolution. The changes in the economic foundation lead, sooner or later, to the transformation of the whole, immense, superstructure. (in Bottomore & Rubel 1976, p. 67)

This paragraph reveals Marx's structuralism in his argument that free will is constrained by economic arrangements. People enter into relations determined by the objective arrangements of society. Although qualified by some of his earlier philosophical writings, here Marx claims that the economy shapes all other aspects of society, including politics, law, culture and even the beliefs and consciousness of humans and the ideas they have.

Modes of production and evolutionary social change

Marx believed that all societies can be defined by their mode of production, with societies evolving progressively from one form to another. He identified five modes of production that had existed, or would eventually exist, in Europe. In the ancient societies of Greece and Rome slavery formed the basis of the mode of production, with slaves and slave owners forming the two main classes. This was replaced by feudalism, which existed in medieval Europe. The mode of production was based on the development of arable land, with technology limited to human and animal power. The two main classes were the landed aristocracy, who owned most of the land, and the serfs, who provided the labour power. The landowners' power was supported by Christianity, whose beliefs suggested the social hierarchy was ordained by God. There was some mutuality in the relationship between serfs and the landowners who exploited them but also protected them and resolved disputes.

By the end of the 18th century, capitalism had replaced feudalism as the dominant economic system. Technology was the new source of energy and a new class of factory owners replaced the landed aristocracy as the dominant class. Factories required an urban workforce, willing to travel to the cities and prepared to work for a wage, breaking the social relationship between landlord and serf. Marx described these two new classes as capitalists or *bourgeoisie*, and **proletariat** or *working class*. He also recognised a middle class, divided into a *petite bourgeoisie* comprising small-business and shop owners and an emerging professional class, but believed this would disappear as capitalism developed.

Marx believed that capitalism contained inherent contradictions that would lead the working class to develop a revolutionary social movement that would overthrow capitalism and establish socialism. The profits of the bourgeoisie rely on paying the proletariat as little as possible, while the proletariat always seek to earn more. Yet the bourgeoisie also require a market to purchase their goods. If workers are too impoverished to purchase them, then the economy goes into a depression. Marx argued this inherent dynamic would lead to prolonged periods of economic depression and in these conditions of pauperisation the working class would form a revolutionary social movement and eventually seize power and control from the upper class. In the socialist state that follows capitalism the state will take over production and redistribute the wealth for the benefit of everyone. Once this has been achieved the need for centralised control will disappear, the state will eventually wither away and each citizen will look after their own affairs.

Marx described the final stage of social evolution as communism. Marx believed that this would be a classless society in which the exploitation of one human over another would be replaced by the exploitation of nature. Wealth would be distributed according to need and exploitation would not exist. The population would be able to engage in any activity they chose, since 'society regulates the general production, making it possible for me to do one thing today and another tomorrow, to hunt in the morning, fish in the afternoon, breed cattle in the evening, criticize after dinner, just as I like, without ever becoming a hunter, fisherman, a herdsman or a critic' (Marx & Engels 1970 [1845–6], p. 53).

Class, class consciousness and the state

Marx's theory of surplus value was concerned with the source of the profits made by capitalists that provided the basis of their domination over other social groups. He argued that the profits they made were the result of the exploitation of the labour power of workers. Instead of returning to workers the full value of their labour, they were given only what was required for bare subsistence; the surplus value was returned to the capitalists as profit. This exploitation of the working class was especially acute because, unlike serfs who owned their own tools and some land, workers had no alternative means of meeting their needs other than by selling their labour. This made them vulnerable to the demands of the capitalists—they might starve if they did not work.

Marx believed that the economically dominant class was also a **ruling class** because its economic power enabled it to dominate politics. In *The Communist Manifesto* it is stated that 'the executive of the modern state is but a committee for managing the common affairs of the whole bourgeoisie' (Marx & Engels 1967, p. 82). This power also extends to control over ideas. *Ruling ideology* is a term used in Marxist theory to describe the complex set of ideas, such as the Divine Right of Kings, which justifies inequality. This ideological dominance was described by Marx as a form of **false consciousness** because it blinds the working class to their exploitation.

To challenge false consciousness Marx believed that the working class had to develop class consciousness and transform themselves from a *class in itself* to a *class for itself*. By class consciousness Marx meant an awareness of shared interests. Marx saw the trade union movement as the main form that opposition to the ruling class would take. He believed that as the inherent crises of capitalism developed, the gap between rich and poor would become more visible and the working class would see through the false ideology of the ruling class and understand their systematic exploitation. They would eventually overthrow the ruling class and establish socialism, the precursor to the final stage of communism.

Criticisms of Marx

Marx's theories have important weaknesses. They are deterministic, teleological and scientistic. There is an overemphasis on the role of material conditions in determining all other aspects of society, including politics and culture. Implicit in the assumption of evolutionary development is a teleological assumption that social change is progressing in a particular direction, towards the ultimate goal of communism. Yet the one thing we know is that the future is unpredictable. There do not appear to be any laws of human development, and certainly none taking us in a specific direction. Marx also believed that his discovery of social evolution would provide guidance on how we should act. This was a common error among 19th-century social theorists who believed that scientific knowledge would be a source of social values. This scientism was challenged by Weber, who pointed out that science can only tell us *what is*, it cannot tell us what *should be* or how we should behave.

At the empirical level, Marx's ideas have been falsified by the direction of history. His model of class identifies just two social classes defined by their relationship to the means of production. Although Marx acknowledged the existence of a middle class, he believed that the crises inherent within capitalism would lead to its eventual absorption into the working class. Instead, the reverse has happened, so that it is sometimes claimed 'we are all middle class now'. Marx's theory has difficulty accounting for the significance of the middle class in contemporary society because it provides only for the role of property as a source of social position, not intellectual skills.

Marx believed that socialism and communism would take place only *after* nations had undergone the capitalist stage of development and that socialist working-class movements would be most widespread in capitalist economies. But in the 20th century socialism and communism appeared in pre-industrial nations such as China and Russia not industrial ones, and it was the peasantry that developed a revolutionary consciousness, not the working class. Marxist politics have been of only limited influence in Western liberal democracies.

Although Marx recognised capitalism's transformative power, he underestimated its capacity to absorb and accommodate conflict. He believed that the inherent contradictions of capitalism would lead to its demise. But capitalism has proved remarkably resilient. Although the cycles of economic boom and bust identified by Marx still occur, they have not been as severe as he predicted and have taken place within a context of welfare provision, political and ideological control and increased affluence, which has prevented the development of a revolutionary working-class movement and the overthrow of the capitalist ruling class in capitalist economies. Although transformed by globalisation, capitalism is not only still in existence but also has proved triumphant in a way that severely challenges Marxist theory.

The legacy of Marx

The weaknesses of Marx's ideas derive from his positivist philosophy, but such ideas were revolutionary in his day. Nor is Marx the only great social theorist whom events have proved wrong. Today we understand how perilous it is to attempt to predict the future trajectory of social development. In Marx's time the opposite was believed. The new science of society was heralded precisely because of its capacity for social engineering towards a desirable and predictable goal. Western affluence has reduced the salience of Marx's theory of exploitation in the developed world, although it has enduring relevance for the developing world. Marx's analysis of the role of the state in ensuring capitalism's survival, both by checking its excesses and through political manipulation of the masses, remains an important reference point for political theory. Today the atrocities associated with communist and socialist regimes, the global dominance of capitalism as an economic system and the decline in size and influence of the working class have pushed Marxism aside both as a political movement and a social theory. Yet Marx's ideas continue to be foundational for the study of social inequality.

WEBER'S MULTIDIMENSIONAL THEORY OF INEQUALITY

Max Weber's model of inequality differs from Marx's in its identification of power as the underlying source of all forms of inequality. Although Weber acknowledged class as being of great significance, especially in capitalist economies, it was only one of three sources of power, the other two being status and party. For Weber, *class* referred to economic factors such as wealth and income, *status* referred to social honour and *party* referred to political organisation and influence. Weber's insight into the multiple dimensions influencing social hierarchy and division is well described by Parkin:

> *Impoverished Brahmins and down-at-heel aristocrats could confidently expect to be deferred to by others better off than themselves, while men of new wealth were generally looked down upon by families of breeding and pedigree. Moreover, even where wealth and social honour were roughly on a par, the relationship between them was not always in the same causal direction. Sometimes social honour flowed from material possessions, sometimes it was more like a springboard to the attainment of such possessions (1982, pp. 96–97).*

Weber insisted on the independent influence of class and status on social inequality, but recognised the tendency for power in one area to lead to power in another. Material possessions tend to lead to high social status, and high social status is an important source of wealth.

Class as market position

Weber shared with Marx a definition of class in terms of the economic factors that influence an individual's or group's life chances. However, as well as recognising the importance of property, Weber also identified the importance of the marketplace in determining the distribution of economic resources. It is in markets—such as financial, real estate and employment markets—that people exchange goods in return for money. Weber therefore expanded the bases of economic inequality beyond property ownership to include skills and credentials.

Weber describes classes as groups of people, such as doctors or dock workers, who possess skills or goods that reap a similar reward in the market and result in similar life chances. This definition provides for the advantaged position of the middle class in contemporary society, many of whom owe their position to possession of educational qualifications.

Weber's model of social class identifies four main groups:

1. the bourgeoisie, whose position is based on ownership of productive property
2. the petty bourgeoisie, comprising self-employed small-business owners and shopkeepers whose wealth is based on possession of relatively small amounts of productive property
3. salaried non-manual workers, including professionals, managers and white-collar workers, who owe their position to their possession of credentials
4. manual workers, whose source of wealth is their labour power and, at the higher levels, their possession of credentials.

Status groups and social closure

Weber acknowledged that social honour, or prestige, is an important source of social position. He defined *status groups* as those groups whose life-fate is determined by a similar specific—positive or negative—social estimation of honour. Weber argued that in some societies status is the foundation of social inequality, using the caste system of India as an example of this. Unlike classes, which may lack any shared group identity, status groups, by definition, always form a community and so share a common lifestyle.

Weber described status groups as forming a vertical structure of power and domination that is separate to the horizontal structure formed by class. Classes share a common economic position and can be conceived visually as a hierarchy of horizontal bands. Status groups cut across these economic groups. In Australia, some migrant communities, such as the Vietnamese, for example, may share a common cultural identity but their possession of different amounts of economic capital places them in different classes. Weber's point is especially relevant in multicultural societies where ethnic divisions have fragmented the working class and reduced its political power.

Weber noted that status groups often operate a process of social closure in which they restrict access to resources and opportunity to their own members. Weber developed this concept in his analysis of the exclusionary cultural practices of Jews and Muslims, such as their dietary restrictions, but observed that it also applied to the way occupational groups restricted entry to their ranks through the requirement for credentials. Weber observed that in modernity this type of social closure was becoming increasingly significant.

Parties

Weber described parties as voluntary associations that are systematically organised for the collective pursuit of interests. The concept acknowledges the importance of collective social action in the distribution of resources. It includes formal and informal political organisations, such as professional associations and pressure groups, as well as political parties, such as the Australian Labor

Party. Weber regarded parties not as an independent source of power but as based on status and class groups. The concept is not well developed in Weber's writings but is important for its acknowledgement that organised social action influences the distribution of resources.

The legacy of Weber

In the 1950s and 1960s, under the influence of the conservative theory of structural functionalism, Weber's ideas were interpreted as opposing those of Marx. But in the 1970s the work of the conflict theorists, Gerth and Mills (1948), led to a reappraisal of Weber's ideas and today he is understood as a conflict theorist who extended Marx's ideas. Although he challenged Marx's economic determinism and the evolutionary theory of social change, he regarded ownership of property and classes, defined in terms of economic position, as central to any account of inequality.

Weber's ideas on social closure have been used to examine the role of credentialism in generating privilege and disadvantage within the occupational order (Parkin 1982). His ideas have also given rise to market-based explanations of inequality and influenced neo-Marxist theories that acknowledge the role of knowledge in explaining the privileged class position of the middle classes in contemporary Western economies.

DURKHEIM AND THE DIVISION OF LABOUR

The French sociologist Emile Durkheim was a contemporary of Weber, but while Weber asked how societies change, Durkheim asked how society is possible. He wanted to explain the 'social glue' that binds social groups together. Durkheim argued that cooperation is made possible through the establishment of a moral order that members of society are socialised into accepting as normal. Durkheim assumed that human sociability requires explanation. His ontological assumption about the innate characteristics of humans follows that of the economist Thomas Hobbes, who believed that were it not for society, humans would engage in a war of all against all. This is quite different from Marx, who believed that humans are fundamentally cooperative and it is social conflict that requires explanation.

Durkheim shared the positivism of Marx, and believed in the existence of laws of social development that sociology would uncover. His evolutionary theory of social change argued that social development occurred as a result of increasing specialisation and differentiation. In *The Division of Labour in Society* (1933 [1893]), Durkheim argued that the basis of sociality changes as societies become more complex. Durkheim used the term *social solidarity* to describe the social forces that make society possible. He argued that mechanical solidarity prevailed in traditional society, and organic solidarity prevailed in modern ones. Durkheim's analysis of traditional societies was based on 19th-century ethnographic accounts of Australian Aboriginal societies. He believed that the level of social differentiation in traditional cultures was low, and that because people shared similar social experiences they also developed shared beliefs and values that formed the basis of cooperation. Religion plays a unifying role in establishing a common value system that binds together the members of traditional society. For Durkheim this social aspect of religion was so powerful that he regarded the real purpose of religious ritual as the establishment of social cohesion.

Durkheim contrasted mechanical solidarity with the organic solidarity of modern societies. Here high levels of specialisation create social diversity so people develop different understandings, values and beliefs. The basis of social cohesion changes from one based on similarity to one based on difference. The basis of social solidarity in these societies is mutual dependence because no-one can exist without the contribution of other members. It is only by being tolerant and cooperative that people will ensure their needs are met.

Durkheim believed that hierarchy was both inevitable and necessary in complex societies. The problem was not its existence, but its legitimation. The basis of inequality needed to be seen as fair, so this required a system that was transparent and meritocratic. Where these requirements are not met, as in societies with high levels of inequality or corruption, then inequality is dysfunctional and leads to social conflict. He wrote:

> *What is needed if social order is to reign is that the mass of men be contented with their lot. But what is needed for them to be content is not that they have more or less, but that they be convinced that they have no right to more.* (cited in Aron 1977, p. 91)

Like Weber, Durkheim argued that in modern industrial economies credentials provide the objective measure of talent and knowledge and are the most appropriate foundation for the distribution of resources.

The legacy of Durkheim: the functions of inequality

Although Durkheim was quite radical in his political views, his concern with how social order is established in society and his belief that society has needs that must be met if it is to survive supported the conservative approaches of structural functionalism in the 1950s and 1960s. The most influential functionalist theorist was Talcott Parsons (1902–79), whose ideas on inequality suggested that because it was universal it must be serving some useful purpose.

The most influential expression of this argument is Davis and Moore's article 'Some principles of stratification' (1967). Davis and Moore argued that in contemporary society roles are highly specialised and differentiated, with some requiring more skills and ability than others. Since talent is not evenly distributed, the stratification system operates to sort individuals into the location that best suits their abilities. Those who are most talented take the most demanding and responsible positions, while the less talented are placed in less difficult jobs. There is a hierarchy of rewards attached to these positions, since the more specialised and demanding jobs require longer training, are more difficult to perform and carry more responsibility. Individuals require encouragement to take on these more demanding positions and so must be rewarded more highly. Davis and Moore argued that in a democracy where positions are open to talent and equal access to education and health services ensures equality of opportunity, this system is efficient and fair and works for the good of society as a whole.

The difficulty with this argument is the assumption that democracies are meritocratic (Tumin 1967). There is no recognition of the role of inherited privilege and the capacity of the wealthy to pass this on to their offspring. The argument also ignores the non-economic rewards associated with high levels of responsibility. These jobs provide opportunities for self-fulfilment, high status and independence. The assumption that the prevailing system of rewards is rational and based on value consensus is also problematic. Corporate lawyers can achieve very high financial rewards while foster carers receive very little, yet it is debatable as to which role contributes more to society. Yet Davis and Moore's argument is important because it reflects mainstream assumptions about the operation of meritocracy in contemporary democracy. What happens to individuals is understood only in terms of their individual capacities rather than being located in the broader social environment.

Pierre Bourdieu: class and culture

The French sociologist Pierre Bourdieu laid the groundwork for a more culturally based understanding of social hierarchy. Bourdieu reworked Marx's notion of economic capital as the source of inequality, to take account of the full range of resources that are implicated in its existence. Bourdieu identified four types of capital as the basis of social position:

- *economic capital (material resources: wealth, income, property)*
- *cultural capital (cultural knowledge, educational credentials)*
- *social capital (social connections, networks, patronage)*
- *symbolic capital (symbolic legitimation, respect, reputation). (Bottero 2005, p. 148)*

In *Distinction* (1984) Bourdieu demonstrates how class is expressed through taste practices so that cultural capital acts as an independent resource. Like economic capital, cultural capital generates position in the stratification order. In contemporary economies possession of cultural capital has become a marketable commodity, because in the services industry cultural competence and social connections are important. To work in the field of the media, social work, retail or finance requires particular kinds of cultural expertise. The significance of cultural capital today is most clearly manifested in the centrality of education to social advancement. It is through the provision of a good education to their offspring that the upper class reproduce their social position across the generations. This extends beyond possession of formal qualifications to the establishment of social networks and informal cultural knowledge, expressed in lifestyles and taste preferences. People invest in cultural capital to establish economic capital.

Bourdieu's research on cultural taste and lifestyle in France found that taste distinctions were systematic and he used this to propose a model of inequality in which differences in the amount of cultural and economic capital determine social position. He retained the usual three-class division of working, middle and upper class, but subdivided these on the basis of social boundaries within these major groups. In the upper class, the bourgeoisie (business owners and financiers) have high levels of economic capital but lower cultural capital, while the reverse is true of intellectuals (writers, artists, university professors). Professionals and senior managers have a more equal balance of both. Similar distinctions exist in the middle class, while the working class is characterised by lower levels of both cultural and economic capital. Shopkeepers and primary school teachers both belong to the middle class, but the former have modest amounts of economic capital and lower levels of cultural capital, whereas the reverse is true for teachers.

Cultural tastes and preferences play a critical role in social relationships, from whom we accept as sexual partners to the kinds of jobs we choose. Bourdieu pointed out that what we like and dislike is powerfully influenced by our social background. In this way taste is not merely a matter of personal preference but locates us in the social order.

The legacy of Bourdieu

Bourdieu's theories established a new wave of research into cultural aspects of inequality. The 'Australian Everyday Culture Project' (AECP) surveyed 2700 Australians in the late 1990s (Bennett, Emmison & Frow 1999). Drawing on the class schemes of Wright and Goldthorpe, it identified an eightfold class structure comprising:

1. never employed
2. manual workers
3. sales and clerical workers
4. supervisors
5. paraprofessionals
6. professionals
7. managers
8. self-employed and employers (3+ workers).

The study contradicted Bourdieu's finding of the close relationship between economic position and taste practices. Although cultural practices were implicated in processes of social division and social exclusion, these operated independently of class. Two important taste cultures were described as 'inclusive' and 'restrictive'. Inclusive taste cultures primarily consisted of 'cultural omnivores' and were characterised by tertiary education, urbanity, youth and women. They were drawn from high-status groups, especially managers and professionals and, to a lesser extent, paraprofessionals and employers. Cultural omnivores had a wide-ranging appreciation of cultural forms encompassing both 'high' and 'low' cultural practices. The study therefore unhinged the connection Bourdieu made between high culture and high class on the one hand, and low culture and low class on the other.

Restrictive taste cultures were the opposite, reflecting a narrow selection of consumption practices. Individuals in this grouping tended to have low levels of education and a rural or regional location. They consisted primarily of manual and sales/clerical workers, the self-employed and the unemployed and were more likely to be men as well as older people.

The analysis of Australian political beliefs produced a similarly complex picture. The study identified three main groupings: 'conservatist welfarist', 'progressive feminist' and 'conservative pro-market'. Each grouping had a distinct social base but it was not reducible either to class or to inclusive or restrictive taste cultures. Conservatist welfarists tended to be drawn from older, less well-educated groups and from the working class and self-employed. Progressive feminists were predominantly well-educated, young women. Conservative pro-marketers were predominantly from the oldest and least-educated members of the community, as well as from managers and employers.

Like Bourdieu, Bennett and associates concluded that different taste cultures serve as a basis of social distinction. They articulate with social variables, such as gender and social class. While taste cultures cannot be reduced to economic location, cultural competence is nonetheless related to access to resources.

In a subsequent work, Emmison develops the idea of cultural mobility (2003). This concept incorporates and develops the idea of the cultural omnivore and expresses the idea that some social groups are able to utilise cultural forms as a strategic resource in a highly flexible way. The data from the AECP suggest that the culturally mobile are able to navigate taste cultures according to the requirements of their particular situation. They may not necessarily like the different cultural practices but they are knowledgeable about them and can therefore traverse the same cultural universe as others who do like them. Emmison argues that, in the fluid conditions that characterise modernity, this gives the culturally mobile the competitive edge over the 'culturally sedentary'. Emmison also stresses that the culturally mobile are not free-floating social groups but are instead predominantly drawn from the 'knowledge classes'—that is, professional groups. Cultural mobility remains a restricted commodity and therefore a restricted advantage.

> **Reflective questions:** What are the bases of your sense of identity? What role does consumption play in this and how does this relate to your economic position and that of your family background?

MATERIAL INEQUALITY IN AUSTRALIA

Research consistently demonstrates that the amount of economic resources possessed by individuals and families is statistically associated with variables related to our life chances. Health, educational achievements, where we live and our wellbeing are all linked to possession of material resources (Vinson 2007; Walter & Woerner 2007; Headey & Wooden 2007; Bennett, Emmison & Frow 1999). Even though we live in an open society, our economic circumstances remain a constraint. It takes money to buy the best education, to live in a well-resourced neighbourhood and to buy the lifestyle of the wealthy.

MEASURING ECONOMIC RESOURCES

Any measure of economic resources is imperfect because it is not possible to take account of every source of material advantage. This is especially true in a globalised economy where wealth is highly diversified and can be spread across complex international structures. Accurate identification of the wealth held by those at the top of the ladder is particularly difficult for this reason.

Economic resources are usually identified as comprising wealth and income. *Wealth* consists of total assets minus total liabilities and includes any capital assets such as shares, cash, artworks, cars, property and pension funds. *Income* consists of any flow of money over a given period of time and includes wages, interest and dividends, and rents from investment properties. Wealth generates income and income generates wealth. Rental income, for example, can be used to buy capital assets such as shares, and this in turn produces income in the form of dividends. Opportunities for wealth creation increase as individuals climb further up the ladder of economic resources since they have a surplus they can invest. Those at the bottom of the ladder often have negative wealth in the form of debts.

Wage income, taxable income and equivalent family income are just three examples of some of the ways in which income can be assessed. Each has its limitations. *Wage income* excludes income from sources other than paid employment, such as investment income, and therefore undercounts the income of the wealthy. *Taxable income* is based on tax returns and inadequately accounts for those whose income is below the tax threshold. Schemes for tax minimisation and the potential for tax avoidance mean that estimations based on income tax returns almost certainly underestimate the economic resources of the wealthy. *Equivalent family income* is a widely used measure that adjusts income for differences in family size.

The Gini coefficient is a widely used index of inequality. It expresses inequality as a number between 0 and 1, with 0 being a situation of perfect equality where every income unit receives equal income, and 1 being a situation of perfect inequality, where one income unit receives all income. The decile ratio compares the ratio between the income of those in the top 10 per cent and those in the bottom 10 per cent.

The social wage

Data on the distribution of wealth and income need to be interpreted in a way that accounts for the social and economic context. Living standards influence social expectations about what is a good life and also influence the experience of inequality, as do such things as the cost of housing and employment opportunities. State provision also influences the value of individual, family and household resources. The social wage refers to the state's redistribution of economic capital through the taxation system via cash payments or service provision. Services may be universal or targeted. For example, in 2009 the First Home Owner Scheme was a universal benefit available to anyone purchasing a home for the first time, but the age pension was available only to people who met the age criteria *and* whose income and assets fell below a specified level.

The contribution of the social wage to economic security can be seen in Table 7.1, which shows how economic status varies over the life cycle. As people enter the labour force and before they start a family, their mean disposable income is relatively high ($666 per week). It remains high if they do not have children, especially if they are 'dinkies' (double income, no kids). If they form a couple and start a family, the decline in income is compensated by government pensions and allowances, cushioning the effects of the partial withdrawal of one partner, usually the woman, from the labour market. This table explains the overrepresentation of women among low-income groups. If the couple separate, mean disposable income declines sharply to $363 per week. In the absence of affordable child care these parents, who are overwhelmingly women, rely heavily on government support, making them vulnerable to changes in these benefits.

Changes in economic inequality

The distribution of income and wealth changes under different economic conditions. Living standards can increase for all economic groups, but if growth at the top outpaces growth at the bottom, then economic inequality will increase. Over the 20th century, economic inequality fluctuated. Australia became more unequal between 1915 and 1933 (McLean & Richardson 1986)

SOCIOLOGY

TABLE 7.1

Income and household characteristics for selected life-cycle groups, 2005–06

	Number of households	Average number of persons	Average number of employed persons	Average number of dependent children	Proportion with government pensions and allowances as PSI [a]	Mean equivalised disposable household income per week	Proportion owning home without a mortgage
	'000	no.	no.	no.	%	$	%
Lone person aged under 35	369.3	1.0	0.9	–	10.8	666	*3.5
Couple only, reference person under 35	423.5	2.0	1.9	–	*2.0	888	*2.7
Couple with dependent children only							
Eldest child under 5	429.9	3.4	1.5	1.4	3.8	683	6.0
Eldest child 5 to 14	859.4	4.1	1.5	2.1	8.1	642	13.0
Eldest child 15 to 24	469.3	4.2	2.3	2.2	7.0	660	29.5
Couple with							
Dependent and non-dependent children only	264.4	4.7	3.0	1.5	*5.9	695	25.3
Non-dependent children only	449.3	3.3	2.3	–	11.4	740	50.2
Couple only, reference person 55 to 64	506.8	2.0	1.2	–	19.2	729	61.1
Couple only, reference person 65 and over	678.8	2.0	0.2	–	67.6	458	86.4
Lone person 65 and over	744.3	1.0	0.1	–	77.6	363	74.0
One-parent, one-family households with dependent children	538.6	3.0	0.8	1.7	50.9	446	12.8

* estimate has a relative standard error of 25% to 50% and should be used with caution
– nil or rounded to zero (including null cells)
(a) Principal source of income (PSI)
Source: ABS (2007e, p. 8).

but by 1968–69 inequality had decreased (Jones 1975). There was a sharp decrease in the proportion of wealth held by the top 1 per cent of the population, from about 37.8 per cent in 1915 to 19.7 per cent in 1969, although some of this decrease may be attributable to estate-duty avoidance practices (Piggott 1984, p. 261). In the 1980s the top 10 per cent maintained or slightly increased their share of wealth, while the bottom 50 per cent remained the same or slightly decreased their share (Piggott 1984, p. 263). In this period, the biggest increase was in the bottom of the top 50 per cent, so that the redistribution that occurred was primarily from the very wealthy to the moderately wealthy.

The more recent picture is one of increasing prosperity, but with some groups at the bottom caught in worsening conditions of poverty. The period 1994–2008 was one of exceptional global economic expansion from which Australia benefited. The availability of cheap credit, together with economic growth in China and other parts of the developing world, created a demand for resources such as zinc, copper and oil, which Australia was able to supply. As the price of resources skyrocketed, Australian companies reaped rich rewards. Between 2004 and 2006 the ASX 200, an index of the Australian Stock Market, grew annually by more than 16 per cent (Treasury 2007, p. 1). This was reflected in real net disposable national income per capita, which grew by 3 per cent per year between 1994–95 and 2004–05 (see Figure 7.1), a rate almost double that of the previous 20 years. Australia's real net private wealth at market value also grew, with some years experiencing leaps of more than 10 per cent on the previous year. Since 1992 real net wealth per Australian increased annually to 2008, with growth of $150 000 between June 2001 and June 2006. In June 2006 Australian net private sector wealth was $7464 billion at market value.

This prosperity was not distributed evenly. In 2004–05, in real terms, average equivalised disposable household income was $644 per week. The mean income of the lowest quintile was $255 per week, while the top quintile (the top 20 per cent) received $1239 per week (ABS 2007e, p. 13). The disparities were even greater in relation to net household worth. In 2004–05 the bottom 20 per cent of households owned $27 368, which is one-twelfth the worth of the middle 40–60 per cent of households and 62 times less than the top 20 per cent of households, whose mean net worth averaged $1 720 680 (ABS 2007e, p. 20) (see Table 7.2). As a percentage, the bottom 20 per cent of the population owned just 1 per cent of privately owned wealth.

It seems that despite this period of economic expansion, inequality at best remained static and at worst grew. Although the income of all wage earners grew in real terms, the income of those at the bottom of the ladder increased more slowly than those in the middle, resulting in higher poverty rates and rising income inequality. Between 2003–04 and 2005–06 the income of households in the bottom and middle income groups grew by 8 per cent, while income growth in high-income groups was 13 per cent (ABS 2007e) (see Figure 7.2).

This distribution leaves more than one million Australians with an equivalised disposable household income

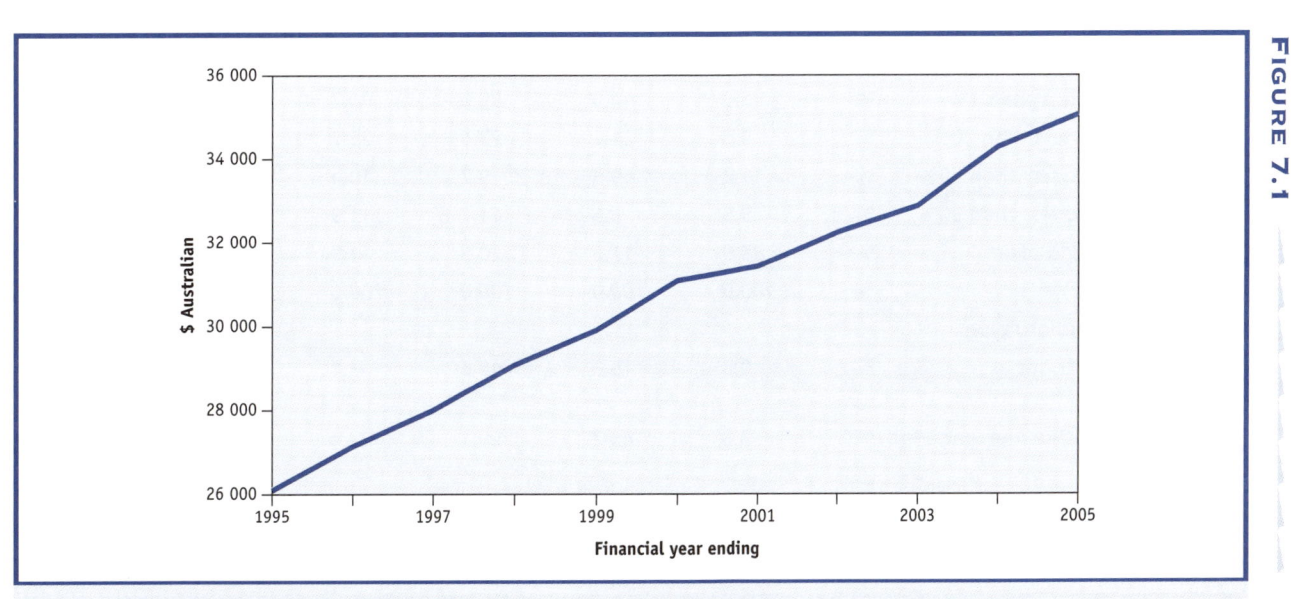

FIGURE 7.1

Real net national disposable income per capita   *Source:* ABS (2006e, p. 60).

SOCIOLOGY

TABLE 7.2

Household net worth quintile							
Household characteristics		**Lowest**	**Second**	**Third**	**Fourth**	**Highest**	**All**
Income per week							
Gross household income							
Mean income	$	769	1 173	1 122	1 363	2 098	1 305
Median income	$	640	1 054	994	1 214	1 722	1 040
Equivalised disposable household income							
Mean income	$	445	597	566	642	908	644
Median income	$	384	556	513	592	775	563
Mean household net worth	$	27 368	160 595	341 745	564 294	1 720 680	562 859
Proportion of households with characteristic							
Principal source of household income							
Zero or negative income	%	*1.0	*0.6	**0.2	*0.3	*0.5	0.5
Wages and salaries	%	50.2	68.4	57.1	62.0	58.7	59.3
Own unincorporated business income	%	2.7	4.9	6.2	5.4	11.2	6.1
Government pensions and allowances	%	43.3	24.2	32.4	24.0	6.7	26.1
Other Income	%	2.8	1.9	4.1	8.3	22.9	8.0
Total	%	*100.0*	*100.0*	*100.0*	*100.0*	*100.0*	*100.0*
Conrtibution of government pensions and allowances to gross household income							
Nil or less than 1%	%	35.0	44.9	35.6	40.2	63.0	43.7
1% to less than 20%	%	9.8	21.2	22.4	25.2	22.6	20.2
20% to less than 50%	%	11.2	9.3	9.7	10.4	7.1	9.5
50% to less than 90%	%	9.5	6.5	11.7	11.9	3.6	8.6
90% and over	%	33.5	17.5	20.5	11.9	3.2	17.3
Total [a]	%	*100.0*	*100.0*	*100.0*	*100.0*	*100.0*	*100.0*
Tenure and landlord type							
Owner without a mortgage	%	*0.8	16.0	40.6	53.1	61.0	34.3
Owner with a mortgage	%	3.3	43.7	50.1	42.4	35.4	35.0
Renter							
State/territory housing authority	%	20.4	2.4	**0.1	*0.3	–	4.7

Household net worth quintile cont'd

Household characteristics		Lowest	Second	Third	Fourth	Highest	All
Private landlord	%	65.9	31.6	7.1	2.6	2.8	22.0
Other landlord type	%	5.4	2.4	*0.6	*0.5	*0.3	1.9
Total renters	**%**	**91.7**	**36.5**	**7.8**	**3.4**	**3.1**	**28.5**
Other tenure type	%	4.2	3.8	1.4	1.1	*0.5	2.2
Total	**%**	**100.0**	**100.0**	**100.0**	**100.0**	**100.0**	**100.0**
Family composition of household							
One family households							
Couple family with dependent children	%	12.6	26.7	29.3	30.7	31.9	26.2
One parent family with dependent children	%	16.8	7.1	4.5	3.4	2.2	6.8
Couple only	%	13.9	22.0	26.9	30.6	35.5	25.8
Other one family households	%	8.4	8.6	10.7	14.2	15.6	11.5
Multiple family households	%	*0.8	*0.9	*0.7	*1.2	1.6	1.0
Non-family households							
Lone person	%	39.3	31.1	26.6	18.9	12.3	25.7
Group households	%	8.1	3.6	1.3	1.0	*0.8	3.0
Total	**%**	**100.0**	**100.0**	**100.0**	**100.0**	**100.0**	**100.0**
Average number in household							
Employed persons	no.	0.9	1.3	1.2	1.4	1.6	1.3
Dependent children	no.	0.6	0.6	0.6	0.7	0.7	0.6
Persons							
Under 18 years	no.	0.6	0.6	0.6	0.6	0.6	0.6
18 to 64 years	no.	1.4	1.6	1.5	1.7	1.9	1.6
65 years and over	no.	0.2	0.2	0.4	0.4	0.4	0.3
Total	**no.**	**2.2**	**2.4**	**2.5**	**2.7**	**2.8**	**2.5**
Estimated number in population							
Households	'000	1 586.3	1 584.4	1 585.2	1 585.3	1 584.9	7 926.2
Persons	'000	3 429.4	3 792.0	3 987.1	4 277.6	4 444.5	19 930.7
Number of households in sample	no.	1 979	2 021	2 046	2 020	1 895	9 961

TABLE 7.2

* estimate has a relative standard error of 25% to 50% and should be used with caution

** estimate has a relative standard error greater than 50% and is considered too unreliable for general use

– nil or rounded to zero (including null cells)

(a) includes households with nil or negative total income

Source: ABS (2007e, p. 20).

FIGURE 7.2

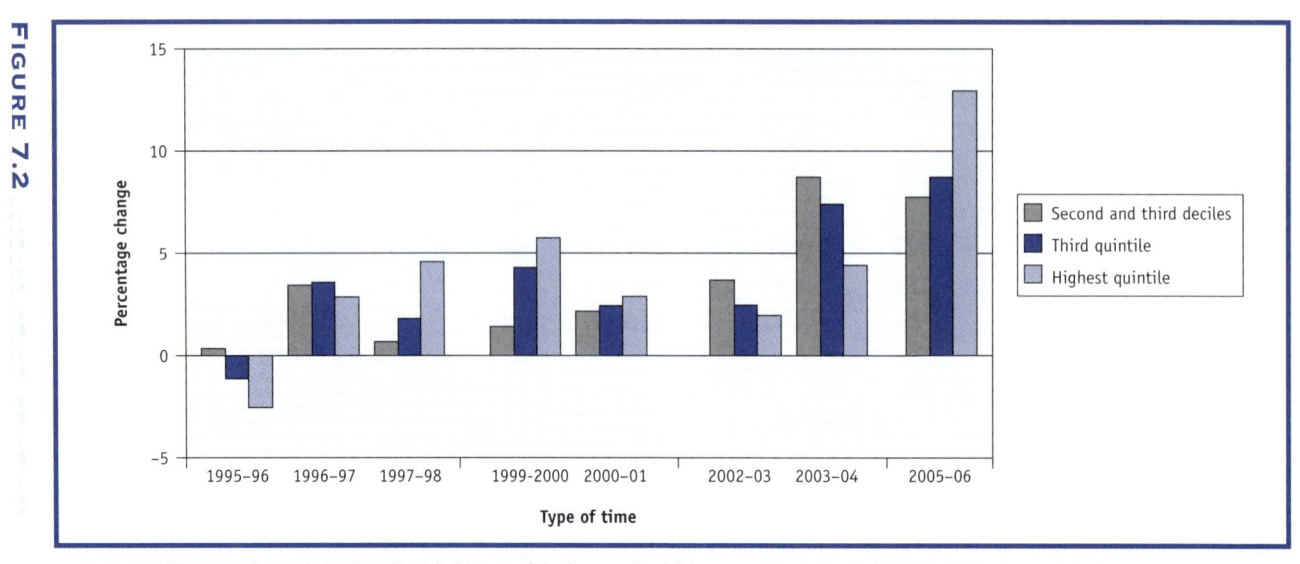

Changes in mean real equivalised disposable household income[a]   *Source:* ABS (2007e, p. 6).

[a] Change from previous year.

of less than $100 per week, and 2.75 million on less than $300 per week. At the other end of the scale, 215 200 Australians received an income of $2000 per week or more (ABS 2007e, p. 14). These figures show that the flow of Australia's wealth leaves behind large numbers of people whose economic circumstances are severely constrained.

Wilkins (2007) argues that differences in income growth that explains the growth in income poverty between 1981–82 and 2001–03. Taking half the median of annual disposable equivalised income as his measure, he identified that the rate of poverty had grown from 11.1 per cent to 12.9 per cent over this period. The global economic crisis that began in 2008 has further increased the hardship experienced by low income groups.

Winners and losers

The growth that took place in the boom years occurred primarily in business and dwelling assets. In 2006, more than half of average net private wealth was held in business assets and more than one-third in dwelling assets (Treasury 2007, p. 1). The beneficiaries of the boom years were therefore those who owned investment properties or investments in financial markets or were senior executives in the private sector. In the ten years since 1995, the value of dwellings grew 60 per cent (Treasury 2007, p. 90). This benefited home owners, especially those who owned investment properties and so were able to liquidate these assets while prices were high. For Australians in the rental market or those whose income provided no surplus for investment, there were few benefits. The real estate boom also reduced housing affordability. Between 1993 and 2003 the median price of a detached home more than doubled (Bond 2003). In 2007, the purchase price of a typical first home was more than $420 000, requiring an income of $100 000 to service it (Australian Council of Social Services 2007, p. 7). Despite the availability of government support to first-time home buyers, today many Australians on low incomes are locked out of the housing market.

The cost of housing is also responsible for the dramatic increase in the level of household debt that has occurred since the 1980s. At that time the ratio of debt to household income was around 45 per cent, but by December 2007 it had increased to 157 per cent, with household debt accounting for most of this (Davies 2009, p. 19). This makes many individuals and families vulnerable to losing their homes or investments in periods of global recession.

The benefits that flowed to those at the top of the economic hierarchy were exceptionally high during this period. From the 1980s the share of private income held by those in the top 5 per cent grew rapidly, so that by 2002 it was at its highest point since 1949 (Atkinson & Leigh 2006). Much of this growth derived from the huge salaries given to Australian business leaders. In 2007 the then CEO of Telstra, Sol Trujillo, received a salary package of $8.7 million. This kind of excessive reward, sometimes unrelated to the performance of the company, was common across the developed world. One study comparing the annual pay of CEOs in the United States with that of average workers found that it was 411 times higher than that of average workers (Lever 2007). The groups that benefited least from this period of prosperity were single parents, early school leavers and Indigenous peoples.

The groups most vulnerable to poverty today are single parents, Indigenous peoples, foreign-born persons and those without post-school qualifications (Wilkins 2007). In 2006 the mean equivalised disposable household income of single parents was $466 per week, with 44 per cent of them falling in the bottom three deciles of the total distribution of income and wealth (ABS 2007e, p. 164). In numerical terms, this meant that 822 000 children aged 0–14 were living in situations of financial hardship. The disadvantage experienced by Indigenous households is even more extreme. They comprise 40 per cent of households in the bottom decile of income distribution, living on a gross weekly equivalised income of $294 or less.

Early school leavers are vulnerable to poverty because their lack of skills reduces their success in the labour market. For most Australians, wages and salaries form the primary source of income. On average, low-income households had 0.6 employed persons, compared with middle- and high-income households which had 1.5 and 1.9 employed persons, respectively (ABS 2007e, p. 4). But even here many Australians are at risk of poverty. The casualisation of the labour market, the decline of collective bargaining and the gradual reduction in the minimum wage have created a new pool of low economic resource workers. In 2007 the value of minimum wages had only just caught up with what they were worth in 1986, leaving many Australians, especially those with low skills, such as recent migrants and young early school leavers, with insufficient resources to meet their needs (Australian Council of Social Services 2007, p. 10). Figure 7.3 illustrates the decline in real weekly minimum wages since 1984–85.

Disadvantage is also distributed unevenly across regions. Urbanisation is linked to economic reward, with average incomes in capital cities 16 per cent higher than those outside capital cities. The less urbanised states have the lowest incomes, with Tasmania and South Australia below the national average by 15 per cent and 6 per cent, respectively. But even within cities extreme social disadvantage is concentrated in particular locations. Just 1.7 per cent of postcodes and communities account for more than seven times their share of top rank positions for the major factors that cause intergenerational poverty, such as low income, poor school attainment, long-term unemployment and imprisonment (Vinson 2007).

International comparisons of social inequality

International comparisons of income distribution are regularly undertaken by the Luxembourg Income Study (LIS). This uses both the Gini coefficient and the decile ratio as indicators of income inequality. Table 7.3 shows that the differences are quite high, with the Scandinavian nations (Denmark, Norway, Finland and Sweden) having Gini coefficients almost half that of the United States (Brandolini & Smeeding 2007, p. 30). At the beginning of the 21st century, Australia ranked 16th out of 26 high-income nations, with a Gini coefficient of 0.317 and a decile ratio of 4.2, compared with Denmark's figures of 0.225 and 2.8. This is still much lower than the level of income inequality that exists in

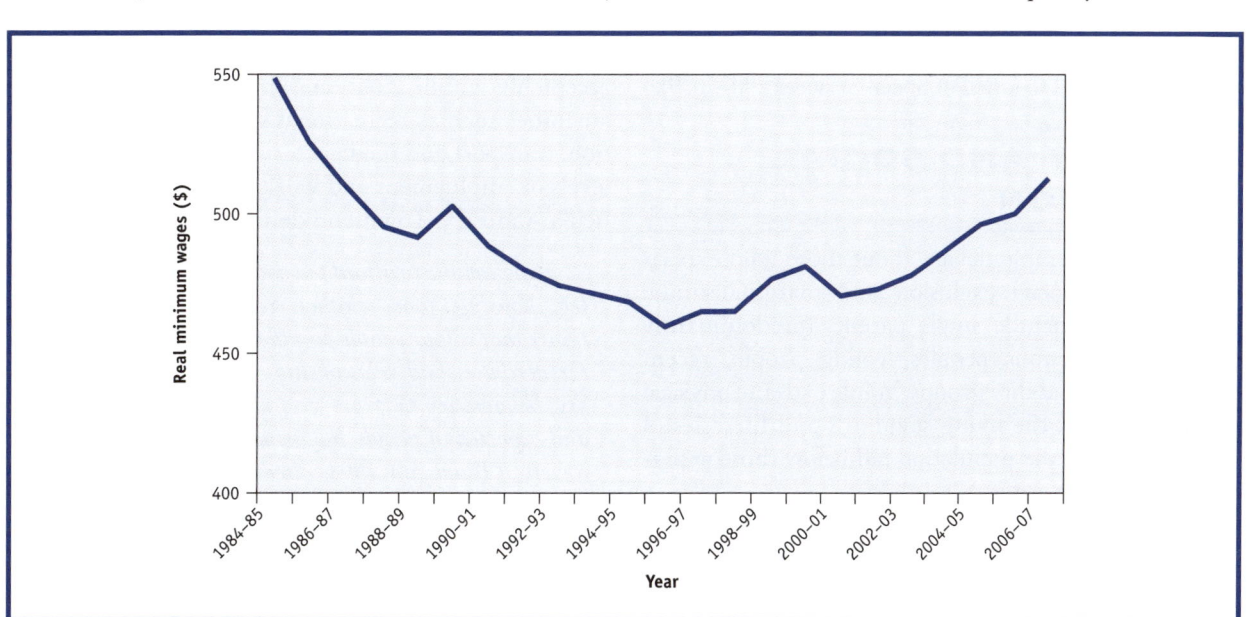

FIGURE 7.3

The decline in real minimum wages, 1984–05 to 2006–07 Source: Australian Council of Social Services (2007, Figure 58, p. 49).

TABLE 7.3 — The distribution of equivalent disposable income in high- and medium-income economies

High income by country	Decile ratio P90/P10	Gini index
Norway 2000	2.8	0.251
Sweden 2000	3.0	0.252
Germany 2000	3.4	0.275
France 2000	3.4	0.278
Canada 2000	3.9	0.302
Japan 1992	4.2	0.315
Australia 2001	4.2	0.317
Italy 2000	4.5	0.333
United Kingdom 1999	4.6	0.343
Spain 2000	4.8	0.340
United States 2000	5.7	0.370

Source: Brandolini & Smeeding (2007, p. 30). © 2008 Russell Sage Foundation, 112 East 64th Street, New York 10065. Reprinted with permission.

Mexico, where income is more than 11.5 times higher at the top than at the bottom. There is, then, a considerable range of income inequality between rich and poor in the rich and medium-income nations.

A study by the Australian Council of Social Services also found a high level of income inequality relative to other countries (2007). Taking the international poverty line, which uses a measure of 50 per cent of median income as a poverty line, it found that Australia ranked 14th out of 18 wealthy nations, suggesting that although we see ourselves as the nation of a 'fair go', there is a high level of inequality. This is partly because relative to GDP, Australia spends far less than most OECD countries on income support, ranking 24th out of 30 countries surveyed (Australian Council of Social Services 2007, p. 9).

Poverty and social exclusion

There is considerable debate about those who experience poverty, social exclusion and marginalisation. These groups include single parents (predominantly women), Indigenous peoples, young people, recent migrants and disability groups. While extreme physical hardship is rare, the living standards and lifestyles of some sections of the population fall below those generally accepted as normal.

Poverty, social exclusion and citizenship

Although inequality and poverty are related, poverty is different from inequality in that it implies that the groups at the bottom of the economic hierarchy not only are relatively poorer than those above but also experience some degree of hardship. Absolute poverty refers to an absence of the material resources necessary for individuals and families to meet their basic needs. The United Nations defines it as:

severe deprivation of basic human needs, including food, safe drinking water, sanitation facilities, health, shelter, education and information. It depends not only on income but also on access to services. (1995, p. 57, cited in Harris, Nutbeam & Sainsbury 2001, p. 260)

Relative poverty refers to a situation where living standards and lifestyles are below those deemed acceptable within a nation. This includes community amenities such as recreational space, quality of education, transport and medical services, as well as regional levels of employment and work practices within a particular industry. Townsend defines relative poverty as:

... being unable to afford the goods, services and activities (eg, housing, food, clothes, recreation, social obligations) that allow people to play the roles, participate in the activities and relationships and follow the customary behaviours that are considered normal in society and expected of people by virtue of their membership of society. (Townsend 1993, cited in Harris, Nutbeam & Sainsbury 2001, p. 260)

Although most poverty in Australia is relative poverty, some Indigenous households lack basic requirements for food, sanitation and housing. The 105 500 individuals who were homeless in 2006 would also count as being in absolute poverty (Chamberlain & MacKenzie 2009).

The concept of social exclusion has recently come into prominence as a way of understanding how some groups are unable to participate in mainstream social and economic life. The term also recognises that the responsibility for social exclusion does not rest only on the excluded but also on those groups that benefit from limiting access to resources (Atkinson [1998], cited in Fincher & Saunders 2001, p. 12). The dimensions of social exclusion have been conceptualised as:

- impoverishment or exclusion from adequate income or resources
- labour market exclusion
- service exclusion
- exclusion from social relations (Gordon et al. 2000).

Social exclusion is a relative concept linked to the idea of citizenship. Marshall (1950) argues that one of the core principles of democracy is that all citizens should have equal access to fulfilment, not just of their basic needs but also to the range of practices and the standard of living that are regarded as the norm for the nation. By virtue of membership of a political community individuals are granted a range of entitlements. Marshall distinguishes between political, civic and social citizenship. *Political citizenship* refers to such things as involvement in political decision making, such as the right to hold political office and to influence the political processes of the nation. *Civic citizenship* expresses the idea of access to basic freedoms such as the right to vote, and freedom of speech and assembly. *Social citizenship* expresses the idea that all citizens should be able to live according to the norms of the broader community and implies the existence of a welfare net to help the economically and socially disadvantaged. This concept helps to focus questions on the extent to which specific-interest groups, such as migrants or Indigenous peoples, have been able to access these rights, and also on their struggles with the state to claim them.

Measuring poverty

Australia's first survey of poverty was conducted in Melbourne in 1966 (Henderson, Harcourt & Harper 1970). The 1966 survey took the **poverty line** as the point at which income fell below the minimum wage, which in 1966 was $33 per week, plus the child endowment payment. A follow-up national study converted this figure into a percentage of average earning, which was 56.6 per cent, and used this as the poverty line. This measure remains in use today (Melbourne Institute of Applied Economic and Social Research 2009).

Income-based poverty lines are problematic not only because of their sensitivity to small changes in where the line falls, but also because they do not take into account expenditure or the social wage. Another approach has been to broaden the concept of poverty by focusing on social exclusion. In his analysis of the ABS Household Expenditure Survey, 1998–99, Saunders (2003b) divides social exclusion into three domains:

1. lack of social interaction
2. domestic deprivation
3. extreme consumption hardship.

Each of these is defined in terms of three or four measures, such as being unable to afford a night out once a fortnight (lack of social action), going without meals (domestic deprivation) and pawning or selling something (extreme consumption hardship) (Saunders 2003b). This approach recognises the complexity behind disadvantage and seeks to understand the processes behind its creation and reproduction. Longitudinal studies are also important in tracing pathways into poverty. These studies may include variables such as wellbeing, government transfers and access to services (e.g. housing, health and child care) as well as regional differences (Fincher & Saunders 2001, p. 9).

Evidence on the extent of poverty is always contested because there is no objective way of deciding at what point an individual or groups should be counted as poor, or which variables should be included in the measure. Such questions have real political consequences, since even minor variations in the way poverty is measured could lead to the identification of opposing poverty trends (Trigger 2003). Table 7.4 shows the extent to which findings can vary, with percentages ranging from 5 per cent to 23 per cent. But even the lower figure reveals that in one of the wealthiest nations in the world at least one million individuals are living in a situation of significant hardship.

The United Nations *Human Development Report 2004* (United Nations Development Program 2004) ranked Australia third in the world for human development (behind Norway and Sweden) but the second worst in the highly developed world for the number of people living in poverty. According to the report, some 14.3 per cent of Australians are living below the poverty line. This compares with 17 per cent in the United States.

Reflective question: Imagine someone told you that people who are poor have only themselves to blame—what would you say to challenge this view?

TABLE 7.4

Estimates of poverty in Australia

Estimation source	Year of estimate	Percentage in poverty	Numbers estimated to be in poverty (million)
Henderson Poverty Line	1999	20–23	3.7–4.1
St Vincent de Paul Society	—	—	3
Australian Council of Social Services (ACOSS)	2000	15	2.5–3.5
The Smith Family	2000	13–19	2.4
The Brotherhood of St Laurence	2000	13	1.5
The Australia Institute	—	5–10	1–2
The Centre for Independent Studies	—	5 (in 'chronic poverty')	1

Source: Adapted from *A Hand Up not a Hand Out: Renewing the fight against poverty*. Report on poverty and financial hardship. Senate Community Affairs References Committee, March 2004. Reproduced with permission.

CLASSES IN AUSTRALIAN SOCIETY

This section examines classes in Australian society from two main perspectives. The first explains sociological debates about the major class groupings of working, middle and upper class. The defining features of each grouping and the boundaries and relationships between them, including relations of domination and subordination, are examined. The second attempts to delineate the class structure of Australian society. Drawing on the theories of Marx and Weber, these 'maps' of class quantify the main classes and their constituent subgroups while also examining how the boundaries between them are changing.

Changes in the occupational structure

The occupational order forms the backbone of arrangements for inequality in contemporary society. Many maps of the class structure use occupational categories as their starting point. Occupation is not only the primary source of material wellbeing in society but also influences social standing. As well as being rewarded by high income, a medical practitioner receives considerable respect. Shared occupational position is a source of social solidarity and serves as the basis of political action. The trade union movement was built on this, and professional and labour associations continue to operate as pressure groups. Occupation is associated with lifestyle and the workplace is increasingly important as a source of friendship. Understanding how the occupational order has changed therefore has direct relevance to the study of class and inequality generally. It impacts on debates about meritocracy since social mobility is influenced by changes in the occupational order. As the size of the service sector has increased, so have opportunities for the offspring of manual workers to move into occupations traditionally regarded as middle class.

Figures 7.4 and 7.5 divide the occupational order into seven main groups. Professional, managerial and clerical categories involve non-manual labour, while those working in trades, semi-skilled and manual labour or as labourers and farmers are manual workers. This division does not necessarily overlap completely with the categorisation of these groups into working and middle class, since there are differences between stratification theorists on the categorisation of these groups. For example, because some tradespeople are small-business owners and earn high incomes they can be classified as middle class, even though they work with their hands.

Figures 7.4 and 7.5 show a drastic shift in the occupational order between 1911 and 2004. In 1911 just over a quarter of the workforce worked in a white-collar setting, while the rest of the employed population were manual workers. Over the course of the 20th century the growth of the service sector transformed this distribution and today most people work in offices. This is especially true for women who dominate employment in clerical, sales and service, where their percentage increased from 12.7 per cent in 1911 to nearly 50 per cent in 2004. Women now outnumber men in the clerical, sales and service sector by a ratio of more than 3:1. The other area of growth for women has been in professional occupations, where their presence has swelled from 11.4 in 1911 to 33.9 in 2004. This has been accompanied by a drastic decline in the number of women employed in trades, farming and labouring.

FIGURE 7.4

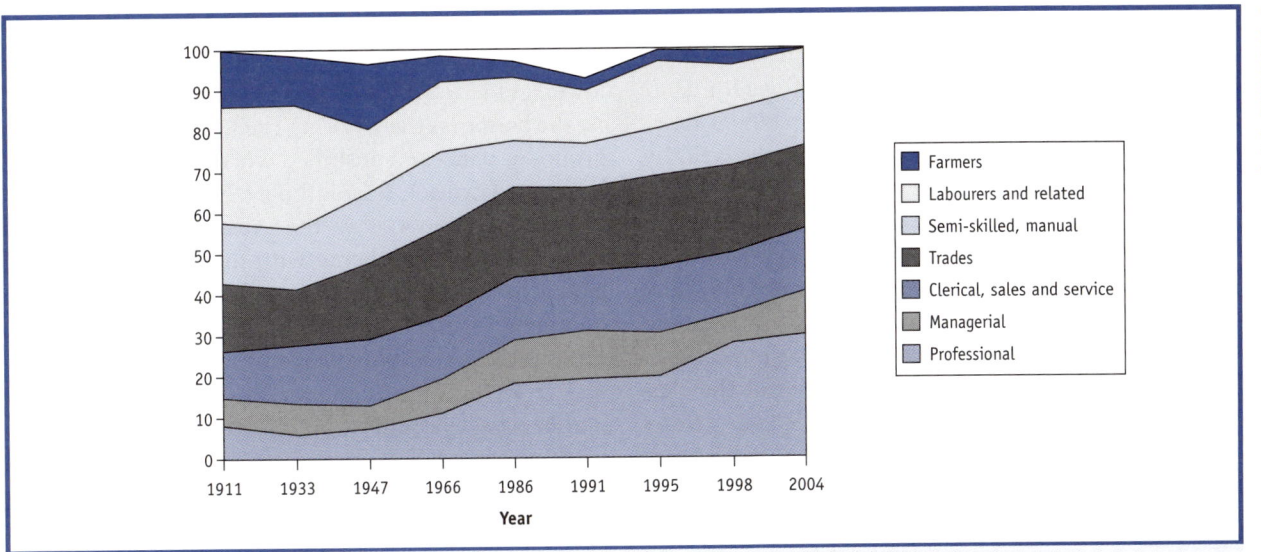

Structure of the male workforce, 1911–2004 *Source:* Broom & Jones (1976); ABS (1989; 1993h; 1995c; 1998b; 2004b).

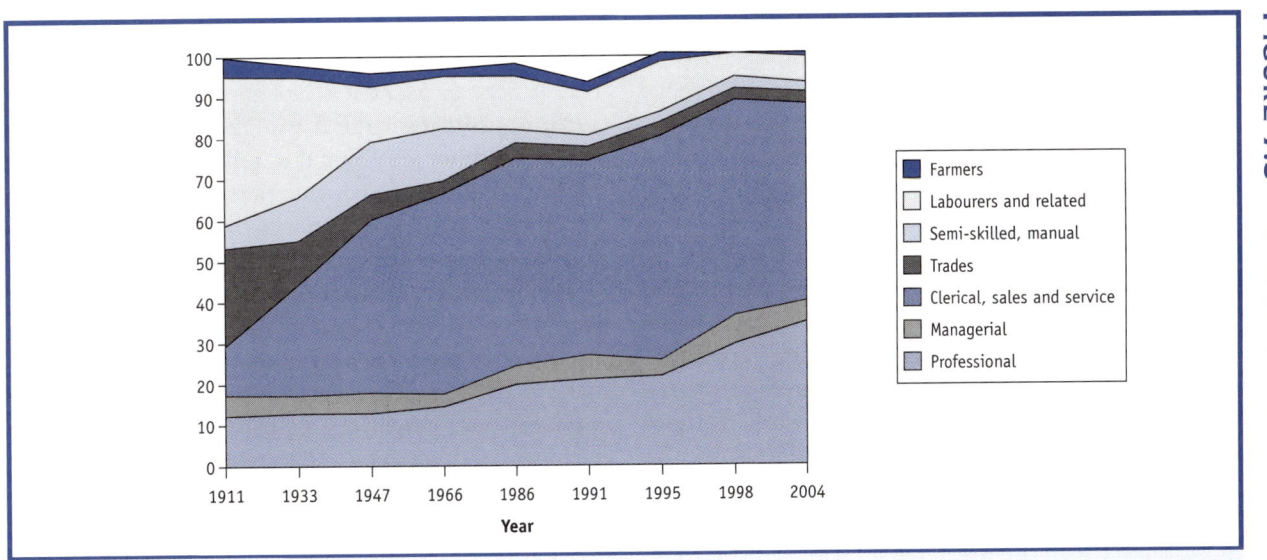

FIGURE 7.5

Structure of the female workforce, 1911–2004 *Source:* Broom & Jones (1976); ABS (1989; 1993h; 1995c; 1998b; 2004b).

For men, there has been an overall decline in manual labour from just over two-thirds to just under 50 per cent, although there has been growth in the proportion of men working in skilled labour. The greatest growth has been in the professions, while labouring jobs and farming have experienced large declines.

The significance of these changes is complex, partly due to changes in the categorisation of occupations, and partly because the nature of work has changed. In 1911, low levels of literacy meant that clerks enjoyed good working conditions, high status and good pay relative to most manual workers, but today many clerks are employed in the secondary labour market and have low pay, job insecurity and low status, raising questions about whether clerks should still be classified as middle class.

Mapping the class structure

The classification of a population into classes and the quantification of this are useful because this provides information about changes in the relative size of the different groups, the relationship between class position and life chances, and the relationship between class position and social action. Mapping the class structure

245

involves identifying the variables determining class position. The occupational order is widely used for this purpose, but it has its limitations. If wealth is not included as a separate variable, occupational-based class schemes fail to account adequately for the wealthy. Jackie Kennedy, for example, was employed as a book editor but her personal wealth located her in the top 1 per cent of the United States' hierarchy of personal wealth. Occupational-based class schemes may also exclude those not in the labour force, such as pensioners and homemakers. In the past this was regarded as unimportant and until the 1980s analyses of the class structure excluded women altogether. Today gender differences are regarded as essential for an understanding of arrangements for social inequality.

The classification of occupational groups into classes can become a sterile exercise without the provision of meaningful insights into the relationship between social position and class formation and class action (Bottero 2005; Connell & Irving 1992). For Marxists, the interesting question is not the classification but the extent to which that classification forms the foundation of social action—that is, whether, and under what conditions, a social group demonstrates characteristics of being a class for itself as well as a class in itself.

Weberian maps—Goldthorpe

Goldthorpe's (1980) scheme uses Weberian theories and applies them to the occupational order in what is known as the Nuffield 'employment aggregate' approach. Rather than ownership or non-ownership of property, this scheme uses market situation and work relationships to group occupational categories into classes on the grounds that how we earn our living is fundamental to our life chances. **Market situation** is defined as those aspects of an occupation that relate to the market, including source and level of income, employment conditions and career prospects. *Work situation* refers to the relations of authority and control associated with the position (Goldthorpe 1980, p. 40). Goldthorpe distinguishes between employers, the self-employed and employees, but divides employees into a number of subcategories. This provides the foundation of a three-class model of class, which can also be presented as a seven- or 11-class model. At the top is the service class, subdivided into an upper group of large proprietors, administrators, managers and professionals, and a lower group of higher grade technicians and supervisors of manual workers. Next is the intermediate class, which consists of four subgroups: routine non-manual workers and sales personnel, a petty bourgeoisie of small proprietors and artisans; farmers and others employed in primary production; and skilled workers including lower grade technicians and skilled manual workers. At the bottom is the working class, subdivided into two groups of semi- and unskilled workers and agricultural labourers (Erikson & Goldthorpe 1993).

Table 7.5 shows how the Australian occupational order fits into this scheme with the gender division of labour being one of the most striking features. Women dominate in the areas of routine non-manual labour, reflecting their employment in the lower levels of the service sector. Men dominate in the highly rewarded service class (Classes I and II) and the less well rewarded working class (Class 7) as well as the skilled manual class. Goldthorpe's scheme produces a very large middle class and a relatively small working class because of the location of both routine non-manual workers and the skilled working class in the Intermediate class.

Wright's models of contradictory class locations

The American Marxist sociologist Erik Olin Wright (1985) argues that a major flaw in neo-Weberian schemes such as Goldthorpe's is that they rely on a classification of occupations in order to discuss class, when class relations actually cut across occupational divisions. Occupations refer to different positions within a technical division of labour, whereas classes are defined by their different positions within a set of social relations surrounding the sphere of production. Goldthorpe's scheme does not make it possible, for example, to distinguish between employers and employees, or between those who own the means of production and those who do not.

Wright follows Marx in seeing the ownership or non-ownership of productive property as the primary class division in capitalist society, but also draws on Marx's theory of exploitation to identify two additional asset classes that provide similar advantages: skills and credentials, and control over the labour of others. In this way he accounts for the privileges associated with professionals and managers. Taking into account whether the number of employees controlled is many, few or none, Wright derives a 12-class scheme based on possession of these assets. Capitalists, for example, own property and employ large numbers of workers, while the petty bourgeoisie own property but employ no workers. Experts do not own property but they possess skills and are further differentiated by how many employees they control. Unskilled workers possess none of these assets and are closest to Marx's definition of the working class.

TABLE 7.5

Distribution of workforce by Goldthorpe classes and sex (column and row %)

Class		Men	Women	Total
I	Upper service, higher professional administrative and managerial, large proprietors	14.8	5.0	10.5
		79.0	*21.0*	
II	Lower service, lower professional administrators, managers etc.; higher grade technicians, supervisors of non-manual employees	21.1	26.6	23.5
		50.3	*49.7*	
IIIa	Routine non-manual higher grade	4.1	18.2	10.3
		22.2	*77.8*	
IIIb	Routine non-manual lower grade: personal service workers	3.5	22.3	11.8
		16.5	*83.5*	
IVabc	Small proprietors, own account workers, non-agricultural, farmers, smallholders	12.0	8.7	10.6
		63.8	*36.2*	
V	Lower grade technical, manual supervisory	8.9	6.4	7.8
		64.1	*35.9*	
VI	Skilled manual workers	18.4	2.8	11.5
		89.3	*10.7*	
VII	Semi-skilled and unskilled manual workers	17.1	10.0	14.0
		68.5	*14.0*	

Note: Figures in italics are added across columns rather than down.
Source: Emmison 1991, p. 43 (adapted from Goldthorpe 1983).

Table 7.6 (p. 248) applies this scheme to Australian society in 1991. This shows that Marx's bourgeoisie—owners of the means of production—are tiny, comprising only 1 per cent of the sample, while the working class, whose only asset is their labour, are the largest group in the sample. In between these two are the remaining ten groups, located according to their ownership of credentials, property and control over labour (organisational assets).

An analysis of weekly income using this scheme shows the extent to which it overlaps with income groups. In Marx's day manual workers would have been at the bottom of the income ladder, but today it is white-collar workers. Most these are women working in the heavily casualised, low-paid secondary labour market. In contrast, the earnings of the male-dominated blue-collar workers are close to those of managers.

THE UPPER CLASS

We have already seen the extent to which both income and wealth are concentrated in the hands of a small minority of the population, and it is this wealthy 5–10 per cent of the population that is usually regarded as the upper class. Their position is based on their exceptionally high concentration of wealth, usually in the form of ownership and control of productive property and capital, and their control over people. Implicit in the term 'upper class' is the assumption that economic and political power are interlinked and that there is also some degree of cohesion among members so that they act together to maintain and develop their material interests.

Interlocks and networks

It is one thing to demonstrate that wealth is concentrated in the hands of the few and another to show that there is a degree of cohesion among this elite group. One of the ways in which this has been examined is to identify the extent to which a small group of individuals controls the economy through multiple directorships. These studies extend back to the 1960s and they suggest a trend of increasing concentration (Rolfe 1967; Stening & Wai 1984; Alexander 1998). Malcolm Alexander's

Sociology

TABLE 7.6

Class and occupation in Australia (column and row %)

Class location	Managers/administration		Professionals		Clerical and sales		Skilled		Semi-skilled/unskilled	
Owners/Self-employed	24	*21*	8	*12*	11	*24*	25	*28*	9	*14*
Employers	15	*38*	2	*9*	5	*6*	3	*11*	2	*7*
Petty bourgeoisie	9	*12*	7	*14*	5	*18*	23	*39*	7	*17*
Experts	26	*31*	37	*70*	0	*0*	0	*0*	0	*0*
Expert managers	24	*47*	17	*53*	0	*0*	0	*0*	0	*0*
Expert supervisors	1	*10*	8	*91*	0	*0*	0	*0*	0	*0*
Expert non-supervisors	1	*7*	12	*94*	0	*0*	0	*0*	0	*0*
Non-expert managers and supervisors	49	*19*	29	*18*	37	*37*	29	*14*	18	*13*
Skilled managers	37	*43*	19	*35*	1	*4*	13	*20*	0	*0*
Skilled supervisors	12	*23*	10	*32*	1	*6*	16	*38*	0	*0*
Unskilled managers	0	*0*	0	*0*	16	*74*	0	*0*	8	*26*
Unskilled supervisors	0	*0*	0	*0*	19	*74*	0	*0*	10	*26*
Workers	1	*1*	25	*11*	52	*38*	45	*15*	74	*36*

Source: Baxter (1991, p. 70). Reproduced by permission from Macmillan Education Australia.

---

analysis of the top 250 companies found that the mean number of interlocks had increased from 5.6 in 1959 to 21 in 1992 (1998). At the same time, this concentration of control over the Australian economy is weakened by the extent to which Australia's economy is owned by non-Australian interests. Today, many company directors are from overseas parent companies.

Unity and division

Raewyn Connell (1977) argues that the evidence relating to concentration of business control and share ownership is primarily an indication of the potential for control, without showing that control is in fact being exercised. She makes the same point about interlocking directorates and family networks—they provide evidence of the potential for organised action, but not of organised action itself (pp. 45–6). Connell goes on to show that there is, in fact, considerable conflict between members of the upper class. This conflict arises from:

- the competition between entrepreneurs and companies, which persists over and above the heavy concentration of ownership

- the conflict between different areas of capital accumulation, different industries and different sources of capital (pp. 108–9).

Historically, Australia's wealthy were a relatively identifiable group of families, such as the Fairbairns, Baillieus, Darlings, Robinsons, Fairfaxes, Lysaghts and Knoxes, who tended to intermarry and who dominated Australian economic life through interlocking networks of ownership and control (Encel 1970). Encel found that the Baillieus alone were connected with seven of the top 16 companies in 1967. This would support the argument that they are a cohesive social group who share a common background and recognise their shared economic interests.

There is a popular image of a greater potential for movement from 'rags to riches' in Australia, heavily promoted in the media, in which the role of inheritance is presented as insignificant. Business acumen, determination and enterprise are given primary credit for the creation of wealth. This portrayal of Australia's self-made millionaires often focuses on the family background of European and Asian immigrants who made their fortunes in business and investment in housing and retail property after arriving in Australia as penniless refugees. This creates an image of Australian society as one where all individuals, no matter what their family background, can become wealthy if they work hard and effectively enough.

There is evidence that the wealthiest people in Australia include a growing number of self-made individuals and families. Gilding's (2004) analysis of the individuals and families who make up the 200 wealthiest people identified in *Business Review Weekly*'s Rich 200 list found that 90 per cent had made their wealth since World War II, suggesting a dilution in the dominance of inherited wealth. Yet it is also true that many of these individuals and families, such as James Packer, Rupert Murdoch and the Holmes à Courts, inherited considerable wealth, which they subsequently multiplied.

Gilding also explored the power relationships among Australia's elite (2004). The minimum point of entry to the Rich 200 list was ownership of $72 million, with the largest fortune being $6.8 billion. Gilding conducted interviews with 43 individuals (22 per cent of the Rich 200 list), most of whom were self-made millionaires. Their median wealth was $128 million, 39 were men and their median age was 56. A total of 39 (91 per cent) had fortunes that were built up after World War II, and 38 (88 per cent) were born in Australia. Gilding found evidence that there was a significant degree of institutional unity among the established elite. They had predominantly Protestant Anglo-Saxon backgrounds and sent their children to the same schools, married one another, were members of the same exclusive social clubs, shared the same political views and sat on the same company boards as directors. They described a past world in which a common culture had created an environment of trust within the elite and felt that this had been destroyed by the intrusion of the new wave of entrepreneurs. Instead of relying on personal relationships in their business transactions, they were now increasingly dependent on formal sanctions. Although they had not been able to keep the newcomers out of the business elite they still operated a system of social closure based on religion and ethnicity. Most members of the 'new money' elite came from Irish Catholic, Jewish and Mediterranean backgrounds and they described being locked out of the dominant social institutions of Melbourne, Sydney and Adelaide. As one respondent put it:

You don't have the real wealth that Europe and America have at the top. But there is still a class thing. There still is the odd English mentality. There still is the Melbourne Club. There still is the upper crust in Sydney. They're the ones who run politics; they're the ones who run the social activities; and they're the ones who run the money in Melbourne and Sydney. (2004, p. 138)

Although the influence of the newcomers did not necessarily extend beyond their immediate business sphere, they regarded the social closure operated by the established elite as an irrelevant anachronism. It did not prevent them from accumulating wealth and some were forming links with the institutions that were the traditional preserve of the established elite. There was also evidence that their involvement in business was propelling them into new business, industry and political relationships. 'New money' respondents also described relatively specialised and far-flung interconnections based on ethnic diversity, political pragmatism and globalisation. Gilding concluded that this suggests that the upper class is undergoing a radical configuration whereby connections, trust and solidarity are being forged differently from what they were in earlier times.

This account of the competitive nature of the global economy challenges any simplistic assumption of the concentration of power and wealth by a small group of self-interested super-rich, suggesting instead that there are frequent conflicts of interest among them. However, Connell and Irving (1980) point out that because the economy is based on private ownership of property, the dominant institutions necessarily support private capital, and it is only when capitalism, and the institution of private property itself, is threatened that the upper class will mobilise to defend it. This happens very rarely but when it has happened, as when the former Labor Prime Minister Ben Chifley wanted to privatise the banks in the 1960s, it was met with a rapid and swift response from Australia's super-rich.

THE MIDDLE CLASS

Traditional stratification theory was more concerned with the working class than the middle class because of its role in Marxist theory as the political movement that would oppose capitalism. But as the middle class grew in size and significance, sociological attention turned to the middle class. Darhendorf (1959) describes the middle class as being 'born decomposed' because it consists of two groups: small self-employed businesspeople who owe their position to their ownership of a small amount of property, and professionals whose position is based on their control over knowledge. But despite this diversity the groups that comprise the middle class have in common individualism, relative affluence, control over knowledge, status, respectability and cultural influence.

The size and characteristics of the middle class help buffer the extremes of inequality because the material success of the middle class hides the wealth of the 'super-rich' by legitimising the democratic ideal of meritocracy. As a large, affluent group who demonstrate the qualities of hard work and self-responsibility, promote user-pays principles by paying for private health and education, and reproduce their position in their offspring by passing on their values and privileges through private education and social capital, the middle class establish a benchmark for other Australians. Their success proclaims that this lifestyle is open to anyone who applies themselves to achieving the rewards that Western culture offers. It establishes individualism as a normative principle that validates the meritocratic principles that underpin liberal democracy, suggesting that those who fail to achieve this have only themselves to blame. This is despite contrary evidence of the processes of inclusion and exclusion that operate to advantage some and privilege others.

Middle or working class?

The decline in the size and significance of the working class, the increased economic power of the skilled working class and the decreased economic power and feminisation of the lower end of the service workers (clerical workers and shop assistants) has meant that the line between the middle and working classes has become blurred (Braverman 1974; Goldthorpe & Lockwood 1968). Although shop assistants and clerical workers identify as middle class and their employment involves intellectual labour, their income and level of skill are often as low as or even lower than that of many manual workers. The scarcity of skilled labour has also meant that many tradespeople earn high incomes and this, together with their years of training, bring them closer to the middle class. It is only in the higher levels of the middle class that a sharp income difference between manual and non-manual labour appears. Consequently, today membership of the middle class is more likely to be defined in terms of relatively advantaged ownership of economic, social and cultural resources. Sociologists also differ in how they categorise the class position of low-grade clerical workers, with Marxist-influenced schemes tending to include them in the working class and Weberian schemes often locating them in the middle class.

The professions and cultural power

Professional occupational groups have expanded considerably over the last 100 years as the economy has created a demand for specialised knowledge. Although divided into higher and lower professions, the groups have in common high levels of cultural capital, professional training and high status. Possession of credentials is the basis of their power and this is associated with job security, pleasant working conditions, including self-regulation and autonomy, and relatively high material rewards, especially in the case of higher professionals. The professions also operate an organisational structure that establishes rules, standards and codes of practice, restricting entry and controlling behaviour through a system of rewards and sanctions. This assists in controlling the market by limiting the availability of expert knowledge so that the rewards associated with the skills and training are limited to its members. While the standards are legitimised on the grounds of the protection of the public from inadequate or harmful service provision, professionalisation also operates as a system of social closure, which contributes to social inequality.

Cultural power is central to the elevated position of the professions and this is the basis of their distinctive lifestyle as well as their capacity to influence public debate. Professionals are a source of expert knowledge that is highly valued and influential. Economists, sociologists, psychologists and professionals engaged in policy formulation and the administration and delivery of services play a critical role in shaping intellectual debate, policy formulation and implementation. Jamrozik (1991) explains that:

they are all important social actors who are engaged in what is referred to as mental production. How they perceive society, how they interpret social issues, the area and issues on which they place emphasis and which they neglect to consider, are all activities which define, often in an authoritative fashion, social reality. (p. xiii)

The question of how they use their influence has been the subject of some debate. In the 1960s and 1970s many intellectuals were influenced by Marxism and adhered to a radical agenda concerned with creating a more egalitarian society. By the 1980s and 1990s, however, left-wing activism had declined. Crompton (1998) argues that this is partly because of the increasingly fragmented nature of the middle class, making it unlikely that its members will develop a collective class identity and consciousness. The extent to which the middle class has developed forms of collective organisation has usually related to protection of their individual interests, as in, for example, the activities of professional groups (p. 157). Crompton argues that this trend is occurring against a background of growing job insecurity as corporations become leaner, working hours become longer and performance appraisals become more widespread, further exacerbating the processes of individualisation.

THE WORKING CLASS

For Marx the working class occupied a unique place in human history as the basis of a revolutionary political movement that would overthrow capitalism. He saw the working class as an exploited group whose adverse working conditions were the direct responsibility of the capitalist upper class who benefited from their labour. Today this historical legacy has faded as traditional industries have declined, average living standards for manual workers have improved, and the social barriers between manual and non-manual labour have dissolved. Their revolutionary potential has also been dissipated through the institutionalisation of industrial conflict via state-sponsored systems of industrial arbitration. These bring capital and labour together to negotiate the wages and conditions of workers.

In Australia the almost constant labour shortage throughout most of the country's history since the 1850s has given the Australian working class a particular strength within society as a whole and a greater inclination to become incorporated into capitalist society rather than oppose capitalism in principle (Wild 1978). Australia was one of the first nations to establish a system of industrial arbitration, which Wild believes has undermined the development of a revolutionary working-class consciousness. Although Australian workers have been relatively highly unionised, union-based conflict has generally centred on improvements within the capitalist economy, rather than making any serious challenge to the institution of private property.

Australia's working class has always had strong racial and gender differences within it. These often overlap with divergent segments of the labour market, segments that also correspond to the distinction between skilled and unskilled manual labour. Women and recently arrived migrants tend to dominate low-wage, unskilled manual work and Indigenous individuals tend to be excluded from employment altogether. This fragments the working class, reducing its political unity.

Lois Bryson's study of 'Newtown', a working-class suburb on the fringes of Melbourne, explores the effects of globalisation and national political trends on the lives of working people in the 30-year period between the 1960s and 1990s (Bryson & Thompson 1972; Bryson & Winter 1999). In the late 1960s the town was an attractive place surrounded by lush open countryside. The welfare net cushioned people from the harsher effects of inequality. Many of the homes in Newtown were public housing. Although on low incomes, few residents lacked employment and most remained in the same job for life. Three-quarters of male residents were unskilled and skilled manual workers. Sons' careers often followed those of their fathers. Family ties were strong and a significant source of support. Although many families experienced serious financial difficulties, most expressed a sense of optimism and were satisfied with their jobs and where they lived.

Thirty years later, Bryson and Winter found that, despite economic growth nationally, Newtown families had not fared well (1999). They were at the 'sharp, uncomfortable end of change' with high levels of unemployment, deteriorating work conditions and increased fragmentation and polarisation (1999, p. 5). A total of 25 per cent of families had at least one member who was unemployed and 53 per cent reported financial strains. Insecurity also undermined those who had jobs. Welfare support had declined, increasing their vulnerability. While the rights of women and Indigenous Australians had improved, overall conditions in the suburb had declined. The public housing that had formerly been for the 'ordinary' working Australian was now welfare housing, serving only those in serious need. In the absence of state support, family connections had become even more important, but the optimism that characterised the suburb in the 1960s had declined.

The comparison of the two populations, separated by more than a generation, documents how change at the national and global level intersects with the lives of people at the local level. The shrinking of the welfare state, the decline in the manufacturing sector, and the disappearance of secure employment and affordable housing had made Newtown a less secure and less hopeful place than in the past. Bryson and Winter argue that the interests of business and the better-off have pushed the needs of those at the lower end of the scale off the social agenda. Their study supports the argument that the last decades of the 20th century saw a growth of inequality and social exclusion in Australian society.

SOCIAL MOBILITY

Social mobility can be defined as the movement of individuals up or down the hierarchy of inequality. Measuring the amount of social mobility is important for assessing how open or closed is a nation's stratification system. The extent of social mobility is also important for understanding the relationship between class and class consciousness since there needs to be a certain amount of stability within a social group for distinctive class cultures to develop. Social mobility is usually measured in terms of occupational position. *Intragenerational mobility* refers to the social mobility that takes place within a single generation, while *intergenerational mobility* refers to mobility across two or more generations. A society in which social mobility is inherited is characterised as having ascribed social mobility, while one in which social mobility results from the individual characteristics of its members is characterised as having achieved social mobility.

Measuring social mobility

Estimates of the amount of social mobility that takes place within a nation are always imperfect. Occupational position is usually taken as the indicator of social position, but this excludes all those not in the workforce, including the very wealthy who do not need to work, and the unemployed. These groups are precisely those of greatest interest to stratification theorists since in a truly open society their position of extreme advantage and disadvantage would not be a barrier to movement up or down the occupational hierarchy.

Until the 1980s many studies of social mobility also excluded women. This was justified on the grounds that most women were married and their social position was dependent on men. This assumed that most women did not participate in the workforce, and in so far as they did, this was secondary to their primary role as homemaker. Such a view is problematic, not only in its assumption of women's dependence but also because it renders women invisible to the researcher and the wider academic and public audience. With the entrance of women into the workforce this view became untenable and today mobility research always includes women. The differences in the mobility patterns of men and women that these studies reveal provide evidence of the extent to which gender is implicated in arrangements for inequality.

Measures of mobility also need to take account of the effects of changes in the occupational structure. The expansion of the service sector has greatly increased the opportunities for individuals to cross the manual/non-manual divide, with corresponding implications for changes in class location. In his analysis of social mobility in the United Kingdom following World War II,

Glass (1954) identified a great deal of this movement and argued that the United Kingdom had an open stratification system. This claim was challenged by Goldthorpe (1980), who drew a distinction between structural and circulation mobility. Structural mobility arises when the occupational structure of a nation changes, thereby creating higher levels of mobility. Circulation mobility occurs when the stratification system is open and permits free movement up or down the occupational hierarchy regardless of the position an individual is born into. Goldthorpe argued that the change identified by Glass was structural and therefore the United Kingdom was no more equal in the 1950s than it had been at the time of World War I. While many people experienced social mobility, the nation had not really loosened its class structure. People born into the top ranks still had a greater chance than those born beneath them of reproducing their parents' privileged position. Those born into the bottom ranks were still more likely to stay there even if they were employed in a white-collar job.

The shift across the manual/non-manual divide is one shared by the working class in general. As well as contributing to arguments about whether the United Kingdom is an open or a closed society, this finding explains why people perceive society to be more open than in the past.

Social mobility in Australia

Studies of social mobility suggest that there is a great deal of social reproduction across the generations. Although there are not many studies of intergenerational mobility, they are consistent in showing that intergenerational mobility is limited and relatively stable (Broom & Jones 1976; Graetz & McAllister 1994; Leigh 2007). While the amount of mobility between manual and non-manual occupations has increased since the 1970s (Graetz & McAllister 1994), most of this has been structural rather than circulation mobility. Leigh concludes that young Australians today have an equal likelihood of reproducing, or not reproducing, the position of their parents, and that change does not necessarily mean upward mobility. Current young Australians are as likely to reproduce the class position of their parents as they are to change it and the social mobility direction of contemporary Australian youth is not necessarily up. Argy (2005) argues that Australia is similar to the United States, where economic liberalisation has not necessarily resulted in an increase in equality of opportunity.

The pattern of intergenerational social mobility for women is different from that of men. Women are more likely to move from manual to non-manual positions, but this is because they are overrepresented in the secondary labour market of casual, low-paid jobs in the service sector as low-grade clerks and shop assistants. While the working environment of these positions might be an improvement on manual labour, the pay is often as low or lower than in the manual sector.

STRATEGIES FOR SOCIAL REPRODUCTION

The studies examined so far have been quantitative descriptions of occupational mobility. They reveal that, were it not for changes in the occupational structure, there would be relatively little movement across the generations and that social reproduction remains a powerful force. Qualitative studies of the strategies used by businesspeople and professionals explain how those with high levels of social and cultural capital can mobilise it to give their offspring the best chance of reproducing the social position of their parents. Fiona Devine's (2004) study of GPs and teachers examined how they used their social networks to ensure that their children received an excellent education. When asked how they chose what school to send their children to they explained that they asked their friends and colleagues for information and advice about the qualities of schools and universities, how to ensure that their children were accepted and the types of subjects they should take. This kind of assertive inquiry and use of social capital extended to the first years of employment where they drew on their cultural knowledge and social networks to select jobs that would provide strong opportunities for advancement and high economic reward. Although parents were not always successful, they recognised the importance of strong educational performance and passed these values onto their children, increasing the likelihood that their children would be educationally successful.

Gilding's (2005) interviews with wealthy Australians also identified the significance of social capital within the family. He found that family relationships were central to the accumulation of capital and succession planning between generations. Prominent families drew on their social networks to access promising employment positions. But they also established family business institutions that assisted family members to maximise and manage their inheritance.

Among the middle classes, the pattern of wealth transmission is shifting away from the direct transfer of economic wealth through inheritance to the transfer of cultural capital. The longevity of Australians as well as changing attitudes to inheritance and consumption mean that baby boomers are less likely to benefit from inheritance than their parents. Instead, parents today place less emphasis on leaving a substantial nest egg for their children and more on ensuring that their offspring achieve strong educational outcomes to help ensure they are well placed when they enter the labour market (Kelly & Harding 2007; Gilding 2005).

Conversely, there is evidence that just as advantage is inherited, so is disadvantage. While some people born into low socioeconomic positions will successfully escape it, others will not, so that intergenerational poverty is part of the landscape of inequality in liberal democracies (Vinson 2007; d'Addio 2007).

Tutorial exercise

Work out your family tree going back to your grandparents. Which members of your family have been upwardly or downwardly mobile over that time? Explain these patterns, using the concepts of class, gender, ethnicity, structural and circulation mobility, and economic, social and cultural capital. What other factors help to account for the changes you have identified?

For activity suggestions, learning aids, revision of key concepts and access to self-study material, visit: **www.pearson.com.au/highered/vankrieken4e**

Further reading

Bottero, W. 2005, *Stratification: Social Division and Inequality*, Routledge, London.

Connell, R. W. & Irving, T. H. 1992, *Class Structure in Australian History*, 2nd edn, Longman Cheshire, Melbourne.

Devine, F., 2004, *Class Practices: How Parents Help Their Children Get Good Jobs*, Cambridge University Press, Cambridge.

Habibis, D. & Walters, M. 2009, *Social Inequality in Australia: Discourses, Realities and Futures*, Oxford University Press, South Melbourne.

Pakulski, J. 2004, *Global Inequalities: New Patterns of Privilege and Disadvantage*, Allen & Unwin, Sydney.

Wilkins, R. 2007, *The Changing Socio-Demographic Composition of Poverty in Australia: 1982–2004*, Melbourne Institute Working Paper Series, Working Paper No. 12/07, The Melbourne Institute of Applied Economic and Social Research, University of Melbourne, <www.melbourneinstitute.com/wp/wp2007n12.pdf>.

Wright, E. O. 1997, *Class Counts: Comparative Studies in Class Analysis*, Cambridge University Press, Cambridge.

Websites

Australian Bureau of Statistics:
www.abs.gov.au
This site contains many reports on surveys relevant to the issues of class, inequality and poverty. Relevant topics include Australian Social Trends (cat. no. 4102.0), Labour Market Statistics (cat. no. 6106), Household Income (cat. no. 6523), Expenditure (cat. nos 6530 and 6535) and Government Benefits, Taxes and Household Income (cat. no. 6553).

The Australian Social Science Data Archive:
www.assda.anu.edu.au
This site contains many quantitative studies on social issues, including inequality.

National Centre for Social and Economic Modelling:
www.natsem.canberra.edu.au
This centre provides detailed quantitative analysis of trends in economic and social wellbeing, including the distribution of wealth, and income and poverty.

Policy Online:
www.apo.org.au/index.shtml
This is one of the best sources of online Australian social, economic, cultural and political research. It covers nearly 120 member centres and institutes.

The Social Policy Research Centre (SPRC):
www.sprc.unsw.edu.au
The Social Policy Research Centre is a leading centre for research and discussion of issues relating to social inequality and the policy issues that arise from this.

The University of Queensland Social Research Centre (QSRC):
www.uqsrc.uq.edu.au/index.html?page=17037
Social inequality is one of the QSRC's core areas of research as part of its agenda to develop an evidence base to address key problems surrounding social and economic change.

8

Identities: Indigenous, National, Ethnic and Racial

The concept of identity refers to who people think they are and also how we see others. Sociologists have spent a lot of time exploring the process through which people come to belong to groups with particular characteristics, to imagine themselves to be members of groups or to project group identities onto others. They also look at the results of this activity, for example how it might lead to racism or inequality. This chapter explores sociological understandings of group belonging and the ways that these structure social inclusion and exclusion.

By the end of the chapter, you should have a better understanding of:
— the forms of disadvantage to which Aboriginal people have been subjected since colonisation
— the history and cultural systems of Australian national identity
— the process of migration and the history of migration to Australia
— the basic ways that racism operates in Australia today.

INTRODUCTION	**256**
AUSTRALIAN ABORIGINES AND ABORIGINALITY	**257**
Australian Aborigines and racial oppression since 1788—a brief history	257
Australian Aborigines and Torres Strait Islanders as 'fourth world peoples'	258
The survival of Australian Aboriginal culture in everyday life	258
Whitefella Comin'—David Trigger	259
The camp at Wallaby Cross—Basil Sansom	259
Kinship ties among Adelaide Aborigines—Fay Gale and Joy Wundersitz	260
Aboriginal life in a rural small town—Gillian Cowlishaw	260
Aboriginal culture and everyday life—summary	260
Australian Aboriginal land rights, Mabo, Wik and the new cultural identity	261
The Mabo decision and other issues in Aboriginal politics	261
Social disadvantage and Australian Aboriginality today	262
Employment, income and education	262
The criminal justice system	263
ETHNICITY	**265**
MIGRATION	**266**
Migrant decision making	266
Structural aspects of migration	266
Outcomes of migration	266
Migration to Australia—a historical overview	267
Migration and multiculturalism	270
Postmodern ethnicity	271
NATIONALISM AND NATIONAL IDENTITY	**272**
Ethnic and civic nationalism	273
Australian national identity	273
Australian national identity in historical perspective	274
Popular culture and national identity—Fiske, Hodge and Turner: *Myths of Oz*	274
Quantitative research on Australian national identity	275
Multiculturalism and the end of traditional nationalism—Castles et al.	277
RACISM	**278**
Old and new racism—historical shifts	278
Institutional racism	279
Racism in Australia	279
Racism and Australia's Indigenous communities	280
Racism in the Australian media	280
Tutorial exercise	282
Further reading	282
Websites	282

INTRODUCTION

Over recent years themes related to race and ethnicity, immigration and multiculturalism, and national identity and globalisation have moved to the centre of the political and cultural stage in Australia. They have created intense political polarisation and passionate emotional responses. Consider how much controversy and angst have surrounded each of the following:

- The 1990s Mabo and Wik decisions by the High Court giving Indigenous Australians limited land rights. Some saw this as justice long overdue, others as a dangerous land grab that would prevent investment in farming and mining and take away backyards.
- The repeated violent confrontations between Aborigines and the police in Redfern, Sydney. To many this is a protest against injustice, to others simply more evidence that Aborigines are trouble.
- The former Howard Government's policies of detaining asylum seekers, illegal immigrants and refugees for extended periods of time in what were alleged to be prison-like conditions and often in remote areas. Was this inhumane and cruel, or simply a fair, effective and rational policy?
- The word 'multiculturalism'. Does this mask political correctness and threaten a core Australian national identity? Is it an empty motherhood statement that nobody cares about? Does it presage a more inclusive future for Australia? The jury is out on this one, but the Australia First Party argues that it is turning Australia into a 'nation of tribes'.
- The rise of Pauline Hanson's One Nation Party in the 1990s with its warnings about 'Asian ghettos' and the allegedly wasteful 'Aboriginal Industry'. Was this a 'racist' organisation as some claimed, or simply a voice for 'ordinary Australians' asking for a fair go?
- The world-beating athlete Cathy Freeman celebrating her Sydney 2000 Olympic Games achievements by wrapping herself in the Aboriginal flag. Was this a positive gesture for Aboriginal recognition or a slap in the face for white Australia?
- The 2005 decision that it was not appropriate for an 'Aussie legend', singer John Farnham, to perform at an official Anzac Day commemoration at Anzac Cove. Did this reflect or disrespect the true spirit of the Anzacs?
- The 2005 Cronulla riots in which Anglo- and Lebanese-Australians fought for control of the beach area, each group blaming the other for inciting the conflict. Why can't people just get along?

As these examples show, Australians seem to really care about issues related to race, ethnicity, national identity and migration. Why do they care so much? In this chapter we will find some answers.

Who am I? Who are we? These are perhaps the two most fundamental questions that people face in their lives. Without adequate answers, life might be meaningless. Society provides us with various tools to answer these questions. For example, some might refer to their kinship role: 'I am a mother.' Or their religion: 'I am a Muslim.' Others might speak of their work: 'I am a doctor.' Often, however, we define ourselves in terms of our belonging to a large-scale group defined by ethnicity, race or nationality. We also define others through these categories. Broadly speaking, each of these terms refers to collectivities marked out by a shared culture, way of life or ancestry. The members of the collectivity will never all meet at the same time and place. Nevertheless, there is a sense of belonging to something bigger than ourselves—something more general and powerful than our circle of family and friends. Whether a group really exists or is simply imagined, these classifications play a major role in social and political life. They can define inequality and opportunity, shape cultural activities and offer a sense of meaning.

AUSTRALIAN ABORIGINES AND ABORIGINALITY

Before starting this section it is worth noting that the term **Aborigine** is a problematic one. First, it encompasses hundreds of linguistic and tribal groups spread out over the continent. As such, it can obscure the variety of cultural identities and ways of life held by Indigenous Australians in much the same ways that the terms 'European' and 'Asian' can be unhelpful. Second, and more importantly, the concept of the Aborigine as a category of person is one that originated under colonial conditions, in part as a tool of social control. For this reason, the word today has a peculiar double-edged character. It is simultaneously an important source of identity for a dispossessed people and a relic of colonial domination. Third, given two centuries of intermarriage between Aboriginal and white Australians, it is by no means clear where the boundary between Aboriginal and non-Aboriginal Australians can be drawn.

Nevertheless, the term 'Aborigine' (or 'Aboriginal') is the best we have. It has been widely adopted in the official documents and policies of the Australian government and deployed in social science research and its literature. It is also used by many of Australia's Indigenous peoples as a form of self-definition and as part of their struggle for social rights. In this chapter we continue to use the term, but with some attention to its embedded ironies and contradictions.

Australian Aborigines should not be considered as just another ethnic group. This is because, along with Torres Strait Islander peoples, they are the original inhabitants of Australia rather than one of many migrant minorities who have come here. Despite, or perhaps because of this special status, there is little doubt that they have been subject to greater levels of racism and oppression than any other group in Australian society. In order to understand the predicament of Australian Aborigines it is necessary to look at the past 200 years of Australian history.

AUSTRALIAN ABORIGINES AND RACIAL OPPRESSION SINCE 1788—A BRIEF HISTORY

Upon arrival in Australia the British colonists declared the land *terra nullius*—meaning an unowned wasteland that could legitimately be colonised. This legal fiction attests to the way that Aborigines were perceived—as not fully human. During the 19th century this view was maintained in part by prevalent (racist) beliefs about the hierarchy of races. Such theories provided a pseudo-scientific charter for colonialism and the appropriation of lands belonging to dark-skinned 'Aboriginals' by 'civilised' Europeans.

Traditional Australian history as taught in schools argued that the country had been colonised peacefully. Australian Aborigines were written out of this history in what the anthropologist W.E.H. Stanner (1979) called a 'cult of disremembering'. For the past three decades history has been re-evaluated. Historians such as Henry Reynolds (1981) have accumulated significant evidence that the frontier was created through violent conflict, with an estimated 20 000 Aborigines killed by violence (and many thousands more killed by imported diseases). Throughout Australia skirmishes took place as Aborigines attempted to defend their lands with spears against encroaching white farmers armed with guns. Although much of the conflict was covert, in some circumstances the police and military were called in to hunt down Aborigines accused of breaking the law. This was especially the case in Tasmania, where the Aboriginal people were systematically imprisoned or exterminated under a condition of martial law.

From the mid-1800s onwards, policies of segregation and exclusion began to replace violence as the basis of racial oppression. Perhaps this was because Aboriginal people no longer posed a significant military threat in frontier regions. Around this time beliefs abounded that drew upon Darwinian ideas about social evolution. In the Australian context these argued that Aborigines were biologically inferior to white colonists and that they were a dying race doomed to extinction. A policy of paternalistic protectionism arose that sought to shelter Aboriginal people from outside influences by establishing Aboriginal reserves under the control of missionaries and other Europeans. Many Aborigines were forcibly taken there, ostensibly for their own good. In these institutions Aborigines were denied many basic rights and freedoms. Children were often removed from their families and brought up by foster parents or in orphanages. Mission stations often set out to systematically destroy Aboriginal culture, giving Aboriginal people European names and clothing and 'educating' them in Western customs and behaviours.

Although this policy of institutional confinement eventually was to break down, other racist policies and practices remained in place. One of these was the doctrine of **assimilation**, which came to replace the policy of protection. The doctrine was founded on the belief that Aboriginal people should lose their own culture and become as much like white Australians as possible. This can be seen as a racist policy because it was premised on the alleged superiority and desirability of the non-Aboriginal dominant culture.

Notwithstanding rhetoric about encouraging assimilation, segregationist policies abounded that were reminiscent of South Africa under apartheid or the history of the Deep South of the United States. Aborigines often had separate hospital wards, or they could not use public swimming pools, or they had separate areas in cinemas and bars—if they were allowed in at all. In addition, Aborigines were unable to vote. As traditional Aboriginal social structures were destroyed and Aboriginal people became dependent on the colonisers, they were stereotyped as lazy, stupid, irrational, dirty and drunken. However, many Aboriginal people took up paid employment, men often working on cattle stations and women taking up positions as domestic labourers. They were usually paid only a fraction of the white person's wage for the equivalent job, despite being in many cases more skilled than their European bosses and co-workers.

From the 1960s onwards things began to change. In May 1967 a referendum endorsed changes to the Constitution that gave Aborigines citizenship and the right to vote in what was, after all, their own land. Legal reforms were put in place that advocated equal rights and made racial discrimination illegal. However, cultural and institutional racism towards Aborigines remains prevalent today. Some of the continuing inequality suffered by Aborigines in such areas as employment, housing, education, criminal justice and health may be attributable to racism in the form of individual prejudice or insensitive and inadequate policies. We look at this issue later in the chapter.

Australian Aborigines and Torres Strait Islanders as 'Fourth World peoples'

Although the history of Australia's Aborigines is unique, it is important to note that there are parallels with human experiences of colonialism and exclusion around the globe. The term Fourth World peoples (Dyck 1995) captures some of this and so has often been applied to Aborigines and Torres Strait Islanders. The concept has been used in a number of ways, but essentially refers to groups with the following characteristics:

- The people in question are an indigenous group rather than a migrant group.
- The people have been subsumed into a modern nation-state and have had their sovereignty and territory appropriated against their will during a period of colonial expansion.
- The people are economically and politically marginalised. Even in First World countries such as Australia, these groups can be living in Third World conditions.
- The indigenous culture is stigmatised by the dominant culture.
- There is a struggle for social justice and for a right to self-determination and control over traditional lands and resources. These struggles are often linked with environmental concerns, such as rainforest logging, mining and hydroelectric power schemes.
- The Fourth World people constitute a tiny minority of the population of a nation. Aborigines make up only 2 per cent of the Australian population and this contributes to their political powerlessness, even in the democratic electoral process.

In addition to Aborigines and Torres Strait Islanders, other notable examples of Fourth World peoples include Native Americans and Canadians, Amazonian Indians and Pacific Islanders. The concept of Fourth World peoples is useful in drawing sociological attention to fundamental similarities in the problems that confront native peoples in different parts of the globe.

The survival of Australian Aboriginal culture in everyday life

Despite this Fourth World status with its history of brutal oppression and neglect, aspects of traditional Aboriginal culture still survive. Studies of Aboriginal life by sociologists and anthropologists suggest that this survival can be seen in part as a creative and adaptive response to the current social, economic and political position of Aborigines. The following sociological studies show that Aboriginal customs and identity remain of central importance in a range of contexts, both urban and rural. They are a resource for building up solidarity, identity and respect in a difficult situation.

Whitefella Comin'—David Trigger

During the 1970s and 1980s, anthropologist David Trigger (1992) conducted extensive ethnographic research in a community on the Gulf of Carpentaria. His interest was in how Aboriginal people in a remote and rural area had adapted to the political and economic structures of colonialism. Trigger's findings suggest that the mode of colonial domination had changed over time. As we discussed above, during the period of early pastoral settlement, domination in the Gulf region was founded on physical force or the threat of physical force. Aboriginal resistance to colonialism also took a physical form, such as cattle raiding and skirmishing. However, the decentralised nature of Aboriginal life and its breakdown under the pressure of invasion made effective military resistance difficult. In the period following this, control over Aborigines was guaranteed by their sedentarisation and by making them dependent on rations provided by missions and cattle stations.

Trigger argues that during the 20th century domination progressively became more cultural or hegemonic and less based on coercive force. Attempts were made by missionaries and others to change the ways that Aboriginal people thought and to instil imported ideas of what constituted work and obedience. Trigger claims that although Aboriginal people have often complied with this authoritarian rule and taken on some imported values and behaviours, there are still pockets of resistance in their everyday lives. This is manifested in the maintenance of a 'Blackfella domain': 'The maintenance by Aboriginal people of a socially closed Blackfella domain constitutes a degree of resistance to the intrusive administrative and evangelical access sought by the white staff' (1992, p. 221).

This 'domain' is characterised by distinctive cultural practices and modes of thought, and in the case of the community Trigger studied a separate spatial locus, 'the village', where Aboriginal people lived away from the whites of the mission. The Blackfella domain is the place for domestic life, traditional knowledge and practices relating to the land, religious rituals, folk healing, gambling and alcohol consumption. This area of Aboriginal knowledge and behaviour is controlled by the Aboriginal people themselves. Whenever possible, whites and administrative power are excluded from this sphere. Aborigines monitored movements so that preparations could be made, and behaviour adjusted, if the whites entered the Blackfella domain. Trigger suggests that the collective maintenance of a Blackfella domain has 'dulled the full impact of colonial forces which would otherwise become all encompassing and result in the homogenisation of Aboriginal people into Australian society' (p. 222). Put another way, it is a small island for the day-to-day preservation of Aboriginal identity.

The camp at Wallaby Cross—Basil Sansom

Like Trigger's ethnography, Basil Sansom's (1980) earlier study of life in Wallaby Cross, an Aboriginal encampment on the fringes of Darwin, showed that aspects of the traditional way of life had survived into the present. The importance of these dimensions of life can be understood, in part, as a response by Aboriginal people to white Australian culture. Like other fringe camps, Wallaby Cross operated as a kind of hostel for rural Aborigines from outlying cattle stations making periodic visits to the city. Sansom argues that members of the Wallaby Cross community thought of themselves as a 'mob'. The mob was a flexible grouping whose members come and go over time, and who may well belong to different linguistic and tribal groups. However, it still provided a form of collective identity and social support for its members. It can be seen as an adaptation of traditional culture that provided a way of establishing a community in a context of high levels of seasonal mobility with workers moving from the city to the cattle stations.

Other aspects of camp life also reflected traditional Aboriginal culture. Drinking, for example, was often a collective and ritualistic activity. Comparable with Kapferer's study of Anzac Day (discussed below), Sansom argued that group drinking was governed by traditional rules of sharing, equality and reciprocity:

- Never drain the beaker.
- Accept the beaker from any co-drinker.
- Maintain the right to thrust the beaker upon any person.
- See that each person gets a fair share.

Like the Blackfella domain described by Trigger, the Aboriginal inhabitants of Wallaby Cross considered it to be a place where they could relax and live in a style of their own. The 'ease' of life there was contrasted with the 'hard' life in the 'Whitefella domain' of mission settlements and cattle stations. In addition, Wallaby Cross became a place where traditional Aboriginal culture was celebrated and upheld. Sansom writes:

An aspect of Wallaby Cross style is the ostentatious commitment to expressive cultural forms. The fringe dwellers count noted dancers, singers and instrumentalists among their number. In their several talents, the home camp commands the means to stage fun corroborees, public ceremonies and secret cult performances. The camp's holding of sacred objects is another set of symbolic cultural properties and the leading men who, when drinking, adopt a masterful style, are masters of ceremony as well. (p. 74)

The inhabitants and visitors of Wallaby Cross, then, had managed to retain and make use of aspects of their traditional culture and identity within a wider colonial context.

Kinship ties among Adelaide Aborigines—Fay Gale and Joy Wundersitz

While Trigger and Samson are anthropologists using ethnographic methods to study Aboriginal culture, Fay Gale and Joy Wundersitz (1982) are sociologists who used survey research methods to look at the lives of Adelaide Aborigines. Their research was particularly concerned with the issues of housing, work and poverty. Among their most important findings was the discovery that traditional kinship relations continue to play a role in the lives of urban Aboriginal people. While white Australian family life is centred on the nuclear family of parents and children, Aboriginal family life revolves around an extended family that includes grandparents, uncles, aunts and cousins. Gale and Wundersitz found that the Aboriginal household was on average one-third larger than households within the population in general. They argued that larger households provided multiple sources of income. Traditional values of sharing and kinship allowed a limited and uncertain income to be distributed among the largest possible number of people.

They also found that kinship ties often played a key role in a family's decision on where to live. New arrivals migrating from reserves in the country to the city would often move to areas already inhabited by their relatives. These relatives provided a source of social support and knowledge for the new arrivals. Gale and Wundersitz argue that such ties were renewed in everyday life. Funerals would bring together members of a particular regional or kin group and reinforce solidarity. During school holidays children were often sent back to the reserves in the bush or outback, thus building links between children, their kin and their homeland.

High levels of residential mobility (frequent moves from one house to another, even in the same suburb) were another aspect of traditional life that had been transferred to an urban context. This pattern of mobility, which had been important in rural areas, was also influenced by kinship. In general, people tried to move so that they could be as close as possible to those they regarded as 'close kin'. Gale and Wundersitz concluded by asserting that:

The urban Aboriginal population exhibits a definite and growing identity both as a community and as a series of sub-cultural groups. Strong inter-dependence amongst kin appears to be increasing rather than abating, as was first assumed to be inevitable with settlement in the city. (p. 181)

Aboriginal life in a rural small town— Gillian Cowlishaw

Gillian Cowlishaw's book *Black, White or Brindle* (1988) looks at relations between Aboriginal and Anglo-Celtic people in a rural community in western New South Wales. She found that in comparison with the Aboriginal residents, whites are relatively advantaged. They enjoy better housing, better employment and better access to the facilities and recreation opportunities provided by clubs, pubs and voluntary associations. Notwithstanding this social advantage, many white residents were hostile towards Aborigines. They did not like groups of Aboriginal people drinking in public, they objected to welfare housing being damaged by Aboriginal people and to 'cash handouts' by the government.

Cowlishaw argues that the cultural and everyday life of Aborigines in 'Brindletown' can be understood as a reaction to such a judgemental and racist-dominant culture. According to her, the 'oppositional culture' of Brindletown Aborigines can be seen as 'their defiant reaction to rejection, and their haven from the indignities meted out to them' (1988, p. 232). Cowlishaw interprets rowdy public behaviour, drunkenness and cheering for the visiting football team as a gesture against white ostracism and domination. She also shows that a failure by whites to understand Aboriginal culture and values was a source of friction. For example, a white businessman resented the way that Aboriginal employees would frequently leave town to attend funerals, interpreting this as demonstrating a poor attitude towards the responsibility of work. Cowlishaw suggests that this person did not understand the significance of kinship, family ties and mourning in Aboriginal culture. This lack of knowledge was common in a town where contact between whites and Aborigines was often limited to casual encounters in the street.

Aboriginal culture and everyday life— summary

Looking in from the outside, many people feel either dismayed or affronted by visible features of Aboriginal life such as drinking, hanging out in public spaces and living in shanty towns. Studies such as those discussed above suggest that these opinions are usually misguided and result from a lack of understanding about the cultural, historical and social context in which Aboriginal Australians live. We can draw several conclusions from the work of scholars such as Trigger, Sansom, Gale and Wundersitz, and Cowlishaw:

- Aspects of Aboriginal life need to be understood from the perspective of Aboriginal people before judgements are made.
- Many activities and behaviours that may appear to be without value can be seen as a creative response to oppressive social relations—a response that helps to maintain a sense of dignity and identity.
- Although the maintenance of some traditional values and behaviours can be a cause of friction with white society, these often provide an essential resource for Aboriginal people, given their highly marginal social location.

Australian Aboriginal land rights, Mabo, Wik and the new cultural identity

Although academic studies, such as those discussed above, show that Aboriginal culture remains a powerful force in the lives of Aboriginal people, it is perhaps the struggle of Aboriginal people for land rights that has done most to remind other Australians of the continuing vitality of Australian Aboriginal identity.

Richard Broome (2001) argues that during the 1970s a pan-Aboriginal feeling emerged for the first time. This pan-Aboriginal consciousness and collective identity overcame regional,tribal and urban/rural divisions within the Aboriginal community. As Wesley Wagner Lanhupuy stated at a National Land Rights Conference in Sydney in 1977: 'Aborigines—whether urban or tribal—who have a spiritual awareness of themselves as Aborigines and identify themselves as Aborigines are Aborigines' (Broome 2001, p. 188).

Along with this recognition of a common identity came a new tactic of direct protest and mass mobilisation. As a result, the land rights struggle came firmly onto the political agenda and a new sense of confidence and pride allowed Aboriginal people to stand up for what they believed to be their due. Throughout the 1970s and 1980s numerous battles took place in the courts and the media between Aboriginal people and mining companies, and Aboriginal groups lobbied state and federal governments for the return of their traditional lands and greater levels of autonomy and self-determination. This new sense of pride had other consequences. There was an efflorescence in the arts, and Aboriginal dance groups, artists and musicians flourished and attained greater recognition in the wider community. In addition, Aboriginal-initiated community welfare projects and organisations such as the Aboriginal Legal Service and Aboriginal Medical Service came into being.

The Mabo decision and other issues in Aboriginal politics

On 3 June 1992 the doctrine of *terra nullius* was overturned in the High Court of Australia. As noted above, *terra nullius* was the legal fiction that argued that Australia at the time of colonisation was a land belonging to no-one and that it could therefore be taken and owned by the British. The High Court ruling is popularly known as the *Mabo decision*, after Eddie Mabo. Mabo was one of five Torres Strait Islanders who went to court in 1982 arguing that colonial annexation had not extinguished existing traditional or common law land rights. The High Court ruling argued that a group was entitled to claim native title so long as it had an abiding connection with the land in question through laws, customs, activity, beliefs and ceremonies.

The federal government passed the *Native Title Act 1993* as a response to the High Court decision. It established a process through which native title could be attained. This involved Native Title Tribunals to which Australian Aboriginal and Torres Strait Islander peoples could present their claims. The enactment of the Native Title Act aroused some controversy. Mining and pastoral sectors in particular argued that their interests would be affected. Suburban Australians, provoked by the media, expressed fear that their homes and gardens would be taken away from them. These concerns were unfounded as the Native Title Act does not contain a provision for overthrowing existing title to land. The vast majority of claims under the Mabo legislation are for lands that currently belong to the Crown, such as Aboriginal reserves and national parks, often in remote areas.

A further important aspect of the Native Title Act was the establishment of a National Aboriginal and Torres Strait Islander Land Fund. Many Aboriginal people, especially urban Aborigines, have been dispossessed of their traditional lands. The idea of this fund was to provide money so that Aboriginal people who had no realistic prospect of attaining land rights could buy land or housing for themselves and their families (Council for Aboriginal Reconciliation 1994).

In 1996 the *Wik decision*, named after Cape York's Wik people who brought the case to court, extended the concept of native title to include lands currently under pastoral and mining leases from the Crown. The idea here was one of coexistence. Rights to pastoral and mining activity would continue as specified in any leases, but the land itself would belong to its traditional owners. This decision caused anxiety among these industry sectors, with claims being made that they required security of tenure if they were to have enough certainty to invest in long-term projects such as major new mine developments. There followed a period of intense and passionate debate about then Prime Minister John Howard's 'Ten Point Plan'. This was pitched as an effort to make the Wik decision workable, although critics described it as an attempt to severely roll back Aboriginal rights. More recently the struggle has moved on to the topic of 'sea rights'. Many Indigenous groups, especially in the north, claim rights to coastlines, fisheries and other marine resources. The legal situation here remains unresolved.

Aside from Mabo and Wik, there have been a number of other noteworthy and contentious public issues in recent years surrounding Aboriginal matters:

- What is commonly known as 'The Stolen Generations Report' of 1997 was an official inquiry into the policy of forcibly removing Aboriginal children from their families. The report documented the reality of this only half-acknowledged activity and stated that the practice was not only wrong but also deeply hurtful to Aboriginal people. After the release of the report, much attention focused on the matter of official apologies, with some state governments and politicians apologising, but others not. For legal and cultural reasons many of the apologies that did emerge were feeble, qualified and half-hearted. However, in 2008 Prime Minister Kevin Rudd issued a historic full apology to the Stolen Generations.
- Uranium mining operations at Jabiluka in the World Heritage-listed Kakadu National Park are also an ongoing contentious issue. Mining has been opposed by a coalition of Aboriginal, Green and Peace groups, and themes relating to Aboriginal control over their own lands have been central to the debate.
- Despite a Royal Commission in the 1980s, and various remedial steps being taken as a consequence, the issue of Aboriginal deaths in custody is yet another theme that continues to cause friction between Aborigines and the criminal justice system.
- More recently, attacks on Aborigines from the political right have been a cause of concern. In the 1990s groups such as Pauline Hanson's One Nation Party claimed that organisations such as the Indigenous-controlled Aboriginal and Torres Strait Islander Commission (ATSIC) were a wasteful 'Aboriginal industry' and that affirmative action programs discriminate against other (i.e. white) Australians. To some extent these views were shared in other political parties. Embattled by scandal and allegations of corruption, and also widely seen as a failed experiment, ATSIC was abolished in 2005. ATSIC was significant because it recognised the importance of 'self-determination' for Indigenous Australians—that is, that they should have a say in decisions about their lives and social problems. Without ATSIC there is no high-visibility and influential umbrella organisation with which an Indigenous perspective can be voiced.

Social disadvantage and Australian Aboriginality today

Aborigines are the most disadvantaged group in Australia. Here we look at some measures of inequality: employment, income, education and involvement with the criminal justice system. Another important indicator of current disadvantage is Aboriginal health, which is discussed in Chapter 10.

Employment, income and education

Data on employment, income and education provide a useful way of measuring social disadvantage. Available data indicate that Aboriginal people are far more disadvantaged than both Anglo-Australians and ethnic migrant groups. Calculating Aboriginal unemployment from routine statistics is difficult due to the numbers of persons siphoned off into training and 'make work' schemes such as Community Development Employment Projects. These people do not appear in official unemployment statistics, even though they are receiving unemployment benefits and are looking for meaningful work. An analysis of the 2001 Census offers one statistical snapshot that allows us to get around misleading ways of counting (ABS 2008c). This shows an Aboriginal unemployment rate of 20 per cent, a rate about three times higher than for the non-Indigenous population. Labour force participation is also much lower: the 2001 Census shows that some 46 per cent of all Indigenous people aged 15–64 were not in the labour force ('labour force' meaning people undertaking paid work or intending to work), in contrast to just 27 per cent of the non-Indigenous population. There could be many reasons for not being in the labour force, including illness, family responsibilities or simply giving up hope of finding a job. Various attempts have been made over the years to boost Aboriginal work outcomes, but these have had limited impact.

Incomes at household and individual levels are also far lower than for the general population. This reflects lower paying jobs, higher rates of unemployment, higher reliance on government benefits and lower labour force participation. The 2001 Census shows that the median gross individual income for Indigenous people was $226 per week, in contrast to $380 for other Australians. In general Aboriginal people work further down in the occupational hierarchy and are paid less even within the same occupation category—for example, Indigenous managers received 81 per cent of the median income for non-Indigenous managers and Indigenous labourers received just 56 per cent of what their non-Indigenous peers were receiving.

When it comes to education there is a similar story (ABS 2008d). Retention rates through school Years 10, 11 and 12 are lower across the board for Indigenous people than for the general population. Figure 8.1 shows that just 36 per cent of Indigenous people aged 18–24 have completed Year 12, compared to nearly 80 per cent for the non-Indigenous population of the same age. The good news, however, is that retention rates have improved slowly over time—as the figure shows older Indigenous Australians are much less likely to have a Year 12 education. Furthermore, we can see that the gap between Indigenous and non-Indigenous educational attainment is closing with each generation. However, the margin remains substantial and the situation is not so good when it comes to higher education. In 2002 some 17 per cent of the non-Indigenous population had a bachelor degree, compared with only 3.7 per cent of the Indigenous community (Australian Human Rights Commission 2006).

The criminal justice system

Statistics repeatedly show that Aboriginal people are overrepresented in the criminal justice system. In June 2005 Indigenous people made up some 22 per cent of all prisoners. Depending on the state, the rate of overrepresentation relative to the population ranges from four (Tasmania) to 19 times (Western Australia) (ABS 2008e). There has been a very high increase in the imprisonment rate for Indigenous women: between 1993 and 2003 the number of Indigenous women in prison increased by 420 per cent and in 2004 they were imprisoned at a rate around 20 times that of non-Indigenous women (Australian Human Rights Commission 2006).

The argument could be made that such statistics might simply reflect higher rates of serious offending by the Indigenous population. Against this the case

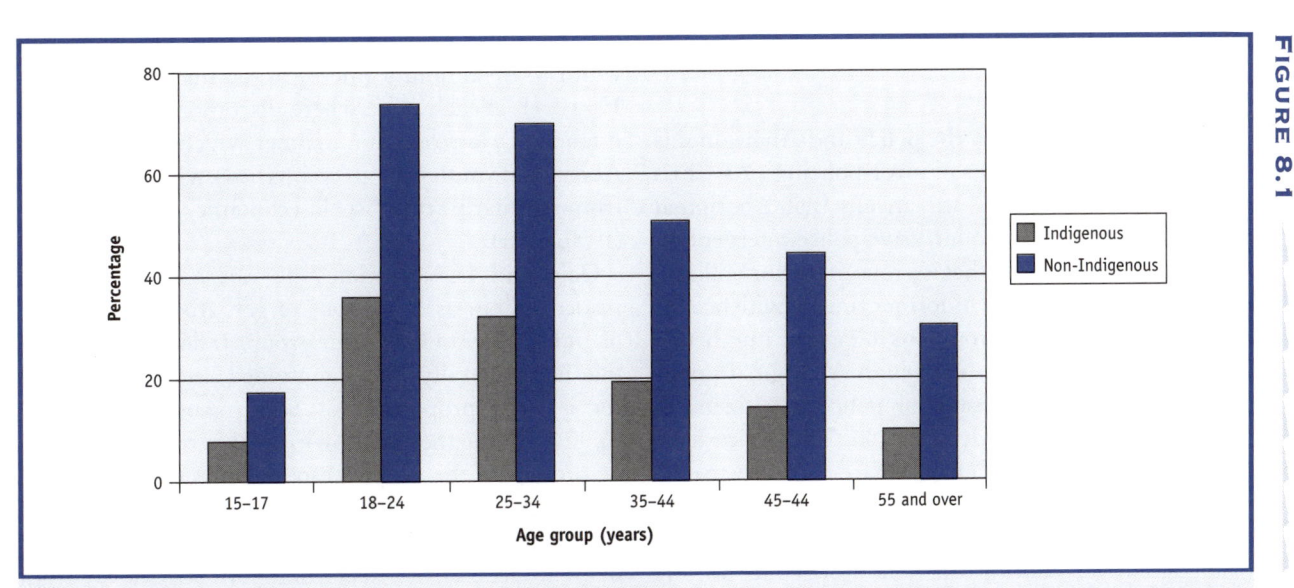

FIGURE 8.1

School completion to Year 12 by Indigenous status, 2006 *Source:* ABS 2008d, 4704.0 The Health and Welfare of Australia's Aboriginal and Torres Strait Islander Peoples.

could be put that Aboriginal people lack the financial and cultural resources to successfully negotiate police interviews and courtrooms. Furthermore, the crimes that are committed reflect entrenched social problems such as poverty, alcohol abuse and despair rather than just 'bad behaviour'. Looked at in this way, the imprisonment statistics are evidence of a systemic failure to give Aboriginal people the kind of adequate life opportunities that lead away from crime.

Importantly, Aboriginal inequality in criminal justice cannot be summed up simply through prison statistics. There is a qualitative or experiential dimension to this. The *Report of the National Inquiry into Racist Violence in Australia* (HREOC 1995) found that complaints against police officers were an 'overwhelming feature' of evidence submitted to the Inquiry by Aboriginal and Torres Strait Islander peoples. Typical complaints included:

- irrational and unprovoked attacks on Aborigines, sometimes during arrest
- assault or threats of force when in custody
- disrespectful language
- harassment of community organisations and the Aboriginal Legal Service
- the use of spotlights by night-time police patrols
- allegations that Aboriginal women had been abused or raped by police officers.

Whether true or not, the prevalence of these kinds of complaints suggests that there are serious problems with police attitudes and methods in dealing with Aboriginal and Torres Strait Islander peoples. One of the most important issues for concern is over-policing.

Over-policing

The relationship between the police and Aborigines is often understood in terms of 'over-policing'. As Chris Cunneen (2001) explains, this means that Aboriginal populations are subject to intrusive police intervention into their lives—a policy that is a relic of the surveillance and containment policies of former times. Evidence for this proposition comes from looking at the number of police stationed in towns with high Aboriginal populations. Sometimes the ratio of police to citizens in these towns is in the order of 1:100. The police have responded that such policing levels are necessary to deal with the levels of crime in such communities. However, it is quite possible that perceived levels of crime are a result of the over-policing. First, the more police officers there are, the more trivial offences will be detected and arrests made. (In contrast, under-policing often leads to culprits being let off with a police caution, due in part to time constraints and the volumes of paperwork needed to process even trivial offences.) Second, over-policing itself creates a climate of hostility and fear that in turn generates a lack of respect for the law and the police. As a result, an 'us against them' mentality might emerge among both police and Aboriginal people, leading in turn to Aboriginal people being caught up in the net. Arrests for swearing, for example, can eventuate as Aborigines voice their resentment at cruising police patrols. It is arguably the case, for example, that such dynamics are at play in Redfern and contribute to the ongoing problems between police and its Aboriginal inhabitants.

Aboriginal youth and the criminal justice system—Fay Gale, Rebecca Bailey-Harris and Joy Wundersitz

One of the most thorough analyses of the criminal justice system and Aborigines is by Fay Gale, Rebecca Bailey-Harris and Joy Wundersitz (1990). They used official statistics from the police and courts to look for differential outcomes between Aborigines and other Australians at various stages in the juvenile justice system. The results suggest that Aborigines are clearly disadvantaged. Aboriginal youths are more likely than non-Aboriginal offenders to be apprehended, arrested, taken to court and detained. Gale and her associates emphasise the role of discretion in the juvenile justice system. Police, for example, can caution, summons or arrest people. Similarly, screening panels can decide whether to send the juvenile offender to court or to implement some form of constructive intervention (e.g. counselling). Courts can decide whether to sentence a youth to detention, a fine or a good-behaviour bond. However, at each stage where discretion was exercised it tended to 'operate in a manner which disadvantages Aboriginal youth even in comparison with white youth from similarly poor socio-economic circumstances' (1990, p. 91).

Gale and her associates do not see the juvenile justice system as being 'out to get' Aboriginal youth, or indeed any other youth group. Indeed, they argue that it is generally well-intentioned and 'operates well for a large proportion of South Australian youth' (p. 124). While they acknowledge that racism may well be present in the system, especially among the police, they argue that discretion is exercised on the basis of criteria that are not appropriate for the Aboriginal population. Decisions to steer young offenders away from harsher options depend upon the presence of a stable nuclear family and employment:

The system requires middle-class characteristics such as parental care in nuclear households and employment status in order for it to operate to the benefit of the child. The Western middle-class concept on which the system is based requires various characteristics that simply do not apply to many Aboriginal families. (p. 124)

High levels of unemployment, residential mobility and large multi-unit households were used by administrators in the juvenile justice system to justify the differentially harsher treatment of apprehended Aboriginal youth. The findings of this work raise interesting questions about the nature of racism in the criminal justice system. It suggests that cultural insensitivity can allow a system to operate in a racially discriminatory fashion even when people have good intentions. This finding is consistent with the 'unintended consequences' model of institutional racism, which is discussed later in this chapter.

Reflective questions: How are Aboriginal Australians disadvantaged today? How did colonisation impact on Aborigines? How has their culture survived and adapted?

ETHNICITY

Sociologists often speak of the **ethnic group**. The concept generally refers to a population that is marked out by its everyday way of life, its language, nationality, religion and customs. The idea is often used by sociologists in contrast to the concept of **race**, which generally refers to groups defined on the basis of visible physical characteristics, most notably skin colour. Sociologists are generally more comfortable with the concept of ethnicity rather than race, in part because the sociological enterprise has spent a long time debunking biological and racist arguments. These have often been associated with extremist politics, colonial attitudes and cruelty. We must note, however, some basic problems and issues that often emerge in studies of race and ethnicity:

- The way that a group sees itself might not correspond to the way that outsiders or government see it. Often outsiders aggregate people into generic ethnic categories, when the members might see themselves as belonging to quite different communities. For example, the white community in Australia might speak of an Iraqi ethnic group or 'Iraqi community'. Yet in Iraq there are Shi'a and Sunni Muslims, Christians and Kurds. Much of the recent civil war and fighting within Iraq has been between these groups as each looks for autonomy or safety. This being the case, it seems laughable to speak of an 'Iraqi' ethnicity with a common identity.
- Groups defined in terms of ethnicity might also be part of a visible racial minority. In Australia migrants from South Asia, East Asia, Africa and the Middle East often fall into this category. Does substituting the term 'race' with 'ethnic group' simply omit the fact that these populations are caught up in racial politics?
- There is often a complex interplay of race and ethnic identity. In the United States, for example, there are African-Americans who have been in the country for generations (many being the descendents of slaves) and there are also Africans who live in America (such as recent migrants from places like Nigeria or Ghana). These Africans-in-America can experience a common set of racial problems (racism, stereotyping etc.) with African-Americans yet have very different ethnic customs and lifestyles from the African-American community. They might think of themselves as distinctive from African-Americans, yet when filling in official forms such as the census they might have to call themselves 'African-American'. Furthermore, ethnic groups sometimes define themselves in terms of real or imagined racial characteristics, such as lines of descent from ancestors or foundational myths. In this case the category of 'race' is the one that is meaningful to them in their own religion, culture or life world, not 'ethnicity'.
- Drawing neat boundaries around ethnic groups can be impossible. Over time there are varying degrees of assimilation to the host culture, including intermarriage. When does a group stop being 'ethnic'? To speak of Irish-Australians seems a little problematic today, yet to speak of Greek-Australians seems less so. Why should this be?
- People can switch into and out of ethnic roles depending on context. At a wedding or funeral they might behave in 'ethnic' ways, but in other aspects of life—such as at work—they might behave no differently from anyone else. At a more macro-level, ethnic ties are often strengthened during periods of hardship, struggle or war.
- We tend to see and research 'ethnicity' only in migrant or minority populations, and especially in those with highly visible customs and traditions. Low-key groups tend to be left out. We don't think of a German-Australian ethnic group. Nor do we speak of being English as an ethnicity or

of afternoon tea with cucumber sandwiches as an 'ethnic activity'.

All that said, theories of ethnicity are often useful for exploring ways of life, customs, political inclusion and exclusion. In the Australian context these themes are very closely linked to the nation's history and in particular to its qualities as a nation of immigrants. We turn to this next.

MIGRATION

Migration is generally used by sociologists to refer to long-term movements of people over large distances. Over past centuries millions have travelled the globe. Usually this movement is voluntary and is driven by the search for work, education, opportunity or a better lifestyle. However, it is important to remember that some migrations are forced. The plight of those taken from Africa to the Americas during the slave trade and of current refugees from war zones exemplifies this pattern.

Migrant decision making

Theories of migration often discuss the decision to migrate in terms of push, pull and hold factors that influence a potential migrant's decision-making process.

- *Push factors* are reasons to leave a place of origin. These can include unemployment, poverty or war.
- *Pull factors* are attractive features of the destination. These can include such things as job opportunities, a warm climate, a developed education and health system, or simply political stability and physical security. Research has repeatedly shown that one of the most important pull factors is the presence of friends or relatives in the destination country. These offer a source of information and social support to new migrants. Chain migration arises when a few migrants from a particular area are followed by others from the same village or region due to informal ties. This process has been especially important, for example, to the Greek, Lebanese and Italian communities of Australia and helps explain the spatial clustering of particular ethnic groups in certain suburbs or regions.
- *Hold factors* are things that prevent people from moving even if they would otherwise wish to. These might include government quotas on immigrant numbers, the fact that older children might be in the middle of a school program leading to exams, the inability to get a passport, or the need to wait and save money to pay taxes and fees associated with moving.

Structural aspects of migration

An analysis of push, pull and hold factors is a useful way of thinking about migrant choices. However, this individualistic focus can often obscure the fact that wider structural forces are at work in society that influence migration patterns and outcomes. These forces can determine the distribution of incentives and disincentives to migrate—or, put another way, they allocate the pushes, pulls and holds. Prospects for employment and unemployment, for example, are linked to changes in the economy and cannot be explained in purely individual terms. Migration from the bush into the cities of Australia is tied to long-term shifts in the Australian economy—the move from primary production towards manufacturing and now a services- and finance-based economy. In the United States the changing economic fortunes of the 'rustbelt' and the 'sunbelt' have seen large numbers of people moving south from places such as North Dakota and Detroit to other places such as California, Texas, Georgia and Florida. This movement is linked to a decline in traditional heavy industrial manufacturing (e.g. cars in Detroit) and the rise of new high-tech employment (e.g. computer programming in Silicon Valley).

Immigration and citizenship policies can also operate as significant macro-variables that shape population movements and migrant outcomes. In Australia, for example, the government sometimes offers incentives for migrants to settle outside the major metropolitan centres in the form of extra 'points' on the visa application. In addition, there are strong cultural forces driving migration patterns. These are also structured and non-individual. For example, fantasies about big city life often attract young Australians to London. Many older Australians have 'sea change' aspirations and seek to retire on the coast. These wishes might seem natural to us now, but they are also relentlessly propagated in popular culture and the mass media. Such cultural forces can shape choices and preferences at the individual level just as sharply as economic factors.

Outcomes of migration

One outcome of migration can be cultural change. We might find the preservation or the loss of distinctive ethnic cultures. Generally the research shows that with each passing generation the arriving group becomes more like the host group in terms of way of life and values. However, some groups assimilate faster than others. Particularly important for this process are experiences outside the home. The workplace and the school are key arenas in which friendships are formed across ethnic lines and new customs, values and languages are learnt.

Aside from culture, another core focus for sociological research has been the linkage between migration and various dimensions of social inequality. Taken as a whole, statistical analyses of census and other numerical information show that it is important to avoid making sweeping, general statements about the social status of migrants and ethnic groups. Most research in this area has focused on occupation and income data. This demonstrates that although some migrant and ethnic groups occupy the lower end of the socioeconomic scale, others can do better than native-born Australians. Research by Toni Makkai and Ian McAllister (1993) is typical in that it demonstrates that there are wide differences between the experiences of migrants from different geographical origins. Their study found that northern European and Asian migrants have occupational characteristics similar to, if not better than, those of people born in Australia. On the other hand, southern and eastern Europeans and Middle Eastern migrants tend to be disadvantaged. Educational criteria tell a similar story, with migrants from northern Europe and Asia tending to have better educational backgrounds—a factor that to some extent has driven their labour market success. Such accounts focusing on 'human capital' are useful but are also vulnerable to critique because they fail to pay attention to discrimination and perhaps give the inadvertent impression that there is a level playing field when in fact some migrant groups do rather badly.

Research shows that racism and cultural exclusion can be a cause of inequality in outcomes for migrant people. Refugee status might compound this disadvantage. Milicia Markovic and Leonore Manderson (2000) conducted an interview study of female refugees from the then war-torn former Yugoslavia and found that these women faced special problems of adjustment. Many experienced a profound sense of loss or ambivalence as they settled into Australia. They had been uprooted from their homes, lost the social networks and financial and social status that they had enjoyed before, and were uncertain about whether or not they belonged in their new home.

The work of Val Colic-Peisker (2002) suggests that language problems are also a major predictor of migrant inequality. Colic-Peisker shows that migrants from a non–English-speaking background (NESB) are particularly likely to experience discrimination and feel a subjective outsider status in Australia when they are working class and lack the social capital that might help them fit in and obtain mobility. Colic-Peisker compared working-class Croatian migrants from the 1960s with professional Croatian migrants from the 1980s in Western Australia. Although both groups had experienced some 'outsider' status as a result of their accent and lack of 'Anglo' cultural competence, the working-class migrants had experienced significantly greater barriers to occupational and residential mobility. By contrast, the professional Croatian migrants had implemented more successful strategies to overcome these barriers, even if they still reported 'accent-ceiling' effects in their professions.

This argument for the centrality of language is confirmed by the work of Christina Ho and Caroline Alcorso (2004), who draw on the Longitudinal Survey of Immigrants to Australia to suggest that English-speaking background (ESB) migrants do much better than NESB migrants in employment outcomes. Whereas 49 per cent of NESB arrivals had been in management, administration or professional jobs in their home nation, some three and a half years into their Australian residency the number had dropped to 32 per cent. By contrast, the ESB migrants had managed to haul themselves up from 47 per cent to 49 per cent. Similarly, 57 per cent of the NESB group reported that they had used their educational or professional credentials 'all the time or very often' before migration, but this dropped to 31 per cent in Australia (ESB = 52 per cent and 37 per cent). Ho and Alcorso suggest that the 'human capital' approach that focuses on the skills and credentials of migrants is inadequate. It fails to look at the subtle forms of discrimination and evaluation by employers that can operate as barriers to success. These often focus on 'soft skills' such as a perceived cultural competence or the ability to fit into a team or deal with the public.

MIGRATION TO AUSTRALIA—A HISTORICAL OVERVIEW

Investigations of migration to Australia, such as those by Geoffrey Sherington (1990) and Gary Freeman and James Jupp (1992), have repeatedly shown that Australia is a country where this process has played a crucial role in the history of the nation. Like the United States, Canada and New Zealand, Australia is sometimes described as a 'nation of immigrants' or a 'settler society'. The patterns of both past and present migration have a profound impact on the ethnic composition and culture of Australia as we know it today.

According to the archaeological record, the first migrants to Australia were the Aboriginal people. Aborigines are thought to have arrived in a series of waves from the north, the first of these taking place around 40 000 years ago. Over the following millennia Aboriginal people spread out and eventually occupied the entire continent. (It must be noted that Aboriginal traditional knowledge often disputes this claim: it is believed that Aborigines have always been here.) The next major episode of migration took place in 1788, when the First Fleet arrived at Port Jackson after a long sea voyage from Britain. There were around 1000 migrants—about 75 per cent of these were convicts sentenced to transportation and the rest were administrators, soldiers and gaolers. Most of the convicts had been convicted of petty criminal acts, and almost all of them were male and from the lowest and most deprived classes of British society. From 1788 to 1852 about 170 000 convicts were sent to eastern Australian states, and from 1850 to 1868 10 000 convicts were sent to Western Australia. The first free settlers arrived in New South Wales in 1793, and during the first half of the 19th century the number and proportion of free migrants and women rose. After 1836 the numbers of free migrants completely outstripped the number of convicts. During the middle of the 19th century, voluntary migrants to Australia, almost all from Britain, were attracted by the availability of land in Australia, opportunities for social advancement in contrast to blocked mobility at home and assisted-passage schemes. These offered subsidies and other forms of support and encouragement to potential British migrants. Other contributing factors influencing people to migrate to Australia were problems of poverty and unemployment, especially among the peasants of Scotland and Ireland who were being dispossessed of their land.

The discovery of gold in Australia in the 1850s provided further impetus to migrating people and Australia's population increased almost threefold in a short period. With the other gold rushes in the latter part of the century came large numbers of non-British migrants, most notably Chinese and Germans. Chinese and Pacific Islanders also came to Australia to work as indentured labourers in the north Queensland cane fields.

An implicit ideology underlying much early Australian migration policy was the strengthening of the British Empire. This was to be achieved by ensuring the racial and cultural characteristics of Australia were as similar as possible to those of Britain. In 1901 this so-called White Australia Policy gave birth to the *Immigration Restriction Act 1901* which was used to exclude non-European migrants. A dictation test was used to screen out people with 'undesirable' characteristics. Although this test was usually in English, examiners were free to choose another language such as Welsh or Gaelic. This meant that people from 'undesirable' backgrounds could be excluded even if they spoke perfect English.

Despite a policy of assisted migration for British people, numbers of unassisted migrants from southern Europe increased during the late 19th century and the first half of the 20th century. The most notable groups establishing a presence in Australia at this time were Italians and Greeks. Economic expansion after World War II provided another spur to migration as labour shortages in Australia were met by large numbers of displaced refugees from a war-ravaged Europe. The result was assisted migration for a cross-section of new European migrant groups from 1947 onwards. Many of these migrants were from eastern and central Europe and the Baltic region. Significant numbers of other migrants arrived as the result of deals between the Australian government and various European governments (Malta, Italy, The Netherlands, the former West Germany, Austria, Greece, Spain, Turkey and the former Yugoslavia) that guaranteed a flow of workers to meet Australian labour needs, especially in manufacturing. So, although postwar migration to Australia was still largely British, a more ethnically diverse population began to emerge.

Despite the multiethnic nature of this postwar migration the assimilationist ideology underlying immigration remained—that the new settlers should become like the host population as soon as possible and acquire their traits and customs. Preferred migrant groups were those that most closely resembled the dominant Anglo-Celtic population of Australia. The initial aim was to bring out ten British people for every one non-British. When not enough British people volunteered, migrants were sought in northern Europe (The Netherlands, Germany and Scandinavia) and, as a last resort, southern Europe. Many of the non-British European newcomers tended to be from poor backgrounds and they entered the bottom of the labour pool in Australia. Perhaps the most significant trend during the past quarter-century has been the steady rise in Asian and South Asian migration and a steady decrease in the proportion of British migrants.

The changing composition of migration to Australia and its impact on the birth of a multicultural nation is clearly discernible in Table 8.1. This shows the countries of birth for the Australian population between 1954 and 2006. Note first that around one-third of Australia's current population was born overseas. Back in 1954 the United Kingdom/Ireland were the dominant contributors of non-Australian-born people. Migration from Europe was also proportionally strong during the period up to about 1981. Observe how migration from Asia picks up rapidly between 1971 and 1981, in part due to less racist immigration policy (see below). Today the United Kingdom and New Zealand remain the major contributors of overseas-born migrants, but the spread of migrants from other nations is much more balanced than before.

As the ethnic balance of migrants changed in the period after World War II the idea of a white, Anglo-Celtic Australia began to look absurd. In 1972 the Whitlam Government responded to these changes by introducing a policy of multiculturalism, which is marked by a belief in pluralism and encourages ethnic and cultural diversity. In 1973 the more or less racist policy of excluding non-European migrants was officially ended. Simultaneous changes to government policy also took place. Previously it had been assumed that migrants would more or less automatically assimilate with the mainstream (Anglo-Celtic) Australia once they learned English and entered the workforce. However, social research from the 1960s onwards began to show that many migrant groups were severely disadvantaged. Consequently, government policies in the 1970s began to recognise the difficulties that migrants faced. Provision was made for multilingual facilities in areas such as health and schooling, and ethnic representation was encouraged on various policy-formulating bodies and in government institutions. In the period since the early 1970s a number of other factors have consolidated this new multicultural policy, most notably closer economic and political ties with Asia, along with declining support for the British monarchy. The closer links with Asia have been reflected in the growing proportion of Asian migrants since the 1980s (as documented in Table 8.1).

TABLE 8.1

Main countries of birth of Australia's population

	1954[a] '000	1961[a] '000	1971[a] '000	1981[a] '000	1996[b] '000	2001[b] '000	2006[b] '000
United Kingdom[c]	664.2	755.4	1 081.3	1 075.8	1 164.1	1 126.9	1 153.3
New Zealand	43.4	47.0	74.1	160.7	315.1	394.1	476.7
Italy	119.9	228.3	288.3	275.0	259.1	238.5	220.5
China[d]	10.3	14.5	17.1	25.2	121.1	157.0	203.1
Vietnam	n.a.	n.a.	n.a.	40.7	164.2	169.5	180.4
India	12.0	14.2	28.7	41.0	84.8	103.6	153.6
The Philippines	0.2	0.4	2.3	14.8	102.7	112.2	135.6
Greece	25.9	77.3	159.0	145.8	141.8	132.5	125.8
South Africa	6.0	7.9	12.2	26.5	61.7	86.9	118.8
Germany	65.4	109.3	110.0	109.3	120.8	117.5	114.9
Malaysia	2.3	5.8	14.4	30.5	83.0	87.2	103.9
The Netherlands	52.0	102.1	98.6	95.1	95.3	91.2	87.0
Lebanon	3.9	7.3	23.9	49.4	77.6	80.0	86.6
Hong Kong (SAR of China)	1.6	3.5	5.4	15.3	77.1	75.2	76.3
Total overseas-born	1 285.8	1 778.3	2 545.9	2 950.9	4 258.6	4 482.1	4 956.9
Australian-born	7 700.1	8 729.4	10 173.1	11 388.8	14 052.1	14 931.2	15 648.6
Total population[e]	8 986.5	10 508.2	12 719.5	14 516.9	18 310.7	19 413.2	20 605.5

Notes: n.a. = not available.
[a] Census counts.
[b] Estimated resident population at 30 June.
[c] Includes Ireland in 1954, 1961 and 1971.
[d] Excludes SARs and Taiwan Province.
[e] Includes country of birth 'Not stated' and 'At sea'.

Source: ABS, *Migration, Australia.*

Migration and multiculturalism

Sociologists have given a lot of attention to the connections of migration with group and individual identity. Disputes have arisen concerning the extent to which migrants lose or preserve their identity as time passes in a new land. Those speaking of assimilation suggest that given two or three generations newcomers take on the characteristics of the host nation. They become indistinguishable from the locals in terms of attitudes and behaviours. An alternative vision is promoted by theorists of the melting pot. The vision here is of a new culture and identity emerging from the fusion of various migrant cultures. In the multicultural scenario each new group retains its core identity and way of life. The result is a society characterised by multiple ethnic identities.

Although proposed as analytic and descriptive models of what really goes on, these terms have also taken on political dimensions. In formulating migrant policy, governments—and indeed social activists—have often advocated one or another of these outcomes as a desirable state of affairs and as a goal of immigration policy. This is clearly seen in the case of Australia.

Stephen Castles (1992) argues that Australia has gone through several stages of migrant policy since World War II. These stages are detailed as follows:

- **Assimilationism**. This policy lasted from 1947 until the mid-1960s. It argued that 'immigrants could/should be culturally and socially absorbed and rapidly become indistinguishable from the existing Anglo-Australian population' (pp. 184–5). Government policies for helping migrants included help in finding work, initial accommodation and English language lessons. Ethnic enclaves in employment or residential segregation were not encouraged and emphasis was placed on schooling as a way of turning children into 'Australians'.
- *Integration*. This stage lasted from the mid-1960s to 1972. It emerged because of an obvious contradiction between the doctrine of assimilation and empirical reality. Non-Anglo migrants tended to be segregated in both employment and social spheres. They were heavily concentrated in working-class manufacturing jobs and had overwhelmingly settled in industrial suburbs. Moreover, migrant children were not doing as well at school as had been expected. Large numbers of migrants were leaving Australia and it was becoming harder to attract new migrants. Realising that the *laissez-faire* policy of assimilationism was failing, a number of active measures were introduced by the government between 1965 and 1972. These included an Integration Branch in the Department of Immigration, grants to community agencies and an extended program of English language courses.
- *Multiculturalism phase 1*. This lasted from 1972 to 1975 and was prompted by a growing realisation that NESB migrants formed a part of society with special needs. At the same time the Whitlam Government did away with the so-called White Australia Policy, abolished privileges for British migrants and introduced non-racist immigration policies. In 1973, Immigration Minister Al Grassby introduced the concept of multiculturalism in a speech on the 'family of the nation'. During this early phase, multiculturalism focused on the provision of welfare and education to NESB groups in areas such as pensions, housing and health.
- *Multiculturalism phase 2*. This lasted from 1972 to the mid-1980s. Castles argues that the Fraser Government, which was not attracted to welfare spending but wished to capitalise on the large ethnic vote, redefined multiculturalism in cultural terms and linked it to the issue of national identity.
- *Multiculturalism phase 3*. This started around 1983. The Hawke and Keating Governments continued the Fraser policy of stressing the cultural contribution of multiculturalism, but tried to combine this with an emphasis on issues of equity framed largely in terms of access and individual rights. The most important statement of this multilevel policy was the National Agenda for a Multicultural Government, which was produced in 1989. It identified three areas of multicultural policy:

1. cultural identity—the right of Australians to express and share their cultural heritage
2. social justice—the right of Australians to equal treatment and opportunity
3. economic efficiency—the need to maintain and develop the skills of all Australians, regardless of their background.

While multiculturalism has become more important over recent years, it is very important to remember that since the 1980s its legitimacy has been repeatedly questioned. Back in 1984 the historian Geoffrey Blainey warned against the Asianisation of Australia (1984). Blainey's attack found widespread support among many sections of the Anglo-Australian community, especially the working class and members of the Returned Services League (RSL). The then Labor government responded by stressing the positive aspects of multiculturalism, especially in the context of growing economic and social links with Asia. It also shifted its migration policies, emphasising the need to attract affluent and skilled migrants who would invest in Australian business and contribute to economic growth. Notwithstanding this policy, the majority of migrants are 'family migrants' who come to Australia to be reunited with their relatives.

From the mid-1990s the kinds of arguments made by Blainey were picked up by the political right. Members of Pauline Hanson's One Nation Party, in particular, suggested that multicultural policies devalued 'traditional' (Anglo) Australian culture and wasted taxpayer's money on what they perceived as special-interest groups. Some commentators suggested that such opinions were silently condoned by the then Prime Minister John Howard, who (initially at least) did little to speak out against them. To many, Howard's own statements eulogising the Menzies-era Australia of the 1950s also suggested a lingering nostalgia for a pre-multicultural past. More recently the Australia First political party has carried the torch, insisting on the need for multiculturalism to be abolished as an official policy.

In contrast to Blainey and Hanson, who saw multiculturalism as having gone too far, a number of radical sociologists and cultural commentators argue that it has not gone far enough. They suggest that Australian multiculturalism plays a mostly ideological role and does not come to terms with fundamental and enduring issues of economic inequality and power. Andrew Jakubowicz (1981), for example, was quick off the mark in asserting that in the Australian case multiculturalism functions to maintain a bourgeois hegemony, or false cultural consensus, that benefits the dominant class. He argues that relationships between the Anglo-Celtic core and ethnic groups have a strong class character with ethnic groups constituting a substantial proportion of the working class. However, the concept of multiculturalism serves to obscure these differences by proposing a 'family of the nation' and emphasising cultural, rather than social and economic, equality. In Jakubowicz's analysis, the ideology of multiculturalism was proposed by the state to defuse possible ethnic-based working-class protest. This new ideology emerged following the collapse of the assimilationist ideology as an effective hegemonic tool. Multiculturalism is attractive as it seemingly embraces ideas of equality, but at the same time diverts policy into an innocuous cultural direction. As Jakubowicz puts it: 'The implicit potential of multiculturalism to assert the priority of ethnicity over class marked its transformation into a means of social control' (1981, p. 9). Whatever the merits of such an argument, it is clear that multiculturalism is not just a contested policy, but also a contested symbol. It is an icon in Australia's culture wars that raises strong sentiments on all sides.

POSTMODERN ETHNICITY

Sociologists have traditionally argued that ethnic identity was something that people automatically had by virtue of primordial ties that went back to days immemorial, the manipulative strategies of the politician playing on ethnic themes or the workings of everyday life and culture. More recently attention has been given to the role of the mass media, individual choice and hybridity. Ethnicity is seen as something that is deployed instrumentally, that is flexible, that comes and goes or that is a superficial but fun aspect of everyday life. John Hughson's (1997) work (discussed below), for example, points to a kind of strategic essentialism among his Croatian football fans. They depict themselves as Croatian when it suits their needs—for example, to get money from the government.

Likewise, Zuleyka Zevallos (2003) interviewed young Latin-American women living in Australia and found that their ethnicity was to some extent constructed and chosen, with negotiation and agency playing a crucial role in their self-identity. The young women had the option of seeing themselves as Latin-American or Australian. In fact they saw themselves as both. Expressions of a Latin self in areas such as dance, food or dress were adopted as a form of resistance to the dominant (Anglo-Celtic) Australian culture. In the Australian context cultural differences between South- and Central-American communities were papered over so that the women could share a common Latin identity. On the other hand, the women were proud to endorse or 'use' their 'Australian side' from time to time. They saw themselves as Australian when themes of gender relations or sexuality were involved. They tended to reject traditional Latin-American gender roles and construct a model of their femininity around 'Australian' notions of equality and independence.

Over recent years processes of globalisation and cultural commodification have intensified a process in which ethnicity becomes a kind of choice or game, rather than something deeply felt. People construct multiple identities as they seek to understand or display who they truly are. The pivotal case of novelist Helen Demidenko provides a useful illustration of this process. Demidenko's award-winning 1993 book, *The Hand that Signed the Paper*, dealt with the Holocaust, allegedly from a Ukrainian perspective. Demidenko presented herself to the media as being an ethnic Ukrainian, even performing folk dances for the cameras. In fact she was an Anglo-Australian (real name: Helen Darville) who had somewhat briefly studied Ukrainian culture and chosen to take on a Ukrainian identity for the purpose of writing and marketing her work. The ease with which Demidenko/Darville appeared to be able to slip into another ethnic identity is suggestive of the way that this is for some just another lifestyle option. It should be noted, however, that Demidenko/Darville was hounded by the media as a fake and a fraud, suggesting that there are commonsense limits to what people can get away with.

A similar process can be seen elsewhere. A few white Australians have chosen to take on an Aboriginal identity and have rejected their own Anglo-European background. Some of these people have been accepted by Aboriginal groups as legitimate members of their communities. Many Australian, Japanese and British teenagers are attracted to an African-American ghetto identity and enthusiastically adopt the language and clothing of an oppressed group that most of them have only ever encountered on television. This is a kind of pseudo-racial lifestyle identification. The fictitious television character Ali-G lampoons this trend. Invented and portrayed by a British-Jewish comedian, it is not really clear who Ali-G is. Some say he is Pakistani-British, others that he is white. What is certain is that with his baggy designer clothes, street slang and stylised gestures he can be taken as an effective parody of gangsta-wannabes across the globe.

Does it make sense to talk of Ali-G and those whom he parodies in terms of race and ethnicity, or consumerist fantasy? We can argue the case each way, but like the Demidenko/Darville case, Ali-G highlights the significance of the global mass media and subcultural lifestyle choices in providing and reproducing a range of possible identities that individuals might find attractive. Far from being condemned to an ethnicity by birth, people seem to be selecting an identity and a self-image with which they feel comfortable—even if this is a pseudo-ethnicity that has been subject to commodification by media and culture industries.

Reflective questions: What does the concept of 'ethnicity' try to capture? What is problematic about this concept? What is 'multiculturalism', and how does its emergence connect to Australia's immigration history? What are some of the critiques that have been made of this concept/policy?

NATIONALISM AND NATIONAL IDENTITY

Over the past 15 or so years sociologists have become aware of the close links between ethnicity, race, nationalism and national identity. Indeed the academic journals are clogged with articles trying to sort out where one of these terms ends and the next begins. For our purposes, **nationalism** can be defined as a set of more or less consciously formulated political and militaristic beliefs that argue for the superiority or unique value of one's own country, its people, landscape and traditions. It is often associated with political movements related to either struggles for self-determination or, on the other hand, imperialist conquest. **National identity** is a more general concept. It refers to a broad set of shared understandings within a nation about its people and values and also to common languages, symbols and practices that help to constitute them as a nation. While nationalistic beliefs are usually formulated deliberately by intellectuals, conceptions of national identity often remain grounded in commonsense thinking and everyday life. In the world today, nationalism and national identity provide an important source of collective identity alongside ethnicity.

Benedict Anderson (1983) famously captures the power of national belonging in his concept of **imagined community**. He points out that people feel themselves to be members of a collectivity and to share a 'deep comradeship' with others whom they have never met face to face. According to Anderson the print media of the 19th century played a major role in the manufacture of an imagined community of nation. It connected people to events distant from their home towns, spoke of 'national' issues and united them in common rituals, such as opening the paper in the morning.

There is resonance here with Michael Billig's (1995) idea of **banal nationalism**—the idea that nationalism, or the sense of belonging to a nation, is reinforced in low-key ways in our lives. It does not depend on major events and big civic ceremonies but rather slips in through the back door. Every time we use a coin or banknote, put a postage stamp on an envelope or read about the national cricket team in the paper the idea that we live in a nation to which we belong becomes a little more automatic or naturalised.

Another influential concept for nationalism studies has been that of the invented tradition. The idea here is that nations do not have primordial origins, but rather emerged quite recently in modernity, making use of manufactured myths and rituals or attributing new values to something ongoing. Sometimes such traditions appear to have been around for centuries, when in truth they are cobbled together by cultural entrepreneurs and intellectuals or are the outcome of pure accident. The 'Scottish' tradition of wearing a kilt, for example, is somewhat bogus. The original highlanders wore large woollen blankets and did not think of this as a 'national dress'. The modern, shorter, skirt-style kilt was invented only in the 19th century as part of a more general and somewhat nostalgic or romantic revival of Scottish nationalism.

Many sociologists argue that today nationalism might be increasing in strength. This is something of a surprise for sociology. It was assumed that the progress of modernity would erode national borders and ways of thinking. More recently, theorists of globalisation assert that national boundaries and identities are being broken down by global communications technologies such as the internet, by transnational corporations and economic integration, and by international political organisations such as the United Nations, the European Union and the Asia-Pacific Forum. Despite these theoretical predictions, recent world events confirm that visceral nationalism remains a strong force in world affairs and people's lives. In the United States, for example, there was a patriotic reaffirmation of national unity in the wake of the terrorist attacks on the World Trade Center and Pentagon on 11 September 2001.

ETHNIC AND CIVIC NATIONALISM

One of the most basic distinctions in academic work has been between ethnic and civic nationalism. For scholars such as Leah Greenfeld (1993) and Rogers Brubaker (1992) ethnic nationalism is characterised by an emphasis on a shared, deeply rooted culture, language and way of life and particularly on the possession of a common blood line as criteria for membership within a national community. Such forms of national identity tend to be exclusionary towards outsiders. If you are not born into a community, you can never join with full rights. Civic nationalism, by contrast, emphasises the subjective, voluntary and contractual allegiance of citizens to institutions (e.g. parliament), beliefs (e.g. democracy) and laws. In a sense civic nationalism is more 'modern' in that it is more universalistic and builds upon conceptions of active citizenship that have arisen over the past 200 years. Countries with civic conceptions of nationalism are often newer, multicultural states such as Australia, Canada and the United States that have been historically characterised by high levels of migration and ethnically heterogeneous populations. In Europe, France is often cited as an exemplar of a civic nationalist country. To some extent this reflects the universalistic and democratic beliefs that arose during the French Revolution. Germany, by contrast, exhibits a strong ethnic nationalism.

As Brubaker (1992) points out, these various conceptions of what it takes to be a member of a nation can have consequences for migrants and migration policy. It is very difficult to obtain German citizenship unless you come from German stock. As a result, the children of Turkish migrants might not be able to obtain citizenship, even though they have lived in Germany all their lives, speak perfect German and are completely assimilated with the way of life. In France, by contrast, Algerian migrants have found it far easier to obtain citizenship rights, thanks to the influence of a civic conception of national identity.

AUSTRALIAN NATIONAL IDENTITY

Australian national identity has been extensively studied by historians, sociologists and cultural studies scholars. We can perhaps see it as having been historically formed around a distinctive Anglo-Celtic ethnic core of early migrants. But at the same time it can be understood as an 'invented tradition' or 'imagined community' in which a variety of disparate phenomena have been thrown together to create a national mythology, a sense of common identity and a sense of the Australian nation. During its history Australia has slowly moved towards a civic conception of national identity as its population has become more diverse. At naturalisation ceremonies where immigrants attain their citizenship status, for example, great emphasis is placed upon feeling Australian and upon the significance of Australian institutions. Australia's officially multicultural identity today downgrades the importance of belonging to an Anglo-Celtic ethnic core as a feature of being Australian, and instead argues for commitment to a shared civic solidarity that can be layered on top of the diverse ethnic identities that citizens carry. Yet for all this talk about ethnic and civic forces, it is perhaps at the level of popular culture that we should seek the roots of Australian national identity.

Australian national identity in historical perspective

Historians and cultural studies scholars such as Richard White (1981) and Catriona Elder (2008) frequently argue that Australian national identity has less to do with ethnic ties or government-sponsored policies and more to do with popular culture. It has been constructed over the past 200 years from popular images and myths. White claims that the way people think about or 'imagine' Australia has changed over and over during this time. During convict days Australia was seen as a sort of hell on earth. However, during the 19th century Australia came to be identified as a land of opportunity and as a 'lucky country' where migrants could build a better life. In this period Australians understood Australia as a classless society characterised by what the historian Russel Ward (1958) called 'egalitarian individualism'. It was a society that defined itself (as distinct from a stereotyped Britain) as the land of the 'fair go' where 'mateship' cut across distinctions of rank and class. This myth found its expression in a series of male archetypes. These included bushrangers such as Ned Kelly, pioneer farmers and, during the 20th century, the Anzacs who fought at Gallipoli and in the Pacific. Other symbols of the quintessential Australia were found in the imagery of the outback and its fauna, in natural disasters and in its membership of the British Commonwealth.

During the post-World War II period a new identity emerged. For a brief time Australia had the highest standard of living in the world, and consequently a consumerist identity was formed focusing on the quality of the Australian lifestyle. The quarter-acre block, the FJ Holden, the Hills Hoist and the barbecue all became iconically associated with 'Australia'. At the same time sports heroes, such as cricketer Donald Bradman, came to replace farmers and bushrangers as the truest expression of the Australian character. Achievements in the arts by figures such as opera singer Joan Sutherland and artists Sidney Nolan and Arthur Boyd have also been important in shaping a postwar image of Australia as cosmopolitan and sophisticated rather than just populist in its culture.

In contemporary Australia the orthodox conception of national identity has been challenged by intellectuals in recent years. Feminists have pointed out that women have been excluded from the masculinist definitions of the Australian type, and Marxists have argued that ideas of egalitarianism and the 'fair go' obscure systematic class and ethnic inequality. Works such as *Myths of Oz*, discussed below, suggest that such critiques have had little impact on the average Australian—most people love Australia and see little wrong with its popular culture. However, there can be little doubt that Australian national identity is slowly changing due to wider social forces. The republican movement; multiculturalism; closer economic ties with Asia; the growing social, economic and political power of women; the recognition of Aboriginal rights; and the passing of the Digger generations are all contributing to the emergence of a new national identity. At the moment it is unclear what the central values and symbols of this identity will be. However, it is remotely possible that events such as Sydney's Gay and Lesbian Mardi Gras, environmental attractions such as the Tasmanian wilderness areas and people such as Indigenous activist Eddie Mabo will replace older icons such as Anzac Day and the bushranger.

Popular culture and national identity— Fiske, Hodge and Turner: *Myths of Oz*

Cultural studies is an interdisciplinary field attracting scholars from such areas as history and English as well as sociology in recent years. Since the 1980s it has conducted perhaps the most influential research into Australian national identity. Scholars in the field place great emphasis on the role of both popular and high culture in creating a sense of Australian national identity and in allowing people to feel 'Australian'. Pivotal here is the idea that the 'Australian' is reproduced through the circulation of symbols and practices in the media and in everyday life.

John Fiske, Bob Hodge and Graeme Turner, for example, conducted a semiotic analysis of contemporary Australian identity. Their book, *Myths of Oz* (1987), was in its day an influential attempt to show how a sense of being Australian is reproduced in everyday life and popular culture. The book consists of the analysis of a number of 'sites' that Fiske, Hodge and Turner treat as 'texts' that can be 'read' for essential Australian meanings. The pub, for example, is a place where values of egalitarianism and mateship are reproduced. The family camping trip is an expression of a continuity of identity with an older, pioneering Australia. Uluru and the Sydney Opera House are seen as locations that capture, for Australians, some quintessential characteristic of their country. In the case of Uluru it is the mystical, sacred power of nature. The Opera House, on the other hand, represents the dynamic, progressive qualities of modern Australia. In addition, it reflects Australia's egalitarian ethos in so far as it is an 'elite' building that everybody likes.

The theoretical impetus for the work of Fiske, Hodge and Turner came from the work of French semiotician Roland Barthes. Barthes (1973) argued that items of everyday culture can be decoded for hidden meanings and that these meanings often play an ideological role. For this reason the analyses of Fiske, Hodge and Turner further claim that the core symbols of Australian identity often reproduce power and inequality—but perhaps without our being aware of this. The pub, for example, is the bastion of male chauvinism and Uluru presents a sanitised and depoliticised version of Australian Aboriginal culture.

Myths of Oz is an imaginative work that has been influential in demonstrating the deep links between popular culture and national identity in contemporary Australia. Criticisms of the work usually focus on methodology. Fiske and his associates drew upon the methodological traditions of literary theory and cultural studies. While these are perfectly adequate in other research traditions, such as those of the humanities, they can appear rather impressionistic to orthodox sociologists. It is never really clear why Fiske and his colleagues selected certain 'sites' for investigation and not others. Perhaps, more importantly, there is little or no attempt to verify the accuracy of their interpretations. They offer virtuoso readings of forms of data such as newspaper reports, postcards, television programs, advertisements and tourist brochures but do not check whether these correspond to the way Australians actually interpret their own world.

This said, recent sociological research suggests that Fiske, Hodge and Turner as well as Australian studies scholars such as Richard White were more or less correct. In a qualitative research project Timothy Phillips and Philip Smith (2000b; Smith & Phillips 2001) asked focus groups to nominate what seemed to them to be 'Australian' and 'un-Australian' people, places and activities. The results suggest that the dominant cultural codes were indeed widely shared. Although the groups were stratified by age, gender and class they all produced remarkably similar results. For example, 'Australian' people nominated included the actor Paul Hogan (*Crocodile Dundee*), diverse sports stars and noted humanitarians such as eye doctor Fred Hollows. 'Australian' places included the beach and the bush. 'Australian' activities included sport and helping other people. By contrast the 'un-Australian' person was selfish or arrogant rather than matey; an 'un-Australian' place was a China Town; and an un-Australian activity a selfish one. Importantly, the groups did not have to struggle to come up with material and engaged in vehement affirmations of the Australian ('I like …') and denunciations of the un-Australian ('I don't care much for …'). This suggests that the codes of the Australian and un-Australian are widely known, shared and endorsed in Australia today and that popular culture plays a major role in creating a sense of belonging and its associated moral boundaries.

Quantitative research on Australian national identity

So far we have been looking at qualitative inquiries into the 'Australian'. Australian national identity has also been investigated using large-scale data sets and statistical techniques—indeed Australian sociology is at the forefront of such investigations globally. This developed literature has explored two key issues:

1. specifying the sociodemographic variables that impact upon national identification
2. developing typologies that define various kinds of national identifier.

Timothy Phillips (1998) conducted a meta-analysis of 12 quantitative studies that had touched on the question of who held a traditional sense of Australian national identity. He found strong evidence that a number of variables are repeatedly and positively associated with having an attachment to a traditional Australia. Being older, Christian, less educated and born in Australia all predict a strong attachment. By contrast younger people, migrants and those with tertiary education are less likely to subscribe to such an orthodox national identity. Evidence for the effects of class, sex, political affiliation and occupation is weak or nonexistent. These statistical effects hold up well in more developed typologies, showing that there are many ways that people can think of themselves as 'Australian'. For example, Frank Jones (1997) looked at responses to a survey question asking people how important various criteria were to being 'truly Australian'. He located four kinds of identifier and argued that persons with particular sociodemographic characteristics will tend to be attracted to each of these:

- *Dogmatic nativists* (15 per cent of the population) believe it is very important that people should

SOCIOLOGY

Case Study
The Anzac myth and national identity

Anzac Day parades are a familiar event for most Australians. They are held on the anniversary of the landings in 1915 at Gallipoli, Turkey, which are shown in the photo. What do Anzac Day parades mean? How are they linked to a sense of being Australian?

Bruce Kapferer (1988) is an anthropologist who uses participant observation methodology to try to answer these questions. Drawing upon Durkheim's late work, *The Elementary Forms of Religious Life* (1965), Kapferer argues for the importance of ritual and the sacred in contemporary Australian national identity. For Kapferer the Anzac tradition constitutes a sacred foundational myth for the Australian people. This myth celebrates the prowess and egalitarianism of the Australian troops as well as their blood sacrifice for the nation. His ethnographic fieldwork suggests that the ceremonies of Anzac Day are a rite in which the links between nationalism and egalitarian individualism are renewed. Anzac Day also expresses the solidarity of the people and marks out popular limits to the power of what is perceived to be an authoritarian and bureaucratic state. On Anzac Day people gather in the streets and take over central areas of the city. Officials and marshals from the various RSL clubs help direct spectators and events while the police take a back seat. Drinking serves to demonstrate not just camaraderie and mateship but also the prowess and autonomy of the Australian male who can consume liquor without getting drunk. Associated with drinking is the egalitarian institution of the 'shout':

> *Pub drinking groups are egalitarian groups par excellence. The institution of the shout—less commonly, 'round'—is directed against any social differentiation, or distinction, conceived of as derived from the ordinary working world. Quite simply, the shout involves one person buying the drinks for all others in the group. It defines membership in the drinking group. (1988, p. 159).*

The ability of the people to play two-up and drink without being arrested is another dramatisation of the power of the people and the limits to the power of the state. Similarly, during the march the Anzacs march in unison, but in a way that 'gives full expression to their individuality'. They might wave to friends in the crowd, for example. In addition, the Anzacs rarely march in an order according to military rank. Kapferer suggests that: 'Anzac Day conforms perfectly with Durkheim's argument about religion as society worshipping itself' (p. 168). By this he means that core values and solidarities are expressed in the quasi-religious rituals of Anzac Day. The overall message of the Anzac Day ritual is to reaffirm the ideal of Australia as a nation characterised by egalitarian individualism. A subsidiary message demonstrates that the Australian people constitute a moral community, the 'nation', which is autonomous from, and more important than, the government or state.

The Anzacs landing at Gallipoli, 1915

Although Anzac Day remains important to many Australians, some people suggest that it is losing the significance it once had. They argue that for many younger citizens the events of World War I and the Anzac mythology seem very distant from their experience. Other groups, such as feminists and pacifists, have critiqued the ceremony for glorifying war and for marginalising women. These views are not widely shared and consequently Anzac Day ceremonies continue to be well attended. The sociological research of Brad West (2005) on the backpacker pilgrimage to Gallipoli further demonstrates the continuing relevance of the Anzac commemoration. West reports that backpackers were deeply moved on touring the battlefields in Turkey where the original landings took place. They found their sense of national identity surprisingly strengthened by the encounter with the sacred soil.

have been born in Australia and have lived here a long time (nativism). They also see links to civic culture (e.g. respecting laws and institutions, feeling Australian) as important.
- *Literal nativists* (8 per cent) believe strongly in nativistic criteria as aspects of national identity, but have a somewhat weaker belief in the importance of institutions and civic commitment for being 'truly Australian'.
- *Civic nationalists* (38 per cent) have a strong commitment to civic culture, but a weaker belief in nativism.

- *Moderate pluralists* (38 per cent) are weak identifiers on both dimensions. National identity is not really that important for them.

Looking at his survey data, Jones argues that nativists tend to be most committed to traditional Australian identity. They are more likely to be opposed to immigration, are more xenophobic and more monarchist. In terms of sociodemographic characteristics his findings are similar to those of Phillips. Nativists tend to be older, less educated, rural, active churchgoers and less likely to vote Labor. Civic nationalists and pluralists, by contrast, tend to be younger, have a diploma or degree, vote Labor and be less religious. Jones suggests that the two nativist groups are most likely to be supporters of right-wing parties. He disputes, however, the claim of Pauline Hanson and others on the right that they were the 'mainstream' of Australia. Nativists make up about one-quarter of the population—a significant constituency, but not a majority. Jones, like Phillips (1996a), also saw their form of traditional identity being superseded by the open, more inclusive forms that seem to be held by younger generations. As older generations die, Australian national identity will probably shift towards a form that is weaker (in terms of strength of effect), more civic in orientation and less closely tied to a core Anglo-Celtic culture.

A parallel study by Jan Pakulski and Bruce Tranter (2000) using data from the 1995 International Social Science Program (ISSP) survey reinforces these findings. Their 'civic identifiers' have a strong belief in Australia as a 'voluntary association of people sharing major social institutions and commitments' (p. 209)—for example, believing in the importance of the law and 'feeling Australian'. They made up about 38 per cent of survey respondents. On the other hand, an enthnotional Australian identity (30 per cent) gives priority to being born in Australia or having lived here a long time and thus sharing its customs and values. This is a less inclusive understanding. A denizen identity (only 6 per cent) contrasts with both of these in that there is only a weak sense of belonging to any collectivity—denizens don't really care that much about 'Australia'. Even though they live in the country and might even enjoy being here they simply don't identify as Australian. The sociodemographic correlates of Pakulski and Tranter's analysis fall out in the same pattern as Jones and Phillips found. The ethnonationalists are older, more religious and less educated; the civic nationalists are baby boomers, secular and better educated. Denizens were harder to pin down, but many had lived overseas or were recent migrants to Australia. These forms of identity could be correlated to political attitudes. When compared with the other groups, the ethnonationalists tended to be more strongly in favour of economic and cultural protectionism and opposed to migration.

The 'denizen' identity hints at current theoretical interest in 'cosmopolitans'. Recently Timothy Phillips and Philip Smith (2008) discovered that open and cosmopolitan orientations in Australia prevail among those born in the baby boomer and X generations, among those with tertiary education and among the non-Christians. Another factor associated with the cosmopolitan outlook is simply doing lots of things that connect the individual to the world outside Australia. These include taking overseas trips, phoning friends abroad and using the internet for one or two hours per day.

Multiculturalism and the end of traditional nationalism—Castles et al.

In their book *Mistaken Identity* (1988), Stephen Castles, Bill Cope, Mary Kalantzis and Michael Morrissey argue that traditional Australian national identity of the kind held by Jones' 'dogmatic nativist' or Pakulski and Tranter's 'ethnonationalist' is dying under the influence of multiculturalism. This policy has advanced a more open and more progressive concept of national identity. Critics suggest that the optimistic position of Castles et al. was made possible by the fact that they tended to focus on the discourses, ideologies and logical implications of multiculturalism as a basis for their conclusions about the end of an orthodox, exclusionary Australian identity. According to Timothy Phillips, this kind of approach could be misleading:

There has been an understandable tendency amongst some researchers to gauge or 'read off' patterns of stability and change in popular views about Australian identity from either popular or impressionistic accounts, textual analysis, or social and political shifts and continuities. However, the danger of treating human behaviour and reactions as 'obvious' in the absence of empirical research has been well documented. (1998, p. 282)

Phillips calls for more data to explore the extent to which official beliefs about Australia (e.g. bureaucratic statements about multiculturalism in government policy documents) are actually shared among citizens. The quantitative research that we have just reviewed suggests that for the time being large numbers of Australians remain attracted to traditional conceptions of national identity that are lukewarm about multiculturalism. Pakulski and Tranter (2000, p. 216) found remarkably low levels of support for multicultural policies across the board. Looking at the ISSP data they found that only about 25 per cent of Australians thought that 'different ethnic and racial groups should maintain their distinct customs and traditions' and, conversely, about 75 per cent believed such groups should 'blend into the larger society' (i.e. assimilate). Amazingly these findings held true for denizens and civic nationalists as well as for hard boiled ethnonationalist Australians.

John Hughson's qualitative work also questions the optimistic conclusions about multiculturalism as advocated by Castles et al. Hughson (1997) conducted ethnographic research with Croatian soccer supporters in Sydney. The group in question used soccer as a vehicle for fighting, held neo-Nazi beliefs, made racist taunts of the opposition and engaged in aggressive displays of Croatian nationalism. The particular cultural beliefs of the group he studied, then, were ones that both expressed their ethnic culture and attacked the culture of others (especially that of Serbians). Hughson argues that the group has used Australia's multicultural policies in a manipulative way to further Croatian nationalism. One of his informants saw multiculturalism as a 'big mumbo jumbo kind of thing' but went on to say that 'it's good, like we can use it ... the Australian government wants it ... we'll take advantage of it' (1997, p. 181).

Hughson's study demonstrates that there is no necessary link between expressions of cultural identity in a multicultural society and peaceful and tolerant coexistence within that society. Hughson suggests that the theorist Homi Bhabha can provide a way of explaining this situation. According to Bhabha (1990, p. 208) multicultural societies are constructed from 'a range of different sorts of interests and different kinds of cultural histories', giving rise to the very real possibility of 'potentially antagonistic cultural identities'. For Bhabha, then, a major problem with multiculturalism is that it all too easily overlooks possible incommensurabilities between divergent cultures that have to coexist. Hughson suggests that the optimistic view of Castles et al. fails to take adequate account of this possibility.

In thinking about these somewhat pessimistic findings, however, it is important to remember that the quantitative work we have reviewed here had very robust findings about the influence of age and education. As older generations pass on and as more and more Australians go to tertiary institutions it is very likely that support for an open, inclusive and cosmopolitan form of national identity will increase. A change looks very likely, although this will perhaps have very little to do with policy documents on multiculturalism coming out of Canberra.

Reflective questions: What does sociological research say about Australian national identity? Isolate some key findings. How has Australian national identity changed over time? What are some of the social, political and economic forces driving these changes?

RACISM

In discussing Aboriginality, Australian national identity and immigration, we have at times come close to engaging with the idea of racism. Back in the 19th century racism was anchored in pseudo-scientific beliefs about the hierarchy of races and evolutionary differences between whites and blacks. Today only a minority of lunatics and extremists believe this sort of nonsense. This does not mean, however, that racism does not exist. Indeed for people of colour it is often a daily reality in their lives. Recently, for example, there have been racist incidents on Sydney's beaches in which Anglo-Australians have tried to drive off Middle Eastern and Asian Australians.

OLD AND NEW RACISM—HISTORICAL SHIFTS

The old racism that emerged most strongly in the 19th century was grounded in biological metaphor and linked to colonial expansion. What is sometimes called the *new racism* is remarkably different. It has arisen in an era of globalisation and is in some ways a defensive reaction to migration from developing to developed nations rather than an aggressive accomplice of colonialism. Scientific language has gone, to be replaced by language that speaks of the need to preserve the cultural identity of the host nation. As Robert Manne (2002) points out, often this is accompanied by talk of the incompatibility of different cultures or religions—for example, that Islam does not belong in Western democratic contexts. Arguments about the superiority of races have also disappeared and have been replaced by arguments that call for equality for all. The point is no longer that dominant groups deserve special treatment, but rather that all groups should be treated equally. In the eyes of the new racism, affirmative action programs and multicultural funding jeopardise basic norms of equality because they favour non-white minorities. We should allocate money on the basis of 'race-free' criteria like poverty or ability. A new world of 'political correctness' operates as a kind of censorship on free speech and rational policy evaluation. A curious feature of the new racism is that it is very difficult to attack. This is because its advocates speak in terms that are remarkably similar to those of postmodernists and the New Left. They talk about the need to preserve identity, difference, traditions and culture. They also speak about the need to maintain standards of equality, fair play and so on. Who can disagree with any of this? Only rarely is anything unambiguously racist said.

INSTITUTIONAL RACISM

Another term that we often hear is institutional racism (or its synonym structural racism). It is frequently used, for example, in policy papers, inquiries and documents on the failure of the police. The idea here is that racism is more than something to be found in scattered individual minds, but rather is embedded in organisations and has a systemic quality. Indeed, institutional racism does not necessarily require malicious thoughts and attitudes at all. Aspects of institutional racism can include the following:

- Insensitivity and lack of understanding towards the customs and beliefs of a particular group—for example, the police locking up Aboriginal people in solitary cells. For Aborigines, being with others in groups is really important.
- Not trying hard enough to look after particular groups or failing to take their concerns, needs and worries seriously—for example, shallow investigations of crimes against Aborigines.
- A culture within an institution that tolerates or turns a blind eye to racist talk or the more actively racist activities of a small minority—for example, a police service without an explicit policy banning racist jokes on the job.
- Stratification within an organisation such that racial minorities never get to the top—for example, when did you last see an Aboriginal police inspector?

Those labelled with the term 'institutional racism' are rarely happy. Commentators from a police union, for example, might suggest that it is an elusive term that unfairly denigrates all members of the institution. The argument is that even if its application is to issues of policy and sensitivity, the public do not understand this. It pollutes symbolically by hinting that negative or racist sentiments exist in the members of the organisation. Still, for all its ambiguities the term does usefully capture the ways that racial disparities and even racist thinking can creep in through the back door.

RACISM IN AUSTRALIA

Despite popular images of Australia as a country in which everyone gets a fair go, Australian history is full of both institutional and popular racism. Racism has also played a key role in migration policy. As discussed earlier, the White Australia Policy underlay attempts to keep Australia as British as possible in its ethnic composition. Discrimination in terms of who was let into Australia was perhaps the single most important form of racism against migrants. Once here, however, the racism did not stop. The *Report of the National Inquiry into Racist Violence in Australia* (HREOC 1995) documents 19th-century racism against Irish migrants, Chinese goldfield workers and Melanesian workers in the cane fields and then again 20th-century racism against southern and eastern Europeans. Critics of the earlier assimilationist paradigm have argued that it was essentially racist in that it denied the validity of non-Anglo cultures and identities.

The *Report of the National Inquiry into Racist Violence in Australia* highlights three factors that contribute to the level of racism directed against a group:

1. *The visibility of members of the group.* People and groups that are visibly different from the white Anglo-Australian norm are more likely to experience racism. This visibility can come from dress (e.g. the traditional Muslim headscarf for women) or from physical appearance.
2. *The ethnic identity of the group.* Some ethnic groups are perceived with greater hatred than others. Jews have been the target of racism throughout Australia's history, as have Asians. Racism directed towards groups may vary over a short period. Germans, for example, experienced far greater levels of racism during the two world wars. Other ethnicities such as the Scottish and Irish have been perceived more favourably in Australia.
3. *The social, economic and political context of the group.* Patterns of unemployment and job competition, international conflict and media reporting can trigger racism towards the group.

Submissions to the *Report of the National Inquiry into Racist Violence in Australia* suggest that the most acute racism among migrants tends to be experienced by Jewish, Asian, Arabic, Maori and Pacific Islander, and Central and South American people (National Inquiry into Racist Violence in Australia 1991, p. 139). Typically this process of ethnic hatred is reinforced by stereotypes about such groups. They are seen as having a negative impact on Australia by 'taking our jobs', 'taking over the country', 'bludging on welfare' or as having 'unAustralian' values and customs. Racist acts in Australia have taken on a number of forms including arson attacks on ethnic schools and places of worship, sexual harassment, verbal harassment, school bullying, physical assault, the desecration of graves, attacks on property and graffiti. But, in addition to these more visible forms of racism, it is probable that racism works in a number of silent ways to exclude ethnic Australians from opportunities in housing, work and education.

Racism and Australia's Indigenous communities

As the earlier historical discussion showed, Australian Aborigines have been subject to racism for the past 200 years and this racism continues today. Former examples of racism directed against Aborigines include:

- in December 1989, shotgun blasts directed at the offices of the Northern Land Council
- fire-bombings of the offices of the Committee to Defend Black Rights
- harassment when using public parks
- security guards and bouncers denying Aboriginal people access to hotels, nightclubs and casinos (National Inquiry into Racist Violence in Australia 1991).

One of the most shocking recent acts of racist violence was the desecration of the grave of land-rights activist Eddie Mabo.

In her study of 'Brindletown' in rural New South Wales, Gillian Cowlishaw (1988) argues that few of the white inhabitants thought of themselves or the town as racist. This was because they understood racism in terms of individual feelings of hatred rather than institutional structures and cultural biases. The white inhabitants asserted that their negative views towards Aborigines were a response to unruly behaviour by Aborigines rather than racial hatred. They asserted that they would respect the Aboriginal population if its people behaved in more appropriate ways—for example, if public drinking was stopped.

Cowlishaw argues that this seemingly universalistic view shows 'no appreciation of the way power and wealth have accumulated in the hands of whites only' (1988, p. 212). Moreover, it did not recognise that the whites were using their own (Eurocentric) norms to evaluate behaviours by the town's Aborigines that might be acceptable under the Aborigines' own set of cultural values. Cowlishaw also shows that institutional racism was rife in 'Brindletown'. For example, policing methods were often intrusive, the organisation of the health system and hospital lacked cultural sensitivity, and Aboriginal studies was given a marginal place in the school curriculum.

Jan Pettman (1992) claims that women are often forgotten in analyses of racism. She argues that racism and sexism have often combined and that women are frequently the greatest victims of both racist beliefs and contexts of institutional racism. She argues that for the past two centuries Aboriginal women have been the victims of colonialism. White colonisation 'ruptured the close association with kin and place, including the places where Aboriginal women's ceremonies made sense' (1992, p. 27). As the colonial frontier expanded, Aboriginal women were often the victims of sexual violence and other forms of exploitation, such as state interference in Aboriginal families, which saw children forcibly taken away from their mothers (the Stolen Generations), and the use of Aboriginal women as domestic servants.

Pettman also suggests that migrant women have been especially disadvantaged. For many women the experience of migration has been one of isolation, exhaustion and anxiety, particularly for those without English language skills. Migrant women have also been located at the bottom of the employment structure, occupying jobs with the worst conditions and pay. Pettman argues that concerns about racist/sexual violence often restrict the mobility of migrant women—for example, preventing them from using public transport or from going out at night.

Racism in the Australian media

The mass media are understood by sociologists to be a major vehicle for the transmission of racist beliefs and prejudices. Many ethnic groups in Australia consider themselves to have been the victims of media stereotyping. It has been argued that stories about 'Filipino mail-order brides', 'increased numbers of Asian students' and 'Arab extremists' have all been associated with increases in racial and ethnic hatred. However, it is media coverage of Australian Aborigines that has aroused the greatest controversy. Aboriginal groups claim that they are persistently portrayed in a negative light by the media and that the media reinforce popular prejudice about them. As an example, Aborigines in the Sydney suburb of Redfern were outraged by a July 1989 *Sixty Minutes* program (National Inquiry into Racist Violence in Australia 1991), which depicted Redfern from a police perspective. Viewer identification with the police was promoted by the fact that much of the footage was taken from within a patrol car at night, while Aborigines on the streets were spotlighted like wild animals.

More recently, critics on the left (e.g. Kelly 2004) have pointed to media coverage of 'riots' in Redfern such as those in February 2004 following the death of T. J. Hickey, a 17-year-old Aboriginal youth who was impaled on a metal fence following a bicycle crash. It has been alleged that Hickey was being chased by police at the time of the accident. Coverage of the riots focused on questions of individual moral responsibility and the failure of the Aboriginal leadership to control young people. There was little sustained discussion of the economic and social contexts that formed a background to the unrest, such as colonialism, racism and unemployment. Moreover, Aborigines continued to be represented as 'the problem', when arguably it was the police force or the broader social system that needed fixing.

More than half of the allegations of racial and ethnic bias adjudicated by the Australian Press Council between 1977 and 1984 concerned Aboriginal items. It is important to realise that racism in the media is not simply important because it can offend and upset people. As the Royal Commission into Aboriginal Deaths in Custody found, it can have very real consequences in contributing to a climate of distrust and racial oppression.

During the 1980s David Trigger (1995) conducted one of the most systematic investigations of the coverage of Aboriginal issues in the Australian media. Trigger looked at 2408 items in the *West Australian* and five rural newspapers between 1984 and 1988. He coded the items according to whether stories featuring ethnic groups or members of ethnic groups had a generally positive or negative message. Criteria for coding a story in a positive way included 'the attractive features of a group or individual'. This might include stories about sporting or cultural achievements, community development or community leadership. Negatively coded stories usually referred to criminal activity and, in the case of Aborigines, the 'threat' presented by land rights claims. The results indicated that Aboriginal groups received far more negative coverage than any other group, and that the ratio of good to bad coverage was exceeded only by stories about Asians.

In discussing the actual topics covered in the stories, Trigger writes:

Overall, the Aboriginal affairs content of both the metropolitan and five selected rural newspapers was disproportionately negative and focused on Aboriginal criminality. Aboriginal subjects were virtually unique among items covering ethnic groups in their focus on alcohol and drunkenness. Items concerning Aborigines were much more likely to portray conflict with other sections of Australian society than to indicate a cooperative relationship. There was also much more treatment of conflict than cooperation among Aboriginal people themselves. (1995, p. 109)

Because it uses quantitative methods David Trigger's study of racism in the Australian media is somewhat unusual. The most common approach has been to interpret and decode media texts from a cultural studies perspective (see also the discussion of *Myths of Oz* above). *Racism, Ethnicity and the Media*, edited by Andrew Jakubowicz (1994) and written by Heather Goodall, Andrew Jakubowicz, Jeannie Martin, Tony Mitchell, Lois Randall and Kalinga Seneviratne, argues that the media perpetuate racist myths and stereotypes and homogenise cultural differences. This theme is exemplified in their analysis of images of Aboriginal Australians. Positive images of Aborigines (often found in advertising) typically placed them in remote and rural settings and as engaged in 'traditional' roles and activities. By contrast, negative images of Aboriginal Australians (usually found in the news) spoke of fighting, crime and disorder in urban contexts.

According to Jakubowicz et al., this coverage separated Aboriginal and non-Aboriginal people and made Aborigines the objects of a white gaze. They argue that these images confirm popular ideas about Aboriginal people as an 'other' who do not belong in a modern society and fix them as 'distant and iconic, rather than people here and now and real!' (1994, p. 60). According to Jakubowicz et al., Aboriginal Australians remain marginal in television in other ways as well. The vast majority of soaps and advertisements feature no Aboriginal actors and very few 'ethnic' Australians either. By contrast, most actors are white, Anglo-Celtic Australians who are used to promote Eurocentric images of Australia. For Jakubowicz et al. series such as *Neighbours* do little for multiculturalism and instead present imaginary images of Australia as it might have been without postwar migration.

Reflective questions: What forms does racism take in Australia today? Look through the text to find examples of racist outcomes based on (a) nasty attitudes and sentiments, (b) benevolent but lazy thinking, (c) unintended consequences to action and (d) institutional racism.

Tutorial exercise

You have the misfortune to find yourself sitting next to a racist on the bus from Adelaide to Perth. This person just won't stop talking and there's not a lot to look at outside except for desert—then it gets dark. She goes on and on about what is wrong with Aborigines and migrants. To alleviate your boredom you decide to enter into a debate with her. Drawing on this chapter, in groups assemble a number of talking points that can be used to change her perspective. (Note: This is a very long bus trip, but you should be able to find a lot of arguments to throw against her.)

For activity suggestions, learning aids, revision of key concepts and access to self-study material, visit: **www.pearson.com.au/highered/vankrieken4e**

Further reading

Broome, R. 2001, *Aboriginal Australians*, 3rd edn, Allen & Unwin, Sydney.
Castles, S., Foster, W., Iredale, R. & Withers, G. 1998, *Immigration and Australia*, Allen & Unwin, Sydney.
Cowlishaw, G. 2004, *Blackfellas, Whitefellas and the Hidden Injuries of Race*, Blackwell, Malden, Mass.
Elder, C. 2008, *Being Australian: Narratives of National Identity*, Allen & Unwin, Sydney.
Fenton, S. 2003, *Ethnicity (Key Concepts)*, Polity Press, Cambridge.
Solomos, J. 2002, *Theories of Race and Racism: A Reader*, Routledge, London.

Websites

Australian Human Rights Commission:
www.hreoc.gov.au/Social_Justice/statistics/index.html
This organisation has done an outstanding job collecting and presenting information from various sources, and the section on Aboriginal and Torres Straight Islander issues is excellent.

Links to Resources in Ethnic/Racial Movements:
www.ssc.wisc.edu/~oliver/soc220/ethniclinkssorted.htm
Coordinated by Professor Pamela Oliver of the University of Wisconsin, Madison, this site has links to various other websites dealing with race, racism and ethnic issues.

Migration Information Source:
www.migrationinformation.org
This useful site contains news items, current data and research.

The Nationalism Project:
www.nationalismproject.org
This website intends to further our understanding of nationalism, and has various resources and links that might be helpful.

# Gender and Sexuality

The examination of gender and sexuality has moved from being a marginal concern to one of the most dynamic fields of sociological theorising and research. This chapter outlines the main theoretical perspectives and core research concerns in the sociology of gender and sexuality.

By the end of the chapter, you should have a better understanding of:
— the sociological definitions of sex, gender and sexuality
— biological approaches to sex, and how sociological approaches differ
— the key sociological perspectives on gender identity, including those of role theory, Nancy Chodorow, Bronwyn Davies and R. W. Connell on 'masculinities'
— the main approaches to sexual identity, including Rich on 'compulsory heterosexuality', Kinsey, social constructionist approaches, Foucault and queer theory
— proposals and suggestions for transforming gender relations, particularly the women's movement/feminism, the gay and lesbian movement, and queer sexual politics.

INTRODUCTION	**284**
Sex, gender and sexuality	285
BIOLOGY, CULTURE, SEX AND GENDER	**285**
Sociobiology—the evolution of human behaviour	286
Criticisms of sociobiological theories	286
Sex roles—Talcott Parsons	287
Sigmund Freud	288
The problem of cultural diversity	289
Gender as 'expression'—Erving Goffman	289
Sociology, biology and the body	290
GENDER IDENTITY	**291**
Role theory	291
Criticisms of role theory	292
The Reproduction of Mothering—Nancy Chodorow	293
Male gender personality	293
Female gender personality	293
Criticisms of Chodorow	294
Frogs and Snails and Feminist Tales—Bronwyn Davies	295
Masculinities—Raewyn Connell	296
Active bodies	296
Hegemonic masculinity	297
Men's life histories	297
The history of masculinities	299
The 'gender order'	301
TRANSFORMING GENDER AND SEXUALITY	**301**
The women's movement/feminism	302
The gay and lesbian movement	302
SEXUAL IDENTITY AND BEYOND—HETEROSEXUAL, HOMOSEXUAL, QUEER	**303**
Criticisms of 'categorical' theory	303
Compulsory heterosexuality—Adrienne Rich	304
Criticisms of Rich	304
Continuums of sexual behaviour—Alfred Kinsey et al.	305
Criticisms of Kinsey	306
The psychology of gender and sexuality after Kinsey	307
Sexual Conduct—John Gagnon and William Simon	308
Sexual scripts	308
Sex as a powerful 'natural' drive	310
Scripting theory	310
An ethnomethodological approach—Suzanne Kessler and Wendy McKenna	311
Sexuality and power—Michel Foucault	312
Beyond sexual 'identity'—queer sexuality	312
Critiques of queer theory	313
Queer sexual politics	314
SOCIOLOGY AND THE FUTURE OF GENDER AND SEXUALITY	**315**
Tutorial exercises	317
Further reading	317
Websites	317

INTRODUCTION

A central figure in the sociology of gender and sexuality is Agnes, an American woman probably born around 1939 (it's hard to tell from the literature on her). As Raewyn Connell puts it, she 'would have grown up with Vivien Leigh, Grace Kelly, *I Love Lucy*, and Elvis Presley when he could still sing. She would have married about the time Betty Friedan published *The Feminine Mystique*, would have been rising 30 when women's liberation began' (Connell 2009, p. 105). Agnes had been born a boy, but had deliberately learnt how to live as a girl and then as a woman, actively transforming her body by ingesting female hormones. Her experience was a reference point for a number of important studies of gender and sexuality by Robert Stoller, Harold Garfinkel, Kessler and McKenna, and West and Zimmerman, as well as a number of controversies around those studies. As what came to be known as a 'transsexual', Agnes represented for many social scientists a number of fundamental things about everyone's gender and sexual identity—the fact that it is not simply natural, but something that is achieved through focused effort, and constantly performed in everyday interactions. The experiences of transsexual and intersexed people show that we are all caught up in the politics of differing ways of ordering gender relations, and in the requirement to produce and perform our gender and sexual identity.

One is not born a woman, but becomes one. (de Beauvoir 1972, orig. 1949)

Alongside race and ethnicity, one of the most pervasive ways in which human beings categorise each other is by **gender** and **sexuality**. From the moment we are born, we are understood and treated as male or female. By the time we become teenagers, we are treated and understand ourselves as straight, gay or some mixture of the two. It is possible to speak of 'sexual citizenship', in that our sexual identity underpins a range of legal, social and political rights, entitlements and obligations (Evans 1993). Although sociology as a discipline has not always paid a great deal of attention to gender and sexuality, from about the middle of the 20th century onwards more and more sociologists, especially symbolic interactionists, have analysed the social construction of gender and sexual identity.

There is cultural and historical variation in approaches to homosexuality, but certainly in Western cultures gay men and lesbians have to struggle for social recognition and are often refused access to basic rights of citizenship. The current concern about gay marriage is just one example of this kind of social and political struggle. With the development of women's, gay and lesbian liberation movements, and 'queer' sexual politics, as well as some doubts among heterosexual men about masculinity, the explanation for such differences has been hotly debated. The HIV/AIDS epidemic also gave additional significance to the understanding of the forms taken by human sexual practices. There are, then, a number of reasons for the study of gender and sexuality having increasingly become a focus of sociological research.

There are three dimensions or aspects of sexual identity around which this research has been organised:

1. **sex**—the biological dimensions of human gender and sexual identity
2. gender—the social organisation of those biological dimensions, generally into something recognisable as masculinity or femininity
3. sexuality—the sexual practices associated with sex and gender, which are then understood in terms of categories such as homosexuality, heterosexuality, bisexuality or queer sexuality.

The term **sexual identity** will be used to refer to all three dimensions. Most research focuses on one or two of these dimensions at a time, and there is no necessary relationship between them. It is certainly necessary to avoid seeing issues related to sexuality as simply equivalent to those concerning gender. As Gayle Rubin has pointed out, 'although sex and gender are related, they are not the same thing, and they form the basis of two distinct arenas of social practice' (1984, p. 308).

However, at the same time it also remains important to see all three as interlinked. Feminine or masculine gender identity exists only within the framework of experiences of a body sexed as female or male, and within the context of sexual practices understood as expressing that feminine or masculine identity. One of the most important lines of debate is the extent to which it is accurate to see human beings as placed within discrete categories in relation to each of these dimensions. For example, should people be regarded as either homosexual or heterosexual, or perhaps as bisexual, 'metrosexual' or 'queer'? Should we see ourselves and each other as either masculine or feminine, or as placed somewhere on a continuum of intermediate categories?

Sex, gender and sexuality

The distinction between *sex* and *gender* is often used as a starting point for the analysis of sexual identity. Sigmund Freud laid its foundations when he argued that the terms 'masculinity' and 'femininity' had three different types of meaning—biological, psychological and sociological—and that human sexuality was formed more within social (familial) relationships than derived from biology. John Money began using the term 'gender' in 1955 to refer to the sexual identity of patients with indeterminate genital organs. This point was further developed into a sex/gender distinction by American psychoanalyst Robert Stoller (1968). In his study of varieties of sexual identity, Stoller began with the observation that the majority of the population can clearly be categorised as physiologically male or female, with differences that enable women and not men to bear and suckle children. These differences are what the term 'sex' refers to. However, argued Stoller:

Gender is a term that has psychological or cultural rather than biological connotations. If the proper terms for sex are 'male' and 'female', the corresponding terms for gender are 'masculine' and 'feminine'; these latter might be quite independent of (biological) sex. (1968, p. 9)

As John Money (1990) formulated it, gender is 'Barbie and Ken doll' sex, 'without the dirty part that belongs to the genitalia and reproduction'. In other words, there is no necessary association between being biologically female and being 'feminine', or between being biologically male and being 'masculine'. Just as we can perceive Barbie as obviously female and Ken as obviously male without anything between their legs, girls and women are not caring and compassionate simply because of their female anatomy, and boys are not aggressive and competitive simply because of their male anatomy.

Anthropologists such as Margaret Mead gathered a body of evidence in the 1930s and 1940s that indicated an enormous variety in sexual identities in different cultures around the world. As Peter Berger and Thomas Luckmann (1971) summed up the discussion:

Human sexuality is characterized by a very high degree of pliability . . . relatively independent of temporal rhythms, it is pliable both in the objects towards which it may be directed and in its modalities of expression. Ethnological evidence shows that, in sexual matters, man is capable of almost anything. (p. 67)

Although each culture patterns sexual behaviour into definite configurations, the immense variety of those configurations, their 'luxurious inventiveness, indicate that they are the products of man's own sociocultural formations rather than of a biologically fixed human nature' (1971, p. 67).

This is still the most widely accepted view in sociology today, but the issue is far from settled in the public arena. The belief that it is 'natural' for men and women to behave in particular ways, that it is 'natural' for their sexuality to take particular forms, is very persistent and seems to enjoy considerable 'scientific' support. This is partly because a central feature of the understanding of sexuality throughout the history of Western Christianity has been to attribute its essential characteristics to the realm of 'nature'. This first section will outline the various approaches to sex and gender in terms of 'natural difference'.

BIOLOGY, CULTURE, SEX AND GENDER

Raewyn Connell commented that frequently 'the notion of natural sex difference forms a limit beyond which thought cannot go' (1987, p. 66). The idea that sex differences have a basis in biology finds adherents from a variety of perspectives. An appeal to nature is attractive to those who wish to argue against feminist and gay critiques of existing gender arrangements, to feminists wishing to assert what is specific about female identity, and to homosexuals hoping to find a solid, indisputable base for their sexual identity in biology.

Connell identified two major versions of 'the doctrine of natural difference':

1. In the first version, society is regarded as an epiphenomenal superstructure built on top of a material, biological basis.
2. In the second, society is seen as complementary or 'additive' to biology.

In the first type, the biologically based approach, gender is determined by biology.

Sociobiology—the evolution of human behaviour

The sociobiological approach to gender and sexuality is essentially an application of Darwin's theory of biological evolution through the process of natural selection to the development of human behaviour over time. Proponents of sociobiology like Edward Wilson (1975a) and David Barash (1979) argue not just that human behaviour undergoes evolutionary change, but that this evolution is driven by the same principles as natural selection, by a concern to maximise the survival chances of the species. Gender differences in behaviour are thus interpreted as manifestations of strategies for maximising the passing of genes from one generation to the next.

More recently, similar types of explanations of gender differences have been routinely discussed in the popular media, referring to biological differences such as the production of testosterone in males and oestrogen in females, or differences in brain function. More recent versions of the approach include Steven Pinker's *The Blank Slate: The Modern Denial of Human Nature* (2002) and Randy Thornhill and Craig Palmer's *The Natural History of Rape: Biological Bases of Sexual Coercion* (2000).

Both Wilson and Barash argue that if we look at one basic biological difference between men and women—males produce trillions of sperm in their lifetime, whereas women produce far fewer ova, only one per menstrual cycle, and the foetus gestates in the woman's body—this can be seen as the basis of many aspects of gender differences. Men are simply biologically programmed to impregnate as many women as possible, whereas women are more concerned with the care of their offspring. This then explains why men are likely to be more promiscuous, while women are likely to be more circumspect in their pursuit of the best possible genetic partner. Any male 'will profit more if he can inseminate additional females, even at the risk of losing that portion of exclusive fitness invested in the offspring of his first mate' (Wilson, 1975a, p. 314). Wilson said that 'the courted sex, usually the female, will … find it strongly advantageous to distinguish the really fit from the pretended fit' (p. 320) and that females improve their ability to discriminate between males through coyness.

From a sociobiological perspective, these evolutionary mechanisms are meant to underpin a greater tolerance for infidelity by their partners among women than men. The fact that motherhood is more certain than fatherhood means, for sociobiologists, that female infidelity is more of a concern for males than male infidelity is for females. From this perspective, it is also perfectly understandable why polygamy (more than one woman married to one man) is more frequently practiced than polyandry (more than one man married to one woman). A woman's search for the best male to father her children also leads her to see males of a higher social status and income as particularly desirable. Much of social and political life, from a sociobiological perspective, can be explained in terms of males competing with each other for the benefits of female reproductive capacity. Although Wilson (1975a) conceded that humans may in fact be guided by different principles in their behaviour, it remained the case that in terms of efficient biological reproduction, the rules governing gender and sexuality were clear.

Criticisms of sociobiological theories

There are a number of serious conceptual problems with such an explanation of differences between males and females based on the supposed 'requirements' of successful evolution. First, it is not clear that there is any close linkage between the 'interests' of biological survival and human behaviour without the intervention of social learning—in other words, whether humans can 'know' what they are 'supposed' to do without learning it from each other. Janet Sayers has pointed out that even in the baboon societies studied by sociobiologists, dominance behaviour was learned and not determined biologically:

> *If dominance behaviour is a learned phenomenon among non-human primates, then it is more than likely also to be learned among humans—that is, a response to environmental and social factors rather than mechanistically determined by biology. (1982, p. 75)*

Indeed, human behaviour is more likely to be based on learning. Rose, Kamin and Lewontin noted that, unlike most animals:

The human infant is born with relatively few of its neural pathways already committed. During its long infancy connections between nerve cells are formed not merely on the basis of specific epigenetic programming but in the light of experience. (1984, p. 145)

As Connell summarised, this means that human action cannot be regarded as determined by biological dispositions, because it is 'highly structured in a collective sense; it is constituted interactively' (1987, p. 69).

Second, human behaviour is approached simply in terms of what is assumed to be characteristic of Western societies. Animal behaviour is analysed using concepts and imagery derived from human society, describing females as 'coy' and males as 'aggressive', without any awareness of different societies or the range of actual behaviour exhibited by men and women in Western societies. The anthropological evidence shows that there are many societies in which women are the sexual aggressors and men are 'coy', and social psychological studies of Western societies indicate that aggression depends more on the structure of social relations than on gender.

Connell referred to sociobiology as 'pseudo-biological', because it interprets animal behaviour in terms of loose analogies culturally derived from the writers' own gender stereotypes. Thus the conceptions that sociobiologists reflect to their readers—although packaged as 'science' and based in biology—are themselves social constructions and what many readers already assume and wish to believe.

Third, evidence from the animal world is used selectively, ignoring examples of animal species where males are not aggressive and dominant, and disregarding the learning that takes place among animals. Bleier (1984) noted that in some species of ape and monkey there are no dominance hierarchies at all. In others, such as Japanese macaques, the rank of a male within the troop depends on the rank of his mother. There are examples of female apes who 'protect territory, fight for their own or other mothers' young, take food from males, and bond with other females to fight aggressive males' (Bleier 1984, p. 31).

Leonard Rosenblum also emphasised that non-human primates exhibit possibly the greatest variety of sexual behaviours in the animal world; males and females can spend most of their time with either sex, and they engage in the copulatory postures of either sex, and under a variety of conditions:

It is by no means unusual to observe ... males mounting males, females mounting females, and even females mounting males in a manner that to the casual observer may be indistinguishable from reproductively successful male–female coitus. (1990, pp. 170–1)

In short, in the sociobiological account of human behaviour, the evidence that contradicts a dichotomised model of gender behaviour is ignored. This is why most sociologists will regard sociobiological approaches as tended too much towards attempting to reduce the very complex phenomenon that is gender and sexuality to an oversimplified conception of human 'nature'.

Sex roles—Talcott Parsons

Biologically based explanations of the behaviour of men and women have not been confined to those that have located differences in hormones, brains or genes. Other writers have approached gender roles in terms of more obvious biological differences between males and females, especially in relation to the fact that women give birth. This approach was identified by Connell as the second general type of 'natural difference theory', which sees society not as constrained by biology but as additive to biology. From this perspective, society 'culturally elaborates the distinction between the sexes' (1987, p. 73).

We saw in Chapter 4 that Talcott Parsons regarded the nuclear family as having two basic functions—the socialisation of children and the stabilisation of personality in adults—and that he saw gender in terms of complementary roles required to fulfil these two functions. On the one hand, the father's 'instrumental' role is to compete in the world of work and maximise his ability to provide financial support and protection for the family as a whole. On the other hand, the mother's 'expressive' role is providing emotional warmth, security and support for both the children and their father. Children require emotional care, and fathers need emotional sustenance and support in the 'haven in a heartless world' (Lasch 1977) for which women are responsible.

Parsons claimed that there were two reasons for this differential allocation of roles between women and men within family life. First, he stated:

The fundamental explanation of the allocation of roles between the biological sexes lies in the fact that the bearing and early nursing of children establish a strong presumptive primacy of the relation of mother to the small child. (1955a, p. 23)

SOCIOLOGY

Because mothers bear and nurse children, they have a closer and stronger relationship with them. This is particularly so in modern industrial society because the isolation of the nuclear family:

> *focuses the responsibility of the mother role more sharply on one adult woman ... furthermore, the fact of the frequent absence of the husband-father from the home premises so much of the time means that she has to take the primary responsibility for the children. (1955a, p. 23)*

Second, he pointed out that this linkage of women to the mothering role produces an asymmetry of sex-role identification processes between boys and girls, which in turn lays the foundations for the later differentiation between instrumentalism and expressivism. In the course of the Oedipus complex, the boy is meant to:

> *substitute a new identification with an unfamiliar and in a very important sense threatening object, the father, at the expense of his previous solidarity with his mother. (Parsons 1955b, p. 98)*

The boy is thus supposed to give up his emotional dependency in 'a more radical sense' than the girl because he is meant to change identification, while the girl can more or less happily continue her sex-role identification with her mother, although she is supposed to change object-choice (see Figure 9.1). Male instrumentalism is thus attained only in the course of a movement away from an original expressiveness within the mother–child relationship, a movement that Parsons believed subjects boys to 'greater strain' and produces a 'tenderness taboo'.

Although Parsons moved further away from biology than the sociobiologists, he saw the sexual division of labour as closely related to biological differences between the sexes, presuming that biological considerations automatically make child-rearing primarily a female task.

So far we have examined the major arguments that approach gender identity in terms of biological differences between the sexes. Although these arguments allow some variation in the way gender roles are played, they all utilise the idea of 'natural' difference to portray gender identities as relatively constant and unalterable.

However, reliance on the concept of more or less 'natural' gender differences has been challenged by a range of psychologists, anthropologists and sociologists. We look first at Sigmund Freud, then the studies of cultural diversity, and finally examine Erving Goffman's critique of the idea of an 'essential' gender or sexual identity.

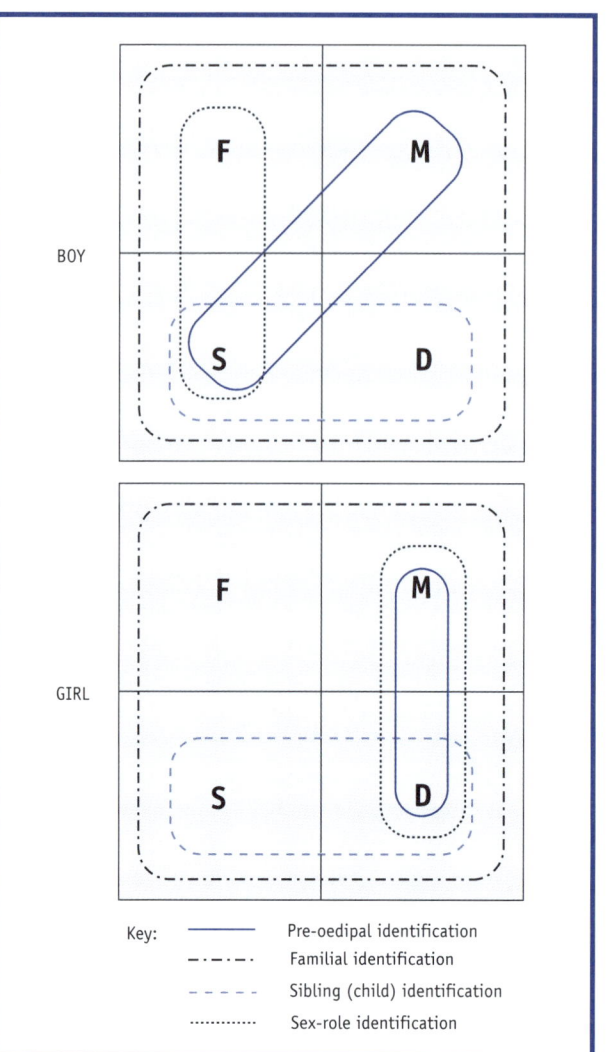

FIGURE 9.1

The basis of sex-role identification in the nuclear family *Source:* Parsons (1955b, p. 99).

SIGMUND FREUD

Sigmund Freud (1856–1939) always hoped to uncover the biological foundations of human behaviour, and he is often seen as arguing for a presocial, 'natural' sexual instinct that opposes social conventions. This is the interpretation of Freud preferred and promoted by writers such as Parsons.

However, Freud's account of the development of sexuality is one of a social rather than a biological process. For Freud, masculinity and femininity had no basis whatsoever in biology, and emerged only in social interaction within family life. Placed within the context of his whole theory of sexuality, it becomes clear that Freud's famous comment 'Anatomy is destiny' was meant to capture the significance that was socially attributed to physical sex differences in the cultural formation of gender identity, not to assert that sexual identity was biologically derived.

His understanding of sexuality itself is better captured by the word 'drive' than 'instinct'; he saw only a vague 'drivenness' as being biologically based, and felt that the two other 'components' of the sexual drive—its 'object' (the person or thing eroticised) and its 'aim' (what one wishes to do with erotic tension: relieve, delay, heighten or displace it)—could emerge only in the course of a person's development as a social being. For Freud there was thus only a drive towards some sort of sexual activity, but no instinct for anything in particular—the form taken by human sexuality could only be determined at the level of society and culture.

Freud saw humans at birth as **polymorphously perverse**, able to gain physical pleasure from an enormous range of bodily activities, and as essentially bisexual, with a particular sexual orientation being constructed within familial relations. For Freud, the basis of sexual orientation was defined in negative rather than positive terms, more strongly an aversion towards one sex than a positive sense of desire for the other.

THE PROBLEM OF CULTURAL DIVERSITY

Another very basic problem with seeing gender differences as 'natural' is the enormous diversity of gender roles across human cultures, a diversity that should not be possible if gender were based on biological nature. The cross-cultural evidence gathered by anthropologists, beginning with Malinowski, Benedict and Mead, indicates that there is no natural or inevitable division of labour or allocation of social roles on the basis of biological sex.

In relation to the sexual division of labour, Claude Lévi-Strauss (1956) argued that what was universal was that every culture had some division of labour organised along gender lines, but the form it took was almost infinitely variable. As he put it, the very fact that the sexual division of labour:

varies endlessly according to the society selected for consideration shows that ... it is the mere fact of its existence which is mysteriously required, the form under which it comes to exist being utterly irrelevant, at least from the point of view of any natural necessity. (p. 275)

The sexual division of labour was thus 'nothing else than a device to institute a reciprocal state of dependency between the sexes' (p. 276).

Ann Oakley (1974a) pointed out that when one looks at the anthropological and cross-cultural evidence about gender behaviour around the world, the sheer variety of gender roles across different cultures, despite the shared basic biological dispositions, makes it difficult to grant biological differences very much of an explanatory status in comparison to cultural divergences. For example, if there are a number of cultural contexts where women engage in heavy physical labour, this undermines the argument that they are simply biologically incapable of such activity (1974a, p. 170). Even mothering is approached in very different ways in different cultural settings, making it impossible to identify a 'natural' way to be mother that is found in all human groups.

For Oakley, Parson's analysis said a lot more about his own beliefs and values, and those dominant in American society, than it did about the reality of gender experience. She suggested that the 'expressive' female role was less an essential function of the family and more a matter of convenience for men. Overall, she thought it was more accurate to see gender roles as determined by culture, and therefore as variable depending on the values and beliefs prevailing in any particular historical period or social context.

GENDER AS 'EXPRESSION'— ERVING GOFFMAN

There are also a number of basic logical problems in the notion that gender is a manifestation of a biological nature. Erving Goffman (1979) pointed out that the appeal to biology in relation to gender reflects the general assumption that any 'object' of analysis must be the 'expression' of something underlying it, some 'essential nature'—hence the widespread belief that one of the most deep-seated human characteristics is gender; 'femininity and masculinity are in a sense the prototypes of essential expression—something that can be conveyed fleetingly in any social situation and yet something that strikes at the most basic characterization of the individual' (1979, p. 7).

Goffman identified three problems with this notion of gender as a manifestation or expression of an essential nature:

1. In any situation where any entity or trait is expressed, what is expressed 'is not so much the character or overall structure of an entity (if such there be) but rather particular, situationally bound features relevant to the viewer' (p. 7). Any

particular man or woman will thus display their supposedly essential masculinity or femininity only in the ways appropriate to the immediate social context, not in ways somehow 'true' to their essential maleness or femaleness.

2. The means by which humans express anything are themselves 'not instinctive but socially learned and socially patterned' (p. 7). Indeed, Goffman argued that one of the most important things we learn is how to present ourselves as natural, unfaked, spontaneous; we learn:

> to be objects that have a character, that express this character, and for whom this characterological expressing is only natural. We are socialized to confirm our own hypotheses about our natures. (p. 7)

3. The social situations in which gender is expressed are more than simply 'a convenient field' for the 'natural expression' of gender; they are not established for that purpose. The configuration of gender expression is 'intrinsically, not merely incidentally, a consequence of what can be generated in social situations' (p. 7). In other words, gender expresses the requirements of social situations, not an 'essential human nature'.

Sociology, biology and the body

Social scientists now generally agree that biological sex differences are a poor guide to the range of human behaviour. Indeed, a moment's reflection would show that the role of biology must be a relatively minor one—a very elaborate cultural machinery of instruction (including sociobiology itself), example, imitation, rehearsal, supervision and inspection, constantly backed by sanctions varying from social disapproval to physical violence, seems to be necessary to anchor masculinity and femininity into our recalcitrant natures. More often, the evidence indicates a varied continuum of behaviours that fit badly into the dichotomous categories of masculine or feminine.

As Gayle Rubin argued, a large part of the problem has been the creation of gender, the very insistence on seeing men and women as somehow 'essentially' different from each other, at the expense of noticing the similarities:

> Men and women are, of course, different. But they are not as different as night and day, earth and sky, yin and yang, life and death. In fact, from the standpoint of nature, men and women are closer to each other than either is to anything else—for instance, mountains, kangaroos, or coconut palms. The idea that men and women are more different from one another than either is from anything else must come from somewhere other than nature ... the idea that men and women are two mutually exclusive categories must arise out of something other than a non-existent 'natural' opposition. Far from being an expression of natural differences, exclusive gender identity is the suppression of natural similarities. It requires repression: in men, of whatever is the local version of 'feminine' traits; in women, of the local definition of 'masculine' traits. (1975, pp. 179–80)

The general tendency today in social scientific studies of sex and gender is to try to move beyond an either/or debate about whether biology or society determines human behaviour, and to see sex and gender as interacting with each other. David Morgan, for example, emphasised 'the intimate interplay between the biological and the cultural' (1975, p. 157). What matters most is the meaning attached to differences, real or imagined, in a society.

John Money (1990) has also pointed out that socialisation itself has a biological dimension, in that learning has effects that can be permanently 'cemented into the brain'. One of the mistakes of too simple an opposition between biology and society is the assumption that whatever human beings learn they can always unlearn. In fact, the acquisition of culture (e.g. language) has effects on human physiology that very much resemble those of biological inheritance.

As Money summarised it, debates about sex and gender used to be organised around an opposition between biology and society, between nature and nurture. The paradigm he argued for is that of three elements, often stages, in human development:

1. nature or biology; for example, genitals, hormonal make-up and so on
2. a 'critical period' of interaction between biological and social factors, which can produce irreversible and immutable effects—the most famous example is Konrad Lorenz's ducklings demonstration, where the ducklings became imprinted, as if it were 'biological', not to a real duck, but to Lorenz, because he squatted and waddled like a duck during the ducklings' critical post-hatching period
3. nurture or socialisation; for example, learning the social rules and patterns governing masculinity

versus femininity, or heterosexuality versus homosexuality—patterns that can also be unlearned.

Because socialisation itself has effects that resemble closely the determinant character so often sought in biology, Money argued that the crucial issue then becomes not whether sexual identity is biologically innate or socially acquired, but the extent to which it is mutable (changeable) or immutable.

Nonetheless, at least two problems remain unresolved for a sociological understanding of sexuality and sexual identity, as we shall see in the following sections.

1. The first is that the notion of biology as a possible 'bedrock' of human sexual identity still has enormous appeal, and often structures the logic used by researchers who would otherwise claim to reject the concept of biological determinism.
2. Second, in the process of rejecting any reduction of social actions and relation to biological facts, sociologists have tended towards a kind of **sociological determinism**, where the body and biology are seen as simply the product of social relations. In his book *The Body and Society*, Bryan Turner argues that 'the social sciences have often neglected the most obvious "fact" about human beings, namely that they have bodies and they are embodied' (1984, p. 227).

There have been some discussions of the body in social relations, including anthropologist Marcel Mauss' 1935 article 'Techniques of the body' (1973), and Norbert Elias' 1939 study of the historical development of the relations between psychic structure, bodily experiences and social relations in his book *The Civilizing Process* (1994). However, such inclusions of the body into social analysis have until recently tended to remain on the margins of sociological thought.

This general orientation began to shift in the 1970s, when Italian Marxist Sebastiono Timpanaro (1975) argued for an extension of the Marxist understanding of the 'material base' of society, to go beyond economic conditions and include natural or biological conditions. At the time, wrote Michèle Barrett, his argument represented 'what is currently regarded as a reprehensible determinist position', introducing 'a biological bogeyman into our all too cerebral disputes' (1981, p. 344).

However, more and more sociologists (e.g. Turner 1984; Shilling 1993; 2005; the journal *Body and Society*) are developing an analysis of social relations and interaction that treats the human body as more than a blank canvas upon which an infinite variety of social relationships can be painted.

Reflective question: Sociologists have generally been concerned to 'denaturalise' gender and sexuality. What does this mean?

GENDER IDENTITY

Whatever influence biology does exert on human sexuality, it achieves meaning and significance only within socially and culturally defined relationships. From an *interactionist perspective*, it can be argued that sexual identity should be seen as the outcome of human practices that continually transform, re-create and give meaning to both biological sex and socially defined models of gender.

For Erving Goffman (1979), gender consisted primarily of the practice of *portraying* gender. He argued that the nature of males and females consists of:

a capacity to learn to provide and to read depictions of masculinity and femininity and a willingness to adhere to a schedule for presenting these pictures, a capacity they have by virtue of being persons, not females or males. (p. 8)

In summary:

One might just as well say there is no gender identity. There is only a schedule for the portrayal of gender ... And what these portraits most directly tell us about is not gender, or the overall relationship between the sexes, but about the special character and functioning of portraiture. (p. 8)

In this section we examine role theory, Nancy Chodorow's analysis of gender socialisation as the 'reproduction of mothering', Bronwyn Davies' account of the importance of language in the social construction of gender, and one of the more important accounts of the social construction of masculinity.

ROLE THEORY

Probably the most frequently used framework for the analysis of masculine and feminine identities in sociology is **role theory**. Connell sketched the logical core of role theory as having five features. The first two, he stated, identify the basic dramaturgical analogy of an actor and a script, and the other three elaborate on how the 'drama' unfolds:

1. there is an analytical distinction between the person and the social position (role) they occupy
2. to which there is attached a set of behaviours
3. roles are accompanied by expectations or norms appropriate to them

4. which are represented by people in the *counter-positions* surrounding the role
5. who reinforce them with *sanctions*—rewards and punishments (1987, p. 47).

In relation to gender, this means that being male or female is approached in terms of acting out the 'gender role' (sometimes 'sex role') socially defined as appropriate to one's sex: either masculine or feminine. The objects of sociological analysis then become the processes by which individuals, first, play their gender roles and, second, come to internalise those gender roles in the form of a gender identity, usually captured by the concept of socialisation.

Ann Oakley (1972) summarised the role theory approach to how socialisation in modern industrial societies shapes the identity and behaviour of girls and boys from an early age. Socialisation into particular gender roles takes place in a variety of ways. For example, children are responded to in differing ways, which communicates the idea of gender differences—girls' appearance is given more attention than boys' appearance, and boys are more encouraged in physical activity than girls. Any visit to a toy store will make it crystal clear that boys and girls do very different things in different colour schemes. Language is also an important arena of the construction of gender difference, with differing applications of words such a 'naughty', 'good', 'nice', 'strong', 'graceful', 'delicate' and so on. Boys and girls are directed to different activities in the home, and of course they cannot help but notice the gendered differences in adult behaviour, with obvious implications for their own.

Criticisms of role theory

There are six main criticisms of a role theory approach to gender, the first five identified by Connell and the sixth suggested by Goffman's critique of the notion of 'essential nature' (see pp. 289–90):

1. *Neglect of power.* Role theories assume a complementary relationship between masculine and feminine roles. They thus overlook the relations between males and females, and make it impossible to see the power dimensions of those relations. There is a notion of a **gender apartheid**, theoretically different but equal, and, like apartheid in practice, this masks the real relations of power between men and women.
2. *Voluntarism.* Roles appear to revolve around the voluntary, chosen actions of socialising agents (parents, teachers). This has two effects. First, it leaves only a weak explanation for why socialising agents insist on particular roles (by applying sanctions, for instance)—namely, that they were socialised in that way themselves. Second, it cannot explain how roles persist even when people appear to choose not to maintain them—for example, when parents or teachers attempt to raise children in a non-sexist manner. This failure then paves the way for a return to biological explanations.
3. *Biology.* The structural context of roles implicitly becomes biological sex differences. The assumption that there can be only two gender roles is built on a continuing reliance on biological dichotomy, and:

    the underlying image is an invariant biological base and a malleable social superstructure ... The implicit question in sex-role analysis is what particular superstructure has been created in such-and-such circumstances, and how far the biological dichotomy still shows through. (Connell 1987, p. 50)

4. *Normative orientation.* The orientation in role theories is towards what is 'normal', expected or approved role behaviour, rather than towards the way people actually conduct themselves. Variations from what roles are supposed to be can only be conceived of in terms of 'deviance', rather than as normal diversity or as resistance against normative expectations (see Chapter 13). Role theories:

    create the impression that the conventional sex role is the majority case, and that departures from it are socially marginal and likely to be the result of some personal eccentricity, produced by imperfect or inappropriate socialization. (Connell 1987, p. 52)

5. *Inability to grasp the history of gender.* Connell also felt that role theories had a poor sociological understanding of how gender roles develop over time. Changes in gender roles are interpreted as something that happens to people from the outside, a consequence of exogenous social, economic, political or demographic developments, and not in terms of the 'interplay' between the practices and social structures of gender.
6. *Back-door essentialism.* In principle, role theory should allow for the possibility of multiple roles attached to particular social situations. However, the notion of a unified gender role contradicts this principle, because it presupposes a gender role that remains relatively constant and consistent across different social situations. People who have been

socialised into the masculine gender role are thus presumed to remain 'masculine' no matter what social situation they are in. In this sense, the way in which role theory has been applied to gender comes very close, as Connell remarked, to the biological model of an 'essential nature', and the logic of biology or nature is smuggled in through the back door. Goffman's point about this approach is that it neglects the extent to which behaviours are in fact elicited by social situations, rather than somehow emerging from or being expressed by an underlying nature—or acquired gender role.

THE REPRODUCTION OF MOTHERING—NANCY CHODOROW

Margaret Mead remarked in 1949 on a regular asymmetry in sexual psychological development in all cultures: a girl identifies with her first primary caregiver, laying the basis for a 'simple and uncomplicated' identification, whereas a boy's identity is based on a separation from his mother. As she put it: 'at the very start of life, effort, an attempt at greater self-differentiation, is suggested to the boy, while a relaxed acceptance of herself is suggested to the girl' (1949, p. 148). This structural requirement of boys and men to develop their specifically male identity through differentiation from females (the mother) explained a greater orientation towards achievement than among girls and women. Mead felt that the asymmetry was largely based on the fact that women breastfeed, and 'the carry-over into social patterns that, because women breastfeed children, they are also the ones to care for them' (p. 149). If that were to change, states Mead, if 'father and brothers were to take over an equal responsibility for the child … the preoccupations of the developing child would alter, and so might the whole psychology of the sexes' (p. 149). A few years later Parsons made similar comments on the differential development of males and females.

Nancy Chodorow (1978) linked these kinds of observations on the workings of gender socialisation, the arguments about women's social location in the domestic sphere and Rubin's identification of the sex/gender system as the organisation of 'sex, gender, and babies' into a comprehensive account of women's identification as mothers. Feminist studies of sex/gender systems had tended to concentrate on relations between men and women both within and outside family life, but Chodorow extended the analysis to the most important 'products' of sexual interaction between men and women and perhaps the central focus of family life: children.

The starting point of Chodorow's analysis was the psychoanalytic understanding of psychic development from infancy. The infant and mother initially feel themselves as psychically fused with each other, followed by a process of separation and individuation from each other. This process of separation from the mother is central to the formation of an autonomous sense of self. However, the social fact that women are primarily responsible for caring for children, as Mead and Parsons argued, means that this process takes place in very different ways for boys and girls, producing distinct 'gender personalities'.

Male gender personality

Boys and mothers experience themselves as different from each other from the child's birth. Masculine identity is defined negatively, as being not female, based on the ongoing repudiation of boys' initial merging with the mother. Masculinity is thus more precarious than femininity because its role model is more abstract and, because of men's general absence from family life, without a foundation in interaction with real males. Like Parsons, Chodorow saw this characteristic of male psychic development as laying the foundations for the 'instrumental' roles expected of them as they grow up.

Female gender personality

Girls, on the other hand, share with their mothers a sense of having the same gender identity, and retain their identification with their mother in the course of their psychic development. Girls do not have to negate their initial identification with their mother in order to develop a sense of femininity, and they grow up with the sense of interconnectedness with others (similar to their fusion with their mother as infants) required by their 'expressive' gender role.

In summary, Chodorow argued that there is a cyclical relationship between a particular sexual division of labour and corresponding feminine and masculine gender personalities, as shown in Figure 9.2.

The central element of gender differences was, for Chodorow, the development of different forms of relational potential in males and females. The only way to break this cycle, she believed, was for men to take greater responsibility for child care. This would 'degender' the basic process of separation/individuation from the child's initial caregiver, and generate more similar relational patterns among men and women. Janet Sayers

FIGURE 9.2

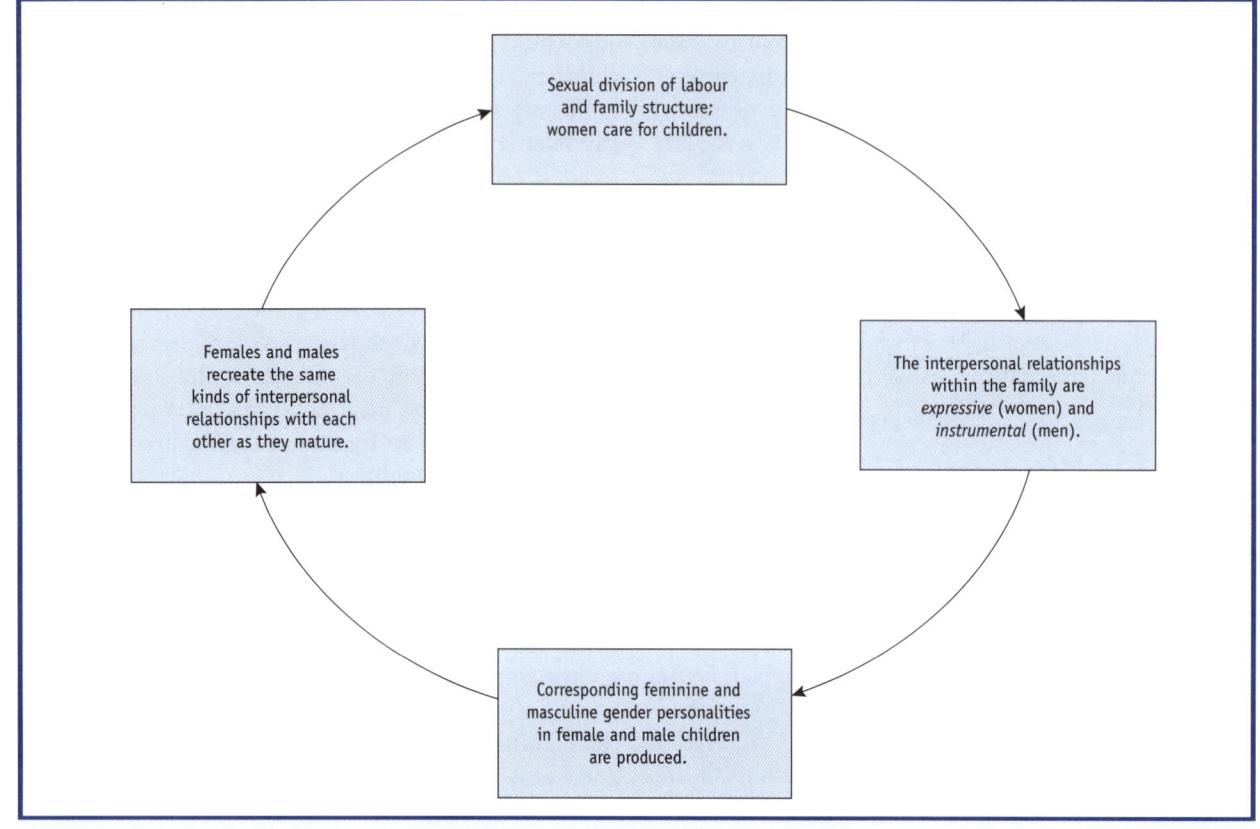

Chodorow's model of gender reproduction

(Cycle: Sexual division of labour and family structure; women care for children. → The interpersonal relationships within the family are *expressive* (women) and *instrumental* (men). → Corresponding feminine and masculine gender personalities in female and male children are produced. → Females and males recreate the same kinds of interpersonal relationships with each other as they mature. → [back to start])

(1986) pointed out that Chodorow's (1978) ideas have 'received widespread acclaim' (p. 71), and are echoed in the work of Carol Gilligan (1982) on gendered styles of morality, the general literature on gender differences and feminist explanations of women's experience of themselves as 'other' to society.

Criticisms of Chodorow

There are a number of problems with Chodorow's analysis. Sayers pointed out that her account seems to be of a self-enclosed process with no exit, and does not explain why some women choose not to merge themselves with their children:

> If women were simply content to be the immanent objects of men's transcendence they would not now be struggling to realize themselves as transcendent, autonomous beings. (1986, p. 76)

In fact, women do 'experience themselves as separate and individuated from others' (p. 76) and it is precisely this experience that underlies feminist thought and action itself. Chodorow's theory does not explain the various forms of women's resistance against oppressive sexual divisions. The obvious extension of this point is that it also seems impossible to explain why and how men might ever become interested in, or even capable of, taking care of children. If they can become male only by negating and denying their connectedness with other human beings, they will be unable to respond to an infant's emotional needs. Chodorow, argued Jennifer Somerville, 'is ultimately guilty of the functionalism from which she set out to escape' (1989, p. 296).

The prescription of shared parenting is a little trite, because it begs the question of how such a goal is to be achieved. Sayers emphasised that it is not simply a matter of 'choosing' to make men more responsible for child care (who would make such a choice?) but of the social organisation of work, the operation of the labour market, men's and women's wages, and child-care provisions. In terms of possible changes to the sex/gender system, Chodorow's analysis eventually collapses into a voluntarism unable to grasp the social dynamics of gender relations.

Chodorow's approach takes no account of possible cultural differences or historical development. There are cultures where women are not primarily responsible for mothering, but where there is still an oppressive sexual division of labour. Several writers have also argued that the notion that biological mothers should have an intense emotional relationship with their children is relatively recent, but this did not prevent the emergence of patriarchal social and economic arrangements.

Her conception of masculine and feminine 'gender personalities' assumes that they are unified psychic (as opposed to social) entities with more difference between than within them. Males and females are put into separate categories of personality structure, with no sense of what differences might exist within the categories, how they might develop and change over time, or possible intermediate positions between the two poles. In this respect, her work has the same problems that haunt psychologists' attempts to measure masculinity and femininity—whether relatively unified psychic entities, recognisable as masculinity and femininity, exist at all (see pp. 000–000).

FROGS AND SNAILS AND FEMINIST TALES— BRONWYN DAVIES

Australian sociologist of education Bronwyn Davies (1989) outlined the ways in which gender differences are produced through a surrounding linguistic context that encourages children's cognition and thought in the direction of a bipolar division of the world into the two categories: male and female.

Davies' research had two components: First, she studied how a group of eight 4–5-year-old children understood and spoke about four feminist stories being read to them. The stories were *The Paper Bag Princess*, *Oliver Button Is a Sissy*, *Rita the Rescuer* and *The Princess and the Dragon*. Second, she observed, recorded and analysed children's behaviour in four different preschools and child-care centres in Armidale, Sydney and Melbourne. A core concern of the study was to explain why it was that attempts to reshape children's gender consciousness through avenues such as feminist rewritings of fairy tales appeared to have so little effect.

Davies' critique of role theory was that there was insufficient recognition of children as active agents, or of the importance of language in setting the scene for children's development of their gendered identity. She observed that language played a crucial role in the maintenance of particular understandings of masculinity and femininity, because 'within the discursive practices made available to children, the only comprehensible identity available to them is as "boy" or "girl", "male" or "female"' (1989, p. 141). The tools that children have at their disposal to signify their position in this duality include 'dress, hairstyle, speech patterns and content, choice of activity' (p. 1). She emphasised that gender is to a large extent 'embedded in the language, in the discursive practices and the social and narrative structures through which the child is constituted as a person, as a child and as a male or female' (p. 4). These discursive practices generally allow only two possibilities, and contain within themselves a range of rules about the correct positioning in one or the other category, which children learn intuitively rather than explicitly.

Davies emphasised that an important foundation of the division of the world into male and female, masculine and feminine, was the very idea of a dual division itself. Gender functions to reduce the complexity of diverse human identities to a much simpler two-category schema, which has enormous force and weight largely because of its simplicity. As Davies put it:

The idea of bipolar maleness/femaleness is something which itself has material force ... One of the ways in which the idea of bipolarity functions is to reduce the actual diversity (non-polarity) of individual behaviour to a bipolar model. This can involve ignoring or not seeing 'deviations' or actually managing to construe behaviour and categories of behaviour as bipolar, even though they would appear to lend themselves more readily to a non-polar perception. (1989, p. 18)

Davies gives the example of a boy whose father occasionally wears a sarong vigorously denying that males could ever wear skirts or dresses, simply redefining his father's sarong as consistent with always wearing pants.

For Davies, then, an important element of the ongoing reproduction of gender differences was the expectation that children form a singular, unified and coherent 'identity' itself. She argued that children 'need the freedom to position themselves in multiple ways, some of which will be recognisably "feminine", some "masculine" as we currently understand these terms, and some totally unrelated to current discursive practices' (p. 141).

Another [boy] ... told me that because he was a boy he was stronger than girls, and gave as an example the fact that he helped his sister, who was weak, over puddles. Shortly afterwards one of the girls of the same age hitched herself up on to a fairly high window sill behind her in order to sit on it. Hamid made a feeble attempt to do the same thing, then whinged for me to lift him up too, knowing that he did not have the strength and agility to match the girl's feat. Once up, however, he continued in his domineering manner, utterly unshaken by this contrary evidence to his earlier assertion. (1989, p. 20)

MASCULINITIES— RAEWYN CONNELL

In the same way that feminist sociologists needed to make visible what was specific about women's experience and social position, the specific character of men's experiences have until recently been correspondingly 'invisible' in sociology. While most research has been conducted by men and the subjects of the research have been men, few have actually drawn attention to this fact and identified their object of study as masculinity. Michael Kimmel (1990) argues that sociology 'was, in part, responsible for the reproduction of gender relations that kept masculinity invisible and rendered femininity problematic' (p. 94). Women were seen as a deviation from the norm (men) and their behaviour therefore was worthy of explanation in terms of their gender. Since men were taken as the norm, they did not need to be researched as men. The maleness of sociological subjects is simply taken for granted; men are assumed to constitute the norm and their behaviour is not explained in terms of gender or compared with that of women.

In this section we examine one of the major studies of the social construction of masculinity, the work of Raewyn Connell. In *Masculinities*, Connell (1995) extended the earlier work on sexuality and power to develop a more specific focus on the sociology of masculinity.

Active bodies

One of Connell's opening points is to suggest that social scientists have so far been faced with three alternatives in thinking about gender and the human body:

1. *biological determinism*, in which masculinity and femininity are regarded as the products or effects of sex-differentiated biological characteristics
2. *sociological determinism*, in which masculinity and femininity are seen as having nothing to do with biology at all, and the human body is treated as 'a more or less neutral surface or landscape on which a social symbolism is imprinted' (1995, p. 46)
3. a 'compromise' position, in which sexual identity is understood as resulting from some kind of *interaction* between biology and social relations.

However, neither sociological nor biological determinism adequately captures the reality of sexual identity and experience, and the notion of an interaction has so far failed because it remains unclear how the processes of interaction actually work.

Connell suggests that we can identify how bodies and social processes interact by conceptualising bodily experiences as active elements of any social situation. For example, being an athlete is more than simply a social position—it revolves around particular things being done to the body and, more importantly, it concerns how the body responds to what is done to it: performing as expected, failing to do so or becoming injured. In relation to gender, Connell maintains that the 'physical sense of maleness and femaleness is central to the cultural interpretation of gender' (p. 52), so that physical experiences and sensations trigger and form the foundation of gendered social action. Connell states:

It is not enough to assert the significance of bodily difference, important as this has been in recent feminist theory. We need to assert the activity, literally the agency of bodies in social processes ... where bodies are seen as sharing in social agency, in generating and shaping courses of social conduct. (p. 60)

Connell gives the example of how a young boy throwing a ball 'like a girl' affects how other males, especially his own father, perceive him (as an 'unsuccessful' male), which then lays the foundation for his own sense of his masculinity. The way the boy's *body* behaved— untutored in the art of masculine ball throwing—had an active effect on the *social* process of gender construction.

In order to capture this idea of bodies being active within social relations, Connell suggests the concept of 'body-reflexive practices':

Through body-reflexive practices, bodies are addressed by social process and drawn into history, without ceasing to be bodies. They do not turn into symbols, signs or positions in discourse. Their materiality (including material capacities to engender, to give birth, to give milk, to menstruate, to open, to penetrate, to ejaculate) is not erased, it continues to matter. (p. 64)

Gender is thus 'a social practice that constantly refers to bodies and what bodies do' (p. 71). The task for the sociological study of sexual identity is then to identify the range of body-reflexive practices and how they operate at different levels of social reality: individual experience, social interaction, social institutions and organisations, and larger scale arenas of social organisation such as the economy and the state.

Source: Gesell (1940, pp. 85–9). Reproduced with permission.

Hegemonic masculinity

Connell emphasises both that there are *multiple* forms of masculinity to be found in any society and also that the relationships between these different masculinities are characterised by *inequality*. It is possible to identify a hegemonic masculinity that will dominate other types of masculinity in any particular historical and social context. Connell defines it as follows:

> *Hegemonic masculinity can be defined as the configuration of gender practice which embodies the currently accepted answer to the problem of the legitimacy of patriarchy, which guarantees (or is taken to guarantee) the dominant position of men and the subordination of women.* (p. 77)

There will then be relations of dominance and subordination between different groups of men, with the clearest example in Western societies being the dominance of heterosexual over homosexual men.

In addition to relations of subordination, Connell suggests that there are also relations of *complicity* between those men less typical of hegemonic masculinity and those who are typical. This means that many men occupy a kind of transitional, compromise zone between hegemonic masculinity and women and more subordinated men; they express sympathy for feminist arguments and gay liberation, while still displaying enough of the characteristics of hegemonic masculinity to survive in those arenas where hegemonic masculinity still dominates, such as the world of work.

However, hegemonic masculinity does not always stay the same and it is always subject to challenge, either from women or subordinated groups of men, or through its interconnections with the material, social and economic bases that make it possible. As those interconnections with the surrounding society change, hegemonic masculinity can undergo a range of crises that can result in its transformation. The conception of the male role as 'provider', for example, is dependent in an advanced capitalist society on the availability of employment, and the existence of structural unemployment creates a crisis situation for many men hoping to achieve hegemonic masculinity. Similarly, the 'impregnator' role has a different significance in a social context where women wish to have either fewer babies or none at all.

Men's life histories

Connell explored the interplay of social and historical processes in different forms of masculinity through a study of the life histories of four groups of men, each of which is positioned differently in relation to hegemonic masculinity:

1. young working-class men
2. counter-cultural men sympathetic to feminism
3. young gay men
4. men of the 'new middle class', occupying professional and technical positions.

Here we look at the first two groups.

Live fast, die young

Eight men aged between 17 and 29 years were interviewed; five were unemployed and three were office workers. All were children of manual workers, and most of their mothers had jobs while they were young. Connell suggests that for these young men the concept of 'male breadwinner' was irrelevant. Only one was uncomfortable about women earning an income, and they did not regard women as 'emotional specialists' in contrast to men. There was minimal emotional investment in a traditional domestic division of labour. Connell gives the example of Jack Harley:

> *a biker with a history of violence and a criminal record, feels no unease about staying at home to do the child care if his wife can get a better-paying job than he can. Several of his mates do just that. He hopes to get trained to do bar work. What he likes in it is the human dimension, the chance to meet people and hear their troubles. Not exactly super-masculine; indeed this could easily be seen as women's work, the classic function of a barmaid. (p. 109)*

A common element of the working-class masculine orientation towards child-rearing is: 'If you're man enough to make babies, you should be man enough to look after babies.' This attitude to the domestic division of labour is partly related to the precarious position these men occupy in the labour market; with few marketable skills, they take short-term work whenever they can.

Masculinity revolved around violence, mostly among themselves, and a general hostility to homosexuality, although one respondent had started cross-dressing and living as a woman. Connell describes their gender identity as a form of 'protest masculinity'. Their class position deprived them of the usual benefits of patriarchy for men, such as better earnings and status, which they compensated for with the display of their masculinity through violence and a celebration of their marginal, deviant status.

Connell refers to 'significant tensions' in their sexual ideology: 'A thin, contemptuous misogyny, in which women are treated basically as disposable receptacles for semen, coexists with a much more respectful, even admiring view of women's strength' (p. 108). Despite denouncing feminism in general, there was a pragmatic support given to equality between the sexes and a genuine interest in investing energy in their children so that they would achieve greater success in their lives.

Towards non-sexist masculinity

Another group of six men aged between 22 and 50 years active in a range of occupations was also interviewed: one was unemployed and there was a trainee nurse, an office worker for an environmental group, an occasionally employed photographer, a public servant and an occasionally employed journalist. What they had in common was an attempt to reform their masculinity in response to feminist criticism.

According to Connell, their interview responses indicated an 'active appropriation' of the hegemonic masculinity that characterised their childhood and youth. They consciously and deliberately set about becoming different kinds of men in response to their awareness of what was problematic about the dominant form of masculinity. Although this meant a positive evaluation of femininity, both in women and within themselves, they still continued to value the physical experience of being male. One respondent said:

> *I'm still really masculine and I feel definitely male and I like that too. I like some aspects of being male, the physical strength I really like. I really like my body; that sort of mental strength that men learn to have whereby they can choose to put aside their feelings for the moment, which I think is great. (p. 123)*

Their active engagement with hegemonic masculinity arose from some of the contradictions *within* what Connell called 'the gender order', in particular their practical experience of female strength in the course of their own personal development. When they encountered feminism, argues Connell, 'feminist images of women's strength could resonate with something in their own experience' (p. 125).

The path taken by their individual biographies, however, first went through an engagement with the environmental movement, which 'engaged their lives at more than one level and met a variety of needs—for solidarity with others, for moral clarity, for a sense of personal worth' (p. 126). Connell points out that this social movement has tended to challenge hegemonic masculinity through a number of its core features:

- the practice and ideology of *equality*, through an emphasis on democracy and a critique of authoritarianism
- collectivity and solidarity, with its emphasis on working in groups rather than on individualism
- the ideology of personal growth, establishing a link between a concern for the external world and personal development—an important part of the movement's activities is its promotion of group therapy, conferences and workshops
- an ideology of organic wholeness, with its critique of violence and mechanisation.

Connell suggests that these core features made the environmental movement 'fertile ground for a politics of masculinity' (p. 128), which springs to life with the impact of feminism. The ethos of the environmental movement was to aim for two qualities: the capacity, first, to be expressive and, second, to have feelings worth expressing, an emotional depth and the capacity to care for people and for nature. The manifestations of these aims included being in the bush, caring about partners and unselfishness.

When they came into contact with feminist ideas and arguments, whether through friends or lovers, or reading books, the effect was to produce powerful feelings of *guilt* about their personal relationships to women. One respondent, states Connell:

took feminism aboard as an accusation. The language for gender politics that he learned centred on the term 'sexism', by which he understood men's personal attitudes towards women. His task, in responding to feminism, was therefore to change his head, to adopt more supportive attitudes towards women, and to criticize other men's attitudes. (p. 129)

Responding to this combination of the ethos of environmentalism and the guilt induced by feminist ideas, these men set about shaping their identities and relations so that they could distance themselves from hegemonic masculinity, 'to reconstruct personality to produce a new, non-sexist self' (p. 130). Connell identifies a central theme of 'renunciation' in the way they went about the development of non-sexist masculinity, especially renunciation of traditional male career paths, which separated them from the masculinising practices of the workplace and gave them a lower income; like the working-class young men, this blocked their access to many of the privileges of hegemonic masculinity. Poverty feminises. Anti-sexist renunciation, states Connell, 'also means giving up everyday masculine privileges and styles of interaction, for instance, by consciously trying not to dominate discussions and decisions' (p. 131).

Within relationships, it meant feelings of guilt about taking the initiative, which tended to be seen as the imposition of yet another male demand on women, so that generally 'The moment of separation from hegemonic masculinity basically involves choosing passivity' (p. 132). In practice, this tendency towards passivity could be contradictory, so that even renunciation could be engaged in as a 'heroic' act, bringing back to life an aspect of the hegemonic masculinity being rejected. Connell also points out that this form of non-sexist masculinity was as resolutely heterosexual as that of the young working-class men, perhaps more so because it allowed for flexibility in the boundaries between masculinity and femininity, and it was characterised by a persistent current of homophobia. This was a boundary over which their reform of hegemonic masculinity would not go—men were still meant to direct their sexual energies towards women, perhaps as the most basic expression of their valuation of women and femininity.

The history of masculinities

In looking at the historical development of different forms of masculinity in Western culture, Connell makes two points: first, that masculinities should be seen as constantly changing; second, that they are integral to larger scale processes of social change. An examination of the history of masculinity thus helps to illustrate and develop the more general sociological point made by the Frankfurt School and Norbert Elias—that there is a relationship between larger scale, long-term social development and the development of personality and the structures of everyday interaction.

Building empires

Connell attaches particular significance to the interconnections between masculinity and the Western nations' development of colonial empires:

The fundamental point is that masculinities are not only shaped by the process of imperial expansion, they are active in that process and help to shape it ... We cannot understand the connection of masculinity and violence at a personal level without understanding that it is also a global connection. European/American masculinities were deeply implicated in the worldwide violence through which European/American culture became dominant. (pp. 186–7)

In the period between 1450 and 1650, argues Connell, there were four developments that were central to the construction of a particular type of hegemonic masculinity:

1. *Cultural change* produced 'new understandings of sexuality and personhood' in urban Europe. The decline of the institutional Church led to greater emphasis on the conjugal household and 'compulsory heterosexuality'. Emphasis on rationality as the bearer of civilisation encouraged the opposition to 'nature' and the utilisation of the gender distinction as an embodiment of that opposition.
2. Development of *overseas empires* occurred in three historical waves: first, Portugal and Spain; then

the Netherlands, France and England; and then Germany, Italy and Japan, with Russia and the United States also expanding into their surrounding territories. 'Empire was a gendered enterprise from the start', with men as seafarers, soldiers, conquerors, explorers, administrators and settlers, and women as wives, mothers and servants.

3. The *growth of cities*, especially Amsterdam, Antwerp and London, created an urbanised form of everyday life that 'was both more anonymous, and more coherently regulated, than the frontier or the countryside' (p. 188). The administrative requirements of cities demanded a precisely defined individual identity that could be exactly located in the overlapping networks of the social relations characterising urban life. There was a gender dimension to the corresponding administrative concern with classification and categorisation, making it important to be able to specify exactly the differences between males and females, and where any individual stood in relation to those differences. Cities also encouraged the division of social life into public and private, again drawing on a hardening gender distinction to embody that division, with public life treated as a masculine domain and private life as a feminine one.

4. A number of large-scale European *civil wars* developed, from which emerged more powerful, centralised nation-states based on military force, providing 'a larger-scale institutionalization of men's power than had been possible before' (p. 189).

The hegemonic masculinity that emerged at the end of the 18th century—Connell calls it 'gentry masculinity'—was resolutely heterosexual, emphasising violence, hierarchical authority, control over women, the rational domination of the natural world and a heroic honourability in the face of threats to the social order, whether they came from the disorderly working class, the colonial natives, homosexual men or women and children.

Processes of transformation

Over the past two centuries, suggests Connell, we can observe 'the splitting of gentry masculinity, its gradual displacement by new hegemonic forms, and the emergence of an array of subordinated and marginalized masculinities' (1995, p. 191). Connell sees three developments underlying the transformation of hegemonic masculinity up to the present day, arising to a large extent from contradictions internal to this gender order itself:

1. *The challenge from women.* There was a gradual emergence of gender politics and social movements around women's political, economic and social rights. In an important sense this was a corollary to the individualism of post-Reformation Western culture and the liberal conception of citizenship. Once the concept of individual rights and citizenship was granted, it became increasingly difficult to deny those rights to any section of the population.

2. *The logic of capitalist development.* In the course of the 19th century, capitalist economic relations became increasingly organised around the rational, bureaucratic management of production and even warfare, gradually rendering obsolete the spectacular heroism of gentry masculinity. A polarity thus emerged between violent, heroic, dominant masculinity and settled, ordered rationality, between 'real men' as cowboys, explorers and farmers on the one hand, and men as experts, technicians, computer programmers and managers on the other. Connell believes that these two versions of masculinity exist alongside each other in contemporary societies, 'sometimes in opposition and sometimes meshing' (p. 194).

3. *The empire strikes back.* The sexual identities of colonised peoples have not simply been reprogrammed by the Western gender order. As time has passed, the varieties of masculinities existing in the countries colonised by the West have reasserted themselves and had a feedback impact on the possible forms taken by masculinity throughout the world. The very complex position of male homosexuality and the different attitudes to female strength and assertiveness in Arabic, Asian, African, Mediterranean and South American countries, in particular, have had a destabilising effect on hegemonic masculinity in former colonial nations.

The result of these processes of transformation is now a situation where men negotiate all these contradictory forces through a variety of forms of masculine sexual identity, in a context where 'hegemonic heterosexuality cannot now monopolize the imagination in the way it once did' (p. 202).

Reflective questions: Some people suggest that masculinity is changing all the time and that perhaps the ways in which males can 'be' male are less dominated by hegemonic masculinity than they used to be. Do you think this is true? What are the arguments for and against the idea that masculinity is changing significantly?

THE 'GENDER ORDER'

A useful theoretical framework for the sociological analysis of gender inequalities was provided by Connell in *Gender and Power* (1987). Connell suggests that it is possible to identify three substantially distinct 'structures of relationship' between men and women, constituting what she calls the 'gender order' or the 'gender regime':

1. Labour (or production)—'the organization of housework and child-care, the division between unpaid and paid work, the segregation of labour markets ... discrimination of training and promotion, unequal wages and unequal exchange' (p. 96).
2. Power structures—relations of 'authority, control and coercion: the hierarchies of the state and business, institutional and interpersonal violence, sexual regulation and surveillance, domestic authority and its contestation' (pp. 96–7).
3. Cathexis relations—involving emotions and desire, 'the patterning of object-choice, desire and desirability ... the production of heterosexuality and homosexuality and the relationship between them ... the socially structured antagonisms of gender (woman-hating, man-hating, self-hatred) ... trust and distrust, jealousy and solidarity in marriages and other relationships ... the emotional relationships involved in rearing children' (p. 97).

Although these can be identified as separate structures, Connell emphasises that they 'interweave all the time', sometimes resonating with each other and sometimes conflicting, as a result of their historical development. The task for the sociological understanding of gender is, argues Connell, to analyse exactly how these structures operate, interweave and conflict with each other in particular historical and social contexts.

The overall conclusion that can be drawn from the research discussed in this section is that a sociological understanding of gender is not simply a matter of substituting a 'social' approach for a 'biological' one. The implications of the arguments examined here are that the sociology of gender needs to go beyond seeing gender or sexuality as something to do with personality traits or characteristics, with ways of being an individual person. This is because the psychic features of masculinity/femininity are in practice extremely sensitive to the character of the social situations within which they exist. The 'overwhelming evidence' produced in many years of research on gender establishes that gender differentiation 'is best explained as a social construction rooted in hierarchy, not in biology or in internalization, either through early experiences, as described by psychoanalysts, or through socialization, as described by psychologists and sociologists' (Epstein 1988, p. 15).

The sociological approach to gender requires seeing the social apparatuses surrounding gender as precisely that, as a *social structuring of relationships and practices* around the relatively minor (in modern industrialised societies) reproductive distinction between sperm carriers and egg carriers. As Connell (1987) puts it, gender is 'practice organized in terms of, or in relation to, the reproductive division of people into male and female' (p. 140). It is 'a linking concept ... about the linking of other fields of social practice to the nodal practices of engendering, childbirth and parenting' (p. 140). Gender is thus transformed from a relatively trivial aspect of people's varied lives into criteria for organising social relationships of hierarchy, status, power, domination and subordination, and exclusion and inclusion.

The mistake often made in the psychology of gender is to assume that gender actually has a real referent within people's psyches with an existence independent of social relations. Gender as an independently existing psychological phenomenon melts away under any close scrutiny, leaving only the social relations constituting gender. Masculinity and femininity are, argue Segal (1993), 'fictions' that do have real psychic effects, but whose power and meaning are constituted socially.

TRANSFORMING GENDER AND SEXUALITY

There is continual debate about how the gender order might be transformed as well as analysed. Connell (1987) identifies two possibilities for the transformation of gender relations:

1. either the abolition of gender or
2. its 'reconstitution on new bases' (p. 286).

Firestone (1972) expresses the strongest support for the first position by advocating androgyny with her suggestion that babies should be conceived and developed outside the womb. David Fernbach (1981) puts a similar type of argument for the 'modernisation' of reproduction, liberating us from our internal nature in the same way that we have transcended the limitations of external nature.

However, Connell suggests that such positions misunderstand the social construction of gender, continuing to rely on the assumption that gender is based on biological differences. If gender is to be abolished, writes Connell, it is the social structure of gender that requires attention, not human reproductive biology.

Connell thus sees the possibilities for the reconstitution of gender as lying in 'disconnecting' or 'uncoupling' the array of social practices surrounding sexual identity from what she calls the 'reproductive division', the obvious biological differences between males and females in relation to bearing children. The biological differences between the sexes would then play a far more limited role, rather than being the focal point around which all sexual identity is organised. The different biological make-up of males and females need not be denigrated or artificially transformed.

However, suggests Connell, at the same time there would be no reason for biology 'to structure emotional relationships, so the categories heterosexual and homosexual would become insignificant. There would be no reason for it to structure character, so femininity and masculinity would depart' (1987, p. 287).

THE WOMEN'S MOVEMENT/FEMINISM

In 1869 John Stuart Mill said:

> *If the principle [of democracy] is true, we ought to act as if we believed it, and not to ordain that to be born a girl instead of a boy, any more than to be born black instead of white, or a commoner instead of a nobleman, shall decide the person's position throughout life.* (p. 33)

The fight for basic civil rights, legal equality between men and women, equal pay, the right to vote and a reduction in discrimination characterised what is often called the 'first wave' of the women's movement around the turn of the 20th century. A 'second wave' emerged in the 1960s, in response to the other social and political movements that became active at the time. Juliet Mitchell (1971) pointed to the various civil rights organisations that campaigned for the rights of ethnic minority groups, the Black Power Movement that spearheaded the demands of more militant blacks, the Youth Movement represented by organisations such as Students for a Democratic Society, and the Peace Movement that coordinated protest against the war in Vietnam and later in Cambodia. All of these social movements, observed Mitchell, provided a large part of the impetus and philosophy for the Women's Liberation Movement. Women increasingly realised that they needed a movement of their own since, even as members of other radical movements, they were often treated in terms of their traditional stereotypes.

By the 1970s and 1980s, then, feminism had become an influential force in Western societies generally and in sociology in particular. However, in the 1990s the role of feminism in society and in social thought came under challenge. Some observers, such as Susan Faludi (1991), have argued that there has been a backlash against feminism from those who believe that the movement has either gone too far or that it has already substantially achieved its objectives. The women's movement itself has become more diverse and differentiated, with particular subgroups concerned with race, the environment or lesbian identity, for example, so that today it is more difficult to identify a single, coherent and unified women's movement.

THE GAY AND LESBIAN MOVEMENT

There were attempts to improve the rights of homosexuals beginning in Europe in the late 19th century and in the United States in the 1920s. The public presence of what came to be called **gay liberation** has, however, been quite different from that of the early women's movement. The piecemeal liberalisation of legislation concerning homosexuality before the 1970s was achieved without the clear mobilisation of homosexuals as part of a mass movement. Until then the general legislative and social climate in relation to homosexuality was repressive, with popular attitudes towards homosexuality confined to denigrating stereotypes. David Greenberg cited a 1970 Kinsey Institute study, where 49 per cent of respondents agreed that 'homosexuality is a social corruption which can cause the downfall of civilization' (1988, p. 457); and Jeffrey Weeks (1985) pointed out that the public visibility of a gay (male) subculture in the 1950s and 1960s was confined largely to the bar and disco scenes in cities such as San Francisco and New York.

In the United States, that gay subculture turned militant, assertive, self-confident and very visible with the 1968 Stonewall riots in New York. The riots were a response to an attempt by New York Police to raid a gay bar, and the resultant mobilisation can be identified as the beginning of the gay liberation movement. The growth of gay liberation after the 1950s was also encouraged by changing attitudes towards sexuality generally, which had begun in the 1920s and were fuelled by research such as Kinsey's that undermined the notion of homosexuality as a 'deviant' identity.

Once it was accepted that heterosexual activity was not essentially sinful and that its primary purpose is the expression of pleasure, love and affection rather than reproduction, much of the rationale for repressing homosexuality was removed. As Greenberg argued, the post-1970s easing of hostility towards homosexuality was part of a general relaxation of attitudes towards divorce, premarital sex, contraception, abortion and pornography (1988, p. 462).

Greenberg also considered the contribution of sociology itself to have been significant. Beginning with studies such as Kenneth Plummer's *Sexual Stigma* (1975), a body of research emerged that provided 'a picture of homosexuality, not as a medical or psychological condition, but as a component of a way of life with distinctive manners, customs, and institutions' (Greenberg 1988, p. 464). In Greenberg's view, this growing literature and its popularisation had a humanising effect, overcoming much of the ignorance upon which repressive and stigmatised views of homosexuality were based.

Connell (1987, pp. 274–5) identified three major differences between the women's and gay liberation movements. First, women's liberation was the radical end of a broad continuum of women's organisations that had been publicly visible since the late 19th century. These forms of organisation emerged within existing organisations, such as churches and political parties, and often expressed women's interests without necessarily defining themselves as part of a women's movement. The interests of homosexual women and men did not achieve the same kind of public presence until the 1970s, and their movement is the primary arena for the articulation of their interests.

Second, gay liberation has been characterised by a fundamental division between the interests and concerns of lesbians and homosexual men. Lesbians are subject to the dual oppression of being women as well as homosexual, producing different types of political and reformative concerns. Lesbians who define themselves as feminists often have a stronger commitment to women's liberation as a movement than to an alliance with men within the gay liberation movement. As a result, the term 'gay' does not usually include lesbians, and the political relationship between lesbians and male homosexuals is often uneasy.

Third, the relationship between the gay political movement and the community from which it emerges is different from women's liberation. The gay community has been organised around the expression of a particular sexual identity, based on activities such as gay bars and dance events. The primary concern that gay liberation has had with the behaviour of the rest of society has been to be left more or less in peace, and as a movement it has been less concerned to transform social structures and sexual behaviour generally. This aspect of gay liberation has been referred to by Dennis Altman (1982) as the conceptualisation of the gay community as a 'minority group' with the same legitimate civil rights as other social and ethnic groups.

Reflective question: Sexuality is meant to be a particularly private and intimate aspect of our lives—is it?

SEXUAL IDENTITY AND BEYOND—HETEROSEXUAL, HOMOSEXUAL, QUEER

It is often assumed that heterosexuality is simply 'natural' and that other forms of sexual identity are 'unnatural'. However, several studies have shown how homosexuality is often institutionalised rather than defined as abnormal or deviant (Herdt 1984; Money & Ehrhardt 1972). More importantly, homosexuality is often institutionalised as a form of 'sequential bisexuality' and presumed to be characteristic of a particular period in a young man's life prior to marriage, after which homosexual activity either stops or becomes sporadic (Money 1990). Indeed, for the Sambia people of New Guinea, a period of homosexual activity is seen as essential to the formation of an adequate heterosexual identity, and it is non-participation in homosexuality that would be stigmatised as deviant (Herdt 1981).

As Rubin argued:

Like gender, sexuality is political. It is organized into systems of power, which reward and encourage some individuals and activities, while punishing and suppressing others. (1984, p. 309)

In other words, just as humans learn how to be masculine/feminine within their society, they also learn what it means and feels like to be homosexual/heterosexual. Whatever the physiological differences between people, male and female, the organisation of actual sexual practices in terms of categories such as homosexual also needs to be understood in cultural, historical and social terms.

CRITICISMS OF 'CATEGORICAL' THEORY

Although there are many differences between the approaches examined in the previous sections, Connell (1987) has identified a number of shared features, which together constitute an overarching orientation she calls 'categorical' theory:

- Societies are seen in terms of a few, usually two, central categories of people 'related to each other by power and conflict of interest' (p. 54).
- Categories are analysed as a closed unit, with little or no attention paid to either the processes by which categories are constituted or the elements of which they are composed.
- Opposed interests in sexual politics are seen as matching particular categories of people. Dominance, for example, is linked with men, and subordination with women (p. 54).

The problem Connell found with this approach to gender is that the general dichotomous picture that emerges is very similar to the approaches based on the idea of biologically based gender differences. It also overlooks major differences within each of the categories—male/masculine and female/feminine—and treats them as homogeneous wholes. This means that categorical theory is unable to understand 'divisions that arise within the field of gender itself', divisions that are central to the development of gender differentiation. For example, the construction and maintenance of particular forms of femininity/masculinity depend precisely on the conflictual dynamics between stereotypical and marginal femininities/masculinities (see also the examination of Kinsey, pp. 305–7).

Compulsory heterosexuality— Adrienne Rich

Heterosexuality is usually assumed to be the 'normal' path of sexual development that most people follow, leading them relentlessly into marriage and having children. Homosexuality, in contrast, is presumed to be a sidetrack off that main thoroughfare, a deviation from the highway of life that requires explanation. Adrienne Rich (1980) argues against this understanding of heterosexuality. She regards it as a social and political institution that constructs female sexuality in terms of a compulsory heterosexuality.

Compulsory heterosexuality overlays a prior and more fundamental female bonding that she calls the 'lesbian continuum'. She gives the term 'lesbian' a broad meaning that captures women's resistance against patriarchy, their identification with other women, and their sexual and emotional independence from men, rather than simply referring to a particular type of sexual conduct. Instead of seeing lesbianism as requiring explanation, Rich argues that it is the development of heterosexuality that demands analysis and understanding.

She points out that heterosexuality is generally assumed to be most women's sexual orientation, without examining the processes by which women come to live heterosexual lives. The assumption of 'a mystical/biological heterosexual inclination, a "preference" or "choice" which draws women toward men' obscures 'the covert socializations and the overt forces which have channelled women into marriage and heterosexual romance' (p. 68). If women (as mothers) are the first source of love and tenderness, Rich asks why women would ever redirect their emotional energies towards men, why species survival and reproduction should be so rigidly identified with emotional/erotic relations, and why social arrangements emerge 'to enforce women's total emotional, erotic loyalty and subservience to men' (p. 68)—arrangements ranging from outright violence to simply obscuring the option of lesbianism.

Failing to see heterosexuality as a social institution, states Rich:

is like failing to admit that the economic system called capitalism or the caste system of racism is maintained by a variety of forces, including both physical violence and false consciousness. (p. 88)

She argues further that:

The lie of compulsory female heterosexuality ... creates a profound falseness, hypocrisy, and hysteria in the heterosexual dialogue, for every heterosexual relationship is lived in the queasy strobelight of that lie. However we choose to identify ourselves, however we find ourselves labelled, it flickers across and distorts our lives. (p. 88)

She contends that the identification of heterosexuality as socially constructed and maintained, rather than as an individual preference or choice, would lead to 'a freeing-up of thinking, the exploring of new paths, the shattering of another great silence, new clarity in personal relationships' (p. 79).

Criticisms of Rich

The critique of Rich's arguments by Ferguson, Zita and Addelson (1982) includes the following four points:

1. Rich's argument is ahistorical, tending to treat both the social institution of heterosexuality and lesbian identity as universal features of women's experience, neglecting their historical development and the ways in which they varied across cultures.

2. The concept of the 'lesbian continuum' does not make enough distinction between female bonding generally, which includes heterosexually active women and sexually active lesbians, who are placed in a very different social position.
3. To the extent that Rich assumes that compulsory heterosexuality is the key mechanism maintaining patriarchy, there are obvious problems about the neglect of other arenas and mechanisms of patriarchal power, such as the state and the economy. Some lesbians are not particularly resistant to patriarchy, and some heterosexual women are effective feminists. As Ferguson and associates argue:

Such women would deny that their involvements are coercive, or even that they are forced to put second their own needs, their self-respect, or their relationships with women. (1982, p. 159)

4. Identifying heterosexuality as a social institution seems to suggest that there is such a thing as a pre-social, non-institutionalised female identity, and implies a return to a notion of women's 'essential nature'—that is, women-directed. But if the fact that women mother is itself a social institution, then 'neither lesbianism nor heterosexuality can be said to be women's natural (uncoerced) sexual preference' (p. 159).

Another point of criticism is that Rich assumed that the relationship between mother and child is unambiguously positive, that it is the only such emotionally positive relationship, and that only a social institution could tear women away from close emotional bonds to women. This neglects the 'darker' aspects of such close bonding, the need for separation/individuation from the mother, and the emotional bonds formed with fathers, brothers and male friends. All these are equally important aspects of women's psychosexual development, aspects that make their attachments to men far less mysterious, and far less dependent on the institutionalisation of compulsory heterosexuality, than Rich assumed.

One also needs to be cautious about what is 'compulsory' about heterosexuality, because, as Rosemary Pringle puts it: 'rather than being yanked screaming into "compulsory heterosexuality", most women actively seek it out and find pleasure in it' (1989, p. 165). Nonetheless, these criticisms do not take anything away from Rich's arguments about the assumption of heterosexuality as 'normal', and the analytical neglect of its formation within the development of sexuality. In order to go beyond the notion of an 'essential nature', it is necessary to analyse all forms of sexual conduct as socially constructed, so that heterosexuality is subjected to the same analytical scrutiny as homosexuality.

CONTINUUMS OF SEXUAL BEHAVIOUR—ALFRED KINSEY ET AL.

When the biologist Alfred Kinsey (1894–1956), together with Wardell Pomeroy and Clyde Martin, turned his taxonomic skills to human sexuality in the 1940s and 1950s, the resulting studies had a major impact on both academic and popular understandings of sexual identity. Three features of Kinsey's approach stand out as particularly significant.

- *Sexuality and 'nature'*. Kinsey's (1948; 1953) extensive study of sexual behaviour suggested that all human sexual response is learned, and he rejected the notion that there is any innate foundation for sexual conduct. In fact, he found that when one did look closely at the animal world, homosexuality, masturbation and oral sex were common among mammals. For Kinsey, writes John Gagnon, the tension between nature and culture rested on:

  a distinction between the bounty and variety of the natural world (read here the diversity of species in an unmanaged nature) as opposed to a civilized world of agriculture in which nature is pruned and limited. In much the same way as agriculture gives the fields over to monocrops, sexually repressive cultures cultivate procreative heterosexuality as their sole flower, treating all else as weeds ... it is in the biology of abundance and adaptation that he found the template for the normal, not in the individual organismic views that characterize the defect-finding traditions in psychiatry, psychology and biology. (1990, p. 189)

- *Sexual practice*. Kinsey focused primarily on what people actually did sexually, 'completely divorced from questions of moral value and social custom' (1948, p. 3). People's sense of what *ought* to exist in the sexual realm appeared to interfere with their ability to perceive what *did* exist. The object of his study was thus to catalogue, in minute detail, people's actual sexual experiences, to take sexual behaviour from the realm of morality and custom into that of 'an accumulation of scientific fact' (p. 5).

- *The importance of sexual fantasy*. Kinsey gathered information on people's erotic fantasies and dreams as well as their activities—what he called their 'psychosexual reactions'. Kinsey regarded sexual imagery as a crucial aspect of sexual identity: even though someone might only have sexual relationships with someone of the opposite sex, it was significant for their sexual identity if they were primarily aroused by images or fantasies concerning the same sex.

For Kinsey, people's sexual identity was thus not a unified and consistent feature of their personality—masculine, feminine, homosexual, heterosexual—but a fluid constellation of whatever sexual activities and fantasies happened to occupy their minds and bodies at any particular time. He argued against the assumption that there are clear-cut divisions between those who are heterosexual and those who are homosexual, as well as against the idea that there are consistent relationships between someone's choice of sexual partners and other aspects of personality, such as masculinity/femininity, temperament, body type or occupation.

The terms 'masculine' or 'feminine', 'homosexual' or 'heterosexual' should thus not be used as nouns to identify groups of people, but as adjectives to describe types of behaviour. Rather than being either heterosexual or homosexual, Kinsey found that humans arranged their sexual behaviour along a continuum, with no clear divisions between discrete groupings.

Kinsey found that a significant proportion of the population combined homosexual with heterosexual experiences and fantasies. Nearly half (46 per cent) the male population and just over one-quarter (28 per cent) of the female population either engaged in both homosexual and heterosexual activities or responded erotically to people of both sexes in the course of their adult lives. This meant that people 'do not represent two discrete populations, heterosexual and homosexual. The world is not to be divided into sheep and goats' (1948, p. 639). Kinsey's scale identified only the balance between homosexual and heterosexual experiences and erotic fantasies, not the actual amount of either.

These arguments were later to find their way into sociology through, for example, Mary McIntosh's (1968) article on 'the homosexual role'. McIntosh took what Kinsey regarded merely as an unfortunate impediment to scientific thought—the inclination to see sexual activity in terms of a dichotomy between homosexuality and heterosexuality—as the object of her analysis. She developed Kinsey's basic argument by observing that what is socially constructed as homosexuality should be regarded as a historically and culturally specific homosexual role that does not match the non-dichotomous diversity of sexual behaviour identified by Kinsey.

Another study by the Kinsey Institute found that of a group of 262 self-identified lesbians, 75 per cent had had sexual relations with men since the age of 18, as had 43 per cent of those who had always seen themselves as lesbian (Sanders, Reinisch & McWhirter 1990, p. xxiv). It is thus unclear what relationship there is between one's sexual *identity* (heterosexual, homosexual, bisexual, asexual) and one's sexual *conduct* (extent of sexual contact with same- or opposite-sex partners) (see Cass 1990).

Criticisms of Kinsey

John De Cecco (1990) provides an overview of the limitations of Kinsey's approach to human sexuality. He points out that sexuality is conceived of primarily as a *physical* phenomenon. Kinsey focused on physiological processes of arousal, culminating in orgasm, and in his scientific concern to avoid the 'distortions' of morality and custom wanted to approach sexuality solely in terms of its objective, 'material' manifestations. This makes it impossible to attend to the patterns of subjective meaning that are socially constructed around sexual conduct. For example, male prisoners may rape each other—that is, have a Kinseyan homosexual 'outlet'—without for an instant defining their behaviour as homosexual. Indeed, it would be interpreted and experienced as a confirmation of their masculine, heterosexual identity. As De Cecco argues, Kinsey made no distinction 'between objective *sexual* performance and subjective *erotic* experience' (p. 372), nor could he identify the relationship between the two. What makes a human encounter erotic goes well beyond a mere counterpositioning of one body to another (or to several bodies, or an object); it depends on a process of defining what is erotic in the first place, and the place of sexual 'behaviour' within that process can vary enormously.

Freud pointed out how apparently non-sexual behaviour could have erotic components, and studies of 'organisational sexuality' also show how 'sexualised' everyday life in any workplace containing both men and women can be (Game & Pringle 1983a; Hearn & Parkin 1987; Hearn et al. 1989; Pringle 1988). In her study of secretaries, for example, Rosemary Pringle argues that the boss–secretary relationship is 'the most visible aspect of a pattern of domination based on desire and sexuality' (1988, p. 84), with secretaries' sexuality consumed at either a real or fantasy level by their bosses and also by other male workers.

Kinsey approached the acquisition of particular patterns of sexual behaviour in terms of a mechanical learning process, the outcome of conditioning. This made it impossible to examine the complex psychological processes by which a sexual identity is constructed, the subjective experiences that lie behind overt 'behaviour'. Kinsey's approach thus overlooks the relationship between sexual *behaviour* and sexual *identity*. A central element of Kinsey's argument—the idea of a 'balance' between homosexual and heterosexual behaviours—has thus disappeared almost without trace, finding no resonance in people's actual experience of their sexual identity, 'engulfed by the idea of the gay identity'. (On all the above points, see the discussion of the social interactionist approach in Chapter 15.)

Kinsey's definition of sexuality in terms of achievement, frequency of encounters and number of orgasms suggested an admiration for 'robust performance'. Those with 'low outlet' were described, states De Cecco, 'as being in poor health, physically incapacitated, sexually apathetic, slow starters, deprived … or sexually timid and inhibited' (1990, p. 370). Kinsey's perspective thus contributed to the identification of maximum sexual 'performance' as an essential aspect of a 'healthy' personality, and encouraged the development of a sexual 'performance principle' without much understanding of the relationship between the aspects of people's lives defined as sexual, non-sexual or somewhere in between.

Kinsey's position suggested that sexuality could be regarded as the pursuit of largely physical pleasure uncomplicated by any social or political concerns. De Cecco points out that one primary purpose for sexual activity—reproduction—was replaced with another—pleasure, in a manner where the supposedly 'natural' was seen as the foundation of human sexual relations. However, most historical and sociological studies of sexuality reject such a naturalistic approach and suggest that the promotion of 'the sexual' as a central organising principle of human life is itself socially constructed, with political and moral dimensions.

The psychology of gender and sexuality after Kinsey

There is also a massive body of psychological research into gender and sexual orientation that has, since the 1970s, been subjected to increasing criticism, from psychologists themselves as well as from other social scientists. Most of this research has been concerned with identifying the features, origins and developmental processes of masculinity and femininity, homosexuality and heterosexuality. Despite the impressive persistence with which the possibility of identifying these aspects of sexual identity as psychological entities has been pursued, however, the psychologists engaged in this quest are no closer to their target today than they were a century ago.

In relation to gender, Florence Geis (1993) has argued that it is primarily a system of self-fulfilling prophecies. Gender stereotypes construct both the perception and treatment of men and women, and the resultant sex differences in behaviour are then held to confirm the original stereotypes. Whatever has been defined as masculine or feminine is in fact the product of 'social expectations and the situational opportunities and constraints of high- versus low-status social roles and power' (p. 38). The history of gender testing, and the seemingly limitless flexibility with which particular traits fluctuate between being masculine or feminine (displaying too much knowledge about a topic, for example, used to earn you masculinity points), indicates that gender is a purely social construct.

Ideal gender roles are almost impossible to attain for the majority of the population; they operate more as models against which we all measure ourselves, usually to be found wanting.

Joseph Pleck (1981) has argued that gender roles (he called them 'sex roles') are by definition unattainable. Pleck suggested that there is persistent tension and conflict both *within* the gender roles we are supposed to play and *between* those ideals of gender and our real personalities, as well as the requirements of other aspects of our lives as workers, parents and so on. This tension, strain and conflict is not simply a malfunctioning in the gender system or the result of individual 'deviance' from established norms, but actually an essential feature of the social construction of gender.

With respect to sexual orientation, there is no identifiable 'pathway' to homosexual orientation and it correlates with no other aspect of personality. The only strong predictor is the sex of the people in the sexual imagery who are found to be arousing, particularly during adolescence (Storms 1980; Bell, Weinberg & Hammersmith 1981); and for Money (1990), erotic orientation is defined by whom we fall in love with, irrespective of whom we have sex with. Pat Califia (cited in Money 1990, p. 195) noted further that it is curious that sexual orientation is defined only in terms of the sex of our partners, when eroticism may be defined by quite different concerns—types of sexual activity, body type or particular social contexts. Money added that there is no reason to assume that erotic desire is the only

> ## Case Study
> ### Unblushing sexual identity
>
> In 1963, Erving Goffman wrote:
>
> *In an important sense there is only one complete unblushing male in America: a young, married, white, urban, northern, heterosexual Protestant father of college education, fully employed, of good complexion, weight, and height, and a recent record in sports... Any male who fails to qualify in any one of these ways is likely to view himself—during moments at least—as unworthy, incomplete, and inferior. (p. 128)*
>
> 1. How have things changed since that time?
> 2. Is there only 'one complete unblushing male in Australia today' and, if so, how would you describe him? And is there 'one complete unblushing female'?
> 3. What is it that makes men and women feel as though they might be 'unworthy, incomplete, and inferior' in their gender and sexual identity?

possible motive for sexual activity. Sexual conduct is also based on an almost infinite variety of motives and desires, which are not in themselves erotic (Gagnon 1990) and only become so through the activities of people making the linkage; desire for power, danger, affection, tenderness, social recognition, psychological acknowledgement, defying social convention, social mobility, assuaging anxiety, earning money, the wish to have children—all are possible candidates. As Gilbert Herdt summed it up:

Nowadays, we might more properly say that there are multiple heterosexualities and homosexualities, which are neither simple nor 'natural' but rather complicated developmental pathways to varied outcomes. (1990, p. 228)

SEXUAL CONDUCT— JOHN GAGNON AND WILLIAM SIMON

The interactionist perspective on sex, gender and sexuality extends the anthropological argument about the cultural relativity of human sexuality to emphasise that sexual conduct enters human relations only within the framework of the social meaning given to it.

In a critique of Kinsey's approach to sexuality, which seemed to regard 'sexual response' as a fairly straightforward set of physiological reactions, M. H. Kuhn (1954) was the first to identify some of the main elements of an interactionist perspective on sexuality. He argued that human physiology itself gives no reliable clue to the patterns of activities that will be associated with that physiology. Summarising what was essentially one of the key points of Freud's theory of sexuality, Kuhn pointed out that physiology itself 'does not supply the motives, designate the partners, invest the objects with preformed passion, nor even dictate the objectives to be achieved. Sex acts, sexual objects, sexual partners (human or otherwise), like all other objects towards which humans behave, are *social objects*; that is, they have meanings because meanings are assigned to them' by human social groups (p. 123).

John Gagnon and William Simon gave this idea more concrete form with the argument that human sexual conduct is organised, like a theatre piece, into a variety of different sexual *scripts* that define the situation, identify the actors and outline the plot. Without such scripts nothing sexual will happen. Biological drives are not sufficient. Thus, argued Gagnon and Simon:

combining such elements as desire, privacy, and a physically attractive person of the appropriate sex, the probability of something sexual happening will, under normal circumstances, remain exceedingly small until either one or both actors organize these behaviors into an appropriate script. (1973, p. 19)

Ironically, the belief that sexuality is biologically based is itself a powerful common element of sexual scripts in Western societies, producing what Gagnon and Simon called 'collective blindness' to the idea that sexuality is scripted. Rather than sexual impulses being expressed within social roles, the relationship is actually the reverse, with sexuality a vehicle for the expression of social roles.

Sexual scripts

Gagnon and Simon developed two basic arguments in their book *Sexual Conduct*:

1. *What* situations and behaviours are defined as sexual is socially determined.
2. *How* those situations and behaviours unfold as specifically 'sexual' events is subject to more or less organised 'scripts', which provide a framework of

meaning. Without such scripts the sexual character of the interaction collapses, almost wholly unsupported by any biological sexual drives.

They identified a range of different scripts that organise human sexuality, including different stages of the average life course from childhood to mature adulthood, prostitutes, prisoners, and homosexual men and women. Middle age and old age were given little attention, and the discussions of sex and the elderly can be seen precisely as an attempt to overcome the fact that the elderly have no easily identifiable script other than that of 'decline'.

Childhood sexual scripts

In relation to childhood sexual scripts, Gagnon and Simon discussed two important areas. First, the gendering of identity occurs both at the *nonverbal level*—through physical contact, differential responses to aggression in boys and girls, and frequency of father–child as opposed to mother–child interaction—and at the *verbal level*, through the naming of behaviour and the verbal reactions to behaviour defined as either sexual or non-sexual.

The definition of what is sexual/non-sexual, approved/disapproved occurs within a process of placing sexuality within a particular universe of meaning—production of children (child itself, siblings), love, marriage, faithfulness, visibility, relation to more visible activity and so on. Gagnon and Simon gave the example of how children's fondling of their genitals might be constructed as 'masturbation' by the adults around them. They argued that the real attractiveness of the behaviour, which virtually all children know to be something that is disapproved of, 'will not derive from anything that resembles sexual pleasure, but from the mysterious and unnamed qualities that are ascribed to the behaviour by the adult world' (1973, p. 36).

Second, Gagnon and Simon pointed out that childhood verbal references to sexuality exist almost completely independently of children's experience and understanding of what adults presume sexual vocabulary refers to. Sexual concepts thus 'develop a complexity of meanings and associations long before they are ultimately applied to the realm of sexual behaviour' (p. 38). A sexual vocabulary loaded with emotion, much of it aggression, composed of words such as 'fuck', 'cunt', 'prick', 'screw', 'motherfucker' and 'wanker', is constructed prior to the experience of the sexual activity they are supposed to refer to, and 'in these nonsexual and often aggressive and hostile applications, become another shaping force when they are applied to the sexual experience itself' (p. 38).

Adolescence and post-adolescence

It is at the onset of adolescence—roughly between 11 and 14 years of age—that a person's sexual character is explicitly recognised and all the previous sexual discourse comes together in a script that is applied to the self. During this period it becomes important to achieve a 'sexual status', not only because of the possible intrinsic attractions of sexual activity, but also because of the role that sexuality plays as a focal point for the organisation of what Gagnon and Simon called 'heterosocial' and 'homosocial' relationships.

In homosociality, 'valuation of the self is more keyed to those of like gender than those of opposing gender' (p. 68). They noted that the most common pattern among adolescent males was a combination of strongly emphasised heterosexuality and homosociality, with heterosexual activity playing a secondary role to homosociality, a focus for bonding among males rather than between males and females. Sex is scripted as a form of achievement for young men and a form of 'social service' for young women; males are scripted to take the initiative, and females are scripted to act reactively as 'gate-keepers'.

The need for sexual scripts is made particularly strong by the cultural expectation that sexual activity takes place largely with minimal discussion, which is part of the model of sex as a 'powerful natural drive'. A stream of practical questions—What's actually going to happen? Should I get undressed now? and so on—have to be answered almost completely wordlessly, a formidable feat of nonverbal communication. The fact that sexual partners are so heavily restricted in their verbal communication makes them heavily dependent on pre-designated scripts to tell them what to do, at least in broad outline.

The sources of scripts are various: most powerfully, our own biography, but also novels, films, magazines, pornography, sex manuals, peers, previous experience and our own imagination. Scripts are also not 'trivial' in the sense that one can easily rewrite them or move around from one script to another at will; often they become experienced as central to our personality. One important pattern is the combination of repetition of previous (pleasant) experience—and avoidance of previous unpleasant experience—with possible variations on that experience, into the realm of innovatory activities.

There is also historical development in sexual scripts, so that there is considerable variation even in what is perceived and experienced as 'erotic' (Simon & Gagnon 1986). John Gagnon (1990) remarked on how difficult it is, even for those who lived through the period between the world wars, to recollect accurately 'the pleasures and pains of sexual life' in that period, and impossible to imagine for those who did not. New 'social forms of desire' were emerging, dancing to jazz and swing, 'double-dating in cars while listening to the sounds of Glenn Miller and Guy Lombardo, the exquisite pleasures and anxieties of truly forbidden and dangerous unbuttonings and touchings' (p. 185). Gagnon sounds almost nostalgic when he says: 'A sexuality created out of glimpses, denials, fears, going only part of the way, and waiting for true love, certainly had its appeal' (p. 185).

Today, in contrast, oral sex, which in the 1930s was regarded in much the same way as sodomy, is considered a relatively unremarkable part of sexual interaction: 'Practices that were once examples of the perverse, the infantile, the abnormal, the deviant are now, among many social groups, mostly matters of convention or taste' (Gagnon 1990, p. 179).

Sex as a powerful 'natural' drive

Gagnon and Simon went beyond simply criticising the idea that sexual identity has a biological base and argued that this idea itself—that sex is a product of some 'essential nature'—is a crucial part of the way in which sexuality is socially constructed in Western societies. Sexuality tends to be regarded as 'a beast held in check only by the application of immense societal sanctions' (1968, p. 121). The tension between a biologically based sexual drive and civilisation is seen to be responsible for both the destructiveness and the creativity of human society. The possibility of liberating sexuality is then seen both as the basis for human freedom and as leading to social disintegration. However, Gagnon and Simon regarded this concept of sexuality as being produced by our perception of it, and argued that 'without the imagery of power and danger, the sexual impulse is no more potent than any other biological component' (1968, p. 121).

It is precisely the notion that sexuality is driven by presocial, natural, biological forces that underlies most of its appeal. As Gagnon and Simon stated:

> It is the possibility of transgression and normative violation that gives sex a status beyond gourmet cooking—it is the possibility of believing that one is controlling a powerful drive that allows a sense of virtue to arise from conformity and the observation of norms, and a sense of sin to arise from their violation. The wisdom of the body (at the risk of being metaphysical) is a consequence of consciousness and culture. (1973, p. 108)

Gagnon and Simon noted 'There is a sense of dismay when one makes the suggestion that sex is really just like everything else' (1973, p. 108) or that there might not be a Promethean struggle between the demands of nature and the requirements of civilisation. The notion that civilisation makes us discontented generates the possibility of delicious, uncivilised, forbidden pleasures, and to suggest otherwise 'tends to undermine the dramatic and powerful images of sex and leaves in its wake a sense of relatively simple and pleasant capacity that cannot fulfil the promises that have been made for it' (1973, p. 108).

Scripting theory

In response to the studies that emerged after *Sexual Conduct*, Simon and Gagnon (1986) developed the notion of sexual scripts to distinguish between their operation in different ways at three different levels of social reality:

1. **cultural scenarios**—operating at the level of social institutions and 'collective life', they 'instruct in the normative requirements of particular roles' (p. 98)
2. **interpersonal scripts**—'the application of specific cultural scenarios by specific individuals in a specific social context', 'the ordering of representations of self and other that facilitate the occurrence of a sexual act' (p. 97)
3. **intrapsychic scripts**—the management of desire within individuals, 'the ordering of images and desires that elicit and sustain sexual arousal' (p. 97).

In other words, sexual scripts are oriented in three directions: towards society, towards others and towards one's self. All social conduct involves all three levels of scripting, although in different historical and cultural

> *An interactionist view of the self provides a means of conceptualizing how we come to be embodied gendered and sexual individuals who nonetheless have the capacity to renegotiate gender divisions and resist dominant constructions of sexuality. It can help to explain why gender is so central to our sense of self without there being a single way of being male or female and why it is so fundamental to the development of a sexual self without positing a deterministic link between gender and sexuality. It provides a basis for analyzing how the reflexivity entailed in the construction of our gendered and sexual selves can be mobilized into particular forms of self-understanding and self-telling in late modernity. (Jackson 2006, pp. 12–13)*

contexts one level can be more significant than the others.

For more recent mobilisations of scripting theory, see the collection in Kimmel (2006).

Reflective question: How would you explain Gagnon and Simon's theory of sexual scripts? Give your own examples of sexual scripts.

AN ETHNOMETHODOLOGICAL APPROACH—SUZANNE KESSLER AND WENDY MCKENNA

In the sex/gender distinction, the argument that gender is socially constructed often relegates sex entirely to the realm of biology and treats it as somehow 'presocial'. The American ethnomethodologists Suzanne Kessler and Wendy McKenna (1978), however, examined the social construction of sex differences, drawing on Harold Garfinkel's (1967) notion of 'cultural genitals', which is based on a distinction between the possession of a penis or a vagina as a *biological* or *cultural* event. They considered that it is not just such gender roles that are socially produced, but also the very way in which a person is regarded as male or female, which they termed **gender attribution**.

Most people hold to what Garfinkel called the 'natural attitude' to gender, assuming that whether someone is male or female is an independent 'fact' based in the real world, that gender is invariant and that the essential signs of someone's sex are the biological 'facts'—that is, the genitals. Kessler and McKenna argue that in reality we differentiate between men and women on the basis of evidence other than biological differences, and that the biological evidence itself is socially constructed.

For example, in biological terms human beings are not divided simply into two mutually exclusive categories, male and female. Some people can have a male genetic make-up but still experience themselves as female. Others may have a particular chromosomal make-up known as Turner's syndrome, whereby they have a single X chromosome instead of the usual male XY or female XX configuration. They look and feel female, but register as male in tests for gender employed in sporting competitions. Yet others have both sets of genitals (**hermaphrodites**) and some have a complex hormonal make-up that does not clearly constitute them as either male or female.

Kessler and McKenna went on to examine how individuals who do not 'fit' the standard gender categories experience their gender identity, interviewing **transsexuals**—individuals who experience themselves as different from their apparent biological sex, sometimes to the point of undergoing medical treatment to alter their hormones and genitals. Our sense of a person's genital make-up is usually 'read off' from their external appearance. Show people a picture of someone flat-chested with short hair and wearing a suit, and they will all presume that this person has a penis and no breasts. But this is not the case for transsexuals, which raises the question of how we actually determine another person's gender.

Kessler and McKenna believe that gender attribution, with particular reference to transsexualism, works in the following four ways:

1. Public physical appearance, or what Kessler and McKenna call **secondary sexual characteristics**, includes breasts, facial and body hair, width of hips, length of hair, distribution of body fat, breadth of shoulders and so on. (The **primary sexual characteristics** are the genitals.) For example, female-to-male transsexuals may disguise their breasts by wearing baggy clothing or by using strapping.
2. Facial expression, movement, body posture, clothing and voice—the **tertiary sexual characteristics** through which gender is displayed—form probably the most important element of gender attribution. Some male-to-female transsexuals have trained themselves to put more inflection in their voices and to have more mobile facial movements when talking.
3. What people say about their life history and current situation is also central to the process of gender attribution. Much of our everyday conversation contains clues about our gender identity, and transsexuals need to incorporate a re-gendering of their biographies in order to 'pass' as the opposite sex. In one case, a female-to-male transsexual attributed pierced ears to belonging to a tough street gang. Others introduce themselves as 'Miss' to settle any doubt.
4. Finally, the most obvious element is the person's **private body**, which gives clues about the genitals. Situations that expose more of the body—medical examinations, going to the beach or swimming pool, public showers, sharing rooms with others and urinating in the presence of others—are important indicators of sex. Transsexuals who have not had their physical body altered need to negotiate such situations carefully.

Kessler and McKenna also found an asymmetry in the gender attribution process: any single sign of male gender is sufficient for a person to be regarded as male, despite contrary indications of femaleness. The general schema by which members of Western society identify people as male or female is: see someone as female only when you cannot see them as male. This is why it is easier for female-to-male transsexuals to pass as males than it is for male-to-female transsexuals: a single male sign is sufficient to be identified as male. Such a principle is currently having significant influence in the sporting world, where female athletes who are given genetic tests and show any sign of XY chromosomes are disqualified as 'really' male.

For transsexuals, taking on the identity of a sex to which they do not belong biologically is clearly difficult and demanding. But Kessler and McKenna's essential point is that this is true for everyone—we all have to learn how to be masculine or feminine, and the mechanisms involved in the attribution of gender identity are social and cannot simply be read off from biology.

Sexuality and power—Michel Foucault

One of the most influential contributions to the 'denaturalisation' of sexuality has been the work of French philosopher and historian of ideas Michel Foucault (1926–84). Like Gagnon and Simon, in *The History of Sexuality* Foucault (1978) argued that sexuality should not be seen as a potentially liberating 'natural' force held in check by social repression, but as itself socially produced.

He observed that there was a tendency to see sexuality as repressed in late 19th- and 20th-century Western societies, as somehow contrary to, and subversive of, power and social order. This idea was what Foucault referred to as the *repression hypothesis*. Its corollary was the idea that those forms of sexuality that did not conform to the norm should also be seen as subversive of existing social relations of power.

However, Foucault argued for a different conception of power, seeing it not simply as restrictive or repressive, but also as productive:

> *If power was never anything but repressive, if it never did anything but say no, do you really believe that we should manage to obey it? What gives power its hold, what makes it accepted, is quite simply the fact that it does not simply weigh like a force which says no, but that it runs through, and it produces, things, it induces pleasure, it forms knowledge, it produces discourse; it must be considered as a productive network which runs through the entire social body much more than as a negative instance whose function is repression.* (2000, p. 120)

In the context of this overall understanding of power, Foucault's study of the history of sexuality showed that the historical evidence indicates more an *encouragement* and *incitement* of discourses of sexuality. These discourses were manifested in the writings and activities of a wide range of professionals—doctors, social workers, psychologists and psychiatrists, social scientists, criminologists and statisticians—and state agencies.

In this way, Foucault extended Gagnon and Simon's initial argument about sexual scripts well beyond the sexual realm and individuals engaged in sexual conduct to the broader range of professional and state activities and structures that formed the surrounding social and political context for sexual scripts. In *Sexual Conduct* (Gagnon & Simon 1973), the source of sexual scripts was unclear, but Foucault provided a picture of the historical development of sexual scripts as located within a wider system of power relations.

An important element of Foucault's analysis, then, was the demonstration that *all* sexual identities are social and discursively produced, including supposedly deviant and oppressed ones such as homosexuality. This meant that even the critique of sexual oppression 'is … in fact part of the same historical network as the thing it denounces (and doubtless misrepresents) by calling it "repression"' (1978, p. 10). For Foucault, marginal groups (such as gay men and lesbians) do not escape or stand outside the operation of power relations, and the identity of 'the homosexual' or 'the lesbian feminist' is itself produced by power relations.

Beyond sexual 'identity'—queer sexuality

This kind of critique of the concept of homosexual or gay and lesbian identity, alongside more general shifts in social theory accompanying social constructivism, helped to lay the foundations for the development of 'queer' theory. Initially the primary impetus for queer theory came from outside sociology, in the work of scholars such as Judith Butler (1990), Eve Kosofsky Sedgwick (1990; 1992) and Diana Fuss (1991). The ideas developed by queer theorists arose to a large extent in response to a number of problems associated with the way in which sexuality had been understood in the social constructionist approach.

First, there were difficulties concerning what was 'unexpected' about actual sexual activity, inconsistencies and instabilities in sexual identities. For example, instead of all gay men conforming to any particular 'identity', there are in fact a variety of forms of gay masculinity (Brekhus 2003). The boundary between heterosexual masculinity and femininity had also become less clear. In relation to sexual practices, the HIV/AIDS epidemic revealed that not all apparently straight men restricted themselves to heterosexual sex, and that people actually seemed to pursue mixtures of different forms of sexual practice. It appeared that there are many straight men who like to dress as women, transsexuals who conform to traditional gender roles, lesbians who are not feminist and so on. As Dennis Altman put it, 'The idea that people are either "straight" or "gay" is a convenient fiction, which ignores the far more fluid nature of sexual desire and fantasy' (1997, p. 107).

Second, following Foucault's arguments, the idea of a gay or lesbian 'identity' itself appeared to operate as a vehicle for power relations. Steven Seidman, for example, suggested that: 'Identity constructions function as templates defining selves and behaviours and therefore excluding a range of possible ways to frame the self, body, desires, actions, and social relations' (1996, p. 12). The concept of identity, while constituting the focus and basis of political action, is also, as Gamson observed, 'the basis for oppression' (1995, p. 393).

Third, the attention of social constructivist writers had focused largely on homosexuality, but little analytical attention had been paid to heterosexuality as being equally socially constructed, equally a product of a variety of social practices and institutions.

The idea of queer sexuality was to a large extent a response to these kinds of conceptual problems. Stein and Plummer (1996, p. 134) highlight the following features of what was put forward as a queer perspective on sexuality:

1. Sexuality is a form of power pervading all aspects of society, particularly through the construction of boundaries and binary oppositions.
2. Gender and sexual categories are unstable and often inconsistent and incoherent.
3. Political activity need not be restricted to the existing accepted forms, but can include activities focused on cultural production, public festivals and carnivals, parody and so on.

4. Almost everything in social life has a sexual dimension, so that a 'queer' reading of any social, cultural, political or economic issue is possible.

Ken Plummer has pointed out that in many respects the development of queer theory, in its questioning of the 'grand narratives' of sexuality, can be understood as the 'postmodernization of sex'. 'Queer theory', writes Plummer, 'is really poststructuralism (and postmodernism) applied to sexualities and genders' (2003, p. 520).

Critiques of queer theory

There are a number of criticisms of queer theory as a novel approach to understanding human sexuality. First, many of its arguments simply repeat those already present in the sociological critique of naturalism. As Stein and Plummer put it, 'the idea that sexuality is socially constructed was promoted by interpretive sociologists and feminist theorists at least two decades before queer theory emerged on the intellectual scene' (1996, p. 136).

Second, reflecting the origins of queer theory in literary and cultural studies, there is a tendency to concentrate on various kinds of texts—literature, film, art—at the expense of studying human beings and what they do. For Stein and Plummer, 'there is a danger for the new queer theorists to ignore "real" queer life as it is materially experienced across the world, while they play with the free-floating signifiers of texts ... Sociology's key concerns—inequality, modernity, institutional analysis, can bring a clearer focus to queer theory' (1996, pp. 137–8).

Third, queer theorists are often criticised for the sheer density and conceptual difficulty of their writing. The effect of this is that queer theory 'limits its audience to only the most theory-literate' (Stein & Plummer 1996, p. 141). Dennis Altman points out: 'The rhetorical flourishes of queer deconstruction have little meaning for groups in Bombay, Buenos Aires or Budapest who have seized on the idea of lesbian/gay identities as a way of carving out certain social and political space in rapidly changing societies' (1997, p. 113).

Fourth, it is possible that the argument for the instability and fluidity of sexual identities has been overstated. Ken Plummer has argued that while the argument might apply to some groups of people, 'empirically I have found it very rare indeed to come across people who live their lives in such fleeting, fragmentary and unstable ways'. In general terms, Plummer suggests that 'sexualities and genders tend to be organized very deeply indeed'. He goes on to argue that:

Gender pervades almost every aspect of our lives, and seems to have a very deep structure. It cannot be lightly changed, performed or wished away very quickly. Likewise, patterns of sexual desire also seem subject to deep routinization. This is not, of course, to say that gender or desire cannot be changed over lives or over cultures, or that they do not vary over time and space—all the constructionist writings point to the fact that they can and they do. Those who argue that there are universal women and men, universal homosexuals or universal transvestites striding around history and across cultures simply miss the importance of precarious and contingent social organization. But with the exception of some radically sexual transgressors, changes do not happen that easily or quickly. And the unstable, identity-less, utterly fractured sexual and gender identity seems to be largely a myth created by social science! (Plummer 2003, p. 525)

Queer sexual politics

In the 1990s the politics of the gay and lesbian movement shifted significantly towards increasing use of the concept of 'queer' sexual politics, as part of activist responses to HIV/AIDS, especially in the United States, and the activist groups 'Queer Nation' and 'ACT UP'. This shift was based on the critique of a reliance on conceptual dualisms such as straight/gay and acceptance of 'minority' status in relation to the dominant sexual groupings. As Teresa de Lauretis puts it, in the queer approach to sexual politics:

Homosexuality is no longer to be seen simply as marginal with regard to a dominant, stable form of sexuality (heterosexuality) against which it would be defined ... it is no longer to be seen as transgressive or deviant vis-à-vis a proper, natural sexuality (i.e. institutionalized reproductive sexuality) according to the older pathological model, or as just another, optional 'lifestyle' according to the model of contemporary North American pluralism. (1991, p. iii)

Following Foucault's analysis of the history of sexuality, the categories that had been the focus of attempts to transform gender and sexuality, such as gay and lesbian, were themselves increasingly 'criticized for functioning as disciplining political forces' (Seidman 1996, p. 10). By using the very word that had been used in a negative way to refer to homosexuality, the reorganisation of gay and lesbian politics in the form of queer politics 'opposes society itself', resisting 'not just the normal behaviour of the social, but the *idea* of normal behaviour' (Warner 1993, p. xxvii).

Just as queer theory has been criticised, there are also some reservations about the turn to queer sexual politics. First, the shift away from identity politics may be accompanied by a number of problems. Dennis Altman, for example, points out that political action generally requires some sort of 'identity' as a foundation for that action:

Without the invention of certain forms of identity and community, the creation of alternative sites of power and expertise, of dissident voices to those of the recognized orthodoxies, would be impossible. The assertion of identity by marginalized and stigmatized groups strengthens the definitions which can be used to control them, but at the same time creates the possibilities to address those factors which maintain their stigmatization. (1997, p. 106)

Whatever the problems with identity as a disciplinary mechanism, argues Altman, it has also been important as an element of self-assertion and self-esteem in the face of a negative broader social construction of people's particular activities and practices. For Altman, 'As long as considerable homophobia exists, as long as people fear rejection, persecution, even violence from others because of their sexuality, there is a need for a political concept of lesbian/gay identity which cannot be easily assimilated under "queerness"' (1997, p. 110).

Second, it may be that queer political activity attempts to pull together groups that actually have little in common. 'Most homosexuals', believes Altman, 'do not feel any particular community with sex-workers, transsexuals, or straight fetishists' (1997, p. 110). For example, there is currently a strong concern among gays and lesbians with the idea of gay marriage, which from a queer perspective is largely a normalising and disciplinary tendency (Warner 1999).

Third, rather than being inherently critical of establishing social institutions and opposing dominant power relations, it may be that queerness is sometimes rather easily incorporated within existing power structures. For example, one could see the rise of the image of masculinity known as 'metrosexuality' ('men who moisturise') as consistent with the queer approach to sexuality, since it rejects the bipolar distinctions between masculine/feminine and heterosexual/homosexual. The term 'metrosexual' was first introduced by British journalist and author Mark Simpson in a 1994 article in *The Independent* titled 'Here come the Mirror Men', but its usage became especially widespread after Simpson posted an article in the American online magazine, *Salon.com*, in 2002 entitled 'Meet the metrosexual'.

Simpson's argument is that the sense of particular forms of dress, speech, physical comportment and appearance as being indicative of gender and sexual identity is being increasingly weakened, rendering sexual identity less stable and fixed, and indeed less significant than the achievement of an image as an object of desire for its own sake. This new configuration of masculinity 'queers' the old form in three ways, writes Simpson: 'It's passive where it should always be active, desired where it should always be desiring, looked at where it should always be looking' (Simpson 2004). Simpson's initial leading examples of metrosexuality were David Beckham, Brad Pitt and Spiderman, but later he also identified Tom Cruise ('he uses all the technology of beauty and fashion to remain a desirable, smooth-skinned, buffed boy with a tarty grin') and Arnold Schwarzenegger—'an example of (early) metrosexuality, proto-metro if you will, because ... he became devoted to his physique, turning himself into a spectacle, a sign, a commodity, one that was eventually noticed and bought by Hollywood—and used to seduce hundreds of millions of other boys around the world into turning themselves into commodities' (Simpson 2004).

However, this kind of construction of male sexual identity is also a powerful marketing tool and an avenue for increased male consumption in cosmetics, hair products, clothing, gym memberships and so on. There may be some sort of gender equality in male bodies being treated the same as female bodies, but the underlying power dynamics remain those of commodification and commercialisation. As Mark Simpson observed, 'it might be said that metrosexuality represents a certain kind of liberation of the male, but I suspect it's another kind of enslavement, albeit a better-dressed variety' (Simpson 2004). To the extent that it requires new consumption patterns to sustain it, queer sexuality is in at least some respects an ideal capitalist sexuality.

> **Reflective questions:** What are the arguments for and against use of the concept 'identity' to think about gender and sexuality? To what extent would it be true to say that 'we are all queer now'?

SOCIOLOGY AND THE FUTURE OF GENDER AND SEXUALITY

Sociological problems and issues have often been defined in terms of the concerns and perspectives of a particular male-centred culture. That culture has been both strongly gendered—in the sense of insisting on major differences between the capacities and social positions of men and women—and simultaneously gender-blind—in the sense of pretending that what was being analysed was a 'human' rather than a specifically male-dominated social world. As a result, for much of its history, sociology has, in many respects, been the sociology of heterosexual men, without much awareness of the specifically masculine and heterosexist character of its perspective on the human social world.

One of the effects of the masculinist and heterosexist culture of Western societies has been that gender- and sexuality-conscious sociological studies have been slow to emerge. A number of factors have contributed to the development of an expanding sociology of gender and sexuality:

1. The definition of women's position in society as a social problem, in relation to social changes such as their increasing participation in education, paid employment, the declining birth rate and so on.
2. The pervasive workings of a liberal ideology of equality and democracy, which make it difficult to sustain social arrangements and ideas that fail to treat women, gay men and lesbians as individuals or citizens who are basically equal to heterosexual men. The general orientation of politically liberal, economically capitalist and industrial societies towards 'achievement' thus, at least, has the tendency to undermine gradually ascriptive categories such as gender and sexual identity.

> I feel it is my duty to let the world know that David Beckham, role model to hundreds of millions of impressionable boys around the world, heartthrob for equal numbers of young girls, is not heterosexual at all. No, ladies and gentlemen, the captain of the England football squad is actually a screaming, shrieking, flaming, freaking metrosexual ... How do I know? ... to determine a metrosexual, all you have to do is look at them. In fact, if you're looking at them, they're almost certainly metrosexual. The typical metrosexual is a young man with money to spend, living in or within easy reach of a metropolis—because that's where all the best shops, clubs, gyms and hairdressers are. He might be officially gay, straight or bisexual, but this is utterly immaterial, because he has clearly taken himself as his own love object and pleasure as his sexual preference ... The stoic, self-denying, modest straight male who didn't shop enough ... had to be replaced by a new kind of man, one less certain of his identity and much more interested in his image—that's to say, one who was much more interested in being looked at (because that's the only way you can be certain you actually exist). A man, in other words, who is an advertiser's walking wet dream. (Simpson 2002)

3. The dissatisfaction that men themselves have felt with existing gender models. As Connell points out, homosexual and non-traditional heterosexual men also suffer under the current gender regime; also, in their everyday lives, heterosexual men are interdependent with women as wives, lovers, daughters, sisters and colleagues.

In many areas of sociology, a subject and its treatment are influenced more by what happens in society than by developments within the discipline itself. In the case of gender and sexuality, a variety of economic, social and political changes have led to the emergence of the sociology of gender and sexuality as subject areas in their own right. This work has opened up the discipline of sociology so that it no longer ignores more than half the human race and takes the realm of private life, intimate relations and sexual desire seriously.

One of the major difficulties that a political concern with overcoming the oppression of women and homosexuality can produce for an accurate sociological understanding of gender and sexuality is the tendency to think in dichotomous terms: male/female, homosexual/heterosexual, normal/deviant. It is clearly important to recognise and analyse the ways in which these polar oppositions have become embodied in social institutions, but also to move beyond them. One of the more important contributions of queer theory has been to stimulate sociological theory and research into a new ways of thinking about gender and sexuality.

When sociological thought remains captured by such dichotomies, the effect is to reproduce and maintain the very organisation of diverse human relationships into oppressive oppositions that sociologists are concerned to criticise. As Theodor Adorno (1981) put it:

Hope cannot aim at making the mutilated social character of women identical to the mutilated social character of men; rather, its goal must be a state in which the face of the grieving woman disappears simultaneously with that of the bustling, capable man, a state in which all that survives the disgrace of the difference between the sexes is the happiness that difference makes possible. (p. 82)

In being critical of oppression organised around sexual identity, the danger to be kept constantly in mind is that of overlooking how much all human beings—male, female, homosexual, heterosexual, transvestite, transsexual—have in common with each other and, as Connell puts it, 'the riotous exuberance of motive and imagination that is a possibility in sexual life' (1987, p. 175).

Tutorial exercises

1. What are the ways in which heterosexuality is made 'compulsory' in Australian society? Do you think the experience of homosexuality has changed over time? What impact has the idea of queer sexuality had on gender and sexual identity?
2. Can you give examples of the ways in which sexuality is bound up with relationships of power? Did it matter that Sarah Palin was a woman, for example? In what ways does it make a difference if primary school teachers are male or female?
3. Imagine a world without gender distinctions. What difference would it make to the character of social relationships, or the way in which social life is structured and organised?
4. Explain what the concept of metrosexuality refers to. Look through some recent newspapers to find some examples of metrosexuality. Do you think that the primary concern is stimulating male consumption patterns, or is there a real change taking place in the nature of masculine identities and male–female relationships?

For activity suggestions, learning aids, revision of key concepts and access to self-study material, visit: **www.pearson.com.au/highered/vankrieken4e**

Further reading

Atlman, D. 2001, *Global Sex*, Allen & Unwin, Sydney.
Beasley, C. 2005, *Gender and Sexuality: Critical Theories, Critical Thinkers*, Sage, London.
Connell, R. W. 1987, *Gender and Power*, Allen & Unwin, Sydney.
Connell, R. W. 2002, *Gender*, Polity Press, Cambridge.
Evans, D. T. 1993, *Sexual Citizenship*, Routledge, London.
Jackson, S. & Scott, S. (eds) 2002, *Gender: A Sociological Reader*, Routledge, London.
Jackson, S. & Scott, S. 2010, *Theorising Sexuality*, Open University Press, Milton Keynes.
Kimmel, M. (ed.) 2006, *The Sexual Self: the Construction of Sexual Scripts*, Vanderbilt University Press, Nashville, TN.
Matthews, J. J. (ed.) 1997, *Sex in Public: Australian Sexual Cultures*, Allen & Unwin, Sydney.
Oakley, A. 2005, *The Ann Oakley Reader: Gender, Women and Social Science*, Policy Press, Bristol.
Richters, J. & Rissel, C. 2005, *Doing it Down Under: The Sexual Lives of Australians*, Allen & Unwin, Sydney.
Seidman, S. 1996, *Queer Theory/Sociology*, Blackwell, Cambridge, MA.
Seidman, S., Fischer, N. & Meeks, C. (eds) 2006, *Handbook of the New Sexuality Studies*, Routledge, London.

Websites

Christine Jorgenson's website:
www.christinejorgensen.org

Morgan Centre for the Study of Relationships and Personal Life:
www.socialsciences.manchester.ac.uk/morgancentre

SocioSite's Sex-Gender and Queer Studies section:
www.sociosite.net/topics/gender.php

TASA's Families, Relationships and Gender:
www.tasa.org.au/thematic-groups/families-relationships-and-gender

The Kinsey Institute for Research in Sex, Gender and Reproduction:
www.kinseyinstitute.org

Voice of the Shuttle, Gender Studies:
http://vos.ucsb.edu/browse.asp?id=2711

10 Health

In this chapter we explore health and illness from a sociological vantage point. This entails moving away from the biological and individualistic perspective of medical science and looking to the intersection of culture and social structure with the human body. The new vantage point provides a surprising amount of analytic purchase on questions as basic as: Who gets sick? How do we manage illness? How do we think about disease?

By the end of the chapter, you should have a better understanding of:
— the distinctive qualities of Western 'biomedicine' relative to traditional medical knowledge and practice
— the diverse sociological arguments challenging modern Western medicine
— medical professions, medical institutions and the organisation of health-care systems
— the importance in our society of popular definitions of health and illness, as well as official 'medical' ones
— the causes of death and the impact of culture on the management of death
— the social distribution of illness along race, class and gender lines
— current challenges and transformations to the health-care system and to biomedicine, including alternative therapies.

INTRODUCTION	**320**
THE RISE OF MODERN MEDICINE	**320**
THE SOCIOLOGICAL CRITIQUE OF MODERN MEDICINE	**321**
Michel Foucault and the medical gaze	321
Marxist views on health, class and capitalism	322
Feminist perspectives—controlling women's bodies	322
Micro-perspectives	323
Erving Goffman on the asylum	324
The moral evaluation of patients—Julius Roth	324
THE HOSPITAL	**324**
DOCTOR–PATIENT INTERACTION	**326**
Empirical studies on doctor–patient interaction	327
HEALTH, WELFARE AND THE COMMUNITY	**328**
Community ties and health	329
The decision to see a doctor—Irving Zola	329
Lay definitions of disease	330
THE POLITICAL ECONOMY OF HEALTH AND WELFARE	**330**
Types of health-care systems	330
The health care system in the United States	331
The Australian health-care system	332
The unexpected consequences of Medicare	332
THE MEDICAL OCCUPATIONS—DOCTORS, NURSES AND ALLIED HEALTH PROFESSIONS	**333**
Doctors	334
Nurses and allied health professions	335
Recent changes to the medical professions	335
Medical training	336
DEATH AND DYING	**337**
Dealing with death	337
EPIDEMIOLOGY AND THE SOCIAL CORRELATES OF HEALTH AND ILLNESS	**338**
Causes of death	338
Health in the developing world	339
Sickness, health and social inequality	339
Sickness, health and gender	341
Sickness, health, ethnicity and migration	342
Sickness, health and Aboriginal people	342
CURRENT TRENDS—THE END OF BIOMEDICINE AND MEDICAL DOMINANCE?	**343**
The rise of alternative therapies	343
Feminist interventions and the women's health movement	345
Health promotion and preventive medicine	345
Self-help movements	346
Managerialism, consumerism and the end of medical autonomy	346
CONCLUSION	**347**
Tutorial exercise	348
Further reading	348
Websites	348

INTRODUCTION

In March 2004 the Fred Hollows Foundation demanded a summit on Aboriginal health, claiming that the health of Indigenous Australians was worse than in much of the developing world. Levels of malnutrition, it argued, were similar to that found in Sudan or Sierra Leone. This lamentable state of affairs was hardly news. Report after report has indicated that a major gap exists between Aboriginal health and that of the wider Australian population. In 2002 the former head of the Australian Medical Association, Kerryn Phelps, spoke of the situation as scandalous.

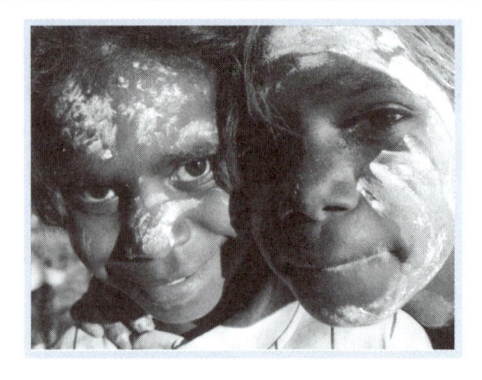

1. Why are Aboriginal health outcomes so poor?
2. What does this tell us about the role of social factors versus biological factors in the distribution of illness and other life chances?

As the case of Aboriginal health shows, health and illness are profoundly social in character. The very basic question 'Who gets sick?' can in part be answered with reference to factors like income. Quality of care can depend on wealth. For example, rich people can afford to pay for better service or opt out of stressful activities. Other social inputs are more subtle. For instance, doctor–patient interactions might seem 'natural' to us, but they are generally shaped by power and by norms about deference to authority. The hospital, with its bureaucracies, hierarchies and technologies, is a product of modernity. The quality of the health-care system can depend on ideology rather than evidence about efficiency and outcomes. Beliefs about the nature of illness and disease are profoundly cultural. They vary from society to society and so influence how people feel about being ill and who treats them—doctor or traditional healer. On the economic front, health and illness are big business. They make up one of the largest employment sectors in Australia. As debates over public health care in the United States show, they are also a crucial factor in political life. Health, then, is about culture, power and institutions as much as it is about genes, bacteria and bodies.

THE RISE OF MODERN MEDICINE

In order to comprehend the unique nature of the modern health-care system and modern health knowledge, it is necessary to examine the conditions of its historical emergence and to identify the ways in which it differs from traditional health knowledge.

In traditional societies, health is closely linked to the religious sphere. The application of traditional remedies is often accompanied by religious interventions such as prayers and meditation. In such societies there is usually a holistic approach to the person, which means that the mind and body are considered to be closely interlinked. According to George Forster and Barbara Anderson (1978), theories of illness in traditional medical knowledge fall into two camps:

- *Personalistic systems* see sickness as the result of malicious action on the part of other people, gods or spirits.
- *Naturalistic systems* argue for the need for balance and harmony in the person. Sickness comes when key substances or forces in the person are out of balance. In traditional Chinese medicine, for example, the key forces are yin and yang.

The central knowledge base of modern medical science is usually known as biomedicine. Biomedicine is a comparatively recent form of medical knowledge, emerging only over the past 300 years. Its core beliefs and practices contrast sharply with those of traditional medicine:

- Science and the scientific method are held to be central to understanding and curing illness. There is no place for folk beliefs and religious knowledge.
- The mind and body are seen as separate and unable to influence each other. For this reason the emotions and desires of the patient are understood as being of little importance in effecting a cure, except in the case of psychological illness.

- The body is like a machine that is made up of separate systems—the nervous system, the circulatory system, the musculoskeletal system and so on. Medical interventions are to be targeted at particular systems rather than at the whole person.
- Biomedical knowledge is supported by a particular complex of social structures. These include hospitals and clinics for the treatment of patients, an organised and regulated medical profession, the pharmaceuticals industry and various research institutions. The complex infrastructure through which modern biomedicine performs its work contrasts with the community organisation of traditional health care.

The rise of biomedicine and biomedical institutions can be explained via a number of the core processes in the emergence of modernity that were theorised by Max Weber, Emile Durkheim and others (see pp. 469 and 475–6). For example there has been *rationalisation* or the rise of scientific knowledge; *secularisation* with the removal of religious thinking on causes and cures for illness; and *differentiation*, which explains both the separation of religion from medicine and the emergence of a specialised medical profession with jurisdiction over medical issues.

THE SOCIOLOGICAL CRITIQUE OF MODERN MEDICINE

Over the years numerous sociologists in the field of health have looked at medical professions and institutions and have argued that they have too much power. Writing in the 1970s, in *Limits to Medicine: Medical Nemesis*, Ivan Illich (1999) launched one of the most influential attacks on the medical profession of recent decades. His thesis centres on the key process of medicalisation and on the dominance of the medical profession. Medicalisation is the process through which more and more aspects of life are defined as medical problems, requiring specialist medical intervention. Illich argues that any possible health benefits of medicalisation are outweighed by the invasion of human freedom and the loss of power to engage in self-care. Additionally, Illich asserts, the process of medicalisation has drained human life of much of its meaning. People no longer have the resources to think of the processes of birth, pain and death in a more holistic, non-medical way. Through medicalisation, suffering becomes meaningless.

MICHEL FOUCAULT AND THE MEDICAL GAZE

The French thinker Michel Foucault provides a complementary perspective to Illich. In his work on the history of mental asylums and medical clinics, he argues that the rise of the medical profession and the modern medical institution is linked to the emergence of new forms of discourse. For Foucault, a discourse is a way of talking about something, organising knowledge and thereby classifying and regulating people. Foucault sees discourses as intimately linked to the forms that power takes in society and argues that they make up a power/knowledge complex. In his book *The Birth of the Clinic* (1973), Foucault shows that the modern clinic or hospital emerged at the end of the 18th century, along with a new discourse on the need for a 'medical gaze' to evaluate the patient. This discourse gives the physician a central role in the process defining health and illness, while devaluing the subjective experiences and interpretations of the patient and the lay community. The clinic, with its rows of beds and collection of patients with different maladies, emerged because it provided the ideal spatial environment for medical training and the development of the gaze.

Likewise in his work *Madness and Civilization* (1965), Foucault argues that the modern asylum for the insane emerged with the Enlightenment in the 18th century. During the Enlightenment, philosophers were praising the power of reason and science. The invention of 'the mad' as a category of person, and their confinement in the asylum, allowed potentially subversive discourses to be controlled and at the same time provided a point of contrast with the triumph of reason.

The broad thesis behind Foucault's work is to suggest that modern medical knowledge is in effect a form of repression and domination in which people are defined by dominant discourses and swept into repressive institutions. Here they are monitored, regulated and subjected to invasive treatment.

Importantly, Foucault sees medical knowledge as symptomatic of wider trends in Western society. In his vision, the world in which we now live is one where discipline, surveillance and control over the body are widespread. This can be seen throughout the core institutions of society—from prisons to schools to the military. In Foucault's understanding of modernity, medical knowledge forms part of an ensemble of discourses aimed at disciplining and controlling populations.

Marxist views on health, class and capitalism

As might be expected, Marxist writers on the modern health system see this as reflecting capitalist interests, processes and social system dynamics. Howard Waitzkin (1983) provides a useful summary of Marxist perspectives on the health system. In his view, Marxist approaches have demonstrated the following:

- Wage inequalities are persistent in the health system. Doctors earn many times more than nurses or cleaners and porters. The health system is therefore just as class-ridden as the rest of society.
- There is little occupational mobility. Few doctors ever come from working-class backgrounds.
- There has been a concentration of wealth in core institutions and hospitals. This reflects the general movement in society towards 'monopoly capital' replacing true market forces, with big corporations squeezing out the competition. The emergence of large medical institutions and corporations has led to the growth of a multibillion dollar medical–industrial complex consisting of health providers, insurance companies, and pharmaceuticals and medical equipment manufacturers. These constitute a powerful lobby group with a vested interest in promoting expensive medical procedures and the general process of medicalisation, which provides an ever-expanding market.
- Medicine is used as a form of social control through the certification of illness and by providing a minimum level of health for the workforce so that there is an adequate supply of workers for the needs of the dominant class.

This last point has been expanded upon by a number of Marxist scholars who argue that modern biomedical beliefs play an essentially ideological role. For example, Steven Kelman (1975) argues that health has been defined in a narrow way related to the ability of the individual to perform a productive role, rather than in holistic terms that include a conception of the need for individual growth and fulfilment. In Kelman's view, such a narrow definition corresponds to the need of capitalism to maintain a productive workforce at the minimum cost.

Feminist perspectives— controlling women's bodies

Feminists argue that the modern medical system is a patriarchal institution that it is run by men and serves male interests. Perhaps the most influential early statement of this hypothesis is by Barbara Ehrenreich and Deirdre English (1973), who suggest that the main victims of medicalisation have been women. For Ehrenreich and English, whereas patriarchy (the rule of men over women) used to be supported by religious legitimation, it is now supported by scientific and medical justification and knowledge. In their empirical work they show how a male-dominated medical profession has marginalised traditional women healers, while at the same time appropriating their traditional skills in areas like midwifery. By defining issues such as childbirth and menstruation as 'medical problems', women have lost important autonomy and control over their own lives and bodies. Feminist scholars have also claimed that the process of medicalisation is often counterproductive from the health point of view, with new interventions often jeopardising women's health rather than improving it. Over recent years, feminist scholars have documented the process of medicalisation in areas as diverse as pregnancy and childbirth, abortion, contraception, ageing, premenstrual syndrome, diet and weight, and mental illness and depression.

While feminist theorists generally portray a top-down process in which medical science dominates women who are passive victims, Catherine Kohler Riessman (1980) suggests that women have often actively participated in this process of medicalisation because of their own needs. Such a perspective may at first glance seem like blaming the victim, but Riessman's point is that these needs and wants have been shaped by a particular set of class/gender relations. Her discussion of contraception provides a good example of this thesis. She argues that contraception offered women a new sense of womanhood that did not require sexual passivity or taking on the maternal role. It also offered the promise of reproductive freedom and the ability to control their own bodies in a patriarchal society. In short, women demanded contraception, and the development of new technologies was pushed by this popular demand. Riessman maintains that while women gained some freedoms from the development and distribution of contraceptive technology, they lost others. Control over contraceptive technology has remained in the hands of the medical profession. As a result, contraception has become medicalised and partially stripped of its potential to transform political relations between women and men.

Riessman also provides an interesting discussion of the reasons women are so often the subjects of medicalisation. She suggests the following:

- Women's bodies produce external 'markers' of biological processes, such as menstruation and milk, whereas these are more hidden in men. These markers make women an attractive target for a medical system based on the biomedical paradigm, because cause and effect can often be clearly measured.
- Women are more likely to come into contact with the medical system. First, they often accompany kin to see the doctor. Second, research suggests that they tend to visit their doctor more often than men (see the discussion on sickness, health and gender below). Many medical problems are accompanied by periodic tests to look for possible implications for the reproductive system. Thus a regular sequence of tests and check-ups is initiated, which sees women become the objects of intense medical attention.
- Women are more structurally vulnerable in a patriarchal society. This vulnerability spills over into the medical system, when male doctors treat female patients.

In addition to attacking the ways that the modern medical system controls women's bodies, feminists have also pointed to the way that gender inequality permeates the medical professions. They argue that the more prestigious and better paying positions are occupied by men, while women are typically positioned in inferior locations as assistants to men or as 'carers' to patients. We can see this pattern in Table 10.1 (see p. 334).

MICRO-PERSPECTIVES

While most critiques of medical dominance have been made at the level of the social system and the dynamics of power between social groups, micro-sociologists argue that we need to look in more detail at the interactions, procedures and definitions of the situation that people use within the health system. One of the most influential of these perspectives has been labelling theory.

Thomas Scheff's (1966) work on mental illness is perhaps the best illustration of the labelling approach in the area of medical sociology. Scheff argues that people who are classified as mentally ill have usually broken a rule of taken-for-granted behaviour. For example, they might talk to themselves in a loud voice while travelling in a lift. Scheff argues that we all break these sorts of rules from time to time, but not everyone is considered mentally ill. One becomes mentally ill only when the behaviour is reported to the authorities (the police or a doctor) and they begin to label and certify the behaviour. Scheff claims that those most marginal to society, such as the homeless or single mothers, are most likely to be reported and that these powerless people are the least likely to be able to address the charges in an adequate way.

A celebrated (if perhaps ethically problematic) experiment conducted by D. L. Rosenhan (1973) seemingly confirmed such insights. Completely sane volunteers presented themselves at psychiatric institutions, complaining of hearing voices. Immediately after admission they ceased simulating any symptoms of abnormality and behaved as 'normally' as possible. A subsequent check of hospital records showed that in no case was the sanity of the pseudopatients detected by the staff. Rosenhan argues that this resulted from the 'stickiness' of labels, which tend to colour the way in which the behaviour of the inmate is viewed. For example, the field-note-taking activities of the researchers were interpreted as compulsive writing behaviour.

In an interesting reverse experiment, a psychiatric hospital was informed that over the subsequent three months several pseudopatients would attempt to gain entry. Staff and psychiatrists were asked to rate all people on a 10-point scale according to the likelihood of their being pseudopatients. Out of 193 people who were admitted, 41 were alleged with high confidence to be pseudopatients by at least one member of staff, and 19 were suspected of being pseudopatients by one psychiatrist and one other staff member. In fact, there were no pseudopatients. These experiments suggest that diagnoses of mental illness are strongly influenced by expectations and prejudices about the nature of the patients and that there is no clinically reliable way of diagnosing 'sanity' and 'insanity'.

Sociological work in the labelling tradition is complemented by work from radical psychologists on mental illness. Thomas Szasz (1971) suggests that the label of 'mental illness' is applied for political reasons to those who do not conform. It is a form of extra-judicial social control and punishment for morally aware dissidents and political agitators, allowing them to be locked away and drugged without due process. Szasz argues that core psychiatric concepts such as 'schizophrenia' do not stand up to rigorous examination, but rather provide a scientific mask for the political control of 'dangerous agitators'. Importantly, the process of labelling someone 'mentally ill' allows basic human rights to be suspended, enabling intervention by authorities that is perhaps more boundless than in the simple case of criminal deviants and political prisoners.

Erving Goffman on the asylum

Erving Goffman's work on mental illness and medical institutions has played an important role in furthering such critique of health settings and their activity. Goffman took a symbolic interactionist approach to life in an asylum and attempted to discover the lived experience of the inmate through intensive fieldwork. Goffman's analysis in *Asylums* (1962) focuses on the way that the asylum systematically attacks the 'self' of the patients, stripping each person of their old identity and imposing a new inmate identity at the time of entry through a complex rite of passage. This involves patients removing their old clothes, showering, putting on institutional clothes, being photographed and then being shown to their quarters. The new inmate identity is subsequently reinforced by the strict rules and timetables of the total institution. A total institution differs from an everyday institution in that every aspect of the life of members is controlled. The ability of inmates to leave the institution is dependent on their compliance with regulations, a compliance motivated by a series of sanctions and rewards ranging from release at one end to solitary confinement at the other. Goffman paints an overall picture of the asylum as an institution where people are destroyed and repressed by an alien institutional regime.

Despite being in this grim situation, Goffman shows that inmates have creative strategies for maintaining a sense of self. These range from intransigence to authority, to cooperation with authority, to withdrawal into a world of books and television. Similarly, Goffman demonstrates how inmates can creatively adapt to the institution through illicit and secret activities such as gambling and drinking. Goffman's ethnographic work also highlights the 'negotiated' order of the asylum. Rather than just following and implementing the hospital rules, staff and inmates reach tacit understandings about permitted and inappropriate forms of behaviour.

The moral evaluation of patients— Julius Roth

Although the labelling and interactionist approaches have been most successfully applied to mental illness, Julius Roth (1972) contends that moral evaluations and labelling processes also take place in the treatment of routine physical conditions. Roth and his associates conducted observational studies of American hospital emergency rooms and explored how perceptions of the 'social worth' of patients had implications for their treatment. Roth found that those who were young, affluent, middle class and white were more likely to be seen as 'deserving'. The old, minorities, the dirty and those on welfare who were 'sponging off' the taxpayer were usually seen as 'undeserving'. A similar process went on with the classification of medical conditions. Cases that were thought to be too minor or too hard to diagnose on the spot, or that could have been dealt with in an outpatient clinic, were considered less deserving of attention in the emergency ward than conditions requiring surgical intervention, such as accidents and stabbings. Psychiatric cases, venereal and gynaecological problems and drunks were also unpopular and stigmatised. Roth concludes that the quality of treatment received is determined by the intersection of these two dimensions, with 'deserving' people and conditions receiving more careful, complete and immediate treatment and higher levels of courtesy from the staff than the 'undeserving'.

THE HOSPITAL

The hospital is the central institutional base of modern medicine. The hospital is still the place where most people are born and die and where the most powerful and prestigious medical positions—those of the specialist, the surgeon, the consultant and the researcher, for example—are generally located.

Early hospitals were small-scale institutions offering little in the way of care that could not be provided in the home (Rosenberg 1987). Their major function was pedagogical and charitable, and they had strong ties to the local community. In contrast, modern hospitals are complex bureaucracies offering the kinds of care that are not available in the home. Most scholars agree that modern hospitals bear a close resemblance to Max Weber's ideal type of bureaucracy. They have hierarchical offices, rules and regulations, record keeping, salaried staff and so forth. At the same time it is acknowledged that there are some important respects in which they differ from the Weberian model (Turner 1987). Perhaps the most interesting of these is a dual structure of power and authority consisting of both bureaucratic/managerial personnel on the one hand and professional/medical personnel on the other. As a result, there is sometimes conflict and tension between these two groups. Those in less powerful positions, such as nurses, often find their jobs are made harder by being subject to twin sources of control. Managers, for example, might pressure nurses to finish work on time to avoid having to make overtime payments, while doctors might require the nurses to stay on duty until a particular medical procedure is completed satisfactorily. In addition to this dual structure of authority, it is far from clear how the role, status and responsibilities of patients fit into the Weberian paradigm. Patients are part of the organisation only temporarily—they receive no pay and have few fixed duties.

While the majority of organisational theorists have looked at the formal structure of hospitals, interactionists have argued for the fluid and dynamic nature of hospital life. Anselm Strauss and his associates (1978) first suggested that the hospital should be considered as a **negotiated order**. They argued that rules could never really be precise enough to cover every contingency (e.g. what exactly counts as an 'emergency'?). As a result, staff and patients continually have to work out the limits of authority and responsibility, and permitted and illicit behaviours. Although useful in explaining some aspects of hospital life, this perspective has been

Case Study
Medical sociology in practice: an interview

Glenn Gardner is Professor and Director of the Centre for Clinical Nursing at the Royal Brisbane and Women's Hospital and Queensland University of Technology. In addition to her nursing and education qualifications she also has a PhD in sociology.

Professor Gardner, what kinds of things do you investigate in your job?

My research covers a range of clinical and health service topics. In the hospital, for example, I conduct clinical trials testing treatment interventions; I investigate patients' experience of surgery, illness and health care; and I conduct large-scale surveys of nursing and health services.

What brought you to realise the importance of sociology?

One of my early projects was about hospital-acquired wound infections. In my study I came to see that this topic is traditionally understood in terms of medical epidemiology and microbiology—that is, the action and spread of the bacteria—with little attention to the profound impact of these chronic infections on the patients, their families, their work life and the community. By using a sociological research approach I was able to investigate the patient dimension and from this suggest ways to improve both patient care and health service delivery.

What kinds of sociological approach have been most useful for you?

In the health setting, methods such as ethnography and theories like symbolic interactionism are particularly useful. They allow us to gain a deeper understanding of what is going on in patient-care environments. Also, we can use body theory. This interpretive framework has uncovered the 'body work' that health professionals take for granted. In my view the diversity of experiences inherent in being a patient can be fully examined only by combining medical and sociological perspectives.

Can you give an example of how sociological research can make a real difference in the medical field?

There is so much that we do not know about health care, treatment modalities, health communication and literacy and so forth. Sociological research provides the intellectual tools to investigate these phenomena. It builds our knowledge and theory base. We can then draw upon this knowledge to develop intervention studies and build the evidence base for more effective nursing, medicine and health care—in short, to improve objective health outcomes as well as the way that people feel about the illness experience.

For example, my team used ethnographic methods to study the practice of moving patients around hospitals. This practice happens all day and every day in large acute hospitals—really sick people are moved from ward to ward and to and from treatment and diagnostic areas. They are stared at in lifts and bumped along on trolleys and we don't know anything about how this affects them. Our study found that transporting patients is an activity that is perceived as marginal to the real business of the hospital. As such the patients, visitors, nurses and orderlies involved enter and exit (what is interpreted as) the 'real world of the hospital' at either end of the journey. Thanks to shared informal definitions of place and activity, patient monitoring and care is likely to be suspended during the journey and patients frequently 'travel' without being accompanied by a health professional. These findings have important implications for any hospital's quality and safety agenda.

criticised. Robert Day and Jo Anne Day suggest it does not take into account the different levels of power and authority that people have in the hospital hierarchy (Day & Day 1977). They argue that more powerful people have more resources with which to negotiate than those who are in less powerful positions.

Drawing on the more general sociological critique of modern medicine, numerous sociological critiques have been made of hospitals and hospital life. In general these critiques, of which those of Foucault and Goffman are representative, have focused on the role of the hospital in cementing relations of power. But as Bryan Turner (1987) points out, the hospital has also been subjected to political, popular and medical criticism. It has been argued by politicians, of both right and left, that hospitals are expensive to run and that money could be better spent on preventive or community medicine. Consumers and activist groups have argued that hospitals are alienating for patients, involving unnecessary degradation and petty rules. Finally, various clinical studies have shown that levels of iatrogenesis are very high in hospitals. Iatrogenesis is the process in which illness or other negative consequences are incurred as a result of medical treatment. Examples might include the side effects of drugs or, as is often the case in hospitals, post-operative infections such as 'golden staph', which may be resistant to antibiotics. Some clinical studies suggest that bringing sick people together into one place might not be the best way of helping them to get better.

DOCTOR–PATIENT INTERACTION

The study of doctor–patient interactions lies at the heart of medical sociology because this is the interface where treatment occurs and where major decisions are taken as to whether and how to treat a complaint. Parsons' concept of the sick role provides a crucial starting point for investigating this issue. Talcott Parsons (1951) argued that health was necessary if individuals were to fulfil their social role and contribute to the wellbeing of society as a whole. If society were to work efficiently it would have to define the role of the sick person in such a way as to limit the possible disruption to society. In consequence, a number of expectations, rights and obligations were placed on people who wished to be relieved of their normal responsibilities on the basis of being sick:

- People should not wish to be sick or try to become sick, and should not be responsible for their condition.
- They should recognise that being ill is undesirable and do something about it.
- They should accept the help of others, especially qualified doctors and other medical professionals.

Parsons argued that doctors, for their part, have a reciprocal role responsibility to try to cure the sick and to treat them in an impartial way, following a norm of universalism (all people should be treated equally). In Parsons' view, the doctor–patient interaction is one in which doctor and patient cooperate in bringing about a cure.

Parsons' essay on the sick role has been very influential, usually as a point of reference for other, more critical perspectives on interactional aspects of the health system. Candace West (1984) and Bryan Turner (1987) provided the following useful summaries of these critiques of Parsons' sick role theory:

- Parsons' focus on the doctor–patient interaction did not take account of the roles of other actors in the health-care process. In particular, lay people such as family members, friends and workmates are likely to play a crucial role in defining sickness, and may tell the person whether he or she should see a doctor in the first place.
- Parsons argued that doctors were motivated by values of universalism and affective neutrality. Empirical studies of real doctors show a variety of motivations, including selfishness and particularism (e.g. favouritism to particular patients). Julius Roth's study of the 'moral evaluation of patients', discussed above, provided an illustration of the varying attitudes of doctors to differing types of patient. In effect, Parsons mistook a professional norm (the medical profession's idea of how a doctor should behave) for real personal motivations.
- Parsons' argument did not take sufficient account of negotiation and interaction between doctors and patients.
- Parsons' argument placed too much emphasis on patient passivity. In fact, we find a range of patient behaviours—from highly active (e.g. diabetics injecting themselves on a regular basis) to completely passive (such as the patient in a coma).
- Parsons argued that the hierarchical nature of the doctor–patient relationship is necessary for the smooth functioning of the medical system. Others have asserted that this is not so much necessary as a product of medical dominance.
- Parsons did not address the issue of whether all sick roles are equally legitimate in the eyes of

society, or the impact of patients' social characteristics on their entitlement to the privileges of the sick role. The exemption from the expectation of undertaking paid work given to the 'respectable married woman' who is pregnant is unlikely to be given as willingly to the 'single welfare mother'.

Although Parsons' concept of the sick role has been roundly criticised, it is important to realise that it was in many ways a brilliant example of sociological insight that offered a starting point for a number of the ongoing empirical inquiries of medical sociology. As Bryan Turner himself points out, Parsons' theory 'indicated the theoretical grounds for an interdisciplinary approach to the nature of illness by combining elements of Freudian psychoanalysis with the sociological analysis of roles and a comparative cultural understanding of the importance of illness in industrial societies' (1992, p. 137). While theoretical critiques have pointed to shortcomings of Parsons' vision, it is far from clear that they are necessarily superior. Kathleen Fahy and Philip Smith (1999) suggest that interactionist approaches can encompass negotiation and contingency in medical encounters, but at the expense of a workable understanding of social structural constraints on social action in medical contexts and their links to a wider social order. Marxist and Foucauldian critiques of Parsons invert this problem. Here there are robust theories of social structure, but insufficient attention is given to questions of motivation. According to Fahy and Smith, the model provided by Parsons is in many ways more rounded and complete than those provided by his critics, even if it has some theoretical blind spots.

Empirical studies on doctor–patient interaction

A crucial insight of empirical sociological research in the area of doctor–patient interaction has been to argue that health outcomes are directly related to the quality and nature of doctor–patient interaction. In particular, it is important for patients to put their case in an appropriate and forceful way. Studies of doctor–patient interaction have shown that when people visit a doctor they often have quite a deal of autonomy in deciding the outcome of the consultation. For example, the implications of a test might be ambiguous. Doctor and patient might then argue over what to do next. This is often the case when a child is ill and the parents are anxious that the problem is taken seriously.

Studies have also shown that patients expend a good deal of time thinking about what to say to the doctor on consultation. This is often oriented towards making certain they get serious attention from the doctor, as well as ensuring that they describe their symptoms correctly. Often patients seek to validate why they are taking up the doctor's time, feeling embarrassed lest they be seen as time-wasting hypochondriacs. Doctors, on the other hand, seek to maintain their authority and status. They will try to obtain information about symptoms while at the same time limiting the possibility of the patient taking over the interaction. In consultations, the superior knowledge of doctors often combines with role expectations that give them legitimate authority. This means that they often have the last word, making summarising statements and concluding the interaction.

The contributions of Eliot Freidson (e.g. 1970) argue that doctor–patient interactions are characterised by a 'clash of perspectives'. Patients want information and tend to understand their own problems as serious and needing immediate attention. Doctors, on the other hand, are inclined to see relatively few medical problems as serious. Importantly, Freidson criticised the Parsonian view that patients are passive and uncritical of the medical profession; he showed how they would often reject treatment proposed by the doctor or struggle to obtain information. Freidson argued that the active or passive nature of patient behaviour is determined by two factors: first, where doctor and patient are similar in cultural and social background, it is more likely that the patient will have some autonomy; and second, where patients have substantial freedom over their choice of doctor (e.g. in self-referral to specialists), they are in a better position to bargain and negotiate over their treatment.

A similar emphasis on the issue of power has been made by Thomas Scheff (1968), who claimed that doctor–patient interactions are marked by a hidden agenda. This agenda consists of control over the medical knowledge about the patient's condition. This knowledge is the source of the doctor's power. Typically, doctors will attempt to limit the ability of patients to access this information. Detailed studies have uncovered some of the techniques by which doctors manage to control interactions. These include:

- asking questions requiring a yes/no type of answer in order to prevent patients from taking control of the interaction (patients might want to make comments about their symptoms, provide the doctor with candidate diagnoses or tell the doctor about

SOCIOLOGY

a new cure they heard discussed on the radio; however, the yes/no question makes it difficult to introduce these issues into the dialogue)
- ignoring comments and suggestions from patients
- establishing consultation routines and timetables that prevent patients from participating (the most common of these methods is to have five-minute consultation sessions—when booked back-to-back these short sessions provide doctors with an excuse to keep interactions brief and the information flow one-sided; moreover, patients may feel inhibited from raising issues if they think they will be taking up the time of the next patient)
- using persuasive rhetorical techniques to convince patients that compliance with medical authority is in their own best interests.

Over recent years patients have become more demanding and critical of doctors and medical authority—a move linked to the rise of consumerist orientations to health that are discussed at the end of this chapter. Surveys reveal that many patients are unhappy with the quality of their interactions with medical professionals. Complaints typically focus on:

- the amount of information they get from their doctor—this might include not discussing possible side effects of medication, or vague and evasive communication of the diagnosis, especially in the case of terminal conditions
- impersonal care
- an unwillingness to listen to descriptions of their condition or to negotiate on treatment.

In many places the medical profession is now trying to deal with this problem through the implementation of training in interaction skills. A major impetus behind this new direction has been a desire to improve health outcomes as much as patient satisfaction. It is slowly being recognised in the medical profession that patient compliance with 'doctor's orders' depends on the quality of interaction and communication between doctor and patient.

Reflective questions: What exactly is 'modern' about modern medicine in contrast to traditional medicine? What are some of the ways that power manifests in the medical system? 'The hospital and the medical encounter are more about expressing power than curing the sick': are you able to defend this seemingly outrageous statement?

HEALTH, WELFARE AND THE COMMUNITY

From what we have looked at so far in this chapter it would seem that the sociology of health and illness is all about doctors, hospitals and medical power/knowledge. Yet issues of health and illness must also be understood in the context of wider social relations.

Although the doctor–patient interaction is a crucial factor in health outcomes, it is important to remember that a consultation with a doctor is really the end of another sequence. This is the process that people go through when deciding whether or not to visit a doctor. Surveys have shown that people experience symptoms of illness far more frequently than they go to a doctor. Most symptoms and problems are dealt with by a trip to the pharmacy or bathroom medicine cabinet, staying at home and resting, or trying to ignore the problem and waiting for it to go away. A. Scambler, G. Scambler and D. Craig (1981) had British women keep diaries of their symptoms and consultations. Some of the ratios of symptom events to consultations were:

- backache—60 symptoms to 1 consultation
- colds/flu—12:1
- stomach pains—11:1
- nerves/depression—74:1.

Similar results have been found in Australian studies. The Australian Health Survey of 2004–05 found that 77 per cent of Australians had one or more long-term medical conditions, yet only 23 per cent had consulted a doctor or specialist in the two weeks prior to the survey (ABS 2006b).

It would seem that many people have known conditions, perhaps have them diagnosed and take regular medication, but then simply put up with them and get on with life rather than bugging the doctor every time the same old problem crops up. Most conditions are dealt with in the community. It is important to know, therefore, how people understand and cope with illness and why they might decide sometimes to go to a doctor and other times not. Studies of community care suggest that most problems are dealt with either by self-care or by the use of others in the community. People will usually seek 'expert advice' from older friends or family members before consulting a doctor. Scambler, Scambler and Craig (1981) suggest a ratio of 11 informal consultations to one formal consultation with a medical professional. Research on the impact of networks on the decision to seek a formal consultation is inconclusive at present. However, it appears that people embedded in dense, traditional, kin-based networks are less likely to consult doctors than those who have several loose networks based around friendship.

COMMUNITY TIES AND HEALTH

A number of sociologists have studied the role of informal and family networks in providing for health-care needs. Most elderly and chronically sick people are cared for by kin rather than institutions, and government policies now encourage 'community care'. Although this policy is often explained in terms of the improved quality of care, there is little doubt that governments have also been enthusiastic because it offers a way of economising on health expenditure by the state.

In an early paper on the sick person and the family, Talcott Parsons and Renee Fox (1952) suggested that over-caring for the sick individual in the family could have negative social consequences, largely because the 'affective neutrality' of the doctor–patient relationship was absent. The sick person might possibly be encouraged to remain sick, due to the sympathy and attention received in the family. Alternatively, some family members might be jealous of the rights and privileges given to the family member in the sick role (e.g. not doing the dishes, not going out to work) and respond with hostility or sanctions. In this case, the individual's recovery might be hampered by unrealistic expectations that would push him or her out of the sick role too early. In general, sociological studies have confirmed the part of Parsons and Fox's argument that stated that negative family attitudes and lack of support can hamper recovery. The other part of Parsons and Fox's argument about the dangers of obsessive care has received less validation. Many studies have shown that positive family involvement and concern tend to produce more rapid recovery rather than encouraging people to remain in the sick role.

Recent feminist studies on the role of informal support have diverted attention away from the patient and towards the (usually female) caregiver. Typically, it is the mother of a sick child or the daughter of an elderly parent who takes on the burden of caring. The role of carer usually brings with it severe disruption to the education and employment prospects of the carer, as well as interfering with leisure time and opportunities to engage in self-fulfilling activities. Importantly, the mental and physical health of the carer may also suffer as a result of participation in caring activities. These findings are consistent with a wider feminist tradition that sees the traditional family as a locus of gendered oppression.

Sociological studies of the role of the community have followed in the footsteps of Durkheim's *Suicide* (1970) in suggesting that the nature of the social ties surrounding individuals might influence their proneness or susceptibility to mental and physical health problems. Once again, the general finding has been that people with good social ties have better health. L. Berkman and L. Syme (1979) looked at a random sample of 5000 British adults over a nine-year period. At the beginning of the test period the nature of their social ties was evaluated along with information collected on marital status, membership of informal associations and churches, and the amount of contact with friends and relatives. Men with the weakest social ties had age-adjusted mortality (death) rates 2.3 times higher than men with the strongest ties; and women with the weakest ties had age-adjusted mortality rates 2.8 times higher than women with the strongest ties. Myfanwy Morgan, Michael Calnan and Nick Manning (1991) suggest that the mechanism through which social ties influence health may be related to the process of 'coping'.

There are several dimensions to this process. First, supportive family members and friends help to give meaning to health-threatening life events, such as bereavement, divorce or unemployment, and enable them to be interpreted as non-catastrophic and transient. Second, social networks offer a source of self-esteem for the individual. They enable a robust sense of self to emerge, which can head off depression. Finally, networks can provide material and physical support in times of crisis, such as housing for the victim of domestic violence or spare cash in times of financial need. The ability to access these basic resources can have significant repercussions for both physical and mental health.

THE DECISION TO SEE A DOCTOR—IRVING ZOLA

Commonsense tells us that it is the seriousness of a medical condition that determines whether or not a person goes to the doctor. But as we saw in the previous section, social factors play a role in this complex equation.

Access to medical services can be explored in terms of barriers, which may be real or perceived. These include the potential cost of treatment, ethnic or class-based linguistic and cultural difficulties, lack of information about available services, geographical distance (especially in outback Australia) and psychological barriers such as fear of looking stupid for having wasted the doctor's time or embarrassment at having a particular condition (e.g. venereal disease). So there are many factors at work that might prevent people from consulting a doctor. For a person to report to the doctor, it is usually necessary for the perceived benefits to outweigh these barriers. But, in addition to these factors, sociological research suggests that the way sick people perceive their symptoms and evaluate their impact plays a key role in their decision.

One of the most influential studies of the role of these non-medical factors was by Irving Kenneth Zola (1973). Zola argued that the decision to go to the doctor often had little to do with the objective seriousness of the illness or the level of pain and more to do with social factors. These include:

- the occurrence of an interpersonal crisis, such as a family dispute involving the sick person
- the medical condition interfering with personal or interpersonal relations, such as not being able to go to a party because of a persistent headache
- sanctioning of the sick person by other members of the family by telling the sick person that he or she should go to the doctor
- the condition interfering with the ability to conduct work.

Zola argued that what patients were responding to was more often a perceived implication of the symptom rather than any worsening of the symptom per se.

Lay definitions of disease

While Zola's work looked at how social interaction and social life play a role in people's courses of action, another research tradition investigates lay definitions of disease. Folk definitions of illness might influence whether or not the patient visits the doctor. Some conditions might not be recognised as serious in some cultures—or even recognised at all.

Arthur Nudelman and Barbara Nudelman (1972) showed that Christian Scientists tended to go to the doctor for 'mechanical' failures (e.g. a broken leg) but to seek spiritual solutions elsewhere to afflictions that were considered to be the result of impure thoughts. Margaret Clark (1959) found that Mexican Americans in the south-west United States considered diarrhoea, sweating and coughing as inevitable and somewhat trivial. Therefore they tended to ignore these possibly serious symptoms rather than report them to the doctor. Similarly, many non-Western cultures define hallucinations and visions as a special prophetic gift rather than as an indication of profound psychosis requiring immediate medical attention. The cultural mores of some societies encourage the expression of pain, while others prefer that it be hidden. Mark Zborowski (1952) discovered that Italian Americans were more inclined to express pain than Anglo-Americans. Significantly, the mostly Anglo-American staff at the hospital Zborowski studied did not look favourably on the vociferous Italians, whom they saw as play-acting or as possibly psychologically disturbed.

It is important to realise that folk understandings of illness influence the kinds of treatment given in the home and in other locations outside the formal medical system. For example, Lenore Manderson and Megan Mathews (1985) looked at definitions of disease in the Vietnamese community of Sydney. The Vietnamese see illness as the result of an imbalance between yin (cold) and yang (hot) forces. Treatment in the Vietnamese home often consists of giving foods that are classified as symbolically 'hot' or 'cold'. By giving these foods it is hoped to restore balance within the patient.

THE POLITICAL ECONOMY OF HEALTH AND WELFARE

In the last section we saw that an understanding of health requires attention to the role of meanings and communities. But health-care delivery is also very much about politics and money: in Australia today, health expenditure by individuals and government runs at around 8 per cent of gross GDP. For this reason, the sociology of health is also concerned with exploring the role of the state and the market in providing and regulating health services.

Types of health-care systems

Health-care systems vary widely between nations, as does the level and type of state involvement. Milton Roemer (1976) usefully identified four kinds of health system:

1. *Free enterprise*. Health care is provided by the private sector. Consumers, who might purchase health insurance, are entirely responsible for the costs of treatment. Doctors charge for their services. The government provides a means-tested

safety net only for those who are most seriously disadvantaged. The United States corresponds most closely to this model.
2. *Social insurance.* This is a mixed system consisting of government contributions, employer contributions and some worker contributions. Doctors are usually salaried by hospitals or other health organisations and a fee is charged for services. This system is found in most European countries and in Japan.
3. *Public assistance.* In this model the government provides only very basic health care and doctors are salaried. The affluent will usually pay for the convenience of private care or might be excluded from the free care by a means test. Such a system is common in developing countries.
4. *Universal service.* The government takes full responsibility for health funding and services, and the provision of health care is funded through tax revenue. Doctors are employees of the state and are paid a salary. The United Kingdom, with its National Health Service, comes closest to this model.

As with all typologies, it is rare to find a case that fits neatly into any one classification. Australia, for example, has characteristics of the universal service, social insurance and free enterprise models.

The health care system in the United States

As Australian health-care costs escalate, some people assert that we should look to the United States model for a solution. The United States has never had a strong welfare state and health-care needs have been provided for almost entirely by a private insurance and hospital system. This is attractive to governments as it allows the costs of health care to be shifted from state revenues to the consumer or their employer in company-sponsored health plans.

Sociological analysis, however, suggests that the market-based solution to health care in the United States has produced dysfunctional outcomes. Consumers have been dismayed by the escalating costs of insurance premiums. However, hospitals have little incentive to cut costs and consumers rarely look for the lowest price when both know that the insurance company will foot the bill. In addition, the prevalence of litigation in the United States has pushed up the fees charged by hospitals, as they need to be able to cover themselves against multimillion-dollar suits for medical malpractice. These costs have been pushed back to consumers through higher premiums. The biggest losers in this equation are those at the bottom of the socioeconomic ladder, who cannot afford even the minimum health-care premiums. The result is a health-care system characterised by gross inequality of access and care. In addition, the total cost of health care per capita increases under such a system. Far from producing a more 'efficient' health-care system, the free market approach in the United States has produced a system that soaks up a higher proportion of GDP than the more collectivistic solutions in such countries as the United Kingdom, Australia and Canada.

Donald Light (1986) shows that since the late 1960s, health in the United States has become increasingly corporatised and oriented towards profit. Significantly, Jack C. Massey, one of the founders of the Hospital Corporation of America, had a background in the fast-food industry, having turned KFC into a national chain. Before this move towards private and corporate hospitals, they had been mostly run by not-for-profit corporations such as religious denominations and universities. Numerous criticisms have been made of the United States corporate model. It has been argued that the profit motive encourages doctors to undertake unnecessary procedures and tests and that the hospitals neglect loss-making functions such as teaching, research and treating the poor. In order to compete, not-for-profit hospitals have responded by adopting some for-profit characteristics, including charging higher fees to pay for capital investment. Furthermore, a new managerial/corporate ethos has replaced an older ethic of care.

The United States experience is in many ways a salutary warning for Australia, where considerable pressures exist for the increased commercialisation of the health-care system. It suggests that even if the health system in Australia is opened up to greater levels of competition and free market intervention, the process might have to be carefully managed in order to prevent adverse outcomes for both the providers and the users of health-care services. Fran Collyer (1998) makes just this point in her critique of the marketisation of the public health sector in Australia, for example in partnerships between the state and private hospital corporations. She indicates that the privatisation of health around the world has usually been accompanied by rising health costs (not cost reductions through efficiencies) and the exclusion of the poor. Job satisfaction and quality of care can decrease as health-care workers are enjoined to have a business focus rather than a patient focus in their decision making. Ironically, private corporations are often able to make money only because of state support that is offered through tax rebates, low-cost loans or the parasitic use of publicly funded health infrastructure.

THE AUSTRALIAN HEALTH-CARE SYSTEM

According to Alan Davis and Janet George (1998), the Australian health-care system is extremely complex due to the involvement of Commonwealth, state and local government and the private sector in the funding, provision and regulation of services. The majority of health funding comes from Commonwealth sources and is supplemented by limited amounts of state funds. The public makes a contribution towards the costs of this health care through the Medicare levy on income. However, the private sector still plays an important role. Affluent people usually subscribe to health insurance schemes and most dental work is conducted in the private sector. The provision of services, such as building hospitals, is usually the responsibility of state governments, with local governments responsible for public health issues such as immunisation and the inspection of food suppliers. The regulation of health services is mostly the task of state governments, which oversee the workings of both public and private medical institutions and determine appropriate standards for medical practice.

Alan Davis and Janet George provide a useful discussion of the way that the history of health care in Australia has been one of increasing government involvement. Leaving aside state provision of health care during the convict era, health care in the 19th century was usually paid for and provided privately. Many people joined insurance schemes run by 'Friendly Societies' or hospitals. In the first half of the 20th century, the Commonwealth's attempts to introduce a system of universal health insurance were fought off by the medical profession. By the early 1970s the need for reform was clear. Despite government hopes, some 2 million people carried no health insurance. In 1972 the Whitlam Government introduced the Medibank universal insurance scheme, despite the opposition of the Australian Medical Association, which was publicly concerned about standards and regulation, but some say privately worried about government intervention into fees and charges. Medibank was dismantled by the Fraser Government soon afterwards. By the early 1980s, 2 million people were again uninsured.

The current Medicare system was introduced in 1984. It is funded by a levy (currently 1.5 per cent) on top of ordinary income tax. Although the levy raises around $5 billion, this covers only about one-fifth of the Australian government's health expenditure. Medicare provides universal access to basic health care with heavily subsidised consumer costs. It has been especially helpful to those on low incomes (e.g. pensioners, youth and the unemployed) who would not be able to pay the price of health insurance. Debate about Medicare has been fierce and often emotionally loaded on both sides. Critics of Medicare argue that the system encourages waste and medifraud and that it has eroded the profits of private sector health funds. They also assert that it is unfair that people who take out private health insurance should have to pay the Medicare levy for services they do not use. Advocates of Medicare counter that fraud is just as rampant in the private sector, with doctors making bogus claims on health insurance companies rather than the public purse. They also argue that access to basic health care is a human right and that this right is more important than the profits of shareholders and the bank balances of more affluent individuals.

The unexpected consequences of Medicare

In some ways Medicare has become a problem due to its own success in providing quality affordable healthcare. When the system was set up it was envisaged that around 40–50 per cent of Australians would retain private health insurance. However, by 1999 this figure stood at 31 per cent as the middle classes defected to Medicare. As a result, more demand is being placed on the public system than was expected, creating a drain on funds.

There are several suggested reasons behind this shift towards the public system. First, people do not like spending money on things they do not want to use. It is easy to sell an attractive product such as a new car, but much harder to sell something associated with pain, misery and death such as health insurance. Second, health insurance premiums are quite expensive for most Australians. This means that some people simply cannot afford them. Others can pay the premium but choose not to. For older, affluent people who are likely to get ill, health insurance may be a good idea. Younger people, by contrast, tend to get sick less often. Many of these people find it more rational to pay off the mortgage or buy investments with the money they save by using Medicare. There is also the related option of self-insuring. This might involve placing money into a savings account or investment portfolio that is set aside for medical bills. This will compound over the years. Because the bureaucratic costs and shareholder profits of the medical insurance industry are sidestepped, for some this can be a more effective way of 'going private'. Finally, and perhaps most importantly, it has yet to be demonstrated that there are any substantial health benefits to being in a health plan as opposed to the public system. To some consumers, then, health insurance might offer a little more choice, a shorter waiting list and a private room in a hospital with designer decor, but this is really not enough to tip the balance and open the cheque book. Why pay for something that you can get for free, or that you are already paying for through tax and the Medicare levy?

Neither major political party is able to fundamentally challenge the Medicare system. It is so popular with the electorate that support for the Medicare system is a mandatory aspect of policy, even among the Liberals who initially opposed its introduction. Yet as the cost of Medicare continues to rise, both the ALP and the Coalition have been looking for ways to draw people towards private health funds. For several years John Howard's governments introduced policies designed to subtly shift the balance of incentives to take out health insurance. High earners who do not belong to a qualifying plan are liable to pay a special Medicare surcharge. There is a tax rebate of 30 per cent on health insurance payments, which is designed to provide an incentive for going private that will lighten the overall burden on the public system. A 'lifetime health cover policy' has also been introduced—the idea being to penalise those who take out private health insurance late in life by allowing insurance companies to charge them higher premiums than those who have been longstanding members. These policies saw participation increase from 31 per cent in 1999 to around 44 per cent in 2003 (ABS 2008a). There has since been a levelling off and the numbers holding private health insurance remain around this mark. Critics charge that the incentive policy is simply a subsidy for the rich—especially for those who are going to belong to a private scheme regardless of any rebate—and that the money would be better spent on directly bolstering the coffers of Medicare.

Ann Daniel (1995) argues that concern over rising costs is a spectre that will continue to haunt future Australian governments. She identifies several factors that, in addition to the continued public support for Medicare, will fuel this concern:

- There are continual medical advances that require investment in expensive machinery and skilled staff.
- With Medicare there are no 'user-pays' controls on people going to the doctor and demanding treatment.
- An ageing population means that more and more people will become heavy users of health system resources.
- The autonomy of the medical profession makes it difficult to impose accountability measures or external reviews of expenditure.

Fears of a health-cost blowout are not totally unfounded. Since 1990 total health expenditure in Australia from all sources (the national and state governments, households, insurance policies and individuals) has grown by around 5 to 9 per cent per annum depending on how this is measured. It is now around $4200 per person—$84 billion in total or about 9 per cent of the GDP (ABS 2008a). The state itself has to pick up 70 per cent of this tab by paying for Medicare, infrastructure, salaries and so forth. Systems of bulk-billing, which reduce administrative costs, and fixed schedules of fees have been one way of trying to control expenditure, as have the incentives used to attract people into private health insurance that we have just been discussing. The shift towards managerialism and the creation of internal markets in the health system is another, more recent, response which is discussed later in this chapter.

Reflective questions: Explain the role that community values and popular beliefs about illness play in shaping health-care decisions and health outcomes and provide examples of these. How are health-care systems linked to the wider themes of political economy, such as 'states' versus 'markets'? Why is Australia a hybrid system in this context?

THE MEDICAL OCCUPATIONS—DOCTORS, NURSES AND ALLIED HEALTH PROFESSIONS

An important area in the sociology of health concerns the study of the medical occupations. Table 10.1 shows that in 2006–07 some 423 000 Australians had jobs in health occupations. Put another way, about 4 per cent of the national workforce today is directly employed in health (e.g. as doctors, nurses, radiographers and chiropractors), with 74 per cent of these being female (ABS 2008a). It is important to remember that many people are also indirectly employed

SOCIOLOGY

TABLE 10.1

Employed persons in health occupations, 2006–07[a]

	Persons ('000)	Males (%)	Part-time workers (%)
Health professionals[b]			
Generalist medical practitioners	37.0	61.8	18.8
Specialist medical practitioners	19.8	68.8	18.2
Registered nurses	169.8	7.8	47.6
Registered midwives	14.1	0.7	59.1
Physiotherapists	15.0	33.0	31.5
Other health professionals[b]	110.6	32.7	30.1
Health associate professionals			
Enrolled nurses	27.7	12.2	40.3
Ambulance officers and paramedics	11.7	79.3	1.6
Aboriginal and Torres Strait Islander health workers	1.5	33.0	14.3
Other health associate professionals	16.2	34.1	47.6
Total employed in health occupations[c]	423.4	25.9	37.1
Total employed in all occupations	10 302.4	55.0	28.4

Source: KOF Index of Globalization (http://globalization.kof.ethz.ch/).

Notes:

[a] Annual average of quarterly data.

[b] Includes health service managers; excludes veterinarians.

[c] Includes health professionals, health service managers, health associate professionals.

---

in the health part of the economy (e.g. workers for pharmaceuticals and medical supply companies, shop assistants in pharmacies, health insurance workers, hospital porters and kitchen workers), so the full number is arguably much higher. Sociologists studying health occupations usually emphasise the role of power and occupational culture in understanding the activities and job experiences of different groups of medical practitioners.

Looking at Table 10.1, we see that gender plays a major role in structuring career outcomes in the health field. Men are in a minority in the health occupations, yet they make up more than 60 per cent of general and specialist practitioners (doctors). With the exception of ambulance officers and paramedics, the other health occupations such as nursing and midwifery are staffed mostly by women. We also find a high proportion of part-time employment in these female occupational positions. The picture we have is broadly consistent with feminist theory. Men control the highest status, most powerful and best paid fields.

DOCTORS

Doctors, like lawyers, may be said to constitute a profession. Eliot Freidson (1970), along with many other scholars, argues that professions consist of groups that have managed to attain self-regulation, autonomy and legally enforced monopolies on certain kinds of work. In combination this amounts to a situation known as **professional closure** in which other people and groups are excluded by the state and by law from performing certain kinds of tasks and entering certain occupations. In the case of the medical profession, this closure arose in tandem with the rise of universities and teaching hospitals and the formalisation of medical training. The lengthy process of accreditation has served to legitimise claims to expert healing knowledge.

Evan Willis (1994) argues that the power of the medical profession has three core aspects:

- *Autonomy* refers to the fact that the medical profession is not under the direction and control of any other occupation.

- *Authority* refers to its power to direct other health workers, such as nurses.
- *Medical sovereignty* refers to the fact that doctors are considered to be the legitimate experts on health-related matters.

In his study of the Australian medical profession, Willis (1989) gives special emphasis to the role of the state in passing legislation that gives doctors a monopoly on certain types of medical intervention. Willis argues that today this medical dominance is underpinned by an ideology of professionalism claiming that doctors have the public interest at heart and that only they have the expertise to advance this interest. In addition, doctors promulgate the view that only they are fit to fully understand and use modern medical technology. This ideology legitimates a complex division of labour in which doctors have authority not only over patients, but also over other health workers. As a result, only doctors (such as radiologists) are legally allowed to interpret the results of some medical procedures, such as x-rays. In this way the levels of autonomy, remuneration and training available to non-doctors (such as radiographers) are severely limited.

Ann Daniel (1995) points to the fact that beliefs about medical knowledge help to reproduce this dominance. Medical practitioners often highlight the importance of individual discretion, judgement and experience in making diagnoses and decisions. Somewhat contradicting the logic of biomedicine, they also argue that each case is unique and that there can be no generic cure for a given condition. Daniel calls this emphasis on the almost mystical and intuitive powers of the doctor 'the signification of indetermination over technicality' (p. 73), a concept that is reminiscent of Foucault's arguments about the discourse of the 'medical gaze' (discussed above) as a source of institutional power. Daniel suggests that doctors have resisted their knowledge being reduced to a set of technical procedures (e.g. computer diagnosis) that can be used by the 'less skilled', because this would threaten their monopoly or lead to deprofessionalisation and deskilling. Daniel also argues that emphasis on the individual nature of each patient case and the need for medical judgement has helped the medical profession to 'exclude surveillance' (p. 73) from outside.

Nurses and allied health professions

The powerful position of (mostly male) doctors contrasts with that of (mostly female) nurses. Nurses are generally subject to supervision by doctors, are held accountable to timetables and standard procedures, and are paid less. Typically, there is little room for autonomous decision making in the nursing profession, even though nurses often have a more intimate knowledge of patient needs than the doctor. Bryan Turner (1987) suggests that many of the problems confronting nurses arise from the continuing devaluation of nursing as 'women's work' with a focus on care and nurturing rather than medical intervention. This is in many ways a legacy of the Florence Nightingale tradition, which saw nursing as a woman's role that was concerned with service, caring and unquestioning obedience to the authority of male doctors. It is hardly surprising, then, that research such as Neville Millen's (1989) shows that Australian nurses experience considerable discontent in their jobs. This is due to a number of factors, including poor pay and conditions, lack of recognition for the quality of care given, hours of scheduled work shifts, and stress. In addition, many nurses feel alienated by the technical and impersonal nature of work in modern hospitals and would like greater interpersonal contact and communication with patients.

Allied health professions include groups such as dentists, occupational therapists and podiatrists. In general, these provide ancillary expertise to the core medical knowledge of doctors and have failed to attain the same level of professional closure. Their history can be largely summed up as a series of failed attempts to attain full professional status. For example, Bryan Turner (1987) offers a useful discussion of pharmacy. He argues that pharmacists' attempts to attain a monopoly on drug distribution and compounding (mixing and manufacturing) were initially threatened by the petit bourgeois image of pharmacy and the lack of a sufficiently arduous system of formal training. During the 20th century the growth of major pharmaceuticals companies further undermined this position, with pharmacists reduced to counting pills and putting them into bottles according to doctors' instructions. Such deskilling of labour is not conducive to attempts at monopoly formation, because it appears that almost anyone could do the job. Moreover, the division between profit-motivated retail pharmacists and highly skilled, vocationally oriented pharmacists (e.g. medical research chemists at universities) has undermined attempts to form a collective identity or undertake collective action.

Recent changes to the medical professions

Over recent years this occupational structure of professionalised doctors and subordinate nurses has begun to change. The monopolistic claims to legitimate medical knowledge of the medical profession have been challenged in a number of ways.

First, there is the consumer movement towards 'alternative therapies' (discussed later in this chapter). This has had repercussions within the medical profession, with many doctors experimenting with these cures. As a result, the authority of the biomedical knowledge base, a pillar of medical dominance, has been threatened. Second, debate on medical issues has moved into a more public arena. Widespread discussion of contentious issues such as euthanasia and abortion has made it clear that there cannot be a simple 'medical' answer to every health-related issue. Third, ongoing efforts at professionalisation by allied health professionals and practitioners of alternative therapies have flattened out the hierarchy between doctors and other purveyors of medical knowledge.

Finally, there has been emerging dissent within the medical profession towards the hierarchical, bureaucratic and impersonal nature of modern health care. While the power of doctors has to some extent been threatened, the situation of nurses has improved. Nursing has begun stripping itself of its female image, with old titles such as 'matron' and 'sister' being replaced by gender-neutral terms such as 'charge nurse'. Nursing has also begun a process of professionalisation, offering nursing degrees and defining the role of nurse in ways other than as nurturer or doctor's assistant. Nursing leaders have been outspoken in defending the skills and knowledge of nursing practitioners. With these changes in status and self-definition, wages have risen and (as often happens when an occupation rises in status) men have begun to enter nursing in increasing numbers.

Neville Millen (1989) shows that support for the process of professionalisation and change in nursing is mixed. Millen's study of Queensland nurses identified a generation gap. Younger nurses are more likely to be militant and supportive of professionalisation, while older nurses tend to be more passive and see strikes and innovations as a threat to their job security. In addition, Millen suggests that a small group of senior nurses, such as nursing academics, is most committed to higher levels of professionalisation in the vocation.

The full impact of these changes to nursing remains to be seen. At present it is not known how relations with doctors will be renegotiated. Nor are the implications clear of the accelerating entry of men into nursing following these recent status changes. One distinct possibility is the reproduction of a gendered hierarchy within nursing, with men taking the senior and managerial positions.

Medical training

Becoming a doctor, nurse or health professional involves a long process of training. The manifest purpose of medical training is to impart medical skills and knowledge. However, sociologists argue that it also has a number of more or less unintended or hidden consequences related to its function as a means of socialisation into the medical role. These include imparting the values of the medical profession, creating a sense of collective identity for medical practitioners and disseminating attitudes that enable medical staff to deal with traumatic situations without suffering undue anxiety.

Sociological studies of doctors' education have shown how the system of examinations in medical training favours the memorisation of facts. Such training often leads to a loss of idealism and increased pragmatism or cynicism (Shapiro 1995) in medical students, alongside the development of conservative attitudes to healthcare reform. A major reason for this is work overload and a rigorous system of examinations. Students have to learn so much in the early years that a narrow focus on cramming a biomedical curriculum becomes an essential survival strategy. Anatomy classes, which require students to dissect human corpses, are introduced early in training. As well as imparting knowledge, these tend to produce an objective and dispassionate view of the human body—a view that is radically divorced from that held in everyday life. Subsequent contact with patients during 'rounds' reinforces this behaviour. As the trainee doctors follow their more senior colleagues around the ward they learn to see and treat patients in an objective way. The patient is 'interesting' not as a person but rather as a collection of symptoms and maladies from which the trainee doctors can learn.

It has been argued that this objective attitude is beneficial. First, it enables doctors to deal with patients from an attitude of 'affective neutrality' (see discussion above, pp. 326–7). This means that personal feelings will not interfere with treatment. Second, it helps doctors to deal with the trauma of hospital life (e.g. amputating a leg, telling parents their child has died) without risking personal psychological collapse. However, critics maintain that orthodox medical training is too one-sided. Doctors are undertrained for many core aspects of their work, including making ethical decisions and communicating with patients. In addition, doctors are relatively undereducated about the social context of disease and patient care, and the need for effective strategies for illness prevention.

Although changes in doctors' attitudes during medical school have been well explored, questions remain as to whether these persist after graduation. Margaret Shapiro (1995) used survey research methods to examine a cohort of medical school graduates from Melbourne, Monash and Queensland medical schools. There were three data points: at time of entry to medical school, during training and 11 years after graduation. She discovered that attitudes formed in medical school persisted in the workplace. At entry to medical school the doctors had rated status and financial rewards as of little importance. This changed to a more materialistic orientation by the time of graduation and persisted in the workplace. Levels of professional conservatism strengthened during medical school and in the workplace, while the level of concern for patient care diminished. For example, Shapiro found that 47 per cent of her sample had a high concern for patient care at entry to medical school, but only 30 per cent had this outlook after 11 years in the workplace. Conversely, interest in the status rewards of being a doctor increased over time. Although only 40 per cent of medical students reported a high level of concern for status rewards on entry to medical school, by the time the cohort had been 11 years in the workplace this had increased to 81 per cent.

While humanistic and altruistic value orientations seem to be eroded by doctors' socialisation, they are valued in the socialisation of nurses. Nurses are trained to acquire the objective knowledge and skills of their profession, but at the same time to retain a concern for the patient. The reason for this lies in the gendered nature of the nursing profession and the way a patriarchal ideology sees nurses as fulfilling a nurturing role in the hospital. This symbolic status has justified low wages and poor conditions for nurses. Bryan Turner writes:

> *Women are exploited as nurses because they are socialised into a doctrine which equates nursing with mothering and the hospital ward as merely an extension of the domestic sphere of labour.* (1987, p. 149)

Nurses typically have to learn to cope with the contradiction between these ideals about caring and the realities of ward life, where they are pressured for time and subject to bureaucratic control.

DEATH AND DYING

Death and dying are inevitable aspects of human existence. Like illness, death is a profoundly social phenomenon even though there are clearly biological processes involved in dying. Studies in psychology have suggested that the 'will to live' is important in prolonging life. David Phillips and Kenneth Feldman (1973) provide sociological support for this hypothesis with their discovery of the 'death dip' phenomenon. In their analysis of large datasets they discovered that there are fewer deaths than usual before key ceremonies such as a person's birthday, a presidential election or a key religious festival. Phillips and Feldman suggest that Durkheim's theory of social integration through ritual can explain this. The proximity of a ritual strengthens social bonds and feelings of connectedness, thereby enabling people (in a way that is not fully understood) to postpone death.

DEALING WITH DEATH

Sociological studies of death and dying have usually focused on the ways that death is managed by the dying and those who survive them. Elisabeth Kübler-Ross (1969) identifies five stages for coping with dying: denial, anger, bargaining, depression and acceptance. Denial consists of continuing to believe that a cure can be found and refusing to believe in the terminal diagnosis. Once death can no longer be denied, the terminally ill often express anger and lash out at medical staff, family members and friends and sometimes even God. This can be a traumatic experience for people who find themselves inexplicably subject to hatred from a person they love and care for. In the next stage, bargaining, the dying person does various good deeds in the hope of receiving some kind of divine reprieve. Depression sets in once death is seen as inevitable. Kübler-Ross argues that most patients finally come to a stage of acceptance in which they are almost devoid of feelings.

The research of Barney Glaser and Anselm Strauss (1965) suggests that this is not always the case. They argue that, although some patients in this final stage are resigned to their fate in a passive way, others are more active. They might start investigating religion or organising their will, attempt to live life to the full by doing things they have always wanted to do, or avoid a protracted, painful and expensive death by committing suicide.

A more cultural and less psychological approach is taken by Allan Kellehear (1990). Kellehear conducted a study of 100 terminally ill people in Newcastle and Sydney. He argues that in modern industrial societies there is a cultural norm of the 'good death'. This involves making financial and legal preparations, renegotiating relationships with the family through talk, locating sources of support and care, providing indications about the funeral and burial, maintaining an active and world-engaged self as long as possible, and making last farewells. The dying use these criteria to follow a 'correct' line of conduct and the survivors use them to evaluate whether or not the dying person was socially responsible. What all these studies show is that dying is a profoundly social experience. People do not simply die according to the nature of their disease, but rather go through a regular pattern of social behaviour.

Sociological studies of hospitals have further shown how dying is socially managed by health workers in complex organisations. In his ethnographic work David Sudnow (1967) demonstrates that death and dying were considered routine by the hospital staff. By defining death in this way, the possible psychological impact of being surrounded by death could be controlled. Care was also taken to shield other patients and visitors from death. The morgue was tucked away in an obscure part of the hospital and bodies were not moved around the ward during visiting hours.

Studies of physicians have confirmed that medical personnel try to avoid confronting the emotional side of death. Donald Oken (1961) shows that doctors preferred to use euphemisms in telling people about their fatal condition. Words such as 'cancer' and 'terminal' were avoided, and attempts were made to cheer up the patient. Glaser and Strauss (1965) looked at interactions between medical staff and patients with respect to patients' knowledge of their medical condition. They too found that doctors did not like to disclose to patients that they were dying, and that nurses were not allowed to do so without consent from the doctor. As a result, the onus was placed on the patients to find out that they were going to die.

Glaser and Strauss identify several interaction patterns characterising these sorts of episodes. In 'closed awareness', patients are not aware that they are dying but the staff know. In 'open awareness' everyone knows and openly acknowledges and discusses the death. There are two intermediate conditions. 'Suspected awareness' arises when patients think they are terminally ill but have not been told so. Patients would then have to try to extract necessary information from the staff, thus moving on to a situation of open awareness. 'Mutual pretence' occurs when both parties know the condition is terminal but neither wishes to talk about it openly.

EPIDEMIOLOGY AND THE SOCIAL CORRELATES OF HEALTH AND ILLNESS

Although most of the work discussed in this chapter has been strongly theoretical in character, perhaps the largest single area of sociological research into health today is more quantitative in orientation. **Epidemiology** is concerned with the distribution of disease in human populations. It usually relies on the collection and statistical analysis of large bodies of data from surveys or medical records. Epidemiologists are interested in the following kinds of questions:

- What is the spatial distribution of particular diseases (e.g. in cities or the country; developed world or developing world)?
- Who tends to get the disease? This can include social or biological characteristics, although sociologists tend to be more interested in social characteristics or their interaction with biological factors. Social variables of interest might include class, habits such as smoking and drinking, and occupation. Biological variables might include age, gender, blood type and genetic make-up.
- Has there been an increase or a decrease in the disease (e.g. has a drop in the number of deaths from lung cancer accompanied the decline in cigarette smoking in Australia)?
- Which cures or public health interventions appear to be most effective in dealing with the disease (e.g. surgery or occupational therapy in the case of heart disease)?

These types of questions can be answered fully only through the analysis of large data sets, especially when analysing the interactions between a number of possible risk factors.

CAUSES OF DEATH

One of the major areas of study for epidemiology is the causes of death. These have changed with the social and economic development of society. A considerable proportion of the prestige of biomedicine comes from its claims to have brought about a major reduction in human mortality rates. Although human life expectancy has increased dramatically over the past 200 years, this is largely due to the decline in the number of deaths caused by infectious diseases such as cholera, typhoid, plagues and tuberculosis. In the past these were major killers. Sociologists generally argue that we can account for the victory over such diseases in terms of improved social and economic conditions, rather than the successes of biomedicine. Thomas McKeown (1979) shows that improved sanitation and water supplies, a knowledge of basic hygiene, improved diet and reduced family size all contributed to a major drop in the potency of such diseases long before antibiotics and cures were available for most of them. Today, infectious diseases remain a serious problem only in the developing world, where poverty and rapid urbanisation prevent the supply of adequate nutrition and sanitation as well as adequate health care.

Epidemiology shows that in industrialised countries most people die from either congenital diseases such as cancer, or lifestyle-related diseases. Lifestyle-related diseases are the so-called diseases of affluence and include smoking-related lung cancer and diet-related heart disease and stroke. Medical science can do little about either congenital or lifestyle diseases at present. Although this state of affairs is partly the result of the modern lifestyle, it is also the result of people living longer than ever before. Anthropologists suggest that the average life span for much of human prehistory was something like 30–40 years. In modern societies many people live to twice that age. As a result, the body is pushed beyond its 'designed' life span and its component organs and systems begin to fail.

For this reason Randall Collins (2004) argues that the attribution of specific cause of death often does not make sense. Although 'old age' is no longer a legitimate medical diagnosis, the fact is that many old and weak people die of conditions that would not be terminal in younger, healthier individuals. He remarks that 'the bodies of people by their late eighties have broken down to the point at which the system gives out and they die'. Hence 'cancer becomes more prevalent at older ages primarily because aging bodies lose their defences against it' (p. 334). The proximate cause of death in a given individual might be cancer or pneumonia, but the background condition is simply being old. Even when this slow deterioration does not result in immediate death, doctors and patients are often faced with the management of long-term chronic conditions, such as arthritis, diabetes, osteoporosis or Alzheimer's disease, which prevent people from participating actively and fully in social life. These are diseases of age as much as affluence.

Bryan Turner (1987, p. 8) suggests that this shift in the types of disease afflicting people has been in part responsible for the rise of interest in the contributions of medical sociology. In the past, medical advances could be made simply by waging war on bacteria or developing new technologies, whereas today the medical system increasingly has to deal with the social and welfare problems created by long-term illness. Doctors, for example, need to understand the causes of stress-related illness or the importance of family dynamics in the care of the elderly. Similarly, an increasing number of medical institutions, such as nursing homes, have social welfare as well as narrow medical responsibilities.

HEALTH IN THE DEVELOPING WORLD

Despite the changes that have come to developed nations, health in the developing world is a different story. Deaths from infectious diseases remain significant and life expectancy remains far below developed world levels. Over the past 50 years rapid urbanisation and environmental degradation have added to the burden of providing adequate health care. Current strategies to improve health focus on a struggle to obtain an adequate diet, clean water, sanitation and primary health care. As with Aboriginal health, scholars in the area of developing world health argue that a simple medical response to these issues is not enough and that the most important factors are poverty and social injustice. These are contexts that call for social and political solutions rather than just medical and sanitary reforms.

SICKNESS, HEALTH AND SOCIAL INEQUALITY

A major research area in social epidemiology concerns the impact of social factors on morbidity (sickness). One of the most consistent findings of studies conducted throughout the world is that, in general, people from higher social and economic groupings have better health. Similarly, those from groups with the lowest socioeconomic status (SES) exhibit higher levels of almost every major illness associated with morbidity and mortality. Australia is no exception to this general pattern.

Ian Burnley and Mine Batiyel (1985) found, for example, that local government areas in Australia that are socially disadvantaged (such as Sydney's western suburbs) tend to have higher mortality (death) rates than more affluent areas (such as Sydney's North Shore). Mortality rates also correlate with occupational categories so that, in general, manual workers have higher mortality rates than those in the professions.

Sociology

Similarly, Australian Health Survey (ABS 2002c) data show that morbidity is inversely correlated with income. Both males and females in low-income households have poorer health than those in high-income households. Numerous reasons have been put forward for this finding. These include class differences in:

- choice of diet (the working class eats more 'junk food' and food high in fat and sugar)
- ability to pay for elite medical services
- levels of knowledge about the benefits of exercise and a 'healthy lifestyle'
- rates of smoking and drinking
- levels of competence and assertiveness in doctor interactions
- levels of exposure to environmental pollution in both the workplace and the home.

It is difficult, however, to pin down exactly which causal forces are at work here. The factors involved are very closely interconnected and sometimes hard to measure. This makes it hard to arrive at statistically valid findings with the existing, routinely collected data sets that do not contain information on all necessary variables. The situation is further complicated by the possibility of a health selection process being at work. Here the usual causal arrows are reversed and it is ill-health that causes social disadvantage. An example might be a person with a chronic condition who is too sick to hold down a job.

One of Australia's leading epidemiologists, Jake Najman (1994), argues that existing Australian research points to the central importance of lifestyle and behavioural choices in explaining class differences in health. He suggests that lower SES groups are less likely to engage in preventive activity (e.g. regular check-ups), yet more likely to engage in unhealthy behaviour. For example, lower income Australians tend to have higher cholesterol levels thanks to poor dietary choices, and they are more likely to be overweight.

Gavin Turrell (1995) suggests that we can find support for Najman's argument by looking at a breakdown of the causes of death in relation to class. Those in the lower SES groups are more likely to die of lifestyle-related respiratory and digestive diseases than people in higher social classes. By way of contrast, the class gradient for cancers (which are less closely related to behaviours and more closely related to genetic factors) is less steep. Data from the National Health Survey confirm this general picture. Figure 10.1 is taken from the useful annual report put out by the Australian Institute of Health and Welfare (2008, p. 65). Here we see that cancer rates are similar for those in the lowest and highest income quintiles. With the exception of heavy alcohol use, however, it is poor people who engage in unhealthy lifestyles and who seem to have more health problems.

Much the same story is told for obesity, as shown in the case study opposite.

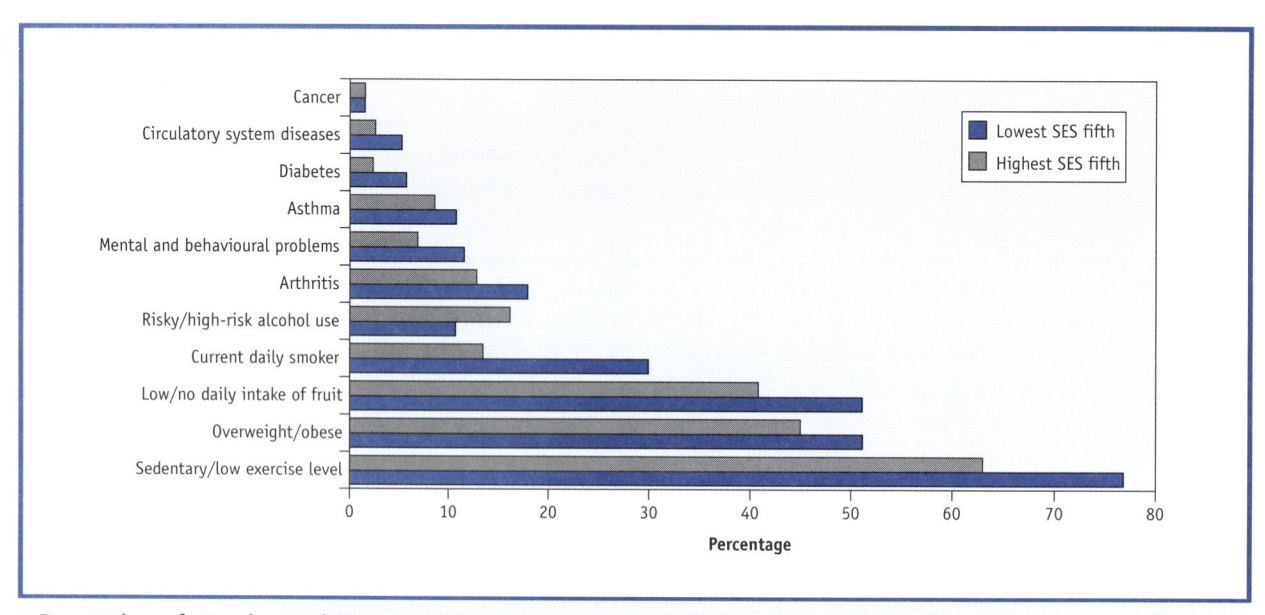

FIGURE 10.1

Proportion of people aged 18 years and over reporting selected health risk factors and long-term conditions, by socioeconomic status, 2004–05 *Source: Australian Institute of Health and Welfare* (2008, p. 65).

340

Case Study
The obesity epidemic

Like many developed nations, Australia is experiencing rising levels of obesity. One major cause of this disease is a diet high in fat and sugar, which is cheap in a developed world context. Not having enough exercise can also contribute to the problem. In other words, there is a strong correlation with lifestyle.

Table 10.2 shows that nearly 50 per cent of Australian adults are either overweight or obese. The table also shows the correlation with two dimensions of inequality. Those who are better educated and make more money are significantly less likely to be obese. Prejudice against 'fat' people is growing in our society and, according to the ABS, obesity costs Australia more than $20 billion every year.

TABLE 10.2

Socioeconomic characteristics of adults and body mass index, 2004–05

		Normal	Overweight	Obese	Total
Highest non-school qualification					
Degree/diploma or higher qualification	%	49.4	34.8	12.9	100.0
Other qualification	%	41.9	36.9	19.3	100.0
No non-school qualification	%	41.3	35.5	20.4	100.0
Household income					
Low income	%	43.3	32.3	20.6	100.0
Middle income	%	44.0	35.7	17.3	100.0
High income	%	45.8	37.6	14.9	100.0
All persons aged 18 years and over	%	44.1	35.4	17.9	100.0
All persons aged 18 years and over	'000	6037.0	4888.0	2478.0	13760.6

Note: The rows do not add up to 100 because the table does not show people whose BMI was 'underweight' or people whose BMI was not stated or was unknown in the data set.

Source: Adapted from ABS (2008a, Table 11.11).

1. What can be done to deal with obesity?
2. Given that obesity is a condition with a strong social component, what do you think could or should be done to get the problem under control?
3. Now reflect on sociological ideas about medicalisation and medical power that were discussed earlier in the chapter. How might these lead you to think in new ways about the so-called obesity epidemic?

SICKNESS, HEALTH AND GENDER

Research in the area of health and gender shows that women have a better life expectancy than men. For example, assuming that current age-specific death rates hold during the future (in reality, they are likely to decline), the Australian life tables suggest that the current life expectancy at birth is 83.3 for a baby girl and 78.5 for a baby boy (ABS 2008a). The causes of death among men and women are more or less the same, with circulatory-system problems and cancer accounting for most deaths. However, for any given age the death rates for men are higher than for women. Debate is ongoing as to whether this is due to biological and genetic differences between the sexes or is a product of differing activities and lifestyles. Some evidence seems to be pointing towards the latter, more sociological hypothesis. It is well established that men are more likely to engage in risky activities, consume alcohol and tobacco, and be exposed to toxins and hazards in the workplace. Particularly noteworthy is the fact that males are much more likely than females to die a violent death while young. Additionally, the gap in life expectancies between men and women has been closing over the past quarter-century in Australia—a finding that is hard to reconcile with ideas of a genetically encoded fate.

Issues of life expectancy aside, the health picture is not at all one-sided in women's favour. Many studies have shown that women tend to get sick more often than men. But, although women get sick more frequently, men tend to be more likely to contract a life-threatening or chronic disease. Debate continues as to whether this finding reflects genuine differences in morbidity between the sexes, is an artefact of gender-specific differences in willingness to report illness or is a product of the way the medical system treats and defines the two sexes.

Sickness, health, ethnicity and migration

Together with socioeconomic status and gender, ethnicity is another important variable along which states of health can vary. Data from countries around the world suggest that it is often the case that minority and migrant groups have poorer than average health. In understanding the Australian case it is important to separate out the relative influences of migration and ethnicity.

Migrants to Australia tend to have better health than Australian-born people. This is due to the selective nature of the migration process. Potential migrants to Australia are screened on a number of criteria, including health. The concern of the Australian government is to avoid admitting chronically sick people who might place demands on the health system and become a 'burden to the taxpayer'. In consequence, migrant populations tend to consist of relatively healthy people. However, people of a non–English-speaking background often have poorer health than Anglo-Australians. One reason for this is that minority groups form disproportionate numbers of the poor. Consequently, they often find themselves engaged in low-status, health-endangering employment and living in crowded housing. These structural conditions common to low SES groups are compounded by the particular problems faced by ethnic minorities in interacting with the health system.

Erica Bates and Susie Linder-Pelz (1987) list four groups of major complaints that ethnic groups have about the health system in Australia:

1. *Communications breakdown.* Migrants face language problems when interacting with the health system and health professionals. There is a need for trained interpreters to confront this problem.
2. *Lack of information and access.* The health-care system is complex. Migrants often lack basic information about obtaining health insurance, signing up for Medicare, registering with a doctor and making full use of the range of services provided by the health system.
3. *Prejudice.* Migrants often confront prejudice from health workers, who might see them as stupid, lazy or hard to deal with. In addition, the Australian health-care system is culturally biased in more subtle ways. For example, the food preferences of ethnic groups might not be catered for by a hospital kitchen, and cultural expectations about the central role of the family in the healing process are hard to meet when there are strict hospital visiting hours.
4. *Inadequate involvement of ethnic groups in service improvement.* Representatives of ethnic groups have traditionally been excluded from health policy formulation, a factor that has contributed to the problems outlined above. Recently, attempts have been made in Australia to develop more appropriate and culturally sensitive services for minority groups. These have included the recruitment of interpreters and ethnic health workers, and the establishment of new operational guidelines that take account of religious and cultural differences.

Sickness, health and Aboriginal people

As a group, the Aboriginal population clearly has the poorest health in Australia, exhibiting patterns of morbidity and mortality that many scholars believe to be similar to those of the Third World. Some representative statistics are as follows:

- Twice as many Indigenous Australians report psychological distress as non-Indigenous Australians.
- Some 57 per cent of the Aboriginal and Torres Strait Islander population aged 15 and over are overweight or obese.
- Life expectancy is 59 years for Indigenous men and 65 years for Indigenous women. This contrasts with the Australian norms of 77 and 82, respectively.

- Hospitalisations for dialysis for Indigenous Australian adults are around 14 times the rate for non-Indigenous adults. (ABS/AIHW 2008)

Today the major killers in the Indigenous population are chronic diseases such as circulatory or respiratory problems and diabetes. In many but not all cases these causes of higher morbidity and mortality are related to smoking, alcohol consumption and diet. Geographical isolation from essential services can also be an important factor in negative health outcomes for rural/remote communities. Aboriginal health should be understood not only in the context of social and economic deprivation, but also in terms of two centuries of colonisation and conquest that have created extreme social and cultural marginalisation.

Dennis Gray and Sherry Saggers (1994) argue that in the Australian context the links between colonialism and poor Aboriginal health go back 200 years. The arrival of white settlers saw the Aboriginal population decimated by introduced infectious diseases such as smallpox, influenza and venereal diseases, as well as by war. A population of somewhere between 300 000 and 1 250 000 at the time of first contact was reduced to 74 000 by 1930, due in large part to lack of inherited resistance to these diseases. Over the past 200 years Aboriginal health has been threatened by economic poverty, exploitative work and insanitary living conditions. The medical problems arising from the use of alcohol, tobacco, amphetamines and petrol- and glue-sniffing must be understood as a response to boredom, unemployment, despair and the breakdown of traditional social structures following colonisation.

For this reason, research on Aboriginal health has pointed to the need to address issues not simply in health terms but through policies designed to bring social and economic justice. Central to this project is the need to re-establish meaning, a sense of purpose in life and a strong community. Aboriginal activists argue that land rights are essential to this process, providing the basis for both economic stability and spiritual sustenance. Aboriginal groups also face an array of cultural problems in dealing with the health system that are similar to, even perhaps more severe than, those experienced by ethnic groups. In particular, Aboriginal people see illness, death and healing as issues that should involve the whole community rather than just the individual (Bates & Linder-Pelz 1987). So the isolation of the patient in a hospital is extremely inappropriate and, possibly, counterproductive in terms of health outcomes, as the patient is cut off from kin support (see the discussion on p. 329 on the role of family support in healing).

Since the poor status of Aboriginal health was recognised in the early 1970s, systematic attempts have been made to address the situation. Health-promotion and education strategies have been central to these policies, coupled with increased spending on housing and other infrastructure by the Commonwealth. Particularly important have been efforts by the Aboriginal people themselves to provide culturally appropriate health care for their fellows. These have included Aboriginal-controlled Aboriginal medical services and the recruitment and training of Aboriginal and Torres Strait Islander health workers. However, significant future advances in the area of Aboriginal health will probably depend, some say, on structural changes in the economic, political and social status of Aboriginal people rather than just health and welfare policy.

Reflective questions: How does culture come into the picture when we think of illness, death and dying? In what kinds of ways does inequality have an impact on health?

CURRENT TRENDS—THE END OF BIOMEDICINE AND MEDICAL DOMINANCE?

Although the biomedical model of disease, and its associated professional and institutional forms, remains dominant in modern society, it is increasingly coming under scrutiny and attack. Pressure for change is coming from several directions at once. This concluding section of the chapter looks at some of these signs of challenge.

THE RISE OF ALTERNATIVE THERAPIES

Since the 1960s the biomedical paradigm has been under attack from medical consumers. There has been a dramatic rise in interest in **alternative therapies** such as homeopathy, chiropractic, acupuncture, herbalism, yoga, meditation and forms of religious intervention such as faith-healing. Consumers are frustrated by the inability of biomedicine to find cures to everyday problems such as smoking addiction, arthritis, the bad back and the common cold. Many are also critical of what they perceive to be the impersonal and authoritarian nature of modern medical practice and its neglect of the total wellbeing of the person. Finally, in the wake of the thalidomide scandal and debates about silicone breast implants, many are suspicious about the benefits of modern pharmaceutical products.

Evan Willis (1994) provides some useful data illustrating the increasing demand for alternative medicine in Australia. Listings of acupuncturists, herbalists and homoeopaths in the Melbourne *Yellow Pages* trebled between 1975 and 1980 and again between 1980 and 1986. Around 400 000 Victorian adults per annum visited natural therapists in the mid-1980s. As long ago as 1983 the Australian Health Survey (ABS 1984) showed that 2 per cent of the population had visited a chiropractor, osteopath, naturopath, herbalist or acupuncturist in the two weeks prior to the survey. Willis argues that a rapprochement, or convergence, is now taking place between 'alternative' and 'orthodox' medicine. Practitioners of alternative medicine are now likely to incorporate some orthodox techniques, such as measuring blood pressure, in their examinations. Both alternative and orthodox practitioners are referring patients to each other. Additionally, orthodox medical practitioners such as GPs are beginning to practise one or more alternative therapies. The trend Willis observed is continuing today. Between 1996 and 2006 there was an 80 per cent increase in the number of people working in complementary health therapy. According to the National Health Survey of 2004–05, some 3.8 per cent of the adult population had visited a complementary health therapist in the two weeks prior to the survey (ABS 2008g).

An emerging trend in the field, particularly in Australian health sociology, is to interpret the rise of alternative therapies in terms of a theory of postmodernity. Heather Eastwood (2000) argues that, while biomedicine is linked to the rise of modernity, more holistic approaches to healing are closely linked to a process of postmodernisation and a growing cultural critique of modern, industrial society. This complex process has seen a renewed interest in working with nature as opposed to dominating it (e.g. the ecology movement). It has also seen a renewed interest in the role religion can play in all aspects of life. There is, moreover, a general shift towards self-empowerment and self-actualisation as core life goals. In combination, these sorts of cultural shifts have created a new type of medical consumer who is likely to be suspicious of modern, scientific biomedicine and medical power, but favourably disposed towards traditional therapies that emphasise the natural, sacred and holistic dimensions of healing and that empower the self. Eastwood's study of Queensland GPs demonstrated that some were adapting to this consumer demand by offering alternative therapies such as acupuncture. However, they were not simply 'calculating economic rationalists' (2000, p. 152) but rather had begun to shift their own values such that they expressed opinions during her interviews with them that were 'more compatible with the holistic health paradigm than with the orthodox biomedical paradigm'.

This position that there has been a value shift finds empirical support in the survey research of Mohammad Siahpush (1998). Siahpush conducted a telephone survey of 209 adults in the Albury region. He found that demographic variables (age, gender and so on) did not seem to have much impact on attitudes towards alternative medicine. Dissatisfaction with conventional medicine was also not a significant predictor, but dissatisfaction with the medical encounter (face-to-face meetings with the doctor) was associated with a turn away from orthodoxy. Far and away the strongest influence on positive attitudes towards alternative therapies was 'postmodern values'. Siahpush defined these as belief in nature, holism, consumer choice and individual responsibility, and rejection of medical authority.

Likewise, in a content analysis of alternative medication advertising and through interviews with consumers in pharmacies in Tasmania, Lisa Rayner and Gary Easthope (2001, p. 175) conclude that the consumption of alternative medicines has 'all the features of postmodern consumption'. These include the niche marketing of products to particular demographics, strong ties between the products and symbolism related to nature, and the use of the products in a process of self-identity formation. Interestingly, they observed that this process was gendered. Women seemed to be the major purchasers of alternative medicine and products were aimed at age/gender-niche markets.

The full implications of the rise of alternative, or complementary, medicine on the health-care landscape remain to be seen. It is possible that a more consumerist or market-driven health system will emerge in which the public choose from a variety of available treatment modalities and 'expert systems'. Such a system might challenge the dominance of biomedicine and the medical profession.

Fran Collyer (2003) urges that we remain sceptical that such outcomes will eventuate. She argues that in recent years complementary and alternative medicine (CAM) has moved out of a cottage industry phase and been co-opted by mainstream health providers and medical capitalism. Products, services and techniques have been appropriated in this upsizing process, but there has been no real challenge to biomedical dominance and authority structures. CAM is valued only as a way of making money and expanding the total size of the medical economy through innovative marketing. The autonomy of formerly independent CAM practitioners has been reduced as they become employees of health corporations rather than front-parlour small businesses. She argues that costs to consumers will escalate too, given that mainstreaming has been linked to the search for profit and that big-business market-based medicine is usually more expensive than state-administered systems.

FEMINIST INTERVENTIONS AND THE WOMEN'S HEALTH MOVEMENT

While the movement towards alternative therapies is in many ways related to individual consumer choices, the feminist movement has mounted a more collectivistic critique of medical dominance. Information sharing is a pivotal strategy in the women's health movement. The idea here is to take away the power/knowledge base of the patriarchal medical system by making available to women health information about their bodies and women's issues.

An early milestone in this process was the Boston Women's Health Collective's 1973 publication of *Our Bodies Ourselves*. This best-selling work was particularly influential because it included women's own stories and experiences as legitimate forms of knowledge alongside those of biomedicine. This focus remains important today, with feminists arguing that women's commonsense and experiential knowledge are tragically undervalued by the orthodox medical system.

Feminists have also argued that:

- Caring is undervalued in a biomedical paradigm that emphasises 'heroic', masculinist technological interventions and measures medical achievement in terms of statistics such as mortality rates. Health services should be delivered in a personal way that respects the dignity of the individual and their choices.
- There should be greater equity in health care. Subsidised women's health clinics in poor areas, for example, are a strategy for addressing this.
- Women should try to influence public policy through advocacy. This might make use of political lobbying, demonstrations or the mass media.

HEALTH PROMOTION AND PREVENTIVE MEDICINE

The biomedical model emphasises the individual level of analysis and the biological causes of disease, but ignores the social and environmental factors that put people at risk. In consequence, the biomedical model has tended to favour resources being concentrated in hospitals, with a focus on cure, rather than dispersed into a program of community preventive medicine. However, epidemiologists and others in the area of social and preventive medicine have long argued that the causes of morbidity are not simply biological diseases. Today their message is beginning to be heard and what has been called the new public health has emerged. The essence of this approach is to take a broader perspective on health and illness, sometimes known as the 'health field concept' (Government of Canada 1974). The four main elements of this are:

1. *Human biology.* This is essentially the human body and its genetic composition—the traditional territory of biomedicine.
2. *Environment.* This consists of the physical world that people inhabit. It is claimed that damage to the broader environment from pollution and urbanisation, as well as the quality of specific workplace and home environments, has a significant impact on health.
3. *Lifestyle.* This concept refers to the way of life and the health-related behaviours of people within the community.
4. *Health-care systems.* This deals with the form and quantity of health-care delivery systems such as clinics, hospitals and medical personnel.

This paradigm argues for a broad-based attack on disease that is concerned more with the community and prevention than the individual and cure. There is a strong focus on health education and the need to target and educate groups that are at risk as a consequence of poor diet, lack of exercise, too much stress or excessive drinking or smoking. In Australia, the 'Slip, Slop, Slap' campaign about the dangers of skin cancer, featuring media advertising and promotional work in schools, is a good example of this preventive approach. The Australian approach to HIV/AIDS is another notable success story for the new public health (Ross 1994). During the 1990s HIV/AIDS-related deaths dropped rapidly, from 666 in 1995, to 568 in 1996 and then 279 in 1997 (ABS 1999f). This decline was partly due to information campaigns about safe sex and drug use, the distribution of free condoms and needles, and health system policies that empowered and worked with community and activist groups.

There are also new initiatives aimed at encouraging people to conduct self-examinations for breast cancer and testicular cancer and to persuade them to have regular medical check-ups. Medical service delivery institutions have also been evaluated and reformed, with a new attention to the development of user-friendly community and mobile clinics aimed at particular groups (e.g. women, Aboriginal people) as an attractive alternative to large, intimidating general-purpose hospitals. Finally, there is a renewed interest in health and safety in the workplace and the environment in general. Indeed, health-based issues have become perhaps the major factor in legislation designed to protect the environment. For example, new cars sold in Australia today must be able to run on unleaded petrol. This policy was prompted largely by concerns about the dangers of lead, especially for children's health. Similarly, legislation about airborne pollution is driven mainly by concern for respiratory disease.

Self-help movements

Over the past 50 years, self-help groups have become an increasingly significant factor in the provision of health-related services. They can be seen as popular movements that have taken the control of medical issues away from the professions and into the community. Alfred Katz and Lowell Levin (1980) argue that self-help groups are an antidote to 'passivity, apathy and dependency in the health care area' (p. 333). As such, they can be seen as challenging the power of the biomedical professions and institutions as described, for example, by Ivan Illich (above). The best known self-help group is Alcoholics Anonymous, which has more than 100 000 branches and 2 million members. However, the range of self-help groups is vast. Alfred Katz (1979) shows that some are organised around attempts to deal with personal problems (e.g. substance abuse, depression or psychological problems arising from sexual abuse as a child) while others are collective efforts to help others through social advocacy and group enterprise (e.g. community groups organising activities for people with disabilities).

Managerialism, consumerism and the end of medical autonomy

John Germov (1995) argues that managerialism is an important threat to medical dominance, especially in Australia. Germov defines managerialism as 'the introduction of private sector management techniques into the public sector' (p. 51). With strong government support, managerialist approaches are now being introduced into the health system. Aspects of the approach include:

strategic planning, results orientation, client focus, program budgeting and evaluation, management by objectives, contract or fixed-term employment, performance-based appraisal and payment of workers, performance indicators and user pays. (p. 58)

Managerialism (which has also been introduced into Australian universities, schools and various public service agencies) focuses on the needs of the 'consumer' (e.g. student, patient etc.) and the cost-effective delivery of services (e.g. staff–student ratios, number of patients treated per day). Often managerialism is accompanied by the creation of artificial internal markets, so different state-run hospitals, for example, will compete with each other for patients and operating grants by trying to meet government-set 'benchmarks' and target 'performance indicators'. Funding depends on efficiency, which is measured in terms of outcomes relative to these artificial standards. As Germov puts it: 'The central idea is to make the providers compete for government funds by attracting more patients and displaying greater efficiency and quality in the delivery of services' (p. 60).

Germov sees two possible advantages to managerialism. One is that it might help stamp out medical fraud, which he estimates as costing up to $500 million per annum in public money. Medical fraud can take a number of forms, such as charging for work never done, exaggerating the severity of a case and performing unnecessary procedures. The second advantage might be an end to medical dominance:

Health managerialism represents a significant challenge to medical autonomy (economic, political and clinical). Managerialism involves a form of control that has the potential to place severe restrictions on medical autonomy through pervasive accountability and quality assurance measures. (p. 61)

Germov argues that, thanks to managerialism, the professional activities and beliefs of doctors will be subject to unparalleled scrutiny in terms of criteria relating to efficiency and cost-effectiveness.

Although Germov sees managerialism as having some possible positive benefits, he gives it only cautious approval. Germov raises a number of concerns:

- Hospitals might abandon necessary but unprofitable areas of service.
- Consumers/patients might be discharged prematurely. This might happen, for example, in an effort to attain a good performance indicator score for the number of days in hospital per patient.
- There is a possibility that tailoring services to meet individual needs might disadvantage marginalised groups.
- An obsessive concern with economic efficiency might lead to the neglect of broader 'public interest and community service objectives' (p. 62) that cannot be quantified or given a dollar value.

A study of day surgery in Australia (Markovic et al. 2004) documents some of the problems that might arise from such policies from the perspective of patients. In recent years funding model policies have favoured day surgery, in which the patient is discharged soon after the procedure rather than occupying a hospital bed overnight. Yet the patients interviewed by Milica Markovic and her colleagues reported concerns over lack of information and contact with the surgeons. They were also disconcerted by production-line processes that were not strongly individuated. Additionally, having to walk to the operating theatre themselves rather than being wheeled in on a trolley resulted in exposure to medical settings and technologies. Some found it worrying to see the tools and machines that would later be used for their surgery. Regardless of the economic or medical benefits it might have, day surgery can have a potential downside for patients.

Running in parallel to managerialism and in some ways complementary to it has been a consumerist movement in the health area. This threatens medical autonomy and authority by empowering patients, allowing them to shop around or choose health-care providers according to their needs and experiences. It further manifests in consumerist social movements and lobby groups that pressure the medical and pharmaceutical establishments over products and services. This consumerist ideology, as we have just seen, has been a significant factor in the rise of alternative medicine in Australia and elsewhere.

Maria Zadoroznyj (2001) has documented this in the context of pregnancy and childbirth through an interview study of Australian women. The 'birth narratives' showed that the women—albeit to varying degrees—made consumerist choices informed by their own risk-management preferences, core values, and emotional and interpersonal concerns. When locating maternity services or a gynaecologist women weighed up their options and undertook diverse strategies to avoid certain clinics or clinicians and to get on the books of others. Pivotal here was a concern to locate a doctor or midwife whom they could 'trust', with whom they did not experience fear or embarrassment and who would recognise their full personhood. Such activist patterns were particularly marked with women who were having their second or third child. Here prior experiences had given them firm ideas about how they wanted to manage their pregnancy and birth. Zadoroznyj (2001, p. 137) concludes that the pattern she identified marked a 'small but significant challenge to medical dominance'. Likewise, Karen Willis (2004) found that the agency of women is pivotal to the uptake of mobile breast-screening services in rural Tasmania. Her interview study explored how the personal management of choice and risk were central to the decision to participate in screening. Furthermore, many women made use of the service because doing so would support their self-definition as a healthy and responsible person.

Reflective questions: What are the various ways in which the knowledge base and activities of modernist, bureaucratic biomedicine are being changed and challenged? What forces and players are behind each initiative?

CONCLUSION

We have seen in this chapter that health and illness are about much more than bacteria and genes, doctors and nurses, big-ticket technology or whatever else commonsense and popular iconography tells us they are about. Health and illness are social in every possible way: inequality shapes who gets sick; modernity influences how we think about illness and how hospitals are run; power runs through doctor–patient interactions; the decision to seek help is informed by practical needs and folk models of sickness; and ongoing transformations of medicine are driven by wider social currents like feminism, managerialism and consumerism. Sociology's contribution is to analyse this complex interplay and to suggest ways that we might do things better.

Tutorial exercise

'Death and illness are social.' Imagine this is the title of a public lecture to be given in Australia by a leading epidemiologist. In your group, make a list of the themes you think the epidemiologist would talk about. Now make a list of the themes that a critical sociologist (someone influenced by Marxism, feminism, Foucault and labelling theory, for example) would talk about when giving a public lecture with exactly the same title. What would be similar and different about the content, rhetorical style and mood of the two talks?

For activity suggestions, learning aids, revision of key concepts and access to self-study material, visit: **www.pearson.com.au/highered/vankrieken4e**

Further reading

Davis, A. & George, J. 1998, *States of Health*, Longman, Melbourne.

Germov, J. 2005, *Second Opinion: An Introduction to Health Sociology*, Oxford University Press, Melbourne.

Turner, B. 1987, *Medical Power and Social Knowledge*, Sage, Beverly Hills.

Weiss, G. L. & Lonnquist, L. E. 2008, *Sociology of Health, Healing and Illness*, 6th edn, Prentice Hall, New York.

Websites

Australian Institute of Health and Welfare:
www.aihw.gov.au
This is an excellent source of varied information on health in Australia, such as the social distribution and prevalence of particular diseases.

Hobart Women's Health Centre:
www.hwhc.com.au
The information here provides a representative insight into the way that feminist values have influenced the provision of health care in Australia.

Women's Health Australia:
www.alswh.org.au
The Women's Health Australia research project is a massive longitudinal study hosted at the University of Newcastle and the University of Queensland. Clicking around will provide insight into a representative large-scale investigation that is informed by sociological and epidemiological thinking as well as narrowly medical parameters.

11 Religion

This chapter explores the relationship between religious beliefs and practices and other social phenomena such as culture and politics. It explains that religion is experienced as involving ultimate truths but is always socially grounded. Understanding this helps us to stand back from everyday assumptions about beliefs and the role of religion in society, as well as our own choices about religion and spirituality.

By the end of the chapter, you should have a better understanding of:
— sociological theories of religion
— the relationship between science and religion
— religion and social change
— whether secularisation has taken place
— the different forms of religion in late modernity, especially fundamentalism and new forms of religious expression
— the future of religion.

INTRODUCTION	**350**
Definitions of religion	351
Religion and spirituality	351
THEORIES OF RELIGION	**352**
Functionalist theories of religion	352
Durkheim	352
Civil religion	353
Materialist theories of religion	353
Marx	353
Phenomenological theories of religion	355
Religion as a sacred canopy	355
Criticisms of Berger and Luckmann	356
Feminist theories of religion	356
The deconstruction of religious traditions	356
Religion as an instrument for the oppression of women	356
The feminist reconstruction of religion	357
The influence of feminism on the Christian church	357
SCIENCE AND RELIGION	**357**
RELIGION AND SOCIAL CHANGE	**358**
Religion as the source of social change	358
The Protestant Ethic and the Spirit of Capitalism—Max Weber	359
Religion as a conservative influence on society	359
The effects of religious beliefs on political and social attitudes	360
Religion as a radical influence on society	361
Liberation theology	361
SECULARISATION	**361**
Evidence in support of secularisation	362
Problems with the secularisation thesis	363
Secularisation or post-secularisation?	365
EXPLAINING THE RESURGENCE OF RELIGION	**366**
The search for moral guidance	366
CONTEMPORARY RELIGIOUS EXPRESSION	**367**
Fundamentalism	367
Christian fundamentalism in the United States	367
Islamic fundamentalism	368
Explanations of the appeal of fundamentalism	370
New forms of religiosity	371
New Age movements	371
Neo-paganism	372
Locating new forms of religiosity in modernity	373
THE FUTURE OF RELIGION	**373**
Tutorial exercise	375
Further reading	375
Websites	375

INTRODUCTION

- Pet cemeteries and crematoriums are a growth industry. They exist in all of Australia's major cities and are becoming so mainstream that even traditional funeral companies offer them. Services offered may include counselling, a chapel ceremony, supply of an urn, a plaque or monument and pet memorabilia such as photo frames. Publicity for the company Pets at Peace, for example, emphasises the last act of respect and care of the dead animal and the permanence of the memorial. On the company's website you can find books with titles such as *Loss of a Pet*, as well as poems and prayers. Poems sometimes describe the pet's continued existence in the afterlife:

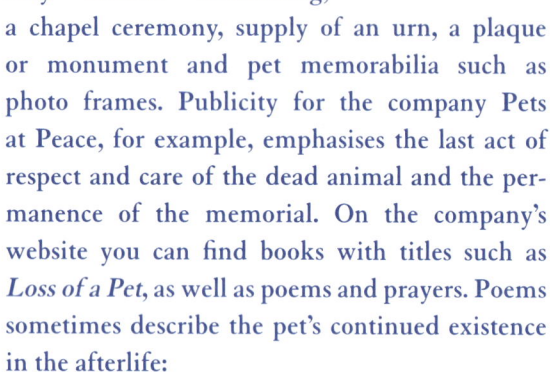

  Through life's journey we took a ride
  The times you spent by my side
  You always were there as my best friend
  But we knew one day, there would be an end.
  Heavens doors are open, just walk through the gates,
  In this Animal Kingdom sunshine awaits.
  (www.petsatpeace.com.au/petprayers.php)

- North Korea is a single-party state, ruled by the Eternal President, Kim Il-sung, who died in 1994. Formally established as the Democratic People's Republic of Korea in 1948 and committed to Marxism-Leninism, its political ideology today is *Juche*, which is a component of *Kimilsungism*. Kim Il-sung's son, Kim Jong-il, is Chairman of the National Defence Commission and the de facto head of state. The anti-God activist, Christopher Hitchens, has described North Korea as a 'celestial state' in which a political religious ideology, centring on the cult of the personality of Kim Il-sung, is used to enslave people. He argues that God is the author of totalitarianism, presiding over a 'celestial North Korea in the sky that subjects us to constant survey ... while we are asleep, after we are dead' (cited in Moore 2008).

1. How might these two examples of the intersection of religion into everyday life and politics be used to support or challenge arguments that religion today is an anachronism?
2. What do they suggest about the role of religion in contemporary social life, including its relationship with democracy?

Religious beliefs exist in all societies, and even in apparently secular societies their influence is so pervasive that no-one escapes their effects. Christianity has been central to the development of Western civilisation and many of its cherished beliefs, such as the belief in human rights, can be traced back to its influence. In Australia, where religion is a private matter, the different traditions and values of Catholics and Protestants played a central role in the nation's politics throughout much of the 20th century. In countries where church and state are united, the influence of religion is more obvious. In fundamentalist Muslim countries such as Iran, for example, religious beliefs shape the political system, attitudes to the use of knowledge, forms of economic investment, and social and sexual relations between men and women.

Religion is integral to culture, binding people in a symbolic universe that shapes how they view their place in the cosmos and their relationships with one another. The association between religion and social identity serves as one of the most important sources of social solidarity and collective association. In shaping our worldview, religion creates both social cohesion and social distance. Throughout history political conflicts have often had an important religious dimension.

The sociological approach to religion is different from everyday understandings. Rather than being concerned with the historical accuracy of religious beliefs, or whether rituals and practices are personally meaningful, sociologists examine religion as a socially constructed phenomenon, linked to a society's culture. Whether religious beliefs are true or not is not of interest. What sociologists seek to discover is the relationship between religion and sociality. This includes examining how religious movements form and their contribution to social stability and change, the meanings that people give to their religious behaviour, and the relationship between religion and other social institutions and forms. Religion is examined both as an external phenomenon that influences behaviour regardless of people's subjective understandings and as a source of social meaning that people use to complement their social identity.

Definitions of religion

Defining religion is surprisingly difficult. Clearly it is concerned with a belief in metaphysical forces that makes our existence meaningful, but this description excludes many other aspects of religion. Religion has an organisational aspect to it, and the wide variety of beliefs that might fall under the term 'religious' make it difficult to provide a definition that would satisfy everyone's understanding of the term. The High Court of Australia defined religion as:

a complex of beliefs and practices which point to a set of values and an understanding of the meaning of existence. (cited in ABS 2005g)

The advantage of this definition is its inclusiveness, but it makes no mention of institutional aspects of religion, or of a belief in the supernatural, which for some is a core aspect of religion.

Definitions of religion vary in their emphasis. The range of features that definitions encompass includes:

- beliefs about the existence of superhuman beings or forces
- the practice of rites and rituals
- the institutional forms that religion takes
- the power relationships believed to be involved between human beings and suprahuman beings
- the provision of answers to questions of meaning
- the explanation of tragic or uncontrollable events
- the legitimation of the status quo
- the linking of individuals and groups with nature and/or the supernatural
- the projection of human ideals and objectives onto an idealised suprahuman order.

Definitions that focus on the first four of these features are described as *substantive definitions* because they emphasise what religion actually is and the forms it takes. Definitions that focus on the last five features are described as *functional definitions* because they focus on what religion does and on the role it plays in social formations.

Some definitions encompass both what religion is and what it does, as in the case of Durkheim's classic definition of religion. For Durkheim religion is:

a unified system of beliefs and practices relative to sacred things, that is to say, things set apart and forbidden—beliefs and practices which unite into one single moral community called a Church, all those who adhere to them. (1965, p. 62)

According to Durkheim, the central feature of religion is not belief in the supernatural or in some divine force, but the division of the world into the sacred and the profane. He is therefore telling us something about what religion is. But his definition also emphasises the role that religion plays in society. As a functionalist theorist, Durkheim stresses its contribution to social order and stability through the provision of a unifying set of religious beliefs and rituals that provide the social glue of a society.

The choice of definition depends on the objectives of the sociologist. Functional definitions are more useful when the goal is to develop a general theory of religion. Substantive definitions are helpful when applied to specific social phenomena. As well, the choice of definition will reflect the views of the researcher about what constitutes 'religion' and its relationship with other social phenomena.

Religion and spirituality

Sociologists have debated the relationship between religion and spirituality, and how these should be defined, since the 1980s when New Age religions became a prominent form of religious expression. The traditional definition of religion had understood spirituality in terms of a set of external beliefs, organisations and practices. This became increasingly inadequate as institutional religion declined and religious expression became individualised. This distinction is reflected in the statement that 'religion is structure, an institution. It limits you. Spirituality is something you are' (Wuthnow 2001, p. 306). This account distinguishes between religion as an institution and spirituality as an expression of self-identity. From this perspective religion is externally imposed on the individual, while spirituality is derived reflexively from within. This distinction can be seen in the contrast between Durkheim's definition of religion and Wuthnow's definition of spirituality as 'a state of being related to a divine, supernatural or transcendent order of reality, or, alternatively, as a sense of awareness of a suprareality that goes beyond life as ordinarily experienced' (Wuthnow 2001, p. 307). Some sociologists regard the two terms as mutually exclusive, but others see them as overlapping. The point is not that one view is correct and the other incorrect, but that the meaning given to each term varies according to the context.

THEORIES OF RELIGION

Sociological theories of religion provide explanations of the relationship between religion and society. They can be divided into four main groups: functionalist, materialist, phenomenological and feminist. Each of these theories contains assumptions about how society works and the relationship between the individual and society.

FUNCTIONALIST THEORIES OF RELIGION

Functionalist theory starts with the assumption that any social phenomenon that is pervasive and enduring must be making a positive contribution to the ongoing existence of the society in which it occurs. Consequently, functionalists examine religion in terms of its role in establishing social cohesion, focusing especially on the role of religion in providing a shared belief system of moral values, rituals and rules.

Durkheim

For Durkheim the study of religion was an essential part of the sociological project. He believed that most of a society's institutions had their foundation in religious beliefs and that by uncovering the social roots of religious phenomena he could help establish the credentials of sociology as a 'positive science' that would add to human knowledge (1965 [1912], p. 62). Durkheim's interest in the study of religion was part of his attempt to explain how society was possible. He saw religion as an expression of human sociality and, in traditional societies, the means by which the existence of society itself was made possible. Although religion was experienced as directed at an external object that existed outside, above and beyond human beings, its real purpose was to establish a collective moral consciousness. What appeared to be worship of God or some other supernatural being was actually the worship of society.

Durkheim's view of the role of religion assumed that human sociability does not exist *a priori* but requires explanation. He argued that in any society social solidarity is established through the establishment of a moral universe, which he called the *collective conscience*. This provides the basis for a society's values and beliefs that enable its existence and provide the taken-for-granted assumptions about the nature of life itself and fundamental concepts such as time. For Durkheim religious beliefs were a primary source of these values and beliefs.

Durkheim examined religion in the traditional societies of Australia and North America, arguing that understanding religious practice in these societies would shed light on its expression in more complex ones. In *The Elementary Forms of Religious Life* (1965 [1918]) Durkheim argued that religion created a primary distinction between the sacred and the profane. By sacred he meant 'things set apart and forbidden' that are associated with rituals and positive and negative sanctions. For example, in Christianity the Eucharist is believed to be the body of Christ. It is treated reverentially, used in the ritual of the Mass and kept in a special object called the Tabernacle. Only those in a state of ritual purity may swallow it. Profane objects are the opposite of this. They are ordinary, everyday objects that relate to this world and lack an association with religion. A loaf of bread is profane but the Eucharist is sacred. Sacred objects have other-worldly symbolic meaning, whereas profane objects belong to this world.

For Durkheim, the social role of sacred objects was to establish common understandings and beliefs within a community of individuals. They expressed the collective interests of the group. But to make ideas and beliefs a social reality they needed to be embedded in actual experiences. Durkheim argued that this was achieved through religious ritual. The feelings generated by religious rituals allowed participants to sublimate their individuality through a process of 'collective effervescence'. The shared feelings associated with religious expression helped establish a common commitment to a collective moral universe. It is through ritual that abstract ideas of morality become socially real. For Durkheim, the real purpose of religion is a social one. It establishes social connections and so 'is society in action' (1965 [1912], p. 465). Its real object is not the external object of God but the external object of society.

As well as establishing a collective moral conscience, Durkheim argued that religion also helped people to make sense of their experiences and to provide them with the strength to deal with suffering and the trials of existence. He observed: 'The believer who has communicated with his god is not merely a man who sees new truths of which the unbeliever is ignorant; he is a man who is *stronger*' (1965 [1912], p. 465 emphasis in the original). Religion helps people to make meaning of major life events, both happy and sad. Marriages, funerals and christenings acknowledge major transitions. They bring communities together to share in these important events and provide a common understanding of their significance.

Civil religion

Durkheim's theory of religion has been criticised because it assumes that religion takes only one major form of expression. This weakness is especially apparent in an age of globalisation in which religious uniformity has been replaced by **religious pluralism**. Multicultural societies such as those in Australia, Europe and Asia are characterised by many different religions that exist alongside one another. Religious differences are now the norm rather than the exception. The functionalist writer Robert Bellah counters this criticism by arguing that religious pluralism coexists with a form of public religion that transcends religious diversity and helps to integrate the nation.

Bellah draws on the ideas of Durkheim, who believed that in modern societies civil rituals such as memorial days are essentially similar to religious rituals in their public affirmation of shared cultural values and beliefs. Bellah uses the term **civil religion** to describe the rituals, symbols and language used by the state, that are often religious in nature and which promote a homogeneous or uniform national culture and identity. Civil religion includes the symbolism of images that express values that are integral to society, such as the Statue of Liberty in the United States. Such symbols are 'sacred' to a nation in much the same way as such religious symbols as the cross are sacred to Christians. In the United States these symbols are often closely associated with Christianity, so that on national occasions, such as the inauguration of a new government or the celebration of a national holiday, public figures will use them to convey their image of an ideal American society 'united under God'. The phrase 'In God we trust' is inscribed on the American currency and the pledge of allegiance describes America as 'one nation under God'. In these ways, God is linked with notions of liberty and democracy, and with the greatness of America. Civil religion functions as a form of nation building. It conveys an image of a nation whose diverse population is united under a single cultural umbrella (Bellah 1967; 1975).

Critics of the concept of civil religion point out that public forms of religious expression are not at all uniform but express a range of images of American society. They suggest that if civil religion does exist it has not succeeded in unifying American society. Despite this, other writers have applied the theory outside of American society.

Gary Freeland (1985) points out that the architecture and symbolism of the Australian War Memorial is religious in nature and represents the celebration of a civic culture based on the sacrifices made by the Anzacs. The Anzac 'cult' itself is seen by Freeland as a central element of Australia's image of itself as an independent and heroic nation. He points out that whereas American civil religion remains linked to Protestantism, this is not true of Australian civil religion. The Anzac celebrations have little or no distinctively Christian teaching or symbolism, and the clergy do not usually participate in the services. He concludes that Australian civil religion differs from its American counterpart since it is 'largely independent of the dogmas and attitudes of any particular segment of the Australian religious spectrum' (p. 113).

A similar analysis is made by Kapferer (1988), who agrees that Anzac Day is a celebration of core Australian cultural values, including mateship, egalitarian individualism and freedom from state interference. By celebrating Anzac Day, Australians are doing more than honouring their war heroes. They are honouring Australian society and Australian culture in a way that reinforces their solidarity and membership of the nation. (Kapferer's ideas are examined in greater detail in Chapter 8.) Kapferer's cultural analysis pushed the concept of civil religion beyond the framework of functionalism by injecting into it notions of power and social struggle.

MATERIALIST THEORIES OF RELIGION

Materialist theories of religion share with functionalists an emphasis on the influence of the social structure on religious expression. But while functionalists stress the integrative aspects of religion, materialists regard religion as a source of division and exploitation. The materialist perspective is rooted in the work of Karl Marx, who argues that all forms of cultural expression, including religion, are influenced by economic forces.

Marx

Marx's view of religion focused on its contribution to social conflict. For Marx religion was a major source of false consciousness. He regarded religion as an illusion in which people projected what belonged to them onto a mythical being. This not only denied them their own humanity and self-fulfilment, it also supported political systems in which the majority of the people were subject to oppression and exploitation.

Marx agreed with Durkheim on the importance of religion for society and in its contribution to social solidarity, but did not share Durkheim's view of its benign role. He believed it was a source of alienation in which people lost the connection with themselves and their fellow humans. In accepting false beliefs they lost their inherent humanity.

Marx's view that religion was damaging to the human spirit derived from his observation of its contribution to the legitimation of inequality. Marx argued that in any society power could not rely on coercion but required legitimation so that people came to accept the rightfulness of existing arrangements. He argued that religion was critical to achieving this because it linked relations of domination to a belief system that suggested the social arrangements for inequality were divinely ordained. This meant that no matter how unjust they might be in reality, to reject them was to challenge God and religion.

In medieval Christianity this association with acceptance of the status quo and religious belief was expressed in the idea of The Great Chain of Being. This established an image of a hierarchy of creation in which every created being had its place (see photo in box opposite). This justified the inegalitarian social order by suggesting that those at the top were deserving of their wealth and prestige, while those ranked below them were equally deserving of their disadvantage. To challenge this order was to threaten the natural harmony of the universe (Tillyard 1952). Should hierarchy or 'degree' be challenged, then chaos will ensue. This view of the relationship between God, nature and social inequality reveals itself in the following passage from the 16th-century play *Troilus and Cressida* by English playwright William Shakespeare:

> Oh, when degree is shak'd,
> Which is the ladder to all high designs
> The enterprise is sick. How could communities,
> Degrees in schools and brotherhoods in cities,
> Peaceful commerce from dividable shores,
> The primogeniture and due of birth,
> Prerogative of age, crowns, sceptres, laurels,
> But by degree stand in authentic place?
> Take but degree away, untune that string,
> And hark, what discord follows. (act 1, scene 3)

Hierarchy, religion and social order: *The Great Chain of Being.* **This drawing from the 1579 work,** *Rhetorica Christiana,* **by Dedacus Valades portrays the prevailing European worldview in which all creation is ranked between heaven and hell, according to its divinely ordained status.**

The political implications of this portrayal of the relationship between religion and society are inherently conservative. Any threat to the political and social order threatens the natural and divine order. It is a challenge to God and will disrupt peace and harmony and spread disease and sickness. To defend the political order is therefore to defend humanity and life as a whole.

Marx suggested that religion also contributed to oppression because it encouraged meekness and passivity and deflected people from resisting suffering in this world by suggesting that they would be compensated in the next. Beliefs such as 'the meek shall inherit the earth' and 'It is easier for a camel to go through the eye of a needle, than for a rich man to enter into the kingdom of God' encouraged an acceptance of inequality and injustice rather than revolutionary resistance. In one of his most famous passages Marx wrote:

Religious suffering is, at one and the same time, the expression of real suffering and a protest against real suffering. Religion is the sigh of the oppressed creature, the heart of a heartless world, and the soul of soulless conditions. It is the opium of the people. The abolition of religion as the illusory happiness of the people is the demand for their real happiness. (cited in Bottomore & Rubel 1976, pp. 41–2)

In this analysis Marx expresses his sympathy for those who turn to religion as a way of compensating for the pain of living in 'soulless conditions' but argues that this mistakes the problem for the solution. By accepting the prospect of an afterlife, people forsake the prospect of a good life in the real world.

PHENOMENOLOGICAL THEORIES OF RELIGION

Phenomenological theories of religion start with the assumption that social life is socially constructed through the establishment of shared subjective understandings of the world. These are not static but must be constantly negotiated, re-created and maintained. The task of the sociologist is to examine how this is achieved.

Phenomenological theories of religion are influenced by the work of the Austrian philosopher Alfred Schutz. Schutz pointed out that our daily existence has a taken-for-granted quality that we do not question—it just *is* (1967). We do not normally question how or why things came to be this way but just accept them as the they are. He suggests this is based on the existence of a shared world of meaning in which we bracket out phenomena that do not fit within this world or threaten to disrupt it. The aim of the sociologist is to remove the brackets and expose the underlying rules and assumptions that support our everyday social life.

In *The Social Construction of Reality* (1971/1966) Berger and Luckmann argue that social life is actively created in an ongoing process of negotiation and interpretation. We experience the world as external and real, but it is always limited by our individual subjectivity. It is a world of our imaginings. We exist physically in a world of concrete objects but mentally our world is populated by people and places that are not immediately accessible to us (p. 36). Our world is an intersubjective one with our actions oriented towards other human beings. Our negotiations of daily life are based on an array of assumptions that are shared with others and this forms the 'commonsense' understanding of the world as an ordered, 'natural' place. It is only when this order is disrupted, such as when those around us breach our expectations so that we cannot 'make sense' of them, that we discover our dependence on this shared universe of meaning.

Berger and Luckmann argue that it is not enough that people develop shared understandings of how the world works. Since there are potentially as many interpretations as there are people, the shared meanings also need to be legitimated. It is this process of legitimation that establishes the social world as external and objective. This takes place gradually and dialectically as our subjective understandings of the world are projected onto external reality and then act back on us in concrete ways so that they are experienced as real, objective and independent social forces. Berger and Luckmann describe this process as involving three stages in which intersubjective meanings are expressed in a way that *externalises* them, these meanings then become *objectified* by being integrated into society's institutions and then they are *internalised* into our consciousness through the process of socialisation (p. 149).

Religion as a sacred canopy

Berger and Luckmann argue that religion is one of the principal mechanisms through which common understandings are established and legitimated. Like a sacred canopy, religious understandings provide the ground rules for existence by providing answers to the unanswerable questions of existence. Human constructions are always precarious, but those that deal with ultimate questions of meaning and purpose are especially so. There is no objective answer to questions about the meaning of life, such as 'What purpose does our existence serve?', 'How should I live my life?' and 'What happens to someone when they die?' This is uncomfortable for us as individuals and socially problematic because social order can be established only if it is accepted as morally legitimate. Berger and Luckmann argue that religious belief and religious institutions are the means by which this is achieved, through the creation of shared understandings that become integral to a community's culture.

This idea of the role of religion in establishing a moral universe has similarities with functionalism, but in phenomenological accounts the precarious status of the sacred canopy is emphasised. Religious beliefs require constant reinforcement and can and are challenged. Neither are they uniform. Different groups have different beliefs and most communities have to acknowledge that their religious beliefs are contestable. This is especially so in conditions of modernity where multiculturalism makes the relative nature of religious beliefs an inescapable fact and science also provides an alternative, secular way of locating oneself in the world.

Criticisms of Berger and Luckmann

Berger and Luckmann's explanation of the role of religion in the establishment of social order has some similarities to functionalist explanation, especially in its lack of attention to issues of power and inequality. Furthermore, even though Berger and Luckmann accept the existence of religious diversity and the need for the sacred canopy to be constantly relegitimated, they pay no attention to how religion has been used as an instrument of oppression. They also have difficulty in accounting for the spread of secularisation, since although science does provide answers to questions of existence it is not a source of moral guidance. Despite this, Berger and Luckmann's ideas have been very influential in drawing attention to the social construction of religious beliefs and their centrality to the establishment of social order.

FEMINIST THEORIES OF RELIGION

There is a feminist joke that 'when God created Adam, she was only testing'. This is a light-hearted expression of a serious claim made by feminists that nearly all the world's major religions are patriarchal. The Scriptures of the three monotheistic religions of Christianity, Judaism and Islam all include passages that identify women as inferior to, and dependent on, men (Armstrong 1994). For example, the Book of Genesis describes man as the first human being, with woman being an afterthought created from Adam's rib, and only for the purpose of being his companion.

Feminists such as Luce Irigaray (1986; 1987) and Carol Christ (1980; 1992) argue that the male-centred symbolism of most religions is damaging to women, influencing their psychology and encouraging them to regard dependence and inferiority as the normal status of the female gender. Religion legitimates male domination in the home and society (Christ 1992, pp. 273–6).

The feminist critique of religion has taken three main forms:

1. a deconstruction of religious traditions from a feminist perspective—that is, the writing of her story rather than history
2. an analysis of the ways in which religious doctrines, practices and structures have oppressed women
3. the reconstruction of religion in a way that acknowledges women's experiences, autonomy and spirituality.

The deconstruction of religious traditions

Feminist writers argue that patriarchy in religion is not a universal phenomenon as there have been religions in which women are revered as deities. The art historian and sculptor, Merlin Stone, refers to the existence of matriarchal religions, arguing that in the Upper Palaeolithic and Neolithic periods in the Near and Middle East a mythical female figure was revered as the creator and supreme deity (1978). Women were perceived as givers of life who gave the gifts of civilisation to humanity, and Stone suggests that these societies were probably matrilineal, tracing descent through the female line. Figurines portraying women at various stages of their life cycle, including pregnancy, suggest that a mother-cult existed in the region at this time. This worship of female deities lasted in various forms until the time of the Roman Empire, only being suppressed in about 500 AD.

Feminists theologians have also sought to deconstruct the portrayal of women within the church (Daly 1968; 1973; 1978; Reuther 1983; Fiorenza 1983; 1984; Thiering 1973). They argue that Jesus lived in a society that oppressed women but he himself had a liberated attitude towards them that was reflected in the church before it became the official religion of the Roman Empire. At that stage male domination reasserted itself and Christian doctrine asserted that only men were created in God's image, while women, according to St Jerome, were 'the devil's gateway'. This hostility was associated with the ethos of celibacy and the repression of sexuality. Women were portrayed as the 'weaker sex' who used their bodies to tempt men into a denial of their godliness. The biblical story of Eve was used to illustrate women's culpability. Eve's deceit is the cause of Adam's downfall and the banishment of humanity from paradise. For women their only salvation lay in passive submission to the will of their husband and to the authority vested in men.

Religion as an instrument for the oppression of women

According to the feminist philosopher Simone de Beauvoir (1972), 'Religion is an instrument of deception' because it encourages women to accept their secondary status on earth by promising them equality in heaven. The symbolism of the church also supports women's exclusion from the public sphere of work and politics, leaving them to the invisible world of reproduction and domesticity, with the Virgin Mary providing a model for female submissiveness and a denial of their sexuality (p. 633).

Jan Mercer's (1975) analysis of the role of the Christian church in Australia draws a similar conclusion. She argues that it has encouraged sexist attitudes (p. 262) and the subjugation of women. By preaching a doctrine of submission it 'stifles and oppresses women in the name of humanity', discriminates against women within its hierarchy and 'has nothing to offer women's liberation' (p. 271).

Mary Daly argues that the central message of Christianity is sadomasochism that is especially directed against women. Religion has been used to legitimate violent and cruel practices against women the world over, including witch burning, genital mutilation, Indian suttee (the burning of the widow on the husband's funeral pyre) and Chinese foot binding. She argues that these are 'sado-rituals' that embody 'the murder of the Goddess, the "Self-affirming being of women"' (1978, p. 111).

The feminist reconstruction of religion

A number of feminists have argued for the creation of new religions that embrace women's lived experiences and that will act as a source of power for them (Hein 1992; Puttick 1997; Adler 1986; 1989; Starhawk 1982; 1989). The Muslim feminist Nawal El Saadawi (1980) uses Islam as her example, arguing that it began as an egalitarian religion but patriarchal arrangements soon became established. She encourages women to struggle for their own liberation following the lead of their ancestors, who insisted the Qur'an develop more-inclusive language. She suggests that women should support socialist revolutions and that these can coexist with non-oppressive religious practices.

The influence of feminism on the Christian church

Feminist theologians and academics within the Christian church have sought to change it from within through their writings and through organisations such as the Movement for the Ordination of Women, which challenges the traditional liturgy and the exclusion of women from office within the church hierarchy (Franklin 1986, p. vii). Some churches have responded positively to these challenges. Women have been ordained in the Uniting Church since its inception in 1977 and it has taken a generally proactive stance on women's issues, including establishing an affirmative action program for women. The Anglican Church initially resisted this development but by the 1990s most Anglican provinces accepted the ordination of women as priests and a number—including in Australia, New Zealand, the United States and Canada—accept the consecration of women as bishops. In the Catholic Church it remains the case that women may not practice as priests.

> **Reflective question:** In your view, which theory of religion best explains the role of Christianity in Australia today?

SCIENCE AND RELIGION

Berger and Luckmann explain that religious beliefs historically have been important in providing a sacred canopy that provides the ground rules for the establishment of shared meanings. They also point out that in contemporary conditions this canopy has become increasingly difficult to sustain because secularisation is changing the foundations of knowledge from religion to science. Berger (1967) observes that in the developed world the supernatural assumptions that are integral to religious beliefs are fundamentally incompatible with the rational–scientific culture of today.

Religious truth is based on knowledge rooted in the Scriptures and in oral traditions that are not open to external validation. It is not possible to prove objectively the existence of God, the infallibility of the Pope or that the Dalai Lama is the reincarnation of his predecessor. In most religious traditions sacred knowledge is entrusted to a religious elite and is not open to challenge—it must be accepted without question. Criticism takes place within the narrow confines of religious dogma that, if overstepped, can lead to exclusion from the religious community.

Scientific truth is based on principles of objectivity and rationality. Its claims to knowledge are based on a logical, rational process of hypothetico-deduction based on the establishment of 'facts'. These are established through observable, empirical and measurable techniques designed to test their accuracy. Far from discouraging criticism, science is based on it, expanding knowledge through critical thinking. It is an open system of knowledge that is objective and non-elitist.

The Enlightenment was the period in which religion was first seriously challenged by science as the new foundation of Western knowledge. This took place in Europe in the 18th and 19th centuries, as rationality began to replace religion as the criterion for assessing what should be accepted as truth. Supernatural beliefs were rejected because they could not meet this requirement. This marked both a cultural and a social revolution, because the challenge to religion also threatened the Church and its institutional domination. As scientific thinking became prominent, so the link between the Church and institutions such as education, politics and the family became uncoupled. This was the context in which sociology itself was born, with the classical theorists including Comte, Marx and Durkheim arguing that the new social sciences would replace religion as the source of wisdom and guidance.

The claim that science deals with objective truth in a way that religion cannot has been called into question by writers such as Michael Polyani (1958), who argue that both science and religion are belief systems that operate according to an internal set of rules. A **belief system** is an interrelated set of beliefs and ideas that helps people to make sense of, and to interpret, their world. Within the system, logic and rational argument prevail, but the rules themselves are not open to external scrutiny. Instead, they are legitimated with reference to the other components—in other words, a circular logic applies. Their claim to truth is accompanied by a refusal to accept the validity of alternative belief systems based on different premises. They are therefore closed systems of knowledge that are supported by a community of believers, in much the same way as religion is. It is the commitment of the believers to the system that supports it, rather than any external criteria of validity.

Polyani's arguments about the conceptual similarities between science and religion were strengthened by the work of Thomas Kuhn (1962), who documented the way in which scientific knowledge is socially constructed. Kuhn points out that scientists are not objective but become attached to their theories to the extent that they ignore or play down evidence that contradicts them. They operate within a framework that lays out the 'rules of the game' and is accepted as a 'given' rather than being open to scrutiny. Kuhn uses the term 'paradigm' to refer to these ground rules that scientists operate within. Their commitment to their paradigm means that, instead of objectively assessing the 'facts', scientists operate within a closed frame of reference and try to fit the data within this. Science therefore has its dogmas in much the same way as religion does.

Science's claim to being an open system of knowledge has also been challenged. Like religion, science has its community of experts possessing specialised knowledge and language that can be understood only by them. Membership of the community is highly selective, so that it is akin to an exclusive club that is not open to outsiders.

Writers such as Polyani and Kuhn agreed with Berger and Luckmann that all knowledge—even scientific knowledge—is socially constructed. It is legitimated according to the prevailing cultural conceptions and is therefore subject to the problem of relativity. From this perspective scientific 'certainty' is diminished and instead it takes its place alongside other belief systems that are used to interpret and make sense of the world. Both systems lay claim to the truth, but their means of arriving at it are different. There are also strands within Western culture that bring science and religion closer together—for example, some New Age religions use scientific knowledge to explain religious phenomena and to enhance religious experiences (Hess 1993).

RELIGION AND SOCIAL CHANGE

The relationship between religion and social change first came to sociological attention with the work of Max Weber, who investigated the relationship between a particular religious orientation and the emergence of capitalism as an economic system. In this work, Weber was concerned to demonstrate the power of religion as a source of social action, partly in response to the economic determinism of the versions of Marxism that prevailed at the time he was writing. But the question of the relationship between religion and social change has also been examined in relation to whether it has been used to support or challenge the status quo. Because religion often has been used by dominant groups to legitimate the arrangements that justify their position, it has been portrayed as a conservative social force. This is the argument of both feminists and Marxists, with feminists arguing that religion supports male dominance and Marxists arguing that it supports the power of the dominant class to oppress everyone else. But this is not the full story, and religion can and has been used to challenge existing arrangements, including being used to provide the ideological foundation of radical social movements.

RELIGION AS THE SOURCE OF SOCIAL CHANGE

Today it seems fairly obvious that religion can be a source of social change, but in the early 20th century

Marxist theorists drew on a rather crude interpretation of Marx's ideas to suggest that ideas were not an independent force but were determined by the economic infrastructure of society. It was against this background that Weber wrote his influential account of the emergence of capitalism in Europe in the 17th century.

The Protestant Ethic and the Spirit of Capitalism—Max Weber

Weber's interest in religion was partly initiated by his observation of family members whose behaviour was deeply influenced by their attachment to Calvinism. This influenced his argument that social action was not always calculated rationally or instrumentally but sometimes derived from traditional or emotional foundations. His early work on aspects of Roman history also resulted in an awareness of the complex relationship between the economy and other aspects of social life, leading him to argue that ideas could operate as an independent source of social change (Giddens 1979a).

Weber demonstrated this in a study of urbanisation in 19th-century Germany. He argued that the movement of peasants to the towns was neither rational nor instrumental. Remaining on the land offered them greater economic wealth and security than moving to the uncertain and alien environment of the city. Yet the peasants were willing to risk this because as serfs they were in servitude, whereas in the cities they were free. Weber pointed out that the *idea* of freedom was so strong that it overrode their concern for economic security.

In this study Weber demonstrated the need for sociologists to account for human subjectivity, because it is the meanings that people bring to their situation that motivates their behaviour. He argued that sociologists need to develop an attitude of *verstehen*, or sympathetic understanding, to the people they are studying so that they develop insight into the way they interpret the world and the relationship between this and the choices they make. It is only by understanding the motives behind social action that a fully sociological account can be provided.

Weber argued that these motives are derived from a wide range of influences, including emotional and cultural factors as well as economic ones. He saw religion as an especially powerful social force that had played a critical role throughout human history. He insisted that this role operated independently of economic determinants and suggested that this could be demonstrated through an examination of the role that a particular set of religious beliefs had on the emergence of capitalism in 17th-century Europe. This claim formed the main argument of his study, *The Protestant Ethic and the Spirit of Capitalism* (1930).

In this study, Weber sought to demonstrate that cultural factors, such as religious beliefs, could influence a society's economy and were an independent source of change in society. Weber argued that the spiritual beliefs of Calvinism resulted in the development of ethics that enhanced the emergence of capitalist activity. Calvinism encouraged a rational and calculated attitude to the world and emphasised asceticism, hard work, thrift and worldly success. According to Weber, these values and attitudes had an elective affinity with capitalism. They promoted practices that led to a sober and entrepreneurial attitude to the world, including the accumulation and investment of capital rather than its careless and wasteful consumption. For Weber it was the combination of religious beliefs and economic realities in 17th-century Europe that led to the emergence of capitalism and the modern, technologically based world. In presenting this argument Weber sought to counterbalance the economic determinism of Marxism with a more flexible view of the relationship between cultural and economic forces. As well, his study suggests the way in which beliefs can influence the social and economic behaviour of social groups.

RELIGION AS A CONSERVATIVE INFLUENCE ON SOCIETY

On the whole, the influence of religion on society is conservative. While this is especially true of fundamentalist movements (see p. 367), it is also true of mainstream religions. Michael Hogan's analysis of the role of religion in Australian history argues that its influence has generally been in a conservative direction (1987, p. 287). He argues that the three-way conflict between Protestant, Catholic and secular forces has strongly influenced Australia. This struggle had a critical effect on the political system after World War II with the split in the Australian Labor Party (ALP) and the formation of a parallel, rival labour party, the Democratic Labor Party (DLP) in 1954. Central to this development was Catholic antagonism to the influence of communism in the ALP. The alignment of the DLP with the National Civic Council, which was a Catholic body, enabled it to exert a powerful, conservative influence on federal politics for the next 20 years. The use of DLP preferences in support of the Liberal–National Party was one of the main factors behind the electoral success of the Liberal–Nationals between 1954 and 1972. Hogan argues that the activities of both Catholics and Protestants have worked to reinforce capitalism, differing primarily in their support for workers (Catholics) or business leaders (Protestants).

Dempsey's analysis of Protestantism in rural Australia also points to the conservative influence of religion. He argues that far from altering existing social inequalities, the main religious organisations tend to reinforce them. He claims:

> *Despite the Church's oft-quoted claim that all men and women are equal in the sight of God, Smalltown churches reinforce rather than challenge the inequitable relationships between the middle and working classes, between men and women and between young and old. It seems that within the churches, people give expression to external social ties and 'secular' values. (1991, pp. 75–6)*

In general, then, Christian religious groups in Australia have tended to be conservative. Organisations such as the Festival of Light, Right to Life and Family First have taken a strong conservative stand on issues such as abortion, immigration, drug legalisation, homosexuality and euthanasia. Prominent individuals with strong religious beliefs, such as former Catholic Tasmanian Senator Brian Harradine, have also used their influence for conservative goals. Christianity has also reinforced the patriarchal nature of Australian society through the symbolism of the church and organisations such as the Anglican Mothers' Union, which was firmly committed to a traditional view of the family (Sturmey 1991, p. 48). This conservative view of the role of women in Australian society still prevails among many Christian groups and is also present in Muslim and Jewish societies. This supports the argument that religion exerts a conservative influence on society.

The effects of religious beliefs on political and social attitudes

Survey research also shows that religion generally influences political and social attitudes in a conservative direction. **Religiosity** refers to the forms that religious expression takes, and in Australia this is positively correlated with support for the more conservative political parties such as the Liberal and National Parties, although historically Catholics have supported the ALP more than Protestant denominations (Bouma & Dixon 1986, pp. 30–50). In their analysis of what survey data reveal about the relationship between religiosity and politics, Evans and Kelley found that there is a strong association between strength of religiosity and political party preference, with 'the most devout Australians being considerably more likely to favour the Liberal–National

Case Study
Hillsong: a contemporary Christian church

Hillsong is a Sydney-based network of Pentecostal churches with a number of centres worldwide, including in London, Paris and Moscow. Pentecostalism is the fastest growing Christian religion in the West and is Australia's second-largest church after Catholicism. As well as prayer and community services, activities focus on the development of life skills, social connections and entertainment, with extensive use of contemporary media. Music, TV shows, environmental activism and social networking technologies are combined with ideals of community, leadership, individual responsibility, material wealth and social service. The church has a special appeal to young people, although it also targets families and primary and senior secondary schoolchildren. Its use of the media is notable, with many of the CDs released by its media arm, Hillsong Music Australia, achieving gold and platinum sales.

Hillsong is fundamentalist in its religious beliefs, which are based on a literal interpretation of the Bible. Creationism rather than evolutionary theory is accepted as an accurate account of the origins of existence. On social matters the church is conservative, with homosexuality being regarded as unnatural and abortion and stem cell research rejected. The church has been politically active, providing its support to Liberal Party candidates and attracting the involvement of high-profile Liberal politicians.

The church has also attracted controversy through its political activities and claims that its use of the media, its wealth and a 'prosperity theology' make it similar to American-style tele-evangelism. These claims are denied and the focus on material prosperity has been discarded.

Coalition over Labor, people of middling religiosity being evenly split and the most secular Australians tending to favour Labor rather than the Liberal–National Coalition' (2004, p. 9). Kelley and Evans suggest that while this can be partly explained by continuity from generation to generation and because of the overlap between religious views, moral judgements about social and economic issues and political party preferences, it is also likely to be because religious people believe that the values of the Coalition are more in tune with their views.

Religiosity also influences attitudes towards morality, with Christian belief being a strong factor in opposition to abortion and homosexuality (Evans et al. 2004, p. 162).

Reflective question: What explanation can you offer for the conservative role that religion has often played in society?

RELIGION AS A RADICAL INFLUENCE ON SOCIETY

While religion often exerts a conservative influence, it can also threaten the status quo and promote progressive social change.

- Marion Maddox (2001) challenges the claim that religion has generally been a conservative influence in Australia. She says that if one looks beyond the Protestant–Catholic divide there is considerable evidence that religion has often challenged right-wing orthodoxies and has been a source of social change. In her view, religious matters have consistently broken through the secularism of Australian politics, often challenging political orthodoxy. Her views are supported by the role of religious organisations, such as the National Council of Churches, challenging government policies such as mandatory detention and the erosion of workers' rights during the Howard Government years (1996–2007).
- Angela Davis (1995) argues that Marx underestimated the extent to which religion can play a transformative role in society. She points out that the religion of African slaves in the United States was a source of resistance to white domination and did not always encourage false consciousness. African sacred music not only helped to preserve African cultural memory but also encouraged resistance to revolutionary activity through the 'sacred articulation of freedom battles' among African-Americans (pp. 234–5).

Liberation theology

The combination of Marxism and Christianity in the form of liberation theology provides one of the best examples of religion exerting a radical influence on society. Friedrich Engels, unlike Marx, did realise that in some circumstances religion could be a force for change. He argued that groups that turned to religion as a way of coping with oppression could develop into political movements seeking change on earth rather than salvation in heaven. Otto Maduro (1982), a contemporary neo-Marxist, agrees with Engels that religion can be a revolutionary force and can help oppressed groups in their battle for liberation from the bourgeoisie. While he accepts that the Catholic Church in Latin America has tended to side with the rich and powerful, he argues that in recent years Catholic priests have demonstrated their autonomy from the bourgeoisie by criticising them and acting against their interests. Maduro believes that members of the clergy can develop revolutionary potential when oppressed members of the population have no outlet for their grievances. They pressure priests to take up their cause, and theological disagreements within a church provide interpretations of a religion that are critical of the rich and powerful. All these conditions have been met in Latin America and have led to the development of a church-based liberation theology.

SECULARISATION

New Age crystals, born-again Christians, Jewish Buddhists, twelve-step recovery groups, holistic health, goddess worship and concern for planetary healing—these are just a few examples of religious expression in the 21st century. While 19th-century sociologists regarded religion as an anachronism that would inevitably disappear as modernity progressed, today the claim is more likely to be that it is not religion that is dead but the debate about secularisation (Lyon 1996, p. 14). Yet secularisation theorists refuse to lie down and argue that there is a fundamental incompatibility between modernity and religion (Wilson 1982; Wallis 1984; Bruce 2002).

The term secularisation refers to a decline in religiosity at both an individual and institutional level. One of the assumptions of modernity was that industrialisation and the scientific approach to knowledge would lead to secularisation. This formed part of Max Weber's thesis in *The Protestant Ethic and the Spirit of Capitalism* (1930), in which he argued that industrialisation would bring about the 'disenchantment of the world' (Gerth

& Mills 1948, p. 155). Weber believed that capitalism was associated with a rational worldview that was opposed to a religious one. Rational action rejects the guidelines provided by emotion, tradition or religion, instead basing action on intellectual reasoning. Weber suggested that in modernity spirituality is reduced to a 'ghost' that prowls around the 'iron cage' of rationality. Modernity had pushed magic and religion to the periphery of social life.

Debate about whether this portrayal accurately describes the contemporary social condition has been ongoing since this time. Some analysts argue that science and rationality, individualism, the decline of traditional values and the increasingly specialised division of labour undermine religion in particular, and faith and non-rational beliefs in general (Bruce 2002; Wilson 1982; Wallis 1984). Others accept that institutionalised religion has declined but argue that it has been replaced by new forms of religion and spirituality so that we now live in an age of post-secularisation (Davie 1995; Heelas 1996).

Evidence in support of secularisation

When religious expression in contemporary Western democracies is compared with the past it seems obvious that religion has ceased to occupy the central place that it once did. Prior to the Enlightenment, mainstream religious groups were closely integrated with social, political and economic institutions and systems. Public policies, such as the treatment of Australian Aborigines or immigration policies, were often supported by religious beliefs. Nowadays, while religious activities are still evident, their public role is diminished and, with the important exception of the United States, it is rare to hear politicians or public servants supporting their actions with reference to religious beliefs.

Participation in institutionalised religion, measured in terms of factors such as church attendance, church membership and participation in ceremonies performed in church, has also declined. Table 11.1 shows that between 1901 and 2006 Christianity as a whole declined by 32 per cent in Australia. Although the pattern varies between the different denominations, the overall movement is downwards. The variation between the denominations is primarily explained by the link between religion and ethnicity. The increase in Catholicism in the period following World War II is related to the arrival of migrants from countries such as Greece and Italy. Catholics also have a higher birth rate than Protestants (ABS 2004c).

The religions that are currently experiencing growth, albeit from a very low base, are Buddhism and Islam, also due to migration. Between 1996 and 2006 Buddhism grew from 1.1 per cent of the population to 2.1 per cent and Islam grew from 1.1 per cent to 1.71 per cent, making Buddhism the fastest growing religion in Australia. But the most striking change shown in Table 11.1 is the growth in the number of people declaring that they have no religion. The number of Australians declaring no religion has grown from 0.3 per cent in 1947 to 18.7 per cent in 2006.

TABLE 11.1

Religious affiliation, 1901–2006 (%)

	1901	1947	1971	1996	2006
Church of England/Anglican	39.7	39.0	31.0	22.0	18.7
Catholic	22.7	20.9	27.0	27.0	25.8
Methodist	13.0	11.0	9.0	—	—
Presbyterian and Reformed	11.0	10.0	8.0	3.8	3.0
Uniting	—	—	—	7.5	5.7
Other Christian	9.7	7.1	11.2	10.6	10.6
Total Christian	96.1	88.0	86.2	70.9	63.9
Non-Christian	1.4	0.5	0.8	3.5	5.6
No religion	0.4	0.3	6.7	16.6	18.7
Not stated[b]	2.0[a]	11.1	6.2	9.0	11.9

[a] Includes 'object to state'.

[b] Comprises 'Religious belief, nfd', 'Not defined', 'New Age, so described' and 'Theism'. In 1996 and 2001, 'Religious affiliation, not defined' was called 'Inadequately described'.

Source: ABS (2005g; 2009d).

The argument for secularisation is further strengthened when age is taken into account. As can be seen from Table 11.2, it is among younger people that religious disaffiliation is growing most strongly. Between 1996 and 2006 the number of 15–34-year-olds stating they had no religion increased from 1 087 516 to 1 262 394, amounting to nearly one in four individuals in this age group. This compares with four out of five people aged 65 and over identifying as Christian in 2006. This pattern is reversed among non-Christians, where religious affiliation is growing most strongly among the younger age groups. For example, the number of 15–34-year-olds identifying as Muslims grew from 75 837 in 1996 to 127 587 in 2006. This is principally due to the predominance of younger people in Australia's migration program and the high birth rate of Australia's Muslim population.

Church attendance rates halved in the three decades between the early 1980s and the early 2000s (Evans et al. 2004, p. 36). Participation in formal Christian religious ceremonies is also in decline. Instead of Church weddings, Christian burials and baptisms, many people are turning to civil celebrants to mark major life-cycle transitions (ABS 2003h). This pattern is typical of other Western nations. In the mid-1990s a cross-national study of religion in ten Western nations including Australia and the United States concluded that 'religious establishments—whether legal or cultural—have substantially weakened if not collapsed' (Roof, Carroll & Roozen 1995, p. 244), while the number of people claiming to have no religion has grown.

PROBLEMS WITH THE SECULARISATION THESIS

While it is clear that institutional religion has declined in Western countries, it is equally clear that irrational beliefs and religious practices are far from dead.

- Although formal Christianity has declined in Australia, non-Christian religions have grown (see Tables 11.1 and 11.2).
- There has been a substantial growth in new religious movements in both Christian and non-Christian countries. This supports Rodney Stark and William Bainbridge's (1985) argument that, while some established churches may have lost part of their emphasis on the supernatural,

Religious affiliation by age, 1996 and 2006

TABLE 11.2

	1996 15–34 Number	%(b)	1996 65+ Number	%(b)	2006 15–34 Number	%(b)	2006 65+ Number	%(b)
Buddhism	76 437	1.4	10 212	0.5	139 314	2.6	25 777	1.0
Christianity	3 550 283	66.8	1 788 484	83.2	3 021 963	56.2	2 096 202	79.3
Hinduism	24 154	0.5	2 133	0.1	63 313	1.2	5 565	0.2
Islam	75 837	1.4	4 411	0.2	127 587	2.4	10 201	0.4
Judaism	18 642	0.4	15 860	0.7	21 326	0.4	16 727	0.6
Other religions	26 274	0.5	3 326	0.2	42 220	0.8	5 791	0.2
No religion	1 087 516	20.5	140 087	6.5	1 262 394	23.5	207 990	7.9
Other religious affiliation(a)	19 798	0.4	3 829	0.2	62 873	1.2	4 890	0.2
Religious affiliation not stated	436 531	8.2	182 553	8.5	639 673	11.9	271 227	10.3
Total	5 315 472	100.1	2 150 895	100.1	5 380 663	100.2	2 644 370	100.1

(a)Comprises 'Religious belief, nfd', 'Not defined', 'New Age, so described' and 'Theism'. In 1996 and 2001, 'Religious affiliation, not defined' was called 'Inadequately described'.
(b)Percentages do not total 100 per cent due to rounding.
Source: ABS (2007f).

Journeys out of faith

What are the reasons for people rejecting the religion of their parents? A study of individuals who rejected their parents' Christian faith when they grew up was conducted by Zina O'Leary (1999). She interviewed 80 individuals about their experience of 'apostasy', the rejection of Christian faith. In order to locate her findings in the context of cultural change she divided her sample into two cohorts: one group leaving before 1967 and the other leaving after 1982. However, she found few differences between the two groups.

O'Leary draws on Durkheim's notion of egoism and anomie (see Chapter 14) to identify three principal pathways out of belief:

The Anomic Apostate (30%)
For the members of this group the journey was characterised by a tone of weariness, anger or 'irritated disgust' with God or religion. The journey was one of reaction or rebellion against the religion of their birth. It was often tied to a pivotal event such as the one described in the following story:

> I was twenty-three when I lost my first child. Cot death they call it now. Well, it was a cruel blow, something that I never got over. It shattered my world, and it shattered my belief in God. The death of my daughter made me so angry with God and . . . um . . . the church provided me with nothing. I cannot believe in a cruel God . . .

The Egoistic Apostate (29%)
For this group withdrawal stemmed, not from feelings of anger about religion but from a quest for knowledge driven by emotional need. They felt they needed to make sense of the world and of themselves and found that religion was not providing the answers. The following story was typical:

> My life at times has not been easy . . . I have been depressed . . . It's hard to believe in anything when you do not believe in yourself and I wanted to turn to God but he didn't reach out. I often felt that God was not there for me . . . It made me wonder whether he existed at all.

In this type of disaffiliation the focus is on the self and feelings of emptiness are associated with religious doubt.

The Postmodern Apostate (41%)
For the postmodern apostate, the path away from Christianity was a rational one. Leaving was part of an ongoing quest for knowledge or meaning. It was an intellectual journey, lacking the emotional intensity of the other two types. It often took place over a relatively short time span. Catalysts for departure were quite mundane and reflected the plurality and relativism of belief in a postmodern world.

> . . . it struck us that God really makes about as much sense as Santa or the bloody Easter bunny. It still amazes me that you can believe in the most ridiculous things if you are told they are true often enough. The same people who think reincarnation is crazy think the concept of heaven and hell makes sense. Like I mean . . . how can you have a closed mind to aliens and UFOs, yet believe in the Devil!

For the postmodern apostates belief in God is just one more myth amongst the many possible beliefs available.

Yet O'Leary does not conclude that her findings spell the death knell for religious belief. Instead she finds evidence of a society in which reflection and evaluation of faith are accepted and encouraged. She argues that the openness of postmodern society means that just as religious belief can be rejected, so it can be rediscovered. In this sense the study supports Bruce's argument that secularisation does not necessarily mean a rejection of the search for meaning (2002).

---

secularisation never proceeds far because new religious groups with more emphasis on the supernatural constantly emerge (pp. 430–1).

- Although the increase in the number of people claiming to have no religion indicates a move away from organised religion, it does not necessarily mean a lack of interest in religious matters. A 2007 survey of religiosity in Australia found that 72 per cent of young people believe in God or a divine power and/or life after death, while almost half of those under 30 said they pray more or less regularly (Morris 2008). Practices such as meditation are also relatively widespread. A 2002 representative survey of the American adult population found that 10.2 per cent of participants had used meditation at some time—this equates to approximately 20 million adults. Of these, 7.6 per cent had practised meditation in the previous 12 months (Burke et al. 2006). Grace Davie (1995) describes this as 'believing without belong-

ing', suggesting that religious affiliation and attendance may be declining, but religious beliefs are not.
- Numerous conflicts and political movements around the world have a strong religious element. Examples include the conflicts in East Timor, Western China, Afghanistan, Israel, Chechnya, Sudan and Iraq. Far from declining in political significance, it seems that religion is increasingly important as an ethnic marker and continues be a focal point of political division both between and within nations.
- Christianity has declined in the West but continues to grow in Africa, Latin America and Asia. According to the *World Christian Encyclopaedia*, statistics from around the world estimate that between 2000 and 2050 the number of Christians globally will increase by 33.4 per cent, taking into account both natural increase and new conversions (Barrett, Kurian & Johnson 2001).

Secularisation or post-secularisation?

It seems, then, that there is evidence on both sides for the argument on secularisation. The enduring strength of religious belief and expression has led some sociologists to argue that we live in a post-secular age in which religion has experienced a resurgence (see below). But it is also clear that, in the West at least, the established religions are in decline and religion has been individualised, playing only a marginal role in the public sphere.

One of the reasons for the contrasting views on the future of religion in advanced economies is that the term 'secularisation' has been used inconsistently, so that proponents have sometimes been focusing on different phenomena. The empirical record is also a factor because of the poor quality of statistical data on religion. Those gathering the data can be biased, and there are often problems of statistical validity and reliability. Definitions of religiosity vary, and comparisons over time may involve different criteria for the same religious phenomenon.

Putting the case for secularisation, Bruce argues that he takes the term to mean:

1. a decline in the importance of religion for the operation of non-religious roles and institutions such as the state and the economy
2. a decline in the social standing of religious roles and institutions
3. a decline in the extent to which people engage in religious practices, display beliefs of a religious kind and conduct other aspects of their lives in a manner informed by such beliefs. (2002, p. 3)

For Bruce and other secularisation theorists, it is almost self-evident that in Western nations religion has become so individualised as to make it irrelevant to anything but individual identity (Berger 1970; Wilson 1982; Wallis 1984; Bruce 2002). The rise of new forms of religious expression, such as meditation and paganism, is not evidence of increasing religiosity but of the declining power of religion over social life. Although individuals may turn to spiritual beliefs as a source of meaning and guidance, the social impact of this is limited. They do not lead to social movements or impact on public life.

Bruce explains that to argue for secularisation is *not* to say:

- Everyone will eventually become an atheist or cease to have irrational beliefs. To not be religious is not the same as being an atheist. There may still be an interest in religious matters but religious belief is likely to be fragmented and, in so far as it continues to exist, its social impact will be minimal.
- Secularisation is a universal phenomenon that will, over time, apply to all nations. Secularisation needs to be understood as a process that has occurred in Western countries. It 'is not so much a universal phenomenon as one that relates to the European disintegration of what Martin calls the religious monopoly' (Lyon 1996, p. 19).

Despite maintaining that religion is in decline, Bruce argues there are two circumstances in which religion will remain socially significant:

- When religious belief is implicated in group identity, especially of an ethnic or national character. Religion provides powerful resources to groups seeking to defend themselves against perceived cultural or political invasion. This is what explains the significance of religion in countries such as Ireland, Croatia and Iraq.
- In situations of 'cultural transition'. Marginalised social groups tend to use religion and religious institutions as a means of negotiating major cultural changes in their environment. Thus, religion is often very important to migrants for whom it provides a mechanism for smoothing the transition between their old and their new homeland. It also explains the significance of religion in the process of modernisation.

It could be argued that these qualifications to Bruce's claim that 'God is dead' effectively defeat his argument. While few would argue that the first two of his three aspects of secularisation have taken place in Western democracies, the jury is still out on the last.

EXPLAINING THE RESURGENCE OF RELIGION

Whether or not secularisation has occurred, the religious landscape in most countries has undergone significant transformation. Established religions are in decline but there is an increase in New Age religions, which offer a form of individualised spiritual expression that serves as a moral compass for individuals. Christianity remains influential in global, political and social issues, and in Latin America, Africa and Asia its membership is growing. Fundamentalism is now also a powerful social and political force, both in its Islamic form and among Christians in the United States.

The resurgence of religion has led some sociologists, such as Heelas, to argue that we live in a post-secular age, characterised by religious privatisation and pluralism, in which belief becomes an individual project and all beliefs are tolerated, and by religious commodification involving the commercialisation of religion through consumption. This development is linked to processes of detraditionalisation and individualisation associated with globalisation. The next section examines these arguments.

THE SEARCH FOR MORAL GUIDANCE

A recurrent theme is that religion offers a solution to the moral uncertainties of contemporary existence.

Zygmunt Bauman argues that modernity tried to put ethical problems on one side. Ethical problems were reduced to, or replaced by, rules or laws. People were encouraged to behave in particular ways because the rules (for example, of bureaucracies) or laws of society said they should. The rules and laws were justified on rational grounds as providing the best means for achieving given ends. Thus, Bauman says, 'Modernity was, among other things, a gigantic exercise in abolishing individual responsibility other than that measured by the criteria of instrumental rationality and practical achievement' (1992, p. xxii). However, once postmodernity has torn away the belief that there can be a rational basis for perfecting society, it leaves individuals with no external rules to govern their lives. This leads to a renewed emphasis on the ethical and the moral, but now it is personal ethics and morality that are important. With a multitude of choices available, and with individuals responsible for their own morality, people turn to experts in morality—religious leaders—for some guidance. The appeal of religion therefore lies in the 'increased attractiveness of agencies claiming expertise in moral values' (1992, pp. 202–3).

A similar argument is put forward by Anthony Giddens, who argues that religion is a pre-modern source of ontological security that, along with tradition, is threatened by globalisation. In a world structured mainly by human-created risks there is 'little place for divine influences' (Giddens 1990, p. 111). However, religion becomes revitalised partly in a response to the uncertainties and doubt generated by contemporary conditions and partly because modern institutions cannot provide the moral guidance necessary for managing daily life. Giddens writes:

In 'high modernity' certainty is undermined; doubt is institutionalized; everything, including science itself, seems open to revision. Consequently many individuals experience the world as bereft of the all-encompassing traditions and certainties that sustained earlier generations. We are increasingly thrown back on ourselves, on our own subjective choices to deal with doubt, uncertainty, stress, fragmentation and the threat of meaninglessness characteristic of high modernity. In many ways the religiosity of the post-war generation . . . can be understood as a response to these perils. (1991a, p. 254)

Giddens describes this revitalisation of religion as 'the return of the repressed', because the earlier period of modernity has pushed it aside. But the inability of modern institutions to address issues of moral meaning opens the door to religion and spirituality once again. This takes place not at the level of society's institutions, which remain secular, but at the level of the individual. Because we are forced to reflexively manage our self-identity we have to deal with moral questions, but we do so in the absence of the formal religious supports of the past. Consequently we turn to individualised forms of religion to provide us with guidance on who we should become and how we should act.

As the institutional foundations of religion have weakened, a huge number of alternative religious groups catering for a wide range of individual needs have emerged. The decline of tradition therefore accounts for the plurality and eclecticism of contemporary religious expression (Giddens 1996).

This argument is similar to that put forward by Robertson (1992c), although Robertson focuses more on the role of religion in the establishment of self-identity rather than on its role as a source of moral guidance. Globalisation has seen the decline of the significance of collective sources of identity such as the family, community and class, freeing people to find their own sources of identity. Religion is one of the options available for selection. Today's commodified religion has become an expression of individual lifestyle and of signifying who we are and what we stand for. By answering questions of meaning, it compensates for the fragility of identity.

Reflective questions: Why is the secularisation thesis difficult to assess? In your view, how relevant is religion to contemporary Australia?

CONTEMPORARY RELIGIOUS EXPRESSION

The diverse forms of religious expression defy any simplistic argument about religion's contemporary role and direction. But although forms of religiosity are almost as varied as human beings themselves, there do appear to be two poles around which religious expression revolves: fundamentalist and pluralist. Fundamentalist forms of religious expression involve adherence to an external source of guidance and belief and, when allied with politics, can form powerful, oppositional, social movements. Pluralist forms represent more immanent understandings of religion and are characterised by their individualism.

FUNDAMENTALISM

Fundamentalist groups are found in all the major religions including Christianity, Hinduism, Islam, Judaism and Sikhism. Although often associated with the developing world they also have a strong presence in the developed world, including the United States and Japan. Fundamentalists have in common a belief that the founding religious doctrines and scriptures are literally true and valid for all times and places. In some cases this belief is associated with a political movement that seeks the radical reformation of society along lines believed to be ordained by God. Fundamentalists sometimes seek to reinstate a past golden age of religiosity, which critics argue probably never existed in the form portrayed. Their relationship with mainstream institutions varies from being closely integrated, as in Iran, to being rather marginalised, as occurs in Australia.

The influence of fundamentalist groups can be considerable. Because fundamentalists have an immutable vision of God's plans for this earth and of the place of human beings within it, there is a tendency for them to divide communities into believers and the 'rest'. The 'rest' includes not only atheists and agnostics but other, non-fundamentalist, religious groups. Where there is a focus on fulfilling God's word on this earth, fundamentalists are active on social issues.

Christian fundamentalism in the United States

Fundamentalist Christianity has considerable influence on American society, where it cuts across denominations. Roof's (1994) study of baby boomers found that one-third of the sample were either fundamentalists or revivalists and that, although they were not economically marginal or disprivileged compared with the rest of the sample, they were less likely to be college educated, were more likely to be female and were politically conservative.

In *Culture Wars: The Struggle to Define America* (1991) James Davison Hunter argues that the strength of fundamentalism in the United States contradicts its image as the most advanced nation in the world. The image that the country projects of a society based on democratic principles of consensus does not reflect the reality of a strong fundamentalism movement (1991). The struggle between the two different interpretations of America is portrayed by Hunter as a 'culture war' with religion, tradition and morality forming the battleground. These conflicts are not just ideological but have also involved acts of violence by both sides of the political divide.

Fundamentalism is especially strong in the southern and mid-western states (known as the Bible Belt), where its influence is overwhelmingly conservative. The New Christian Right has supported policies that favour free trade, anti-communism, increased military spending, less central state control, reduced welfare spending and fewer controls on business. It has tended to defend the interests of the rich and powerful at the expense of other groups in the population (Bruce 1990; Green, Rozell & Wilcox 2003). It played an important part in ensuring the presidential election of Ronald Reagan in 1984 and George W. Bush in 2000 and 2004. There is general agreement that the New Christian Right grew in the period when George W. Bush was president, with some moderates claiming that it took over the Republican Party (Apple 2001, p. 161). Bush is a Methodist and born-again Christian and made many statements testifying to his strong belief in the importance of 'a relationship with the Lord' (Harris 2005).

Critics have objected to what they see as a trend within the Republican Party to unite the church and the state. Pat Robinson, one of the most influential figures in the New Christian Right, has argued that the current separation of church and state is an 'intellectual scandal' and that 'for the sake of our children we must bring God back into the classrooms, homes and businesses of America' (cited in Apple 2001, p. 170). During Bush's presidency a Federal Office of Faith-Based and Community Initiatives was established, which some liberals interpreted as a step in this direction. According to Parent, it represents potentially the most comprehensive integration of government and religion in the United States since prohibition (2003, p. 20). By 2009 the program had come directly under the Executive Office of the President, who by then was Barrack Obama. However, there are guidelines to ensure that it does not breach constitutional requirements for the separation of church and state.

Claims of the influence of the New Christian Right are contradicted by analysts such as Bruce (2002) and Green, Rozell and Wilcox (2003), who believe that although the New Christian Right is highly visible in American politics, its influence on public policy has been limited. A case study of the influence of the New Christian Right in 12 states found 'no evidence of extensive success in achieving the movement's substantive goals' (Green, Rozell & Wilcox 2003, p. 4). Bruce also points out that the group has not succeeded in reducing the number of abortions, making divorce more difficult, restoring male hegemony or putting religious ceremonies back into state schools (2002, p. 214). Bruce argues that the success of the New Christian Right in politicising socio-moral issues is explained by the greater openness of the American political structure. This provides opportunities for well-organised minorities to have a public impact, but equally there is enormous resistance to theocracy within the United States, so that while they may win in the short term they often lose further down the track.

Islamic fundamentalism

There are as many forms of Islam as there are of Christianity, but it is fundamentalist Islam that has dominated the engagement between Muslim and Western countries. For Westerners the words 'Islam', 'fundamentalism' and 'terror' have become almost synonymous. Images of suicide bombers and hooded terrorists threatening kidnap victims have become part of the landscape of Western culture. As a political movement in the Muslim world, fundamentalist Islam has roots that go back to the 19th century. But by the 21st century, especially following September 11, it had become the dominant paradigm through which the Islamic world was understood in Western politics and culture. The events that followed September 11 added a second strand of conflict between the West and the Islamic world, with conflicts in Iran, Iraq and Afghanistan joining the longstanding conflict between Israel and most of the Arab world.

There have been many attempts to explain the current conflicts between the West and Islam; some of these stress economic and political factors, while others emphasise cultural factors.

Huntington and the clash of civilisations

Political analyst Samuel P. Huntington argues that in the 21st century the main conflict will take place between the West and Islam, and its basis will be cultural rather than economic or political. In 'The clash of civilizations' (1993), he describes civilisation as 'the highest cultural grouping of people and the broadest level of cultural identity people have short of that which distinguishes humans from other species' (p. 24). Membership of a civilisation is defined by a number of objective factors including language, history, culture, tradition and 'most important, religion' (p. 24).

According to Huntington, globalisation is bringing different cultures into closer contact and this is leading to an increase in 'civilisation consciousness'. Cultural differences will cause 'often violent' struggles between social groups and states from different religious and ethnic backgrounds. Religion will play an important part in the 'civilisation rallying' that is now uniting people from diverse nations and that may form the basis for new political alliances (p. 39). Huntington suggests that the main fault line will be between 'the West and the Rest' as non-Western countries, especially those influenced by Islamic fundamentalism, seek to oppose the economic and military might of Western countries. For Huntington, the clash between Islam and the West will play a critical part in the national and international conflicts of the future.

Huntington's thesis has been influential but it has also been criticised. His portrayal of Islam is schematic and lacks historical specificity. It reifies a particular kind of Islamic fundamentalism as typifying the whole of the Muslim world. It also fails to recognise the cultural and political diversity that exists in the Muslim world and the extent of religious and political division both within and between Muslim nations. In addition, Huntington's emphasis on cultural differences ignores the economic issues that are implicated in many of the political conflicts between Muslim and Western nations. Muslim countries have been the object of Western imperialism for centuries and in the 19th and 20th centuries many were subject to Western political and economic domination. Explaining conflicts in the Middle East and other regions of the Islamic world in terms of culture is simply inadequate (Encel 2002, p. 225).

Carroll and the meaning of September 11

Carroll's (2002; 2004) analysis of the meaning of September 11 offers an alternative cultural interpretation of the conflicts between Islamic fundamentalist movements and the West. He argues that contemporary Western culture is fundamentally flawed because it has turned away from the great narratives that have sustained it since the Ancient Greeks. For Carroll, any culture must be able to answer three fundamental existential questions:

- Where do we come from?
- How do we live our lives?
- Where do we go when we die?

The rational foundations of Western thought have provided enormous material benefits but they are unable to answer questions of meaning. Western cultures are morally bankrupt, and material excess masks the hollowness of Western life.

Carroll argues that Osama bin Laden's attack on the West was motivated not by a desire to spread Islam but rather to expose the amorality of Western culture. The attack on the World Trade Center in New York was as much a symbolic act as a physical one. It demonstrated the vulnerability of a culture that substitutes knowledge for belief. Bin Laden is the 'enemy within' because he revealed something that Western citizens already understand and experience. It is this that explains the intensity of the emotional impact of September 11 on Western consciousness. It was more than a reaction to the physical horror of Ground Zero. It was also a shocked response to the realisation of the power of religion versus the impotence of a culture that has no basis for belief. For Carroll the answer is not that people in the West should return to religion, or that they should follow their habitual path of decisive political action. Instead, we need to turn our gaze on ourselves and develop detachment through *being*. This, he suggests, will enable us to move beyond the greed and selfishness of contemporary culture so that we start to share our knowledge and wealth with the rest of the world.

Achcar and the class origins of Islamic fundamentalism

The political theorist and Marxist intellectual Gilbert Achcar presents a radical explanation of the clash between the West and Islam. He points out that because Islam is a religion that does not separate church and state, Islam and politics are always inseparable (1981). In Christianity church and state are usually separate because of the principle established by Jesus to 'Give to Caesar what is Caesar's, and give to God what is God's' (Caesar being the secular ruler of the Ancient world). So in the West the disruption caused by secularisation was limited, as the retreat of religion from the public sphere did not threaten its presence in the private sphere. However, in Islam the establishment of a secular society challenges religion itself.

As a socialist, Achcar shares Marx's view of religion as 'the opium of the people'. For him Islamic fundamentalism is a conservative social and political movement that is reacting against modernity. It seeks to 'roll back the wheels of history' (1981). But Achcar also recognises that it plays an important role as a source of comfort to people experiencing exploitation and is an expression of cultural identity. He is critical of the efforts of countries seeking to ban some forms of Muslim religious expression—most notably France, where the wearing of religious symbols, largely understood as directed against the *hijab* (the headscarf or veil), has been banned. Like the Turkish sociologist Nilufer Gole (1996), Achcar argues that this denial of freedom of religious expression is a form of political oppression. For Muslim peoples living in the West, their religious practices are an important expression of identity and cultural integrity. What can be understood as a form of female servitude in Muslim nations may be an expression of resistance to religious discrimination in the West. The denouncement of the veil follows 'a tradition of colonial contempt' in its suggestions that, as a culture, Islam is 'intrinsically unfit for modernity' (2006).

In his analysis of Islamic fundamentalism Achcar points out the absurdity of simplistic analyses that lack historical and social specificity. Achcar suggests that the roots of Islamic fundamentalism do not lie in the tenets of the religion of Islam, but in the political and social impact of modernity on the Muslim world. He locates the resurgence of a militant form of Islam in the context of racism and the long history of Western imperialism. It is a political rather than a religious movement and represents a form of resistance to the political, economic and social oppression by Western nations in the countries of the Middle East and Asia that commenced in the 18th and 19th centuries.

Achcar argues that the form of Islamic fundamentalism that came into prominence in the 1970s was assisted by Western policies. Although modern forms of Islamic fundamentalism came into existence in the 19th century, they were not a global social force until the 1970s partly because there were alternative forms of secular political expression, including left-wing and nationalist movements. What fed the rise of Islamic fundamentalism was the elimination of these alternatives by Western powers and their support of Islamic fundamentalism movements as a strategy for curtailing the growth of communism and secular nationalism in the Islamic world. At that time these were seen as the threat to Western global dominance, not religious fundamentalism. The most notable example of this was the support given to the *mujaheddin* by the United States and other Western nations in Afghanistan during the Soviet occupation in the 1980s. This simultaneously assisted the propagation of Islamic fundamentalism and crushed the organic growth of a political alternative in the form of left-wing and progressive nationalist movements. It 'freed up the space for political Islam as the only ideological and organisational expression of popular resentment' (2006).

For Achcar, Islamic fundamentalism has its roots not in religion but in class politics. It is above all a movement of the petite bourgeoisie, for whom communism and corporate capitalism are the enemy and for whom both imperialism and communism are to be resisted, because both threaten their existence. Islamic fundamentalism developed in countries such as Iran and Pakistan where capitalist competition led to a decline in middle-class living standards and communism failed to provide a credible political alternative.

Explanations of the appeal of fundamentalism

The last section examined the causes of Islamic fundamentalism in the context of its resistance to the West. This section undertakes a broader analysis of the relationship between Islamic fundamentalism and contemporary society, locating its origins in globalisation and in the conditions of postmodernity.

The impact of globalisation

One of the explanations for the rise in fundamentalism is that it is a consequence of the political and cultural impact of globalisation. Robertson (1991) argues that the globalisation of culture and threats to national autonomy have created a need for nations 'to produce their own unique accounts of their places in world history' (p. 290). Religion contributes to this because of its role in cultural revitalisation. Robertson suggests that this is one of the reasons behind the 'religion–state tensions and the politicization of religion', which have become a familiar feature of global relations (1992c, p. 43). Religion serves as a vehicle for nations to express their distinctive national identity, defining them in relation to the rest of the world. This has been especially important in countries outside Europe, such as Iran and Japan. The process occurs within political parties and social movements as well as nationally.

Fundamentalism and the conditions of postmodernity

Zygmunt Bauman (1997) locates the rise of fundamentalism in the context of the uncertainty associated with postmodernity. It is appealing because of its offer of certainty in an uncertain world. Bauman argues that the benefits of modernity involved giving up individual freedom for the securities offered by civilisation. Modernity offered order and security but its corollary was the loss of freedom to do as one wished. But the conditions of postmodernity transform the relationship again. While modernity meant order and regulation, in postmodernity deregulation reigns, opening up new possibilities for freedom and the pursuit of pleasure. The individualism and relativism that characterise postmodernity create the space for individual freedom and choice. The right of individuals to pursue their desires is now the principle that governs social life.

But Bauman argues everything carries a cost and, in this case, the price we pay for freedom is the loss of certainty. For Bauman, *'postmodern men and women exchanged a portion of their possibilities for security for a portion of happiness'* (1997, p. 3; italics in original). Yet the conditions that create this uncomfortable choice also permit its reverse. While the 'default' position of postmodernity is freedom, it is still possible to choose security if one is willing to trade it for freedom. This is where the appeal of fundamentalist religions resides. While New Age religions look to the inner redoubt of individual consciousness as the solution to uncertainty, fundamentalist religions turn outwards to an external source of authority that is an immutable source of truth. By offering access to a single source of incontestable truth, fundamentalist religions remove the uncertainty and doubt that accompany freedom and choice. There is only one way, one truth and they know which path will lead to it. All other paths are in error.

This is a powerful offer. If the freedom to choose what

to believe comes at the expense of not knowing whether the choice is 'right' and, even more unsettling, the rejection of the possibility of 'rightness', then exchanging it for the security of 'truth' is a fair deal. Bauman sees this offer as particularly appealing to those who dwell at the hard edge of global change and who form the constituency of fundamentalist movements. The deprived and impoverished are the 'flawed consumers' of contemporary society. For them the offer of freedom is hollow because they lack the resources to purchase its rewards. It is this link with the social conditions of our times that makes fundamentalism a 'thoroughly contemporary, postmodern phenomenon' (p. 182). The poor of today experience only the downside of freedom. The pleasures of consumption are minimal; the risks, uncertainties and fears are maximal. Their personal exposure to the frailty of human individuality creates a sense of insufficiency. This then opens the door to fundamentalism's offer of external direction and guidance. In this sense fundamentalism is the extreme expression of the search for expert knowledge that characterises the postmodern condition. As such, it belongs to 'the wider family of totalitarian or proto-totalitarian solutions offered to all those who find the burden of individual freedom excessive and unbearable . . . (including) . . . ethnic, race-oriented, or tribal fundamentalisms' (p. 184).

For Bauman fundamentalism is a misguided solution to the discontents of the postmodern condition. Nonetheless, he argues that the problems of solitude and abandonment that characterise contemporary life are real. The critical question, then, is how to find solutions that are free from the totalitarianism of fundamentalist movements.

NEW FORMS OF RELIGIOSITY

Since the 1950s a wide variety of forms of religious expression have appeared, some representing the importation of ancient, often Eastern, religious traditions, others being entirely new or syncrestic forms of spirituality. These represent an important cultural shift. They are not integrated into mainstream institutions and they manifest a wide variety of attitudes towards mainstream society, ranging from acceptance of it to a concern with its radical transformation.

New Age movements

New Age movements are religious or spiritual movements that are new to the country of their practice and that are characterised by an emphasis on individual and planetary spiritual growth. Catherine Albarese provides the following description of the New Age movement:

To evoke the New Age is, in some sense, to reify a mood, a moment, or—in what is perhaps the best description—a language; for the New Age is above all a religious discourse community that elicits certain forms of action. The New Age has no central church or organization. It possesses no authoritative denominational officialdom, no creedal platform, no sectarian tests for inclusion or exclusion . . . its identity is elusive. (1992, p. 73)

New Age movements are characterised by:

- a belief in spiritual immanence—that is, the belief that God (or some spiritual equivalent) exists within all human beings and in all creation
- a belief in self-spirituality—the objective of human existence is to become consciously aware of the spirituality that lies within each individual and to achieve spiritual transformation in the here and now
- an emphasis on individual experiential learning as the only way of achieving spiritual development
- the freedom of individuals to choose their own spiritual path
- a concern with healing, spiritual and physical, both of the self and the environment
- a belief that achieving self-realisation requires overcoming the veiling or contaminating effects of the ego or lower self
- an emphasis on spiritual practices, such as meditation, healing, dance or magical rituals
- a tolerance of the diversity of forms of religious expression since all are expressions of the one ultimate truth—this is often expressed in an eclectic approach to diverse religious and spiritual traditions
- the use of science to both express and validate spiritual beliefs
- an optimistic outlook both for the individual adherent (often expressed in terms of material success) and for the environment (Heelas 1996; Lewis 1992, pp. 6–9; Albarese 1992).

What motivates people to become New Agers? Adam Possamai's (2000) qualitative study of 35 New Agers living in Melbourne identified two main motives: a life crisis prompting them into an active search for meaning; or a more gradual process through exposure to New Age ideas through consumption of products and practices such as crystals or yoga. Most had explored a range of religious practices before eventually specialising in one specific activity (such as astrology, Buddhism, channelling or urban shamanism). None had followed the spiritual inheritance of their upbringing, which was more often a source of rebellion, even when it was an alternative form of religion. They were instead 'individualists of religion' with a rather cynical attitude towards establishment religion. They rejected the idea of an imposed religion, preferring an 'à la carte' menu to a 'set' one.

Questioning New Age patterns of commitment

The idea that adherents to New Age forms of religious involvement are characterised by free-floating forms of religious commitment is challenged by Tim Phillips and Haydn Aarons (2005). Buddhism is one of the fastest growing forms of spirituality in Western nations. There are numerous Buddhist centres in Australia whose adherents are predominantly drawn from parents born in Australia or another English-speaking country. One of these, a large Western Buddhist centre in a major regional city, was the subject of a survey by Phillips and Aarons. Their investigation into patterns of commitment revealed that 60 per cent of respondents (N = 333) demonstrated long-term commitment to Buddhism. They argue that this challenges the portrayal of Western Buddhism as a New Age style of reflexive spiritual involvement entailing a range of different beliefs. For most adherents Buddhism was the sole source of spiritual interest. Phillips and Aarons argue that their findings suggest that the New Age assumption that spiritual searching is an ongoing process may be wrong. Instead, people may eventually find what they are looking for or, alternatively, they may give up through disenchantment, boredom or ambivalence.

Neo-paganism

The term **neo-paganism** has been used to describe a range of spiritual beliefs and practices that have come into prominence in the past two decades. Hume defines it as 'any earth-centred or nature-based religion with roots in a pre-Christian past' (1997, p. 42). Alternative terms include witchcraft, Wicca, the Old Religion, Goddess Spirituality, the Craft, Nature Religion, Earth Religion, Ecofeminist Spirituality and Euro-American Shamanism. Although all these movements locate their roots in ancient, non-Christian practices and beliefs, their current appearance can be dated to the late 1970s. Neo-paganism has many of the features of New Age movements and is also characterised by the identifica-

New Age witchcraft and the re-enchantment of everyday life

The renaissance of witchcraft as a form of religious expression has seen its entrance into mainstream culture through movies, magazines, websites and novels. Spellbooks, with titles such as *How to Turn Your Ex-Boyfriend into a Toad and Other Spells for Love, Wealth, Beauty and Revenge* (Starwoman & Gray 1996), have become a popular form of consumption for teenagers, especially young women and girls. Although witchcraft practitioners and some academic studies have rejected the argument that witchcraft is part of the New Age, Ezzy's study of a sample of spellbooks found they had many of its characteristics (2003). These include a self-ethic, a this-worldly orientation, holism, evolutionary development and ephemeral participation. Spellbooks have become a commodified 'cultural and practical resource' (Heelas 1993, in Ezzy 2003) typical of the spiritual technologies of the New Age. Yet while the focus on the self leads away from the experience of the sacred as mysterious, other aspects reaffirm the magical and mystical. The use of spellbooks may also lead towards the re-enchantment of everyday life and the sacralisation of the sensuous through such things as body confidence spells. Teenage witchcraft is therefore a site in which central contemporary identity issues are contested.

tion of the divinity as female and the use of magic as a means of controlling everyday life (Lewis 1996, pp. 3–4; Kelly 1992, p. 139).

In Australia, according to census data, the number of people identifying as either pagan or Wiccan increased dramatically between 1991 and 2001 (increasing from 2667 to 19 632), but since then growth has slowed (to 23 730 in 2006), with women heavily overrepresented. Berger and Ezzy (2007) argue that for teenagers, witchcraft provides a feeling of self-empowerment and is a source of meaning and belonging.

The appeal of neo-paganism is explained by Carpenter as residing in the similarity between its views and features of our everyday world (1996). Carpenter observes that 'many of the themes within postmodern spirituality appeared similar to those within contemporary Paganism' (p. 37). Drawing on the work of Griffin (1998a; 1998b), Carpenter points out that modernism is characterised by individualism and dualism. The Creator is conceived as separate from creation and humans are seen as separate from Nature. Mind and body are split and non-human life is portrayed as without spirituality. Carpenter argues that it is these features that lie behind modernity's willingness to exploit Nature. In contrast, 'constructive' or 'revisionary' postmodernism is characterised by 'a creative synthesis of modern and premodern truths and values' (p. 39). It stresses the interconnectedness of all life and a non-dualistic conception of the relationship between humans, Nature and Divinity; it is post-patriarchal; materialism is rejected; time is immanent (i.e. past and future are recognised as influencing the present); creativity is central; the importance of community is stressed; and religion is egalitarian, non-institutional and pluralistic. Carpenter argues that these same features are characteristic of neo-paganism and that there is therefore a 'fit' between contemporary social conditions and neo-paganism. Neo-paganism gives expression to the cultural experiences of its adherents.

Locating new forms of religiosity in modernity

Carpenter's arguments about the positive association between neo-paganism and 'postmodern spirituality' represent a new wave of sociological thinking that contrasts with earlier arguments that these movements are antagonistic to modernity. The two most prominent exponents of this view are Peter Berger (1967) and Bryan Wilson (1982), who argue that the pluralisation and privatisation that typify contemporary religious expression reflect their marginal relevance to mainstream society. In the work of these writers religion is portrayed as a protest against the alienating conditions of contemporary life. As such it offers little of real and lasting significance to society. While it may offer individuals comfort and compensation, it has only minimal impact on the organisation and structure of social life.

However, writers such as Heelas (1996) and Lewis (1992) point out that while new forms of religiosity superficially appear antagonistic to modernity, they actually give expression to mainstream values and assumptions, albeit in a more radicalised form. Heelas and Lewis agree with Carpenter that people turn to new forms of religiosity because they exemplify beliefs and values that form part of their everyday experience. While it is certainly true that new forms of religiosity have, in the words of Beckford, 'come adrift from their former points of social anchorage' (cited in Dawson 1998, p. 10), this renders them neither trivial nor marginal to mainstream social life. The same point is made by Lorne Dawson in her analysis of the relationship between new forms of religiosity and modernity. Dawson argues that instead of seeing new forms of religiosity as opposed to modernity we should see them as part of an ongoing dialectic between religion and society in which each accommodates the other (p. 10). Following Beckford she suggests that new forms of religiosity should not be understood as institutions but as cultural resources of enormous symbolic power (p. 14). In a society in which traditional sources of allegiance and security have become unglued, religion provides an alternative source of individual and collective identity whose potential to influence society has actually increased, because religious sentiments are now the result of personal conviction rather than mere social conformity.

THE FUTURE OF RELIGION

Predicting the future role of religion in social formations is not an easy task. This chapter has noted that, while surveys suggest that religious belief and practice are declining in Western nations, there are also signs of its resurgence. In many ways religion has become more relevant both as a source of moral guidance and as a resource for individual and collective identity. The assumption that the rational foundations of modernity exclude religion has come unstuck in an era in which religion continues to be a mobilising social force.

The paradox of late modernity is that as the conditions that led to the departure of established religion in the West continue to unfold, so they are leading to a demand for its return. The moral gulf and ontological uncertainty of contemporary life have led a number of sociologists to call for a return of religion because of religion's ability to provide social cohesion in a world that is increasingly relativised, uncertain and ever-changing.

Even a rationalist such as Gellner calls for the creation of a 'constitutional religion' (1992). He argues that neither fundamentalism nor the romantic relativism of postmodernism can sustain us in the future. He suggests the creation of a socially contained constitutional religion that will offer a nation ritualised legitimation of social arrangements without interfering in the application of rational principles to the organisation of daily life (1992). Giddens argues that although religion is largely incompatible with the detraditionalised contemporary world, there is a need for a 'remoralization of social life' to which privatised forms of religion could contribute (1991a). In these accounts religion may continue to have a role as either a source of symbolic power for use by the state in the establishment of social order or as a source of individualised moral guidance.

This optimistic view of the future role of religion contrasts with the view of theorists such as Huntington and Hunter. For them religion is far more likely to be a source of social division than social harmony. Its role as an expression of culture, its symbolic power and its ability to mobilise communities make it a powerful carrier of social movements which as well as rekindling old antagonisms can also generate new divisions.

Whether either of these possibilities is likely in Western nations is, however, questionable. The organic link between religious and other social institutions such as the political system and the family, which was so notable a feature of pre-industrial Western society, has been broken. In most Western countries, including Australia, religion has become unhinged from this social nexus. The religion of the future in many Western countries, including Australia, is likely to be pluralistic and commodified. Whether this will apply to the United States remains an open question. Equally important is the question of whether this Western pattern will be exported globally or whether some religions, such as Islam, will retain their hold on the culture and institutions of some non-Western nations and communities.

Tutorial exercise

Commpare the case study of Hillsong Pentecostal Church (p. 360) with the rise of neo-Paganism (p. 372). Using the material examined in this chapter, what do you think these examples suggest about the extent to which secularisation is growing?

For activity suggestions, learning aids, revision of key concepts and access to self-study material, visit: **www.pearson.com.au/highered/vankrieken4e**

Further reading

Aldridge, A. 2000, *Religion in the Contemporary World*, Polity Press, Cambridge.
Berger, H. & Ezzy, D. 2007, *Teenage Witches: Magical Youth and the Search for the Self*, Rutgers University Press, Brunswick, NJ.
Bouma, G. 2006, *Australian Soul: Religion and Spirituality in the Twenty-first Century*, Cambridge University Press, Melbourne.
Davie, G. 2007, *The Sociology of Religion*, Sage, London.
Heelas, P. & Woodhead L. 2005, *The Spiritual Revolution: Why Religion is Giving Way to Spirituality*, Blackwell, Carlton, Vic.
Hunt, S. 2005, *Religion in Everyday Life*, Routledge, Oxford.
Kurtz, L. R. 2007, *Gods in a Global Village: The World's Religions in Sociological Perspective*, 2nd edn, Pine Forge Press, CA.

Websites

The Association of Religion Data Archives:
www.thearda.com
This clearing house for quantitative data on religion in the United States provides free access to survey data on religious groups and organisations, as well as summaries of the main findings. It also provides links to other relevant websites.

British Sociological Association Sociology of Religion Study Group:
www.socrel.org.uk
As well as providing information on conferences, this website provides links to other helpful sites and relevant journals, information on recent publications and an email list that is open to non-members.

Center for Spirituality, Theology and Health, Duke University:
www.spiritualityandhealth.duke.edu
This website explores the intersection of health, spirituality and faith. As well as providing details on the Society for Spirituality, Theology and Health, the website also includes publications and research in the area.

Christian Research Association:
www.cra.org.au
This non-denominational Christian-based research organisation undertakes secondary data analysis of surveys such as the Census, as well as conducting its own studies on religious expression in Australia. Some of these studies are available as free downloads from the website; others are available for a fee. Although the association is primarily concerned with Christianity in Australia, it also provides information about non-Christian organisations and other forms of religious expression. For example, a CD-ROM containing information on religious groups in Australia is available for purchase.

Opinion.com:
www.onlineopinion.com.au
Online Opinion is an influential Australian e-journal for political and social debate and regularly has topics on religious matters. Membership and access to articles are free.

Religious Research Association:
http://rra.hartsem.edu
This organisation is concerned with the academic study of religion and is based in the United States. As well as providing details of the organisation, the website has information about conferences, links to other relevant sites and a members' discussion board. It also provides some lectures on religion that are freely available to be downloaded in PDF format.

12
Power and the State

The concept of power is central to all sociological accounts of human society, social interaction and behaviour. The questions that run through discussions of power and the operation of power relationships are:
— What is power? How should it be defined and distinguished from other kinds of relationships, such as affection, love or care? Should we even think of 'it' as a thing, or as a particular kind of relationship? Can it be 'concentrated' or does it only exist in networks?
— How does power work? What mechanisms and techniques characterise the workings of power relations, and how are these changing over time? Is it concentrated in particular social groups and institutions, or spread throughout society in a wide variety of social relationships?

By the end of the chapter, you should have a better understanding of the following topics and issues:
— central foundational definitions of power
— how we should understand the way in which power is exercised through the state, with specific reference to Australia
— the different perspectives on who exercises power, particularly pluralism, elite theory, conflict theory and neo-Marxism
— the more recent works on rethinking power in contemporary society, including that of Lukes on the 'three faces' of power: Elias, Foucault and Latour
— the question of power operating 'beyond the state', the postmodernisation of politics and the impact of new social movements.

INTRODUCTION	378
DEFINING POWER	378
Max Weber	378
Charismatic authority	378
Traditional authority	379
Rational–legal authority	379
Types of social action	380
Elite theory	380
The power elite—C. Wright Mills	380
Elite theory in Australia	381
Power is like money—Talcott Parsons	382
Pluralism	383
Who Governs?—Robert Dahl	385
BUREAUCRACY, DISCIPLINE AND THE STATE	386
The 'technical superiority' of bureaucracy, or TINA	386
Bureaucracy, discipline and power	386
Stateless societies	387
The emergence of the modern state and bureaucracy	387
The sources of social power—Michael Mann	388
The Australian state	388
The Constitution and the High Court	388
The federal structure	389
A Weberian approach to the Australian state—Sol Encel	389
RETHINKING POWER	390
The three faces of power—Steven Lukes	390
Neo-pluralism	391
The power of hegemony—Antonio Gramsci	391
Class and the Australian state—Raewyn Connell	392
POWER AND THE SELF	394
The Civilising Process—Norbert Elias	394
Court society—representational power	395
Power and meetings	396
A micro-ritual theory of power—Randall Collins	396
Knowledge, discipline and government—Michel Foucault	397
Knowledge, discourses and power	397
The history of sexuality	397
Modern individuality and power	398
Disciplinary power	399
Governmentality	400
Power as effect—Bruno Latour	402
BEYOND THE STATE?	402
New social movements and postmodernisation	402
Critique—how 'new' is the new politics?	403
Australian social movements and globalisation—Verity Burgmann	404
Tutorial exercise	406
Further reading	406
Websites	406

INTRODUCTION

In 1990, Dario Melossi closed his book, *The State of Social Control*, with this image:

> There is, in the Museum of Anthropology in Mexico City, a statuette of a man carrying on his back an idol, in human form. Because the man is so bent under the weight of the idol, his face is hardly discernible. One can see little more than the beaming face of the idol and the hunched body of the man who is carrying it. The power of the idol lies entirely with the man, but he does not know it. He thinks it is an honor to carry such an important and powerful idol. (p. 185)

What is important about this illustration is that while the man carrying the idol can be seen to constitute the power of the idol, he is also presented as being unaware of that power. He is thus ultimately at the mercy of the idol, its *object*, because of that lack of knowledge.

1. Is this a useful way to represent the operation of power in human social groups, or does it capture only some aspects of power relations?

The study of power and politics brings sociology together with other disciplines such as political philosophy and political science. In political science, there is a tendency to concentrate on the state and the various institutions of government, such as parliament and the judiciary, and the processes by which governments get elected. Sociologists are more inclined to supplement this kind of analysis with broader examinations of the workings of power throughout society, 'beyond the state'.

As you work through the chapter, it is worth keeping in mind a distinction between two different approaches to power, one that emphasises 'power to' or power as a capacity (e.g. Parsons, Mann, Foucault's 'governmentality') and the other that emphasises 'power over' or power as constraint (e.g. Bachrach & Baratz, Lukes, neo-Marxism, conflict theory, pluralism, Foucault's 'sovereign' power). There is also a theoretical issue whether power is best understood as a capacity or resource that institutions, groups or individuals 'have' more or less of, or as a 'relation' that operates differently in different historical contexts and social situations (e.g. Elias, Latour).

DEFINING POWER

MAX WEBER

The sociological analysis of power has been strongly influenced by Max Weber's early understanding of power as a capacity of an individual or a group to 'realize their own will in a communal action even against the resistance of others who are participating in the action' (1948, p. 180). One important corollary of this definition was that, for Weber, power should be seen as a fixed amount of some resource or entity, so that if some individuals 'have' more power, then others must have less. Often this is referred to as the '**zero-sum' concept of power**. The exercise of power is also closely linked to the conflicting 'interests' of individuals and groups engaged in collection action, which constitute the 'motor' of power.

Weber's analysis of power operated within the framework of the concept of *herrschaft*, which has been translated as either 'authority' or 'domination' that is granted a degree of legitimacy, although one could also use concepts such as 'rule' or 'governance'. He distinguished three different types of authority: (1) charismatic, (2) traditional and (3) rational–legal authority. In practice, these three forms of authority overlap in particular individuals or organisations, which means that they are best understood as dimensions or aspects of power rather than entirely distinct types.

Charismatic authority

When particular leading individuals have unique qualities that persuade their followers to feel devoted to them as unique individuals, then one can speak of the exercise of **charismatic authority**. These individuals' charisma is based on their capacity to appeal to the emotions of large groups of people, and to convey a sense of possessing qualities, talents, abilities and strengths that go beyond the average person in the street. The most recent example of a leader with charismatic authority is the current US president, Barack Obama, but there have been many other embodiments of this kind of authority—John F. Kennedy, Adolf Hitler, Josef Stalin, Napoleon, Alexander the Great, Fidel Castro, Mao Tse-Tung, Charles Manson, Martin Luther King. It can also play a role at a more local level, so that school or university teachers, mid-level managers and sports coaches can base their authority and ability to direct people's behaviour on their charisma.

The role of charismatic authority on its own is limited to the lifespan of the charismatic leader, since it depends on their personal qualities, and any organisation or movement based on such authority can survive only if it draws on other forms of authority as well.

Traditional authority

At other times, observed Weber, people simply believe that doing things in a particular way, according to tradition and custom, is the 'right' thing to do, and this is what he called **traditional authority**. People in leadership positions are given or assume authority over others on the basis of their established social status and position, or on the basis of appeals to customary beliefs and values. The authority granted to monarchs or lords and barons is the leading example, but it also includes the authority of Church leaders and, within family life, patriarchs as masters of their households. If one believes, for example, that husbands have authority over their wives and children simply by virtue of their status as 'head of the household', this is an example of traditional authority.

Traditional authority also underpins what Weber called 'patrimonial bureaucracy', which he said is 'a special case of patriarchal domination—domestic authority decentralised through assignment of land and sometimes equipment to sons of the house or other dependents' (1948, p. 1011). Individuals' duties are prescribed by customs that are articulated orally and can be redefined according to the preferences of the particular ruler or lord. The appropriate performance of traditionally defined roles takes precedence over the pursuit of agreed-upon tasks and goals.

Rational–legal authority

Authority that rests on a system of impersonal written rules is different again, observed Weber, and he called this **rational–legal authority**. The written rules, laws, by-laws, resolutions and guidelines that underpin rational–legal authority are designed to achieve particular goals, and they constitute the basis for the appeal to people's conformity to those rules. The authority of a police officer, for example, is based to a large extent on the legal construction of the position of 'police officer', granted particular powers by legislation that has passed through parliament.

This type of authority is most fully expressed in a particular kind of organisation: rational–legal bureaucracy. Weber defined organisations as any 'social relationship which is either closed or limits the admission of outsiders' (1948, p. 48), and formal organisations as any 'association with a continuous and rationally operating staff' (p. 52). Weber identified an ideal type of the rational–legal bureaucratic organisation. Several of its characteristics are found in the state administrations of ancient Egypt and China and the later stages of the Roman Empire. However, the ideal type is most closely approximated in capitalist industrial society, where Weber thought it had become the most widespread form of organisational control. Weber proposed that the basic principles underlying the modern bureaucracy, to a greater or less extent, were as follows (but in reality, not every organisation will conform to all of them):

1. *Division of labour.* Organisations are divided into distinct 'jurisdictional areas' (1948, p. 956), with clearly distinguished competencies and aims. A university, for example, is divided into faculties, schools, and departments with responsibility for different fields of knowledge, each with a range of staff with specific duties within an overall division of labour.
2. *Hierarchy.* There is 'a clearly established system of super- and subordination in which there is a supervision of the lower offices by the higher ones' (p. 957). There is also the possibility of 'appealing, in a precisely regulated manner, the decision of the lower office to the corresponding superior authority' (p. 957).
3. *Written documents.* The activities of the bureaucratic organisation are consistently written down and stored in 'the files'. This written documentary record is in turn used as the basis and reference point for future organisational activity.
4. *Specialised training and knowledge.* Staff are not elected, but are appointed on the basis of their skills and knowledge as appropriate to their particular position in the organisation. Weber said: 'Bureaucratic administration means fundamentally domination through knowledge. This is the feature of it which makes it specifically rational' (p. 225).
5. *Full-time, salaried work.* Officials are full-time paid employees and their occupation constitutes a career. Promotion is based on seniority or achievement, or

a combination of both. There is a strict boundary drawn between private and official income, and between private and official time. 'Bureaucracy', wrote Weber, 'segregates official activity from the sphere of private life' (p. 957).

6. *General, impersonal rules.* The operations of a bureaucracy are governed by 'a consistent system of abstract rules' (p. 217). These rules clearly define the limits of the authority held by various officials in the hierarchy. The 'ideal officials' perform their duties in 'a spirit of formalistic impersonality … without hatred or passion, and hence without affection or enthusiasm' (p. 225). The activities of the bureaucrat are governed by the rules, not by personal considerations such as feelings towards colleagues or clients, 'without regard for persons' (p. 975).

Types of social action

The distinctions between different forms of authority or domination overlap with Weber's typology of different types of social action. He argued that in order to understand and explain human action, it is important to appreciate that it is always directed by meanings, which in turn need to be analysed. Weber (1978) thought that human action could be seen as falling into the following four types:

- **Affective or emotional action** is motivated by people's emotions in response to the situation they are in. Fear, anxiety, anger and euphoria are examples of drivers of this type of action.
- **Traditional action** is the product of custom and tradition, when people do what they believe has always been done in their culture or society without reflecting on its reasons or possible alternatives.
- **Value–rational action** arises from a clear formulation of a set of values and 'the consistently planned orientation of its detailed course to these values' (1978, p. 25). The examples Weber gave included devotion to duty, a religious calling, personal loyalty, the pursuit of beauty and devotion to a cause.
- **Instrumentally rational action** involves a clear awareness of a goal, and a systematic assessment of the various means of attaining a goal and the selection of the most appropriate means. It is instrumentally rational since, in Weber's words, 'the end, the means, and the secondary results are all rationally taken into account', and it involves 'rational consideration of alternative means to the end, of the relations of the end to the secondary consequences, and finally of the relative importance of different possible ends' (1978, p. 26).

The types of action are related to his forms of authority, although without mapping perfectly onto them. Affective action is the motivation for charismatic authority, traditional action for traditional authority, instrumentally rational action for rational–legal authority, and value–rational action for both traditional and rational–legal authority. Weber thought that the long-term historical tendency was towards instrumentally rational action underpinning rational–legal authority. He referred to this as the long-term process of rationalisation, and he felt that one could see its impact in all areas of social life, beginning with monasteries and the army, then government and business administration, education, science, sport, and even in family life, art and music. For Weber the spread of modern, instrumental rationality was most obviously manifested in the bureaucratisation of social life, which we will turn to later in the chapter.

> **Reflective question:** Outline Weber's typology of different forms of authority, and try to find examples of each.

ELITE THEORY

The picture of social life that quickly emerges once one begins to think about the operation of power is one that is hierarchical, divided between an elite that exercises power and authority and the rest of the population. Two early leading figures in the elite theory of power were the Italian sociologists Vilfredo Pareto (1848–1923) and Gaetano Mosca (1858–1941). They both thought that the people who were part of the elite had psychological qualities that set them apart from the rest of the population. For Pareto this was simply cunning and intelligence, but for Mosca it was also organisational skill. An important difference between Pareto and Mosca was that Pareto saw elites as more or less stable, with power and status handed down from one generation to the next, whereas Mosca thought that elites 'circulated' in the process of competition between different powerful groups and there was an inevitable tendency for any one dominant group to have to give way to new groups over time.

The power elite—C. Wright Mills

The American sociologist C. Wright Mills also thought that power was organised around a division between elites and the rest of the population, but he attributed this to institutional structures rather than the distribution of personal traits and skills. Mills focused attention on the organisations that have monopoly control over the exercise of power, with the power elite being those who occupied the 'command posts' in those organisations. He identified three institutional arenas as especially important:

1. the major corporations
2. the military
3. the federal government.

The individuals who occupy the command posts in these arenas constitute distinct elites, but they are also interrelated in ways that make up a more or less coherent 'power elite'. For Mills, the power elite is the product of the 'coincidence of economic, military, and political power' (1956, p. 278). Business corporations, government and the military are all interconnected and overlapping, so that business and government 'cannot now be seen as two distinct worlds' (p. 274).

For Mills a key element of the cohesiveness of the power elite is the fact that the different leading groups share similar social backgrounds, and individuals move quite freely between the different arenas of power. They went to the same schools, are members of the same clubs, play golf together and take care of each other's children. This means that they tend to see the world in the same way and share values and sympathies. The elite are also active across a number of different arenas. Mills observed that 'on the boards of directors we find a heavy overlapping among the members of these several elites' (1956, p. 283), such as 'the admiral who is also a banker and a lawyer and who heads up an important federal commission' (p. 288).

Mills thought that American society is dominated by a power elite that feels little need to be accountable to the rest of the population. The really crucial political decisions are made quite independently of what the general population think, and ordinary people are seen simply as 'the masses' needing to be manipulated to produce the outcomes that the power elite is sure is 'best' for the nation—which usually means best for them. Mills regarded the supposed democratic choice that is meant to be exercised at election time between Republicans and Democrats as a charade, so that there is a deep division between ordinary people concerned primarily with their own families, communities and workplaces, and an elite exercising power as it sees fit, subject to little or no accountability.

Elite theory in Australia

Many aspects of Mills' view of elites in the United States can also be applied to Australia. Although there is no comparable military elite, several researchers have found that the majority of those who occupy elite positions in Australia are recruited from the minority of the population with privileged backgrounds. This appears to apply to a wide range of Australian elites, including politicians, judges, higher public servants, senior military officers and the directors of large companies and major banks. There are high levels of elite self-recruitment: the children of elite members are particularly likely to be recruited to elite positions.

There is also evidence that there may be some degree of cohesion within and between the various elites. Individuals may occupy positions within more than one elite: cabinet ministers and other members of parliament may hold directorships in large companies. Individuals may move between elites, so that former politicians often become active at an elite level in business, diplomacy or the law. Directors may also sit on the boards of a number of different companies (Encel 1970).

Michael Pusey has argued, in relation to elite Commonwealth public servants, that their privileged social and educational backgrounds survive 20 years of experience in the workplace, shaping their current social and political attitudes. In addition to a commitment to the status quo, the more privileged the background of members of Australia's bureaucratic elite, the more likely they are to be 'the most ungenerous, individualistic, tough, and "anti social"' (1991, p. 74).

Higley, Deacon and Smart

Higley, Deacon and Smart (1979) at the Australian National University began by identifying elites as arising in any society requiring complex forms of organisation. They shared the basic premise of elitist theory that all complex organisations concentrate decision-making power in their uppermost positions, and elites are the persons in those positions, with 'power to affect organizational outcomes individually, regularly and seriously' (p. 3). This means that their viewpoints are often regarded by others as 'important factors' in making decisions.

Types of elite structure

Higley and his colleagues distinguished three different types of elite structure. The first is the **disunified elite** structure, where there are persistent, apparently irresolvable and often violent conflicts between different elites. This structure is characteristic of societies with military dictatorships and frequent military coups or other dramatic changes of government, and is a basically unstable elite structure. The second type, an

ideologically unified elite structure, is far more stable. There is usually a single political party to which all elite persons belong and that organises all political viewpoints into a unified whole, often coercively. Italian and German fascism of the 1930s and the former Union of Soviet Socialist Republics (USSR) are typical examples. The stability of the third type, a **consensual unified elite** structure, is based on the elites' ongoing commitment to the stability of existing social and political institutions—a commitment that consistently outweighs the real ideological and material conflicts between them. Such an elite structure arises 'only when elites calculate that it is in their personal interest to avoid destructive conflicts and to preserve existing institutions and procedures' (p. 12). This is the type of elite structure that Higley, Deacon and Smart saw operating in Australia.

Elite networks and elite integration

The research conducted by Higley and his colleagues consisted of interviews with 370 persons in leadership positions in business, trade unions, federal politics, state politics, the Commonwealth public service, media, voluntary associations and academe. In addition to identifying elite ideology, opinions and social backgrounds, their research attempted to deal with the degree and type of integration among elite groups. Respondents were asked to identify their most 'important interaction partners' in relation to the one political issue they were most active about during 1975 when the Whitlam Labor Government was dismissed by the Governor-General, Sir John Kerr (see the case study below). In this way, it was possible to identify a relatively small circle of people who most frequently interacted with the respondents.

Higley and his colleagues found that the fathers of elite persons 'were heavily concentrated in the most prestigious, best educated, most affluent and influential occupational categories' (p. 79). One-third of all elite fathers were business owners or managers and a quarter were in the professions—occupations that together accounted for only 10 per cent of the workforce in the 1940s, when these elites began working. They also found that Australian elites were characterised by highly educated fathers and mothers in leading positions in business, politics and the professions, although to a far less extent in the Australian Labor Party (ALP), trade unions and left voluntary associations (Higley, Deacon & Smart 1979).

Elites were also likely to have a common educational background: the majority attended private or elite state secondary schools and held specialised university degrees. More than half (52 per cent) of all elite persons in the study attended Catholic or non-Catholic private secondary schools. In addition, 43 per cent of all Australian-educated elites attended 23 schools, and 18 of those schools educated one-third of the Australian-educated elite. There was a further concentration in the first 12 schools, which educated 27 per cent of the elite (Higley, Deacon & Smart 1979, p. 88).

On the one hand, their results undermined the pluralist position (see below, pp. 383–385), in that there was far greater integration and contact through informal networks than the pluralist model would suggest (1979, p. 262). They found that a core of three elite groups—politicians, businesspeople and public servants—were regarded as central by all the elite respondents. This central circle consisted of 70 people, including 23 political leaders, 22 business leaders and 11 public servants.

On the other hand, Higley and his colleagues were unwilling to agree that their evidence indicated the existence of a power elite or ruling class, for a number of reasons. First, it seemed difficult to believe that such a small group of people could dominate Australian society, requiring 'a belief in conspiracy beyond what is reasonable to conclude' (p. 263). Second, despite the apparent power of this small core group, the researchers believed there could only be said to be a power elite, or a ruling class, if the business and government elites were insulated from other elites and able to impose policies favouring their own interests relatively unhindered (p. 221)—and their analysis did not produce such a picture. Third, they observed that the three central elite groups—politics, business and public service—were sharply divided over issues in 1975, and that this indicated there was no unity of interests and opinions among the power elite.

In sum, Higley and his colleagues believed that Australia's elites were more integrated than pluralists allow and too loosely integrated to be regarded as either a power elite or a ruling class.

Reflective question: To what extent is it fair to see Australian society as dominated by a power elite? Who constitutes this elite, and what is the basis of their power?

POWER IS LIKE MONEY— TALCOTT PARSONS

Talcott Parsons (1960; 1967) provided a different perspective on power, seeing it more as 'a generalised

Case Study
Gough Whitlam's dismissal

The Australian Labor Party, led by Gough Whitlam, was elected to government on 2 December 1972, after Australia had been governed by the Liberal/Country Party coalition for 23 years. Whitlam pursued a resolutely reformist agenda, abolishing university fees, ending conscription and withdrawing from the Vietnam war, promoting equal rights for women, establishing universal health insurance in the form of Medibank, making divorce no-fault in the Family Law Act, extending maternity leave and child-care provisions, expanding social welfare, opening up relationships with China, supporting Aboriginal land rights, and preventing racial and sexual discrimination. However, in response to rising inflation and unemployment, as well as a number of scandals, especially the 'Overseas Loans Affair', the Liberal/Country Party coalition, led by Malcolm Fraser, refused to allow the passage of the Supply Bill in the Senate until Whitlam had called an election, which he refused to do. To resolve the constitutional crisis the Governor-General, Sir John Kerr, sought the advice of the Chief Justice of the Supreme Court, Sir Garfield Barwick, the result being that he dismissed Whitlam on 11 November 1975, dissolving both houses of parliament and appointing Fraser as caretaker prime minister in the lead-up to a double-dissolution election, which Fraser won easily.

Many see this event as an example of the workings of an Australian 'power elite', with established groups and interests uniting in their opposition to genuine social and economic change. From this perspective, political power was exercised to remove a duly-elected government and then manipulate public opinion in the mass media so as to ensure a return to the established distribution of power. Do you think this is a fair assessment of Whitlam's dismissal, and can you see examples of this sort of exercise of power in the world today?

facility or resource in the society'. He defined power as 'the capacity to mobilize the resources of the society for the attainment of goals for which a general "public" commitment has been made' (1960, p. 221). The exercise of power in society does not take place simply for the benefit of some (the powerful) and at the expense of others (the powerless), but it mobilises resources in ways that benefit everyone in society. His approach is known as the **'variable-sum' concept of power**, because it is not seen as a fixed 'quantity', where an increase in the power of some individuals or groups necessarily means a decrease in others. For Parsons, there is no reason why power does not operate in a win–win way, so that the exercise of power by some individuals or groups can be accompanied by a related improvement in the capacity of others to exercise power. He drew an analogy between power and money (Parsons 1964), and both are capable of increasing in absolute terms. Parsons saw the operation of power within the context of a set of shared values and collective goals—such as increased material prosperity, democracy and individualism—which 'drive' the exercise of power.

The central problem with Parsons' approach was the presumption that there was indeed a consensus on shared values and goals. As Stewart Clegg and his colleagues remark, his theory of power was 'at odds with the experiences of liberal democracies in the 1960s characterized by civil rights demonstrations, race riots, student demonstrations, and the 'Paris Events of 1968' which marred General de Gaulle's last year as president of France' (Clegg, Courpasson & Phillips 2006, p. 197). Anthony Giddens (1968) argued that power is more 'zero-sum' than Parsons was willing to recognise and that power 'is always exercised by someone' (1968, p. 24). Rather than seeing society as being characterised by consensus, Giddens was more responsive to the view of conflict theorists like Mills that there are always clashes between the interests of different social, political and economic groups in society. As he wrote, '[h]owever much it is true that power can rest upon "agreement" to code authority which can be used for collective aims, it is also true that interests of power-holders and those subject to that power often clash' (Giddens 1968, p. 24).

PLURALISM

Pluralist theorists of power, such as the French philosopher Alexis de Tocqueville (1805–59) and the American political scientist Robert Dahl (1961), take up a position somewhere between elite theorists and Parsons. They agree with Parsons that it is incorrect to see power as especially concentrated in particular groups of institutions and that liberal democracies do allow their populations to participate in the exercise of political power. However, they also agree with elite theorists that power should be seen in 'zero-sum' terms, so that the gain in the power of some groups takes place at the expense of others; and they agree with the conflict theorists' argument that there is not really a coherent consensus on values across the whole of society.

There may be agreement on some issues; for example, **pluralism** would assume that most Australian citizens share a commitment to the country's Constitution, its political institutions such as parliament and the electoral system, and a particular set of values such as egalitarianism and fairness. However, modern society is highly differentiated with a complex division of labour, composed of a wide variety of social groups with diverse social and cultural backgrounds. Indeed, the core characteristic of complex, industrialised, urbanised modern societies is precisely that *diversity* of value orientation, rather than the existence of a unified worldview, which is more characteristic of pre-modern social life.

The pluralist position still diverges from that of conflict theorists, however. First, in the sense that they see all these differences and divergences as *cutting across* rather than *lining up* with each other, making it impossible to identify a single 'working class', 'Aboriginal' or 'women's' value orientation. The pluralist picture of liberal democracies, then, is of an assembly of competing interest groups, none of which absolutely dominates the others, with no really dominant coalition among them, and with power constantly shifting across and among the different groups. Second, pluralists also question *whether* there will always be a power structure in every human community and argue that this needs to be empirically established rather than simply assumed. As Nelson Posby argued:

> *... nothing categorical can be assumed about power in any community. It rejects the stratification thesis that some group necessarily dominates a community. If anything, there seems to be an unspoken notion among pluralist researchers that at bottom nobody dominates in a town, so that their first question to a local informant is not likely to be, "Who runs this community?," but rather, "Does anyone at all run this community?" It is instructive to examine the range of possible answers to each of these questions. The first query is somewhat like, "Have you stopped beating your wife?,", in that virtually any response short of total unwillingness to answer will supply the researchers with a "power elite" along the lines presupposed by the stratification theory.* (1960, p. 476)

Pluralists also argue that one should not assume that power relations are stable over time, or that a group that has a reputation for being powerful is necessarily so, and this is a question that has to be empirically tested (Posby 1960).

An important manifestation of this dissipation of power is, in the view of pluralist theorists, the competition between different political parties in a liberal democracy. Using Rodney Smith's definition, political parties are 'organisations that aim to influence public policy in favour of an ideology or set of interests primarily by attempting to gain control of public office' (1993a, p. 130). The pluralist position is evident in Seymour Martin Lipset's definition of democracy:

> *Democracy in a complex society may be defined as a political system which supplies regular constitutional opportunities for changing the governing officials, and a social mechanism which permits the largest possible part of the population to influence major decisions by choosing among contenders for political office.* (1981, p. 27)

Political parties make it possible for the power of governing groups to be held in check, and elections allow for 'turn-taking' in the government of society in response to the population's values and preferences. The emergence of new parties, such as the Greens, is evidence of the way in which the political system is responsive to shifts in ideas about how society ought to be governed.

In addition to the variety of political positions embodied by political parties, there is also additional scope for the expression of divergent views by **interest groups**, which seek to influence the political process and policy formulation without necessarily aiming to participate directly in the mechanics of government. Interest groups are often classified in terms of their aims as either **'protective' groups** or **'promotional' groups**. Protective groups defend the interests of a particular section of society. Trade unions such as the Australian Workers' Union, professional associations such as the Australian Medical Association (AMA) and employers' organisations such as the Australian Chamber of Commerce and Industry (ACCI) are classified as protective groups. Promotional groups support a particular cause rather than guard the interests of a particular social group. Organisations such as the Royal Society for the Prevention of Cruelty to Animals (RSPCA), the 'new social movements' (see below) including environmental groups such as Greenpeace and the Wilderness Society, women's, gay and civil rights movements and the anti-globalisation movement are all promotional groups. Membership of promotional groups is potentially larger and usually more varied than that of protective groups, since promotional groups require only a commitment to their cause as a qualification for joining. By comparison, membership of protective groups is usually limited to individuals of a particular status—for example, only doctors can be members of the AMA.

In Australia, representatives of interest groups have permanent places on a wide range of government advisory committees. In 1972, Dowse and Hughes observed that:

> *interest groups constitute a continuous mandate for the government and without them no government could conceivably be regarded as democratic. More to the point, no government could begin to operate without the assistance of interest groups. (pp. 396–7)*

This is even more true today than it was over three decades ago.

The activities of interest groups are an important part of the pluralist conception of how liberal democracy ought to work. They do not believe that, in Australia for instance, voting once every three years is an adequate level of participation. Interest groups provide the opportunity for many individuals who are not members of political parties to participate in politics. For example, members of the environmental movement generally limit their active interest in politics to participation in the activities of organisations such as the Wilderness Society and Greenpeace. Fathers' rights groups pursue their goals through letter-writing campaigns, public meetings and other forms of lobbying outside the normal electoral process.

Who Governs?—Robert Dahl

In his famous study of local politics in New Haven, Connecticut, *Who Governs?*, Robert Dahl (1961) found that power was indeed spread across a number of different groups. In a direct critique of Mills' arguments concerning a 'power elite', Dahl argued that one could not observe financial or corporate interests as having a dominant influence on New Haven politics:

> *Economic Notables, far from being a ruling group, are simply one of many groups out of which individuals sporadically emerge to influence the policies and acts of city officials. Almost anything one might say about the influence of Economic Notables could be said with equal justice about a half dozen other groups in the New Haven community. (1961, p. 72)*

Political action was the outcome of a complex process of bargaining, negotiation and compromise that did not give the upper hand automatically to any particular group or interest, and this is the essence of the pluralist conception of power.

The theory of power that Dahl developed, as Andrew McFarland (2007) has summarised it, had four elements. First, power was defined in terms of causation, the ability to change people's behaviour and actions, so that 'A has power over B to the extent that A causes changes in B's behavior in the direction of A's intentions' (p. 47). So money and military capacity are not, in this view, 'power', but 'resources', which may or may not be used in the pursuit of power.

Second, the exercise of power is seen as a political process, which unfolds over time in a complex interaction between all the relevant actors. McFarland identifies the following elements of Dahl's political process model of power:

1. Empirical observation indicates agents acting within a policy system.
2. These agents are seen as groups and individuals representing group interests.
3. The agents interact and affect one another's behaviour.
4. The agents pursue their interests, defined according to the agents' own definitions of interest, although sometimes these must be inferred from their behaviour.
5. Interests frequently change in the process of interaction among the agents over time.
6. Implicit in the foregoing, empirical observation should continue over a period sufficient to understand fluctuations in power, interest groups and policymaking activities. (2007, p. 48).

Third, the analysis of power needs to engage with separate realms of politics and policy making, which do not necessarily correspond with each other, and this can be determined only by careful empirical example. This point was a caution against the inclination of elite theorists to presume that the power elite is always dominant in every context. Fourth, interests should not be 'second-guessed' and 'researchers should accept the definitions of interest given by the subjects themselves, or perhaps as inferred from observations of subjects' patterns of behavior' (2007, p. 49).

We will engage with the critique of the elite, Parsonian and pluralist conceptions of power in a later section, but first it is useful to turn to possibly the core settings for the exercise of power: the state and bureaucracy.

BUREAUCRACY, DISCIPLINE AND THE STATE

Weber observed that bureaucratic organisations had become the dominant institutions of all industrial societies, both capitalist and socialist. Government departments, banks, churches, political parties, business corporations, schools, armies and sporting clubs are all organised more or less on bureaucratic lines. He was convinced that an understanding of the process of bureaucratisation is essential to a proper appreciation of the nature of modern society. It is bureaucratic organisations that enable the pursuit of clearly defined goals, and embody the precise calculation of the means to attain these goals and the systematic elimination of those factors standing in the way of the achievement of these objectives. Bureaucracy is the institutional embodiment of rational, calculative action.

The 'technical superiority' of bureaucracy, or TINA

For Weber, the increasing dominance of bureaucracy is due to its 'technical superiority' compared with organisations based on charismatic and traditional domination. Weber argued: 'The decisive reason for the advance of bureaucratic organization has always been its purely *technical* superiority over any other form of organization' (1978, p. 973). This superiority stems from the combination of specialist skills subordinated to the goals of the organisation and the exclusion of private, personal emotions and interests that might detract from the attainment of those goals. As Weber put it: 'Precision, speed, unambiguity, knowledge of the files, continuity, discretion, unity, strict subordination, reduction of friction and of material and personal costs—these are raised to the optimum in the strictly bureaucratic organization' (p. 973). In its ideal form, bureaucracy eliminates 'from official business love, hatred, and all purely personal, irrational and emotional elements which escape calculation' (p. 975).

Weber argued that when anyone tries to escape the influence of existing bureaucracies 'this is normally possible only by creating an organization of their own which is equally subject to bureaucratization' (p. 224). This is why it is possible to speak of 'the bureaucratisation of the world' (Jacoby 1973). Stewart Clegg has nicely captured the essence of the argument for the inescapability of rational–legal rationality and bureaucracy by referring to it as the TINA tendency: *There is No Alternative* (1990, p. 58).

Bureaucracy, discipline and power

Weber regarded bureaucratic organisation as central to the exercise of power in modern societies in three ways. First, he saw the hierarchical and specialised structure of bureaucracy as a key form of *power as domination*. The uniform and rational procedures of bureaucratic routine tend to undermine spontaneity, creativity and individual initiative, confining these human capacities within what he called the 'iron cage' of rationality. The impersonality of official conduct produces 'specialists without spirit' (1930, p. 182) and it was 'horrible to think that the world would one day be filled with little cogs, little men clinging to little jobs and striving towards the bigger ones'. For Weber, the only real basis for any sort of opposition to bureaucracy's restriction of human freedom lay in the realm of values and politics. Weber saw the 'great question' as how we can 'oppose this machinery in order to preserve a vestige of humanity from this fragmentation (*Parzellierung*) of the soul, from this absolute domination of bureaucratic ideals of life' (Weber 1924, p. 414).

Second, bureaucracy had become the central way in which human psychology was *disciplined* in modern social life. As we are increasingly subjected to impersonal routines, exercises, procedures and rules, they become built into our 'psycho-physical apparatus'. He wrote that 'the individual is shorn of his natural rhythm as determined by his organism; in line with the demands of the work procedure, he is attuned to the new rhythm through the functional specialization of muscles and through the creation of an optimal economy of physical effort' (1978, p. 1156). The disciplinary effects of modern organisations also include the production of a particular emotional orientation. As Merton states:

> *Discipline can be effective only if the ideal patterns are buttressed by strong sentiments which entail devotion to one's duties, a keen sense of the limitation of one's authority and competence, and methodical performance of routine activities. The efficacy of social structure depends ultimately upon infusing group participants with appropriate attitudes and sentiments (1940, p. 562).*

Weber commented that once it was established, this 'settled orientation of man for observing the accustomed rules and regulations' possesses its own reality and stability, enabling it to outlive the social organisation, which produced a calculative, disciplined orientation to the world (1978, p. 988).

Third, the production of a disciplined orientation to the world within bureaucracies was both *preceded* and *accompanied* by the more general ideological development of Christian asceticism's methodical, calculative organisation of conduct. Christian asceticism encouraged the rejection of all that was based on emotion, in favour of 'the alert, methodical control of one's own pattern of life and behaviour' (Weber 1978, p. 544). The disciplined orientation to the conduct of everyday life, which could first be found in armies and monasteries, 'strode into the market-place of life, slammed the door of the monastery behind it' and began to permeate the 'naturally spontaneous character of daily life in the world' with its 'methodicalness' (Weber 1930, p. 154). This in turn meant that at least some workers already possessed an 'adequate lifestyle' through which capitalist work organisations 'gained massive control over life in the manner that [they have]' (Weber 1978), so that Protestant asceticism unintentionally prepared the foundations for the development of organisational discipline (van Krieken 1989).

The most important bureaucracy was, for Weber, **the state**, defined as 'a human community that [successfully] claims the monopoly of the legitimate use of physical force within a given territory' (in Gerth & Mills 1948, p. 78). In Australia today, for example, it is clear that the state rules over a clearly defined geographical area. For Weber, state-formation was precisely the development of a monopoly over the right to use force by a legitimate central authority, making other forms of the exercise of violence illegitimate and subject to state control. So only the state is meant to wage war or have the capacity to restrain people's liberty and put them in prison.

At the very least, for Weber, the state consists of a number of institutions, including the legislature which decides on law-making, a government administration to administer those laws, a judiciary, and a legal system and police force to interpret and enforce the law, as well as a military force responsible for the protection of the state from external, and sometimes internal, threats such as terrorism. Often sociologists will include other publicly administered institutions in their definition of the state, such as the education, health and welfare systems, public transport, urban planning and development, sanitation, water management and so on.

STATELESS SOCIETIES

States as Weber defined them are not especially new, but it is true to say that nation-states such as Australia, the United States, the United Kingdom and the countries making up the European Union—centralised authorities that have sovereign control over a bounded territory—are a relatively recent phenomenon in human history. To understand the nature of the state, it is useful to take a brief look at those forms of human society that have existed across history and across cultures without any institution that could be called a 'state'.

The Australian anthropologist L. R. Hiatt (1996, pp. 78–99), for example, outlines how Europeans regarded Australian Aborigines as a 'people without politics' (Sharp 1958), their social order based entirely on custom and kinship ties rather than anything resembling 'government' in the Weberian sense of enduring institutions and organisations controlling a bounded territory and monopolising the legitimate use of force. Hiatt uses the example of a book written in 1886 by the Australian pastoralist E. M. Curr, *The Australian Race*, where Curr argues that Aboriginal tribes could be seen as not possessing any form of government. For Curr, 'government' meant the 'habitual exercise of authority, by one or a few individuals, over a community or a body of persons' (1886, p. 60). Hiatt points out that European observers have almost always seen social order among the Aborigines as based not on the authority, backed by force, of leaders or political institutions which could be said to resemble a 'state', but on the constraints of custom, superstition and a complex and constraining kinship system. This has, in Hiatt's view, played an important role in helping 'to make assimilation of Aboriginal communities into the imported structures of British government a task of notorious difficulty' (p. 99).

THE EMERGENCE OF THE MODERN STATE AND BUREAUCRACY

In the history of Western Europe, the operation of power can be understood only in terms of the emergence, from a quite different structure of power relations, of a centralised state and the structuring of human relations by various types of organisations and bureaucracies.

A central feature of *feudalism*, which reached its most developed form in the 12th and 13th centuries, is that the legitimate use of force was not in fact concentrated in the hands of a centralised authority. Although kings and queens ruled in theory from their palaces and courts, in reality the control of any given territory was in the hands of local lords and barons. Poggi has argued that the king was usually only a 'dimly perceived, politically ineffective figure' (1978, p. 26) and the governance of feudal society relied on linking together a number of separate centres of power.

The more centralised state as we know it began to emerge in the 17th century in France, as the balance of power between the monarch and the aristocracy shifted towards the former. This shift in the balance of power towards the centre accelerated in the 19th and 20th centuries, as developments in transport and communications facilitated the capacity of central state agencies to control all of their territory.

In Australia, the establishment of a convict colony by the English government in 1788 constituted the importation of a completely state-run enterprise—a prison—into Aboriginal Australia. Since then the state has continued to play a particularly strong and influential role, especially from the late 19th century and throughout the 20th century, when the state greatly extended its involvement in, and control over, economic affairs, as well as the provision of welfare, health care and education. The importance of the state in industrial societies has prompted sociologists to devote considerable attention to it. In particular, they have debated which groups in society control the state and in whose interests the state is run.

THE SOURCES OF SOCIAL POWER—MICHAEL MANN

Michael Mann (1986; 1993) draws a detailed examination of the history of state formation to argue that distinctions need to be made between four different types of power, drawing on different kinds of resources: economic power, political power, military power and ideological power. They do not necessarily overlap with each other, and most of human history is, for Mann, the story of how the clashes between different forms of power are played out, or how institutions that have managed to combine different types of power deal with them being uncoupled by entities competing for one or more of them.

Mann also argued, in contrast to Weber's emphasis on the nation-state, that these forms of power and their 'containers' should be seen as cutting across national boundaries, so that they do not simply 'sit inside' the nation-state. As Mann observed, 'human beings do not create unitary societies but a diversity of intersecting networks of social interaction' (1986, p. 16). Any given 'society', then, is 'constituted of multiple overlapping and intersecting sociospatial networks of power' (p. 1).

THE AUSTRALIAN STATE

Several features of the Australian state distinguish it from other forms of government and set the framework for the operation of power in Australian society in a particular way. The origins of white Australian society as a convict colony placed the state at the centre of both society and the economy, rather than emerging alongside these two separate spheres. Economic activity has thus consistently been closely tied to state intervention, and economic development would have been impossible without state activity. This is one of the reasons the state has always been assigned a central role in Australian political culture, as the avenue through which most issues should be dealt with, generating what Encel (1970) referred to as an underlying authoritarianism in Australian culture. Michael Pusey (1993) thus referred to the Australian state as an example of a 'strong' state compared with nations such as the United Kingdom or the United States.

The Constitution and the High Court

A central element of the framework within which Australian state action takes place is the Constitution, which establishes the ground rules for the ways in which various political institutions relate to each other, the relationship between the Commonwealth government and state governments, the powers of the state over the population and how the law is to be interpreted in relation to contemporary Australian society. Although it is possible for the Constitution to be changed, the requirements are very strict and very few proposals for amendment have been passed. Any proposal for change must:

- be initiated by the Commonwealth Parliament
- pass both houses of parliament by absolute majorities
- receive a majority in a national yes/no referendum and
- receive majorities in a majority of states (four out of six).

As a result, in terms of its Constitution, Australia has been characterised as 'the frozen continent' (Sawer 1967, p. 208).

Any changes in the relationship between the Constitution and a changing Australian society have thus been effected by the institution responsible for interpreting it, the High Court. Elaine Thompson (1993) has commented that, although the Australian High Court presents its judgements primarily in terms of conformity to legal principle, its interpretations and judgements are often based on particular political positions, and they certainly have political effects.

For example, the High Court prevented the Chifley Labor Government from nationalising banks and stopped the Menzies Liberal Government from banning the Communist Party. It made it possible for the Commonwealth to control the gathering of income tax, to prevent the Tasmanian government from building a dam across the Franklin River, and to stop state governments from practising racial discrimination. More recently, in the Mabo and Wik decisions, it has reinterpreted the rights of Aboriginal peoples to the possession of land. Over time, the High Court's decisions have had the general effect of granting increased powers to the Commonwealth government at the expense of state governments, particularly in the area of taxation and state borrowing. The control that the Commonwealth has over state income and expenditure has the subsequent effect of granting it indirect control over almost everything the state governments do.

The federal structure

Australia's federal system of government is similar to that of the United States, Germany and Canada. It is characterised by a distribution of powers between a national government and a number of state or provincial governments, with the relationships between them specified in a Constitution. Australian government is divided into three levels—Commonwealth, state and local or municipal government—and the precise relationship between the different tiers can have far-reaching consequences, depending on the political complexion of the parties in power. The Commonwealth raises between 70 and 80 per cent of total public revenue, with much of this income distributed to state and local governments (Groenewegen 1995, p. 178). Since the introduction of the goods and services tax in 2000, this government income has flowed directly to the states.

The Constitution specifies the Commonwealth's powers and responsibilities to include trade and commerce, post, telegraph and telephone, currency, marriage and divorce, railways and external affairs. Since then its responsibilities have extended to immigration, income taxation, social security, public sector borrowing and civil aviation (Head 1983, p. 8). The states' responsibilities were left unspecified, but were to include education, health, roads, housing and police. Today they have extensive powers over 'industry, energy supply, prices, courts, mineral exploration and development, land use, environment, welfare services, consumer affairs, ports, water resources, and most aspects of criminal, civil and commercial law' (Head 1983, pp. 8–9). Some of these responsibilities, such as community services, urban development and land use, are in turn devolved to local government, but its powers are generally determined by state government. However, because of the Commonwealth's control over customs and excise duties, income tax and public sector borrowing, as well as the High Court's interpretation of many of its responsibilities, the Commonwealth in fact now exercises extensive control over many of the areas originally designated as the states' responsibility, especially health, education, housing and Aboriginal affairs.

One central enduring effect of federalism on Australian politics and democracy is the very particular meaning of the concept of state 'sovereignty', since both state governments and the Commonwealth government possess sovereign powers that can relate to each other in a variety of ways. Each state, for example, also has its own Constitution. In a sense the Australian and state Constitutions, the High Court, the Commonwealth government and the state governments are the most visible political 'actors' on the Australian political stage, alongside (less visible) private economic interests, the media and the electorate.

Groenewegen (1983, p. 189) concludes his discussion of Australian federalism by arguing that the continued existence of the federal system can be attributed to the special advantages gained by particular social groups who are able to exploit the division of powers to produce outcomes favourable to their interests. In particular, the states' responsibility for industry benefits business, because the states are driven to compete with each other to attract investment and employment, to the detriment of other concerns that have to be taken up by the Commonwealth, such as the environment, social welfare and social justice. In this sense, the relationship between the Commonwealth government and the state governments is a vehicle for the overall relationship between state, economy and society in Australia.

A Weberian approach to the Australian state—Sol Encel

A key figure in the development of the sociological analysis of power in Australian society has been Sol Encel. For Encel, it was Weber's approach that provided 'the necessary corrective to the fashionable Marxist simplifications which were all the rage among my fellow students' (1991, p. 76). Encel built on Weber's analysis of bureaucracy as a key source of power in modern societies, as well as on the Weberian distinction between class, status and party as lines of division in capitalist society. He argued that the public service bureaucracy should be seen as central to the operation of power in Australia. Drawing on the work of Noel Butlin (1959), Encel emphasised the dependence of private economic development on state action and intervention. Although the concept of 'free enterprise' may be applied to the development of capitalism in Western Europe and North America, Australia's economic history 'only makes sense if government action is put at the centre of the picture ... It is much nearer the truth to conceive of the Australian economy as having been dependent, throughout its history, on government action and government regulation' (Encel 1970, p. 324).

A large part of Encel's work consisted of an analysis of how the Australian public service has developed historically into a powerful, independent political force—what he referred to as 'the bureaucratic ascendancy'. The essence of his argument against some Marxist interpretations of the state is the assertion that the state is not simply a reflection of the economic power of leading capitalists but an independent source of power and authority in its own right. He also drew attention to the long-term effects of the use of bureaucratic action to encourage equality, identifying the 'paradox' of egalitarianism in Australia as follows: 'the search for equality of the redistributive kind breeds bureaucracy; bureaucracy breeds authority; and authority undermines the equality which bred it' (1970, p. 57).

Within the Australian cultural and historical context, Encel argued that the state had come to be regarded and constructed in terms of its utility for the achievement of ends, responsive not to any central philosophy or ruling class, but operating largely as 'a machine, or perhaps a collection of pieces of machinery, available for manipulation by sufficiently powerful interested groups or syndicates' (1968, p. 44). Encel did see Australia as populated by elites—indeed, much of his major work, *Equality and Authority* (1970), argued against the myth of Australia as an egalitarian society by indicating the close integration, interconnectedness and exclusivity of Australian elites. However, like Higley, Deacon and Smart (1979), he did not see those elites as constituting a ruling class; he saw them simply as 'a loose collection of elite groups linked together by what may be called a governing consensus' (1970, p. 4).

Because of what he called the 'primitive Benthamism' (1968, p. 44) of the Australian state (its orientation to the utilitarian philosophy of Jeremy Bentham), Encel did not regard its political parties as particularly class-based; he saw them as more responsive to the pragmatic material concerns of their constituencies than as either defending or attacking capitalism as an economic system.

RETHINKING POWER

An important characteristic of sociological thinking about power until the 1970s was the emphasis on decision making, on active intervention into social life. However, in a path-breaking article entitled 'Two faces of power', the American political scientists Peter Bachrach and Morton Baratz (1962; also 1970) argued that in addition to the **first 'face' of power**, when A participates in the making of decisions that affect B:

power is also exercised when A devotes his energies to creating or reinforcing social and political values and institutional practices that limit the scope of the political process to public consideration of only those issues which are comparatively innocuous to A. (1962, p. 948)

They suggested that 'non-decision making' (p. 952) was an equally important **second 'face' of power** that set the agenda for the ways in which decisions were made 'safe' for powerful and established interests. Even more problematic was the fact that the exercise of this sort of power can coexist with an impression being created of democratic decision making in which all interests carry equal weight, when in fact the deck has been stacked in favour of particular social groups from the outset.

THE THREE FACES OF POWER—STEVEN LUKES

In his book *Power: A Radical View*, Steven Lukes (1974) took Bachrach and Baratz's critique of pluralism one step further, arguing in his 'radical' view of power that power in fact has *three* 'faces' or dimensions. As well as decision making and non-decision making, or agenda-setting, Lukes argued that the exercise of power is also evident in the way that people's preferences and desires can be socially shaped and moulded—the **third 'face' of power**. This draws attention to social institutions such as the education system and the mass media, and the way in which identity is shaped and formed in particular ways, as equally important arenas for understanding the operation of power in society.

On this basis, Lukes defined power as follows: 'A exercises power over B when A affects B in a manner contrary to B's interests' (1974, p. 27). This definition uncoupled the analysis of power from evidence of harm being inflicted, suggesting the importance of looking at the myriad other ways in which power functions without people necessarily being aware of being harmed or dominated. Hearn has recently summed up both Lukes' 1974 book and the 2005 second edition, stating that Lukes proposed:

> ... that power is not just about manifest conflicts over 'the actual', but also about latent conflicts over 'the possible', and that social researchers may sometimes be better able to survey the relevant range of possibilities, and to reasonably imagine alternative historical paths, than those subject to those possibilities. (Hearn 2008, p. 38)

Lukes was thus moving away from the concentration on elites to examine the effects of power on the powerless, saying that 'people's wants may themselves be a product of a system which works against their interests, and, in such cases, relates the latter to what they would want and prefer, were they able to make the choice' (Lukes 2005, p. 38).

In the 2005 second edition of his book, however, Lukes makes an important departure from his 1974 account. He concludes that:

> It was a mistake to define power by 'saying that A exercises power over B when A affects B in a manner contrary to B's interests'. Power is a capacity not the exercise of that capacity (it may never be, and may never need to be, exercised); and you can be powerful by satisfying and advancing others' interests: PRV's topic, power as domination, is only one species of power (2005, p. 12).

Drawing on the work of Spinoza (in Lukes 2005, pp. 73, 85–87, 114–116), Lukes argues that it is more accurate to say that 'power as domination is the ability to constrain the choices of others, coercing them or securing their compliance, by impeding them from living as their own nature and judgement dictate' (2005, p. 85). Rather than being persuaded to act contrary to one's interests, although this also happens often enough, the more subtle aspect of the operation of power is the very construction of what our interests are, in ways that, for Lukes, are not necessarily consistent with our 'real' needs or aspirations.

Reflective question: Explain the differences between the three 'faces' of power, and give examples of each. Are there ways in which power operates that can be seen as more than one face of power at the same time?

NEO-PLURALISM

Pluralist approaches to power have responded to criticisms to combine the insights of the original pluralist model with subsequent developments in social and political theory. David Marsh (1983) referred to many such attempts as elite pluralism, and the overall approach has more recently been termed 'neo-pluralism' (McFarland 2004; 2007). While retaining the original idea that power should be seen as dispersed, this approach:

1. is more responsive to the uneven distribution of power
2. recognises the role of elites—that although there may not be a single unified 'power elite', there are still concentrations of individuals with disproportionate control and influence in society
3. acknowledges that the state is not simply an umpire adjudicating among the different interests, but itself is an active 'player' in power relationships
4. incorporates an analysis of Bachrach and Baratz's second 'face' of power.

However, there is still little response to Lukes' third 'face' of power, which has found more resonance in the neo-Marxist adaptations of Mills' elite theory developing the concept of 'hegemony', to which we now turn.

THE POWER OF HEGEMONY— ANTONIO GRAMSCI

The Italian sociologist and activist Antonio Gramsci (1891–1937) has been enormously influential in the development of sociological understandings of power, by drawing attention to the complex relationship between political, social and economic structures. For Gramsci, the state should be understood as:

> the entire complex of practical and theoretical activities with which the ruling class not only justifies and maintains its dominance, but manages to maintain the active consent of those over whom it rules. (1971, p. 244)

Hegemonic power should be distinguished from 'domination', which Gramsci confined to the exercise of coercion or armed force. As Fontana observes, 'A group is hegemonic to the extent that it exercises intellectual and moral leadership over other groups such that the latter become "allies" and "associates" of the former' (2002, p. 159). Power also operates through 'leadership', the formation of alliances that require concessions and securing—often reluctant—consent from the parties to the compromise. Such consent is achieved in the realm of civil society—the family, the education system, everyday life, voluntary associations, political parties, social movements, churches and religious associations.

Power is thus not restricted to the sphere of economics or even politics, but also operates in the realm of ideas and the formation of consciousness. Gramsci argued that power could generally be exercised only through compromises and strategic concessions among different social groups. As he put it, 'Undoubtedly the fact of hegemony presupposes that account be taken of the interests and the tendencies of the groups over which hegemony is to be exercised' (1971, p. 161). It involves the formation of a particular worldview, political grammar or 'way of seeing' the world that, like Bacharach and Baratz's second 'face' of power, sets the agenda for what is even 'thinkable' in public debate, excluding other ways of approaching particular issues and problems. And, like Lukes' third 'face' of power, hegemony also involves the formation of a particular kind of self and identity with defined preferences and desires; it is, as Fontana observes, 'the proliferation throughout the people of a particular conception of the world and of a particular way of life' (2002, p. 166).

> One of the key arenas for shaping desires and preferences is marketing, advertising and the realm of consumption. Many observers of advanced industrial societies have said that this is one of the primary ways in which power is exercised over individuals, creating the illusion that they are free because they are free to choose between McDonald's and KFC, between Coles and Woolworths or between different sizes of television set. Some consumers of McDonald's hamburgers, for example, have sued McDonald's for having been responsible for their obesity.

Reflective questions: To what extent do you think it is useful to see the world of consumption as a site of power relations, and how do you think it relates to other types of power operating in different contexts, such as the economy or politics? How would you use the various theories of power that we have examined so far to account for differing explanations for the workings of the advertising and public relations industry?

Class and the Australian state—Raewyn Connell

Before examining Connell's extension of Gramsci's ideas in relation to Australian society, it is important to identify Connell's concept of the ruling class and the role of the state bureaucracy. Connell understood the ruling class very specifically as those who live off the profits generated by the ownership of property, defined broadly to include 'profits of personal entrepreneurship; dividends, rents and interest; and corporate profit appropriated as salaries' (1977, p. 51). Connell recognised leading public servants and politicians as being among the most powerful people in the country, with their decisions affecting most people in more serious ways than the executives of leading private corporations (1977, p. 56). However, their base of power, the resources they mobilise to exercise their power, is fundamentally different from those of leading capitalists: their power base is their legal and administrative authority, rather than the power arising from ownership of property. Connell argued that the exercise of power by politicians and bureaucrats, despite the extensive impact it has, is nonetheless 'superimposed on a social dynamic whose roots lie elsewhere' (1977, p. 59).

Because of this difference in the power sources of politicians and bureaucrats on the one hand and business leaders on the other, Connell did not see them as part of the same ruling class or power elite. For her, the ruling class remained that group whose power derives from the private ownership of property (1977, p. 57). The term 'ruling class', Connell argued, does 'not imply "rule" in the sense of executive control (no one, and no group, rules a capitalist society in that sense)'. Instead, the term was intended to refer to 'a collective domination, the maintenance of an institutional structure within which the class appropriates benefits, the choking off of alternatives—the only sense in which a *class* can intelligently be said to rule' (1977, p. 58).

Most importantly, Connell did not see the power of state bureaucrats as competing with, or undermining, that of private capitalists. In Connell's later work with Terry Irving, she referred to the similarity in social background of leading politicians, bureaucrats and business leaders, and the movement and interaction between the upper echelons of the various elites. There is, argued Connell and Irving, 'enough common outlook to make the idea of this being a *competing* social system absurd' (1980, p. 84).

Australian hegemony

Connell began by arguing that Gramsci's concept of hegemony related best to particular social historical situations, and that it was necessary to extend his concepts in order to analyse highly industrialised societies with well-developed working-class movements. Connell also thought it necessary to examine other mechanisms of control that had been identified by writers after Gramsci—in particular, Wilhelm Reich, Herbert Marcuse and Louis Althusser.

Hegemony can be analysed at three levels, according to Connell (1977):

1. *The level of individual consciousness and social attitudes.* This is the most usual sense in which sociologists analyse ideology and the manipulation of consciousness to generate consensus. Sociological studies of the media and their role in promoting particular beliefs and attitudes provide the most striking examples. Connell gave a variety of examples of 'ideological warfare' in Australian history, including the construction and treatment of the 'communist threat', which helped to keep ideas about alternatives to capitalism off the political agenda.
2. *The level of unconscious mental processes.* Connell referred in particular to the development of unconscious 'threat schema'—that is, apprehensions of external dangers and threats that then justify particular political arrangements. Such unconscious ideas had been analysed by Reich in his study of the psychological foundations of German fascism, and Marcuse in his analysis of the American working class's lack of interest in social change. These 'threat schema' can operate at two different 'degrees' of unconsciousness: a relatively accessible level where the ideas are unconscious in the sense that they are implicit or inferred, and a less accessible level where they are associated with more powerful emotions. Connell gave the example of the emotive power and effectiveness of ALP leader Arthur Calwell entertaining Labor Party gatherings in 1966 with images of Chinese junks and sampans invading Australia at the same time that realistic discussions of Chinese military capability got little coverage or response. More recent examples could include former American President Ronald Reagan and his portrayal of the former Soviet Union as the 'evil empire', the depiction by former British Prime Minister Margaret Thatcher and the British media of the 'heroic' battle against Argentina in the 1982 Falklands War, the characterisation of Saddam Hussein or the image of terrorists.

   Connell also mentioned Marcuse's ideas on 'repressive desublimation', the idea that the effect of the loosening of social restrictions can be to render social control more effective, because the desires set free actually feed into a greater demand for consumer goods, and channel energy and interest away from changing the social order. Mass consumerism also has a particular gender order built into it, promoting the consumption of goods operating in the public sphere for men (cars, travel), and goods operating in the private sphere for women (fashion, cosmetics, domestic goods). However, Connell pointed out that this process can have counter-hegemonic effects: for example, sexual liberation laid much of the foundations of the contemporary women's movement (p. 213).
3. *The level of the practical, material structuring of everyday life and routine interactions.* Connell referred to Althusser's work on ideology 'as a system of social practices, as regular patterns of action by which people are constrained' (p. 208).

   Pursuing the example of sexual divisions, Connell argued that they are also maintained by particular material patterns of interaction, 'a division of labor that is most clearly expressed in the daily life of suburban households where the wife-mother stays at home and does the housework and child care while the husband-father drives off to a paid job' (p. 215).

   Equally influential is the structure of housing and the material organisation of urban life (or, in Australia's case, suburban life), which has a range of effects on people's attitudes to social stability and change: 'To buy the "little piece of earth with a house and a garden" that former Australian Prime Minister Robert Menzies apostrophised in a famous wartime speech normally sent a man into debt for most of his working lifetime. To fill the house with appliances and buy the car that derisory public transport often made necessary meant a further debt load. Merely to sustain the basic way of life the husband was locked into his job' (p. 216). The wife was still locked into unpaid household labour (with a slowly growing tendency to add a part-time or unskilled job to it), now in a situation where the labour was much more isolated than in the higher diversity inner districts.

For Connell, the status division between workers, which Weberian writers draw attention to, was part of the mechanism of hegemony, producing a cultural segmentation of the working class that undermines their perception of themselves as a class and redirects their activities towards the maintenance and improvement of their status position (p. 217).

Intellectuals and counter-hegemony

Connell followed Gramsci in regarding intellectuals (broadly defined) as central to both the maintenance and erosion of hegemony. She drew particular attention to teachers, journalists and social workers. Social workers play an important role because their work often has the effect of defining poverty and suffering as individual aberrations in the social order rather than an integral part of it (1977, p. 219).

Connell ended on an optimistic note by indicating the various forms of counter-hegemonic activity that have appeared in Australian society. The examples she referred to are opposition to the Vietnam War, the green ban movement, alternative lifestyles and the resistance still shown on occasion by some workers (strikes, sabotage); she concluded that there is always the possibility of resistance to hegemony (pp. 221–2).

Reflective question: Explain Gramsci's concept of hegemony and give examples using Connell's work.

POWER AND THE SELF

In addition to Parsons' arguments for a 'variable-sum' concept of power, there are also other critiques of the 'zero-sum' concept, which revolve around seeing power as a *social relationship*, rather than a 'thing' that some people, groups or institutions possess to a greater or lesser degree. The problem with the 'zero-sum' concept is that people who are powerless do not simply exist as objects of the powerful. In reality, they continue to act and have agency, so that even domination is a process of interaction. Georg Simmel made this point eloquently in 1908:

Within a relationship of subordination, the exclusion of all spontaneity whatever is actually rarer than is suggested by such widely used popular expressions as 'coercion', 'having no choice', 'absolute necessity', etc. Even in the most oppressive and cruel cases of subordination there is still a considerable measure of personal freedom ... Interaction ... exists even in those cases of superordination and subordination ... where according to popular notions the 'coercion' by one party deprives the other of every spontaneity, and therefore of every real 'effect' of contribution to the process of interaction. (Simmel 1971, pp. 97–8)

Anthony Giddens echoed this approach in an argument for the concept of a 'dialectic of control'. He wrote that 'all relations of autonomy and dependence are reciprocal; however wide the asymmetrical distribution of resources involved, all power relations express autonomy and dependence "in both directions"' (Giddens 1982, p. 39). Even the powerless or 'less powerful' have some agency and play their own particular role in the operation of power relationships.

THE CIVILISING PROCESS— NORBERT ELIAS

Like Weber, the German sociologist Norbert Elias also thought that human psychology had been tending towards a self-disciplined, methodical and calculative mode of conduct. However, he had a different explanation. For Elias it was changes in the nature of social relationships, in social figurations, that produce different forms of behaviour, different personality structures. As functional differentiation increases, the sheer number of people each individual is interconnected with also increases.

As more and more people must attune their conduct to that of others, the web of actions must be organized more and more strictly and accurately, if each individual action is to fulfil its social function. The individual is compelled to regulate his conduct in an increasingly differentiated, more even and more stable manner ... the more complex and stable control of conduct is increasingly instilled in the individual from his earliest years as an automatism, a self-compulsion that he cannot resist even if he consciously wishes to. (1994, p. 445)

The foresight required by this increasing interdependency in turn makes it necessary for every individual to develop increasing constraint of their drives, impulses and affects. Increasing social interdependence thus produces a development from external to internal constraint, or a 'social constraint towards self-restraint', which becomes part of human personality structure: 'The web of actions grows so complex and extensive, the effort required to behave "correctly" within it becomes so great, that beside the individual's conscious self-control, an automatic, blindly functioning apparatus of self-control is firmly established' (1994, pp. 445–6). Elias referred to this long-term process as the *civilising process*.

Power, ladies and gentlemen, is understood today in everyday speech as if it were something that one owns, that one could put in one's pocket, so to speak, like a coin or a piece of soap. But power is nothing of the kind. Power, ladies and gentlemen, is a relationship. We really need language which is much more detached and differentiated to express the fact that power always consists in a relationship of balance between control and dependence, and not only in extreme cases when one side has total superiority. (2008, pp. 136-7)

The 'motive force' of the change in personality structure 'is provided ... by pressures arising out of the manifold intertwining of human activities ... bringing about shifts in the form of relationships and in the whole social fabric' (1994, p. 518). Elias thus saw a fairly direct, unmediated relationship between a particular social figuration and the personality structures of its members. He wrote that 'to an increasing degree, the complex functioning of Western societies, with their high division of labour, depends on the lower agrarian and urban strata controlling their conduct increasingly through insight into its more long-term and more remote connections' (1994, p. 459). Elias regarded social conditions in themselves as explaining the change in personality and behaviour, in particular the development towards increasing self-discipline and the subjection of emotional life to a calculative rationality. For Elias the question of why behaviour and emotions change 'is really the same as the question of why their forms of life change' (1994, p. 168).

Court society—representational power

For Elias, the logic of many aspects of contemporary power relations can be seen as rooted in the emergence of the aristocracy and court society from the Middle Ages onwards. 'By studying the structure of court society and seeking to understand one of the last great non-bourgeois figurations of the West', argued Elias, 'we indirectly gain increased understanding of our own professional-bourgeois, urban-industrial society' (Elias 1983, p. 40). Elias added to Weber's list of different types of action and rationality that of 'courtly rationality' as a precursor to, and foundation for, legal–rational rationality.

Elias pointed out that among the bourgeoisie the means of exercising power revolves around the acquisition of predominantly *economic* capital, whereas in court society power revolved around the acquisition of *symbolic* capital, status and prestige, often at the expense of economic capital.

> *Bourgeois-industrial rationality is generated by the compulsion of the economic mesh; by it power-opportunities founded on private or public capital are made calculable. Court rationality is generated by the compulsion of the elite social mesh; by it people and prestige are made calculable as instruments of power. (1983, p. 111)*

In court society, individual existence and identity were profoundly *representational*—they consisted of how one exhibited one's position and status to everyone else, and this process of exhibition and performance was highly competitive and constantly fluctuating. There was no real division between public and private life—one's public position was heavily dependent on all aspects of one's relations with others. Behaviour at any time and place could decide a person's place in society, could mean social success or failure, and 'society encompassed the whole being of its members' (Elias 1983, p. 115). This is in contrast to Weber's argument about the 'impersonal' character of bureaucracy.

The operation of this type of power relationship demanded continuous observation of both others and one's self, as well as the constantly fluctuating relations between various members of court society. One observed others in order to ascertain their true motives and desires, but also, more importantly, to search for any point of leverage to gain some advantage over them. The superiority of one's position was heavily dependent on how one displayed that superiority to subordinates.

> *[La Bruyère said:] 'A man who know the court is master of his gestures, of his eyes and of his face; he is profound, impenetrable; he dissimulates bad offices, smiles at his enemies, controls his irritation, disguises his passions, belies his heart, speaks and acts against his feelings'. (Elias 1983, p. 105)*

Authenticity was to be avoided at all costs, for it simply gave competitors advantages in the constant struggle for psychological dominance. Social status was dependent on the extent to which others recognised it, and unless one was in a structurally central position, such as the king, it disappeared when that recognition evaporated. The king's superiority lay in the fact that 'each individual noble depended on the king far more than the king depended on each individual noble' and 'there was always a "reserve army" of nobles from which he could pick a replacement' (Elias 1983, p. 207). As a *collective* entity the nobility could usurp the king, but their competition with each other constantly undermined such a possibility, to the advantage of the central actor managing the tensions among them, the king, who would assist this or that group in their competition with one another. 'The king', wrote Elias, 'appeared over and again as the ally and helped of each class or corporation against the threats from other groups which they could not master on their own' (1983, p. 168). But even Louis XIV, the Sun King, 'proves on closer scrutiny to be an individual who was enmeshed ... in a specific network of interdependencies'. The power of kings was not a possession that simply lay 'in' themselves, for they could preserve their power 'only by a carefully calculated strategy which was governed by the peculiar structure of court society in the narrow sense, and more broadly by society at large' (1983, p. 3).

Court society 'was shot through with the countless rivalries of people trying to preserve their position by marking it off from those below while at the same time improving it by reducing the demarcation from those above' (1983, p. 76). It was the competition between various social groups for advantages over others that generated both the willingness to submit to the demands of etiquette and the process of 'courtisation', where the body, emotions and desires were increasingly subjected to stringent controls and ever more demanding forms of self-discipline. Competition also drove the spread of many aspects of courtly rationality first to the higher bourgeois strata, in their attempts to enter court society, and then in turn to the strata below them.

For Elias, much of the dynamics of court society can still be seen in social interaction today, with power and status heavily dependent on adept display, performance and representation.

Power and meetings

The Dutch sociologist Wilbert van Vree has given a useful example of how Elias' ideas can be utilised by highlighting the role of meetings in embodying the 'social constraint towards self-restraint' that Elias outlined. As well as developing general behavioural prescriptions, for example, the Protestant church once organised its members' behaviour through a strict set of meeting rules, which were 'aimed at the development of more comprising and stricter discipline during meetings than most people of the middle and lower classes were used to until that time' (van Vree 1999, p. 288). Everyday life outside the church might be turbulent, but 'the Protestant church bound its members to act, talk or think in a less violent manner during meetings' (p. 288).

The historical development of meetings as a central aspect of interaction within and between organisations can thus be seen as 'an aspect of the long-term process of social interdependency':

> Meetings in which people talk with each other about changes in their mutual relations and decide what they are to do are 'nodal points' of plans and intentions of individual people. The development of meetings can be considered and further investigated as a process in which people, via orientation to ever-longer, stable and more differentiated chains of action, constrain each other towards control of their mutual relations and thus also of their selves. (1999, p. 281)

Meetings thus play a key role in the operation of power in everyday life in contemporary societies. They function as the arena where individuals are encouraged to coordinate their activities with others in their 'network of interdependency'. In the first place this coordination takes place with those people the individuals are in direct contact with. However, each meeting is itself a part of a larger network of meetings, all of which are interrelated with each other, and which constantly intensify and make more complex the demands and expectations placed on individuals to regulate their emotions and behaviour so as to better coordinate with an ever-expanding network of social interdependencies.

Reflective question: Meetings have been used here as an example of Elias' concept of the civilising process and its role in the exercise of power. Can you think of other examples? What role does anger management, for example, play in the operation of power?

A micro-ritual theory of power— Randall Collins

Although Randall Collins (2004) does not refer to Elias, he has gone on to argue in a very similar way that power emerges from within groups and, more specifically, from the process of their face-to-face interaction. This approach draws attention to the ways in which power is *created* in addition to the way it is used or mobilised. Collins draws explicitly on Durkheim's analysis of the motivating power of religious rites as well as Goffman's focus on the rules and forms governing everyday life. Collins suggests that successful interactions, including in everyday life, are rituals that empower the members of groups. They give them a sense of belonging, being valued and being important. He calls this 'emotional energy'. Even a conversation can give people an emotional charge. According to Collins, powerful groups are often characterised by a repertoire of ongoing interaction rituals that manufacture this energy.

We see this in armies in activities like parades, in sports teams where there are half-time pep talks and high fives, and in academic life where currently fashionable theories are supported by cliques who engage in intensive discussion. The creation of this kind of energy and power requires entrepreneurial individuals, like social movement leaders, to provide a driving force and organisational focus, by organising events and gatherings where emotional energy is created through intensive human interaction. The absence of this kind of energy creation, in contrast, can be seen as an example of powerlessness.

Collins also analyses the distribution of power more broadly. He argues that it is important to examine the operation of power in ordinary social interaction, which does not always lend itself to analysis in terms of broad categories such as class, race or gender. What is very often important in everyday life, for example, is the boundary between 'insiders' and 'outsiders'. In places like high schools and nightclubs, interactions and power relations are organised around the shifting border between those cliques who are 'cool' and part of the 'in' crowd and those who are not. Such cliques, argues Collins, can be seen everywhere, including in business, politics, the church and the world of academia. Power relations are, for Collins, to a large extent about people seeking membership of cliques that confer status rewards and high levels of emotional energy. They want to be in physical co-presence with people characterised by high status and high emotional energy, and to engage in rewarding interaction rituals with them. The status of such groups depends on their exclusivity—the maintenance of a boundary around the ritually integrated group—so that individuals are constantly struggling for admission and pursuing strategies to settle for lower status interactions, or trying to set up new counter-rituals.

KNOWLEDGE, DISCIPLINE AND GOVERNMENT— MICHEL FOUCAULT

Since the late 1970s a central influence on sociological approaches to power has been the studies of the French philosopher Michel Foucault on the history of prisons, psychiatric institutions and sexuality, as well as social and political thought generally. His work has played a central role in rethinking power in at least three key respects:

- encouraging an understanding of power as closely linked with the production of *knowledge*, and with developing ways of thinking, talking and writing about people and social relations, which can be referred to collectively as *discourses*
- moving sociological research away from seeing power as a *capacity* that individuals, groups or institutions 'have' more or less of, and towards regarding it more as a *relation*, with different power relations displaying both similarities and differences in disparate social contexts
- moving away from seeing power simply in terms of coercion and restriction, and including an understanding of power as *enabling* people to do particular things.

Knowledge, discourses and power

For Foucault, the formation of *persons*, of *subjectivity*, within relations of *power*, is an essential part of the development of modern societies. He saw the characteristics of various forms of scientific knowledge and their construction of 'truth' about human beings as constituting a form of power, and this was why he saw it as important to undertake what he called an 'archaeology' of knowledge. His aim was:

> *To determine, in its diverse dimensions, what the mode of existence of discourses and particularly of scientific discourses (their rules of formation, with their conditions, their dependencies, their transformations) must have been in Europe since the seventeenth century, in order that the knowledge which is ours today could come to exist, and, more particularly, that knowledge which has taken as its domain this curious object which is man. (1991, p. 70)*

Foucault saw the nature of the various forms of knowledge or discourses about human beings—medicine, psychology, psychiatry, sociology, law, education, theology and so on—as laying the foundation for political authority and as having social effects. Such discourses should not, for Foucault, be seen as simply a reflection or expression of what they refer to—human beings—but as actually constructing or constituting what it means to be a human being. For example, our actual psychological experiences are transformed over time in association with the bodies of scientific knowledge produced about human psychology; it makes a difference whether we call an experience 'madness' or 'mental illness', 'vice' or 'child abuse'. The point of this kind of analysis was to challenge:

1. the power that discourses wield over human life, by analysing their rules of formation and demonstrating their contingent nature
2. the notion of original or fundamental aspects of human life, such as 'freedom' or 'the individual', because power is organised around such concepts.

Foucault's examination of the rules of formation of various authoritative discourses, and their relations to each other and to their objects—the human body, psyche, social relations—fits within a general 'constructivist' perspective in sociology which emphasised the *constitutive* role of knowledge.

The history of sexuality

One major example that Foucault (1978) uses is the discourse surrounding *sexuality*. The most widely held assumption in Western societies is that sexuality stands in an *oppositional* relation to society—for example, Freud's opposition of the 'pleasure' to the 'reality principle'. Sex is seen as 'natural', requiring 'restraint' or 'repression'. The implication is that the more sex is released from this repression, the more truly free or liberated we become. As Foucault put it, the new discourse surrounding sexuality around the beginning of the 20th century said:

> Our sexuality, unlike that of others, is subjected to a regime of repression so intense as to present a constant danger; not only is sex a formidable secret ... not only must we search it out for the truth it conceals, but if it carries with it so many dangers, this is because ... we have too long reduced it to silence. (1978, pp. 128–9)

The idea around which this discourse was organised was referred to by Foucault as the *repressive hypothesis*.

However, Foucault argues that this notion of sexual 'liberation' was born of the middle classes' attempts in the 19th century to generate a symbolic 'sexual body' in their own image. These attempts were later given intellectual support by doctors, social workers, psychoanalysts and so on, especially in the 1920s and 1930s as Freud's work gained in influence. 'This whole "sexual revolution", this whole "anti-repressive" struggle', argued Foucault, was 'nothing more, but nothing less ... than a tactical shift and reversal in the great deployment of sexuality' (1978, p. 131). Sexual 'liberation' was thus itself a technique of power relations, a means by which power relations could operate deep within us. The discourse of sexual liberationists presents sex as something authentically 'natural' and essential, thereby drawing attention away from its *social* production and social organisation. Rather than revealing the 'truth' of sexuality, then, what the discourse surrounding sex does is *construct* sex, and indeed the whole of our lives, in a very particular way, a way that Foucault argued integrates us very firmly within established relations of power.

Modern individuality and power

Foucault distinguished between two overall historical developments in Western social and political life:

1. an increasing centralisation of political power in the state
2. a corresponding emergence of technologies (techniques) of power oriented towards individuals.

His emphasis was on the latter, because he felt that concentration on the state as a central source of power has led to a neglect of the finer networks of power that have spread throughout society. These finer networks of power would also tend to be reproduced at the micro-level if political change occurs only at the level of the state. We cannot understand contemporary society or our own lives, Foucault argued, unless we closely examine not state or class or corporate power, and not the working class or the people or the ruling class, but hospitals, schools, prisons, armies and factories, and patients, children, criminals, conscripts and workers. He argued for a closer examination of the real location of the everyday exercise of power, in seemingly mundane and ordinary practices.

One of Foucault's objectives, then, was to establish a critique of the way modern societies control and discipline their populations through the **human sciences**—medicine, psychiatry, psychology, criminology, sociology and so on, and the institutional practices associated with them. He argued that these human sciences have changed radically the way in which social power operates and helped institute a new regime of power, a **disciplinary society**.

In his studies of the history of social thought, prisons and the treatment of insanity ('madness'), he suggested that, until the 18th century, the exercise of power was based on a rather loose **discipline** at the micro-level: habitual rules and customary routines operated with little more than intermittent coercion. Political interventions were dramatic but infrequent—like the dramatic opening section of his book *Discipline and Punish* (1977):

> On 2 March 1757 Damiens the regicide was condemned 'to make the amende honorable before the main door of the Church of Paris', where he was to be 'taken and conveyed in a cart, wearing nothing but a shirt, holding a torch of burning wax weighing two pounds'; then, 'in the said cart, to the Place de Grève, where, on a scaffold that will be erected there, the flesh will be torn from his breasts, arms, thighs and calves with red-hot pincers, his right hand, holding the knife with which he committed the said parricide, burnt with sulphur, and, on those places where the flesh will be torn away, poured molten lead, boiling oil, burning resin, wax and sulphur melted together and then his body drawn and quartered by four horses and his limbs and body consumed by fire, reduced to ashes and his ashes thrown to the winds'.
>
> 'Finally he was quartered' ... 'This last operation was very long, because the horses used were not accustomed to drawing; consequently, instead of four, six were needed; and when that did not suffice, they were forced, in order

to cut off the wretche's thighs, to sever the sinews and hack at the joints'. (p. 3)

The point of this kind of public punishment and extreme cruelty was to make royal power very visible, and thus to work in an *exemplary* way to enforce the law, even though most criminals would, in practice, be able to escape its operation. In this context power was exercised primarily in a *negative* fashion, to restrict and confine the population within certain limits.

From around the 16th century onwards, suggested Foucault, the ways in which power has been exercised has gradually changed to a more *positive* form, in which there are attempts to produce certain long-term effects within individuals—for example, education, rehabilitation in prisons, pastoral care in the church and so on. In the traditional form of exercising power, the 'light' shines on the sovereign and his or her subjects are in the shade; but in the operation of modern, disciplinary power the 'light' is thrown onto the sovereign's subjects as individuals, so that everyone becomes a potential or actual case for observation and analysis. Foucault emphasised that it is precisely *through* individualisation that power is exercised, rather than individuality being a source of opposition to powerful individuals or organisations.

Disciplinary power

Foucault stated that what made **disciplinary power**, as opposed to **sovereign power**, distinct was that:

this form of power cannot be exercised without knowing the inside of people's minds, without exploring their souls, without making them reveal their innermost secrets. It implies a knowledge of the conscience and an ability to direct it. (1982, p. 214)

He connected this argument with what had been said about sexuality by theorists such as Wilhelm Reich, who assumed that power was exercised over sexuality through its repression (repression hypothesis). Foucault argues in *The History of Sexuality* (1978) that, in fact, sexuality in a certain form is positively encouraged and produced in modern society. Consequently, we cannot escape sex; it permeates all aspects of our lives, individual and social, and we are constantly urged to *confess* our 'real' sexual natures, although they are only allowed to fall within specific parameters—outside of these it becomes 'perversion'.

Foucault argued that it was primarily in the course of the 18th century that 'discipline'—the methods of observation, recording, calculation, regulation and systematic training, which had already been in operation in monasteries, armies and factories—became what he called a 'general formula' throughout society. The new methods provided a means of mutual influence that extended throughout society further and more effectively than the previous, more negative forms of power. For example, the school not only produced trained and docile children, but also was a means of supervising parents. The manifest function of the school may have been the training of children, but in so doing it also extended a form of supervision over their parents, gathering information on their morality, material resources and lifestyles. This is what Foucault means when he says that disciplinary strategies 'spread' throughout the social body.

Foucault's primary concern was with a particular *style* of exercising power, rather than particular institutions or 'sites' of power. 'Discipline', he wrote, 'may be identified neither with an institution nor with an apparatus; it is a type of power ... comprising a whole set of instruments, techniques, procedures, levels of application, targets; it is a "physics" or an "anatomy" of power, a technology' (1977, p. 215). His emphasis was on the 'ordinariness' and dispersal of power, making it all the more difficult to change its operation:

Power relations are rooted deep in the social nexus, not reconstituted 'above' society as a supplementary structure whose radical effacement one could perhaps dream of ... A society without power relations can only be an abstraction. (1982, pp. 222–3)

The focus of his analysis, then, was on *how* the various strategies of power actually operated. The model he used to demonstrate one of the strategies was that of the prison design developed by Jeremy Bentham, the panopticon (see Figure 12.1):

[It] consists of a large courtyard, with a tower in the center, surrounded by a series of buildings divided into levels and cells. In each cell there are two windows: one brings in light and the other faces the tower, where large observatory windows allow for the surveillance of the cells. The inmate ... is visible to the supervisor alone. (Rabinow 1984, p. 19)

This new form of power is uniquely *individualising* and *continuous*. Even when there is no supervisor present, the inmate *thinks* that the supervisor is there, constantly observing. Foucault's argument was that the discipline of a prison, an army, a factory, a school or a hospital represents a continuation and an intensification of what goes on in everyday life—in fact it would not be possible if it didn't. So the panopticon is a metaphor for the ways in which our lives are organised in modern society from one day to the next, from the cradle to the grave—what other writers have called the 'administered society'.

Although Foucault spoke of the disciplinary society, he did not assume that a disciplined society has, in fact, come about. He gave two reasons for this:

1. The existence of disciplinary strategies does not necessarily imply their *realisation*. In fact, the history of strategies of the more rational control and management of people and their relationships is more often characterised by their failure to realise their aims, or by the achievement of completely different aims.
2. There is also *resistance* to disciplinary strategies and techniques, which contributes to the lack of correspondence between aims and effects, although Foucault did not explain what the source of this resistance is.

Governmentality

Although this discipline-resistance approach to power is the aspect of Foucault's work that has received the greatest attention in social research, Foucault eventually felt it was insufficient in itself because, as many of its critics had said, it tended to encourage a view of power simply as domination over individuals. Above all, his conception of disciplinary power did not account for the place of individual freedom.

In the late 1970s Foucault suggested using the concepts of government, governmentality or governmental rationality as a way of capturing the linkage between power and freedom. He suggested that forms of governmental power link the disciplinary strategies of various organisations, the knowledge produced about human beings by the human sciences, and the active projects and independent strategies of individuals and groups. Foucault roughly equated governmental rationality with liberal political thought, and contrasted it with the earlier concepts of police, cameralism or sovereignty as a central principle for the organisation of society.

In 16th- and early 17th-century political thought, the aim was to extend the state's management of society (at various levels) to the maximum possible. In this understanding of the 'Reason of State', which Foucault also called the model of sovereignty, governing was modelled on family life, with the relations between rulers and their subjects equated with those between a patriarch and his family, aimed at the achievement of a unified common good.

However, towards the end of the 16th century the liberal argument developed that greater prosperity and stability would be achieved by a different style of ruling—one where families were the instrument rather than the model of government. This conception of government has a dual significance for Foucault. First, it concerns the government of 'things' rather than 'subjects'.

> *The things with which ... government is to be concerned are ... men in their relations, their links, their imbrication with those other things which are wealth, resources, means of subsistence, the territory with its specific qualities, climate, irrigation, fertility, etc.; men in their relation to that other kind of things, customs, habits, ways of acting and thinking, etc.; lastly, men in their relation to that other kind of things, accidents, and misfortunes such as famine, epidemics, death, etc. (1979, p. 11)*

Liberal government deals with relations between subjects and their material world, then, rather than simply with subjects themselves.

Second, the notion of 'convenience implies a plurality of specific aims' rather than a single 'common good' (Foucault 1979). 'Convenience' is the mediating concept that allows the widest possible variety of individuals, groups, and organisational and state strategies to be linked together and coordinated around aims such as

FIGURE 12.1

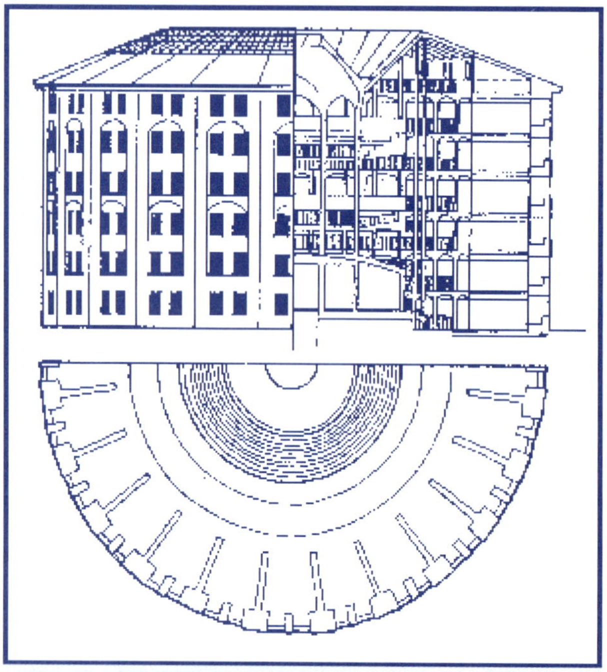

Prison design developed by Jeremy Bentham, the panopticon *Source:* Bentham Papers, UCL Library Services, Special Collections. Reprinted with permission.

prosperity, health, stability, moral virtue, some regional or national identity or a combination, and wellbeing. Government could thus be regarded as a linking concept, tying together all 'techniques and procedures designed to direct the conduct of men. Government of children, government of souls or of consciences, government of a home, of a state, or of oneself' (cited in Keenan 1982, p. 37). Foucault argued that the historical shift to liberalism constituted a shift to the organisation of state and society around the **disciplined autonomy** of subjects (citizens), rather than simply their 'discipline'.

The apparent independence of demographic and economic dynamics from sovereign action meant that it seemed necessary to manage those processes by making the aim of government the welfare, health, wealth and moral virtue of the population, rather than the simple maintenance of sovereign power. Rather than simply ruling populations, bodies of citizens and so on, state authorities shifted their attention to processes within the population itself. As well as continuing to act directly on the population through, say, educational campaigns, governments began acting 'indirectly through techniques that will make possible, without the full awareness of the people, the stimulation of birth rates, the directing of the flow of population into certain regions or activities, etc.' (Foucault 1979, p. 18). Populations become both the subject of needs and aspirations and the object of governmental rationality, 'aware, vis-à-vis the government, of what it wants, but ignorant of what is being done to it' (1979, p. 18).

The management of demographic and economic processes also relied on the provision of knowledge about them. The emergence of disciplines such as political economy and sociology was thus an essential aspect of the governmentalisation of state and society, for it was only with the knowledge of economic, social and demographic processes that state authorities could begin to act upon them.

Foucault contrasted a relationship of violence, coercion or domination with one of power. A relationship of violence 'acts upon a body or upon things; it forces, it bends, it breaks on the wheel, it destroys, or it closes the door on all possibilities. Its opposite pole can only be passivity, and if it comes up against any resistance it has no other option but to try to minimize it' (1982, p. 220). A relationship of power, on the other hand, 'is a mode of action which does not act directly and immediately on others. Instead it acts upon their actions', on both present action and possible future action. Power thus depends on the recognition of those over whom power is exercised as possessing agency, and then on the opening up of 'a whole field of responses, reactions, results, and possible inventions' (1982, p. 220).

Government takes place 'where the way individuals are driven by others is tied to the way they conduct themselves'. It is 'not a way to force people to do what the governor wants; it is always a versatile equilibrium, with complementarity and conflicts between techniques which assure coercion and processes through which the self is constructed or modified by himself' (cited in Keenan 1982, p. 38). Government concerns the structuring of 'the possible field of action of others'. Governmental power, argued Foucault, 'is exercised only over free subjects, and only insofar as they are free'.

By this we mean individual or collective subjects who are faced with a field of possibilities in which several ways of behaving, several reactions and diverse comportments may be realized ... In this game freedom may well appear as the condition for the exercise of power (at the same time its precondition, since freedom must exist for power to be exerted, and also its permanent support, since without the possibility of recalcitrance, power would be equivalent to a physical determination). (1982, p. 221)

Government thus presumes rather than undermines both freedom and resistance, and works through freely chosen human agency, by coordinating, linking, setting frameworks and establishing rules of action. Governmental rationality depends on the active participation of the governed in their own government, even their resistance.

Foucault was not simply arguing, as Weber did, that freedom and bureaucracy are linked in the sense that the rational self-discipline expands our realm of possible action, but made the stronger point that government and social discipline presupposes and works on the basis of free human agency. As Ian Hunter has put it for schooling, the object of 'pastoral pedagogy' characterising Christian schools from about the 17th century onwards, and which is still a central aspect of contemporary schooling, 'was not to produce docile workers or social automatons ... it was to form the capacities required for individuals to comport themselves as self-reflective and self-governing persons' (1994, p. 57).

Foucault illustrated this argument by looking at the concerns of most contemporary political struggles; he identified the women's movement, anti-psychiatry, critiques of medicine and critiques of parental authority over children. All these forms of political opposition are concerned, he argued, with similar techniques of governmental power, a particular form of power that 'applies itself to immediate everyday life which categorizes the individual, marks him by his own personality, attaches him to his own identity, imposes a law of truth on him which he must recognize and which others have to recognize in him' (1982, p. 212). Foucault identified two possible meanings of the word *subject*: 'subject to someone else by control and dependence, and tied to his own identity by a conscience or self-knowledge. Both meanings suggest a form of power which subjugates and makes subject to' (1982, p. 212). Resistance to power in itself thus does not guarantee escape from its workings, because the subjective identity around which resistance can be organised can itself be a basis of governmental power.

As far as the role of the intellectual and analyst of power is concerned, Foucault believed that power relations are characteristic of all societies, and that striving for 'freedom' from power was an illusion. But this does not mean that the exact form that power relations take is somehow necessary, or that we should simply resign ourselves to their constant presence. Instead, he wrote, 'I would say that the analysis, elaboration, and bringing into question of power relations and the "agonism" between power relations and the intransitivity of freedom is a permanent political task inherent in all social existence' (1982, pp. 222–3). In other words, he urged constant analysis and resistance to power without ever assuming that one can actually transcend it or escape *some* form of power relation. The issue for Foucault was not whether or not power relations exist, but the particular *form* that they take.

> **Reflective question:** What aspects of the operation of power relations are captured by Foucault's conception of government? Give examples.

POWER AS EFFECT—BRUNO LATOUR

The French sociologist Bruno Latour (1986) also argues against the 'zero-sum' concept of power by making a distinction between a 'diffusion' model of power and a 'translation' model of power. In the diffusion model, a person or group is endowed with power that enables them to diffuse their will—in the form of what Latour calls a 'token', orders, claims or artefacts—throughout the surrounding social space, which is regarded as a medium with greater or lesser resistance, such as poor conviction, inertia, opposing interests and so on. The existence of power is explained in terms of the power of those who possess it, with the objects of that power acting only to transmit it (through obedience) or to resist it. Latour argues against this way of thinking about power by observing that the 'medium' of this transmission of power—the individuals upon which it acts—are not a medium at all, but constitute the very stuff of whatever is happening. They are all doing something essential for the existence and maintenance of power, and they all 'shape it according to their different projects' (p. 268). As he puts it:

> *'Power' is always the illusion people get when they are obeyed; thinking in terms of the diffusion model, they imagine that others behave because of the master's clout without ever suspecting the many different reasons others have for obeying and doing something else; more exactly, people who are 'obeyed' discover what their power is really made of when they start to lose it. They realise, but too late, that it was 'made of the wills of all the others'. (pp. 268–8)*

Power, argues Latour, is not the *cause* of the things people do, but the *consequence* or simply an aspect of them. The causes need to be sought in something more complex, namely the collision and combination of a constellation of different projects and strategies, even if they are all unequally resourced and unequally successful and effective in practice.

BEYOND THE STATE?

The work of Lukes, Gramsci, Elias, Foucault and Latour has already highlighted the extent to which we need to look beyond the state to understand the operation of power. A key example of this arena for the exercise of power is that of the changing role of social movements in contemporary politics.

NEW SOCIAL MOVEMENTS AND POSTMODERNISATION

In their book *Postmodernization*, Stephen Crook, Jan Pakulski and Malcolm Waters (1992) argue that postmodernity has been accompanied by new forms of political activity, which redefine the operation of power in contemporary social life. For Crook and his colleagues, the nature of politics has shifted from a modern to a postmodern form in the following five areas:

1. The relationship between political parties and particular socioeconomic groups has become looser and less predictable. The Australian Labor Party, for example, can no longer rely on the support of the working class, nor can the Liberal Party assume that it has the support of the middle and upper classes.

2. The relationship between socioeconomic groups and particular political issues has also become weaker. Whereas a concern for environmental issues, for example, used to be a characteristic of the middle class, now the approach to political issues cannot be 'read off' from an individual's socioeconomic position.
3. The elites of social and political groups and movements are seen less frequently as representing the interests of those groups and movements, and there is greater democratic participation by those at the 'grass roots'.
4. The state's role as the arena of political activity has become weaker, and various political groups have developed a more direct relationship with the population at large.
5. The realm of politics has become less distinct and more closely linked to other aspects of people's lives, such as their lifestyle and consumer preferences.

Overall the different aspects of people's lives—their occupation, where they live, their consumption patterns, their political and moral values—become uncoupled from each other, and social movements are driven by a much broader variety of social groups.

An important aspect of the postmodernisation of politics is the changing role of the *mass media*. Politics has become more and more about the representation of issues and positions, and less about any kind of 'reality' of a political position or practice. As Crook and his colleagues write, political issues are:

> *always contextualized, and linked with the global issues and general values, often in the form of such doom scenarios as nuclear holocaust and greenhouse disaster. This dramatizes them, adds a sense of urgency, and generates mass anxiety which proves to be an exceptionally potent propellant for action. (Crook, Pakulski & Waters, 1992, p. 156)*

The impact of the 'mediatisation' of politics, then, is to establish the links between the local and the global (see Chapter 2, p. 64) in a more dramatic and urgent way, such as in relation to global warming or poverty in developing countries, rather than political orientations being confined to immediate, directly experienced concerns.

Reflective question: Watch an episode of the ABC program *The Hollowmen* and reflect on whether this is an accurate representation of postmodern politics and the emphasis on representation and 'spin'.

Some sociologists, like Alberto Melucci (1989), believe that we are now witnessing the emergence of new types of social movement in contemporary society. These movements are said to be novel because they attempt to retain some degree of autonomy from the state and conventional political actors. They are also said to be examples of new movements in that they transcend the former preoccupation with the politics of social class—they are apparently unconcerned with the 'old' class-based politics of the past that sought to harness the political power of the state. To some extent, the older social movements, such as the labour or trade union movement, have gone a long way towards achieving this goal. The social security or welfare state is a product of the success of workers' struggles for greater rights and entitlements. In the new social movements, people are less concerned with material wellbeing and more concerned with 'post-material' issues such as self-identity, lifestyle, the environment and cultural values. Consequently, a number of social movements now focus on 'identity politics' or issues relating to gender, sexuality, environmental issues, disability, and race and ethnicity.

CRITIQUE—HOW 'NEW' IS THE NEW POLITICS?

New social movement theory has been criticised on a number of fronts. Craig Calhoun (1994) points out that the women's movement, for example, cannot be considered a new movement, since it has roots stretching back to the early 19th century. It is also argued that the novel characteristics of the new movements are features of *all* social movements during their nascent period. In other words, all social movements have a radical grassroots organisation and are distrustful of the political establishment when they start out.

In addition, critics argue that new social movement theorists have failed to recognise the multidimensional nature of past movements, which were not solely concerned with issues of class and inequality. Calhoun (1995) says the working-class movement in the 19th and early 20th centuries was not entirely unified and univocal: '[i]t did not constitute just one collective actor in a single drama. There was mobilization over women and children working, community life, the status of immigrants, education, access to public services, and so forth' (p. 179). Similarly, Tucker (1991) has shown how during the 19th century the formation of a collective identity was just as important as securing workers' rights for trade unionists who 'had shared experiences and traditions of autonomy at the work place related to their possession of skill' (p. 85).

Verity Burgmann (2003) argues that some sociologists may have been a little too hasty in their attempt to 'bail out of the ship of class' (p. 29) as the discipline's accepted concern with class became unfashionable in the 1990s. In the United Kingdom, John Westergaard (1995) argues against the idea that class structure has 'decomposed', suggesting that, far from dying, class differences became even stronger in the late 20th century. The stridency of the claims of postmodernists and politicians' rhetoric concerning the *declining* importance of class seems to be almost directly proportional to the entirely contrary objective reality of class divisions becoming *more* significant. What has declined, suggests Westergaard, is class consciousness, but not the economic realities of capitalist social inequality. As Burgmann suggests, 'the most remarkable aspect of the decline of class analysis was that it occurred at a moment in history when socio-economic inequalities were widening, in Australia as elsewhere' (p. 30).

Australian social movements and globalisation—Verity Burgmann

Verity Burgmann points out that the success of social movements has generally been measured in terms of the extent to which their concerns have been addressed by governments. However, if the nation-state is itself increasingly subject to transnational economic and political forces, this changes in a corresponding way the 'playing field' that social movements need to operate on. Whether one regards globalisation as undermining or working in tandem with the power of the state (see Chapter 2), in both approaches there is a presumption that ordinary people are relatively passive and powerless in the face of whatever transformation is taking place, and it is this presumption that a range of social movements seeks to challenge.

Burgmann restricts her study to movements for 'progressive' social change, excluding the New Right and neo-fascist movements, or anti-immigration movements. Those she regards as most significant today are:

- the Aboriginal movement, concerned with Indigenous civil rights, land rights, autonomous political identity, the Stolen Generations, improved health and reduced imprisonment
- the women's movement, engaging with issues such as equal pay and opportunity in employment, child care, abortion, education, the cultural construction of gender differences, women's sexuality and lesbianism
- the green movement, protecting the environment—forests, rivers, the sea—from unsustainable development, opposition to nuclear power, 'green' consumerism and renewable energy sources
- the anti-capitalist and anti-corporate globalisation movements—in one sense the heirs of the labour movement—opposing the increasing power of global corporations over nation-states and their citizens, and resisting the destructive effects of global free trade on social and community life, particularly as expressed in the activities of the World Trade Organization.

All of these movements, as well as challenging the supposed 'inevitability' of the processes of globalisation, are also themselves subject to globalising forces. To the extent that the nation-state has to make way for other political actors, this changes the way in which social movements are required to operate. For example, Greenpeace has to address its arguments and actions not just to governments but also directly to the corporations whose activities it seeks to modify. The forms of organisation and mobilisation characterising contemporary social movements have also been transformed, drawing on new technologies such as the internet, email and faxing to develop more extensive and faster means of communication and a wider range of strategies and tactics. Furthermore, as Burgmann observes, without completely displacing the usual forms of social movement political practice (leaflets, posters, stalls, graffiti, press conferences and lectures) 'the new technology has provided the movement with novel means to organise, mobilise and communicate its views directly to the public it seeks to influence' (2003, p. 297). For example, in Australia the internet campaigns of the organisation GetUp were instrumental in undermining the influence of neoliberalism (see Chapter 2).

Maddison and Martin (2010) consider the ways that progressive Australian social movements were restrained by neoliberalism and the neoconservative politics of the Howard Coalition Government (1996–2007). Their volume tells the story of the survival strategies (and successes) of social movements during this period. They show how some social movements accommodated or even embraced neoliberalism, but also how some resisted it, surviving via global, social and virtual networks or achieving small victories through other artful or novel means. Some movements emerged or re-emerged and subsequently flourished as a direct response to government policy, while others were adversely affected by the constraints on democratic expression and hence were suppressed, silenced or marginalised. However, as with social movements in other countries and at other times, many Australian movements operating during the Howard years tended to combine these characteristics.

Reflective question: Should we focus on the state when we think about power, or should we look further afield? Taking the latter approach, what other elements would we include in our understanding of power, and what difference would this make?

Tutorial exercise

Looking at the September 2001 attacks on the World Trade Center in New York and the actions that followed, especially the American and British invasion of Iraq (with assistance from Australia, Poland and Denmark), explain how the sequence of events can be analysed sociologically in terms of the power relationships that underpinned and drove it. For example, to what extent were the attacks on the World Trade Center the product of global power relations and attempts to realign them in particular ways?

The invasion of Iraq was subsequently justified with a range of arguments about the relationship of Saddam Hussein's regime to terrorism, as well as the need to protect the Iraqi population from his autocratic excesses. In the light of the critical accounts of these justifications that have emerged since that time, to what extent can you use the concept of hegemony to analyse the political consensus that the governments of George W. Bush, Tony Blair and John Howard achieved in their respective countries?

How could this example be approached using Lukes' concept of the three 'faces' of power? Can you see evidence of a power elite?

For activity suggestions, learning aids, revision of key concepts and access to self-study material, visit: **www.pearson.com.au/highered/vankrieken4e**

Further reading

Castells, M. 1997, *The Information Age: Economy, Society and Culture, Volume 2: The Power of Identity*, Blackwell, Oxford.

Clegg, S. 1989, *Frameworks of Power*, Sage, London.

Courpasson, D. 2006, *Soft Constraint: Liberal Organizations and Domination*, Copenhagen Business School Press, Copenhagen.

Foucault, M. 2000, *The Essential Works of Foucault 1954–1984, Vol. 3: Power*, ed. J. D. Faubion, New Press, New York, pp. 1–89.

Goldfarb, J. C. 2006, *The Politics of Small Things: The Power of the Powerless in Dark Times*, University of Chicago Press, Chicago.

Hindess, B. 1996, *Discourses of Power: From Hobbes to Foucault*, Blackwell, Oxford.

Janoski, T., Alford, R., Hicks, A. & Schwartz, M. A. (eds) 2005, *The Handbook of Political Sociology: States, Civil Societies, and Globalization*, Cambridge University Press, Cambridge.

Mann, M. 1986, *The Sources of Social Power*, Vol. 1, Cambridge University Press, Cambridge.

Mann, M. 1993, *The Sources of Social Power*, Vol. 2, Cambridge University Press, Cambridge.

McFarland, A. S. 2004, *Neopluralism: The Evolution of Political Process Theory*, University of Kansas Press, Lawrence.

Nash, K. 2000, *Contemporary Political Sociology: Globalization, Politics and Power*, Blackwell, Malden, MA.

Nash, K. & Scott, A. (eds) 2001, *The Blackwell Companion to Political Sociology*, Blackwell, Oxford.

Pusey, M. 1991, *Economic Rationalism in Canberra*, Cambridge University Press, Melbourne.

Websites

Australianpolitics.com:
www.australianpolitics.com
This site outlines the structure of the Australian political system.

Freedom House:
www.freedomhouse.org
This site critically surveys the state of democracy around the world.

Government, Law and Society:
http://eserver.org/govt/theory.html
This site has classical (Machiavelli, Hobbes, Mill) and modern (Foucault, Habermas) resources, as well as links to documents on (inter)national conflicts and liberation movements.

Political Resources on the Net:
www.politicalresources.net
This worldwide listing of political sites is sorted by country, with links to parties, organisations, governments and media.

SocioSite's Activism and Power sections:
www.sociosite.net/topics/activism.php and
www.sociosite.net/topics/power.php
These two sites have a collection of materials on a wide range of social movements and other political science resources.

The Whitlam Dismissal:
http://whitlamdismissal.com
This site is devoted to the events surrounding the dismissal of the Whitlam Government in 1975.

13

Crime and Deviance

This chapter approaches the study of crime and deviance from both a theoretical and an applied perspective. It provides a critical review of the main theories of crime, as well as the patterns and trends of crime in Australia. The chapter emphasises the connections between crime and deviance and social control, and points out that differences in power contribute to which groups are identified as criminal. Marginalised groups such as young people and Indigenous individuals are especially vulnerable to criminalisation.

By the end of this chapter, you should have a better understanding of:
— sociological arguments about the social construction of crime and deviance, including the social construction of official crime records
— the difference between biological and psychological explanations of crime and deviance and sociological explanations
— the strengths and weaknesses of the main theories of crime and deviance, including functionalist, social control and New Right theories, Marxist and New Left theories, and feminist and reintegrative shaming theories
— debates about sociology's contribution to the social construction of crime and deviance
— the sources of crime data and their limitations
— patterns and trends of crime in Australia and their social context
— the relationship between the criminal justice system, young people, women, Indigenous peoples and powerful groups such as politicians, professionals and businesspeople
— the effect of demographic changes on the future direction of crime, and the links between this and the creation of a socially divided society.

INTRODUCTION	**408**
DEFINING CRIME AND DEVIANCE	**409**
THE SOCIAL CONSTRUCTION OF OFFICIAL CRIMINAL STATISTICS	**409**
The dark figure of crime—undetected and unreported crime	409
Changing definitions of crime	410
Changing resources of law and order	410
The influence of discretionary decisions within the criminal justice system	410
THEORIES OF CRIME AND DEVIANCE	**411**
Biological and psychological theories of crime and deviance	411
Sociological theories of crime and deviance	411
Deviance—a functionalist perspective	412
Traditional functionalists	412
Anomie theory	412
The Chicago School	413
The ecology of deviance	413
The ethnography of deviance	413
Criticisms of the Chicago School	413
Social control theory	414
Wilson and Herrnstein	414
Social control theory—an assessment	415
Crime control and the New Right	415
Deviance—an interactionist perspective	416
Primary and secondary deviance—Edwin Lemert	416
Labelling theory—Howard Becker	416
Deviance amplification; moral panics and collective reactions	417
Deviance and the interactionist perspective—criticisms and evaluation	417
Deviance and power—conflict perspectives	417
Deviance—the conventional Marxist perspective	418
The second wave—neo-Marxist and 'socialist' perspectives	418
Left realism—the new reformism?	419
Feminist theories of crime and deviance	419
Women and social control—Heidensohn	419
Masculinities and the accomplishment of gender through crime—Messerschmidt	420
Feminist theory—an evaluation	420
Crime, shame and reintegration	420
THE FUTURE OF THE SOCIOLOGY OF CRIME AND DEVIANCE	**421**
PATTERNS OF CRIME IN AUSTRALIA	**422**
Crime rates in Australia over time	424
Community attitudes towards crime	426
Offenders	426
Young people and crime	428
Young people and gangs	429
Young people and the police	430
Offending women	431
Victims	432
Violence against women	433
Indigenous people and crime	433
The Royal Commission into Aboriginal Deaths in Custody	434
Crimes of the powerful	435
Class and crime	436
The costs of crimes of the powerful	437
Class and the criminal justice system	438
Tutorial exercise	440
Further reading	440
Websites	440

INTRODUCTION

In November 2004 the tropical paradise of Palm Island in Far North Queensland was the scene of violent confrontation between Indigenous individuals and the police. About 300 Indigenous people marched on the local police station, pelting the police with rocks and setting the complex on fire. The riot started after the local residents questioned the results of an autopsy conducted on the body of an Aboriginal man who had died in police custody a few days previously. The Queensland government declared a state of emergency on Palm Island, closing the airport, evacuating government personnel and calling in reinforcements, including 80 Tactical Response Group commandos armed with semiautomatic weapons. By 2 December, 28 people had been charged with 64 offences including riot, arson, being armed with intent to cause fear, serious assault on police, burglary, wilful damage and unlawful assembly.

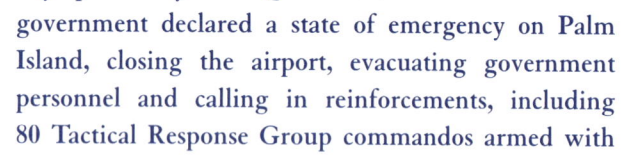

1. Look up the history of Palm Island on the internet. What contribution do you think it made to the events described above?
2. What measures could have been taken to reduce the tension between the police and local Indigenous groups following the death of the Aboriginal man?
3. Review the material on theories of crime. Which theory best explains these events?

Many people would agree that street riots are a form of deviant, sometimes criminal, behaviour. Yet many would also recognise that this is only one way of looking at the issue. The violence on Palm Island was sparked by the death in custody of an Aboriginal man whose only crime appeared to be that of being drunk on the streets. His death was one of a number of Aboriginal deaths in custody that had occurred in Palm Island over the years. Palm Island is stunningly beautiful but it is also one of the poorest regions of Queensland, with a high rate of unemployment among the local Indigenous population and a long history of conflict between blacks and whites. The riot was one of many clashes between the police and local Aborigines over the years. For some observers it was the heavy-handed actions of the police and the Queensland government that caused the problem, rather than the Indigenous population.

This example shows that what is perceived to be criminal or deviant depends on the prevailing values and norms. Deviance and crime are *socially constructed*. This understanding of the relative nature of crime and deviance is relatively recent and can be traced back to the 1960s and 1970s. Prior to that, sociologists, like the wider society, accepted official definitions of deviance and crime at face value. Those identified as 'deviant' or criminal were regarded as having done something wrong and whose behaviour needed correction and control. This was especially true of criminology, which was concerned with the search for definitive answers to social problems such as drug use and motor vehicle theft. The change towards a relative understanding of crime and deviance occurred as part of a broader understanding of the diversity that exists within human cultures, such that it is impossible to identify any absolute standards or norms. This moved the focus away from questions about how to control deviant or criminal behaviour to questions about why some social groups attract the label 'criminal' or 'deviant' and others do not. Today the political nature of the identification of crime and deviance is understood. Although crime is condemned there is also an awareness that the criminal or nonconformist of today could become tomorrow's hero or political leader.

The identification of behaviour as deviant and/or criminal is linked to issues of power and social control. This control may be official and enforced through the criminal justice code, or unofficial and imposed through informal condemnation such as gossip, ridicule and social exclusion. Some individuals and groups have the power to define behaviour as acceptable or deviant, while others have limited capacity to influence these processes of social control.

A sociological focus on crime and deviance is therefore concerned with:

- documenting the nature and extent of rule-breaking behaviour
- challenging conventional understandings about crime, such as who the criminal or deviant is, why people commit crime and deviance, and the fairness of our criminal justice system
- how understandings of crime and deviance change over time
- the relationship between crime and other aspects of a society, such as the family and the economy.

DEFINING CRIME AND DEVIANCE

Deviance can be defined as norm- or rule-breaking behaviour that is usually subject to negative social sanctions. Deviants are the nonconformists who transgress a community's normative standards and are condemned by other, influential social groups. Deviants are not necessarily minority social groups. Mental illness affects one in ten of the population, yet people with a mental illness are often regarded with suspicion by the rest of the population. Illegal drug use is widespread, yet doing drugs still attracts public disapproval and potential criminal prosecution. In some nations black individuals and families outnumber white ones, yet from a normative point of view it is the black population who are the deviants. To be deviant is therefore to violate a social norm rather than a statistical one.

Crime can be defined as behaviour that is proscribed and punishable by law. Yet crime exists only in so far as certain forms of behaviour are identified by the state as against the law. Like deviance, its existence is dependent on a community's notions of right and wrong. For this reason, some sociologists and criminologists take a broader approach to the definition of crime and include acts that harm other human beings or the environment but that do not transgress criminal codes. For example, inadequate health and safety practices may result in the death of an employee but may not violate any criminal laws.

The identification of some acts as criminal is always political because of the centrality of the role of the state. Although the media often plays a central role in debates about crime and deviance, ultimately it is the state that decides what form official reaction will take. This includes deciding what types of behaviour should be criminalised and the type and level of sanctions they attract. Because Australia has a federal political system it is possible for some behaviours to be criminalised in some states but not in others. For example, operating a brothel is a crime in Tasmania but not in Victoria.

While deviance and crime are overlapping concepts, deviance is a more inclusive concept than crime because it includes behaviour that is not proscribed by law. For example, some forms of sexual activity may break social conventions, but they may not be criminal. There are also some crimes that are not widely regarded as deviant. For example, illegal downloading of music is a criminal act but, because it is widespread, social disapproval of it is limited.

THE SOCIAL CONSTRUCTION OF OFFICIAL CRIMINAL STATISTICS

Data on crime patterns are notoriously unreliable, especially when different criminal jurisdictions make nationwide figures difficult to establish. Four factors reduce the reliability of crime data:

1. the dark figure of crime—undetected and/or unreported crime
2. changing definitions of crime
3. changing resources of law and order
4. the influence of discretionary decisions within the criminal justice system.

THE DARK FIGURE OF CRIME—UNDETECTED AND UNREPORTED CRIME

Most criminal statistics represent only a percentage of the actual incidence of that type of behaviour. The difference between the actual and the officially recorded incidence is known as the dark figure of crime and results from many crimes being undetected or unreported. Victims of cybercrime may be unaware that their computer network has been invaded. Undetected crimes usually involve property, whereas unreported crimes include both property crimes and crimes against the person. Figure 13.1 shows reporting rates for different crimes. Less than one-third of attempted break-ins and assaults are reported.

There are many reasons for low reporting rates. Victims may feel that the incident is too trivial or they may be reluctant to involve the police in what they see as a private matter, as in the case of domestic violence and among male victims of assault. Perceptions that a successful prosecution is unlikely can influence the decision not to report (such as can occur among victims of sexual assault) and intimidation can also be a factor (as can occur with child abuse victims).

FIGURE 13.1

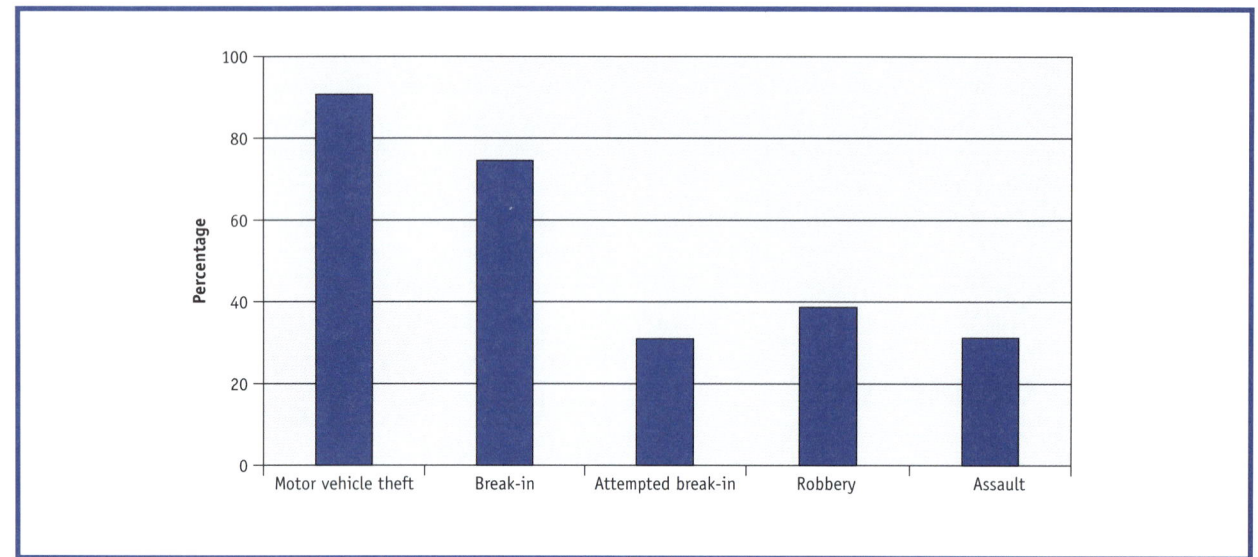

Rate of reporting to police of selected crimes, 2005 *Source:* Australian Institute of Criminology (2008, p. 48). Used with permission from Australian Institute of Criminology (AIC) 2009.

The reporting authority must also agree that a crime has been committed. Crimes such as theft, sexual assault and tax evasion may not be recorded unless there is some evidence to support the victim's claim. When a person dies or goes missing the event must be classified by the police or coroner. The 1984 shooting death of a Victorian woman, Jennifer Tanner, was treated as suicide by the police and it was only 14 years later that a second inquest returned a verdict of murder, overturning the open verdict of the original inquest.

Changing definitions of crime

The law is not static but changes over time, affecting rates of recorded crime. For example, Australian legal jurisdictions now recognise sexual assault within marriage but this has not always been the case, and this must be taken into account when compiling crime data. Definitional differences between legal jurisdictions also affect official data, especially when most criminal law is enacted at a state level. International comparisons are even more difficult.

Changing resources of law and order

Changes in the level of law enforcement influence official crime rates. Increases in police resources often increase apprehension and charge rates. Greater attention to drink-driving will draw resources away from other areas such as organised crime and be reflected in recorded crimes. Such changes cannot be accounted for methodologically, even though they affect official data.

The influence of discretionary decisions within the criminal justice system

At every point in the criminal justice process, from the reporting of a crime to prosecution and sentencing, agents of the state engage in a process of negotiation with the alleged perpetrator, victims and other state and private agents on what the official response to the original event will be. Whether or not the police make an arrest; whether someone is charged, referred to another agency or released; whether someone is placed in custody or given bail; whether plea bargaining results in a case being dropped or a lesser charge (and therefore lesser sentence) being made—are all decisions that affect the official data. The data are therefore the outcome of a social process open to variation and interpretation.

The phrase social construction of crime and deviance is a recognition of this. Criminal justice statistics are the outcome of a social process rather than an absolute reflection of the incidence of crime in the community, and this has important implications for perceptions of who is the criminal.

> **Reflective question:** In your own words, explain what is meant by the social construction of crime and deviance. Find three examples to illustrate this.

THEORIES OF CRIME AND DEVIANCE

In the past explanations of crime and deviance often drew on theological or supernatural explanations. Such explanations relied on notions of innate wickedness, humanity's fallen state, the wrath of supernatural beings and human degeneracy as the source of deviant activity. Today the idea of deviant behaviour as sin or transgression has been superseded by explanations based on secular moralities and personal character failings. Biology, medical science, personal psychology and social factors are referred to for insight into the causes of criminal and deviant behaviour.

BIOLOGICAL AND PSYCHOLOGICAL THEORIES OF CRIME AND DEVIANCE

Biological and psychological theories of crime differ from sociological theories in their identification of the causes of crime as in the individual characteristics of the criminal or deviant person. From this perspective crimes result from a personality or biochemical defect, such as a hormonal imbalance or deprivation of maternal love. The role of the social context in which criminal or deviant behaviour take places is unexplored, such as opportunities for crime or the effects of income. An understanding of crime and deviance as relative is also ignored, so that they are instead understood as reflecting an absolute set of moral standards.

Both biological and psychological theories regard deviants as abnormal. For psychological theories, while the cause of this abnormality may be biological, it is the person's mental functioning or individual experience that is the primary explanation of their deviant behaviour. Psychological explanations often regard inadequate socialisation as a cause of crime and deviance. Eysenck (1979) argues that extroverts are difficult to socialise into mainstream norms and values, while Bowlby (1946) argues that people who are deprived of maternal love in the early years of childhood are more likely to develop psychopathic personalities.

Today, criminal profiling represents an influential area of psychology in the area of crime. This involves identification of potential suspects of a criminal act based on analysis of the nature of the offence. There are doubts about the reliability of this approach, but it continues to be used in some jurisdictions. Criminal profiling may draw on theories of personality but does not in itself constitute an explanation of crime.

There are many criticisms of biological and psychological theories. First, they tend to reduce explanations of crime to a single factor, such as maternal deprivation, or to a personality trait linked to a biochemical imbalance. This is deterministic, suggesting that individuals have no choice but to be criminal, and fails to explain why only some individuals with these characteristics become criminals. It also ignores the multidimensional causes of crime and deviance. Biological and psychological factors work in interaction with their social environment. Even the effects of many genetic predispositions are influenced by factors such as social class.

Second, biological and psychological theories operate with a narrow definition of crime, which fails to problematise the label 'criminal'. Instead of understanding crime and deviance as a process, involving interaction between different groups in society, they are explained as objective phenomena, whose causes reside in the, often innate, characteristics of particular individuals. The reasoning behind this approach is circular, as criminals are those who are labelled 'criminal'. There is no attempt to problematise the process of criminalisation itself. This approach can lead to the labelling of whole groups as inherently criminal and so lead to social discrimination.

Contemporary explanations of crime and deviance therefore regard social factors as of greater significance than biological ones. Social inequality, limited social opportunities, social stereotyping and bias in the policing and judicial process provide better explanations of the pattern of crime and deviance than do biological arguments about chemical imbalances and physical characteristics.

SOCIOLOGICAL THEORIES OF CRIME AND DEVIANCE

As is the case with all social thought, the development of theories of crime and deviance reflects the social environment in which they emerged. The earliest theories, which appeared around the end of the 19th century, sought the cause of crime in the pathological characteristics of the individual. They were located within a modernist, positivist model in which scientific analysis was believed to hold the key to improving society. This position gradually shifted and by the 1960s and 1970s it reached the opposite pole in the form of labelling theory and early versions of Marxist theory. These theories argued that it was society rather than the deviant that was the problem. They operated with a relative definition of deviance, pointing out that since deviance exists only in the eye of the beholder, it is a creation of society itself. In later developments the notion of power became central, so that crime and deviance were seen as mechanisms by which those in power and control maintained the status quo. More recently, theories have recognised the harm done by all forms of crime, whether committed by the powerful or the powerless. There is also concern that the concepts of crime and deviance are themselves problematic and contribute to the problem they seek to resolve, an issue examined later in this chapter.

DEVIANCE—A FUNCTIONALIST PERSPECTIVE

Functionalist theories explain deviance as the result of inadequate integration or cultural disaffiliation—lack of attachment to the culture. These theories operate with an absolute definition of crime and deviance and accept that 'social control mechanisms' (the police, the courts and so on) are necessary to keep deviance in check to ensure social order.

Functionalist explanations of deviance can be divided into two main schools: traditional functionalists and anomie theorists. Traditional functionalists argue that since crime and deviance are present in all societies, a certain level of crime is necessary and contributes to social stability and order. This view is not shared by anomie theorists, who instead argue that some cultural values create problems for society.

Traditional functionalists

Traditional functionalists argue that a certain amount of deviance is normal and performs positive functions by defining and clarifying the boundaries between right and wrong. Durkheim (1938) argues that crime and deviance perform the following functions:

1. *Crime and deviance serve a boundary maintenance function.* They establish the moral boundaries of a community by publicly identifying the limits that are acceptable. When crime occurs, the social reaction warns people where the boundaries of acceptable behaviour lie and what will happen to those that breach them.
2. *Crime and deviance are an important source of social change.* For change to occur, yesterday's deviance must become today's normality. For Durkheim, crime and deviance can prefigure the future moral order of society. Terrorists or freedom fighters may represent a future established order. Since a certain amount of change is necessary for a society's development, so is deviance.
3. *Crime strengthens social solidarity through the reinforcement of collective sentiments.* Collective sentiment of any kind binds people together, reinforcing their social ties and confirming their shared view of the world. For Durkheim, the community outrage that follows a serious deviant or criminal event, such as an apparently senseless act of violence, strengthens social ties. This explains why the suicide rate tends to decrease in times of crisis, such as war. Social solidarity is strengthened by the social reaction to deviant behaviour.

Durkheim's view that crime was functional for society was tempered by his view that excessively high levels of crime and deviance indicate a weakness in the culture that, if not dealt with, threatens the maintenance of order and stability within it. He believes that a harmonious society is one in which people have a firm sense of their place in it, socially, morally and psychologically. High levels of crime are an indication of anomie or social dislocation and suggest that society is in danger of disintegration. The key to preventing this is to improve the attachment of people to their society through better socialisation.

Anomie theory

Robert Merton's development of Durkheim's argument about the effects of anomie on crime has been an influential theory of crime and deviance (1968). The theory is also known as *strain theory* because it argues that deviance results from the tension that arises from dysfunctional social arrangements.

Merton's understanding of anomie differs from that of Durkheim, but he agrees that cultural values are implicated in the genesis of criminality. For Merton, anomie does not result from an absence or ambiguity of cultural values, as Durkheim suggests, but from a discrepancy between cultural goals and their means of achievement. His argument is a critique of the American dream, which normalises excessive material success without providing the means for its achievement.

Merton argues that both goals and means are learned

through the process of socialisation. In the United States people are encouraged to aspire to great wealth. All Americans are exposed to the expectation that they must own a large home, have more than one car, keep up with fashions in clothing and home wares and own the latest consumer goods. Being a good American citizen involves being materially successful and engaging in conspicuous consumption. Merton argues that the difficulty with this is that the opportunities for achieving these goals are not equally distributed. For most Americans this dream is an unachievable fantasy. But the pressure to achieve it is very strong and this leads some Americans to resolve it by resorting to illegal means of achievement. Merton argues 'By impinging similarly upon persons differentially equipped to meet it, a cardinal American virtue—ambition—promotes a cardinal American vice—deviant behaviour' (1968, p. 20). For Merton, the severe disjunction between goals and means produces anomie and strain for individual citizens. No society can hold out a common goal to all its members and simultaneously block off access to its attainment. Merton describes this problem as one of 'structural dysfunction' and identifies a fivefold typology of response to this situation:

- *conformism*, in which individuals accept the demands and spend their lives in a futile struggle to achieve material success
- *innovation*, in which individuals create novel ways of achieving material success, including criminal ones
- *ritualism*, in which individuals appear to accept the goals and attempt to achieve them, but in reality have given up trying; rule-following bureaucrats are an example
- *retreatism*, in which individuals reject the goal of material success and make no attempt to achieve it—Merton regarded substance users as retreatists
- *rebellion*, in which individuals resist both the goals and their means of attainment. These are the revolutionaries who seek to change the rules of engagement. Left-wing revolutionaries and eco-warriors fit this definition.

THE CHICAGO SCHOOL

According to official data, the distribution of crime and deviance is not spread evenly throughout the community but is concentrated in particular geographical areas. The significance of this observation was first recognised in the social ecological model of crime developed by the **Chicago School** in the 1920s.

The ecology of deviance

The Chicago School combined a structural approach that focused on urban social processes with a subcultural one that focused on the local environment and the subjective experiences of the deviant. Charles Darwin's notion of 'ecological interdependence' was used to apply concepts such as the web of life and biotic communities to the influence of geographical boundaries on human behaviour. Statistical analysis of the male delinquency rates in Chicago and other American cities resulted in *zone maps* which portrayed the distribution of crime across five circular zones steadily decreasing from Zone I, next to the central business district, to Zone V on the outskirts of the city (see Figure 13.2). This led to an understanding of crime as caused by social and economic processes rather than individual pathology.

These ideas were linked to a theory of social disorganisation. Deviance was explained as the result of processes associated with the transformation from rural to urban society. The rapid social change associated with industrialisation, urbanisation and immigration weakened the social control formerly exerted by the family, community and church. Into this moral vacuum new values and behaviours appeared which challenged traditional norms and led to an increase in deviance.

The ethnography of deviance

This structural approach of the Chicago School was combined with an interactionist approach. Techniques such as participant observation, the case study, the life history and ethnography were employed to provide qualitative accounts of subcultures and an early portrayal of deviance as difference. But this emerging relative definition of deviance was not integrated with the ecological studies, which operated with an absolute definition of deviance. It was not until **labelling theory** appeared that the relative definition of deviance was integrated into a theory.

Criticisms of the Chicago School

Three main criticisms have been made of the Chicago School:

1. The emphasis on social disorganisation tends to underplay the degree of organisation in criminal and delinquent subcultures.
2. There is a tendency for the theory to be tautological—that is, saying the same thing twice in different words. Since crime and delinquency are evidence of social disorganisation, social disorganisation cannot be used to explain them.

SOCIOLOGY

FIGURE 13.2

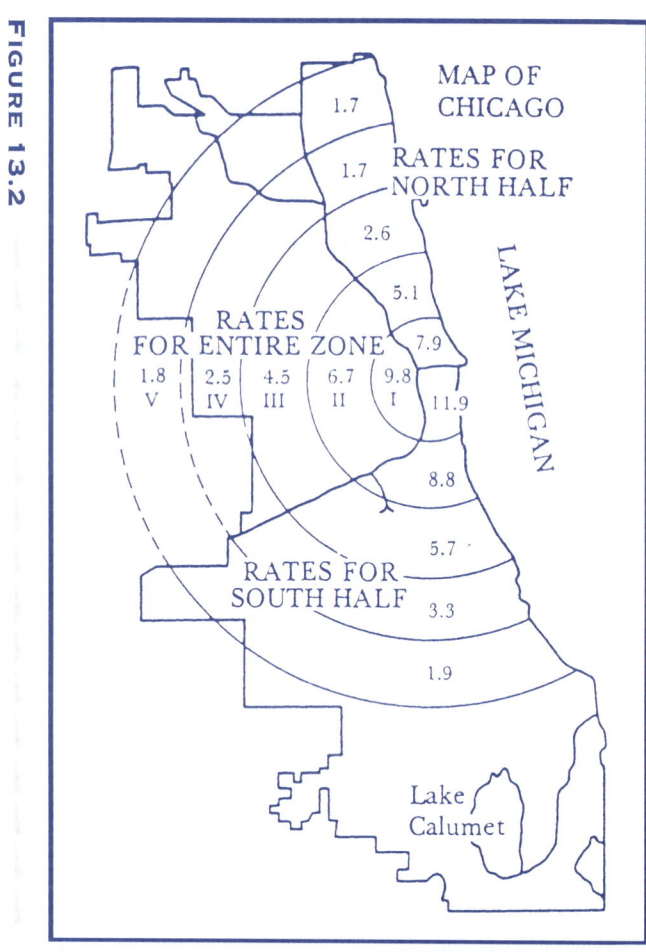

Map of Chicago showing the distribution of crime
Source: Shaw & McKay (1969).

3. The scientific terminology of the theory provides a misleading portrayal of social relationships as natural and inevitable. This positivist approach fails to acknowledge the extent to which differences of power explain social arrangements. For example, there was no attempt to consider the relationship between crime and the effect of public policy on low income and high unemployment.

SOCIAL CONTROL THEORY

Social control theory follows Durkheim in arguing that it is only socialisation that leads people to behave in ways that are socially acceptable. Social control theorists do not ask 'Why do people break norms?' but 'Why do people conform?' They see mainstream norms and values as the principal source of social control. They assume that if social control breaks down, deviance will increase and society as a whole will suffer. They dismiss the possibility that the subculture is a source of deviance because only some members of a subculture become deviant. Instead they see inner and outer controls as the explanation of social order. Some writers, such as Charles Murray (1990; 1994) and Walter C. Reckless (1961), stress the existence of inner controls, while others, such as Michael Gottfredson and Travis Hirschi (1990), stress both. In all cases the role of traditional sources of socialisation, such as the family, are central to their explanation of who becomes deviant.

Wilson and Herrnstein

One of the most influential social control theorists is James Q. Wilson. *Crime and Human Nature* (1985), written with Richard Herrnstein, provides the most developed account of the theory. It explains crime as the result of three influences:

1. *Biological influences.* Most crimes are committed by young men. This suggests that the biological constitution of young men predisposes them towards involvement in crime.
2. *Psychological influences.* The way that social institutions respond to individuals patterns their behaviour through the process of operant conditioning. Our patterned responses to situations are learned according to the inputs we receive from our social environment. If 'bad' behaviour is positively reinforced by our social environment, then that behaviour will flourish; conversely, if it is punished through negative sanctions, it will diminish. The same principle applies to 'good' behaviours.
3. *Strength of conscience.* Wilson and Herrnstein argue that strength of conscience interacts with the other two elements to determine who will and who will not break the law. If the conscience is strong, even if biological and psychological factors favour law breaking, the individual may still not break the law.

It is the combination of these three factors that explains why some people break the law and others do not. Individuals may not have internalised the value of adhering to the law but if biological factors do not predispose them towards breaking it then they may be law-abiding. This may be the case with many women who constitutionally seem to be more law-abiding than men. The social policy implications of the theory are a focus on the treatment or punishment of the individual and a concern with controlling areas with high official rates of crime.

Social control theory—an assessment

Many of the criticisms of social control theory stem from its unquestioned acceptance of the values and moral standards of conventional society. First, it offers a limited, individualistic explanation of crime. It has no concept of structural inequality and its relationship with patterns of crime. Second, it accepts definitions of deviance as unproblematic, ignoring the way in which powerful groups are able to impose their views on society. For example, it has nothing to say about the way the law criminalises female sex workers but not their male clients. Finally, it deals only with identified deviants, confirming the conventional view that most deviants are young, working class and black. This ignores the extent to which middle-class people commit crime, including the high levels of corporate crime committed by older, white middle-class males.

CRIME CONTROL AND THE NEW RIGHT

Official data on rising crime rates have fuelled public concerns and are associated with a shift in social policy dating back to the mid-1970s. Prior to this period social policy had been influenced by the welfare model as the universal solution to social problems including crime. Welfare provision was linked to the rising crime rate and blamed for producing a dependent underclass. Murray (1984) explained the rise in crime as the result of poverty, unemployment and welfare dependence, and the absence of a male role model. The political response to this situation included a retreat from the welfare state, a refocusing on family and community, and a 'no nonsense' approach to crime. The response of the right was to shift attention away from social explanations of crime back to the individual and the use of social control theory, especially in the United States, as the principal model for dealing with crime. This model, variously described as Right Realism or the New Right, argues that individuals must be held accountable for their actions and the state must develop programs that punish, control and change their behaviour.

One of the most influential New Right theories was the 'broken windows' thesis (Wilson & Kelling 1982). This argues that visible evidence of physical and social decay in a neighbourhood, such as vandalism, fighting and graffiti, sends a signal to criminals that the neighbourhood is an easy target because it lacks social control. As the area becomes subject to petty crime, a destructive spiral of increasing fear among residents, rising crime and neighbourhood decline takes place. Wealthier, more mobile residents move out of the district, leaving the more vulnerable ones behind, and an influx of criminals, drug addicts and sex workers causes further deterioration. According to Wilson and Kelling, the solution to this problem is in increasing levels of control through the aggressive policing of petty crime, surveillance of the environment and other forms of control. In the United States the theory was used to support the introduction of zero tolerance policing in the 1990s in which minor incivilities were treated as serious crimes to prevent the development of more serious offences.

Research on the effectiveness of such forms of social control is mixed (Grabosky 1998), and writers such as Crawford (1998, p. 133) point out that the groups that need most help, such as the poor and drug addicts, are the ones that tend to be criminalised. Some of the behaviours identified by Wilson and Kelling as indicators of community decline are not only common in many public places widely regarded as 'safe', but also are practised by 'respectable' citizens. Research by Phillips and Smith (2003) on everyday incivility challenges the binary opposition between law-abiding and criminal citizens implicit in the broken windows thesis. Instead, they found that dominant social groups are perpetrators of incivilities that are confronting and disturbing for recipients. Despite these criticisms, the broken windows thesis remains an influential theory informing policymakers and law-enforcement agencies.

Rather than explaining and dealing with the sources of crime, the influence of the New Right has resulted in debates about the relative merits of various harsh measures to control it. Law and order policies promoted by politicians often use military analogies—'the war on drugs', 'combating crime' or 'target hardening'. There has been a move towards use of paramilitary-style units and tactics that have led, in Victoria, to offenders being shot by the police. These tactics have led to sharp increases in expenditure on crime and on incarceration rates.

Social policy influenced by the New Right has also been associated with the introduction of youth curfews, mandatory sentencing and increasing surveillance of public spaces. Since the 1980s in some states the police have been empowered to remove juveniles from the streets even though they may not have committed an offence (Cunneen & White 1995, p. 264).

Cunneen and White (2007) question both the morality of these developments and their effectiveness. They argue that young people are unfairly identified as the principal source of the 'crime problem' and that the harsh measures offer nothing in the way of rehabilitation. Most importantly, they fail to address the underlying issues of structural disadvantage and social exclusion. Policies based on deterrence not only diminish civil liberties but increase rather than decrease criminal behaviour. These views are shared by Innes and Jones (2006), whose analysis of crime rates in the United Kingdom suggests that many of the factors behind high rates of youth crime relate to urban decay and that higher levels of investment would see a reduction in crime.

DEVIANCE—AN INTERACTIONIST PERSPECTIVE

The work of interactionist theorists such as Becker (1963) and Goffman (1962) is quite different from that of social control theorists and the New Right. The latter utilise an absolute definition of deviance and see the individual as the problem. Interactionists use a relative definition and see society as the problem. Interactionists apply symbolic interactionism to the study of crime and deviance, and see these as the outcome of a social process in which the definition of deviance is negotiated by the actors involved. They side with the underdog, portraying the deviant as one who has been wronged by society so that it is society, not the deviant, that needs to change how it acts. *Labelling theorists* are sociological partisans who deliberately champion deviants and criminals as powerless victims of the values and social arrangements of mainstream society.

Primary and secondary deviance—Edwin Lemert

Writing in the early 1950s, the criminologist Edwin Lemert distinguished between primary and secondary deviance. He argued it was society's attempt to control primary deviance that led to secondary deviance. Lemert defined secondary deviance as 'a special class of socially defined responses which people make to problems created by the social reaction to their deviance' (Lemert 1967, p. 40). He assumes that if there was no reaction, secondary deviance would not take place. It is the reaction to primary deviance that hardens the initial norm violation and makes it difficult for individuals to retrace their steps. He argues that application of the deviant label has three main effects that create the deviant identity, in the areas of structured opportunities, interpersonal networks and self-concept (see Figure 13.3):

- *Structured opportunities.* Being labelled deviant creates social stigma that compromise the individual to meet their economic needs through legitimate avenues, such as employment.
- *Interpersonal networks.* Social reaction to deviance changes the individual's social relationships. Feeling excluded from mainstream society, fraternal feelings of solidarity develop within the deviant subculture.
- *Self-concept.* The reinforcement of a deviant identity is further strengthened through self-labelling. The deviant person comes to accept as their own the identity that was initially imposed on them from outside.

Labelling theory—Howard Becker

Lemert's ideas were developed by Howard Becker. In *Outsiders* (1963), Becker wrote:

Social groups create deviance by making the rules whose infraction constitutes deviance, and by applying those rules to particular people and labelling them as outsiders. From this point of view, deviance is not a quality of the act the person commits, but rather a consequence of the application by others of the rules and sanctions to an 'offender'. The deviant is one to whom the label has been

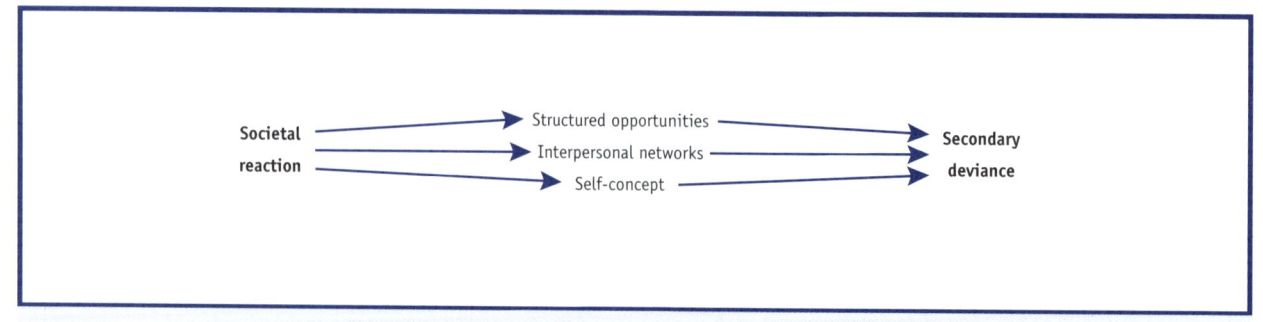

FIGURE 13.3

Societal reaction → Structured opportunities → Secondary deviance
Societal reaction → Interpersonal networks → Secondary deviance
Societal reaction → Self-concept → Secondary deviance

The effect of societal reaction on secondary deviance *Source:* Liska (1987, p. 125). © 1987 Prentice-Hall, Inc. Reproduced with permission of Pearson Education, Inc.

successfully applied; deviant behaviour is behaviour that people so label. (1963, p. 9)

In asking how and why deviance comes about, Becker shifts attention from the behaviour identified as deviant to the process by which it comes to be labelled. Deviance is caused by the interaction between social groups, with one group having power to impose its label on another. Arising during the birth of the civil rights movement in the United States, labelling theory argued that the law does not treat all groups equally but selects out some groups rather than others, often based on skin colour. Both black and white young people engage in drinking in public places, but black young people are more likely to face social control than young white people. Each group has its own set of values, which are valid within their subcultures. The relationship between these different values is always subject to negotiation, and it is differences in power that result in the values of some groups being undesirable and/or criminal. These ideas led labelling theorists to regard the criminal and deviant as victims of an unjust system. It is not the deviant that is the problem but the apparatus of social control that seeks conformity.

Deviance amplification; moral panics and collective reactions

Deviance amplification is a concept developed by labelling theorists to describe the spiral of action and reaction in which the response to the initial act of deviance structures and escalates its development (Wilkins 1964). The initial act that causes attention can be relatively trivial, such as differences in dress or leisure preferences. Where the social reaction to deviance is stereotyped, oversimplified or based on incorrect information, the social reaction is likely to cause greater social isolation of the deviants. Each further reaction of misunderstanding or inappropriate response produces greater distortion of information, for example through media stereotyping, which raises the level of public anxiety and encourages greater alienation and deviancy. Stereotypes encourage punitive responses that further push the deviant into playing the deviant role.

Cunneen et al. (1989) used these ideas in their analysis of the clashes between bikies and police at the Bathurst motorcycle races in New South Wales in the 1980s. Cunneen et al. argue that the antagonism between the two groups was amplified by a process of action and reaction that occurred over two decades. Drawing on labelling and Marxist theory, they argue that the participants were predominantly younger working-class men and women who came from a subculture characterised by anti-police grievances and activity. There was also a history of conflict with authority over their use of public space for leisure purposes as capitalism gradually commercialised spaces formerly available to working-class people, including the Bathurst races (Cunneen et al. 1989, pp. 81–4). Policing practices had also changed, relying less on policing by consent and more on technology and physical coercion. Cunneen et al. argue that the riots were an expression of a more deeply held and enduring antagonism between young working-class males and the police as representatives of a middle-class mainstream culture that excluded them from the use of public space.

Deviance and the interactionist perspective—criticisms and evaluation

In the 1960s interactionist theory became the principal paradigm for the analysis of crime and deviance but by the late 1980s it was critiqued by both the political left and the right (Plummer 1979, p. 99). For the left it did not go far enough in critiquing existing social arrangements. For the right it went too far by siding with the deviant and ignoring issues of morality and natural justice.

Its definition of deviance was excessively relative, implying that no acts caused harm or were morally wrong. Even left-wingers such as Taylor, Walton and Young (1973) pointed out that although deviance is not a sociological category, it is a *social* category and we all have a good idea of what is and is not acceptable behaviour. The focus was always on 'soft' areas of crime, while violent crimes received little attention.

In addition, labelling theory ignores the question of where deviance comes from in the first place, explaining it only as a response to social control. It cannot account for crimes that continue despite the absence of social reaction, such as corruption and professional fraud.

Furthermore, the empirical evidence only partially supports the labelling perspective. While the effects of stigma, lack of opportunity and self-definition have been shown to make it difficult for people to shrug off the label 'deviant' or 'criminal', there is contradictory evidence. There is little evidence to suggest that those people who receive the most severe sanction of incarceration are the most negatively labelled and most likely to reoffend (Box 1981). Nor is there much support for the idea that labelling creates deviance (Gove 1980).

DEVIANCE AND POWER— CONFLICT PERSPECTIVES

The previous section has pointed out that interactionists acknowledged that differentials of power were a key aspect of why some groups were criminalised and others were not. However, interactionist theory operated within an essentially pluralist conceptual framework and said little about the material basis for these differences of power. It was only with Marxist theory that a fully developed analysis of the role of power on crime and deviance emerged.

Deviance—the conventional Marxist perspective

Many Marxists see crime as a natural outgrowth of capitalist society. They argue that a capitalist economic system generates crime for the following reasons:

- The capitalist mode of production emphasises the maximisation of profits and the accumulation of wealth.
- Economic self-interest rather than public duty motivates behaviour.
- Capitalism is based on the private ownership of property.
- Personal gain rather than collective wellbeing is encouraged.
- Capitalism is a competitive system. Mutual aid and cooperation for the betterment of all are discouraged in favour of individual achievement at the expense of others.
- Competition breeds aggression, hostility and, particularly for the losers, frustration.

These ideas are reflected in the work of the American sociologist William Chambliss.

Chambliss (1964) examined how laws on vagrancy were used to defend the interests of the English ruling class in the 14th century. These laws made it illegal to provide or to receive any financial or other form of assistance for beggars, making it impossible for the poor to travel. This forced them to seek work in their local parish, providing the local landowners with the labour force they needed. The laws were passed at a time when the labour force was halved as a result of the Black Death and the Crusades. Chambliss argues that the real motive behind the laws was not concern for the parish purse, but to ensure that the aristocracy had labour for their agricultural estates.

In other work, Chambliss shows that crime is not unique to the working class but exists within all levels of society. His ten-year study of crime in Seattle demonstrated the links between organised crime and the ruling class, such that 'organised crime is not merely the servant of the ruling class but rather an integral part of it' (1978). Given that few of the ruling class are apprehended or punished for their criminal activities, Chambliss concludes that this is because differences in wealth and influence determine whether or not the law will be enforced. Chambliss presents a political economy of crime that reveals the links between the economic interests of the ruling class and the creation and enforcement of laws.

Chambliss' work was influential, but was criticised for portraying too direct a relationship between the economic organisation of society and its criminal activities. British Marxists responded by trying to retain many of Marx's insights, while acknowledging the exercise of individual agency.

The second wave—neo-Marxist and 'socialist' perspectives

In the 1970s British criminologists developed a second wave of Marxist theories of crime that attempted to demonstrate that although criminals were in control of their life, they were also victims of an unjust social system.

Mugging, the state, and law and order—policing the crisis

In the early 1970s the United Kingdom was subject to a moral panic about violent crime, particularly the crime of mugging (bashing). Stuart Hall et al. (1979) argue that the panic was not based on a real law and order crisis but was related to the economic and political crisis that British capitalism was facing at the time. Recession was raising unemployment and reducing wages, thereby creating industrial unrest at a time when businesses were facing intense competition and the threat of collapse. Hall et al. argue that the moral panic of a decline in law and order was used by the state to assert its authority over the working class. This was assisted by the media's association of violent street crime with West Indian immigrants so that they became the scapegoats for the stress ordinary people experienced due to the economic arrangements of capitalism.

Hall et al. avoided developing a conspiracy theory as the explanation for how the ruling class translated the crisis into police action by arguing that there was no agreement by police, government, media and the courts to act together. Rather, the media tended to report mugging in much the same way as its sources, basing stories on police evidence, court statements by magistrates and judges and so on. It therefore reproduced statements defining the situation as a 'crisis', a 'war' or a 'mindless crime' that needed to be stamped out like other disorderly social behaviour.

Although influential, the study was criticised for failing to provide any evidence for its claim that the moral panic was caused by a crisis of British capitalism. There is also a contradiction in the argument that the apparent rise in street crime was due to deviancy amplification and yet it was bound to rise as a result of unemployment.

Left realism—the new reformism?

Left realism is distinguished from earlier left-wing theories of crime in its acknowledgement of the social harm caused by crime, much of which affects the working class. It shifts attention from the perpetrators of crime and deviance to the victims. It criticises right-wing theories for their positivism and left-wing theories for their utopian suggestion that in a socialist society there would be no crime. Instead of revolutionary politics, Left realists accept a reformist approach that emphasises the need to relieve ordinary people of the 'problem' of law and order.

Lea and Young (1984) argue that crime among working-class people is due to **relative deprivation**, subcultural influences and marginalisation.

- *Relative deprivation.* Relative deprivation occurs when cultural norms of affluence make individuals and groups feel disadvantaged compared with others they regard as having the same attributes and deserving of the same rewards as them.
- *Subculture.* Lea and Young link the idea of relative deprivation to that of the subculture, arguing that groups that share a sense of relative deprivation will develop countercultures to overcome this. These solutions will vary from one group to another and may result in criminal activities.
- *Marginalisation.* Those who lack power due to marginalisation are most likely to resort to violent resistance to their situation. This generates police responses, creating further community breakdown. Improving employment opportunities is an important strategy for reducing crime.

Lea and Young's work is similar to the ideas of **subcultural theory** and suffers from some of its criticisms, including being unable to be conclusive about the extent to which police policies influence the figures on the involvement of different classes and ethnic groups in crime. They are also criticised by feminists. Naffine (1997) shares with Walklate (1998, pp. 63–4) the view that, despite their claims to the contrary, Lea and Young's work demonstrates masculinist positivist concerns that pay only lip-service to the insights of feminist criminology and have little concern for female victims of crime (pp. 65–7). Despite these limitations, left realism has issued an important challenge to left-wing sociologists of crime and deviance to take street crimes as seriously as crimes of the wealthy.

FEMINIST THEORIES OF CRIME AND DEVIANCE

Feminist criminology is concerned with the role of gender in shaping the treatment of women by the criminal justice system. It argues that gender stereotypes mean that men and women are treated differently according to the way notions of masculinity and femininity are constructed. Feminists point out that criminology itself is a positivist discipline, from which women are largely absent, and this has led to a framework that regards scientific rationality as the only way of apprehending the social world. It ignores more subjective accounts of crime and deviance. The exclusion of women as practitioners, perpetrators, victims and members of the criminal justice system has also been largely ignored by criminology, even though understanding the role of gender is critical to understanding crime itself.

Until the arrival of feminist analyses in the 1970s virtually all explanations of female crime relied on stereotypes about women. Often untested assumptions were made about the links between female biology and their involvement in crime (Pollak 1950). Feminist criminologists such as Carlen (1988), Smart (1976) and Heidensohn (1986) seek to explain their involvement in terms of both structural and cultural forces.

Women and social control—Heidensohn

Heidensohn (1986) seeks to explain why women are less involved in crime than men. She argues that women are subject to greater levels of social control than men. Control over women is exerted in the home, where domesticity is valued as evidence of the fulfilment of the traditional female role. The rounds of housework and child care leave little opportunity for illegal activity. Economic dependency also reinforces such control. At work women are often in service industries that are extensions of the domestic caring role or process industries in which the top positions are occupied by males and the bottom ones by unskilled women. Discipline is maintained by supervisors, often male, who combine gender power with positional power in the organisation to ensure that women know their place and stay in it.

Masculinities and the accomplishment of gender through crime—Messerschmidt

James W. Messerschmidt (1986; 1993; 1997) has developed the concept of masculinity to explain the role of gender in crime, using Giddens' concept of 'structured action', which attempts to examine how gender, race and class are enacted in the social settings in which crime is realised. Messerschmidt argues that 'gendered power is central to understanding why men commit more crimes and more serious crimes than women' (1993, p. 84). He reverses the usual argument that crime is an expression of masculinity, instead suggesting that masculinity is established through engagement in crime—'it is a strategy of masculinity', a 'way of enacting masculine gender' (Connell in Messerschmidt 1993, p. xi).

Messerschmidt builds on Connell's argument that gender is structured through the hegemonic power of normative heterosexuality (Connell 1987). For men, the values and norms of white heterosexual males constitute a **hegemonic masculinity** that sets the standard against which all other forms of masculinity are measured. This structural force coexists alongside other structural forces, especially those of class and race. However, gender still involves an act of agency as it has to be accomplished in daily life and takes different forms in different settings.

> *Because masculinity is a behavioural response to the particular conditions and situations in which men participate, different types of masculinity exist in the school, the youth group, the street, the family and the workplace. In other words, men do masculinity according to the social situation in which they find themselves.* (Messerschmidt 1993, p. 84)

Messerschmidt argues that among disadvantaged black groups one way of 'being a man' is through an aggressive heterosexuality that is played out in violent gang behaviour. For these men violence is a source of status that is unavailable through employment. For Messerschmidt, crime is an arena in which the accomplishment of masculinity is performed. Hegemonic masculinity is characterised by independence, by toughness and aggression, by uncontrollable sexuality and by the assertive subordination of women. It is this association that explains men's extreme overrepresentation in crime, especially crimes of violence and against women.

Feminist theory—an evaluation

The analysis of the role of gender on crime and deviance has opened up new avenues for research, generating new theories and challenging old ones. It has identified new concerns in areas such as sexual discrimination, gender bias within the criminal justice system and the need to account for victims of crime. Although it has not succeeded in changing the masculine nature of criminology itself, it has provided a range of alternative perspectives that have changed the nature of criminological debate.

CRIME, SHAME AND REINTEGRATION

An attempt to bring together some of the ideas covered in this section can be found in Braithwaite's (1989) argument that the way that justice systems punish people who commit crimes does not lead to an outcome that aids rehabilitation of the offenders. Instead, it pushes offenders into subcultures that put them beyond the reach of moral education. Braithwaite reached this position by reviewing the current state of criminological knowledge, arguing that many of the theories outlined above have valuable elements worth retaining.

Braithwaite argues that punishment should be done in a way that does not stigmatise offenders and proposes that in some cases this can be achieved through a form of public shaming in which offenders are forced to confront the effects of their actions. Braithwaite suggests that **reintegrative shaming** is most likely to be effective in crimes where there is a high degree of value consensus about the unacceptable nature of the offence. In these cases there is a chance that shaming will succeed in making the offender repent their offence and rejoin the moral community. Shaming is likely to be least effective where there is a high degree of dissension, for example when conflicts generated by inequalities of class, ethnicity, gender or race result in the formation of subcultures whose members espouse values that support the criminal activity in opposition to the values of mainstream society.

For Braithwaite, shaming will therefore be effective only when both offenders and agents of social control have a high level of interdependency and belong to communities with shared values and activities. Shaming is also most effective when the sanctions are wielded by those who are important figures in the offender's life. For this reason families are efficient sanctioners because the relationships in them may be intense ones of dependency, trust and love, so punishment takes place within this context. Braithwaite argues that where punishment and shaming are separated from each other they lose their legitimacy, because they are seen as just another part of an unjust, oppressive system of power and brutality.

Braithwaite's ideas have been influential. Legislation now exists that diverts juveniles away from the courts towards forms of family conferences in which offenders who admit their offence are required to confront the victims of their crimes in front of their parents, police and others. They are forced to hear from their victims the effects of their crime and to discuss with the group the most appropriate forms of punishment or compensation (O'Connell & Moore 1992). Community service orders can also have some of these effects, attempting to enmesh the offender in a network of social relationships that will promote other values and provide ways in which self-esteem can be built up.

Braithwaite was clear that his arguments applied only to predatory crimes in societies where there is a strong social consensus. Some societies are now so socially segregated, individualistic in ideology and unequal in wealth and power that shaming is not a feasible strategy. It is most likely to work with first offenders, those not involved with deviant subcultures and articulate people with social skills—in other words, middle-class juvenile delinquents or people whose position in society is at stake.

His theory has been criticised for not clarifying whether the shaming/reintegration is a result of rather than a cause of societies with low crime rates (Potter 1992). The theory does not give much scope for individual choice and action either. By pitching the explanation at the level of networks and structures, Braithwaite does not have to develop a theory of action in which it is possible for people to choose actions others judge to be against the law.

Reflective question: Find a newspaper cutting that provides a detailed description of a criminal act, for example public rioting, sexual assault or corporate fraud. Which social theories are most helpful in understanding these events?

THE FUTURE OF THE SOCIOLOGY OF CRIME AND DEVIANCE

In the 1990s the study of the sociology of crime and deviance came under attack as a discipline area that was no longer relevant to a postmodern world. Writers such as Sumner (1994) and Young (1998) explained that both criminology and the sociology of deviance were part of the Enlightenment project that located criminology within the modernist project of 'solving' society's problems and that accepted mainstream definitions of crime and deviance uncritically. Young writes:

The old certainties of the obvious nature of crime, the central role of the criminal justice system in its control, and the possibility of realising by government intervention a social contract that embraced all citizens have come, one by one, to be cast in doubt. (1998, p. 262)

Young identifies four reasons for this crisis:

1. *The rise in the rate of recorded crime.* This challenged the validity of left-wing theories that argued that social conditions such as unemployment and deprivation caused crime, thereby allowing for the rise of the New Right.
2. *The revelation of invisible victims.* Partly as a result of feminist research it was acknowledged that violent crimes, such as assault, occur at all levels of society and in its most intimate and private settings. This challenged the modernist notion that most crime is committed by working-class male strangers who attack their victims in public settings. Traditional criminology had ignored the family as a site of violence.
3. *The problematisation of crime.* Traditional criminology accepted data relating to crime and deviance as empirical 'facts' and developed universal theories to explain their occurrence. This view was challenged by labelling theory, which suggested that crime and deviance were the result of a process of social labelling. This meant that the behaviour identified as 'criminal' or 'deviant' therefore required no explanation—by sociologists or anyone else.

   A range of social movements rendered the notions of crime and deviance even more opaque. Feminism, environmentalism, drug legalisation and child protection movements sought to recategorise crimes and to redefine social problems. Modernist notions of crime and deviance became contested phenomena. If the object of the sociologists' study is now so muddied, how is it possible to contemplate the development of a universal explanation for its occurrence?
4. *The universality of crime and the selectivity of the social justice system.* Recognition of crimes of the powerful, including state crime, revealed the flaws in traditional criminology's argument that crime was a working-class phenomenon. This challenge was further heightened by feminist theory's exposure of the inability of criminology to explain female patterns of crime. Young explains that 'theory after theory ... breaks down when

women are put into the explanatory equation' (Young 1998, p. 276). The fact that middle-class men engage in crime while working-class women do not makes positivist notions about the link between poverty, unemployment and crime difficult to sustain.

The work of Foucault has also contributed to this sense of crisis by exposing the complicity of academics in relations of power and domination (1974; 1977). Foucault argued that knowledge and power are intimately related, and that no-one is free from the constituting effects of knowledge. This made criminologists consider their role in perpetuating discourses that contributed to the surveillance and regulation of criminalised populations. Consequently, they have become more reflexive and less optimistic about their role in society as bringers of positive change.

The responses of sociologists to these developments have been influenced by their politics. Sociologists on the left of the political spectrum, such as Messerschmidt (1997), Young (1998) and Braithwaite (1998), tend to reject modernist notions of the past while seeking to retain a concern with the reality of the problem of crime. They see the solution as lying in the creation of a more just society, which balances state responsibility (but not control) for the wellbeing of its citizens with community vitality and empowerment. For Young this takes the form of recognising the role of relative deprivation and problems of citizenship. For Braithwaite it involves extending communitarian control and using measures such as reintegrative shaming, with the state becoming involved only 'to mop up the failures' (1998, p. 60). For Messerschmidt a focus on the intersection of gender, class and race remains central (1997, pp. 113–19).

This view contrasts with that of sociologists on the political right who do not see a crisis of sociology but rather a crisis of society. Analysts such as Murray (1990; 1994) and Wilson and Herrnstein (1985) continue to focus on official crime data and portray crime as a working-class problem that is increasing. They continue to use the terms 'crime' and 'deviance' unproblematically and to seek solutions within a universal theory of crime that to a great extent pathologises the deviant and the criminal. They share with the left an idealisation of the community, as well as a concern with problems of citizenship, political marginalisation, the loss of coherent social values and excessive individualism, but their solution is different. While left-wing writers emphasise the need for social justice and an empowered citizenship, writers on the right seek an increase in social control and intolerance, and exclusion of the nonconformist.

Today the study of deviance is in decline, but the study of crime is a growth industry. Law and order issues remain hot topics and politically important. This reflects rising expectations about what is acceptable within a community, as well as anxiety that beneath the apparent harmony of a global culture lies an increasingly divided and 'decivilised' society.

Reflective question: Why do some sociologists argue that criminology and the sociology of crime and deviance are in a state of crisis?

PATTERNS OF CRIME IN AUSTRALIA

When analysing crime data care has to be taken to account for the way that the information has been derived. National data need to account for differences between jurisdictions, including differences in legislation and how crimes are enumerated. Figure 13.4 shows the relative volume of recorded crime for six categories of major offences in Australia in 2007, amounting to a total of 1 025 491 offences. Property offences account for nearly 80 per cent of these major crimes, with petty theft ('Other theft') being the most commonly recorded crime, accounting for just under 50 per cent of the total. The violent crimes of homicide and kidnapping amount to less than 1 per cent of the eight major categories of offences and do not appear in the figure. In 2007, 282 homicides and 730 kidnappings were recorded. Homicide, kidnapping, sexual assault and robbery are the least common crimes, although high levels of fear are associated with these violent crimes.

In comparison with other countries, Australia has had a relatively high rate of crime (Van Kesteren et al. 2001) but since 2000 its position has improved. Figure 13.5 shows crime victimisation rates in the top 15 countries of 30 that were surveyed in 2003–04, with previous survey results also shown. In 2003–04 the countries with the highest rates were Ireland, England and Wales, New Zealand and Iceland, with Australia 14th, behind Belgium, the United States, Canada and Sweden. Levels of victimisation are closely related to levels of affluence and levels of urbanisation. The countries ranked at the bottom, including Spain, Japan, Hungary and Portugal (not shown in the figure), are relatively less urbanised and have relatively lower levels of affluence than the other countries surveyed. Other factors influencing declining victimisation rates are examined in the next section.

FIGURE 13.4

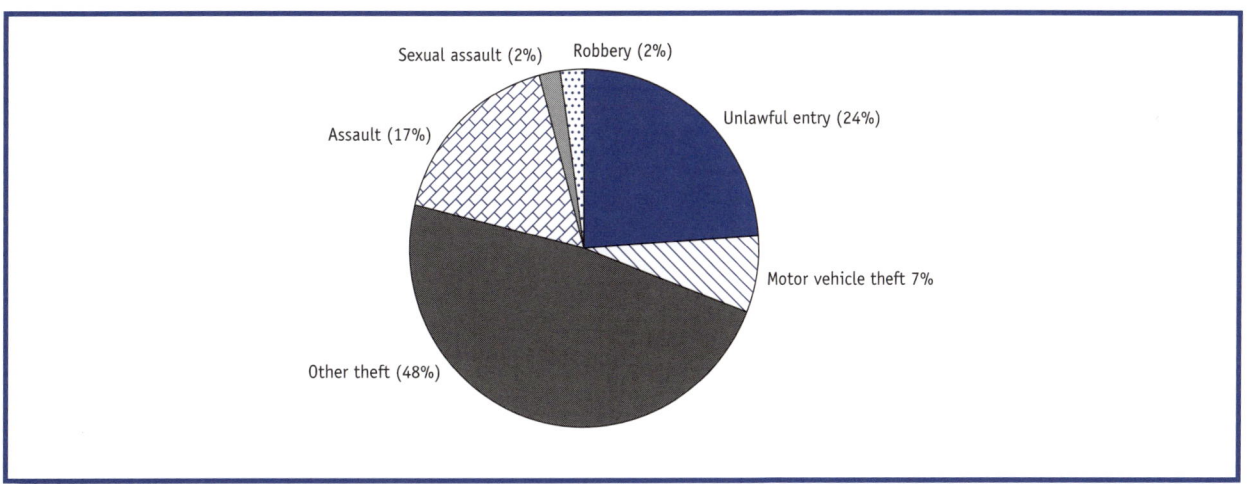

[Pie chart: Recorded crime in Australia, 2007]
- Unlawful entry (24%)
- Motor vehicle theft 7%
- Other theft (48%)
- Assault (17%)
- Sexual assault (2%)
- Robbery (2%)

Recorded crime in Australia, 2007 *Source:* Australian Institute of Criminology (2008). Used with permission from Australian Institute of Criminology (AIC) 2008.

FIGURE 13.5

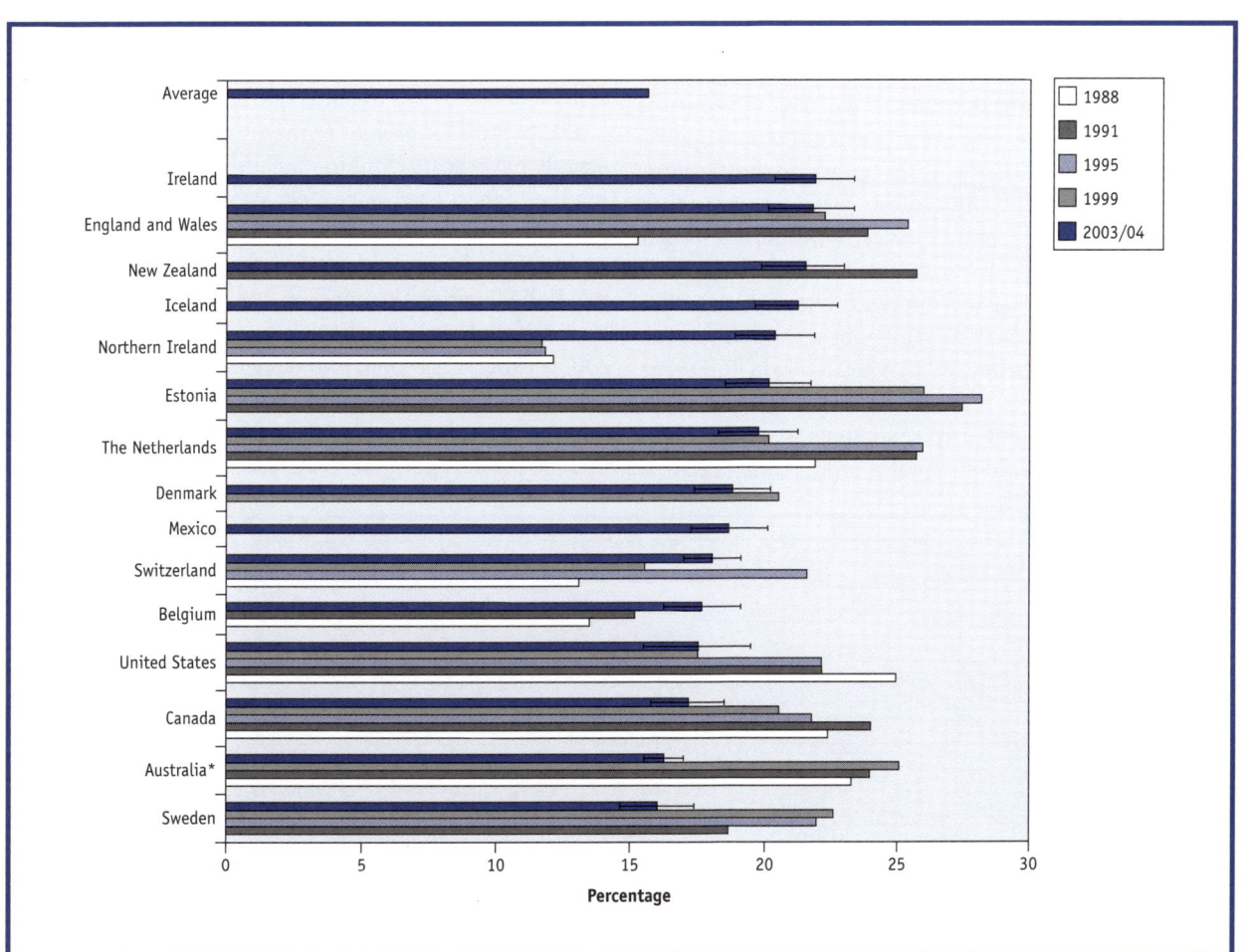

[Bar chart comparing crime victimisation rates across countries for years 1988, 1991, 1995, 1999, 2003/04. Countries listed: Sweden, Australia*, Canada, United States, Belgium, Switzerland, Mexico, Denmark, The Netherlands, Estonia, Northern Ireland, Iceland, New Zealand, England and Wales, Ireland, Average. X-axis: Percentage, 0 to 30.]

Comparison of crime victimisation rates in 15 countries, 2003–04 and earlier surveys

* The Australian victimisation rate is based on nine crimes, because the question about sexual victimisation was omitted. If this had been included, the overall victimisation rate would a percentage point higher (est. 16.5 per cent).

Source: Van Dijk, Van Kesteren & Smit (2007, p. 43). Reproduced with permission.

Crime rates in Australia over time

It is difficult to assess long-term trends in crime rates because of the scarcity of reliable data for the 18th and 19th centuries and the different methods of recording crime. Nonetheless, it can confidently be said that since the 19th century the volume of crime has increased, but there are also periods when crime rates have declined (see Figure 13.6). According to Mukherjee (1981), the dip in offences that occurred around the 1890s can be linked to the recession of that time, while similar dips occurred around the times of the Depression and World War I as well as World War II. These were primarily due to declines in petty offences such as vandalism and disguise the growth in property crime that was occurring in the same period. The end of World War II saw a rapid escalation in the volume of crime, largely explained by demographic changes and the expansion of opportunities for consumption.

The growth in crime that occurred in the 20th century is largely due to rising levels of affluence and new opportunities for crime. In the 19th century drunkenness, gambling and other public order offences, including homosexuality, were major issues, while crimes such as social security or cheque fraud, motor vehicle theft and computer hacking did not exist. Other crimes that concern us today, such as child abuse and domestic violence, were regarded as private matters (Graycar 2001).

Research on violent crime suggests that the 19th century was more violent than it is today. Court records suggest that the homicide rate in Victoria between 1871 and 1875 was more than double the rate a century later (Mukherjee, Walker & Jacobsen 1986). Since then, long-term trends suggest that the homicide rate has remained within a relatively stable range of between just under 1 and 2.4 per 100 000 population (Indermaur 1996).

More recently, official crime rate data suggest that rates for some offences have declined, while others continue to increase. The number of crimes gives an indication of the volume of crime, but the rate of crime provides the best indication of trends since it accounts for changes in the size of the population. Figure 13.7 shows rates of property crimes recorded by the police between 1996 and 2007, for other theft, unlawful entry with intent and motor vehicle theft. There has been a marked decrease in each of these, with 2007 representing the lowest recorded property crime rate since 1996. Between 2001 and 2007 other theft dropped by one-third, while motor vehicle theft decreased by more than 50 per cent. The rate of unlawful entry was relatively stable between 1996 to 2001, but has since declined.

The picture for violent crimes is more mixed. Rates of assault have been climbing steadily, with 2007 recording the highest level since 1996 at 840 crimes per 100 000 persons per year. Rates of sexual assault have also continued to rise, although less dramatically—from 78 crimes per 100 000 persons per year in 1997 to 94 in 2007. Other forms of violent crime have been declining: in 2007 the robbery rate was 86 per 100 000 persons per year, a 38 per cent decline from its peak in 2001; and the homicide rate has been trending downwards from its peak of 2.0 per 100 000 persons per year in 1999 to 1.3 in 2007.

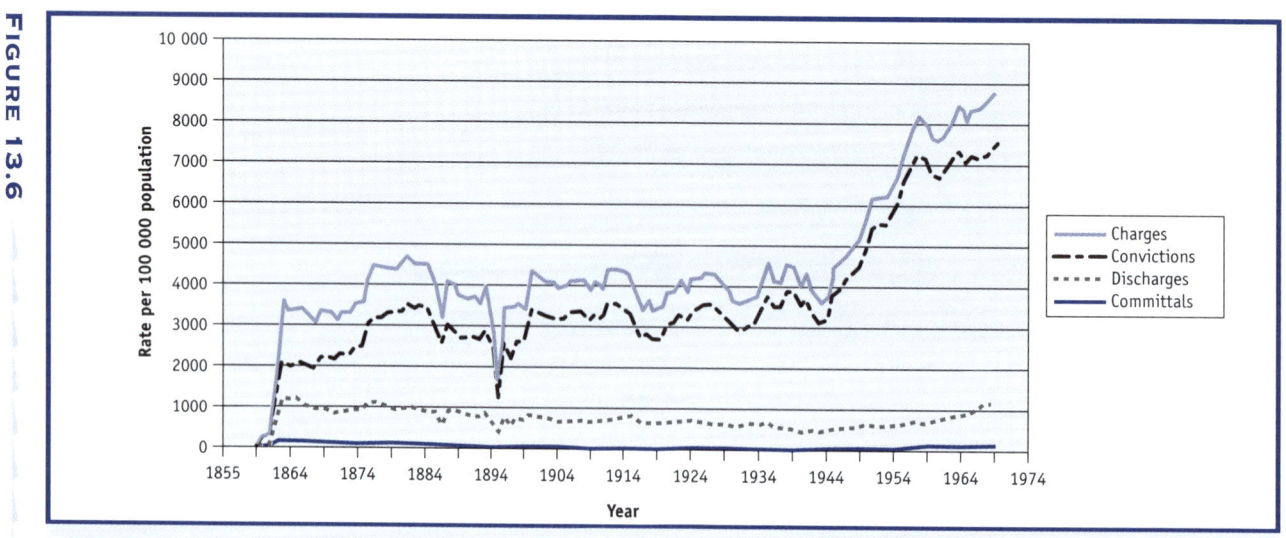

FIGURE 13.6

All offences heard and determined at Magistrates' Courts, Australia, 1859–1971 *Source:* Mukherjee (2000, pp. 45–62). Reproduced with permission of LexisNexis.

FIGURE 13.7

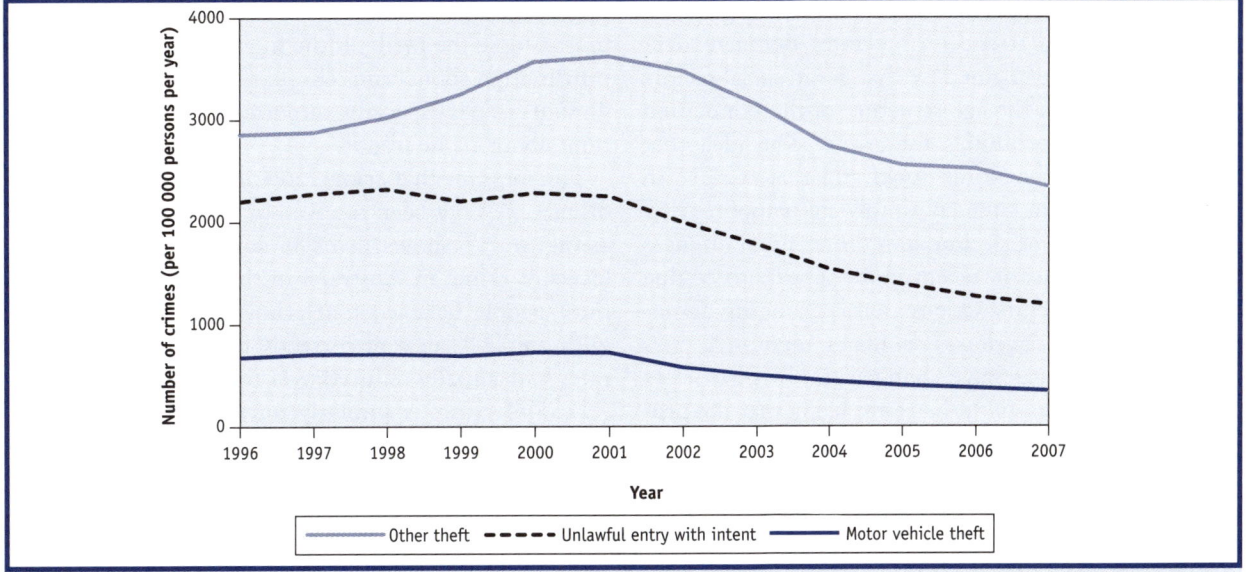

Property crimes, 1996–2007 *Source:* Australian Institute of Criminology (2008, p. 7). Used with permission of the Australian Institute of Criminology (AIC), 2009.

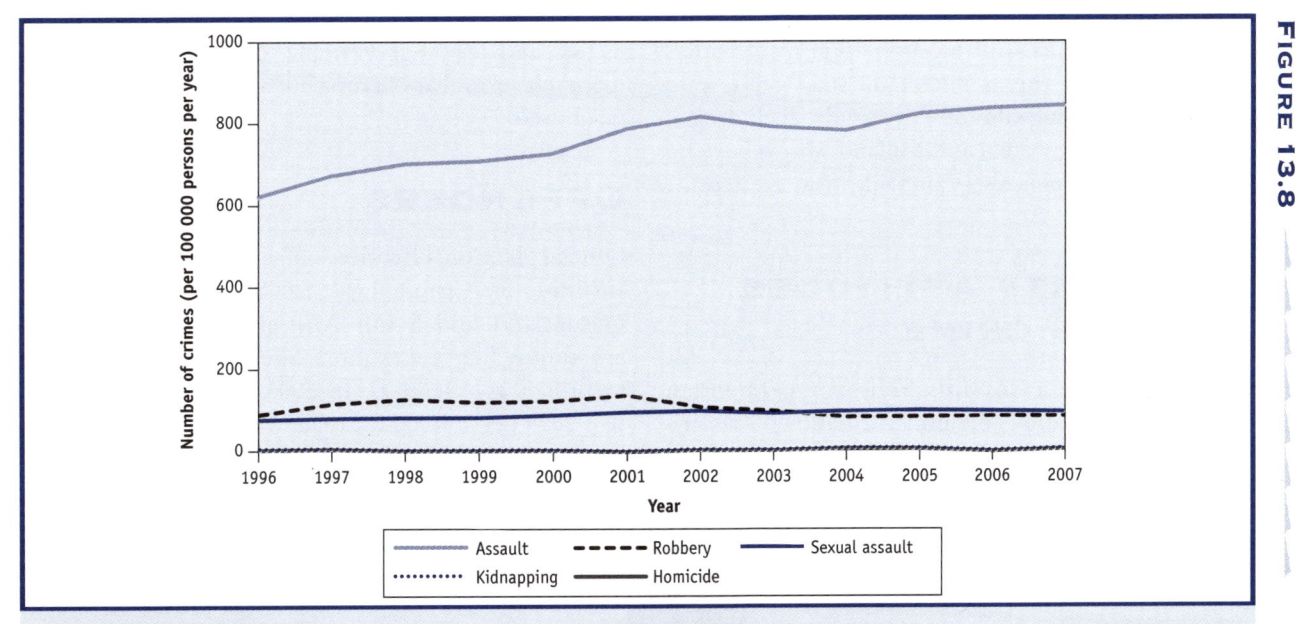

FIGURE 13.8

Violent crimes, 1996–2007
Note: Homicide and kidnapping each occur at a rate less than 5 per 100 000 persons per year and so are difficult to distinguish on this chart.
Source: Australian Institute of Criminology (nd, p. 6). Used with permission of the Australian Institute of Criminology (AIC).

Victim surveys are a more reliable indicator of crime trends than official records because they are less subject to changes derived from the shrinking of the dark figure rather than real increases in the incidence of offences. For example, the rise in sexual assault rates has been influenced by the increased willingness of women and the police to report and prosecute an incident, partly as a result of changes in legislation. The Australian Bureau of Statistics conducts a biannual survey of crime victimisation asking people about their experiences of criminal victimisation. The findings of the 2005 survey correlate with those of official data in showing an overall decline in rates of victimisation, but with some crimes increasing (ABS 2006f). Prevalence rates for break-ins, attempted break-ins, robbery and motor vehicle theft have declined, whereas rates for assault and sexual assault have increased.

The evidence suggests that far from being on an inexorable upward trend, crime rates fluctuate over time and are best explained by changes in social factors such as changes in the age structure of the population or increased opportunities for crime. The idea that law and order is breaking down and that we live in increasingly violent times is simply not supported by careful analysis. The decline in most criminal offences that has taken place in recent years appears to be due to a number of factors. One reason is changing demographics. In most developed countries, high birth rates and high death rates have changed to low birth rates and low death rates, with the result being that the proportion of young people in the population has been in decline since around the 1970s. Since young males are responsible for most recorded crime, this has had the effect of reducing levels of recorded crime. A second reason is improved security measures, which have reduced opportunities for crime. There are claims that tougher policing and more severe sentencing have been responsible for the decline in crime, through a combination of deterrence and incapacitation of offenders. The evidence for this is uncertain, since crime rates have been declining almost universally, including in countries such as Sweden and Finland, which have not introduced such policies (Van Dijk, Van Kesteren & Smit 2007, pp. 102–3).

Community attitudes towards crime

Community attitudes towards crime play an important role in the formulation and implementation of criminal justice policy. Public concern that offenders are 'getting off too lightly' or that crime is out of control can put pressure on politicians to 'do something about it'. For most people the media is the most important source of information about crime (Roberts & Indermaur 2009, p. 9), so its role is especially important in creating perceptions about crime trends.

The message that crime rates are declining for many offences has not been received by most people. Instead, as Figure 13.9 shows, in a 2007 survey about changes in levels of crime in Australia in the previous two years most people believed that crime rates had increased, with only 2.9 per cent correctly identifying that crime rates had actually reduced over this period.

Fear of crime is similarly unrelated to reality, with people having a far higher level of fear than is justified by crime rates. The 2007 Survey of Social Attitudes (Roberts & Indermaur 2009) showed that the percentage of respondents who were worried or fairly worried about victimisation was relatively high, ranging from 20 per cent (physical attack in the home) to more than 50 per cent (credit card used illegally via internet) (see Table 13.1). There is also little relationship between risk factors and fear. For example, older people have the highest level of fear of crime but are the least likely to be victimised.

Offenders

Official data on offenders collated by the Australian Institute of Criminology (2008) covering Victoria, Queensland and South Australia shows that males are almost four times more likely than females to be identified as offenders. In 2006–07 the offender rate was 2699 per 100 000 for males compared with 747 for females, while the offender rate for homicides was 2.3 per 100 000 for males compared with 0.5 for females

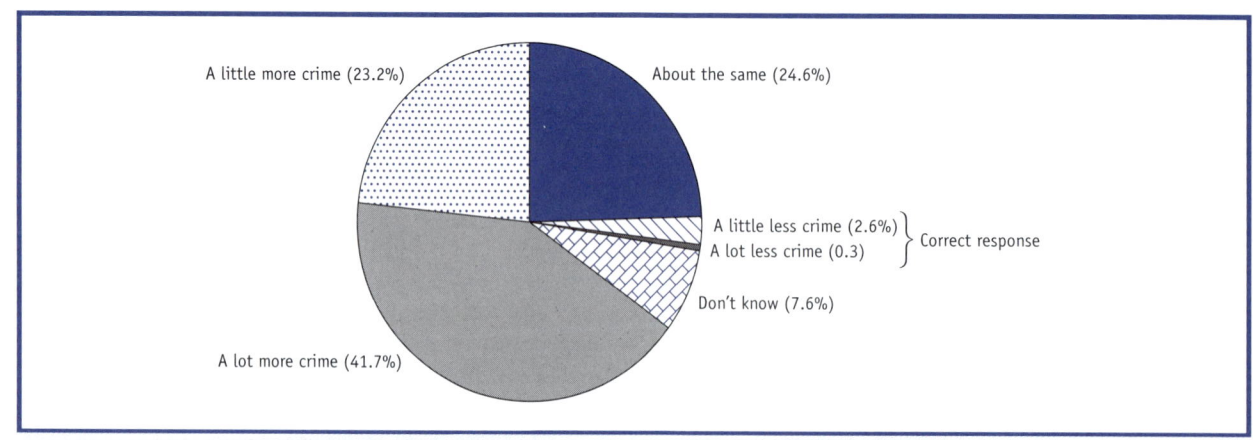

FIGURE 13.9

A little more crime (23.2%)
About the same (24.6%)
A little less crime (2.6%) } Correct response
A lot less crime (0.3)
Don't know (7.6%)
A lot more crime (41.7%)

Perceptions of crime trends over the past two years Source: Roberts & Indermaur (2009, p. 10). Used with permission of the Australian Institute of Criminology (AIC), 2009.

(Dearden & Jones 2008, p. 12). For males, offender rates were highest for other theft, assault and unlawful entry with intent and lowest for robbery, sexual assault and homicide. For females, offender rates were highest for other theft, fraud/deception and assault.

Since 1996–97 offending rates for juvenile females has increased by 14 per cent, but for juvenile males it has declined by 17 per cent. However, female juvenile offenders comprise only 24 per cent of all juvenile offenders. Official data show that offenders are more likely to be young, with juveniles heavily overrepresented. Offending rates are highest for persons aged between 15 and 19 and decline thereafter. In 2006–07 the offending rate for persons aged 15–19 was 5735 per 100 000, four times the rate of 1305 per 100 000 for offenders aged 19 or more.

Official crime data suggest that crime is concentrated among disadvantaged sections of the population. Figure 13.10 shows that in 2007 nearly half of male detainees and more than 40 per cent of female detainees were early school leavers having completed Year 10 or less, one-fifth of males and 24 per cent of females had completed Year 11 or 12, and only 5 per cent of detainees had obtained a university qualification. Furthermore, only one-fifth of adult male detainees and less than 10 per cent of adult female detainees were in full-time employment, with one-third of adult males and almost half of adult females receiving a welfare or government benefit as their main source of income (Australian Institute of Criminology 2008, p. 67).

This portrayal of crime as an offence of young, low-income males needs qualification, especially in relation to property crime:

- The dark figure for property crimes is very high and clearance rates are low. In 2007 in New South

TABLE 13.1

Concern about becoming a victim of crime							
	Physical attack —home %	Physical attack —street %	Sexual assault %	Home broken into %	Identity stolen via internet %	Credit card stolen %	Credit card used illegally via internet %
Very worried	6.0	8.3	6.0	14.9	15.9	17.5	23.0
Fairly worried	13.6	22.3	12.5	34.6	24.4	28.0	27.9
Not very worried	49.9	52.3	41.3	41.6	328	37.5	27.1
Not worried at all	30.5	17.1	40.2	8.9	26.9	17.0	22.0
Total	100.0	100.0	100.0	100.0	100.0	100.0	100.0

Source: Roberts & Indermaur (2009, p. 15). Used with permission of the Australian Institute of Criminology (AIC), 2009.

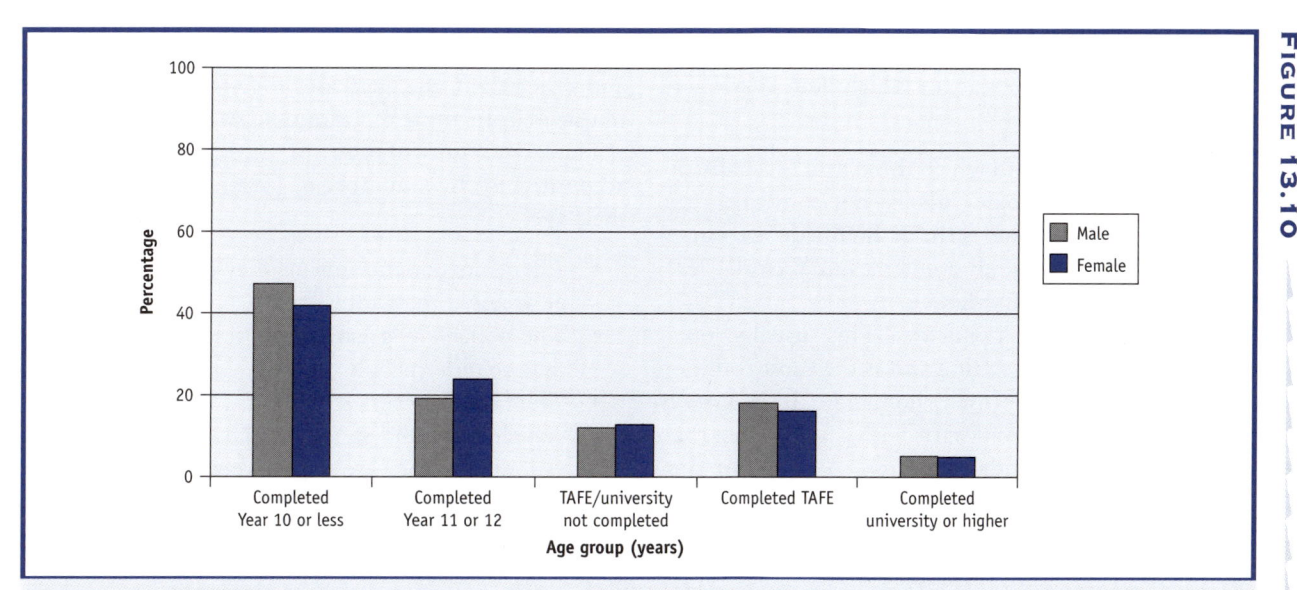

FIGURE 13.10 Education level of adult police detainees, 2007 Source: Australian Institute of Criminology (2008, p. 66). Used with permission of the Australian Institute of Criminology (AIC), 2009.

Wales, 30-day clearance rates were 13.7 per cent for robbery, 6 per cent for break and enter, and 5 per cent for motor vehicle theft (Welch 2008). Often the perpetrator remains unknown and professional criminals are less likely to be caught than amateurs.

- The crimes of the rich and powerful tend to be invisible. Inadequate workplace safety standards, tax evasion, many cyber crimes, state corruption and identity fraud are examples of acts that cause significant social harm, but that may not be defined as criminal and, even if they are, may be hard to detect or control.
- Certain groups are targeted more frequently by the police, including young people and Indigenous individuals (Blagg & Wilkie 1995; Cunneen & White 2007; Youth Justice Coalition et al. 1994).
- Juveniles are more likely to be caught than older people. This is not only because of their lack of experience but also because they are more visible. They often work in groups and so multiple offenders may be charged for a single offence.

The evidence on violent street crimes such as homicide, assault, sexual assault and robbery is more conclusive and suggests that the violent criminal is typically a young, working-class male. In a high percentage of incidents of violent crime alcohol is involved (Adams et al. 2008).

Social constructions of masculinity are an important element in the explanation of violent crime. Ken Polk's analysis of homicides in Victoria between 1985 and 1989 identifies four distinctive 'masculine scenarios' of lethal violence (1994). The first is primarily male perpetrator/female victim homicide, while the remaining three are male on male homicide (i.e. in which both victim and perpetrator are male):

- Sexual homicide in which the victim is usually the perpetrator's female partner but sometimes the victim's rival. This form of homicide accounted for 32 per cent of all homicides in Victoria. Jealousy is the primary motive.
- Confrontational homicide. This usually takes place in a public setting and is the most common form of male-on-male homicide. It is usually unpremeditated and starts with a fight rather than deliberate homicidal intention. A crowd of supporters is often present and it is not unusual for one of these to become the unintended victim of the homicide. Alcohol is often implicated as well as provocation and anger. The violence occurs in defence of the honour of the males concerned. Ironically, the incident leading to the homicide is often of a trivial nature.
- Homicide as part of engagement in another crime, such as armed robbery.
- Homicide as the resolution of a personal conflict such as non-payment of a drug debt.

Like many criminologists, Polk sees masculinity as an essential element in the explanation of crime, especially violent crime.

Young people and crime

The term *young people* can include a range of ages, such as individuals between 16 and 24 years. The term juvenile is used in criminal law to refer to individuals under the age of 17 or 18 years, depending on the legal jurisdiction. Juvenile offender rates have generally been twice as high as adult rates, but there has been variation over time. Between 1996–97 and 2003–04 juvenile offender rates decreased, but they have been increasing since 2005–06. In contrast, adult offender rates have been declining consistently since 2001–02. In 2006–07 adult offender rates were less than half the juvenile rate (1492 per 100 000 persons for adults compared with 3532 for juveniles).

There have also been changes in the pattern of juvenile offending. Compared with young adults, juveniles are more likely to be involved in property crime than violent crime, but since 1996 offence rates for property crimes have been declining while those for violent crime have been increasing (Australian Institute of Criminology 2008, p. 59). Figure 13.11 shows changes in offence rates among juveniles, with declines in the rate of offences for motor vehicle theft, burglary, fraud and other theft and increases for assault and robbery (Australian Institute of Criminology 2008).

The overrepresentation of juveniles is partially accounted for by a number of features associated with their age:

- Their inexperience means they are more likely to be arrested than adults.
- The police pay greater attention to young people than to older people.
- The types of crimes they commit, such as motor vehicle theft and shoplifting, have a high level of visibility, so they are more likely to be caught.
- They tend to commit crimes in groups. This increases the likelihood that they will be caught and also means that more than one individual will be counted against the same offence, thereby inflating their representation.

FIGURE 13.11

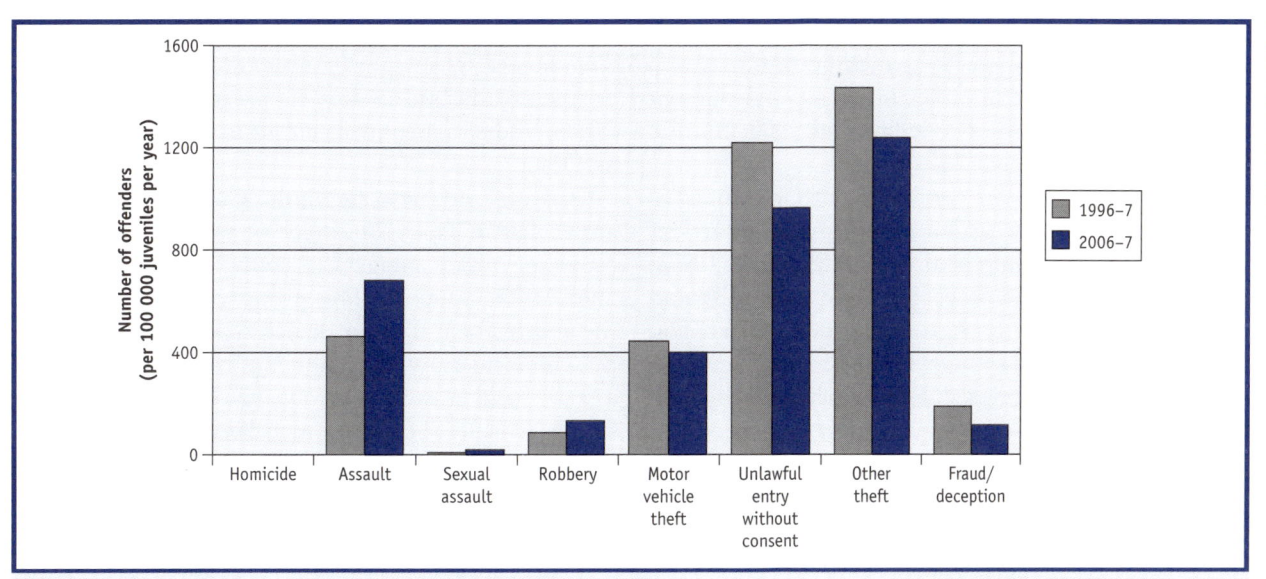

Juvenile offenders by offence type, 1996–97 and 2006–07 *Source:* Australian Institute of Criminology (2008, p. 59). Used with permission of the Australian Institute of Criminology (AIC), 2009.

- They are more likely to commit crimes in their own neighbourhood, increasing the likelihood that they will be seen, identified and reported.

The risk factors that predict which young people are most likely to be involved in crime are closely correlated with marginalisation and exclusion. They include:

- coming from a low socioeconomic background
- using drugs or alcohol
- being reared in a single-parent family
- wagging school
- poor school performance
- experiencing parental neglect or rejection
- having parents who are involved in crime (White & Habibis 2005, p. 295).

Cunneen and White (2002) point out that there is a strong connection between class situation, youth engagement in crime and the criminalisation of marginalised young people. Changes in patterns of employment and social expectations relating to consumption occur at a critical time in the life cycle of young people as they establish their identity as adults. Yet these forces are not distributed evenly throughout the population but are mediated by class, impacting most powerfully on those with the least resources.

Numerous studies have shown that while many juveniles have some contact with the justice system, the majority do not offend very often. A small percentage of juvenile offenders have multiple contacts and account for a disproportionate amount of crime. Cain's (1998) analysis of juvenile offenders in New South Wales found that 9 per cent of juvenile offenders were responsible for almost one-third of all criminal appearances and less than 2 per cent of juvenile offenders were responsible for almost 10 per cent of all criminal appearances. Nonetheless, those who did reoffend, including persistent offenders, were likely to commit a property crime rather than a violent crime and so did not escalate to more serious offences. These studies confirm the view that most juveniles grow out of offending behaviour as they mature.

Young people and gangs

A **gang** can refer to a number of different groups, including organised crime gangs and street gangs. White (2002) defines a gang as a group of people who see themselves, and are seen by others, as a gang primarily because of their illegal activities. He argues the critical feature of gang membership is not engagement in crime but a shared characteristic, such as similar social interests, ethnic identity or the need for social belonging (White et al. 1999). Messerschmidt (1995; 1997) argues that young people join gangs as a way of gaining a sense of belonging and identity, especially when they are excluded from conventional pathways such as a job and family. For both young men and young women the gang provides an environment in which they can establish and enact their masculinity and femininity in ways that are recognised within their communities but that are not otherwise so easily available to them. For disempowered young people, belonging to a gang is accessible and inexpensive and offers an otherwise elusive source of prestige. Gang membership may also be important for mutual protection in an environment of violence and uncertainty (Collins et al. 2000; Gordon & Foley 1998; White et al. 1999).

When these factors are combined with membership of an ethnic minority group they provide a particularly potent mix (Collins et al. 2000; McDonald 1999a; White et al. 1999). Some people from culturally and linguistically diverse backgrounds, such as Lebanon or Vietnam, experience high levels of social marginalisation. This is expressed both structurally in high levels of unemployment and culturally in a pervasive racism that permeates their daily experience.

The reporting of a series of sexual assaults in Sydney in 2001 illustrates the ease with which the links between being a member of an ethnic minority (in this case, Lebanese Arab) and being criminal, immoral and dangerous are made. These sexual assaults attracted widespread media attention both for their brutality and because of suggestions that they involved a form of reverse ethnic domination, as the male attackers were from an ethnic minority while the young women were all white Australians. In *Bin Laden in the Suburbs* Poynting et al. (2004) argue that media reporting follows a long tradition within mainstream Australian culture of creating Arab migrants as 'folk devils' who threaten the social fabric of Australian communities. Poynting et al. point out that in the moral panic that followed the first reports the stories were immediately racialised. The sexual assaults were explicitly linked to the ethnic background of the perpetrators so that Arab culture itself was on trial. To be of Arab descent was to be inherently suspect, uncivilised and treacherous. Poynting et al. offer the following portrayal of media representations of the Arab 'threat':

> *They invade our shores, take over our neighbourhood and rape our women. They are all little bin Ladens and they are everywhere: explicit bin Ladens; closet bin Ladens; conscious bin Ladens and unconscious bin Ladens; bin Ladens on the beach and bin Ladens in the suburbs. Within this register, the Arab, like the Jew or the Nazi, is intolerable as such. Even a single Arab is a threat.* (2004, p. 4)

Whole communities were subjected to this form of ideological denigration. Yet there was no evidence that the sexual assaults were in any way linked with the values, beliefs and traditions of the local Arab communities or with Arab culture in general. Nor was there any evidence that racial hatred was the primary motive. The effect was to marginalise and exclude Arab migrants. Young, second-generation Australians from non–English-speaking backgrounds may identify as Australians, but they are subjected to an ideology of racism and social control that insists on treating them as 'Other'.

Drawing on Messerschmidt, Collins et al. (2000) argue that in these conditions of social exclusion and economic disadvantage the young men turn to one another for support. The group becomes a site for the construction of a particular type of working-class masculine identity that values physical prowess and assertiveness as well as group loyalty in a seemingly hostile world. The young men become vulnerable to engagement in acts of collective violence against, and resistance to, both Anglo-Australians and other ethnic groups. But rather than resolving the problem, this response exacerbates it by further reinforcing the negative stereotyping and social reaction that produced it in the first place. Racism, economic marginalisation and a particular type of masculinity combine with the young men's struggle for identity and social space to reinforce their disadvantage. For Collins et al. it is these structural forces that shape ethnic violence rather than the cultural factors suggested by the media.

Public fears about the growth of American-style gangs in Australia appear to be misplaced. Research by White and Perrone (2000) found no evidence of American-style gangs appearing in Australian cities. They do argue, however, that the social conditions that give rise to such gangs are present. These include negative stereotyping of young ethnic minorities by the police and the media, police harassment, and economic and social exclusion. They warn that failure to address these conditions could cause problems in the future.

Young people and the police

White's study of young people (1990) analyses the motives behind young people's use of public space and their interaction with the police. He points out that young people lack both physical and cultural space. They have low material resources and power, and also receive little support from the state or civil society as they experience the transition from childhood to adulthood. Their use of public spaces, particularly shopping centres, is a response to their structural situation. Hanging out in shopping centres provides them with a sense of excitement and interest, where they can see and be seen by their peers. It offers them space to develop their own identity away from the restrictions of the private sphere of home and school. It provides a degree of empowerment not available elsewhere. For some young people this may include involvement in loud, unruly behaviour, shoplifting, petty vandalism and fights. Interaction between police and youth in shopping centres is inherently fractious because of the conflict between the needs of shop owners and traders and those of the young people who 'hang out' there. The shopping centre is ostensibly a public space but is designed for the consumption of consumer goods. The young people present a social order 'problem' for retailers and the police, who see their presence as an intrusion. The police face pressures to be seen to be 'doing their duty' and to 'protect the public', and respond by controlling, and often excluding, young people. White argues that rather than meeting the needs of young people this excludes them further, with the most marginalised groups being most vulnerable to this (White 1990; 1994, p. 122).

Research shows that the police do target young people. Studies of police–youth relations point to persistent and ongoing problems and conflicts between law enforcement officers and young people (White & Alder 1994; Blagg & Wilkie 1995; Collins et al. 2000). Research by Phillips and Smith (2000a) on complaints of police violence found that three in five incidents involved only young people under 25 years. In 26 per cent of the incidents there was no evidence of any form of provocative behaviour by the civilian, and in a further 26 per cent the behaviour consisted of the civilian being disrespectful towards the officer. The physical force used by the police in the incidents ranged from pushing and poking (53 per cent of incidents) to punching (44 per cent of incidents), kicking (23 per cent of incidents) and hitting with a baton (15 per cent of incidents).

In their analysis of the time–space dynamics of the incidents Phillips and Smith found that incidents that occurred at night and in public space were more likely to involve major physical force (punching, kicking, baton-hitting) than those that occurred during the day or in other locations. They argue that this can be explained in terms of the different perceptions that the police and civilian users bring to public spaces at night. For civilians, many public spaces at night are interpreted as an area for fun and playful activity, whereas for the police they are defined as a zone of danger, 'where hidden threats lurk and where potentially threatening characters and incidents tend to be found' (2000a, p. 490). This mismatch of understandings and expectations goes some way towards explaining the problematic encounters between the police and young people.

OFFENDING WOMEN

According to all available statistics, women commit fewer crimes than men. In Australia men outnumber women in every category of serious crime. The few areas where women do predominate as offenders are in those that relate to their female gender role. They relate to their sexuality (prostitution and promiscuity), to their domestic role (shoplifting and social security offences) and to their roles as child-rearers (crimes against children and infants, and illegal abortion). Crimes such as promiscuity, ungovernability and running away from home similarly reflect our society's endeavour to ensure that women conform to conventional notions of the good, passive woman. The profile of female offenders is also quite different from that of men. Female homicide offenders are usually older than male offenders and are likely to have been victims of domestic violence.

Although it is widely accepted that women's engagement in crime is less than that of men, some theorists have argued that women are treated more leniently by the police and the courts. Pollak called this the chivalry factor (1950). Although there is evidence that white middle-class women do benefit from such a factor, there is also considerable evidence that in so far as there is an ethos of chivalry and 'protection', it results in many women receiving harsher treatment than males. Stereotypes about appropriate sexual behaviour for women mean that women who do not conform to these are treated harshly. Evidence for this claim is found in the fact that while fewer girls than boys are placed in juvenile correctional institutions, proportionally fewer are there as the result of a criminal act. Young girls in the care of the state are much more likely to enter the juvenile justice system than the rest of the female juvenile population (Alder 1997). Girls in welfare placements or foster care are particularly vulnerable to being charged with criminal offences and being characterised as a 'serious offender' in situations where they may be acting out as a result of their difficult circumstances (Alder 1997).

Alder makes the point that in the case of young girls the line between welfare and justice tends to become blurred. Dominant discourses about girls' sexuality lead to attempts to control their behaviour, to protect them against both potential abuse and their own desires. The result is that the decision to place young women in custodial care is reached far more readily than for boys. While in Australia this pattern has changed in the past decade as a result of the separation of juvenile criminal offences from welfare, in the United States the pattern remains unchanged (Alder 1998, p. 55).

VICTIMS

Until the 1970s little attention was paid to victims. Feminism, victims' movements and left- and right-realist arguments changed this so that today the perspectives and needs of victims receive greater recognition within both criminology and the criminal justice system.

Like perpetrators of crime, victimisation rates are socially patterned. Most people experience the effects of a criminal act on a fairly regular basis, but some groups are victimised with much greater frequency than others. For most violent crimes—including robbery, attempted murder, blackmail and extortion, and murder—men are more likely than women to be victims (ABS 2009c). In 2008, 72 per cent of victims of attempted murder and 61 per cent of victims of murder were males, with nearly two-thirds killed by non-family members (ABS 2009c, p. 8; Dearden & Jones 2008, p. iii). Table 13.2 shows victimisation prevalence rates for assault and robbery (ABS 2006f). For assault, men have higher prevalence rates than women, but because the figures include domestic violence, the differences are not great. For both groups single, employed individuals aged under 45 years have the highest risk, but here the similarity ends. Men are most likely to be assaulted in a public place, whereas women are more likely to be assaulted in the home. Prevalence rates are higher for 15–19-year-old women compared with 20–24-year-olds. For robbery the group with the highest risk is young, single, employed men living in a capital city and out on the street.

Men who are victims of other men therefore form one of the main categories of victims of violence. The two other main categories are women victimised by their male ex- or current partners (with children also forming part of this group) and Indigenous individuals, both of which are considered below. It is also important to recognise the vulnerability of children to violence: 10 per cent of all homicide victims are children aged under 15 years, nearly all of them killed by their parents (Dearden & Jones 2008, p. iii).

TABLE 13.2 Prevalence rates for victims of robbery and assault—selected characteristics, 2005

	Assault ('000)		Robbery ('000)	
Age group	**Males**	**Females**	**Males**	**Females**
15–19	68.1	65.4	13.4	3.3
20–24	66.9	45.3	9.2	2.0
25–34	97.8	89.2	6.2	2.8
35–44	80.7	69.8	6.5	0.9
45–54	59.7	57.8	np	np
55–64	30.5	19.5	5.1	2.8
Marital status				
Married	173.8	136.6	6.9	4.6
Not married	238.8	221.3	37.1	10.3
Labour force status				
Employed	319.3	233.4	28.7	9.5
Unemployed	25.6	23.6	4.0	1.2
Area of residence				
Capital city	254.6	58.7	29.7	9.8
Other	158.0	41.3	14.3	5.1
Location of incident				
Home	89.6	148.8	5.8	4.6
Work/study	106.4	91.9	6.1	1.5
Street	63.1	28.4	16.2	5.1
Place of entertainment	75.1	26.6	np	np

np = not available for publication but included in totals where applicable, unless otherwise indicated.
Source: Adapted from ABS (2006c, pp. 19–23).

VIOLENCE AGAINST WOMEN

The pattern of violence against women is quite distinct from that against men. Whereas men are more likely to experience violence in a public place, most often at the hand of a friend, an acquaintance or a stranger, women are more likely to be victimised in their home by a current or former intimate male partner. More than one million Australian women are estimated to have experienced violence from a former partner since the age of 15 (ABS 2006c, p. 35)—this represents 15 per cent of women aged 18 years and over.

Nearly one-quarter of homicides in 2006–07 were intimate homicides involving current or former sexual partners, with women usually the victims (Dearden & Jones 2008, p. iii). Polk's study of homicides in Victoria in the 1990s found that possessive jealousy, combined with a determination to control the victim at all costs, was the motivating factor in most cases. The words 'If I can't have you, no one will' occur with tragic regularity (Polk 1994). Separated women are especially vulnerable to violent crime and have a violent crime victimisation rate that is higher than that of any other population group. In 2006–07, 43 per cent of homicides between intimates had a history of domestic violence with police involvement (Dearden & Jones 2008, p. 2).

Although all violent crimes, with the exception of homicide, are seriously underreported, the problem is especially acute for women. International surveys show that sexual incidents are the least frequently reported crimes (on average, 15 per cent are reported), and even though sexual assault is more frequently reported the figure is less than one-third of all mentioned incidents (28 per cent) (Van Dijk, Van Kesteren & Smit 2007). Patterns of reporting vary according to the nature of the relationship with the offender, with reporting being highest when the offender is a stranger and lowest when the offender is a current intimate partner.

Indigenous women are particularly vulnerable to domestic violence. In New South Wales in 2008, 7 per cent of victims of sexual assault were Indigenous, with the Indigenous victimisation rate nearly 3.5 times higher than the non-Indigenous rate. The perpetrators of assault are more likely to be known to Indigenous victims than to non-Indigenous victims. In the Northern Territory over half of Indigenous victims of assault identified a family member, usually a partner, as the offender, compared with 10 per cent for non-Indigenous victims of assault (ABS 2009c, pp. 22–3).

The extent of intimate violence has led to policy developments at the state and federal level, with changes in legislation and policing practices designed to apprehend perpetrators and protect victims. It is no longer the case that family violence is regarded as a private matter. But for Indigenous women and children there remains much to be done. Although violence within Indigenous homes is the subject of considerable public debate, this has not yet resulted in a similar level of policy change, despite its urgency as a social issue.

INDIGENOUS PEOPLE AND CRIME

The relationship between Indigenous people and the law has been an issue of ongoing public concern since the 1990s. It was first placed on the political agenda with the Royal Commission into Aboriginal Deaths in Custody (1991), followed by the 'Stolen Generations' Report (NISATSIC 1997) and the Northern Territory Emergency Intervention in 2008.

Indigenous people are overrepresented at every stage of the criminal justice system. They are arrested, charged and incarcerated at rates far in excess of their number in the population. Moreover, the overrepresentation is not limited to particular states or offences but occurs in every state, for almost every offence and at every level of the criminal justice system, from arrests through to imprisonment. The overrepresentation is particularly severe in Western Australia and Queensland.

In 2001, 40 per cent of Indigenous males aged between 20 and 24 years appeared before the New South Wales courts charged with a criminal offence, compared with 8.4 per cent for the male population as a whole (Weatherburn, Lind & Hua 2003). In 2008 Indigenous people in Western Australia were 20 times more likely to be imprisoned than non-Indigenous people. Nationally, Indigenous prisoners represented 24 per cent of the total prisoner population in 2007, with the Indigenous imprisonment rate being 16 times as high as the non-Indigenous rate (Australian Institute of Criminology 2008, p. 95).

A key recommendation of the Royal Commission into Aboriginal Deaths in Custody (1991) was a reduction in the rate of Indigenous incarceration. Figure 13.12 shows instead that Indigenous imprisonment rates have been steadily increasing since that time, with an overall increase of 10 per cent since 1992 and with the greatest growth occurring between 2006 and 2007.

Indigenous women are also severely overrepresented in the criminal justice system. In 2001 more than 6 per cent of the female Indigenous population appeared

FIGURE 13.12

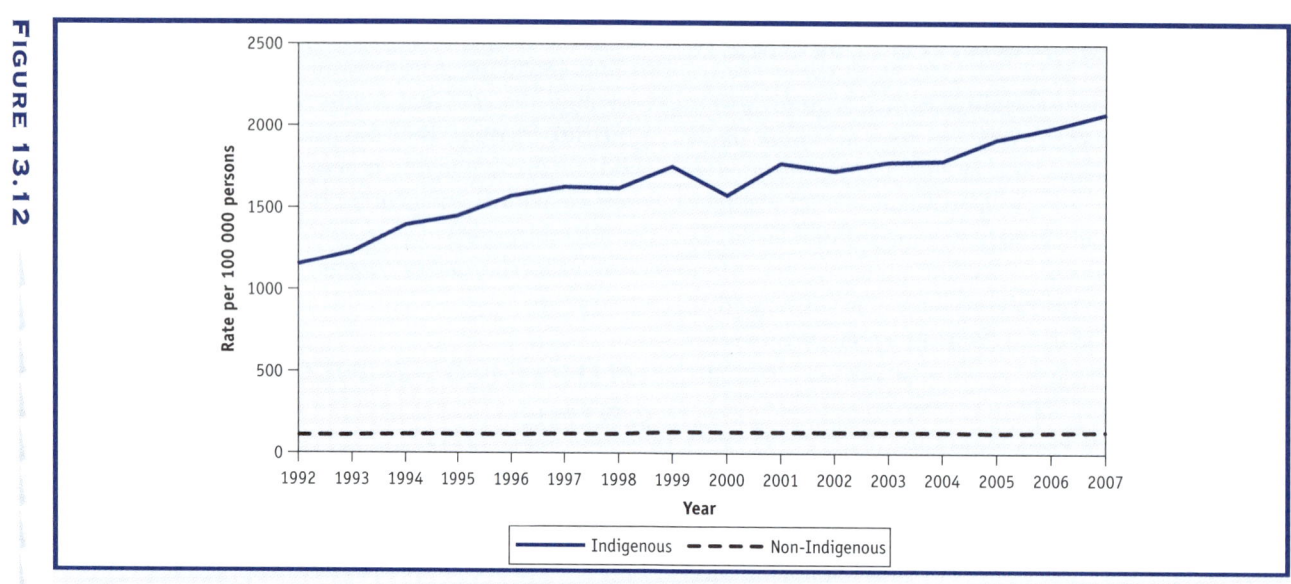

Indigenous and non-Indigenous imprisonment rates, 1992–2007 (*Note:* Increases may be due to alterations in data collection methods and the willingness of individuals to identify as Indigenous.) *Source:* Australian Institute of Criminology (2008, p. 95). Used with permission of the Australian Institute of Criminology (AIC).

before the New South Wales courts, compared with 0.7 per cent for the female population as a whole. For Indigenous women in the 20–24 age group, the rate of court appearance was eight times higher than the corresponding rate for women in the general population (Weatherburn, Lind & Hua 2003). Figures for other states present similar patterns. Indigenous women represent the fastest growing group of prisoners, with incarceration rates increasing by 34 per cent between 2002 and 2006. Indigenous women are 23 times more likely to be imprisoned than non-Indigenous women.

For all prisoners, re-incarceration rates are very high, but for Indigenous men and women the rates are even higher: 74 per cent of Indigenous prisoners have previously been imprisoned, compared with 52 per cent of non-Indigenous prisoners (Australian Institute of Criminology 2008, p. 95). Young Indigenous men and women are especially vulnerable to criminalisation. A survey of juvenile detention from 1981 to 2002 found that Indigenous juveniles were 19 times more likely to be detained than the non-Indigenous juvenile population (Cahill & Marshall 2002). By 2002, 89 per cent of Indigenous males on supervision orders had entered the adult corrections system, with 71 per cent having served at least one term of imprisonment; and for those juveniles on care and protection orders the likelihood was that 91 per cent would have some contact with the adult corrections system (Lynch, Buckman & Krenske 2003, p. 2).

The overrepresentation of Indigenous people in official crime statistics needs to be placed in the context of their social disadvantage and exclusion, as well as the differential application of social control by official agencies. Over-policing leads to a high proportion of Indigenous people having recurrent, hostile encounters with police, the courts and custodial institutions. It also increases the likelihood that young Indigenous individuals will be in conflict with the law before they reach adulthood (Cunneen 2001).

Indigenous individuals and families are simultaneously offenders and victims, with the criminal justice system playing a critical role in this construction. Table 13.3 shows the extreme levels of violence experienced by Indigenous people compared with the non-Indigenous population. These figures for New South Wales reveal victimisation rates for serious violent crimes between two and six times the levels for non-Indigenous people for all offences except robbery and blackmail/extortion. This takes place against a background of high unemployment, inadequate housing and high levels of substance use. A process of deviance amplification and social polarisation takes place that, together with mandatory sentencing and social exclusion, helps to explain the overrepresentation of Indigenous people in the criminal justice system.

The Royal Commission into Aboriginal Deaths in Custody

Concern at the unacceptably high number of Indigenous people who died in prisons or lock-ups eventually

TABLE 13.3

Indigenous and non-Indigenous victimisation rates, New South Wales, 2008		
	Indigenous ('000)	**Non-Indigenous ('000)**
Murder	5.3	0.9
Attempted murder	2.0	0.9
Assault	3.79	1.03
Sexual assault	309.3	90.2
Kidnapping/abduction	14.6	7.2
Armed robbery	3.3	29.9
Unarmed robbery	42.4	70.0
Blackmail/extortion	—	1.3

Source: Burawoy (2005a, p. 16).

led to a Royal Commission into the deaths that took place between 1980 and 1989 (Royal Commission into Aboriginal Deaths in Custody 1991). To emphasise the significance of these deaths, Lincoln and Wilson point out that 'if non-Aboriginal people had been imprisoned at the same rate as Aborigines, then over 8500 non-Aboriginal people would have died in custody' (1994, p. 85).

The inquiry established that Aboriginal prisoners were dying in custody at the same rate as non-Aboriginal prisoners. However, as larger numbers of Aboriginal males than non-Aborigines were held in custody, the numbers were larger, even though the rates were the same. When these rates were compared with those of other countries, they were shown as relatively high (House of Representatives Standing Committee on Aboriginal and Torres Strait Islander Affairs 1994, p. 9; Biles 1990). The inquiry argued that the principal reason for the overrepresentation of Indigenous people was their extreme structural disadvantage. It focused on empowerment and self-determination as the means of overcoming this. It also highlighted the inadequacy of the existing methods of dealing with Aboriginal offenders.

The recommendations included diverting Aboriginal people away from the courts and gaol, assisting them to achieve greater levels of empowerment and self-determination, improving education and employment, and decriminalising public drunkenness together with establishing detoxification centres (House of Representatives Standing Committee on Aboriginal and Torres Strait Islander Affairs 1994, pp. 9–12). Yet few of these recommendations have been implemented and, if anything, Indigenous criminalisation is growing and remains one of the Australia's most significant social issues.

Reflective question: To what extent is the 'problem of crime' in Australia caused by young males?

CRIMES OF THE POWERFUL

Since the 1940s there has been a recognition that the middle and upper classes commit crimes that are at least as serious as the crimes of marginalised social groups. This was first recognised by Edwin Sutherland in the 1930s when he pointed to the phenomenon of **white-collar crime**—crimes committed by non-manual workers, often in the course of their employment (1949). Sutherland emphasised that crime in the business sector is just as real as crime among the disadvantaged and is arguably more damaging in terms of the sums involved and the damage to trust in society's institutions. Yet prisons are not filled with corporate executives. This can be partly explained by the relative invisibility of the crimes of the wealthy and the normalisation of their criminal activities.

Corporate crime refers to the activities of businesses—both large and small—that break the law, often on a routine basis. It can be defined as criminal acts committed by corporate executives and managers in the course of their employment that are intended to benefit the corporation and that, directly or indirectly, also benefit them.

Environmental crime refers to unauthorised or irresponsible acts or omissions that negatively impact on people and their environments. For example, in the 1980s and 1990s the Broken Hill Proprietary Company Limited (BHP) poured the waste from its Ok Tedi mine in Papua New Guinea into the local rivers, causing serious environmental damage, including widespread deforestation, the destruction of the local waterways and the loss of wildlife habitats. Lawsuits resulted in BHP's agreement to repair the damage and compensate local people.

State crime refers to crimes involving the state acting against its own citizens or against the citizens of another state. It includes corruption of state officials, dissemination of false and misleading statements to citizens, and illegal participation in the overthrow of other sovereign regimes.

An important definitional issue when considering the crimes of the powerful is that some acts described in the criminological literature as 'criminal' break civil and administrative, rather than criminal, laws. Yet they are considered crimes because of the moral issues they raise and the social harm they cause. By drawing attention to the different set of moral judgements that is applied to the activities of the rich, compared with those of the poor, criminologists can question everyday assumptions about why some acts are defined as criminal and subject to close scrutiny by law-enforcement agents, while others are ignored or treated much more lightly (Clinard & Yeager 1980).

The controversy over the response of transnational building materials company James Hardie Industries to compensate its employees who developed asbestosis is an example of this. As the cost of this compensation became apparent, the company restructured between 1995 and 2000 so that its assets went offshore, while its subsidiary companies (which carried legal liability for its employees' health) remained within Australia. The company then moved to the Netherlands, having assured the Australian courts that it had provided adequate money to a compensation fund to cover its liability for asbestosis claims. The fund turned out to be severely inadequate and in 2004 a judicial inquiry was very critical of the extent of this underfunding—the company had provided only $286 million, well short of the $1.573 billion that was estimated would be required. However, the company's restructuring meant that it had no legal obligation to provide compensation, and it was only after concerted efforts by politicians, trade unions and victims as well as new legislation that the company eventually provided adequate compensation. Efforts by the Australian Securities & Investments Commission to bring civil and criminal charges against James Hardie executives have failed (ACTU 2009).

Class and crime

Crimes of the powerful challenge traditional notions of crime, which rely on arguments that crime is a working-class phenomenon and is causally related to inequality. Crime is committed by all social groups. What differs are the motives, opportunities, resources and consequences of criminal behaviour. This is illustrated in Table 13.4, which summarises the association between

TABLE 13.4

The relationship between crime, power and motivation

Source of power	Social Position	Motivation	Types of crime
Control of economic and cultural resources	High/Medium	Maximisation of profit	Environmental crime, breaches of corporate law, occupational health and safety violations, violation of labour laws, fraud
		Maximisation of personal wealth	Tax evasion, insider trading, computer fraud
	Low	Subsistence: using illegal means to meet basic income needs or supplement low income	Burglary, theft, robbery, shoplifting, social security fraud, illegal prostitution
		Alienation, rooted in marginalisation from mainstream institutions	Public order crimes, such as vandalism; some violent crimes, such as rape, assault
Political	High/Medium	Maintenance of status quo	State crimes, such as police brutality, civil rights abuses, government corruption
		Maximisation of personal wealth	Embezzlement of public funds, 'jobs for the boys'
	Low	Attempted usurpation of status quo	Strikes, workplace sabotage, violent political protest

Source: Adapted from Cunneen & White (1995).

FIGURE 13.13

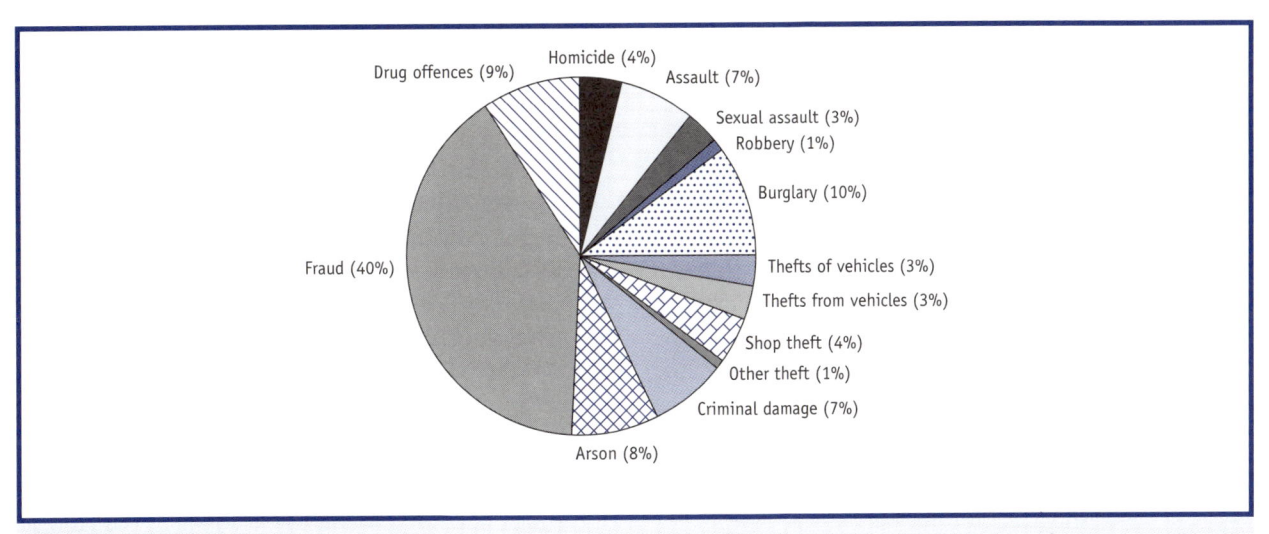

The costs of crime by major category Source: Rollings (2005, p. xi). Used with permission of the Australian Institute of Criminology (AIC).

Homicide (4%)
Assault (7%)
Sexual assault (3%)
Robbery (1%)
Burglary (10%)
Thefts of vehicles (3%)
Thefts from vehicles (3%)
Shop theft (4%)
Other theft (1%)
Criminal damage (7%)
Arson (8%)
Fraud (40%)
Drug offences (9%)

types of crime, motivation and the class position of the perpetrators, and how access to political, economic and cultural resources shapes who gets involved in what type of crime, and why. Box's (1983) explanation of corporate crime in terms of the pressure to engage in illegal activity in the face of competing demands of the profit imperative and external constraints such as government regulations explains both the motive and the nature of environmental crimes or fraud. This is quite different from the explanation of crime by young people as being due to economic marginalisation and the demands of consumer capitalism (Cunneen & White 2002).

The costs of crimes of the powerful

The financial costs of the crimes of the powerful are enormous. The Ponzi scheme operated by Bernie Madoff in the United States was estimated by federal prosecutors to have cost his clients almost US$65 billion (Bray 2009). The scheme involved paying clients profits from their own money, or from other clients' money, rather than from actual profit. It collapsed when Madoff was unable to maintain the payments. In Australia, when insurance giant HIH collapsed in 2001 it cost the public and stakeholders $5.3 billion (Elias 2003).

Estimates of recorded crime suggest that it comprises by far the largest component of all crime at $8516 million. In 2005, fraud cost $5.88 billion, four times the cost of the next largest category, burglary (see Figure 13.13) (Rollings 2005, p. xii).

The costs also involve physical damage to individuals and the environment, as well as to levels of trust within the community. Practices such as the inadequate testing of products, failure to acknowledge or release research results because they would harm sales of a commodity, and poor industrial safety standards can affect millions of people and whole communities. The hurried release of the drug thalidomide resulted in the births of an estimated 10 000 tragically deformed babies in at least 20 countries (Clinard & Yeager 1980, p. 266; Braithwaite 1984). Attempts by tobacco companies to produce research studies that deny the link between smoking and cancer affect an inestimable number of individuals (Chapman 1997). In 2006 the New South Wales government banned fishing in Sydney Harbour because it had found levels of dioxin in fish almost 100 times the World Health Organization's recommended dosage. Dioxins have been linked to serious health disorders including cancer, skin lesions and reproductive and immune system disorders. Investigations linked the dioxins to industrial pollution caused by dumping of pesticides, including Agent Orange, by chemical companies located at Homebush Bay between the late 1940s and the mid-1970s. Commercial fishing in the harbour was stopped and a multimillion dollar clean-up operation was undertaken (White 2008, pp. 103–5).

When a major business collapses, such as occurred with the telco One.Tel in 2001, it is not just that thousands of innocent victims lose their money; there is also a demoralising effect on public confidence in both business corporations and the regulatory powers of government. Misrepresentation in advertising leads to widespread cynicism about values and motives of business leaders. State crimes, such as the use of waterboarding on terror suspects by the US government in the aftermath of September 11, or the complicity of France and other Western powers in the attempted genocide of Tutsis in Rwanda in 1994 (Melvern 2006), have immeasurable effects on foreign relations and community perceptions about the integrity of politicians.

Far from being victimless, the crimes of the powerful are certainly as destructive as traditional crime. They appear victimless only because the relationship between the well-off offender and the victim is an indirect one, giving white-collar crimes an insidious quality that can be more dangerous than the violence we associate with traditional crimes. The reprehensible morality of the perpetrator may be obvious, especially to the victim; the illegality may not be and the corporation may successfully defend itself against prosecution.

Class and the criminal justice system

Middle- and upper-class criminals rarely suffer for their crimes for a number of reasons:

- *The invisibility of many crimes of the powerful.* For example, the only physical trace of a crime may be a computer record. Often prosecuting authorities face an enormous tangle of complex and highly specialised paperwork, which they need to track down and analyse.
- *Legal complications.* These include legal problems arising from the fact that the law is based on the guilt of individuals not corporations and on inappropriate legal responses because the case is heard under administrative rather than criminal law. For example, many occupational health and safety omissions are not regarded as criminal acts; and it is difficult to find evidence of illegality when companies are operating within a global network.
- *The immense resources that are often available to corporations.* For example, in 1999 the transnational oil company Esso hired a team of five barristers to present its case to the Royal Commission into the explosion at its Longford plant in Victoria.

The crimes of the powerful are coming under increasing scrutiny. In the wake of the economic crash of 2008 government leaders in Australia and the United States spoke of the need to increase regulation of corporations and to facilitate an enlightened capitalism that would develop business ethics that pay more attention to social and moral issues. According to the philosopher John Armstrong, a new business ethic is emerging that will be more socially responsible (2009). Whether or not capitalism can develop in this way is debatable given the pressures of global competition, but failure to do so may be equally costly.

Reflective question: Outline the arguments for and against the view that Australia is becoming a more violent society than it was a hundred years ago.

Case Study
The future of crime and deviance

If the face of the criminal in the year 2000 was that of a young male engaged in street crime, by the year 2050 this profile is likely to have been transformed. By that time population ageing will have reversed our current demographic profile of relatively few older people and many young people. As the age distribution in the population inverts, so the volume of crimes and acts of deviance typically committed by young people is likely to decline. This factor is probably part of the explanation for the decline of crime in some American cities, including New York (King & Mauer 2001).

So what will the profile of the 21st-century criminal look like? Probably, much more middle class. Crime has not escaped the effects of the transition from a manufacturing to a service economy. It has also been affected by globalisation. Global terrorism, environmental crimes, cyber crime, people smuggling and identity crime are emerging as the main areas in which law-breaking will occur. The explosion of information technology offers new possibilities of surveillance and social control, while simultaneously affording new forms of law-breaking, many of which are transnational. Telecommunications fraud, copyright infringement and 'phishing' are already increasingly prevalent. Phishing, for example, involves obtaining information about people through the internet in order to commit fraud. Phony emails from banks seeking personal passwords are one example. The Nigerian bank scam is another. This involved unsolicited emails purporting to be from a bank seeking an overseas partner to share in the proceeds of a large bank account owned by someone who had died leaving no heir. Email recipients were offered the opportunity to participate in the proceeds in return for an initial payment. Sophisticated technologies make identification of perpetrators difficult, and in many cases the perpetrators are based overseas, so any attempt to apprehend them involves negotiating complex international treaties and multiple agencies.

Just as the face of the criminal is likely to change, so is the face of the victim. Older people will be especially vulnerable. A significant proportion will not have children, and this, combined with high divorce rates, means that many will lack the security provided by close family support. While older people have an unfounded fear of becoming the victim of violent youth crime, in the future it is probable that the real threat will come from men in suits. The greater wealth of the baby boomer generation may make them a target for unscrupulous lawyers, insurance brokers and financial advisers.

Fear of crime is also likely to see a growth in gated communities. As the baby boomers enter old age, some will have sufficient wealth to retreat to an enclosed 'island' of security surrounded by high fences and electronically controlled gates.

Such trends may contribute to an increase in social division. In *The Exclusive Society* Jock Young (1999) argues that the conditions of late modernity are leading away from inclusiveness to exclusiveness, with the fault lines occurring along the lines of race and class. While the white middle class are becoming increasingly wealthy, those at the bottom of the social hierarchy are increasingly marginalised. Black people, 'single mothers and feckless fathers' (p. 20) and other members of the underclass are subject to economic exclusion from the labour market, social exclusion within civil society and excessive social control through an expanding criminal justice and welfare system. In Young's view we are in the process of creating an 'exclusive dystopia' in which no-one wins. He asks, 'Can one part of a room remain forever warm whilst the other half is perpetually closed off and cold?' (p.19). His answer is a cautious 'no'. Young argues that there is nothing inevitable about the process, as there are forces that undermine the creation of such a divided world. Greater exposure to, and understanding of, the social conditions that create such social divisions are likely to lead to attempts to discover a politics that reincorporates those who are excluded. For him the creation of such a politics and new forms of community are imperative if we are to avoid the creation of a socially divided world.

Tutorial exercise

Review the material on the response of James Hardie Industries Ltd to the development of asbestosis and mesothelioma among its employees. What features of crimes of the powerful does it reveal?

For activity suggestions, learning aids, revision of key concepts and access to self-study material, visit: **www.pearson.com.au/highered/vankrieken4e**

Further reading

Anleu, S. 1999, *Deviance, Conformity and Control*, 2nd edn, Longman, Melbourne.
Carrington, K. & Hogg, R. 2002, *Critical Criminology: Issues, Debates and Challenges*, Federation Press, Sydney.
Goldsmith, A., Israel, M. & Daly, K. 2003, *Crime and Justice: An Australian Textbook in Criminology*, 2nd edn, Thomson Lawbook Co., Sydney.
Graycar, A. & Grabosky, A. 2002, *The Cambridge Handbook of Australian Crime and Criminology*, Cambridge University Press, Cambridge.
Stenson, K. & Sullivan, R. 2000, *Crime, Risk and Justice: The Politics of Crime Control in Liberal Democracies*, Federation Press, Sydney.
Walklate, S. 2003, *Gender, Crime and Justice*, Federation Press, Sydney.
White, R. & Habibis, D. 2005, *Crime and Society*, Oxford University Press, Melbourne.
White, R. & Haines, F. 1996, *Crime and Criminology: An Introduction*, Oxford University Press, Melbourne.

Websites

Aboriginal and Torres Strait Islander Social Justice:
www.hreoc.gov.au/social_justice/index.html
The Australian Human Rights Commission provides information, reports and data on Aboriginal issues (including native title, customary law and the Stolen Generations), as well as links to useful resources.

Australian Bureau of Statistics:
www.abs.gov.au
The ABS produces regular reports on levels and patterns of crime, including annual reports on crimes reported, victim surveys, and court and prison data.

Australian Domestic & Family Violence Clearinghouse:
www.austdvclearinghouse.unsw.edu.au
This is a national resource for the collection and dissemination of policies, practice and research on issues relating to domestic and family violence. It also provides links to other sources.

Australian Government Crime Prevention Initiatives:
www.crimeprevention.gov.au
The Australian government's crime prevention and community safety website outlines some of the federal government's major initiatives aimed at reducing the incidence of violence and other crime in Australia.

Australian Institute of Criminology:
www.aic.gov.au
Australia's principal criminology research organisation is funded by the Commonwealth. It collects and compiles data and publishes numerous reports on crime. It also organises conferences, with many of the papers available online.

International Victimology Website:
www.tilburguniversity.nl/intervict
This site was established by the United Nations and other organisations with the aim of facilitating implementation of the United Nations Declaration of Basic Principles of Justice for Victims of Crime and Abuse of Power. It provides information on victim research and policy, and on the prevention of crime and abuse of power.

National Criminal Justice Reference Service Information Centre:
www.ncjrs.org
This US Department of Justice website provides information on crime, criminal justice and victims in the United States and internationally.

New South Wales Bureau of Crime Statistics & Research:
www.lawlink.nsw.gov.au/bocsar
The New South Wales Attorney-General Department's crime statistics and research agency provides summary data on levels of crime in New South Wales. Its research publications are also valuable.

Research Development and Statistics Directive, Home Office, United Kingdom:
www.homeoffice.gov.uk/rds/pubsintro1.html
This website provides publications, policy, research and statistics on crime in the United Kingdom.

14

Methods of Social Research

This chapter deals with the central features of social research methods, both in *principle* and in *practice*.

By the end of the chapter, you should have a better understanding of the following key concepts and issues:

— *positivism and quantitative methodology*, the nature of a positivist approach to sociological research and the role of quantitative methods, the utility of statistics, the distinction between inductive and deductive methodologies, cultural relativism, the comparative method and the importance of scientific paradigms

— the example of the *sociology of suicide* as a useful reference point for these methodological debates, as well as the conflict between quantitative and qualitative approaches

— *interpretive and qualitative methodology*, beginning with Max Weber and going on to symbolic interactionism, phenomenology, ethnomethodology, the realist concept of science and feminist research methods, as well as the possibilities of combining quantitative and qualitative methods in methodological pluralism

— the case of *street corner society* to illuminate issues and debates over conducting ethnographic field research, including prospects for activist research and questions as to the authority of social researchers.

INTRODUCTION	**442**
POSITIVISM AND QUANTITATIVE METHODOLOGY	**443**
Positivist sociology	443
Social facts as 'things'	443
Statistics	443
Laws of human society and inductive methodology	443
Falsification and the hypothetico-deductive model—Karl Popper	444
Paradigms and scientific revolutions—Thomas Kuhn	444
Paradigms	445
Scientific revolutions	445
Anti-positivism and relativism—Peter Winch	445
The comparative method	446
THE SOCIOLOGY OF SUICIDE	**446**
Suicide rates	446
Types of suicide	447
Criticisms of Durkheim's study	448
Categorising death as suicide—J. Maxwell Atkinson	449
Suicide in Australia—Riaz Hassan	450
INTERPRETIVE AND QUALITATIVE METHODOLOGY	**450**
Qualitative data and the interpretive approach	451
Verstehen sociology—Max Weber	452
Symbolic interactionism	452
Applications and criticisms of symbolic interactionism	453
Phenomenology	454
Ethnomethodology	454
The realist view of science	455
Scientific research 'systems'	455
Studying the unobservable	455
Causation	455
Sociology as science	456
Feminist research	456
Triangulation or methodological pluralism	457
STREET CORNER SOCIETY	**459**
Cornerville revisited	460
Boelen's critique of Whyte	460
Whyte's reply	461
The wider significance of street corner society	461
Possibilities for action research	462
A note on representation	462
Tutorial exercises	464
Further reading	464
Websites	464

INTRODUCTION

On studying the Nuer people of the Sudan, the English social anthropologist E. E. Evans-Pritchard commented:

> *Since my tent was in the midst of homesteads or windscreens and my inquiries had to be conducted in public, I was seldom able to hold confidential conversations and never succeeded in training informants capable of dictating texts and giving detailed descriptions and commentaries. This failure was compensated for by the intimacy I was compelled to establish with the Nuer. As I could not use the easier and shorter method of working through regular informants I had to fall back on direct observation of, and participation in, the everyday life of the people. (1940, p. 15)*

A number of observations flow from these comments.

First, it is often thought that **participant observation** was the preferred method of anthropologists, but as Evans-Pritchard makes clear it was a technique he resorted to only when he found it impossible to interview key informants. Second, this hindrance actually revealed something significant about the culture or way of life of the Nuer, namely that they are gregarious and lack a conception of private space. Thus, a point to bear in mind when reading this chapter is that carrying out research among human beings is a messy business. It is not like conducting a **laboratory experiment** on rats; it is never neat. This is because the conditions of social research cannot be controlled. All sorts of contingencies play upon the social researcher largely because, unlike rats, both they and their subjects are people with feelings, emotions and values.

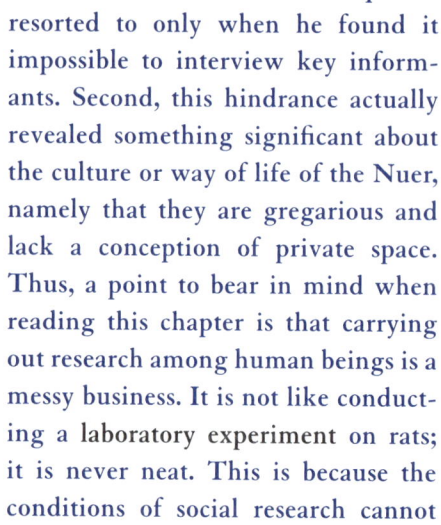

All academic disciplines require a **methodology** or approach. **Methods** provide a means of gathering as well as analysing information and data to produce knowledge. Unless knowledge is produced in a systematic manner, observations about social life may only amount to conjecture or be based on simple commonsense.

Methodology is concerned with both:

1. the practical methods through which data are collected; and
2. the more general **epistemologies** (theories of knowledge) upon which the collection and analysis of data are based.

Like most areas of sociology, there is little consensus as to the best methodological approach to social research, and there is much debate in the 'philosophy of social science' regarding the most appropriate epistemology. Perhaps the most contentious area to do with methodology in the social **'human' sciences** has been whether sociology should utilise the methods of the natural 'physical' sciences. Some sociologists have attempted to apply scientific methods to produce 'objective' or impartial knowledge about society, much as natural scientists try to produce objective knowledge about the natural world. However, other sociologists have argued that adopting the methods of science to study the *social* world is not satisfactory, since the subject matter of the human and natural sciences is so fundamentally different. Human beings have culture, possess values and have emotions. Thus, sociology requires a very different approach to that of the natural sciences.

Three broad approaches to the methodology of social research can be identified:

1. those who favour the methods of the natural sciences and tend to advocate the use of **quantitative methods**
2. those who believe social science methodology should be quite distinct and support the use of more humanistic and **qualitative methods**
3. those who question the need for, or sense of, such a division between quantitative and qualitative methods, suggesting a *combination* of quantitative and qualitative methods.

Common to all three positions, however, is a concern with developing improved understandings of human social life through an engagement with **empirical evidence** about actual social interactions, structures, relations and behaviour. This orientation towards what counts as *substantiation* of what one says is generally what distinguishes the social or human sciences from other, equally influential, commentaries on the human condition, such as literature, philosophy and art.

POSITIVISM AND QUANTITATIVE METHODOLOGY

Some of the earliest attempts to use quantitative methods in sociology can be found in the work of Comte and Durkheim, under the general umbrella of positivism.

Positivist sociology

It was the French thinker Auguste Comte who first coined the term 'sociology' during the early nineteenth century. For Comte, sociology was the most important of all scientific disciplines, capable of contributing *positively* to the betterment of human society without interference from non-rational forms of belief such as religion. Emile Durkheim continued this 'positivist' approach to the study of society, which he set out in his book, *The Rules of Sociological Method*, and then applied in his study, *Suicide*.

Social facts as 'things'

Durkheim believed that sociology should be distinguished from psychology. Psychologists study an individual person's innermost feelings, thoughts and subjective states, which cannot be observed directly. Conversely, the object of study for sociologists should be society itself or 'social facts', which can be observed empirically.

Durkheim argued, 'The first and most fundamental rule is to consider social facts as things' (1938, p. 14). Thus, social facts should be treated as objects in their own right, and should constitute the subject matter of sociology just as objects and events in the natural world constitute the subject matter of science. Social facts are external to the individual. Since social facts exist independently and outside of individuals, they can be studied objectively.

According to Durkheim, 'society' is more than the sum of its parts; it is reality *sui generis*—that is, it has a life of its own. Individuals do not act independently or of their own free will. Rather, people's actions and behaviour are constrained by what in *The Division of Labour in Society* Durkheim called the *conscience collective* (or belief system of a society) as well as by social facts. Thus, in his study of suicide (discussed below) Durkheim was concerned to show how social facts might influence that most individual of all acts, suicide. For example, he discovered there was an apparent link between a certain branch of Christianity, Protestantism, and high rates of suicide.

Statistics

Durkheim wanted to discover 'laws' about the workings of society. To that end, he believed that sociology should mimic the natural sciences in quantifying the social world through classification, counting and measurement. That meant there should be a central place for statistics, which reveal the existence of social facts. Thus, in his study of suicide, Durkheim claimed that suicide rates were social facts. The fact that the number of individuals committing suicide remains more or less constant across a population year after year demonstrated to Durkheim the influence that social forces have upon the individual.

Statistics are useful for revealing causality between social phenomena or, indeed, a correlation or connection between two or more things. However, statistical data have limitations and may provide only a partial picture of social reality. Official crime statistics, for example, might be used to demonstrate the existence of crime 'hot spots' or to show how particular crimes or crimes in particular neighbourhoods are declining. However, statistical data on crime are of limited use in other respects.

For example, crime statistics reflect only *reported* crime and so do not reveal the full extent of crime in society. Certain crimes are less likely to be reported to the police in the first place, which means they will never appear as 'official' crime statistics. This includes crimes that take place behind closed doors and in private, such as domestic violence and sex crimes. Such crimes are likely to be *underreported* because the victims may feel that they will not be believed or taken seriously if they go to the police, or they may feel a sense of guilt or shame in coming forward. It is argued that the real extent of crime across a society is better sought via 'victim surveys', which allow victims to reveal experiences of crime they might not otherwise disclose.

Laws of human society and inductive methodology

For positivists, a major achievement of the natural sciences has been to establish definite 'laws' about the natural world—laws that explain, predict and govern processes and events in the natural world everywhere and all of the time. The aim of positivism is similarly to establish social laws about society and human behaviour. For example, rising rates of suicide at the extremities of the economic cycle (i.e. in boom times or slumps) constituted, for Durkheim (1970), a law about suicide rates.

Positivists believe that laws can be established by observing the social world empirically and by gathering enough evidence to support general propositions. This type of approach is based on an inductive methodology. The starting point for this approach is the direct observation and collection of data, which are then analysed and tested so eventually a law can be established *based on the evidence*. Inductive reasoning proceeds from the specific to the general, postulating a series of premises (based on experience and observation) before reaching a conclusion. Take the following example: iron nails rust in water; iron washers rust in water; iron knives rust in water; therefore, all iron objects rust in water. While that great fictional sleuth, Sherlock Holmes, famously used a variant of inductive reasoning to solve crimes, the inductive method has been subject to criticism.

Falsification and the hypothetico-deductive model—Karl Popper

The 18th-century Scottish philosopher David Hume was critical of science's claim to be able to establish laws using an inductive methodology. Just because something has always happened in the past, it does not logically follow that it will continue to occur in the future. Hume claimed that scientific reasoning is flawed in so far as it claims to produce universal laws from observation of only a limited number of examples. Hume called this the 'problem of induction'.

A deductive approach is the polar opposite of an inductive methodology. The deductive approach was made famous during the 17th century by the French rationalist philosopher René Descartes in his phrase '*Cogito, ergo sum*', often translated as 'I think, therefore I am'. Contrary to inductive reasoning, deduction moves from the general to the specific. Take the Cartesian example: whatever thinks, exists. I think; therefore, I exist. Descartes used the logic of this argument to establish specifically *his* certainty in *his* own existence.

Karl Popper supported a version of the deductive method in his book, *The Logic of Scientific Discovery* (1959). According to Popper, the purpose of science is not to establish indomitable laws. Rather, science should progress in a piecemeal fashion, slowly generating theories that are capable of being tested and scrutinised against the evidence. Popper's 'hypothetico-deductive' method followed a set procedure. First, the scientist makes a precise statement or hypothesis as to what is to be tested and under what circumstances. Hypotheses are not derived from observation but might come about in a moment of inspiration or originate as *a priori* knowledge—that is, knowledge independent of one's experience. Second, it should then be possible to deduce a consequence of the hypothesis. Third, through observation and experimentation the scientist determines whether that consequence in fact occurs. Fourth, if it does not occur, the hypothesis must be false, so a new hypothesis is required. Fifth, if the consequence does occur, the hypothesis is verified, although to further verify the hypothesis further consequences should be deduced and subject to observation and experimentation to determine whether those consequences actually occur.

For Popper, the hallmark of scientific endeavour consists of the capacity to test theories and, ultimately, falsify them or prove them wrong. The hypothesis, 'all ravens are black', is a scientific statement because it makes a precise prediction about what colour to expect a raven to be should you encounter one. But however many times you observe a black raven, that does not elevate the statement, 'all ravens are black', to the status of a law, because that proposition is always capable of being refuted or falsified.

For these reasons, Popper was critical of the Marxist account of history and Freud's theory of psychoanalysis. According to Popper, psychoanalysis had more in common with primitive myth than genuine science. Psychoanalytic theory is too imprecise to be subject to falsification, since it claims to explain all forms of human conduct, much like a universal law. Similarly, when Marxist predictions about the historical trajectory of society (i.e. the shift from capitalism to communism) were not realised, the theory was reformulated to fit the facts.

Paradigms and scientific revolutions— Thomas Kuhn

Thomas Kuhn developed an analysis of science that sees it as being far from the objective pursuit of knowledge. In *The Structure of Scientific Revolutions* (1962), Kuhn argued that science is characterised by a commitment by the scientific community to a scientific paradigm.

Rather than seeing science as evolving in a piecemeal fashion *à la* Popper, Kuhn argued that science changes via radical or revolutionary shifts of paradigm.

Paradigms

A **paradigm** consists of a set of beliefs shared by a group of scientists about what the natural world is composed of, what counts as true and valid knowledge, what sort of questions should be asked and what sort of procedures should be followed to answer those questions. A paradigm is a complete theory and framework within which scientists operate. It guides what evidence is collected, how that evidence is collected, and how it should be analysed and explained. When scientists work within a paradigm, they tend to look for data that support and refine that paradigm. The way that scientists perceive the world around them is also governed by the paradigm—they see the world in ways that are consistent with the paradigm.

Kuhn did not believe that the same methods and procedures are found throughout scientific history; rather they are specific to particular sciences at particular times. Nor did Kuhn believe that scientists are entirely objective—paradigms are not accepted or rejected on the basis of evidence alone. Each paradigm has a social base in that it is grounded in a community of scientists committed to a particular view of the world or some part of it. Older scientists trained to think within the framework provided by an established paradigm find it difficult to see the world in any other way. Furthermore, they have a vested interest in maintaining it, for their academic reputations and careers rest upon the work they have done within that paradigm. Consequently, scientists may ignore evidence that does not fit 'their' paradigm.

Scientific revolutions

Scientific beliefs do change but, according to Kuhn, rather than changing gradually they are changed by 'scientific revolutions'. In a scientific revolution one scientific paradigm is replaced by another; for example, when Newton's paradigm in physics was replaced by Einstein's. Change in science is not a gradual process of accumulating new knowledge, but a sudden move or shift from one paradigm to another. This occurs when an accepted paradigm is confronted by so many 'anomalies', or things it cannot explain, that a new paradigm is developed that does not suffer from the same anomalies. A community of scientists may resist the change, but once a new generation of scientists who have been trained within the new paradigm start practising, the new paradigm is accepted. A science then returns to its 'normal' state in which the paradigm is elaborated and developed, but the framework that it lays down is largely unquestioned.

Kuhn's work raises serious questions about the other views of science. To Kuhn, a scientific subject is one in which there is, most of the time at least, an agreed paradigm. There is no guarantee, however, that the accepted paradigm is correct: it may well be replaced by a new paradigm in the future. Scientific training has more to do with learning to see the physical world in a particular way than it has to do with a commitment to discovering the truth through objective research.

If Kuhn's view of science is accepted, it is doubtful whether sociology can be seen as a science. The sociological community has not accepted one paradigm, or in sociological vocabulary one 'perspective'. Marxists, functionalists, interactionists and ethnomethodologists see the social world in different ways: they ask different questions and get different answers. Even within one perspective there is a lack of consensus. There are many variations within Marxism, while within functionalism Durkheim and Parsons reached different conclusions on many issues, and they did not analyse societies in the same ways. In this situation, sociology can be regarded as 'pre-paradigmatic': a single paradigm has not yet been accepted, and as such sociology is 'pre-scientific'. It could, of course, become scientific if sociologists were to agree upon a perspective that all practitioners of the subject could accept. Given the present state of the subject, such an outcome seems highly unlikely.

Whether it is desirable for sociology to become like a science is questionable. Sociology seems to exist almost in a permanent state of revolution, but the constant conflict may help to push the subject forward at a rapid pace.

ANTI-POSITIVISM AND RELATIVISM—PETER WINCH

The British philosopher Peter Winch was a vehement critic of positivism who also 'had a sort of underground influence in sociology, rarely acknowledged by sociologists' (Craib 1992, p. 101). Winch was influenced by Ludwig Wittgenstein's linguistic philosophy. Wittgenstein developed the notion of 'language games' to describe the way the world is explained and understood in different contexts. Scientists, for example, use particular words to make sense of the world around them and their use of a *scientific* language or language game defines a certain reality. According to this view, different languages constitute different realities.

In a famous essay, Winch (1970) applied Wittgenstein's ideas to Evans-Pritchard's (1937) anthropological study of the role played by witchcraft in the lives of the Azande people of central north Africa. Winch objected to Evans-Pritchard's **ethnocentric assumptions** about the Azande belief in witchcraft, which were based on Western scientific notions about **rationality** and the existence of an objective reality that could be discovered and explained by scientific means. For Winch, it mattered not whether witchcraft worked in any rational or logical sense. The most important thing was that witchcraft made the world intelligible to the Azande. The language of science could not be used to explain Azande witchcraft, since the language of science defines a different reality to the reality that the language of witchcraft defines for the Azande. As for Wittgenstein, language is the key for Winch when he says, 'What is real and what is unreal shows itself *in* the sense that language has' (1970, p. 82).

Winch's position was one of **cultural relativism**: 'all realities are real in the context of the language that defines them as such' (Benton & Craib 2001, p. 98). One implication that flows from Winch's position is that we cannot make moral judgements as to different 'forms of life'—a position that might be problematic in respect of what might be considered disagreeable aspects of other cultures, such as female circumcision.

A second implication flowing from Winch's arguments relates to Kuhn's concept of the scientific paradigm. Are we able to translate or even judge between paradigms? Winch's position thus 'raises the question of whether we can translate from one form of life to another in any meaningful way' (Benton & Craib 2001, p. 98). That, in turn, might cause us to contemplate the utility of the comparative method.

Reflective question: What are the benefits and drawbacks of adopting a relativistic position?

THE COMPARATIVE METHOD

Usually involving cross-societal or cross-cultural analysis, the **comparative method** is integral to all sociology as well as being the principal province of anthropology. Durkheim's work sometimes straddled those two disciplines and in *The Rules of Sociological Method* he observed that, 'Comparative sociology is not a special branch of sociology; it is sociology itself, insofar as it ceases to be purely descriptive and aspires to account for facts' (1982, p. 157). Thus, each of the founding fathers of sociology—Marx, Weber and Durkheim—employed the comparative method, although all in different ways.

Marx compared different societies throughout history to show how each has been dominated by a central conflict or class struggle (see pp. 471–3). Durkheim used a comparative analysis to show how social organisation has changed from mechanical to organic solidarity (see Chapter 15 for further details). Similarly, in his study of suicide (considered below) he used statistics (suicide rates) to compare different societies, different populations within a society and differences across time to establish a taxonomy or **typology** of suicide. In *The Protestant Ethic and the Spirit of Capitalism* (1930), Weber compared societies of the West with those of the East. That enabled him to explain why the doctrines of a particular religious sect, Calvinism, had what he called an 'elective affinity' with the development of capitalist forms of economic organisation (see p. 359).

Contemporary sociologists continue to employ the comparative method. While there are numerous examples throughout this book, in the Australian context, Raewyn Connell et al.'s (1982) comparison of working- and middle-class schooling is a case in point (see p. 183). More recently, though, Connell (2007) has argued that sociologists of the global south, which includes Australia, should resist transposing the theories and approaches of the northern 'metropole' into their research and studies. According to Connell, 'southern theory' should reflect the unique experiences of southern nations and societies, such as the experiences of colonialism—an argument that appears to chime with Winch's relativism (discussed above).

THE SOCIOLOGY OF SUICIDE

Durkheim used his book *Suicide: A Study in Sociology* (1970) as a vehicle to showcase his methodological approach. Although subsequent commentators on suicide have been critical of his pioneering study (as discussed below), it remains a sociological classic. Durkheim was concerned to establish sociology as the queen of the social sciences, which meant: first, demonstrating it could be as methodologically rigorous as the natural sciences; and, second, distinguishing it from psychology. In order to distinguish sociology from psychology, Durkheim set out to show how that most individual of all acts, suicide, had social origins and could not be explained fully by psychologists.

SUICIDE RATES

Although people may have personal reasons for committing suicide, for Durkheim individual circumstances could not explain the *rate* of suicide; a rate per thousand, for instance, is by definition a collective phenomenon and is therefore a *social* fact. Contrary to psychological analyses of suicide, Durkheim showed that there was no connection between insanity and the suicide rate. For example, insanity and the suicide rate were inversely related among the Jewish population—that is, the incidence of insanity was high but the suicide rate was low. Durkheim concluded that even though it did not forbid suicide, the Jewish religion was an important factor here, notwithstanding the fact that Jews were relatively well educated—education being another factor that could shake people's value systems, thus affecting an individual's propensity to commit suicide. Hence Durkheim discovered that the suicide rate among different social groups within a particular society was relatively stable.

Durkheim's task was made easier by the increased availability of statistical data in European societies at the time of his study. As previously discussed, Durkheim believed that statistics were social facts, which he thought he could use to establish the social *causes* of suicide. He established correlations between variables, used the comparative method and discovered patterns or trends, claiming these revealed the sociological origins of suicide rates. Accordingly, he showed how suicide rates across certain European countries and over time were relatively stable, as Table 14.1 illustrates. He argued, 'The suicide rate is therefore a factual order, unified and definite, as is shown by both its permanence and its variability' (1970, p. 51).

Other factors that correlated with suicide included religion, marriage and periods of political turbulence. Thus, Protestants were more likely to commit suicide than Catholics, and Jews were even less likely than Catholics to take their own lives. People who were married were less likely to commit suicide than those who were unmarried. Interestingly, Durkheim discovered that the suicide rate fell after the *coup d'état* of Louis Napoleon Bonaparte in France in 1851. The suicide rate also fell during times of war, dipping 14 per cent in Austria and Italy after war broke out in 1866.

'Nationality' was also a variable that affected the suicide rate in particular countries and certain regions of countries, although it interrelated with religion, which Durkheim regarded as the most influential factor of all. In the Bavarian region of Germany, for example, there was a high concentration of Catholics and a low incidence of suicide. Moreover, although a high level of education correlated with a high suicide rate, Durkheim again found that religion was most significant, which, as suggested above, accounted for the low suicide rate among the Jewish population.

TYPES OF SUICIDE

Durkheim's interest in suicide not only reflected his concern to establish sociology as a science. It was also grounded in his theory of society as a self-sustaining social organism, which to function properly or 'normally' necessarily requires both the *integration* and *regulation* of its members. Durkheim's method enabled him to distinguish between different types of suicide, as illustrated in Figure 14.1, based on the degree to which individuals were integrated into social groups and society, as well as the extent to which social groups and society regulated a person's behaviour.

TABLE 14.1

The rate of suicides per million inhabitants in the different European countries

	Period			Numerical position in the		
	1866–70	1871–75	1874–78	1 period	2 period	3 period
Italy	30	35	38	1	1	1
Belgium	66	69	78	2	3	4
England	67	66	69	3	2	2
Norway	76	73	71	4	4	3
Austria	78	94	130	5	7	7
Sweden	85	81	91	6	5	5
Bavaria	90	91	100	7	6	6
France	135	150	160	8	9	9
Prussia	142	134	152	9	8	8
Denmark	277	258	255	10	10	10
Saxony	293	267	334	11	11	11

Source: Durkheim 1970, p. 50. Reproduced with permission from Taylor and Francis.

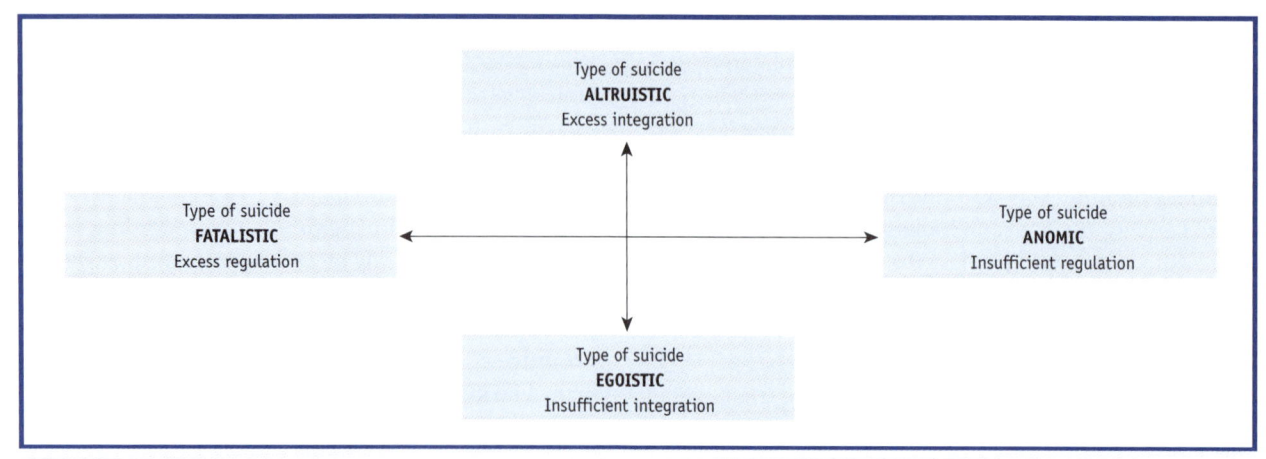

FIGURE 14.1 Suicide types and the balance of society *Source:* Lee & Newby (1983). Reproduced with permission.

Egoistic suicide was committed by individuals who experienced *insufficient integration*. This explained the disparity in the rate of suicide between Catholics and Protestants. The Protestant religion encourages individualism, whereas Catholicism tends to integrate its members into a more or less homogeneous community and fosters a strong set of beliefs. Protestants tend to be free thinkers, or as Durkheim put it, 'The Protestant is far more the author of his faith' (1970, p. 158). The consequence is that Protestants are more likely to commit egoistic suicide than Catholics on account of Protestantism 'being a less strongly integrated church than the Catholic Church' (1970, p. 159). Similarly, those who were less integrated into the family unit or were unmarried or childless tended to be inclined to egoism and thus more likely to commit suicide.

Anomic suicide occurred when individuals experienced *insufficient regulation*. Durkheim believed this to be the major type of suicide of industrial societies, which was associated with the disturbance of established norms as a consequence of rapid social change and economic upheaval. Thus, periods of economic boom or depression both equally create uncertainty and instability, which lead to anomie and, in turn, increased rates of suicide. Durkheim's study of suicide reflected his general sociological concern with transformations of social solidarity across societies. Accordingly, he believed egoism and anomie were 'social ills' associated with industrial societies, which engendered specialisation and the division of labour, leading to insufficient integration and regulation. Pre-industrial societies, on the other hand, tended to suffer obverse problems.

Altruistic suicide was the consequence of *excessive integration* whereby an individual was submitted to the 'general will' and made the ultimate sacrifice for the sake of others. Examples include the practice of Hindu widows committing suicide at their husband's funeral and acolytes of the king in Ashanti society killing themselves upon the death of the monarch.

Fatalistic suicide happened when individuals suffered *excessive regulation*. Durkheim thought that this type of suicide was not of contemporary relevance, but was important historically for explaining the high incidence of suicide among slaves. It was the kind of suicide committed by 'persons with futures pitilessly blocked and passions violently choked by oppressive discipline' (1970, p. 276).

CRITICISMS OF DURKHEIM'S STUDY

In accordance with what Popper said about the essential characteristic of science, Gibbs and Martin (1964) believed that Durkheim's work remained vague and could not be tested. For example, his notion of 'social integration' lacked precision and measurability. Gibbs and Martin refined Durkheim's work in accordance with positivist principles, concluding that their tests of the theory demonstrated its predictive power. Halbwachs (1930) claimed that where a person lived had a greater influence on the suicide rate than religion. For example, cities have higher rates of suicide than rural areas, although in Durkheimian terms that might be seen as a function of the degree of integration and regulation individuals experience in those different settings.

Writing from an interpretative sociological perspective and using qualitative methods, Jack Douglas in his book, *The Social Meanings of Suicide* (1967), disputed Durkheim's use of official statistics. As we saw above with the example of crime statistics, official statistics do not tell the whole story, which calls into question their reliability. Despite pretensions to be scientifically informed, a coroner's decision as to whether a death is suicide is not an objective and dispassionate one: it is influenced by the deceased's family and friends whose sentiments might, in turn, be seen to reflect wider norms and social mores.

A person who has close family ties and a tight-knit circle of friends might be better integrated than individuals without those connections. Although the degree of integration may well affect suicide rates, Douglas' point is that the death of a person who was supposedly well integrated is less likely to be *recorded* as a suicide. That is because family and friends in those circumstances might feel personally responsible and therefore guilty. They may also be in a state of denial as to the possibility that a friend or family member could contemplate, never mind commit, suicide. Douglas' argument is that these sentiments are transmitted to the coroner and influence his or her judgement accordingly. So, just as crime statistics are influenced profoundly by people underreporting certain crimes out of feelings of guilt or shame, so too human emotions come into play with respect to official statistics around suicide.

Another of Douglas' arguments against Durkheim is that he failed to recognise the *social meanings* attached to acts of suicide across different cultures. For example, suicide in Japan would be considered quite differently compared to suicide in Australia. Also, just as victim surveys demonstrate the limitations of official statistics, which tend not to reveal the reality or true extent of crime in a society or across a population, so too can statistics on suicide produce a false impression of social reality. That is why Douglas proposed the use of case studies to discover the meanings of particular suicides, which included conducting interviews with persons close to the deceased, as well as analysing suicide notes and the diaries of the deceased persons. Others have also questioned the factual reality of suicide rates.

CATEGORISING DEATH AS SUICIDE—J. MAXWELL ATKINSON

Positivists believe that an external or objective social 'reality' is out there, waiting to be 'discovered' using scientific methods. That view is rejected by adherents of ethnomethodology, who argue that imposing a scientific view upon the social world distorts it. Indeed, Michael Phillipson (1972) has suggested that the scientism of social researchers 'rides roughshod over the very social reality they are trying to comprehend' (p. 86). According to Ian Craib (1992), the ethnomethodological perspective regards society as a conspiracy in which we all collude to create the impression of stability and certainty. Thus, for ethnomethodologists like Atkinson (1978), suicide is a *construct* of social actors—namely, coroners and their officers, who are responsible for defining certain deaths as suicide, which is also an interpretive task crucial to the generation of official statistics. Whether official statistics are inaccurate or biased or skewed is irrelevant to ethnomethodologists. Rather, it is important to identify the *processes* by which sudden deaths become categorised as suicide.

Accordingly, in his study *Discovering Suicide* (1978), Atkinson examined the methods used by coroners and coronial officers in determining whether a death was suicide. He elicited information via unstructured observational techniques such as observing and asking questions of coroners and their officers while they worked. He also examined the records of one particular coroner. Atkinson concluded that coroners are involved in the business of 'commonsense theorising' about suicide. This means that if a suicide seems to them to be indicated by the biographical history of the deceased, that death will be classified as suicide. In other words, theories are developed to fit the facts.

According to Atkinson, 'the theorizing of coroners, their officers and others could be seen simply as a way of making sense of potentially senseless and disorganized occurrences in society' (p. 172). It is, in other words, their means or 'method' of imposing order on the social world. Evidence coroners draw upon to conclude that a sudden death was suicide include whether the deceased left a suicide note, had a history of mental illness, was recently divorced or suffered financial difficulties or had problems at work, and the mode of death (e.g. gassing, drug overdose etc.). Weighing up such evidence enabled coroners and coronial officers to draw upon their take-for-granted, commonsense stock of knowledge to formulate a theory as to whether the person had or had not committed suicide. In other words, there was little that was 'scientific' about the process. Instead, the verdict of suicide was arrived at via the coroner's own interpretation of what constituted suicide. As Atkinson put it, 'coroners and their officers are engaged in analysing features of the deaths and the biographies of the deceased according to a variety of taken-for-granted assumptions about what constitutes a "typical suicide", a "typical suicidal biography", and so on' (pp. 104–1).

The implication of Atkinson's study is that official statistics on suicide ought not, as Durkheim posited, to be treated as 'facts'. Rather, they are the result of some interpretive process. Indeed, that is a point made about statistics themselves—statistics, taken at face value, are meaningless: they need to be interpreted.

Interestingly, Atkinson found coroners' theories of suicide bore a remarkable resemblance to those of sociologists and psychologists. While that is unsurprising on one level, since coroners use social scientific theories about the causes of suicide to generate their own theories of suicide, on another level it suggests that social scientific theories about the social or psychological origins of deaths officially classified as suicide may actually reflect the commonsense theories of coroners and coronial officers. It is not difficult, then, to see why ethnomethodologists treat society as a conspiracy (Craib 1992).

Suicide in Australia— Riaz Hassan

In his study of suicide in Australia, *Suicide Explained* (1995), Riaz Hassan charted a path between Durkheimian analysis and the criticisms of writers such as Atkinson. Hassan argued that it is possible to develop an understanding of suicide that merges sociological and psychological approaches and that, despite the problems associated with the official statistics, one can develop meaningful analyses of both the patterns taken by suicides and what those patterns say about the development of Australian society.

A number of additional factors are included in Hassan's account which extends Durkheim's original analysis: age, ethnicity, marital status, social isolation, the nature of social integration, occupation, temporal cycles, economic cycles and modernisation. However, Hassan accepted the essential thrust of Durkheim's work—that the patterns taken by suicides tell us something useful and relevant about long-term trends in social integration, social tension and social cohesion.

It is true, suggested Hassan, that there are significant problems in the way official statistics about suicides are produced, especially in the way deaths are classified by coroners as 'accidental', 'undetermined' or 'suicide'. He pointed to the variation among Australian states, with South Australian coroners most likely to classify an unexpected death as suicide; New South Wales coroners most likely to classify an unexpected death as 'undetermined' or 'suicide' rather than 'accidental'; and Northern Territory coroners most likely to classify an unexpected death as 'accidental' and least likely as 'suicide'. Very few motor accidents are classified as 'suicide', even though most researchers agree that it is a common method for committing suicide. Particular close-knit ethnic groups or smaller rural communities will often be anxious to define a death in some other way, so that generally it is highly likely that suicides are indeed underreported and that some changes in the rates are attributable to changes in coronial practices and perceptions.

However, Hassan ended up agreeing with the position adopted by Pescosolido and Mendelsohn (1986) in the United States, that the errors pointed to by critics of official statistics 'are generally not large enough to preclude meaningful sociological analysis' (p. 25). Suicides among the young, argued Hassan, are related to unemployment, changes in family, substance abuse, interpersonal violence and access to mental health facilities. Among the aged, they are connected with declining health, dependence, poverty, loneliness and institutional care. The higher rates among males, and especially among unemployed males, also tell us something about the particular significance of employment and instrumental orientations for masculine roles, and the relative decline among females is connected with 'modernisation' and the changed social position of women.

INTERPRETIVE AND QUALITATIVE METHODOLOGY

Quantitative approaches to sociological analysis are only one alternative. Other social researchers prefer to use methods and techniques that enable them to adduce qualitatively rich data—or produce what Clifford Geertz (1973) has termed 'thick description'. Still others argue that blending research methodologies is the best way forward, since it is a technique most apt to painting a holistic picture. For example, using semi-structured interviews and/or participant observation to supplement or 'fill out' the thin data obtained in large-scale social surveys in order to find out 'why' people do what they say they do.

However, for some, qualitative methods are simply the best means of understanding social life. After all, human beings and those who research human society are all involved in a daily pursuit of *interpreting* the world about them. Phenomenologists, for example, reject the view that the methods of the natural sciences are appropriate to sociology. To phenomenologists, objective observation and measurement of the social world is not possible. The social world is classified by members

Case Study
Bowling alone: the erosion of social capital

In a significant study, Robert Putnam (1995) used statistical data taken from social surveys to show how over recent decades American society has been marked by the declining influence of 'social capital' or 'features of social organizations such as networks, norms, and social trust that facilitate coordination for mutual benefit' (p. 67).

For example, Putnam shows how Americans' engagement in politics and government has fallen, with the number of people reporting that they had 'attended a public meeting on town or school affairs' dropping by more than one-third, from 22 per cent in 1973 to 13 per cent in 1993. Involvement in trade unionism has also declined: since the 1950s, when union membership peaked, membership in non-agricultural industries had fallen from 32.5 per cent in 1953 to 15.8 per cent in 1992. Similar trends were discernible in respect of parent–teacher associations (participation dropping from 12 million in 1964 to barely 5 million in 1982) and the number of people volunteering for mainline civic organisations such as the Scouts (down by 26 per cent since 1970) and the Red Cross (down by 61 per cent since 1970). In sum, says Putnam, 'after expanding throughout most of this century, many civic organizations have experienced a sudden, substantial, and nearly simultaneous decline in membership over the last decade or two' (p. 70).

The most discomforting evidence of social disengagement adduced by Putnam is his finding that while more Americans are bowling than ever before, they are not doing so in organised leagues—they are bowling alone. Between 1980 and 1993, the total number of bowlers in the United States increased by 10 per cent, but league bowling *declined* by 40 per cent. For Putnam, the broader social significance of the rise of solo bowling 'lies in the social interaction and even occasionally civic conversations over beer and pizza that solo bowlers forgo' (p. 70).

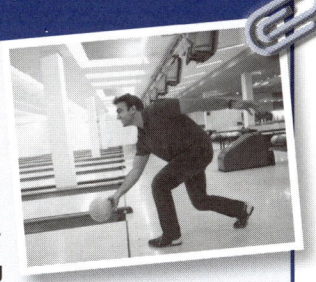

Lest we forget the starkest reminder of bowling as a metaphor for the malaise of contemporary American society examined by Michael Moore in his documentary film, *Bowling for Columbine*, where he notes that at six o'clock in the morning on 20 April 1999, two students calmly went bowling … before going on to carry out the massacre at Columbine High School.

1. Even though Putnam concentrates on American society, he says that the developments he portrays could easily characterise many contemporary societies. Are Putnam's examples also relevant to Australia?
2. How would you go about researching the erosion of social capital across Australian society? What research tools and resources would you use to provide evidence for your findings?
3. Why might social capital be declining in Australia?

---

of society in terms of their own stereotypes and taken-for-granted assumptions. In these circumstances, the social world cannot be measured objectively; statistics are simply the product of the categorisation procedures used. The best that sociologists can hope to do is study the way that members of society categorise the world around them. They cannot collect meaningful statistical data and establish correlations, causal connections and laws. Indeed, phenomenologists reject the whole possibility of finding laws of human behaviour.

The influence of Peter Winch's linguistic philosophy on sociology was discussed above. For Winch, science is simply a language game whereby the rules of the game define and limit the world as scientists define and study that world. This leads to a relativistic view of the world in as much as no one language game or 'form of life' is privileged above others. Accordingly, it is fallacious for scientists to claim, as positivists do, that they can establish universal 'laws' of human society as well as posit the existence of an objective reality that operates as an external constraint upon individual behaviour.

QUALITATIVE DATA AND THE INTERPRETIVE APPROACH

Whereas numbers, often presented in the form of statistical data, are an important indicator of 'social facts' for sociologists employing quantitative methods, words and language are equally significant for those using qualitative techniques. The data might be presented in the form of interview transcripts or excerpts from field notes jotted down during a researcher's direct observations of a particular social or cultural scene. Sociologists who adopt an **interpretive approach** use qualitative data to discover the motives and meanings that lie behind social action. Since the subject matter of the natural sciences is very different to that of the social sciences, it would be futile for sociologists to imitate scientific methods. To do so only provides a 'thin' depiction of society and social life. For interpretive sociologists, *subjectivity* rather than objectivity is key. The most appropriate way to study human society and reveal its richness is to uncover the subjective intentions of social actors; how they assign meaning to their own individual experience, how they actively construct and reconstruct social reality—rather than it being something imposed upon them—through social action and interaction.

Verstehen sociology— Max Weber

Much qualitative or interpretative sociology owes a debt to the work of Max Weber. For Weber, interpretive sociology 'considers the individual and his action as the basic unit' (Gerth & Mills 1948, p. 55). In order to understand the individual person, Weber said sociologists should develop a **verstehen** approach, whereby they attempt to empathise with their subjects to understand the intentions and meanings behind their actions. Importantly, Weber recognised that just as the subjects have values and beliefs, so too do sociologists. This suggests that the dichotomy often drawn between objectivity and bias is in fact false. Weber (1949) distinguishes between 'value freedom' or 'value neutrality' and 'value relevance', arguing that sociologists will inevitably be guided by their values or will make value judgements when choosing research topics for their 'ethical interest'. Thus 'objectivity' (which he always put in inverted commas) is only possible if sociologists declare, at the outset, their values within the chosen frame of reference.

Another of Weber's important contributions to interpretive sociology was his formulation of 'ideal types'. These are concepts devised or constructed by sociologists, which 'cannot be found empirically anywhere in reality' (Weber 1949, p. 90). Researchers form mental constructs, pure or ideal types, which they may then use to interpret the motives and meanings behind people's actions. So, in *The Protestant Ethic and the Spirit of Capitalism*, Weber was able to talk of the ideal typical capitalist entrepreneur who was 'not any empirical average type' (Weber 1930, p. 200) and who, among other things, 'gets nothing out of his wealth for himself, except the irrational sense of having done his job well' (Weber 1930, p. 71). For Weber, the 'elective affinity' between Protestantism and the emergence of capitalist forms of economic organisation could be explained by examining the motivations of Calvinist believers, who strived to accumulate wealth not out of greed, but because they saw success in business as a sign of God's grace and, ultimately, as a sign they were predestined for salvation (see p. 475).

Symbolic interactionism

Weber's *verstehen* approach whereby researchers attempt to develop an empathic understanding of their subjects compares in many ways to what symbolic interactionists call 'taking the role of the other' or imagining what it would be like to be in someone else's shoes. *Symbolic interactionism* has its roots in American pragmatism and Charles Horton Cooley's notion of the 'looking glass self'—the idea that the self is socially constituted, formed in response to interactions and the perceptions of others.

Although Herbert Blumer was the first to use the term 'symbolic interactionism' in 1937, it was George Herbert Mead (1934) who was its principal architect. For Mead, what sets human beings apart from other animals is the ability to interact and communicate with one another using symbols. Animals relate to one another through a process of stimulus-response. For example, one dog provides the stimulus by barking, baring its teeth and snarling at another. In response, the other dog may simply walk away or it may reciprocate and start a fight. Interaction and communication between the two dogs is done through gestures. Their behaviour is unconscious and mechanistic, not symbolic and reflective.

However, as Mennell (1980, p. 10) shows, people are able to distinguish between, for instance, the act of punching someone and shaking a fist at them. The latter conveys the *idea* of aggression. People are able to share and communicate meaning via the use of symbols by putting themselves in the place of the other or, as symbolic interactionists say, taking the role of the other. Thus, we know what the fist-shaker means when he shakes his fist at us because we are able to *imagine* what message he is trying to convey by shaking a clenched fist at us. Mead regarded language as the most important symbol of all. Through verbal communication people can *learn* indirectly from others.

Human beings also learn to 'take the role of the generalised other'. This is a crucial aspect of the socialisation processes and moral development of young children. Initially, children take the role of the other. For instance, a little girl might pretend to be a mother to her cuddly toys, which she treats as her babies. Role-playing of this nature is relatively simple when compared to the more complex team games children eventually engage in at school. Such participation enables children to adopt imaginatively the roles and perspectives of the other participants in the game and hence comprehend the part they play in a far bigger game. For Mead, the game was a microcosm of society (Mennell 1980, p. 12). By taking the role of the generalised other, children become aware of their place in a wider context and develop 'a sort of social conscience' (Craib 1992, p. 88).

Applications and criticisms of symbolic interactionism

Howard Becker (1963) used an interactionist perspective to show how people learn to become drug users in a social context. For Becker, becoming a marijuana user is less a consequence of the pharmacological properties of the drug than an outcome of social processes whereby people learn the techniques of smoking marijuana and how to experience the drug's effects in interactive settings. The process of 'labelling' someone a marijuana user, and hence a deviant, is also essentially interactive. For labelling theorists, acts are not inherently deviant. Rather, 'moral entrepreneurs' play a crucial role in determining who is deviant. In Becker's words, 'The deviant is one to whom that label has successfully been applied' (1963, p. 9). However, labelling can also produce self-fulfilling prophecies, such that people in social groups or subcultures may assume a label as the basis for forming a deviant identity. Sometimes this is done in an effort to neutralise the negative connotations of a label. (For details of labelling theories, see Chapter 13.)

Symbolic interactionism has been criticised for stressing consensus and focusing on micro-level relations and social encounters, which do not take seriously wider questions of how power, conflict and inequality operate in a society. To an extent, labelling theory answers this charge by considering the power that moral entrepreneurs have to define acts as deviant. Others have combined a symbolic interactionist approach with a critical perspective. For example, Pat Carlen (1976) provides an account of the workings of a courtroom based on her ethnographic observations. She shows how in magistrates courts the symbolic odds are stacked against the defendant, despite claims as to 'equality before the law' and the 'right to a fair trial'. Key to this is the spatial arrangement of the courtroom, wherein dominance is achieved by structural elevation—the magistrate is raised up from the rest of the court; the defendant is raised up in the dock, but the dock is set lower than the magisterial seat. The railings surrounding the dock symbolise the defendant's captive state and therefore guilt. The defendant is also the one protagonist who is placed farthest from the magistrate.

Between the defendant and the magistrate sit clerk, solicitors, probation officers, social workers, press reporters, police, and any others deemed to be assisting the court in the discharge of its duties. Spatial arrangements, however, which might signify to the onlooker a guarantee of an orderly display of justice, are too often experienced by participants as being generative of a theatrical autism with all the actors talking past each other. (Carlen 1976, p. 50)

Carlen's focus on the drama of judicial proceedings—the staging of magistrates' justice in a surrealist play or 'the theatre of the absurd' (p. 49)—reflects the 'dramaturgical perspective' in sociology, which was most famously developed by Erving Goffman (1959) in his book, *The Presentation of Self in Everyday Life*. Taking a step further the Shakespearean metaphor that 'all the world's a stage, and all the men and women merely players', Goffman showed how the 'interaction order' is held together by social actors performing 'impression management'. This involves, for instance, 'front of stage' and 'backstage' roles and social relations as well as *rituals* of 'face-work', whereby interacting parties collude with one another to ensure that any potential social *faux pas* does not result in the transgressor 'losing face'. An example of such a social encounter might be when a person tells a tasteless joke in polite company. This is followed by a pregnant pause, which enables the offending party to correct the indiscretion, after which either he or she or someone else changes the subject.

The implications of symbolic interactionist thought for sociological research methods was developed by Blumer (1962), who was against positivist procedures, which he saw as distorting social reality by imposing categories and meaning upon actors. Applying to social research the notion of taking the role of the other, Blumer argued that it was essential to see the world from the actor's perspective. To do that, sociologists must immerse themselves in the actor's social world in an effort to grasp their ways of understanding and making sense of social reality. That should entail 'feeling one's way inside the experience of the actor' (p. 188). As actors assign meaning to action,

Blumer believed sociologists have to 'catch the process of interpretation through which they construct their action' (p. 188). Thus, the social researcher 'must take the role of the acting unit whose behaviour he is studying' (p. 188). This is no mean feat, as the following quotation suggests:

> *It is a tough job requiring a high order of careful and honest probing, creative yet disciplined imagination, resourcefulness and flexibility in study, pondering over what one is finding, and a constant readiness to test and recast one's views and images of the area. (Blumer 1969, p. 40)*

From this short exposition, it should be apparent that the influence of symbolic interactionism on sociological methods, and sociology generally, has been far and wide. A similar 'naturalistic' approach was adopted by David Matza (1969, p. 5), who strove to remain true to the phenomena under study or, quite simply, to 'tell it like it is'. Glaser and Strauss' **grounded theory** is another variant of that approach, whereby theory is largely *generated* from data. In other words, the researcher attempts to be faithful to the data, rather than forcing them to fit a theory (Glaser & Strauss 1967, p. 34).

PHENOMENOLOGY

Alfred Schutz (1967) was a social phenomenologist who drew upon the Weberian tradition as well as the phenomenology of Edmund Husserl. Schutz's principal concern was with how we come to understand one another on a daily basis. In other words, he was interested in how 'intersubjectivity' worked in everyday life. Schutz believed that all people acquire their own unique 'stock of knowledge' via biographical processes of socialisation. However, individuals also have the capacity to exchange their everyday stock knowledge with each other. Therefore, they are able to develop a 'reciprocity of perspectives', similar, in a way, to the symbolic interactionist notion of taking the role of the other.

Schutz believed that people interact with one another by forming 'typifications', or classifying and categorising the social world on the basis of similar experiences. The stability of daily life rests on people's ability to comprehend, in social interactions, 'typical situations', 'typical actors', 'typical motives', 'typical actions' and so forth. (This issue was examined earlier in the chapter, when we saw how Atkinson looked at coroners' assessments of sudden deaths according to their taken-for-granted assumptions about what constitutes a 'typical suicide' etc.)

For Schutz, the crucial question became: how does sociological scientific knowledge distinguish itself from people's everyday stock of knowledge? The answer is that social scientists have to make sense of people's essentially incoherent and meaningless experiences by imposing clear and consistent explanations on their behaviour and actions. Much like positivists, sociologists have to construct a rational and thus objective account of the social world. To do so, they must generate *second-order constructs*: 'typifications of our common-sense typifications which order the social world in a rational way' (Craib 1992, pp. 99–100). There are clear similarities between this enterprise and Weber's urging of sociologists to devise ideal types.

Schutz's sociological phenomenology was developed further and popularised by Berger and Luckmann in *The Social Construction of Reality* (1971). In that book, Berger and Luckmann posit that human beings actively create social institutions that arch over individuals and gradually become established external realities. Over time, these institutions undergo a process of 'objectification' and become sources of socialisation, which in turn enables people to acquire different forms of knowledge. In so far as Berger and Luckmann's approach attempts to reconcile an individual-micro account with a holistic-macro explanation, it resembles Anthony Giddens' (1984) structuration theory, which itself borrows something from ethnomethodology.

ETHNOMETHODOLOGY

Ethnomethodology was a radical brand of sociological thought that started in the United States during the 1960s and took phenomenology as its point of departure. Harold Garfinkel, who is widely regarded as the founder of ethnomethodology, first published his *Studies in Ethnomethodology* in 1967. Ethnomethodologists are concerned with understanding how social interaction is *achieved by doing*. They are interested in studying (*ology*) the methods (*method*) people (*ethno*) use for establishing and maintaining social order (Craib 1992, p. 103). For ethnomethodologists, the stability of social life is the outcome of some kind of conspiracy to create the impression of shared commonsense knowledge. People produce the appearance of a stable order. Conventional sociology stands accused of ignoring the fragile and ephemeral nature of social situations wherein meaning is subject to continual exploration and renegotiation.

Ethnomethodologists' critique of conventional sociology is that it takes as a resource what ought to be taken as a topic. Moreover, sociologists conspire with the people they study to produce the impression of social stability.

That is why ethnomethodologists are sceptical about the techniques of qualitative sociology, which depend on the researcher's supposed ability to develop an empathic understanding of subjects' motives and to intuit meaning from observations and interviews.

Ethnomethodologists are therefore equally critical of Weber's *verstehen* approach and symbolic interactionists' method of taking the role of the other. Garfinkel often said, if you want to understand what goes on inside someone's head, you should become a brain surgeon, not a sociologist (Dingwall 2002, p. 230). However, ethnomethodologists accept Schutz's idea that social order depends on people's ability to form typifications, although Garfinkel set out to show what would happen if this assurance in the apparent order of things was shaken.

Thus, during his early work in particular, Garfinkel conducted 'breaching experiments' to demonstrate how we rely on 'background expectancies' or taken-for-granted forms of commonsense knowledge. For example, he told his students to bargain for goods in stores instead of simply paying for them and to pretend to be lodgers in their family homes. He regarded the ensuing social disorder as proof of his point—namely, that social order is inherently flimsy and transitory.

THE REALIST VIEW OF SCIENCE

In some respects, ethnomethodologists want to uncover the true nature of social reality, which they say is intrinsically fragile and ephemeral. A distinction is made here between the *essence* or essential character of social life and the *appearance* or impression of society as stable and certain. In some ways, then, ethnomethodology proffers a 'realist' perspective whereby it seeks to delve beneath the (orderly) surface of things to discover the underlying (disorderly) nature of social reality. Ethnomethodological realism would stress the dissimilarities between sociological endeavours and the pursuits of positivism and the natural sciences, which focus, among other things, on generating and falsifying theories with recourse to observable phenomena. However, the **realist theory of science** emphasises the similarities between the social and natural sciences. Thus, realists would say the question of whether sociology is a science is incorrectly posed, and that positivists are simply mistaken as to the nature of science.

Scientific research 'systems'

Andrew Sayer (1984) argues that scientific studies that conduct laboratory experiments and thus are able to control and measure all relevant variables use 'closed' systems of scientific inquiry. However, numerous areas of science are not able to measure all variables or control complex processes to make exact predictions, as Karl Popper believed genuine science should be able to do. We know only too well that meteorologists are not always able to predict the weather with absolute certainty. Likewise, although there are now many early-warning systems in place across the globe, seismologists and geophysicists are never able to predict precisely the occurrence of earthquakes and tsunamis. Sociology suffers a similar fate, in that society and social life throw up so many imponderables as to make prediction impossible. Sociologists have to try to deal with highly complicated 'open' systems and consequently they are not able to make precise predictions, such as extrapolating about the incidence of suicide in five years' time.

Studying the unobservable

For positivists, interpretative sociology does not constitute science, since it concerns itself with comprehending people's individual motives and the meanings they assign to social action, rather than studying the observable world that is external to the individual. However, realists argue that natural scientists themselves do not limit their studies to what can be observed empirically. Keat and Urry note that scientists might 'postulate the existence of entities which have not been observed, and may not be open to any available method of detection' (1982, p. 35). For example, some processes in the physical world take place too slowly to be observed—like continental drift and evolutionary processes. Similarly, notions such as radioactive half-life and the human genome, studied in the disciplines of physics and biology, respectively, are not directly observable but are nonetheless subject to scientific scrutiny and experimentation.

Causation

Since both the natural and social sciences are about uncovering and explaining the *causes* of phenomena and events in respect of underlying and frequently unobservable structures and processes, realists argue that the distinction between the two realms of study is essentially false. An example of realist approaches in the natural sciences would be Charles Darwin's ideas about natural selection or, more recently, Richard Dawkins' selfish gene theory, both of which postulate underlying causal mechanisms for human behaviour. In sociology, the concentration of capital and the pauperisation of the proletariat provide examples (see Chapter 7).

Importantly, for realists, *structures* are key to understanding the operation of phenomena and events in the social world. Keat and Urry (1982) propose that a structure is a 'system of relationships which underlie and account for the sets of observable social relationships and patterns of social consciousness' (p. 21). Similarly, Sayer has defined structures as 'sets of internally related objects or practices' (1984, p. 84). Using the relationship between a landlord and a tenant to illustrate his point, Sayer says, 'The landlord–tenant relation itself presupposes the existence of private property, rent, the production of an economic surplus and so on; together they form a structure' (p. 84). While structures constrain and limit objective relations between people, they do not determine the way actual situations play out. Thus, the structure of the relationship between landlord and tenant dictates, in broad terms, that the tenant will pay the landlord rent, but it will not determine which particular tenant will occupy the landlord's rental property.

Although structures are not capable of being observed directly, social and natural scientists can tell they exist by their consequences. For example, Durkheim argued that even though we cannot see it, 'society' has an influence on individuals that we are able to determine via statistical data, such as suicide rates. Likewise, Marxists argue that social classes exist and are real, even though we cannot observe them. Paul Willis (1977) demonstrated this in his classic study, *Learning to Labour*. He showed how the educational system disadvantaged working-class children, such that schools, as essentially middle-class institutions, militated against working-class children obtaining qualifications that would help them to get white-collar jobs and instead prepared them for blue-collar work (see pp. 182–3). In Willis' study we see quite clearly the underlying mechanism and structure of class in action in the school system, operating through its consequences or effects, despite us not being able to actually 'see' social class as such.

Sociology as science

As will be apparent from the above, the realist view of science comprises the notion that there is very little difference between natural science and social science; both attempt to comprehend underlying structures, mechanisms and processes at work in the physical and social worlds. It follows, then, that realists do not reject interpretative sociology, on the ground that it deals with subjective meanings and individual motives, which are unobservable and thus not capable of being studied 'scientifically'. While some branches of the physical sciences use 'closed' systems of scientific inquiry, others are simply not able to control and measure all relevant variables to derive precise predictions. Sociology is faced with the prospect of having to deal with complex 'open' systems.

Although both the natural and social sciences strive, in some form or other, to generate 'objective' or impartial explanations, in sociology (and in the social sciences and humanities more broadly) the ideal of objectivity has been challenged profoundly by feminist analyses of society and social research methods.

FEMINIST RESEARCH

It is often said that there is no single feminist methodology in social science. However, there are a number of themes and issues around which the debates on feminist approaches to social research have been organised, even though different writers will take up differing positions on each of them:

1. *The ubiquity of gender as a dimension of social life.* Probably the most obvious contribution of feminist social research has been to focus attention on the gendered nature of every sociological topic—class, family life, the state, organisations, education, health, work and so on. Until the 1970s, the tendency was to undertake sociological research without very much specific attention being paid to the differences between the experiences of men and women, and feminist scholars opened up new research territory by treating gender as a significant independent dimension. A central influence of a feminist approach to social research has therefore been on the choice and definition of *topics* of research.

2. *The critique of objectivity and 'reason'.* Feminist sociologists have also been highly critical of the goal of value-freedom or a neutral objectivity in social science, arguing that the construction of an ideal objectivity actually privileges particular social groups and oppresses others. Feminist writers tend to argue for a rejection of the opposition between reason and emotion, or between knowledge and experience. As Stanley and Wise put it, 'a feminist social science should begin with the recognition that "the personal", direct experience, underlies all behaviours and actions ... we need to construct our own social science, a social science which starts from women's experience of women's reality' (1993, p. 164). All research, it is argued, is undertaken from the particular social

position of the researcher, and gender is a crucial feature of that social position.
3. *The politics of research, research as emancipation.* The goal of social research is usually treated by feminists as being emancipation or liberation (from patriarchy) and the empowerment of women. Given the existence of power relations in society, research either leaves those power relations unchallenged, tacitly remaining part of them, or attempts to transform them, and writers such as Caroline Ramazanoglu argue in favour of feminists' 'immensely ambitious project' of 'seeking ways of knowing which avoid subordination' (1992, p. 210).
4. *Overcoming researcher/researched opposition.* Social researchers tend to see themselves as entirely distinct from the people they study, and feminist researchers have argued that this reproduces and extends existing relations of power in ways that are inconsistent with feminism as a social theory and political philosophy. Stanley and Wise remark that 'social scientists frequently cannot or will not enter into the world as it is experienced by the people who are its subjects' (1993, p. 164), and Harding has put it, 'The best feminist analysis ... insists that the inquirer her/himself be placed in the same critical plane as the overt subject matter' (1987, p. 9). Hammersley (1992) has argued that there are three supports for this position: first, a political concern with equality and non-hierarchical relations, which feminist writers often argue should extend to the research relationship; second, a methodological concern that a power relationship between researcher and researched undermines the **validity** of the data gathered; and third, a political concern that if research is to be part of the process of social transformation, this will not be achieved while researchers retain an aloof distance from the people they study.

All these issues are the subject of considerable debate, both among feminists and between feminists and non-feminist writers (e.g. Hammersley 1992). Consequently, there is no settled position on what constitutes a feminist approach to social research, whether there is such a thing as feminist science and whether there is such a thing as a feminist methodology or only feminist epistemologies. Many of the arguments put by feminist researchers—such as the critique of objectivity—can also be found in the work of ethnomethodologists and other earlier critics of positivism such as Weber, so that sometimes it is unclear what is actually specific to a feminist approach. However, many sociologists organise their research around the particular position they take up on these four issues, and a large proportion of current sociological research is defined and presented as feminist, not least because of an ongoing concern with the experience and politics of gender relations.

TRIANGULATION OR METHODOLOGICAL PLURALISM

Alan Bryman (1988) has argued that the most fruitful approach to sociological research is to combine quantitative and qualitative methods. Indeed, both have advantages and disadvantages. By adopting a 'mixed methods' approach, the social researcher, in theory at least, has the best of both worlds. Quantitative data produce a somewhat static view of the social world, but they are also inclined to depict the social world in broad brushstrokes. Qualitative methods do not produce a big picture but they can provide rich, detailed and nuanced data via techniques such as participant observation and **semi-structured interviews**. Furthermore, by combining qualitative and quantitative research methods, some disadvantages specifically associated with qualitative methods can be minimised, namely problems to do with qualitative data deriving from small-scale studies that draw on a limited **sample**, which means qualitative sociologists often have difficulty claiming their findings are **representative** of and therefore **generalisable** across a population. Bryman proposed there be a 'division of labour' between the two methodologies whereby 'quantitative research may be conceived of as a means of establishing the structural element in social life, qualitative research the processual' (p. 140).

Is it still useful, then, to make a distinction between quantitative and qualitative methods? Often the disputes concern what constitutes useful or genuinely meaningful research, rather than really being about the quantitative/qualitative distinction, for the following reasons:

1. Advocates of *either* quantitative *or* qualitative methods do not always stick rigidly to their guns in practice. For instance, Douglas (1967) has shown how Durkheim did not focus solely on examining social facts in his study of suicide, but also attempted to understand individuals' mental states. In an exercise reminiscent of Weber's *verstehen* approach, Durkheim sought to discover what it might feel like to be a Catholic or a

Protestant to determine how suicide rates should differ so significantly among these two religions. At the other end of the research methods spectrum, Aaron Cicourel (1976) has been a fierce opponent of quantitative approaches. Yet in his study of juvenile justice, he compared statistical data of law enforcement across two Californian cities to explain differences in crime rates. Martyn Hammersley also reminds us that 'ethnographers regularly make quantitative claims in verbal form, using formulations such as "regularly", "frequently", "often", "sometime", "generally", "in the main", "typically", "not atypically" etc.' (1992, pp. 161–2).

2. An opposition between quantitative and qualitative approaches has little practical significance; most sociologists get on with actually doing research without worrying too much about the epistemological basis of that research. To be sure, practical difficulties have at least as much influence on the choice of research methods as philosophical or theoretical considerations. Many sociologists advocate what is termed *methodological pluralism* or **triangulation**, whereby a mixture of quantitative and qualitative methods is used.

3. Finally, disagreements between positivists and interpretative sociologists are rendered virtually obsolete when one considers the realist theory of science (see pp. 455–456), which proposes that both sociology and science are concerned with understanding and explaining unobservable structures, mechanisms and processes at work in the social and natural worlds. Such a concept of science allows for the prospect that qualitative methods may constitute *scientific* modes of sociological inquiry.

Hammersley summed up the issue by suggesting that the real methodological problems are quite different ones, to do with the practicalities of undertaking particular research projects, the type of questions being asked, the data available and the particular trade-offs that any particular researcher makes between comprehensiveness on the one hand and detail and accuracy on the other:

What is involved is not a cross-roads where we have to go left or right. A better analogy is a complex maze where we are repeatedly faced with decisions, and where paths wind back on one another. (1992, p. 172)

In reality, then, the degree to which quantitative and qualitative approaches differ has been exaggerated. In fact, Bryman states, 'Most researchers rely primarily on a method associated with one of the two research traditions, but buttress their findings with a method associated with the other tradition' (1988, p. 128). To be sure, the practice of using a plurality of methods was advocated long ago by Max Weber. Bryman proposes that it can be useful for a variety of reasons, including:

1. The accuracy of conclusions drawn from quantitative and qualitative data can be crosschecked against one another.
2. A **pilot study** can be carried out using qualitative research techniques, the results of which can then be used to generate hypotheses to be tested using quantitative methods.
3. Quantitative and qualitative approaches can be used in tandem to produce a more complete picture of the social setting or social group under study.
4. Qualitative approaches can be used to explore why quantitative data show certain variables as correlated statistically.

There are numerous examples of research in the sociological literature that can be cited to support the merit of combining quantitative and qualitative techniques. For example, Eileen Barker's (1984) study of the Unification Church, or the Moonies, uses participant observation, **questionnaires** and in-depth interviews. Barker purports that this enabled her to 'see how the movement as a whole was organised and how it influenced the day to day actions and interactions of its members' (p. 17). She claims this technique also allowed her to test hypotheses she had generated out of qualitative data. Sara Delamont (1976) used quantitative methods to scrutinise data derived from observational techniques and participant observation. She timed and classified different forms of interaction between school pupils to reveal differing experiences of education for girls and boys. She then used qualitative data to explicate the quantitative relationships she had discovered.

However, researchers not only employ a mixture of methods when using **primary sources** of data, they also do so using **secondary sources**. For example, in his study of secondary schools in the United Kingdom, Paul Corrigan (1981) used interviewing and observation in combination with an analysis of contemporary and **historical documents**. In his study of a Western Australian high school, Martin Forsey (2006) used principally participant observation complemented by small-scale surveys and semi-structured interviews of school staff, as well as interrogation of state government policy texts.

After this brief excursus on methodological pluralism, we turn now to examine a sociological classic and look at how William Foote Whyte conducted **ethnographic research** using the technique of participant observation in his study, *Street Corner Society* (1955).

STREET CORNER SOCIETY

Whyte first published his study in 1943. It consisted of an account of the social organisation of an Italian 'slum' district located in the North End of the American city of Boston. He carried out **fieldwork** for the study during the tail end of the Depression years of the 1930s. Methodologically speaking, his study provides an early illustration of what has become known as 'at-home ethnography'—that is, a sociologist employing the technique of participant observation to study his or her own society rather than a 'foreign' or exotic culture, as a social anthropologist might do. On the face of it, such an approach would seem to be less fraught with difficulties than immersing oneself in some alien place. However, as Whyte's reflections on his method reveal, the use of such a technique to research a relatively familiar social setting poses its own problems.

Whyte freely admitted that his method of finding what he came to name 'Cornerville' as his study area was far from scientific. He simply wandered the streets searching for what looked to him like a run down and derelict part of the city. As is often the case in research of this nature, Whyte had a number of false starts before his research got going. At first, he carried out door-to-door inquiries, asking people prescribed questions about housing problems in the district, but he felt embarrassed intruding into people's homes and was not convinced of his findings. So, on the advice of another researcher, he decided to go into a hotel and attempt to engage people in conversation to elicit information over drinks. However, when he approached a table where two girls and a young man were sitting and asked whether he could join them, they appeared ready to throw him out of the hotel! So, he abandoned that idea too.

His breakthrough came when he visited a settlement house on Norton Street, in the heart of Cornerville. There he encountered a 29-year-old man native to Cornerville who went by the name of 'Doc'. Doc was the leader of the Norton Street gang. On their first meeting, Doc asked Whyte, 'Do you want to see the high life or the low life?' (p. 291). Whyte responded by saying, 'I want to see all that I can. I want to get as complete a picture of the community as possible' (p. 291). Doc replied that he would take Whyte anywhere, anytime. He said Whyte would not have to explain himself—all he needed to do was to say that he was Doc's friend. Given Whyte's previous setbacks, this seemed too good to be true, but over the coming months Whyte was able to use a version of the technique of **snowballing**—the use of personal contacts to build up a sample of people to be studied—to gain the acceptance of a variety of social groups because of Doc's patronage.

Whyte also experienced the force of personal introductions when he was given a room to rent in a family-run Italian restaurant, but only after he had been introduced to the proprietor as a friend of the editor of a local newspaper. Over the course of his study, the restaurant became a refuge for Whyte after long hard days in the field conducting social investigations, meeting strangers and visiting people's homes. In methodological terms, these two examples demonstrate how Whyte gained 'access' to Cornerville, his field of study. They also show how he came to use the technique of participant observation to obtain information and data about the social setting.

Significantly, Whyte's failed attempts to gain access to Cornerville, as well as his subsequent successes, revealed something important about the nature of the slum—namely, that contrary to wider perceptions of such areas being disorganised, it was a cohesive community with its own social structures and friendship ties. As Hammersley and Atkinson (1983, p. 54) put it, 'the discovery of obstacles to access, and perhaps of effective means of overcoming them, themselves provide insights into the social organisation of the setting'.

Whyte's study illustrates the importance of securing the trust of 'gatekeepers' or influential players in the social setting under investigation. Since Whyte had gained the trust of Doc, he did not need to explain himself to other members of the group. In fact, this became a strategy whereby Whyte would volunteer far more information about himself and his study to group leaders than he would to average gang members.

Nonetheless, Whyte found that people in Cornerville were initially suspicious of him, since they thought he had come to criticise them. He found that one way to satisfy their curiosity was to engage in what Goffman calls 'telling practices', whereby 'You have to anticipate being questioned by people whom you study so you engage in providing a story that will hold up should the facts be brought to their attention' (1989, p. 126). Whyte found his own story was too elaborate to mean anything to the people of Cornerville and after explaining it there would be an awkward silence (p. 300).

However, he soon discovered that people had begun to develop their own stories about his research—that he was writing a book—which seemed too vague to him but he was happy to accept.

The relationship between Whyte and Doc changed over the course of Whyte's study. Among other things, Doc became more self-conscious. On one occasion, Doc commented, 'You've slowed me up plenty since you've been down here. Now, when I do something, I have to think what Bill Whyte would want to know about it and how I can explain it. Before, I used to do things by instinct' (p. 301). This quotation provides a perfect illustration of the impact (often unintentional) that social researchers may have on the people and places they study.

Part way through his research, Whyte began to wonder whether hanging out on street corners with Doc and his mates constituted real research. So, one night he resolved to ask more questions. On that occasion, he and Doc went to a gambling joint, where a man Whyte had been told was a big gambling operator was regaling the party with tales of organised gambling activities. Given his interest in such things, Whyte felt he ought to say something in order to be part of the group and said, 'I suppose the cops were all paid off?' The gambler's jaw dropped and he glared at Whyte. He denied vehemently that any policemen had been paid off and changed the subject. Whyte continued to feel uncomfortable for the rest of the evening. The next day, when he and Doc were alone, Doc said to him, 'Go easy on that "who", "what", "why", "when", "where" stuff, Bill. You ask questions, and people will clam up on you. If people accept you, you can just hang around, and you'll learn the answers in the long run without even having to ask the questions' (p. 303).

Becoming part of the furniture in this way is what distinguishes participant observation from more interventionist forms of research. Despite minor setbacks, such as the night at the gambling joint, after only a few weeks of living in Cornerville Whyte seemed to have fitted in quite well. In fact, he was flattered when Doc said to him, 'You're just as much of a fixture around this street corner as that lamppost' (p. 306). However, a dilemma for social researchers is not to try too hard to be accepted. Indeed, a balance has to be struck between *participation* on the one hand and *observation* on the other. Social researchers do not want to remain too aloof and detached but, equally, they do not want to compromise their studies by immersing themselves too deeply in the social setting or, as it is termed in the jargon, by 'going native'. Whyte confronted this problem one evening when he was walking down the street with some corner boys and tried to enter into the spirit of small talk, cutting loose with a string of obscenities and profanities. The walk stopped abruptly and the gang members looked at Whyte in surprise. Doc shook his head and said, 'Bill, you're not supposed to talk like that. That doesn't sound like you' (p. 304).

Although Whyte's study did not cover all of Cornerville, he was able to build up a picture of 'the structure and functioning of the community through intensive examination of some of its parts—*in action*' (p. 358, original emphasis). Moreover, he was able to connect parts by observing events between groups, group leaders and the bigger institutional structures and activities of politicians and racketeers. In short, he says, 'I was seeking to build a sociology based upon observed interpersonal events' (p. 358).

While researchers ought to consider carefully what it is they intend to study and how they wish to go about the business of conducting social research before they set out, Whyte's study shows that it is not necessarily a bad thing if research deviates from its intended course. Indeed, *Street Corner Society* stands as testament to the fact that a great deal can be gleaned about a social setting from the trials and tribulations experienced by the researcher, or by engaging in what Van Maanen (1988) calls 'confessional tales'. Above all, Whyte's study is as an exemplar for 'flexibility, alertness for the unexpected observation, and the exploitation of unforeseen opportunities—these are the signs of a good researcher and not merely of an erratic one' (Madge 1963, p. 225).

Reflective questions: Is it possible to over-plan a research project? Do those researchers who follow precisely what they set out to do necessarily produce the best research?

CORNERVILLE REVISITED

In 1992, nearly 50 years after Whyte's original study was published, the *Journal of Contemporary Ethnography* published a special issue entitled, '*Street Corner Society*: Cornerville revisited'. In that volume Marianne Boelen discusses how her research methods and findings differ significantly from those of Whyte.

Boelen's critique of Whyte

Boelen's principal criticism of Whyte is that he imposed value judgements on situations he was unfamiliar with and thereby presented a distorted image of Cornerville. Unlike Whyte, Boelen had lived in Italy for four years and she understood Italian culture and society far better than Whyte. Thus, what Whyte identified as 'gangs' of young men hanging around on street corners was, according to Boelen, a habit of Italian men brought over to the United States from the old country. It was not a consequence of being uprooted and influenced by American society.

Boelen also remarks that Whyte ultimately failed to give voice to his subject population. He did not seek feedback from the people he had studied. For instance, he did not take the book manuscript back into the field to elicit people's comments on his interpretations and conclusions. During her visits to Cornerville to interview some of the protagonists of Whyte's study, Boelen found that people felt aggrieved about the book. Not only did they disagree with some of the things Whyte presented as fact, but they were also hurt by his labelling of the area as a 'slum' populated by 'gangs' of young men socialising on street corners. They felt that Whyte had placed too much stress on the role of racketeers and overlooked the role of the family as a fundamental institution in Italian society. Moreover, although Whyte claimed to have informed people that he was writing a book about Cornerville, Boelen discovered that had not been clear to many people. They considered the book a breach of confidence because after he had accepted their friendship and been welcomed into their homes he went on to write an unflattering book.

In addition, Boelen questions whether Whyte was really considered an 'insider'. For example, he did not feel the need to master the Italian language because he was mixing mainly with second-generation migrants, many of whom had nevertheless spent their formative years in Italy. This meant that he missed and likely misinterpreted a lot of the conversations that took place in the Italian language in people's homes, at work and on street corners. Furthermore, as most people during that time of economic depression were concerned with survival, worrying about having no job and no food to put on the table, they told Boelen that they felt a great gulf between themselves and Whyte, who had secure income from his university fellowship. Whyte's lack of understanding of Italian culture and value systems combined with his upper middle-class background tended to distance him from the people of Cornerville and caused him to impose his own normative judgements on what he observed. All of this meant that Whyte presented a rather stereotypical picture of Italians and Italian community:

It is here that the borderline between science and fiction starts blurring. Whyte felt that Cornerville best fit his picture of a slum, and he looked for all the characteristics that made up a slum in a modern American city. He placed the numbers game—a legitimate pastime in the Italian villages—in this framework and labeled it a 'racket'. He considered the grocer who collected the dimes for the numbers games 'a racketeer', and placed him in contact with the politician, who both in turn controlled the 'gangs'. (Boelen 1992, p. 49)

Whyte's reply

In response to Boelen, Whyte mounted a vigorous defence of his conduct and research practices (1992). He cites a number of correspondences with informants who wrote to him in glowing terms about his book. One of the street corner men, for instance, wrote to tell him that his book was excellent. It was sincere and would cast Cornerville in a new light to outsiders, showing them that human beings inhabited the district. Whyte accuses Boelen of taking things out of context and at one point describes a conversation she claims took place between him and some corner boys as 'sheer fantasy' (p. 58).

Whyte also disputes Boelen's suggestion that he committed a cardinal ethical sin by not taking his manuscript back to the field so that his subjects could check its contents. Whyte argues that this principle is stated nowhere in the literature. Indeed, it is worth noting Gary Alan Fine's (1993) observation that ethnographic work, like all other work, has an 'underside', consisting of compromises one frequently makes with the idealised ethical standards. Finally, to Boelen's charge that he leaned on his own values and belief system and did not give voice to his subject population, Whyte retorts, 'It would be hard to find a book that devoted such a large proportion of the text to quotations from people in the community studied' (p. 68). Ultimately, what these disagreements highlight is that two researchers can study the same social setting yet arrive at very different conclusions, which is not at all unusual in the social sciences.

THE WIDER SIGNIFICANCE OF STREET CORNER SOCIETY

Notwithstanding these internal debates, which go to the **credibility** of Whyte's study, the concept of street corner society remains relevant and applicable in other arenas. For instance, MacDonald and Shildrick (2007) show how young people in poor neighbourhoods in the

United Kingdom hang out on street corners because they are unable to afford to participate in more mainstream leisure pursuits such as going to nightclubs.

An example perhaps more pertinent to Whyte's study is Philippe Bourgois' book, *In Search of Respect* (2003).

Possibilities for action research

Like Whyte's study, Bourgois' book is a piece of 'at-home ethnography', in which he documents some of his experiences of living with and researching Puerto Ricans in the El Barrio area of Harlem, New York City, a district renowned for crack, poverty, ethnic segregation and social marginalisation. Among other things, Bourgois is concerned to connect the street culture and experiences of the people he studied to the wider political economy to consider how and why the richest nation on earth can also impose racial segregation and economic marginalisation on so many of its citizens.

Bourgois lived in El Barrio for three and a half years. He spent hundreds of nights on the streets and in crack houses observing drug dealers and addicts. He often tape-recorded conversations and **life histories**, he visited families, attended parties and intimate reunions (e.g. Thanksgiving dinners), interviewed local politicians and attended institutional meetings. He also exercised 'self-conscious reflexivity', meaning that he was mindful he was 'an outsider from the larger society's dominant class, ethnicity, and gender categories who was attempting to study the experience of inner-city poverty among Puerto Ricans' (p. 13).

While ethnographers have a tendency to present the societies or cultures they study as hermetically sealed from the larger environment, Bourgois' study is unusual in that it attempts to place the self-destructive daily lives of those surviving on the streets within the wider context of 'the particular history of the hostile race relations and structural economic dislocation they have faced' (p. 17). For Bourgois, the merit of the ethnographic method is it 'allows the "pawns" of larger structural forces to emerge as real human beings who shape their own futures' (p. 17). Nevertheless, Bourgois says he is worried 'that the life stories and events presented in this book will be misread as negative stereotypes of Puerto Ricans, or as a hostile portrait of the poor' (p. 11).

In the spirit of cultural relativism, of the sort discussed by Peter Winch (see above), Bourgois does not treat the culture he studied as good or bad. Equally, he says he does not wish to succumb to 'a pornography of violence that reinforces popular racist stereotypes' (p. 15). But he also does not want to sanitise what he has witnessed. Thus he resolves, 'I feel it imperative from a personal and ethical perspective, as well as from an analytical and theoretical one, to expose the horrors I witnessed among the people I befriended, without censoring even the goriest details' (p. 18). Bourgois sees his ethnographic writing as a 'site of resistance' and, in this way, it might be thought of as a form of activist or **action research**, which has a concern for human rights (Speed 2006). Accordingly, it answers C. Wright Mills' (1959) call for sociologists to relate biography to history and connect 'personal troubles' to 'public issues'.

Although Bourgois recognises that there are no easy solutions to long-term structural problems such as inner-city poverty, substance abuse, racism and class segregation that are integral to the suffering of the people in his book, he concludes by offering some short-term public policy recommendations (pp. 319–24). Those include: destroying the profitability of narcotic trafficking by decriminalising drugs; aggressive political intervention to promote economic opportunities for the marginal working class; dismantling the hostile bureaucratic maze that punishes the poor for working illegally and providing incentives for them to engage in legitimate careers (e.g. allowing unemployed workers to enrol in education programs); and, finally, remedying the unequal distribution of public funds and services along class and race lines through, for example, tax reform and streamlining access to social welfare benefits (e.g. affordable health-care coverage), and democratising educational institutions (e.g. equalising per capita funding for schools and universities).

A NOTE ON REPRESENTATION

A chapter on social research methods contained in a textbook such as this could conclude by presenting an orderly and procedural account of the *research process*. But the fact that many researchers use a plurality of methods, and their research is seen frequently to deviate from the ideals presented in methods textbooks, indicates that we are unlikely to find one model that fits all kinds of social research. Indeed, it ought to be apparent by now that conducting social research can be a somewhat haphazard affair, although that does not excuse sloppiness in either research design or execution. It is also not possible to provide a complete picture. Both quantitative and qualitative researchers and those using a combination of methods should realise that it is only ever possible to produce a partial account. Furthermore, as Whyte opines, social research is not an entirely logical process:

I am convinced that the actual evolution of research ideas does not take place in accord with the formal statements we read on research methods. The ideas grow up in part out of our immersion in the data and out of the whole process of living. Since so much of this process of analysis proceeds on the unconscious level, I am sure that we can never present a full account of it. (Whyte 1955, p. 280)

Importantly, however, beyond those many and varied 'how-to-do-social-research' manuals sold in university bookshops, broader issues are at stake. While positivist sociology has been critiqued for imposing a scientific framework on social phenomena, the authority of qualitative social researchers has been questioned since, it is argued, they are inclined to impose their cultural values and beliefs, albeit unwittingly, on those they study. It seems wise, then, for sociologists to heed Weber's advice and declare their values at the beginning of a research project. In more recent parlance, that means social researchers have to be 'self-reflexive' and recognise the influence on their studies of their social background and life experiences. Even so, that is not such a simple exercise.

At the time of Whyte's research, this may have been couched in terms of juggling the dual role of participant-observer. There were occasions, for instance, when Whyte's role was more that of an observer than a participant, and vice versa. That, in turn, meant he sometimes confronted an ethical dilemma that presents itself to many social researchers doing this type of fieldwork. For example, to gain an inside view of politics he resolved to align himself with a particular political organisation, but he felt by doing so he might compromise his future research endeavours with those in Cornerville who were not of that particular political persuasion. In this case, the problem solved itself: Whyte went to work for a politician who, although corrupt, had a reputation for being a friend to the poor and the Italian community. After spending three and a half years in a slum district Whyte also developed a concern for the problems people faced there, saying 'it is difficult to remain solely a passive observer' (p. 337). He thus orchestrated a march on town hall to petition local politicians and the mayor to change things in Cornerville.

Writing some years on from Whyte, Bourgois relates similar dilemmas to what he calls the 'politics of representation' (p. 13). The 'crisis of representation' (Denzin 2002) in the discipline of anthropology derives in large part from practitioners recognising and problematising the colonial roots from whence the discipline came. Among other things, that has affected a 'literary turn' in anthropology whereby ethnographies are treated as (ethnocentric) 'texts', such that, 'What once seemed only technically difficult, getting "their" lives into "our" works, has turned morally, politically, even epistemologically, delicate' (Geertz 1988, p. 130). It is no longer possible to naively 'tell it like it is' as David Matza suggests we should (see p. 454). Thus, while the eminent sociologist Howard S. Becker (1986) has produced an excellent guide to help social scientists write for publication, it must be recognised too that writing in the social sciences is not a neutral exercise—a point evidenced by Bourgois himself when he talks of how he made conscious decisions about what material to include in his final manuscript (p. 13).

Lastly, although it may be apt that the chapter finishes on an anthropological note, as it started, the final word shall go to the Australian sociologist Raewyn Connell (2007), who has cast doubt on the whole enterprise of applying theories and methods originating in the global metropole of North America and Western Europe to countries of the south such as Australia. That involves acknowledging the part played by colonialism in shaping not only contemporary Australian culture and society but also the discipline of sociology. Connell argues, 'The comparative method and grand ethnography deleted the actual practice of colonialism from the intellectual world built on the gains of empire' (p. 16), which has led ultimately to, 'The most important erasure in globalisation theory [which] concerns colonialism' (p. 65):

Sociology was formed within the culture of imperialism, and embodied an intellectual response to the colonised world. This fact is crucial in understanding the content and method of sociology, as well as the discipline's wider cultural significance. (Connell 2007, p. 9)

Tutorial exercises

1. Is it possible to talk of sociology as a social *science*? Are quantitative research approaches best suited to a scientific methodology and, if so, why? How might triangulation help researchers overcome the rigid division between quantitative and qualitative methods? Does it pose any problems?
2. How would you set about conducting fieldwork in your own neighbourhood? What techniques would you use? What ethical dilemmas might you face?
3. Draw up a list of the pros and cons of quantitative and qualitative research methods.

For activity suggestions, learning aids, revision of key concepts and access to self-study material, visit: www.pearson.com.au/highered/vankrieken4e

Further reading

Babbie, E. 2002, *The Basics of Social Research*, 2nd edn, Wadsworth, Belmont.

Babbie, E. 2004, *The Practice of Social Research*, 10th edn, Wadsworth, Belmont.

Denzin, N. K. & Lincoln, Y. S. (eds) 2003, *Collecting and Interpreting Qualitative Materials*, Sage, Thousand Oaks.

de Vaus, D. A. 2002, *Surveys in Social Research*, 5th edn, Allen & Unwin, Sydney.

Gilbert, N. (ed.) 1993, *Researching Social Life*, Sage, London.

Grotty, M. 1998, *The Foundations of Social Research: Meaning and Perspective in the Research Process*, Allen & Unwin, Sydney.

Kellehear, A. 1993, *The Unobtrusive Researcher: A Guide to Methods*, Allen & Unwin, Sydney.

Layder, D. 1993, *New Strategies in Social Research*, Polity Press, Cambridge.

Sarantakos, S. 1998, *Social Research*, 2nd edn, Macmillan, Melbourne.

Stanley, L. & Wise, S. 1993, *Breaking Out Again: Feminist Ontology and Epistemology*, Routledge, London.

Websites

Intute's Education and Research Methods page:
www.sosig.ac.uk/roads/subject-listing/World-cat/meth.html

Research Resources for the Social Sciences:
www.socsciresearch.com

Social Sciences Virtual Library:
www.vl-site.org/sciences/index.html

SocioSite's Methodology section:
www.sociosite.net/topics/research.php

WWW Virtual Library Sociology:
http://socserv2.mcmaster.ca/w3virtsoclib

15

Sociological Theory

In this chapter we provide an introduction to the basic elements of sociological theory organised very roughly into four categories based on the ideas of the 'classical' sociological theorists—Emile Durkheim, Karl Marx, Max Weber and Georg Simmel. We also outline a 'sample' of more recent sociological theory that has developed and extended the work of each of these theorists, in order to give some examples of how the classical theorists' ideas have been used by later writers. Finally, we look at two of the more important extensions of sociological theory: feminism, and the arguments concerning how the sociological conceptualisation of modernity needs to change in response to contemporary social conditions.

By the end of the chapter, you should have a better understanding of:

- the ideas of the 'classical' sociological theorists—Emile Durkheim, Karl Marx, Max Weber and Georg Simmel
- the work of Parsons, Western Marxists, conflict theorists, and symbolic interactionist and ethnomethodological theorists
- the feminist critique of classical sociology, and the concept of postmodern society, in particular the work of Lyotard and Baudrillard
- Ulrich Beck's alternative to the idea of postmodernity—his concept of modern society's development towards a 'second', reflexive modernity.

INTRODUCTION	**466**
DURKHEIM AND THE SOCIAL	**468**
Social facts	468
The collective conscience and moral order	468
The division of labour, differentiation of society and social solidarity	469
Anomie and justice	469
Talcott Parsons and the problem of social order	469
MARX AND WESTERN MARXISM	**470**
Ideology	470
Alienation	471
Social change	471
Western Marxism	472
Antonio Gramsci	472
The Frankfurt School	473
WEBER AND CONFLICT SOCIOLOGY	**474**
Capitalism and ascetic Protestantism	475
The Protestant ethic	475
The spirit of capitalism	476
Conflict sociology	476
Authority and conflict—Ralf Dahrendorf	477
Conflict Sociology—Randall Collins	477
SIMMEL AND SOCIAL INTERACTIONISM	**477**
Simmel's concept of society and sociology	478
Relationism and reciprocal working	478
Social relations—forms and types	479
The philosophy of money and objective culture	480
Simmel—an evaluation	481
Interactionism and interpretive sociology	481
Symbolic interactionism	482
Ethnomethodology	483
BEYOND CLASSICAL SOCIOLOGY?	**484**
Feminist sociology	484
Anna Yeatman—beyond public and private	484
Modernity, the Enlightenment and beyond	485
Postmodernism and knowledge—Jean-François Lyotard	485
Simulations—Jean Baudrillard	486
Second modernity and 'zombie' sociology—Ulrich Beck	487
SOCIOLOGY TODAY	**488**
Tutorial exercises	490
Further reading	490
Websites	490

INTRODUCTION

The question of climate change is now very high on the political and economic agenda—Australia appears to be getting hotter and drier; tsunamis, hurricanes and floods are destroying people's lives; and Pacific Islands are threatening to disappear under the rising ocean waves. Much of the discussion on climate change revolves around the facts, such as whether the earth's temperature has really risen in recent decades, by how much and so on. Yet the debate also concerns how we should understand the relationship between any rises in temperature in different parts of the world and human behaviour. For example, a recent British government report by economist Lord Stern (2006) indicates that the cost of failing to halt the rise in global temperatures could cost between 20 and 30 per cent of the world's wealth. Yet some, such as the Danish environmental scientist Bjorn Lomborg (2001), question a number of aspects of the reasoning behind both the idea that temperatures are rising and the relationship of temperature changes to human economic and social activity.

These two opposing positions on global warming cannot simply be reconciled by an appeal to the 'facts'. The problem with attempting to identify objective facts in the absence of any theoretical discussion is that we can only observe 'facts' through some conceptual lens. Both descriptions and explanations of facts always have some kind of theory embedded within them. A theory is simply the conceptual framework for the way we organise our perceptions of the world around us and then explain it. A theory is a 'way of seeing' (Berger 1972) and there are a number of different ways of seeing the social world, expressed in a variety of theoretical perspectives in sociology. The differing positions on global warming rest on different theories of how facts about climate change should be understood and how they should be related to what human beings do.

Facts do not speak for themselves. As Peter Worsley pointed out, 'if there is one thing that facts never do it is to speak'—instead, people 'select certain facts, interpret them, and then take actions which may or may not be closely dependent upon the analysis they have made' (1970, p. 41).

Theory is as necessary as it is unavoidable. Without it, it would be impossible to learn or to act in a consistent fashion; without generalizations and abstractions, the world would exist for us only as a chaotic patchwork of discrete, disconnected experiences and sensory impressions. (Joas 2009, p. 5)

In any recent introductory sociology textbook, whether written in the United States ... or on the other side of the world ... there will almost certainly be, in the first few pages, a discussion of founding fathers, focused on Karl Marx, Emile Durkheim, and Max Weber. The introductory chapter will probably, though not certainly, also mention Auguste Comte, Herbert Spencer, and Georg Simmel. It will sometimes mention members of a second team: Ferdinand Tonnies, Friedrich Engels, Vilfredo Pareto, William Graham Sumner, Charles H. Cooley, and G. H. Mead. (Connell 1997, p. 1511)

When we look at the range of theoretical approaches or perspectives in sociology, one distinction that is very frequently made is that between 'classical' and 'contemporary' sociological theory. It is not always very clear, however, where the boundaries are meant to be drawn, or which writers should be categorised as 'classical' and therefore making up the 'foundations' or central 'canon' of current sociological thought.

Over time, the canon of sociological theory has come to crystallise, more or less, around Karl Marx, Max Weber and Emile Durkheim, with occasionally the addition of

Georg Simmel. We say 'more or less' because there are also frequently arguments about the inclusion, or even substitution, of others. The ideas of August Comte are important, as are those of Herbert Spencer and the 'second team' referred to by Raewyn Connell. We can go back further in time to include Adam Ferguson and Adam Smith, or identify the proto-sociological aspects of de Tocqueville, John Stuart Mill or Aristotle. Alongside the European sociologists, there are good arguments for including the early American writers Sumner, Ross, Albion Small, Ward, W. I. Thomas, Du Bois, Giddings and Dewey. Recently a movement has emerged for a return to the work of Gabriel Tarde, the historic 'loser' in debates with Durkheim about the nature of 'the social', who is now seen by some as developing a more accurate understanding of the complexity of social life (Latour 2001). Those included are generally presented as representing a distinctively sociological way of seeing the world, and as such, observes Connell, 'they influence what kind of discussion counts as sociological theory, what theoretical language sociologists are to speak in, and what problems are most worth speaking about' (1997, p. 1512).

Connell has outlined the problems with the whole idea of 'classical' or 'foundational' sociological thought. First, the classics are honoured more in the breach than the observance, in the sense that although they are declared to constitute sociology's canon, when sociologists get on with their research they make very little use of their ideas (Connell 1997, p. 1513). Second, in the period of classical sociology itself, things were seen very differently. Connell points out that Franklin H. Giddings, the first professor of sociology at Columbia University, named Adam Smith as the founding father of sociology, and Marx was often ignored. Earlier textbooks had completely different configurations of founding sociological theorists, often ignoring Weber and Marx. Third, until the 1920s, sociologists had what Connell calls an 'encyclopaedic' rather than a 'canonical' view of sociological theory, by which she means that there was 'a sense of a broad, almost impersonal, advance of scientific knowledge with the notables being simply leading members of the pioneering crew' (1997, p. 1514). The writers now identified as 'classical' were certainly included, but alongside 'literally hundreds of other theorists and researchers, carefully abstracted and classified by nationality, date, and school' (Connell 1997, p. 1514).

Most of the early writers had a strong emphasis on the concept of progress, but the two world wars weakened the coherence of sociologists' view of their discipline. Connell argues that this, combined with the transformation of American universities in particular into a system of mass education, stimulated the identification of a smaller, more coherent classical core of theorists who would better convey the essence of the sociological imagination to a steadily expanding audience of sociology students.

This classical core was the outcome of the intense, focused labour of a number of leading American sociologists, including Talcott Parsons, Lewis A. Coser, Robert Nisbet, Randall Collins, Reinhard Bendix, Robert Merton and C. Wright Mills. The canon that emerged was the product of compromise. Parsons' own choice was Alfred Marshall, Pareto, Weber and Durkheim; Mills focused on Marx, Durkheim and Weber, but also Spencer, Mannheim and Veblen; Coser mounted the argument for Simmel; and Bendix and Collins promoted Weber. The narration of an origin story of sociology's classical period 'provided not only an intellectual but also a symbolic solution to the internal disintegration and cultural marginalization that had overtaken sociology before the midcentury. Inheritors of a golden age, bearers of the insights of great thinkers, sociologists had weight in the world—in their own eyes and, increasingly, in the eyes of students' (Connell 1997, pp. 1540–1). In one sense, then, the selection of classical sociological theorists was the outcome of which sociologists got the most 'votes', or at least consistent and ongoing support from leading American sociologists in the 1930s, 1950s and 1960s. Today reference to the classics also has the function of establishing one's membership of the sociological community.

Any examination of classical sociological theory needs, then, to be accompanied by the general caveat that it remains important to be conscious that these writers are only the tip of the sociological iceberg and that their work is only part of an enormous variety of sociological theorising and research. As Connell remarks, the classical sociologists themselves did not think in terms of a canon, they 'had a sense of adventure, a skepticism about authority, and a breadth of interest, which we could still do with' (1997, p. 1546).

Having said that, it is also true that much contemporary sociological analysis has some kind of relationship to the work of one or some combination of the ideas of the four early sociologists most frequently referred to in sociology—Durkheim, Marx, Weber and Simmel—so in this chapter we begin by outlining their approaches to sociological theory. This is followed by a discussion of some of the extensions of later sociological theory, as well as a selection of the attempts to move beyond classical sociology in feminist sociology and postmodernist theory, and efforts to rethink core sociological categories such as 'modernity' and 'the social'.

DURKHEIM AND THE SOCIAL

A central aspect of Durkheim's approach to sociology, as Cuff, Sharrock and Francis suggest, is his critique of an individualistic understanding of social life (1998, p. 63). For Durkheim, it was a misconception to see society simply as the sum of all the individuals in that society. Human beings are born into an already-existing social structure, language, culture, tradition and worldview, and indeed the very concept of 'the individual' itself does not exist in the same way across time and in differing cultural contexts. In many respects his conception of sociology as a way of thinking was, as Bryan Turner observes, 'a sustained criticism of nineteenth-century individualism, especially utilitarian doctrines of the egoistic self' (2006, p. 140).

Social facts

For Durkheim (1938), society cannot be explained simply in terms of individual behaviour, because that behaviour takes place within the framework of social facts, by 'every way of acting, fixed or not, capable of exercising on the individual an external constraint . . . while at the same time existing in its own right independent of its individual manifestations' (p. 13). Human beings only become human in the context of beliefs, moral codes and ways of doing things that exist prior to their entry into the world. From this point of view individual behaviour is not directed by those individuals themselves, but by common beliefs, ideas and moral sentiments that exist outside of individuals and shape their thinking and conduct.

In this respect Durkheim wanted to establish a way of thinking that was distinct from psychology or biology. The sociologist, he wrote,

> must give up making psychology in some way the focal point of his operations, the point of departure to which he must always return after his adventurous incursions into the social world. He must establish himself at the very heart of social facts in order to observe and confront them totally, without any mediating factor, while calling upon the science of the individual only for a general preparation and, if needs be, for useful suggestions. (1982[1895], p. 135)

For Durkheim this meant that one had to 'seek the explanation of social life in the nature of society itself' (p. 102). Durkheim referred to society as the realm of social facts:

> a category of facts with very distinctive characteristics, which ... consists of ways of acting, thinking and feeling, external to the individual, and endowed with a power of coercion, by reason of which they control him ... since their source is not in the individual, their substratum can be no other than society, either the political society as a whole or some one of the partial groups it includes such as religious denominations, political, literary and occupational associations, etc. (1982 [1895], p. 3)

What he was trying to capture here was the constraint that all individuals feel being exercised by the world around them, embodying patterned expectations about conduct, values, beliefs, dress, language, appearance and so on.

> If I do not submit to the conventions of society, if in my dress I do not conform to the customs observed in my country and in my class, the ridicule I provoke, the social isolation in which I am kept, produce, although in an attenuated form, the same effects as punishment ... I am not obliged to speak French with my fellow-countrymen nor to use the legal currency, but I cannot possibly do otherwise. (Durkheim 1982 [1895], p. 5)

Despite the political and philosophical commitment to individual autonomy and freedom characterising liberal democratic societies, Durkheim argued that one cannot ignore the restrictions placed upon that autonomy by social relations, nor indeed the fact that the very idea of individuality is itself the product of a particular kind of polity and society.

The collective conscience and moral order

Durkheim argued that since social life could not be explained in terms of individual motivations and concerns, it also constituted a moral force that either held groups of individuals, all with distinct concerns and conceptions of the world, together, or drove them apart with conflicting moral representations. He suggested that one can clearly observe a particular social consensus, a 'collective conscience' consisting of common beliefs and sentiments. Social life could not be explained simply in terms of the rational individual pursuit of self-interest, one also had to take into account the emotional and non-rational dimensions of social order.

Religion was, for Durkheim, a key example of the way in which society is held together through the expression, maintenance and reinforcement of the sentiments or values that form the collective conscience. As Berger (1967) observed in his commentary on Durkheim, one can understand social practices such as marriage, work and serving in the army by noting that 'To marry becomes a sacrament, to work becomes a duty pleasing to the gods, and to die in war, perhaps, becomes a passport to a happier afterlife' (p. 340). Religious forces, wrote Durkheim, 'dominate us; they are, so to speak, something superhuman and, at the same time, they bind us to objects, which are outside of our temporal life. They appear to us as an echo of a force which is foreign to us and which is superior to that which we are' (1938, p. 100). The concept of a supernatural, religious power was for Durkheim a proxy for the principle of 'the social' itself—that is, a power or concern over and above individuals that binds them together, gives them a shared identity and legitimately demands sacrifices to the social good at the expense of individual advantage, sometimes at the expense of life itself.

The division of labour, differentiation of society and social solidarity

Durkheim observed that social life was characterised by a progressive division of labour—that is, the work and activities people engaged in gradually became more and more specialised—and increasing in complexity and differentiation—that is, it was characterised by an ever-expanding variety of interlocking social groups with differing concerns, aims, beliefs and values bound together primarily by their interdependence rather than their similarity to each other. He would often refer to different types of social solidarity to capture this historical development from **mechanical solidarity**, based on people's basic similarity of beliefs and values, to **organic solidarity**, characterising a form of social life held together by people's need for each other's services, support and activities—their interdependence.

As an illustration, Durkheim argued that the role of law can be seen to be different in the two types of solidarity. Under mechanical solidarity, the aim of law is to repress deviation from the social norm, whereas under organic solidarity it is to reconcile differences and distinctions. Individualism is precisely a product of a form of social life characterised by organic solidarity, whereas the idea of the individual is entirely alien to social groups structured around mechanical solidarity.

Anomie and justice

A key problem that accompanied the increased differentiation of society was, felt Durkheim, the possibility of individuals becoming dissociated from their social context and a decline in social cohesion and moral regulation, which he referred to as *anomie* (1933[1893], p. 5). The effects of anomie in a complex and highly differentiated society could be counteracted by a developed principle of justice and organised attempts to compensate for the inequalities and injustices that characterise a society of disparate individuals competing for rational advantage without the constraints of a shared moral order (p. 409). Durkheim's concept of justice asks only 'that we be thoughtful of our fellows and that we be just, that we fulfil our duty, that we work at the function we can best execute and receive the just reward for our services' (p. 407).

For Durkheim, there were two important expressions of the pursuit of social justice, beginning with the arena of contract law, because it imposed (in principle at least) equal constraints on all parties to a transaction or an interaction, no matter what their status or power position (Cotterrell 1999, pp. 119–20). The second arena is that of what Durkheim called *occupational groups*, which are formed when people 'have ideas, interests, sentiments and occupations not shared by the rest of the population' (1933[1893], p. 14), at which point they form associations around those shared interests or concerns, such as bowling clubs, bird-watching groups, historical re-enactment groups, online gaming groups, car clubs—the possibilities are endless. What was sociologically significant for Durkheim about such groupings was that they occupy the space between the state and the individual in ways that help constrain social inequality and the unjust exercise of power.

Talcott Parsons and the problem of social order

Durkheim's theoretical orientation was given strong support by Talcott Parsons, who wanted to highlight the ways in which social life is held together, to a large extent as part of an argument with the Marxist emphasis on identifying the sources of social, political and economic conflict. Like Durkheim, Parsons felt that it was not possible to understand human sociability if one assumed that people simply pursued their own individual interests in a purely rational way. Even in a business transaction—presumably the most calculative, rational and self-motivated transaction of all—in reality people's behaviour is governed by shared norms and values concerning what is correct and appropriate business behaviour. Economic transactions in fact rely on trust to an enormous extent, which in turn is based on shared moral rules and norms. Australian entrepreneurs attempting to do business in China, for example, will quickly discover the importance of this to the success of their enterprise. For Parsons this meant that it is fundamental to social order that there be some means by which people can align their values and moral principles, so that they can cooperate and work towards shared goals.

Like Durkheim, Parsons also felt that social cohesion and order was made problematic by the dynamics of increasing specialisation and social differentiation. For example, he observed how many of the functions of the family, such as raising children and managing intimate relationships, had become transferred to other social institutions, such as the education system and the welfare system. This made it increasingly important for societies to develop integrating systems of norms and values as a kind of morally integrative umbrella under which the diverse forms of existence in modern society could coexist. Much of Parsons' work concerned the analysis of exactly how this worked.

> **Reflective questions:** What do you think of the idea that the pursuit of justice can compensate for the anomie of modern society? Are there examples of how a concern for legality and justice can be seen as fulfilling this function in contemporary social life, and do you think they can be seen as supporting Durkheim's general approach to the critical analysis of society?

MARX AND WESTERN MARXISM

The approaches to sociology found in Marx and Marxist writers share with Durkheim and Parsons, despite their differences, the use of a model of 'society as a whole'. Where they differ is in their use, in one form or another, of the notion that societies are composed of groups that have fundamentally different and conflicting interests. Sociologists influenced by Marxism also have a particular approach to the relations of power that exist between different social groups, in which they argue that social arrangements tend to benefit some groups at the expense of others. Because of the existence of different interests and power relations, the potential for, and likelihood of, conflict is always present. This is in contrast to the image of societies as more or less harmoniously integrated wholes. Durkheim and Parsons, for example, tended to stress what the members of any society share, and focused their attention on what they saw as an overarching consensus over 'society's' values.

The work of Karl Marx (1818–83) can be interpreted in various ways, especially when one focuses on one part of his extensive writings at the expense of looking at all his sociology as a whole. As a result, there are often arguments about the 'correct' interpretations of Marx, and although the boundaries between the different positions are often blurred, one should be sensitive to the overlaps that exist between them.

IDEOLOGY

A central feature of the distinction between Marx and his collaborator Friedrich Engels on the one hand and sociologists such as Durkheim on the other is that Marx saw the realm of culture, beliefs, ideas and social institutions as anchored in *economic* relationships. If there are relationships of power and domination built into the structure of economic relationships, argued Marx, then they would flow through to the corresponding social, legal and political institutions. As he put it, 'The existing relations of production between individuals must necessarily express themselves also as political and legal relations' (in Bottomore & Rubel 1963, p. 92).

For Marx, if there is a dominant social group or ruling class that owns and controls the means of production, this economic position will get translated into a political and legal one, so the formulation and enforcement of the laws governing private property, economic relations, political action and crime will be framed in such a way that its overall position of dominance will be maintained and indeed constantly extended.

Members of the ruling class 'rule also as thinkers, as producers of ideas' (Marx & Engels 1970, p. 64). Marx and Engels referred to the prevailing ideas of each epoch as its dominant ideology, which serves the interests of the ruling class. As they put it, 'the ideas of the ruling class are in every epoch the ruling ideas' (p. 64). Ideology is a misrepresentation of society, operating usually through the device of a partial truth, rather than simple falsehood. It overlooks or glosses over the contradictions and conflicts that are built into social relationships. As a result, we tend to accept our situation as normal and natural, right and proper, given and unchangeable. This false consciousness of reality helps to maintain the existing system, much as value consensus is meant to maintain the social system in consensus theory.

> One upon a time a valiant fellow had the idea that men were drowned in water only because they were possessed with the idea of gravity. If they were to knock this notion out of their heads, say, by stating it to be a superstition, a religious concept, they would be sublimely proof against any danger from water. His whole life long he fought against the illusion of gravity, of whose harmful results all statistics brought him new and manifold evidence. This honest fellow was the type of the new revolutionary philosophers in Germany.

Under capitalism, for example, the ideas of equality and freedom operate to disguise the basic inequality between those who work for a wage or salary and those who gain their income from the possession of capital in various forms (property, companies, stocks and shares and so on). Workers are defined as free agents since they have the freedom to choose their employers. In reality, this freedom and equality is an illusion: the employer–employee relationship is neither free nor equal. Workers are not free because they are forced to work in order to survive. The only freedom they have is to exchange one form of 'wage slavery' for another.

For Marx and Engels, ideas and the realm of belief and culture should not be seen as the motor of social change, because the realm of material—that is, real and objective—social relations always determines or underpins what goes on in people's minds. 'It is not the consciousness of men that determines their being, but, on the contrary, their social being that determines their consciousness' (Marx & Engels 1951, p. 329).

ALIENATION

In terms similar to Durkheim's account of anomie in a complex division of labour, Marx also felt that the development of capitalist society was accompanied by increasing alienation, although he focused on different aspects of the experience. For Marx, alienation concerned the ways in which the products of human labour and activity appear to people as entirely alien objects existing outside of themselves. Although social, economic and political institutions are human creations, because they appear to have an existence independent of the people that comprise them—exactly what Durkheim identified as the constraints of 'social facts'—they are experienced as controlling us and not subject to our own capacity to remake and redesign them. In this sense people become alienated from the world around them and dissociated from the processes of social creation and development that actually make their social environment.

The two key examples of alienation in modern capitalist societies were religion and work. Marx's approach to alienation produced a very different understanding of religion from Durkheim's. They both saw religion as socially produced, but for Marx religion was also a key example of human alienation. As he put it, 'Man makes religion, religion does not make man' (Marx 1975, p. 244). The fact that people see religious doctrine or the word of God as something external to them subjects them to particular relations of power without developing the capacity to analyse those relations critically or to change them.

The realm of work constituted for Marx perhaps the most important expression of alienation in capitalist society. He saw productive labour as central to the formation of the human self, a key way for humans to express themselves in the world, to realise their very being. However, if workers never really enjoy the realisation of the final product, and never have any strategic or creative control over the production process, 'the object produced by labour, its product, now stands opposed to it as an alien being, as a power independent of the producer' (in Bottomore & Rubel 1963, p. 178). In this crucial sense, workers become alienated from themselves in capitalist society if they are never able to control or even influence their own production process—which for Marx constituted the production of self and identity. As he put it, 'The more the worker expends himself in work, the more powerful becomes the work of objects which he creates in face of himself, and the poorer he himself becomes in his inner life, the less he belongs to himself' (in Bottomore & Rubel 1963, p. 178).

Under capitalism 'the social character of men's labour appears to them as an objective characteristic' (1954, p. 77), what Marx called the **commodity form** taken by human labour. However, the capitalist world of commodities and impersonal, objective market forces is 'a definite social relation between men, that assumes, in their eyes, the fantastic form of a relation between things' (1954, p. 77). For Marx, an end to alienation required a radical change in the economic infrastructure.

SOCIAL CHANGE

For Marx, the major contradictions that propel change were to be found in economic relations. At the dawn of human history, when humans supposedly lived in a state of primitive communism, economic contradictions did not exist. The means of production and the products of labour were communally owned. Since each member of society produced both for themselves and for society as a whole, there were no conflicts of interest between individuals and groups. However, with the emergence of private property and, in particular, private ownership of the means of production, the fundamental contradiction of human society was created. Through its ownership of the means of production, a minority is able to control, command and enjoy the fruits of the labour of the majority. Since one group gains at the expense of the other, a conflict of interest exists between the minority who own the means of production and the majority who perform productive labour. The tension and conflict generated by this contradiction is the major dynamic of social change.

Marx often portrayed history as divided into a number of time periods or epochs, each being characterised by a particular mode of production. Major changes in history can then be seen as the result of new **forces of production**. The change from feudal to capitalist society stemmed from the emergence, during feudalism, of the forces of production of industrial society. This resulted in a contradiction between the new forces of production and the old feudal **relations of production**. Capitalist industrial society required relations of production based on wage labour rather than the traditional ties of lord and vassal. When they reach a certain point in their development, the new forces of production lead to the creation of a new set of relations of production. Then, a new epoch of history emerges, which sweeps away the social relationships of the old order.

However, Marx also pointed out that not all social change is driven by economic change. Engels once observed that although he and Marx believed that 'the ultimately determining element in history is the production and reproduction of real life',

> ... if somebody twists this into saying that the economic element is the only determining one, he transforms that proposition into a meaningless, abstract, senseless phrase. The economic situation is the basis, but the various elements of the superstructure ... also exert their influence upon the course of the historical struggles and in many cases preponderate in determining their form. (Marx & Engels 1962, p. 488)

Marx saw social change as the product of human action operating within the constraints of the 'raw materials' of history available to them—the political, legal and economic institutions, the ideas that the population are responsive to, the particular charismatic individuals who happen to be on the public stage. As he wrote, 'It is not "history" which uses men as a means of achieving—as if it were an individual person—its own ends. History is nothing but the activity of men in pursuit of their ends' (in Bottomore & Rubel 1963, p. 78). It was the development of this aspect of Marx's work that lay at the heart of the emergence of the new strands of Marxist thought usually referred to as Western Marxism.

WESTERN MARXISM

Western Marxism is the term used to refer to the general perspective on Marxism that developed in Western Europe from the 1920s among writers whose work was inspired by Marx's ideas and theories, but who, to a greater or lesser extent, placed heavier emphasis on the role of culture and ideas than the more orthodox Marxism promoted from within the former USSR. The basic problem that the Western European Marxists faced was how to explain the continued political support for capitalism, or at least a lack of enthusiasm for alternatives, among the working class, despite their exploitation and oppression. The first generation of Western Marxists included Walter Benjamin (1892–1940), Ernst Bloch (1885–1977), Karl Korsch (1889–1961), Georg Lukács (1885–1971), Antonio Gramsci (1891–1937) and the Frankfurt School theorists such as Max Horkheimer (1895–1973), Theodor Adorno (1903–69), Herbert Marcuse (1898–1979) and others. In one way or another they broke with the Soviet interpretations of Marx and their supporters in order, as they saw it, to understand contemporary society more adequately. Here we focus on the work of Gramsci and some selected aspects of the Frankfurt School.

Antonio Gramsci

Gramsci drew out the implications of the fact that social change is driven by human action for the Marxist conception of culture and the realm of ideas. Marx and Engels had argued that the dominant ideas are those of the dominant class, but what Gramsci noted was that this ideological dominance did not emerge automatically—it had to be worked at and sustained—and that times of radical social change were precisely those when the dominance of particular ideas was called into question. He argued that the dominance of the ruling class is based on ideological hegemony—that is, the fusion of contradictory and conflicting ideological orientations into a relatively stable framework of functioning ideas, worldviews, beliefs and values. For capitalism to function with any degree of effectiveness, it needed to secure the loyalty and support of the working class as much as any other social group—it could not rely on mere force or deception. The aim of Marxism, argued Gramsci, should be to provide arguments and new ideas that unsettle the ideological hegemony of any particular epoch or period in social history. A central part of Gramsci's approach, then, was to pay more attention than Marx and Engels themselves had to the realm of culture and ideas and to institutions such as the Church, the mass media and the education system in understanding why and how capitalist societies are maintained or changed.

The Frankfurt School

The term 'Frankfurt School' refers to an interdisciplinary group of social scientists in the Institute for Social Research established at the University of Frankfurt in 1923. Many members of the group moved to the United States in the 1930s when the Nazis came to power, and some returned to Germany in the 1950s. The school referred to its work as critical theory. As part of their greater responsiveness to culture and ideas, members worked towards establishing linkages between the work of psychoanalyst Sigmund Freud and Marx, as well as more broadly between the disciplines of sociology, history and psychology.

This meant that the Frankfurt School theorists were especially interested in fleshing out the Marxist theme of alienation and identifying the psychological costs of capitalist society, as well as its non-rational and irrational aspects. Like Gramsci, they thought that social order was maintained primarily in the ideological sphere, and they saw developments such as the mass media as a central element of the control exercised over the general population. Marx saw religion as the 'opiate of the masses', but for the Frankfurt School theorists this role had been taken over by what they referred to as the 'culture industry'—popular radio, mass circulation magazines, film and later television. In their analysis, the mass media had taken the place of Durkheim's occupational associations, playing the role of generating meaning in every individual's life in ways that community or work-based associations were decreasingly able to engage with.

Shaped by their experience of German fascism in the 1930s, the Frankfurt School theorists developed an important critique of the ideas of reason and enlightenment as simply the opposite of myth, tradition and emotion. They highlighted the ways in which the supposed pursuit of increased rationality can lead to highly irrational outcomes, and how the pursuit of enlight-

> There are powerful reasons to question the supposed liberty that arises from our culture of consumerism. Do so-called lifestyle statements—Apple iPods, Gucci watches, Mont Blanc pens—really satisfy our deeper personal strivings, or are they just a further stimulus to a society that cannot stop desiring to desire? How may online shoppers find that they really have more quality time available in their lives—for family, friends or meaningful pursuits? How many parents avoid spending time with their children as a result of the culture of shopping? And do today's consumer industries—from travel agencies selling pre-packaged holidays to IKEA-inspired firms selling pre-packaged living—promote new freedoms or new insecurities? (Elliott 2009, p. 19)

Case Study
Irrational rationality?

During 2009, a large number of employees at the French mobile and internet company Orange-France Telecom committed suicide, citing workplace stress and management bullying. In the 18 months to September 2009, 23 employees killed themselves and another 13 attempted suicide. In 2002, 29 Orange workers committed suicide, and in 2000 the number was 28 (Chrisafis 2009, p. 25). Many employees say that managers at Orange are pursuing a reduction in the workforce by repeatedly sending them messages suggesting they find work elsewhere, transferring them frequently from one part of the company to another, requiring them to ask permission to go the toilet and to file written explanations if they are a minute late after lunch, and imposing unworkable time limits on their interactions with customers. As one employee put it, 'only money and marketing count, not the quality of our work' (Chrisafis 2009, p. 25).

1. Do you think this style of management is common in other companies in other countries?
2. To what extent can it be seen as an example of the 'irrationality of rationality'?

enment can itself take on mythological dimensions. Rather than science taking the place of religion, science had become the new religion of the modern world, requiring as much unquestioning faith as religious doctrine, and placing as much ideological and cultural power in the hands of scientists as witch-doctors, priests or cardinals.

For the Frankfurt School theorists, Nazism and the Holocaust were not the product of some deviation from rationality and enlightenment, driven by non-rational emotional forces such as anti-Semitism. They saw them more as the outcome of a kind of hyper-rationality, the application of pure reason to problems of complex society in the absence of any kind of critical or moral concern about the value of human life. The Holocaust was not to be explained as the product of moral orientations specific to German culture, but as one very plausible outcome of the very ideas of enlightenment and rationality, especially if rationality was seen simply as the sensible pursuit of purely instrumental goals. With the concept of 'the dialectic of enlightenment', they aimed to encourage a sense of the double-sidedness of human action—the idea that every worthwhile political or social ideal also has a 'dark side' if pursued in too abstract a way without constant critical reflection on its impact on real human beings. Today this argument would apply, for example, to the pursuit of economic growth and expanding GDP, or increased economic productivity.

WEBER AND CONFLICT SOCIOLOGY

Max Weber (1864–1920) is widely regarded as one of the most significant sociologists. In 1998 members of the International Sociological Association voted his books *Economy and Society* (1978) and *The Protestant Ethic and the Spirit of Capitalism* (1930) to be the most influential and the fourth most influential sociological books, respectively, of the 20th century. Weber's major concerns included explaining how capitalism came into existence, why it appeared in the West and not in other parts of the world (particularly in China, India and Islamic countries), the operation of different forms of rationality in modern societies, the role of ideas in social change and the importance of bureaucratic forms of organisation. Previous chapters have examined Weber's work on class, status and party (see Chapter 7) and rationalisation (see Chapter 12); this section focuses on his understanding of **social action** and social change.

In many respects Weber had a very different approach to sociology from either Durkheim or Marx, in that he emphasised social life as the product of human action. He was not as enthusiastic as Durkheim about thinking in terms of abstractions such as 'society', preferring to attempt to identify how a range of different courses of action among different groups intersected with each other. Even if society is composed of social institutions and groups, Weber insisted that they are nonetheless constituted by real human beings engaging in social action. As he wrote, 'When reference is made in a sociological context to a state, a nation, a corporation, a family or an army corps, or to similar collectivities, what is meant is . . . only a certain kind of development of actual or possible social actions of individual persons' (1978, p. 14).

In *Economy and Society*, he attempted to outline the specific object of sociological analysis when he said that 'Sociology . . . is a science concerning itself with the interpretive understanding of social action and thereby with a causal explanation of its course and consequences' (1978, p. 4). He argued that human activity is always social to the extent that people attach meanings to their actions and that each action 'takes account of the behaviour of others and is thereby oriented in its course'. This meant that an important aim for sociological analysis was the understanding (*verstehen*) of human action. Weber distinguished between *aktuelles verstehen*, or 'immediate understanding', which simply describes what is happening (e.g. a car has collided with a bicycle), and *erklärendes verstehen*, or 'explanatory understanding', which aims to explain the event (e.g. the bicycle accident resulted from the absence of a bicycle path, the cyclist's erratic riding or failure to use lighting, the motorist's negligence, or some combination of all of these factors). To a large extent this is an act of imagination and creativity, involving putting oneself in the place of the relevant actors and trying to imagine how and why they would act as they do.

Given the importance that Weber attached to social action, it is not surprising that he also attached considerable importance to the role of ideas in shaping social life. Weber maintained that both material factors and beliefs were important in explaining social change. He believed that religious beliefs could develop quite independently of material factors, for example through theological arguments within a church. On the other hand, new beliefs would be taken up and become socially effective only if circumstances made them likely to thrive. Thus, material circumstances might affect whether or not ideas became widely accepted, but they did not determine what ideas were produced in the first place.

Weber adopted a similar type of argument to explain the role of religion in the advent of capitalism. To Weber, before capitalism could fully develop it was necessary to have both the appropriate beliefs and the appropriate material circumstances. In a simple tribal society neither would be present. According to Weber, many oriental societies had the economic conditions that could have led to capitalism, but they lacked a 'spirit of capitalism' that encouraged rational economic activity. Western Europe and the United States had both the material conditions and the rationalised belief system that were necessary preconditions for the development of modern capitalism.

Capitalism and ascetic Protestantism

In his most famous book, *The Protestant Ethic and the Spirit of Capitalism*, Weber (1930) examined the relationship between the rise of certain forms of Protestantism and the development of Western industrial capitalism. He tried to demonstrate that a particular form of Protestantism, ascetic Calvinist Protestantism, preceded particular types of development in capitalist economic activity, and that specific forms of capitalism developed initially in areas where this religion was influential. Other areas of the world displayed many of the preconditions for capitalist development, yet they were slow to move in that direction. For example, India and China had technological knowledge, labour to be hired and individuals engaged in making money. What they lacked, according to Weber, was a religion that encouraged and facilitated a particularly rational psychological orientation to the role of work in human life. The first vigorously capitalist nations emerged among the nations of Western Europe and North America, argued Weber, which had Calvinist religious groups. Furthermore, most of the earliest capitalist entrepreneurs in these areas came from the ranks of Calvinists.

In the version of Protestantism derived from the beliefs of Martin Luther, it was believed that individual Christians could affect their chances of reaching heaven by the way that they behaved on earth. It was very important for Christians to develop faith in God and to act out God's will on earth. In order to do this they had to be dedicated to their calling in life. Whatever position in society God had given them, they had to conscientiously carry out the appropriate duties. The practical effect of Lutheranism was to encourage people to produce or earn no more than was necessary for their material needs. It attached more importance to piety and faith than to the accumulation of great wealth.

Calvinist Protestantism, in contrast, originated in the beliefs of John Calvin in the 16th century. Calvin held to a 'doctrine of predestination', the idea that there was a distinct group of the 'elect': those chosen to go to heaven. They had been chosen by God even before they were born, and those who were not among the 'elect' could never gain a place in heaven however well they behaved on earth.

This religious orientation seems as unlikely as Lutheranism to encourage the accumulation of wealth. If certain individuals are destined for heaven regardless of their earthly behaviour—and the rest were equally unable to overcome their damnation—there would be little point in hard work on earth. However, Weber pointed out that Calvinists had a psychological problem: they did not know whether they were among the elect. They suffered from a type of inner loneliness or uncertainty about their status; their behaviour was not an attempt to earn a place in heaven, but rather to convince themselves that they had been chosen to go there. They reasoned that only the chosen people of God would be able to live a good life on earth. If their behaviour was exemplary they could feel confident that they would go to heaven after death.

The Protestant ethic

The Calvinist 'inner loneliness' produced what Weber called the 'Protestant ethic' in the course of the 17th century in Western Europe. The ethic was ascetic (encouraging abstinence from life's pleasures), an austere lifestyle and rigorous self-discipline. It produced individuals who worked hard in their careers or 'callings', in a single-minded manner. Success in one's calling meant the individual had not lost grace in God's sight. Making money was a concrete indication of success in one's calling. John Wesley, a leader of the great Methodist revival that preceded the expansion of English industry at the close of the 18th century, wrote:

For religion must necessarily produce industry and frugality, and these cannot but produce riches. We must exhort all Christians to gain what they can and to save all they can; that is, in effect to grow rich. (quoted in Weber 1930, p. 175)

According to the ethic, these riches could not be spent on luxuries, fine clothes, lavish houses and frivolous entertainment, but in the glory of God. For

475

entrepreneurs this meant, in effect, reinvesting profits in the business.

The Protestants at the time attacked time wasting, laziness, idle gossip and more sleep than was necessary—six to eight hours a day at the most. They frowned on sexual pleasures—sexual intercourse should remain within marriage and then only for the procreation of children (a vegetable diet and cold baths were sometimes recommended to remove temptation). Sport and recreation were accepted only for improving fitness and health, and condemned if pursued for entertainment. The impulsive fun and enjoyment of the pub, dance hall, theatre and gaming house were prohibited to ascetic Protestants. In fact, anything that might divert or distract people from their calling was condemned. Living life in terms of these guidelines was seen as an indication that the individual had not lost grace and favour in the sight of God.

The spirit of capitalism

Weber maintained that the origins of the spirit of the particularly rational, modern form of capitalism were to be found in this general ethical orientation. There had been no shortage in history of those who sought money and profit. Pirates, traders and moneylenders in every corner of the world had always pursued wealth. However, according to Weber, both the manner and purpose of their pursuit of money were at odds with the spirit of modern capitalism. Traditionally, money seekers engaged in speculative projects: they gambled in order to gain rewards. If successful they tended to spend money frivolously on personal consumption. Furthermore, they were not dedicated to making money for its own sake. To Weber, labourers who had earned enough for their family to live well, and merchants who had secured the luxuries they desired, would feel no need to press themselves harder to make more money. Instead, they sought free time for leisure.

The ascetic Protestant had a quite different attitude to wealth, one that became characteristic of modern capitalism. Weber argued that in modern, rationalised capitalism 'Man is dominated by the making of money, by acquisition as the ultimate purpose of his life (1930, p. 53). Capitalist enterprises are organised on rational bureaucratic lines. Business transactions are conducted in a systematic and rational manner with costs and projected profits being carefully assessed. (Weber's views on 'rational action' are examined in Chapter 12, p. 380.)

Weber claimed that ascetic Protestantism was a vital influence in the creation and development of the spirit and practice of modern capitalism. A methodical and single-minded pursuit of a calling encourages rational capitalism. He wrote:

The Puritan wanted to work in a calling; we are forced to do so. For when asceticism was carried out of the monastic cells into everyday life, and began to dominate worldly morality, it did its part in building the tremendous cosmos of the modern economic order. (1930, p. 181)

Making money became both a religious and a business ethic. The Protestant 'interpretation of profit-making justified the activities of the businessman' (p. 163).

Weber argued that two major features of capitalist industry (standardisation of production and the specialised division of labour) were encouraged by Protestantism. The Protestant 'uniformity of life ... immensely aids the capitalist in the standardization of production' (p. 169). The emphasis on the 'ascetic importance of a fixed calling provided an ethical justification of the modern specialized division of labour' (p. 163).

Finally, Weber noted the importance of the creation of wealth and the restrictions on spending it, which encouraged saving and reinvestment:

When the limitation of consumption is combined with this release of acquisitive activity, the inevitable result is obvious: accumulation of capital through an ascetic compulsion to save. The restraints which were imposed on the consumption of wealth naturally served to increase it, by making possible the productive investment of capital. (p. 172)

The ascetic Protestant way of life had led to the accumulation of capital, investment and reinvestment. It produced the early businesses, which expanded to create capitalist society.

Although Weber saw religious beliefs and practices as influential in social and economic change, it should be stressed that Weber did not discount the importance of the economy and material factors. He wrote, 'it is, of course, not my aim to substitute for a one-sided materialistic an equally one-sided spiritualistic causal interpretation of culture and of history' (p. 183). Capitalism was made possible not just by Calvinist Protestantism, but also by the technology and economic system of the countries in which it developed. Material factors were as important as ideas in its development; neither could be ignored in any explanation.

CONFLICT SOCIOLOGY

As Chapter 7 indicated, class was not the only important social division—social status and position in relation to organised political interests were also significant dimensions of an individual's overall position in society. Weberian conflict theorists thus agree with Marxists that conflict should be given greater attention than is found in Durkheim and Parsons, but they go on to suggest that the possible sources of conflict are multi-dimensional, often cutting across and conflicting with each other.

This section examines the work of the German sociologist Ralf Dahrendorf (1929–2009), who first proposed an integration of Marxist and Weberian approaches to conflict in contemporary capitalist societies, and of the American sociologist Randall Collins, who extended conflict sociology to include both the study of social interaction and a fuller examination of the historical development of capitalist societies.

Authority and conflict—Ralf Dahrendorf

In the 1950s, Dahrendorf developed an amalgam of Marx and Weber's sociological approaches in his analysis of postwar capitalist countries. For Dahrendorf (1959) the nature of capitalist societies had changed so much since Marx and Weber's day that it had become necessary to speak of them as 'post-capitalist'. Those changes included an increase in the proportion of skilled and semi-skilled workers in the workforce, the growth of the middle class and the increasing control of capitalist production by managers rather than owners of the means of production. This shifted the basis of conflict in contemporary societies away from economic concerns to those related to **authority** and **power**.

A consequence of this is that conflict is organised around a number of different types of issue, with an ever-changing variety of groups forming to pursue their particular interests, with no clear divisions between one part of society and another. As Dahrendorf wrote, 'Since domination in industry does not necessarily involve domination in the state, or a church, or other associations, total societies can present the picture of a plurality of competing dominant (and, conversely, subjected) aggregates' (pp. 171–2).

Conflict Sociology—Randall Collins

In 1975 Collins developed conflict theory to include the dimensions of subjective experience and everyday interaction. In his book, *Conflict Sociology*, he 'tried to show that stratification and organization are grounded in the interactions of everyday life' (1975, p. 72). In this sense Collins attempted to extend conflict sociology by building a bridge between the perspectives of the symbolic interactionists and ethnomethodologists (see pp. 481–4), who were criticised for neglecting the structural dimensions of social interaction, and the broader theories of social structures developed by Marxists and Weberians.

Collins suggested that Dahrendorf's argument about authority being the central focus of conflict in late-capitalist societies led to an examination of how authority relations actually operate, making the research of writers such as Erving Goffman necessary to illuminate that question. 'If', wrote Collins, 'the fundamental reality of classes is the division between giving and taking orders, that points us to the social psychology of just how those experiences take place' (p. 72). These themes are examined in greater detail by the theorists discussed in the next section.

Reflective question: Do you see Weber's approach to sociological theory as radically different from that of either Durkheim or Marx, or is it possible that he combines aspects of their approaches in different ways? Use an example to illustrate your argument.

SIMMEL AND SOCIAL INTERACTIONISM

The German sociologist Georg Simmel (1858–1918) was central to the foundation of sociology as a distinct way of thinking about the social world. He taught and exerted a strong influence on Mannheim and Lukács, and Weber said that he 'deserves his reputation as one of the foremost thinkers, a first-rate stimulator of academic youth and academic colleagues' (Weber 1972, p. 158). George Ritzer remarked that Simmel actually had a stronger influence on early American sociology than Marx, Weber or Durkheim (Ritzer 1996, p. 155). His influence came to be marginalised after Talcott Parsons defined the sociological canon around the other three writers, who even today provide the focus of most textbooks on 'classical sociology'. Nonetheless, we can see strong traces of his ideas in the Chicago School, symbolic interactionism and Goffman, and his book *The Philosophy of Money* (1990) anticipated many of the more recent developments in social theory, particularly the attention paid to the importance of abstract representation (postmodernism) and the gradually increasing significance of the logic of competition and the market, as well as the 'social meaning of money' (Zelizer 1994).

Simmel's concept of society and sociology

Simmel argued against seeing 'society' as a unified, supra-individual entity or organism; indeed, he wrote that 'there is no such thing as society "as such" ... for there is no such thing as interaction "as such"—there are only specific kinds of interaction' (1971, p. 27). Rather, what we call 'society' is actually the combination of the social interactions that individuals and groups engage in. He wrote that sociology investigates the rules by which human beings live 'insofar as they form groups and are determined by their group existence because of interaction' (in Coser 1977, p. 179). Society is seen as consisting of a 'web' of relationships between ceaselessly active, interacting individuals. As David Frisby put it,

> *In contrast to Durkheim, who viewed society as a 'system of active forces' operating upon individuals, Simmel ... sees society as constituted by interactional 'forces' between individuals. This enables him to reflect upon our experience of society in every single social interrelation in which we engage. (1992, p. 14)*

Sociology was, for Simmel, the study of the 'delicate, invisible threads' of interaction binding individuals together:

> *On every day, at every hour, such threads are spun, dropped, picked up again, replaced by others, or woven together with them. Herein lie the interactions between the atoms of society ... which support the entire tenacity and elasticity, the entire variety and uniformity of this so evident and so puzzling life of society. (in Frisby & Featherstone 1997, p. 110)*

Social institutions are the 'crystallisations' of the various forms of human behaviour and social interaction, but they exist only because of that interaction. The question for Simmel was then the *forms* taken by these relationships, associations and interactions; and what makes sociology distinct from other disciplines, such as history and psychology, is 'the investigation of the forces, forms and developments of sociation, of the cooperation, association and co-existence of individuals' (in Frisby 1984, p. 53).

The particular conceptual contribution that Simmel felt could be made by sociology was to identify the structural similarities between apparently unconnected social situations, to go beneath surface characteristics and analyse the structure and dynamics of distinct forms of social interaction and association. As Lewis Coser explained this feature of Simmel's approach, 'Although there is little similarity between the behaviour displayed at the court of Louis XIV and that displayed in the main offices of an American corporation, a study of the forms of subordination and superordination in each will reveal underlying patterns common to both' (1977, p. 179). Later, the American sociologist Everett Hughes passed on this basic orientation to sociology by arguing that sociologists should set about 'learning about doctors by studying plumbers, and about prostitutes by studying psychiatrists' (1971, p. 316).

In a related way, for Simmel sociologists are not concerned with individuals, no matter how powerful or influential they may seem, but the structured networks of interaction within which they are located. As Coser said:

> *The sociologist does not contribute to knowledge about the individual actions of a King John, or a King Louis, or a King Henry, but he can illuminate the ways in which all of them were constrained in their actions by the institution of kingship. The sociologist is concerned with* King *John, not with King* John. *On a more abstract level, he may not even be concerned with the institution of kingship, but rather with the processes of conflict and cooperation, of subordination and superordination, of centralization and decentralization, which constitute the building blocks for the larger institutional structure. (1977, pp. 179–80)*

Simmel explained his approach to sociology, particularly his concern with social 'form' rather than 'content', as being similar to geometry, and it is useful to see his work as either a 'geometry' or a 'grammar' of social life.

Relationism and reciprocal working

Bryan Turner (1986) pointed out that, for Simmel, every aspect of social life has to be understood as inter-related with every other aspect. Turner referred to this as the 'relationism' of Simmel's approach. This means that nothing is trivial for a sociologist, because everything human beings do has a particular place within the 'totality' of forms of association and interaction. Simmel analysed money as a social institution in detail in this regard (see below), but 'fashion', wrote Turner, 'the rules of chess or the use of knives at table would be as appropriate as money for understanding this totality' (p. 95).

An important outcome of Simmel's relationism is a sensitivity to the fact that social relations work in more than one direction, and that all social relationships should be understood as *inter*actions, even when they do not look like it. For example, we tend to think of 'power', 'domination' and 'subordination' in terms of one person or institution imposing their will, unilaterally, on others who acquiesce to their power. But Simmel wrote:

> *Within a relationship of subordination, the exclusion of all spontaneity whatever is actually rarer than is suggested by such widely used popular expressions as 'coercion', 'having no choice', 'absolute necessity', etc. Even in the most oppressive and cruel cases of subordination there is still a considerable measure of personal freedom... Interaction... exists even in those cases of superordination and subordination... where according to popular notions the 'coercion' by one party deprives the other of every spontaneity, and therefore of every real 'effect' of contribution to the process of interaction. (1971, pp. 97–8)*

Power thus 'conceals an interaction, an exchange ... which transforms the pure one-sidedness of superordination and subordination into a *sociological* form' (Wolf 1950, p. 186). Coser pointed out that approaching power without seeing it as a *relationship* (rather than a 'thing' that the powerful possess) 'would have been rejected by Simmel as examples of what he called the *fallacy of separateness*' (1977, p. 185; see also the discussion on Foucault and power in Chapter 12).

Social relations—forms and types

Simmel's argument in favour of 'formal' sociology, or a sociology concerned with the forms of association and interaction, was that underneath the dizzying disparity of human conduct, there are related basic forms that tell us a great deal about the rules governing those particular situations. Coser gave the examples of 'how both war and profit-making involve cooperation. Inversely, identical interests and purposes may crystallize into different forms. Economic interests may be realized in competition as well as in planned cooperation, and aggressive drives may be satisfied in various forms of conflict from gang warfare to legal battles' (1977, p. 180).

His forms of interaction and types of person were not meant to capture all aspects of social reality completely, but to operate as 'pure', conceptual versions of the real world. The concept of 'the stranger', for example, was not meant to account for each and every situation where there are strangers, but to identify the most significant features of the relationship between 'strangers' and the surrounding social world that tend to reappear in a wide variety of specific situations. They emphasise or exaggerate 'so as to bring out configurations and relations which underlie reality but are not factually actualized in it' (F. H. Tenbruck, cited in Coser 1977, p. 181).

Simmel examined a wider variety of forms and types of social interaction, including the 'mediator', the 'man in the middle', urban life, domination and subordination, conflict, exchange, group interaction, secrets and lies, prostitution, the dude, the miser and the spendthrift, the adventurer, love and sexuality, faithfulness and gratitude. Here we examine, as examples, his analysis of the stranger and fashion.

The stranger

Simmel developed the concept of 'the stranger' in order to capture the combination of distance and remoteness, being both near and far at the same time, which can be seen in some individuals, arguing that this combination of characteristics played a clearly defined role in modern social life. The stranger, for example, is considered both part of the social group and yet able to stand outside it, and 'is therefore assigned a role that no other members of the group can play' (Coser 1977, p. 182). The fact that the stranger has one foot outside the group means that he or she is regarded as more objective and may be called upon to play the role of judge or mediator in conflicts. Being less constrained by social ties, which would affect his or her perception and understanding, the stranger 'is the ideal intermediary in the traffic of goods as well as in the traffic of emotions' (p. 182). People will also often confide in the stranger, because they feel that there will be fewer consequences of revealing their secrets to him or her, rather than a more closely related, regular member of the group.

Fashion

The starting point for Simmel's account of fashion is to indicate a tension between the tendency of individuals to separate themselves from their social group and to merge or identify with it. Fashion is a way of resolving this tension, by allowing one to both be part of a group and yet somehow distinguish oneself from the 'crowd'. It 'represents nothing more than one of the many forms of life by the aid of which we seek to combine ... the tendency towards social equalization with the desire for individual differentiation and change' (1971, p. 296). This is more significant in highly differentiated societies, where individuality is more central to social life. Being ephemeral is also essential to its function, since there is a continuous need for renewing the mechanism of distinction. Fashion also has little to do with aesthetics or a desire for beauty: 'Judging from the ugly and repugnant things that are sometimes in vogue, it would seem as though fashion were desirous of exhibiting its power by getting us to adopt the most atrocious things for its sake alone' (1971, p. 297).

Fashion's leaders appear to be exercising a heightened form of individuality, since they always appear to be standing out from the group. As Ian Craib put it, 'The dude does this to perfection, always slightly exaggerating the dominant fashion, wearing the baggiest trousers, the shortest skirt, or whatever—employing the fashion in the most individualistic way' (1997, pp. 170–1). However, Simmel pointed out that in fact 'the leader allows himself to be led' (1971, p. 305) in that he (or she) is merely exaggerating group-defined norms.

It is not really possible to avoid the effects of fashion, because in rejecting what is fashionable we are as bound to it as when we slavishly follow it. It is striking, for example, how strict the dress codes are of groups devoted to political radicalism or social non-conformity. 'Similarly', wrote Simmel, 'atheism has been made into a religion, embodying the same fanaticism, the same intolerance, the same satisfying of the needs of the soul that are embraced in religion proper' (p. 307).

Simmel also drew attention to the fact that fashion operated differently for men and women. Given that women's social position makes it more difficult for them than it is for men to achieve an autonomous individual identity, Simmel felt that fashion was a more important means for women to distinguish themselves as individuals. 'It seems', said Simmel, 'as though fashion were the valve through which woman's craving for some measure of conspicuousness and individual prominence finds vent, when its satisfaction is denied her in other fields' (p. 309). He argued that men are less concerned with fashion because they are generally 'rather unfaithful' (p. 310) and express their individuality in all of the rest of their lives, whereas 'woman is a more faithful creature than man', creating a need for change, diversity and individuality that is then met by fashion.

Reflective questions: Do you think that the gender dimensions of fashion have changed since Simmel's day? Are men more concerned about fashion than they used to be? How would you explain your answer?

The philosophy of money and objective culture

Simmel's observations on money in modern societies emerge from his analysis of *exchange* as a particular form of social interaction, although they expanded into a more general account of the psychological dimensions of capitalism. He defined 'value' in terms of use value, but this is made 'objective' through the process of exchange. As Craib put it, 'valued objects are brought into relation to each other through exchange—if I want to buy books, then I have to give up something else that I might buy with the money—say, food, or furniture. In this way I equate a sociology textbook with two McDonald's meals' (1997, p. 152).

Exchange was, for Simmel, the model for all forms of social relations. Society is a collection of exchange relations, and money symbolises all social interaction, a reference point for all human activity:

The philosophical significance of money is that it represents within the practical world the most certain image and the clearest embodiment of the formula of all being, according to which things receive their meaning through each other, and have their being determined by their mutual relations. (1990, pp. 128–9)

Money takes on an independent existence, and vastly expands the range of possible human activities, allowing for long-range planning and long-distance coordination. The stability of money allows for 'long-range calculations, large-scale enterprises and long-term credits'; it has 'developed ... the most objective practices, the most logical, purely mathematical norms, the absolute freedom from everything personal' (pp. 125, 128).

Simmel wrote that money is 'the purest example of the tool' (p. 210); money in the bank, for example, has a utility that unsold goods or unemployed labour do not. It is the most powerful means of translating human activity into abstract quantities. As Craib remarked,

Simmel suggests that money is the purest example of the tendency in modern culture, particularly in the sciences, to the reduction of the qualitative to the quantitative ... The concern of many twentieth-century sociologists with small-scale quantitative studies perhaps explains why Simmel has been neglected by later generations of sociologists. (1997, p. 154)

Money makes it possible to create objective values and 'things'—books, art, ideas, institutions, products—which everyone can share, which 'reduces the human tragedy of competition', and this is the 'civilizing influence of culture' (Simmel 1990, p. 291).

A money economy also encourages the calculative character of modern life, and in this respect Simmel's ideas are closely related to Weber's analysis of rationalisation which, as Turner remarked, is essentially 'an elaboration and extension of Simmel's account of money' (1986, p. 105). In Ritzer's words,

> *Money allows us to reduce the most disparate phenomena to numbers of dollars, and this allows them to be compared to each other. In other words, money allows us to relativize everything. (1996, p. 176)*

A maxim of the modern world, and one of its defining features, has become: 'Everything has a price'; and this concept reflects a central dimension of Simmel's analysis. Calculative rationality thus pervades more and more areas of social interaction, reducing quality to quantity.

A money economy undermines 'the enigmatic unity of the soul' (1990, p. 296), said Simmel, because people 'enter into relationships with each other only by virtue of a single activity, such as the delivery of goods, the lending of money', without taking account of the qualities that make each other unique individuals. 'The general tendency … undoubtedly moves in the direction of making the individual more and more dependent upon the achievements of people, but less and less dependent on the personalities that lie behind them' (p. 296). The greater the range of people we depend on, the more anonymous and interchangeable they all become, and the more one is thrown back onto one's own, autonomous emotions and personality. We thus gain in individual freedom, but at the expense of fragmenting and 'thinning out' our relationships with the ever-increasing number of people we encounter in modern, urban social life.

Simmel distinguished between *subjective culture* and *objective culture*. Subjective culture refers to the direct, unique experiences of individuals, while objective culture refers to the products of the transformation of those experiences into objects accessible to every individual and beyond the influence of any single person. For example, Simmel referred to the way in which the concept of pedagogy as the 'formation of man' and the development of 'a personal internal value' was transformed in the 19th century into 'the concept of "education" in the sense of a body of objective knowledge and behavioural patterns' (1990, p. 449). Simmel suggested that the discrepancy between subjective and objective culture was constantly widening:

> *Every day and from all sides, the wealth of objective culture increases, but the individual mind can enrich the forms and contents of its own development only by distancing itself still further from that culture and developing its own at a much slower pace. (p. 449)*

In other words, the overall historical tendency was for the two to separate from each other more and more, increasing human 'alienation', to use Marx's terminology, and this was what Simmel regarded as the 'tragedy of culture'.

There were a number of advantages to a money economy and objective culture, however. Ritzer (1996, p. 177) summarises these as follows:

- A money economy makes it possible to interact with ever-larger numbers of people.
- Mutual obligations are specific and task-oriented, rather than generalised and all-encompassing.
- Objective culture enables pleasures and activities that are not possible without it.
- A money economy promotes greater individuality, lessens constraint from social groups and enables greater attention to individual subjectivity.

A money economy was essentially the driving force or 'reference point' of modernity, and it would be impossible to think of how modern social life would be possible without it. Nonetheless, like Weber's bleak view of the 'iron cage' of bureaucracy and rationalisation, and Marx's general negative assessment of the impact of capitalism, Simmel's primary emphasis in analysing the expansion of the money economy and the widening disparity between subjective and objective culture was on its problematic impact on everyday human experience.

Simmel—an evaluation

Simmel is often regarded as a flighty essayist rather than a systematic theorist, but Donald Levine has pointed out that this is based on fairly superficial readings of his work. Levine argues instead that 'the way is open to reconsider Simmel's sociological writings not merely as occasional sources of catchy hypotheses but as the matrix of one of the most sophisticated perspectives on social interaction that we possess' (1997, p. 202). We now turn to examine one of the areas of sociological theory where Simmel's influence has been felt—symbolic interactionist and interpretivist approaches.

INTERACTIONISM AND INTERPRETIVE SOCIOLOGY

Like Simmel, sociologists who adopt social action, interactionist or interpretive perspectives usually reject the view that society has a clear structure that directs individuals to behave in certain ways. Some social action theorists do not actually *deny* the existence of social structure and social institutions, but see this structure as based on the action of individuals. Weber, who to a large extent spans the distinction between the structural and social action perspectives, acknowledged the existence of classes, status groups and parties, but challenged Durkheim's argument that society exists independently of the individuals who make it up. Symbolic interactionists accept the existence of social roles, but deny that these roles are fixed and inflexible, or determined by the supposed 'needs' of the social system. Ethnomethodologists represent a much more radical rejection of structural perspectives. They deny the existence of any sort of social structure. All of these perspectives argue that sociologists need to understand and interpret human behaviour and discover the meanings that lie behind it. Ethnomethodologists claim that sociology can go no further than reaching an understanding of the meanings individuals attach to the world around them.

Symbolic interactionism

The term **symbolic interactionism** is used to refer to a conceptual orientation emerging from the work of American philosopher George Herbert Mead (1863–1931) and the translation of his ideas into sociological theory by one of his students, Herbert Blumer (1900–1987). Other important influences include the work of W. I. Thomas and John Dewey, as well as the fieldwork-oriented approach to sociology championed in the sociology practised at the University of Chicago in the 1930s, 1940s and 1950s, often termed the Chicago School, led by Robert Park, Ernest Burgess and Everett C. Hughes. A central feature of symbolic interactionism is the focus, like Simmel's work, on small-scale interactions, with relatively less attention being paid to large-scale social change.

George Herbert Mead

Mead emphasised the ways in which human social interaction is dependent on its symbolisation, the use of language and the communication of meaning between people. Language and symbols do not just represent objects; people construct particular meanings for those objects, which then function to orientate and organise the human activity related to those objects. For Mead, the human self is essentially social in that it only develops through engagement with the realm of language and symbols, in interaction with key people in one's environment—hence the term symbolic interactionism. Children, for example, begin to learn through imitation of those around them in the form of play, taking on particular roles and then shifting to others. Over time, they learn how others see them and tailor their 'presentation of self' accordingly, and they learn how to take on the role of another by imagining themselves in that role.

For Mead, the development of the self is organised around the process of role-taking, through which people acquire the social capacity to see themselves as others see them, and act accordingly. Mead identified two aspects of the self: the 'me' refers to your direct experience of yourself as 'your self' in particular contexts and settings; and the 'I' encompasses the reactions of others to you, and the incorporation of those reactions and perceptions in your own self-concept. For example, the 'me' will experience success in a university exam simply in its own terms as a relatively pleasant relief after the stress involved in taking the exam, whereas the 'I' will include what this event means for your identity as a 'clever' or 'hard-working' student.

Mead saw the self as developing through a number of stages:

- In the first stage, the **play stage**, children play at occupying a variety of roles that they see around them. They do not yet have a clear sense of their own self.
- In the second stage, the **game stage**, children learn to develop strategies for interacting with other players in the pursuit of particular goals. They also learn to see how others see them, and they develop a sense of what Mead called 'the generalised other'. This refers to a kind of 'averaging out' of the perceptions of particular other people, to form a sense of how 'people in general' or 'society' views them.

Mead argued that human thought is only possible 'by taking the attitude of the generalized other' towards oneself, 'for only then can thinking—or the internalized conversation of gestures which constitutes thinking—occur' (1934, p. 156). The fact that people are always reflecting in an ongoing 'inner conversation' on what 'the generalised other' thinks and expects of them is an important means by which human conduct is regulated and organised. As Mead put it, 'It is in the form of the generalized other that the social process influences the behaviour of the individuals involved in it ... that the community exercises control over the conduct of its individual members' (p. 155).

Herbert Blumer

Herbert Blumer developed Mead's ideas more systematically into a particular approach in sociology. In contrast to Durkheim's emphasis on the constraints of 'the social', Blumer argued that social action and interaction are ongoing processes that are dependent on the exact form taken by the meaning-attribution process in any given situation within which people take an active role. Blumer (1969) identified the following three core elements of a symbolic interactionist approach:

1. Human behaviour is not the product of either biology or external social constraints, but of the meanings that people attach to the world around them.
2. Those meanings do not exist prior to the process of interaction, but emerge within it. People do not simply act out a pre-existing script; they write and rewrite the script for their role as they go along.
3. This process of meaning creation depends on a variety of approaches to interpretation of the social world utilised by people, in which they take on the role of the other and imagine how they are perceived, modifying their conduct accordingly.

Blumer's critique of other approaches to sociology revolved around the failure to see 'the social actions of individuals in human society as being constructed by them through a process of interpretation. Instead, action is treated as a product of factors which play on and through individuals' (p. 84). He thought, in contrast, that 'It is the social process in group life that creates and upholds the rules, not the rules that create and uphold group life' (p. 19).

This does not mean that Blumer thought there were no constraints on human action, or that it was not framed by existing social institutions. He recognised that much human action unfolds according to a formula, so that 'In most situations in which people act towards one another they have in advance a firm understanding of how to act and how other people will act' (p. 17). But it remained necessary to be sensitive to the extent to which people improvised on such formulas and used their creativity and imagination to play with social rules and expectations. Even in the situations where people appear to be behaving in a standardised way, we do not know the extent to which they are conscious of that and decide to follow the rules because they want to, rather than because they 'have no other choice'. As Blumer observed:

The participants still have to build up their lines of action and fit them to one another through the dual process of designation and interpretation ... Repetitive and stable joint action is as much a result of an interpretative process as is a new form of joint action that is being developed for the first time. (p. 18)

Ethnomethodology

An even more radical version of this understanding of the social world being the product of a constant process of creation and re-creation appears in the theoretical perspective referred to as **ethnomethodology**. The term was introduced by Harold Garfinkel in 1967, and it means simply the study of the methods that people use to give meaning to the world around them.

Ethnomethodologists see social order as primarily a fiction that people use to behave 'as if' their world has a structure to it and thus make it more manageable. What sociologists see as social order is primarily a highly contingent narrative consistency that is imposed on the real world, not a reflection of that world. Zimmerman and Weider (1971) describe the task of sociology as being to explain 'how members of society go about the task of seeing, describing, and explaining order in the world in which they live' (p. 289).

For example, Garfinkel (1967) argued that people take aspects of their situation and impose a pattern on them, and then further manifestations of the same pattern are used to indicate its 'real' existence. He referred to this as the 'documentary method', which:

consists of treating an actual appearance as 'the document of', as 'pointing to', as 'standing on behalf of' a presupposed underlying pattern. Not only is the underlying pattern derived from its individual documentary evidences, but the individual documentary evidences, in their turn, are interpreted on the basis of 'what is known' about the underlying pattern. Each is used to elaborate the other. (p. 78)

This means that social life is 'essentially reflexive'—in other words, accounts of the social world do not just make sense of and explain that world, they actually produce that world.

Garfinkel gave an example of how the documentary method works with an experiment he conducted with his students. The students were invited to participate in what was described as a new type of psychotherapy. Each student was asked to speak with a counsellor, who was in another room, via an intercom about a personal problem or issue. Although the students did not know it, the counsellor gave only random 'yes' or 'no' responses that had no substantial relationship to their situation at all. Despite this, the students felt that the advice they received made sense of their problem and was reasonable and useful. For Garfinkel, this was an illuminating illustration of his argument, in that the students imposed their own meaning on what was essentially meaningless, and their account of the interaction ended up constituting it—that is, giving it shape and meaning where there had in fact been none.

Garfinkel also extended this argument to suggest the concept of 'indexicality'—the idea that human behaviour is 'indexed' to the particular situation one is in, rather than being the product of human nature or even a socialised self or identity that exists across all situations. This approaches human behaviour as almost entirely 'situation-driven', making the situations the object of sociological analysis and rendering almost meaningless concepts like 'status', 'race', 'class' or 'gender'.

In broad terms Garfinkel was critical of the tendency among sociologists, especially those influenced by Durkheim and Marx, to see humans as what he called 'cultural dopes'—puppets dancing to the tune determined by a puppeteer referred to as 'society'. As he put it, 'By "cultural dope" I refer to the man-in-the-sociologist's-society who produces the stable features of society by acting in compliance with pre-established and legitimate alternatives of action that the common culture provides' (1967, p. 68). Garfinkel and the ethnomethodologists prefer to see humans as 'skilled' and 'knowledgeable', constantly creating their social world in response to the demands and expectations of the social institutions around them.

> **Reflective questions:** What are the arguments for and against seeing sociological thinking as characterised by a tendency to treat people as 'cultural dopes'? How would you characterise the alternative? Is Garfinkel's approach the only way to do things differently?

BEYOND CLASSICAL SOCIOLOGY?

> *All fixed, fast-frozen relations, with their train of ancient and venerable prejudices and opinions, are swept away, all new-formed ones become antiquated before they can ossify. All that is solid melts into air, all that is holy is profaned, and man is at last compelled to face with his sober senses, his real conditions of life, and his relations with his kind.*
> *(Marx & Engels, 1967, p. 36)*

The fact that a variety of important changes are taking place in contemporary societies that distinguish them from earlier phases in the modern era has had a number of effects on sociological theory. Here we focus on three of them: the arguments for a particular feminist approach to sociological theory, one that is better equipped to capture the profoundly gendered dimensions of social life; the move to approach recent social changes in terms of the concept of postmodernity; and the interest in developing new understandings of the ways in which modernity itself has been transformed into a 'second' or 'reflexive' modernity.

FEMINIST SOCIOLOGY

The very simple observation that feminists in sociology made about the structure of sociological theory was that it was a misrepresentation of reality to talk simply in terms of 'individuals' or 'members of society', because human social life is made up of men and women, girls and boys, husbands and wives, mothers and fathers. This means that there is in fact a gender dimension to all human social life that may have more or less significance in particular situations, and may itself be the product of a process of social construction, but should not be ignored altogether. However, up until the 1960s gender played no clear role at all in sociological theory. Many sociologists argued that this was a fundamental problem requiring correction through the incorporation of gender into all the categories that were used in sociological theorising. Feminist sociologists agued that it should be impossible to speak of social inequality, social mobility, the education system, the mass media, socioeconomic status or the social construction of the self without being conscious of the significant differences between males and females.

Beyond public and private—Anna Yeatman

The Australian sociologist Anna Yeatman went one step further to identify the crucial difference that the incorporation of a feminist perspective can make to the way in which all social life is understood. Although Yeatman (1986) argued that gender has become a central topic of sociological analysis alongside class, ethnicity and occupation, the challenge remains to accommodate 'the distinctive world of women ... what we refer to variously as domestic life, family life, or personal life ... the world of love relations and parenting' (p. 158).

Yeatman maintained that there is still a primary emphasis in sociology on the public domain of the state, the economy, work and organisations, and that work in those areas remains divorced from the study of domestic life, the private sphere and family life. Yeatman argued:

> *It is not just that 'the economy' looms larger in theoretical terms than 'love' but that 'love disappears altogether from*

theoretical view ... It is accordingly, virtually impossible to bring them together within a logically coherent and consistent account of social life. (pp. 156–60)

The aim of a feminist sociology, then, would be to integrate all of the various topics covered in this book, such as class, family life, state and politics, sex, gender and sexuality, rather than allowing theory and research in each of these areas to proceed independently of each other.

Yeatman admitted that a potential weakness of feminist sociology is to see the gender division of labour and the public/private division as one and the same thing. 'If men and women are the starting point', wrote Yeatman, the tendency will be to see them 'as interest groups engaged in some form of competitive, albeit asymmetrical, power relation' (p. 172). There is some value in this form of analysis for Yeatman, but she believed that 'it adds nothing to the extant theoretical agenda of sociology' (p. 172). However, she suggested that the strength of a feminist concern with an integration of the sociology of the public and private domains is that it may overcome the individual/society dichotomy that has consistently plagued sociological thought, by placing the development of personal relations at the heart of social life rather than adding it as an afterthought.

Reflective question: What impact do you think feminism has had on sociological thought?

Modernity, the Enlightenment and beyond

The understanding of the kind of society being examined in the work of sociologists up until about the 1970s was organised to a large extent around the concepts of modernity and the Enlightenment. To differing extents one might be critical of aspects of capitalist or urbanised social life, but contemporary social forms were seen relatively consistently as having a range of features in common that distinguished modern from traditional or pre-modern societies. The origins of a specifically modern way of seeing the world are often seen to lie in the 18th-century intellectual movement known as the Enlightenment, which David Harvey (1990) sums up as follows:

The idea was to use the accumulation of knowledge generated by many individuals working freely and creatively for the pursuit of human emancipation and the enrichment of daily life. The scientific domination of nature promised freedom from scarcity, want, and the arbitrariness of natural calamity. The development of rational forms of social organisation and rational modes of thought promised liberation from the irrationalities of myth, religion, superstition, release from the arbitrary use of power as well as from the dark side of our own human natures. (p. 12)

The French Revolution, and the understanding of society and social progress that it encouraged, is one example of this way of thinking, but more broadly it has become a central feature of the worldview of everyone in countries and regions like Australia, North America and Western Europe.

However, as we have seen in the discussion of the ideas of the Frankfurt School theorists, in the course of the second half of the 20th century it became clear that the Enlightenment 'project' (the aim of Enlightenment thinkers) was itself characterised by a number of problems. Rationality was revealed to have its irrational sides; and progress did not turn out to be either inevitable or unambiguously a good thing. From the 1960s onwards there was greater pessimism about the future and less willingness to believe that the truth could be found in grand, unified theories, or even that there was a clear relationship between theory and reality.

Postmodernism and knowledge—Jean-François Lyotard

A modernist conception of knowledge is to see it as reflective of some 'reality', with the real world being the most important consideration, and knowledge (understood as scientific knowledge) important only in the sense of how well it captures and understands what is being talked about. This is in contrast to the forms of knowledge in pre-modern societies, where it served different functions, such as the indication of social status or the maintenance of cultural tradition.

However, Lyotard (1984) observed that with changing technology, knowledge had become a more independent variable, something produced for its own sake and turning into a productive force in its own right, of increasing significance in an 'information age'. In addition, the 'grand narratives' of progress, the Enlightenment and socialism had tended to function as 'shells' for a variety of forms of action, many contradicting the supposed overall aim of the larger 'meta-narrative'. So in the pursuit of equality, democracy and freedom, the French Revolution in practice brought about the oppression of new categories of people. But a healthy scepticism had developed in relation to these grand narratives, argued Lyotard, and for him this was a central feature of 'the postmodern condition'. 'I define postmodern', wrote Lyotard, 'as incredulity towards meta-narratives' (1984, p. xxiv). Knowledge can therefore been seen only as emerging from particular social positions, with no general 'truth' worth searching for. This also encourages a greater emphasis on the uses to which knowledge can be put, rather than whether it is interesting, profound or truer to reality than previous accounts.

Simulations—Jean Baudrillard

Although Jean Baudrillard did not especially want to be seen as a postmodern theorist, as Bryan Turner remarked, 'Baudrillard is widely regarded in sociology as the postmodernist *par excellence*' (1993, p. 75). The particular significance of his work for sociologists is his argument that the sociological claim to study a distinct domain—'the social' or 'society', as opposed to 'the political' or 'the economic'—no longer makes any sense. For Baudrillard, in the postmodern world the 'social' did not exist as an objective reality waiting to be studied by sociologists. Sociology, he argued, 'can only depict the expansion of the social and its vicissitudes ... The hypothesis of the death of the social is also that of its own death' (1983, p. 3).

Like Lyotard's account of knowledge, Baudrillard also argued that images, signs and symbols are no longer closely linked to some objective, material reality, but have an independent existence and salience. For example, one might think that the imagery surrounding bottled water is meant to convey something about the water itself and that this is what consumers are buying. However, from Baudrillard's perspective, the symbol for, say, Fiji bottled water is not simply a representation of that water, it is itself what is being sold and bought. The story about the water becomes more important and more significant than the water itself.

He used the term simulacrum to refer to an image of something that does not exist and has never existed, and he argued that social life is increasingly organised around such simulacrums. To Baudrillard, postmodern society is based on the production and exchange of free-floating signifiers (words and images) that have no connection with what is signified (the things that words and images refer to).

The recent US election, for example, can be analysed in this way. A 'modernist' approach would be to look for the social groups that supported either the Republicans or the Democrats for reasons to do with their appreciation of the different party policies and orientations. Obama and McCain are then seen as 'standing for' or 'representing' other dimensions of people's lives. But from Baudrillard's perspective there is no relationship to an external reality: the US election was a kind of public drama entirely contained within itself, a simulacrum of a political contest driven by the mass media's concern to entertain and to generate audiences for itself.

In many respects, Bryan Turner (1993) has shown how Baudrillard's work as a philosophy actually reinforces and resonates with a variety of arguments that have been developed in sociology since Weber and Simmel. His critique of the concept of 'the social' is, argued Turner, related to Weber's caution about the use of terms such as 'social' and 'sociology'. The critique of objective social knowledge has also been a point of debate in the social sciences since the late 19th century. Baudrillard's analysis of postmodern culture, maintained Turner, has its roots in Georg Simmel's analysis of everyday life in modern urban centres, and in Daniel Bell's analysis of contemporary culture in *The Coming of Post-Industrial Society* (1973) and *The Cultural Contradictions of Capitalism* (1976). Bell argued that since the 1920s there has been a contradiction between the culture of capitalism, with its media-promoted emphasis on pleasure and consumption, and the real demands of capitalist economies, requiring the asceticism and discipline of Weber's Protestant ethic. He also argued that the realm of culture and signs was autonomous from the economy in the 1970s.

Zygmunt Bauman (1992) pointed out that the roots of postmodern sociology can be traced back to Harold Garfinkel's (1967) efforts 'to expose the fragility and brittleness of social reality, its "merely" conversational and conventional groundings, its negotiability, perpetual use and irreparable underdetermination' (p. 40). However, one can also argue, suggests Turner, that the idea that the features of contemporary societies highlighted by writers such as Lyotard and Baudrillard are particularly new is historically incorrect, and that 'the simplistic periodization of modernity/postmodernity should be abandoned' (p. 84). He argued that modernity has its origins in the Protestant Reformation, the development of agrarian capitalism and the expansion of the colonial world economic system, but that there was a reaction against the 'meta-narrative' of Protestant modernism in 18th-century Baroque culture. He described Baroque culture as one that 'had a strong sense of the fragmented and constructed nature of the social, which developed an articulate sense of the anxiety and subjectivity of the self, and which practised parody and irony as rhetorical styles' (pp. 83–4). It was a 'mixture of high, low and kitsch culture, which was designed to trap the masses in a simulated culture' (pp. 83–4).

Second modernity and 'zombie sociology'—Ulrich Beck

A number of sociologists have responded to the challenges posed by the idea of postmodernity by developing new theoretical approaches to the changing forms taken by modern social life. The German sociologist Ulrich Beck has been particularly influential in suggesting revisions to sociological theory that adequately encompass the character and dynamics of what he calls 'second modernity', his proposed alternative to the concept of postmodernity.

Beck observes that 'postmodernist theory only tells us what is *not* the case', what is wrong with old approaches to modernity, but does not go beyond that to engage with the task that this critique makes necessary, namely 'a fundamental self-critique, a redefinition—we might even say a reformation—of modernity and modern society' (Beck & Willms 2004, p. 25). For Beck, the social changes taking place today do not reflect a movement 'beyond' modernity, or the 'end' of an era, but a radical modernisation of modernity itself and the beginning of a new type of society.

First and second, reflexive modernity

Instead of seeing modernity as having evolved into postmodernity, Beck, Bonß and Lau (2003) emphasise a distinction between 'first' and 'second' modernity. They suggest that in what sociologists have understood as modern society, social change took place with 'a stable system of coordinates' (p. 2). Modernity is underpinned by the following premises (pp. 4–5):

1. Society is organised in terms of the nation-state.
2. Society is based on pre-existing collective identities.
3. There is full employment.
4. Society is distinct from nature, and the relationship is one of exploitation.
5. Society is characterised by an ongoing process of rationalisation and increasing instrumental control, informed by ever-improving scientific knowledge.
6. Society is organised in terms of functional differentiation, and progressive specialisation leads to ever-improving articulation of ends and means.

For Beck the emergence of a 'second' modernity concerns all of these premises being called into question, and the framework of modernisation itself is also subjected to change. The first premise has been called increasingly into question by globalisation; the second by individualisation; the third by the fragmentation and diversification of the labour market; the fourth by intensifying ecological risks and bio-technology; the fifth by challenges to the scientific monopoly on 'truth', the unintended consequences of rational action and the 'irrationality of rationality'; and the sixth by a range of side effects of increasing social differentiation.

Beck and his colleagues also refer to the emergence of 'second' modernity as 'reflexive modernisation'. They explain this concept as follows:

The hypothesis of a 'reflexive' modernisation of modern societies examines a fundamental societal transformation within modernity. Modernity has not vanished, but it is becoming increasingly problematic. While crises, transformation and radical social change have always been part of modernity, the transition to a reflexive second modernity not only changes social structures but revolutionises the very coordinates, categories and conceptions of change itself. (2003, p. 2).

Their argument is that social change has 'moved up a level', turning into a kind of 'meta-change' with a variety of highly unpredictable and contingent effects. Beck suggests that reflexive modernisation appears to be producing 'a new kind of capitalism, a new kind of labour, a new kind of global order, a new kind of society, a new kind of nature, a new kind of subjectivity, a new kind of everyday life and a new kind of state' (Beck 2000c, p. 81).

Beck emphasises that he is not attempting to describe a simple evolution from first to second modernity—the one does not just replace the other. As he puts it, 'they exist simultaneously, and completely interpenetrate each other' (Beck & Willms 2004, p. 31). Second modernity is better understood as first modernity being subjected to its own processes of modernisation, with unpredictable outcomes.

Sociological theory and society beyond the nation-state

Beck observes that since sociological theory arose within first modernity, it developed in the context of the nation-state, and the concept 'society' tends to be equated with the nation-state. He refers to this as 'methodological nationalism' (see Chapter 2). All of the other central concepts in sociology—family, class, education, work, identity and so on—also presume that 'society' is to be understood within the 'container' of particular nation-states. The vast majority of the data used in social science, particularly statistical data, are organised in terms of the nation-state. This means that sociologists can think only in terms of national societies—Australian society, British society, Japanese society and so on.

> ... the social-scientific stance is rooted in the concept of nation-state. A nation-state outlook on society and politics, law, justice, and history governs the sociological imagination. To some extent, much of social science is a prisoner of the nation-state. (Beck 2003, p. 454)

However, to the extent that social life has been subjected to various forces of social change, including globalisation, the categories of classical sociological theory may be less and less capable of grasping the reality of social relations, structures and processes. Beck argues that many sociological concepts have turned into 'zombie' categories, in the sense that the reality they originally captured has died, but the concepts live on, a kind of theoretical 'living dead'.

He gives the example of the 'household': the reality of family life that this concept is meant to refer to has changed so much—with divorce, remarriage, single parenthood, multiple careers, geographical mobility—that the idea of a 'household' now does a very poor job of representing that reality. Beck argues that sociologists now need to ask themselves 'To what extent are our fundamental categories based on assumptions that have become historically obsolete?' (Beck & Willms 2004, p. 21).

Another example is the sociological analysis of social inequality. Beck argues that methodological nationalism produces a tendency to focus on inequalities within nation-states ('small inequalities'), which are then explained away in terms of 'merit'. He identifies four central features of this 'national' perspective on inequality:

1. The accountability for global inequalities is fragmented. 'The nation-state principle is the analytical key to understanding why the connection between globalization and poverty has been so seldom researched in the social sciences' (2003, p. 461).
2. Inequality is seen as bounded by national forms of citizenship organised internally on principles of equality.
3. Inequality is analysed only within and not across national boundaries. This makes it hard to perceive the 'large' inequalities across nation-states.
4. An ongoing lack of action on large inequalities is legitimised because they are seen as irrelevant.

The consequences of approaching inequality in this way are, on the one hand, that the sociological understandings of inequality within nation-states are subtle and detailed; and on the other hand, this methodological nationalism 'effaces global inequalities—a form of legitimisation through neglect'.

> Large inequalities are thus invisible from the national perspective; they can both grow and be 'legitimized' via a form of institutional irrelevance and unreality ... the national perspective functions like a microscope. But focusing on small internal inequalities, the bigger global ones are left out. (Beck 2003, p. 460)

There remains a range of poorly understood 'large' inequalities that cut across national boundaries and that Beck believes underpin much of the social and political instability characterising contemporary global society.

For Beck, then, one of the more important challenges facing contemporary sociological theory is to identify the extent to which the categories of earlier theorists may have become 'zombie' categories because the social reality they were meant to capture has changed beyond recognition. The difficulty facing sociological theory is that second modernity is characterised by a transformation of most of sociology's core concepts. The umbrella sociological concept of 'society' is especially problematic because it is anchored so firmly in methodological nationalism and equated with the nation-state, making it difficult to develop theoretical categories capable of understanding a global civil society. 'If the social sciences want to avoid becoming a museum of antiquated ideas', writes Beck, all of its concepts—family, class, inequality, democracy, power, the state, public and private, community and so on—have to be reworked and reconfigured 'within the framework of a new cosmopolitan social and political science' (2003, p. 458).

Reflective question: Give some examples of 'zombie' categories in sociology, and explain why you would see them in this way.

SOCIOLOGY TODAY

It is clear that there are a variety of reasons to reject the view put by postmodern philosophers unfamiliar with sociological theory and research that the Enlightenment project, of which sociology is a part, either has been or should be abandoned. Modern societies can be systematically studied and understood, and ways of improving them and the lives of those who live in them can be identified, even if translating those ideas into practice often proves difficult. Human social life consists of more than language games or simulacrums, and includes real relations between living human beings and a variety of forms of real resistance to existing relations of power and domination. This makes the study of those social relations through disciplines such as sociology worthwhile, indeed essential, and makes it important to understand the variety of theoretical perspectives from which the study of human social relations can be undertaken.

When we look at the field of sociological theory and research, we do not see the 'death' of the social accompanied by sociology's demise. What we see is a diverse and exciting range of vigorous theoretical and empirical work, including:

- new understandings of earlier sociological theorists, including Weber, Durkheim, Simmel, Parsons, the Frankfurt School and others, utilising their ideas in new ways to analyse contemporary social conditions and their historical roots in preceding eras
- the development of fresh sociological perspectives, most of which we have not had the space to examine in any detail here, including:
  - the utilisation of Michel Foucault's work on power and government, Touraine's action theory and the study of contemporary social movements
  - Pierre Bourdieu's reformulation of sociological methodology and the sociological understanding of culture, language, power, action and social reproduction
  - the work of Ulrich Beck and his colleagues on second or reflexive modernity and the ways in which established sociological concepts and theories are to be reconceptualised in order to grasp a truly global society
  - the utilisation of Norbert Elias' work on 'the civilising process' and his 'process' sociological approach in the study of topics ranging from the changing management of emotions to the globalisation of culture and state formation, and the changing forms taken by organised and individual violence
  - the continuing transformation of sociological theory by feminist debates and the integration of a feminist perspective into mainstream sociological theory and research
- empirical research on:
  - the historical processes underlying contemporary social conditions
  - transformations in class relations, state formation, education, sexuality and gender
  - globalisation and its relation to locally based social and political identities
  - culture and ethnicity, and their relation to state formation
  - the shifting relations between economy, civil society and the state
  - changes in family life
  - the nature of the network society, and the role of changing communications technology in reshaping social relationships
  - the variety of ways in which social life can be 'modern', particularly through the concept of 'multiple modernities'
  - the question of processes of individualisation in contemporary societies and the impact of market forces on social relations
  - the nature of knowledge—scientific, literary and popular—and its social construction.

These are only a few of the questions and issues being explored by sociologists, in conjunction with other disciplines such as history, anthropology, economics, psychology and geography. Indeed, one of the more exciting features of the social sciences today is their increasing integration and cross-fertilisation, so that the supposedly postmodernist decline of disciplinary meta-narratives seems to be reinvigorating *all* of the social science disciplines and increasing the importance of each of their contributions.

Many of these topics have been central to sociology since its emergence in the 19th century and remain significant in the 21st century. Others are new concerns reflecting the changing nature of social life. All of them indicate the profound importance of the contribution that a sociological understanding can make to a deeper awareness of the human world and how it is changing.

Tutorial exercises

1. Look at any feature of social life around you—for example, alienation at work, the state of family life or the education system—and explain how it would be approached differently by each of the four major approaches to sociology outlined in this chapter—Durkheim and functionalism, Marxism, Weber and conflict sociology, and Simmel and social interactionism.
2. Find three examples of social analysis from recent newspaper or television reports, books you've read or films you've seen and identify their underlying sociological 'theory'. What connections can you see with the theorists examined in this chapter?
3. What does it mean to approach contemporary society as being characterised by second modernity, and how does this relate to the ideas of the 'classical' sociologists?

For activity suggestions, learning aids, revision of key concepts and access to self-study material, visit: **www.pearson.com.au/highered/vankrieken4e**

Further reading

Bauman, Z. 2000, *Liquid Modernity*, Polity Press, Cambridge.

Beck, U., Giddens, A. & Lash, S. 1994, *Reflexive Modernization: Politics, Tradition and Aesthetics in the Modern Social Order*, Polity Press, Cambridge.

Bottomore, T. B. & Nisbet, R. A. (eds) 1978, *A History of Sociological Analysis*, Basic Books, New York.

Caine, B. & Gatens, M. (eds) 1998, *Australian Feminism: A Companion*, Oxford University Press, Melbourne.

Calhoun, C. et al. (eds) 2002, *Contemporary Sociological Theory*, Blackwell, Oxford.

Elliott, A. & Ray, L. 2003, *Key Contemporary Social Theorists*, Blackwell, Oxford.

Giddens, A. 1971, *Capitalism and Modern Social Theory*, Cambridge University Press, Cambridge.

Hughes, J. A., Martin, P. J. & Sharrock, W. W. 1995, *Understanding Classical Sociology*, Sage, London.

Ritzer, G. & Goodman, D. J. 2004, *Sociological Theory*, 6th edn, McGraw-Hill, Boston.

Ritzer, G. & Smart, B. (eds) 2003, *Handbook of Social Theory*, Sage, London.

Waters, M. 1999, *Modernity: Critical Concepts*, Routledge, London.

Websites

Intute's Sociology page:
www.intute.ac.uk/sociology

Marxists Internet Archive:
www.marxists.org

Sociology Central:
www.sociology.org.uk

Sociology Online:
www.sociologyonline.co.uk

SocioSite's Famous Sociologists section:
www.sociosite.net/topics/sociologists.php

SocioSite's Theory section:
www.sociosite.net/topics/theory.php

The Mead Project:
http://spartan.ac.brocku.ca/%7Elward

Theory.org.uk:
www.theory.org.uk

Bibliography

Abbott, P., Wallace, C. & Tyler, M. 2005, *An Introduction to Sociology: Feminist perspectives*, Routledge, London.

Abercrombie, N., Hill, S. & Turner, B. S. 2000 [1994], *The Penguin Dictionary of Sociology*, 4th edn, Penguin Books, London.

Abrahams, J. 1995, *Divide and School: Gender and Class Dynamics in Comprehensive Education*, Falmer Press, London.

ABS (Australian Bureau of Statistics) 1984, *Australian Health Survey, 1983*, cat. no. 4311.0, ABS, Canberra.

——1986, *Australian Health Survey, 1983*, AGPS, Canberra.

——1988a, *Year Book Australia*, cat. no. 1301.0, ABS, Canberra.

——1988b, *Deaths in Australia*, AGPS, Canberra.

——1989, *Census 86—Summary Characteristics of Persons and Dwellings Australia*, cat. no. 2487.0, ABS, Canberra.

——1991a, *Census 86—Australia's One Parent Families*, cat. no. 2511.0, ABS, Canberra.

——1991b, *Census*, Commonwealth of Australia, Hobart.

——1992a, *Social Indicators No. 5*, AGPS, Canberra.

——1992b, *Schools Australia, 1991*, cat. no. 4221.0, ABS, Canberra.

——1993a, *Year Book Australia*, cat. no. 1301.0, ABS, Canberra.

——1993b, *Australia's Aboriginal and Torres Strait Islander Populations, 1991 Census*, cat. no. 2740.0, ABS, Canberra.

——1993c, *Australia's Families—Selected Findings from the Survey of Families in Australia March 1992 to May 1992*, cat. no. 4418.0, ABS, Canberra.

——1993d, *Divorces Australia, 1992*, cat. no. 3307.0, ABS, Canberra.

——1993e, *Women in Australia*, cat. no. 4113.0, ABS, Canberra.

——1993f, *Census Characteristics of Australia, 1991*, cat. no. 2710.0, ABS, Canberra.

——1993g, *Crime and Safety Australia, 1993*, cat. no. 4509.0, ABS, Canberra.

——1993h, *Labour Force*, cat. no. 6203.0, ABS, Canberra.

——1994a, *Projections of the Population of Australia, States and Territories, 1993 to 2041*, cat. no. 3222.0, ABS, Canberra.

——1994b, *Year Book Australia*, cat. no. 1301.0, ABS, Canberra.

——1994c, *Crime and Safety Australia, April 1993*, cat. no. 4509.0, ABS, Canberra.

——1995a, *Employed Wage and Salary Earners Australia*, cat. no. 6248.0, ABS, Canberra.

——1995b, *Government Finance Statistics Australia, 1993–94*, cat. no. 5512.0, ABS, Canberra.

——1995c, *Labour Force*, cat. no. 6203.0, ABS, Canberra.

——1995d, *Schools Australia*, cat. no. 4221.0, ABS, Canberra.

——1995e, *Year Book Australia*, cat. no. 1301.0, ABS, Canberra.

——1995f, *Marriages and Divorces Australia, 1994*, cat. no. 3310.0, ABS, Canberra.

——1995g, *Social Trends*, cat. no. 4102.0, ABS, Canberra.

——1996a, *Census*, Commonwealth of Australia, Hobart.

——1996b, *Year Book Australia*, cat. no. 1301.0, ABS, Canberra.

——1996c, *Schools, Australia, Preliminary*, cat. no. 4220.0, ABS, Canberra.

——1997a, *Family Characteristics*, cat. no. 4442.0, ABS, Canberra.

——1997b, *Schools Australia*, cat. no. 4221.0, ABS, Canberra.

——1997c, *Wage and Salary Earners*, cat. no. 6248.0, ABS, Canberra.

——1997d, *Expenditure on Education, Australia, 1996–97*, cat. no. 5510.0, ABS Canberra.

——1997e, *Year Book Australia*, cat. no. 1301.0, ABS, Canberra.

——1998a, *Government Finance Statistics, 1996–97*, cat. no. 5512.0, ABS, Canberra.

——1998b, *Labour Force Australia*, cat. no. 6203.0, ABS, Canberra.

——1998c, *Schools Australia*, cat. no. 4221.0, ABS, Canberra.

——1998d, *Social Trends*, cat. no. 4102.0, ABS, Canberra.

——1998e, *Wage and Salary Earners*, cat. no. 6248.0, ABS, Canberra.

——1998f, *Year Book Australia*, cat. no. 1301.0, ABS, Canberra.

——1998g, *How Australians Use Their Time, 1997*, cat. no. 4153.0, ABS, Canberra.

——1998h, *Divorces*, cat. no. 3307.0.55.001, ABS, Canberra.

——1998i, *Marriage and Divorces*, cat. no. 3310.0, ABS, Canberra.

——1999a, *Government Finance Statistics, 1997–98*, cat. no. 5512.0, ABS, Canberra.

——1999b, *Labour Force*, cat. no. 6203.0, ABS, Canberra.

——1999c, *Social Trends*, cat. no. 4102.0, ABS, Canberra.

——1999d, *The Health and Welfare of Australia's Aboriginal and Torres Strait Islander Peoples, 1999*, cat. no. 4704.0, ABS, Canberra.

——1999e, *Year Book Australia*, cat. no. 1301.0, ABS, Canberra.

——1999f, *Causes of Death, Australia*, cat. no. 3303.0, ABS, Canberra.

——1999g, *Education and Training in Australia, 1998*, cat. no. 4224.0, ABS, Canberra.

——1999h, *Marriages and Divorces, Australia, 1998*, cat. no. 3310.0, ABS, Canberra.

——1999i, *Divorces*, cat. no. 3307.0.55.001, ABS, Canberra.

——2000a, *Year Book Australia*, cat. no. 1301.0, ABS, Canberra.

——2000b, *Use of the Internet by Householders, Australia*, cat. no. 8147.0, ABS, Canberra.

——2000c, *Births, Australia, 1999*, cat. no. 3301.0, ABS, Canberra.

——2002a, *Australian Social Trends, 2002*, cat. no. 4202.0, ABS, Canberra.

——2002b, *Education and Training Indicators, Australia 2002*, cat. no. 4230.0, ABS, Canberra.

——2002c, 'Health—mortality and morbidity: mortality of Aboriginal and Torres Strait Islander Peoples' in *Australian Social Trends, 2002*, cat. no. 4202.0, ABS, Canberra.

——2002d, *Marriages and Divorces, Australia, 2001*, cat. no. 3310.0, ABS, Canberra.

——2002e, *National Health Survey, 2001*, cat. no. 4364.0, ABS, Canberra.

——2002f, *Social Trends*, cat. no. 4102.0, ABS, Canberra.

——2002g, *Year Book Australia*, cat. no. 1301.0, ABS, Canberra.
——2003b, *Census of Population and Housing: Selected Social and Housing Characteristics, Australia*, cat. no. 2015.0, ABS, Canberra.
——2003c, *Crime and Safety: Australia, April 2002*, cat. no. 4509.0, ABS, Canberra.
——2003d, *Divorces, Australia*, cat. no. 3307.0.55.001, ABS, Canberra.
——2003e, *Family Characteristics*, cat. no. 4442.0, ABS, Canberra.
——2003f, *Labour Force Australia*, 6202.0, ABS, Canberra.
——2003g, *Marriages*, cat. no. 3306.0.55.001, ABS, Canberra.
——2003h, *Marriages and Divorces, 2002*, cat. no. 3310.0, ABS, Canberra.
——2003i, *Year Book Australia*, cat. no. 1301.0, ABS, Canberra.
——2004a, *Australian Historical Population Statistics*, cat. no. 3105.0.65.001, ABS, Canberra.
——2004b, *Australian Labour Market Statistics*, cat. no. 6105.0, ABS, Canberra.
——2004c, *Australian Social Trends*, www.abs.gov.au/Ausstats/abs@.nsf/0/FA58E975C470B73CCA256E9E00296645?Open, accessed 2 April 2005.
——2004d, *Australian Social Trends, 2004*, cat. no. 4202.0, ABS, Canberra.
——2004e, *Births, Australia, 2003*, cat. no. 3301.0, ABS, Canberra.
——2004f, *Family Characteristics, 2003*, cat. no, 4442.0, ABS, Canberra.
——2004g, *Labour Force Status of Aboriginal and Torres Strait Islander Peoples*, www.abs.gov.au/Ausstats/abs@.nsf/0/bc6a7187473c6fb6ca256dea00053a29?OpenDocument, accessed 7 January 2005.
——2004h, *Marriages, Australia, 2003*, cat. no. 3306.0.55.001, ABS, Canberra.
——2004i, *Prisoners in Australia, 2004*, cat. no. 4517.0, ABS, Canberra.
——2004j, *Recorded Crime—Victims, 2003*, cat. no. 4510.0, ABS, Canberra.
——2004k, *Schools Australia*, cat. no. 4221.0, ABS, Canberra.
——2004l, *Social Trends*, cat. no. 4102, ABS, Canberra.
——2004m, *Year Book Australia*, cat. no. 1301.0, ABS, Canberra.
——2005a, *Australian Historical Population Statistics*, cat. no. 3105.0.65.001, ABS, Canberra.
——2005b, *Causes of Death, Australia, 2001*, cat. no. 3303.0, ABS, Canberra.
——2005c, *Divorces, Australia, 2003*, cat. no. 3307.0.55.001, ABS, Canberra.
——2005d, *Government Finance Statistics, Australia, 2003–2004*, cat. no. 5512.0, ABS, Canberra.
——2005e, *Labour Force, Australia, Detailed*, cat. no. 6291.0.55.001, ABS, Canberra.
——2005f, *Schools Australia, 2004*, cat. no. 4221.0, ABS, Canberra.
——2005g, *Year Book Australia*, cat. no. 1301.0, ABS, Canberra.
——2005h, *Prisoners in Australia 2005*, cat. no. 4517.0, ABS, Canberra.
——2006a, *How Australians Use Their Time*, cat. no. 4153.0, ABS, Canberra.
——2006b, *National Health Survey, 2004–2005. Summary of Results*, cat. no. 4364.0, ABS, Canberra.
——2006c, *Population Characteristics, Aboriginal and Torres Strait Islander Australians*, cat. no. 4713, ABS, Canberra.
——2006d, *Family Characteristics and Transitions, 2005–2006*, cat. no. 4442.0, ABS, Canberra.
——2006e, *Measuring Australia's Progress 2006*, cat. no. 1370.0, ABS, Canberra.
——2006f, *Crime and Safety Australia 2005*, cat. no. 4509.0, ABS, Canberra.
——2007a, *Work in Selected Culture and Leisure Activities*, cat. no. 6281.0, ABS, Canberra.
——2007b, *Family Characteristics and Transitions, 2006–2007*, cat. no. 4442.0, ABS, Canberra.
——2007c, *Marriages, Australia*, cat. no. 3306.0.55.001, ABS, Canberra.
——2007d, *Divorces, Australia 2007*, cat. no. 3307.0.55.001, ABS, Canberra.
——2007e, *Household Income and Income Distribution, 2005–06*, cat. no. 6523, ABS, Canberra.
——2007f, *2006 Census of Population and Housing, Australia*, cat. no. 2068.0, ABS, Canberra.
——2008a, *Year Book Australia*, cat. no. 1301.0, ABS, Canberra.
——2008b, *How Australians Use Their Time*, cat. no. 4153.0, ABS, Canberra.
——2008c, *Population Characteristics: Aboriginal and Torres Strait Islander Australians*, 2001, cat. no. 4713.0, ABS, Canberra.
——2008d, *The Health and Welfare of Australia's Aboriginal and Torres Strait Islander Peoples*, cat. no. 4704.0, ABS, Canberra.
——2008e, *Prisoners in Australia*, cat. no. 4517.0, ABS, Canberra.
——2008f, *Household Use of Information Technology, 2007–08*, cat. no. 8146.0, ABS, Canberra.
——2008g, *Australian Social Trends: Complementary Therapies*, cat. no. 4102.0, ABS, Canberra.
——2008h, *Australian Historical Population Statistics*, cat. no. 3105.0.65.001, ABS, Canberra.
——2009a, *Australian Social Trends 2009*, cat. no. 4102.0, ABS, Canberra.
——2009b, *Labour Force, June 2009*, cat. no. 6202.0, ABS, Canberra.
——2009c, *Recorded Crime: Victims 2008*, cat. no. 4510.0, ABS, Canberra.
——2009d, *2006 Census of Population and Housing, Australia*, cat no. 2068.0, ABS, Canberra.
ABS/AIHW 2008, *Health and Welfare of Australia's Aboriginal and Torres Straight Islander Peoples*, cat. no. 4704.0, ABS, Canberra.
ABS & Office of the Status of Women (OSW) 1995, *Australian Women's Year Book 1995*, ABS & OSW, Canberra.
Achcar, G. 1981, 'Eleven theses on the resurgence of Islamic Fundamentalism', *International Marxist Review*, 2(3), www.internationalviewpoint.org/spip.php?article1132, accessed 1 August 2009.
——2006, *The Clash of Barbarisms: The Making of the New World Disorder*, Paradigm, Boulder, Co.
Acker, J. & van Houten, D. R. 1974, 'Differential recruitment and control: the sex structuring of organizations', *Organization Studies*, 19(2), 152–3.
Acker, S. 1994, 'Feminist theory and the study of gender and education', *International Review of Education*, 33(4), 419–435.
Ackroyd, S. & Hughes, J. 1981, *A Data Collection in Context*, Longman, London.
ACTU 2009, 'James Hardie', www.actu.asn.au/Campaigns/

PastCampaigns/JamesHardie/default.aspx, accessed 18 August 2009.

Adams, K., Sandy, L., Smith, L. & Triglone, B. 2008, *Drug Use Monitoring in Australia: 2007 Annual Report on Drug Use Among Police Detainees*, Australian Institute of Criminology Research & Public Policy Series No. 93, www.aic.gov.au/documents/7/E/8/{7E8D4A8E-A5AF-4D3B-8821-ED8A1BA489B6}rpp93.pdf, accessed 20 July 2009.

Adler, M. 1986, *Drawing Down the Moon Witches, Druids, Goddess-Worshippers, and Other Pagans in America Today*, rev. edn, Beacon Press, Boston.

——1989, 'The juice and the mystery' in *Healing the Wounds: The Promise of Ecofeminism*, ed. J. Plant, New Society Publishers, Philadelphia, 151–4.

Adorno, T. W. 1981 [1967], *Prisms*, MIT Press, Cambridge, Mass.

Adorno, T., Frenkel-Brunswick, E., Levinson, D. J. & Sanford, R. N. 1950, *The Authoritarian Personality*, Harper, New York.

Adorno, T. & Horkheimer, M. 1972, *Dialectic of Enlightenment*, Herder & Herder, New York.

AIC (Australian Institute of Criminology) 1998, *Australian Crime: Facts and Figures 1998*, AIC, Canberra.

——2002, *Facts and Figures 2002*, AIC, Canberra.

——2003, *Indigenous Juvenile Detention Rates: Crime Facts Info No. 60*, www.aic.gov.au/publications/cfi/cfi060.html, accessed 7 January 2005.

——2004, *Australian Crime: Facts and Figures 2004*, AIC, Canberra.

Alanen, L. 1988, 'Rethinking childhood', *Acta Sociologica*, 31(1), 53–67.

——1994, 'Gender and generation: feminism and the "child question"' in *Childhood Matters*, eds J. Qvortrup, M. Bardy, G. Sgritta & H. Wintersberger, Avebury, Aldershot, 27–42.

Alanen, L. & Mayall, B. (eds) 2001, *Conceptualizing Child–Adult Relations*, Routledge/Falmer Press, London.

Albarese, C. 1992, 'The magical staff: quantum healing in the New Age' in *Perspectives on the New Age*, eds J. R. Lewis & G. Melton, State University of New York, Albany, 68–86.

Albrow, M. 1970, *Bureaucracy*, Pall Mall Press, London.

——1996, *The Global Age: State and Society Beyond Modernity*, Blackwell Publishing, Oxford.

——2000, 'Globalization after modernization: a new paradigm for development studies' in *Globalization and Development Studies*, ed. F. J. Schuurman, Thela Thesis, Amsterdam, 21–30.

Alder, C. 1997, 'Young women and juvenile justice: objectives, frameworks and strategies', paper presented at the Australian Institute of Criminology Conference: Towards Juvenile Crime and Juvenile Justice: Towards 2000 and Beyond, Adelaide.

——1998, 'Young women and juvenile justice: objectives, frameworks and strategies' in *Juvenile Crime and Juvenile Justice*, ed. C. Alder, Australian Institute of Criminology, Canberra.

Alexander, J. C. & Colomy, P. 1990, 'Neofunctionalism today: reconstructing a theoretical tradition' in *Frontiers of Social Theory*, ed. G. Ritzer, Columbia University Press, New York, 33–67.

Alexander, M. 1998, 'Big business and directorship networks: the centralisation of economic power in Australia', *Journal of Sociology*, 34(2), 107–34.

Allan, G. 1985, *Family Life*, Blackwell Publishing, Oxford.

Alloway, N., Freebody, P., Gilbert, P. & Muspratt, S. 2002, *Boys, Literacy and Schooling: Expanding the Repertoires of Practice*, Report to the Department of Education, Science and Training, Australia.

Alston, P., Parker, S. & Seymour, J. (eds) 1992, *Children, Rights and the Law*, Clarendon, Oxford.

Althusser, L. 1969, *For Marx*, Penguin, London.

——1971, *Lenin and Philosophy, and Other Essays*, New Left Books, London.

Altman, D. 1982, *The Homosexualization of America, the Americanization of the Homosexual*, St Martin's Press, New York.

——1997, '(Homo)sexual identities, queer theory and politics' in *The Politics of Identity in Australia*, ed. G. Stokes, Cambridge University Press, Melbourne, 105–14.

Ambert, A.-M. 1986, 'Sociology of sociology. The place of children in North American sociology', *Sociological Studies of Child Development*, 1, 11–31.

Amin, A. 1993, 'The globalization of the economy. An erosion of regional networks?' in *The Embedded Firm*, ed. G. Grabner, Routledge, London, 278–95.

Anderson, B. 1983, *Imagined Communities*, Verso, London.

——1991, *Imagined Communities*, 2nd edn, Verso, London.

Anderson, D. 1990, 'Access to university education in Australia 1852–1990: changes in the undergraduate social mix', *Australian Universities Review*, 1 & 2, 37–50.

Anderson, D., Boven, R., Fensham, P. J. & Powell, J. P. 1978, *Students in Australian Higher Education*, Tertiary Education Research Unit, University of New South Wales, Sydney.

Anderson, D. S. & Vervoorn, A. 1983, *Access to Privilege*, ANU Press, Canberra.

Anderson, M. 1972a, 'Household structure and the industrial revolution; mid-nineteenth-century Preston in comparative perspective' in *Household and Family in Past Time*, eds P. Laslett & R. Wall, Cambridge University Press, Cambridge, 215–35.

——1972b, 'The study of family structure' in *Nineteenth-century Society: Essays in the Use of Quantitative Methods for the Study of Social Data*, ed. E. A. Wrigley, Cambridge University Press, Cambridge, 47–81.

Anderson, N. 1923, *The Hobo: The Sociology of the Homeless Man*, University of Chicago Press, Chicago.

Ang, I. 1985, *Watching Dallas*, Methuen, London.

Annan, K. 2004, 'The role of the state in the age of globalization' in *The Globalization Reader*, 2nd edn, eds F. J. Lechner & J. Boli, Blackwell Publishing, Oxford, 240–3.

Appadurai, A. 1990, 'Disjuncture and difference in the global cultural economy', *Theory, Culture & Society*, 7(2), 295–310.

——1996, *Modernity at Large: Cultural Dimensions of Globalization*, University of Minnesota Press, Minneapolis.

Apple, M. W. 2001, 'Bringing the world to God', *Discourse: Studies in the Cultural Politics of Education*, 22(2), 149–72.

Argy, F. 2005, 'Equality of opportunity: is it a fact or an illusion?', *On-Line Opinion*, 7 September, www.onlineopinion.com.au/print.asp?article=228, accessed 13 February 2006.

Ariès, P. 1962, *Centuries of Childhood*, Capre, London.

——1974, *Western Attitudes Toward Death*, Johns Hopkins University Press, Baltimore.

——1980, 'Two successive motivations for the declining birth rate', *Population & Development Review*, 64, 645–50.

Armitage, C. 1995, 'Higher learning no guarantee of higher earning', *Australian*, 6 September.

Armstrong, K. 1994, *A History of God: The 4000 Year Quest of Judaism, Christianity and Islam*, Alfred A. Knopf, New York.

——2001, *Islam: A Short History*, Modern Library, New York.

Armstrong, J. 2009, *In Search of Civilization: Remaking a Tarnished Idea*, Penguin, Harmondsworth.

Armstrong, P. 1984, 'Competition between the organizational professions and the evolution of management control strategies' in *Work, Employment and Unemployment*, ed. K. Thompson, Open University Press, Milton Keynes, 97–120.

Arnold, M. 1935 [1869], *Culture and Anarchy*, Cambridge University Press, Cambridge.

Arnot, M. 2002, *Reproducing Gender? Essays on Educational Theory and Feminist Politics*, RoutledgeFalmer, London.

Arnot, M., David, M. & Weiner, G. 1999, *Closing the Gender Gap: Post-war Education and Social Change*, Polity Press, Cambridge.

Arnot, M. & Whitty, G. 1982, 'From reproduction to transformation: recent radical perspectives on the curriculum from the USA', *British Journal of Sociology of Education*, 3(1), 93–103.

Aron, R. 1977, *Main Currents in Sociological Thought 2*, Penguin, Harmondsworth.

Aronson, J. 2001, 'The communication and Internet revolution' in *The Globalization of World Politics*, eds J. Baylis & S. Smith, Oxford University Press, Oxford, 540–58.

Askew, K. & Wilk, R. R. 2002, *The Anthropology of Media: A Reader*, Blackwell, Malden, Mass.

Atkinson, A. & Leigh, A. 2006, *The Distribution of Top Incomes in Australia: Using Income Taxation Statistics to Study Income Distribution*, Centre for Economic Policy Research, Australian National University, Canberra.

Atkinson, J. 1985, 'The changing corporation' in *New Patterns of Work*, ed. D. Clutterbuck, St Martin's Press, New York.

Atkinson, J. M. 1978, 'Societal reactions to suicide' in *Discovering Suicide*, ed. J. Atkinson, Macmillan, London.

Atkinson, P. 1985, *Language, Structure and Reproduction: An Introduction to the Sociology of Basil Bernstein*, Methuen, London.

Austin-Broos, D. 1984, *Australian Sociologies*, George Allen & Unwin, Sydney.

Australian Council of Social Services 2007, *A Fair Go for All Australians: International Comparisons, 2007 10 Essentials*, Australian Council of Social Services, Strawberry Hills.

Australian Government Actuary 2004, *Australians Living Longer*, media release.

AVCC 2003, AVCC fact sheet, 'Public investment in higher education', www.avcc.edu.au/content.asp?page=/publications/facts/index.htm.

Australian Human Rights Commission 2006, 'A statistical overview of Aboriginal and Torres Strait Islander peoples in Australia', www.hreoc.gov.au/Social_Justice/statistics/index.html#toc7, retrieved 19 February 2009.

Australian Institute of Criminology n.d. *Violent Crime Statistics*, www.aic.gov.au/en/statistics/violent%20crime.aspx. Australian Institute of Criminology, Canberra.

Australian Institute of Criminology 2008, *Australian Crime Facts and Figures 2008*, www.aic.gov.au/publications/current%20series/facts/1-20/2008.aspx, accessed 20 June 2009. Australian Institute of Criminology, Canberra.

Australian Institute of Health and Welfare (AIHW) 2008, *Australia's Health 2008*, cat no. Aus 99, AIHW, Canberra.

——2009, *Child Protection in Australia, 2007–2008*, Child welfare series no.45, cat. no. CWS 33, AIWH, Canberra.

Axford, B. 2001 [1995], 'Beyond the nation state (extract from *The global system: economics, politics and culture*)' in *Globalization: The Reader*, eds J. Beyon & D. Dunkerley, The Athlone Press, London, 256–60.

Bachrach, P. & Baratz, M. S. 1962, 'Two faces of power', *American Political Science Review*, 56(4), 947–52.

——1970, *Power and Poverty*, Oxford University Press, New York.

Bakan, J. 2004, *The Corporation: The Pathological Pursuit of Profit and Power*, The Free Press, New York.

Baker, D., Epstein, G. & Pollin, R. 1998, *Globalization and Progressive Economic Policy*, Cambridge University Press, Cambridge.

Baker, W. E. & Coleman, K. M. 2004, 'Racial segregation and the digital divide in the Detroit metropolitan region' in *The Network Society: A Cross-Cultural Perspective*, ed. M. Castells, Edward Elgar, Cheltenham, UK, 249–68.

Bala, N. 2008, 'An historical perspective on family violence and child abuse: comment on Moloney et al., Allegations of Family Violence, 12 June 2007', *Journal of Family Studies*, 14(2–3), 271–8.

Baldock, C. V. 1994, 'Sociology in Australia and New Zealand' in *International Handbook of Contemporary Developments in Sociology*, eds R. P. Mohan & A. S. Wilke, Greenwood Press, Westport, Conn., 587–622.

Balnaves, M., Mayrhofer, D. & Shoesmith, B. 2004, 'Media professions and the new humanism', *Continuum: Journal of Media & Cultural Studies*, 18(2), 191–203.

Barash, D. 1979, *The Whisperings Within*, Harper & Row, New York.

Barber, B. 1963, 'Some problems in the sociology of professions', *Daedalus*, 92, 669–88.

——1992, 'Jihad Vs. McWorld', *The Atlantic Monthly*, 269(3), 53–65.

——2004 [1995], 'Jihad vs. McWorld' in *The Globalization Reader*, 2nd edn, eds F. J. Lechner & J. Boli, Blackwell Publishing, Oxford, 29–35.

Barbour, I. 1960, 'The methods of science and religion' in *Science and Religion*, ed. H. Shapley, Appleton-Century-Crofts, New York, 196–215.

Barcan, A. 1990, 'The school curriculum and the national economy' in *Issues in Australian Education*, eds V. D'Cruz & P. Langford, Longman Cheshire, Melbourne, 3–38.

Barker, E. 1984, *The Making of a Moonie*, Blackwell Publishing, Oxford.

——1995, 'The postwar generation and establishment religion in England' in *The Postwar Generation and Establishment Religion: Cross-Cultural Perspectives*, eds W. C. Roof, J. W. Carroll & D. A. Roozen, Waterview Press, Boulder, Co., 1–25.

Barnard, C. I. 1938, *The Functions of the Executive*, Harvard University Press, Cambridge, Mass.

Barrett, D. B., Kurian, G. T. & Johnson, T. M. 2001, *World Christian Encyclopedia*, www.bible.ca/global-religion-statistics-world-christian-encyclopedia.htm, accessed 1 July 2009.

Barrett, M. 1980, *Women's Oppression Today*, Verso, London.

——1981, 'Timpanaro: materialism and the question of biology', *Sociology of Health & Illness*, 33, 337–45.

Barrett, M. & McIntosh, M. 1982, *The Anti-social Family*, Verso, London.

Bartelson, J. 2000, 'Three concepts of globalization', *International Sociology*, 15(2), 180–96.

Barthes, R. 1973, *Mythologies*, Granada, London.
Bates, E. & Linder-Pelz, S. 1987, *Health Care Issues*, Allen & Unwin, Sydney.
Baudrillard, J. 1983, *Simulations*, Semiotexte, New York.
Bauman, Z. 1982, *Memories of Class: The Pre-History and After-Life of Class*, Routledge & Kegan Paul, London.
——1989, 'Hermeneutics and modern social theory' in *Social Theory of Modern Societies: Anthony Giddens and His Critics*, eds D. Held & J. B. Thompson, Cambridge University Press, Cambridge, 34–55.
——1990, *Thinking Sociologically*, Basil Blackwell, Oxford.
——1992, *Intimations of Postmodernity*, Routledge, London.
——1997, *Postmodernity and Its Discontents*, Polity, Oxford.
——1998, *Globalization: The Human Consequences*, Polity Press, Cambridge.
——1999, *In Search of Politics*, Polity Press, Cambridge.
——2000, *Liquid Modernity*, Polity Press, Cambridge.
——2001a, *Community: Seeking Safety in an Insecure World*, Polity Press, Cambridge.
——2001b, *The Individualized Society*, Polity Press, Cambridge.
——2002, *Society Under Siege*, Polity Press, Cambridge.
Bauman, Z. & Tester, K. 2001, *Conversations with Zygmunt Bauman*, Polity Press, Cambridge.
Baxter, J. 2002, 'Patterns of change and stability in the gender division of household labour in Australia, 1986–1997', *Journal of Sociology*, 38(4), 399–424.
Baxter, J. et al. 1986, 'The class structure of Australia', paper presented at the Annual Conference of the Sociological Association of Australia & New Zealand, University of New England, Armidale.
Baxter, J. H., Emmison, M. C., Western, J. S. & Western, M. C. (eds) 1991, *Class Analysis and Contemporary Australia*, Macmillan, Melbourne.
Bean, C., Gow, D. & McAllister, I. 2001, 'Australian Election Study, 2001', User's Guide to the Machine-Readable Data File, Social Science Data Archives, Canberra.
Beck, U. 1992, *Risk Society: Towards a New Modernity*, Sage, London.
——1995, *Ecological Politics in an Age of Risk*, Polity Press, Cambridge.
——2000a, 'Living your own life in a runaway world: individualisation, globalisation and politics' in *On the Edge: Living with Global Capitalism*, eds W. Hutton & A. Giddens, Vintage, London.
——2000b, 'Risk society revisited: theory, politics and research programmes' in *The Risk Society and Beyond*, eds B. Adam, U. Beck & J. van Loon, Sage, London, 211–29.
——2000c, 'The cosmopolitan perspective: sociology of the second age of modernity', *British Journal of Sociology*, 51(1), 79–105.
——2000d, *What is Globalization?*, Polity Press, Cambridge.
——2003, 'Toward a new critical theory with a cosmopolitan intent', *Constellations*, 10(4), 453–68.
——2005, *Power in the Global Age: a new Global Political Economy*, Polity Press, Cambridge.
——2006, *Cosmopolitan Vision*, Polity Press, Cambridge.
Beck, U. & Beck-Gernsheim, E. 1995, *The Normal Chaos of Love*, Polity Press, Cambridge.
——2002, *Individualization: Institutionalized Individualism and Its Social and Political Consequences*, Sage, London.

Beck, U. & Willms, J. 2004, *Conversations with Ulrich Beck*, Polity Press, Cambridge.
Beck, U., Bonß, W. & Lau, C. 2003, 'The theory of reflexive modernization: problematic, hypotheses and research programme', *Theory, Culture & Society*, 20(2), 1–33.
Beck, U., Giddens, A. & Lash, S. 1994, *Reflexive Modernization: Politics, Tradition and Aesthetics in the Modern Social Order*, Polity Press, Cambridge.
Beck, U. & Sznaider, N. 2006, 'Unpacking cosmopolitanism for the social sciences: a research agenda', *British Journal of Sociology*, 57(1), 1–23.
Becker, H. S. 1963, *Outsiders*, The Free Press, New York.
——1970, *Sociological Work*, Transaction Books, New Brunswick.
Becker, H. 1986, *Writing for Social Scientists: How to Start and Finish Your Thesis, Book, or Article*, Chicago University Press, Chicago.
Beckford, J. A. 1985, *Cult Controversies*, Tavistock, London.
Beck-Gernsheim, E. 1998, 'On the way to a post-familial family: from a community of need to elective affinities', *Theory, Culture & Society*, 15(3–4), 53–70.
Beck-Gernsheim, E. 2002, *Reinventing the Family: In Search of New Lifestyles*, Polity Press, Cambridge.
Beilharz, P. 1992, *Social Theory: A Guide to Central Thinkers*, Allen & Unwin, Sydney.
——(ed.) 2001, *The Bauman Reader*, Blackwell, Malden, Mass.
Beilharz, P., Considine, M. & Watts, R. 1992, *Arguing about the Welfare State: The Australian Experience*, Allen & Unwin, Sydney.
Bell, A. P., Weinberg, M. S. & Hammersmith, S. K. 1981, *Sexual Preference*, Indiana University Press, Bloomington.
Bell, D. 1947, 'Adjusting men to machines: social scientists explore the world of the factory', *Commentary*, 3(1), 79–88.
——1973, *The Coming of Post-Industrial Society*, Basic Books, New York.
——1976, *The Cultural Contradictions of Capitalism*, Heinemann, London.
Bell, D. R. & Ditton, P. 1980, *Law: The Old and the New*, Aboriginal Legal Aid Service, Canberra.
Bellah, R. 1965, 'Religious evolution' in *Reader in Comparative Religion*, 2nd edn, W. A. Lessa & E. Z. Vogt, Harper & Row, New York.
——1967, 'Civil religion in America', *Daedalus*, 96, 1–21.
——1975, *The Broken Covenant: American Civil Religion in Time of Trial*, Seabury, New York.
Bello, W. 2002, 'Pacific panopticon', *New Left Review*, 16, 68–85.
——2004, *Deglobalization: Ideas for a New World Economy*, Zed Books, London.
——2007, 'Sand in the wheels', *New Internationalist*, 400.
Bendle, M. 2002, 'Trajectories of anti-globalism', *Journal of Sociology*, 38(3), 213–22.
Bennett, T., Emmison, M. & Frow, J. 1999, *Accounting for Tastes: Australian Everyday Cultures*, Cambridge University Press, Cambridge.
Benston, M. 1972, 'The political economy of women's liberation' in *Woman in a Man-Made World*, eds N. Glazer-Malbin & H. Y. Waehrer, Rand McNally, Chicago, 119–28.
Bentley, P. & Hughes, P. 1998, *Australian Life and the Christian Faith*, Christian Research Association, Victoria.
Benton, T. & Craib, I. 2001, *Philosophy of Social Science: The Philosophical Foundations of Social Thought*, Palgrave, Houndsmill.

Beresford, Q. & Omaji, P. 1996, *Rites of Passage: Aboriginal Youth, Crime and Justice*, Fremantle Arts Centre Press, Fremantle.

Berger, B. & Berger, P. L. 1983, *The War Over the Family*, Hutchinson, London.

Berger, H.A. & Ezzy, D. 2007, *Teenage Witches: Magical Youth and the Search for Self*, Rutgers University Press, Piscataway.

Berger, J. 1972, *Ways of Seeing*, Penguin, Harmondsworth.

Berger, P. 1963, *Invitation to Sociology: A Humanistic Perspective*, Penguin, Harmondsworth.

Berger, P. L. 1967, *The Sacred Canopy*, Doubleday, New York.

——1970, *A Rumour of Angels*, Allen Lane, London.

Berger, P. L. & Kellner, H. 1974, 'Marriage and the construction of reality' in *The Family: Its Structures and Functions*, ed. R. L. Coser, Macmillan, London, 157–74.

Berger, P. L. & Luckmann, T. 1969, 'Sociology of religion and sociology of knowledge' in *Sociology of Religion*, ed. R. Robertson, Penguin, Harmondsworth, 61–73.

——1971 [1966], *The Social Construction of Reality*, Penguin, Harmondsworth.

Berkman, L. & Syme, L. 1979, 'Social networks, host resistance and mortality', *American Journal of Epidemiology*, 10(9), 186–204.

Berman, H. J. 1995, 'World law', *Fordham International Law Journal*, 18(5), 1617–22.

Bernard, J. 1957, *Social Problems at Mid Century*, Holt, Rinehart & Winston, New York.

——1972, *The Future of Marriage*, World Publishing, New York.

Berndt, C. H. 1963, 'Art and aesthetic expression' in *Australian Aboriginal Studies*, ed. H. Sheils, Oxford University Press, Melbourne, 256–77.

Berndt, R. M. & Berndt, C. H. 1968, *The World of the First Australians*, Ure Smith, Canberra.

Bernstein, B. 1961, 'Social class and linguistic development: a theory of social learning' in *Education, Economy and Society*, A. H. Halsey, J. Floud & C. A. Anderson, The Free Press, New York, 288–314.

——1970a, 'A socio-linguistic approach to social learning' in *Modern Sociology*, P. Worsley, Penguin, Harmondsworth, 195–204.

——1970b, 'Education cannot compensate for society', *New Society*, 26, 344–347.

Bernstein, B. 1971, *Class, Codes and Control, Volume I: Theoretical Studies Towards a Sociology of Language*, Routledge & Kegan Paul, London.

——1972, 'Language and social context' in *Language and Social Context*, ed. P. P. Giglioli, Penguin, Harmondsworth, 157–78.

——1975, *Class, Codes and Control, Volume III: Towards a Theory of Educational Transmissions*, Routledge & Kegan Paul, London.

——1990, *Class, Codes and Control, Volume IV: The Structuring of Pedagogic Discourse*, Routledge, London.

——1996, *Pedagogy, Symbolic Control and Identity: Theory, Research, Critique*, Taylor & Francis, London.

——1999, 'Vertical and horizontal discourse: an essay', *British Journal of Sociology of Education*, 20(2), 157–73.

——2000, *Pedagogy, Symbolic Control & Identity: Theory, Research, Critique*, 2nd edn, Rowman & Littlefield, London.

——2001, 'From pedagogies to knowledges' in *Towards a Sociology of Pedagogy: The Contribution of Basil Bernstein to Research*, eds A. Morais, I. Neves, B. Davies & H. Daniels, Peter Lang, New York.

Berry, J. W. 1966, 'Temme and Eskimo perceptual skills', *International Journal of Psychology*, 1, 207–29.

——1971, 'Ecological and cultural factors in spatial perceptual development', *Canadian Journal of Behavioural Science*, 3, 324–36.

Best, J. 1990, *Threatened Children. Rhetoric and Concern about Child Victims*, University of Chicago Press, Chicago.

Beyon, J. & Dunkerley, D. 2000, *Globalization: The Reader*, The Athlone Press, London.

Bhabha, H. 1990, 'The third space: interview with Mommi Bhabba' in *Identity: Community, Culture, Difference*, ed. J. Rutherford, Lawrence & Wishart, London, 207–21.

Biles, D. 1990, *International Review of Deaths in Custody*, Research Paper no. 15, Royal Commission into Aboriginal Deaths in Custody, AGPS, Canberra.

Billig, M. 1995, *Banal Nationalism*, Sage, London.

Birdsall, N. 2002, 'A stormy day on an open field: asymmetry and convergence in the global economy' in *Globalisation, Living Standards and Inequality: Recent Progress and Continuing Challenges, Proceedings of a Conference Held in Sydney on 27–28 May 2002*, eds D. Gruen, T. O'Brien & J. Lawson, Reserve Bank of Australia and Australian National Treasury, Canberra, 66–87.

Birke, L. 1986, *Women, Feminism and Biology*, Wheatsheaf, Brighton.

Birrell, B. 1999, 'Residential location in Sydney and the NSW coast over the period 1991 to 1996', *People and Place*, 7(2), 33–47.

Birrell, B. & Seol, B. 1998, 'Sydney's ethnic underclass', *People and Place*, 6(3), 16–29.

Bittman, M. 1991, *Juggling Time*, Office of the Status of Women, Department of the Prime Minister and Cabinet, Canberra.

Bittman, M. & Lovejoy, F. 1993, 'Domestic power: negotiating an unequal division of labour within a framework of equality', *Australian & New Zealand Journal of Sociology*, 29(3), 302–21.

Bittman, M. & Pixley, J. 1997, *The Double Life of the Family*, Allen & Unwin, Sydney.

Bittman, M. & Wajcman, J. 2000, 'The rush hour: the character of leisure time and gender equity', *Social Forces*, 79(1), 165–89.

Black, A. & Kaldor, P. 1999, *1998 Australian Community Survey*, Edith Cowan University and National Church Life Survey Research.

Blackledge, D. & Hunt, B. 1985, *Sociological Interpretations of Education*, Croom Helm, London.

Blagbrough, J. & Glynn, E. 1999, 'Child domestic workers: characteristics of the modern slave and approaches to ending such exploitation', *Childhood*, 6(1), 51–6.

Blagg, H. & Wilkie, M. 1995, *Young People and Police Powers*, Australian Youth Foundation, Sydney.

Blainey, G. 1966, *The Tyranny of Distance*, Sun Books, Melbourne.

——1984, *All for Australia*, Methuen Haynes, North Ryde, NSW.

Blau, P. M. 1963, *The Dynamics of Bureaucracy*, 2nd edn, University of Chicago Press, Chicago.

——1974, *On the Nature of Organizations*, John Wiley & Sons, New York.

Blau, P. M. & Duncan, O. D. 1967, *The American Occupational Structure*, Wiley, New York.

Blau, P. M. & Schoenherr, R. A. 1971, *The Structure of Organizations*, Basic Books, New York.

Blauner, R. 1964, *Alienation and Freedom*, University of Chicago Press, Chicago.

Bleier, R. 1984, *Science and Gender*, Pergamon Press, New York.

Block, F. 1977, *The Origins of International Financial Disorder: A Study of United States International Monetary Policy from World War II to the Present*, University of California Press, Berkeley, CA.

Blombery, T. & Hughes, P. 1987, *Combined Churches Survey for Faith and Mission: Preliminary Report*, Christian Research Association, Wangaratta.

Blumer, H. 1962, 'Society as symbolic interaction' in *Human Behaviour and Social Processes*, ed. A. Rose, Prentice Hall, Englewood Cliffs, NJ, 179–92.

——1964, 'Industrialization and the traditional order', *Sociology & Social Research*, 48, 129–38.

——1969, *Symbolic Interactionism: Perspective and Method*, Prentice Hall, Englewood Cliffs, NJ.

——1990, *Industrialization as an Agent of Social Change: A Critical Analysis*, Aldine de Gruyter, New York.

Boelen, W. A. M. 1992, '*Street Corner Society*: Cornerville revisited', *Journal of Contemporary Ethnography*, 21(1), 11–51.

Bond, J. 2003, *Recent Developments in the Australian Housing Market*, Domestic Economy Division, Australian Treasury, Canberra.

Boorstin, D. 1964, *The Image*, Harper, New York.

——1987 [1961], *The Image: A Guide to Pseudo-Events in America*, Vintage Books, New York.

Bordua, D. 1962, 'A critique of sociological interpretations of gang delinquency' in *The Sociology of Crime and Delinquency*, eds M. E. Wolfgang, L. Savitz & N. Johnston, John Wiley & Sons, New York.

Borland, J., Gregory, R. & Sheehan, P. 2001, *Work Rich, Work Poor: Inequality and Economic Change in Australia*, CFES, Sydney.

Boston Women's Health Collective 1973, *Our Bodies Ourselves*, Simon & Schuster, New York.

Bottero, W. 2005, *Stratification: Social Division and Inequality*, Routledge, London.

Bottomley, G. 1979, *After the Odyssey*, University of Queensland Press, St Lucia.

Bottomore, T. B. & Rubel, M. (eds) 1976 [1963], *Karl Marx: Selected Writings in Sociology and Social Philosophy*, Penguin, Harmondsworth.

Boudon, R. 1974, *Education, Opportunity, and Social Inequality; Changing Prospects in Western Society*, Wiley, New York.

Bouma, G. 1992, *Religion: Meaning, Transcendence and Community in Australia*, Longman Cheshire, Melbourne.

Bouma, G. & Dixon, B. 1986, *The Religious Factor in Australian Life*, Marc Australia, Melbourne.

Bourdieu, P. 1973, 'Cultural reproduction and social reproduction' in *Knowledge, Education and Cultural Change*, ed. R. Brown, Tavistock, London, 71–112.

——1974, 'The school as a conservative force: scholastic and cultural inequalities' in *Contemporary Research in the Sociology of Education*, ed. J. Eggleston, Methuen, London, 32–46.

——1977, *Outline of a Theory of Practice*, Cambridge, Cambridge University Press.

——1978, 'Sport and social class', *Social Science Information*, 17, 819–40.

——1984, *Distinction: A Social Critique of the Judgement of Taste*, Routledge, London.

——1988, *Homo Academicus*, Polity Press, Cambridge.

——1990, *The Logic of Practice*, Polity Press, Cambridge.

——1993, *Sociology in Question*, Sage, London.

——1996, *The State Nobility*, Polity Press, Cambridge.

——1999, *The Weight of the World: Social Suffering in Contemporary Society*, Stanford University Press, Stanford.

——2007, *Distinction*, Harvard University Press, Cambridge, Mass.

Bourdieu, P. & Passeron, J. 1990 [1977], *Reproduction in Education, Society and Culture*, Sage, London.

——1977, *Reproduction in Education, Society and Culture*, Sage, London.

——1979, *The Inheritors: French Students and their Relation to Culture*, University of Chicago Press, London.

Bourdieu, P. &. Wacquant, L. J. D 1992, *An Invitation To Reflexive Sociology*, Polity Press, Cambridge.

Bourgois, P. 2003, *In Search of Respect: Selling Crack in El Barrio*, 2nd edn, Cambridge University Press, Cambridge.

Bourke, H. 1988, 'Social scientists as intellectuals: from the First World War to the Depression' in *Intellectual Movements and Australian Society*, eds B. Head & J. Walter, Oxford University Press, Melbourne, 47–69.

Bourne, J. 2003, 'Vertical discourse: the role of the teacher in the transmission and acquisition of decontextualised language', *European Educational Research Journal*, 2(4), 496–521.

Bowlby, J. 1946, *Forty-four Juvenile Thieves*, Tindall & Cox, London.

Bowles, S. & Gintis, H. 1976, *Schooling in Capitalist America*, Routledge & Kegan Paul, London.

Box, S. 1981, *Deviance, Reality and Society*, 2nd edn, Holt, Rinehart & Winston, London.

——1983, *Power, Crime and Mystification*, Tavistock, London.

——1987, *Recession, Crime and Punishment*, Barnes & Noble, Totowa, New Jersey.

Boyle, M. & McKay, J. 1995, 'Leave your troubles at the gate', *Gender & Society*, 9(5), 556–75.

Bradley, D., Noonan, P., Nugent, H. & Scales, B. 2008, *Review of Australian Higher Education: Final Report*, Commonwealth of Australia, Canberra.

Bradley, H. 1996, *Fragmented Identities: Changing Patterns of Inequality*, Polity, Cambridge.

Bradshaw, J. & Mayhew, E. (eds) 2005, *The Well-Being of Children in the United Kingdom*, Save the Children, London.

Braithwaite, J. 1984, *Corporate Crime in the Pharmaceutical Industry*, Routledge, London.

——1989, *Crime, Shame and Reintegration*, Cambridge University Press, Cambridge.

——1998, 'Reducing the crime problem' in *The New Criminology Revisited*, eds P. Walton & J. Young, Macmillan, London, 47–63.

——2002, *Restorative Justice and Responsive Regulation*, Oxford University Press, Oxford.

——2005, 'For public social science', *British Journal of Sociology*, 56(3), 345–53.

——2008, *Regulatory Capitalism: How it Works, Ideas for Making it Work Better*, Edward Elgar, Cheltenham.

Brake, M. & Hale, C. 1992, *Public Order, Private Lives*, Routledge, London.

Bramble, T. 2006, '"Another world is possible": a study of participants at Australian alter-globalization social forums', *Journal of Sociology*, 42(3), 287–309.

Brandolini, A. & Smeeding, T. 2007, *Inequality Patterns in Western-Type Democracies: Cross-Country Differences and Time Changes*, Luxembourg Income Study Working Paper Series, www.lisproject.org/publications/liswps/458.pdf.

Braudy, L. 1986, *The Frenzy of Renown: Fame and Its History*, Oxford University Press, New York.

Bray, C. 2009, 'Madoff pleads guilty to massive fraud', *The Wall Street Journal*, 12 March.

Braverman, H. 1974, *Labor and Monopoly Capital*, Monthly Review Press, New York.

Brekhus, W. 2003, *Peacocks, Chameleons, Centaurs: Gay Suburbia and the Grammar of Social Identity*, University of Chicago Press, Chicago.

Brierley, P. (ed.) 2001, *Religions Trends 3, 2002/2003*, Christian Research, London, 1.2.

Brooks, A. 1997, *Postfeminisms: Feminisms, Cultural Theory and Cultural Forms*, Routledge, London.

Broom, D. H. 1991, *Damned if We Do: Contradictions in Women's Health Care*, Allen & Unwin, Sydney.

Broom, L. & Jones, F. L. 1976, *Opportunity and Attainment in Australia*, Stanford University Press, Stanford.

Broome, R. 2001, *Aboriginal Australians*, 3rd edn, Allen & Unwin, Sydney.

Brown, P. 1997, 'Cultural capital and social exclusion: some observations on recent trends in education, employment, and the labour market' in *Education, Culture, Economy, Society*, eds A. H. Halsey, H. Lauder, P. Brown & A. S. Wells, Oxford University Press, Oxford.

Brown, R. (ed.) 1976, 'Women as employees: some comments in research in industrial sociology' in *Dependence and Exploitation in Work and Marriage*, eds D. L. Barker & S. Allen, Longman, London, 21–46.

Brubaker, R. 1992, *Citizenship and Nationhood in France and Germany*, Oxford University Press, Oxford.

Bruce, S. 1990, *The Rise and Fall of the New Christian Right*, Clarendon, Oxford.

——2002, *God Is Dead: Secularization in the West*, Blackwell Publishing, Oxford.

Bruns, A. 2008, *Blogs, Wikipedia, Second Life, and Beyond: From Production to Produsage*, Peter Lang, New York.

Bryman, A. 1988, *Quantity and Quality in Social Research*, Unwin Hyman, London.

Bryson, L. 1972, *An Australian Newtown: Life and Leadership in a Working-class Suburb*, Penguin, Melbourne.

——1992, *Welfare and the State: Who Benefits?*, Macmillan, London.

Bryson, L. & Thompson, F. 1972, *An Australian Newtown: Life and Leadership in a New Housing Suburb*, Penguin, Ringwood.

Bryson, L. & Winter, I. 1999, *Social Change, Suburban Lives: An Australian Newtown 1960s to 1990s*, Australian Institute of Family Studies and Allen & Unwin, Sydney.

Budapest, S. 1992, 'Self-blessing ritual' in *Womanspirit Rising*, eds C. Christ & J. Plaskow, Harper, San Francisco, 269–72.

Bühler-Niederberger, D. 1998, 'The separative view. Is there any scientific approach to children?' in *Children and Childhood in our Contemporary Societies*, ed. D. K. Behera, Falmer Press, London, 51–66.

——2003, 'The needy child and the naturalization of politics' in *Hearing the Voices of Children: Social Policy for a New Century*, eds C. Hallett & A. Prout, Falmer Press, London, 89–105.

Burawoy, M. 1979, *Manufacturing Consent*, University of Chicago Press, Chicago.

——2004, 'Public Sociologies: Contradictions, Dilemmas, and Possibilities', *Social Forces*, 82(4), 1603–18.

——2005a, 'For public sociology', *British Journal of Sociology*, 56(2), 259–94.

——2005b, 'For public sociology', *American Sociological Review*, 70(1).

Bureau of Tourism Research 2003, *The Economic Value of Tourism*, accessed at www.tourism.australia.com.

——2004, *Tourism Industry Yield 2002–2003*, accessed at www.tourism.australia.com.

Burgmann, V. 2003, *Power, Profit and Protest: Australian Social Movements and Globalisation*, Allen & Unwin, Sydney.

Burke, A., Upchurch, D., Dye, C., Chyu, L. & Levine, E. 2006, *A National Health Interview Survey (NHIS) Report on Meditation Use in the US*, 134th Annual Meeting and Exposition of the American Public Health Association, 4–8 November, http://apha.confex.com/apha/134am/techprogram/paper_129275.htm, accessed 1 August 2009.

Burke, G. & Spaull, A. 2001, 'Australian schools: participation and funding 1901 to 2000' in *Year Book Australia*, ABS, Canberra, 433–509.

Burbank, V. K. 1988, *Aboriginal Adolescence*, Rutgers University Press, New Brunswick.

Burnley, I. & Batiyel, M. 1985, 'Indicators of changing mortality in Sydney and Adelaide' in *Living in Cities*, eds I. Burnley & J. Forrest, Allen & Unwin, Sydney, 128–39.

Burns, A. 1980, *Breaking Up*, Nelson, Melbourne.

——1986, 'Why do women continue to marry?' in *Australian Women*, eds N. Grieve & A. Burns, Oxford University Press, Melbourne, 210–32.

Burns, T. 1973, 'Leisure in industrial society' in *Leisure and Society in Britain*, eds M. Smith, S. Parker & C. Smith, Allen Lane, London.

Burns, T. & Stalker, G. M. 1994, *The Management of Innovation*, 3rd edn, Oxford University Press, Oxford.

Burrell, G. & Hearn, J. 1989, 'The sexuality of organisation' in *The Sexuality of Organizations*, eds J. Hearn, D. L. Sheppard, P. Tancred-Sheriff & G. Burrell, Sage, London, 1–28.

Burton, A. 1989, 'Looking forward from Aries? Pictorial and material evidence for the history of childhood and family life', *Continuity & Change*, 4(2), 203–29.

Busch, A. 2000, 'Unpacking the globalization debate: approaches, evidence and data' in *Demystifying Globalization*, eds C. Hay & D. Marsh, Macmillan, Houndsmill, Basingstoke, 21–48.

Butler, J. 1990, *Gender Trouble: Feminism and the Subversion of Identity*, Routledge, New York.

Butlin, N. G. 1959, 'Colonial socialism in Australia, 1860–1900' in *The State and Economic Growth*, ed. H. H. J. Aitken, SSRC, New York.

Butsch, R. 2007, *Media and Public Spheres*, Palgrave Macmillan, Basingstoke.

Butt, R. 1981, 'Economics are the method: the object is to change the soul', *Sunday Times*, 3 May, 33–5.

Cahill, L. & Marshall, P. 2002, *Statistics on Juvenile Detention in*

Australia: 1981–2001, Technical and Background Paper Series No. 1, Australian Institute of Criminology, Canberra.

Cain, M. 1998, 'An analysis of juvenile recidivism' in *Juvenile Crime and Juvenile Justice*, ed. C. Alder, Research & Public Policy Series, No. 14, Australian Institute of Criminology, Canberra, 12–15.

Caldwell, J. C. 1982, *Theory of Fertility Decline*, Academic Press, London.

Caldwell, J. C. & Ruzicka, L. T. 1978, 'The Australian fertility transition: an analysis', *Population & Development Review*, 41, 81–103.

Caldwell, J. C. & Schindlmayr, T. 2003, 'Explanations of the fertility crisis in modern societies: a search for commonalities', *Population Studies*, 57(3), 241–63.

Calhoun, C. 1994, 'Social theory and the politics of identity' in *Social Theory and the Politics of Identity*, ed. C. Calhoun, Blackwell, Oxford, 9–36.

——1995, '"New social movements" of the early nineteenth century' in *Repertoires and Cycles of Collective Action*, ed. M. Traugott, Duke University Press, Durham, 173–215.

Callinicos, A. 2003, *An Anti-Capitalist Manifesto*, Polity Press, Cambridge.

——2007, 'Globalization, imperialism and the capitalist world system' in *Globalization Theory: Approaches and Controversies*, eds D. Held & A. McGrew, Polity Press, Cambridge, 62–78.

Carcach, C. 1997 (March), *Reporting Crime to the Police*, Trends and Issues in Crime and Criminal Justice, Australian Institute of Criminology, Canberra.

——1997 (September), *Youth as Victims and Offenders of Homicide*, Trends and Issues in Crime and Criminal Justice, Australian Institute of Criminology, Canberra.

Carcach, C. & James, M. 1998, *Homicide between Intimate Partners in Australia*, Trends and Issues in Crime and Criminal Justice, Australian Institute of Criminology, Canberra.

Cardoso, G. 2006, 'Societies in transition to the network society' in *The Network Society: From Knowledge to Policy*, Centre for Transatlantic Relations, The John Hopkins University, Washington, DC, 23–67.

Carey, J. W. 1968, 'Harold Adams Innis and Marshall McLuhan' in *McLuhan: Pro and Con*, ed. R. Rosenthal, Penguin, Baltimore, Maryland, 270–308.

Carey, J. W. 2004, 'Introduction to the Rowman & Littlefield Edition' in *Changing Concepts of Time*, H. A. Innis, Rowman & Littlefield Publishers, Lanham, Maryland, vii–xx.

Carlen, P. 1976, 'The staging of magistrates' justice', *British Journal of Criminology*, 16(1), 48–55.

——1988, *Women, Crime and Poverty*, Open University Press, Milton Keynes.

Carmichael, G. 1990, 'Analysis of marriage and informal cohabitation', *Australian & New Zealand Journal of Sociology*, 27(1), 53–72.

Carmichael, G. & McDonald, P. 1986, 'The rise and fall of divorce in Australia' in *Proceedings of the Australian National Population Association, 3rd National Conference, Vol. 1*, Flinders University, Adelaide, 1–32.

Carpenter, A. 2004, *Creating the Future for Our Young People: Raising the School Leaving Age: A Consultation Paper*, Government of Western Australia, Perth.

Carpenter, D. D. 1996, 'Emergent nature spirituality' in *Magical Religion and Modern Witchcraft*, ed. J. R. Lewis, State University of New York, Albany, 35–72.

Carroll, J. 1993, *Humanism: The Wreck of Western Culture*, Harper-Collins, London.

——2002, *Terror: A Meditation on the Meaning of September 11*, Scribe Publications, Melbourne.

——2004, *The Wreck of Western Culture—Humanism Revisited*, Scribe Publications, Melbourne.

Carruthers, S. L. 2001, 'International history 1900–1945' in *The Globalization of World Politics*, 2nd edn, eds J. Baylis & S. Smith, Oxford University Press, Oxford, 51–73.

Cashmore, E. E. 1984, *Dictionary of Race and Ethnic Relations*, Routledge, London.

——2002, *Beckham*, Polity Press, Cambridge.

Cass, B. 1987, 'Family' in *Selected Readings in Australian Society*, eds S. Encel & M. Berry, Longman Cheshire, Melbourne, 11–41.

——1994, *Creating the Links*, AGPS, Canberra.

Cass, B. & Radi, H. 1981, 'Family, fertility and the labour market' in *Australian Women: Feminist Perspectives*, Oxford University Press, Melbourne, 190–204.

Cass, V. C. 1990, 'The implications of homosexual identity formation for the Kinsey model and scale of sexual preference' in *Homosexuality/Heterosexuality*, eds D. P. McWhirter, S. A. Sanders & J. M. Reinisch, Oxford University Press, Oxford, 239–66.

Castells, M. 1996a, 'The Net and the self: working notes for a critical theory of the informational society', *Critique of Anthropology*, 16(1), 9–38.

——1996b, *The Information Age: Economy, Society and Culture, Volume 1: The Rise of the Network Society*, Cambridge, Mass., Blackwell.

——1997, *The Information Age: Economy, Society and Culture, Volume 2: The Power of Identity*, Malden, Mass., Blackwell.

——1998, *The Information Age: Economy, Society and Culture, Volume 3: End of Millenium*, Malden, Mass., Blackwell.

——1999a, 'Grassrooting the space of flows', *Urban Geography*, 20(4), 294–302.

——1999b, 'An introduction to the Information Age' in *The Media Reader: Continuity and Transformation*, eds H. Mackay & T. O'Sullivan, Sage, London, 398–410.

——2000a, *The Rise of the Network Society*, 2nd edn, Blackwell Publishing, Oxford.

——2000b, *End of Millennium*, 2nd edn, Blackwell Publishing, Oxford.

——2000c, 'Materials for an exploratory theory of the Network society', *British Journal of Sociology*, 51(1), 5–24.

——2001, *The Internet Galaxy: Reflections on the Internet, Business, and Society*, Oxford University Press, New York.

——2004a, *The Power of Identity*, 2nd edn, Blackwell Publishing, Oxford.

——(ed.) 2004b, *The Network Society: A Cross-Cultural Perspective*, Edward Elgar, Cheltenham, UK.

Castells, M. & Cardoso, G. (eds) 2006, *The Network Society: From Knowledge to Policy*, Johns Hopkins Center for Transatlantic Relations, Washington, DC.

Castells, M., Fernandez-Ardevol, M., Qiu, J. L. & Sey, A. 2007, *Mobile Communication and Society: A Global Perspective*, MIT Press, Cambridge, Mass.

Castells, M. & Ince, M. 2003, *Conversations with Manuel Castells*, Polity Press, Cambridge.

Castells, M., Tubella, I., Sancho, T., de Isla, M. I. D. & Wellman, B. 2004, 'Social structure, cultural identity, and personal autonomy in the practice of the internet: the network society in Catalonia' in *The Network Society: A Cross-Cultural Perspective*, ed. M. Castells, Edward Elgar, Cheltenham, UK, 233–48.

Castles, S. 1992, 'Australian multiculturalism' in *Nations of Immigrants*, eds G. Freeman & J. Jupp, Oxford University Press, Melbourne.

——1999, 'The future of Australian citizenship in a globalising world', paper presented at the 50th Anniversary of Australian Citizenship Conference, 21–23 July.

Castles, S. & Miller, M. J. 1993, *The Age of Migration*, Macmillan, London.

Castles, S., Cope, B., Kalantzis, M. & Morrissey, M. 1988, *Mistaken Identity*, Pluto Press, Sydney.

Cerami, C. A. 1962, 'The US eyes Greater Europe', *The Spectator*, 5 October, 495–6.

CGA (Commonwealth Government of Australia) 2003, *Educating Boys: Issues and information*, www.deewr.gov.au/Schooling/BoysEducation/Pages/publications_conferences_websites.aspx.

Chamberlain, C. 1983, *Class Consciousness in Australia*, George Allen & Unwin, Sydney.

Chamberlain, C. & MacKenzie, D. 2009, *Counting the Homeless 2006*, AIHW cat no. HOU 213, Australian Institute of Health & Welfare, Canberra.

Chambliss, W. J. 1964, 'A sociological analysis of the law of vagrancy', *Social Problems*, 12, 67–77.

——1978, *On the Take*, Indiana University Press, Bloomington.

Chang, H. 1998, 'Globalization, transnational corporations, and economic development: can the developing countries pursue strategic industrial policy in a globalizing world economy?' in *Globalization and Progressive Economic Policy*, eds D. Baker, G. Epstein & R. Pollin, Cambridge University Press, Cambridge, 97–113.

Chapman, S. 1997, 'Passive smoking memo reveals passive smoking strategy', *British Medical Journal*, 314, 31 May, 1569.

Chase-Dunn, C., Kawano, Y. & Brewer, B. D. 2000, 'Trade globalization since 1795: waves of integration in the world system', *American Sociological Review*, 65(1), 77–95.

Chen, R., Bennett, S. & Maton, K. 2010, 'Absenting discipline: non-disciplinarity in online learning' in *Disciplinarity: Systemic Functional and Sociological Perspectives*, eds F. Christie & K. Maton, Continuum, London.

Chen, S. & Ravallion, M. 2008, 'The developing world is poorer than we thought, but no less successful in the fight against poverty', Policy Research Working Paper No. 4703, The World Bank, Washington, DC.

Cherlin, A. J. 2004, 'The deinstitutionalization of American marriage', *Journal of Marriage and Family*, 66, 848–61.

Chesher, C. 2004, 'Connection unbound by location', *Griffith Review*, 3, 189–200.

Child, J. & Macmillan, B. 1973, 'Managers and their leisure' in *Leisure and Society in Britain*, M. Smith, S. Parker & C. Smith, Allen Lane, London.

Chiricos, T. 1987, 'Rates of crime and unemployment: an analysis of aggregate research and evidence', *Social Problems*, 34(2), 187–212.

Chodorow, N. 1978, *The Reproduction of Mothering*, University of California Press, Berkeley.

Chomsky, N. 1996a, *Power and Prospects: Reflection on Human Nature and the Social Order*, Allen & Unwin, Sydney.

——1996b, *World Orders Old and New: With an Update on the Palestinian Predicament*, Columbia University Press, New York.

——1999, *Profit over People: Neoliberalism and Global Order*, Seven Stories Press, New York.

——2003, *Hegemony or Survival: America's Quest for Global Dominance*, Allen & Unwin, Sydney.

Chossudovsky, M. 1998a, *The Globalisation of Poverty: Impacts of IMF and World Bank Reform*, Pluto Press, Sydney.

——1998b, 'Global poverty in the late 20th century', *Journal of International Affairs*, 52(1).

Chrisafis, A. 2009, 'Stress and worker suicides mean the future's not bright at Orange', *The Guardian*, 18 September, 25.

Christ, C. 1980, *Diving Deep and Surfacing: Women Writers on Spiritual Quest*, Beacon Press, Boston.

——1992, 'Why women need the goddess: phenomenological, psycho logical and political reflections' in *Womanspirit Rising*, eds C. Christ & J. Plaskow, Harper & Row, San Francisco, 273–86.

Christensen, T. 2001, 'European and regional integration' in *The Globalization of World Politics*, 2nd edn, eds J. Baylis & S. Smith, Oxford University Press, Oxford, 494–518.

Cicourel, A. V. 1976, *The Social Organization of Juvenile Justice*, Heinemann, London.

——1982, 'Interviews, surveys, and the problem of ecological validity', *American Sociologist*, 17(1), 11–20.

Cicourel, A. V. & Kitsuse, J. I. 1971, 'The social organization of the high school and deviant adolescent careers' in *School and Society*, eds B. R. Cosin, I. R. Dale, G. M. Esland & D. F. Swift, Routledge & Kegan Paul, London.

Clarricoates, K. 1980, 'The importance of being Ernest ... Emma ... Tom ... Jane: the perception and categorisation of gender conformity and gender deviation in primary schools', in *Schooling for Women's Work*, ed. R. Deem, Routledge & Kegan Paul, London.

Clark, M. 1959, *Health in Mexican American Culture*, University of California Press, Berkeley.

Clarke, J. & Critcher, C. 1985, *The Devil Makes Work*, Macmillan, London.

Clegg, S. 1989, *Frameworks of Power*, Sage, London.

——1990, *Modern Organizations*, Sage, London.

Clegg, S. R., Courpasson, D. & Phillips, N. 2006, *Power and Organizations*, Sage, London.

Clegg, S. & Dunkerley, D. 1980, *Organization, Class and Control*, Routledge & Kegan Paul, London.

Clinard, M. B. & Yeager, P. 1980, *Corporate Crime*, The Free Press, New York.

Coad, D. 2008, *The Metrosexual: Gender, Sexuality, and Sport*, State University of New York Press, Albany, NY.

Coates, K. & Silburn, R. 1970, *Poverty*, Penguin, Harmondsworth.

Coeuré, B. 2002, 'Discussion' in *Globalisation, Living Standards and Inequality: Recent Progress and Continuing Challenges, Proceedings of a Conference Held in Sydney on 27–28 May 2002*, eds D. Gruen, T. O'Brien & J. Lawson, Reserve Bank of Australia and Australian National Treasury, Canberra, 88–91.

Cohen, A. K. 1955, *Delinquent Boys*, Free Press, Glencoe.

Cohen, H. 2000, 'Revisiting McLuhan', *Media International Australia*, 94, 5–12.

Cohen, M. G. 2004, 'Globalization's challenge to feminist political economy and the law: a socialist perspective' in *New Socialisms: Futures Beyond Globalization*, eds R. Albritton, S. Bell, J. R. Bell & R. Westra, Routledge, London, 33–49.

Cohen, R. & Kennedy, P. 2000, *Global Sociology*, Palgrave, Houndsmill, Basingstoke.

Cohen, S. & Young, J. 1971, *Psychological Survival*, Penguin, Harmondsworth.

Cole, C. & Andrews, D. L. 2000, 'America's new son: Tiger Woods and American multiculturalism', *Cultural Studies*, 5, 109–24.

Coleman, J. S. 1966, *Equality of Educational Opportunity*, Government Printing Office, Washington, D.C.

Colic-Peisker, V. 2002, 'Croatians in Western Australia', *Journal of Sociology*, 38(2), 149–66.

Collins, C., Kenway, J. & McLeod, J. 2000, *Factors Influencing the Educational Performance of Males and Females in School and their Initial Destinations after Leaving School*, Department of Education, Training and Youth Affairs (DETYA), Canberra.

Collins, J. 1978, 'Fragmentation of the working class' in *Essays in the Political Economy of Australian Capitalism, Vol. 3*, eds E. L. Wheelwright & K. Buckley, Australia & New Zealand Book Co., Sydney, 42–85.

Collins, J., Noble, G., Poynting, S. & Tabar, P. 2000, *Kebabs, Kids, Cops & Crime: Youth, Ethnicity and Crime*, Pluto Press, Sydney.

Collins, L. & Ali, M. 2003, *Deaths in Custody in Australia: 2002 National Deaths in Custody Program Annual Report*, Research and Public Policy Series No. 50, Australian Institute of Criminology, Canberra.

Collins, R. 1975, *Conflict Sociology*, Academic Press, New York.

——1986, *Weberian Sociological Theory*, Cambridge University Press, Cambridge.

——1992, 'The romanticism of agency/structure versus the analysis of micro/macro', *Current Sociology*, 40(1), 77–97.

——1997, 'A sociological guilt trip: comment on Connell', *American Journal of Sociology*, 102(6), 1558–64.

——2004, *Interaction Ritual Chains*, Princeton University Press, Princeton, NJ.

Collyer, F. M. 1998, 'Privatisation on the agenda: policy directions in health care', *Australian Journal of Hospital Pharmacy*, 28(2), April, 108–11.

——2003, 'The corporatisation and commercialisation of complementary and alternative medicine' in *The Mainstreaming of Complementary and Alternative Medicine in Social Context: An International Perspective*, eds P. Tovey, G. Easthope & J. Adams, Routledge, London, 81–99.

Commission of Inquiry into Poverty 1975, *Poverty in Australia*, Government Printer, Canberra.

Committee of Review of NSW Schools 1989, *Report of the Committee of Review of NSW Schools*, Carrick Report, Department of Education and Youth Affairs, Sydney.

Committee of the Ministry of Education and Youth Affairs NSW 1989, *Excellence and Equity*, White Paper on Curriculum Reform, Ministry of Education and Youth Affairs, Sydney.

Commonwealth of Australia 2004, *Higher Education for the 2004–2006 Triennium*, Commonwealth of Australia, Canberra.

Commonwealth Department of Education 1975, *Report of the Inquiry into Schools of High Migrant Density*, AGPS, Canberra.

Comte, A. 1986, *The Positive Philosophy*, Bell & Sons, London.

Connell, R. W. 1970, 'Australia: dilemmas of sociology', *Politics*, 52, 201–9.

——1977, *Ruling Class, Ruling Culture*, Cambridge University Press, Cambridge.

——1983, *Which Way Is Up?*, George Allen & Unwin, Sydney.

——1985, *Teachers' Work*, George Allen & Unwin, Sydney.

——1987, *Gender and Power*, Allen & Unwin, Sydney.

——1988a, 'Class inequalities and "just health" strategy', *Community Health Studies*, 12(2), 212–17.

——1988b, 'Cool guys, swots and wimps: the interplay of masculinity and education', *Oxford Review of Education*, 153, 291–303.

——1991, 'A thumbnail dipped in tar or: can we write sociology from the fringe of the world?', *Social Analysis*, 30, 68–76.

——1994, 'Poverty and education', *Harvard Educational Review*, 64(2), 125–49.

——1995, *Masculinities*, Allen & Unwin, Sydney.

——1997, 'Why is classical theory classical?', *American Journal of Sociology*, 102(6), 151–7.

——2007, *Southern Theory: The Global Dynamics of Knowledge in Social Science*, Allen & Unwin, Sydney.

——2009, 'Accountable conduct: "doing gender" in transsexual and political retrospect', *Gender & Society*, 23(1), 104–11.

Connell, R. W. & Irving, T. H. 1980, 'Yes, Virginia, there is a ruling class' in *Australian Politics: A Fifth Reader*, eds H. Mayer & H. Nelson, Longman Cheshire, Melbourne, 78–84.

——1992, *Class Structure in Australian History*, 2nd edn, Longman Cheshire, Melbourne.

Connell, R. W., Ashenden, D. J., Kessler, S. & Dowsett, G. 1982, *Making the Difference*, George Allen & Unwin, Sydney.

Connell, R. W., White, V. M. & Johnston, K. M. 1990, *Poverty, Education and the Disadvantaged Schools Program*, School of Behavioural Sciences, Macquarie University, Sydney.

Connell, W. F. et al. 1975, *12 to 20: Studies of City Youth*, Hicks, Smith & Sons, Sydney.

Cooley, C. H. 1902, *Human Nature and the Social Order*, Charles Scribner's Sons, New York.

Coontz, S. & Henderson, P. 1986, 'Introduction: "Explanations" of male dominance' in *Women's Work. Men's Property*, eds S. Coontz & P. Henderson, Verso, London, 1–42.

Corrigan, P. 1981, *Schooling the Smash Street Kids*, Macmillan, London.

Corsaro, W. A. 1992, 'Interpretive reproduction in children's peer cultures', *Social Psychology Quarterly*, 55, 160–77.

Coser, L. A. 1977, *Masters of Sociological Thought*, 2nd edn, Harcourt Brace Jovanovich, New York.

Cotterrell, R. 1999, *Emile Durkheim: Law in a Moral Domain*, Edinburgh University Press, Edinburgh.

Cottle, S. 2006, 'Mediatized rituals: beyond manufacturing consent', *Media, Culture & Society*, 28(3), 411–432.

Couldry, N. 2000, *The Place of Media Power: Pilgrims and Witnesses of the Media Age*, Routledge, London.

——2003, *Media Rituals: A Critical Approach*, Routledge, London.

——2006, *Listening Beyond the Echoes: Media, Ethics, and Agency in an Uncertain World*, Paradigm Publishers, Boulder, Co.

Couldry, N. & Curran, J. (eds) 2003, *Contesting Media Power: Alternative Media Power in a Networked World*, Rowan & Littlefield, Lanham, MD.

Couldry, N. & McCarthy, A. (eds) 2004, *Mediaspace: Place, Scale and Culture in a Media Age*, Routledge, London.

Couldry, N., Livingstone, S. & Markham, T. 2007, *Media Consumption and Public Engagement: Beyond the Presumption of Attention*, Palgrave Macmillan, New York.

Coumarelos, C. 1994, *Juvenile Offending: Predicting Persistence and Determining the Cost-Effectiveness of Interventions*, NSW Bureau of Crime Statistics and Research, Sydney.

Council for Aboriginal Reconciliation 1994, *Walking Together*, AGPS, Canberra.

Cowlishaw, G. 1988, *Black, White or Brindle*, Cambridge University Press, Cambridge.

Cox, O. C. 1970 [1948], *Caste, Class and Race*, Monthly Review Press, New York.

Cox, M. 2001, 'International history since 1989' in *The Globalization of World Politics*, 2nd edn, eds J. Baylis & S. Smith, Oxford University Press, Oxford, 111–40.

Craib, I. 1992, *Modern Social Theory*, 2nd edn, Harvester Wheatsheaf, Hemel Hempstead.

——1997, *Classical Sociological Theory*, Oxford University Press, Oxford.

Craik, J. 1991, *Resorting to Tourism*, Allen & Unwin, Sydney.

Crawford, A. 1998, *Crime Prevention and Community Safety: Politics, Policies and Practices*, Longman, London.

Critcher, C., Dicks, B. & Waddington, D. 1992, 'Portrait of despair', *New Statesman & Society*, 23 October, 16–17.

Crockatt, R. 2001, 'The end of the Cold War' in *The Globalization of World Politics*, 2nd edn, eds J. Baylis & S. Smith, Oxford University Press, Oxford, 92–110.

Crompton, R. 1998, *Class and Stratification: An Introduction to Current Debates*, 2nd edn, Polity Press, Cambridge.

Crompton, R. & Mann, M. 1986, *Gender and Stratification*, Polity Press, Cambridge.

Crook, S., Pakulski, J. & Waters, M. 1992, *Postmodernization: Change in Advanced Society*, Sage, London.

Crotty, M. 1998, *The Foundations of Social Research: Meaning and Perspective in the Research Process*, Allen & Unwin, Sydney.

Crough, G. 1980, 'Small is beautiful but disappearing: a study of share ownership in Australia', *Journal of Australian Political Economy*, 8, 3–14.

Cuff, E. C., Sharrock, W. W. & Francis, D. W. 1998 [1979, 1990], *Perspectives in Sociology*, 4th edn, Routledge, London.

Cummins, J. 1978, 'Educational implications of mother tongue maintenance in minority language groups', *Canadian Modern Language Review*, 34(3), 395–416.

——1979, 'Linguistic independence and the educational development of bilingual children', *Review of Educational Research*, 49(2), 222–51.

——1980a, 'The entry and exit fallacy in bilingual education', *NABE Journal*, 43, 25–60.

——1980b, 'The crosslingual dimensions of language proficiency: implications for bilingual education and the optimal age issue', *TESOL Quarterly*, 14(2), 175–87.

——1984, *Bilingualism and Special Education*, Multilingual Matters, Clevedon.

Cunneen, C. 2001, *Conflict, Politics and Crime: Aboriginal Communities and the Police*, Allen & Unwin, Sydney.

Cunneen, C. et al. 1989, *The Dynamics of Collective Conflict*, Law Book Company, Sydney.

Cunneen, C. & White, R. 2002 [1995], *Juvenile Justice: Youth and Crime in Australia*, Oxford University Press, Melbourne.

——2007, *Juvenile Justice: Youth and Crime in Australia*, Oxford University Press, South Melbourne.

Cunningham, S. & Jacka, E. 1996, *Australian Television and International Mediascapes*, Cambridge University Press, Melbourne.

Curr, E. M. 1886, *The Australian Race: Its Origin, Languages, Customs, Place of Landing in Australia, and the Routes by Which It Spread Itself Over That Continent*, John Farnes, Melbourne.

Cutler, A. C. 2001, 'Globalization, the rule of law, and the modern law merchant: medieval or late capitalist associations?', *Constellations*, 8(4), 480–502.

d'Addio, A. 2007, 'Intergenerational transmission of disadvantage: mobility or immobility across generations? A review of the evidence for OECD countries', http://econpapers.repec.org/paper/oecelsaab/52-en.htm, accessed 23 February 2008.

Dahl, R. A. 1961, *Who Governs?*, Yale University Press, New Haven.

——1973, 'A critique of the ruling elite model' in *Power in Britain*, eds J. Urry & J. Wakeford, Heinemann, London, 282–90.

Dahlberg, L. & Siapera, E. (eds) 2007, *Radical Democracy and the Internet: Interrogating Theory and Practice*, Palgrave Macmillan, Basingstoke.

Dahlgren, P. 2001, 'The public sphere and the Net: structure, space and communication' in *Mediated Politics: Communication in the Future of Democracy*, eds W. L. Bennett & R. M. Entman, Cambridge University Press, Cambridge, 33–55.

——2002, 'The public sphere as historical narrative' in *McQuail's Reader in Mass Communication Theory*, ed. D. McQuail, Sage, London, 195–200.

——2005, 'The internet, public spheres and political communication: dispersion and deliberation', *Political Communication*, 22(2), 147–62.

Dahrendorf, R. 1959, *Class and Class Conflict in an Industrial Society*, Routledge & Kegan Paul, London.

Daly, M. 1968, *The Church and the Second Sex*, Geoffrey Chapman, London.

——1973, *Beyond God the Father: Towards a Philosophy of Women's Liberation*, Beacon Press, Boston.

——1978, *Gyn/Ecology: The Metaethics of Radical Feminism*, Beacon Press, Boston.

Daniel, A. 1995, 'The politics of health' in *Sociology of Health and Illness*, eds G. Lupton & J. Najman, Macmillan, Melbourne, 57–76.

Davie, G. 1995, *Religion in Britain since 1945: Believing without Belonging*, Blackwell Publishing, Oxford.

Davies, B. 1989, *Frogs and Snails and Feminist Tales*, Allen & Unwin, Sydney.

Davies, M. 2009, 'Household debt: implications for monetary policy and financial stability', *Bank for International Settlements*, BIS Papers No. 46, May, www.bis.org/publ/bppdf/bispap46e.pdf, accessed 2 June 2009.

Davis, A. 1995, 'I used to be your sweet mamma: ideology, sexuality and domesticity in the blues of Gertrude "Ma" Rainey and Bessie Smith' in *Sexy Bodies*, eds E. Grosz & E. Probyn, Routledge, London, 231–65.

Davis, A. & George, J. 1998, *States of Health*, Longman, Melbourne.

Davis, F. 1975, 'Deviance disavowal' in *Readings in Social Psychology*, 2nd edn, eds A. R. Lindesmith, A. L. Strauss & N. K. Denzin, Dryden, Hinsdale.

Davis, K. 1937, 'Reproductive institutions and the pressure for population', *Sociological Review*, 29(3), 289–306.

——1940, 'Extreme isolation of a child', *American Journal of Sociology*, 45(4), 554–65.

——1959, 'The myth of functional analysis as a special method in sociology and anthropology', *American Sociological Review*, 24, 757–82.

——1984, 'Wives and work: the sex role revolution and its consequences', *Population and Development Review*, 10(3), 397–417.

Davis, K. & Moore, W. E. 1953, 'Some principles of stratification' in *Class, Status and Power*, eds R. Bendix & S. M. Lipset, Routledge, London.

——1967, 'Some principles of stratification' in *Class, Status, and Power*, 2nd edn, eds R. Bendix & S. M. Lipset, Routledge & Kegan Paul, London, 47–53.

Dawe, A. 1970, 'The two sociologies', *British Journal of Sociology*, 21, 207–18.

Dawson, L. 1998, 'Anti-modernism, modernism and post modernism: struggling with the cultural significance of new religious movements', *Sociology of Religion*, 59(2), 131.

Day, L. 1979, 'Those unsatisfactory statistics on divorce', *Australian Quarterly*, 51(4), 26–31.

Day, R. & Day, J. 1977, 'A review of the current state of negotiated order theory', *Sociological Quarterly*, 18, 126–42.

Dayan, D. 2008, 'Beyond media events: disenchantment, derailment, disruption' in *Owning the Olympics: Narratives of the New China*, eds M. E. Price & D. Dayan, University of Michigan Press, Ann Arbor, 391–401.

Dayan, D. & Katz, E. 1992, *Media Events: The Live Broadcasting of History*, Harvard University Press, Cambridge.

D'Cruz, J. V. & Langford, P. (eds) 1990, *Issues in Australian Education*, Longman Cheshire, Melbourne.

Deal, T. & Kennedy A. 1988, *Corporate Cultures*, Penguin, London.

Dean, M. 1991, *The Constitution of Poverty: Towards a Genealogy of Liberal Governance*, Routledge & Kegan Paul, London.

——1999, *Governmentality: Power and Rule in Modern Society*, Sage, London.

Dearden, J. & Jones, W. 2008, *Homicide in Australia: 2006–07 National Homicide Monitoring Program Annual Report*, Australian Institute of Criminology Monitoring Reports, www.aic.gov.au/documents/F/F/B/{FFB9E49F-160F-43FC-B98D-6BC510DC2AFD}mr01.pdf, accessed 5 August 2009.

de Beauvoir, S. 1972, *The Second Sex*, Penguin, Harmondsworth.

De Cecco, J. P. 1990, 'Sex and more sex: a critique of the Kinsey conception of human sexuality' in *Homosexuality/Heterosexuality*, eds D. P. McWhirter, S. A. Sanders & J. M. Reinisch, Oxford University Press, Oxford, 367–86.

DEET (Department of Employment, Education & Training) 1993, *Retention and Participation in Australian Schools 1967 to 1992*, AGPS, Canberra.

de la Fuente, E. & West, B. 2008, 'Cultural sociology in the Australian context', *Journal of Sociology*, 44(4), 315–19.

Delamont, S. 1976, 'Beyond Flanders' fields: the relationship of subject matter and individuality to classroom style' in *Explorations in Classroom Observation*, eds M. Stubbs & S. Delamont, Wiley, Chichester.

de Lauretis, T. 1991, 'Queer theory: lesbian and gay sexualities', *Differences*, 3, iii–xviii.

de Lemos, M. M. 1975, *A Study of the Educational Achievement of Migrant Children*, Australian Council for Educational Research, Melbourne.

de Mause, L. (ed.) 1974, *The History of Childhood*, Harper & Row, New York.

Demidenko, H. 1993, *The Hand that Signed the Paper*, Allen & Unwin, Sydney.

Dempsey, K. 1983, *Conflict and Decline: Ministers and Laymen in an Australian Country Town*, Methuen, Sydney.

——1988, 'Exploitation in the domestic division of labour: an Australian case study', *Australian & New Zealand Journal of Sociology*, 24(3), 420–36.

——1989, 'Is religion still relevant in the private sphere?', *Sociological Analysis*, 50, 247–63.

——1990, *Smalltown*, Oxford University Press, Melbourne.

——1991, 'Inequality, belonging and religion in a rural community' in *Religion in Australia*, A. Black, Allen & Unwin, Sydney.

——1992, *Man's Town*, Oxford University Press, Melbourne.

Dennis, N. 1975, 'Relationships' in *The Sociology of Modern Britain*, rev. edn, eds E. Butterworth & D. Weir, Fontana, Glasgow.

Denzin, N. K. 2002, 'Confronting anthropology's crisis of representation', *Journal of Contemporary Ethnography*, 31(4), 478–516.

de Sousa Santos, B. 1995, *Toward a New Common Sense: Law, Science and Politics in the Paradigmatic Transition*, Routledge, London.

DEST (Department of Education, Science and Training) 2000, *Higher Education Students Time Series Tables: Selected Higher Education Student Statistics*, Canberra.

de Tocqueville, A. 1846, *Democracy in America*, Oxford University Press, London.

DETYA (Department of Education, Training and Youth Affairs) 2000, 'The education of boys', Submission to the House of Representatives Standing Committee on Employment, Education and Workplace Relations, Canberra.

de Vaus, D. 1984, 'Workforce participation and sex differences in church attendance', *Review of Religious Research*, 25, 247–58.

de Vaus, D. & McAllister, I. 1987, 'Gender differences in religion: A test of the structural location theory', *American Sociological Review*, 52, 472–81.

de Vaus, D. & Gray, M. 2004, 'The changing living arrangements of children 1946–2001', *Journal of Family Studies*, 10(1), 9–19.

Devine, F. 2004, *Class Practices*, Cambridge University Press, Cambridge.

Devine, F. & Savage, M. 2000, 'Conclusion: renewing class analysis' in *Renewing Class Analysis*, eds R. Crompton, F. Devine, M. Savage & Y. Scott, Blackwell Publishing, Oxford.

Dezalay, Y. 1990, 'The Big Bang and the law: the internationalization and restructuration of the legal field', *Theory, Culture & Society*, 7(2), 279–93.

Dezalay, Y. & Garth, B. 1996, *Dealing in Virtue: International Commercial Arbitration and the Construction of a Transnational Legal Order*, University of Chicago Press, Chicago.

——2006, 'From the Cold War to Kosovo: the rise and renewal of

the field of international human rights', *Annual Review of Law & Social Science*, 2, 231–55.
Dicken, P. 1992, *Global Shift: The Internationalization of Economic Activity*, 2nd edn, Paul Chapman Publishing Limited, London.
Dilnot, A. W. 1990, 'The distribution and composition of personal sector wealth in Australia', *Australian Economic Review*, 89, 33–40.
Dingwall, R. 2002, 'Ethnomethodology and law' in *An Introduction to Law and Social Theory*, eds R. Banakar & M. Travers, Hart Publishing, Oxford, 227–44.
Djilas, M. 1966 [1957], *The New Class*, Unwin, London.
Dollar, D. 2002, 'Global economic integration and global inequality' in *Globalisation, Living Standards and Inequality: Recent Progress and Continuing Challenges, Proceedings of a Conference Held in Sydney on 27–28 May 2002*, eds, D. Gruen, T. O'Brien & J. Lawson, Reserve Bank of Australia and Australian National Treasury, Canberra, 9–36.
Dollar, D. & Kraay, A. 2004 [2002], 'Growth is good for the poor' in *The Globalization Reader*, 2nd edn, eds F. J. Lechner & J. Boli, Blackwell, Oxford, 177–82.
Dollard, J., Miller, N. E., Doob, L. W., Mowrer, O. H. & Sears, R. 1957, *Frustration and Aggression*, Yale University Press, New Haven.
Domingues, J.M. 2009, 'Global modernization, "coloniality" and a critical sociology for contemporary Latin America', *Theory, Culture & Society*, 26(1), 112–33.
Donzelot, J. 1979, *The Policing of Families*, Hutchinson, London.
Douglas, J. D. 1967, *The Social Meanings of Suicide*, Princeton University Press, Princeton.
Downes, D. & Rock, P. 1988, *Understanding Deviance*, 2nd edn, Clarendon Press, Oxford.
Dowse, R. E. & Hughes, J. A. 1972, *Political Sociology*, John Wiley & Sons, London.
Drahos, P. & Braithwaite, J. 2001, 'The globalisation of regulation', *Journal of Political Philosophy*, 9(1), 103–28.
Drainville, A. C. 2008, 'Resistance to globalisation: the view from the periphery of the world economy', *International Social Science Journal*, 59(192), 235–46.
Dreher, A. 2006, 'Does globalization affect growth? Evidence from a new index of globalization', *Applied Economics*, 38(10), 1091–110.
Dreher, A., Gaston, N. & Martens, P. 2008, *Measuring Globalization. Gauging its Consequence*, Springer, New York.
Duke, C. & Sommerlad, E. 1976, *Design for Diversity*, Education Research Unit, ANU, Canberra.
Dunne, T. & Schmidt, B. C. 2001, 'Realism' in *The Globalization of World Politics*, 2nd edn, eds J. Baylis & S. Smith, Oxford University Press, Oxford, 141–61.
Dunning, E. 1999, *Sport Matters: Sociological Studies of Sport, Violence and Civilization*, Taylor & Francis, London.
Durkheim, E. 1912, 'Review of Levy-Bruhl's "Les Fonctions Mentales dans les Societes Inferieures"', *Annes Sociologique*, 12, 33–7.
——1915, *The Elementary Forms of Religious Life*, George Allen & Unwin, London.
——1933 [1893], *The Division of Labour in Society*, The Free Press, New York.
——1938, *The Rules of Sociological Method*, The Free Press, Glencoe.
——1961 [1925], *Moral Education*, The Free Press, Glencoe.
——1964, 'Sociology' in *Emile Durkheim: Essays on Sociology and Philosophy*, ed. K. H. Wolff, Harper & Row, New York.
——1965 [1912], *The Elementary Forms of Religious Life*, The Free Press, New York.
——1970 [1952, 1897], *Suicide: A Study in Sociology*, Routledge & Kegan Paul, London.
——1982 [1895], *The Rules of Sociological Method*, trans. W. D. Halls, The Free Press, New York.
Dyck, N. 1995, *Indigenous Peoples and the Nation State*, Institute of Social and Economic Research, St Johns, Newfoundland.
Eagleton, T. 1986, 'Capitalism, modernism and postmodernism' in *Against the Grain*, Verso, London.
Easteal, P. 1994, 'Violence against women in the home', *Family Matters*, 37, 86–93.
Eastwood, H. 2000, 'Why are Australian GPs using alternative medicine? Postmodernisation, consumerism and the shift towards holistic health', *Journal of Sociology*, 36(2), 133–56.
Eccles, S. 1984, 'Women in the Australian labour force' in *Unfinished Business*, ed. D. H. Broom, George Allen & Unwin, Sydney, 80–93.
Edwards, C. & Read, P. (eds) 1989, *The Lost Children*, Doubleday, Sydney.
Ehrenreich, B. 1994, 'Divorce spawns extended families', *Sydney Morning Herald*, 6 July, 12.
Ehrenreich, E. & English, D. 1973, *Complaints and Disorders: The Sexual Politics of Sickness*, Feminist Press, New York.
Elder, C. 2008, *Being Australian: Narratives of National Identity*, Allen & Unwin, Sydney.
Elias, D. 2003, 'HIH chiefs facing jail terms', *The Age*, 17 April, www.theage.com.au/articles/2003/04/16/1050172650638.html?oneclick=true, accessed 11 March 2005.
Elias, N. 1983 [1969], *The Court Society*, Pantheon, New York.
——1994 [1939], *The Civilizing Process*, Blackwell Publishing, Oxford.
——2008, 'Power and civilisation', *Journal of Power*, 1(2), 135–42.
Elliott, A. 2009, *Contemporary Social Theory: An Introduction*, Routledge, London.
El Saadawi, N. 1980, *The Hidden Face of Eve*, Zed Books, London.
Emmison, M. 1991, 'Wright and Goldthorpe: constructing the agenda of class analysis' in *Class Analysis and Contemporary Australia*, eds J. H. Baxter, M. C. Emmison, J. S. Western & M. C. Western, Macmillan, Melbourne, 38–65.
——2003, 'Social class and cultural mobility', *Journal of Sociology*, 19(3), 211–30.
Encel, S. 1968, 'The concept of the state in Australian politics' and 'The political elite in Australia' in *Readings in Australian Government*, ed. C. A. Hughes, University of Queensland Press, St Lucia, 34–49, 86–105.
——1970, *Equality and Authority*, Cheshire, Melbourne.
——1991, 'Sociology, politics and social democracy' in *Social Democracy and Social Science*, ed. A. Daniel, Longman Cheshire, Melbourne, 75–94.
——2002, 'September 11 and its implications for sociology', *Journal of Sociology*, 38(3), 223–7.
Engels, F. 1962 [1884], 'The origin of the family, private property and the state' in *Selected Works, Vol. 2*, K. Marx & F. Engels, Foreign Languages Publishing House, Moscow, 170–327.

Epstein, C. F. 1988, *Deceptive Distinctions*, Yale University Press, New Haven.

Erikson, E. 1950, *Childhood and Society*, Imago, London.

Eriksen, T. H. 1993, *Ethnicity and Nationalism*, Pluto Press, London.

Erikson, R. & Goldthorpe, J. 1993, *Class Mobility in Industrial Societies*, Clarendon Press, Oxford.

ESCAP 1982, 'Marriage and divorce in Australia' in *Population of Australia Vol. 1*, United Nations, New York, 183–98.

Etzioni, A. 1964, *Modern Organizations*, Prentice Hall, Englewood Cliffs, NJ.

Evans, D. T. 1993, *Sexual Citizenship: The Material Construction of Sexualities*, Routledge, London.

Evans, G. T. & Poole, M. E. 1975, 'Relationships between verbal and non-verbal abilities for migrant children and Australian children of low socio-economic status: similarities and contrasts', *Australian Journal of Education*, 19(3), 209–30.

Evans, M.D.R., Kelley, J. & Headey, B. 2004, 'Attitudes to abortion: Australia in comparative perspective' in M.D.R. Evans & J. Kelley, eds, *Australian Economy and Society 2002: Religion, Morality and Public Policy*, Annandale, NSW, Federation Press, 136–68.

Evans-Pritchard, E. E. 1937, *Witchcraft, Oracles and Magic among the Azande*, Oxford University Press, Oxford.

——1940, *The Nuer: A Description of the Modes of Livelihood and Political Institutions of a Nilotic People*, Oxford University Press, New York.

Eysenck, H. 1971, *Race, Intelligence and Education*, Sun Books, Melbourne.

——1979, *Crime and Personality*, Paladin, London.

Ezzy, D. 2003, 'New Age Witchcraft? Popular spell books and the re-enchantment of everyday life', *Culture and Religion*, 4(1), 47–65.

Fahy, K. & Smith, P. 1999, 'From the sick role to subject positions: a new approach to the medical encounter', *Health*, 3, 1, 71–93.

Faludi, S. 1991, *Backlash: The Undeclared War against American Women*, Crown, New York.

Fantasia, R. 1995, 'Fast food in France', *Theory & Society*, 24(2), 201–43.

Fausto-Sterling, A. 2000, *Sexing the Body: Gender Politics and the Construction of Sexuality*, Basic Books, New York.

Featherstone, M. 1990, 'Global culture: an introduction', *Theory, Culture & Society*, 7(2), 1–14.

——1995, *Undoing Culture: Globalization, Post modernism and Identity*, Sage, London.

Feeley, D. 1972, 'The family' in *Feminism and Socialism*, ed. L. Jenness, Pathfinder Press, New York.

Ferguson, A., Zita, J. N. & Addelson, K. P. 1982, 'On "compulsory heterosexuality and lesbian existence": defining the issues' in *Feminist Theory*, eds N. O. Keohane, M. Z. Rosaldo & B. C. Gelpi, Harvester Press, Brighton.

Fernbach, D. 1981, *The Spiral Path*, Gay Men's Press, London.

Field, J. 2006, *Lifelong Learning and the New Educational Order*, Trentham Books, Stoke on Trent.

Fielding, H. 1996, *Bridget Jones's Diary: A Novel*, Picador, London.

Fincher, R. & Saunders, P. (eds) 2001, *Creating Unequal Futures? Rethinking Poverty, Inequality and Disadvantage*, Allen & Unwin, Sydney.

Fine, G. A. 1993, 'Ten lies of ethnography: moral dilemmas of field research', *Journal of Contemporary Ethnography*, 22(3), 267–94.

Fiorenza, E. S. 1983, *In Memory of Her: A Feminist Theological Reconstruction of Christian Origins*, Crossroad, New York.

——1984, *Bread not Stone: The Challenge of Feminist Biblical Interpretation*, Beacon, Boston.

Firestone, S. 1972, *The Dialectic of Sex*, Paladin, London.

Fiske, J. 1987, *Television Culture*, Routledge, New York.

Fiske, J., Hodge, B. & Turner, G. 1987, *Myths of Oz*, Allen & Unwin, Sydney.

Fiss, P. C. & Hirsch, P. M. 2005, 'The discourse of globalization: framing and sensemaking of an emerging concept', *American Sociological Review*, 70(1), 29–52.

Fisse, B. & Braithwaite, J. 1993, *Corporations, Crime and Accountability*, Cambridge University Press, Cambridge.

Fitzgerald, R. T. 1976, *Poverty and Education in Australia*, Commission of Enquiry into Poverty Fifth Main Report, AGPS, Canberra.

Fletcher, R. 1966, *The Family and Marriage in Britain*, Penguin, Harmondsworth.

Flew, T. 2005, *New Media: An Introduction*, 2nd edn, Oxford University Press, Melbourne.

Flew, T. & S. McElhinney 2002, 'Globalization and the structure of new media industries' in *Handbook of New Media: Social Shaping and Consequences of ICTs*, eds L. H. Lievrouw & S. Livingstone, Sage, London, 304–19.

Flood, J. 2002, 'Globalisation and law' in *An Introduction to Law and Social Theory*, (eds) R. Banakar & M. Travers, Hart, Oxford, 311–28.

Folds, R. 1987, *Whitefella School: Education and Aboriginal Resistance*, Allen & Unwin, Sydney.

Fontana, B. 2002, 'Gramsci on politics and state', *Journal of Classical Sociology*, 2(2), 157–78.

Forbes, E., Knight, A. & Turner, G. W. (eds) 1984, *The Australian Oxford Mini Dictionary*, Oxford University Press, Melbourne.

Forsey, M. 2006, *Challenging the System? A Dramatic Tale of Neoliberal Reform in an Australian High School*, Information Age Publishing, Greenwich, CT.

Forster, G. & Anderson, B. 1978, *Medical Anthropology*, John Wiley & Sons, London.

Foster, L. & Harman, K. 1992, *Australian Education*, 3rd edn, Prentice Hall, Sydney.

Foucault, M. 1965, *Madness and Civilization*, Pantheon, New York.

——1973, *The Birth of the Clinic*, Routledge, London.

——1974, *The Archaeology of Knowledge*, Tavistock, London.

——1977, *Discipline and Punish*, Allen Lane, London.

——1978, *The History of Sexuality*, Vol. 1, Pantheon, New York.

——1979, 'Governmentality', *Ideology & Consciousness*, 6, 5–21.

——1982, 'The subject and power' in *Michel Foucault: Beyond Structuralism and Hermeneutics*, eds H. L. Dreyfus & P. Rabinow, Harvester, Brighton, 208–26.

——1991, 'Politics and the study of discourse' in *The Foucault Effect: Studies in Governmentality*, ed. G. Burchell, C. Gordon & P. Miller, Harvester, London, 53–72.

——2000, 'Truth and power' in *The Essential Works of Foucault 1954–1984, vol. 3: Power*, ed. J. D. Faubion, New Press, New York, 111–33.

Fourcade-Gourinchas, M. 2002, 'The rebirth of the liberal creed:

paths to neoliberalism in four countries', *American Journal of Sociology*, 108(3), 533–79.

Fowler, R. & Grabosky, P. 1989, 'Lead pollution and the children of Port Pirie' in *Stains on a White Collar: Fourteen Studies in Corporate Crime or Corporate Harm*, eds P. N. Grabosky & A. Sutton, Federation Press, Sydney.

Frankfurt Institute for Social Research 1973, *Aspects of Sociology*, Heinemann, London.

Franklin, A. & Crang, M. 2001, 'The trouble with travel and tourism theory', *Tourist Studies*, 1(1), 5–22.

Franklin, M. A. 1986, *The Force of the Feminine*, Allen & Unwin, North Sydney.

Franko, K. 2007, 'Analysing a world in motion: global flows meet "criminology of the other"', *Theoretical Criminology*, 11(2), 283–303.

Fraser, N. 1999, 'Rethinking the public sphere: a contribution to the critique of actually existing democracy' in *The Cultural Studies Reader*, ed. S. During, Routledge, London, 518–36.

Fraser, S. 1995, *The Bell Curve Wars: Race, Intelligence and the Future of America*, Basic Books, London.

Freeland, G. 1985, 'Death and Australian civil religion' in *Essays on Mortality*, eds M. Crouch & B. Huppauf, Faculty of Arts, University of New South Wales, Sydney, 105–20.

Freeman, G. & Jupp, J. 1992, *Nations of Immigrants*, Oxford University Press, Melbourne.

Freeman, M. 1983, *The Rights and Wrongs of Children*, Frances Pinter, London.

——1997, *The Moral Status of Children: Essays on the Rights of the Child*, Martinus Nijhoff, The Hague.

——1998, 'The sociology of childhood and children's rights', *International Journal of Children's Rights*, 6(4), 433–44.

Freeman, J. & Hutchins, B. 2009, 'Balancing the digital democratic deficit: e-government', *Media International Australia*, 130, 17–27.

Friedan, B. 1963, *The Feminine Mystique*, Penguin Books, Harmondsworth.

Friedman, L. M. 2001, 'Erewhon: the coming global legal order', *Stanford Journal of International Law*, 37(2), 347–64.

Freidson, E. 1970, *The Profession of Medicine*, Dodd, Mead, New York.

Frisby, D. P. 1984, *Georg Simmel*, Ellis Horwood/Tavistock, Chichester.

——1992, *Simmel and Since: Essays on Georg Simmel's Social Theory*, Routledge, London.

——2002, *Georg Simmel*, rev. edn, Routledge, London.

Frisby, D. P. & Featherstone, M. (eds) 1997, *Simmel on Culture: Selected Writings*, Sage, London.

Frow, J. 1998, 'Is Elvis a god? Cult, culture, questions of method', *International Journal of Cultural Studies*, 1(2), 197–210.

Fukuyama, F. 1992, *The End of History and the Last Man*, The Free Press, New York.

Fulcher, J. 2000, 'Globalisation, the nation-state and global society', *Sociological Review*, 48(4), 522–43.

Fuller, M. 1984, 'Black girls in a London comprehensive school' in *Life in School*, (eds) M. Hammersley & P. Woods, Open University Press, Milton Keynes.

Fuss, D. (ed.) 1991, *Inside/Out: Lesbian Theories, Gay Theories*, Routledge, New York.

Gagnon, J. H. 1990, 'Gender preference in erotic relations' in *Homosexuality/Heterosexuality*, eds D. P. McWhirter, S. A. Sanders & J. M. Reinisch, Oxford University Press, Oxford, 177–207.

Gagnon, J. H. & Simon, W. (eds) 1968, 'Sexual deviance in contemporary America', *Annals of the American Academy of Political & Social Science*, 37(6), 106–22.

——1973, *Sexual Conduct*, Aldine, Chicago.

Gale, F. 1981, 'Adjustment of migrants in cities: Aborigines in Adelaide, Australia' in *Population Mobility and Development*, eds G. W. Jones & H. V. Richter, Development Studies Centre, ANU, Canberra.

Gale, F. & Wundersitz, J. 1982, *Adelaide Aborigines*, Australian National University Press, Canberra.

Gale, F., Bailey-Harris, R. & Wundersitz, J. 1990, *Aboriginal Youth in the Criminal Justice System*, Cambridge University Press, Sydney.

Gale, F., Jordan, D., McGill, G., McNamara, N. & Scott, C. 1987, 'Aboriginal education' in *Australian Education*, ed. J. P. Keeves, Allen & Unwin, Sydney.

Game, A. 1991, *Undoing the Social*, Open University Press, Milton Keynes.

Game, A. & Pringle, R. 1983a, *Gender at Work*, George Allen & Unwin, Sydney.

——1983b, 'The making of the Australian family' in *The Family in the Modern World*, eds G. Bottomley & P. Jools, George Allen & Unwin, Sydney, 80–102.

Gamson, J. 1995, 'Must identity movements self-destruct? A queer dilemma', *Social Problems*, 42(3), 390–407.

Garfinkel, H. 1967, *Studies in Ethnomethodology*, Prentice Hall, Englewood Cliffs.

Garrett, G. 2004, 'Partisan politics in the global economy' in *The Globalization Reader*, 2nd edn, eds F. J. Lechner & J. Boli, Blackwell Publishing, Oxford, 231–9.

Gates, B. 2000, 'The network (extract from *The Road Ahead*, 1995)' in *Globalization: The Reader*, eds J. Beyon & D. Dunkerley, The Athlone Press, London, 216–17.

Geertz, C. 1973, *The Interpretation of Cultures*, Basic Books, New York.

——1988, *Works and Lives: The Anthropologist as Author*, Stanford University Press, Stanford, CA.

Geis, F. L. 1993, 'Self-fulfilling prophecies: a social psychological view of gender' in *The Psychology of Gender*, eds A. E. Beall & R. J. Sternberg, Guilford Press, London, 9–54.

Gellner, E. 1983, *Nations and Nationalism*, Blackwell Publishing, London.

——1992, *Postmodernism, Reason and Religion*, Routledge, London.

George, V. & Wilding, P. 2002, *Globalization and Human Welfare*, Palgrave, Houndsmill, Basingstoke.

Germov, J. 1995, 'Medi-fraud, managerialism and the decline of medical autonomy', *Australian & New Zealand Journal of Sociology*, 31(3), 51–66.

Gerth, H. H. & Mills, C. W. (eds) 1948, *From Max Weber*, Routledge & Kegan Paul, London.

Gesell, A. 1940, *The First Five Years of Life: A Guide to the Study of the Preschool Child*, Methuen & Co, London.

Gessner, V. & Schade, A. 1990, 'Conflicts of culture in cross-border legal relations: the conception of a research topic in the sociology of law', *Theory, Culture & Society*, 7(2), 253–77.

Gibbs, J. & Martin, W. 1964, *Status Integration and Suicide*, University of Oregon Press, Oregon.

Gibson, R., Wilson, S., Denemark, D., Meagher, G. & Western, M. 2003, *The Australian Survey of Social Attitudes*, ASSDA Study No. 1070, Australian Social Science Data Archive, Australian National University, Canberra.

Giddens, A. 1968, '"Power" in the recent writings of Talcott Parsons', *Sociology*, 2, 257–72.

——1971, *Capitalism and Modern Social Theory*, Cambridge University Press, Cambridge.

——1973, *The Class Structure of the Advanced Societies*, Hutchinson, London.

——1979a, *Capitalism and Modern Social Theory*, Cambridge University Press, Cambridge.

——1979b, *Central Problems in Social Theory: Action, Structure and Contradiction in Social Analysis*, Macmillan, London.

——1981, *A Contemporary Critique of Historical Materialism*, Macmillan, London.

——1982, *Profiles and Critiques in Social Theory*, Macmillan, London.

——1984, *The Constitution of Society*, Polity Press, Cambridge.

——(ed.) 1986, *Durkheim on Politics and the State*, Polity Press, Cambridge.

——1990, *The Consequences of Modernity*, Stanford University Press, Stanford.

——1991a, *The Consequences of Modernity*, Polity Press, Cambridge.

——1991b, *Modernity and Self-Identity: Self and Society in the Late Modern Age*, Polity Press, Cambridge.

——1992, *The Transformation of Intimacy: Sexuality, Love and Eroticism in Modern Societies*, Polity Press, Cambridge.

——1995, *Beyond Left and Right*, Polity Press, Cambridge.

——1996, 'Living in a post-traditional society' in *In Defence of Sociology*, ed. A. Giddens, Polity Press, Cambridge, 8–77.

——2000, *Runaway World: How Globalisation Is Reshaping Our Lives*, Routledge, London.

Gilbert, R. & Gilbert, P. 1998, *Masculinity Goes to School*, Allen & Unwin, Sydney.

Gilding, M. 1997, *Australian Families: A Comparative Perspective*, Longman, Melbourne.

——2001, 'Succession planning among the super rich', paper presented at the TASA Conference, University of Sydney, 13–15 December.

——2004, 'Entrepreneurs, elites and the ruling class: the changing structure of power and wealth in Australian society', *Australian Journal of Political Science*, 39(1), 127–143.

——2005, 'Families and fortunes: accumulation, management succession and inheritance in wealthy families', *Journal of Sociology*, 41(1), 29–45.

Gillborn, D. & Mirza, H. 2000, *Educational Inequality: Mapping Race, Class and Gender*, Commission for Racial Equality, London.

Gillespie, M. 1995, *Television, Ethnicity and Cultural Change*, Routledge, London.

Gillespie, R. 1991, *Manufacturing Knowledge: A History of the Hawthorne Experiments*, Cambridge University Press, Cambridge.

Gillies, V. 2003, 'Families and intimate relationships: a review of the sociological research', Families & Social Capital ESRC Research Group Working Paper No. 2, Families & Social Capital ESRC Research Group, London.

Gilligan, C. 1982, *In a Different Voice*, Harvard University Press, Cambridge, Mass.

Giulianotti, R. & Robertson, R. 2004, 'The globalization of football: a study in the glocalization of the "serious life"', *British Journal of Sociology*, 55(4), 545–68.

——2007, 'Forms of glocalization: globalization and the migration strategies of Scottish football fans in North America', *Sociology*, 41(1), 133–52.

Glaser, B. & Strauss, A. 1965, *Awareness of Dying*, Aldine, Chicago.

——1967, *The Discovery of Grounded Theory*, Aldine, Chicago.

Glass, D. 1954, *Social Mobility in Britain*, Routledge & Kegan Paul, London.

Glock, C. Y. & Stark, R. 1965, *Religion and Society in Tension*, Rand McNally, Chicago.

Glover, D. & Strawbridge, S. 1985, 'The sociology of knowledge' in *Sociology: New Directions*, ed. M. Haralambos, Causeway Press, Ormskirk.

Glueck, S. & Glueck, E. 1956, *Physique and Delinquency*, Harper, New York.

Goddard-Spear, M. 1989, 'Differences between the written work of boys and girls', *British Educational Research Journal*, 15, 271–7.

Goffman, E. 1959, *The Presentation of Self in Everyday Life*, Anchor Books, New York.

——1962 [1961], *Asylums*, Aldine, Chicago.

——1963, *Stigma*, Prentice Hall, Englewood Cliffs.

——1979 [1976], *Gender Advertisements*, Macmillan, London.

——1989, 'On fieldwork', *Journal of Contemporary Ethnography*, 18(2), 123–32.

Goggin, G. 2006, *Cell Phone Culture: Mobile Technologies in Everyday Life*, Routledge, London.

——(ed.) 2008, *Mobile Phone Cultures*, Routledge, London.

Goggin, G. & McLelland, M. 2009, *Internationalizing Internet Studies*, Routledge, London.

Goldthorpe, J. E. 1987, *Family Life in Western Societies*, Cambridge University Press, Cambridge.

Goldthorpe, J. H. 1973, Review article, 'A revolution in sociology?', *Sociology*, 7, 449–62.

——1974, Correspondence, 'A rejoinder to Benson', *Sociology*, 8, 131–3.

——1980, *Social Mobility and Class Structure in Modern Britain*, Clarendon Press, Oxford.

——1983, 'Women and class analysis: in defence of the conventional view', *Sociology*, 17(4), 465–88.

——2000, *On Sociology*, Oxford University Press, Oxford.

Goldthorpe, J. & Marshall, G. 1992, 'The promising future of class analysis', *Sociology*, 26(3), 381–400.

Goldthorpe, J. & Lockwood, D. 1968, *The Affluent Worker in the Class Structure*, Cambridge University Press, London.

Goldthorpe, J. H., Lockwood, D., Bechhofer, F. & Platt, J. 1968a, *The Affluent Worker: Industrial Attitudes and Behaviour*, Cambridge University Press, Cambridge.

——1968b, *The Affluent Worker: Political Attitudes and Behaviour*, Cambridge University Press, Cambridge.

——1969, *The Affluent Worker in the Class Structure*, Cambridge University Press, Cambridge.

Gole, N. 1996, *The Forbidden Modern: Civilization and Veiling*, Michigan University Press, Michigan.

Goode, W. J. 1963, *World Revolution and Family Patterns*, The Free Press, New York.

——1971, 'A sociological perspective on marital dissolution' in

Sociology of the Family, ed. M. Anderson, Penguin, Harmondsworth, 301–20.
Goody, J. 1983, *The Development of the Family and Marriage in Europe*, Cambridge University Press, Cambridge.
Gordon, D., Adelman, L., Ashworth, K., Bradshaw, J., Levitas, R., Middleton, S., Pantazis, C., Patsios, D., Payne, S., Townsend, P. & Williams, J. 2000, *Poverty and Social Exclusion in Britain*, Joseph Rowntree Foundation, York.
Gordon, L. 1984, 'Paul Willis—education, cultural production and social reproduction', *British Journal of Sociology of Education*, 5(2), 105–15.
Gordon, R. & Foley, S. 1998, *Criminal Business Organisations, Street Gangs and Related Groups in Vancouver: The Report of the Greater Vancouver Gang Study*, Ministry of Attorney-General, Vancouver.
Goss, M. E. W. 1969, 'Influence and authority among physicians in an outpatient clinic' in *A Sociological Reader on Complex Organizations*, 2nd edn, ed. A. Etzioni, Holt, Rinehart & Winston, New York, 275–91.
Gottfredson, M. & Hirschi, T. 1990, *A General Theory of Crime*, Stanford University Press, Stanford, CA.
Gough, K. 1972, 'An anthropologist looks at Engels' in *Woman in a Man-Made World*, eds N. Glazer-Malbin & H. Y. Waehrer, Rand McNally, Chicago, 107–18.
——1975, 'The origin of the family' in *Toward an Anthropology of Women*, ed. R. R. Reiter, Monthly Review Press, New York, 51–76.
Gouldner, A. W. 1954, *Patterns of Industrial Bureaucracy*, The Free Press, Glencoe.
——1955a, 'Metaphysical pathos and the theory of bureaucracy', *American Political Science Review*, 49, 496–507.
——1955b, *Wildcat Strike*, Routledge & Kegan Paul, London.
——1962, 'Anti-minotaur: the myth of value-free sociology', *Social Problems*, 9(3), 199–213.
——1970, *The Coming Crisis of Western Sociology*, Heinemann, London.
Gove, P. B. (ed.) 1981, *Third New International Dictionary of the English Language*, G & G Merriam Co., Springfield, Mass.
Gove, W. R. 1980, *The Labelling of Deviance*, Sage, Beverley Hills.
——1984, 'Gender differences in physical and mental illness', *Social Science & Medicine*, 19(2), 77–91.
Government of Canada 1974, *A New Perspective on the Health of Canadians*, Ottawa.
Grabosky, P. 1998, *Crime in a Shrinking World*, Australian Institute of Criminology, Canberra.
Graetz, B. 1988, 'The reproduction of privilege in Australian education', *British Journal of Sociology*, 39(3), 358–76.
Graetz, B. & McAllister, I. 1988, *Dimensions of Australian Society*, Macmillan, Melbourne.
——1994, *Dimensions of Australian Society*, 2nd edn, Macmillan, Melbourne.
Gramlich, E. M. 2002, 'Discussion' in *Globalisation, Living Standards and Inequality: Recent Progress and Continuing Challenges, Proceedings of a Conference Held in Sydney on 27–28 May 2002*, eds. D. Gruen, T. O'Brien & J. Lawson, Reserve Bank of Australia and Australian National Treasury, Canberra, 92–4.
Gramsci, A. 1971, *Selections from the Prison Notebooks*, Lawrence & Wishart, London.

Gray, D. & Saggers, S. 1994, 'Aboriginal ill health' in *Just Health*, eds C. Waddell & A. Petersen, Churchill Livingstone, Melbourne, 119–33.
Gray, J. 2002a, *False Dawn: The Delusions of Global Capitalism*, Granta Books, London.
——2002b, 'The true limits of globalization', *Ethical Perspectives*, 9(4), 191–9.
Graycar, A. 2001, 'Crime in twentieth century Australia' in *Year Book Australia 2001*, cat. no. 1301.0, ABS, Canberra, 477–95.
Green, E., Hebron, S. & Woodward, D. 1990, *Women's Leisure, What Leisure?*, Macmillan, London.
Green, J. C., Rozell, M. J. & Wilcox, C. (eds) 2003, *The Christian Right in American Politics: Marching to the Millennium*, Georgetown University Press, Washington, DC.
Green, N. 1982, 'The classroom teacher's influence on the performance of Aboriginal children' in *Aboriginal Education*, ed. J. Sherwood, Creative Research, Perth.
Green, P. 1985, 'Multi-ethnic teaching and the pupils' self-concepts', Annexe B in Swann Report, 1985.
Greenberg, D. F. 1988, *The Construction of Homosexuality*, University of Chicago Press, Chicago.
Greene, S. 2004, 'Biological determinism: persisting problems for the psychology of women', *Feminism & Psychology*, 14(3), 431–5.
Greenfeld, L. 1993, *Nationalism: Five Roads to Modernity*, Harvard University Press, Cambridge.
Greenfield, S. M. 1961, 'Industrialization and the family in sociological theory', *American Journal of Sociology*, 67, 312–22.
Gregory, B. & Hunter, B. 1996, 'Is there an Australian underclass?', *Urban Futures: Issues for Australian Cities*, 18(95), 14–24.
Gregory, L. & Hutchins, B. 2004, 'Everyday editorial practices and the public sphere: analysing the Letters to the Editor page of a regional newspaper', *Media International Australia*, 112, 186–200.
Greider, W. 2004 [1997], 'Wawasan 2020 (extract from Wawasan 2020)' in *The Globalization Reader*, 2nd edn, eds F. J. Lechner & J. Boli, Blackwell Publishing, Oxford, 160–6.
Grenfell, M. & James, J. 1998, *Bourdieu and Education: Acts of Practical Theory*, Falmer Press, London.
Griffin, D. R. 1998a, 'Introduction: postmodern spirituality and society' in *Spirituality and Society*, ed. D. R. Griffin, State University of New York Press, Albany, NY.
——1998b, 'Introduction to SUNY series in constructive post modern thought' in *Sacred Interconnections*, ed. D. R. Griffin, State University of New York Press, Albany, NY.
Grimshaw, P. & Willett, G. 1981, 'Women's history and family history: an exploration of colonial family structure' in *Australian Women*, eds N. Grieve & P. Grimshaw, Oxford University Press, Melbourne, 134–55.
Grint, K. 1991, *The Sociology of Work*, Polity Press, Cambridge.
Gripsrud, J. 1995, *The Dynasty Years: Hollywood Television and Critical Media Studies*, Routledge, London.
Groenewegen, P. D. 1983, 'The political economy of Federalism, 1901–81' in *State and Economy in Australia*, ed. B. W. Head, Oxford University Press, Melbourne, 169–95.
——1995 'The political economy of Federalism since 1970' in *State, Economy and Public Policy*, eds S. Bell & B. Head, Oxford University Press, Melbourne, 169–93.
Guggenheim, M. 2005, *What's Wrong with Children's Rights?*, Harvard University Press, Cambridge, Mass.

Guillén, M. F. 2001, 'Is globalization civilizing, destructive or feeble? A critique of five key debates on the social science literature', *Annual Review of Sociology*, 27, 235–60.

Gunter, B. G. & van der Hoeven, R. 2004, 'The social dimension of globalization: a review of the literature', *International Labour Review*, 143(1–2), 7–43.

Guttmann, A. 1978, *From Ritual to Record: The Nature of Modern Sports*, Columbia University Press, New York.

Habermas, J. 1976, *Legitimation Crisis*, Heinemann, London.

——1984, *The Theory of Communicative Action*, Vol. 1, Heinemann, London.

——1987, *The Theory of Communicative Action*, Vol. 2, Beacon Press, Boston.

——1989 [1962], *The Structural Transformation of the Public Sphere*, Polity Press, Cambridge.

——1992, 'Further reflections on the public sphere' in *Habermas and the Public Sphere*, ed. C. Calhoun, MIT Press, Cambridge, Massachusetts, 421–61.

——1996, *Between Facts and Norms: Contributions to a Discourse Theory of Law and Democracy*, MIT Press, Cambridge, Mass.

——1997, 'The public sphere' in *Contemporary Political Philosophy: An Anthology*, eds R. E. Goodin & P. Pettit, Blackwell, Oxford, 105–8.

Habibis, D. & Walter, M. 2009, *Social Inequality in Australia: Discourses, Realities and Futures*, Oxford University Press, Melbourne.

Hacking, I. 1999, *The Social Construction of What?*, Harvard University Press, Cambridge, Mass.

Haebich, A. 1988, *For Their Own Good*, University of Western Australia Press, Perth.

Hagan, J. 1996, 'The class and crime controversy' in *Criminological Controversies: A Methodological Primer*, eds J. Hagan, A. Gillis & A. & D. Brownfield, Westview Press, Boulder.

——2003, *Justice in the Balkans: Prosecuting War Crimes in the Hague Tribunal*, University of Chicago Press, Chicago.

Hagan, J. & Levi, R. 2005, 'Crimes of war and the force of law', *Social Forces*, 83, 1499–1534.

Hagan, J., Schoenfeld, H. & Palloni, A. 2006, 'The science of human rights, war crimes, and humanitarian emergencies', *Annual Review of Sociology*, 32, 329–49.

Hajnal, J. 1982, 'Two kinds of preindustrial household system', *Population & Development Review*, 8(3), 449–94.

Halbwachs, M. 1930, *Les Causes de Suicide*, Alcan, Paris.

Hall, S. 1981, 'Notes on de-constructing "The Popular"' in *People's History and Socialist Theory*, ed. R. Samuel, History Workshop Series, Routledge & Kegan Paul, London, 227–40.

——1990, 'Encoding, decoding' in *The Cultural Studies Reader*, ed. S. During, Routledge, London, 507–17.

——1991, 'Old and new identities, old and new ethnicities' in *Culture, Globalisation and the World System*, ed. A. D. King, Macmillan, Basingstoke.

——1992, 'Our mongrel selves', *New Statesman & Society*, 19 June, 6–8.

Hall, S. & Jefferson, T. 1976, *Resistance through Rituals: Youth Subcultures in Post-war Britain*, HarperCollins Academic, London.

Hall, S., Critcher, C., Jefferson, T., Clarke, J. & Roberts, B. 1979, *Policing the Crisis*, Macmillan, London.

Halliday, T. C. & Osinsky, P. 2006, 'Globalization of law', *Annual Review of Sociology*, 32, 447–70.

Halsey, A. H., Heath, A. F. & Ridge, J. M. 1980, *Origins and Destinations: Family, Class and Education in Modern Britain*, Clarendon Press, Oxford.

Halsey, A. H., Lauder, H. Brown, P. & Wells, A. S. (eds) 1997, *Education, Culture, Economy, Society*, Oxford University Press, Oxford.

Hamilton, P. 2002, 'The practice of sociology: mapping the field' in *The Uses of Sociology*, (eds) P. Hamilton & K. Thompson, Blackwell Publishing, Oxford, 1–29.

Hammersley, M. 1992, 'On feminist methodology', *Sociology*, 26(2), 187–206.

Hammersley, M. & Atkinson, P. 1983, *Ethnography: Principles in Practice*, Routledge, London.

Hannerz, U. 1992, *Cultural Complexity*, Columbia University Press, New York.

——1996, *Transnational Connections*, Routledge, London.

Harbury, C. D. & Hitchens, D. M. W. M. 1979, *Inheritance and Wealth Inequality in Britain*, Allen & Unwin, London.

Harding, A. 2005, *Recent Trends in Income Inequality*, Online Conference Paper CP0505, National Centre for Social and Economic Modelling, www.natsem.canberra.edu.au/publication.jsp?titleID=CP0505, accessed 14 April 2005.

Harding, A., Lloyd, R. & Warren, N. 2004, *Income Distribution and Redistribution: The Impact of Selected Government Benefits and Taxes in Australia in 2001–02*, Online Discussion Paper CP2004_04, www.natsem.canberra.edu.au/publicationsByYear.jsp?year=2004, accessed 3 May 2004.

Harding, A. & Richardson, S. 1998, *Unemployment and Income Distribution*, NATSEM paper DP32, www.natsem.canberra.edu.au/publicationsByYear.jsp?year=1998, accessed 3 May 2005.

Harding, S. (ed.) 1987, *Feminism and Methodology*, Indiana University Press, Bloomington.

Hardman, C. 1973, 'Can there be an anthropology of children?', *Journal of the Anthropological Society of Oxford*, 4, 85–99.

Hardt, M. & Negri, A. 2000, *Empire*, Harvard University Press, Cambridge, Mass.

Hareven, T. K. 1987, 'Historical analysis of the family' in *Handbook of Marriage and the Family*, eds M. B. Sussman & S. K. Steinmetz, Plenum Press, New York, 37–57.

Harris, C. C. 1983 [1969], *The Family and Industrial Society*, Allen & Unwin, London.

Harris, E., Nutbeam, D. & Sainsbury, P. 2001, 'Does our limited analysis of the dimensions of poverty limit the way we seek solutions?', in *The Social Origins of Health and Well-Being*, eds R. Eckersley, J. Dixon & B. Douglas, Cambridge University Press, Melbourne, 259–68.

Harris, F. 2005, 'Presidents need contact with God, says Bush', *The Age*, 14 January, www.theage.com.au/news/World/Presidents-need-contact-with-God-says-Bush/2005, accessed 14 January 2005.

Harrison, M. 1989, 'Who's to blame?', *Family Matters*, 24, 46–9.

Hart, C. W. M., Pillig, A. R. and Goodale, J. C. 1988, *The Tiwi of North Australia*, 3rd edn, Holt, Rinehart & Winston, New York.

Hart, N. 1976, *When Marriage Ends*, Tavistock, London.

Hartley, J. 1992, *The Politics of Pictures: The Creation of the Public in the Age of Popular Media*, Routledge, London.

——1996, *Popular Reality: Journalism, Modernity, Popular Culture*, Arnold, London.

———1999, 'What is journalism? The view from under a stubbie cap', *Media International Australia*, 90, 15–33.

———2000, 'Communicative democracy in a redactional society: the future of journalism studies', *Journalism: Theory, Practice & Criticism*, 1(1), 39–48.

Hartman, P. & Husband, C. 1974, *Racism and the Mass Media*, Davis-Poynter, London.

Hartman, T. 2007, 'On the Ikeaization of France', *Public Culture*, 19(3), 483–98.

Hartmann, H. 1981, 'The unhappy marriage of Marxism and Feminism: toward a more progressive union' in *Women and Revolution*, ed. L. Sargent, Black Rose Books, Montreal, 1–41.

Harvey, D. 1990, *The Condition of Postmodernity*, Blackwell, Cambridge.

Harvey, D. 2005, *A Brief History of Neoliberalism*, Oxford University Press, New York.

Hassan, R. 1995, *Suicide Explained: The Australian Experience*, Melbourne University Press, Melbourne.

Hassan, R., Healy, J. & McKenna, R. B. 1985, 'Lebanese families' in *Ethnic Family Values in Australia*, ed. D. Storer, Prentice Hall, Sydney, 173–98.

Hawken, P. 2001, 'Seattle' in *Take It Personally: How Globalization Affects You and Powerful Ways to Change It*, ed. A. Roddick, Thorsons, London, 22–9.

Hay, C. & Marsh, D. 2000, 'Introduction: demystifying globalization' in *Demystifying Globalization*, eds C. Hay & D. Marsh, Macmillan, Houndsmill, Basingstoke, 1–17.

Hayek, F. 1976, *Law, Legislation and Liberty, Vol 2: The Mirage of Social Justice*, University of Chicago Press, Chicago.

Hayes, S. 1996, 'Minorities as victims and offenders' in *Crime and Justice*, ed. K. Hazlehurst, Law Book Company, Sydney, 317–48.

Hazlehurst, K. 1992, 'Aboriginal and police relations' in *Policing Australia*, eds P. Moir & H. Eijman, Macmillan, Melbourne.

Hazlehurst, K. M. & Braithwaite, J. 1993, 'Crime in Australia' in *A Sociology of Australian Society*, eds J. Najman & J. Western, Macmillan, Melbourne, 369–401.

Head, B. W. 1983, 'The Australian political economy' in *State and Economy in Australia*, ed. B. W. Head, Oxford University Press, Melbourne 3–21.

Headey, B. & Wooden, M. 2007, in *Rethinking Wellbeing*, L. Manderson, API Network, Perth.

Healy, J., Hassan, R. & McKenna, R. B. 1985, 'Aboriginal families' in *Ethnic Family Values in Australia*, ed. D. Storer, Prentice Hall, Sydney, 291–332.

Hearn, J. 2008, 'What's wrong with domination?', *Journal of Power*, 1(1), 37–49.

Hearn, J. & Morgan, D. H. J. 1990, 'Men, masculinities and social theory' in *Men, Masculinities and Social Theory*, eds J. Hearn & D. H. J. Morgan, Unwin Hyman, 1–18.

Hearn, J. & Parkin, W. 1987, *'Sex' at 'Work'*, St Martin's Press, Brighton.

Hearn, J., Sheppard, D. L., Tancred-Sheriff, P. & Burrell, G. (eds) 1989, *The Sexuality of Organizations*, Sage, London.

Heelas, P. 1996, *The New Age Movement*, Blackwell Publishing, Oxford.

Heidegger, M. 1971, 'The thing' in *Poetry, Language, Thought*, Harper & Row, New York, 165–82.

Heidensohn, F. 1986, *Women and Crime*, Macmillan, London.

———1989, *Crime and Society*, Macmillan, London.

Hein, H. 1992, 'Liberating philosophy: an end to the dichotomy of spirit and matter' in *Women, Knowledge and Reality*, A. Garry & M. Pearsall, Routledge, London, 293–311.

Held, D. et al. n.d., *What is globalization?*, www.polity.co.uk/global/whatisglobalization.asp.

Helleiner, E. 1994, 'Freeing money: why have states been more willing to liberalize capital controls than trade barriers?', *Policy Sciences*, 27(4), 299–318.

———1996, *States and the Re-emergence of Global Finance*, Cornell University Press, Ithaca, NY.

Henderson, R., Harcourt, A. & Harper, R. 1970, *People in Poverty: A Melbourne Survey*, University of Melbourne, Melbourne.

Hendrick, H. 1997, *Children, Childhood and English Society, 1880–1990*, Cambridge University Press, Cambridge.

Henry, M., Knight, J., Lingard, R. & Taylor, S. 1988, *Understanding Schooling*, Routledge, London.

Hepburn, J. 1977, 'The impact of police intervention upon juvenile delinquents', *Criminology*, 15, 235–62.

Herdt, G. (ed.) 1981, *Guardians of the Flutes*, McGraw-Hill, New York.

———1984, *Ritualized Homosexuality in Melanesia*, University of California Press, Berkeley.

———1990, 'Developmental discontinuities & sexual orientation across cultures' in *Homosexuality/Heterosexuality*, eds D. P. McWhirter, S. A. Sanders & J. M. Reinisch, Oxford University Press, Oxford, 208–36.

Herlihy, D. 1985, *Medieval Households*, Harvard University Press, Cambridge, Mass.

Hermassi, E. 1978, 'Politics and culture in the Middle East', *Social Compass*, 25(3–4), 445–64.

Hermes, J. 2006, 'Citizenship in the age of the internet', *European Journal of Communication*, 21(3), 295–309.

Herrnstein, R. & Murray, C. 1994, *The Bell Curve: Intelligence and Class Structure in American Life*, Simon & Schuster, London.

Hess, D. J. 1993, *Science in the New Age*, University of Wisconsin Press, Madison, Wisconsin.

Heydebrand, W. 2000, 'Globalization and the rule of law at the end of the 20th century', *European Yearbook for the Sociology of Law*, 25–128.

Heywood, A. 1998, *Political Ideologies: An Introduction*, 2nd edn, Macmillan, Houndsmill, Basingstoke.

Hiatt, L. 1985, 'Maidens, males and Marx: some contrasts in the work of Frederick Rose and Claude Meillassoux', *Oceania*, 56, 34–46.

Hiatt, L. R. 1996, *Arguments about Aborigines: Australia and the Evolution of Social Anthropology*, Cambridge University Press, Cambridge.

Hickox, M. 1982, 'The Marxist sociology of education: a critique', *British Journal of Sociology*, 33(4), 563–78.

Higgins, K. 1997, *Exploring Motor Vehicle Theft in Australia*, Trends and Issues in Crime and Criminal Justice, Australian Institute of Criminology, Canberra.

Higley, J., Deacon, D. & Smart, D. 1979, *Elites in Australia*, Routledge & Kegan Paul, London.

Hill, B. 1990, 'Who should control schools?' in *Issues in Australian Education*, eds V. D'Cruz & P. Langford, Longman Cheshire, Melbourne, 55–81.

Hindess, B. 1987, *Politics and Class Analysis*, Blackwell Publishing, Oxford.

—— 1996, *Discourses of Power: From Hobbes to Foucault*, Blackwell Publishing, Oxford.

Hindess, B. & Dean, M. (eds) 1998, *Governing Australia: Studies in Contemporary Rationalities of Government*, Cambridge University Press, Melbourne.

Hirschi, T. 1969, *The Causes of Delinquency*, University of California Press, Berkeley.

Hirst, P. 2000, 'Why the nation still matters' in *Globalization: The Reader*, eds J. Beyon & D. Dunkerley, The Athlone Press, London, 241–6.

Hirst, P. & Thompson, G. 1992, 'The problem of "globalization": international economic relations, national economic management and the formation of trading blocs', *Economy & Society*, 21(4), 357–96.

—— 1995, 'Globalization and the future of the nation-state', *Economy & Society*, 24(3), 408–42.

—— 1999 [1996], *Globalization in Question*, 2nd edn, Polity Press, Cambridge.

Hirst, P., Thompson, G. & Bromley, S. 2009, *Globalization in Question*, 3rd edn, Polity Press, Cambridge.

Hitchner, R. B. 2008, 'Globalization avant la lettre: globalization and the history of the Roman Empire', *New Global Studies*, 2(2), 1–12.

Ho, C. & Alcorso, C. 2004, 'Migrants and employment', *Journal of Sociology*, 40(3), 237–60.

Hobbes, T. 1914 [1651], *Leviathan*, J. M. Dent, London.

—— 1983, *De Cive*, Clarendon Press, Oxford.

Hobhouse, L. T. 1906, *Morals in Evolution: A Study in Comparative Ethics*, Holt, New York.

Hochschild, A. R. 1983, *The Managed Heart*, University of California Press, Berkeley.

Hogan, M. 1984, *Public vs. Private Schools*, Penguin, Melbourne.

—— 1987, *The Sectarian Strand: Religion in Australian History*, Penguin, Melbourne.

Hogan, T. 1996, 'Globalisation: experiences and expectations' in *Social Self, Global Culture: An Introduction to Sociological Ideas*, ed. A. Kellehear, Oxford University Press, Melbourne, 275–88.

Holland, J. 1981, 'Social class and changes in orientation to meaning', *Sociology*, 15(1), 1–18.

Holm, J. (ed.) 1994, *Women in Religion*, Themes in Religious Studies Series, Pinter, London.

Holmes, D. 2005, *Communication Theory: Media, Technology and Society*, Sage, London.

Holmwood, J. 2007, 'Sociology as public discourse and professional practice: a critique of Michael Burawoy', *Sociological Theory*, 25(1), 46–66.

Hoogenboom, M. & Ossewaarde, R. 2005, 'From iron cage to pigeon house: the birth of reflexive authority', *Organization Studies*, 26(4), 601–19.

Hooper, M. 1998, 'Up, up and away', *Business Review Weekly*, 20(19), 72–3.

Hopkins, A. 1980, 'Power, elites and ideology: a commentary on elites in Australia', *Australian & New Zealand Journal of Sociology*, 16(1), 73–8.

—— 2006, *Global History: Interactions between the Universal and the Local*, Palgrave Macmillan, Basingstoke.

Hopkins, T. K. & Wallerstein, I. 1996, 'The world-system: is there a crisis?' in *The Age of Transition: Trajectory of the World-System 1945–2025*, eds T. K. Hopkins & I. Wallerstein, Zed Books, London, 1–10.

Horkheimer, M. 1982, *Critical Theory*, Continuum, New York.

Horton, D. & Wohl, R. 1956, 'Mass communication and parasocial interaction: observations on intimacy at a distance', *Psychiatry*, 19, 215–29.

Hosokawa, S. 1999, '"Salso No Tiene Frontera": Orquest de la Luz and the globalization of popular music', *Cultural Studies*, 13(3), 509–34.

House of Representatives Standing Committee on Aboriginal & Torres Strait Islander Affairs 1994, *Justice under Scrutiny: Report of the Inquiry by Governments of the Recommendations of the Royal Commission into Aboriginal Deaths in Custody*, AGPS, Canberra, November.

Hout, M., Brooks, C. & Manza, J. 1996, 'The persistence of classes in post-industrial societies' in *Conflicts about Class*, eds J. Lee & B. Turner, Longman, Harlow.

HREOC (Human Rights and Equal Opportunities Commission) 2004, *A Statistical Overview of Aboriginal and Torres Strait Islander Peoples in Australia*, www.hreoc.gov.au/social_justice/statistics/, accessed 7 January 2005.

—— 1995, *Racist Violence: Report of the National Inquiry into Racist Violence in Australia*, AGPS, Canberra.

Hughes, E. E. 1971, *The Sociological Eye: Selected Papers*, Aldine-Atherton, Chicago.

Hughes, J. A. 1984, 'Bureaucracy' in *Applied Sociological Perspectives*, eds R. J. Anderson & W. W. Sharrock, Allen & Unwin, London, 106–24.

Hughes, J. A., Martin, P. J. & Sharrock, W. W. 1995, *Understanding Classical Sociology*, Sage, London.

Hughes, P. & Bond, S. with Bellamy, J. & Black, A. 2003, *Exploring What Australians Value*, Research Paper No. 5, Christian Research Association and NCLS Research, Openbook Publishers, Adelaide.

Hughson, J. 1997, 'Football, folk dancing and Fascism', *Australian and New Zealand Journal of Sociology*, 33, 2, 167–86.

Hugo, G. 1986, *Australia's Changing Population*, Oxford University Press, Melbourne.

—— 1992, 'Australia's contemporary and future fertility and mortality: trends, differentials and implications' in *Population Issues and Australia's Future*, ed. National Population Council, AGPS, Canberra.

—— 2001, 'A century of population change in Australia', *Year Book Australia 2001*, cat. no. 1301.0, ABS, Canberra, 169–210.

Huizinga, J. 2003, *Homo Ludens: A Study of the Play Element in Culture*, Taylor Francis, London.

Hume, L. 1997, *Witchcraft and Paganism in Australia*, Melbourne University Press, Melbourne.

Humphrey, M. 1984, 'Religion, law and family disputes in a Lebanese Muslim community in Sydney' in *Ethnicity, Class and Gender in Australia*, eds G. Bottomley & M. de Lepervanche, George Allen & Unwin, Sydney, 183–98.

Hunter, I. 1994, *Rethinking the School: Subjectivity, Bureaucracy, Criticism*, Allen & Unwin, Sydney.

Hunter, J. D. 1991, *Culture Wars: The Struggle to Define America*, Basic Books, New York.

Huntington, S. P. 1993, 'The clash of civilizations', *Foreign Affairs*, 72(3), 22–49.

——2004 [1993], 'The clash of civilizations' in *The Globalization Reader*, 2nd edn, eds F. J. Lechner & J. Boli, Blackwell Publishing, Oxford, 36–43.

Hutchins, B. 2002, *Don Bradman: Challenging the Myth*, Cambridge University Press, Melbourne.

Hutchins, B. & Lester, L. 2006, 'Environmental protest and tap-dancing with the media in the Information Age', *Media, Culture & Society*, 28(3), 433–51.

Hutchins, B. & Mikosza, J. 1998, 'Australian Rugby League and violence 1970 to 1995: a case study in the maintenance of masculine hegemony', *Journal of Sociology*, 34(3), 246–63.

Hutchins, B., Rowe, D. & Ruddock, A. 2009, '"It's fantasy football made real": networked media sport, the internet and the hybrid reality of MyFootballClub', *Sociology of Sport Journal*, 26(1), 89–106.

Hyman, R. 1984, *Strikes*, 3rd edn, Fontana, Aylesbury.

Ikenberry, J. 1992, 'A world restored: expert consensus and the Anglo-American post-war settlement', *International Organization*, 46(1), 289–321.

Illich, I. 1971, *Deschooling Society*, Harper & Row, New York.

——1999 [1975], *Limits to Medicine: Medical Nemesis, The Expropriation of Health*, Marion Boyars, London.

Imray, L. & Middleton, A. 1983, 'Public and private: marking the boundaries' in *The Public and the Private*, eds E. Gamarnikow et al., Heinemann, London.

Indermaur, D. 1996, *Violent Crime in Australia: Interpreting the Trends*, Trends and Issues Paper No. 61, Australian Institute of Criminology, Canberra, October.

Innes, M. & Jones, V. 2006, *Neighbourhood Security and Urban Change: Risk, Resilience and Recovery*, Joseph Rowntree Foundation, York.

Innis, H. A. 1950, *Empire and Communications*, Clarendon Press, Oxford.

——1951, *The Bias of Communication*, University of Toronto Press, Toronto.

——2004, *Changing Concepts of Time*, Rowman & Littlefield Publishers, Lanham, Maryland.

International Monetary Fund 2004, *The IMF at a Glance: A Fact Sheet*, www.imf.org, accessed 22 March 2005.

Internet Worldwide Stats 2009, www.internetworldstats.com/stats.htm, accessed 20 February 2009.

Irigaray, l. 1986, 'Women, the Sacred, and Money', trans. D. Knight & M. Whitford, *Paragraph*, 8 (October), 6–18.

——1987, *Sexes et Parentés*, Minuit, Paris.

Ironmonger, D. (ed.) 1989, *Households Work*, Allen & Unwin, Sydney.

Irwin, J. 1970, *The Felon*, Prentice Hall, Englewood Cliffs.

Jackson, S. 2006, 'The sexual self in late modernity' in *The Sexual Self: the Construction of Sexual Scripts*, ed. M. Kimmel, Vanderbilt University Press, Nashville, 3–15.

Jacoby, H. 1973, *The Bureaucratization of the World*, University of California Press, Berkeley.

Jakubowicz, A. 1981, 'State and ethnicity', *Australian & New Zealand Journal of Sociology*, 17(3), 4–13.

——(ed.) 1994, *Racism, Ethnicity and the Media*, Allen & Unwin, Sydney.

James, A. & Prout, A. (eds) 1997 [1990], *Constructing and Reconstructing Childhood*, 2nd edn, Falmer Press, London.

James, A., Jenks, C. & Prout, A. 1998, *Theorising Childhood*, Polity Press, Cambridge.

James, A., James, A. L. & McNamee, S. 2004, 'Turn down the volume? Not hearing children in family proceedings', *Child & Family Law Quarterly*, 16(2), 189–203.

James, M. & Carcach, C. 1997, *Homicide in Australia: 1989–96*, Research and Public Policy Series No. 13, Australian Institute of Criminology, Canberra.

James, R., Anderson, M., Bexley, E., Devlin, M., Garnett, R., Marginson, S. & Maxwell, L. 2008, *Participation and Equity: A Review of the Participation in Higher Education of People from Low Socioeconomic Backgrounds and Indigenous People*, Universities Australia, Canberra.

James, R., Baldwin, G., Coates, H., Krause, K. L. & McInnis, C. 2004, *Analysis of Equity Groups in Higher Education, 1991–2002*, Department of Education, Science and Training, Centre for the Study of Higher Education, University of Melbourne.

Jamieson, L. 1999, 'Intimacy transformed? A critical look at the "pure relationship"', *Sociology*, 33(3), 477–94.

Jamrozik, A. 1991, *Class, Inequality and the State: Social Change, Social Policy and the New Middle Class*, Macmillan, Melbourne.

Jayasuriya, K. 2001, 'Globalization, sovereignty, and the rule of law: from political to economic constitutionalism?', *Constellations*, 8(4), 442–60.

Jencks, C. 1972, *Inequality: a Reassessment of the Effect of Family and Schooling in America*, Basic Books, New York.

Jenkins, H. 2004, 'The cultural logic of media convergence', *International Journal of Cultural Studies*, 7(1), 33–43.

——2006a, *Convergence Culture: Where Old and New Media Collide*, New York University Press, New York.

——2006b, *Fans, Bloggers, and Gamers: Exploring Participatory Culture*, New York University Press, New York.

Jenkins, R. 1992, *Pierre Bourdieu*, Routledge, London.

Jenks, C. 1982, 'Constituting the child' in *The Sociology of Childhood: Essential Readings*, ed. C. Jenks, Batsford Academic and Educational, London, 9–24.

Jensen, A. 1969, 'How much can we boost IQ and scholastic achievement?', *Harvard Educational Review*, 39, 2–51.

——1973, *Educational Differences*, Methuen, London.

Jessop, B. 1990, *State Theory*, Polity Press, Cambridge.

Joas, H. 2009, *Social Theory: Twenty Introductory Lectures*, Cambridge University Press, Cambridge.

Johnson, L. 1988, *The Unseen Voice: A Cultural Study of Early Australian Radio*, Routledge, London.

Johnson, T. J. 1972, *Professions and Power*, Macmillan, London.

Johnson-Woods, T. 2002, *Big Bother*, University of Queensland Press, Brisbane.

Jones, A. 2006, *Dictionary of Globalization*, Polity Press, Cambridge.

Jones, F. 1991, 'Economic status of Aboriginal and other Australians: a comparison' in *Aboriginal Employment Equity by the Year 2000*, ed. J. C. Altman, Academy of the Social Sciences in Australia and Centre for Aboriginal Economic Policy Research, Australian National University, Canberra, 27–46.

——1993, 'Unlucky Australians: labour market outcomes among Aboriginal Australians', *Ethnic and Racial Studies*, 16, 420–58.

——1997, 'Ethnic diversity and national identity', *Australian and New Zealand Journal of Sociology*, 33, 3, 285–305.

Jones, F. L. 1975, 'The changing shape of the Australian income distribution, 1914–15, and 1968–69', *Australian Economic History Review*, 15(1), 21–34.

Jones, S. 1993, 'We are all cousins under the skin', *The Independent*, 12 December.

Julian, R. 1998, 'I love driving', *Race, Class and Gender*, 5(2), 112–24.

Jupp, J. 1986, *Don't Settle for Less*, AGPS, Canberra.

Kalantzis, M. & Cope, B. 1984, 'Multiculturalism and education policy' in *Ethnicity, Class and Gender in Australian Society*, eds G. Bottomley & M. de Lepervanche, George Allen & Unwin, Sydney, 82–97.

Kalyvas, A. 2003, 'Feet of clay? Reflections on Hardt's and Negri's *Empire*', *Constellations*, 10(2), 264–79.

Kamin, L. J. 1974, *The Science and Politics of IQ*, John Wiley & Sons, New York.

Kanter, R. M. 1977, *Men and Women of the Corporation*, Basic Books, New York.

Kapferer, B. 1988, *Legends of the People*, Smithsonian Institution Press, Washington.

Karmel, P. 1973, *Schools in Australia: Report of the Interim Committee for the Australian Schools Commission*, AGPS, Canberra.

Karon, T. 2002, 'Adieu, Ronald McDonald', *Time*, 24 January.

Katz, A. 1979, 'Self-help groups, some clarifications', *Social Science & Medicine*, 13a, 491–4.

Katz, J. E. & Aakhus, M. (eds) 2002, *Perpetual Contact: Mobile Communication, Private Talk, Public Performance*, Cambridge University Press, New York.

Katz, A. & Levin, L. 1980, 'Self-care is not a solipsistic trap', *International Journal of Health Services*, 10, 329–36.

Katz, J., Rice, R. E. & Acord, S. 2006, 'Uses of the internet and mobile technology in health systems: organizational and social issues in a comparative context' in *The Network Society: From Knowledge to Policy*, eds. M. Castells & G. Cardoso, John Hopkins Center for Transatlantic Relations, Washington, DC, 183–214.

Kautsky, K. 1953, *Foundations of Christianity*, Russell, New York.

Kawai, M. 2002, 'Discussion' in *Globalisation, Living Standards and Inequality: Recent Progress and Continuing Challenges, Proceedings of a Conference Held in Sydney on 27–28 May 2002*, eds D. Gruen, T. O'Brien & J. Lawson, Reserve Bank of Australia and Australian National Treasury, Canberra, 93–5.

Kay, T. 1989, 'Unemployment' in *Developments in Sociology*, Vol. 5, ed. M. Haralambos, Causeway Press, Ormskirk.

Keat, R. & Urry, J. 1982, *Social Theory as Science*, 2nd edn, Routledge & Kegan Paul, London.

Keating, P. 1999, 'Globalisation: Australia in the global context' in *Globalisation: Issues in Society*, ed. J. Healey, The Spiney Press, Sydney, 10–12.

Keefe, K. 1992, *From the Centre to the City: Aboriginal Education, Culture and Power*, Aboriginal Studies Press, Canberra.

Keenan, T. 1982, 'Translator's afterword: Foucault on government', *Philosophy & Social Criticism*, 9(1), 35–40.

Kellehear, A. 1990, *Dying of Cancer*, Harwood, Melbourne.

Kelley, J., Cushins, R. G. & Headey, B. 1987, *Australian Social Science Data Archives*, Australian National University, Canberra.

Kellner, D. 1992, 'Popular culture and the construction of postmodern identities' in *Modernity and Identity*, eds S. Lash & J. Friedman, Basil Blackwell, Oxford, 141–77.

Kelly, A. (ed.) 1981, *The Missing Half: Girls and Science Education*, Manchester University Press, Manchester.

Kelly, A. A. 1992, 'An update on neopagan witchcraft in America' in *Perspectives on the New Age*, eds J. R. Lewis & G. Melton, State University of New York Press, Albany, NY.

Kelly, H. E. 1979, 'Biosociology and crime' in *Biology and Crime*, ed. C. R. Jeffery, Sage, Beverley Hills.

Kelly, L. 1987, 'The continuum of sexual violence' in *Women, Violence and Social Control*, eds J. Hanmer & M. Maynard, Macmillan, London.

Kelly, R. 2004, *Australia: Government and Media Attack Aboriginal Community after Redfern Riot*, www.wsws.org/articles/2004/feb2004/redf-f20.shtml, accessed 3 June 2005.

Kelly, R., Holborn, M. & Makin, J. 1983, 'Unit 2: Positivistic theories' in Open College of the North West, *Criminology Distance Learning Course*, Preston Polytechnic.

Kelly, S. 2001, 'Trends in Australian wealth: new estimates for the 1990s', paper presented at the 30th Annual Conference of Economists, University of Western Australia, online conference paper CPO108, NATSEM, www.natsem.canberra.edu.au/publication.jsp?titleID=CP0108, accessed 14 April 2005.

Kelly, S. & Harding, A. 2007, *Don't Rely on the Old Folks' Money*, National Centre for Social and Economic Modelling, Canberra, www.apo.org.au/linkboard/results.chtml?filename_num=130881, accessed 23 February 2008.

Kelman, S. 1975, 'The social nature of the definition of a problem in health', *International Journal of Health Services*, 5, 625–42.

Kemeny, J. 1980, 'Dependent economy, dependent ruling class' in *Australia and World Capitalism*, eds G. Crough, E. L. Wheelwright & E. Wilshire, Penguin, Melbourne, 191–6.

Kempe, C. H., Silverman, F. N., Steele, H. F., Droegemuller, W. & Silver, H. K. 1962, 'The battered child syndrome', *Journal of the American Medical Association*, 181, 17–24.

Keohane, R. O. & Nye, J. S. Jr. 2000a, 'Globalization: What's new? What's not? (And so what?)', *Foreign Policy*, 118, 104–19.

——2000b, 'Introduction' in *Governance in a Globalizing World*, eds J. S. Nye and J. D. Donahue, Brookings Institution Press, Washington, DC, 1–44.

Kerr, C. & Siegel, A. 1954, 'The inter-industry propensity to strike' in *Industrial Conflict*, eds A. Kornhauser, R. Dubin & A. M. Ross, McGraw-Hill, New York.

Kessler, S. J. & McKenna, W. 1978, *Gender: an Ethnomethodological Approach*, John Wiley & Sons, New York.

Key, E. 1909, *The Century of the Child*, Putnams & Sons, New York.

Kiely, R. 2005, 'Globalization and poverty, and the poverty of globalization theory', *Current Sociology*, 53(6), 895–14.

Kildea, G. & Leach, J. 1979, *Trobriand Cricket*, video, Ronin Films.

Kilmartin, C. 1989, '"Traditional" families', *Family Matters*, 24, 48.

Kilminster, R. 1997, 'Globalization as an emergent concept' in *The Limits of Globalization: Cases and Arguments*, ed. A. Scott, Routledge, New York, 257–26.

Kimmel, M. 1990, 'After fifteen years: the impact of the sociology of masculinity on the masculinity of sociology' in *Men, Masculinities and Social Theory*, eds J. Hearn & D. H. J. Morgan, Unwin Hyman, 93–109.

——(ed.) 2006, *The Sexual Self: The Construction of Sexual Scripts*, Vanderbilt University Press, Nashville, TN.

King, A. 1998, 'Income poverty since the early 1970s' in *Australian Poverty: Then and Now*, eds R. Fincher & J. Nieuwehuysen, Melbourne University Press, Australia.

King, R. S. & Mauer, M. 2001, *Ageing Behind Bars: 'Three Strikes' Seven Years Later—The Sentencing Project*, www.sentencing project.org/pubs_10.cfm, accessed 11 June 2005.

Kinsey, A. C., Pomeroy, W. B. & Martin, C. E. 1948, *Sexual Behaviour in the Human Male*, W. B. Saunders, Philadelphia.

Kinsey, A. C., Pomeroy, W. B., Martin, C. E. & Gebhard, P. H. 1953, *Sexual Behaviour in the Human Female*, W. B. Saunders, Philadelphia.

Klein, N. 2000, *No Logo: No Space, No Choice, No Jobs*, Flamingo, London.

Klineberg, O. 1951, *Race and Psychology*, UNESCO, Paris.

Klug, H. 2005, 'Transnational human rights: exploring the persistence and globalization of human rights', *Annual Review of Law & Social Science*, 1, 85–103.

Knowles, R. D. 2006, 'Transport shaping space: differential collapse in time–space', *Journal of Transport Geography*, 14(6), 407–25.

Koch, C. H. 2004, 'Envisioning a global legal culture', *Michigan Journal of International Law*, 25(1), 1–76.

Koedt, A. 1971, 'The myth of the vaginal orgasm' in *Voices from Women's Liberation*, ed. L. B. Tanner, New American Library, New York, 158–66.

Kohn, H. 1971, 'Nationalism and internationalism' in *History and the Idea of Mankind*, ed. W. W. Wagar, University of New Mexico Press, Albuquerque, 119–34.

Korzeniewicz, M. 2004 [1994], 'Commodity chains and marketing strategies: Nike and the global athletic footwear industry' in *The Globalization Reader*, 2nd edn, eds F. J. Lechner & J. Boli, Blackwell Publishing, Oxford, 167–76.

Kössler, R. 2000, 'Globalization and human rights: some developmental reflections' in *Globalization and Development Studies: Challenges for the 21st Century*, ed. F. J. Schuurman, Thela Thesis, Amsterdam, The Netherlands, 83–98.

Kübler-Ross, E. 1969, *On Death and Dying*, Macmillan, London.

Kuhn, M. H. 1954, 'Kinsey's view on human behaviour', *Social Problems*, 1, 119–25.

Kuhn, T. S. 1962, *The Structure of Scientific Revolutions*, University of Chicago Press, Chicago.

Kurtz, L. R. 1995, *Gods in a Global Village*, Pine Forge Press, CA.

Lafferty, Y. & McKay, J. 2004, 'Suffragettes in satin shorts?', *Qualitative Sociology*, 27(3), 249–76.

Laing, R. D. & Esterson, A. 1964, *Sanity, Madness and the Family*, Tavistock, London.

Lamont, A. & Maton, K. 2008, 'Choosing music: exploratory studies into the low uptake of music GCSE', *British Journal of Music Education*, 25(3), 267–82.

Lane, D. 1970, *Politics and Society in the USSR*, Weidenfeld & Nicolson, London.

Lang, M. 2006, 'Globalization and its history', *Journal of Modern History*, 78(4), 899–931.

Lapchick, R. E. 1999, *Racial and Gender Report Card*, Center for the Study of Sport and Society, Northeaster University.

Lareau, A. 1997, 'Social-class differences in family-school relationships: the importance of cultural capital' in *Education, Culture, Economy, Society*, eds A. H. Halsey, H. Lauder, P. Brown & A. S. Wells, Oxford University Press, Oxford.

Lasch, C. 1977, *Haven in a Heartless World*, Basic Books, New York.

Lash, S. 2002, *Critique of Information*, Sage, London.

Lash, S. & Urry, J. 1987, *The End of Organized Capitalism*, Polity Press, Cambridge.

——1994, *Economies of Signs and Spaces*, Sage, London.

Laslett, P. 1972, 'Mean household size in England since the sixteenth century' in *Household and Family in Past Time*, eds P. Laslett & R. Wall, Cambridge University Press, Cambridge, 125–58.

——1983, 'Family and household as work group and kin group: areas of traditional Europe compared' in *Family Forms in Historic Europe*, eds R. Wall, J. Robin & P. Laslett, Cambridge University Press, Cambridge, 513–63.

——1984, 'The family as a knot of individual interests' in *Households*, eds R. M. Netting, R. R. Wilk & E. J. Arnould, University of California Press, Berkeley, 353–79.

Latour, B. 1986, 'The powers of association' in *Power, Action and Belief: A New Sociology of Knowledge?*, ed. J. Law, Routledge & Kegan Paul, London, 264–80.

——2001, 'Gabriel Tarde and the end of the social' in *The Social in Question. New Bearings in History and the Social Sciences*, ed. P. J. Joyce, Routledge, London, 117–32.

——2005, *Reassembling the Social: An Introduction to Actor-Network Theory*, Oxford University Press, Oxford.

Lavalette, M. 1994, *Child Employment in the Capitalist Labour Market*, Avebury, Aldershot.

——1996, 'Thatcher's working children: contemporary issues of child labour' in *Thatcher's Children?*, eds J. Pilcher & S. Wagg, Falmer Press, London, 172–200.

Lawrence, E. 1982a, 'Just plain common sense: the roots of racism' in *The Empire Strikes Back*, eds Centre for Contemporary Cultural Studies, Hutchinson, London.

——1982b, 'In the abundance of water the fool is thirsty' in *The Empire Strikes Back*, eds Centre for Contemporary Cultural Studies, Hutchinson, London.

Lawton, D. 1975, *Class, Culture and the Curriculum*, Routledge & Kegan Paul, London.

Lazarsfeld, P., Berelson, B. & Gaudet, H. 1968, *The People's Choice: How the Voter Makes up His Mind in a Presidential Campaign*, Columbia University Press, New York.

Lea, J. & Young, J. 1984, *What Is to be Done about Law and Order?*, Penguin, Harmondsworth.

Leach, E. R. 1968a, *A Runaway World?*, BBC Publications, London.

——1968b, 'The cereal packet norm', *The Guardian*, 29 January, 8.

Lechner, F. J. 1990, 'Fundamentalism revisited' in *In Gods We Trust: New Patterns of Religious Pluralism in America*, eds T. Robbins & D. Anthony, Transaction Books, New Brunswick, NJ.

Lechner, F. 2009, *Globalization: The Making of World Society*, Wiley-Blackwell, Malden, MA.

Lechner, F. J. & Boli, J. (eds) 2004, *The Globalization Reader*, 2nd edn, Blackwell Publishing, Oxford.

Lee, D. & Newby, H. 1983, *The Problem of Sociology*, Hutchinson, London.

Lee, N. 1998, 'Towards an immature sociology', *Sociological Review*, 46(3), 458–82.

Lees, S. 1997, *Ruling Passions: Sexual Violence, Reputation and the Law*, Open University Press, Buckingham, UK.

Leigh, A. 2007, 'Intergenerational mobility in Australia', *The B.E. Journal of Economic Analysis & Policy*, www.bepress.com/bejeap/vol7/iss2/art6, accessed 30 December 2007.

Leiner, B., Cerf, V., Clark, D., Kahn, R., Kleinrock, L., Lynch, D., Postel, J., Roberts, L. & Wolff, S. 2000, *A Brief History of the Internet*, www.isoc.org/internet/history/brief.shtml.

Lemert, E. 1972 [1967], *Human Deviance, Social Problems and Social Control*, Prentice Hall, Englewood Cliffs, NJ.

Leonard, E. 1982, *Women, Crime and Society*, Longman, London.

Lepenies, W. 1988, *Between Literature and Science: the Rise of Sociology*, Cambridge University Press, Cambridge.

Lester, L. & Hutchins, B. 2009, 'Power games: environmental protest, news media and the internet', *Media, Culture & Society*, 31(4), 579–95.

Lever, R. 2007, 'CEO pay sparks backlash', *Sydney Morning Herald*, 13 February, www.news.com.au/adelaidenow/story/0,22606,21219412-5005962,00.html, accessed 30 December 2007.

Levine, D. 1997, 'Simmel reappraised: old images, new scholarship' in *Reclaiming the Sociological Classics*, ed. C. Camic, Blackwell, Oxford, 173–207.

Levinson, P. 1999, *Digital McLuhan: A Guide to the Information Millennium*, Routledge, London.

Lévi-Strauss, C. 1956, 'The family' in *Man, Culture, and Society*, ed. H. L. Shapiro, Oxford University Press, London, 261–85.

——1969, *The Elementary Structures of Kinship*, Beacon Press, Boston.

Levitt, T. 1983, 'The globalization of markets', *Harvard Business Review*, 61(3), 92–102.

Levy, M. J. 1965, 'Aspects of the analysis of family structure' in *Aspects of the Analysis of Family Structure*, eds A. J. Coale et al., Princeton University Press, Princeton, 1–63.

Lewis, J. 2009, 'What's the point of media studies?', *Television & New Media*, 10(1), 91–3.

Lewis, J. R. 1992, 'Approaches to the study of the New Age' in *Perspectives on the New Age*, eds J. R. Lewis & G. Melton, State University of New York Press, Albany, NY, 1–12.

——1996, 'Introduction' in *Magical Religion and Modern Witchcraft*, ed. J. R. Lewis, State University of New York, Albany, NY, 1–5.

Liazos, A. 1972, 'The poverty of the sociology of deviance: nuts, sluts and perverts', *Social Problems*, 20, 103–20.

Licht, B. G. & Dweck, C. S. 1987, 'Sex differences in achievement orientations' in *Gender and the Politics of Schooling*, eds M. Arnot & G. Weiner, Hutchinson, London, 95–107.

Liebel, M. 2003, 'Working children as social subjects: the contribution of working children's organizations to social transformations', *Childhood*, 10(3), 265–85.

Liebes, T. & Katz, E. 1990, *The Export of Meaning: Cross-Cultural Readings of Dallas*, Oxford University Press, New York.

Light, D. 1986, 'Corporate medicine for profit', *Scientific American*, 255(6), 38–45.

Lincoln, R. & Wilson, P. 1994, 'Aboriginal offending: patterns and causes' in *The Australian Criminal Justice System: The Mid-1990s*, eds D. Chappell & P. Wilson, Butterworths, Sydney, 61–86.

Lindroos, M. 1995, 'The problems of "girls" in an educational setting', *Gender and Education*, 7, 175–84.

Lingard, B., Martino, W., Mills, M. & Barr, M. 2002, *Addressing the Educational Needs of Boys*, Report to the Department of Education Science and Training, Australia.

Lipset, S. M. 1981 [1959], *Political Man* (expanded edn), Johns Hopkins University Press, Baltimore.

Liska, A. E. 1987, *Perspectives on Deviance*, 2nd edn, Prentice Hall, Englewood Cliffs, NJ.

Livingstone, S. M. & Lunt, P. K. 1994, *Talk on Television: Audience Participation and Public Debate*, Routledge, London.

Loh, N. & Ferrante, A. 2003, *Aboriginal Involvement in the Western Australian Criminal Justice System: A Statistical Review, 2001*, University of Western Australia for the Department of Indigenous Affairs, Perth.

Lomborg, B. 2001, *The Skeptical Environmentalist*, Cambridge University Press, Cambridge.

Lombroso, C. 1876, *L'Uomo Delinquente*, Hoepli, Milan, translated Ferrero, G. 1911, *Criminal Man*, G. P. Putnam & Sons, New York.

Loos, N. 1988, 'Concern and contempt: church and missionary attitudes towards Aborigines in North Queensland in the nineteenth century' in *Aboriginal Australians and Christian Missions: Ethnographic and Historical Studies*, eds T. Swain & D. B. Rose, Australian Association for the Study of Religions, Adelaide, 100–20.

Luhmann, N. 1997, 'Globalization or world society? How to conceive of modern society', *International Review of Sociology*, 7(1), 67.

Luke, C. 1989, *Pedagogy, Printing and Protestantism: the Discourse on Childhood*, State University of New York Press, Albany, NY.

Luke, T. W. 1991, 'Touring hyperreality: critical theory confronts informational society' in *Critical Theory Now*, ed. P. Wexler, Falmer Press, London, 1–26.

Lukes, S. 2005 [1974], *Power: A Radical View*, Macmillan, London.

Lupton, D. 1994, *Moral Threats and Dangerous Desires*, Taylor Francis, London.

Lynch, M., Buckman, J. & Krenske, L. 2003, *Youth Justice: Criminal Trajectories*, Trends and Issues in Crime and Criminal Justice No. 265, Australian Institute of Criminology and Queensland Crime and Misconduct Commission, Canberra.

Lyon, D. 1988, *The Information Society: Issues and Illusions*, Polity Press, Cambridge.

——1996, 'Religion and the postmodern: old problems, new prospects' in *Postmodernity, Sociology and Religion*, eds K. Flanagan & P. C. Jupp, Macmillan, London, 14–29.

Lyotard, J. F. 1984 [1979], *The Postmodern Condition*, Manchester University Press, Manchester.

Macan Ghaill, M. 1994, *The Making of Men: Masculinities, Sexualities and Schooling*, Open University Press, Milton Keynes.

MacCannell, D. 1976, *The Tourist*, Macmillan, London.

MacDonald, R. & Shildrick, T. 2007, 'Street corner society: leisure careers, youth (sub)culture and social exclusion', *Leisure Studies*, 26(3), 339–55.

Macfarlane, A. 1986, *Marriage and Love in England: Modes of Reproduction 1300–1840*, Basil Blackwell, Oxford.

Maddison, S. & Martin, G. (eds.) 2010, *Surviving Neoliberalism: The Persistence of Australian Social Movements*, special issue of *Social Movement Studies*, 9(2).

Maddock, K. 1972, *The Australian Aborigines*, Allen Lane, London.

Maddox, M. 2001, *For God and Country: Religious Dynamics in Australian Federal Politics*, Department of the Parliamentary Librarian, Information and Research Services, Commonwealth of Australia, Canberra.

Madge, J. 1963, *The Origins of Scientific Sociology*, Tavistock Publications, London.

Maduro, O. 1982, *Religion and Social Conflicts*, Orbis Books, New York.

Maher, I. 2002, 'Competition law in the international domain: networks as a new form of governance', *Journal of Law & Society*, 29(1), 111–36.

Makkai, T. & McAllister, I. 1993, 'Immigrants in Australian society' in *A Sociology of Australian Society*, eds J. Najman & J. Western, Macmillan, Melbourne, 178–212.

Manderson, L. & Mathews, M. 1985, 'Care and conflict' in *Immigration and Ethnicity in the 1980s*, eds I. Burnley, S. Encel & G. McCall, Longman, Melbourne, 248–60.

Mann, M. 1986, *The Sources of Social Power*, Vol. 1, Cambridge University Press, Cambridge.

——1993, *The Sources of Social Power*, Vol. 2, Cambridge University Press, Cambridge.

Manne, R. 2002. 'Beware the new racism', *The Age*, 16 September.

Marchand, P. 1989, *Marshall McLuhan: The Medium and the Messenger*, MIT Press, Cambridge, Mass.

Marcuse, H. 1964, *One Dimensional Man*, Routledge & Kegan Paul, London.

Marginson, S. 1993, *Education and Public Policy in Australia*, Cambridge University Press, Cambridge.

——1997, *Educating Australia: Government, Economy and Citizen Since 1960*, Cambridge University Press, Cambridge.

Markovic, M. & Manderson, L. 2000, 'Nowhere is at home', *Journal of Sociology*, 36(3), 315–28.

Markovic, M., Bandyopadhyay, M., Manderson, L., Allotey, P., Murray, S. & Vu, T. 2004, 'Day surgery in Australia', *Journal of Sociology*, 40(1), 74–84.

Marks, G. 2007, *Completing University: Characteristics and Outcomes of Completing and Non-completing Students*, Longitudinal Surveys of Australian Youth (LSAY) Research Report 51, Australian Council for Education Research.

Marks, G. N. & Jones, F. L. 1991, 'Changes over time in father–son mobility', *Australian & New Zealand Journal of Sociology*, 27(3), 315–31.

Marks, S. 2003, 'Empire's law', *Indiana Journal of Global Legal Studies*, 10, 449–66.

Marsh, D. (ed.) 1983, *Pressure Politics*, Junction Books, London.

Marshall, G. 1982, *In Search of the Spirit of Capitalism*, Hutchinson, London.

Marshall, P. D. 1997, *Celebrity and Power: Fame in Contemporary Culture*, University of Minnesota Press, Minneapolis.

Marshall, T. H. 1950, *Citizenship and Social Class and Other Essays*, Cambridge University Press, Cambridge.

Martin, A. 2001, 'The student motivation scale: a tool for measuring and enhancing motivation', *Australian Journal of Guidance and Counselling*, 11, 1–20.

Martin, A. J. & Marsh, H. 2005, 'Motivating boys and motivating girls: does teacher gender really make a difference?', *Australian Journal of Education*, 49(3), 320–34.

Martin, D. 1978, *A General Theory of Secularisation*, Blackwell, Oxford.

Martin, J. 1967, 'Extended kinship ties: an Adelaide study', *Australian & New Zealand Journal of Sociology*, 3, 44–63.

Martin, J. I. & Meade, P. 1979, *The Educational Experience of Sydney High School Students*, AGPS, Canberra.

Marx, K. 1954, *Capital*, Vol. 1, Progress, Moscow.

——1975, *Early Writings*, trans. R. Livingstone & G. Benton, Penguin, Harmondsworth. (See also under Bottomore & Rubel; Tucker.)

Marx, K. & Engels, F. 1951, *Selected Works, Vol. 1*, Foreign Languages Publishing House, Moscow.

——1962, *Selected Works, Vol. 2*, Foreign Languages Publishing House, Moscow.

——1967, *The Communist Manifesto*, Penguin Books, Harmondsworth.

——1970 [1845–6], *The German Ideology, Part One*, International Publishers, New York.

Mason, D. 1982, 'After Scarman, a note on the concept of institutional racism', *New Community*, 10(1), 338–45.

Mathews, R. L. 1968, 'Finance for education', *Economic Papers*, 27, June.

Maton, K. 2000, 'Languages of legitimation: the structuring significance for intellectual fields of strategic knowledge claims', *British Journal of Sociology of Education*, 21 (2), 147–67.

——2005, 'A question of autonomy: Bourdieu's field approach and policy in higher education', *Journal of Education Policy*, 20(6), 687–704.

——2007, 'Knowledge-knower structures in intellectual and educational fields' in *Language, Knowledge and Pedagogy: Functional Linguistic and Sociological Perspectives*, eds F. Christie & J. Martin, Continuum, London, 87–108.

——2008, 'Habitus' in *Pierre Bourdieu: Key Concepts*, ed. M. Grenfell, Acumen, London, 49–66.

——2009, 'Cumulative and segmented learning: exploring the role of curriculum structures in knowledge-building', *British Journal of Sociology of Education*, 30(1), 43–57.

Maton, K. & Moore, R. 2010a, 'Coalitions of the mind', in *Social Realism, Knowledge and the Sociology of Education: Coalitions of the Mind*, eds K. Maton & R. Moore, Continuum, London, 1–13.

——(eds) 2010b, *Social Realism, Knowledge and the Sociology of Education: Coalitions of the Mind*, Continuum, London.

Matza, D. 1969, *Becoming Deviant*, Prentice Hall, New York.

Maurício Domingues, J. 2009, 'Global modernization, "coloniality" and a critical sociology for contemporary Latin America', *Theory, Culture & Society*, 26(1), 112–33.

Mauss, M. 1973 [1935], 'Techniques of the body', *Economy & Society*, 2(1), 70–88.

Maxwell, R. 2003, 'The marketplace citizen and the political economy of data trade in the European Union' in *Critical Cultural Policy Studies: A Reader*, eds J. Lewis & T. Miller, Blackwell, Malden, Mass., 149–60.

Mayhew, P. 2003, *Counting the Costs of Crime in Australia*, Trends and Issues in Crime and Criminal Justice No. 247, Australian Institute of Criminology, Canberra.

McCallum, D. 1990, *The Social Production of Merit*, Falmer Press, London.

McCarthy, J. R., Edwards, R. & Gillies, V. 2000, 'Moral tales of the child and the adult: narratives of contemporary family lives under changing circumstances', *Sociology*, 34(4), 785–803.

——2003, *Making Families: Moral Tales of Parenting and Step-Parenting*, Sociology Press, Durham.

McDonald, K. 1999a, *Struggles for Subjectivity: Identity, Action and Youth Experience*, Cambridge University Press, Cambridge.

———1999b, 'Watch him burn', *Meanjin*, 4, 107–21.
———2002, 'From s11 to September 11', *Journal of Sociology*, 38(3), 229–36.
McDonald, P. F. 1984, 'The baby-boom generation as reproducers' in *Proceedings of the Australian Family Research Conference, ANU, Canberra, 23–25 Nov. 1983, Vol. 1: Family Formation, Structure, Values*, ed. Institute of Family Studies, Australian Institute of Family Studies, Melbourne.
———1988, 'Families in the future: the pursuit of personal autonomy', *Family Matters*, 22, 40–47.
———1991, 'Migrant family structure' in *Images of Australian Families*, ed. K. Funder, Longman Cheshire, Melbourne.
———1992, 'Extended family in Australia', *Family Matters*, 32, 5–9.
———1994, 'Household and family trends in Australia' in *Year Book Australia, 1994*, No. 76, cat. no. 1301.0, ABS, Canberra, 149–65.
———1995, *Families in Australia: a Socio-Demographic Perspective*, Australian Institute of Family Studies, Melbourne.
———2000, 'Gender equity, social institutions and the future of fertility', *Journal of Population Research*, 17(1), 1–16.
———2003, 'Transformations of the Australian family' in *The Transformation of Australia's Population: 1970–2030*, eds S. Khoo & P. McDonald, University of New South Wales Press, Sydney, 77–103.
McDonough, R. & Harrison, R. 1978, 'Patriarchal relations of production' in *Feminism and Materialism*, eds A. Kuhn & A. M. Wolpe, Routledge & Kegan Paul, London, 11–41.
McFarland, A. S. 2004, *Neopluralism: The Evolution of Political Process Theory*, University of Kansas Press, Lawrence.
———2007, 'Neopluralism', *Annual Review of Political Science*, 10, 45–66.
McGillivray, A. (ed.) 1997, *Governing Childhood*, Dartmouth, Aldershot, 1–24.
McGrew, A. 1992, 'A global society?' in *Modernity and its Futures*, eds S. Hall, D. Held & A. McGrew, Polity Press, Cambridge.
———2007, 'Organized violence in the making (and remaking) of globalization' in *Globalization Theory: Approaches and Controversies*, eds D. Held & A. McGrew, Polity Press, Cambridge, 15–40.
McGuire, M. B. 1981, *Religion, the Social Context*, Wadsworth, Belmont.
McIntosh, M. 1968, 'The homosexual role', *Social Problems*, 16(2), 182–92.
McIntyre, D. 1994, 'Occupational stressors' in *Just Health*, eds C. Waddell & A. Petersen, Churchill Livingstone, Melbourne, 61–72.
McKay, H. 2002, *Media Mania*, University of New South Wales Press, Sydney.
McKay, J. 1982, 'An exploratory synthesis of primordial and mobilizationist approaches to ethnic phenomena', *Ethnic & Racial Studies*, 5(4), 395–420.
———1995, 'Just do it: corporate slogans and the political economy of enlightened racism', *Discourse*, 16(2), 191–201.
McKay, J., Messner, M. and Sabo, D. 2000, *Masculinities, Gender Relations and Sport*, Sage, Thousand Oaks, CA.
McKee, A. 2005, *The Public Sphere: An Introduction*, Cambridge University Press, Melbourne.
McKenzie, R. T. 1969, 'Parties, pressure groups and the British political process' in *Studies in British Politics*, 2nd edn, ed. R. Rose, Macmillan, London, 255–62.

McKeown, T. 1979, *The Role of Medicine*, Oxford University Press, Oxford.
McLean, I. & Richardson, S. 1986, 'More or less equal? Australian income distribution in 1933, and 1980', *Economic Record*, 62(176), 67–81.
McLennan, G. 1989, *Marxism, Pluralism and Beyond*, Polity Press, Cambridge.
McLuhan, M. 1962, *The Gutenberg Galaxy: The Making of Typographic Man*, University of Toronto Press, Toronto.
———1967, *Understanding Media: The Extensions of Man*, Routledge, London.
McNeill, W. H. 2008, 'Globalization: long-term process or new era in human affairs?', *New Global Studies*, 2(1).
McRobbie, A. 2007, 'TOP GIRLS? Young women and the post-feminist sexual contract', *Cultural Studies*, 21(4–5), 718–37.
Mead, G. H. 1934, *Mind, Self and Society*, ed. C. Morris, University of Chicago Press, Chicago.
Mead, M. 1949, *Male and Female*, William Morrow, New York.
Meade, P. 1981, *The Educational Experiences of Sydney High School Students: Teachers and Parents' Perceptions of Schooling: Report No. 2*, AGPS, Canberra.
———1983, *The Educational Experience of Sydney High School Students: A Comparative Study of Migrant Students of Non-English-Speaking Origin and Students Whose Parents Were Born in an English-Speaking Country: Report No. 3*, AGPS, Canberra.
———1984, *Comparative Educational Experiences of Students of Non-English-Speaking Origin and Students of English-Speaking Origin*, Brisbane College of Advanced Education, Brisbane.
Media India 2008, 'Upper caste village in Northern India proud of "honour killing" of couple', 17 May, www.medindia.net/news/Upper-Caste-Village-in-Northern-India-Proud-of-honour-Killing-of-Couple-36797-1.htm, accessed 1 July 2009.
Mehan, H. 1974, 'Accomplishing classroom lessons' in *Language Use and School Performance*, ed. A. V. Cicourel, Academic Press, New York, 76–142.
———1979, *Learning Lessons. Social Organization in the Classroom*, Harvard University Press, Cambridge, Mass.
Mehta, P. B. 2000, 'Cosmopolitanism and the circle of reason', *Political Theory*, 28(5), 619–39.
Melbourne Institute of Applied Economic and Social Research 2009, *Poverty Lines: Australia*, Melbourne Institute of Applied Economic and Social Research, University of Melbourne, Melbourne.
Melossi, D. 1990, *The State of Social Control: A Sociological Study of Concepts of State and Social Control in the Making of Democracy*, Polity Press, Cambridge.
Melucci, A. 1989, *Nomads of the Present: Social Movements and Individual Needs in Contemporary Society*, Hutchinson Radius, London.
Melvern, L. 2006, *Conspiracy to Murder: The Rwandan Genocide*, Verso, London.
Mennell, S. 1980, *Sociological Theory: Uses and Unities*, 2nd edn, Nelson, London.
———1990, 'The globalization of human society as a very long-term social process: Elias's theory', *Theory, Culture & Society*, 7(2), 359–71.
Mercer, J. 1975, *The Other Half: Women in Australian Society*, Penguin, Harmondsworth.

Merton, R. K. 1940, 'Bureaucratic structure and personality', *Social Forces*, 18(4), 560–8.

——1946, *Mass Persuasion: The Social Psychology of a War Bond Drive*, Harper and Brothers, New York.

——1949a, *Social Theory and Social Structure*, Free Press, Glencoe.

——1949b, 'Discrimination and the American creed' in *Discrimination and National Welfare*, ed. R. McIver, Harper & Row, New York.

——1968, *Social Theory and Social Structure*, enlarged edn, The Free Press, New York.

Messerschmidt, J. W. 1986, *Capitalism, Patriarchy and Crime: Towards a Socialist Feminist Criminology*, Rowman & Littlefield, Totowa, NJ.

——1993, *Masculinities and Crime: Critique and Reconceptualization of Theory*, Rowman & Littlefield, Totowa, NJ.

——1995, 'From patriarchy to gender' in *International Feminist Perspectives in Criminology*, eds N. H. Rafter & F. Heidensohn, Open University Press, Buckingham, 175–85.

——1997, *Crime as Structured Action: Gender, Race, Class and Crime in the Making*, Sage, London.

Mewett, P. & Toffoletti, K. 2008, 'Rogue men and predatory women: female fans', *Perceptions of Australian Footballers' Sexual Conduct*, 43(2), 165–80.

Meyer, B. & Geschiere, P. (eds) 1999, *Globalization and Identity: Dialectics of Flow and Closure*, Blackwell Publishing, Oxford, 1–15.

Meyer, J. W. et al. 1997, 'World society and the nation-state', *American Journal of Sociology*, 1003(1), 144–81.

Michels, R. 1915, *Political Parties*, Jarrold & Sons, London.

Middleton, C. A. 2008, 'Illusions of balance and control in an always-on environment: a case study of Blackberry users' in *Mobile Phone Cultures*, ed. G. Goggin, Routledge, London, 28–41.

Mikosza, J. 2003, 'In search of the "mysterious" Australian male: editorial practices in men's lifestyle magazines', *Media International Australia*, 107, 134–44.

Miliband, R. 1969, *The State in Capitalist Society*, Weidenfeld & Nicolson, London.

——1972, 'Poulantzas and the capitalist state', *New Left Review*, 82, 83–94.

Mill, J. S. 1869, *The Subjection of Women*, Longmans, Green, Reader & Dye, London.

Millen, N. 1989, 'The factors behind the emergent militancy of nurses' in *Sociology of Health and Illness*, eds J. Najman & G. Lupton, Macmillan, Melbourne, 236–58.

Miller, D. & Slater, D. 2000, *The Internet: An Ethnographic History*, Routledge, London.

Miller, P. 2005, 'Useful and priceless children in contemporary welfare states', *Social Politics*, 12(1), 3–41.

Miller, T. 2007, *Cultural Citizenship: Cosmopolitanism, Consumerism, and Television in a Neoliberal Age*, Temple University Press, Philadelphia.

Miller, T. & Turner, G. 2002, 'Radio' in *The Media & Communications in Australia*, eds S. Cunningham & G. Turner, Allen & Unwin, Sydney, 133–51.

Millett, K. 1970, *Sexual Politics*, Doubleday, New York.

Mills, C. W. 1943, 'The professional ideology of social pathologists', *American Journal of Sociology*, 49, 165–80.

——1951, *White Collar*, Oxford University Press, New York.

——1956, *The Power Elite*, Oxford University Press, New York.

——1959, *The Sociological Imagination*, Oxford University Press, New York.

Mills, M., Martino, W. & Lingard, B. 2004, 'Attracting, recruiting and retaining male teachers: policy issues in the male teacher debate', *British Journal of Sociology of Education*, 25(3), 355–69.

Mishra, D. 2004, 'Globalisation and market mentality', *Businessline*, 17 March.

Mishra, R. 1999, *Globalization and the Welfare State*, Edward Elger, Cheltenham.

Mitchell, J. 1966, 'Women: the longest revolution', *New Left Review*, 40, 11–37.

——1971, *Woman's Estate*, Penguin, Harmondsworth.

Modelski, G. 1968, 'Communism and the globalization of politics', *International Studies Quarterly*, 12(4), 380–93.

——1972, *The Principles of World Politics*, The Free Press, New York.

——1978, 'The long cycle of global politics and the nation-state', *Comparative Studies in Society & History*, 20(2), 214–35.

Money, J. 1990, 'Agenda and Credenda of the Kinsey Scale' in *Homosexuality/Heterosexuality*, eds D. P. McWhirter, S. A. Sanders & J. M. Reinisch, Oxford University Press, Oxford, 41–60.

Money, J. & Ehrhardt, A. A. 1972, *Man and Woman, Boy and Girl*, Johns Hopkins University Press, Baltimore.

Moore, A. 2008, 'Hitchens takes "New Atheist" gospel to the masses', *WorldNetDailyExclusive*, 12 July 2008, www.wnd.com/index.php?pageId=69456, accessed 13 June 2009.

Moore, R. 2004, *Education and Society: Issues and Explanations in the Sociology of Education*, Polity Press, Cambridge.

——2008, 'Capital' in *Pierre Bourdieu: Key Concepts*, ed. M. Grenfell, Acumen, London, 101–18.

Moore, W. 1966, 'Global sociology: the world as a singular system', *American Journal of Sociology*, 71(5), 475–82.

Morais, A., Neves, I. & Pires, D. 2004, 'The *what* and the *how* of teaching: going deeper into sociological analysis and intervention' in *Reading Bernstein, Researching Bernstein*, eds J. Muller, B. Davies & A. Morais, RoutledgeFalmer, London.

Morgan, D. J. H. 1975, *Social Theory and the Family*, Routledge & Kegan Paul, London.

Morgan, F. 1993, 'Contact with the justice system over the juvenile years' in *National Conference on Juvenile Detention: Conference Proceedings*, eds L. Atkinson & S. A. Gerull, Australian Institute of Criminology, Canberra.

Morgan, M., Calnan, M. & Manning, N. 1991, *Sociological Approaches to Health and Medicine*, Routledge, London.

Morley, D. 1980, *The Nationwide Audience: Structure and Decoding*, British Film Institute, London.

Morris, L. 2008, 'God's ok, it's just the religion bit we don't like', *Sydney Morning Herald*, 11 July.

Morrow, R. A. & Torres, C. A. 1995, *Social Theory and Education: A Critique of Theories of Social and Cultural Reproduction*, State University of New York Press, Albany, NY.

Mortimore, P. 1997, 'Can effective schools compensate for society?' in *Education, Culture, Economy, Society*, eds A. H. Halsey, H. Lauder, P. Brown & A. S. Wells, Oxford University Press, Oxford.

Morton, T. 2004, 'Uncle Sam's bastard children', *Griffith Review*, 3, 179–87.

Mosca, G. 1939, *The Ruling Class*, McGraw-Hill, New York.

Moss, G. 2006, 'Informal literacies and pedagogic discourse' in *Popular Literacies, Childhood and Schooling*, eds J. Marsh & E. Millard, Routledge, London.

Mouzelis, N. P. 1967, *Organisation and Bureaucracy*, Routledge & Kegan Paul, London.

Mouzos, J. & Makkai, T. 2004, *Women's Experiences of Male Violence: Findings from the Australian Component of the International Violence Against Women Survey IVAWS*, Research & Public Policy Series no. 56, Australian Institute of Criminology, Canberra.

Mukherjee, S. 1981, *Crime Trends in Twentieth Century Australia*, Allen & Unwin, Sydney.

——1997, 'The dimensions of juvenile crime' in *Juvenile Crime, Justice and Corrections*, eds A. Borowski & I. O'Connor, Longman, Melbourne, 4–24.

——2000, 'Crime trends: a national perspective' in *Crime and the Criminal Justice System in Australia: 2000 and Beyond*, eds D. Chappell & P. Wilson, Butterworths, Sydney, 45–62.

Mukherjee, S., Carcach, C. & Higgins, K. 1997, *A Statistical Profile of Crime in Australia*, Australian Institute of Criminology, Canberra.

Mukherjee, S. & Dagger, D. 1990, *The Size of the Crime Problem in Australia*, 2nd edn, Australian Institute of Criminology, Canberra.

Mukherjee, S., Neuhaus, D. & Walker, J. 1990, *Crime and Justice in Australia*, Australian Institute of Criminology, Canberra.

Mukherjee, S., Walker, J. R. & Jacobsen E. N. 1986, *Crime and Punishment in the Colonies: A Statistical Profile*, History Project Inc., Sydney.

Mulinari, D. & Sandell, K. 2009, 'A feminist re-reading of theories of late modernity: Beck, Giddens and the location of gender', *Critical Sociology*, 35(4), 493–507.

Muller, J. & Young, M. F. D. 2009, 'Knowledge and truth in the sociology of education' in *Social Realism, Knowledge and the Sociology of Education: Coalitions of the Mind*, eds K. Maton & R. Moore, Continuum, London, 110–30.

Murray, C. 1984, *Losing Ground*, Basic Books, New York.

——1990, *The Emerging British Underclass*, Institute of Economic Affairs (IEA), London.

——1994, *Underclass: The Crisis Deepens*, Institute of Economic Affairs (IEA), London.

Murray, S. 2003, 'Media convergence's third wave: content streaming', *The Journal of Research into New Media Technologies*, 9(1), 8–18.

Myers, W. E. 1999, 'Considering child labour: changing terms, issues and actors at the international level', *Childhood*, 6(1), 13–26.

Myrstad, G. 1999, 'What can trade unions do to combat child labour?', *Childhood*, 6(1), 75–88.

Nader, R. 1999, *Seattle and the WTO*, www.nader.org/interest/12799.html, accessed 12 April 2005.

Naffine, N. 1997, *Feminism and Criminology*, Allen & Unwin, Sydney.

Naficy, H. 1993, *The Making of Exile Cultures: Iranian Television in Los Angeles*, Minneapolis, University of Minnesota Press.

Najman, J. 1994, 'Class inequalities in health and lifestyle' in *Just Health*, eds C. Waddell & A. Petersen, Churchill Livingstone, Melbourne, 27–46.

Narushima, Y. 2009, 'Work–life balance worse for women', *Sydney Morning Herald*, 27 July, 3.

Nash, K. 2000, *Political Sociology: Globalization, Politics, and Power*, Blackwell Publishing, Malden, Mass.

National Centre in HIV Epidemiology and Clinical Research 2003, *Australian HIV Surveillance Update*, 20(2), Sydney.

National Inquiry into Racist Violence in Australia 1991, *Report of the National Inquiry into Racist Violence in Australia*, AGPS, Canberra.

National Population Council 1987, *What's Happening to the Australian Family?*, AGPS, Canberra.

National Social Science Survey 1995, 1993 International Social Survey Programme, Religion, (ISSP) Australia 1991 (computer file), M.D.R. Evans & J. Kelley (Principal Investigators), Social Science Data Archives, Australian National University, Canberra.

Navarro, V. 1980, 'Work, ideology and science: the case of medicine', *Social Science & Medicine*, 14, 191–205.

NBC's 'Complete Olympics' 2008 (9 July), www.nbcolympics.com/newscenter/news/newsid=148556.html, accessed 4 August 2008.

Nederveen Pieterse, J. 1994, 'Globalization as hybridization', *International Sociology*, 9(2), 161–84.

——2004, *Globalization and Culture: Global Mélange*, Rowman & Littlefield, Lanham, MD.

Nielsen Company 2009, *Global Faces and Networked Places: A Nielsen Report on Social Networking's New Global Footprint*, Nielsen.

Nelson, B. J. 1984, *Making an Issue of Child Abuse. Political Agenda Setting for Social Problems*, Chicago University Press, Chicago.

Nelson, G. K. 1986, 'Religion' in *Developments in Sociology*, Vol. 2, ed. M. Haralambos, Causeway Press, Ormskirk.

Nettl, J. P. & Robertson, R. 1968, *International Systems and the Modernization of Societies*, Basic Books, New York.

Nietszche, F. 2003, *Writings from the Late Notebooks*, ed. R. Bittner; trans. K. Sturge, Cambridge University Press, Cambridge.

NISATSIC (National Inquiry into the Separation of Aboriginal and Torres Strait Islander Children from Their Families—Australia) 1997, *Bringing Them Home: Report of the National Inquiry into the Separation of Aboriginal and Torres Strait Islander Children from Their Families* (Wilson, R.D., HREOC Commissioner), Human Rights and Equal Opportunity Commission, Sydney.

Norman, F., Turner, S., Granados, J., Schwarez, H., Green, H. & Harris, J. 1988, 'Look, Jane, look: anti-sexist initiatives in primary schools' in *Just a Bunch of Girls*, ed. G. Weiner, Open University Press, Milton Keynes.

Nowotny, T. 2007, 'Security and power through interdependence: on the morality of globalisation', *Global Society*, 21(2), 179–97.

Nudelman, A. & Nudelman, B. 1972, 'Health and illness behavior of Christian Scientists', *Social Science & Medicine*, 6, 253–62.

Oakley, A. 1972, *Sex, Gender and Society*, Temple Smith, London.

——1974a, *Housewife*, Allen Lane, London.

——1974b, *The Sociology of Housework*, Martin Robertson, Oxford.

——1982, 'Conventional families' in *Families in Britain*, eds R. N. Rapoport, M. P. Fogarty & R. Rapoport, Routledge & Kegan Paul, London, 123–37.

O'Connell, T. & Moore, D. 1992, 'Wagga juvenile cautioning process', *Rural Society*, 2, 16–19.

OECD (Organisation for Economic Cooperation and Development) 1993, *Education in OECD Countries*, OECD, Paris.

OECD (Organisation for Economic Cooperation and Development) 2008, *Tertiary Education for the Knowledge Society—*

Volume 1: special features: Governance Funding, Quality and *Volume 2: Special features: Equity, Innovation, Labour Market, Internationalisation*, OECD, Paris.

OECD (Organisation for Economic Cooperation and Development) n.d., *The OECD*, www.oecd.org/dataoecd/15/33/34011915.pdf, accessed 29 May 2005.

Ohmae, K. 1990, *The Borderless World: Power and Strategy in the Interlinked Economy*, Harper Business, New York.

——2004, 'The end of the nation state' in *The Globalization Reader*, 2nd edn, eds F. J. Lechner & J. Boli, Blackwell Publishing, Oxford, 214–18.

Oken, D. 1961, 'What to tell cancer patients', *Journal of the American Medical Association*, 17(5), April, 1120–8.

O'Leary, Z. 1999, *Reaction, Introspection and Exploration: Diversity in Journeys out of Faith*, Christian Research Association Research Paper No. 4, Christian Research Association, Melbourne.

Olsen, R. 2000, 'Families under the microscope: parallels between the young carers debate of the 1990s and the transformation of childhood in the late nineteenth century', *Children & Society*, 14(5), 384–94.

Omran, A. (ed.) 1974, *Community Medicine in Developing Countries*, Springer, Berlin.

Organisation for Economic Co-operation and Development (OECD) 2008, *Tertiary Education for the Knowledge Society. VOLUME 1: Special Features: Governance, Funding, Quality* and *VOLUME 2: Special Features: Equity, Innovation, Labour Market, Internationalisation*, OECD, Paris.

Ortner, S. B. 1974, 'Is female to male as nature is to culture?' in *Woman, Culture and Society*, eds M. Z. Rosaldo & L. Lamphere, Stanford University Press, Stanford, 67–87.

Oxfam 2004, 'Growth with equity is good for the poor' in *The Globalization Reader*, 2nd edn, eds F. J. Lechner & J. Boli, Blackwell Publishing, Oxford, 183–9.

Packer, R., Caldwell, P. & Caldwell, J. 1976, 'Female Greek group interviews in Melbourne' in *Towards an Understanding of Contemporary Demographic Change*, J. Caldwell et al., Department of Demography, ANU, Canberra.

Pakulski, J. & Tranter, B. 2000, 'Civic, ethnic and denizen identity in Australia', *Journal of Sociology*, 36(2), 205–22.

Pakulski, J. & Waters, M. 1996, *The Death of Class*, London, Sage.

Papacharissi, Z. 2002, 'The virtual sphere: the internet as a public sphere', *New Media & Society*, 4(1), 9–27.

Parent, R. E. 2003, 'The office of faith-based and community initiatives: an ongoing case study of American belief, symbol and ritual', *Journal of Ritual Studies*, 17(1), 19–31.

Pareto, V. 1935, *The Mind and Society*, 4 volumes, ed. A. Livingstone, Jonathan Cape, London.

——1966, *Sociological Writings*, selected and introduced by S. E. Finer, Pall Mall Press, London.

——1991 [1901], *The Rise and Fall of Elites*, Transaction Books, New Brunswick, NJ.

Parker, D. 1977, 'Social agents as generators of crime' in *Aborigines and Change*, ed. R. Berndt, Australian Institute of Aboriginal Studies, Canberra.

Parker, S. 1976, 'Work and leisure' in *The Sociology of Leisure*, eds E. Butterworth & D. Weir, Allen & Unwin, London.

Parkin, F. 1971, *Class Inequality and Political Order*, Holt, Rinehart & Winston, New York.

——1982, *Max Weber*, Horwood, Chichester.

Parry, N. & Parry, J. 1976, *The Rise of the Medical Profession*, Croom Helm, London.

Parsons, T. 1937, *The Structure of Social Action*, McGraw-Hill, New York.

——1951, *The Social System*, Routledge & Kegan Paul, London.

——1955a, 'The American family: its relations to personality and the social structure' in *Family, Socialization and Interaction Process*, T. Parsons & R. F. Bales, The Free Press, New York, 3–33.

——1955b, 'Family structure and the socialization of the child' in *Family, Socialization and Interaction Process*, T. Parsons & R. F. Bales, The Free Press, New York, 35–131.

——1960, *Structure and Process in Modern Societies*, The Free Press, Chicago.

——1961, 'The school class as a social system: some of its functions in American society' in *Education, Economy and Society: A Reader in the Sociology of Education*, eds A. H. Halsey, J. Floud & C. A. Anderson, Collier-Macmillan, London.

——1964, 'The theoretical development of the sociology of religion' in *Essays in Sociological Theory*, The Free Press, New York.

——1965a, 'Religious perspectives in sociology and social psychology' in *Reader in Comparative Religion*, 2nd edn, W. A. Lessa & E. Z. Vogt, Harper & Row, New York, 88–92.

——1965b, 'The normal American family' in *Man and Civilization*, ed. S. M. Farber, McGraw-Hill, New York, 31–50.

——1967, *Sociological Theory and Modern Society*, The Free Press, New York.

——1975, 'Some theoretical considerations on the nature and trends of change of ethnicity' in *Ethnicity: Theory and Experience*, eds N. Glazer & D. P. Moynihan, Harvard University Press, Cambridge, Mass.

Parsons, T. & Fox, R. 1952, 'Illness, therapy and the modern family', *Journal of Social Issues*, 8, 31–44.

Parton, N. 1985, *The Politics of Child Abuse*, Macmillan, London.

Peristiany, J. G. 1976, 'Introduction' in *Mediterranean Family Structures*, ed. J. G. Peristiany, Cambridge University Press, Cambridge.

Pescosolido, B. A. & Mendelsohn, R. 1986, 'Social causation or social construction of suicide? An investigation into the social organisation of official rates', *American Sociological Review*, 51, 80–101.

Peterson, R. & Kern, R. M. 1996, 'Changing highbrow taste: from snob to omnivore', *American Sociological Review*, 61, 900–7.

Pettman, J. 1992, *Living in the Margins*, Allen & Unwin, Sydney.

Phillips, D. & Feldman, K. 1973, 'A dip in deaths before ceremonial occasions', *American Sociological Review*, 38, 678–96.

Phillips, T. 1996a, 'Symbolic boundaries and national identity in Australia', *British Journal of Sociology*, 47, 113–34.

——1996b, Australian National Identity, PhD dissertation, University of Queensland, Brisbane.

——1998, 'Popular views about Australian identity', *Journal of Sociology*, 34, 3, 281–302.

Phillips, T. & Aarons, H. 2005, 'Choosing Buddhism in Australia: towards a traditional style of reflexive spiritual engagement', *British Journal of Sociology*, 56(2), 215–32.

Phillips, T. & Smith, P. 2000a, 'Police violence occasioning citizen complaint: an empirical analysis of time-space dynamics', *British Journal of Criminology*, 40, 480–96.

——2000b, 'What is "Australian"? Knowledge and attitudes

among a gallery of contemporary Australians', *Australian Journal of Political Science*, 35(2), 203–24.

——2003, 'Everyday incivility: towards a benchmark', *Sociological Review*, 51(1), 85–108.

——2004, 'Emotional and behavioural responses to everyday incivility: challenging the fear/avoidance paradigm', *Journal of Sociology*, 40(4), 378–99.

——2008, 'Cosmopolitan beliefs and cosmopolitan practices: an empirical investigation', *Journal of Sociology*, 44(4), 391–9.

Phillipson, M. 1972, 'Theory, methodology and conceptualization' in *New Directions in Sociological Theory*, P. Filmer, M. Phillipson, D. Silverman & D. Walsh, Collier-Macmillan, London, 77–116.

Pieper, U. & Taylor, L. 1998, 'The revival of the liberal creed: the IMF, the World Bank, and inequality in a globalized economy' in *Globalization and Progressive Economic Policy*, eds D. Baker, G. Epstein & R. Pollin, Cambridge University Press, Cambridge, 37–63.

Piggott, J. 1984, 'The distribution of wealth in Australia—a survey', *Economic Record*, 60(170), 252–65.

——1988, 'The distribution of wealth: what is it, what does it mean, and is it important?', *Australian Economic Review*, 83, 35–41.

Pigman, G. A. 2006, 'Civilizing global trade: alterglobalizers and the "Double Movement"' in *Global Standards of Market Civilization*, eds B. Bowden & L. Seabrooke, Routledge, London, 188–204.

Pinker, S. 2002, *The Blank Slate: The Modern Denial of Human Nature*, Allen Lane, London.

Piore, M. 1986, 'Perspectives on labour market flexibility', *Industrial Relations*, 25(2), 146–66.

Platt, A. M. 1969, *The Child Savers*, University of Chicago Press, Chicago.

Pleck, J. H. 1981, *The Myth of Masculinity*, MIT Press, Cambridge, Mass.

Plummer, K. 1975, *Sexual Stigma*, Routledge & Kegan Paul, London.

——1979, 'Misunderstanding labelling perspectives' in *Deviant Interpretations*, eds D. Downes & P. Rock, Martin Robertson, London.

——1982, *Documents of Life: an Introduction to the Problems and Literature of a Humanistic Method*, George Allen & Unwin, London.

——2003, 'Queers, bodies and postmodern sexualities: a note on revisiting the "sexual" in symbolic interactionism', *Qualitative Sociology*, 26(4), 515–30.

Poggi, G. 1978, *Development of the Modern State*, Hutchinson, London.

Polk, K. 1994, *When Men Kill: Scenarios of Masculine Violence*, Cambridge University Press, Cambridge.

Polk, K. & Warren, I. 1996, 'Crimes against the person' in *Crime and Justice*, ed. K. Hazlehurst, Law Book Company, Sydney, 183–203.

Pollak, O. 1950, *The Criminality of Women*, University of Philadelphia Press, Philadelphia.

Pollock, L. 1983, *Forgotten Children. Parent–Child Relations from 1500–1900*, Cambridge University Press, Cambridge.

Polanyi, K. 1944, *The Great Transformation: The Political and Economic Origins of our Time*, New York, Farrar & Rinehart.

Polyani, M. 1958, *Personal Knowledge: Towards a Post-critical Philosophy*, Routledge & Kegan Paul, London.

Poole, M. (ed.) 2005, *Family: Changing Families, Changing Times*, Allen & Unwin, Sydney.

Popenoe, D. 1988, *Disturbing the Nest: Family Change and Decline in Modern Societies*, Aldine de Gruyter, New York.

——1993, 'American family decline, 1960–1990: a review and appraisal', *Journal of Marriage & the Family*, 55, 527–55.

Popper, K. R. 1959, *The Logic of Scientific Discovery*, Hutchinson, London.

Poppi, C. 1997, 'Wider horizons with larger details: subjectivity, ethnicity and globalization' in *The Limits of Globalization: Cases and Arguments*, ed. Alan Scott, Routledge, New York.

Porteus, S. D. 1931, *The Psychology of a Primitive People*, Edward Arnold, London.

Posby, N. W. 1960, 'How to study community power: the pluralist alternative', *Journal of Politics*, 22(3), 474–84.

Possamai, A. 2000, 'A profile of New Agers', *Journal of Sociology*, 36(3), 364–77.

Poster, M. 1995, *The Second Media Age*, Polity Press, Cambridge.

——2001, *What's the Matter with the Internet?*, University of Minnesota Press, Minneapolis.

——2006, *Information Please. Culture and Politics in the Age of Digital Machines*, Duke University Press, London.

Postman, N. 1986, *Amusing Ourselves to Death: Public Discourse in an Age of Show Business*, Heinemann, London.

Potter, R. 1992, 'Crime, shame and integration', *Australian & New Zealand Journal of Sociology*, 28, 224–32.

Poulantzas, N. 1969, 'The problem of the capitalist state', *New Left Review*, 58, 67–78.

——1976, 'The capitalist state: a reply to Miliband & Laclau', *New Left Review*, 95, 63–83.

——1978, *State, Power and Socialism*, New Left Books, London.

Powles, M. 1987, *Women's Participation in Tertiary Education*, Centre for Higher Education Research, University of Melbourne, Melbourne.

Poynting, S., Noble, G. & Tabar, P. 2003, 'Protest masculinity and Lebanese youth in western Sydney' in *Male Trouble: Looking at Australian Masculinities*, eds S. Tomsen & M. Donaldson, Pluto Press, Melbourne.

Poynting, J., Noble, G., Tabar, P. & Collins, J. 2004, *Bin Laden in the Suburbs: Criminalizing the Arab Other*, Institute of Criminology, Sydney.

Price, M. E. 2008, 'On seizing the Olympic platform' in *Owning the Olympics: Narratives of the New China*, eds M. E. Price & D. Dayan, University of Michigan Press, Ann Arbor, 86–114.

Price, M. E. & Dayan, D. (eds) 2008, *Owning the Olympics: Narratives of the New China*, University of Michigan Press, Ann Arbor.

Prigoff, A. 2000, *Economics for Social Workers: Social Outcomes of Economic Globalization with Strategies for Community Action*, Brooks/Cole, Belmont, CA.

Pringle, R. 1988, *Secretaries Talk*, Allen & Unwin, Sydney.

——1989, 'Bureaucracies, rationality and sexuality: the case of secretaries' in *The Sexuality of Organizations*, eds J. Hearn, D. L. Sheppard, P. Tancred-Sheriff & G. Burrell, Sage, London, 158–77.

Project for the New American Century 1997, *Statement of Principles*, http://newamericancentury.org/statementofprincples.htm, accessed 24 March 2005.

Purcell, P. (ed.) 2006, *Networked Neighbourhoods: The Connected Community in Context*, Springer, London.

Pusey, M. 1987, *Jürgen Habermas*, Tavistock Publications, London.

———1991, *Economic Rationalism in Canberra*, Cambridge University Press, Cambridge.

———1993, 'Australia: state and polity' in *A Sociology of Australian Society*, 2nd edn, J. M. Najman & J. S. Western, Macmillan, Melbourne.

———2003, *The Experience of Middle Australia: The Dark Side of Economic Reform*, Cambridge University Press, Melbourne.

Putnam, R. 1995, 'Bowling alone: America's declining social capital', *Journal of Democracy*, 6(1), 65–78.

Puttick, E. 1997, *Women in New Religions: In Search of Community, Sexuality and Spiritual Power*, Macmillan, London.

Putnam, R. 2001, *Bowling Alone*, Simon & Schuster, New York.

Quiggan, P. 1988, *No Rising Generation*, Department of Demography, ANU, Canberra.

Qvortrup, J. 1985, 'Placing children in the division of labour' in *Family and Economy in Modern Society*, eds P. Close & R. Collins, Macmillan, London.

———(ed.) 1993a, *Childhood as a Social Phenomenon: Lessons from an International Project*, European Centre for Social Welfare Policy & Research, Vienna.

———1993b, 'Nine theses about "Childhood as a Social Phenomenon"' in *Childhood as a Social Phenomenon: Lessons from an International Project*, ed. J. Qvortup, European Centre for Social Welfare Policy & Research, Vienna, 11–18.

———1995, 'From useful to useful: the historical continuity of children's constructive participation', *Sociological Studies of Children*, 7, 49–76.

Rabinow, P. 1984, 'Introduction' in *The Foucault Reader*, ed. P. Rabinow, Penguin, Harmondsworth.

Radford, W. C. 1962, *School Leavers in Australia, 1959–60*, Australian Council for Educational Research, Melbourne.

Radway, J. 1991, *Reading the Romance*, University of North Carolina Press, Chapel Hill.

Rahman, M. 2004, 'David Beckham as a historical moment in the representation of masculinity', *Labor History Review*, 69(2), 219–33.

Ramazanoglu, C. 1992, 'On feminist methodology: male reason versus female empowerment', *Sociology*, 26(2), 207–12.

Ramsey, A. 2005, 'Ad cacophony builds to a lengthy silence', *Sydney Morning Herald*, 18 May.

Randall, G. J. 1987, 'Gender differences in pupil–teacher interaction in workshops and laboratories' in *Gender under Scrutiny*, G. Weiner & M. Arnot, Hutchinson, London.

Ranki, V. 1999, 'Nato's bombs fuel dangerous fires for all', *Australian*, 29 April.

Rapoport, R. & Rapoport, R. N. 1975, *Leisure and the Family Life Cycle*, Routledge, London.

———1982, 'British families in transition', *Families in Britain*, eds R. N. Rapoport, M. P. Fogarty & R. Rapoport, Routledge & Kegan Paul, London, 475–99.

Rayner, L. & Easthope, G. 2001, 'Postmodern consumption and alternative medications', *Journal of Sociology*, 37(2), 157–76.

Read, P. 1983, *The Stolen Generations*, NSW Ministry of Aboriginal Affairs, Sydney.

Reckless, W. C. 1961, *The Crime Problem*, 3rd edn, Appleton-Century-Crofts, New York.

Redmond, S. & Holmes, S. 2007, *Stardom and Celebrity: A Reader*, Sage, London.

Reuther, R. A. 1983, *Sexism and God-Talk: Toward a Feminist Theology*, Beacon Press, Boston.

Rex, J. 1996, *Ethnic Minorities in the Modern Nation State*, Macmillan, London.

Rex, J. & Moore, R. 1967, *Race, Community and Conflict*, Institute of Race Relations/Oxford University Press, London.

Reynolds, H. 1981, *The Other Side of the Frontier*, James Cook University, Townsville.

Rheingold, H. 2002, *Smart Mobs: The Next Social Revolution*, Basic Books, Cambridge, Mass.

Rich, A. 1980, 'Compulsory heterosexuality and lesbian experience' in *Women: Sex and Sexuality*, eds C. R. Stimpson & E. S. Person, University of Chicago Press, Chicago, 62–91.

Richardson, I. 2008, 'Pocket technospaces: the bodily incorporation of mobile media' in *Mobile Phone Cultures*, ed. G. Goggin, Routledge, London, 66–85.

Richardson, S. & Harding, A. 1998, *Low Wages and the Distribution of Family Income*, NATSEM paper DP 33, www.natsem.canberra.edu.au/publicationsByYear.jsp?year=1998, accessed 3 May 2005.

Richmond, K. 1974, 'The workforce participation of married women in Australia' in *Social Change in Australia*, ed. D. E. Edgar, Cheshire, Melbourne, 267–305.

Riessman, C. T. 1980, 'Women and medicalization', *Social Policy*, 14, 3–18.

Ritzer, G. 1996 [1992], *Sociological Theory*, McGraw-Hill, New York.

———2004 [2000, 1993], *The McDonaldization of Society*, Revised New Century Edition, Pine Forge Press, Thousand Oaks, CA.

———2008 [2004, 2000, 1993], *The McDonaldization of Society*, 5th edn, Pine Forge Press, Thousand Oaks, CA.

Roach, J. L. & Roach, J. K. (eds) 1972, *Poverty*, Penguin, Harmondsworth.

Roach Anleu, S. & Mack, K. 2005, 'Magistrates' everyday work and emotional labor', *Journal of Law and Society*, 32(4), 590–614.

Roberts, K. 1978, *Contemporary Society and the Growth of Leisure*, Longman, New York.

———1986, 'Leisure' in *Developments in Sociology*, Vol. 2, ed. M. Haralambos, Causeway Press, Ormskirk.

Roberts, L. & Indermaur, D. 2009, *What Australians Think About Crime and Justice: Results from the 2007 Survey of Social Attitudes*, AIC Research and Public Policy Series 101, www.aic.gov.au/documents/4/8/A/{48A3B38B-376E-4A7A-A457-AA5CC37AE090}rpp101.pdf, accessed 9 August 2009.

Roberts, M. 1975, *A Portrait of Europe 1900–1973: The New Barbarism?*, Oxford University Press, Oxford.

Robertson, R. (ed.) 1969, *Sociology of Religion*, Penguin, Harmondsworth.

———1983, 'Religion, global complexity and the human condition' in *Absolute Values and the Creation of the New World, Vol. 1*, International Cultural Foundation, New York.

———1990, 'Mapping the global condition: globalization as the central concept', *Theory, Culture & Society*, 7(2), 15–30.

———1991, 'Globalization, modernization and postmodernization: the ambiguous position of religion' in *Religion and Global Order*, eds R. Robertson & W. Garrett, Paragon House, New York, 281–92.

———1992a, *Globalization*, Sage, London.

———1992b, '"Civilization" and the civilizing process: Elias, globalization and analytic synthesis', *Theory, Culture & Society*, 9(1), 211–27.

———1992c, '"Civilization", civility and the civilizing process' in *Globalization: Social Theory and Global Culture*, Sage, London, 115–28.

———2001, 'Globalization theory 2000+: major problematics' in *Handbook of Social Theory*, eds G. Ritzer & B. Smart, Sage, London, 458–71.

———2003, *The Three Waves of Globalization: A History of a Developing Global Consciousness*, Zed Books, New York.

Robertson, R. & Lechner, F. 1985, 'Modernization, globalization and the problem of culture in world-systems theory', *Theory, Culture & Society*, 2(3), 103–117.

Robertson, R. & White, K. E. 2005, 'Globalization: sociology and cross-disciplinarity' in *The Sage Handbook of Sociology*, eds C. Calhoun, C. Rojek & B. S. Turner, Sage, London, 345–66.

Roche, J. 1999, 'Children: rights, participation and citizenship', *Childhood*, 6(4), 475–493.

Roemer, M. I. 1976, *Health Care Systems in World Perspective*, Health Administration Press, Ann Arbor, Mich.

Roethlisberger, F. J. & Dickson, W. J. 1939, *Management and the Worker*, Harvard University Press, Cambridge, Mass.

Rogers, E. & Dearing, W. 1988, 'Agenda setting research: where it has been, where is it going?' In J. A. Anderson (ed.), *Communication Yearbook II*. (pp. 555–594). Sage Publications: Newbury Park, California.

Rogers, L. J. 1981, 'Biology: gender differentiation & sexual variation' in *Australian Women*, eds N. Grieve & P. Grimshaw, Oxford University Press, Melbourne, 44–57.

Rojek, C. 1989, *Leisure for Leisure*, Macmillan, London.

———2001, *Celebrity*, Reaktion Books, London.

Rolfe, H. 1967, *The Controllers*, Cheshire, Melbourne.

Rollings, K. 2005, *Counting the Costs of Crime in Australia: A 2005 Update*, Research & Public Policy Series No. 91, www.aic.gov.au/documents/9/A/3/%7B9A333836-6275-4855-9C0B-20FB05B05992%Drpp91.pdf, Australian Institute of Criminology, Canberra.

Roof, W. C. 1994, *A Generation of Seekers: The Spiritual Journeys of the Baby Boom Generation*, HarperCollins, New York.

Roof, W. C., Carroll, J.W. & Roozen, D. A. (eds) 1995, *The Postwar Generation and Establishment Religion: Cross-Cultural Perspectives*, Waterview Press, Boulder, Co., Oxford.

Ropers, R. 1973, 'Mead, Marx and social psychology', *Catalyst*, 7, 42–61.

Rosaldo, M. Z. 1974, 'Women, culture and society: a theoretical overview' in *Women, Culture and Society*, eds M. Rosaldo & L. Lamphere, Stanford University Press, Stanford, 17–42.

Rose, S., Kamin, L. J. & Lewontin, R. C. 1984, *Not in Our Genes*, Penguin, Harmondsworth.

Rosenberg, C. 1987, *The Care of Strangers*, Basic Books, New York.

Rosenblum, L. A. 1990, 'Primates, homo sapiens, and homosexuality' in *Homosexuality/Heterosexuality*, eds D. P. McWhirter, S. A. Sanders & J. M. Reinisch, Oxford University Press, Oxford, 171–4.

Rosenhan, D. L. 1973, 'On being sane in insane places', *Science*, 17(9), 250–8.

Rosenthal, R. & Jacobson, L. 1968, *Pygmalion in the Classroom*, Holt, Rinehart & Winston, New York.

Ross, A. M. & Hartman, P. T. 1960, *Changing Patterns of Industrial Conflict*, John Wiley & Sons, New York.

Ross, M. 1994, 'AIDS and the new public health' in *Just Health*, eds C. Waddell & A. Petersen, Churchill Livingstone, Melbourne, 323–35.

Roth, J. 1972, 'Some contingencies of the moral evaluation and control of clientele', *American Journal of Sociology*, 77, 839–56.

Rowbotham, S. 1979, 'The trouble with "patriarchy"', *New Statesman*, 98 (December), 970–1.

Rowe, W. & Schelling, V. 1991, *Memory and Modernity: Popular Culture in Latin America*, Verso, London.

Royal Commission into Aboriginal Deaths in Custody 1991, *National Report* (Elliott Johnston, Commissioner), AGPS, Canberra.

Rubin, G. 1975, 'The traffic in women: notes on the "political economy" of sex' in *Toward an Anthropology of Women*, ed. R. R. Reiter, Monthly Review Press, New York, 157–210.

———1984, 'Thinking sex: notes for a radical theory of the politics of sexuality' in *Pleasure and Danger*, ed. C. Vance, Routledge & Kegan Paul, Boston, 276–319.

Rubinstein, D. M. 2001, *Culture, Structure and Agency: Toward a Truly Multidimensional Society*, Sage, Thousand Oaks, CA.

Rudd, K. 2009, 'The global financial crisis', *The Monthly*, 42.

Ruddock, A. 2001, *Understanding Audiences*, Sage, London.

Ruddock, A. 2007, *Investigating Audiences*, Sage, London.

Ruggie, J. G. 1983, 'International regimes, transaction and change: embedded liberalism in the post-war economic order' in *International Regimes*, ed. S. D. Krasner, Cornell University Press, Ithaca, NY.

Ruggiero, R. 1996, 'Managing a world of free trade and deep interdependence', *WTO News: 1996 Press Releases*, Press/55, 10 September.

Rushdie, S. 1989, *The Satanic Verses*, Viking, New York.

Rushton, J. P. 1995, *Race, Evolution and Behaviour*, Transaction Publishers, New Brunswick.

Ryman, H. & Kean, S. 2002, 'Globalisation: the poor must come first', World Vision internal paper, June 2002.

Sabel, C. 1982, *Work and Politics*, Cambridge University Press, Cambridge.

Sacks, K. 1975, 'Engels revisited: women, the organization of production, and private property' in *Toward an Anthropology of Women*, ed. R. R. Reiter, Monthly Review Press, New York, 211–34.

Sahlings, M. 1972, *Stone Age Economics*, Transaction Publishers, London.

Salam Pax 2003, *The Baghdad Blog*, Atlantic Books, London.

Salaman, G. 1979, *Work Organizations*, Longman, London.

Saldanha, A. 2002, 'Music, space, identity: geographies of youth culture in Bangalore', *Cultural Studies*, 16(3), 337–50.

Samuel, L. 1983, 'The making of a school resister: a case study of Australian working-class secondary schoolgirls' in *Sociology of Education*, 3rd edn, eds R. K. Browne & L. E. Foster, Macmillan, Melbourne, 367–75.

Sanders, S. A., Reinisch, J. M. & McWhirter, D. P. 1990, 'Homosexuality/heterosexuality: an overview' in *Homosexuality/Heterosexuality*, eds D. P. McWhirter, S. A. Sanders & J. M. Reinisch, Oxford University Press, Oxford, xix–xxvii.

Sansom, B. 1980, *The Camp at Wallaby Cross*, Australian Institute of Aboriginal Studies, Canberra.

Sardar, Z. 1982, 'Why Islam needs Islamic science', *New Scientist*, 1 April.
Sargent, M., Nilan, P. & Winter, G. 1997, *The New Sociology for Australians*, 4th edn, Longman Cheshire, Melbourne.
Sassen, S. 1991, *The Global City*, Princeton University Press, Princeton.
——2007a, 'The places and spaces of the global: an expanded analytic terrain' in *Globalization Theory: Approaches and Controversies*, eds D. Held & A. McGrew, Polity Press, Cambridge, 79–105.
——2007b, *A Sociology of Globalization*, W. W. Norton, New York.
Saul, J. R. 1999, 'Globalisation and democracy', lecture presented at University of Sydney: ABC TV, www.abc.net.au/specials/saul/default.htm, accessed 13 August 2003.
Saunders, P. 1992, *Longer-run Changes in the Distribution of Income in Australia*, Centre for Applied Economic Research and the Social Policy Research Centre, University of New South Wales, Sydney.
——2003a, *Examining Recent Changes in Income Distribution in Australia*, Social Policy Research Centre Discussion Paper No. 130, Social Policy Research Centre, University of New South Wales, Sydney.
——2003b, *Can Social Exclusion Provide a New Framework for Measuring Poverty?*, SPRC discussion paper no. 127, October, Social Policy Research Centre, University of New South Wales, Sydney.
Savage, M. 2000, *Class Analysis and Social Transformation*, Open University Press, Buckingham.
Savitch, H. V. 2002, 'What is new about globalisation and what does it portend for cities?', *International Social Science Journal*, 54(172), 179–89.
Sawer, G. 1967, *Australian Federation in the Courts*, Melbourne University Press, Melbourne.
Sayer, A. 1984, *Method in Social Science*, Hutchinson, London.
Sayers, J. 1982, *Biological Politics*, Tavistock, London.
——1986, *Sexual Contradictions*, Tavistock, London.
Scambler, A., Scambler, G. & Craig, D. 1981, 'Kinship and friendship networks and women's demand for primary care', *Journal of the Royal College of General Practitioners*, 26, 746–50.
Scheff, T. 1966, *Being Mentally Ill*, Aldine, Chicago.
——1968, 'Negotiating reality', *Social Problems*, 16, 3–17.
Scheuerman, W. 1999, 'Economic globalization and the rule of law', *Constellations*, 6(1), 3–25.
——1999, 'Globalization and the fate of law' in *Recrafting the Rule of Law: The Limits of Legal Order*, ed. D. Dyzenhaus, Hart, Oxford.
—— 2001, 'Reflexive law and the challenges of globalization', *Journal of Political Philosophy*, 9(1), 81–102.
Schirato, T. & Webb, J. 2003, *Understanding Globalization*, Sage, London.
Schivelbusch, W. 1978, 'Railroad space and railroad time', *New German Critique*, 14, 31–40.
Schneider, D. & Gough, K. (eds) 1961, *Matrilineal Kinship*, University of California Press, Berkeley.
Schneiderman, D. 2006, 'Transnational legality and the immobilization of local agency', *Annual Review of Law & Social Science*, 2, 387–408.
Scholte, J. A. 2001, 'The globalization of world politics' in *The Globalization of World Politics*, 2nd edn, eds J. Baylis & S. Smith, Oxford University Press, Oxford, 13–34.
Schudson, M. 1979, *Discovering the News: A Social History of Newspapers*, Basic Books, New York.
Schuerkens, U. 2003, 'The sociological and anthropological study of globalization and localization', *Current Sociology*, 5(3/4), 209–22.
Schultz, T. W. 1961, 'Investment in human capital', *American Economic Review*, 51, 1–17.
Schutz, A. 1967, *The Phenomenology of the Social World*, Northwestern University Press, Evanston, Illinois.
Scott, J. 1990, *A Matter of Record: Documentary Sources in Social Research*, Polity Press, Cambridge.
Scott, L. 2001, International history 1945–1990' in *The Globalization of World Politics*, 2nd edn, eds J. Baylis & S. Smith, Oxford University Press, Oxford, 73–91.
Scraton, P. (ed.) 1997, *"Childhood" in Crisis?*, Routledge, London.
Scraton, S. 1992, 'Leisure' in *Developments in Sociology*, Vol. 8, ed. M. Haralambos, Causeway Press, Ormskirk.
Scutt, J. 1990, *Women and the Law*, Law Book Company, Sydney.
Seagrim, G. F. & Lendon, R. 1980, *Furnishing the Mind: A Comparative Study of Cognitive Development in Central Australian Aborigines*, Academic Press, Sydney.
Sedgwick, E. K. 1990, *Epistemology of the Closeti*, University of California Press, Berkeley.
——1992, *Between Men: English Literature and Male Homosocial Desire*, Columbia University Press, New York.
Segal, L. (ed.) 1993, 'Changing men: masculinities in context', *Theory & Society*, 22(5), 625–41.
Seidman, S. 1996, 'Introduction' in *Queer Theory/Sociology*, ed. S. Seidman, Blackwell Publishing, Cambridge, Mass., 1–29.
Select Committee on Aboriginal Education 1985, *Aboriginal Education*, AGPS, Canberra.
Selznick, P. 1949 [1966], *TVA and the Grass Roots*, Harper & Row, New York.
Sen, A. 2002, 'How to judge globalism', *American Prospect*, 13(1), A2–A6.
Senate 2004, 'A hand up, not a hand out: renewing the fight against poverty', Senate Community Affairs Reference Committee Report on Poverty and Financial Hardship, Commonwealth of Australia, Canberra, www.aph.gov.au/senate_ca, accessed 2 August 2004.
Sennett, R. 1998, *The Corrosion of Character: The Personal Consequences of Work in the New Capitalism*, Norton, New York.
Servon, L. J. & Pinkett, R. D. 2004, 'Narrowing the digital divide: the potential and limits of the US community and technology movement' in *The Network Society: A Cross-Cultural Perspective*, ed. M. Castells, Edward Elgar, Cheltenham, UK, 319–38.
Sey, A. & Castells, M. 2004, 'From media politics to networked politics: the internet and the political process' in *The Network Society: A Cross-Cultural Perspective*, ed. M. Castells, Edward Elgar, Cheltenham, UK, 363–81.
Sgritta, G. B. 1996, 'The golden age of child poverty. Facts and reasons' in *Children on the Way from Marginality towards Citizenship. Childhood Policies: Conceptual and Practical Issues*, ed. H Wintersberger. European Centre for Social Welfare Policy and Research, Vienna, Austria, Chapter 2.
Shapiro, M. 1993, 'The globalization of law', *Indiana Journal of Global Legal Studies*, 1(1), 37–64.

——1995, 'Doctors learning their trade' in *Sociology of Health and Illness*, eds G. Lupton & J. Najman, Macmillan, Melbourne, 217–35.

——2003, 'The globalization of freedom of contract' in *On Law, Politics, and Judicialization*, eds, M. Shapiro & A. Stone Sweet, Oxford University Press, Oxford.

Sharma, S. D. 2008, 'The many faces of today's globalization: a survey of recent literature', *New Global Studies*, 2(2).

Sharp, L. 1958, 'People without politics' in *Systems of Political Control and Bureaucracy in Human Societies*, ed. V. Ray, University of Washington Press, Seattle, 1–8.

Sharpe, S. 1995 [1976], *Just Like a Girl*, 2nd edn, Penguin, Harmondsworth.

Shaw, C. R. & McKay, H. D. 1969 [1942], *Juvenile Delinquency and Urban Areas*, rev. edn, University of Chicago Press, Chicago.

Sheil, C. 2001, 'Globalisation is ... globalisation: introduction' in *Globalisation: Australian Impacts*, ed. C. Sheil, University of New South Wales Press, Sydney, 1–18.

Sherington, G. 1990, *Australia's Immigrants*, Allen & Unwin, Sydney.

Sherman, R. 2007, *Class Acts: Service and Inequality in Luxury Hotels*, University of California Press, Berkeley, CA.

Shilling, C. 1993, *The Body and Social Theory*, Sage, London.

——2005, *The Body in Culture, Technology and Society*, Sage, London.

Shiva, V. 2004, 'Earth democracy' in *New Socialisms: Futures Beyond Globalization*, eds R. Albritton, S. Bell, J. R. Bell & R. Westra, Routledge, London, 53–70.

Siahpush, M. 1998, 'Postmodern values, dissatisfaction with conventional medicine and the popularity of alternative therapies', *Journal of Sociology*, 34, 1, 58–70.

Sidel, V. & Sidel, R. 1977, 'Primary care in relation to socio-political structure', *Social Science & Medicine*, 11, 145–59.

Silbey, S. S. 1997, '"Let them eat cake": globalization, postmodern colonialism, and the possibilities of justice', *Law & Society Review*, 31(2), 207–35.

Silj, A. 1988, *East of Dallas: The European Challenge to American Television*, British Film Institute, London.

Silverman, D. 1970, *The Theory of Organisations*, Heinemann, London.

——1985, *Qualitative Method and Sociology*, Gower, Aldershot.

Simmel, G. 1968, *Conflict in Modern Culture and Other Essays*, Teachers College Press, New York.

——1971, *On Individuality and Social Forms*, University of Chicago Press, Chicago.

——1990, *The Philosophy of Money*, 2nd edn, Routledge, London.

Simon, W. & Gagnon, J. H. 1986, 'Sexual scripts: permanence and change', *Archives of Sexual Behaviour*, 15(2), 97–120.

Simpson, M. 1994, 'Here come the Mirror Men', *The Independent*, 15 November.

——2002, 'Meet the metrosexual', *Salon.com*, 22 July.

——2004, 'MetroDaddy speaks!', *Salon.com*, 5 January.

Sinfield, A. 1981, *What Unemployment Means*, Martin Robertson, Oxford.

Singer, P. 2002, *One World: The Ethics of Globalisation*, Text Publishing Company, Melbourne.

Sissons, M. 1970, *The Psychology of Social Class*, Open University Press, Milton Keynes.

Skeggs, B. 1997, *Formations of Class and Gender: Becoming Respectable*, Sage, Thousand Oaks, CA.

Skelton, C. 1993, 'Women and education' in *Introducing Women's Studies*, eds D. Richardson & V. Robinson, Macmillan, London.

——2002, 'Typical boys? Theorising masculinity in educational settings' in *Investigating Gender*, eds B. Francis & C. Skelton, Open University Press, Buckingham.

Skidmore, W. 1975, *Theoretical Thinking in Sociology*, Cambridge University Press, Cambridge.

Sklair, L. 1991, *Sociology of the Global System*, Harvester Wheatsheaf, New York.

——1995, *Sociology of the Global System*, 2nd edn, Johns Hopkins University Press, Baltimore.

——1999, 'Competing conceptions of globalization', *Journal of World Systems Research*, 5(2), 143–63.

——2002, *Globalization: Capitalism and Its Alternatives*, 3rd edn, Oxford University Press, New York.

Skocpol, T. 1979, *States and Social Revolutions*, Cambridge University Press, Cambridge.

——1985, 'Bringing the state back in: strategies of analysis on current research' in *Bringing the State Back In*, eds P. Evans, D. Rueschemeyer & T. Skocpol, Cambridge University Press, Cambridge, 3–37.

Skrbis, Z. & Germov, J. 2004, 'The most influential books in Australian sociology (MIBAS), 1963–2003', *Journal of Sociology*, 40(3), 283–303.

Slevin, J. 2000, *The Internet and Society*, Polity Press, Cambridge.

Smart, B. (ed.) 1999, *Resisting McDonaldization*, Sage, London.

Smart, C. 1976, *Women, Crime and Criminology*, Routledge & Kegan Paul, London.

——1999, 'A history of ambivalence and conflict in the discursive construction of the "child victim" of sexual abuse', *Social & Legal Studies*, 8(3), 391–409.

Smart, C., Neale, B. & Wade, A. 2001, *The Changing Experience of Childhood: Families and Divorce*, Polity Press, Cambridge.

Smart, C. & Shipman, B. 2004, 'Visions in monochrome: families, marriage and the individualization thesis', *British Journal of Sociology*, 55, 491–509.

Smeeding, T. M. 1998, 'US income inequality in a cross-national perspective: why are we so different?' in *The Inequality Paradox: Growth of Income Disparity*, eds J. Auerbach & R. Belous, National Policy Association, Washington, 194–217.

——2002, *Globalization, Inequality and the Rich Countries of the G-20: Evidence from the Luxembourg Income Study*, Social Policy Research Centre Discussion Paper No. 122, Social Policy Research Centre, University of New South Wales, Sydney.

Smith, A. 1991, *National Identity*, University of Nevada Press, Reno.

Smith, A. D. 1990, 'Towards a global culture?', *Theory, Culture & Society*, 7(2), 171–91.

Smith, J. 2004, 'The world social forum and the challenges of global democracy', *Global Networks*, 4(4), 413–21.

Smith, P. & Phillips, T. 2001, 'Popular understandings of the unAustralian: A study of the non-national', *Journal of Sociology*, 37(4), 323–39.

Smith, R. 1993a, 'The party system' in *Politics in Australia*, 2nd edn, ed. R. Smith, Allen & Unwin, Sydney, 130–47.

——(ed.) 1993b, *Politics in Australia*, 2nd edn, Allen & Unwin, Sydney.

Smolicz, J. J. 1987, 'Education for a multicultural society' in *Australian Education*, ed. J. P. Keeves, Allen & Unwin, Sydney.

Smyrnios, K. X. & Tonge, B. 1981, 'Immigrant Greek mothers: the anxiety of change', *Australian Social Work*, 34(2), 19–24.

Snooks, G. D. 1994, *Portrait of the Family within the Total Economy*, Cambridge University Press, Melbourne.

Soar, M. 2001, 'Engines and acolytes of consumption', *Body and Society*, 7(4), 37–55.

Solomos, J., Findlay, B., Jones, S. & Gilroy, P. 1982, 'The organic crisis of British capitalism and race' in *The Empire Strikes Back*, eds Centre for Contemporary Cultural Studies, Hutchinson, London, 9–46.

Somerville, J. 1989, 'The sexuality of men and the sociology of gender', *Sociological Review*, 37(2), 277–307.

Speed, S. 2006, 'At the crossroads of human rights and anthropology: towards a critically engaged activist research', *American Anthropologist*, 108(1), 66–76.

Spender, D. 1982, *Invisible Women*, Writers & Readers, London.

——1994, 'Introduction' and 'The ancient history of wifeliness' in *Weddings and Wives*, ed. D. Spender, Penguin, Melbourne, xi–xxiv, 3–63.

Speier, M. 1976, 'The adult ideological viewpoints in studies of childhood' in *Rethinking Childhood. Perspectives on Development and Society*, ed. A. S. Skolnick, Little, Brown, Boston, 168–86.

Stacey, M. 1960, *Tradition and Change*, Oxford University Press, Oxford.

Stanley, L. & Wise, S. 1993, *Breaking Out Again: Feminist Ontology and Epistemology*, Routledge, London.

Stanner, W. E. H. 1963, 'On Aboriginal religion: cosmos and society made correlative', *Oceania*, 33.

——1967, 'Reflections on Durkheim and Aboriginal religion' in *Social Organisation: Essays Presented to Raymond Firth*, ed. M. Freeman, Cass, London.

——1979, *White Man Got No Dreaming: Essays 1938–1973*, Australian National University Press, Canberra.

——1992, 'Religion, totemism and symbolism' in *Religion in Aboriginal Australia*, eds M. Charlesworth, H. Morphy, D. Bell & K. Maddock, University of Queensland Press, St Lucia.

Stanworth, M. 1983, *Gender and Schooling: A Study of Sexual Divisions in the Classroom*, Hutchinson, London.

Stanworth, P. & Giddens, A. (eds) 1974, *Elites and Power in British Society*, Cambridge University Press, Cambridge.

Starhawk 1982, *Dreaming the Dark: Magic, Sex and Politics*, Beacon Press, Boston.

——1989, *The Spiral Dance: A Rebirth of the Ancient Religion of the Great Goddess*, Harper & Row, San Francisco.

Stark, R. & Bainbridge, W. S. 1985, *The Future of Religion*, University of California Press, Berkeley.

Starwoman, A. & Gray, D. 1996, *How to Turn your Ex-Boyfriend into a Toad and other Spells for Love, Wealth, Beauty and Revenge*, HarperCollins, Sydney.

Stehr, N. 1994, *Knowledge Societies*, Sage, London.

Stein, A. & Plummer, K. 1996, '"I can't even think straight": "queer" theory and the missing sexual revolution in sociology' in *Queer Theory/Sociology*, ed. S. Seidman, Blackwell Publishing, Cambridge, Mass., 129–44.

Stening, B. W. & Wai, W. T. 1984, 'Interlocking directorates among Australia's largest 250 corporations 1959–1979', *Australian & New Zealand Journal of Sociology*, 20(1), 47–55.

Stern, N. 2006, *Stern Review on The Economics of Climate Change*, HM Treasury, London.

Stiglitz, J. 2004 [2002], 'Globalism's discontents (extract from *Globalism's Discontents*)' in *The Globalization Reader*, 2nd edn, eds F. J. Lechner & J. Boli, Blackwell Publishing, Oxford, 200–7.

Stinson, R. 1998, *What Jobs Pay 1998: How Much Can You Earn?*, 4th edn, New Hobsons Press, Sydney.

Stinson, T. 2004, *What Jobs Pay 2003–4: Earnings in the Australian Job Market by Occupation and Age*, Yorkcross Pty Ltd, Sydney.

Stoller, R. 1968, *Sex and Gender*, Science House, New York.

Stone, D. 2002, *Policy Paradox—The Art of Political Decision Making*, 3rd edn, W. W. Norton & Co., New York.

Stone, M. 1978, *When God Was a Woman*, Harcourt Brace Jovanovich, New York.

——1981, *The Education of the Black Child in Britain*, Fontana, London.

Storms, M. D. 1980, 'Theories of sexual orientation', *Journal of Personality & Social Psychology*, 38(5), 783–92.

Strange, S. 2004, 'The declining authority of states' in *The Globalization Reader*, 2nd edn, eds F. J. Lechner & J. Boli, Blackwell Publishing, Oxford, 219–24.

Strauss, A., Erlich, D., Bucher, R., Sabshin, M. & Schatzman, L. 1978 [1963], 'The hospital and its negotiated order' in *Modern Sociology*, eds P. Worsley et al., Penguin, Harmondsworth, 394–405.

Strinati, D. 1995, *An Introduction to Theories of Popular Culture*, Routledge, London.

Sturmey, R. 1991, 'Anglicanism and gender in Australian society' in *Religion in Australia*, A. Black, Allen & Unwin, Sydney.

Sudnow, D. 1967, *Passing On*, Prentice Hall, Englewood Cliffs.

Summers, A. 2002, *Damned Whores and God's Police*, rev. edn, Penguin, Melbourne.

Sumner, C. 1994, *The Sociology of Deviance: An Obituary*, Open University Press, Buckingham, UK.

Sutherland, E. H. 1960 [1949], *White Collar Crime*, Holt, Rinehart & Winston, New York.

Synnott, A. 1983, 'Little angels, little devils: a sociology of children', *Canadian Review of Sociology & Anthropology*, 20(1), 79–95.

Szasz, T. 1971, *The Manufacture of Madness*, Routledge, London.

Tait, D. 1994, 'Cautions and appearances: statistics about youth and police' in *The Police and Young People in Australia*, eds R. White & C. Alder, Cambridge University Press, Melbourne.

Tapper, A. 1990, *The Family in the Welfare State*, Allen & Unwin, Sydney.

Tavris, C. 2001, *Psychobabble and Biobunk*, Prentice Hall, Upper Saddle River, NJ.

Taylor, F. W. 1917, *The Principles of Scientific Management*, Harper & Brothers, New York.

Taylor, I., Walton, P. & Young, J. 1973, *The New Criminology*, Routledge & Kegan Paul, London.

Taylor, N. 2002, *Robbery Against Service Stations and Pharmacies: Recent Trends*, Trends and Issues in Crime and Criminal Justice No. 223, Australian Institute of Criminology, Canberra.

Taylor, P. J. 2000, 'Izations of the world: Americanization, modernization and globalization' in *Demystifying Globalization*, eds C. Hay & D. Marsh, Macmillan Press, Houndsmill, Basingstoke, 44–70.

Theall, D. F. 2000, 'Who/what is Marshall McLuhan?', *Media International Australia*, 94, 13–27.

Therborn, G. 1996, 'Child politics: dimensions and perspectives', *Childhood*, 3(1), 29–44.

——2000, 'Globalizations: dimensions, historical waves, regional effects, normative governance', *International Sociology*, 15(2), 151–79.
——2002, 'The world's trader, the world's lawyer', *European Journal of Social Theory*, 5(4), 403–17.
——2004, *Between Sex and Power: Family in the World 1900–2000*, Routledge, London.
Thiering, B. 1973, *Created Second? Aspects of Women's Liberation in Australia*, Family Life Movement of Australia, Sydney.
Thomas, C. 2001, 'Poverty, development, and hunger' in *The Globalization of World Politics*, 2nd edn, eds J. Baylis & S. Smith, Oxford University Press, Oxford, 559–81.
Thomas, C. & Bishop, D. 1984, 'The effects of formal and informal sanctions on delinquency', *Journal of Criminal Law & Criminology*, 75, 1222–45.
Thompson, E. 1993, 'The Constitution' in *Politics in Australia*, 2nd edn, ed. R. Smith, Allen & Unwin, Sydney, 61–77.
Thompson, E. P. 1967, 'Time, work discipline and industrial capitalism', *Past & Present*, 38, 56–97.
Thompson, G. F. 2007, 'Religious fundamentalisms, territories and "globalization"', *Economy & Society*, 36(1), 19–50.
Thompson, J. 1990, *Ideology and Modern Culture: Critical Social Theory in the Era of Mass Communication*, Polity Press, Cambridge.
——1995, *The Media and Modernity: A Social Theory of the Media*, Polity Press, Cambridge.
——2000, *Political Scandal: Power and Visibility in the Media Age*, Polity Press, Cambridge.
——2005, 'The new visibility', *Theory, Culture & Society*, 22(6), 31–51.
Thompson, P. 1993, 'The labour process; changing theory, changing practice', *Sociological Review*, 3(2).
Thompson, P. & McHugh, D. 1990, *Work Organisations*, Macmillan, London.
Thorne, B. 1987, 'Re-visioning women and social change: where are the children?', *Gender & Society*, 1(1), 85–109.
Thornhill, R. & Palmer, C. 2000, *The Natural History of Rape: Biological Bases of Sexual Coercion*, MIT Press, Cambridge, Mass.
Thrift, N. 2000, 'State sovereignty, globalization and the rise of soft capitalism' in *Demystifying Globalization*, eds C. Hay & D. Marsh, Macmillan, Houndsmill, Basingstoke, 71–102.
Tiefer, L. 1990, 'Sexology and the pharmaceutical industry: the threat of co-optation', *Journal of Sex Research*, 37, 273–83.
——2004, 'Biological politics (read: propaganda) remains alive and well in sexology', *Feminism & Psychology*, 14(3), 436–41.
Tiekell, A. & Peek, J. A. 1995, 'Social regulation after Fordism: regulation theory, neo-liberalism and the global–local nexus', *Economy & Society*, 24(3), 357–86.
Tillyard, E. 1952, *The Elizabethan World Picture*, Chatto & Windus, London.
Timpanaro, S. 1975, *On Materialism*, New Left Books, London.
Tinklin, T., Croxford, L., Ducklin, A. & Frame, B. 2001, *Gender and Pupil Performance in Scotland's Schools*, Scottish Executive Education Department, Edinburgh, 2.
Tisdell, C., Svizzero, S. & Lasselle, L. 2004, 'Unequal economic gains of nations from globalisation' in *Economic Globalisation: Social Conflicts, Labour and Environmental Issues*, eds C. Tisdell & R. K. Sen, Edward Elgar, Cheltenham, 71–86.

Torrey, J. 1973, 'Illiteracy in the ghetto' in *Tinker, Tailor… The Myth of Cultural Deprivation*, ed. N. Keddie, Penguin, Harmondsworth, 67–74.
Tittle, C. R. 2004, 'The arrogance of public sociology', *Social Forces*, 82(4), 1639–43.
Touraine, A. 1988, *Return of the Actor. Social Theory in Postindustrial Society*, University of Minnesota Press, Minneapolis.
Travers, P. & Richardson, S. 1993, *Living Decently*, Oxford University Press, Melbourne.
Treasury 2007, *Economic Roundup, Summer 2007*, Commonwealth of Australia, www.treasury.gov.au/documents/1221/PDF/05_private_wealth.pdf, accessed 30 December 2007.
Trigger, D. 1992, *Whitefella Comin'*, Cambridge University Press, Cambridge.
——1995, 'Everyone's agreed, the West is all you need', *Media Information Australia*, 75, 102–22.
——2003, *Does the Way We Measure Poverty Matter?*, NATSEM Discussion Paper No. 59, www.natsem.canberra.edu.au/publications.jsp, accessed 3 May 2005.
Troeltsch, E. 1976, *The Social Teachings of the Christian Churches*, Vols 1 & 2, University of Chicago Press, New York.
Tucker, R. C. 1978, *The Marx–Engels Reader*, Norton, New York.
Tucker, K. H. 1991, 'How new are the new social movements?', *Theory, Culture & Society*, 8(2), 75–98.
Tumin, M. M. 1967, 'Some principles of stratification: a critical analysis' in *Social Stratification: The Forms and Functions of Social Inequality*, R. Bendix & S. Lipset, Prentice Hall, Englewood Cliffs, NJ.
Turk, A. T. 1969, *Criminology and Legal Order*, Rand McNally, Chicago.
Turkle, S. 2000, 'Virtual sex (extract from Turkle, S. (1996). 'Life of the screen: identity in the age of the Internet')' in *Globalization: The Reader*, eds J. Beyon & D. Dunkerley, The Athlone Press, London, 229–30.
Turnbull, S. 2000, 'Figuring the audience' in *The Australian TV Book*, eds G. Turner & S. Cunningham, Allen & Unwin, Sydney, 173–89.
——2002, 'Audiences' in *The Media & Communications in Australia*, eds S. Cunningham & G. Turner, Allen & Unwin, Sydney, 85–98.
Turner, B. S. 1983, *Religion and Social Theory*, Humanities Press, Atlantic Highlands, NJ.
——1984, *The Body and Society*, Basil Blackwell, Oxford.
——1986, 'Simmel, rationalisation and the sociology of money', *Sociological Review*, 34(1), 93–114.
——1987, *Medical Power and Social Knowledge*, Sage, Beverley Hills.
——1989, 'From orientalism to global sociology', *Sociology*, 23(4), 629–38.
——1990, 'The two faces of sociology: global or national?', *Theory, Culture & Society*, 7(2), 343–58.
——1992, *Regulating Bodies*, Routledge, London.
——1993, 'Baudrillard for sociologists' in *Forget Baudrillard?*, eds C. Rojek & B. S. Turner, Routledge, London.
——2006, 'Classical sociology and cosmopolitanism: a critical defence of the social', *British Journal of Sociology*, 57(1), 133–51.
Turner, G. 1993, 'Media texts and messages' in *The Media in Australia: Industries, Texts, Audiences*, ed. S. Cunningham & G. Turner, Allen & Unwin, Sydney, 203–66.

——1996, *British Cultural Studies: An Introduction*, 2nd edn, Routledge, London.

——2004, *Understanding Celebrity*, Sage, London.

Turner, G., Bonner, F. & Marshall, P. D. 2000, *Fame Games: The Production of Celebrity in Australia*, Cambridge University Press, Melbourne.

Turner, J. H. & Maryanski, A. 1979, *Functionalism*, Benjamin/Cummings Publishing, CA.

Turrell, G. 1995, 'Social class and health: a summary of the overseas and Australian evidence' in *Sociology of Health and Illness*, 2nd edn, eds G. M. Lupton & J. M. Najman, Macmillan, Melbourne, 113–42.

Tylor, E. B. 1891, *Primitive Culture: Researches into the Development of Mythology, Philosophy, Religion, Language, Art, and Custom*, 3rd edn, J. Murray, London.

UNCTAD 2007, *Handbook of Statistics, Worldwatch Institute's Vital Signs 2006–2007 Report*, United Nations, Geneva.

UNESCO 1952, *What is Race? Evidence from Scientists*, United Nations Educational, Scientific and Cultural Organisation, Paris.

United Nations Development Program 2004, *Human Development Report 2004: Cultural Liberty in Today's Diverse World*, United Nations, http://hdr.undp.org/reports/global/2004/, accessed 3 May 2005.

United States Department of Homeland Security 2009, *Yearbook of Immigration Statistics: 2008*, US Department of Homeland Security, Office of Immigration Statistics, Washington, DC, 5.

Universities Australia 2008, *Participation and Equity: A Review of the Participation in Higher Education of People from Low Socioeconomic Backgrounds and Indigenous People*, Centre for the Study of Higher Education, University of Melbourne.

Urry, J. 1990, *The Tourist Gaze*, Sage, London.

——2007, *Mobilities*, Polity Press, Cambridge.

van Dijk, T. 1991, *Racism and the Press*, Routledge, London.

van Dijk, J. J. M., Manchin, R., van Kesteren, J. N. & Hideg, G. 2007, *The Burden of Crime in the EU: A Comparative Analysis of the European Survey of Crime and Safety (2005 EU ICS)*, Gallup Europe, Brussels.

van Dijk, J. J. M., van Kesteren, J. N. & Smit, P. 2007 *Criminal Victimisation in Internal Perspectives: Key Findings from the 2004–2005 ICVS and EU ICS*. WODC.

van Kesteren, J., Mayhew, P. & Nieuwbeerta, P. 2001, *Criminal Victimisation in Seventeen Countries: Key Findings from the 2000 International Crime Victims Survey*, Research and Documentation Centre, The Hague.

van Krieken, R. 1989, 'Towards "good and useful men and women": the state and childhood in Sydney, 1840/1890', *Australian Historical Studies*, 23(93), 405–25.

——1991, *Children and the State*, Allen & Unwin, Sydney.

——2005, 'The "best interests of the child" and parental separation: on the "civilizing of parents"', *Modern Law Review*, 68(1), 25–48.

van Krieken, R. & Bühler-Niederberger, D. 2009, 'Rethinking the sociology of childhood: conflict, competition and cooperation between children and adults in contemporary social life' in *New Handbook of International Sociology*, eds A. Denis & D. Kalekin-Fishman, Sage, London, 185–200.

van Maanen, J. 1988, *Tales of the Field: On Writing Ethnography*, University of Chicago Press, Chicago.

van Vree, W. 1999, *Meetings, Manners, and Civilization: The Development of Modern Meeting Behaviour*, Leicester University Press, London.

Veno, A. & Veno, E. 1989, 'The police, riots and public order' in *Australian Policing*, eds D. Chappell & P. Wilson, Butterworths, Sydney.

Vernon, P. E. 1969, *Intelligence and Cultural Environment*, Methuen, London.

Vinson, T. 2007, *Dropping off the Edge: The Distribution of Disadvantage in Australia*, Catholic Social Services Australia and Jesuit Social Services, www.australiandisadvantage.org.au/order.html, accessed 30 January 2008.

Voas, D. & Crockett, A. 2005, 'Religion in Britain: neither believing nor belonging', *Sociology*, 39(1), 11–28.

Vold, G. B. 1958, *Theoretical Criminology*, Oxford University Press, New York.

Volkmer, I. 1999, *News in the Global Public Sphere: A Study of CNN and Its Impact on Global Communication*, University of Luton Press, Luton.

——2002, 'Towards a new world news order? Journalism and political crises in the global network society' in *Journalism After September 11*, eds. S. Allen & B. Zelizer, Routledge, London, 235–46.

——2003, 'The global network society and the global public sphere', *Development*, 46(1), 9–16.

Volkmer, I. & Heinrich, A. 2009, 'CNN and beyond: journalism in a globalized network sphere' in *Broadcast Journalism: A Critical Introduction*, eds. J. Chapman & M. Kinsey, Routledge, London, 49–57.

Voye, L. 1995, 'From institutional Catholicism to "Christian inspiration": another look at Belgium' in *The Postwar Generation and Establishment Religion: Cross-Cultural Perspectives*, eds W. C. Roof, J. W. Carroll & D. A. Roozen, Waterview Press, Boulder, Co., 191–206.

Wade, R. H. 2002, 'Globalisation, poverty and income distribution: does the liberal argument hold?' in *Globalisation, Living Standards and Inequality: Recent Progress and Continuing Challenges, Proceedings of a Conference Held in Sydney on 27–28 May 2002*, eds, D. Gruen, T. O'Brien & J. Lawson, Reserve Bank of Australia and Australian National Treasury, Canberra, 37–65.

Waitzkin, H. 1983, *The Second Sickness*, The Free Press, Glencoe, Ill.

Walby, S. 1990, *Theorizing Patriarchy*, Basil Blackwell, Oxford.

——2003, 'The myth of the nation-state: theorizing society and polities in a global era', *Sociology*, 37(3), 529–46.

Walker, J. 1994, 'Trends in crime and criminal justice' in *The Australian Criminal Justice System: The Mid-1990s*, eds D. Chappell & P. Wilson, Butterworths, Sydney.

Walker, J. & McDonald, D. 1995, *The Over-Representation of Indigenous People in Custody in Australia*, Trends and Issues Paper No. 47, Australian Institute of Criminology, Canberra.

Walker, J. C. 1988, *Louts and Legends*, Allen & Unwin, Sydney.

Walklate, S. 1998, *Understanding Criminology*, Open University Press, Buckingham, UK.

Wall, T. F. 2001, *Thinking Critically about Philosophical Problems: A Modern Introduction*, Wadsworth, Thomson Learning, Melbourne.

Walter, J. & Woerner, J. 2007, *The Well-Being of Australians: Groups with the Highest and Lowest Well-Being in Australia*, Australian

Unity Well-Being Index Survey Special Report, Australian Centre on Quality of Life, Deakin University, Geelong, www.australianunity.com.au/au/info/pdf/Windex_survey17_report.pdf, accessed 30 December 2007.

Wallerstein, I. 1979, *The Capitalist World-Economy*, Cambridge University Press, Cambridge.

——1983, *Historical Capitalism with Capitalist Civilization*, Verso, London and New York.

——1984, *The Politics of the World-Economy, the States, the Movements and the Civilizations, Essays by Immanuel Wallerstein*, Cambridge University Press, Cambridge.

——1987, 'World-systems analysis' in *Social Theory Today*, eds A. Giddens & J. Turner, Polity Press, Cambridge, 309–24.

——1996, 'The global possibilities, 1990–2025' in *The Age of Transition: Trajectory of the World-System 1945–2025*, eds T. K. Hopkins & I. Wallerstein, Zed Books, London, 226–43.

——2000 [1974], 'The world system (extract from The rise and future demise of the capitalist world system)' in *Globalization: The Reader*, eds J. Beyon & D. Dunkerley, The Athlone Press, London, 233–8.

——2002, 'The eagle has crash landed', *Foreign Policy Magazine*, July/August.

——2004, 'The dilemmas of open space: the future of the WSF', *International Social Sciences Journal*, 182, 629–37.

——2005, 'After developmentalism and globalization, what?' *Social Forces*, 83(3), 1263–78.

——2006, 'The curve of American power', *New Left Review*, 40, 77–94.

Wallis, R. 1984, *The Elementary Forms of the New Religious Life*, Routledge & Kegan Paul, London.

Walton, T. 2004, 'Steven Prefontaine: from rebel with a cause to hero with a Swoosh', *Sociology of Sport Journal*, 21(1), 61–83.

Ward, R. 1958, *The Australian Legend*, Oxford University Press, Melbourne.

Warner, M. 1993, 'Introduction' in *Fear of a Queer Planet: Queer Politics and Social Theory*, ed. M. Warner, University of Minnesota Press, Minneapolis.

——1999, *The Trouble with Normal: Sex, Politics, and the Ethics of Queer Life*, Harvard University Press, Cambridge, Mass.

Warrington, M. & Younger, M. 2000, 'The other side of the gender gap', *Gender and Education*, 12(4), 493–507.

Waters, M. 2001, *Globalization*, 2nd edn, Routledge, London & New York.

Waters, R. 1992, 'It's a miracle', from the album *Amused to Death* by Roger Waters, 1992 Sony, Lyrics Copyright, 1988–1991 Roger Waters Music Overseas Ltd/Pink Floyd Music Publishers Inc.

Watson, J. L. 2004 [1997], 'McDonald's in Hong Kong' in *The Globalization Reader*, 2nd edn, eds F. J. Lechner & J. Boli, Blackwell, Oxford, 125–32.

Weatherburn, D. 1996, 'Property crime: linking theory to policy' in *Crime and Justice: An Australian Textbook in Criminology*, ed. K. Hazlehurst, Law Book Company Information Services, Sydney, 205–32.

Weatherburn, D., Lind, B. & Hua, J. 2003, *Contact with the New South Wales Court and Prison Systems: The Influence of Age, Indigenous Status and Gender*, Contemporary Issues in Crime and Justice No. 78, Crime and Justice Bulletin, NSW Bureau of Crime Statistics and Research, Sydney.

Weber, M. 1924, *Gesammelte Aufsätze zur Soziologie und Sozialpolitik*, J. C. B. Mohr, Tübingen.

——1930, *The Protestant Ethic and the Spirit of Capitalism*, Allen & Unwin, London.

——1949, *The Methodology of the Social Sciences*, The Free Press, New York (German orig. 1903–1917).

——1964, *The Theory of Social and Economic Organization*, The Free Press, New York.

——1968, *On Charisma and Institution Building*, ed. S. N. Eisenstadt, Chicago University Press, Chicago.

——1972, 'Georg Simmel as sociologist', *Social Research*, 39, 155–63.

——1978, *Economy and Society*, University of California Press, Berkeley. (See also Gerth & Mills 1948.)

Weedon, C. 1987, *Feminist Practice and Post-Structuralist Theories*, Blackwell, Oxford.

Weeks, J. 1985, *Sexuality and Its Discontents*, Routledge & Kegan Paul, London.

Weiner, G. Arnot, M. & David, M. 1997, 'Is the future female? Female success, male disadvantage and changing gender patterns in education', in *Education, Culture, Economy, Society*, eds A. H. Halsey, H. Lauder, P. Brown & A. S. Wells, Oxford University Press, Oxford.

Weiss, L. 1997, 'Globalization and the myth of the powerless state', *New Left Review*, 225, 3–27.

——2003, *The Myth of the Powerless State*, Cornell University Press, Ithaca, NY.

Welch, A. 1996, *Australian Education: Reform or Crisis?*, Allen & Unwin, Sydney.

Welch, D. 2008 'Clearance rates for NSW cops a shocker', *Sydney Morning Herald*, 7 December 2008.

West, B. 2005, 'Independent travel and international civil religious pilgrimage: backpackers at the Gallipoli battlefields' in *Down the Road: Exploring Backpackers and Independent Travel*, ed. B. West, API Press, Perth.

West, B. 2008, 'Enchanting pasts: the role of international civil religious pilgrimage in reimagining national collective memory', *Sociological Theory*, 26(3), 258–70.

West, C. 1984, *Routine Complications*, Indiana University Press, Bloomington.

Westergaard, J. 1995, *Who gets What? The Hardening of Class Inequality in the Late Twentieth Century*, Polity Press, Cambridge.

Westergaard, J. & Resler, H. 1975, *Class in a Capitalist Society*, Heinemann, London.

Western, J. S. 1983, *Social Inequality in Australian Society*, Macmillan, Melbourne.

——1991, 'Dimensions of the Australian class structure' in Baxter, J., Emmison, M. & Western, J., *Class Analysis in Contemporary Australia*, Macmillan, South Australia, 66–85.

Western, M. C. 1991, 'Class structure and class formation in Australia', unpublished PhD thesis, Department of Anthropology and Sociology, University of Queensland.

Wexler, P. 1992, *Becoming Somebody: Toward a Social Psychology of School*, Falmer Press, London.

Wheelahan, L. 2007, 'How competency-based training locks the working class out of powerful knowledge: a modified Bernsteinian analysis', *British Journal of Sociology of Education*, 28(5), 637–51.

Wheelwright, E. L. 1972, 'Concentration of private economic

power' in *Australian Capitalism*, eds J. Playford & D. Kirsner, Penguin, Melbourne, 65–83.
Wheelwright, E. L. & Miskelly, J. 1967, *Anatomy of Australian Manufacturing Industry*, Law Book Co., Sydney.
Whelehan, I. 1995, *Modern Feminist Thought: From the Second Wave to 'Post-Feminism'*, Edinburgh University Press, Edinburgh.
——2000, *Overloaded: Popular Culture and the Future of Feminism*, Women's Press, London.
White, R. 1981, *Inventing Australia*, Allen & Unwin, Sydney.
——1990, *No Space of Their Own*, Cambridge University Press, Melbourne.
——1994, 'Street life' in *The Police and Young People in Australia*, eds R. White & C. Alder, Cambridge University Press, Melbourne.
——2002, *Understanding Youth Gangs*, Trends and Issues in Crime and Criminal Justice No. 237, Australian Institute of Criminology, Canberra.
——2008, *Crimes Against Nature*, Oxford University Press, South Melbourne.
White, R. & Alder, C. (eds) 1994, *The Police and Young People in Australia*, Cambridge University Press, Melbourne.
White, R. & Habibis, D. 2005, *Crime and Society*, Oxford University Press, Oxford.
White, R. & Perrone, S. 2000, *Young People and Gangs*, Trends and Issues in Crime and Criminal Justice No. 167, Australian Institute of Criminology, Canberra.
White, R. & van der Velden, J. 1995, 'Class and criminality', *Social Justice*, 22(1), 51–74.
White, R., Perrone, S., Guerra, C. & Lampugnani, R. 1999, *Ethnic Youth Gangs in Australia: Do They Exist?*, Overview Report, Australian Multicultural Foundation, Melbourne.
Whyte, W. F. 1955, *Street Corner Society*, 2nd edn, University of Chicago Press, Chicago.
——1992, 'In defense of *Street Corner Society*', *Journal of Contemporary Ethnography*, 21(1), 52–68.
Wild, R. 1974, *Bradstow*, Angus & Robertson, Sydney.
——1978, *Social Stratification in Australia*, George Allen & Unwin, Sydney.
Wilensky, H. L. 1969, 'Work, careers and social integration' in *Industrial Man*, ed. T. Burns, Penguin, Harmondsworth.
Wilensky, H. L. & Edwards, H. 1974, 'The skidder: ideological adjustments of downward mobile workers' in *Social Stratification: a Reader*, J. Lopreato & L. S. Lewis, Harper & Row, New York.
Wilensky, H. L. & Lebeaux, C. N. 1958, *Industrial Society and Social Welfare*, The Free Press, New York.
Wilkins, L. 1964, *Social Deviance*, Tavistock, London.
Wilkins, R. 2007, *The Changing Socio-Demographic Composition of Poverty in Australia: 1982–2004*, Melbourne Institute Working Paper Series, Working Paper No. 12/07, Melbourne Institute of Applied Economic and Social Research, University of Melbourne, Melbourne.
Wilkinson, R. & Pickett, K. 2009, *The Spirit Level: Why More Equal Societies Almost Always Do Better*, Allen Lane, London.
Willetts, P. 2001, 'Transnational actors and international organizations in global politics' in *The Globalization of World Politics*, 2nd edn, eds J. Baylis & S. Smith, Oxford University Press, Oxford, 356–83.
Williams, C. 1981, *Open Cut*, George Allen & Unwin, Sydney.
——1988, *Blue, White and Pink Collar Workers in Australia*, Allen & Unwin, Sydney.

——2003, 'Sky Service: the demands of emotional labor in the airline industry', *Gender Work and Organization*, 10(5), 513–50.
Williams, M. 1986, *Society Today*, Macmillan, London.
Williams, N. 1986, *The Yolngu and Their Land: a System of Land Tenure and the Fight for Its Recognition*, Australian Institute of Aboriginal Studies, Canberra.
Williamson, J. 1990, 'What Washington means by policy reform' in *Latin American Adjustment: How Much Has Happened?*, ed. J. Williamson, Institute for International Economics, Washington, DC.
Willis, E. 1989, *Medical Dominance*, Allen & Unwin, Sydney.
——1994, *Illness and Social Relations*, Allen & Unwin, Sydney.
Willis, K. 2004, 'Personal choice/social responsibility: women aged 40–49 years and mammography screening', *Journal of Sociology*, 40(2), 121–36.
Willis, P. 1977, *Learning to Labour: How Working Class Kids Get Working Class Jobs*, Saxon House, Farnborough.
Willmott, P. 1988, 'Urban kinship past and present', *Social Studies Review*, November.
Wilson, B. R. 1982, *Religion in Sociological Perspective*, Oxford University Press, Oxford.
Wilson, E. O. 1975a, *Sociobiology*, Harvard University Press, Cambridge, Mass.
——1975b, 'Human decency is animal', *New York Times Magazine*, 12 October.
Wilson, J. Q. 1975, *Thinking about Crime*, Basic Books, New York.
Wilson, J. Q. & Herrnstein, R. J. 1985, *Crime and Human Nature*, Simon & Schuster, New York.
Wilson, J. Q. & Kelling, G. L. 1982, 'Broken windows', *The Atlantic Monthly*, 249(3), 29–38.
Winch, P. 1970, 'Understanding a primitive society' in *Rationality*, ed. B. Wilson, Blackwell, Oxford, 78–111.
——1990, *The Idea of a Social Science*, 2nd edn, Routledge, London.
Winston, B. 1998, *Media Technology and Society. A History: From the Telegraph to the Internet*, Routledge, London.
Wiseman, J. 1998, *Global Nation? Australia and the Politics of Globalisation*, Cambridge University Press, Cambridge.
Wilson, W. J. 1991, 'Studying inner-city dislocations', *American Sociological Review*.
Winston, B. 1998, *Media Technology and Society. A History: From the Telegraph to the Internet*, Routledge, London.
Wober, J. M. & Fazal, S. 1994, '*Neighbours* at home and away: British viewers' perception of Australian soap operas', *Media Information Australia*, 71, 78–87.
Wolf, E. R. 1982, *Europe and the People Without History*, University of California Press, Berkeley.
Wolf, K. H. (ed.) 1950, *The Sociology of Georg Simmel*, The Free Press, New York.
Wolf, N. 1991, *The Beauty Myth: How Images of Beauty Are Used Against Women*, William Morrow, New York.
Wolpe, A. M. 1988, *Within School Walls: The Role of Discipline, Sexuality and the Curriculum*, Routledge & Kegan Paul, London.
Wood, S. 1989, 'The transformation of work?' in *The Transformation of Work?*, ed. S. Wood, Unwin Hyman, London.
Woods, P. 1979, *The Divided School*, Routledge & Kegan Paul, London.
Woodward, I. 2003, 'Divergent narratives in the imagining of the

home among middle class consumers', *Journal of Sociology*, 39(4), 391–412.

——2006, 'Investigating the consumption anxiety thesis', *The Sociological Review*, 54(2), 263–82.

Woodward, I. & Emmison, M. 2001, 'From aesthetic principles to collective sentiments: the logics of everyday judgements of taste', *Poetics*, 29(6), 295–316.

Woolgar, S. (ed.) 2002, *Virtual Society? Technology, Society, Reality*, Oxford University Press, Oxford.

——2004, 'Reflexive internet? The British experience of new electronic technologies' in *The Network Society: A Cross-Cultural Perspective*, ed. M. Castells, Edward Elgar, Cheltenham, UK, 125–42.

World Bank 2005, *What Is the World Bank?*, www.worldbank.org, accessed 22 March 2005.

World Trade Organization n.d., *The World Trade Organization*, www.wto.org/english/res_e/doload_e/inbr_e.pdf, accessed 29 May 2005.

Worsley, P. 1970, *Introducing Sociology*, Penguin, Harmondsworth.

Wright, C., Weekes, D., McGlaughlin, A. & Webb, D. 1998, 'Masculinised discourses within education and the construction of black male identities amongst African Caribbean youth', *British Journal of Sociology of Education*, 19(1), 75–88.

Wright, E. O. 1985, *Classes*, New Left Books, London.

——1996, 'Juvenile justice' in *Crime and Justice*, ed. K. Hazlehurst, Law Book Company, Sydney.

Wundersitz, J. 1996, 'Juvenile justice' in *Crime and Justice*, ed. K. Hazlehurst, Law Book Company, Sydney.

Wuthnow, R. 2001 'Spirituality and spiritual practice' in *The Blackwell Companion to Sociology of Religion*, ed. R. K. Fenn, Blackwell Publishers, Oxford, 306–20.

Wynhausen, E. 2004, 'Our hidden families', *Weekend Australian*, 10 July, www.theaustralian.news.com.au/common/story_page/0,5744,10091040%255E28737,00.html, accessed 20 July 2004.

Yeatman, A. 1986, 'Women, domestic life and sociology' in *Feminist Challenges*, eds C. Pateman & E. Gross, Northeastern University Press, Boston, 157–72.

Yinger, J. M. 1981, 'Towards a theory of assimilation and dissimilation', *Ethnic & Racial Studies*, 4(3), 249–64.

Young, C. 1990, *Balancing Families and Work*, AGPS, Canberra.

Young, J. 1971, 'The role of the police as amplifiers of deviancy, negotiators of reality and translators of fantasy' in *Images of Deviance*, ed. S. Cohen, Penguin, Harmondsworth.

——1998, 'Writing on the cusp of change' in *The New Criminology Revisited*, eds P. Walton & J. Young, Macmillan, London, 259–95.

——1999, *The Exclusive Society: Social Exclusion, Crime and Difference in Late Modernity*, Sage, London.

Young, M. F. D. (ed.) 1971, *Knowledge and Control: New Directions for the Sociology of Education*, Collier Macmillan, London.

Young, M. & Willmott, P. 1973, *The Symmetrical Family*, Routledge & Kegan Paul, London.

——1975, *Family and Kinship in East London*, Routledge & Kegan Paul, London.

Youth Justice Coalition, Western Sydney Juvenile Justice Interest Group and Youth Action and Policy Association 1994, *Nobody Listens: The Experience of Contact Between Young People and the Police*, Youth Justice Coalition, Sydney.

Zachary, G. P. 2000 [1999], 'The world gets in touch with its inner American' in *Globalization*, ed. K. Sjursen, 72(5), 146–52.

Zadoroznyj, M. 2001, 'Birth and the reflexive consumer: trust, risk and medical dominance in obstetric encounters', *Journal of Sociology*, 37(2), 117–40.

Zaretsky, E. 1982, 'The place of the family in the origins of the welfare state' in *Rethinking the Family: Some Feminist Questions*, eds B. Thorne & M. Yalom, Longman, New York, 188–224.

Zborowski, M. 1952, 'Cultural components in response to pain', *Journal of Social Issues*, 8, 16–30.

Zelizer, V. 1985, *Pricing the Priceless Child: The Changing Social Value of Children*, Basic Books, New York.

——1994, *The Social Meaning of Money*, Basic Books, New York.

——2002, 'Kids and commerce', *Childhood*, 9(4), 375–96.

——2005, 'The priceless child revisited' in *Studies in Modern Childhood: Society, Agency, Culture*, ed. J. Qvortrup, Macmillan, Basingstoke, 184–200.

Zevallos, Z. 2003, 'That's my Australian side', *Journal of Sociology*, 39(1), 81–98.

Zimmerman, C. C. & Frampton, M. E. 1966, 'Theories of Frédéric Le Play' in *Kinship and Family Organization*, ed. B. Farber, John Wiley & Sons, New York, 14–23.

Zimmerman, D. H. & Weider, D. L. 1971, 'Ethnomethodology and the problem of order: comment on Denzin' in *Understanding Everyday Life*, ed. J. D. Douglas, Routledge & Kegan Paul, London, 285–95.

Zola, I. K. 1973, 'Pathways to the doctor', *Social Science & Medicine*, 7, 677–89.

Zuboff, S. 1988, *In the Age of the Smart Machine*, Basic Books, New York.

Zubrzycki, J. 1971, *The Teaching of Sociology in Australia and New Zealand*, Cheshire, Melbourne.

Zwingle, E. 2000 [1999], 'A world together' in *Globalization*, ed. K. Sjursen, 72(5), 53–64.

Zysman, J. 1996, 'The myth of a "global" economy: enduring national foundations and emerging regional realities', *New Political Economy*, 1(2), 157–85.

Glossary

Aborigine An Indigenous inhabitant of Australia.

Absolute poverty An absence of the material resources necessary for individuals and families to meet their basic needs.

Acceptance of hierarchy The organisation of schools on a hierarchical principle of authority and control—teachers give orders and pupils obey. Students have little control over the subjects they study or how they study them. This prepares them for relationships within the workplace where, if workers are to stay out of trouble, they will need to defer to the authority of supervisors and managers.

Action research Going beyond merely observing, describing and explaining a social setting or group, by intervening in action to promote change in social and cultural practices, politics, public policy and so on.

Affective or emotional action Stems from an individual's emotional state at a particular time.

Alienation Associated with the thinking of Marx, this term refers to the exploitation of workers and their sense that their work is meaningless.

Allocative function The idea that education helps allocate young people to different positions in society through training and qualifications. Different theories describe this function as operating in different ways.

Alternative therapies A term applied in a loose way to encompass the range of procedures, practices and knowledge that are not authorised by, and contend with, Western biomedicine—for example, acupuncture, traditional Chinese medicine and reflexology.

Altruistic suicide Suicide resulting from the individual being so well integrated into society that he or she sacrifices his or her own life out of a sense of duty to others.

Americanisation It is argued that Americanisation occurs through a process of progressive modernisation, in which each locality becomes progressively modernised 'under the relentless force of American cultural imperialism' (Featherstone 1995, p. 87). As locations become more modernised, they move up the modernity hierarchy. Each movement towards complete modernisation inches a locality one step closer to the ultimate realisation of a global America. As such, Americanisation is strongly equated with modernisation and globalisation.

Anomic suicide Suicide resulting from social disorder creating imbalances and contradictions in the regulation of individual behaviour.

Anomie A cultural condition described by Durkheim in which morals and customary constraints on behaviour were weak.

Anomie theorists They argue that crime is the result of a disjunction between the goals and values encouraged by the social order and the opportunities available to citizens to achieve them.

Assimilation The process of particular human groups being absorbed into a larger group, culture or social structure.

Assimilationism The policy holding that migrant groups should come to take on the characteristics of the host culture.

Asymmetry Structural difference between boys' and girls' sexual and psychological development. Mead argued that a girl identifies with her first primary caregiver, her mother, whereas a boy's identity is based on a separation from his mother. This structural requirement of boys and men to develop their specifically male identity through differentiation from females (the mother) may explain a greater orientation towards achievement.

Authority Power understood as being legitimate, and obeyed for that reason, rather than because of the exercise of force.

Banal nationalism Low-key nationalism that becomes a sort of commonsense chain migration—a migration process in which social networks play a major role. This can lead to spatially concentrated populations of migrant groups.

Belief system An interrelated set of beliefs and ideas that help people to make sense of, and interpret, their world.

Biomedicine The form of medicine that emerged in Western modernity. Its characteristics include a mechanistic model of the body and a scientific knowledge base. The term is often expanded to include medical institutions and organisational forms.

Breadwinner system A term used by Davis for the family structure based on the man as the breadwinner and the woman as homemaker.

Calculability One of the four interconnected dimensions in what Ritzer called the 'McDonaldisation' process, in which organisations, their work processes and the human resources and raw materials they work with are made as quantifiable and calculable as possible. *See also* **Control**, **Efficiency** and **Predictability**.

Capitalism A system of production that emerged with modernity, which is characterised by industrial production, private ownership of capital (including property) and wage labour.

Capitalists Those who own the means of production.

Case studies The detailed examination of single examples. A case study could involve the study of a single institution, community or social group, an individual person, a particular historical event or a single social action.

Cathexis relations Relations involving the investment of emotions and desire, 'the patterning of object-choice, desire and desirability … the production of heterosexuality and homosexuality and the relationship between them … the socially structured antagonisms of gender (woman-hating, man-hating, self-hatred) … trust and distrust, jealousy and solidarity in marriages and other relationships … the emotional relationships involved in rearing children' (Connell 1987, p. 97). This is one of the three substantially distinct 'structures of relationship' between men and women, constituting what Connell calls the 'gender order' or 'gender regime'.

Causality How cause and effect are related.

Celebrity An individual, a desired cultural identity and a system for representing a famous person that suits the commercial interests of the media and publicity industries. The fame, talent and/or desirability of the celebrity in the eyes of the audience represent the legitimacy and triumph of individualism. The legitimacy of this value system helps make the celebrity a commodity that attaches cultural significance to brands, products and services.

Chain migration A process in which migrants follow one after another from the same point of origin to the same destination, often due to social networks and kinship ties.

Charismatic authority Power based on the exceptional personal characteristics of particular individuals.

Chicago School A theory that explained crime in terms of the social ecology of the city and the belief that social disorganisation was linked to crime.

Circulation mobility Occurs when the stratification system is open and permits free movement up or down the occupational hierarchy regardless of the position an individual is born into.

Citizenship Refers to the idea that by virtue of membership of a political community individuals are granted a range of political, civic and social entitlements, such as the right to vote, and the fulfilment of basic human needs for food and shelter.

Civic nationalism A form of nationalism that defines belonging in terms of commitment to laws, institutions and subjective belonging. This form of nationalism is generally more open to newcomers than ethnic nationalism.

Civil religion Describes the rituals, symbols and language used by the state, which is often religious in nature and seeks to promote a homogeneous or uniform national culture and identity.

Class A social group, defined in terms of its economic position in a hierarchy of inequality and with material interests that differentiate it from other classes.

Class consciousness A term used by Marx to describe the awareness a class has of its shared interests. When used in relation to the working class this includes an understanding of the exploitative nature of existing social relationships.

Coercion Forms of power not founded primarily on their legitimacy, but on the exercise of force.

Cohabitation Living together as husband and wife without being legally married.

Commodity form The form taken by human labour under capitalism whereby 'the social character of men's labour appears to them as an objective characteristic' (Marx 1954, p. 77).

Communism The classless society that Marx predicted would follow the collapse of capitalism, in which inequality and exploitation would no longer exist and human potential would be fulfilled.

Comparative method The use of comparisons between different societies or groups within one society or more, and comparisons at the same or different points in time.

Compulsory heterosexuality The social and cultural imposition of a heterosexual model of sexual attraction, which Rich thought overlays, for women, a prior and more fundamental female bonding.

Computer-mediated interaction Refers to a wide-range of communications interactions enabled by networked computers, including email, real-time chat, message boards, social networking sites, video calls and videoconferencing. The term signifies an important addition to human communication in modernity, as it encompasses and complicates dimensions of face-to-face communication (e.g. video calls, Skype), mediated interaction (email) and mediated quasi-interaction (live video streaming).

Conflict What is emphasised by sociologists critical of consensus approaches to sociology, paying greater attention to the fundamental differences of interest among different social groups, especially those divided along lines of class, gender and ethnicity.

Conflict theory Explains many aspects of social formations in terms of what is believed are fundamental differences of interest among social groups, which are usually based on economic differences and create unequal relations of power.

Consensual unified elite One of the three different types of elite structure identified by Higley, in which the unity of the elite is based on the elite's ongoing commitment to the stability of existing social and political institutions, despite other divisions between them. *See also* **Disunified elite** and **Ideologically unified elite**.

Consensus What is emphasised by sociologists critical of conflict approaches, paying more attention to questions of social order, stability and cohesion.

Control One of the four interconnected dimensions in what Ritzer calls the 'McDonaldisation' process, whereby there is maximum control over everything that organisations deal with: human beings and their labour, raw materials, labour processes and sometime animals. *See also* **Calculability**, **Efficiency** and **Predictability**.

Convergence A widely used term that refers to the bringing together of formerly discrete media and communications technologies and industry sectors. Whereas the book, television and radio were once distinct objects, the digitisation of information has meant that sounds, data, images and text can all be transmitted via computer-mediated communication. This process has separated content from the restrictions of specific media formats and resulted in the convergence of (a) media content, (b) computing and information technologies and (c) communication networks. An outcome of these developments is the birth of a 'convergence culture' in which longstanding distinctions between the users and producers of media content have blurred and a 'do-it-yourself' participatory media culture has arisen. Sites such as YouTube, fan-produced online videos and fan fiction have grown in popularity in this setting.

Corporate crime Criminal acts committed by corporate executives and managers in the course of their employment that are intended to benefit the corporation and that, directly or indirectly, also benefit them.

Correlation A tendency for two or more things to be found together. It may also refer to the strength of the relationship between them.

Counter-school culture A way of life opposed to the values espoused by the school.

Credibility Refers to the trustworthiness of a researcher's methods and findings.

Crime Behaviour that is proscribed and punishable by the law.

Critical theory The work of the 'Frankfurt School' (a group of sociologists connected to the Institute of Social Research, established at the University of Frankfurt in 1923). Critical theorists aimed to develop the work of Marx to analyse social changes during the 20th century.

Critical thought Critical thinking is central to the sociological perspective and involves challenging commonsense explanations of human behaviour.

Cultural capital A form of value associated with consumption patterns, lifestyle choices, social attributes and formal qualifications.

Cultural diversity Variations in the beliefs, practices, values and symbols that humans learn from their social environment.

Cultural pluralism A situation in which cultural diversity is identified and positively evaluated at an ideological level, without any necessary connection with institutional change.

Cultural relativism An approach that does not evaluate cultures as 'good' or 'bad' but sees each as *different*, having its own internal logic. *See also* **Ethnocentric assumptions**.

Cultural scenarios One of the three levels at which 'sexual scripts' operate, referring to conceptions of sexual identity in social institutions and 'collective life'; they 'instruct in the normative requirements of particular roles' (Simon & Gagnon 1986, p. 98).

Culture Shared values, norms and everyday practices.

Dark figure of crime The number of criminal acts that are not reported to the police and therefore do not appear in official recorded crime rates.

Deductive approach Approach whereby one begins with a theory and tests it against the evidence, rather than developing a theory as a result of examining the data. *See also* **Inductive methodology**.

Deglobalisation The ways in which globalisation processes can also change direction and go into reverse, so that there are times when the world can become *less* integrated across the dimensions of economics politics and culture.

Demographic transition The conceptual framework often used to analyse the change in the size and structure of human populations in the course of industrialisation.

Denomination Religious groups that are accepted as legitimate by the religious tradition to which they belong and by the wider society. Membership is non-exclusive and usually inherited.

Deviance Norm- or rule-breaking behaviour that is usually subject to negative social sanctions.

Deviance amplification The spiral of action and reaction in which the response to an initial act of deviance structures and escalates its occurrence.

Digital divide A term used to capture existing inequalities of access to the internet and information and communications technologies. Communities, nations and continents without access to these networked resources are disadvantaged, as they are the primary sources of productivity and power in the global economy. The risk for such populations is that they will become 'black holes of informational capitalism' (Castells 2000b).

Disciplinary power Power exercised through the establishment of internalised discipline within individuals, rather than through the external imposition of control or domination.

Disciplinary society A society organised around disciplinary power.

Discipline The internalisation of models of conduct within individuals, establishing patterns of behaviour independently of any external imposition of control or domination.

Disciplined autonomy The exercise of personal freedom with self-imposed limits.

Discourse A relatively coherent assembly of particular ways of thinking, speaking and writing about a topic organised around a set of shared presumptions and premises, which varies over time and across social, cultural and political settings.

Discrimination The process by which minorities are disadvantaged. This can apply in areas such as housing, jobs and education.

Dispersed extended families Families characterised by an extended kinship network in which different families cooperate with each other, even though they live some distance apart and do not rely on each other on a day-to-day basis.

Disunified elite One of the three different types of elite structure identified by Higley, in which there are persistent, apparently irresolvable and often violent conflicts between different elites. *See also* **Consensual unified elite** and **Ideologically unified elite**.

Domestic group A family as a household sharing a roof and meals.

Domestic labour Work concerning the home or family, as opposed to wage labour.

Domestic sphere The realm of social life focused on family and interpersonal life. Often also referred to as the 'private sphere' and seen as distinct from the 'public sphere'.

Dominant ideology The prevailing ideas and values of an epoch, often seen as the ideas of the dominant social, political and economic groups.

Economic power Power based on control over financial and productive resources.

Educational knowledge code The principles underlying a set of practices, analogous to the genetic code, which underlies many variations in our appearances.

Efficiency The least costly and most effective means of achieving desired goals. Also one of the four interconnected dimensions in what Ritzer calls the 'McDonaldisation' process. *See also* **Calculability**, **Control** and **Predictability**.

Egoistic suicide Suicide resulting from the individual being insufficiently integrated into the social groups and society to which he or she belonged.

Elaborated code A kind of speech that explicitly verbalises many of the meanings that are taken for granted in a restricted code. It fills in the detail, spells out the relationships and provides the explanations omitted by restricted codes. As such, its meanings tend to be 'universalistic': they are not tied to a particular context or experience.

Elite pluralism An approach to the pluralist understanding of power that allows for the formation of elites.

Emotional labour The work that people have to do to project certain emotions and to generate these in client groups.

Empirical evidence Proof based on observation and experiment as opposed to theory or speculation. *See also* **Rationality**.

Environmental crime Unauthorised or irresponsible acts or omissions that negatively impact on people and their environments.

Epidemiology The study of the distribution of disease through populations. This is often a quantitative activity involving large data sets.

Epistemologies Differing models of the study of the methods and forms of knowledge.

Ethnic group A social group marked out by a distinctive way of life and a set of customary values and beliefs.

Ethnic nationalism   Forms of nationalism that focus on blood lines, primordial culture and language. This form of nationalism often excludes outsiders.

Ethnic politics   The organisation of arguments for changed educational policies, structure and practices around ethnic or cultural identities.

Ethnocentric assumptions   Prejudicial attitudes towards other cultures based on the moral superiority of one's own culture. *See also* **Cultural relativism**.

Ethnographic research   Entails immersion in the life of a community, culture or social setting via the use of the technique of participant observation, often supplemented by informal or semi-structured interviews, to build up as complete a picture as possible and produce a descriptive account of that place and its people. *See also* **Fieldwork, Participant observation** and **Semi-structured interviews**.

Ethnomethodology   A term coined by Garfinkel meaning a study of the methods used by people (or 'members' as ethnomethodologists refer to them) to construct, account for and give meaning to their social world.

Extended family   A family as a social unit made up of parents, children and immediate relatives, sometimes encompassing three generations at a time, living under one roof.

False consciousness   A view of reality that overlooks or glosses over the contradictions and conflicts that are built into social relationships and thereby helps to maintain the existing system.

Falsify   To prove wrong.

Family wage   A wage sufficient for a man or a woman to support a partner and children.

Fatalistic suicide   Suicide resulting from the excessive social regulation of individual behaviour.

Feminist theory   An umbrella term referring to the wide range of theories that place women at the centre of social analysis.

Fieldwork   Investigations carried out 'in the field', rather than under laboratory conditions, in real-life social settings, using unstructured techniques such as participant observation and informal interviewing. *See also* **Laboratory experiment**.

First 'face' of power   Power exercised through decision making. *See also* **Second 'face' of power** and **Third 'face' of power**.

Forces of production   Comprises land, raw materials, tools and machinery, the technical and scientific knowledge used in production, the technical organisation of the production process and the labour power of workers.

Fordism   Industrial production of standardised products on a massive scale, often on production lines.

Fourth estate   A term that emerged in the 19th century referring to the 'watchdog' function of the press. The media stands independent from the first three 'estates'—representative parliament, the executive (the offices and activities of political leaders) and the judiciary—serving to report and check their excesses and wrongdoings. This role is central to the maintenance of democracy. It is questionable as to whether the contemporary news media performs this function consistently.

Fourth World peoples   A politically weak indigenous population 'trapped' inside a modern nation-state.

Functionalism   A theory of society that explains society in terms of the role of culture in establishing consensus between social groups and the contribution each component of society makes to the functioning of the whole.

Fundamentalism   Fundamentalists have in common a belief that the founding religious doctrines and scriptures are literally true and valid for all times and places. In some cases this belief is associated with a political movement that seeks the radical reformation of society along lines believed to be ordained by God.

Game stage   The second stage in the development of self, as identified by Mead, in which children come to see themselves from the perspective of the various participants in a variety of different types of games. In doing so, they see themselves in terms of the collective viewpoint of the other players. *See also* **Play stage**.

Gang   A group of people who see themselves, and are seen by others, as a gang primarily because of their illegal activities.

Gay liberation   A social movement aiming to improve the rights of homosexual men and women.

Gender   The social organisation of the biological dimensions of human gender and sexual identity, generally into something recognisable as masculinity or femininity.

Gender apartheid   A conception of men and women as being different but equal, which in practice masks the real power relations between them.

Gender attribution   The decision to regard another person as male or female.

Gender revolution   The phenomenon whereby the gap in educational achievements between the genders has shifted from boys outperforming girls to girls outperforming boys.

Generalisable   The capacity to apply research findings derived from a small sample across a larger population. *See also* **Representative** and **Sample**.

Gini coefficient   A measure of inequality in which 0 is a situation of perfect equality where every income unit receives equal income and 1 is a situation of perfect inequality where one income unit owns all income.

Global public sphere   A term coined by Volkmer to describe ever-expanding 'transborder' communications via media. This expansion has seen the power of news media addressing predominantly national audiences challenged by the emergence of genuinely global platforms and audiences. Since the 1980s, communications satellites and cable technologies have accelerated this process, contributing to the rise of influential international news 'hubs' such as CNN International, BBC World, Al Jazeera, Zee-TV and Fox News. The internet has further extended this sphere.

Globalisation   The process by which people's daily lives are increasingly influenced by the growing cultural, political and economic integration of communities and nation-states.

Globalism   Robertson states that globalism refers to a 'conscious process of globalization or a set of policies designed specifically to effect greater global rather than international interactions' (2003, p. 4). More specifically, it is associated with 'American globalism', which contains hegemonic goals but also strives to redress the global inequalities and disadvantages left from the wake of colonialism and imperialism characteristic of the second wave of globalisation.

Glocalisation   Stems from the Japanese word *dochakuka*, referring to global localisation, but has also come to mean localised globalisation—that is, the local finetuning of global processes, ideas or institutions. The phrase 'think global, act local' is an example of what the term is aiming to capture.

Governmentality   A term used by Foucault to refer to the structure of power relations based on the linkage of the disciplinary strategies of governing institutions, systems of knowledge and the active projects of individuals and groups. *See also* **Liberalism**.

Grounded theory A term used by Glaser and Strauss to refer to theory, conceptual categories, hypotheses and explanations that emerge from, rather than precede or structure, the data gathered in empirical social research.

Habitus A system of dispositions that are shaped by our previous experiences and that shape our actions and beliefs.

Hegemonic masculinity The values and norms of white, heterosexual males that set the standard against which all other forms of masculinity are measured.

Hegemony The achievement of political stability through the population's acceptance of the political and moral values of the ruling class, rather through the use of force.

Hermaphroditism A condition in which a person has both male and female genitals.

Hidden curriculum A set of values that pupils learn through the experience of attending school, rather than the stated educational objectives of such institutions.

Historical documents Written material relating to past events.

Horizontal segregation Separation of the workforce into different jobs at the same status level.

Household A group sharing a roof and meals.

Human agency The active creation of social formations by human agents.

Human sciences The sciences concerned with human beings: medicine, psychiatry, psychology, criminology, sociology and so on, and the institutional practices associated with them.

Hypothesis An idea or a statement that is to be tested.

Iatrogenesis Illness that arises as a result of medical procedures.

Identity The constellation of characteristics, such as values and beliefs, which people regard as part of their self but that are derived from social forces.

Ideological power Power exercised through ideas and the management of beliefs and values.

Ideologically unified elite One of the three different types of elite structure identified by Higley, usually with a single political party organising all political viewpoints into a unified whole, often coercively. *See also* **Consensual unified elite** and **Disunified elite**.

Imagined community A group whose members feel a shared identity.

Individualism The belief that people should be treated as autonomous free agents rather than according to their membership of any collectivity. Sociologists argue that whereas traditional societies tend to emphasise the collective, contemporary societies stress the freedom and uniqueness of individuals.

Inductive methodology This approach starts by collecting data, which are then analysed to develop a theory. This theory is tested against other sets of data to see whether it is confirmed or not. If it is repeatedly confirmed, one can assume a law has been discovered.

Industrialisation The large-scale use of machines to produce goods.

Infrastructure (of society) The economic base of society, that, in Marx's view, was the most powerful determinant of all other aspects of society, including cultural phenomena.

Institutional racism Racism that is entrenched in organisational process and culture. It does not require malicious thought in individuals, but can arise from lack of sensitivity or interest.

Instrumentally rational action A type of action oriented to a clear goal; a systematic assessment of the various means of attaining a goal and the selection of the most appropriate means.

Intelligence quotient A score derived from tests designed to assess intelligence. Intelligence quotient (IQ) tests have been subject to considerable criticism for their cultural biases.

Interactionist theorists They see crime and deviance as the outcome of a social process in which the definition of deviance is negotiated by the actors involved.

Interest groups A central concept in pluralist theories of power, referring to the organisation of political groups and movements around a shared set of concerns or interests. Pluralist theorists see interest groups as the primary basis of democratic politics.

International Monetary Fund (IMF) First conceived in 1944 to develop an international framework of economic cooperation and monitoring, to avoid a repeat of the 'global' economic depression that took place in the 1930s. The IMF aims to promote and facilitate economic cooperation and expansion of a balanced growth in trade. It does this through a process of surveillance, technical and financial assistance.

Internationalisation Scholte states that internationalisation is sometimes one way of defining globalisation. Internationalisation refers to 'an intensification of cross-border interactions and interdependence between countries' (2001, p. 14). The difference between this and globalisation is that under internationalisation the concepts of borders and nation-states are more or less retained, whereas globalisation implies the progressive blurring and erosion of the meaningfulness of borders and demarcated space.

Internationalism The tendency towards linking nation-states into a global system of states.

Interpersonal scripts The second level at which sexual scripts operate, in which broader cultural models of sexual conduct are mobilised in specific social and interpersonal contexts.

Interpretive approach An approach based on the understanding of social action by interpreting the meanings and motives on which the action is based.

Intrapsychic scripts The third level at which sexual scripts operate, in which desire is managed at the individual level, including 'the ordering of images and desires that elicit and sustain sexual arousal' (Simon & Gagnon 1986, p. 97).

Invented tradition A seemingly 'traditional' activity from the deep past that was in fact made up quite recently.

Juvenile A legal term to describe individuals who are under the age of 17 or 18 years, depending on the jurisdiction.

Kinship group An organisation of people based on blood relationships and marriage.

Knowledge paradox The notion that knowledge is increasingly seen by theorists as crucial to the form of modern societies but is rarely analysed by them.

Labelling theory Argues that social groups create deviance by making the rules whose infraction constitutes deviance and by applying those rules to particular people and labelling them as outsiders.

Laboratory experiment Investigation or test carried out in a controlled environment in which the various independent variables can be controlled and manipulated.

Labour (or production) One of the three substantially distinct structures of relationship between men and women, constituting what Connell calls the gender order or gender regime, referring to 'the organization of housework and child-care, the division between unpaid and paid work, the segregation of labour markets ... discrimination of training and promotion, unequal wages and unequal exchange' (1987, p. 96).

Lay definitions of disease Understandings of illness held by the general public rather than by medical experts.

Left realism A theory of crime developed by left-wing criminologists, which recognised that some crimes were committed by the working class and that these disproportionately affected those with the least resources.

Liberal humanism An educational philosophy that emphasises learning knowledge for its own sake and its civilising effects on learners.

Liberalism An approach to power and government organised around the promotion of individual liberty.

Liberation theology A term developed in the 1960s to describe the use of Christianity and the Church, especially the Catholic Church, to support oppressed groups in their struggles to resist political oppression.

Life chances The chances that individuals and groups have of obtaining those things defined as desirable in their society, such as wealth, power and prestige.

Life histories Biographical accounts of individuals' life stories taken from face-to-face interviews and the analysis of documents such as 'life documents' (e.g. personal diaries). *See also* **Primary sources** and **Secondary sources**.

Liquid modernity A theory proposed by Bauman to describe the interplay of continuity and change that characterises contemporary social life.

Localism Attachment to a particular place.

Market situation The relationship of individuals and groups to the labour market according to their skills and other resources, including capital.

Masculinity The assembly of qualities and characteristics socially ascribed to boys and men.

McDonaldisation A term coined by Ritzer to refer to 'the process by which the principles of the fast-food restaurant are coming to dominate more and more sectors of American society as well as the rest of the world' (2004, p. 1). The term does not simply refer to the spread and global proliferation of McDonald's restaurants, or indeed the global franchising of countless other industries. Instead, Ritzer identifies McDonald's as the paradigm example of modern bureaucratic rationality. The dimensions of this involve efficiency, calculability, predictability and control through non-human technology. Paradoxically, such rationality produces its own forms of irrationality that more often than not undermine any elements of efficiency, calculability etc.

Means of production Marx's term for the resources used to produce goods, such as raw materials and machinery.

Mechanical solidarity Durkheim's term for the morality and collective conscience in societies with little division of labour.

Media events Events broadcast by television on a mass scale that are live, pre-planned and interrupt media routine, and that feature themes of celebration, reconciliation and commemoration. The function of these events is to promote social unity, reaffirm the social and political order and generate 'an upsurge of fellow feeling' between members of a community and/or nation. Examples include the moon landing in 1969, Australia's Bicentennial in 1988 and the first anniversary of September 11 in 2002.

Media rituals Those actions and practices, such as viewing, reading, listening, discussing and appearing in the media, through which people give expression to the belief that they are connected to others.

Media text The purpose of labelling a program such as *Big Brother* a media text is to remove it from its everyday context, thereby opening it up as a subject for critical analysis. This strategy suspends the taken-for-granted meanings and assumptions about the program and permits investigation into what it means in terms of wider social and cultural significance.

Mediated quasi-interaction A term coined by Thompson to help describe the shift from the face-to-face communication and social life of feudal times to the modern experience where communication-at-a-distance is made possible by media and communications technologies, particularly television. Communication has been transformed, as the clear-cut dominance of face-to-face interaction and mediated interaction has been undercut. The effect of this communicative practice is to reshape collective perceptions of space and time and to naturalise a technological mode of interaction that is actually quasi-interaction ('quasi' meaning 'seemingly' but not 'actually').

Medical dominance A term referring to the power of medical institutions, professions and knowledge.

Medical–industrial complex Derived from the idea of the military–industrial complex, this concept refers to the ensemble of pharmaceutical and health-supply companies, hospitals and large health insurance corporations. Generally pejorative, its use often insinuates that vested interests, shady collusions and excessive power are at play.

Medicalisation The process in which medical knowledge and power come to expand their sphere of influence, often by defining something as a 'medical issue'.

Meritocracy The claim that the location of individuals in a system of stratification is not determined by the inherited position of their family but by their own capabilities.

Method A means of gathering and analysing information and data to produce knowledge.

Methodological nationalism The organisation of sociological thinking around the presumption that 'society' is more or less equivalent to, or contained by, the nation-state.

Methodology A way of producing and analysing empirical data so that theories can be tested, accepted or rejected and built upon.

Middle class The group that sits between the upper class and the working class in a system of stratification. Their position is based on their control over knowledge (professionals) or their ownership of small amounts of productive capital (small businesses).

Migration Human movements in time and space; generally long term or permanent.

Military power The exercise of power through the use of organised armed forces.

Mode of production How a society produces its wealth, including both the means of production (comprising the technological knowledge used to produce goods, such as food and clothing) and the social relations of production (the relationships between groups involved in production).

Modernity In sociology this term is used to describe the features that characterise modern, Western social formations. These include an economic system based on capitalism, democracy and the rationalisation of all aspects of social life.

Modified elementary family Inner or 'elementary' family consisting of wives, husbands, their parents, children, brothers and sisters.

Modified extended family Inner or 'elementary' family consisting of wife, husband, their parents, children, brothers and sisters, plus uncles, aunts, nephews, nieces, cousins or more distant kin.

Morbidity Sickness, illness.

Mortality Death.

Multiculturalism An official doctrine holding that a national society should consist of multiple cultures, each making an important contribution to the vitality of its social life. Multiculturalism is often opposed to assimilationism. *See* **Assimilationism**.

Multidimensionality The multiple aspects of any social phenomenon.

Multilateral Agreement on Investment (MAI) This agreement was originally drafted, mostly in secrecy, in 1995 by the OECD. The main aspects involve removing the remaining global barriers to trade, giving foreign companies the same rights as domestic companies, allowing companies the right to sue governments if they block trade of investment opportunities, and the potential removal of domestic conditions and laws that might hurt foreign investment and trade, such as environmental or industrial conditions.

National identity A set of cultural codes about a nation and the sense of belonging that people have towards that nation. This is often reinforced by myths, symbols and everyday practices.

Nationalism A political doctrine and set of beliefs about a nation, usually arguing for its distinctive and superior qualities.

Negotiated order A situation in which social conduct is determined not so much by formal rules as by informal understandings shared by people in a setting.

Neoconservative Often combines with *neoliberalism* in an appeal to nationalism, moral righteousness, family values and antagonism towards progressive social movements.

Neoliberalism A theory of political and economic practices that stresses individual freedom and enterprise. The state plays a crucial but limited role, only putting in place 'those military, defence, police, and legal structures and functions required to secure private property rights and to guarantee, by force if need be, the proper function of markets' (Harvey 2005, p. 2).

Neo-paganism New forms of religiosity that identify with 'earth-centred or nature-based religions whose roots lie in a pre-Christian past' (Hume 1997, p. 42).

Network society A comprehensive social theory developed by Castells that emphasises the interdependent character of technological, communications and social development. The structural logic of the contemporary age is based on adaptable information and communication technology networks that criss-cross the globe, influencing social life and paying limited heed to the national and political boundaries that have governed the past two centuries.

Networked individualism A pattern evident in online social interaction that relates to sociability in offline life, especially with the rise of internet-enabled mobile communications. The range of communications options available online enables individuals to build their networks on the basis of mobile and flexible interests, values, affinities and projects. This mode of communication is individualistic and emphasises diversity, plurality and choice. An outcome of networked individualism appears to be the creation of weak social ties over strong lasting ones.

New Age Movements Religious or spiritual movements that are new to the country of their practice and are characterised by an emphasis on individual and planetary spiritual growth.

New economism Educational ideology that emphasises the role of markets and economic considerations.

New public health A term used for a raft of initiatives aimed at delivering services at local levels, informing people about risks and unhealthy behaviours, and encouraging prevention rather than cure.

New Religious Movements A term commonly used to refer to the wide variety of small religious, spiritual and mystical groups that have sprung up since the 1950s. These groups are not integrated into mainstream institutions and manifest a wide variety of attitudes towards mainstream society, ranging from acceptance of it to a concern with its radical transformation.

Non-government organisation (NGO) Willetts (2001, pp. 369–72) draws from the United Nations' definition of a non-governmental organisation and explains that they should: (1) support the broad aims of the United Nations; (2) have a 'representative body, with identifiable headquarters'; (3) not be for profit; (4) be non-violent; (5) not be a political party or interfere with a nation's internal affairs; and (6) not be the product of intergovernmental agreements. Examples cited by Willetts are Amnesty International, Greenpeace and the Red Cross.

Norms Standards that define the rights and obligations applicable to a particular role.

North American Free Trade Agreement (NAFTA) Initially implemented in 1994, it outlines an agreement of liberalised trade between the United States, Canada and Mexico. Its broad aims are to remove all barriers to trade between these countries, and promote and strengthen regional development, cooperation and trade.

Nuclear family Family as a social unit made up of parents and children.

Omnivore Person with widespread cultural tastes.

Organic solidarity Durkheim's term for the morality and collective conscience in societies with an advanced division of labour.

Organisation for Economic Cooperation and Development (OECD) Formed in 1947 to assist in the postwar reconstruction of Europe, since 1961 it has taken on a broader mandate, aiming to assist all governments to develop sustainable economic growth policies and practices.

Overrepresentation This occurs when the frequency of a social group, such as young people, in social statistics is proportionally greater than their number in the population.

Paradigm The overall model of what counts as true and valid knowledge, what sort of questions should be asked and what sort of methods should be used to answer those questions.

Participant observation A research technique in which the researcher takes part in the activities of the group in the same way as members of the group.

Patriarchal family An extended kinship network exerting a strong influence over marriage and family life, with relatively high fertility, early marriage, infrequent divorce, women's work concentrated in and around the home, and strong paternal authority over women and children.

Patrimonial domination A society in which large households, including apprentices, servants, slaves and soldiers, were the basis of social, economic and political organisation.

Pax Americana A term that basically means American peace, or the idea that global peace can be achieved and maintained by the continual application of American power and authority on a global scale.

Pilot study A small-scale preliminary study conducted before the main research in order to check its feasibility or to improve the research design.

Pink-collar occupations Jobs where women make up a substantial proportion of the workforce, such as teaching or nursing.

Play stage The first stage in the development of self, as identified by Mead, which involves the child playing roles such as mother or father, or doctor or nurse; thus, the idea of a self is developed as the child takes on the role of a make-believe other. *See also* **Game stage**.

Pluralism An approach to the understanding of power, which sees it as spread throughout the population as a whole rather than from an elite or a central institution.

Political power The exercise of power through political institutions and processes.

Polygyny The practice of a man having more than one wife.

Polymorphously perverse Able to gain physical pleasure from a range of different bodily activities.

Positivism The belief that social formations can be studied using the same methods and ideas as those used by natural scientists, including the belief that scientific methods will lead to the discovery of universal laws of human behaviour.

Post-Fordism An economic system that favours flexibility, knowledge-products and worker re-skilling.

Postmodernist One who follows the new social order that is replacing modernity in advanced industrial societies.

Postmodernity In sociology this term is used to describe the new social order that is replacing modernity in advanced industrial societies. While it has continuities with modernity, it also has distinctive features of its own.

Post-secularisation The argument that religion today is flourishing because conditions of individualisation encourage all forms of belief, including religious ones. It is characterised by religious pluralism, the privatisation of religioisity and the commodification of religion through consumption.

Poverty A condition in which individuals or families are unable to meet their basic needs (absolute poverty) or their living standards fall below what is normal for their community (relative poverty).

Poverty line The point at which social researchers consider people to be poor; for example, if they fall below a particular measure such as income.

Power In sociology the word 'power' has many meanings. Defined by Weber as 'the chance of a man or a number of men to realize their own will in a communal action even against the resistance of others who are participating in the action' (in Gerth & Mills 1948, p. 180).

Power structures The third structure of relationship between men and women constituting what Connell calls the gender order or gender regime, referring to relations of 'authority, control and coercion: the hierarchies of the state and business, institutional and interpersonal violence, sexual regulation and surveillance, domestic authority and its contestation' (1987, pp. 96–7).

Predictability One of the four interconnected dimensions in what Ritzer calls the 'McDonaldisation' process, whereby the work done by organisations is predictable and standardised, so that work processes, the organisation's products and even workers themselves remain as similar as possible no matter what the context. *See also* **Calculability**, **Control** and **Efficiency**.

Primary sexual characteristics Male and female genitals.

Primary socialisation The changing of a child's behaviour to what is acceptable in society—this takes place mainly within the family.

Primary sources Data collected by the researchers themselves. Primary sources include questionnaires, interviews and participant observation.

Private body Those parts of the human body usually hidden from public view.

'Process of legitimation' Miliband's term for the means by which the economic power of the ruling class is presented as legitimate and justified.

Production (or labour) *See* **Labour**.

Profane Refers to ordinary, everyday objects that relate to this world and lack an association with religion.

Professional closure The process in which an occupational group obtains a legal monopoly on the provision of certain goods or services.

Proletariat A word for workers that is often used by Marxists.

'Promotional' group A type of interest group supporting a particular cause rather than guarding the interests of a given social group.

'Protective' group A type of interest group that defends the interests of a particular section of society.

Psyche Psychological make-up.

Public sphere The domain of social life where public dialogue occurs and public opinion is formed. The media is central to the operation and condition of this sphere, given its role in the mediation of social communication.

Qualitative methods Social science research methods focusing on the interpretation of the meanings that humans attach to their experiences and actions.

Quantitative methods Social science research methods based on gathering numerical or statistical information about the phenomenon being studied.

Questionnaire A list of pre-defined questions, usually given to respondents in the same order so that the same information can be collected from every member of the sample.

Race A group of people of common descent with distinct physical characteristics.

Racism The belief that the human world consists of distinctive racial groups along with stereotypes about these. Racists generally believe that some 'racial' groups (usually their own!) are superior to others.

Rationality Knowledge of the world is acquired using the mind, logic and reason rather than via sensory experience. *See also* **Empirical evidence**.

Rational–legal authority A type of control based on the acceptance of a set of impersonal rules.

Realist theory of science An approach that stresses the similarities between the social and natural sciences, rejecting the argument that their methodologies are radically distinct.

Reflexive The quality of a property, such as an individual, a theory or a society, reflecting back on itself and modifying its behaviour accordingly.

Reintegrative shaming A form of public shaming of offenders that forces them to confront the effects of their actions while simultaneously encouraging their reintegration into the moral community.

Relational potential The capacity to form particular kinds of relationships, which can vary between men and women.

Relations of power Those aspects of social relationships that need to be understood in terms of differing and unequal resources and capacities.

Relations of production According to Marx, the social and legal relationships surrounding productive economic activity.

Relative autonomy A term used by Poulantzas to refer to the relationship between the state and the ruling class, in which the interests of the ruling class as a whole are protected in broad terms by the state, even though the state is not directly controlled by any members of the ruling class.

Relative deprivation Occurs when a group feels deprived in comparison with other similar groups, or when its expectations are not met.

Relative poverty A situation in which living standards and lifestyles are below those deemed acceptable within a nation.

Reliability Data are seen to be reliable if other researchers produce the same results using the same methods of investigation on the same material.

Religion A complex of beliefs and practices that point to a set of values and an understanding of the meaning of existence.

Religiosity The forms that religious expression takes, such as beliefs, political and social views and church attendance.

Religious pluralism Multicultural societies such as Australia are characterised by a plurality of religions that exist alongside one another. Religious differences are the norm rather than the exception.

Representative Whether research findings are typical of a population. *See also* **Generalisable** and **Sample**.

Restricted code A kind of shorthand speech, with limited use of adjectives or adjectival clauses and adverbs or adverbial clauses. Meaning and intention are conveyed more by gesture and voice intonation, and they are closely tied to the particular context in which the communication takes place.

Role theory A theoretical framework for the analysis of masculine and feminine identities, seeing gender in terms of people playing different gender 'roles' socially defined as appropriate to one's sex, the characteristics of which are internalised through a process of gender socialisation.

Ruling class The dominant social group that owns and controls the means of production.

Sacred Refers to things that are set apart and forbidden, and that are associated with rituals and positive and negative sanctions.

Sacred canopy A concept developed by Berger and Luckmann to describe the role of religion in providing the ground rules for the establishment of shared meanings.

Sample The actual individuals to be studied. A sample is a part of a larger population: those included in the sample are chosen as a cross-section of the larger group. *See also* **Generalisable** and **Representative**.

Schema A broad pattern, scheme or model.

'Second' or 'reflexive' modernity A type of modernity in which the process of modernisation turns on itself, so that modernity is itself modernised.

Second 'face' of power Power exercised through agenda-setting. *See also* **First 'face' of power** and **Third 'face' of power**.

Secondary sexual characteristics Breasts, facial and body hair, width of hips, length of hair, distribution of body fat, breadth of shoulders and so on.

Secondary sources Data that already exist. Secondary sources include official statistics, mass media products, diaries, letters, government reports, other sociologists' work, and historical and contemporary records.

Sects Offshoots of mainstream religious organisations that advocate religious doctrines that are widely regarded as deviant. They claim to have a monopoly on the truth, a strong and often rigid sense of identity and a rejection of the outside world. They are usually exclusive in membership.

Secularisation Refers to a decline in religiosity at the level of both the individual and society's mainstream institutions.

Self-fulfilling prophecy A concept aiming to capture the way in which the making of a prediction (say, by teachers about the future success or failure of students) will tend to come true because of the effects of that prediction itself.

Semi-structured interviews A technique that is halfway between structured interviews and informal unstructured interviews. Typically, the interviewer has a schedule of themes to be covered. Open-ended questions are used, which enables interviewees to express their ideas and opinions. If an interesting issue arises, the interviewer has the flexibility to probe it further, before returning to the schedule.

Sex The biological dimensions of human gender and sexual identity.

Sex/gender system A term used by Rubin to refer to the established and institutionalised linkage of sex and gender distinctions into a single comprehensive construction of gendered identities and relationships.

Sexual identity The three dimensions of sex, gender and sexuality.

Sexuality The sexual practices associated with sex and gender, which are then understood in terms of categories such as homosexuality, heterosexuality, bisexuality or queer sexuality.

Sick role A set of shared understandings about the appropriate behaviour for the sick individual, including such things as trying to get better and taking medical advice. Being in the sick role exempts people from many customary social obligations and expectations.

Simulacrum A term used by Baudrillard to refer to an image of something that does not exist, but which nonetheless is treated as if it does.

Snowballing A type of sampling that involves using personal contacts to build up a sample of the group to be studied.

Social action An action carried out by an individual to which a person attached a meaning and one which, in Weber's words, 'takes account of the behaviour of others and is thereby oriented in its course' (1978). Any action that does not take account of the existence and possible reactions of others is not social.

Social capital The social networks and trust that hold a community together.

Social closure The exclusion of some people from membership of a status group.

Social constructions of crime and deviance The idea that in any community what is identified as crime and deviance is powerfully influenced by social factors; as a result, definitions vary over time and space.

Social control theory A theory that explains crime in terms of an inverse relationship between the strength or weakness of social control and low or high levels of crime.

Social democracy Political ideology that emphasises universalism, equality of opportunity and meritocracy as the basis of inclusion and achievement.

Social differentiation A process whereby the institutions and roles that form the social system become increasingly differentiated and specialised in terms of their function.

Social distance Perceptions of the degree of similarity, relatedness and acceptance between social groups.

Social division Those aspects of inequality that include both horizontal and vertical boundaries between social groups.

Social exclusion The processes by which some groups exclude or include others from participating in the activities and rewards considered to be an essential feature of citizenship.

Social fact A force outside the individual, such as common beliefs, ideas and moral sentiments, which transcends the individual and shapes his or her consciousness.

Social inequality Unequal distribution of social, political and economic resources within a social collective, such as a nation.

Social mobility The capacity of individuals to move up or down the hierarchy of inequality either within a single person's lifetime or across generations.

Social realism A theory of education that views knowledge as being socially produced but having real effects.

Social stratification The existence of a systematic hierarchy of inequality that is usually based on some social variable, such as class or ethnicity, and that persists across generations.

Social structure A concept that expresses the idea that social formations are organised along patterned lines that endure over time and that act as a constraint on those living within them, even though those people may not be aware of this.

Social surveys Research projects that collect standardised data about large numbers of people.

Social wage The state's redistribution of economic capital through the taxation system, cash payments or service provision.

Socialisation The process by which humans learn the socially patterned behaviours that exist within their culture.

Sociobiology The study of evolutionary development applied to human behaviour.

Sociological determinism The explanation of any phenomenon as determined entirely by social structure and social relations.

Sociological imagination Sociology's core task of pointing out the connections between individual behaviour and the social forces that shape it.

Sociology The study of society; the description and analysis of the social forces that shape human behaviour in contemporary social formations.

Sovereign power The exercise of power through command and direct control.

Spirituality A state of being related to a divine, supernatural or transcendent order of reality; a sense of awareness of a suprareality that goes beyond life as ordinarily experienced.

Stabilisation of adult personalities An aspect of the marriage relationship in which the mutual emotional support that partners in a couple give each other has the effect of adding stability to their personalities.

State crime Crimes involving the state acting against its own citizens or the citizens of another state.

State-centred theory of power A theory of power in which power is seen to be exercised primarily through state agencies.

Status A hierarchy of social groups with a shared sense of social honour or prestige that becomes the basis for the unequal distribution of resources.

Structural Adjustment Program (SAP) '[These are] designed by the IMF, supported by the World Bank, and based on "neoliberal" monetary policies originally articulated by Milton Friedman' (Prigoff 2000, p. 121). They are more often than not used in developing countries under the view that an adjustment can be made to restore a nation's balance of payments and promote growth. According to Prigoff, SAPs typically involve a range of policy measures such as privatisation, deregulation, tax breaks, retrenching 'expensive' welfare, devaluing national currency and terminating indigenous land rights or environmental considerations.

Structural mobility Arises when the occupational structure of a nation changes, thereby creating higher levels of mobility.

Structural racism The way that racist outcomes are promoted or facilitated by institutions and organisations; this is sometimes an unintended consequence of action rather than the result of a deliberate racist policy.

Subcultural theory A theory that explains crime and deviance in terms of the existence of social groups whose norms and values differ from those of conventional society.

Superstructure (of society) A Marxist term referring to the political, legal and educational institutions, culture, and the belief and value systems, which he saw as being determined to a greater or lesser extent by economic relations and structures.

Symbolic interactionism A perspective that explains social actions in terms of the meanings that individuals give to them.

Symmetrical family A term used by Young and Willmott to capture a family structure where conjugal roles, although organised around a division between men's work and women's work, still ensure a high degree of sharing of tasks and an equivalence between the contribution each spouse makes to the running of the household.

Systems of stratification Particular arrangements for inequality that have existed historically.

Taylorism The doctrine of scientific management that aims to maximise worker efficiency by testing and measuring. Sociologists generally associate this with alienation and exploitation.

Tertiary sexual characteristics Facial expressions, movements, body posture, clothing, voice and so on.

The public Historically conceived as a grouping of rational, self-determining individuals linked by common interests, such as community, politics, national identity and social practice. The media helps identify and constitute the public on a daily basis.

The state Defined by Weber as 'a human community that [successfully] claims the monopoly of the legitimate use of physical force within a given territory' (in Gerth & Mills 1948, p. 78).

Third 'face' of power Power exercised through the shaping of desires. *See also* **First 'face' of power** and **Second 'face' of power**.

Total institution A formal organisation marked by hierarchy, closed boundaries and strict rules. The hospital is arguably a total institution.

Tourist gaze A term coined by Urry for the voyeuristic, simplistic and ideologically conservative viewpoint of the tourist.

Traditional action A term used by Weber to refer to action based on established custom: individuals act in a certain way because of ingrained habit, because things have always been done that way.

Traditional authority A type of control where authority rests on a belief in the 'rightness' of established customs and traditions.

Transnational corporations (TNCs) Sometimes referred to as multinational corporations (MNCs); however, there are some slight differences. Dicken argues that the transnational corporation is 'the single most important force creating global shifts in economic activity' (1992, p. 47). He defines a transnational corporation as having three distinct features: (1) operates in more than one country; (2) can take advantage of, and exploit, geographical differences, such as differences between nations' policies, resources, workforce, etc.; and (3) is flexible enough to be able to move its operations and resources globally. Multinational corporations meet these criteria; however, while transnational corporations may have an identifiable nation base, multinationals may not be so clearly located in, or responsible to, any particular nation.

Transsexuals People who psychologically feel themselves to be members of the opposite biological sex.

Triangulation Using a plurality of methods and perspectives in relation to the same research question.

Typology A model or set of categories defining basic classes of social phenomena.

Underclass A disadvantaged group, more or less permanently entrenched at the bottom of the social hierarchy, who lack employment skills and are welfare dependent.

Upper class The group at the top of a system of stratification. They owe their position to their high level of wealth and power.

Validity Data are valid if they provide a true, accurate and relatively comprehensive picture of what is being studied.

Value consensus Agreement about what is valuable, important and desirable in society and in individual experience.

Value–rational action Arises from a clear formulation of a set of values and 'the consistently planned orientation of its detailed course to these values' (Weber 1978, p. 25). The examples Weber gave included devotion to duty, a religious calling, personal loyalty, the pursuit of beauty, or devotion to a cause.

'Variable-sum' concept of power An approach to power in which power is not seen as fixed or constant within any given society.

Verstehen The capacity to grasp the meanings that people attach to their experiences and actions by imagining yourself in the position of the person whose behaviour you are seeking to explain and experiencing more or less what that person has experienced.

Vertical segregation The hierarchical separation of the workforce by status; for example, the distinction between managers and workers or doctors and nurses.

Victim surveys Surveys of population groups of their experiences of crime victimisation.

Washington Consensus A term introduced in 1989 by US economist John Williamson to capture the core policy prescriptions for economies in crisis. It subsequently became a shorthand term for neoliberal, market-oriented economic policies and political approaches.

White-collar crime A general term that includes all crimes committed by non-manual workers, from administrators to company directors, political leaders and professional men and women.

Working class The group of people below the middle class who possess no productive capital and rely on manual labour for their livelihood.

World Bank Formed during the closing of World War II in 1945, the World Bank played an important role in the reconstruction of postwar Europe and now has more than 180 members. Its main objective is to reduce global poverty through the provision of loans, grants and other sources of assistance.

World Economic Forum (WEF) Established formally in 1987, the WEF comprises members from some of the world's most wealthy and prominent businesses, as well as politicians and academics. The not-for-profit organisation aims to improve global living conditions, for example by fostering greater private/public business cooperation and developing ways to address some of the world's most pressing social and environmental problems.

World Social Forum (WSF) An annual meeting of the 'alter-globalisation' movement, often held at the same time as the World Economic Forum's gatherings, aiming to provide alternative approaches to the world's economic problems.

World Trade Organization (WTO) Formed in 1995, the WTO has absorbed the GATT as the main global governing organisation with the mandate to ensure that global trade flows as freely as possible. The WTO specific responsibilities include administering trade agreements, settling trade disputes and assisting developing countries in trade policy issues through technical assistance and training programs.

'Zero-sum' concept of power An approach to power that sees it as bound within a fixed amount, so that power held by some can only be at the expense of others.

Zero tolerance A form of crime control that does not distinguish between serious and minor crimes, on the grounds that this prevents the escalation of crime.

Author Index

Aakhus, M. 105
Aarons, Haydn 372
Abbott, P. 179, 181
Abercrombie, N. 6
Abrahams, J. 178
ABS *see* Australian Bureau of Statistics
Achcar, Gilbert 369–70
Acker, S. 176
ACTU 436
Adams, K. 428
Addelson. K. P. 304–5
Adler, M. 357
Adorno, Theodor 91, 117–18, 316, 472
AIC (Australian Institute of Criminology) 423, 425–9, 433, 434, 437
al-Afghani 71
Alanen, Leena 149–50, 151, 152
Albarese, Catherine 371
Albrow, M. 52
Alcorso, Caroline 267
Alder, C. 431
Alexander, Malcolm 247–8
Alloway, N. 170
Alston, P. 151
Althusser, Louis 393
Altman, Dennis 303, 313, 314
Ambert, A.-M. 152
Anderson, Barbara 320
Anderson, Benedict 78, 272
Anderson, Francis 22
Andrews, D. L. 206
Ang, I. 79
Annan, Kofi 53
Appadurai, Arjan 58, 62, 63–4
Apple, M. W. 368
Argy, F. 252
Aristotle 467
Armstrong, John 438
Armstrong, K. 356
Arnold, Matthew 163
Arnot, M. 169, 175, 178, 180
Aron, R. 232
Aronson, J. 42–3
Askew, K. 79
Atkinson 243
Atkinson, A. 240
Atkinson, J. Maxwell 449–50, 454, 459
Atkinson, Meredith 22, 23
Australian Bureau of Statistics (ABS)
    Aboriginal Australians 263
    crime 425, 432, 433
    education 168, 169, 170
    family life 122–3, 129
    health 328, 340, 341, 343, 344, 345

    inequality 236, 237, 238–9, 240, 241, 243
    leisure 194, 195
    medicine 333
    migration 269
    religion 351, 362, 363
    sport 200, 201
    tourism 207
    work 211, 212, 217, 218
Australian Council of Social Services 240, 241, 242
Australian Everyday Culture Project (AECP) 234
Australian Institute of Health and Welfare 340
Axford, B. 49

Bachrach, Peter 378, 390, 392
Bailey-Harris, Rebecca 264–5
Bainbridge, William 363
Baker, W. E. 103, 104
Bala, N. 154
Baldock, C. V. 24
Balnaves, M. 99
Barash, David 286
Baratz, Morton 378, 390, 392
Barbalet, Jack 24
Barber, Benjamin 57, 58, 61
Barcan, A. 166
Barker, Eileen 458
Barrett, D. B. 365
Barrett, Michèle 121, 291
Bartelson, Jens 70
Barthes, Roland 275
Bates, Erica 342, 343
Batiyel, Mine 339
Baudrillard, Jean 7, 13, 14, 66, 96, 486–7
Bauman, Zygmunt 2, 3, 20, 52, 71, 76, 83, 92, 95, 96, 225, 366, 486
    fundamentalism and postmodernity 370–1
Baxter, Janeen 122
Beck, Ulrich 10, 20, 30, 52, 70, 72, 227
    chaos of love 156–8
    second modernity 487–8, 489
Becker, Howard 416–17, 453, 463
Beckford, J. A. 373
Beck-Gernsheim, Elisabeth 156–8
Beilharz, Peter 24
Bell, A. P. 307
Bell, D. 226
Bell, Daniel 486
Bell, D. R. 128
Bellah, Robert 21, 353
Bello, Walden 64, 69
Bendix, Reinhard 467
Benedict 289
Benjamin, Walter 472
Bennett, S. 190
Bennett, T. 197, 234, 235

545

Benston, Margaret 120
Bentham, Jeremy 390, 399–400
Benton, T. 446
Berger, B. 114
Berger, H. A. 372
Berger, John 9
Berger, Peter 3, 7, 285, 355–6, 357, 358, 373, 454
Berger, P. L. 114, 154, 365, 469
Berger J. 466
Berkman, L. 329
Berndt, C. H. 126
Berndt, R. M. 126
Bernstein, Basil 166, 177, 186–8, 189
Best, J. 152
Bhabha, Homi 278
Biles, D. 435
Billig, Michael 272
Birdsall, N. 51
Bittman, Michael 121, 158, 199
Blackledge, D. 183
Blagbrough, J. 153
Blagg. H. 428, 431
Blainey, Geoffrey 270–1
Bleier, R. 287
Bloch, Ernst 472
Block, F. 46
Blumer, Herbert 452, 453–4, 482–3
Boelen, Marianne 460–1
Bonß, W. 487
Bond, J. 240
Boorstin, Daniel 95–6, 208
Boston Women's Health Collective 345
Bottero, W. 223, 233, 246
Botticelli, Sandro 18
Bottomley, Gillian 130
Bottomore, T. B. 228, 355, 470, 471, 472
Boudon, R. 150
Bouma, G. 360
Bourdieu, Pierre 7, 12, 66, 150, 188, 189, 489
    class and culture 233–4
    cultural capital 196–7, 223, 227
    field theory 184–6
    sport and social class 205
Bourgois, Philippe 462, 463
Bourke, Helen 23
Bourne, J. 187
Bowlby, J. 411
Bowles, S. 174–5, 177, 188
Box, S. 437
Boyle, Maree 203–4
Bradley, D. 169, 170, 171, 180
Bradshaw, J. 152
Braithwaite, John 22, 24, 420–1, 437
Bramble, Tom 69
Brandolini, A. 242
Braverman, Harry 214, 250
Bray, C. 437
Brekhus, W. 313
Bromley, Simon 52–3, 54
Broom, L. 245, 252
Broome, Richard 261
Brown, Morven 19, 22
Brown, P. 185

Brubaker, Rogers 273
Bruce, S. 361, 362, 364, 365–6, 367, 368
Bruns, A. 83
Bryman, Alan 457, 458
Bryson, L. 19
Bryson, Lois 251
Bühler-Niederberger, D. 151, 152
Burawoy, Michael 11, 20–2, 212, 214
Burbank, Victoria 126–7
Burgess, Ernest 17, 482
Burgmann, Verity 64, 404–5
Burke, A. 364
Burke, G. 165
Burnley, Ian 339
Burns, Ailsa 121, 147, 149
Burton, A. 150
Busch, A. 64
Butler, Judith 312
Butlin, Noel 390
Butt, R. 47

Cahill, L. 434
Cain, M. 429
Caldwell, John 130, 133, 134–6, 138–9
Caldwell, P. 130
Calhoun, Craig 403
Califia, Pat 307–8
Callinicos, Alex 55, 64, 65–6
Calnan, Michael 329
Calvin, Jean 475
Cannold, Leslie 222
Cardoso, G. 99, 103
Carey, J. W. 100, 106
Carlen, Pat 419, 453
Carlyle, Thomas 95
Carmichael, Gordon 142–3, 144, 148–9
Carpenter, D. D. 372–3
Carroll, J. 363, 369
Cashmore, Ellis 205
Cass, Bettina 122
Castells, Manuel 10, 42, 43, 52, 92, 96, 98, 104, 105, 106, 188
    networked individualism 102–3
    the network society 99–102
    techno-capitalism and inequality 37–8
Castles, Stephen 24, 270, 277–8
Cerami, Charles A. 30
CGA 170
Chamberlain, C. 243
Chambliss, William 418
Chang, H. 45
Chapman, S. 437
Chase-Dunn, C. 38, 39, 53
Chen, M. 49, 50
Chen, R. 190
Cherlin, Andrew J. 159
Chodorow, Nancy 19, 293–5
Chomsky, Noam 57, 66
Chossudovsky, Michael 49, 51
Chrisafis, A. 473
Christ, Carol 356
Cicourel, Aaron 458
Clark, Margaret 330
Clarricoates, K. 179

Clegg, Stewart 24, 383, 386
Clinard, M. B. 436, 437
Coeuré, B. 51
Cohen, H. 100
Cohen, R. 43
Cole, C. 206
Coleman 150
Coleman, K. M. 103, 104
Colic-Peisker, Val 267
Collins, C. 170, 178, 179, 180
Collins, J. 169, 430, 431
Collins, R. 71, 119, 339, 396–7, 467, 477
Collyer, Fran 331–2, 344–5
Comte, August 9, 15, 16, 358, 443, 466, 467
Connell, R. W. 24, 150, 175, 177, 246, 249, 284, 285, 287, 316, 420, 446, 463, 466–7
   class and Australian state 392–4
   gender and power 203–4, 301–2, 303–4
   globalisation as Northern Theory 70–2
   making the difference 163, 183–4
   masculinities 296–300
   role theory 291–3
   ruling class, ruling culture 23, 248
Cooley, Charles Horton 452, 466
Cope, Bill 176, 277–8
Copland, D. B. 23
Corrigan, Paul 458
Corsaro, W. A. 152
Coser, Lewis A. 467, 478, 479
Cotterrell, R. 469
Cottle, S. 85
Couldry, Nick 77, 84–5, 87, 106
   media as social practice 85–6
Courpasson, D. 383
Cowlishaw, Gillian 260, 280
Cox, M. 57
Craib, Ian 445, 446, 449, 450, 453, 454, 480
Craig, D. 328
Craik, Jennifer 209, 210
Crang, Mike 208, 209–10
Crawford, A. 415
Crompton, R. 226, 250–1
Crook, Stephen 24, 402–3
Cuff, E. C. 11, 468
Cunneen, Chris 264, 415–16, 417, 428, 429, 434, 436, 437
Cunningham, S. 79
Curr, E. M. 387
Curran, J. 85
Cutler, A. C. 56

d'Addio, A. 253
Dahl, Robert 383–4, 385
Dahlgren, P. 91, 92
Dahrendorf, R. 477
Daly, Mary 356, 357
Daniel, Ann 333, 335
Darhendorf 249
Darwin, Charles 286, 413, 455
David 169, 175, 178, 180
Davie, Grace 362, 364–5
Davies, A. F. 30
Davies, Bronwyn 295–6
Davies, M. 240

Davis, Alan 332
Davis, Angela 361
Davis, K. 233
Davis, Kingsley 18, 141, 159
Dawe, Alan 7–8
Dawkins, Richard 455
Dawson, Lorne 373
Day, Jo Anne 326
Day, Lincoln 148
Day, Robert 326
Dayan, Daniel 84
   Beijing Olympic Games (2008) 88–9
   Media Events 86–8
D'Cruz, J. V. 166
Deacon 381–2, 390
Dean, Mitchell 24
Dearden, J. 427, 432, 433
Dearing 79
de Beauvoir, Simone 284, 356–7
De Cecco, John 306, 307
de la Fuente, Eduardo 106
Delamont, Sara 458
de Lauretis, Teresa 314
de Mause, Lloyd 150
Demidenko/Darville, Helen 272
Dempsey, Ken 121–2, 360
Dempster, Guy 18
Denzin, N. K. 463
Derrida, Jacques 188
Descartes, René 444
de Sousa Santos 55
de Tocqueville, Alexis 383–4, 467
de Vaus, David 145–6
Devine, Fiona 227, 253
Dewey, John 467, 482
Dezalay, Yves 56
Dicken, P. 36, 42
Dingwall, R. 455
Ditton, P. 128
Dollar, D. 49, 51
Domingues, Mauricio 71
Donzelot, J. 152
Douglas, Jack 448–9, 457–8
Dowse, R. E. 385
Drainville, A. C. 69
Dreher, Axel 31
Du Bois, W. E. B. 21, 467
Duménil, Gérard 47
Dunne, T. 53
Dunning, Eric 202
Durkheim, Emile 5–6, 16, 34, 85, 97, 194, 276, 329, 396, 414, 456, 466–7
   crime and deviance 412
   division of labour 232–3
   egoism and anomie 364
   religion 351, 352–3, 354, 471
   rules of sociological method 443–4, 446
   the social 468–70, 478
   social ritual 84, 337
   suicide 446–50, 457–8
Dyck, N. 258

Easteal, P. 124
Easthope, Gary 344

Eastwood, Heather 344
Eccles, S. 139
Edwards, C. 129, 158
Ehrenreich, Barbara 141, 322
Elder, Catriona 274
Elias, D. 437
Elias, Norbert 12, 202, 291, 299, 378, 402, 489
  civilising process 394–7
Elkin, A. P. 23
Elliott, Anthony 24, 473
El Saadawi, Nawal 357
Emmison, Michael 196–7, 234, 235, 247
Encel, Sol 30, 248, 369, 381, 388
  Australian state 389–90
Engels, Friedrich 28, 34, 116–17, 118, 229, 361, 466, 470, 471, 472, 484
  Communist manifesto 42
English, Deirdre 322
Epstein, C.F. 301
Erikson, Erik 149, 246
ESCAP 147, 148
Evans, D. T. 284
Evans, M. D. R. 360, 361
Evans-Pritchard, E. E. 442, 446
Eysenck, H. 172, 411
Ezzy, D. 372

Fahy, Kathleen 327
Faludi, Susan 302
Fantasia, Rick 64
Featherstone, M. 478
Feldman, Kenneth 337
Ferguson, Adam 304–5, 467
Fernbach, David 301
Field, J. 188
Fincher, R. 243
Fine, Gary Alan 461
Fiorenza, E. S. 356
Firestone, S. 19, 301
Fiske, John 87, 274–5
Fitzgerald, R. T. 175
Fletcher, Ronald 120, 147
Flew, T. 101
Fontana, B. 391, 392
Forsey, Martin 458
Foster, George 320
Foster, L. 165
Foucault, Michel 180, 188, 312, 321, 326, 327, 335, 489
  disciplinary power 399–400
  discourses 397
  governmentality 378, 400–2
  history of sexuality 397–8
  knowledge and power 397–402, 422
  modern individuality and power 398–9
Fourcade-Gourinchas, Marion 47–8
Fox, Renee 329
Franklin, Adrian 208, 209–10
Franklin, M. A. 357
Fraser, N. 87, 91, 92
Fraser, S. 172
Freeland, Gary 353
Freeman, Gary 267
Freeman, J. 103

Freeman, M. 151
Freidson, Eliot 327, 334
Freud, Sigmund 285, 288–9, 306, 308, 327, 398, 444, 473
Friedan, Betty 284
Friedman, Lawrence 56
Friedman, Milton 46, 48
Frisby, David 478
Frow, John 97–8, 197, 234, 235
Fukuyama, Francis 65
Fulcher, James 52, 53, 54
Fuller, M. 181
Fuss, Diana 312

Gagnon, John 305, 308–11, 312
Gale, Fay 128, 176, 180, 260, 264–5
Game, A. 24, 306
Gamson, J. 313
Gardner, Glenn 325
Garfield, Bob 60–1
Garfinkel, Harold 7, 284, 311, 454, 455, 483–4, 486
Garrett, G. 53
Geertz, Clifford 450, 463
Geis, Florence 307
Gellner, E. 373
George, Janet 332
Germov, John 346–7
Gerth, H. H. 95, 223, 232, 361–2, 387, 452
Geschiere, Peter 63
Gibbs, J. 448
Giddens, Anthony 3, 7, 8, 10, 31, 64, 65, 70, 359, 366, 373, 383, 394, 420, 454
  consequences of late-modernity 36–7
  democratisation 155–6
  transformation of intimacy 156
Giddings, Franklin H. 467
Gilding, Michael 124, 154, 249, 253
Gillborn, D. 171, 181
Gillespie, M. 79
Gillies, V. 154, 155, 158
Gilligan, Carol 294
Gintis, H. 174–5, 177, 188
Giulianotti, R. 64
Glaser, Barney 337, 338, 454
Glass, D. 252
Goddard-Spear 179
Goffman, Erving 13, 326, 396, 416, 459, 477
  the asylum 324
  gender as 'expression' 289–90, 291, 292, 293
  presentation of self 453
  sexual identity 308
Goggin, G. 105
Goldthorpe, John 114, 174, 234, 246, 247, 250, 252
Gole, Nilufer 369
Goodale 125, 126
Goodall, Heather 281
Goode, William J. 112, 141
Goody, Jack 114–15
Gordon, D. 243
Gordon, R. 430
Gottfredson, Michael 414
Gouldner, Alvin W. 12–13
Gove, P. B. 417
Grabosky, A. 415

Author Index

Graetz, B. 252
Gramlich, E. M. 51
Gramsci, Antonio 57, 177, 391–4, 402, 472–3
Gray, Dennis 343, 372
Gray, John 45
Gray, Matthew 145–6
Graycar, A. 424
Green, J. C. 367, 368
Green, N. 180
Green, P. 178
Greenberg, David 302–3
Greenfield, Leah 273
Greenfield, Sidney 113
Gregory, L. 92, 93
Greider, W. 45
Grenfell, M. 185
Griffin, D. R. 372
Grimshaw, Patricia 115, 116
Gripsrud, J. 79
Groenewegen, P. D. 389
Guggenheim, M. 151
Gunn, John 22, 23
Guttmann, Allen 200–2

Habermas, Jürgen 14, 90–3
Haebich, A. 129
Hajnal, John 113–14
Halbwachs, M. 448
Hall, Stuart 7, 87, 418–19
Halliday, T. C. 55, 56
Halsey, A. H. 150, 168
Hamilton, Peter 11–13, 20
Hammersley, Martyn 457, 458, 459
Hammersmith, S. K. 307
Harding, S. 457
Hardman, Charlotte 149
Hardt, Michael 54–5
Hareven, T. K. 113
Harris, C. C. 141
Harris, E. 242
Harris, F. 368
Harrison, M. 148
Hart, C. W. M. 125, 126
Hartley, John 77–8, 80, 90
Harvey, David 38, 42, 45–7, 48, 214, 485
Hassan, Riaz 131, 132, 450
Hayek, Friedrich von 46, 47, 48, 225
Head, B. W. 389
Headey, B. 235
Healy, J. 131, 132
Hearn, J. 306, 391
Heelas, P. 362, 366, 371, 372, 373
Heidegger, Martin 29
Heidensohn, F. 419
Hein, H. 357
Held, D. 31
Helleiner, Eric 48
Henderson, Norman 164
Henderson, R. 243
Hendrick, H. 152
Henry, M. 169
Herdt, Gilbert 303, 308
Herlihy, David 114–15

Hermes, J. 90
Herrnstein, Richard 172, 414–15, 422
Hiatt, L. R. 126, 387
Hickox, M. 175
Higley, J. 381–2, 390
Hindess, Barry 24
Hirschi, Travis 414
Hirst, Paul 43, 48, 52–3, 54
Hitchens, Christopher 350
Ho, Christina 267
Hobbes, Thomas 232
Hobhouse, L. T. 29
Hochschild, Arlie 215
Hodge, Bob 274–5
Hogan, Michael 359–60
Holland, J. 186
Holmes, D. 99
Holmwood, John 22
Hooper, Chloe 408
Hopkins, T. K. 35
Horkheimer, Max 91, 117–18, 472
Horton, D. 96
House of Representatives Standing Committee on Aboriginal and Torres Strait Islander Affairs 435
HREOC 264, 279
Hughes, Everett C. 478, 482
Hughson, John 271, 278
Hugo, Graeme 134, 135, 136
Huizinga, Johan 200
Hume, David 444
Hume, L. 15, 372
Humphrey, Michael 131, 132
Hunt, B. 183
Hunter, Ian 175, 401
Hunter, James Davison 367, 374
Huntington, Samuel P. 61–2, 368–9, 374
Husserl, Edmund 454
Hutchins, Brett 81, 92, 93, 100, 101, 103, 203

Ikenberry, J. 46
Illich, Ivan 321, 346
Ince, M. 99
Indermaur, D. 424, 426, 427
Innes, M. 416
Innis, Harold 100
Irigaray, Luce 356
Ironmonger, Duncan 120
Irvine, R. F. 22
Irving, Terry 392
Irving, T. H. 246, 249
ISSP (International Social Science Program) 277–8

Jackson, S. 310
Jacoby, H. 386
Jakubowicz, Andrew 271, 281
James, A. 150, 151, 152
James, R. 169, 171
Jamieson, Lynn 158
Jamrozik, A. 250
Jencks, C. 150
Jenkins, H. 88–9
Jenkins, R. 184
Jenks, C. 151, 152

Jensen, A. 172
Jevons, William Stanley 46
Joas, H. 466
Johnson, L. 81
Johnson, T. M. 365
Jones, F. L. 237, 245, 252, 275–7
Julian, Roberta 210
Jupp, James 267

Kalantzis, Mary 176, 277–8
Kamin, L. J. 172, 286–7
Kapferer, Bruce 276, 353
Karmel, P. 165
Karon, Tony 64
Katz, Alfred 346
Katz, Elihu 79, 84, 86–8
Katz, J. 106
Katz, J. E. 105
Kawai, M. 51
Keat, R. 455, 456
Keating, Paul 29
Keenan, T. 401
Kellehear, Allan 337–8
Kelley, J. 360, 361
Kelly, A. 178
Kelly, A. A. 372
Kelly, Liz 124
Kelly, S. 253
Kelly, R. 281
Kelman, Steven 322
Kempe, C. H. 154
Kenway, J. 170, 178, 179, 180
Keohane, R. O. 31
Kessler, Suzanne 284, 311–12
Key, Ellen 151
Keynes, Maynard 46
Kildea, G. 201–2
Kilmartin, C. 133
Kimmel, Michael 296, 311
King, R. S. 439
Kinsey, Alfred 305–7, 308
Klein, Naomi 43, 52, 66–9
Klug, H. 56
Knowles, R. D. 36
Korsch, Karl 472
Korzeniewicz, M. 59
Kübler-Ross, Elisabeth 337
Kuhn, M. H. 308
Kuhn, Thomas 11, 358, 444–5
Kurian, G. T. 365

La Bruyère 395
Lafferty, Yvonne 204
Lamont, A. 190
La Nauze, L. A. 164
Lanhupuy, Wesley Wagner 261
Lareau, A. 185
Lasch, C. 287
Lash, Scott 34–5, 52, 214
Laslett, Peter 113–14
Latour, Bruno 378, 402, 467
Lavalette, M. 153

Lazarsfeld, P. 79
Lea, J. 419
Leach, E. R. 201–2
Lechner, Frank 31, 34, 49, 54, 55
Lee, D. 448
Lee, N. 150, 152
Leigh, A. 240
Lemert, Edwin 416
Lepenies, W. 13
Le Play, Frédéric 113
Lester, L. 101
Lever, R. 240
Levin, Lowell 346
Levine, Donald 481
Levinson, P. 100
Lévi-Strauss, Claude 126, 289
Levitt, T. 34, 44
Lévy, Dominique 47
Levy, Marion 113
Lewis, J. 371, 372, 373
Liebel, M. 153
Liebes, T. 79
Light, Donald 331
Lincoln, R. 435
Linder-Pelz, Susie 342, 343
Lindroos, M. 179
Lingard et al. 170, 179
Lipset, Seymour Martin 384
Liska, A. E. 416
Locke 15
Lomborg, Bjorn 466
Lorenz, Konrad 290
Luckmann, Thomas 285, 355–6, 357, 358, 454
Luhmann, Niklas 29
Lukács, Georg 472, 477
Luke, C. 150
Lukes, Steven 378, 390–1, 392, 402
Luther, Martin 475
Lynch, M. 434
Lyon, D. 361, 365
Lyotard, Jean-François 14, 188, 485–6

MacCannell, Dean 208
MacDonald, R. 461–2
Macfarlane, A. 114
Mack, Kathy 216
Mackellar, Charles 129
MacKenzie 243
Maddison, S. 404–5
Maddock, K. 126
Maddox, Marion 361
Madge, J. 460
Maduro, Otto 361
Makkai, Toni 267
Malinowski 289
Manderson, Leonore 267, 330
Mann, Michael 226, 378, 388
Manne, Robert 278
Mannheim, 467, 477
Manning, Nick 329
Marchand, P. 100
Marcuse, Herbert 117–18, 393, 472
Marginson 165, 166

Markovic, Milica 267, 347
Marks, G. 169
Marsh, David 179, 391
Marshall, Alfred 46, 467
Marshall, P. D. 96
Marshall, T. H. 243
Martin, A. J. 179
Martin, Clyde 305–7
Martin, D. 176
Martin, Jeannie 281
Martineau, Harriet 13
Marx, Karl 5, 8, 15–16, 19, 28, 66, 194, 222, 231, 232, 233, 246, 327, 389–90, 456, 466–7, 484
   alienation 211, 471
   The Communist Manifesto 34, 42
   comparative method 446
   deviance 412, 418
   family and the reproduction of capitalism 116–18
   health, class and capitalism 322
   ideology 470–1
   materialist theory of religion 353–5, 358, 361, 369
   social change 471–2
   theory of class 227–30
   Theses on Feuerbach 12
   Western Marxism 472–4
   working class 251
   Wright's models of contradictory class locations 246–7
Mathews, Megan 330
Mathews, R. L. 165
Maton, Karl 166, 181, 184, 185, 186, 188–9, 190
   legitimation code theory 189–90
Matza, David 454, 463
Mauss, Marcel 291
Maxwell, R. 100
Mayhew, P. 152
McAllister, Ian 252, 267
McCallum, D. 163, 164, 172
McCarthy, J. R. 85, 158
McDonald, K. 430
McDonald, Peter 129, 130, 132, 133, 136–7, 143–4, 145, 147–9
McFarland, Andrew 385, 391
McGillivray, A. 152
McGrew, A. 31
McIntosh, Mary 121, 306
McKay, H. 79
McKay, Jim 202, 203–4, 206
McKee, A. 92
McKenna, Wendy 131, 132, 284, 311–12
McKeown, Thomas 339
McLean, I. 235
McLeod, J. 170, 178, 179, 180
McLuhan, Marshall 99, 100
McNamee, S. 151
Mead, George Herbert 17, 452–3, 466, 482
Mead, Margaret 285, 289, 293
Media India 224
Mehan, H. 152
Melbourne Institute of Applied Economic and Social Research 243
Melossi, Dario 378
Melucci, Alberto 403
Melvern, L. 438
Mencken, H. L. 132

Mendelsohn 450
Menger, Carl 46
Mennell, S. 452–3
Mercer, Jan 357
Merton, Robert 12, 79, 100, 386, 467
   anomie theory 412–13
Messerschmidt, James W. 420, 422, 429, 430
Messner, Mike 202–3
Mewett, Peter 204
Meyer, Birgit 63
Middleton, C. A. 105
Mikosza, Janine 93, 203
Mill, John Stuart 302, 467
Millen, Neville 335, 336
Miller, P. 152
Miller, T. 81, 89
Mills, C. Wright 2, 3, 77, 95, 223, 232, 362, 385, 387, 452, 462, 467
   power elite 380–3
Mills, M. 179
Mishra, D. 44
Mitchell, Juliet 19, 121, 302
Mitchell, Tony 281
Money, John 285, 290–1, 303, 307–8
Montesquieu 15
Moore, A. 185, 350
Moore, Michael 451
Moore, R. 176, 180, 181, 185, 188–9
Moore, W. E. 173, 233
Moore, Wilbert 34
Morais, A. 187
Morgan, David 116–17, 290
Morgan, Myfanwy 329
Morley, D. 79
Morris, L. 364
Morrissey, Michael 277–8
Morrow, R. A. 177
Mortimore, P. 182
Morton, T. 101
Mosca, Gaetano 380
Moss, G. 187
Mukherjee, S. 424
Mulinari, D. 156
Murray, Charles 155, 414, 415, 422
Myers, W. E. 153
Myrdal, Gunnar 21
Myrstad, G. 153

Naffine, N. 419
Naficy, H. 79
Najman, Jake 340
Narushima, Y. 141
Nash, K. 34, 53
Nederveen Pieterse, Jan 53, 54, 58–9, 62–3, 72
Negri, Antonio 54–5
Nelson, B. J. 152
Nettl, J. P. 36
Nietzsche, Friedrich 29
Nisbet, Robert 467
Nudelman, Arthur 330
Nudelman, Barbara 330

Oakley, Ann 19, 289, 292
O'Connell, T. 421

OECD 172, 173
Oken, Donald 338
O'Leary, Zina 364
Olsen 151

Packer, R. 130
Pakulski, Jan 24, 277–8, 402–3
Palmer, Craig 286
Papacharissi, Z. 92
Parent, R. E. 368
Pareto, Vilfredo 380, 466, 467
Park, Robert 17, 482
Parker (1992) 151
Parkin, F. 231, 232, 306
Parsons, Talcott 17–18, 113, 172, 233, 293, 329, 467, 477
    power like money 382–3
    primary socialisation 120
    problem of social order 469–70
    sex roles 287–8, 289
    sick role 326–7
    mentioned 378, 445
Parton, N. 151, 154
Peristiany, J. G. 130
Pescosolido, B. A. 450
Peterson, Richard 196
Petion, Jerome 78
Pettman, Jan 280
Philipson, Michael 449
Phillips, David 337
Phillips, Timothy 275, 277, 372, 415, 431
Pieper, U. 45
Piggott, J. 237
Pigman, G. A. 69
Pinker, Steven 286
Piore, Michael 214
Pixley, J. 121, 158
Platt, A. M. 151
Pleck, Joseph 307
Plummer, Kenneth 303, 313–14, 417
Poggi, G. 387–8
Polanyi, Karl 47
Polk, Ken 428, 433
Pollak, O. 419, 431
Pollock, L. 150
Polyani, Michael 358
Polybius 29
Pomeroy, Wardell 305–7
Popenoe, David 147–8, 155
Popper, Karl 444, 455
Poppi, C. 70
Porteus, S. D. 172
Posby, Nelson 384
Possamai, Adam 371–2
Poster, Mark 98
Postman, N. 92
Potter, R. 421
Powles, M. 172, 179
Poynting, J. 430
Price, M. E. 84, 88–9
Prigoff, A. 44, 45, 48, 49–51
Pringle, R. 24, 305, 306
Prout, A. 150, 151, 152
Pusey, Michael 23, 24, 77, 90, 381, 388

Putnam, Robert 197–8, 451
Puttick, E. 357

Quiggan, P. 136
Qvortrup, J. 150, 152

Rabinow, P. 399
Radway, Janice 198–9
Rahman, Momin 205
Ramazanoglu, Caroline 457
Randall, G. J. 181
Randall, Lois 281
Rapoport, Rhona 125
Rapoport, Robert 125
Rayner, Lisa 344
Read, P. 129
Reckless, Walter C. 414
Reich, Wilhelm 393, 399
Reuther, R. A. 356
Reynolds, Henry 257
Rheingold, Howard 105
Rich, Adrienne 304–5
Richardson, I. 105
Richmond, K. 139
Riesman, David 21
Riessman, Catherine Kohlier 322–3
Ritzer, George 3, 34, 62, 64, 477, 480, 481
    McDonaldisation of society 59–61
Roach Anleu, Sharyn 24, 216
Roberts, L. 426, 427
Robertson, R. 10, 31, 64, 367, 370
Robertson, Robbie 30, 38
Robertson, Roland 31, 33–4, 38, 64
    compression of the world 35–6
Roche, J. 151
Roemer, Milton 330–1
Rogers, E. 79
Rogers, L. J. 172
Rojek, Chris 95, 96, 97–8, 198
Rolfe, H. 247
Rollings, K. 437
Roof, W. C. 363, 367
Rose, S. 286–7
Rosenberg, C. 324
Rosenblum, Leonard 287
Rosenhan, D. L. 323
Rosenthal, R. 178
Ross, A. M. 467
Ross, M. 345
Roth, Julius 324, 326
Rousseau 15
Rowe, W. 62
Rozell, M. J. 367, 368
Rubel, M. 228, 355, 470, 471, 472
Rubin, Gayle 284–5, 290, 293, 303
Ruddock, A. 76, 79
Ruggie, J. G. 46
Ruzicka, Lado 133, 134–6, 138–9
Ryman, H. 44

Saggers, Sherry 343
Sahlings, Marshall 214
Saint-Simon, Claude Henri 15, 16, 33

Salam Pax 99
Sanders, S. A. 306
Sansom, Basil 259–60
Saunders, P. 243
Savage, M. 227
Sawer, G. 388
Sayer, Andrew 455, 456
Sayers, Janet 286, 293–4
Scambler, A. 328
Scambler, G. 328
Scheff, Thomas 323, 327
Schutz, Alfred 355, 454, 455
Scraton, P. 152
Sedgwick, Eve Kosofsky 312
Seidman, Steven 313, 314
Senate 244
Seneviratne, Kalinga 281
Sennett, R. 166
Servon, L. J. 104
Sey, A. 92
Sgritta, G. B. 152
Shakespeare, William 354
Shapiro, Margaret 336, 337
Sharma, S. D. 31
Sharp, L. 387
Sharpe, S. 178
Sherington, Geoffrey 267
Sherman, Rachel 212
Shilling, C. 291
Siahpush, Mohammad 344
Silbey, Susan 31, 55, 69, 70
Silj, A. 79
Simmel, Georg 6, 9, 11, 13, 34, 87, 394, 466, 467, 486
    concept of society and sociology 478–81
    influence 477
Simon, William 308–11, 312
Simpson, Mark 314–15
Skelton, C. 178, 179
Sklair, Leslie 34, 44–5, 58–9
Slevin 99
Small, Albion 17, 467
Smart, C. 158, 419
Smart, Carol 153–4
Smart, D. 381–2, 390
Smeeding, T. M. 242
Smith 15
Smith, Adam 467
Smith, Philip 275, 277, 327
Smith, Rodney 384
Smyrnios, Kosmas 131
Snooks, Graeme 133, 134, 138, 140–1
Soar, Matthew 206
Somerville, Jennifer 294
Spencer, Herbert 15–16, 70, 466, 467
Spender, Dale 149
Spinoza 391
Stanley, L. 456, 457
Stanner, W. E. H. 257
Stanworth, M. 179
Starhawk 357
Stark, Rodney 363
Starwoman 372
Stehr, N. 188

Stein, A. 313
Stening, B. W. 247
Stern, Lord 466
Stiglitz, Joseph 49–51
Stoller, Robert 284, 285
Stone, D. 44, 52
Stone, Maureen 180–1
Stone, Merlin 356
Storms, M. D. 307
Strauss, Anselm 325–6, 337, 338, 454
Strinati, D. 91
Sturmey, R. 360
Sudnow, David 338
Summers, A. 23
Sumner, C. 421
Sumner, William Graham 466, 467
Sutherland, Edwin 435
Syme, L. 329
Synnott, A. 151
Szasz, Thomas 323–4
Sznaider, Nathan 30

Tapper, Alan 145
Tarde, Gabriel 467
Taylor, Frederick Winslow 214
Taylor, I. 417
Taylor, P. J. 57
Tenbruck, F. H. 479
Theall, D. F. 100
Therborn, Göran 31, 115, 151, 158–9
    globalisation 39–42
Thiering, Barbara 356
Thomas, W. I. 17, 467, 482
Thompson, Elaine 388
Thompson, Graeme 52–3, 54
Thompson, J. 92, 95, 105
Thompson, John B. 106
    conceptual tools 81–4
    Media and Modernity, The 78–84
Thorne, B. 151
Thornhill, Randy 286
Tillyard, E. 354
Timpanaro, Sebastiono 291
Tinklin, T. 179
Tisdell, C. 51
Tittle, Charles 22
Toffoletti, Kim 204
Tonge, Bruce 131
Tonnies, Ferdinand 466
Touraine 151, 489
Tranter, Bruce 277–8
Treasury 237, 240
Trigger, David 243, 259, 281
Tucker, K. H. 403–4
Tumin, M. M. 233
Turkle, S. 42
Turnbull, S. 79
Turner, B. S. 23–4, 33, 291, 324, 326, 327, 335, 337, 339, 468, 480, 486–7
    relationism 478
Turner, G. 79, 96, 97
Turner, Graeme 274–5
Turrell, Gavin 340

Tyler, M. 179, 181
Tylor, Edward 6

Universities Australia 171
UN (United Nations) 242, 243
Urry, John 34–5, 52, 104, 105, 214, 455, 456
   tourist gaze 208–9

Valades, Dedacus 354
Van Dijk, J. J. M. 422–3, 426, 433
Van Kesteren, J. 422–3, 426, 433
van Krieken, R. 151, 152, 153, 387
Van Maanen, J. 460
van Vree, Wilbert 396
Veblen 467
Vinson, T. 235, 241, 253
Volkmer, Ingrid 94
Voltaire 15

Wacquant 186
Wade 51, 153
Waitzkin, Howard 322
Wajcman, Judy 199
Walker, J. 183, 424
Walklate, S. 419
Wallace, C. 179, 181
Wallerstein, Immanuel 10, 34, 35, 57–8, 69
Wallis, R. 361, 362, 365
Walras, Leon 46
Walton, Theresa 206, 417
Ward, Russel 274, 467
Warner, M. 314
Warrington, M. 179
Waters, Malcolm 24, 44, 48–9, 62, 402–3
Watson, J. L. 62
Weatherburn 434
Weatherburn, D. 433
Weber, Max 16–17, 33, 34, 59, 86, 201, 230, 324, 463, 466–7, 477, 480, 481–2
   bureaucracy 386–7, 401
   capitalism and ascetic Protestantism 358, 359, 361–2, 446, 475–6
   charismatic authority 95
   power 223, 378–80
   social action 474–7
   the state 51–2
   theory of inequality 230–2
   theory of the family 112, 118–19
   types of social action 380, 395
   verstehen sociology 452, 474
   Weberian maps (Goldthorpe) 246
Weeks, Jeffrey 302
Weinberg, M. S. 307
Weiner, G. 169, 175, 178, 180
Weiss, L. 53
Welch, D. 428
Wesley, John 475
West, Brad 106, 210, 276, 284

West, Candace 326
Westergaard, John 404
Wheelahan, L. 189
White, R. 274, 275, 415–16, 428, 429, 430, 430–1, 436, 437
Whyte, William Foote 459–63
Wickham, Gary 24
Wilcox, C. 367, 368
Wild, R. 251
Wilensky, H. L. 113
Wilk, R. R. 79
Wilkie, M. 428, 431
Wilkins, L. 417
Wilkins, R. 240, 241
Wilkinson, R. 225
Willett, Graham 115, 116
Willetts, P. 43
Williams, Claire 213–14, 216
Willis, E. 24, 334–5, 344
Willis, Karen 347
Willis, Paul 175, 182–3, 456
Willmott, Peter 116, 121, 122, 156, 158
Wilson, B. R. 373
Wilson, E. O. 286
Wilson, J. Q. 361, 362, 365, 414–15, 422
Winch, Peter 445–6, 451, 462
Winston, B. 77, 100
Wise, S. 456, 457
Wittgenstein, Ludwig 445–6
Wober, J. M. 79
Wolf, K. H. 479
Wolf, Naomi 9, 81
Wolpe, A.M. 176
Woodward, Ian 197
Woolgar, S. 103
Worsley, Peter 466
Wright, C. 179
Wright, Erik Olin 234, 246–7
Wundersitz, Joy 260, 264–5
Wuthnow, R. 351–2

Yeatman, Anna 24, 484–5
Young, C. 139–40
Young, J. 188, 421–2, 439
Young, Michael 116, 121, 122, 156, 158
Youth Justice Coalition 428

Zadoroznyj, Maria 347
Zaretsky, E. 157
Zborowski, Mark 330
Zelizer, Viviana 141, 151, 152–3, 477
Zevallos, Zuleyka 271
Zimmerman, C. C. 113
Zimmerman, D. H. 483
Zita, J. N. 304–5
Zola, Irving 329–30
Zubrzycki, Jerzy 23
Zysman, John 53

Subject Index

Aboriginal and Torres Strait Islander Commission (ATSIC) 262
Aboriginal Australians 272
   crime and 433–5
   criminal justice system
      deaths in custody 262, 281, 408, 433, 434–5
      over-policing 264, 434
      women in 433–4
      youth and juvenile justice 264–5
   education
      disadvantage 263
      students 171, 180
   European views of 387
   family life 125–9
      change in 128
   as Fourth World peoples 258
   health 320, 342–3
   kinship ties (Gale and Wundersitz) 260
   land rights 261–2
      Mabo decision 256, 261, 280, 389
      Wik decision 256, 262, 389
   migration theory (contested) 268
   poverty 241, 242
   racism
      in media 280–1
      in rural Australia 280
      since 1788 257–8, 265
   rural 127–8, 259, 260, 280
   social disadvantage 262–5
      in education 263
      in income 263
      unemployment 262–3
   Stolen Generations 128–9, 176, 262
   survival of culture 258–61
      Blackfella domain study (Trigger) 259
      Wallaby Cross study (Sansom) 259–60
   traditional 125–7, 232
   urban 127–8, 259–60
      in Redfern 256, 280–1
   women
      colonialism and 280
      in criminal justice system 433–4
      violence against 433
Aboriginal Protection Boards 129
Aborigine (term) 257
absolute poverty 242–3
acceptance of hierarchy 174
action *see* social action
action research 462
affective or emotional action 380, 396
Afghanistan 370
Africa 265
agency 7–8
Alcoholics Anonymous 346
Ali-G (TV character) 272

alienation 211, 471
allocative function 173, 184
alternative therapies 336, 343–5
altruistic suicide 448
American Dilemma, An (Myrdal) 21
American hegemony 57–8 *see also* hegemony
Americanisation 57
Amnesty International 55
anomic suicide 448
anomie 364, 412–13, 469
anomie theorists 412
Anzac Day 276, 353
Asian financial crisis 49
Asian migration 271
assimilation 257–8
assimilationism 268, 270
ASX 200 237
Asylums (Goffman) 324
asymmetry 293
AT Kearney/*Foreign Policy* Globalisation Index 31
Australia 203
   airline industry 216
   CEO pay 240
   class 244–53
      mapping 245–7
      occupational structure 244–8
      social mobility 252–3
      the state and 392–4
      wealth 248–9
      working class 251
   communities
      Arab 430
      Croatian 267, 278
      Greek 130–1
      Latin-American 271
      Lebanese Muslim 131–2
      Vietnamese 330
   crime in 422–35
      community attitudes 426, 427
      magistrates courts 216, 453
      offenders 426–8
      offending women 431
      rates over time 424–6
      victims 432
      violence against women 123–4, 433
      young people 428–31
   cultural consumption 196–7
   deglobalisation 69
   divorce 145, 146
   domestic labour 121–4
   education 162–8
      contemporary 167–8
      liberal humanism 163
      marketisation 166

new economism 165–6
social democracy 164–5
'The Australian Way of Life' 176
elite theory 381–2
family life (colonial) 115–16
fertility decline 133–8
demographic transition 134–6
post-1970s 136–8
gender 121–4
globalisation 33, 404–5
health 328
alternative therapies 344
expenditure 333
health care system 330, 331, 332–3
inequality 339–40
Medicare 332–3
new public health 345–6
obesity epidemic 341
suicide 450
inequality
gender 121–4
health 339–40
material 234–43
leisure 194–6
media 80
migration to 267–9
migration within 266
national identity 273–8
Anzac myth 276
historical perspective 274
multiculturalism 256, 269, 270–1, 277–8
popular culture 274–5
research 275–7
political system 359–61
political attitudes 360–1
political beliefs 234
social movements 404–5
poverty 243, 244
racism 256, 279–81
religion 353, 357, 359–61
affiliation 362
affiliation by age 363
social attitudes 360–1
sociology in 19, 22
history 22–3
research 23–4
sport
gender order 202–4
participation 199–202
sexual violence 204
the state 388–90, 392–4
the Constitution 388–9
counter-hegemony 393–4
emergence of 388
Encel (Weberian approach) 389–90
federal structure 389
hegemony 392–3
High Court 388–9
intellectuals 393–4
state 'sovereignty' 389
taste culture 234
tourism 207–8

work 211, 212–14
domestic labour 121–4
occupational order 244–8
unemployment 217, 218
Australia First 271
Australian Aborigines *see* Aboriginal Australians
Australian Constitution 388–9
Australian Family Law Court 132
Australian High Court 388–9
Australian Medical Association 320, 332
Australian Press Council 281
Australian Race, The (Curr) 387
Australian Securities & Investments Commission 436
Australian Society: A Sociological Introduction (Davies and Encel) 30
authority
charismatic 378–9, 380
conflict and (Dahrendorf) 477
rational–legal 379–80
traditional 379, 380

banal nationalism 272–3
Baroque culture 486–7
Beauty Myth, The (Wolf) 9
Beckham, David 205
belief system 358
Bell Curve, The (Herrnstein and Murray) 172
BHP 435
Big Brother (reality TV) 76
Bin Laden in the Suburbs (Poynting et al.) 430
biology 290–1, 292
biological determinism 296
influences on crime 414
theories of crime 411
biomedicine 320–1, 335, 343–7
Birth of the Clinic, The (Foucault) 321
Black, White or Brindle (Cowlishaw) 260, 280
Blair, Tony 65
Blank Slate, The (Pinker) 286
Blue, White and Pink Collar Workers in Australia (Williams) 213
the body 210, 290–1, 320–1
Body and Society (journal) 291
Body and Society, The (Turner) 291
Bowling for Columbine (film) 451
Bradman, Donald 203
brands 66–7
Brazil 58
breadwinner system 141
Brief History of Neoliberalism (Harvey) 45–7
'Brindletown' 260, 280
Britain *see* United Kingdom
Buddhism 362, 372
bureaucracy 9, 16, 386–90
discipline and 386–7
emergence of 387–8
organisations 379–80
patrimonial 379
technical superiority of (Weber) 386
Business Review Weekly's Rich 200 list 249

calculability 59–60 *see also* control; efficiency; predictability
Camp at Wallaby Cross, The (Sansom) 259–60

capitalism 9, 35
   anti-capitalist movement 65–6
   ascetic Protestantism (Weber) 475–6
   capital 233–4
   capitalists 229
   cultural capital 7, 184–5, 196–7, 223, 233–4
   economic capital 7, 233–4, 235–42
   family and reproduction of (Marx) 116–18
   global *see* globalisation
   health (Marx) 322
   inequality (Castells) 37–8
   needs 174–5
   spirit of (Weber) 476
   techno-capitalism (Castells) 37–8
   technology and 31, 42–3
case studies (defined) 449
case studies (examples)
   Anzac myth and national identity 276
   bowling alone: erosion of social capital 451
   caste system in India 224
   future of crime and deviance 439
   gender and identity transformations 18
   Hillsong 360
   letters to the editor 93
   medical 325
   obesity epidemic 341
   Olympic Games Sydney (2000) 200
   Pinochet and global law 46
   rationality 473
   Rudd 187
   sexual identity 308
   Whitlam dismissal 383
   work/life balance 141
'categorical' theory 303–4
cathexis relations 301
causality 443, 455–6
celebrity 94–8
Centuries of Childhood (Ariès) 150
chain migration 266
charismatic authority 378–9, 380
Chicago School 17, 46, 477, 482–3
   criticisms of 413–14
   deviance 413–14
Chifley, Ben 249
children/childhood 115–16, 145–7, 149–54
   abuse and neglect 153–4
   divorce 153
   education *see* education
   gender 293–4
   invention of (Ariès) 150
   lives beyond the family 152–3
   regulation and rights 150–1
   sexual scripts 309
   social construction of 150, 151–4
Chile 46, 48
China 51, 58, 215, 230, 237, 470, 475
Christianity
   Calvinist aceticism (Weber) 387, 475–6
   European family (Goody) 114–15
   fundamentalism 367–8
   kinship 114–15
   marriage 114–15

   parental control 114–15
   property 114–15
   Protestant ethic 443, 475–6
   secularisation 361, 364, 365
   theories of religion 354, 356, 357
circulation mobility 252
citizenship 227, 242–3, 258
civic nationalism 273, 276–7
civil religion 352–3
Civilizing Process, The (Elias) 202, 291, 394–7
clash of civilisations 61–2, 368–9
class, social 13, 20, 404
   in Australia 244–53, 392–4
   class consciousness 229–30
   crime and 436–7
   criminal justice system 438
   cultural capital 7, 184–5, 196–7, 233–4
   defined 223, 231
   in education 168–9, 170, 173–5, 181, 183–4
   fundamentalism 369–70
   global capitalism 44–5 *see also* globalisation
   health (Marx) 322
   inequality
      class and culture (Bourdieu) 233–4
      division of labour (Durkheim) 232–3, 379, 443, 469
      Marx 227–30
      Weber 230–2
   as market position 231
   middle class 226, 249–51
   modernity 225–7
   power 226, 392, 436–8
      power elite 380–2, 383, 385
   ruling class 229, 382, 392, 418, 470
   social mobility 251–3
      in Australia 252–3
      measuring 252
   social reproduction strategies 253
   sport and 205–6
   stratification 223, 225–6
   structure 245–7
      Weberian maps (Goldthorpe) 246
      Wright (contradictory locations) 246–7
   tourism 206
   underclass 104
   upper class 226, 247–9
   work: occupational structure 244–8
   working class 226, 229, 250, 251
climate change 466
Clinton, Bill 65
code theory
   Bernstein's 186–8
   legitimation 189–90
coercion 391
cohabitation 141, 144–5
Cold War 40
collective conscience 468–9
colonialism
   Australia
      Aboriginal health 343
      Aboriginal women 280
      family life 280

masculinity 299–300
modernity 9–10
sociology and 463
Coming of Post-Industrial Society, The (Bell) 486
commodity form 471
Commonwealth Schools Commission 165
communication, globalisation of 80–1
communism 58, 229
Communist Manifesto, The (Marx and Engels) 34, 42, 229
Communist Party of Australia 389
Community Development Employment Projects 262
community ties and health 329
comparative method 446
compression of the world (Roland Robertson) 35–6
compulsory heterosexuality 304–5
computer-mediated interaction 83–4
conflict 6, 198
Conflict Sociology (Collins) 477
conflict theory 18, 19, 20, 380–2
  authority (Dahrendorf) 477
  deviance and power 417–19
  subjective experience (Collins) 477
conformism 413
conscience 414, 443
consensual unified elite 382
consensus 6, 468–9
Consequences of Modernity, The (Giddens) 36–7
conservatism 359–61
consumption 9, 346–7
contraception 322–3
control 60 *see also* calculability; efficiency; predictability
  of crime 415–16
  dialectic of 394
  parental 114–15
  social control theory 414–15
convenience 400–1
corporate crime 435–8
correlation 443
correspondence theories 174–5
counter-school culture 182–3
credibility 461
Crikey.com 80
crime 408–39, 443 *see also* criminal justice system
  in Australia 422–35
    community attitudes 426, 427
    offenders 426–8, 431
    rates over time 424–6
    victims 432, 433
    violence against women 123–4, 433
    women offenders 431
    young people 428–31
  class 436–7
  control 415–16
  criminal (label) 411
  dark figure of 409–10
  definitions of 409, 410
  deviance
    amplification 417
    power and 417–19
    primary and secondary 416
  discretionary decisions 410
  domestic violence 123–4, 433

  future 439
  gender
    masculinities 420
    social control of women 419
  law and order 410, 418–19
  New Right 415–16
  offenders 426–8, 431
  official statistics 409–10, 443
  organised 418
  power and 417–19, 435–8
  shame and reintegration 420–1
  social construction of 408, 409–10, 443
  state 418–19, 435–6
  theories of 411–21
    biological and psychological 411
    Chicago School 413–14
    feminist 419–20, 421–2
    functionalist 412–13
    interactionist 416–17
    labelling theory 416–17, 421, 453
    Left realist 419
    Marxist 418
    neo-Marxist 418–19
    social control 414–15, 419
    socialist 418–19
Crime and Human Nature (Wilson and Herrnstein) 414–15
criminal justice system
  Aboriginal Australians
    deaths in custody 262, 281, 408, 433, 434–5
    juvenile justice 264–5
    over-policing 264
  discretionary decisions 410
  juvenile justice 264–5, 428–31
  power and 438
critical theory 12–13, 21, 91, 473
critical thought 3
Critique of Political Economy, The (Marx) 228
cultural capital 7, 184–5, 196–7, 233–4
  defined 223
Cultural Contradictions of Capitalism, The (Bell) 486
cultural diversity 125, 289
cultural globalisation 58–64
  heterogeneity 62–4
  homogenisation 58–62
    clash of civilisations 61–2
    Jihad vs McWorld 61
    McDonaldisation of society 59–61
    Starbuckisation of society 61
cultural pluralism 176
cultural relativism 189, 446
cultural scenarios 310
culturalism 171, 182–8
  class (Connell) 183–4
  code theory (Bernstein) 186–8
  educational knowledge code 187–8
  field theory (Bourdieu) 184–6
    cultural capital 7, 184–5, 196–7, 233–4
    habitus 184–5
    limitations of **185–6**
  learning to labour **(Willis)** 182–3
  Rudd 187

culture
  class and 233–4
  defined 6–7
  nuclear family 119–20
  of real virtuality 101–2
culture jamming 68–9
Culture Wars: The Struggle to Define America (Hunter) 367

dark figure of crime 409–10
death and dying 337–9
deductive approach 444
deglobalisation 32, 39, 41, 64–9 *see also* globalisation
  anti-capitalist movement 65–6
  defined 10
  no logo (Klein) 66–9
  World Social Forum 69
democracy 164–5, 173–4, 384
Democratic People's Republic of Korea 350
demographic transition 134, 135
denomination 362
developing world 339
deviance 408–39 *see also* crime
  amplification 417
  crime control 415–16
  defined 409
  future 421–2, 439
  gender
    masculinities 420
    social control of women 419
  New Right 415–16
  power and 417–19
  primary and secondary 416
  shame and reintegration 420–1
  social construction of 408, 409–10, 443
  theories of 411–21
    anomie 412–13
    biological and psychological 411
    Chicago School 413–14
    conflict 417–19
    ecology 413
    ethnography 413
    feminist 419–20, 421–2
    functionalist 412–13
    interactionist 416–17
    labelling theory 416–17, 421, 453
    Left realist 419
    Marxist 418
    neo-Marxist 418–19
    social control 414–15
    socialist 418–19
dialectic of control 394
Dialectic of Enlightenment (Adorno and Horkheimer) 91
dialectical materialism 228–9
Diana, Princess of Wales 96
differentiation
  in modern medicine 321
  of society 469
digital divide 103–4
discipline 386–7, 398–9
  defined 398
  disciplinary power (Foucault) 399–400

disciplinary society 398
disciplined autonomy 401
Discipline and Punish (Foucault) 398–9
discourses 180, 189, 312
  defined 321
  history of sexuality (Foucault) 397–8
  knowledge and power (Foucault) 397
Discovering Suicide (Atkinson) 449–50
discrimination 267
Disneyland 60–1
dispersed extended families 125
Distinction (Bourdieu) 196, 233–4
disunified elite 381–2
division of labour 232–3, 379, 443, 469
Division of Labour in Society, The (Durkheim) 443
divorce 141, 145–9, 153
domestic group 112
domestic labour 117–18, 121–5, 433
domestic sphere 293
domestic violence 123–4, 433
dominant ideology 470
domination 378, 386, 391 *see also* authority

economic capital 7, 233–4, 235–42, 470
economic globalisation 31
  class 44–5
  international economy 43–4
  limits 48–9
  neoliberalism 47–8, 404
  poverty debate 49–51
  size and scope of 44
economic inequality *see* material inequality
economic power 381–2, 388
economic rationalism 45–8, 166, 404
Economy and Society (Weber) 474
education 103, 162–90, 222
  in Australia 162–8, 427
    for Aboriginal Australians 263
  class, social 168–9, 170, 183–4
  classroom practices 177–8
  contemporary 167–8
  crime and 427
  disciplinary power (Foucault) 399
  ethnicity 170–1, 176, 180–2
  gender 169–70
  learning to labour (Willis) 182–3, 456
  making the difference (Connell) 183–4
  marketisation of 165–6
  new economism in 165–6
  object of 401
  power elite 382
  rise of knowledge 188–90
  schooling and fertility decline 135–6
  sociology of 171–90
  theories of
    code theory (Bernstein) 186–8
    feminist theory 175–6
    field theory (Bourdieu) 184–6
    labelling theory 177–8
    legitimation code theory 189–90
    liberal humanist 163
    reproduction theories 174–5

social democratic 164–5
    social realist 189
    structural functionalist 173–4
educational knowledge code 186, 187–8
efficiency 59, 331 *see also* calculability; control; predictability
egoistic suicide 448
elaborated code 186
Elementary Forms of Religious Life, The (Durkheim) 276
elite pluralism 391
elite theory 380–2, 383, 385
emotional action *see* affective or emotional action
emotional labour 215–16
empirical evidence 327–8, 442–3
End of Millennium (Castells) 38
End of Organized Capitalism, The (Lash and Urry) 34–5
Enlightenment 227–8, 321, 357–8, 421, 485
environmental crime 435
epidemiology 338–43
    Aboriginal Australians 342–3
    causes of death 338–9
    ethnicity 342
    gender 341–2
    health in developing world 339
    inequality 339–40
    migration 342
epistemologies 442
equality 164, 471 *see also* inequality
Equality and Authority (Encel) 390
essentialism 188–9, 292–3, 455
Esso 438
ethnicity 265–6 *see also* race
    Aboriginal Australians 125–9, 257–65
    education and 170–1, 176, 180–2
    ethnic group 265
    ethnic nationalism 273
    ethnic politics 176
    health 342
    migrant 129–32
    postmodern 271–2
    young people 430
ethnocentric assumptions 189, 446
ethnographic research 413, 459
ethnomethodology 311–12, 449
    defined 483
    ethnoscapes 63
    methods of social research 454–5
    sociological theory 483–4
Europe 447
European Union Common Agricultural Policy 65
exclusion 71
Exclusive Society, The (Young) 439
extended family 113
externalism 171, 173–7
    Australian way of life 176
    criticisms of 176–7
    patriarchal needs 175–6
    reproduction theories 174–5
    structural functionalism 173–4

Fairfax Media 80
false consciousness 229, 470
falsify 444

Family Law Act 1975 (Cwlth) 147, 148
family life 112–59
    in Australia
        Aboriginal Australians 125–9
        colonial 115–16
    children/childhood 149–54
    Christian Church (Goody) 114–15
    cohabitation 141–9
    culture 125–32
    'decline' 155
    diversity 125–32
    divorce 141–9
    domestic violence 123–4, 433
    ethnicity 125–32
    European family (Goody) 114–15
    fertility decline 133–8
    functionalism 119–20
    future 158–9
    gender 121–5
    health 329
    industrialisation 114
    inequality
        within marriage 124–5
        rural (Dempsey) 121–2
    marriage 141–9
    migrant 129–32
    modern 113–16
    nuclear 113–14, 119–20
    parental control 114–15
    power relations 158
    structural change 132–49
    theories of
        democratisation (Giddens et al.) 155–8
        egalitarianism (Giddens et al.) 155–8
        feminism and 'antisocial family' 120–1
        'post-familial' 154–8
        reproduction of capitalism (Marx) 116–18
        sociological 116–21
        symmetrical family (Young and Willmott) 116
        theory of (Weber) 118–19
    work
        division of labour (Baxter) 122
        domestic labour 121–5
        time use 122–3, 124
        women 138–41
family wage 116
fashion 479–80
fatalistic suicide 448
Feminine Mystique, The (Friedan) 284
feminist theory 302–3
    'antisocial family' 120–1
    Christianity, influence on 357
    of crime and deviance 419–22
    development of 19–20
    in education 175–6, 178–80
    gender 13, 198–9, 215–16, 420
    health 329, 345
    inequality 215–16
    interactionist 19
    leisure 198–9
    medicine 322–3
    methods of social research 456–7

public and private (Yeatman) 484–5
   of religion 356–7, 358
   social control of women 419
   sociology 19
   work 215–16
      medical occupations 334
fertility decline in Australia 133–8
feudalism 387–8
fieldwork 459
first 'face' of power 390
First World 34
Focus on the Global South 69
forces of production 472
Ford, Henry 60
Fordism 208, 214, 215
fourth estate 78
Fourth World peoples 104, 258
France 48, 64, 66, 369, 383, 388, 437–8
Frankfurt School 90, 91, 117–18, 299, 472, 473, 485
Fred Hollows Foundation 320
free enterprise 390
freedom 401, 471
Freeman, Cathy 256
French Revolution 15, 77–8
Frogs and Snails and Feminist Tales (Davies) 295–6
From Ritual to Record (Guttmann) 200–2
functionalism 6, 17–18
   anomie theory 412–13
   definitions 351
   deviance, 412–13
   nuclear family 119–20
fundamentalism 366, 367–71
   appeal of 370–1
   Christian 367–8
   clash of civilisations 368–9
   class 369–70
   globalisation 370
   Islamic 368–70
   postmodernity 370–1
   September 11 369

game stage 482
gang 429–30
gay liberation 284, 302–3
gender 284–316
   active bodies 296
   biology and 285–91
   the body and 290–1
   children/childhood 293–4
   crime and deviance 419–20
      victims of crime 432
   culture and 285–91
      cultural diversity 289
      as expression 289–90
      fashion 480
      men's life histories 297–9
   defined 284–5
   education 169–70, 175–6, 181–2
   future sociology of 315–16
   gay and lesbian movement 302–3
   gender apartheid 292
   gender attribution 311, 312

gender personalities 293
gender revolution 169–70
health 341–2
identity 178–80, 291–301
inequality 121–2, 124–5, 215–16, 301
leisure 198–9
methods of social research 456
patriarchal needs 172–3
psychology 307–8
sex 285, 285–91, 308–11, 312
   sex roles 287–8
   sexual conduct (Gagnon and Simon) 308–11
   sexual scripts 308–11, 312
sociobiology 286–7
sociology and 290–1
sport 201–5
   David Beckham and 'new man' 205
   gender order 202–4
theories of
   ethnomethodological approach (Kessler and McKenna) 311–12
   feminist 13, 198–9, 215–16, 456
   Freud 288–9
   language and cognition (Davies) 295–6
   masculinities (Connell) 296–300
   reproduction of mothering (Chodorow) 293–5
   role theory 291–3
transformations 18, 301–3
women's movement 302–3
work 195, 211, 212
   division of labour (Baxter) 122
   domestic labour 121–5
   inequality in 215–16
   medical occupations 334
   occupational order 246–8
   time use 122–3, 124
   workforce structure 244–5, 246, 247
Gender and Power (Connell) 301
generalisable 457
Gerada, Rodriguez de 68
Gini coefficient 235, 241
global warming 466
globalisation 4, 28–72 *see also* deglobalisation
   Australia 33, 404–5
   class 44–5
   of communication 80–1
   compression of the world (Roland Robertson) 35–6
   cultural 58–64
   defined 10, 31
   economic 31, 42–51
   fundamentalism and 370
   global governance 49–51, 53–5, 404
   global law 46, 55–6
   global public sphere 94
   global shrinkage 36
   'global village' 100
   glocalisation 64
   hegemony 45, 57–8
   history of 38–42
   inequality (Castells) 37–8
   international economy 43–4
   KOF Index 31–3, 334

limits of 48–9
measuring 31–3
modernity and 36–7
neoliberalism 47–8, 404
as Northern Theory (Connell) 70–2, 463
political 32, 51–5
postmodernity and 20
poverty debate 49–51
size and scope of 44
sociology and 20
sociology of 33–8
the state, withering away of 52–3
techno-capitalism (Castells) 37–8
technological 31, 37–8, 42–3
trade 38, 39, 45
United States and 32–3, 40
world-systems theory (Wallerstein) 35
globalism 30
glocalisation 64
gold rushes 268
government policies
   Chifley 389
   Fraser 270, 332
   Hawke 270
   Howard 166, 170, 211, 256, 262, 271, 333, 404–5
   Keating 48, 270
   Menzies 389
   Rudd 47, 162, 187, 262
   Whitlam 165, 332, 382, 383
governmentality 378, 400–2
   defined 400
Great Transformation, The (Polanyi) 47
the Greens 384
grounded theory 454
Gutenberg Galaxy, The (McLuhan) 99
Gutenberg, Johan 80

Habits of the Heart (Bellah et al) 21
habitus 184–5
Hand that Signed the Paper, The (Demidenko/Darville) 272
health *see also* modern medicine
   alternative therapies 343–5
   community ties 329
   death and dying 337–8
   in developing world 339
   doctors 329–30
   epidemiology 338–43
   expenditure 330, 333
   health-care systems 330–1
      in Australia 331, 332–3
      in United States 331–2
   health field concept 345–6
   lay definitions of disease 330
   managerialism 346–7
   Marxist views on 322
   Medicare 332–3
   political economy of 330–3
   preventive medicine 345–6
   promotion 345–6
   self-help movements 346
   welfare 328–30
   workforce 333–4

hegemony
   American 57–8
   class 392–4
   counter-hegemony 393–4
   defined 45
   global capitalism and 45
   hegemonic masculinity 203, 297, 420
   levels of (Connell) 393
   power of (Gramsci) 391–4
Hegemony or Survival (Chomsky) 57
hermaphroditism 311
herrschaft 378
Hetherington, Ethel 207
hidden curriculum 174, 179, 187
hierarchy 379
HIH 437
Hinduism 367
historical documents 458
historical materialism 228–9
historical sensibility 3
History of Sexuality, The (Foucault) 312, 399
HIV/AIDS 345
Holocaust 2
homeless 242–3
Homo Ludens (Huizinga) 200
horizontal segregation 211, 212, 215
hospital 324–6
household 112, 118–19, 488
Household, Income and Labour Dynamics in Australia (HILDA) 146
housing market 240
human agency 7–8
human rights 56, 150–1, 162, 225
Human Rights Watch 55
human sciences 398, 442
hypothesis 444

iatrogenesis 326
identity *see also* national identity
   defined 8
   gender 18, 178–80, 291–301
   the self 8–9
   sexual 284–5, 303–15
   socialisation 8–9
ideology 203–4, 335, 393
   dominant ideology 470
   ideological power 388
   ideologically unified elite 382
   ideoscapes 64
   ruling 229
   theory (Marx) 470–1
Imagined Communities (Anderson) 78
imagined community 272
immigration 268, 270, 279
In Search of Respect (Bourgois) 462
income 146, 235, 236, 237, 240, 263
index of inequality *see* Gini coefficient
indexicality 484
India 51, 58, 224, 231, 475
individualism 8–9, 156, 157, 468
   Foucault (power and) 398–9
inductive methodology 444

Subject Index

industrialisation 9, 113, 114
inequality 222–43, 488
   in Australia 252–3
   caste system in India 224
   in a changing world 225–7
   class 225–6, 226–7
   concepts 223–4
   defined 223
   economic *see* material inequality
   in education 168–71
   functions of 232–3
   gender 215–16, 301
   health 339–40
   leisure 196–8
   within marriage 124–5
   migration 267
   modernity 226–7
   power 196–8
   racial *see* racism
   religion 354
   social *see* class, social
   social mobility 251–3
   stratification 223, 225–6
   technology 37–8
   theories of 227–34
      class and culture (Bourdieu) 233–4
      class (Marx) 227–30
      division of labour (Durkheim) 232–3, 379, 443, 469
      Weber 230–2
   work 215–16
Information Age, The (Castells) 188
infrastructure (of society) 228
innovation 413
institutional racism 279
instrumental knowledge 20–1
instrumentally rational action 380
integration 270, 447
intellectuals 393–4
intelligence quotient 172
interactionism 291, 306–7, 308, 325
   criticisms and evaluation of 417
   defined 416, 482
   development of 19–20
   deviance 416–17
   methods of social research 452–4
   sociological theory 481–4
   symbolic 11, 177, 180, 284, 324
interactions, media
   computer-mediated 83–4
   face-to-face 81–2
   mediated 82
   mediated quasi- 82–3
interest groups 384–5
internalism 171, 177–82
   boys, underperformance of 179–80
   classroom practices 177–8
   criticisms of 180–2
   ethnicity 180
   gender 178–80
   identity 178–80
   labelling theory 177–8
International Criminal Court 56

International Monetary Fund (IMF) 48, 49
International Sociological Association 474
internationalisation 33
internet 98–104
   community 102–3
   culture of real virtuality 101–2
   digital divide 103–4
   history of 101
   network society 99–101
   networked individualism 102–3
Internet Galaxy, The (Castells) 99–100, 102–3
interpersonal scripts 310
interpretive approach 17, 450–8, 481–4
   defined 13, 452
intrapsychic scripts 310
invented tradition 273
Iran 58
Iraq 58, 83, 99, 265
Islam 131–2, 356, 362, 367
   fundamentalism 368–70

James Hardie Industries 436
Japan 58
Jihad vs McWorld 61
Journal of Sociology 22, 106–7
Judaism 356, 367
juvenile 428

Kapital, Das (Marx) 211
Kennedy, Jacqui 246
Kentucky Fried Chicken (KFC) 60
kinship group 112, 114–15, 118–19
kinship ties 260
knowledge 162, 166, 222, 379 *see also* education
   constitutive role of 397
   disciplinary power (Foucault) 399–400
   discourses (knowledge) (Foucault) 397
   governmentality (Foucault) 400–2
   history of sexuality (Foucault) 397–8
   individuality and power (Foucault) 398–9
   knowledge paradox 188
   legitimation code theory 189–90
   postmodernism (Lyotard) 485–6
   power (Foucault) 397–402
   power (Foucault) 422
   rise of 188–90
   social realism 189
KOF Index of Globalisation 31–3, 334
Kondratieff cycles 35

labelling theory 453
   of crime and deviance 416–17, 421, 453
   defined 413
   in education 177–8
   in modern medicine 323–4
labour (or production) 263, 301, 472
land holding 114–15
language
   gender and 292, 295–6
   inequality and 267
   language games 445–6, 451
Latin America 361

law *see also* legislation
   global 46, 55–6
   law and order 410, 418–19
   laws of human society 443–4
lay definitions of disease 330
leadership 391
Learning to Labour (Willis) 182–3, 185, 456
Left realism 419
legislation 163, 202, 215, 261, 268, 270, 279, 302, 418, 421 *see also* law
legitimation code theory 189–90
leisure 194–9
   in Australia 194–6
   conflict 198
   gender 198–9
   inequality 196–8
   power 196–8
Lenin, Vladimir 228
liberal humanism 163
liberalism 28, 400–1
liberation theology 361
life chances 223
life histories 297–9, 462
Limits to Medicine (Illich) 321
liquid modernity 225
localism 62–3
Logic of Scientific Discovery, The (Popper) 444
Lonely Crowd, The (Riesman) 21

McDonaldisation 4, 34, 59–61, 64
   calculability 59–60
   control 60
   efficiency 59
   predictability 60
   rationality 60–1
McDonaldization of Society, The (Ritzer) 4, 59–61
McDonald's 68
Madness and Civilization (Foucault) 321
Madoff, Bernie 437
Making the Difference (Connell et al.) 183–4, 185
Managed Heart, The (Hochschild) 215
managerialism 346–7
Mao Zedong 228
market situation 231, 246
marketisation of education 166
marriage 114–15, 119, 141
   child-bearing 142–4
   inequality within 124–5
   marriage rate 142–4
Masculinities (Connell) 296–300
masculinity 296–300, 420, 428
   history of 299–300
mass media *see* media
material inequality 234–43 *see also* social inequality
   in Australia 234–43
   changes in 235–40
   citizenship 243
   effects of 240–1
   international comparisons 241–2
   measuring resources 235–42
   poverty 242–3
   social exclusion 242–3

materialist theories of religion 353–5
The Matrix (movie) 91
means of production 470
mechanical solidarity 232, 469
Médecines San Frontières 55
media 76–107, 403
   audiences 79
   celebrities 94–8
   as commercial concerns 80
   cross-cultural 79
   future, sociology of 106–7
   globalisation of communication 80–1
   interactions 81–4
   internet 98–104
      community 102–3
      culture of real virtuality 101–2
      digital divide 103–4
      history of 101
      network society 99–101
      networked individualism 102–3
   media events 86–9
      Beijing Olympic Games (2008) 88–9
   media rituals 84–5
      formalised action 84
      habitual action 84
      theories of (Couldry) 84–5
   mediascapes 63–4
   mobile network society 104–6
   modernity (Thompson) 78–84
   periodical publications 80
   printing industry 79–80
   the public 89–90
   public sphere
      global (Volkmer) 94
      structural transformation (Habermas) 90–3
   racism in 280–1
      representations of Arabs 430
   as social practice (Couldry) 85–6
Media and Modernity, The (Thompson) 78–84
Media Consumption and Public Engagement (Couldry) 85–6
Media Events: The Live Broadcasting of History (Dayan and Elihu) 86–9
mediated quasi-interaction 82–3
medical dominance 323–4
medical gaze 321, 335
medical occupations 325, 326–30, 333–7 *see also* modern medicine
   allied health professionals 335
   changes to 335–6
   doctor–patient interaction 326–8, 329–30
   doctors 334–5
   nurses 335
   training 336–7
medical–industrial complex 322
medicalisation 321
medicine *see* modern medicine
meritocracy 164, 223, 225
method (defined) 442
methodological nationalism 30, 487–8
methodological pluralism 457–8
methodology 442
methods of social research 442–63
   action 462

comparative 446
feminist 456–7
inductive 443
interpretive 450–8
pluralistic 457–8
positivist 443–4
   inductive methodology 443–4
   laws of human society 443–4
   social facts as 'things' 443
   statistics 443
qualitative 442, 450–8
   data 451–2
   ethnomethodology 454–5
   phenomenology 450–1, 454
   realist view of science 455–6
   symbolic interactionist 452–4, 453–4
   verstehen sociology (Weber) 452
quantitative 275–7, 442, 443–6
   anti-positivism (Winch) 445–6
   falsification (Popper) 444
   hypothetico-deductive model (Popper) 444
   paradigms (Kuhn) 445
   relativism (Winch) 445–6
   scientific revolutions (Kuhn) 444–5
representation 462–3
research process 462–3
sociology of suicide (Durkheim) 446–50
   in Australia 449–50
   criticisms 448–9
   death as suicide (Atkinson) 449–50
   rates 446–7
   types of 447–8
Street Corner Society (Whyte) 459–63
   critique 460–1
   representation 462–3
   significance of 461–2
triangulation 457–8
Mexico 47, 48, 66
middle class 226, 249–51
   cultural power 250–1
   professions 250–1
   working class 250
Middle East 58
migration 41, 129–32, 210
   asylum seekers 256
   to Australia 267–9
   decision making 266
   defined 266
   ethnicity and 265
   multiculturalism 256, 269, 270–1, 277–8
   outcomes 266–77
   sickness and health 342
   structural aspects 266
military analogies to crime 415
military power 381–2, 388
Mistaken Identity (Castles et al.) 277–8
mobile network society 104–6
mode of production 228, 229
modern medicine *see also* health
   hospitals 324–6
   medical fraud 346
   patients 324, 326–8, 329–30, 346–7

rise of 320–1
sociological critique 321–4
   feminist perspectives 322–3
   Foucault (medical gaze) 321, 335
   Goffman (the asylum) 324
   labelling theory 323–4
   Marxism (health, class and capitalism) 322
   Roth (moral evaluation of patients) 324
work *see* medical occupations
modernity
   beyond nation–state 487–8
   class 223, 225–6
   colonialism 9–10
   consequences (Giddens) 36–7
   defined 9
   family 113–16
   first and second, reflexive 487
   globalisation 36–7
   media (Thompson) 78–84
   religiosity 373
   sociological theory 485–8
   sport 200–4
   the state 387–8
   work 214–15
modified elementary family 125
modified extended family 125
morality
   moral guidance 366–7
   moral order 468–9
   moral panics 417
morbidity 339–40
mortality 329
motivation 436
multiculturalism 256, 269, 270–1, 277–8
multidimensionality 32
Multilateral Agreement on Investment (MAI) 45
multinational corporations (MNCs) 43, 80
Myths of Oz (Fiske et al.) 274–5

Napoleon Bonaparte 40
national identity (Australian) 273–8 *see also* nationalism
   Anzac myth 276
   defined 272
   historical perspective 274
   multiculturalism 256, 269, 270–1, 277–8
   popular culture 274–5
   research 275–7
National Population Council 132
nationalism 272, 273 *see also* national identity
nation–state 9, 30–1
Natural History of Rape (Thornhill and Palmer) 286
naturalism 171–3, 313–14
nature versus nurture 172
Nazi ideology 91
needs
   capitalist 174–5
   economic 173
   patriarchal 175–6
negotiated order 325–6
neo-paganism 372–3
neo-pluralism 391
neoconservative 404–5

neoliberalism 45–8, 166, 404
network society 99–101
networked individualism 102–3
New Age movements 371–2
New Christian Right 367–8
new economism 165–6
'new man' 205
new politics 403–4
new public health 345–6
new racism 278–9
new religious movements 363–5
New Right 415–16, 421
new social movements 384–5, 402–3
 in Australia 404–5
News Limited 80
Nike 59, 67, 68, 205–6
9/11 58
No Logo (Klein) 66–9
non-government organisation (NGO) 43, 53
Normal Chaos of Love, The (Beck and Beck-Gernsheim) 156–8
norms 6–7, 292
North American Free Trade Agreement (NAFTA) 45, 66
North Korea 350
Northern Theory (Connell) 70–2, 463
nuclear family 112, 113–14, 119–20, 287–8

Obama, Barack 156
object/objectivity 378, 456–7, 481
OECD (Organization for Economic Cooperation and Development) 173
Olympic Games Beijing (2008) 88–9
Olympic Games Sydney (2000) 200
omnivore 196–7, 234
One Nation Party 256, 262, 271, 277
Open Cut (Williams) 213
Orange-France Telecom 473
organic solidarity 232, 469
organisational theory 325
Organization for Economic Cooperation and Development (OECD) 173
Our Bodies Ourselves (Boston Women's Health Collective) 345
Outsiders (Becker) 416–17
overrepresentation (of juveniles) 428
Oxfam 51, 55

Palm Island 408
Papua New Guinea 435
paradigm 11, 445, 446
participant observation 442, 460
parties (Weber) 231–2
patriarchy 20
 patriarchal family 129–32
 patriarchal needs 175–6
patrimonial bureaucracy 379
patrimonial domination 119
Pauline Hanson's One Nation Party 256, 262, 271, 277
Pax Americana 57–8
phenomenology
 methods of social research 450–1, 454
 theories of religion 355–6

Philosophy of Money, The (Simmel) 477, 480–1
pilot study 458
pink-collar occupations 215
Pinochet, Augusto 46
play stage 482
pluralism 382
 cultural 176
 defined 384
 elite 391
 methodological 457–8
 neo-pluralism 391
 power 383–5, 391
 religious 353
police
 over-policing 264, 434
 young people 430–1
political citizenship 243
political crime 437–8
political economy 401, 418
political globalisation 32, 51–5
political parties 384
political power 381–2, 388
political science 378
politics
 of representation 463
 of social research 457
 sociology as 12
polygyny 126–7
polymorphously perverse 289
popular culture 274–5
positivism 16, 228, 443–6
post-Fordism 208, 214
post-secularisation 365–6
post-structuralism 180
post-tourist 210
postmodernity
 alternative therapies 344
 apostasy 364
 defined 14
 ethnicity 271–2
 fundamentalism 370–1
 globalisation 20
 knowledge (Lyotard) 485–6
 postmodernist, defined 14
 second modernity (Beck) 487–8
 simulations (Baudrillard) 486–7
 sociology and 20
 the state 402–3
 work 214–15
Postmodernization (Crook et al.) 402–3
poverty 17, 237–40, 242–3
 globalisation of 49–51
 measuring 243–4
 social exclusion 242–3
power 292, 321, 378–405
 in Australia 388–90
 authority 378–80, 477
 bureaucracy 386–90
 civilising process (Elias) 394–7
 class 226, 392, 436–8
  power elite 380–2, 383, 385
 conflict 198, 477

crime 435–8
    costs 437–8
    criminal justice system 438
cultural 250–1
defining 223, 378–80, 390–1
deviance 417–19
    discipline 386–7, 398–9
disciplinary (Foucault) 399–400
discourses (Foucault) 397–8
as effect (Latour) 402
elite theory 380–2
faces of (Lukes) 390–1
in family life 158
Foucault (knowledge) 397–402, 422
governance (Dahl) 385
governmentality (Foucault) 378, 400–2
hegemony (Gramsci) 391–4
individuality and 398–9
inequality 196–8, 226
    Weber (theory of) 230–2
knowledge (Foucault) 397, 397–402, 422
leisure 196–8
of medical profession 334–5
in meetings 396
money (Parsons) 382–3
neo-pluralism 391
pluralism 383–5
relations of 470
representational 395–6
rethinking 390–4
the self 394–402
sexuality 312
    history of (Foucault) 397–8
social action 380
social power 388
the state 386–90
'variable-sum' concept 383
'zero-sum' concept 384, 394, 402
Power: A Radical View (Lukes) 390–1
power elite 380–2, 383, 385
predictability 60
Prefontaine, Steven 206
Presentation of Self in Everyday Life, The (Goffman) 453
primary sexual characteristics 311
primary socialisation 120
primary sources 458
printing industry, rise of 79–80
prison design (panopticon) 399–400
private body 311
private sphere 484–5
private troubles 3
process of legitimation 355
production (or labour) 263, 301, 472
professional closure 334–5
professional sociology 21
professions 56, 250–1, 334–5
profit 9
progress 9
projection 71
proletariat 229
'promotional' group 384–5
property 114–15

prostitution 119
'protective' group 384–5
Protestant Ethic and the Spirit of Capitalism, The (Weber) 16–17, 34, 359, 361–2, 446, 452, 474
    Protestant ethic 443, 475–6
    spirit of capitalism 476
psyche 301
psychology
    of gender and sexuality 307–8
    influences on crime 414
    theories of crime 411
the public 89–90
public sociology 3, 20–2
public sphere 90–3, 484–5
purchasing power parity (PPP) 49
push and pull factors 266

Qantas 213
qualitative methods 442, 450–8
quantitative methods 275–7, 442, 443–6
queer sexuality 312–15
    critiques of queer theory 313–14
    sexual politics 314–15
questionnaire 458

race 265 *see also* ethnicity
    sport and 206
racism 265, 267, 278–81
    in Australia 279–81
        Aboriginal Australians 257–8
    defined 278
    institutional/structural 279
    old and new 278–9
Racism, Ethnicity and the Media (Jakubowicz et al.) 281
rationality 9, 60–1, 446
    feminist critique of reason 456–7
    irrationality 473
    rational action 380, 476
    rational organisation of social life 4
    rationalisation 321, 380
    rational–legal authority 379–80
Reagan, Ronald 46–7, 48
the real 208
realist theory of science
    causation 455–6
    defined 455
    scientific research 'systems' 455
    sociology as science 456
    studying the unobservable 455
reality television 76
rebellion 413
reciprocal working 478–9
reflexive 4–5, 20–1, 37, 155–6
reflexive modernisation 487
'reflexive' modernity 487
reformism 419
regulation 150–1, 447
reintegrative shaming 420–1
relationism 478–9
    relational potential 293
    relations of power 470

relations of production 472
relationship of power 401
relativism 189
   relative autonomy 184
   relative deprivation 419
   relative poverty 242
reliability 449
religion 232, 350–74, 468–9 *see also* religiosity
   alienation 471
   apostasy 364
   Calvinist Protestantism (Weber) 387, 475–6
   caste system in India 224
   celebrity and 97–8
   Christian Church and European family (Goody) 114–15
   civil 352–3
   conservativism 359–61
   contemporary expression 367–73
   deconstruction of 356
   definitions of 351
   feminist influence on Christian church 357
   fundamentalism 366, 367–71
     appeal of 370–1
     Christian 367–8
     Islamic 368–70
   future 373–4
   Hillsong 360
   oppression of women 356–7
   political attitudes 360–1
   radicalism 361
   reconstruction of 357
   resurgence of 366–7
   as sacred canopy 355–6
   science and 357–8
   secularisation 361–6
   social attitudes 360–1
   social change and 358–61
   spirituality and 351–2
   theories of 352–7
     feminist 356–7
     functionalist 352–3
     materialist 353–5
     phenomenological 355–6
   tourism and 207
religiosity 360–1, 365 *see also* religion
   in modernity 373
   neo-paganism 372–3
   New Age movements 371–2
   new forms of 371–3
   witchcraft 372
religious pluralism 353
representative
   defined 457
   representation 462–3
   representational power 395–6
repression
   repression hypothesis 312, 398, 399
   repressive desublimation 393
Reproduction of Mothering, The (Chodorow) 293–5
   criticisms of 294–5
reproduction theories 174–5
research process 462–3
resistance 400, 401, 402

restricted code 186
retreatism 413
revolution 15–16
Right Realism 415
Rise of the Network Society, The (Castells) 37–8, 101–2
ritualism 413
role theory 291–3
   criticisms of 292–3
Royal Commission into Aboriginal Deaths in Custody 434–5
rules 380
Rules of Sociological Method, The (Durkheim) 443, 446
ruling class 229, 382, 392, 418, 470
ruling ideology 229, 470–1
Russia 58, 230
Rwanda 437–8

sacred canopy 355–6
sample 457
Sanders, Colonel 60
scheme 312
Schooling in Capitalist America (Bowles and Gintis) 174–5
science 12
   causation 455–6
   realism 455–6
   religion and 357–8
   research 'systems' 455
   revolutions in 445
   sociology as 456
   the unobservable 455
second 'face' of power 390
'second' or 'reflexive' modernity 487
Second World 34
secondary sexual characteristics 311
secondary sources 458
sects 114
secularisation 321, 361–6
   defined 361
   evidence for 362–3
   post-secularisation 365–6
   problems with 363–5
segregation 258
   horizontal 211, 212, 215
   vertical 211, 212, 215
Seinfeld (TV series) 155
the self
   civilising process (Elias) 394–7
   identity 8–9
   meetings 396
   power 394–402
     Collins theory 396–7
     representational 395–6
   social change 4
   socialisation 8–9
   stages (Mead) 482
self-fulfilling prophecy 307
self-help movements 346
semi-structured interviews 450, 457
separation of time and space 37
September 11 369
servants 113–14
sex 119, 284–5
sex as 'natural' drive 310

sex discrimination 215
sex/gender system 293
sexual assault 410, 424, 425, 430
sexual citizenship 284
Sexual Conduct (Gagnon and Simon) 308–11, 312
sexual harassment 216
sexual identity 303–15
   'categorical' theory 303–4
   compulsory heterosexuality (Rich) 304–5
      criticisms of 304–5
   defined 284–5
   power structures 301
   queer sexuality 312–15
   sexual behaviour (Kinsey) 305–7
      criticisms of 306–7
   sexual conduct (Gagnon and Simon) 308–11
   sexual scripts 308–11, 312
      adolescence and post-adolescence 309–10
      childhood 309
      scripting theory 310–11
      sex as 'natural' drive 310
   unblushing 308
Sexual Stigma (Plummer) 303
sexual violence and sport 204
sexuality 210, 284–316
   biology and 285–91
   cultural diversity 289
   culture 285–91
   defined 284–5
   ethnomethodology (Kessler and McKenna) 311–12
   feminism 302–3
   Freud 288–9
   future sociology of 315–16
   gay and lesbian movement 302–3
   gender 285, 285–91
      as 'expression 289–90
      identity 291–301
      transforming 301–3
   heterosexuality 303–15
   history (Foucault) 397–8
   homosexuality 303–15
   metrosexuality 314–15
   power 312
   psychology 307–8
   role theory 291–3
   sex roles 287–8
   sexual conduct (Gagnon and Simon) 308–11
   sexual scripts 308–11, 312
   sociobiology 286–7
   transsexuals 284, 311, 312
shame 420–1
Shell 68
sick role 326–7
Sikhism 367
simulacrum 486
Simulations (Baudrillard) 486–7
Smart Mobs: The Next Social Revolution (Rheingold) 105
snowballing 459
social (term) 6 *see also* culture
social action 8, 380, 395, 474
   affective or emotional 380
   instrumentally rational 380

   traditional 380
   value–rational 380
social attitudes 393
social capital 197–8, 223, 451
social change 471–2
   religion 358–61
   the self and 4
social citizenship 243
social class *see* class, social
social closure 231, 232
social construction
   of childhood 150, 151–4
   of crime and deviance 408, 409–10, 443
   of family 117
   of gender and sexual identity 284
   of madness 321
   of masculinity 428
   of our interests 391
   queer theory 312–13
   of reality 5, 355–6, 454
   second-order constructs 454
   of self *see* interactionism
   of sex 398
Social Construction of Reality, The (Berger and Luckmann) 355–6, 454
social control theory 414–15 *see also* control
   assessment of 415
   feminist 419
   Wilson and Herrnstein 414–15
social democracy 164–5, 173–4
social differentiation 470
social distance 223
social division 223
social exclusion 223, 242–3
social fact 5–6, 443, 468
social globalisation 32 *see also* globalisation
social impacts of tourism 209
social inequality *see* inequality
social institutions 5
social interactionism *see* interactionism
social meanings 449
Social Meanings of Suicide, The (Douglas) 448–9
social mobility 224, 251–3
   in Australia 252–3
   measuring 252
social objects 308
social order 469–70
social power 388
social practice 85–6
social realism 189
social relations—forms and types 479–80
   fashion 479–80
   social relationship 394
   the stranger 479
social reproduction strategies 253
social research methods *see* methods of social research
social solidarity 232, 469
   mechanical solidarity 232, 469
   organic solidarity 232, 469
social stratification 223
social structure 5–6, 8
social surveys 450

social system 5–6, 8
social wage 235, 236
socialisation 152 *see also* class; education; gender; race
   primary 120
   self and identity 8–9
socialist perspectives on deviance 418–19
society (term) 6, 30–1, 478–81 *see also* culture
sociobiology 286–7
   criticisms of 286–7
sociological determinism 291, 296
sociological imagination 2–3
sociological theory 466–87
   classical vs contemporary 466–8
   conflict theory 19, 20, 380–2, 476–7
      authority (Dahrendorf) 477
      deviance and power 417–19
      subjective experience (Collins) 477
   crime and deviance 411–21
   current 488–9
   Durkheim 468–70
      anomie and justice 469
      collective conscience and moral order 468–9
      differentiation of society 469
      division of labour 232–3, 379, 443, 469
      social facts as 'things' 468
      social order (Parsons) 469–70
      social solidarity 232, 469
   ethnomethodology 483–4
   feminist 484–5 *see also* feminist theory
   inequality 227–34 *see also* inequality
   interpretivist 481–4
   Marx 470–4
      alienation 471
      Frankfurt School 473–4
      ideology 470–1
      power of hegemony (Gramsci) 472–3
      social change 471–2
      Western Marxism 472–4
   modernity, the Enlightenment and beyond 485–8
      postmodernism and knowledge (Lyotard) 485–6
      second modernity and 'zombie sociology' (Beck) 487–8
      simulations (Baudrillard) 486–7
   Simmel 477–84
      concept of society and sociology 478–81
      an evaluation 481
      objective culture 481
      philosophy of money 480–1
      relationism and reciprocal working 478–9
      social relations 479–80
   symbolic interactionism 482–3 *see also* interactionism
   Weber 474–7
      capitalism and ascetic Protestantism 475–6
      conflict sociology 476–7
sociology *see also* sociological theory
   agency 7–8
   biology and the body 290–1
   colonialism 463
   critical theory 12–13
   of education 182–8 *see also* education
   emergence of 401
   of family life 116–21 *see also* family life
   of gender 315–16 *see also* gender

   of globalisation 33–8 *see also* globalisation
   history of 15–20
   as interpretation 13
   methods of social research 442–63
   of modern medicine 321–4 *see also* modern medicine
   as politics 12–13
   public sociology 20–2
   reasons to study 2
   as science 12, 456
   of sexuality 315–16 *see also* sexuality
   social change and 15–20
   sociological determinism 291, 296
   sociological imagination 2–3
   sociological perspectives 10–11, 445
   of suicide (Durkheim) 446–50
   theories of inequality 227–34 *see also* inequality
Souls of Black Folk, The (Du Bois) 21
Southern Theory (Connell) 70–2, 446
sovereign power 399
Soviet Union 34, 40, 370
spirit of capitalism (Weber) *see under* capitalism
spirituality 351–2
sport 194, 199–206
   in Australia 199–202
   class 205–6
   gender 201–5
      David Beckham and 'new man' 205
      gender order 202–4
   modernity 200–4
   race 206
   sexual violence 204
   tourism 210
stabilisation of adult personalities 120
stages
   game stage 482
   play stage 482
Starbucks 61, 67
the state 51–3, 128–9
   Australian 388–90
   bureaucracy 386–90, 387–8
   crime and deviance 418–19, 435–6
   defined 387
   disciplinary power (Foucault) 399–400
   discipline 386–7, 398–9
   governmentality (Foucault) 378, 400–2
   individuality and power (Foucault) 398–9
   modern 387–8
   new social movements 384–5, 402–3
   postmodernity 402–3
   power and 378–405
   social power 388
   withering away of 52
State of Social Control, The (Melossi) 378
stateless societies 387
statistics 443
status 223, 231
strain theory 412–13
stranger 479–80
stratification 223, 225–6 *see also* class, social
Street Corner Society (Whyte) 459–63
Structural Adjustment Program (SAP) 48, 49–51
structural change in family life 132–49

structural dysfunction 413
structural functionalism 6, 173–4 *see also* functionalism
structural mobility 252
structural racism 279
Structural Transformation of the Public Sphere, The (Habermas) 90–3
structure 5–6, 8, 456
    elite 381–2
Structure of Scientific Revolutions, The (Kuhn) 11, 444–5
Studies in Ethnomethodology (Garfinkel) 454–5
subcultural theory 419
subject/subjectivity 397, 402, 452
    subjective culture 481–4
substantiation 443
substantive definitions 351
suicide
    in Australia 450
    death as (Atkinson) 449–50
    rates 446–7
    sociology of (Durkheim) 446–50
    types of 446–7, 446–50
        altruistic 448
        anomic 448
        egoistic 448
        fatalistic 448
Suicide: A Study in Sociology (Durkheim) 329, 443, 446–50
Suicide Explained (Hassan) 450
superbrands 67–8
superstructure (of society) 228
symbolic interactionism *see* interactionism
symmetrical family 116
Symmetrical Family, The (Young and Willmott) 116
system 5–6, 8
systems of stratification 223, 225–6 *see also* class, social

Taylor, Frederick 60
Taylorism 214
technology
    globalisation 31, 42–3
    inequality and 38
    techno-capitalism 37–8
    technoscapes 63
Telecom (Telstra) 213
terra nullius 257, 261
tertiary sexual characteristics 311
Thatcher, Margaret 46–7, 48
theory 466
third 'face' of power 390–1
Third Reich of Nazi Germany 2
Third World 34, 65
threat schema 393
Three Waves of Globalisation (Robbie Robertson) 38
TINA 386
Torres Strait Islanders 257, 258 *see also* Aboriginal Australians
total institution 324
tourism 194, 206–10
    future studies 209–10
    importance 207–8
    social impacts 209
    sociological perspectives 207, 208–9
    sports 210
    tourist gaze 208–9

traditional action 380
traditional authority 379, 380
traditional medicine 320–1
transcendent values 84–5
Transformation of Intimacy (Giddens) 156
transnational corporations (TNCs) 43, 80
transportation 268
transsexuals 284, 311, 312
triangulation 457–8
Trobriand cricket 201–2
Troilus and Cressida (Shakespeare) 354
typology 446
Tyranny of Distance, The (Blainey) 81

Uluru 208
UN Convention on the Rights of the Child 151
UN *Human Development Report 2004* 243
underclass 104
unemployment 217–18, 262–3
United Kingdom
    American hegemony 58
    Australian colonies 268
    crime 416
    health 328, 329
    mugging 418–19
    neoliberalism 48
    reality television 76
    social mobility 252
    Stonehenge 198
    Sunday trading 198
United Nations 162
United States
    advertising 67
    African slaves 361
    CEO pay 240
    Chile 46
    civil rights movement 417
    crime control 415
    cultural consumption 196
    deviance 413
    divorce 145, 146
    education 172
    elections 486
    ethnicity 265
        Italians in Boston 459–61, 463
        Puerto Ricans in Harlem 462
    fundamentalism 353, 367–8
    gangs 430
    globalisation 32–3, 40
        global law 56
    health care system 331–2
    hegemony 57–8
    media
        internet history 101
        media effects research 79
    migration to 41
    migration within 266
    poverty 243
    power elite 381
    race 206, 361, 417
    social capital erosion 451
    sociology in 21–2

sport
   gender order 202
   race 206
   subprime mortgage market 28
   Washington Consensus 65
universalism 164
University of Chicago
   neoliberalism 46 *see also* neoliberalism
   theorists *see* Chicago School
upper class 226, 247–9
uranium mining 262
urbanisation 241
Utah Mining Company 213
utilitarianism 390

validity 457
value consensus 470
value-freedom 12–13
value–rational action 380
values 6–7
'variable-sum' concept of power 383
verstehen sociology 452, 474
vertical segregation 211, 212, 215
victim surveys 425, 443
victims of crime 432
Vietnam War 58
violence
   domestic 123–4, 433
   racist, in Australia 264, 279
   relationship of 401
   sexual, in sport 204
   symbolic 184
Virgin Airlines 67
Volcker, Paul 47
voluntarism 292

Washington Consensus 65
Ways of Seeing (Berger) 9
wealth 235, 237, 240, 248–9
Web 98–104
Weddings and Wives (Spender) 149
welfare 328–30 *see also* health
Western Europe 58
Western Marxism 472–4
Westphalian model 54
white-collar crime 435
Whitefella Comin' (Trigger) 259
Who Governs? (Dahl) 385
witchcraft 372, 446
Wiwa, Ken Saro 68
women
   Aboriginal Australian
     colonialism 280
     criminal justice system 433–4
     prison 263
   crime 431
   domestic violence against 123–4, 433
   fertility decline 136
   health 345
   leisure 198–9
   migrant 280
   social control 419
   in workforce 116, 138–41, 226
Woods, Tiger 206
work 194, 211–18, 379–80
   in Australia 211, 212–14
   domestic labour 117–18, 121–5, 433
   experience of 211–13
   gender 215–16
   inequality 215–16
   militancy and strikes 213–14
   modernity/postmodernity 214–15
   occupational groups 469
     legal profession 56
     medical 325, 326–30, 333–7
     occupational order 244–8, 250–1
     pink-collar 215
   unemployment 217–18, 262–3
   women in workforce 116, 138–41
   work/life balance 141
   work situation 246
working class 226, 229, 250, 251
World Bank 49–51
World Economic Forum (WEF) 45, 69
World Health Organization 437
World Social Forum (WSF) 69
world-systems theory 35
World Trade Organization (WTO) 45, 404
World Wide Web 98–104

young people
   adolescent sexual scripts 309–10
   crime 428–31
     Aboriginal Australians 264–5
     juvenile justice 264–5, 428–31
   gangs 429–30
   police 430–1

'zero-sum' concept of power 378, 384, 394, 402
zero tolerance 415
'zombie sociology' (Beck) 488
zone maps 413, 414